Perinatal
Physiology

Perinatal Physiology

Edited by

Uwe Stave

Mailman Center for Child Development
University of Miami Medical School

With a Foreword by

A. Ashley Weech

Late Professor of Pediatrics
University of Cincinnati College of Medicine

PLENUM MEDICAL BOOK COMPANY
New York and London

Library of Congress Cataloging in Publication Data

Main entry under title:

Perinatal physiology.

Published in 1970 under title: Physiology of the perinatal period, entered under Stave.

Bibliography: p.
Includes index.
1. Fetus — Physiology. 2. Infants (Newborn) — Physiology. I. Stave, Uwe, 1923-   Physiology of the perinatal period. [DNLM: 1. Animals, Newborn — Physiology. 2. Fetus — Physiology. 3. Physiology, Comparative. 4. Infant, Newborn. QT4 P445]
RG600.S73 1977   612.6'47   77-12596
ISBN 0-306-30999-8

(Second Edition of Physiology of the Perinatal Period)

© 1970, 1978 Plenum Publishing Corporation
227 West 17th Street, New York, N.Y. 10011

Plenum Medical Book Company is an imprint of Plenum Publishing Corporation

Printed in the United States of America

Contributors

F. John Ballard   CSIRO, Division of Human Nutrition, Adelaide, South Australia 5000, Australia

Ross C. de Belle   McGill University, Montreal Children's Hospital, Montreal, PQ Canada

John Bench   Audiology Unit, Royal Berkshire Hospital, Reading, England

William H. Bergstrom   Department of Pediatrics, State University of New York Upstate Medical Center, Syracuse, New York 13210

Kurt Brück   Institute of Physiology, Justus Liebig University, D63 Giessen, West Germany

José Cara   Department of Pediatrics, Coney Island Hospital, State University of New York Downstate Medical Center, Brooklyn, New York 11235

Joseph Dancis   Department of Pediatrics, New York University School of Medicine, New York, New York 10016

Klaus Dietel   Children's Hospital of the Regional Hospital, Karl-Marx-Stadt, German Democratic Republic

Jean Claude Dreyfus   Institute of Molecular Pathology, University of Paris, Paris, France

Frank Falkner   Fels Research Institute, Yellow Springs, Ohio 45387; and University of Cincinnati College of Medicine, Cincinnati, Ohio 45229

Louis Gluck   Department of Pediatrics, School of Medicine, University of California San Diego, La Jolla, California 92037

Peter Gruenwald   Hahnemann Medical College and Hospital, Philadelphia, Pennsylvania

Peter Hahn   Centre for Developmental Medicine, Department of Obstetrics and Gynaecology and Department of Paediatrics, Faculty of Medicine, University of British Columbia, Vancouver, British Columbia, Canada

Herbert S. Harned, Jr. Department of Pediatrics, The University of North Carolina School of Medicine, Chapel Hill, North Carolina 27514

Williamina A. Himwich Nebraska Psychiatric Institute, University of Nebraska Medical Center, Omaha, Nebraska 68105

Barbara B. Hixon Division of Biostatistics, Washington University School of Medicine, St. Louis, Missouri 63110

Tryphena Humphrey Deceased, Department of Anatomy, The University of Alabama in Birmingham, The Medical Center, Birmingham, Alabama

Martti Kekomäki Department of Pediatric Surgery, University of Helsinki, Helsinki, Finland

Edmund Kerpel-Fronius Department of Pediatrics No. II, University Medical School, Budapest IX, Hungary

Enno Kleihauer Department of Pediatrics, University of Ulm, D79 Ulm (Donau), West Germany

Leonard I. Kleinman Departments of Pediatrics, Physiology, and Environmental Health, University of Cincinnati College of Medicine, Cincinnati, Ohio 45229

Otakar Koldovsky Joseph Stokes' Research Institute, Children's Hospital of Philadelphia and Department of Pediatrics, University of Pennsylvania, Philadelphia, Pennsylvania 19104

Roger Lester University of Pittsburgh School of Medicine, Pittsburgh, Pennsylvania 15261

John Lind Department of Pediatrics, Karolinska Hospital and Wenner-Gren Research Laboratory, Stockholm, Sweden

Maria C. Linder Physiological Chemistry Laboratories, Department of Nutrition and Food Science, Massachusetts Institute of Technology, Cambridge, Massachusetts

James F. Marks The University of Texas Health Science Center, Dallas, Texas 75235

Alvin M. Mauer St. Jude Children's Research Hospital, Memphis, Tennessee 38101

T. Allen Merritt Department of Pediatrics, School of Medicine, University of California San Diego, La Jolla, California 92037

Gaspard de Muralt Department of Perinatology, University Women's Hospital, Bern, Switzerland

Michael Obladen Department of Pediatrics, School of Medicine, University of California San Diego, La Jolla, California 92037

Eduardo Orti Department of Pediatrics, State University of New York Downstate Medical Center, Brooklyn, New York 11203

Niels C. R. Räihä Departments of Obstetrics and Gynecology and Pediatrics, University of Helsinki, Helsinki, Finland

Leonard E. Reisman Departments of Pathology and Pediatrics, Jefferson Medical College, Philadelphia, Pennsylvania 19107

Julius B. Richmond The Judge Baker Guidance Center, Boston, Massachusetts 02115

Klaus P. Riegel University Children's Hospital, D8 Munich, Germany

Mark C. Rogers Departments of Pediatrics and Anesthesia, The Johns Hopkins Hospital, Baltimore, Maryland 21205

Fanny Schapira Institute of Molecular Pathology, University of Paris, Paris, France

Franz J. Schulte Department of Pediatrics, University of Göttingen, D34 Göttingen, Germany

Thomas R. C. Sisson Department of Pediatrics, Obstetrics and Gynecology (Perinatology), Neonatal Research Laboratory, Temple University School of Medicine, Philadelphia, Pennsylvania 19140

Selma E. Snyderman Department of Pediatrics, New York University Medical School, New York, New York 10016

Mark A. Sperling Department of Pediatrics, University of California at Los Angeles School of Medicine, Harbor General Hospital Campus, Torrance, California 90509

Uwe Stave Mailman Center for Child Development and Department of Pediatrics, University of Miami School of Medicine, Miami, Florida 33152

Ronald G. Strauss St. Jude Children's Research Hospital, Memphis, Tennessee 38101

Mildred Trotter Department of Anatomy and Neurobiology, Washington University School of Medicine, St. Louis, Missouri 63110

Hans T. Versmold University Children's Hospital, D8 Munich, Germany

S. Zoe Walsh Department of Pediatrics, Karolinska Hospital; and Wenner-Gren Research Laboratory, Stockholm, Sweden

David S. Walton Massachusetts Eye and Ear Infirmary, Boston, Massachusetts 02114

Margaret L. Williams Department of Pediatrics, State University of New York Upstate Medical Center, Syracuse, New York 13210

Foreword

Living Nature, not dull Art
Shall plan my ways and rule
my heart
—Cardinal Newman
Nature and Art
1868

One of the ineluctable consequences of growth in any field of science is that subjects of inquiry once established tend to give birth to subsubjects and that the subsubjects once established will in time undergo further mitotic division. Not so many years ago, problems surrounding the fetus and newly born infant lay in a realm almost to be described as a "no-man's land." Obstetricians properly gave major consideration to understanding and learning about processes and disorders concerned with maternal health and safety. The welfare of the infant was regarded as of secondary importance. Pediatricians on their part hesitated to invade the nursery, a sanctum regarded as belonging to the domain of the accoucheur. And the pathologist, enveloped in the mysteries of life and death in the adult, found scant time for the neonate and the placenta.

Within little more than a score of years, all these things have changed. Obstetricians led by Nicholson Eastman, pediatricians guided by Clement Smith, pathologists represented by Sydney Farber and Edith Potter, the anesthesiologist Virginia Apgar, and many others have recognized the reward to be gained by exploring a previously neglected field. Numerous treatises are now available for the clinician who must supervise the treatment of disorders of this period of life. Compendiums on pathology are readily found. For the student bent on exploring the physiologic happenings of perinatal life, the volume entitled *The Physiology of the Newborn Infant* by Clement A. Smith has been a bible. With so much material now in convenient reference form, one may wonder why still another book. The answer lies in an expansion of methodology in a way now permitting the utilization of new biochemical techniques in unraveling the entangled threads of perinatal physiology. This compilation is not just another book. Nor is it a treatise for the clinician. But, for the investigator dedicated to understanding the genesis of what takes place at the very start of life, the volume will be a must.

Editor's Note: This Foreword was written for the first edition and newly edited by Dr. Weech for the present volume. Dr. Weech died in August, 1977.

This foreword would be devoid of purpose if it failed to furnish an introduction to the physician who conceived of the need for the volume and at once devoted energy and talent to selecting appropriate authors for each of the 40 chapters, to the writing of two of these chapters himself, to a labor of love involving self-discipline and sacrifice suited for the task. His medical education began in November of 1945 at the University of Hamburg. It is significant that his doctoral thesis was on a subject that presaged future interests. It was entitled (in English translation) "Studies of the Physiology and Pharmacology of the Phrenic-Diaphragm Preparation of the Rat." After an internship, he joined the Department of Pharmacology, where he became engrossed in investigating the reactions of smooth muscle to various newly synthesized drugs. In April 1953, he accepted an invitation to become a staff member at the University of Marburg an der Lahn. Here, he was associated with two pediatricians with collateral experience in the field of metabolic diseases and chromatographic chemistry—Friedrich Linneweh and Horst Bickel. Studies of amino acid metabolism ensued. There followed an opportunity to become affiliated with Theodor Buecher and associates in the Department of Biochemistry, where the young Privat-Dozent became acquainted with the techniques of enzyme chemistry. Published articles over a period of eight and a half years in Marburg reveal a maturing interest in problems of developmental physiology. And, even more important from the standpoint of this foreword, our editor was learning—through his writings and by personal contacts at scientific meetings—to know the scientists of Europe who were making important contributions to the subjects of his interest.

In October 1961, Stave emigrated to the United States in order to join the staff of the Fels Research Institute for the Study of Human Development in Yellow Springs, Ohio. Here he was able to carry on his investigations in an exceedingly stimulating and hospitable environment. In the immediate reaches of a single building, he was associated with colleagues in the fields of anthropology, genetics, psychology, psychiatry, psycho-physiology, and biochemistry—all of them men with a dedicated interest in the overall study of growth. Once again, through writing and travel to scientific meetings, he came to know the productive students in a land over the seas from where his work began.

Enough has been said to justify the statement that the editor of this book was "singularly suited for the task." It is appropriate that in his preface, Doctor Stave himself should say more about his carefully selected contributors. Perhaps the writer of this foreword, who has been for many years a member of the Scientific Advisory Committee of the Fels Research Institute, is also justified in recording his own pleasure in having known Uwe Stave both personally and under circumstances that have permitted familiarity with his work.

A. Ashley Weech, M.D.

Preface

In the sixties a new breed of pediatricians, called neonatologists, emerged, and in this decade the movement has continued beyond neonatology toward perinatology. This innovative new field, perinatal physiology, is the true bonding link that promises to integrate the separate disciplines of obstetrics and neonatology into a unified approach to growth and functional development through the pre- and postnatal periods.

The expansion and revision of *Perinatal Physiology* is in response to the need for an updated source book in this field for teachers, researchers, and students which incorporates a new emphasis on the *human* fetus and newborn. The subject matter of perinatal physiology includes the rapid and important period of development which climaxes with parturition of the fetus from its protective intrauterine environment; this text focuses on the final preparation for birth, the impact of parturition on the biological functions of the newborn, and the establishment of an early postnatal homeostasis. Material on postnatal growth, the skeleton, blood-clotting factors, neonatal nutrition, trace elements, and hearing has been added in this second edition. In some chapters the time frame of the perinatal period, usually defined as the 24th week of gestation through the 28th day of postnatal life, was insufficient and needed to be expanded in order to achieve a more complete understanding of functional changes. While normal function and development are of focal interest, the comprehensive presentation of physiologic functions in this text requires some discussion of pathology. The size of the present volume, however, has limited the inclusion of material in this border area.

Fifty years ago Adalbert Czerny was teaching that "the biggest influence on natural immunity is exerted by nutrition" ("den grössten Einfluss übt auf die natürliche Immunität die Ernährung aus"). The wisdom of this teaching is reinforced in contributions on fetal and neonatal nutrition in this volume. In paying tribute to Ad Czerny, I also want to express my gratitude and appreciation to my teachers, Friedrich Linneweh and the late Klaus Soehring, who both were trained by him.

Since publication of the first edition in 1970, five of those contributing colleagues have passed away: Jörn Gleiss, David Yi-Yung Hsia, Tryphena Humphrey, Lubor Jílek and A. Ashley Weech. In deep respect and appreciation we recognize and will remember these scientists and their work.

I am most grateful for the cooperation and enthusiasm of the contributing authors who have made this publication possible. My sincere thanks to the team of experts at Plenum who, with deft competence, have refined and shaped this volume. I am grateful also to my assistant, Cecilia Ruvalo, and my secretary, Patricia Fernandez, for their most efficient help.

Uwe Stave

Miami

Contents

CHAPTER 4: Postnatal Growth

FRANK FALKNER

CHAPTER 5: The Skeleton

MILDRED TROTTER AND BARBARA B. HIXON

PART II: RESPIRATION, CIRCULATION, AND BLOOD

CHAPTER 6: Respiration and the Respiratory System

HERBERT HARNED, JR.

CHAPTER 7: Lung Maturity and Pulmonary Phospholipid Metabolism

T. ALLEN MERRITT, MICHAEL OBLADEN, AND
LOUIS GLUCK

CHAPTER 8: The Fetal Circulation and Its Alteration at Birth

S. ZOE WALSH AND JOHN LIND

CHAPTER 9: Blood Volume

THOMAS R. C. SISSON

CHAPTER 10: Formed Elements of Human Blood

RONALD G. STRAUSS AND ALVIN M. MAUER

CHAPTER 11: The Hemoglobins

ENNO KLEIHAUER

CHAPTER 12: Respiratory Gas Transport Characteristics of Blood and Hemoglobin

KLAUS P. RIEGEL AND HANS T. VERSMOLD

CHAPTER 18: Protein and Amino Acid Metabolism

SELMA E. SNYDERMAN

CHAPTER 19: Lipids

PETER HAHN

CHAPTER 20: Functions and Metabolism of Trace Elements

MARIA C. LINDER

CHAPTER 21: Heat Production and Temperature Regulation

KURT BRÜCK

CHAPTER 22: Liver Enzymes

UWE STAVE

CHAPTER 23: Bilirubin Metabolism

THOMAS R. C. SISSON

CHAPTER 24: Development of the Ornithine–Urea Cycle

NIELS C. R. RÄIHÄ AND MARTTI KEKOMÄKI

CHAPTER 25: Hepatic Drug Metabolism

ROSS C. DE BELLE AND ROGER LESTER

PART IV: BODY FLUIDS AND RENAL FUNCTION

CHAPTER 26: Electrolyte and Water Metabolism

EDMUND KERPEL-FRONIUS

CHAPTER 27: The Kidney

LEONARD I. KLEINMAN

CHAPTER 28: Calcium and Phosphorus Metabolism

WILLIAM H. BERGSTROM AND
MARGARET L. WILLIAMS

PART V: THE NEUROMUSCULAR SYSTEM

CHAPTER 29: Physiology and Pharmacology of the Central Nervous System

WILLIAMINA A. HIMWICH

CHAPTER 30: Function of the Nervous System During Prenatal Life

TRYPHENA HUMPHREY†

CHAPTER 31: Neonatal Brain Mechanisms and the Development of Motor Behavior

FRANZ J. SCHULTE

CHAPTER 32: Biochemistry of Muscle Development

JEAN CLAUDE DREYFUS AND FANNY SCHAPIRA

CHAPTER 33: The Autonomic Nervous System

MARK C. ROGERS AND JULIUS B. RICHMOND

CHAPTER 34: **The Visual System**

DAVID S. WALTON

CHAPTER 35: **The Auditory Response**

JOHN BENCH

CHAPTER 36: **Morphological and Functional Development of the Skin**

KLAUS DIETEL

PART VI: **THE ENDOCRINE SYSTEM**

CHAPTER 37: **Steroid Hormone Formation and Metabolism**

EDUARDO ORTI

Perinatal
Physiology

CHAPTER 1

Intrauterine Growth

Peter Gruenwald

1. Introduction

The third trimester of pregnancy, when an infant may be born with some chance of surviving, has been considered to be a period in which fetal growth predominates over maturation. This view is true in comparison with earlier periods when developmental changes are strikingly in the foreground, but it is at best a gross oversimplification. Maturation rather than growth accounts for the steadily improving chance of extrauterine survival during the third trimester. While everyone is familiar with the functional handicaps of the preterm infant, knowledge of the week-by-week progress of structural and functional maturation is woefully inadequate. Actually, it is quite impossible to separate growth from maturation; there is no period of life in which the former proceeds without the latter; that is, there is no period in which there is growth without changes in composition or function. With these reservations in mind, and with occasional reference to maturation, this chapter will be devoted primarily to growth as judged by weight or by linear measurements.

1.1. Terminology and Classification

Until recently, it was customary to judge the past progress and present stage of development of the fetus at birth by its body weight, and to recognize prematurity by a birth weight of 2500 g or less. During the past decade, it has become increasingly clear that this practice is not only improper, but has prevented the recognition and study of small size at birth due to slow fetal growth. For this reason, an expert committee of the World Health Organization[64] took an important step in 1961 and recommended that the group of neonates with a birth weight of 2500 g or less be set apart as before because of the need for special care, but under the designation *infants of low birth weight*, since a sizable proportion of them are not truly premature. Infants above that cutoff weight may be designated as "full-size." On the basis of menstrual age independent of weight, "preterm," "full-term," and "postterm" infants may be distinguished by dividing points at 38 weeks (266 days) and 42 weeks (294 days) from the last menstrual period. The Committee on Fetus and Newborn of the American Academy of Pediatrics[1] has recently agreed with this division into gestational age groups, coupled with weight groups designated by the limits used. In addition, each infant may be designated as "small," "appropriate," or "large" for gestational age by arbitrary standards, such as the 10th and 90th percentile, or mean plus or minus 2 standard deviations for the respective week of gestation. Similar recommendations have been made by the Second European Congress of Perinatal Medicine.[52] These suggestions, as well as

Peter Gruenwald · Hahnemann Medical College and Hospital, Philadelphia, Pennsylvania

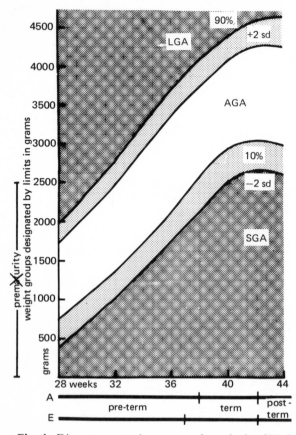

Fig. 1. Diagram comparing suggested standards of birth weight for gestational age. The heavily stippled areas include weights above and below two standard deviations (sd) from the mean; the lightly stippled areas, the additional ranges beyond the 10th and 90th percentiles (10%, 90%) for a middle-class population in Portland, Oregon.[2] (LGA, AGA, SGA) Large, appropriate, and small, respectively, for gestational age. At the bottom, the ranges for preterm, term, and postterm birth are those suggested by (A) the American Academy of Pediatrics[1] and (E) the Second European Congress of Perinatal Medicine.[52] Use of the term "prematurity" to indicate a birth weight below 2501 g, or in any other sense, should be avoided because of past misuse. Reproduced (with added lettering) from Gruenwald[29] by permission of the Ciba Foundation.

their difference in the definition of preterm birth, and the two sets of cutoff lines suggested, are shown in Fig. 1.

Gestational age has customarily been calculated from either of two different starting points. True *conceptional age,* as used particularly by embryologists, is known directly in human subjects only

seldom, such as in cases under close surveillance because of fertility problems. Clinicians usually use the more readily available *menstrual age,* counting from the date of onset of the last menstrual period. In women with a regular, 28-day cycle, this date precedes conception by 2 weeks. Since most of the data in this book are based on this information, menstrual age will be given in most instances. Simply to subtract 2 weeks and then call this information conceptional age may give the erroneous impression that there actually was knowledge of the date of conception. This 2-week difference must be kept in mind, however, particularly when referring to both embryologic and clinical data.

2. Growth and Maturation

2.1. Factors That Control and Influence Fetal Growth

Several types of factors affect growth and, to a lesser extent, maturation of the fetus during the third trimester. These factors may be classified as fetal, placental, maternal, and environmental, but since all of them reach the fetus in one way or another via the mother, arbitrary definitions must be made, taking as the basis the fetus late in the second trimester:

1. The factors inherent in the fetus at that time might be considered as "fetal." They would include genetic factors such as the normal growth potential and abnormal genetic traits, as well as teratogenic, infectious, and similar influences early in embryonic life.
2. Placental factors—i.e., true placental insufficiency—are unlikely to affect the fetus before the third trimester because early in fetal life, the functional capacity of the placenta is far in excess of the needs of the fetus. During the third trimester, true placental insufficiency occurs, but in this case, as in the case of "prematurity by weight," the use of a slogan can impede progress: if all evidence or suggestion of fetal deprivation is laid to placental insufficiency, the study of maternal factors will be neglected.
3. Maternal and environmental factors will be considered together, since in many instances they cannot be separated. Socioeconomic factors, for instance, are partly maternal in

that they influence, at the time of the mother's development, her ability to support fetal growth later on, and partly environmental in that they affect the mother during the pregnancy under study.

During much of the third trimester, unrestrained fetal growth as controlled by the growth potential of the fetus follows a linear course that is basically the same in all populations studied.[22] When the fetal supply line as affected by mother and placenta becomes a limiting factor, growth declines, and the birth-weight curve departs from the straight-line course. This limitation is detectable in the birth-weight curve at about 36–39 weeks of menstrual age; it must therefore have begun somewhat earlier. Each population has a characteristic point at which growth limitation becomes apparent.[22] This refers, of course, to mean values; there is a considerable range of birth weights for each week. Without limitation by maternal or placental factors, growth would continue as characterized by the straight-line birth-weight curve. That it would is evident from the fact that the growth curve returns to that slope when the infant is again adequately supplied after adjusting to extrauterine life.[42] Thus, the extrapolated growth curve has a basic biological significance—it indicates how most populations of fetuses would grow if not limited by their supply line. One may therefore characterize growth of a fetus by relating it to one of two sets of standards: either the empirical birth-weight curve of the population from which it derives or the extrapolated curve, which, if what has just been said is correct, should be the same for all populations. The two should be identical up to 36–39 weeks, except for certain special groups to be discussed below.

The growth potential of the fetus, determined by the total of fetal factors as defined above, appears to provide normally for a weight gain of about 220 g per week during the third trimester. If, as was suggested above, the straight birth-weight curve is indicative of the growth potential, then abnormalities of the growth potential should be evident as shifts of the curve to one side or the other, rather than departure from the straight course. This is true of the sex difference in fetal growth. Lubchenco et al.[39] and Kloosterman[36] found such a shift to be present consistently during the second half of gestation. Malformed fetuses are frequently small, and there is every reason to believe that their smallness is due to a reduced

potential rather than to deprivation. The same growth deficit is seen in experimentally produced malformed mammals and birds. It is likely that not all types of malformation are equally affected, but the birth-weight curve of all malformed fetuses in the material of the National Birthday Trust[28] suggests that the abnormality is indeed of the type suggestive of an altered growth potential, rather than of deprivation; as far as one can tell on the basis of limited material in the early weeks of the third trimester, the birth-weight curve (Fig. 2) shifts to the right at some time during the third trimester, rather than departs from the normal course, as would be the case in deprivation. On the other hand, the birth-weight curve of infants of diabetic mothers is also basically abnormal, but shifted to the left, even early in the third trimester[26] (Fig. 2). The cause is unknown.

Growth support of the fetus comes, along with the needs for current maintenance of body functions, from the mother via the placenta and therefore represents the placental, maternal, and environmental factors as characterized above. Severe limitation by the placenta is unlikely to be caused before term by minor variations or pathologic changes in that organ, since placental adequacy apparently exceeds the fetal needs by a very wide margin early in the third trimester. Placental growth as indicated by weight[20] or DNA content[63] slows and ceases shortly before fetal growth does. This phenomenon suggests a relationship, but there is no compelling evidence that in the presence of adequate maternal supplies a nearly normal placenta effectively limits the fetal supply line; one might conjecture that this limitation would be most likely to occur past term if at all. There are, however, instances of pathologic reduction in the amount of normally functioning placental tissue, and it is difficult to escape the conclusion that in these cases, true placental insufficiency has an adverse effect on fetal growth. At this time, we can only use circumstantial evidence to suggest that in any given pregnancy, either placental or maternal factors have limited fetal growth and well-being.

Confirmation of our supposition that birth-weight curves as shown here are truly representative of fetal growth has recently been obtained. Ultrasound cephalometry, which is as yet the only means of measuring the same fetus repeatedly without disturbing its well-being and growth, yields curves with very similar slopes, and departures from the straight course.[12]

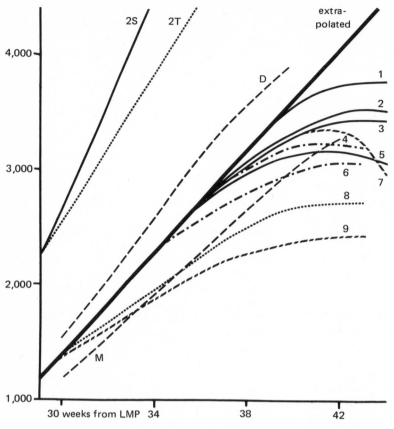

Fig. 2. Graph illustrating fetal growth during the third trimester of pregnancy as derived from birth weights. The curves are approximate and smoothed; most of them are derived from data originally presented in different form. They are intended to illustrate rather than prove a hypothesis described in the text. (1) A Swedish population[38]; (2) British data from the Perinatal Mortality Survey by the National Birthday Trust in 1958[11]; (3) the author's Baltimore data[22]; (4) Japanese birth weights[24]; (5) infants of smokers in a Baltimore Negro population[19]; (6) Japanese birth weights in 1945–1946,[24] 18 years before those shown in curve (4); (7) hypothetical growth curve in subacute fetal distress; (8) surviving twins, National Birthday Trust Survey of 1958[26]; (9) hypothetical growth curve in chronic fetal distress; (D) infants of diabetic mothers; (M) malformed infants among perinatal deaths, National Birthday Trust Survey[26]; (2T) combined birth weights of pairs of twins and, for comparison, (2S) double weights of singletons. The curves for most populations (curves 1–5) depart from the straight, extrapolated curve at 36 weeks or later; in severe deprivation (curves 6, 8, and 9), departure occurs earlier. When the growth potential of the fetus is abnormal, weights differ from normal even before the beginning of the third trimester (curves D and M). Reproduced from Gruenwald[26] by courtesy of Springer-Verlag, Inc., New York.

Maternal factors would most likely be either chemical or circulatory. Little is known about the degree to which the levels of essential nutrients in the maternal organism and bloodstream exceed the needs of the fetus, except perhaps in the case of oxygen, which is discussed in Chapter 6. According to some investigators, but not others, hypoxia of a significant degree exists in those postterm pregnancies in which the fetal outcome suggests deprivation. Knowledge of the adequacy of levels of other essential materials, such as amino acids, specific lipids, carbohydrates, or others, is entirely lacking. Somewhat more suggestive evidence exists with regard to circulatory factors. McLaren and Michie[43] concluded from their work in the mouse that hydrostatic factors determine those differences in fetal growth that have a characteristic relationship to location in certain parts of the uterus. Räihä[51] and Kauppinen[35] found an increased inci-

dence of "prematurity," which is mostly slow fetal growth, when the maternal heart volume as estimated radiographically does not adjust to the demands of pregnancy. This finding has been confirmed elsewhere by some, but not by others. Bieniarz and co-workers[7] demonstrated by angiography that the speed and extent of filling of the uterine arteries with contrast medium during pregnancy bear a significant relationship to the adequacy of fetal growth. They also showed that pressure by the pregnant uterus may reduce circulation in the pelvic vessels in normotensive women, but to a lesser extent in those with hypertension.[8] This finding suggests an explanation of the observation recorded independently in three investigations[3,6,23] that in pregnancies associated with hypertension, there is an excess not only of growth-retarded fetuses, but also of large ones. Poor growth in some of these pregnancies is almost certainly related to the demonstrated reduction in uterine blood flow. It must be kept in mind, however, that regulation of blood flow elsewhere in the body is usually achieved by arterioles; in the pregnant uterus, the arterioles are expanded and their walls are severely altered to the point where their contraction may become ineffective. It is no wonder, then, that the effects of maternal hypertensive conditions are so variable.

Just which maternal characteristics are affected by the mother's own development in relation to socioeconomic conditions so that they, in turn, make this woman less than optimally suited years later to supply her fetus is entirely unknown and needs to be investigated. Clinical evidence for the effect of maternal factors on fetal growth was contributed by Ounsted and Ounsted.[49]

Multiple births offer a fascinating opportunity to study various factors that affect fetal growth. It was suggested by McKeown and Record[41] that the supply line can support unrestricted growth of a litter until the combined fetal weight approaches 3000 g. This author's data on twins are entirely in agreement with this contention. Since it is known that placental weight in twins is larger in proportion to fetal weight than in singletons,[30,42,50] it is most likely that the limitation is maternal. In attempting to evaluate this limitation, however, one must remember that even though twins are individually growth-retarded from the early part of the third trimester, their combined growth far exceeds even that of large singletons (see Fig. 1). Thus, their growth limitation is not an absolute one in terms of supplies utilized. It seems that the supply line can yield far more than the usual amounts when tapped by the needs of more than one fetus. All these aspects, as obvious and challenging as they are, have not been elucidated to any extent.

2.2. Standards and Criteria of Fetal Growth

Normal data may be derived in different ways, depending on one's definition of normal. These standards are needed not only as indicators of fetal growth in population groups, as was discussed above, but also in order to judge the adequacy of postfetal growth in a given infant or group of infants. The choice of data depends on the purpose. Customarily used *empirical* standards are based on normality in a statistical sense, i.e., the mean values in a given population, be it the one under study

or one that is believed to be reasonably similar. Whatever handicaps affect the greater part of this population therefore become normal, and cannot be detected except by reference to other populations. In contrast, use of the *extrapolated* birth-weight curve discussed above would yield universally valid but very high standards that a population would reach under optimal conditions; the highest known, Swedish empirical standards,[38] conform to these extrapolated standards up to term (see Fig. 1). Examples of empirical standards and extrapolated data are given in Table I. Extrapolated standards have not been used extensively; they are particularly useful in the study of prolonged pregnancy, where

Table I. Empirical and Extrapolated Birth-Weight Standards[a]

Gestational age (nearest week from LMP)	Smoothed empirical standards (Sinai Hospital of Baltimore) (g)	Extrapolated standards (g)[b]
28	1050 ± 350	
29	1200 ± 350	
30	1380 ± 370	
31	1560 ± 360	
32	1750 ± 400	
33	1950 ± 420	
34	2170 ± 440	
35	2390 ± 440	
36	2610 ± 440	
37	2830 ± 430	
38	3050 ± 430	
39	3210 ± 430	3250 ± 450
40	3280 ± 440	3460 ± 490
41	3350 ± 450	3670 ± 520
42	3400 ± 460	3880 ± 540
43	3410 ± 490	4090 ± 570
44	3420 ± 520	4300 ± 600

[a] From Gruenwald.[27]

[b] These are arbitrary figures corresponding to an extension of the straight portions of empirical curves. Depending on slight changes in the slope of the straight portion, one may arrive at different values diverging with increasing gestational age. The present figures represent the averages of the regression coefficients, and the intercepts at 39 weeks, of 6 sets of data. The slopes were nearly indentical, and the weights at 39 weeks were all within 190 g. Dr. O. DeLisser made the calculations, and his help is gratefully acknowledged. An equivalent of standard deviation was set arbitrarily at 14% of weight, as it is in the Baltimore data from 39 to 42 weeks. Reproduced from Gruenwald[29] by permission of Ciba Foundation.

increasing degrees of growth deficit are built into any empirical data as normal.[21]

Comparison of empirical data from many sources shows fair conformity at about 38 weeks of menstrual age. Discrepancies above and below that age need some comment. Early in the third trimester, the spread of birth-weights in each week is quite wide. The distribution is asymmetrical with respect to the peak, with considerably more cases and sometimes a secondary peak among the higher weights.[22,47] It is likely that the excess of high-weight infants is contributed by pregnancies with an understated duration, either because the mother's bleeding after conception was mistaken for a menstrual period or because she gave to the interviewer the date of the first missed, rather than the last actual, menstrual period. Whatever the explanation may be, correction made independently by this author[22] and by Neligan[47] aimed at producing a symmetrical distribution of weights on both sides of the peak, and the resulting data fit an overall fetal growth curve much better than do the uncorrected ones. When that is done, most of the differences between birth-weight curves in the early part of the third trimester disappear. The standards given in Table I are corrected in this manner. That the irregularity of birth-weight distribution disappears near term agrees with the explanation of understated gestational age: near term, it becomes increasingly unlikely that a pregnancy 4 weeks older than stated has not yet terminated.

Contrary to this situation early in the third trimester, differences among empirical curves after about 38 weeks are probably true. The distribution of weights about the peak is symmetrical, and the differences correspond to those known to occur among populations with regard to overall mean birth weight. As was briefly mentioned above, these differences are most likely caused by limitation of growth support by the maternal organism. It is becoming increasingly evident that much of what was once attributed to racial (i.e., genetic) differences, e.g., between Caucasians and Negroes in the United States, is in fact socioeconomic and therefore environmentally caused.[33] An example of the rapid response of the birth-weight curve of a population to socioeconomic change was given by this author in collaboration with Japanese colleagues[24] from data in Japanese hospitals over a 20-year period (see Fig. 2). Such a rapid response, however, must not let us forget that socioeconomic changes also affect fetal growth via the mother's own development and ability to support her own pregnancies years later. The full benefits of socioeconomic improvement may therefore not appear until two generations later. That they may not raises the question whether fetal growth will increase indefinitely under improving circumstances. It is very likely that the conclusion reached by Bakwin and McLaughlin[4] after studying growth in childhood, namely, that the end is in sight, applies equally to fetal growth. Growth in accordance with the extrapolated curve should be the limit.

2.3. Pathologic Growth Retardation

Definitely subnormal birth weight in relation to gestational age, as identified by the criteria mentioned above, occurs sporadically in all populations. It carries a high mortality; in fact, Butler and Bonham[11] found that in the weight group of 1500–2000 g, the mortality of infants born between 38 and 41 completed weeks is higher than that of infants born before 38 weeks of menstrual age. The former are growth-retarded and the latter immature. Certain types of pregnancy are overrepresented among growth-retarded survivors and to an even greater extent among perinatal deaths—malformed infants as discussed under growth potential in Section 2.1, pregnancies complicated by hypertension, and multiple births.[20] In many cases, however, there is no association with any known factor. Among perinatal deaths at 33–40 weeks, Gruenwald[20] found 28% with a birth weight below mean minus 2 standard deviations, or about 10 times the expected proportion. Some somatic characteristics of severely growth-retarded infants will be mentioned below.

2.4. Linear Measurements

Linear measurements, particularly body length, have also been used to characterize the growth status at birth. The principal reason for their infrequent use is probably the lack of reliability with which crown–heel length (corresponding to standing height measured in later life) is determined in the newborn unless a special effort is made. This lack of reliability holds true to a lesser extent for crown–rump length, corresponding to sitting height. Much of the detailed information available is based on perinatal deaths. Because of the inordinately high proportion of growth-retarded

Table II. Body Measurements and Ratios for 200-g Weight Groups of Normally Grown and of Growth-Retarded Infants[a]

Body weight	Crown-heel length (CHL)		$10^3 \times$ body wt. / CHL³		Crown-rump length (CRL)		CRL / (CHL − CRL)		Head circumference		$10^3 \times$ head circ. / body wt.		Brain wt. / head circ.	
Score[b]:	0	−2	0	−2	0	−2	0	−2	0	−2	0	−2	0	−2
1000–1199	38.0	38.5	201	193	25.6	23.3	2.06	1.53	25.6	27.4	23	25	6.1	7.0
1200–1399	39.4	38.6	212	226	26.6	25.8	2.08	2.02	27.2	27.9	21	21	7.1	7.8
1400–1599	41.0	41.4	218	211	27.9	27.9	2.13	2.07	28.7	29.6	19	20	7.3	9.1
1600–1799	42.4	43.6	223	205	28.8	28.8	2.12	1.95	29.2	30.3	17	18	8.0	9.0
1800–1999	43.5	45.1	230	207	29.0	29.6	2.00	1.91	30.0	31.1	16	16	7.9	9.9
2000–2199	44.8	46.2	234	214	30.4	30.9	2.11	2.02	31.2	31.8	15	15	9.2	10.7
2200–2399	45.6	47.0	242	221	31.0	31.6	2.12	2.05	31.1	32.6	14	14	9.5	10.5
2400–2599	47.0	48.0	241	226	31.9	33.2	2.12	2.24	32.1	32.8	13	13	10.0	11.0
2600–2799	48.6		234		33.2		2.15		32.9		12		10.6	
2800–2999	48.8		250		33.8		2.25		33.4		12		11.0	
3000–3199	50.3		244		34.8		2.25		34.0		11		11.7	
3200–3399	50.8		251		35.1		2.23		34.7		11		11.6	
3400–3599	51.8		252		35.9		2.26		35.3		10		11.4	
3600–3799	51.6		270		36.5		2.41		35.3		10		12.0	
3800–3999	52.5		270		36.9		2.37		35.3		9		12.2	
4000–4199	54.6		251		38.3		2.35		36.6		9		12.0	

[a] From British Perinatal Mortality Survey of the National Birthday Trust Fund.[28] Data are in grams and centimeters.
[b] Score 0: normally grown neonates (birth weight within 1 S.D. of the mean for gestational age); score −2: severely growth-retarded ones (weight below mean −2 S.D.).

fetuses in this material, certain precautions need to be taken. In determining normal standards, only infants with a birth weight within 1 standard deviation from the mean have been used. Such data from the British Perinatal Mortality Survey[28] are given in Table II by 200-g weight groups for infants of normal weight and for growth-retarded ones.

Crown–rump length bears a fairly constant relationship to crown–heel length throughout the third trimester, crown–rump length being about two-thirds of crown–heel length. Head circumference is more useful for following postnatal growth than for evaluating the status at birth. In view of the great difference in brain weight between preterm and growth-retarded infants of similar birth weight, one might expect head circumference to be helpful in distinguishing the two conditions, but as with crown–heel length (see Section 3), it is not. Data for infants with birth weights within 1 standard deviation from the mean (score 0) and those below mean minus 2 standard deviations (score −2) for 200-g birth-weight groups are given in Table II.

3. Components of Fetal Growth

Since the fetus never grows proportionately, i.e., with all its components increasing at the same increment, the question arises how meaningful the simple determination of total weight or length really is. For some purposes, rather simple refinements may help establish or illustrate trends. The growth rate (weight gain per unit of time in relation to weight at the beginning of the respective time span) must, of course, decrease when absolute gain remains constant over several units of time. Figure 3 shows this relationship in weekly intervals for the empirical Baltimore data and the extrapolated weights in Table I. Various ways of analyzing and interpreting growth data were reviewed in a discussion under the leadership of Zuckerman[65] that ranges over many aspects of animal and plant growth.

Differences in body proportions have been characterized by indices relating various measurements to each other. Illuminating information may be obtained from the index of weight to length, which, when calculated as (grams of body weight $\times 10^3$)/ (cm of crown–heel length)^3, yields values of the order of 20. This index, calculated for weeks of the third trimester from mean values of the British Perinatal Mortality Survey (Fig. 3), shows that a population of fetuses grows stouter up to 33 weeks of menstrual age, and at a somewhat slower rate up to 38 weeks. A plateau is reached at 39–41 weeks, and beyond that time (in prolonged pregnancy), the average fetus becomes thinner again. Chronic fetal distress with severe growth retardation, as characterized by a weight below mean minus 2 standard deviations, does not produce a ratio significantly different from that of normally grown, preterm infants of similar weight. These growth-retarded infants are therefore not long and thin, presumably because their deprivation started before they could accumulate significant amounts of subcutaneous fat; they therefore could not lose weight. In contrast, subacute fetal distress, as exemplified by the malnourished postterm infant, does result in long, thin babies with abnormal weight-to-length ratios.

Data on body composition were recently reviewed by Brans and Cassady.[9] These authors also collected somatic and neuromuscular characteristics of neonates, which are so important in judging maturity and possible deprivation in the absence of a good history or in verifying the history.

One would like to know to what extent body weight is representative of active, living mass. During the third trimester, the proportion of water decreases and that of fat increases. According to Widdowson and Spray,[60] the combined proportion of water and fat remains about the same, as does the proportion of protein, while body weight increases from 1500 to 3500 g. This, of course, does not take into account that part of the water is intracellular and may therefore be considered part of the active, living mass. The data of Fee and Weil[18] on fetuses larger than 400 g are similar to those just cited. Sinclair et al.,[54] on the other hand, concluded from their metabolic studies that active tissue mass comprises body weight minus extracellular water, but including fat. It is possible that white fat, being a store of food material, behaves differently from brown fat, which is a source of body heat. Thus, Dawes[15] points out that in newborn rabbits, brown fat is depleted on exposure to cold, whereas white fat is used up during fasting. Cheek[13] demonstrated that fetal growth increment as measured by the amount of protein and water is linear in the second and third trimesters of human pregnancy, but to a different extent in each trimester, with a break at about 28 weeks of menstrual age.

Stores of glycogen and lipid were discussed by Dawes[15] with a view to the possibility that their

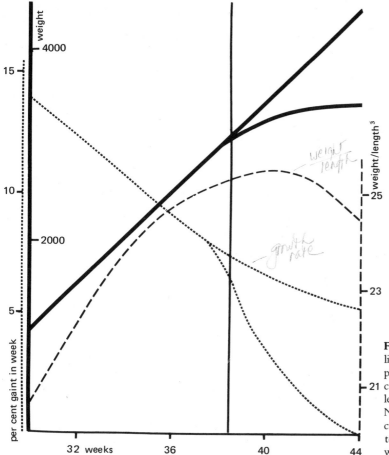

Fig. 3. Birth-weight curves (heavy lines: Baltimore empirical above, extrapolated below), growth rates from these curves (dotted lines), and body weight/length³ (dashed line) from data of the National Birthday Trust Fund. All curves are smoothed and are meant only to indicate trends. Data from Gruenwald.[28]

accumulation may be essential for survival after birth. In the human fetus, accumulation of glycogen in both liver and muscle occurs sufficiently early to be available throughout the period for which survival after preterm birth is possible. It is likely that deprivation of stores during periods of hypoxia is more significant for future function than is failure of storage owing to a premature state. The chronically deprived fetus, on the other hand, may be deficient in glycogen even when born without undue perinatal asphyxia, and this deficiency is assumed to be the cause of the fetus's liability to neonatal hypoglycemia. Fat accumulates more gradually during the third trimester, and is obviously deficient in the early-born as well as in the chronically deprived fetus.

In addition to weights and measurements, functional aspects may. be examined in the living neonate to estimate the degree of maturity at birth and the adequacy of past fetal growth. As might be expected in view of the great structural and functional complexity of development of the nervous system, neurological and electroencephalographic criteria have proved particularly discriminating and valuable (see Chapter 29). Several investigators have examined the reliability and usefulness of a variety of other somatic characteristics of the living neonate.[17,53,58] Prenatal (intrauterine) determinations based on skeletal growth and maturation or examination of amniotic fluid have so far not been very helpful.

At *necropsy*, additional information becomes available along several lines: (1) the pattern of growth of viscera; (2) histological maturity; (3) development of the brain; and (4) variations of cellular growth and multiplication.

Table III. Body Weight and Length and Weight of Placenta and Organs (Mean ± Standard

Placenta weight	Placenta weight, smoothed	Ratio placenta/ fetus	Body weight[b]	Body weight, smoothed	Gestational age[c]
		All births			
270 ± 39	270	1:4.6	1075 ± 305	1050	28
287 ± 36	295	1:4.4	1303 ± 370	1290	29–30
335 ± 45	335	1:5.0	1670 ± 400	1665	31–32
373 ± 60	375	1:5.5	2055 ± 425	2060	33–34
414 ± 64	415	1:6.2	2500 ± 455	2500	35–36
452 ± 58	455	1:6.4	3001 ± 475	2940	37–38
481 ± 68	480	1:6.8	3222 ± 439	3245	39–40
494 ± 74	495	1:6.8	3391 ± 457	3375	41–42
490 ± 62	490	1:7.0	3430 ± 500	3415	43+

[a] From Gruenwald.[24] Only newborn infants with a birth weight within 1 S.D. from the mean for all births (score 0) were included.
[b] Weights up to 36 weeks are corrected as explained by Gruenwald.[22]
[c] Each group extends from 3 days below to 3 days above the stated age from the last menstrual period.

Weight standards of organs in relation to gestational age or to total body weight have been established for the human neonate by several authors. The standards given in Tables III and IV are derived from material limited to birth weights within 1 standard deviation of the mean for the respective week of gestation in order to avoid a bias due to the increased mortality of infants with abnormal birth weights.[20,24] Evidence for abnormal fetal growth may be obtained by com-

Table IV. Body Length and Weight of Placenta and Organs (Mean ± Standard Deviation) of

Placenta weight	Placenta weight, smoothed	Ratio placenta/ fetus	Body weight group[b]	Body length	Heart	Lungs combined
	All births					
			1000	38.0 ± 1.5	7.4 ± 1.6	29 ± 9
272 ± 39	265	1:5.2	1250	38.0 ± 2.7	9.3 ± 2.3	32 ± 8
289 ± 34	295	1:5.5	1500	40.9 ± 2.1	10.9 ± 2.7	32 ± 11
338 ± 40	325	1:5.8	1750	42.9 ± 2.8	12.3 ± 3.2	43 ± 9
342 ± 37	355	1:6.0	2000	44.6 ± 2.3	14.9 ± 3.1	45 ± 8
381 ± 49	385	1:6.2	2250	46.0 ± 2.2	15.8 ± 2.7	51 ± 11
425 ± 51	415	1:6.3	2500	47.5 ± 1.5	17.2 ± 1.9	55 ± 8
439 ± 63	445	1:6.4	2750	48.8 ± 1.8	19.0 ± 2.5	60 ± 14
476 ± 64	475	1:6.6	3000	49.9 ± 3.2	19.2 ± 4.3	57 ± 16
508 ± 65	505	1:6.7	3250	50.8 ± 2.5	21.6 ± 4.9	61 ± 16
518 ± 78		1:7.0	3500	52.6 ± 2.6	22.9 ± 5.7	64 ± 16
525 ± 73		1:7.4	3750	53.0 ± 2.8	25.0 ± 3.6	68 ± 16

[a] From Gruenwald.[24] Only infants with a birth weight within 1 S.D. from the mean for all births (score 0) were included. All
[b] Extending 125 g above and below stated value.

Deviation) in Relation to Gestational Age[a]

				Autopsies				
Body length	Heart	Lungs combined	Spleen	Liver	Adrenals combined	Kidneys combined	Thymus	Brain
37.4 ± 2.5	8.1 ± 2.1	27 ± 7	3.3 ± 1.9	49 ± 13	3.9 ± 1.5	10.9 ± 3.2	4.0 ± 1.5	150 ± 33
39.6 ± 3.2	10.2 ± 3.3	34 ± 11	4.2 ± 1.9	60 ± 21	4.3 ± 1.7	14.7 ± 5.1	5.1 ± 2.5	189 ± 45
42.5 ± 2.4	12.5 ± 3.1	39 ± 11	4.9 ± 2.0	72 ± 22	4.6 ± 2.0	16.4 ± 4.6	8.1 ± 3.3	234 ± 41
45.4 ± 2.7	14.6 ± 2.9	47 ± 12	6.7 ± 2.5	86 ± 22	6.1 ± 2.4	18.3 ± 5.7	8.7 ± 3.5	275 ± 39
47.6 ± 2.3	18.1 ± 4.2	58 ± 11	8.2 ± 3.4	108 ± 28	7.6 ± 3.0	22.3 ± 5.9	9.7 ± 4.0	325 ± 29
49.2 ± 2.8	20.2 ± 4.9	63 ± 17	10.4 ± 3.6	127 ± 27	9.0 ± 3.0	24.8 ± 4.8	12.7 ± 5.0	367 ± 37
50.7 ± 3.1	20.7 ± 4.7	59 ± 16	10.5 ± 3.8	142 ± 35	9.0 ± 2.5	25.9 ± 6.0	11.1 ± 3.7	400 ± 50
52.0 ± 2.8	22.6 ± 5.8	62 ± 16	10.9 ± 4.0	146 ± 34	9.4 ± 3.2	26.0 ± 6.2	10.5 ± 3.7	425 ± 48
52.3 ± 2.7	23.9 ± 3.4	60 ± 15	10.7 ± 3.7	146 ± 28	9.9 ± 3.3	27.8 ± 9.2	9.0 ± 3.7	433 ± 46

All weights are in grams; body length is in centimeters.

paring organ weights of a proband with those normal for the respective birth weight. Fetal growth retardation (chronic distress) due to deprivation shows characteristic deviations in the pattern of organ weights similar to that found in experimental deprivation caused by malnutrition of ewes during the second half of gestation[5] or by ligation of uterine vessels in the pregnant rat.[61]

Compared with organ weights of normally grown, preterm infants of similar body weight,

Neonates in 250-g Body Weight Groups[a]

			Autopsies		
Spleen	Liver	Adrenals combined	Kidneys combined	Thymus	Brain
3.1 ± 1.2	40 ± 13	3.9 ± 1.9	11.8 ± 1.9	3.3 ± 1.5	150 ± 26
3.7 ± 1.9	53 ± 15	4.0 ± 1.4	13.2 ± 3.8	5.3 ± 2.4	173 ± 24
4.4 ± 1.9	64 ± 17	4.6 ± 1.8	14.8 ± 4.2	6.2 ± 2.4	202 ± 34
5.0 ± 2.0	73 ± 19	4.5 ± 1.9	15.6 ± 4.7	6.9 ± 2.9	234 ± 29
6.2 ± 2.1	84 ± 21	5.3 ± 2.0	19.0 ± 5.1	8.8 ± 3.4	259 ± 37
6.7 ± 2.6	89 ± 16	6.3 ± 1.6	19.0 ± 3.9	8.4 ± 3.2	290 ± 25
7.4 ± 2.3	105 ± 15	7.6 ± 2.6	21.4 ± 3.2	9.4 ± 4.3	330 ± 32
9.6 ± 3.1	112 ± 27	7.9 ± 2.4	23.6 ± 4.0	9.8 ± 3.1	355 ± 32
10.6 ± 4.7	133 ± 30	8.4 ± 2.7	24.0 ± 5.4	10.4 ± 4.2	379 ± 47
10.4 ± 3.5	140 ± 31	9.1 ± 2.9	27.6 ± 6.4	10.8 ± 4.6	398 ± 49
11.6 ± 4.3	151 ± 32	9.9 ± 3.3	28.1 ± 7.6	11.8 ± 4.8	413 ± 39
12.2 ± 3.8	176 ± 26	11.0 ± 3.7	30.1 ± 3.4	12.2 ± 3.5	426 ± 58

weights are in grams; body length is in centimeters.

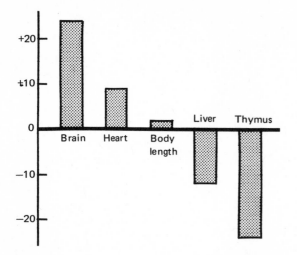

Fig. 4. Body length and organ weights of cases of chronic fetal distress (birth weight below mean minus 2 standard deviations for gestational age) expressed as percentages of values for normally grown infants of similar weight. Reproduced from Gruenwald[25] by courtesy of H. E. Stenfert Kroese, N. V.

growth-retarded neonates have a relatively large (less growth-retarded) brain, a somewhat larger heart, a relatively small liver (even more deficient in weight than the total body), and a very small thymus[25] (Fig. 4). The thymus is involuted as it would be in a child with postnatal malnutrition or chronic disease. This is pathologically the most spectacular demonstration of chronic fetal distress. An example of the usefulness of this information in confirming the existence of chronic fetal distress as opposed to preterm birth is given in Table V.

Histological maturation, much like functional maturity, correlates more closely with gestational age than with birth weight. As an example, sections of kidneys of two infants weighing about 1900 g are shown in Fig. 5. The one from the preterm infant, whose weight is commensurate with its gestational age, has under the capsule a layer of incompletely developed nephrons; the other kidney is that of a growth-retarded infant born at full term and is fully differentiated. It is impossible to tell whether this latter kidney is entirely normal for gestational age or perhaps slightly retarded. Existing

Table V. Weights and Measurements of Two Severely Growth-Retarded Neonates Compared with Values Normal for Their Gestational Age and Birth Weight[a]

	Normal standard for 38 weeks	Case I	Case II	Normal standard for 1750 g
Gestational age, nearest week	38	38	39	32
Body weight (g)	3050[b]	1795	1800	1750
Crown–heel length (cm)	50	44	44	43
Weight/length^3 × 10^3	24	21	22	22
Head circumference (cm)	33	30		30
Heart (g)	20	13	11	12
Liver (g)	130	62	53	73
Thymus (g)	12.5	5.1	4.7	6.9
Brain (g)	380	340	365	234
Placenta (g)	465	260	400	325
Placenta/body weight ratio	1:6.5	1:6.9	1:4.5	1:5.4

[a] Most values of the two cases show the trends characteristic of fetal growth retardation.
[b] Mean −2 S.D.: 2150 g.

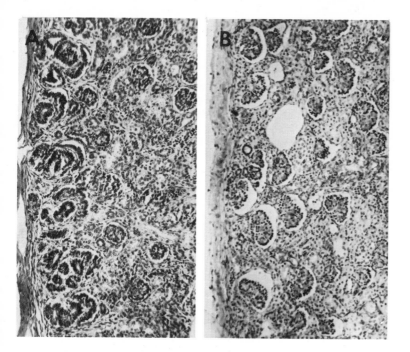

Fig. 5. Kidney sections from two infants weighing about 1800 g: (A) preterm infant with a weight adequate for gestational age; shown are immature nephrons near the capsule; (B) infant born at term and therefore growth-retarded; it has mature nephrons throughout. Each infant is at a stage commensurate with its gestational age. Reproduced from Gruenwald, P., Dawkins, M., and Hepner, P., *Sinia Hosp. J.* 2:54.

standards do not permit the determination of the degree of maturity within very narrow limits such as a single week; the same is true for other criteria.

The study of maturation of the brain occupies a place of special importance because of the great complexity, which should permit fine differentiation of developmental phases, and also because functional maturation is being studied in the living infant in great detail and with considerable success. Beyond simple weighing as discussed above, morphological characteristics of brain development were described by Larroche,[37] and a chemical approach to the assessment of myelination with increasing maturity was used by Davison and Dobbing.[14] All aspects of brain development under normal conditions as well as in states of deprivation need to be investigated in much more detail.

Cellular growth and multiplication are being examined by two methods: *in vitro* determinations of DNA and RNA (or protein) content of the body and its portions, and microscopic morphometry such as line-sampling. Histological visualization of cell multiplication by radioactive tracers has not been used to any extent in the field under consideration here. Winick and Noble[62] studied the growth of the rat before and after birth and found that increase in the amount of DNA is indicative of cell multiplication and stops in various

tissues at a characteristic time after birth, in most instances a few days postnatally. Similar work has not been done in man. Davison and Dobbing[14] illustrated with regard to brain development that processes occurring after birth in one species may occur prenatally in another. This difference surely applies to other parts of the body in principle if not in detail. Naeye[45] used morphometry particularly for comparison of normal and abnormal states in human neonates and found that both cell number and cell size are subnormal in fetal growth retardation, similar to what he saw in postnatal malnutrition.

Chemical criteria of fetal maturity by examination of amniotic and maternal fluids was reviewed in detail by DeVoe and Schwarz.[16]

4. The Placenta

In all considerations of the relationship of fetus and placenta, it is essential to remember that the placenta is a fetal organ. Its fixed tissue is fetal, including those layers that are actively or passively concerned with the transfer of materials between mother and fetus. The same holds true for the vessels and blood within the fixed tissue. Only the blood circulating in the intervillous space is maternal. To use a crude comparison, the fetal placental villi are bathed by maternal blood much as the intestinal villi are bathed by intestinal contents. The composition and circulation of blood in the intervillous space are under maternal control, and their abnormalities should therefore not be considered as placental insufficiency.

4.1. Growth and Structure

The normal ponderal growth of the human placenta during the third trimester of pregnancy in relation to gestational age and birth weight can be determined from Tables III and IV. The weight relationship between the fetus and the placenta is obviously a poor indicator of changes in placental adequacy, since maturation (presumably with increasing functional efficiency) and aging (possibly associated with decreasing efficiency) occur. Placental size correlates better with fetal weight than with gestational age, which must be expected, since the placenta is a fetal organ. Thus, a proportional deficit in the weight of the fetus and the placenta does not permit the conclusion that the small placenta was the cause of poor fetal growth. In fact, such a relationship of placental and fetal growth could exist only if the placenta were normally at the limit of its functional adequacy, which we have no right to assume. On the average, however, placental growth slows before fetal growth does. According to Winick *et al.*,[63] cell multiplication ceases in the human placenta at about 35 weeks of menstrual age. Subsequent growth is by cell enlargement and perhaps deposition of intercellular material.

The functionally most active cells in the placenta are those of the trophoblast, particularly the syncytium covering the villi. To what extent the cytotrophoblast has functions other than that of a source of syncytium is not known. As the placenta matures during the second half of pregnancy, the number of cytotrophoblastic cells on the surface of the terminal villi decreases. In the mature placenta, groups of these cells are conspicuously associated with deposits of fibrin at the border of the intervillous space. Another functionally significant factor of maturation is the increasing number of capillaries in the terminal villi, and their progressively closer proximity to the trophoblast on the surface. Shortly before term, degenerative changes usually appear, particularly fibrin deposition and calcification. The normal and functionally irrelevant limit

of amount and distribution of fibrin has not been determined. Calcification appears in nonfunctional areas, usually in fibrin deposits along the base of the placenta and villous stems, and has no known functional significance.

Placental vessels react to variations in oxygenation[48] and to drugs.[40,56] It is doubtful that the scant innervation that has been demonstrated in the umbilical cord and placenta in recent years is responsible for any of these reactions; they occur in placentas separated from fetuses. The syncytium of terminal villi reacts reversibly to low oxygenation by forming knots and syncytiovascular membranes; the membranes may facilitate exchange.[57]

4.2. "Placental Insufficiency"

It has been mentioned that there are few instances of primary pathologic reduction of the amount of functional placental tissue, such as choriohemangiomas. Other placental lesions such as infarction or long-standing premature separation are secondary to local disturbances in maternal blood supply. It was suggested above that there is no good evidence to suggest that apart from these sporadic cases, the placenta can limit the transmission of materials to the fetus to a physiologically significant extent in the presence of adequate levels in the maternal environment. Dawes[15] analyzed information on man and mammals in detail, and came to the conclusion that maternal as well as placental factors may be involved in limiting fetal growth, but it seems to this author that available information can be fully explained by the action of maternal factors alone. As was mentioned in Section 4 and also by Dawes, the correlation of fetal and placental size may well be due to the fact that the placenta is a fetal organ. One factor in particular that favors the predominant role of maternal factors is the relatively large size of the placenta of growth-retarded twins.[41,50] Whether placental insufficiency, rather than limitation by maternal factors, occurs in prolonged pregnancy in the absence of extensive pathologic changes is also undecided. The decline of exchange function mentioned above, coupled with lagging growth of the placenta relative to the fetus, makes the occurrence of placental insufficiency a possibility.

It is important not to use the term *placental insufficiency* indiscriminately, since true, primary placental insufficiency is probably quite rare. The use of this term distracts from study of the maternal organism that is responsible, often in a manner that is still unknown, for fetal deprivation. Yet, in contrast to the placenta, the mother can be investigated, and this possibility opens a wide field for study.

5. Perinatal Mortality in Relation to Fetal Growth and Maturation

Many studies have substantiated what would be expected, namely, that there is an optimum range of maturity and fetal growth that carries the lowest risk of perinatal death. Karn and Penrose[34] illustrated this by entering on a grid of weight and gestational age circular lines connecting points of equal risk of mortality. When one considers mortality rates, there is a well-known, spectacular drop with increasing weight or gestational age, followed by an increase at very high weights or past term. The number of births in the optimum range is so much greater, however, that in most populations, e.g., that studied in the British Perinatal Mortality Survey of 1958 (Fig. 6), the largest *number* of deaths occurs in the period with the lowest *rate*, namely, at term. With regard to weight, a large decrease in numbers of cases in 500-g groups occurred in the same population only above 3000 g.[28] Thus, the common belief that prematurity is the principal cause or association of perinatal death holds true as far as any given individual is concerned, but not necessarily for populations.

The risk of perinatal death, and with it presumably that of nonfatal damage, is high in preterm infants because of their poor ability to adapt to extrauterine life. It is also high in mature, growth-retarded infants of similar weight because of the damage inflicted by chronic fetal distress and the sudden aggravation of deprivation during the birth process. This explains why birth weight correlates better with mortality than does gestational age.[44] The causes of mortality in immaturity and in

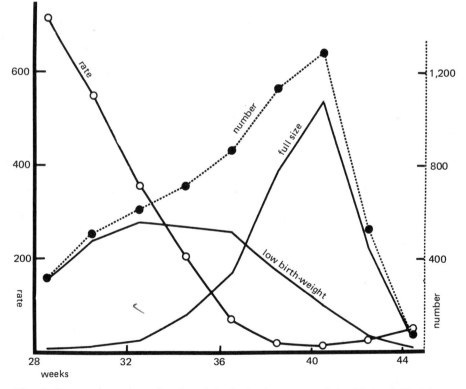

Fig. 6. Rate and number of perinatal deaths in the survey of the National Birthday Trust Fund. The lowest rate and the highest number of deaths coincide at term. Reproduced from Gruenwald[28] by courtesy of E. & S. Livingstone, Ltd.

chronic fetal distress are vastly different, however, and it is fair to suppose that the sequelae in damaged survivors are too. That they are is not well known because in the past, most studies were based on birth weight alone.

It is clear that throughout fetal life, normal or deficient growth and maturation determine the chance of a normal outcome. Maturation is the more basic of the two, in the sense that it is the result of genetically determined developmental processes and is little affected by the environment during the period under consideration here. Growth, on the other hand, while also subject to genetic determinants, varies considerably in response to environmental factors. Also, the ability of a neonate to adjust to extrauterine life depends to a greater extent on past maturation, and therefore on gestational age, than on past growth. In evaluating infants by weight and duration of pregnancy, it is therefore appropriate to vary birth weight on gestational age as most investigators have done, rather than gestational age on birth weight, as suggested by van den Berg and Yerushalmy.[59]

One of the most urgent needs in perinatal physiology is for the development of methods for objectively determining the degree of maturity in the healthy as well as the sick infant. This determination is complicated by the possibility that various aspects of maturation may not always proceed, or be inhibited, at the same rate, as exemplified by differences in neuromotor maturation between Caucasian and Negro neonates.[10]

6. References

1. AMERICAN ACADEMY OF PEDIATRICS, COMMITTEE ON FETUS AND NEWBORN, 1967, Nomenclature for duration of gestation, birth weight and intra-uterine growth, *Pediatrics* **39**:935–939.
2. BABSON, S. G., BEHRMAN, R. E., AND LESSEL, R., 1970, Fetal growth: Liveborn birth weights for gestational age of white middle class infants, *Pediatrics* **45**:944–947.
3. BAIRD, D., THOMSON, A. M., AND BILLEWICZ, W. Z., 1957, Birth weights and placental weights in preeclampsia, *J. Obstet. Gynaecol. Br. Emp.* **64**:370–372.
4. BAKWIN, H., AND McLAUGHLIN, S. M., 1964, Secular increase in height: Is the end in sight?, *Lancet* **2**:1195, 1196.
5. BARCROFT, J., 1947, *Researches on Pre-natal Life*, p. 59, Charles C. Thomas, Springfield, Illinois.
6. BEAUDRY, P. H., AND SUTHERLAND, J. M., 1960, Birth weights of infants of toxemic mothers, *J. Pediatr.* **56**:505–509.
7. BIENIARZ, J., ROMERO-SALINS, G., CURCHET, E., AND YOSHIDA, T., 1966, Evaluacion de la eficiencia funcional placentaria por el metodo de angio et radiografia seriada, *Prog. Obstet. Ginecol.* **9**:367–406.
8. BIENIARZ, J., CROTTOGINI, J. J., CURUCHET, E., ROMERO-SALINAS, G., YOSHIDA, T., POSEIRO, J. J., AND CALDEYRO-BARCIA, R., 1968, Aortocaval compression by the uterus in late human pregnancy. II. An arteriographic study, *Amer. J. Obstet. Gynecol.* **100**:203–217.
9. BRANS, Y. W., AND CASSADY, G., 1975, Intrauterine growth and maturation in relation to fetal deprivation, in: *The Placenta and Its Maternal Supply Line* (P. Gruenwald, ed.), Chapt. 18, Medical and Technical Publishing Co., Lancaster, England, and University Park Press, Baltimore.
10. BRETT, E., 1965, The estimation of foetal maturity by the neurological examination of the neonate, *Clin. Dev. Med.* **19**:105–116.
11. BUTLER, N. R., AND BONHAM, D. G., 1963, *Perinatal Mortality: The First Report of the 1958 British Perinatal Mortality Survey*, under the auspices of the National Birthday Trust Fund, E. & S. Livingstone, Edinburgh.
12. CAMPBELL, S., 1975, Ultrasonic and radiological examination, in: *The Placenta and Its Maternal Supply Line* (P. Gruenwald, ed.), Chapt. 17, Medical and Technical Publishing Co., Lancaster, England, and University Park Press, Baltimore.
13. CHEEK, D. B. (ed.), 1968, *Human Growth: Body Composition, Energy, and Intelligence*, Lea and Febiger, Philadelphia.
14. DAVISON, A. N., AND DOBBING, J., 1966, Myelination as a vulnerable period in brain development, *Br. Med. Bull.* **22**:40–44.
15. DAWES, G. S., 1968, *Foetal and Neonatal Physiology: A Comparative Study of the Changes at Birth*, Year Book Medical Publishers, Chicago.
16. DeVOE, S. J., AND SCHWARZ, 1975, in: *The Placenta and Its Maternal Supply Line* (P. Gruenwald, ed.), Chapt. 16, Medical and Technical Publishing Co., Lancaster, England, and University Park Press, Baltimore.
17. FARR, V., KERRIDGE, D. F., AND MITCHELL, R. G., 1966, The value of some external characteristics in the assessment of gestational age at birth, *Dev. Med. Child Neurol.* **8**:657–660.
18. FEE, B. A., AND WEIL, W. B., JR., 1963, Body composition of infants of diabetic mothers by direct analysis, *Ann. N. Y. Acad. Sci.* **110**:869–897.
19. FRAZIER, T. M., DAVIS, G. H., GOLDSTEIN, H., AND GOLDBERG, I. D., 1961, Cigarette smoking and prematurity: A prospective study, *Amer. J. Obstet. Gynecol.* **81**:988–996.

20. GRUENWALD, P., 1963, Chronic fetal distress and placental insufficiency, *Biol. Neonat.* **5**:215–265.

21. GRUENWALD, P., 1964, The fetus in prolonged pregnancy, *Amer. J. Obstet. Gynecol.* **89**:503–509.

22. GRUENWALD, P., 1966, Growth of the human fetus. I. Normal growth and its variation, *Amer. J. Obstet. Gynecol.* **94**:1112–1119.

23. GRUENWALD, P., 1966, Growth of the human fetus. II. Abnormal growth in twins and infants of mothers with diabetes, hypertension, or isoimmunization, *Amer. J. Obstet. Gynecol.* **94**:1120–1132.

24. GRUENWALD, P., 1967, Growth of the human foetus, *Adv. Reprod. Physiol.* **2**:279–309.

25. GRUENWALD, P., 1968, Growth pattern of the normal and the deprived fetus, in: *Nutricia Symposium: Aspects of Prematurity and Dysmaturity* (J. H. P. Jonxis, H. K. A. Visser, and J. A. Troelstra, eds.), H. E. Stenfert Kroese, Leiden, The Netherlands.

26. GRUENWALD, P., 1968, Deprivation of the human fetus: Forms, causes and significance, in: *Diagnoses and Treatment of Fetal Disorders* (E. Adamsons, ed.), Springer-Verlag, New York.

27. GRUENWALD, P., 1968, Fetal growth as an indicator of socio-economic change, *Public Health Rep.* **83**: 867–872.

28. GRUENWALD, P., 1969, Growth and maturation of the foetus and its relationship to perinatal mortality, in: *Perinatal Problems* (N. R. Butler and E. D. Alberman, eds.), pp. 141–162, E. & S. Livingstone, Edinburgh.

29. GRUENWALD, P., 1974, Pathology of the deprived fetus and its supply line, in: *Size at Birth* (K. Elliot and J. Knight, eds.), *Ciba Found. Symp. (New Ser.)* **27**:3–19.

30. GRUENWALD, P., 1976, Environmental influences on twins apparent at birth, *Biol. Neonat.,* **28**: 125–132.

31. GRUENWALD, P., DAWKINS, M., AND HEPNER, R., 1963, Panel discussion: Chronic deprivation of the fetus, *Sinia Hosp. J.* (Baltimore) **11**:51–80.

32. GRUENWALD, P., FUNAKAWA, H., MITANI, S., NISHIMORA, T., AND TAKEUCHI, S., 1967, Influence of environmental factors on foetal growth in man, *Lancet* **1**:1026–1029.

33. HENDRICKS, C. H., 1967, Delivery patterns and reproductive efficiency among groups of differing socioeconomic status and ethnic origins, *Amer. J. Obstet. Gynecol.* **97**:608–619.

34. KARN, M. N., AND PENROSE, L. S., 1951, Birth weight and gestation time in relation to maternal age, parity and infant survival, *Ann. Eugen.* **16**: 147–164.

35. KAUPPINEN, M. A., 1967, The correlation of maternal heart volume with the birth weight of the infant and prematurity, *Acta Obstet. Cynecol. Scand.* **46**(*Suppl. 6*):1–128.

36. KLOOSTERMAN, G. J., 1966, Prevention of prematurity, *Ned. Tijdschr. Verloskd. Gynaecol.* **66**:361–379.

37. LARROCHE, J. C., 1962, Quelques aspects anatomiques du développement cérébral, *Biol. Neonat.* **4**:126–153.

38. LINDELL, A., 1956, Prolonged pregnancy, *Acta Obstet. Gynecol. Scand.* **35**:136–163.

39. LUBCHENCO, L. O., HANSMAN, C., DRESSLER, M., AND BOYD, E., 1963, Intrauterine growth as estimated from liveborn birth-weight data at 24 to 42 weeks of gestation, *Pediatrics* **32**:793–800.

40. MANCINI, R. T., AND GAUTIERI, R. R., 1964, Effect of certain drugs on perfused human placenta. IV. Detection of specific receptor sites, *J. Pharm. Sci.* **53**:1476–1481.

41. MCKEOWN, T., AND RECORD, R. G., 1952, Observations of foetal growth in multiple pregnancy in man, *J. Endocrinol.* **8**:386–401.

42. MCKEOWN, T., AND RECORD, R. G., 1953, The influence of placental size of foetal growth in man, with special reference to multiple pregnancy, *J. Endocrinol.* **9**:418–426.

43. MCLAREN, A., AND MICHIE, D., 1960, Control of prenatal growth in mammals, *Nature (London)* **187**:363–365.

44. MELLIN, G. W., 1962, Fetal life tables: A means of establishing perinatal rates of risk, *J. Amer. Med. Assoc.* **180**:91–94.

45. NAEYE, R. L., 1965, Malnutrition: Probable cause of fetal growth retardation, *Arch. Pathol.* **79**:284–291.

46. NAEYE, R. L., AND KELLEY, J. A., 1966, Judgment of fetal age. III. The pathologist's evaluation, *Pediatr. Clin. North Amer.* **13**:849–862.

47. NELIGAN, G., 1965, A community study of the relationship between birth weight and gestational age, *Clin. Dev. Med.* **19**:28–32.

48. NYBERG, R., AND WESTIN, B., 1957, The influence of oxygen tension and some drugs on human placental vessels, *Acta Physiol. Scand.* **39**:216–227.

49. OUNSTED, M., AND OUNSTED, C., 1966, Maternal regulation of intra-uterine growth, *Nature (London)* **212**:995–997.

50. PANKAMAA, P., AND ASCHAN, E., 1958, Über das Verhältnis zwischen Frucht und Plazenta bei Zwillingsschwangerschaften, *Chir. Gynaecol. Fenn.* **47**(*Suppl. 81*): 156–159.

51. RÄIHÄ, , C. E., 1956, On the significance of prematurity in pediatrics of today, its causes and possible prevention, *Etud. Neo-Natales* **5**:87–96.

52. SECOND EUROPEAN CONGRESS OF PERINATAL MEDICINE, 1970, Working Party to Discuss Nomenclature Based on Gestational Age and Birth Weight, *Arch. Dis. Child.* **45**:730.

53. SCOTT, K. E., AND USHER, R., 1964, Epiphyseal development in fetal malnutrition syndrome, *New Engl. J. Med.* **270**:822–824.

54. SINCLAIR, J. C., SCOPES, J. W., AND SILVERMAN, W. A., 1967, Metabolic reference standards for the neonate, *Pediatrics* **39**:724–732.

55. STERNBERG, J., 1962, Placental transfers: Modern methods of study, *Amer. J. Obstet. Gynecol.* **84**:1731–1748.

56. THOMSEN, K., 1963, Die Beeinflüssung der Hämo-
    dynamik perfundierter Placenten durch Pharmaka,
    Arch. Gynaekol. **198**:60–64.
57. TOMINAGA, T., AND PAGE, E. W., 1966, Accom-
    modation of the human placenta to hypoxia, *Amer.
    J. Obstet. Gynecol.* **94**:679–691.
58. USHER, R., MCLEAN, F., AND SCOTT, K. E., 1966,
    Judgment of fetal age. II. Clinical significance of
    gestational age and an objective method for its
    assessment, *Pediatr. Clin. North Amer.* **13**:835–848.
59. VAN DEN BERG, B. J., AND YERUSHALMY, J., 1966,
    The relationship of the rate of intruterine growth
    of infants of low birth weight to mortality, morbidity
    and congenital anomalies, *J. Pediatr.* **69**:531–545.
60. WIDDOWSON, E. M., AND SPRAY, C. M., 1951,
    Chemical development *in utero,* *Arch. Dis. Child.*
    26:205–214.

61. WIGGLESWORTH, J. S., 1964, Experimental growth
    retardation in the foetal rat, *J. Pathol. Bacteriol.* **88**:1–13.
62. WINICK, M., AND NOBLE, A., 1965, Quantitative
    changes in DNA, RNA, and protein during prenatal
    and postnatal growth in the rat, *Devl. Biol.*
    12:451–466.
63. WINICK, M., COSICIA, A., AND NOBLE, A., 1967,
    Cellular growth in human placenta. I. Normal
    placental growth, *Pediatrics* **39**:248–251.
64. WORLD HEALTH ORGANIZATION, EXPERT COMMITTEE
    ON MATERNAL AND CHILD HEALTH, 1961, Public
    health aspects of low birth weight, *WHO Tech. Rep.
    Ser.* **217**:1–16.
65. ZUCKERMAN, S. (leader), 1950, A discussion on the
    measurement of growth and form, *Proc. R. Soc.
    London Ser. B* **137**:433–523.

CHAPTER 2

The Placenta: An Overview

Joseph Dancis

1. Introduction

A unique feature of mammalian reproduction is the prolonged protective period afforded to the young, which often extends for years after birth. During the earliest stages of critical development, maximum protection is given by retaining the fetus within the mother. Intrauterine pregnancy marked a major evolutionary departure from previous modes of reproduction, requiring anatomic and physiologic adjustments on the part of the mother and fetus. The development of the placenta by the fetus is unique among these adjustments in that the sole function of this organ is to make intrauterine pregnancy possible.

2. "Growth and Development" of the Placenta

The initial nutrition of the conceptus is from the interstitial fluids. A store of food is not deposited with the embryo, as it is with egg-laying animals, although the fetal membranes that absorb nutrients are developed. Two of these membranes, the chorion and the allantois, are extensively modified to form the placenta. By 17 days of gestation, fetal and maternal circulations are readily visible. The fetal villi erode through the maternal epithelium of the uterus, penetrating maternal vessels and forming a maternal sinusoid into which the villi dip.

In the earliest stages, the placenta is larger than the embryo, but is quickly outstripped in size. The greater nutritive demands developed during growth of the fetus are satisfied by an increasing efficiency within the placenta. An extensive absorbing surface is achieved within limited space by a branching system of chorionic villi capped by microvilli. The terminal villi progressively fill with thin-walled capillaries. This remarkable intimacy between the maternal and fetal circulations permits the efficient exchange of materials. By this mechanism, the maternal blood composition, which is maintained within narrow limits by finely developed homeostatic controls, becomes a major factor in maintaining constancy of fetal blood composition.

The phenomenon of placental senescence appears to vary among mammalian species. In the human, thickening of the basement membranes of endothelium and trophoblast, obliteration of fetal and maternal vessels, and deposition of fibrinoid around the villi suggest diminution of function. This con-

Joseph Dancis · Department of Pediatrics, New York University School of Medicine, New York, New York 10016

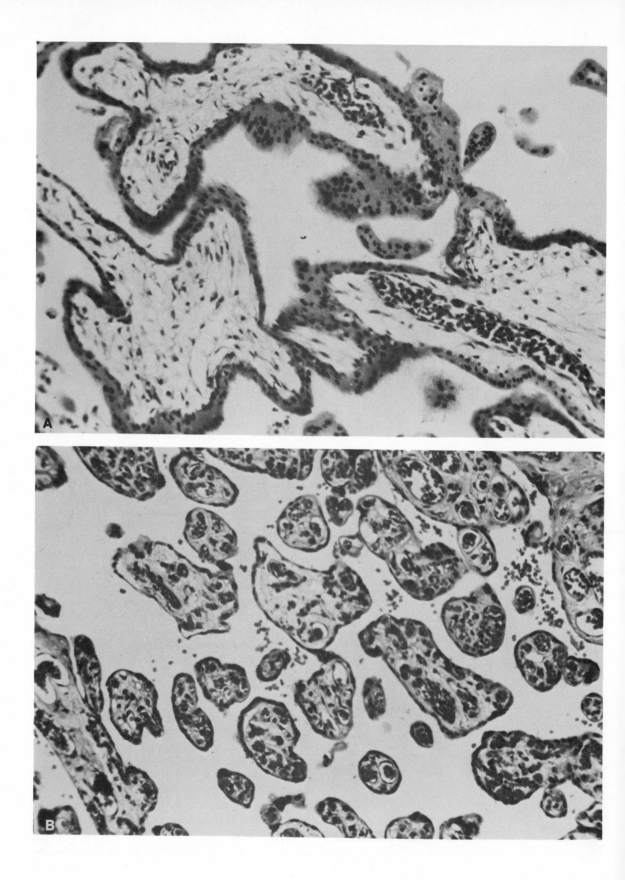

cept is supported by studies of sodium transfer demonstrating a progressive inefficiency during gestation, peaking at about 36 weeks with a decline toward 40 weeks.

3. Placental Metabolism

The emphasis on the placenta as a transport organ tends to obscure the fact that it is very active metabolically. Since it is, it also has significant nutritive requirements that must be derived from the mother. Thus, an estimated 17% of the oxygen directed toward the conceptus at term is preempted by the placenta. Mechanisms for extracting and utilizing nutritive materials are present in the placenta, as they are in other metabolically active organs.

In addition to the expected general catalogue of enzymes and physiologic mechanisms, there are those features that make the placenta unique, or at least unusual. Many of the transport processes have been modified to make nutrients available to the fetus as well as to itself. Conversions by the placenta may facilitate transport or modify the transported substrate. For example, the excretion of fetal estrogen sulfates is greatly enhanced by placental sulfatases, whereas an active insulinase increases the barrier to the transfer of insulin. Maternal cortisol is largely converted to the less physiologically active cortisone before it reaches the fetus. Claude Bernard first called attention to the fact that the first-trimester placenta is rich in glycogen, and that these stores disappear by term. The "purpose" of this metabolic peculiarity of the placenta is still uncertain, despite the persistent inclination to designate the placenta as a fetal liver.

As the largest mammalian endocrine organ, the placenta possesses the machinery for synthesizing liberal amounts of steroids and protein hormones

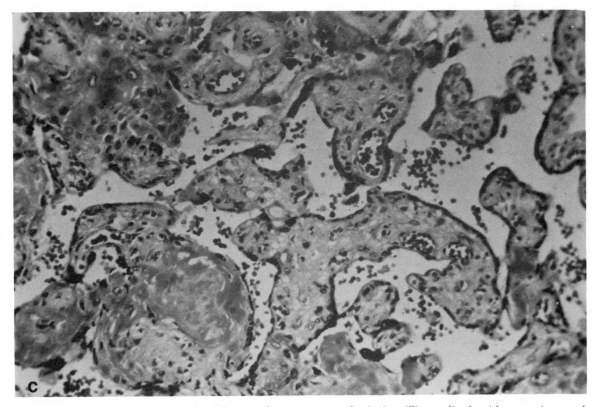

Fig. 1. Cross sections of chorionic villi: (A) first trimester—chorionic villi are lined with syncytium and cytotrophoblast and are sparsely vascularized; (B) third trimester—illustrating extensive vascularization with fetal vessels separated by a thin membrane from maternal vascular channels (the intervillous space); (C) third trimester—another section of the same placenta illustrating senescent changes, including a relative decrease in fetal vessels and partial hyalinization of villi reflecting fibrinoid deposition. By courtesy of Dr. F. Gorstein.

(see Chapter 37). In some respects, as for estrogens, it is incomplete, relying on contributions from the mother or fetus of prefabricated materials or missing enzymatic steps. In some respects, it appears to be amazingly complete, supplying both trophic and target hormones, though these relationships are still indistinct.

The placenta has gained a new prominence as a newly appreciated source of "fetal-type" proteins. Oncologists and biochemists, intent on mapping the metabolic activities of neoplasms for purposes of diagnosis and treatment, are recognizing fascinating parallels to the placenta. For example, the HeLa cell maintained for years in tissue culture from a uterine malignancy still synthesizes placental alkaline phosphatase and human chorionic gonadotropin.

The placenta has become an important subject of study, not only to the reproductive physiologists, but to medical biologists of a wide array of different disciplines.

4. Endocrine Functions

The placenta is the largest and most versatile endocrine organ in the human. It undoubtedly plays a pivotal role in maintaining pregnancy and in inducing many metabolic changes in the mother and fetus. There is general acceptance that the placenta synthesizes four hormones: chorionic gonadotropin (HCG); chorionic somatomammotropin (HCS), also called placental lactogen; progesterone; and the estrogens. Suggestions concerning possible synthesis of other hormones await confirmation.

Endocrine synthesis is in the syncytiotrophoblast. The steroids are secreted in high concentration into the maternal and fetal circulations, inducing significant systemic effects as well as direct effects on the decidua. The peptide hormones are secreted unidirectionally into the maternal circulation, modifying maternal metabolism.

The synthesis of estrogens and progesterone increases rapidly during pregnancy, reaching very high levels by term. Early in gestation, the corpus luteum is the site of synthesis, but by 7 weeks, placental synthesis of steroids is adequate to maintain pregnancy even after oophorectomy. The synthesis of placental steroids requires a cooperative effort on the part of the placenta and fetus (Fig. 2). Placental progesterone, in turn, serves as precursor for fetal synthesis of corticosteroids, androstenedione, and testosterone (see also Chapter 37).

The protein hormones are related biochemically to pituitary hormones. HCG is composed of two subunits, the α subunit being very similar to that in luteinizing hormone, follicle-stimulating hormone, and thyroid-stimulating hormone. Biological specificity appears to reside in the β subunit. HCG production peaks at 60–70 days, and then remains at a low plateau for the rest of pregnancy. The significance of this pattern of production is not understood. Early synthesis is believed responsible for the maintenance of the corpeus luteum of pregnancy. HCG suppresses the response of lymphocytes to mitogens, suggesting that it may contribute to the prevention of immunologic rejection by the mother.

HCS is remarkably similar in amino acid sequence and structure to growth hormone. The amount synthesized increases throughout pregnancy, reaching the relatively enormous amount, for a hormone, of approximately 1 g per day at term. Its biological effect during pregnancy appears to be the reverse of insulin, converting maternal metabolism to increased utilization of lipids and making glucose more readily available to the fetus.

5. Immunologic Functions

An aspect of intrauterine pregnancy that has provoked considerable interest is the suppression of immunologic rejection of the fetus by the mother. The fetus differs genetically from the mother by virtue of the paternal complement of genes. Such dissimilarities should initiate a cellular response in the mother leading to elimination of the fetus. It has become clear that several factors contribute to the protection of the fetus, and that the placenta plays a central role in the phenomenon. The placenta protects the fetus from a major invasion of maternal cells, although transplacental cellular traffic does occur to a limited extent. The trophoblast, which is fetal and is directly exposed to maternal blood, also escapes attack. Several explanations have been offered. It has been suggested that the trophoblast is not antigenically active, that this may be because of a protective coat of sialomucin, or that the antigenic sites may be "masked" by maternal antibodies. Suppression of the maternal immune response by placental hormones has also been described. It is very likely that the outcome of pregnancy depends on the successful operation of more than one of these mechanisms.

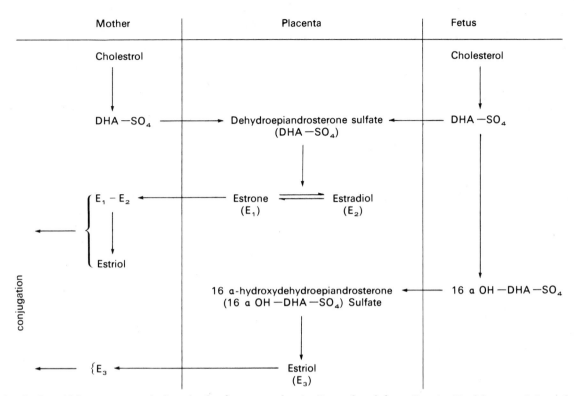

Fig. 2. Steroid hormone metabolism in the fetomaternal unit. Reproduced from Dancis. Used by permission of J. B. Lippincott Co., Philadelphia.

It should be stressed that the immunologic reaction of the mother is not eliminated. The mother does respond to the fetus, but the nature of the response is controlled so that rejection is avoided. In fact, evidence has been presented that the maternal immune reaction may contribute to the vigor of the outbred offspring (see Table I).

A major advantage to the fetus of intrauterine pregnancy is protection against invasion by pathogenic organisms. For pathogens to reach the fetus, they must first breach maternal defense and invade the bloodstream. Even then, microorganisms in any significant numbers are generally excluded from the fetal circulation unless the placenta becomes infected. Cells of the lymphoid series have been described in the placenta that may have originated locally and may contribute an immunologic defense.

During intrauterine gestation, the fetal immunologic system develops so that the infant at birth is capable of both humoral and cellular responses. Because of its insular position prior to birth, however, the newborn infant would be born without circulating antibodies if they were not provided by the mother. In the human, the placenta is provided with recognition sites for IgG, which permit it to selectively bind maternal antibody for transfer to the fetus. Temporary protection is thus provided while the infant further develops its own immunologic defenses (see Chapter 14 for details).

6. Placental Transport

Biological membranes serve to delimit organic units from their surroundings. By selectively controlling transfer of materials, they maintain the identity of the confined unit. In this respect, the placenta is a fetal membrane, albeit a complex one. The placenta is unique among membranes in being exposed on each side to circulating blood (see Chapters 6 and 8). That transfer is to and from protein-rich media influences the characteristics of transport.

Four mechanisms for transfer across membranes are generally recognized. In simple diffusion, transfer

Table I. Theories Propounded to Account for the Invulnerability of the Fetoplacental Unit to Rejection[a]

Altered immunologic responsiveness of mother	Uterus	Trophoblast	Fetus
Nonspecific			
1. Placental protein or steroid hormones	1. Complete separation of fetal and maternal circulations	1. Nonantigenic	1. Antigenic immaturity
2. Plasma factors	2. Immunologically privileged site (decidual tissue)	2. Physiologic barrier	2. Serum factors (fetuin)
		3. Local immuno-suppression by hormones (HCG and HCS)	
Specific			
1. Antibody-mediated suppression			
2. Adult tolerance			

[a] Reproduced from Beer and Billingham.[3] Copyright © 1974 by Year Book Medical Publishers, Inc., Chicago. Used by permission.

occurs when a concentration gradient exists across the membrane. In the placenta, the rate of presentation to the membrane by one circulation and removal by the other circulation exerts a major influence on transfer rates. The physicochemical state of the molecule within the circulation, whether protein-bound (e.g., free fatty acids and divalent ions) or part of large complexes (e.g., neutral fats and certain vitamins), is also influential. Finally, the diffusion resistance within the placenta for the particular substrate affects the rate of transfer (see also Chapter 25).

In facilitated diffusion, transfer is speeded by a mechanism that does not require energy and will not transfer against a gradient. Glucose and apparently oxygen, two nutrients required in large amounts by the fetus, are transferred in this way. In active transport, energy is expended to transfer the material against an electrochemical gradient. For example, amino acids are transferred to the fetus "uphill." The molecular explanation of these transport mechanisms is currently under intense investigation. Large molecules such as proteins are transferred by pinocytosis. Transfer is relatively slow, but can be significant, as it is with antibodies.

Our knowledge concerning placental transfer in the human is very incomplete. Ethical issues prohibit many types of study, forcing a dependence on animal and in vitro experiments. There is reasonable confidence that water diffuses rapidly across the placenta in response to osmotic differences, and that urea and sodium find relatively little resistance to simple diffusion. Free fatty acids are impeded by protein-binding and appear to contribute little to the energy requirements of the human fetus. Three of the nutrients required in large supply, oxygen, glucose, and amino acids, have specific transport mechanisms, as indicated above. The water-soluble vitamins are in higher concentration in the fetal circuit, leading to the simple assumption that active transport occurs. They circulate in multiple forms, however, and alternative explanations of the concentration gradient are possible. In contrast, the lipid-soluble vitamins are in lower concentration in the fetal circulation. Mechanisms and rates of transport are, again, obscure.

Certain generalizations can be made about the transfer of hormones. Steroids are transferred rapidly, whereas the transfer of the protein hormones appears to be too slow to exert significant physiologic effect. The same is true for thyroid hormones.

The divalent cations (iron, zinc, calcium, magnesium) are transferred against concentration gradients. Iron transfer has been studied extensively in the rodent. Specific receptors in the placenta bind the maternal iron–transferrin complex and release iron for transfer to the fetus. Transfer is unidirectional (see Chapter 20 for details).

A common question that arises during the discussion of placental transport is whether a particular substance crosses the placenta. The question is an incomplete one. Given a sufficiently extended time scale and a sufficiently sensitive detection method, it is probably possible to demonstrate some transfer of all circulating materials. Even circulating blood cells regularly cross the placental barrier. The significance of the transfer will vary, however, according to transfer rate and fetal need. For example, it was long questioned whether maternal proteins were transferred to the fetus. The development of radio-active techniques made it possible to detect a slow rate of transfer of γ-globulin. The slow utilization rate by the fetus permits this inefficient transfer mechanism to provide the fetus with the protection of circulating maternal antibodies. In contrast, the short half-life of other plasma proteins coupled with their slow transfer rates makes the maternal contribution insignificant.

7. The Fetal "Parasite"

In the final analysis, the fetus must draw its nourishment from the mother. As a rapidly growing organism, it undoubtedly draws a disproportionate share per unit weight of available nutrients. The concept that the placenta extracts from the mother all its requirements, regardless of maternal need, is, however, an oversimplification. Observa-

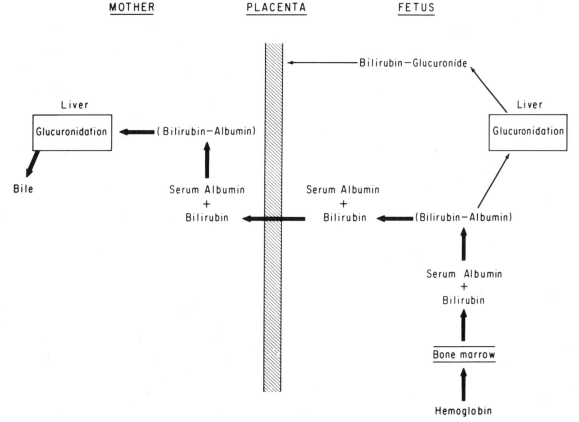

Fig. 3. Excretion of bilirubin. Fetal and maternal pathways for bilirubin excretion are coordinated to dispose of fetal bilirubin through the mother. Reproduced from Dancis. Used by permission of J. B. Lippincott Co., Philadelphia.

tions made during mass starvation in World War II have clearly demonstrated that limited maternal intake has its impact on the fetus, particularly during the third trimester.

Specific nutritional deficiencies in the pregnant rat have given some indication of the complexity of the situation. Restriction of sodium intake resulted in relatively equivalent hyponatremia in mother and fetus, both sharing the limited resources. Nutritionally induced hypokalemia sharply lowered maternal serum and muscle potassium with relatively little effect on fetal composition, more consistent with the notion of "parasitism." Magnesium deficiency during the last 2 weeks of pregnancy had little detectable effect on the mother, clinically or biochemically, but the young were runted and had a severe hemolytic anemia associated with hypomagnesemia. Maternal magnesium was not made freely available to the fetus.

8. Maternal–Placental–Fetal Interaction

A sharply focused inquiry into placental function may be disappointing and even bewildering if the attempt is not made to relate the results to the total maternal–fetal unit. Two examples will suffice to make the point.

It had been known for many years that the human placenta synthesized large amounts of estrogens. Investigators were puzzled because they could not demonstrate synthesis *in vitro* from simple precursors. The solution was not evident until the interplay between fetus and placenta, the "feto-placental unit" of Egon Diczfalusy, was recognized (see Chapter 37).

Hyperbilirubinemia of the newborn is an old observation that gained new prominence when the threat of kernicterus was appreciated. The cause was assumed to be a temporary maturational incompetence in bilirubin excretion. It is now clear that antepartum excretion of fetal bilirubin across the placenta requires suppression of glucuronidation because the conjugate is poorly transferred. This situation must be reversed after birth to make biliary excretion possible (Fig. 3). The problem arises not from a maturational arrest, but from the requirements imposed by finding two different solutions for biliary excretion—one that is appropriate to maintain life prior to birth and the other to an independent existence after birth (see Chapter 23 for details).

9. References

1. Dancis, J., 1975, Feto–maternal interaction, *in*: *Neonatology* (G. W. Avery, ed.), J. B. Lippincott Co., Philadelphia.
2. Dancis, J., and Schneider, H., 1975, Physiology: Transfer and barrier function, *in*: *The Placenta and Its Maternal Supply Line* (P. Gruenwald, ed.), Medical and Technical Publishing Co., Lancaster, England, and University Park Press, Baltimore.
3. Beer, A. E., and Billingham, R. E., 1974, Immunologic coexistence in the maternal–fetal relationship, *in*: *Modern Perinatal Medicine* (L. Gluck, ed.), Year Book Medical Publishers, Chicago.

CHAPTER 3

Maturation, Adaptation, and Tolerance

Uwe Stave

1. Introduction

The physiology of the newborn mammal is much more complex than the physiology of mature animals. By definition, physiology is the knowledge of functions and vital processes of the organism, its parts, and its organs. Neonatal physiology deals with a growing organism that has just suffered from a stressful parturition and is engaged in adjusting its vital functions to extrauterine life. The somatic and functional changes that predominate in this period of life are greater than those at any other time; therefore, neonatal physiology aims to establish a knowledge of the driving forces underlying these functional changes rather than to provide descriptions of functional levels or capacities.

Three factors have been found to be the determining forces for functional changes; maturation, adaptation, and tolerance. *Maturation* will be used[14] here to designate the *genetically determined* (autonomous) *functional and morphological differentiation*. Basically, maturation is, like differentiation, irreversible.

Although adaptation is a basic requirement of life, we usually describe the normal functions of the adult organism without considering adaptation as a determining factor; in neonatal physiology, however, adaptation plays a more decisive role.

The newborn is engaged in a process of transition from the sheltered intrauterine to the exposed extrauterine environment that imposes many new physical and chemical stimuli on the organism. Furthermore, the prenatal maturation prepares the newborn organism for postnatal adaptation. On these premises, Linneweh[15] defined *neonatal adaptation* as *the exogenously accelerated maturation*. Neonatal adaptation prevails in the neonatal period, but soon after birth, other adaptational phenomena can begin to occur if the environment is unusually unfavorable.

If we consider the various stressful events (stressors) that occur during the expulsion period and at birth, and furthermore, if we refer to possible birth traumas as events that may produce shock, we can rightfully use the term *birth stress*.[14,23] The many stimuli that begin to act on the neonate in the immediate perinatal period belong, however, in a group of expected new experiences. Such stimuli will be discussed in detail below. One or the other stimulus can become perilously strong, or even

Uwe Stave · Mailman Center for Child Development and Department of Pediatrics, University of Miami School of Medicine, Miami, Florida 33152

traumatic, and such stressful conditions do not produce the typical alarm reaction as they would in adults. Instead, in the immediate perinatal period, the fetus and newborn disclose a remarkable tolerance for enduring birth hazards. *Neonatal tolerance* has therefore been mentioned as the third major factor in neonatal physiology.

In the following sections, the three major factors of postnatal development—maturation, adaptation, and tolerance—will be analyzed and evaluated. Knowledge of the particular role that is played by each of these factors is indispensable for performing research in neonatology. In addition, this knowledge will be helpful in understanding the specific problems evolving from the study of functional behavior in newborns.

2. Maturation

It might be self-evident that maturation should be regarded as a major factor in neonatal physiology, but in connection with neonatal adaptation, some basic characteristics and examples will be discussed. Perinatal maturation includes physical growth and functional differentiation. Physical growth concerns mainly an increase in cell number and size, but our attention will be focused on functional differentiation. The initiation of a new function or functional units, as, for example, the circulation or renal excretion, might easily be designated as autonomous if it occurs during intrauterine development. At birth, however, the organism is suddenly exposed to many new exogenous stimuli, so that an evaluation as to whether a certain functional change is exogenously accelerated or proceeding at an autonomously set pace can become extremely difficult. Some of the circulatory changes at birth and during the newborn period are predetermined to occur in a certain sequence (see Chapter 8). Simultaneously, at birth, the lung begins to function and subsequently changes its prenatal organization into the postnatal pattern (Chapters 6 and 7). Such rapid functional changes at birth are basically maturational events; they are indispensable for survival, and they are part of the developmental master plan. In addition, however, those systems used as examples are capable of adaptation, and this ability increases quickly after birth.

The postnatal increase of renal functions is predominantly a process of maturation, and several excretory functions were already in existence before birth. The capacity to excrete certain ions or compounds usually serves to evaluate kidney functions; the perinatal changes clearly demonstrate this developmental maturation (Chapter 27). The glomerular filtration rate, for example, increases postnatally as a result of changing hemodynamic factors and because of different regional rates of microstructural development. Moreover, in full-term infants, the renal secretion of phenol red per unit of time increases postnatally at a certain pace, but this process of renal maturation also proceeds in prematurely born infants to the extent that their kidney function is advanced at the time when delivery should have normally occurred according to gestation.[16,30] The initiation of many functions is vitally important for prematurely born infants, but despite successful adaptational efforts, the overall progress of maturation is slowed down by the precocious cessation of intrauterine development.

Enzymologic studies of growing tissues have provided ample examples for the course of functional development. Many tissue enzyme activities increase steadily and are unaffected by birth; certain enzyme activities appear first in the perinatal period, and others reveal sudden increases or decreases in the immediate perinatal period,[19,20] (see also Chapters 17 and 22). The enzymatically active protein demonstrates the developmental differentiation quite clearly. The genetic preposition or readiness, however, often precedes the appearance of the function by a certain period of time. This lag period between the readiness of the genetic material to release the specific information for protein synthesis (derepression of a regulator gene) and the beginning of the specific protein function is the first and most important part of *critical periods*[33] or *sensitive phases*[8] in development. Such phases usually outlast the period of time during which an enzyme activity appears and increases, but the termination is more difficult to define (see below). The immediate perinatal period is an especially critical period[4] during which functional activities begin with "a rapid increase of clusters of enzyme activities."[9]

Along the ontogenetic time axis, many limited sensitive phases occur, and the perinatal period is only one of these phases. It has been speculated that the sensitive phase is the equivalent of transitory activation of genes, a process that has been associated with the puffing phenomenon as observed in the macrochromosomes of chironomus larvae.[2] Specific chromosomal puff spectra have been investigated, and their induction and repression were related to functional and somatic changes of the organism.[12] It seems to be a long way from observations in primitive organisms to applications in mammals. Many phenomena and experimental data, however, support the hypothesis that sensitive phases are genetically determined periods of high interactions not only between the genetic material and all levels of protein synthesis, but also among the intermediary cell metabolism, hormones, and the environment. In the mammalian organism, endogenous and exogenous stimuli produce specific functional phenomena; however, we lack knowledge of the mechanisms involved because of the very different quality and origin of effector molecules that act as derepressors of regulator genes. The multifarious interactions among the genetic material, the intermediary cell metabolism, the hormonal regulatory system, and the environment need intensive investigations in the future. At present, we have to separate maturation and neonatal adaptation phenomenologically, and our definition of adaptation serves this purpose.

3. Adaptation

Dill[3] states in the preface to *Adaptation to the Environment* that "the concept of adaptation has not been standardized among physiologists." Hence, each author interprets the term with slight variation according to the needs in a specific field. This variation in definition resembles the problem of defining and using the term "life," where every scientist adds to the concept by daily exploration of life's manifestations. In developmental physiology, the evidence of adaptation is omnipresent and the approaches to this phenomenon are so varied that it is necessary to extend the definition provided in the introduction.

"Adaptation [as used in the present context implies] physiologic adaptation [and refers to] any property of an organism which favors survival in a specific environment, particularly a stressful one."[22] Our primary concern is with those phenomena that arise at the time of parturition as a result of the changes from the intrauterine to the extrauterine environment and that usually persist throughout the neonatal period. We assume that the healthy fetus is fully adapted to the intrauterine environment. We exclude fetal adaptation from this discussion because it occurs under a different presupposition

at a different developmental stage (e.g., prenatal changes of hemoglobin types have been claimed to be governed by adaptational needs; see Chapter 11) and because its mechanisms are quite unknown and experimental results are controversial.[19] At birth, the neonate is abruptly separated from the maternal nutritional sources, hormones, and other humoral factors, and it loses the placenta as an organ for excretion and for completion of many other metabolic functions of the fetus. At the same time, the neonate leaves a liquid-phase, constant-temperature environment and enters the gas-phase environment with quickly varying temperatures. In addition, the lung function for breathing air and the digestive processes must be established. These events are topped by the need for a neurohumoral regulatory system that never before was similarly flooded with stimuli of all kinds and never had to direct its regulatory efforts toward a new and different homeostasis. The complexity and scope of events in which neonatal adaptation is directly or indirectly involved can only be roughly outlined here, but this outline elucidates the difficulties in fitting the concept of "neonatal adaptation" into the schemes of definitions proposed by Prosser.[22] The crucial point is that the newborn has been developmentally prepared for birth and for the existence in the extrauterine environment. Tissue or cellular adaptation is referred to as a mechanism for the adjustment of the organism to the action of unfavorable factors in the environment.[1] For the newborn mammal, however, *the extrauterine environment represents the goal,* i.e., the final environment for which the organism was designed by its genetic master plan. The sudden change of environments at birth might seem to be drastic and the new environment unfavorable, but we also know that the continuation of the prenatal environment beyond the genetically determined time of delivery becomes quite unfavorable for the fetus.

During gestation, the fetus has created its own homeostasis and is able to maintain internal stability, although supported and buffered by the placental and maternal metabolism. For example, the fetus maintains high plasma levels of amino acids and certain vitamins, produces large amounts of extracellular fluids, and regulates the placental blood flow.[17] Since the organism must achieve internal independence of the environment as soon as it separates from the maternal organism, many functional adjustments must be made to establish a new internal stability. Granted, maturation has created the basis for performing the changeover at birth, but the necessary flexibility and speed can be provided only by neonatal adaptation. This necessity makes neonatal adaptation a major supporting principle in achieving survival with minimum risk.

The last phase of gestation is a period of active metabolic preparations for the change to extrauterine life. The fetus accumulates high amounts of glycogen (Chapter 17) and lipids (Chapter 19), which are both essential for survival after birth. Premature birth interferes with completion of such preparations, or can even occur before appreciable amounts of metabolic fuel have been deposited. This deficiency is a major disadvantage of premature birth, but many other metabolic functions are similarly immature according to the maturational scale at certain gestational stages. The maturation of lung function, and the presence of a specific phospholipid, the surfactant, may serve as a proper example. The high mortality rate of prematurely born infants clearly underlines that fact. Unfortunately, in many fatal cases, knowledge of the underlying metabolic mechanisms remains obscure. The multilevel regulation of the acid–base metabolism (Chapters 6 and 26), the excretory function of the liver (Chapters 23 and 25) and kidney (Chapter 27), and many insufficient functions of regulatory systems in the CNS (Chapters 29 and 31) and the autonomic nervous system (Chapter 33) can each and in combination fail to accomplish the challenge of precocious cessation of intrauterine development.

Premature birth frequently causes a severe metabolic crisis, and such situations exceed by far the capacity of neonatal adaptation. A surprisingly large number of prematurely born infants finally manage, however, to survive the hazardous and critical newborn period, and those infants allow us to evaluate the contribution of the birth process and extrauterine environment to the acceleration of maturation[16] normally seen at that time. Nevertheless, the postnatal struggle for survival may proceed on the level of cell metabolism and last for several days. Such temporary, functional inadequacies limit comparisons between premature and full-term infants. As already mentioned, several vitally important functions must be established after birth, regardless of gestational maturity. During the first week of life, the hepatic conjugation of bilirubin is less effective in premature infants than in full-term infants, but according to gestational age, the

prematures accomplish this conjugation and similar excretory functions well before the normal time of delivery has been reached. The same principle holds true for temperature regulation and heat production (Chapter 21), for some renal functions (Chapter 27), and, to some extent, for the production of immunoglobulins (Chapter 14).

The initiation of physiologic functions is based mainly on the appearance of enzymes or enzyme systems. What can be studied as a functional capacity (e.g., bilirubin clearance) can also be investigated on the level of cell metabolism by measuring enzyme activities (e.g., UDP glucuronyltransferase activity in liver homogenates). Some tissue- or organ-specific functions can be closely pursued by enzymatic studies, whereas functions that employ many or even all tissues of the organism (e.g., those involved in acid–base metabolism) cannot be evaluated from single-tissue examinations. Several examples of the initiation of enzyme activities with respect to the liver are discussed in Chapters 22 and 24. Of special interest are experiments in which birth was either precociously induced or delayed beyond normal term. Several enzyme activities that normally appear at birth could be initiated by premature delivery or delayed until parturition occurred a few days after normal term. Such experimental systems provide a more profound insight into the metabolic mechanisms and the regulatory systems involved; along this line, we will try to apply our definition of neonatal adaptation.

If the mechanism of enzyme initiation is conditioned by the change of environment, we expect a temporary increase of enzyme activity unless the environmental conditions require, and the respective regulatory system of the organism is able to maintain an elevated level of enzyme activity. This might be explained by an example published by Greengard.[5] At 3 days before normal birth, rat liver tyrosine aminotransferase activity can be evoked by a single intraperitoneal injection of glucagon, but 4 or 5 days before term, this hormone has no such effect. The precocious increase of this enzyme activity after a single hormone injection occurs within 4 hr and lasts for approximately 24 hr. This hormone-induced increase can be inhibited by simultaneous application of actinomycin D; this observation leads to the conclusion that this enzyme must be synthesized *de novo*, and that the stimulation must have triggered the enzyme protein synthesis at the DNA or

RNA level. Since it was known that glucagon facilitates the formation of cyclic AMP (cAMP), it remained to be shown whether this compound could act as an effector molecule on the DNA level. In fact, intraperitoneal injection of dibutyryl cAMP into rat fetuses evoked the appearance of liver tyrosine aminotransferase on the third and also on the fourth day before term. Hence, the administration of cAMP to an organism that is still unable to produce glucagon can act as an effector molecule by derepressing the regulator gene for the biosynthesis of a specific enzyme protein. Some evidence exists, however, that hormones can also act directly as effectors on the DNA or RNA level.[27,32] Greengard[5] studied two other enzyme activities in fetal rat liver and their precocious inducibility by other hormones. The author concluded that "the same enzyme in different developmental or physiological states may respond to different hormones." Prior to the stage of possible hormone stimulation, a certain accumulation of effector molecules can apparently evoke the appearance of an enzyme activity. This observation concerns the cAMP experiments, and it still supports the concept of a sensitive phase and the stepwise inauguration of a new metabolic function. This order would be: (1) readiness of the DNA (comparable to the puffing effect); (2) accumulation of effector molecules; and (3) mobilization of the multiple steps of protein synthesis. The latter two steps, as well as many supporting mechanisms, such as the activation of amino acids for peptide formation and other energy-requiring reactions, seem to be governed by hormones. The appearance of the different hormones during prenatal development might well reveal some clues for the beginning of sensitive phases.[6,7,10]

Hence, premature birth and hormone treatment of the fetus directly or via the mother can have the same result on the initiation of enzyme activities. On the basis of this observation, Greengard[5] proposed to advance some of the postnatal adaptation to the late gestational days by prenatal application of hormones to the fetus. Such treatment would stimulate the course of enzyme differentiation and thereby facilitate the metabolic adjustment of prematurely born mammals to extrauterine life. Liggins[13] successfully applied this principle by treating the mother with corticosteroids to stimulate fetal synthesis of lung surfactant.

Preventive adaptation is widely practiced in adults. Why should it not be possible to apply this principle to the fetus in case of imminent or unavoidable premature delivery? This preventive treatment could be directed toward more and other specific functions.

That neonatal adaptation and maturation are interlocked has been expressed in our definition. Future investigations might reveal, however, that the presently used phenomenology is insufficient for defining neonatal adaptation, and that a more precise evaluation can be achieved by using characteristics of the cell metabolism and the regulatory systems.

4. Stimulation

The exposure to the extrauterine environment has a tremendously stimulating effect on the newborn. It is more for didactic than for practical reasons that we separate stimulation from hazardous impacts; however, it is necessary to state that the degree of stimulation and the basic condition of the neonate to deal with stimulation are very important and must be recognized. The degree, strength, and duration of a stimulus, e.g., cold environment, will determine whether the final outcome is beneficial or detrimental for the newborn. For this reason, we will discuss stimulation before we proceed to birth stress and tolerance.

Most environmental stimuli are needed to evoke, initiate, and maintain physiologic functions necessary for extrauterine life. We must also remember that the intrauterine maturation prepared the organism to deal with the new stimuli to be encountered at birth. This line of thought helps us to understand that a prematurely born infant is more prone to suffer from normal environmental stimuli, which consequently become hazards and stresses for these insufficiently prepared infants. Stimuli can thus be compared with potent drugs, which are very helpful in small, correctly applied quantities, given over the right period of time, while overdosage and prolonged application are dangerous and occasionally fatal. A deep but relatively short drop in the arterial oxygen saturation is an excellent (though not exclusive; see Chapter 6) stimulus for the onset of respiration in the newborn; however, prolonged anoxia will damage brain tissue and certainly becomes a serious birth hazard.[20]

Figure 1 lists the major environmental factors and shows the immediate response organ of the newborn. This simplified scheme should aid the understanding of environmental factors and their immediate response and target organs. The interplay between environment and organism includes a multiplicity of secondary effects that go far beyond this scheme. It is a well-known example that the breakdown of hemoglobin in immature (premature) newborns leads to a sometimes hazardous accumulation of unconjugated bilirubin. The liver responds properly with initiation and production of enzymes necessary for conjugating bilirubin, but it takes too long, and the load is too big for immature newborns, compared with full-term and mature babies (see Chapter 23). The induction of specific liver enzyme activities to metabolize barbiturates can even be started before birth (see Chapter 25); this observation underlines the fact that the term *postnatal stimulation* would be inaccurate and the more embracing term *perinatal stimulation* more adequate.

The perinatal stimuli that more often become perilously strong and dangerous are those involving the reduction of tissue oxygenation in the perinatal period. It is beyond the scope of this survey, which is concerned with principles, to discuss the many metabolic effects that accompany perinatal hypoxia and anoxia,[31] or to present the many characteristic metabolic and functional responses to oxygen deficiency in the CNS.[11] A look at the types of hypoxia (Table I) helps to envision the multiplicity of factors involved, but it also shows

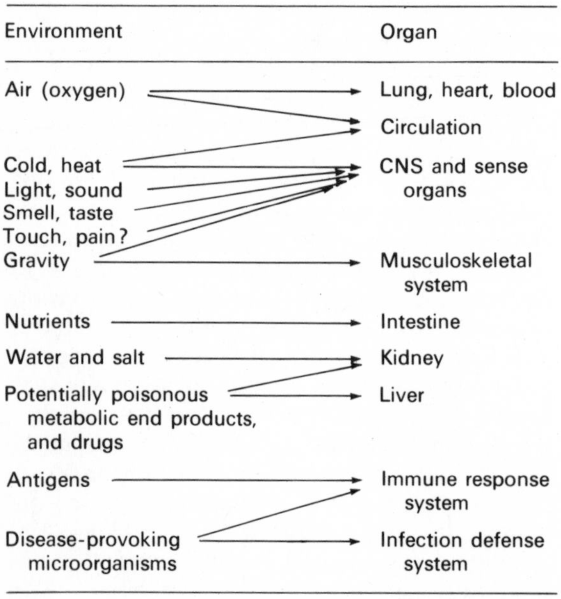

Table I. Types of Hypoxia

Aerogenic hypoxia
  (O_2 does not reach erythrocytes)
Anemic hypoxia
  (insufficient erythrocytes for O_2 transport)
Stagnant hypoxia
  (circulatory disorders)
Histotoxic hypoxia
  (blocking of oxidative cell metabolism)
Hypoxia from excessive O_2 Consumption
  (e.g., seizures, thyroid crisis)

how close physiologic stimulation and hazardous birth stress are. Normal vaginal delivery of a full-term baby is always accompanied by aerogenic and stagnant hypoxia of several minutes' duration. Anemic and histotoxic anemia both develop in babies with blood factor incompatibility, although our therapeutic measures can prevent the serious damage seen in untreated cases. These few examples may suffice to demonstrate the perinatal occurrence of and close relationship between stimulation and damage.

5. Birth Stress and Tolerance

As was outlined above, the hazardously strong stimuli represent stressors that in adults cause systemic stress. Systemic stress denotes "a condition in which extensive regions of the body deviate from their normal resting state."[28] Before 1956, the definition of stress had been either vague or controversial, and the effort of Selye[29] at clarifying this confusion begins with the question whether a biological concept can actually be defined. With some presuppositions, Selye[29] defined stress as "the state manifested by a specific syndrome which consists of all the nonspecifically induced changes within a biologic system." In the newborn, we are dealing with many changes, but we must hesitate to call the situation at birth a state, even if we recognize that the normal newborn discloses a specific "syndrome of the just-born infant." This syndrome is comprised of many characteristic symptoms that are directly or indirectly caused by or related to the process of birth. The homeostasis of the fetus ceases at the time of parturition. At birth, the newborn becomes engaged in a series of profound metabolic and morphological changes,

Environment	Organ
Air (oxygen)	Lung, heart, blood
	Circulation
Cold, heat	CNS and sense organs
Light, sound	
Smell, taste	
Touch, pain?	
Gravity	Musculoskeletal system
Nutrients	Intestine
Water and salt	Kidney
Potentially poisonous metabolic end products, and drugs	Liver
Antigens	Immune response system
Disease-provoking microorganisms	Infection defense system

Fig. 1. The newborn and the extrauterine environment.

and the immediate postnatal period is characterized by temporary internal instability.[18] Selye[29] stated that "the term 'stress' is meaningful only when applied to a precisely delineated biologic system." It seems that the latter term can easily be applied to the newborn's organism as a whole, but if homeostasis is considered as essential to the definition of a "precisely delineated biologic system," the lack of homeostasis in the neonate would prevent the meaningful application of the term *stress*.

Since it is impossible to appraise the state of stress, we must deal with the changes or symptoms produced by stress. This latter process is explained in that "the condition of biologic stress is essentially the development of an antagonism between an agent and the resistance offered to it by the organism."[29] In this context and in regard to the newborn, the "agent" is represented by several nonspecific stimuli or stressors or both. The situation of the newborn, however, deviates in many respects from an adult organism that is exposed to alarming stimuli. It is logical to designate the newborn's endeavor as directed toward adjustment to the extrauterine environment and not, at least not primarily, as directed toward building up resistance to the new condition of life. This adjustment relies on postnatal adaptation, a phenomenon that requires some time to become effective, at least hours to show first effects. During this lag period and overlapping with the beginning of postnatal adaptation, we find the newborn practicing an unusual *tolerance*. This tolerance might be best seen in three examples. First, toward the end of delivery and during the expulsion period, hypoxia or even a short spell of anoxia occurs frequently; this stressor is encountered by a high tolerance to hypoxia. Second, most newborns experience a rapid and marked cooling immediately after birth (even the application of cool water on the back is still in use for initiating the first breath); at this time, the cold-induced increase in oxygen consumption rises very slowly to a moderately elevated level, thus preventing the newborn from an exhausting strain on the energy metabolism (see Chapter 21). Third, most newborns experience a low blood glucose level without obvious disadvantages. These three examples show that tolerance is an important protection for surviving birth hazards. Tolerance seems to be very expedient under the stressful conditions at birth, since the energy metabolism (air, respiration, lung function) first needs some time to be-

come established, and many new metabolic reactions (enzyme activities) must be initiated.

The tolerance of the newborn is frequently explained as being an expression of weakness. McCance[18] therefore raised the question: "Is 'tolerance' merely a lack of response? . . . Can these weak responses and the instability of the steady states conceivably be beneficial, and if so why?" McCance answered by citing Aristotle, "There is a reason behind everything in nature," and this aphorism is a summons to further intensify developmental research.

A sudden discharge of corticosteroids and the resulting high plasma levels of corticoids have frequently been used as criteria for declaring a person to be suffering from stress. Selye,[29] however, did not want to include such specific hormonal reactions in the concept of stress. The discharge of corticosteroids and adrenaline is an early defense reaction that begins during the shock phase but is actually characteristic of countershock; both constitute the alarm reaction.[28] Ample proof has been provided that the administration of a sufficiently high dose of either ACTH or cortisol to a normal person produces symptoms that are typical of the alarm reaction. Schäfer[24] denoted the neonatal stress reaction as "partly passive" because of the great amount of maternal cortisol transferred to the fetus immediately before birth. The same author suspects that "the first postnatal stress-like reaction of the newborn is probably induced to a small extent by the newborn's organism but to a greater extent by the maternal organism via the placenta." The following symptoms were observed and listed by Schäfer[24]: high plasma cortisol level, depression of plasma iron, hemoconcentration, and eosinopenia. Details on the neonatal corticoid plasma level are presented in Chapter 37.

In summary, we have tried to show that the fetus during delivery and the newborn at birth are exposed to stimuli or stressors or both, but that the newborn does not develop an alarm reaction similar to that of older individuals. At birth, the newborn does not possess the basic metabolic and regulatory properties that are required for a stress reaction as defined by Selye.[28]

In the foregoing, we discussed the major stressors, such as anoxia and cooling, but in addition, the fetus and newborn can also suffer from physical impacts that we categorize as *birth trauma*. By definition, birth trauma includes physical injuries as well as shock.

Controversy might arise from the fact that birth traumas belong to pathophysiology rather than to developmental physiology. Granted, we do not want to include massive intracranial hemorrhage, prolonged anoxia, fractures, or similarly severe injuries and claim these traumas to be part of neonatal physiology. Furthermore, we foresee great difficulties in formulating categories of birth traumas, even if we designate them simply as severe, moderate, and minor. Inevitable events accompany the process of parturition, such as physical impacts and some degree of hypoxia; in addition, drastic changes of the blood volume with multiple circulatory and metabolic consequences occur more frequently than they are diagnosed. It does not really seem to be necessary to argue about a sophisticated division between birth injuries of pathologic qualities and minor physical or functional impacts inflicted by events incident to birth. The minor traumas have always been considered as minor risks of the normal process of birth, and they do escape our observation easily, or even normally, unless we apply very carefully selected tests.

Minor injuries or temporarily visible symptoms of birth trauma are frequently regarded as unimportant in terms of survival and later development. Under the conditions of normal delivery, physical injuries to the skin or soft tissues are harmless, but compression during expulsion can cause more severe impacts, such as local hypoxia, edema, or hemorrhage. Minor cerebral traumas are not necessarily caused by mechanical forces during delivery; they sometimes occur in consequence of disturbances in the regulation of vasomotor functions, which, in turn, affect the nutrition and energy metabolism of brain cells.[21,25,26] In this respect, the CNS is more sensitive than other organs. The phylogenetically older structures of the CNS, such as the medulla oblongata and the diencephalon, develop lesions more easily and earlier than do the phylogenetically younger brain structures such as the cortex.[11] Furthermore, the higher permeability of membranes in general and the lack of certain coagulation factors in the blood affect the brain tissue more severely than other tissues of the body. Functional imbalances due to fluid and electrolyte shifts between the intra- and extracellular spaces in brain tissue may eventually influence regulatory functions of the entire organism, while in other tissues, such imbalances may be of local importance only.

Temporary disturbances of this kind will lead to brain lesions in only a small number of newborns, but there is good reason to suspect that such disturbances occur on a subclinical level in a greater number of newborn infants. Although circumscribed cell necrosis may cause brain lesions that are not detectable by readily available clinical methods and instruments, we expect much more frequent derangements in certain brain regions that cause shock to functional units of the CNS. The majority of such events are transient, however, and they are repaired within the first days of life. It is well known that not only severe and moderate but also minor cerebral birth injuries affect prematurely born infants more frequently than full-term babies.

As mentioned in the introduction, shock is considered to be the first phase of the alarm reaction. According to Selye[28] we "consider shock merely as a condition of suddenly developing intense general damage"; furthermore, "shock is a phenomenon of generalized necrobiosis always involving a biologic unit in its entity"; and finally, "any number of qualitatively distinct derangements can lead to shock, hence, it would be futile to search for a single pathogenic mechanism." In adults, the phase of shock is characterized by hypothermia, hypotension, depression of the CNS, decrease in muscle tone, hemoconcentration, deranged capillary and cell membrane permeability, generalized tissue breakdown (catabolism), hypochloremia, hyperkalemia, acidosis, a transitory rise followed by a decrease in blood glucose, leukopenia, and acute gastrointestinal erosions. The discharge of epinephrine and corticosteroids begins in the shock phase, but especially the increase of the latter hormones is actually characteristic of the countershock phase.

This list of shock symptoms is certainly very similar to the syndrome of the just-born infant, but even without evaluating each symptom or sign, we know of quite different underlying mechanisms in the newborn, the basic differences of which will be outlined and discussed in the various chapters of this book. Hazardous stimuli and birth trauma, however, have a certain impact on the organism at birth and during the immediate postnatal period. At present, we cannot prove whether one or the other shock symptom (as in adult physiology) is related to stress or shock, and we must still learn how to differentiate exactly between shock effects and birth-related maturational changes (e.g., conversion of the respiratory and circulatory system). Nevertheless, clinical observations and a limited number of experimental results lead to the conclusion that neonatal tolerance is the prominent mechanism that protects the newborn from stressors and shock.

6. Perspectives

The process of birth is an essential part of the developmental master plan. The early stages of development must proceed in a well-protected aqueous environment, but the genetic design of the mammalian organism is such that life must further proceed in an atmospheric environment. The drastic changeover from the intrauterine to the extrauterine environment is facilitated by numerous stimuli, most of which are of environmental, but some of which are of endogenous, origin. The process of birth still remains the most hazardous event during the entire life span, this hazard being even more pronounced in premature than in full-term infants. We thus find certain factors and mechanisms at work to minimize the risk of failure to survive during the immediate perinatal period.

Maturation prepares the organism for the transition from the intrauterine to the extrauterine environment; the pattern of morphological and functional development is genetically determined and lacks flexibility.

Postnatal adaptation assists the developmental course by accelerating the maturation according to vital needs.

Neonatal tolerance protects the organism from premature exhaustion of energy reserves by rendering birth trauma and potential stressors ineffective.

The potential for postnatal adaptation and tolerance is limited, yet has a remarkably wide range. Furthermore, we can observe that postnatal adaptation becomes more effective with increasing gestational age, while the phenomenon of tolerance diminishes with progressing maturation.

Premature delivery prevents completion of developmental preparations, and only by virtue of a very active postnatal adaptation does the premature infant have a chance to survive precocious parturition. Potent stressors, such as prolonged hypoxia, anoxia, or cooling, fail to evoke systemic stress; similarly, minor birth traumas or transitory functional derangements do not initiate a shock syndrome or alarm reaction in the newborn. Instead, these latter hazards can be tolerated without ensuing perilous effects as long as certain limits of capacity are not surpassed. Unfortunately, we know very little about alarming symptoms that can alert us to the imminent damage of surpassing the capacity of tolerance that would mark the beginning of the formation of permanent damage.

Our knowledge of the metabolic mechanisms that underlie neonatal tolerance is very limited as yet. Tolerance can easily be misinterpreted by conceiving of it as an expression of weakness, immaturity, or simply as lack of response. By definition, tolerance is the natural ability to endure, and endurance in itself requires action, which cannot be achieved by passivity. Thus, it would be inconsequent to define neonatal tolerance as lack of response. In newborns, hypoxia tolerance has been shown to initiate certain metabolic reactions that are, however, basically different from those observed in adults.[31] Nevertheless, we need to investigate further the phenomenon of neonatal tolerance, and we must postpone making a more complete definition until we understand the meaning and mechanism of neonatal tolerance.

7. References

1. BARBASHOVA, Z. I., 1964, Cellular level of adaptation, in: *Adaptation to the Environment: Handbook of Physiology* (D. B. Dill, ed.), Sect. 4, pp. 37–54, American Physiological Society, Washington, D.C.
2. BEERMANN, W., 1963, Cytologische Aspekte der Informationsübertragung von den Chromosomen in das Cytoplasma, in: *Induktion und Morphogenese, 13th Colloquium der Gesellschaft für Physiologische Chemie,* pp. 64–97, Springer-Verlag, Berlin.
3. DILL, D. B. (ed.), 1964, Preface, *Adaptation to the Environment: Handbook of Physiology,* Sect. 4, American Physiological Society, Washington, D.C.
4. FLEXNER, L. B., BELKNAP, E. L., AND FLEXNER, J. B., 1953, Biochemical and physiological differentiation during morphogenesis. XVI. Cytochrome oxidase and succinoxidase in the developing cerebral cortex and liver of the fetal guinea pig, *J. Cell. Comp. Physiol.* **42**:151.
5. GREENGARD, O., 1969, Enzymic differentiation in mammalian liver, *Science* **163**:891–895.
6. GREENGARD, O., AND DEWEY, H. K., 1968, The developmental formation of liver glucose-6-phosphatase and reduced nicotinamide adenine dinucleotide phosphate dehydrogenase in fetal rats treated with thyroxine, *J. Biol. Chem.* **243**:2745–2749.
7. GREENGARD, O., AND DEWEY, H. K., 1970, The premature deposition or lysis of glycogen in livers of fetal rats injected with hydrocortisone or glucagon, *Dev. Biol.* **21**:452–461.

8. HADORN, E., 1958, Role of genes in developmental processes, in: *The Chemical Basis of Development* (W. D. McElroy and B. Glass, eds.), pp. 779–791, The Johns Hopkins Press, Baltimore.

9. HERRMANN, H., AND TOOTLE, M. L., 1964, Specific and general aspects of the development of enzymes and metabolic pathways, *Physiol. Rev.* **44**:289–371.

10. JACQUOT, R. L., PLAS, C., AND NAGEL, J., 1973, Two examples of physiological maturations in rat fetal liver, *Enzyme* **15**:296–303.

11. JÍLEK, L., TRÁVNÍČKOVÁ, E., AND TROJAN, S., 1970, Characteristic metabolic and functional responses to oxygen deficiency in the central nervous system, in: *Physiology of the Perinatal Period* (U. Stave, ed), pp. 987–1041, Appleton-Century-Crofts, New York.

12. KARLSON, P., 1963, Morphogense und Metamorphose der Insekten, in: *Induktion und Morphogenese, 13th Colloquium der Gesellschaft für Physiologische Chemie,* pp. 101–122, Springer-Verlag, Berlin.

13. LIGGINS, G. C., AND HOWIE, R. N., 1974, The prevention of RDS by maternal steriod therapy, in: *Modern Perinatal Medicine* (L. Gluck, ed.), pp. 415–424, Year Book Publishers, Chicago.

14. LINNEWEH, F., 1958, Funktion und Lebensalter, *Muench. Med. Wochenschr.* **100**:616–618.

15. LINNEWEH, F., 1959, Die Faktoren des postnatalen Funktionswandels, in: *Die physiologische Entwicklung des Kindes* (F. Linneweh, ed.), pp. 1 and 2, Springer-Verlag, Berlin.

16. LINNEWEH, F., AND STAVE, U., 1960, Über Anpassungsvorgänge nach der Geburt, *Klin. Wochenschr.* **38**:1–5.

17. McCANCE, R. A., 1959, The maintenance of stability in the newly born. I. Chemical exchange, *Arch. Dis. Child.* **34**:361–370.

18. McCANCE, R. A., 1961, Characteristics of the newly born, in: *Somatic Stability in the Newly Born* (G. E. W. Wolstenholme and M. O'Connor, eds.), pp. 1–4, Churchill, London.

19. MOOG, F., 1965, Enzyme development in relation to functional differentiation, in: *The Biochemistry of Animal Development* (R. Weber, ed.), Vol. 1, pp. 307–365, Academic Press, New York.

20. MOOG, F., 1970, Enzyme development and functional differentiation in the fetus, in: *Fetal Growth and Development* (H. A. Waisman and G. Kerr, eds.), pp. 29–48, McGraw-Hill Book Co., New York.

21. MYERS, R. E., 1972, Two patterns of perinatal brain damage and their conditions of occurrence, *Amer. J. Obstet. Gynecol.* **112**: 246–276.

22. PROSSER, C. L., 1964, Perspectives of adaptation: Theoretical aspects, in: *Adaptation to the Environment: Handbook of Physiology* (D. B. Dill, ed.), Sect. 4, pp. 11–25, American Physiological Society, Washington, D.C.

23. SCHÄFER, K. H., 1952, Die Geburt als Eingriff auf den kindlichen Organismus, *Monatsschr. Kinderheilkd.* **101**:158–160.

24. SCHÄFER, K. H., 1959, Über den Anteil der Stressreaktion am Funktionswandel der ersten Lebenszeit, in: *Die physiologische Entwicklung des Kindes* (F. Linneweh, ed.), pp. 11–17, Springer-Verlag, Berlin.

25. SCHMIDT, H., 1965, Untersuchungen zur Pathogenese und Ätiologie der geburtstraumatischen Hirnschädigungen Früh- und Reifgeborener, G. Fischer, Stuttgart.

26. SCHWARTZ, P., 1961, *Birth Injuries of the Newborn,* pp. 14–85, S. Karger, Basel.

27. SEKERIS, C. E., 1967, Wirkung der Hormone auf den Zellkern, in: *Wirkungsmechanismen der Hormone* (P. Karlson, ed.), pp. 126–157, Springer-Verlag, Berlin.

28. SELYE, H., 1950, *The Physiology and Pathology of Exposure to Stress,* Acta, Montreal.

29. SELYE, H., 1956, What is stress?, *Metabolism* **5**:525–530.

30. STAVE, U., 1956, Beitrag zur funktionellen Reifung der Nierentubuli: Die Phenolrot-Ausscheidung im Säuglingsalter, *Z. Kinderheilkd.* **77**:554–562.

31. STAVE, U., AND WOLF, H., 1970, Metabolic effects in hypoxia neonatorum, in: *Physiology of the Perinatal Period* (U. Stave, ed.), pp. 1043–1088, Appleton-Century-Crofts, New York.

32. TOMKINS, G. M., AND THOMPSON, E. B., 1967, Hormonal control of protein synthesis at the translational level, in: *Wirkungsmechanismen der Hormone* (P. Karlson, ed.), pp. 107–125, Springer-Verlag, Berlin.

33. WADDINGTON, C. H., 1940, *Organizers and Genes,* Cambridge University Press, Cambridge.

CHAPTER 4

Postnatal Growth

Frank Falkner

1. Introduction

From conception, growth is a continuum and by no means a steady process. Particularly in infancy and the preadolescent period, we are inclined to view growth as a concept of size attained. What is the average body weight of healthy full-term infants at 1 year of age? These measures, and their distribution, are valuable, for they indicate progress along a growth curve. Such distance curves, however, are rarely dramatic and may give a false impression of, for example, steady growth.

In any discussion of physical growth, then, it is necessary to study growth patterns in the context of an additional concept—that of growth rates or velocity curves.

2. Velocity

The concept of incremental or velocity growth is not easy to grasp, but it is a vital one. When information is needed on change, or velocity over time, it is inappropriate to use the familiar cross-sectional approach, in which groups of infants or children are measured at specific ages. For velocity

information, it is necessary to use a longitudinal method, in which the same subjects are measured at specific intervals. Thus, incremental, or decremental, information is sought. More accuracy is required than in the cross-sectional approach, for the chance of error is multiplied by the number of times the subject is measured. The time of planning such a study is also a time to think about, and encourage, good techniques and the use of good, practical measuring devices.* No one expects the reader to become necessarily an expert anthropometrist, but easily learned techniques lead to useful and accurate information about physical growth—especially velocity growth, which is much needed, particularly in any discussion of early growth.

A healthy infant seems destined to seek an individual velocity growth curve, and given a reasonable environment, once he is following such a curve, it appears very difficult indeed to deflect him from it permanently. Various insults may deflect and slow him from the curve, but when the conditions are corrected, he will usually exhibit catch-up growth and rise above his own curve before returning to it once again.

Catch-up growth can be studied only by the longitudinal approach, and it is by no means always associated with insults. Once a healthy, full-term,

Frank Falkner · Fels Research Institute, Yellow Springs, Ohio 45387; and University of Cincinnati College of Medicine, Cincinnati, Ohio 45229

---

* A versatile measuring device for recumbent length and stature is available from the Waters Instrument Company, Rochester, Minnesota.

newly born infant has shaken off perinatal factors influencing early growth, he seems to climb onto a largely genetically determined series of individual trajectories and continue along it. Since healthy, full-term, newly born infants vary comparatively little in birth size, it may be asked why and how an infant destined genetically to be a tall adult requires about 2 years of age[6,14] before finally getting on target. The answer, especially if he is a small newly born baby, is that he exhibits catch-up growth and grows at a velocity much greater than the average for the period. His main thrust in catch-up growth is in the first 6 months of life. Hence, the range of total body weight in various samples of healthy infants is not as wide at 6 months as at other ages.[11] There appears to be a control of growth mechanism in action here, because not all small babies exhibit catch-up growth; healthy infants destined genetically to be small adults do not. Growth appears to be aimed at its genetic target of size.

3. Length

Length (and stature) is a good general indicator of human growth, and useful information comes from studying incremental data. The newly born full-term infant is found to be growing at a very rapid rate—at easily the greatest velocity at any time in postnatal life. It can be difficult to appreciate this notable velocity when one realizes that the infant is also rapidly decelerating in growth. As the months pass, growth continues to be rapid, but less and less rapid.

In most children, the velocity curve stops its deceleration somewhat sharply at about 3 years of age, and a comparatively steady and regular velocity curve begins. In other words, the annual increments in length/stature become similar and regular until just before adolescence.

The difficulty in producing such curves is, of course, that children must be measured longitudinally, regularly, and accurately. If incremental measures are plotted at, say, 6-month intervals, the curves will not be smooth. Several factors are responsible, e.g., seasonal influence on growth, illness, and nutrition. Growth curves are often derived from measurements of many different children who are all attaining a great diversity of size measures at various ages. Such curves will notably tend to be smooth and absorb individual peaks. Thus, when the growth curve of an individual child is plotted, it should not be expected to follow the smooth, regular course of such normative curves.

4. Body Weight

The same principles apply for weight, but since body weight is surely the most common measure made of the human being, some comment is necessary. The birth weight of the full-term infant is generally considered to be within normal limits if it is between 2500 and 4200 g (5.5 and 9.5 lb), though obviously there is great need to exclude abnormality beyond either end of this range. If a neonate with a birth weight of 8 lb has doubled his weight at 6 months of age to 16 lb, the increment for his first 6 months is 8 lb. At 3 months of age, however, he may suddenly, for some abnormal reason, have lost, say, 4 lb, had the condition corrected, grown unusually fast in weight for a period, and at 6 months finished up at 16 lb. This example illustrates three points: (1) that weight decrements may occur frequently, thus demonstrating that total body weight is of itself an unstable measure; (2) that a compensatory phase of growth may occur; and (3) that in studying growth, or following it for a particular reason, particularly in the early months of life, it is necessary that the incremental periods be short in order that such patterns emerge and not be hidden. In overall terms, though, we may say that growth as shown by body weight follows the same pattern as that of stature.

5. Other Patterns

This general curve of early normal growth is followed, as might be expected, by many tissues and major organs of the body, e.g., muscle, bone, liver, lungs, spleen, and kidney. It is important to note that there are exceptions. When a particular tissue or body complex is under review, its particular pattern should be known in principle and taken into account. Head circumference is a good overall indicator, in health, of skull size and brain size. The incremental curve of this measure shows a very rapid velocity, and acceleration after birth. This pattern is followed by a sharp deceleration to roughly 10 years of age, after which tiny increments occur until the curve then begins to decline and reaches zero at adulthood.

As can be readily understood, testis, ovary, uterus, and prostate growth, being related to functional needs, has a slowly decelerating incremental curve after birth in relation to percentage of adult size achieved, reaching zero by about 9 years and exhibiting virtually no growth until the start of puberty, when a decided acceleration occurs.

Not only are changes in body composition reflected in patterns of body weight, during infancy in particular, but also the changes themselves are an important part of the growth picture. When weight is lost or gained, we need to ask what is involved in the loss or gain. An example is given in the complicated fat growth curve of early life. Fat increases steadily and rapidly for approximately the first 9 months of life, and indeed in the early months of life represents a large portion of the body weight gain. Then a plateau is reached, and the increments will be zero, muscle and bone growth being then largely responsible for weight gain. After this, a true loss of fat (in percentage of body weight) occurs and continues until about 7 years of age, when once again fat growth is increased. Thus, the growth curve of fat must be able to reflect increments and decrements.

Particularly with so much current concern over, and interest in, the relationship of the overnourished and overfat infant to his later fat growth and status, it is very important to keep the normal patterns of fat growth—in both cell size and number—firmly in mind.

6. Norms

Norms do not evaluate, but they do describe. And provided the all-important dispersion of the measures over age is made available and kept in mind, normative data are useful and contributory, particularly in screening and follow-up.

Ideally, the sample from which the normative data are derived should match the individual subject or group of subjects for whom comparisons are needed in race, geography, and historical time. This is, alas, rarely possible.

For general guidance and referral, appropriate resources are listed in the addendum (Section 8).

7. The Infant of Low Birth Weight (ILB)

It is not all that long ago that the neonate was either a premature or a full-term baby according to whether his birth weight was below or above 2500 g. This tradition of measuring time by weight is ancient and deep-rooted, and does have an obvious practical basis. The next advance was to recognize that low-birth-weight babies are not a homogeneous group and may indeed vary greatly in their needs, prognosis, and postnatal growth. Thus, the term *infants of low birth weight* (ILB) was introduced to cover this heterogeneous group. This step has kept pace with the current interest and advances in knowledge about intrauterine growth and gestation, and has led to the present two large subgroups of ILB: the prematurely born and the small-for-gestational-age (SGA). Neither group, of course, is homogeneous.

There are multiple intrauterine factors involved. Most are related to the conflict of nature–nurture influences, a complexity made more complex by the interaction of genetic and environmental influences themselves. As an illustration of this complexity, the next section describes the postnatal growth of a pair of twins.

7.1. An Example of ILB: Multiple Births

These monozygous male twins were born near term. The placenta was monochorionic–diamniotic. Routine study of the placenta[8] revealed that there was a marked difference in mass between the placental part supplying one twin and the part supplying the other. The first-born twin (Twin A) weighed 1460 g at birth; Twin B weighed 2806 g. The corresponding placental part supplying Twin A weighed 258.5 g wet and 37.40 g dry, and measured $20 \times 7.5 \times 2.0$ cm; Twin B's placental part weighed 551.0 g wet and 85.90 g dry, and measured $30 \times 15.5 \times 2$ cm. In addition to this inequality, there was a small arteriovenous shunt, resulting in a mild transfusion syndrome in the direction of Twin A "transfusing" Twin B. There is a high degree of correlation between these measures and the birth weights of the twins.

The factors specifically responsible for the marked within-pair difference in birth size could be discussed in depth, but the reason for presenting these data here is to make the point that both were full-term infants, yet one was SGA. Since they were genetically identical, it is interesting to follow their postnatal growth pattern. Table I shows the anthropometric measures at various ages. The within-pair weight difference of the smaller Twin A was reduced in the first 9 months, and was lowest of all at 12 months. Note that although the within-pair subcutaneous tissue measurement difference

Table I. Anthropometric Measures of Twins A and B[a]

Measure	Birth A	Birth B	9 Months A	9 Months B	8 Months A	8 Months B	12 Months A	12 Months B	2 Years A	2 Years B	30 Months A	30 Months B	3 Years A	3 Years B	4 Years A	4 Years B	11 Years A	11 Years B
Weight (kg)	1.46	2.81	6.94	8.07	8.21	8.53	8.6	10.1	9.7	10.95	10.36	11.82	11.25	12.96	13.28	15.53	25.57	30.68
	(1.35)		(1.13)		(0.32)		(1.5)		(1.25)		(1.46)		(1.71)		(2.25)		(5.11)	
Length or stature (cm)	43.0	50.0	64.9	68.0	68.7	71.6	75.9	78.6	79.8	82.0	84.2	86.6	87.8	90.8	96.2	99.2	130.81	135.89
	(7.0)		(3.1)		(2.9)		(2.7)		(2.2)		(2.4)		(3.0)		(3.0)		(5.08)	
Head circumference (cm)	30.0	34.0	44.6	44.2	45.6	44.7	47.1	47.4	48.2	48.3	48.6	48.8	49.2	49.2	49.6	50.0		
	(4.0)		(−0.4)		(−0.9)		(0.3)		(0.1)		(0.2)		(0.0)		(0.4)			
Maximum calf circumference (cm)			(2.5)		(0.4)		(2.0)		(1.9)		(2.2)		(2.3)		(2.0)			
Subcutaneous tissue (mm)			(0.2)		(−1.4)		(1.3)		(2.6)		(0.8)		(1.2)		(1.0)			

[a] Figures in parentheses are the within-pair differences of Twin B over Twin A.

remained more or less the same, this age of 1 year was the only time at which this measure for Twin A was greater than that for twin B. After the age of 1 year, the within-pair difference, allowing for greater total body size, remained about the same, though at 11 years there was a 5.11-kg difference.

Length and stature growth patterns are interesting and important. In the first 9 months, Twin A's rate of growth exhibited marked catch-up, and he grew significantly faster in length than Twin B, as though to try to make up the birth-length deficiency of 7.0 cm. Figure 1 shows this catch-up growth; it shows that after that time, the twins continued to grow in length at approximately the same rate—at least until 11 years of age. The smaller twin did not thereafter exhibit sufficient catch-up growth to attain his brother's size curve.

Head circumference measures exhibit the pattern of growth expected from an ILB, namely, very rapid growth compared with a full-term infant within normal size limits in the early months. Twin A was 4.0 cm smaller in this measure than Twin B at birth; yet by 9 months, he became (even if only slightly) larger. From then on, he maintained a head circumference very similar to that of his twin. Other anthropometric measures follow, in general, the overall body size indications already presented.

By 2½ years, the twins should have been virtually free of perinatal influences and onto their genetic growth curves. Was there (at 11 years) an irreversible difference in their lengths and sizes due to the factors already described? Presumably, Twin A was following the growth pattern of a SGA infant, and the illustration of this pair is interesting because we can hold the genetic growth factor constant between the two.

Before discussing the postnatal growth of the ILB in more detail, we need to consider a factor that is complex, yet important.

7.2. Nutritional Factors

There is, of course, much variety in the nutrition of ILB, according to custom, methodology,

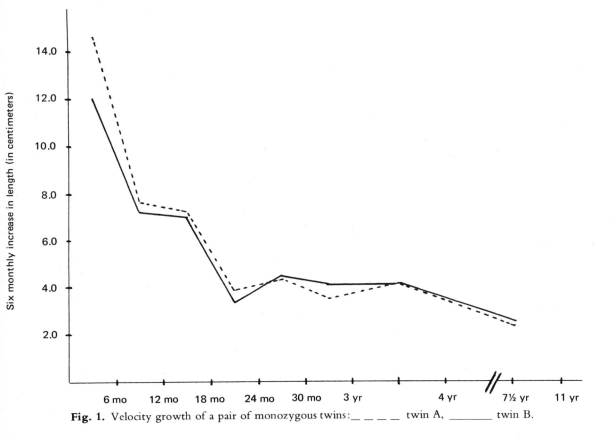

Fig. 1. Velocity growth of a pair of monozygous twins: _ _ _ _ twin A, _____ twin B.

and geography. To what extent will this factor influence the postnatal growth of the ILB? Falkner *et al.*[9] compared the growth of ILB cared for in a newborn nursery. One group had had routine feeding with formulas yielding a mean 26 cal/oz 92 cal/dl, range 20–30 cal/oz) over a 2½-year period. Feeding was then changed in the same nursery so that subsequent ILB received a mean 42 cal/oz (148 cal/dl, range 30–48 cal/oz). The volume of formula taken was not altered, only the concentration. The data clearly showed that in these samples, increased caloric feeding was related to a more rapid gain in weight in all birth-weight groups below 2500 g (and a highly significant shorter hospital stay). Snyderman and Holt[12] described a similar effect and concluded that the "extra weight" was probably due to increased fat deposit. Nitrogen retention studies supported this conclusion. Aside from the obvious advantages of a shorter hospital stay, we did ask at that time whether we were in fact discharging immature infants who simply weighed more due to increased fat deposits.

We of course wished to examine other, possibly more important indicators of growth in the two groups, but only weight was available for those babies fed the original 26 cal/oz (92 cal/dl) formula. The second group (42 cal/oz, 148 cal/dl) did indeed have other somatic growth measures made. After the study described above, the opportunity for a further study occurred. The newborn nursery was directed by a neonatologist for the first time, and the routine feeding of ILB was returned to 26 cal/oz. After a 2-year period, it was possible to compare two groups once again: the 42 cal/oz group already studied and measured anthropometrically and radiographically, and a new 26 cal/oz group that also had similar physical growth measures. Table II summarizes some of the measures in the two birth-weight groups. In the lowest birth-weight groups, not only were the numbers small, but also there were virtually no differences detected. Regarding weight, the 42 cal/oz group gained weight at a slower rate than the 26 cal/oz group, and the 13-week increment is in fact significantly less in one birth-weight group, but not at a very impressive level. In only one measure and in one instance did the 42 cal/oz group grow faster—length in the 13-week increment of one birth weight group. This was significant, but again at an unimpressive level. Fibula length by X-ray measurement showed the 26 cal/oz group always "superior."

There are two points to be made about these results: (1) Careful anthropometry is important in comparing such groups, and here showed no significant difference in growth after hypercaloric feeding. (2) The two groups are in one important way not comparable: The advent of the first neonatologist and his staff in the period of study of the "new" 26 cal/oz group conferred many new and important advantages, one of which was that the perinatal and infant mortality rate in that nursery dropped significantly in that early period. Although it is then not appropriate to compare the two groups, the comparison does demonstrate that hypercaloric feeding of ILB does not appear to increase their growth rate if the overall standard of neonatal care present is high for all infants.

7.3. Subgroups of ILB

There is a need to know the early growth patterns not only of ILB, but also of the subgroups of ILB, particularly whether there are any differences between the prematurely born infant (preterm infant, PTI) and the near full-term infant of low birth weight (SGA infant). This knowledge can be gained only by longitudinal study. Babson[1] and Fitzhardinge and Steven[10] reported the postnatal growth longitudinally of SGA infants. Cruise[3] answered these basic questions for us admirably, using the estimation of velocity growth in a 3-year longitudinal study of healthy ILB divided into two PTI groups (28–32 and 33–36 weeks' gestation), a SGA group (37–42 weeks' gestation), and a fullterm group above 2500-g birth weight for comparative purposes.

Important highlights of the study were that *all* ILB had the highest growth velocity in the first 3 months of life, and that the SGA infants grew significantly less rapidly than the preterm infants.

The SGA infants were the largest of the ILB groups at birth, but by 2 and 3 years of age, they were the smallest. This growth pattern occured because the PTIs grew significantly more rapidly than the SGA infants at each 3-month interval up to 1 year, and tended to do so up to 3 years. By 1 year of age, of course, the PTIs had therefore become larger than the SGA infants—reversing the status at birth—and remained so at 3 years. The full-term infants greater than 2500 g at birth were always larger than all ILB up to 3 years of age, but by this age, the PTIs had approached close to them in mean measurements and closer than the SGA infants.

Table II. Anthropometric Measures in Two Birth-Weight Groups

Measure	Birth-weight group	Age	n	26 cal/oz	n	42 cal/oz	42/26 cal/oz	Student's t test
Weight in lb and (kg)	3.0–3.9 lb (1.4–1.8 kg)	Birth	49	3.36 (1.52)	79	3.40 (1.54)	+0.04 (0.0181)	
		13 weeks	16	8.98 (4.07)	48	8.60 (3.90)	−0.38 (0.1723)	
		13-week increment	33	5.72 (2.50)	48	5.20 (2.35)	−0.52 (0.2358)	$P = < 0.35 > 0.30$
	4.0–5.5 lb (1.8–2.5 kg)	Birth	60	4.21 (1.90)	221	4.70 (2.13)	+0.49 (0.2222)	
		13 weeks	27	10.18 (1.90)	169	10.30 (4.67)	+0.12 (0.0544)	
		13-week increment	41	5.91 (2.68)	162	5.50 (2.49)	−0.31 (0.1406)	
Length (cm)	3.0–3.9 lb (1.4–1.8 kg)	Birth	51	41.48	71	41.40	−0.08	
		13 weeks	19	52.23	48	52.40	+0.17	
		13-week increment	22	10.39	48	11.10	+0.71	$P = < 0.45 > 0.40$
	4.0–5.5 lb (1.8–2.5 kg)	Birth	68	44.01	220	45.20	+0.19	
		13 weeks	36	54.47	168	55.80	+0.33	
		13-week increment	35	10.76	162	10.40	−0.36	
Fibula length (cm)	3.0–3.9 lb (1.4–1.8 kg)	Birth	36	4.89	75	5.01	+0.12	
		13 weeks	8	6.74	46	6.40	−0.34	
		13-week increment	13	1.49	46	1.40	−0.09	
	4.0–5.5 lb (1.8–2.5 kg)	Birth	49	5.37	221	5.47	+0.10	
		13 weeks	37	7.14	169	7.13	−0.01	
		13-week increment	21	1.80	162	1.61	−0.19	

The mean growth rates of all the ILB tended to be mostly above, or very close to, the median rates in the North American norms of Falkner.[7]

Taking ILB as a whole, head circumference growth is unusual and important. By 3 months of age, the head circumference is very similar to that of the full-term infant. At birth, it is very much smaller. This pattern is clearly explained by comparing the 3-month ILB increments to those of the full-term infants. After 3 months of age, both classes of infants are remarkably similar in rate, but the ILB exhibit a markedly greater rate of growth or catch-up.[8] Thus, the ILB who is thought to be developing hydrocephalus is generally not, but rather is exhibiting this catch-up growth.

In Cruise's study,[3] growth in head circumference was the most notable. The growth rate for all ILB was above the 95th percentile in Falkner's norm[7] in the first 3 months; within the ILB, both groups of PTIs had faster rates than SGA infants. Indeed, by 2 and 3 years of age, the head circumference of PTIs was virtually the same as that of full-term infants greater than 2500 g birth weight, but that of the SGA infants remained smaller.

The considerations discussed above are clearly of the utmost importance concerning overall size and head circumference, which is one indication of brain growth. One-third of all infants born weighing under 2500 g are SGA infants. We must understand the need to relate growth to gestational age and to enhance our ability to predict the subsequent growth and development of individual ILB.

7.4. Long-Term Outcome

While there are some good follow-up studies of the outcome for ILB, there are all too few data concerning the outcome for the PTI and SGA subgroups—and this is a real need.

Drillien[4,5] has perhaps the greatest experience in this area, and at this stage, one can do little better than summarize her findings. Of SGA infants, 40% were considered entirely normal at follow-up, compared with 62% of those above the 10th percentile in the Denver studies[2] for weight and gestational age. According to these considerations, ILB can be divided into three groups:

1. Preterm or SGA infants, in whom the causation is developmental fetal abnormality. There is a high following incidence of mental,

neurological, and congenital abnormalities of varying degrees.
2. SGA infants who are growth-retarded *in utero* due to such factors as hypoxia and subnutrition. On follow-up, these infants tend to exhibit mild degrees of mental retardation and neurological abnormalities.
3. PTIs potentially normal at birth who, especially with marked improvement of postnatal care, have prognostically a good outcome.

7.5. Growth Standards

There are various tables and charts available that lend themselves to evaluating the growth status or progress of an ILB. The norms of Cruise[3] already discussed are valuable for incremental growth norms. One good example that embraces all the necessary attributes for growth status and is practical will be presented. Tanner and Whitehouse[13] have presented such charts previously for use in infant welfare clinics. They provide a method of plotting the weights and lengths of ILB. In the case of a PTI, plotting the size at 12 weeks of age of an infant of 32 weeks' gestation at a point 12 weeks after 40 weeks' gestation (the traditional growth chart method for "infants") may make him erroneously appear to be below the 3rd percentile. If he is plotted, as he should be, using the conceptional age notion, at 12 less the 8 weeks (40 − 32 weeks) by which he was prematurely born, then he will be average in size for conceptional age. And it is this conceptional age concept that is so important in evaluating the growth status of ILB. It is a recommended and already widely followed practice to use "corrected age" and chronological age distinctively in all infants of premature birth up to age 24 months (corrected age).

8. Addendum: Normative Growth Data References

National Center for Health Statistics, 5600 Parklawn Building, Rockville, Maryland 20852. A series booklet in preparation. Length, stature, weight, head circumference. Birth to 18 years. Distance data. No velocity data.
The Center for Disease Control, DHEW, 1600 Clifton Road, N.E., Atlanta, Georgia 30333. Charts based on the above in preparation. Birth

to 3 years; 3 years to 18 years. Distance data. No velocity data.

The Fels Research Institute, Yellow Springs, Ohio 45387. Length velocity, weight velocity, head circumference velocity, tables and charts in preparation. Birth to 3 years.

Tanner *et al.* (ref. 15). Standards from birth to maturity for height, weight, height velocity, and weight velocity: British children 1965.

Various charts based on the above obtainable from Creaseys Ltd., Print Division, Bull Plain, Hertford, England.

Falkner (ref. 7). Some physical growth standards for white North American children. Weight, height, height velocity, weight velocity, head circumference, and head circumference velocity. Birth to 3 years. Standards based on combination and pooling of several different studies, largely in the United States.

9. References

1. BABSON, S. G., 1970, Growth of low birth weight infants, *J. Pediatr.* **77**:11–18.
2. BATTAGLIA, F. C., AND LUBCHENCO, L. O., 1967, A practical classification of newborn infants by weight and gestational age, *J. Pediatr.* **71**:159–163.
3. CRUISE, M. O., 1973, A longitudinal study of the growth of low birth weight infants, *Pediatrics* **51**:620–628.
4. DRILLIEN, C. M., 1964, *The Growth and Development of the Prematurely Born Infant*, Livingstone, Edinburgh.
5. DRILLIEN, C. M., 1971, Personal communication; and Prognosis of infants of very low birth weight, *Lancet* **1**:697.
6. FALKNER, F., 1958, Some physical measurements in the first three years of life, *Arch. Dis. Child.* **33**:1–9.
7. FALKNER, F., 1962, Some physical growth standards for white North American children, *Pediatrics* **29**:467–474.
8. FALKNER, F. (ed.), 1966, *Human Development,* W. B. Saunders, Philadelphia.
9. FALKNER, F., STEIGMAN, A. J., AND CRUISE, M. O., 1962, The physical development of the premature infant: I. Some standards and certain relationships to coloric intake, *J. Pediatr.* **60**:895–907.
10. FITZHARDINGE, P. M., AND STEVEN, E. M., 1972, The small-for-date infant. I. Later growth patterns, *Pediatrics* **49**:671–681.
11. KASIUS, R. V., RANDALL, A., IV, TOMPKINS, W. T., *et al.,* 1957, Size and growth of babies during first year of life, *Milbank Mem. Fund Q.* **35**:323–372.
12. SNYDERMAN, S. E., AND HOLT, L. E., JR., 1961, The effect of high calorie feeding on the growth of premature infants, *J. Pediatr.* **58**:237–240.
13. TANNER, J. M., AND WHITEHOUSE, R. H., 1973, Height and weight charts from birth to 5 years allowing for length of gestation, *Arch. Dis. Child.* **48**:786–789.
14. TANNER, J. M., HEALY, M. J. R., LOCKHARD, R. D., *et al.,* 1956, The prediction of adult body measurements from measurements taken each year from birth to 5 years, *Arch. Dis. Child.* **31**:372–381.
15. TANNER, J. M., WHITEHOUSE, R. H., AND TAKAISHI, M., 1966, Standards from birth to maturity for height, weight, height velocity and weight velocity: British children 1965, *Arch. Dis. Child.* **41**:454–613.

CHAPTER 5

The Skeleton

Mildred Trotter and Barbara B. Hixon

1. Introduction

It is possible that noteworthy changes occur in the skeleton and in the associated muscles and joints at the time of birth. Unfortunately, any of these changes—in particular, the biochemical and physiologic changes that may occur—would be difficult to assess.[2] Changes in the osseous skeleton for which most data are available concern such morphologically measurable parameters as the weight of the total osseous skeleton, the weight of its individual components, differentiated growth rates of parts of the skeleton, the gravimetric density of selected bones, and the percentage ash weight of individual bones or bone sets. In what follows, we shall present some findings from data that have been accumulated in our laboratory during the past several years.

Most of the data are derived of necessity from stillborn fetuses or from children who have died shortly after birth from any one of a number of pathologic disorders.[4] Since the extent to which such disorders might have affected the development of the skeleton is not known in these cases, we have attempted to complement the available data for human skeletons in the perinatal period with comparable data derived from the skeletons of a

nonhuman primate, the macaque monkey. Since these skeletons were obtained from animals bred for experimental purposes (in which there is no reason to suspect any pathology affecting the skeleton or any of the other organ systems),[8] we have every reason to believe that we have measured the corresponding parameters of the developing skeleton in an essentially "normal population."

2. Weight of the Total Osseous Skeleton in Relation to Age

The weights of the total osseous portions of our series of human fetal and postnatal skeletons, up to and including $\frac{1}{2}$ year of age, are shown plotted against age in Fig. 1a. It can be seen that weight increases with age approximately exponentially in the fetal period. After birth, there is some indication of an increase in weight with age, although there is a great deal of scatter due to a number of weights that are lower than might be expected. Similar patterns are seen for weights of individual bones or sets of bones, although the rates may differ among bones. There is considerable variation around the curve of best fit for each bone. In general, if a skeleton is exceptionally heavy (or light) for its age, all the bones or bone sets of that skeleton will be heavier (or lighter) than the average for that age.

Mildred Trotter · Department of Anatomy and Neurobiology, and **Barbara B. Hixon** · Division of Biostatistics, Washington University School of Medicine, St. Louis, Missouri 63110

47

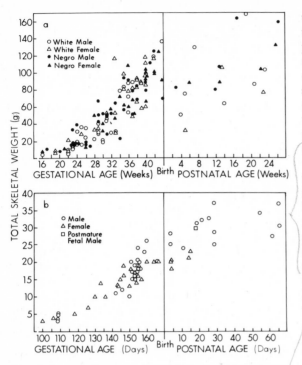

Fig. 1. Scatter diagrams of total skeletal weights plotted against age: (a) Man (age in weeks); (b) *Macaca mulatta* (age in days).

Among the postnatal skeletons, there are some with a total weight much less than might be expected on the basis of the weights of the fetal skeletons. It is known that many of these skeletons with low weights came from individuals who had been ill for some time, perhaps even during the fetal period, and whose skeletal development may have been retarded. Support for this interpretation is suggested by a comparison of the pattern of skeletal weight in relation to age with that of our collection of skeletons of *Macaca mulatta* during corresponding age periods.[8] During the fetal period, the weight of the monkey skeletons (Fig. 1b) also increased approximately exponentially. After birth, the weight continued to increase, but at a decreasing rate, with no skeleton weighing less than might be expected from the trend in the fetal period.

2.1. Proportionate Weights of Four Divisions of the Skeleton

Differential growth rates of anatomic divisions of the skeleton result in changes in the propor-

tionate weights of a given division to the weight of the total skeleton. It is of interest to compare the proportionate weights of the skeleton in four divisions, viz., skull, postcranial axial skeleton, skeleton of superior limb, and skeleton of inferior limb, in sequential age stages during the perinatal period (see Table I) with the corresponding proportionate weights of the adult skeleton. In the youngest age period of the fetal series for which data are available (16–20 weeks), the skull makes up 38% of the weight of the total, increasing slightly during the remainder of the fetal period and continuing to increase after birth to a mean of 46% in the first half year. As the proportionate weight of the skull increases, that of the postcranial division varies slightly, and the proportionate weights of the superior and inferior limb skeletons decrease slightly. With the onset of adolescence and the increased rate of growth, especially of the inferior limbs, the proportionate weights of the skull and of the skeleton of the inferior limbs are markedly altered, and are reversed by adulthood.[4] Thus, little change occurs between birth and $\frac{1}{2}$ year of age, with the exception of the increase in the proportionate weight of the skull, which is believed to result from the developing teeth.

3. Length of Long Limb Bones

The length of each of four long limb bones (humerus, radius, femur, and tibia) increases with age during the fetal period in a pattern that cannot

Table I. Mean Proportionate Weights (%) of Four Divisions of the Skeleton of the Fetus in Sequential Age Periods, of the Neonate from Birth to the First Half Year, and of the Adult in Middle Age

					Age (years)	
	Fetal age (weeks)				Neo-natal	Adult
Division of skeleton	16–20 (6)[a]	21–28 (30)	29–36 (42)	37–44 (39)	B–0.5 (18)	45–64 (46)
Skull	38.2	41.1	42.2	42.1	46.2	19.0
Postcranial	21.3	21.9	22.8	23.1	21.8	17.5
Superior limb	18.0	15.7	14.3	13.6	13.0	18.5
Inferior limb	22.2	21.2	20.9	20.9	18.9	45.0

[a] Figures in parentheses are numbers of skeletons.

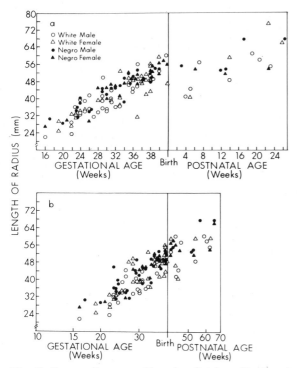

Fig. 2. Scatter diagrams of lengths of right radii plotted against: (a) Age in weeks on an arithmetic scale; (b)logarithm of age (in weeks for the prenatal series, in weeks plus 40 for the postnatal series). Of the prenatal series, 9 are postmature, with gestational ages from 42 to 44 weeks; these are indicated as being 2–4 weeks of postnatal age.

be distinguished from a straight line, because of the great amount of variation. When the lengths for the postnatal series are plotted on the same scatter diagram, however, a power type curve seems to fit the combined data of the pre- and postnatal series (see the scatter diagram of the radii in Fig. 2a as an example). When length is plotted against logarithm of age, a linear relationship is evident, as shown in Fig. 2b, where gestational age for the fetal skeleton is in weeks and for the postnatal series in weeks plus 40, assuming 40 weeks to be the average length of the gestational period. Thus, for these samples, bone length appears to increase on a continuous curve throughout the perinatal period, with no indication of change following birth.

3.1. Intermembral Index

An effect of the differential growth rates of parts of the skeleton is seen in the intermembral index,

which is the ratio of the sum of the lengths of the humeri and radii to the sum of the lengths of the femora and tibiae. In addition to the series of skeletons on which our data are based, the intermembral indices of three younger fetal skeletons (ages 12, 14.5, and 17.5 weeks) from the display specimens in the museum of the department have been included. (The cartilage in these specimens had been distinguished from the osseous parts of the bone by clearing methods, so that it was possible to measure the length of the osseous parts.) The intermembral index was highest, exceeding 1.00, for the two youngest skeletons, and decreased continuously throughout the fetal period to an average of 0.85 for three skeletons at 44 weeks of gestation. During the first year of life, the decrease continued, but at a slower rate. In Fig. 3, the individual intermembral indices are shown plotted against age for the fetal period from 12 weeks of gestation through $\frac{1}{2}$ year of postnatal life. The average intermembral index for four skeletons of 1 year of age is 0.736, which is only 0.04 higher than the mean intermembral index reported by Schultz[1] for 465 adults. There is no evidence to indicate that birth affected the course of reduction of the intermembral index.

4. Density of Long Limb Bones

Gravimetric density, defined as the weight (in grams) of a bone divided by its volume (in cubic centimeters), was determined for a series of each of four long limb bones: humerus, radius, femur, and tibia. The volume was measured by displacement of water with the bone enclosed in a thin rubber sheath.[7]

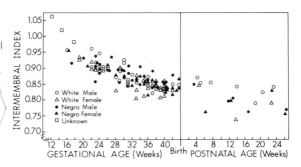

Fig. 3. Scatter diagram of intermembral indices plotted against age from 12 to 44 weeks of gestation and from birth through the first $\frac{1}{2}$ year.

Scatter diagrams of the individual densities for a given bone, when plotted against age in weeks, show a linear increase in the fetal period. In the postnatal period, however, many of the density determinations are found to be lower than even the lowest of those in the late fetal period (as an example, see Fig. 4a for femora). Consideration of the characteristics (weight and volume) from which the density determinations are made shows that in some neonatal skeletons, both weight and volume are lower than might be expected from the pattern found for the fetal period,[7] with weight being more deficient than volume (see Fig. 4b,c). It will be recalled that in relating weight of the skeleton to age, some skeletons were found to have very low weights after birth. Now, it is suggested that whereas the organic portion of the bone has increased in size with age, although perhaps less than expected, the deposition of minerals, the inorganic portion of the bone, has not kept pace. Thus, low density values may be another result of the patho-

logic conditions that caused the death of the individuals from whom this series of skeletons was derived. Is it possible that the condition of a bone with low density is analogous to the condition found in children with rickets or in older individuals with osteomalacia? This hypothesis gains credibility when the densities are compared with densities of the corresponding bones of *Macaca mulatta* during the perinatal period. Although the mean density of the macaque bones is higher than that of the human bones, the pattern of increase of density with age in the fetal period is similar in the two species. After birth, however, the densities of the human bones are markedly lower throughout the first year than are those in the fetal period, whereas in *Macaca mulatta*, the increase continues after birth, although at a somewhat decreasing rate, with the maximum density reached by approximately 4 years of age.[5] It is believed that normal human skeletons would show a pattern of change in density with increasing age in the perinatal period closer to that found for *Macaca mulatta* skeletons than to that of the present human series, which are from individuals who died from illnesses.

5. Percentage Ash Weight of the Total Skeleton and Its Parts

The percentage ash weight of a bone is defined as the weight of the mineral content in percent of the weight of the dry, fat-free bone. The weight of the mineral content was determined after ashing the bone in a muffle furnace at 600° for a period of 20–23 hr.[3] The percentage ash weight during the fetal period is found to increase with age significantly for the total skeleton and for each of 19 individual bones or bone sets (listed in Fig. 5) with the exceptions of cervical vertebrae, thoracic vertebrae, sternum, radius, and hand bones. The mean percentage ash weights of the fetal skeletons are highest for the segments of the vertebral column and sternum and lowest for the hand bones and foot bones. In Fig. 5, the mean percentage ash weights of the 19 bones or bone sets are shown for the fetal series, as well as for the postnatal series from birth to ½ year of age, and for an adult series. During the first 6 months of postnatal life, all bones have lower mean percentage ash weights than have the corresponding fetal bones, except the cranium and mandible, probably due to the development of

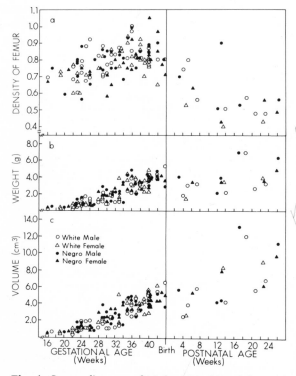

Fig. 4. Scatter diagrams of (a) densities, (b) weights, and (c) volumes of right femora plotted against weeks of gestation for the prenatal series and against weeks of age for the postnatal series.

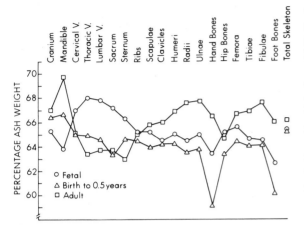

Fig. 5. Distribution of mean percentage ash weights of 19 series of human bones or bone sets and of the total skeletons for the fetal series (mean age, 32.1 weeks), the postnatal series of the first $\frac{1}{2}$ year (mean age, 0.31 year), and an adult series (mean age, 63.0 years).

teeth. The bones that appear to have had the greatest loss in percentage ash weight during the first 6 months after birth are the segments of the vertebral column, the hand bones, and the foot bones. It is possible, as conjectured for the low density values, that the lower percentage ash weights found after birth for all bones except those of the skull are due to the poor quality of the specimens. This explanation gains support when these findings are compared with those found for the adult in an earlier study.[6] The percentage ash weights for 12 of the 19 bones or bone sets of the adult skeleton have been found to be higher than those of either the fetal skeleton or the neonatal skeleton. It is of interest that the segments of the vertebral column and the sternum have much higher percentage ash weights in the fetus than in the adult, and that the ribs and hip bones are nearly equal in percentage ash weights in the two age periods. It is unfortunate that no macaque skeleton of less than 1 year of age has been ashed for comparison with the human skeletons.

6. Conclusions

During the perinatal period, the weight of the total osseous skeleton increases with age but, based on an inference from *Macaca mulatta*, at a somewhat slower rate after birth. The proportionate weights of four parts of the skeleton (skull, postcranial skeleton, superior limb, and inferior limb) to the weight of the total skeleton are not affected by birth.

The length of each of four long limb bones increases on a continuous curve throughout the perinatal period. There is no evidence to indicate that birth affects the course of reduction of the intermembral index.

The density (weight/volume) of long limb bones increases with age in the fetal period. In the neonatal skeletons, many of the densities are lower than those in the late fetal period, but this is believed to be due to pathologic conditions. Evidence from skeletons of *Macaca mulatta* in good physical condition indicates that the density of human skeletons in healthy individuals would continue to increase in the neonatal period.

The percentage ash weight of the osseous skeleton (weight of ash/weight of bone) increases significantly during the fetal period, but is lower for our series of the first 6 months after birth for all bones except the cranium and mandible, for which the increase is probably due to developing teeth. The lower percentage ash weights after birth are believed, as in the case of the lower densities in the same period, to be due to the pathologic conditions that caused death. It is emphasized that the lower values should not be interpreted to mean that for a given individual, either density or percentage ash weight is decreased as a result of birth.

ACKNOWLEDGMENT

This work was supported by grant HD-02619 of the National Institutes of Health, United States Public Health Service.

7. References

1. SCHULTZ, A. H., 1937, Proportions, variability and asymmetries of the long bones of the limbs and the clavicles in man and apes, *Hum. Biol.* **9**:281–328.
2. STAVE, U., 1970, Maturation, adaptation, and tolerance, in: *Physiology of the Perinatal Period* (U. Stave, ed.), pp. 29–40, Appleton-Century-Crofts, New York.
3. TROTTER, M., 1973, Percentage ash weight of young human skeletons, *Growth* **37**:153–163.
4. TROTTER, M., AND HIXON, B. B., 1974, Sequential changes in weight, density, and percentage ash weight of human skeletons from an early fetal period through old age, *Anat. Rec.* **179**:1–18.

5. TROTTER, M., AND HIXON, B. B., 1976, The density of limb bones and the percentage ash weight of the skeleton of *Macaca mulatta*, *Amer. J. Phys. Anthropol.* **44**:223–232.

6. TROTTER, M., AND PETERSON, R. R., 1962, The relationship of ash weight and organic weight of human skeletons, *J. Bone J. Surg.* [*Am*] **44**:669–681.

7. TROTTER, M., AND PETERSON, R. R., 1970, The density of bones in the fetal skeleton, *Growth* **34**:283–292.

8. TROTTER, M., HIXON, B. B., AND DEATON, S. S., 1975, Sequential changes in weight of the skeleton and in length of long limb bones of *Macaca mulatta*, *Amer. J. Phys. Anthropol.* **43**:79–93.

CHAPTER 6

Respiration and the Respiratory System

Herbert S. Harned, Jr.

1. Fetal Respiration

1.1. Introduction

While the fetus is undergoing development of its own respiratory tract and the intricate neural, muscular, and circulatory structures necessary for initiating respiration at birth, it must entirely depend on its mother for the supply of oxygen and release of carbon dioxide, and for the maintenance of a metabolic environment compatible with its well-being. The dramatic substitution of its own respiratory system for that of the placenta is the primary event that occurs at birth, and the failure to perform this respiratory transition is the major cause of death or morbidity in the perinatal period. To visualize the primary significance of this change at birth, it is essential to understand the respiratory state of the fetus *in utero*. To aid in this understanding, the development of the placenta and its function as a respiratory organ will be emphasized in this section, as well as the development of the fetus's own respiratory system.

Herbert S. Harned, Jr. · Department of Pediatrics, University of North Carolina School of Medicine, Chapel Hill, North Carolina 27514

1.2. Respiration of the Ovum and Development of the Placenta

The fertilized ovum must receive its nutrients from its own cell mass or from the fluids surrounding it while it migrates down the fallopian tube and while it lies free in the uterine cavity for several days. By the time of implantation, it has assumed a hollow spherical shape (blastoderm) with an inner cell mass on the side of the sphere attaching to the endometrium. From this region, trophoblastic cells rapidly erode the underlying uterine mucosa, first as irregular strands. By the end of the second week after fertilization of the ovum, these strands form primitive villi with an outer irregular layer of syntrophoblastic cells, an inner, better-defined layer of cytotrophoblastic cells, and a beginning core of mesoderm. Soon, blood vessels appear in the mesodermal core; these vessels will later represent the fetal component of the placental vessels for exchange of gases and nutrients. Simultaneously with this process of extension of the trophoblast, endometrial cells are destroyed, and their contents produce a fluid pool, the embryotroph, which may supply early nutrient for the developing fetus. Also, the trophoblast invades small blood vessels, causing some oozing of blood. A delicate balance must be created as these blood spaces enlarge, because excessive bleeding would result in formation of hematomas, which might result in fetal loss. These blood spaces or lacunae are destined to become the large, coalescent, intervillous spaces of the functioning placenta.

Gas exchange and nutrition from the glycogen-rich endometrium may begin as soon as implantation occurs, but the rapidly growing fetus must develop its own circulation. The oxygen consumption of the embryo appears to increase from the time of fertilization, suggesting that differentiation increases the embryo's energy needs. By estimating the maximum tissue thickness through which oxygen can perfuse at the available P_{O_2}, one can determine when the embryo must develop its own circulation. The 22-day-old human embryo is 2 mm long and curved so that the maximum distance for perfusion is approximately 0.2–0.3 mm. Circulation must develop in the embryo of this size, and indeed blood has been found in the yolk sac on the 20th day and in the chorion on the 21st day. The embryonic heart begins to circulate blood effectively by the onset of the fourth week after fertilization. The villi become increasingly branched, and reduction of the epithelial layers on their surfaces decreases the tissue thickness of the placental membrane. With increasing arborization of the villi, they simulate treelike units that have been designated *cotyledons*. Among these cotyledons, maternal septa remain in the endometrium that has not been so deeply eroded.

Definition of the characteristics of the human placental circulation has resulted from recent studies by Ramsey[220] of the circulation of the rhesus monkey, which is probably very similar. She demonstrated that spiral end-arteries from the uterus spurt blood into the spaces surrounding the cotyledonary fronds, and that venous drainage occurs into openings adjacent to those of the arteries on the maternal side of the intervillous space. This fountain effect produces turbulence in the blood flow and accounts for the sound of the placental souffle, the continuous bruit audible late in gestation. It is believed that not all the arterial jets in the placenta function at all times, some being shut off by contraction of the individual arteries and some closed by myometrial contraction. This arterial constriction may be an important factor in the variation of maternal placental perfusion that is so significant in considerations of maternal–fetal gas exchange.

1.3. Respiration of the Fetus *in Utero*

One of the fundamental questions in fetal physiology has been whether the fetus is sufficiently supplied with oxygen to maintain cellular and organic function similar to that occurring after birth, or whether indeed the fetus survives in a hypoxic atmosphere of "Everest *in utero*." The analogy to the latter state seemed reasonable because the newborn resembles the mountain climber returning to sea level in several respects.[13,106] The hemoglobin concentration and oxygen-carrying capacity of the blood are high at birth, suggesting earlier hypoxic stimulation of blood formation.[261] Also, arterial blood O_2 saturation, content, and tension have been shown to be lower in the fetus than in the adult in all the mammalian species that have been studied.

Recently, increasing evidence indicates that the fetus has sufficient oxygen for all its developmental needs and does not need to mobilize anaerobic glycolysis except under conditions of severe stress. It is capable of converting to an anaerobic state,[255] and probably can survive more successfully than the adult animal under severe asphyxic circumstances.[195] Nevertheless, the energy available from such anaerobic sources is minimal compared to that from aerobic metabolism.[86] Other studies have suggested that the glycolytic pathway of fetal muscle does not respond more effectively to hypoxia than does adult muscle,[35] and that other mechanisms must be found to explain the greater ability of the newborn to survive hypoxia.

The placenta supplies the oxygen needs of the fetus and effectively removes fetal CO_2 from the time of placental differentiation until the infant begins its independent existence. To understand this function, a review of some of the basic physiologic considerations is in order, but it must be realized that information is incomplete even in this area. Later, an evaluation of the relative significance of some of these mechanisms will be made.

1.4. Placental Gas Tensions

Barcroft[24] emphasized that the partial pressures of gases, rather than the concentrations, are fundamental in considering gas exchange at membranes, including the placenta. O_2 and CO_2 pass the placental membrane by simple diffusion from regions of higher pressure to those of lower pressure. Thus, the pressure gradient is readily identified as the driving force for movement of the gas molecules.

In Fig. 1, which is modified from the work of Bartels et al.,[32] representative values that have been determined for human O_2 and CO_2 tensions at important maternal and fetal sites are expressed as partial pressures. These values represent approximations, because sampling disturbs the normal placental circulation. Also, the range of values noted in different studies may indicate physiologic variation.

Maternal arterial blood near term was shown to have a P_{O_2} of approximately 97 mm Hg.[45] The maternal arterial P_{CO_2} of 29 mm Hg is lower than the usual arterial CO_2 tension of the adult because pregnancy is associated with a state of respiratory alkalosis associated with hyperventilation.[133] Döring and Loeschke[103] and Döring et al.[104] proposed that this hyperventilation is an effect of progesterone on the respiratory centers.

The maternal uterine arterial blood divides into a large fraction that actually enters the intervillous spaces and a smaller fraction supplying uterine muscle. From estimates of myometrial and placental weights at term, this shunt may amount to 25% of maternal blood flowing through the uterus. The latter fraction represents enough of a shunt that the uterine venous gas tensions (P_{O_2} of 33 mm Hg and P_{CO_2} of 46 mm Hg; see Fig. 1) do not reflect actual gas tensions of maternal placental veins. Despite this shunt, however, the low value of P_{O_2} and high value of P_{CO_2} in uterine venous blood indicate that much O_2 has been passed to the fetus and much CO_2 gained from it.

Blood sampling of the placenta through the abdominal wall has yielded surprisingly similar mean values of maternal blood from the so-called "intervillous space" [P_{O_2} values of 42–44.5 mm Hg by Rooth and Sjöstedt[230] and Quilligan and Cibils[218]; P_{CO_2} values of 36.5–38 mm Hg by Rooth et al.[231] and Rooth and Sjöstedt[230]]. Blood in this space is undergoing rapid change in gas tensions as active interchange of gases is occurring between the intervillous space and the villous capillaries.[115] Despite the consistency of values for the intervillous gas tensions reported by some investigators, doubt remains that these samples are representative of maternal blood in contact with fetal villi. In fact, if the human placenta does indeed resemble that of the rhesus monkey, minute samplings obtained from many intervillous sites should show a span of gas tensions between those of the uterine artery and those of the maternal placental veins. Quilligan and Cibils,[218] using a needle electrode, noted P_{O_2} values between 22 and 78 mm Hg in the intervillous space.

The umbilical venous P_{O_2} of 30 mm Hg and P_{CO_2} of 40 mm Hg shown in Fig. 1 are also values projected from averaged data (see Table I). The drop from maternal arterial P_{O_2} of 97 mm Hg to umbilical venous P_{O_2} of 30 mm Hg is striking, and might be interpreted as indicating a degree of inefficiency at the placenta for O_2 exchange, but further analysis of this phenomenon is needed. The umbilical arterial P_{O_2} of 20 mm Hg indicates that the blood directed to the fetal tissues supplied by the descending aorta is considerably more hypoxic than umbilical venous blood (as also shown in Fig. 1). The umbilical arterial P_{CO_2} of 55 mm Hg represents hypercapnic blood returning from the fetus to the placenta for elimination of CO_2 by the mother. Because of the shunting of inferior caval blood to the left atrium, the P_{O_2} of carotid arterial blood would be expected to be slightly higher (approximately 22–24 mm Hg) and the P_{CO_2} lower (approximately 40–45 mm Hg) than these values in umbilical arterial blood.

The values of gas tensions shown for the umbilical vessels are illustrative of those obtained from sampling human umbilical cord blood at the time of delivery under a variety of circumstances. Table I reveals other representative values for gas tensions, O_2 saturation, and pH obtained in humans by similar methods. These values may be considerably lower for P_{O_2} and pH and higher for P_{CO_2} than those existing in the human fetus during normal gestation. In fact, Freda and Adamsons,[114] sampling the femoral artery of a human fetus during an exchange transfusion, found the O_2 saturation to vary between

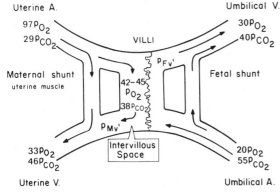

Fig. 1. Diagram of placental circulation. Values of P_{O_2} and P_{CO_2} shown are representative of data obtained from humans during the perinatal period. $P_{M_{V}1}$ (partial pressure in maternal placental veins) and $P_{F_{V}1}$ (partial pressure in fetal placental veins) have not been adequately measured. Reproduced (with modifications) from Bartels et al.[32]

Table I. O_2 **Saturation,** P_{O_2}, P_{CO_2}, **and pH in Blood from Human Umbilical Vessels at Birth (Mean Values)**

O_2 sat. (%)		P_{O_2} (mm Hg)		P_{CO_2} (mm Hg)		pH		References
uv[a]	ua[a]	uv	ua	uv	ua	uv	ua	
		26	12	50	—			Haselhorst and Stromberger[132]
50	16	22	9	36	42	7.36	7.33	Eastman[107]
		29	14	45	60			Beer et al.[36]
62	28			42	53	7.34	7.28	Goodlin and Kaiser[117]
				38	45	7.33	7.26	Rooth et al.[231]
47.5	23			48.5		7.28		MacKinney et al.[171]
64	31							MacKay[170]
				44	49	7.41	7.30	Wulf[264,266]
	60–80		25–28					Freda and Adamsons[114]

[a] uv: umbilical vein; ua: umbilical artery.

60 and 80% and the pH between 7.32 and 7.38; the calculated P_{O_2} was 25–28 mm Hg.

During cesarean section, these values will vary markedly with the type of anesthesia used. Values for P_{O_2} in the umbilical vein (29.1–39.2 mm Hg) and umbilical artery (16.6–22.9 mm Hg) have been noted,[135] with even wider variations in P_{CO_2} and pH depending on the type of ventilatory support.

A fetal arteriovenous shunt has been shown in anatomic studies by Boe[48] and Danesino[83] in the human placenta. Metcalfe et al.[186] estimated such a shunt to be on the order of 19% of total umbilical flow in the sheep. Conspicuously absent from the idealized drawing (Fig. 1) is a representation of the regions of the placenta itself that are engaged in active O_2 uptake and CO_2 production.

The fetal and maternal shunts and the utilization of O_2 by the placenta and fetal membranes make measurements of uterine and umbilical venous blood gases nonrepresentative of true maternal and placental venous values. In addition, this intrinsic metabolism of the placenta must be considered in explaining the large differences in O_2 and CO_2 tensions across the placenta.[67,148] The effect of placental metabolism is more essential in quantitative considerations of placental gas exchange, however, than in nullifying the basic physiological concepts to be described.

1.5. Oxygen Transfer

In blood, O_2 is not simply held in physical solution, but is chemically bound to hemoglobin

located in actively metabolizing red blood cells. The relationship between the O_2 saturation and the P_{CO_2} is shown for maternal and fetal blood in Fig. 2. The pH and temperature of the blood must be accurately controlled to avoid shifting of the curves. The S-shaped characteristics of the curves have certain favorable features for the uptake of O_2 by the maternal lungs and for its release to maternal and fetal tissues.

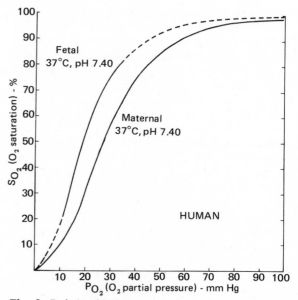

Fig. 2. Relationship between O_2 saturation and P_{O_2} for maternal and fetal blood. Reproduced from Metcalfe et al.[183]

Consideration of the curves in general reveals that at high levels of O_2 tension (e.g., above P_{O_2} of 70 mm Hg), the curves are relatively flat, so that there is little change in O_2 saturation for a large change in P_{O_2}. These levels are not attainable for the fetus even under hyperbaric conditions. Wide variation in maternal alveolar O_2 pressures, however, will result in only small changes in her arterial O_2 saturation. Conditions such as living at moderately high altitude or pulmonary insufficiency from disease of the lungs are compatible with maintenance of the maternal arterial O_2 saturation at a relatively high level. In contrast, at the middle and lower end of the curve, a small drop in O_2 tension is associated with large release of O_2 from hemoglobin.

Also of importance is consideration of the Bohr effect, which relates acidity to the affinity of blood for O_2. Blood with high acidity or high P_{CO_2} has less affinity for O_2 than does blood with lower acidity, and this increased acidity will displace the curves to the right (see Chapter 12 for details).

These principles affect the diffusion of O_2 from mother to fetus, so that favorable and unfavorable factors are operating concurrently, as listed and described in the following sections.

1.5.1. Factors That Favor Diffusion of Oxygen from Mother to Fetus

(a) Characteristics of Oxygen Dissociation Curves. The O_2 dissociation curve for fetal blood, determined by tonometry, lies to the left of the O_2 dissociation curve for maternal blood at the same pH and temperature (Fig. 2). Thus, at all O_2 tensions, the fetal blood has greater affinity for O_2 than has maternal blood. The major role of 2,3-diphosphoglycerate (DPG) in determining hemoglobin O_2 binding was defined by Chanutin and Curnish[70] and Benesch and Benesch.[39] This organic phosphate compound is present in greater quantities than ATP in red cells, and competes with O_2 for binding sites of reduced hemoglobin. Its higher concentration in adult as opposed to fetal erythrocytes is the primary reason for the differing positions of the maternal and fetal curves.[34,199] The present state of knowledge of this clinically important subject is detailed in Chapters 11 and 12.

(b) Fetal and Maternal Hemoglobin Concentrations. The total hemoglobin concentration of the fetus is normally greater than the maternal hemoglobin concentration late in pregnancy. The regulatory mechanism for increasing the fetal hemo-globin concentration to this high level is not understood completely. Additional erythropoesis occurs in animals at high altitude.[158] The importance of this difference in concentration will become apparent in the discussion of the normal quantitative relationships during active O_2 interchange between mother and fetus (Section 1.5.3).

(c) Bohr Effects. Positive and negative Bohr effects are present in the dynamic exchange of O_2 in the human placenta. Thus, as maternal blood gains CO_2 and acid metabolic products, its increased acidity results in less affinity of maternal hemoglobin for O_2 (positive Bohr effect). This effect would promote loss of O_2 from maternal blood to the fetus. Also, the fetus, by releasing CO_2 and acid metabolites to the maternal intervillous blood, decreases the acidity of its own blood. As the fetal blood becomes more alkaline, it will increase its affinity for O_2 (negative Bohr effect), promoting transfer of O_2 from maternal to fetal bloodstreams.

1.5.2. Factors That Oppose Diffusion of Oxygen from Mother to Fetus

(a) Greater Acidity of Fetal Blood. The fetal villous capillary blood is more acid than maternal intervillous blood, which results in a decrease in affinity for O_2 of fetal blood during conditions of actual gestation. This effect is sufficient to partly cancel the advantage of the increased affinity of fetal blood over maternal blood at the same pH, as mentioned above.

(b) Decreased Oxygen-Carrying Capacity of Hemoglobin in Fetal Blood. Gram for gram of hemoglobin, fetal blood may be less capable of carrying O_2 when fully saturated (1.26 ml O_2/g hemoglobin) than is maternal hemoglobin (1.35 ml O_2/g hemoglobin).[188] Any such difference would be offset by the more marked discrepancy usually found between fetal and maternal hemoglobin concentrations that aids fetal oxygenation. Also, except for hyperbaric conditions of mother and fetus, the hemoglobin in their bloodstreams will never be completely saturated with O_2.

1.5.3. Normal Oxygen Exchange at the Placenta

Metcalfe *et al.*,[183] in an outstanding review of the dynamics of gas exchange in the pregnant uterus, calculated representative human fetal and maternal O_2 dissociation curves. The curves shown in Fig. 2

reveal the position of the fetal curve somewhat to the left of the maternal curve when P_{O_2} is related to O_2 saturation. To illustrate the degree of the effect of the higher hemoglobin content of fetal blood, they have constructed fetal and maternal curves relating P_{O_2} to O_2 concentration in milliliters per 100 ml of blood (Fig. 3). In Fig. 3, the units of the ordinate were converted to O_2 concentrations by assuming an O_2 capacity of 20% by volume as representative of fetal blood at term and an O_2 capacity of 15.5% by volume as representative of maternal blood. The wider distance between the curves plotted for O_2 concentrations (Fig. 3) than for those plotted for O_2 saturations (Fig. 2) indicates that under usual conditions of gas exchange at the human placenta, a wide difference in O_2 affinity exists between maternal and fetal blood.

To illustrate the dynamics of placental O_2 exchange, Metcalfe et al.[183] plotted selected values from the literature for maternal uterine artery and vein and for fetal umbilical artery and vein in relation to the curves. In the example shown in Fig. 4, the maternal uterine arterial plot falls on the maternal curve at pH 7.40 and has a P_{O_2} value of slightly over 60 mm Hg. As O_2 is passed to the fetus during circulation through the uterus, a concurrent fall in pH occurs, and the uterine venous plot lies to the right of the maternal curve at 7.36. The small shift

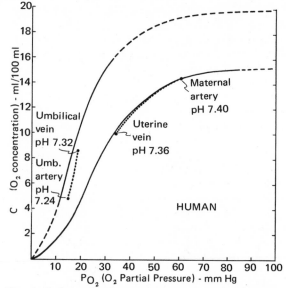

Fig. 4. Relationship between O_2 concentration and P_{O_2} for maternal uterine artery and vein and fetal umbilical artery and vein. Reproduced from Metcalfe et al.[183]

from the pH 7.40 curve suggests that this effect on O_2 affinity is not very large, but a greater deviation would be shown if the illustrative uterine venous pH value were lower. Similarly, the umbilical arterial plot of pH 7.24 and P_{O_2} of approximately 15 mm Hg and umbilical venous value of pH 7.32 and P_{O_2} of approximately 18 mm Hg again indicate a change in O_2 affinity from altered pH. These Bohr effects are both in the direction of widening the distance between the O_2 tension values.

The actual contribution of the Bohr effects relative to those of O_2 capacity and O_2 affinity were estimated by Bartels.[29] He concluded that the major characteristic of blood that contributes to maternal–fetal O_2 exchange in man is the differing O_2 capacities, and that Bohr effects actually play a more important role than differing O_2 affinities.

1.6. Placental Gas-Exchange Systems

Another important consideration in placental gas exchange involves the basic structural features of the placenta. Four basic systems, analogous to heat- and gas-exchange systems used by engineers, were proposed for placental gas exchange, and their relative efficiencies were evaluated.[31,32] The directions of flow of maternal and fetal blood at the regions of gas exchange for such proposed flow systems are diagrammed in Fig. 5.

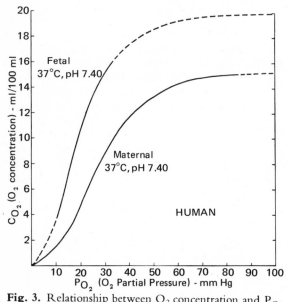

Fig. 3. Relationship between O_2 concentration and P_{O_2} for maternal and fetal blood. Reproduced from Metcalfe et al.[183]

In the concurrent system, maternal and fetal O_2 tensions, far apart in the arteries, would become nearly similar in the veins, but maternal uterine venous P_{O_2} would remain somewhat greater than

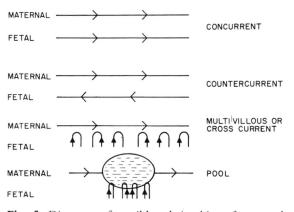

Fig. 5. Diagrams of possible relationships of maternal and fetal vascular patterns in the placenta.

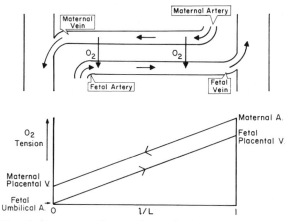

Fig. 6. Dynamics of gas exchange in the countercurrent system. Top: The flow of maternal and fetal blood is shown to be in opposite directions at the region of exchange of oxygen from maternal to fetal streams. Bottom: The changes in oxygen tension occurring along the maternal and fetal vessels are shown, assuming uniform exchange of oxygen throughout the total length L of both vessels in the area of gas exchange. Units on the abscissa are the distance l traveled by fetal blood along its vessel length (L), so that the ratio l/L at any given point on the abscissa indicates the fraction of total distance traveled and the ratio of 1 (at right) indicates that the total length of the vessel has been traversed. Note that with completion of the exposure of fetal to maternal blood, fetal placental venous blood has a higher O_2 tension than that of maternal placental venous blood. Reproduced (with modifications) from Metcalfe *et al.*[183]

fetal umbilical venous P_{O_2}. In the countercurrent system (Figs. 5 and 6), in which maternal and fetal blood flows proceed in opposite directions, a more efficient exchange of O_2 would occur, and umbilical venous P_{O_2} would be higher than maternal venous P_{O_2}. In the so-called "multivillous" or "cross-current" flow system (Figs. 5 and 7), maternal blood would contact fetal capillaries with blood flowing in different directions, and the efficiency of this system

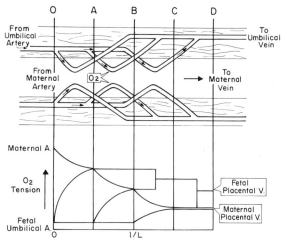

Fig. 7. Dynamics of gas exchange in the multivillous system. Top: Idealized pattern of gas exchange in a multivillous system. The fetal vessels shown above and below the maternal blood channel are observed to dip into the channel at various points and to receive O_2 from the maternal blood. Bottom: Occurrence of the expected changes in O_2 tension as the blood in fetal vessels traverses its region of gas exchange in the maternal vessels. Thus, at point 0, the fetal vessel has a low O_2 tension, but this tension is soon increased as the first fetal vessels dip into the maternal vessel. The magnitude of change in fetal P_{O_2} is greater during the first interchange (length OA) than subsequently (lengths AB and BC) because fetal blood is exposed to maternal blood with higher P_{O_2} than that downstream. The O_2 tension in fetal placental venous blood after exposure of all the villi to maternal blood will be a result of mixture of the many streams of venous blood from the villi. In the diagram, only three such villi are shown for illustrative purposes. Note that the final O_2 tension achieved in the fetal placental vein (far right) is greater than that of the maternal placental vein. Units on the abscissa are expressed as in Fig. 6, but l indicates the distance traveled by all the fetal blood from the beginning of gas exchange in the upstream capillary along the entire length (L) of the region of gas exchange until the capillary emerges downstream from the maternal vessel. Reproduced (with modifications) from Metcalfe *et al.*[183]

would be intermediate between the two systems described above. The blood in the umbilical vein in such a system represents a mixture of blood from different villi that have been exposed to various levels of P_{O_2} between those of the maternal uterine arteries and placental veins. If, on the other hand, fetal villous blood is exposed to a pool of maternal blood (Fig. 5), gas interchange may be less complete than that occurring in the multivillous system, and a mechanism similar in efficiency to a concurrent system would be present.

From the basic description of these systems, it is apparent that the anatomic description by Ramsey[219,220] and Freese[115] of the primate placenta fits most closely with the multivillous mechanism, although some features of the pool system may be present. This so-called "multivillous streambed" placenta appears to have spaces without villi in the centers of the cotyledons, permitting spurting of blood from the centrally placed arteries toward the chorionic plate and peripheral flow into the areas rich in villi.

1.7. Anatomic Characteristics of Placental Membranes

Placentas may also be classified in relation to the anatomic features of their membranes, as shown in Fig. 8, which illustrates five placental types found in several species of mammals. The layers shown between maternal and fetal blood for the epithelio-chorial placenta include maternal endothelium, maternal mesenchyme, uterine epithelium, chorionic epithelium, chorionic mesenchyme, and fetal endothelium. The human has a hemochorial placenta with the villi lying directly in the intervillous maternal blood space. In general, animals with a greater number of tissue layers between maternal and fetal blood have higher mean O_2

tension gradients, lower placental diffusion capacities for O_2, lower coefficients of O_2 extraction in the uterus, and a higher percentage of maternal cardiac output directed through the uterus, as will be delineated in Section 1.8.

1.8. Quantitative Measurements of Oxygen Transfer

To illustrate the physiologic differences among species, the interesting comparative data determined by Metcalfe et al.[183] for the most-studied species are shown in Table II. For complete understanding of the methods and calculations for each species, the reader is referred to Metcalfe's original article. The derivations of these quantitative measurements are of sufficient importance, however, that references and illustrative calculations will be given for the values obtained for the human placenta shown in Table II.

Uterine blood flow (column 4) was estimated by Metcalfe et al.[187] by the nitrous oxide equilibration method to approximate 150 ml/kg fetal weight per min. Using the Fick principle, the average O_2 consumption of the uterus (column 5) was calculated as 24.5 ml/min, or 7.4 ml/kg fetal weight per min.

The coefficient of O_2 extraction (column 6), defined as that percentage of O_2 supplied to the uterus by maternal arterial blood that is removed in transit through the uterus, is calculated from the expression

$$\frac{Ca_{O_2} - Cuv_{O_2}}{Ca_{O_2}} \times 100\%$$

where Ca_{O_2} and Cuv_{O_2} represent the O_2 concentrations in volumes percent of the maternal artery and uterine vein, respectively. Stenger et al.[247] estimated this to be approximately 30% agreeing generally with the calculations of Romney et al.[227]

Metcalfe et al.[187] determined that approximately

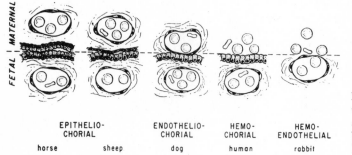

EPITHELIO-   ENDOTHELIO-   HEMO-   HEMO-
CHORIAL   CHORIAL   CHORIAL   ENDOTHELIAL

horse   sheep   dog   human   rabbit

Fig. 8. Anatomic types of placentas. Note that this classification depends on the presence or absence of epithelial and endothelial layers between the fetal and maternal capillaries. Reproduced from Metcalfe et al.[183]

Table II. Comparative Data on Placental Oxygen Transfer[a]

1	2	3	4	5	6	7	8	9	10
Species	Placental type	Term fetal weight (kg)	Uterine blood flow (ml/kg fetus per min)	Uterine V_{O_2} (ml/kg fetus per min)	$\dfrac{C_{aO_2} - C_{uvO_2}}{C_{aO_2}} \times 100\%$	$\dfrac{UBF\%}{Qmat}$	Assumed vascular geometry	$\bar{P}_{mO_2} - \bar{P}_{fO_2}$ (mm Hg)	Dp_{O_2} (ml/kg fetus per min per mm Hg)
Human	Hemochorial	3.3	150	7.4	30	10	Pool	20	0.37
							Multivillous	23	0.32
Macaca mulatta	Hemochorial	0.4	145	10.0	50	5	Pool	20	0.50
							Multivillous	23	0.30
Sheep	Epitheliochorial	3.0	330	9.0	30	20	Countercurrent	40	0.20
Goat	Syndesmochorial?	3.0	325	12.0	28	20	Pool	35	0.23
							Countercurrent	40	0.30
Rabbit	Hemoendothelial		83	7.7	71		Pool	26	0.46
							Countercurrent	10	0.70

[a] A summary of anatomic and physiologic characteristics of the placenta as an organ for gas transfer in each of several species. The mean gradient of oxygen tension between maternal and fetal blood ($\bar{P}_{mO_2} - \bar{P}_{fO_2}$) is given (column 9) for each of the patterns of vascular arrangement suggested on anatomic grounds. The placental diffusing capacity for oxygen, Dp_{O_2}, calculated according to equation 1 is given (column 10) for each value of tension gradient on the basis of the intrauterine oxygen consumption (V_{O_2} uterine) shown in column 5. Column 6 gives the coefficient of oxygen extraction that expresses the percentage of oxygen brought to the uterus in arterial blood (C_{aO_2}) that is removed from blood during its passage through the uterus ($C_{aO_2} - C_{uvO_2}$). C_{uvO_2} represents the oxygen concentration in uterine venous blood. Column 7 presents an estimate of the percentage of maternal cardiac output ($Qmat$) that flows to the uterus in each species (UBF symbolizes the rate of uterine blood flow). All values are based on data obtained near term.[(183)]

10% of maternal cardiac output (column 7) is directed through the human placenta.

Prystowsky[215] and Prystowsky et al.[216] determined the mean O_2 pressure gradient (column 9) at 20–24 mm Hg from data on the O_2 tensions in maternal blood and fetal umbilical vessels. Rooth[228] found a 20 mm Hg difference between intervillous blood P_{O_2} and the mean of the O_2 tensions determined for umbilical venous and arterial blood. The same order of magnitude was found when the gradients were determined assuming each of the four placental systems, such that gradients of 22 mm Hg, 25 mm Hg, 23 mm Hg, and 20 mm Hg were calculated for concurrent, countercurrent, multivillous, and pool systems, respectively.[181] This relatively close agreement indicates that the type of system is not of primary importance in determining placental efficiency. More important are the consistently high values for the P_{O_2} gradient whatever the system, a fact that demands further explanation.

The diffusion capacity for O_2, Dp_{O_2}, defined as that amount of O_2 passing the placental membrane per mm Hg pressure gradient per minute, may be expressed in the following terms:

$$Dp_{O_2} = \frac{V_{O_2}}{\overline{Pm}_{O_2} - \overline{Pf}_{O_2}} \qquad (1)$$

(column 10)

where V_{O_2} equals the rate of O_2 transfer across the placenta per minute, $\overline{Pm}_{O_2}$ equals the average O_2 tension of maternal blood reaching the placental membrane, and $\overline{Pf}_{O_2}$ equals the average P_{O_2} in fetal villous capillary blood.

If 24.5 ml O_2/min is passed across the placenta with a drop of 20 mm Hg in a pool system, $Dp_{O_2} = 24.5/20 = 1.38$ ml/min per mm Hg, or 0.37 ml/kg fetus per min per mm Hg (column 10). Likewise, for a multivillous system, $Dp_{O_2} = 24.5/23 = 1.1$ ml/min per mm Hg, or 0.32 ml/kg fetus per min per mm Hg (column 10).

1.9. Diffusion Equation

The diffusion equation of Fick may be expressed in terms of the difference of partial pressures and may be applied to O_2 transfer:

$$V_{O_2} = Kp_{O_2} \times A \times \frac{\overline{Pm}_{O_2} - \overline{Pf}_{O_2}}{L} \qquad (2)$$

where V_{O_2}, $\overline{Pm}_{O_2}$, and $\overline{Pf}_{O_2}$ are defined as in equation (1); Kp_{O_2} is the placental diffusion coefficient for O_2; A is the total area of placenta for O_2 exchange, or specifically the surface area of fetal villous capillaries; and L is the harmonic thickness of the placental membrane.

It is apparent from this relationship that the larger the surface area and the larger the difference in O_2 pressure between the maternal and fetal circuits, the greater will be the transfer of O_2. Conversely, the greater the distance O_2 has to traverse in its passage from maternal to fetal blood, the less the transfer of O_2.

Metcalfe et al.,[183] Bartels et al.,[32] and Adamsons[7] suggested substitution of various estimates of Kp_{O_2}, A, and L into equation (2) and into an equation for Dp_{O_2} derived by substituting Dp_{O_2} as defined in equation (1) into equation (2):

$$Dp_{O_2} = \frac{Kp_{O_2} \times A}{L} \qquad (3)$$

Serious questions arise about the meaning of the values for Dp_{O_2} derived from such a formula because of the variations in estimates of each of its factors by different investigators. For example, Aherne and Dunnill[11] estimated that the surface area of the placenta may be 12.2 m², while other estimates have ranged from 6.5 m² to 15 m².[101,102,260] The estimate of Aherne and Dunnill[11] for L of 3.5 also differs markedly from the estimate by Adamsons[7] of 10 μm. Kp_{O_2} was estimated from O_2 diffusion constants in brain (3.0×10^{-7} cm²/sec atm) and those in plasma and muscle (3.1×10^{-7} to 6.1×10^{-7}[7]). Even with these limitations, such calculations for Dp_{O_2} have revealed consistently higher values than those listed in column 10 of Table II. For example, Metcalfe et al.[183] determined a Dp_{O_2} from these calculations to be at least 5 times that derived from estimations of the mean pressure gradients for pool and intervillous systems. They concluded that this indicates that a diffusion barrier per se is not the limiting factor in placental O_2 exchange, but rather that the placenta's shunts, its inherent O_2 consumption, and maldistribution of blood flow to the region of gas exchange primarily limit the O_2 transfer from mother to fetus.

Adamsons[7] compared various parameters of O_2 transfer across the human lung and placenta and showed that the placenta compares favorably with the lung as an organ of gas exchange, provided

Table III. Comparison of Oxygen Transfer Across Lung and Placenta[a]

Measure	Lung	Placenta
O_2 concentration in environment (mM/liter)	8.3	8.3
O_2 concentration at site of gas exchange (mM/liter)	5.6	6.7
P_{O_2} at site of gas exchange (mm Hg)	104	45–60
Volume flow through O_2 donor site (ml/ml O_2 absorbed)	18	20–30
Volume flow through O_2 uptake site (ml/ml O_2 absorbed)	23	20–30
Oxygen utilization coefficient (%)	19	10–25

In the above calculations, molal concentration of oxygen in ambient air was calculated assuming an air temperature of 24°C and in maternal blood assuming a hemoglobin content of 13.6 g/100 ml and 100% O_2 saturation. The O_2 concentration in the placenta (intervillous space) was calculated assuming a hemoglobin concentration of 13.6 g/100 ml and 80% O_2 saturation.
[a] Data from Adamsons.[7]

comparison is made on the basis of O_2 requirements. As shown in Table III, estimates of O_2 concentration in the environment (ambient air for lung vs. maternal arterial blood for the placenta) and of O_2 concentration at the site of gas exchange (alveolar space vs. intervillous space) are similar. Also, the volume flow through the O_2 donor site in milliliters per milliliter of O_2 absorbed (alveolar ventilation in milliliters per milliliter of O_2 uptake in lung; intervillous space blood flow in milliliters per milliliter of O_2 absorbed in placenta) are comparable. The volume flow through the O_2 uptake site in milliliters per milliliter of O_2 absorbed (pulmonary blood flow/total body O_2 consumption; umbilical blood flow/fetal O_2 consumption) are also of similar magnitude in lung and placenta. The percentage of O_2 removed during contact with the respective exchange surfaces, listed as the O_2 utilization coefficient, is also of the same order of magnitude.

The major differences observed have been the lung's greater P_{O_2} at the site of gas exchange and the lung's much larger potential area of gas exchange; thus, the lung has a far greater ability than the placenta to increase the amount of O_2 transferred under stress. This advantage of the lung reflects its need to increase O_2 transfer markedly during exercise, when O_2 consumption increases greatly. Fetal O_2 consumption remains more constant because of

the resting state of the fetus in its protected environment, and no similar need exists for marked increase in placental O_2 transfer.

1.10. Oxygen Consumption by the Placenta and Its Membranes

Another approach to answering the question why there is such a large gradient in O_2 tension between mother and fetus was initiated by a series of clever experiments performed on anesthetized sheep near term by Campbell *et al.*[67] Two methods were used to eliminate placental transfer of oxygen. In the first series of experiments, the fetus was replaced by a mechanical pump that circulated blood through the umbilical vessels, and in a second series, the fetus, with intact umbilical circulation, was artificially ventilated with appropriate gas mixtures so that umbilical arterial and venous gas contents were equalized and fetal O_2 uptake from the placenta thereby eliminated. Under both these conditions, the maternal and fetal O_2 tensions did not become equal, and a maternal–fetal decrement of approximately 35 mm Hg remained, while the ewes maintained normal arterial O_2 tensions of 80–90 mm Hg. Also, when the ewes were given high O_2 mixtures to breathe, the gradient increased.

Campbell and co-workers considered that this difference in maternal and fetal O_2 tensions indicated O_2 consumption by the placenta itself, and pursued this point further. By comparing maternal uterine arterial O_2 tensions with those in major uterine veins and in uterine veins from individual cotyledons, they found a significant uptake of O_2 by the placenta and its cotyledons at a time when the exteriorized ventilated fetus was not consuming O_2 from the placenta at all.

The O_2 uptake by the placenta and fetal membranes was derived from several experiments in which the maternal placental blood flow had been eliminated by blocking blood flow through the ewe's aorta. While the intact fetus was being ventilated, its O_2 uptake was measured before and after umbilical cord occlusion; the difference in O_2 usage that was observed thus represented O_2 uptake by the placenta and fetal membranes. These measurements agreed well with calculations of O_2 uptake from umbilical arterial–venous O_2 differences and measured umbilical venous blood flows. The mean values ranged from 6.3 to 8.4 ml/min for O_2 uptake by the placenta and fetal membranes, and appeared to be higher in fetuses maintained more completely *in utero*. The ratios of fetal O_2 consumption to that of the placenta and fetal membranes ranged from 1.3 : 1.0 to 4.5 : 1.0, indicating very substantial O_2 consumption by these latter tissues.

The O_2 consumption of individual cotyledons was determined by fetal arterial–venous differences and flow through the fetal side of the cotyledons determined by an electromagnetic flow meter. The mean cotyledonary O_2 consumption was estimated to be 1.04 ml/100 g wet weight per min. A rough value of O_2 consumption of 0.80 ml/100 g per min was estimated for the O_2 consumption of the fetal membranes.

These studies show clearly that the sheep placenta is a very active metabolic organ, and that the large O_2 gradient across it may be due in part to its own O_2 consumption, as suggested originally by Huggett and Hammond.[149] The question whether this O_2 consumption of placental tissue occurs in series with the area of gas exchange or in parallel with it has not been resolved, but mechanisms considering the possibilities have been proposed by Dawes.[87]

Bartels[30] suggested that gas exchanges occur between the maternal circuit and the placenta both before and after the maternal–fetal transfer. He proposed that gas exchanges also occur between the fetal vascular compartment and placenta both before and after the transfers through the placental membrane. This combined parallel–series model is shown in Fig. 9, with hypothetical P_{O_2} values introduced from data obtained in sheep.

1.11. Evaluation of Placental Gas Exchange by Use of Mathematical Models

As revealed in the foregoing discussion, placental gas exchange involves many factors, and additional complexities are added frequently from new experiments. Many essential measurements, such as end-capillary blood gas values, are simply unavailable, even in animals; other measurements cannot be considered in the human for ethical reasons. The great number of factors that affect placental O_2 transfer were summed up by Longo *et al.*[167] (Table IV).

To evaluate the relative importance of many of these factors, Longo and co-workers developed elegantly conceived mathematical models for placental O_2 and CO_2 transfers.[142,143,167] Certain quite reasonable assumptions had to be made for the O_2 transfer model (i.e., concurrent flow, uniform diameter and equal lengths of the capillary, uniform tissue separating two parallel capillaries, thorough mixing of blood in the capillaries, nonpulsatile flow, constant P_{CO_2} and temperature during transit along the capillary). Despite these limitations, useful conclusions have been formulated relating to the mechanics of placental gas transfers from this prototype. The reader is referred to the series of articles by these authors for more details, but among the conclusions from their model studies and other experiments that may have wide application to O_2 transfer in general are:

1. Maternal and fetal placental end-capillary blood is essentially equilibrated.

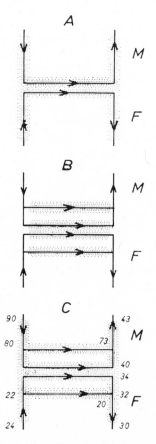

Fig. 9. Diagrams of possible sites of oxygen uptake by the placenta (stippled areas): (A) series and (B) parallel circulations; (C) a combination of series and parallel circulations, which is a probable model. The numbers are P_{O_2} values, similar to those obtained in sheep, which illustrate the effects of gas exchange in this model. Reproduced from Bartels.[30]

Table IV. Principal Factors That Affect Placental Oxygen Transfer[a]

1. Placental diffusing capacity
   Membrane diffusing capacity: area, thickness, solubility, diffusivity of tissues; capillary blood volume
   Diffusing capacity of blood: O_2 capacity, hemoglobin reaction rates, concentration of reduced hemoglobin

2. Maternal arterial P_{O_2}
   Inspired P_{O_2}; alveolar ventilation; mixed venous P_{O_2}; pulmonary blood flow; pulmonary diffusing capacity

3. Fetal arterial P_{O_2}
   Umbilical venous P_{O_2}; fetal oxygen consumption; peripheral blood flow; maternal arterial P_{O_2}; maternal placental hemoglobin flow, placental diffusing capacity

4. Maternal hemoglobin oxygen affinity
   pH; temperature; P_{CO_2}; 2,3-diphosphoglycerate concentration; carbon monoxide concentration

5. Fetal hemoglobin oxygen affinity
   pH; temperature; P_{CO_2}; 2,3-diphosphoglycerate concentration; carbon monoxide concentration

6. Maternal placental hemoglobin flow rate
   Arterial pressure; placental resistance to blood flow; venous pressure; oxygen capacity of blood

7. Fetal placental hemoglobin flow rate
   Umbilical artery blood pressure; umbilical venous blood pressure (or maternal vascular pressure under conditions of sluice flow); placental resistance to blood flow; oxygen capacity of blood

8. Spatial relationship of maternal to fetal flow

9. Amount of carbon dioxide exchange

[a] Adapted from Longo et al.[167]

2. Transient fetal end-capillary P_{O_2} and O_2 exchange rates are most sensitive to uncompensated changes in umbilical arterial P_{O_2} and fetal P_{50}, less sensitive to changes in maternal and fetal placental flow rates, and much less sensitive to changes in maternal P_{O_2} and placental diffusion capacity.

3. When the O_2 exchange rate is constant (as with steady-state constant fetal O_2 consumption), a different pattern of sensitiveness of end-capillary P_{O_2} would be expected. Maternal P_{50}, maternal flow, fetal placental flow, and maternal arterial P_{O_2} changes then have the greatest effects.

4. During normal conditions of oxygenation, uneven distribution of maternal and fetal blood flows may account for 80% of the P_{O_2} difference between uterine and umbilical venous blood.

5. With hypoxia, uneven distribution of such flows probably contributes only 33% of the measured difference. This conclusion confirms previous studies with radioactive labeled macroaggregates of albumin,[209] which had indicated more even distribution of flows during hypoxia.

6. Uneven distribution of diffusing capacity to blood flow also limits O_2 transfer.[208]

Concern has been expressed about the validity of models, because they will provide correct answers only when good data are entered into their formulas. Holland[145] used models for pool and multivillous systems and concluded that oxygen diffusion is limited at the placental capillary, which is in contrast to Longo's view. Rankin[221] established a physical model to evaluate the effects of maternal alkalosis on fetal oxygenation. Panigel[202] emphasized the use of *in vivo* "models," such as the bidiscoid rhesus placenta, in which comparisons of uteroplacental O_2 consumption can be made between a placental area still occupied by an undelivered twin and another area where the placenta has been removed with the other fetus.

1.12. Possible Facilitated Transport of Oxygen Across the Placenta

Also of great concern in evaluating the multiple factors responsible for O_2 transfer is the provocative recent evidence that O_2 might be transported across the placenta. Gurtner and Burns,[63,120,121] noting that argon has physical properties similar to those of O_2, but has a different ability to cross the placental barrier, set up an extremely interesting experiment. The fetus was delivered from term ewes by severing the umbilical cord, and the whole placenta was perfused by a pump primed with adult sheep's blood that had been equilibrated with argon. The partial pressures of argon and O_2 were measured in the umbilical artery and vein and in the maternal artery and uterine vein by mass spectrometry. Maternal uteroplacental flow was calculated measuring argon transfer from fetus to mother and using the argon values obtained as described above. The uteroplacental O_2 consumption was determined from this derived flow and maternal arterial and uterine venous O_2 contents. Several drugs known to bind cytochrome P450, including SKF-525A, analine, morphine, and meperidine, were administered through the "fetal" circulation, and their effects on argon and O_2 transfer were evaluated. A large drop in O_2 transfer was noted with administration of these drugs, but no significant fall in argon transfer occurred. There was usually concurrent fall in uteroplacental O_2 consumption, so that diversion of blood flow to the placental tissues and myometrium was not shown, and increased O_2 use by these tissues could not explain the diminished O_2 transfer. These observations led the authors to propose that O_2 transfer might be facilitated in the placenta by O_2 binding with cytochrome P450, as occurs in the liver.[168] This study also provides a reason for morphine-addicted females having smaller infants, since morphine would interfere with such O_2 transport, and fetal oxygenation might be compromised.

Obviously, this work needs confirmation before active O_2 transport must be considered in the models and calculations detailed above. If active O_2 transport exists, a major reorientation of ideas about placental gas exchange will have to take place. Possible new therapeutic approaches can be developed for improving fetal oxygenation. Evaluation should be made of clinical conditions, other than morphine addiction, in which defective O_2 transport may be involved.

1.13. Carbon Dioxide Transfer

The diffusion of CO_2 from fetus to mother also involves complex physiologic mechanisms, some of which have not been completely delineated. CO_2 is far more soluble than O_2, and one would expect the placental diffusion coefficient for CO_2 to be approximately 20 times that for O_2. If this were the case, one might expect a very small gradient of CO_2 across the placenta. The data shown in Fig. 1 indicate that this is not the case, but it must be emphasized again that these illustrative P_{CO_2} gradients may be greater than those present under

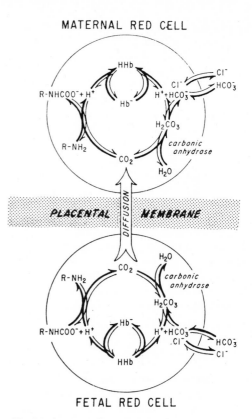

Fig. 10. Mechanisms for carriage of carbon dioxide by maternal and fetal blood. Reproduced from Metcalfe et al.[183]

more basal conditions,[228] and do not represent end-capillary measurements (see also Chapter 12).

The mechanisms for carriage of CO_2 by the fetal blood are the same as those for maternal carriage (Fig. 10). In the fetal red cell, a portion of CO_2 is in solution, and the remainder is present in the form of H_2CO_3 or HCO_3^-, or as carbaminohemoglobin. Diffusion of the gas proceeds into the maternal bloodstream, where similar combinations occur within the red cell and plasma. An important consideration is that the enzyme carbonic anhydrase acts as a catalyst in the interconversion between CO_2 and H_2CO_3 or any of its ionic species. Carbonic anhydrase speeds this reaction, probably sufficiently so that it may be nearly completed during the time needed for maternal blood to pass through the region of gas exchange in the placenta. In the fetal blood, however, this enzyme is in low concentration, and there has been some question whether there is insufficient time during the passage of fetal blood past the region of gas exchange for the reaction to reach equilibrium. Recent experiments in sheep indicate that this low concentration of carbonic anhydrase in fetal erythrocytes does not limit placental CO_2 exchange, and indeed, when the fetal Pa_{CO_2} was lowered below maternal levels by administration of THAM, CO_2 moved from maternal to fetal blood.[166] Carbonic anhydrase is not involved in the reaction of CO_2 with the amino groups of hemoglobin. Also shown in Fig. 10 is the exchange of HCO_3^- ions of the red cells with plasma Cl^- ions, which aids in conversion of CO_2 to HCO_3^- in the cells. At equilibrium in maternal blood, approximately 8% of the total CO_2 is dissolved in blood, 30% exists as carbaminohemoglobin, and 62% is bound as bicarbonate. Certain physiologic mechanisms favor CO_2 release from fetus to mother, including the characteristics of the CO_2 dissociation curves.

In Fig. 11, sections of the curves for CO_2 dissociation are shown over the usual physiologic range for nonpregnant, pregnant, and fetal humans. These curves are composed from blood samples obtained under resting conditions from women not in labor and from cord blood samples of fetuses, and thus may not accurately reflect differing affinities. Nevertheless, the fetal curve, lying to the right and below the maternal curve, indicates an apparent lower affinity for CO_2 than that of the mother.

The CO_2 dissociation curve is influenced by oxygenation of the blood. With increased oxygenation of fetal blood, as occurs during placental O_2 exchange, the fetal blood develops decreased affinity for CO_2, and the fetal curve tends to shift downward and to the right. Concurrently, with decreased oxygenation of maternal blood during placental passage, the maternal blood increases its affinity for CO_2 and tends to shift upward and to the left. These so-called "Christiansen–Douglas–Haldane effects" both favor release of CO_2 from the fetal to the maternal blood.[113] Two mechanisms have been described that are involved in this effect whereby release of O_2 increases the affinity of blood for CO_2; one involves the dissociation of the acid groups in the globin–heme linkage of hemoglobin, and the other involves binding of CO_2 by the amino groups of hemoglobin.

Not all factors are favorable for fetal CO_2 release at the placenta. For example, the higher hemoglobin content of fetal blood will tend to maintain CO_2 as fetal carbaminohemoglobin.

Under normal conditions of gestation, maternal hyperventilation with production of respiratory alkalosis is compensated by a decrease in renal excretion of fixed acids with decreased blood HCO_3^- and shifting of the maternal toward the fetal curve. Also, during the exercise of labor, the mother may develop increased levels of lactic acid,[136] which would also be expected to shift her curve toward that of the fetus.

Hill, Power, and Longo developed a mathematical model of CO_2 placental transfer and its interaction with O_2.[143,167] With certain assumptions similar to those of their O_2 transfer model, they projected several useful conclusions concerning placental CO_2 transfer. They found that CO_2 transfer is very rapid, but plasma CO_2 reactions are much slower. The Christiansen–Douglas–Haldane effect appears to play an important role in CO_2 transfer, accounting for 46% of the CO_2 exchanged. They also found that CO_2 exchange was most sensitive to uterine and umbilical arterial P_{CO_2} changes and capillary blood flow rates, as well as to the amount of O_2 exchanged and hemoglobin buffering.

The presence of the significant fetal–maternal P_{CO_2} gradient, which has been observed by actual measurements, again causes one to look for factors other than those purely related to CO_2 affinities and diffusion characteristics that might be involved in the

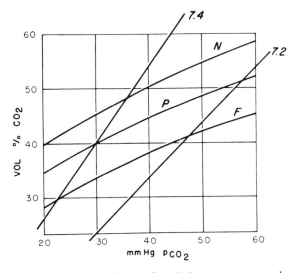

Fig. 11. Sections of CO_2 dissociation curves over the usual physiologic range for nonpregnant (N), pregnant (P), and fetal (F) humans. Iso-pH lines for pH's of 7.4 and 7.2 are also shown. Reproduced from Bartels *et al.*[32]

transfer of CO_2 from fetus to mother. As in the case of O_2, significant factors may be (1) fetal and maternal shunts, (2) placental metabolism, and (3) unequal maternal and fetal perfusions of the placental membrane. In addition, the low fetal carbonic anhydrase may limit significantly the elimination of CO_2 during passage through the fetal placental circuit.

1.14. Regulation of Placental Gas Transfer

1.14.1. Changes with Gestational Age

Only a few measurements of uterine and umbilical blood flow and fetal O_2 consumption have been made in the human, but several interesting observations from sheep studies have indicated changing relationships of these measures as gestation proceeds. Uterine blood flow increases in volume, and early studies suggested that this increase did not keep pace with fetal growth.[27] Even so, Meschia et al.[178] showed that the transfer of O_2 and the diffusion

capacity of the placenta increase in proportion to fetal weight in the later weeks of pregnancy. Representative determinations of uterine blood flows are shown in Table V.

Fetal umbilical blood flow increases with advancing gestation, but when it is related to kilograms of fetal body weight, there may be some decline (see Table VI). Early in gestation, the increase in flow may result from decreased umbilical resistance, but later, increased umbilical arterial pressure may be important.[84] Values for umbilical blood flow derived by several methods are shown in Table VI.

With advancing gestation, fetal O_2 consumption was noted by several observers to fall slightly when related to fetal weight (Table VII). There is considerable disagreement among investigators concerning the absolute values of fetal O_2 consumption of various animals near term. Indirect methods, using α-aminoantipyrine and urea infusions and with the animals unanesthetized, have given higher values[178,179] than those measurements using a flow

Table V. Uterine Blood Flow

Species	Age of gestation	Flow (ml/kg tissue weight per min), mean or range	Method	References
Human	10–28 weeks	94–127	Cuff electro-magnetic flow meter[a]	Assali et al.[17]
Human	Term	124	N_2O equilibration	Metcalfe et al.[183]
Human	Term	150	N_2O equilibration	Assali et al.[15]
Rhesus; pigtail monkeys	Last month of pregnancy	146[b]	4–Aminoantipyrine equilibration	Parer et al.[203]
Sheep, goats	102–139 days	276	Antipyrine equilibration	Meschia et al.[179]
Sheep	Term	186–252	Electromagnetic flow meter[a]	Assali et al.[14]
Goat	Term	354	Antipyrine equilibration (methoxyflurane)	Cotter et al.[77]
Macaca mulatta monkey	132–154 days	213	Antipyrine equilibration (N_2O or halothane)	Behrman et al.[38]

[a] Measurements were made on a single uterine artery. The uterine arterial flow was estimated by multiplying the value obtained by 2.
[b] Estimate from highest values obtained.

Table VI. Umbilical Blood Flow

Species	Age of gestation	Mean flow (ml/kg per min)	Method	Anesthetic	References
Human	9–28 weeks	110	Cuff electromagnetic flow meter	Hysterotomy, spinal or i.v. barbiturate	Assali et al.[17]
Human	35–42 weeks; less than 100 sec from normal delivery	75	Thermodilution	Normal delivery	Stembera et al.[244]
Sheep	135–146 days	104	Velodyne flow meter	Chloralose	Dawes and Mott[91]
Sheep	87–95 days	217	Electromagnetic flow meter	Chloralose	Dawes and Mott[93]
Sheep	137–141 days	170			
Sheep	Near term	183	Cuff electromagnetic flow meter	Spinal	Assali (personal communication to Dawes)
Sheep, goat	102–139 days	233	α-Aminopyrine infusion	Spinal	Meschia et al.[179]
Sheep	121–140 days	175 ± 8	Antipyrine	None—chronic preparation	James et al.[150]
Sheep	110–135 days	199 ± 20	Microsphere indicator dilution	None—chronic preparation	Faber and Green[112]
Macaca mulatta monkey	132–154 days	212	Antipyrine	N₂O or halothane	Behrman et al.[38]

Table VII. Fetal Oxygen Consumption

Species	Age of gestation (days)	Calculated fetal O_2 uptake (ml/kg per min ± S.E.)	Method of flow determination	Anesthetic	Sources
Human	Term	5.0	N_2O infusion	Cesarean section, spinal	Romney et al.[227]
Sheep	79–87	4.0 ± 0.9	Venous occlusion plethysmograph	Pentobarbitone	Acheson et al.[1]
	117–138	3.7 ± 1.0			
Sheep	85–90	4.8 ± 0.7	Velodyne flow meter	Chloralose	Dawes and Mott[91]
	135–146	4.2 ± 0.5			
Sheep	87–95	5.4 ± 0.5	Cannulated electro-magnetic flow meter	Chloralose	Dawes and Mott[93]
	137–141	4.6 ± 0.3			
Sheep	81–94	8.8 ± 0.3	Fick principle—urea	None	Meschia et al.[178]
	123–136	5.9 ± 0.4			
Sheep, goat	102–139	7.1 ± 0.4	Fick principle—anti-pyrine equilibration	None	Meschia et al.[179]
Sheep	121–140	5.99 ± 0.15	Fick—antipyrine	None—chronic preparation	James et al.[150]
Macaca mulatta monkey	132–154	7.73	Fick—antipyrine	N_2O or halothane	Behrman et al.[38]

meter to record blood flow through the intra-abdominal segment of the fetal umbilical vein.[91,93] It was suggested[179] that manipulation of the uterus may have compromised the fetal basal state during the latter experiments, particularly when they have been performed near term. Nevertheless, the estimate by Romney et al.[227] of fetal O_2 consumption of the human at term (5.0 ml/kg per min) agrees quite closely with the estimates by Dawes and associates of the fetal lamb's O_2 consumption of 3.7, 4.2, and 4.6 ml/kg per min obtained by three different direct methods for measuring blood flow.[1,91,93,97]

Recently, techniques have been developed that allow chronic implantation of sophisticated instruments into the fetus, permitting observations in a relatively basal state. Use of flow meters, ECGs, EEGs, intravascular pressure recordings, injections of radioactive microspheres, and sampling of blood from various sites in the fetus has opened up multiple new prospects for research, as well as permitting reevaluation of earlier investigations.

Meschia et al.[177] found no major changes in blood O_2 saturations and O_2 and CO_2 contents in fetal sheep and goats in which periodic samplings were taken during gestation. Others found decreases of fetal Pa_{CO_2},[45] but this decrease was minimal from the fourth month of gestation to term.

Since the placental/fetal weight ratio decreases during pregnancy, the placenta must increase its efficiency to maintain the stable fetal blood gas levels. Several factors may explain this increase, including (1) an increase in the number of fetal villi associated with enlarged placental exchange area,[248,260] (2) a decrease in the diffusion distance,[146] (3) an increase in placental perfusion that has been shown to occur on the maternal side,[1] and (4) an increase in the fetal O_2 capacity.

The distribution of uterine blood flow has been shown to change during gestation, with greater flow to cotyledons occurring as fetal weight increases. Flows to endometrium and uterine muscle remain quite constant.[173]

1.14.2. Effects of Hypoxia

In considering the effects of hypoxia on the fetus, one needs to differentiate between fetal hypoxia from compromised umbilical blood flow and that secondary to maternal hypoxia. In the former state, certain compensatory mechanisms may be brought into play by the fetus that may combat progression of this asphyxiation that interferes with CO_2 loss as well as O_2 gain. These mechanisms include: (1) lowering of oxygen tensions in the umbilical vessels, which, by creating a larger diffusion gradient for O_2 from mother to fetus, may favor maternal–fetal transfer; (2) increased umbilical blood flow occurring transiently as a result of the rise in fetal arterial blood pressure early during acute hypoxemia; (3) a redistribution of blood flows in the fetus that tends to maintain blood supply to the fetal brain, heart, and placenta and maintenance of effective cardiac output[37,66,156,159]; (4) a possible decrease in fetal O_2 consumption during hypoxia; and (5) fetal use of anaerobic glycolysis, under which circumstances excess lactic acid may be transferred from fetus to mother.[148] Unfortunately, severe fetal asphyxiation results in metabolic and respiratory acidosis with decreased cardiac output, and these compensatory mechanisms will be overcome. Also, decreased umbilical blood flow may compromise fetal circulation, initiating other detrimental and at times fatal conditions.

An interesting study was done evaluating the effects of maternal exercise on sheep fetuses, some of which had compromised umbilical circulation from tying off one umbilical artery.[109] In this chronic preparation, initial blood gases of the uncompromised lambs (P_{O_2}, 19.7 mm Hg; P_{CO_2}, 42.8 mm Hg; pH 7.41) were altered to values of P_{O_2}, 14.2 mm Hg; P_{CO_2}, 37 mm Hg; and pH, 7.45, but recovery was soon complete. In contrast, the lambs with the single functional umbilical artery were hypoxic during the preexercise period (P_{O_2}, 13.9 mm Hg; P_{CO_2}, 48.1 mm Hg; pH, 7.39) and showed additional hypoxia (P_{O_2}, 9.6 mm Hg) with slower recovery. The fetal hypoxia probably resulted from reduced uterine blood flow during exercise.

On the other hand, severe acute maternal hypoxia also involves maternal compensatory mechanisms. For example, (1) uterine blood flow may increase and (2) maternal hyperventilation may result in decreased maternal and fetal Pa_{CO_2} early during the hypoxic episode, and may prevent marked fall in maternal Pa_{CO_2} under certain conditions. Other mechanisms that the fetus initiates may be similar to those found when the umbilical cord is compromised. An additional possible compensatory mechanism was suggested by Tominaga and Page,[253] who showed thinning of the placental membrane during anoxia, which presumably would permit increased gas transfer.

Myers[197] quantitated the degree of hypoxia that produces brain damage in fetal monkeys. Falls in fetal aortic P_{O_2} from 26 to 30 mm Hg (normal during barbiturate anesthesia) to 15 or 16 mm Hg are not associated with brain injury if sustained for up to 2 hr, even though bradycardia and hypotension may occur. On the other hand, a fall to P_{O_2} of 11 or 12 mm Hg for 10–15 min can result in brain damage. Myers speculated that such O_2 deprivation results in decreased energy of brain tissue, but that this deprivation does not appear to be mediated through high-energy phosphate depletion. He showed a pathologic picture of brainstem involvement in acute, severe hypoxia, whereas prolonged partial asphyxia results in swelling of the brain, hemispheral tissue necrosis, porencephaly, and cystic brain degeneration.

The physiologic adaptations during chronic maternal hypoxia were studied extensively in Andean sheep,[28,180,184,185,217] and inferences were drawn from these studies about chronic hypoxia in humans. Since many women live at high altitude and appear to be adequately reproductive after long acclimatization,[31] maternal and fetal adaptation to such conditions must be favorable. The umbilical O_2 tensions remain similar in sheep living at high altitude to those found in animals at sea level, despite decreased maternal O_2 tensions. Fetal O_2 consumption and fetal growth are also similar. Uterine blood flow was found to increase by 35%, but this increase was not great enough to explain the persistence of normal O_2 tensions in the fetal vessels, and an improved placental diffusion capacity was inferred.[28] Pregnant women hyperventilate at high altitude and thus improve their Pa_{O_2} while lowering Pa_{CO_2} levels. Their hemoglobin contents and O_2 capacities also increase, as do those in the fetus. Despite these adaptations, there appears to be increased neonatal mortality in infants born at high altitude.[119]

In contrast, rapid movement from low to high altitudes results in different adaptations.[172] Using indwelling catheters to sample umbilical arterial and venous blood as well as maternal arterial and uterine venous blood of sheep, Makowski et al.[172] moved their animals rapidly from an altitude of 5280 feet to one of 14,260 feet above sea level. The acute exposure to high altitude of these unacclimated sheep resulted in a marked reduction in P_{O_2}, O_2 saturation, and O_2 content in the umbilical vessels. After several days, adaptation to the higher altitude was observed, as fetal total hemoglobin content

increased and an increase in uterine venous P_{O_2} suggested increased uterine blood flow.

Exposure of ewes with indwelling catheters and flow meters to a 15% O_2 environment for 10 min enabled Makowski et al.[172] to evaluate short-term changes in uterine blood flow (decrease of 2.4%), uterine hemoglobin flow (increase of 3.7%), and hemoglobin concentration (increase of 6.4%). The magnitude of these effects was not great enough to explain the maintenance of P_{O_2} levels in the uterine and umbilical veins under these conditions.

Mothers with cyanotic congenital cardiac disorders with right-to-left shunts have a low fertility rate[64,182] and may have small-for-date infants, but the fetus appears much less threatened by this condition of pregnancy than the mother. The mother with Eisenmenger's syndrome appears to be especially endangered after delivery, perhaps resulting from increasing pulmonary hypertension.

1.14.3. Effects of Hyperoxia

Of interest is the observation that maternal hyperoxia is not associated with significant change in fetal O_2 consumption,[33] an observation that strengthens the argument that normally the fetus is not living under hypoxic conditions.

Administration of 80–100% O_2 mixtures to mothers may produce a large rise in maternal Pa_{O_2}, but only a small rise in the fetal O_2 tension.[265] In sheep, this P_{O_2} increase may be in the range of 10 mm Hg in the umbilical vein and carotid artery.[131] This small rise protects the fetus from deleterious effects of hyperoxia such as ductal closure[262] or retrolental fibroplasia.

1.15. Effects of Labor and Delivery on Placental Gas Exchange

Studies of the changes in placental gas exchange during labor and delivery are especially difficult to perform in humans, but with the advent of fetal scalp sampling and other techniques, some information is becoming available. It appears that humans, like cows and sheep,[75] normally show little fall in Pa_{O_2} until the second stage of labor. Decreases of approximately 4–6 mm Hg in P_{O_2} have been noted in the cow shortly before birth, and considerably larger vacillations have been noted during the strong contractions of the second stage of labor. During labor, uterine blood flow falls prior to uterine contraction, then recovers during the early part of the contraction until intrauterine pressure builds up to 30 mm Hg, at which time uterine flow decreases again.[59] Strong uterine contractions "throttle" maternal placental blood flow, resulting in a decrease in placental O_2 transfer. Martin (cf. Moll[191]) estimated that uterine conductance falls linearly with uterine pressure in the rhesus monkey, and human uterine blood flow may be reduced by half during a strong contraction.

Power and Longo[207] also studied these "sluice-flow" characteristics in the sheep, using perfusion of an isolated cotyledon. They showed that conditions that raise the uterine venous pressure by 30 mm Hg will increase cotyledonary inflow pressure and can result in fetal bradycardia. Uterine contractions and blocking of maternal venous return by pressure of the uterus would be expected to produce these effects. Umbilical blood flow is affected by coiling of the cord around the fetal neck, which results in spasm of the cord, perhaps mediated through nerves to the umbilical vessel walls.[246] Severe hypoxia was shown to be associated with decreased cord flow.[245]

Interestingly, during normal deliveries, serial umbilical arterial samples taken 2–8 sec after birth and then 5–46 sec later showed a pH drop of 0.02 unit/10 sec and increasing P_{CO_2} whether the infant had started breathing or not. Thus, the initial, apparently effective breaths may not alter the trend toward asphyxia.[254]

1.15.1. Methods of Improving Placental Gas Exchange and Fetal State

Although the fetus does not show a large increase in Pa_{O_2} when maternal oxygenation is augmented, a critical improvement from a fetal hypoxic state can occur, and there is little evidence that the fetus is harmed by this procedure.[116,160] Augmentation of maternal oxygenation appears to be more effective in relieving fetal pulmonary vasoconstriction and bradycardia than administration of boluses of $NaHCO_3$ periodically to fetal and neonatal lambs.[156] To obtain maximum effect from $NaHCO_3$ administration, constant infusions that will raise plasma tonicity and increase plasma volume seem to be needed. In difficult deliveries with maternal metabolic acidosis, $NaHCO_3$ has been administered intravenously to mothers with

the intention of combating concurrent fetal metabolic acidosis.[229]

1.15.2. Effects on the Fetus of Severe Maternal Hyperventilation

Although maternal hyperventilation during pregnancy maintains fetal acid–base conditions close to those of the adult, and moderate hyperventilation may increase fetal Pa_{O_2}, severe hyperventilation, especially by mechanical ventilators, may have deleterious effects on the fetus.

Morishima et al.[192,193] mechanically hyperventilated pregnant guinea pigs and observed that this procedure produced a profound state of metabolic acidosis in their fetuses. This effect appeared to be due in part to use of the mechanical ventilator, since only slight fetal acidosis was produced when maternal hyperventilation was evoked by α-lobelline. These interesting findings were extended by Motoyama et al.,[194] who observed that hypocapnia of the mother caused decrease in umbilical arterial blood flow, as determined by a cuff electromagnetic flow meter in the fetal sheep. Maternal hyperventilation was found to cause fetal metabolic acidosis if the associated maternal hypocapnia was not corrected; when three ewes were given 3–5% CO_2 mixtures to breathe while being hyperventilated and were thus maintained in a eucapnic state, fetal metabolic acidosis did not develop.

This deleterious effect of maternal hyperventilation was not confirmed in recent sheep experiments by Baillie et al.,[23] and has not been found to occur during normal deliveries.[251]

The clinical implications of hyperventilation during delivery were reviewed by Lumley and Wood.[169] In the conscious patient during labor, deliberate maternal hyperventilation does not result in fetal hypoxia unless maternal hypocapnia is very severe, and the data obtained from fetal scalp sampling[235] show much variance. Under most conditions of delivery, maternal hyperventilation should not endanger the fetus.

Of more concern is hyperventilation associated with maternal anesthesia, as at cesarean section, which can result in fetal hypoxia; fortunately, fetal hypoxia under these conditions is usually not associated with threatening fetal acidosis.[73] Also, excessive hyperventilation should be avoided in the presence of adverse clinical complications, such as diminished uterine or umbilical blood flow. Fetal acidosis has been detected during these conditions of labor.[196]

1.16. Conclusions

In addition to the classic considerations of O_2 and CO_2 dissociation curves, one must include Bohr effects and Christiansen–Douglas–Haldane effects, concepts of active placental metabolism, anatomic arrangements of the blood vessels in the placentas of the particular animal species, variation in uterine and umbilical blood flows, and the size of the area of gas exchange between the maternal and fetal circuits in a unitary hypothesis of placental gas exchange. The gradients in gas tensions across the placenta do not result from a large diffusion barrier *per se*, but instead are caused by the differences in affinities for O_2 and CO_2 of maternal and fetal blood, and by the important factors of active metabolism of the placenta itself and of incomplete perfusion of the area of gas exchange by the maternal and fetal placental circuits.

The complexities of maternal fetal gas transfer may require further use of mathematical models with sophisticated computer-based calculations to evaluate the importance of the component mechanisms. The possibility that active O_2 transport may be involved in placental O_2 transfer needs to be evaluated thoroughly because of the major reorientation such an involvement would have on present concepts of placental gas exchange.

Normally, the fetus is not living in an oxygen-deprived state, and the placenta, like the lung, provides a mechanism for gas exchange with a rather wide margin of safety. In fact, it is useful to consider the analogies between the gas-exchange mechanisms of the placenta and the lung, such as perfusion/perfusion relationships (analogous to ventilation/perfusion relationships), gas-exchange areas, gradients in gas tensions, and diffusion gradients. When such comparisons are made and related to O_2 requirements, the placenta compares favorably with the lung.[7]

2. Development of the Fetal Respiratory System

The fetal respiratory apparatus, including the lungs and respiratory tract, the respiratory muscles and their nerves, and the reflex regulatory mecha-

nisms, must be in a state of readiness for the extraordinary demands of the transition to independent respiration at birth. Although it is not within the purview of this book to detail the morphogenesis of this apparatus, certain anatomic changes in the fetal respiratory tract that have important functional implications will be described. The functional development of the fetal respiratory system will also be reviewed.

2.1. Development of the Fetal Lung

2.1.1. Morphological Changes

Early in gestation, the fetal lung develops as a glandular organ. At 3.5 weeks of gestation, the lung bud appears as a protrusion from the gut and several days later begins its first branching. This endodermal tree is surrounded by mesenchyme that may later differentiate into the nonepithelial and connective tissue components of the alveolar structures, pleura, interlobar septa, and bronchial cartilage. Lobar bronchi, present at the 6th week of gestation, continue to branch, and between the 10th and 16th weeks, most of the bronchial branching has been completed. Acini of varying size have been observed as discrete terminal units as early as 17 weeks' gestation.[50]

At about the 20th week, canals begin to develop in the bronchial tree,[61] and since the inner lining of epithelial cells proliferates more rapidly than the stroma,[242] infoldings of the terminal divisions of the lung buds occur to form primitive air sacs. By the 28th week, blood vessel structures invade the mesenchyme so that gas exchange between these structures and the canals of the bronchial tree is possible. This anatomic event is obviously very important, because it determines to a considerable degree the potential of the fetus for independent survival. At this stage, an additional limitation of the fetal lung to providing adequate air exchange in the event of birth is the incomplete development of alveoli.[222] Some flattening of the alveolar epithelium may occur *in utero* before air has been introduced into the alveoli.[204,242] It is important to realize, however, that development and proliferation of the alveoli continue for many months after birth, so that even the term infant may be handicapped in gas exchange after birth by this structural immaturity.[252]

The branching of pulmonary vessels corresponds

structurally to bronchial branching to a certain extent, but many supernumerary vessel branches that communicate with adjacent respiratory units are formed. These alternative vessel networks will be of great importance after birth in maintaining gas exchange when individual respiratory units are nonfunctioning.

The range of muscularity in small pulmonary arteries is great,[108] but the small arteries are relatively more muscular than larger ones, and therefore are potentially more capable of increasing pulmonary vascular resistance by contraction.

Exposure of the small fetal pulmonary arteries to low O_2 tension is probably the main reason fetal pulmonary vascular resistance is so high.[233] Fetal hypoxia increases this resistance even more. Also of clinical importance, in the premature infant, the media of the pulmonary arteries is poorly developed, so that the postnatal drop in pulmonary vascular resistance occurs more rapidly than in the term infant. This drop permits cardiac failure to occur early in prematures with left-to-right cardiovascular shunts, such as patent ductus arteriosus and ventricular septal defect.

Mucus-secreting glands of the trachea appear at 8 weeks' gestation,[243] goblet cells at 13 weeks, and cilia at 13 weeks in the peripheral air passages.[18] The hyperacidity of the tracheal fluid of the newborn[4] may be a result of the acid mucopolysaccharide secretions of the mucous glands.

During fetal life, alveolar lining cells show osmiophilic inclusions that may be the source of the surfactant material that is so important in maintaining the stability of alveoli by altering surface tension during expansion and contraction of the airspaces. Campiche et al.[68] detected these inclusions in a small human fetus weighing 840 g, but deficiency of surfactant material was observed in premature infants with hyaline membrane disease.[20] The vital role of deficiency of surfactant in this clinical disorder is emphasized in the more detailed discussion of the alveolar lining cells in Chapter 7.

The process of fetal lung development may be accelerated by administration of corticosteroids to fetal animals. Administration of corticosteroids hastens the development of surfactant-producing cells, and was suggested as an approach to preventing or ameliorating respiratory distress syndrome in humans.[163] Clinical trials in which corticosteroids have been administered to mothers undergoing premature labor indicated a possibly lower incidence of respiratory distress syndrome, but there were side effects from this treatment.[19,163]

2.1.2. Functional Development

From the foregoing discussion of anatomic changes, it is apparent that the lung will usually not be functional in the human of less than approximately 26 weeks of gestation. Also, for weeks thereafter, the fetal lung will be ill prepared for its role in gas exchange because of limited development of terminal air spaces closely adjacent to pulmonary vessels.

Early in gestation, the glottis is closed, but as the airways develop, they fill with fluid, which later will be passed through the upper respiratory tract to the pharynx, where it will be swallowed.[3] In full-term fetal lambs, drainage of this fluid immediately after the trachea has been cannulated can amount to as much as 50 ml. The fluid has been found to be acid (pH 6.43), to have an osmolality similar to maternal and fetal blood (302 mOsm/liter), to have a low CO_2 concentration (4.4 mEq/liter), and to contain surfactant activity at term in the lamb.[2,4,5] Under usual circumstances, it is unlikely that much of this fluid enters the amniotic fluid pool.

The fetal sheep normally swallows 20–200 ml of amniotic fluid in 2–7 random episodes daily, each lasting 1–9 min.[51,52] This swallowing appears to be related to the functioning of taste buds in the last trimester,[53] and may have clinical implications as a route of offering oral medications to the fetus. Fetal acidosis has been treated by introducing $NaHCO_3$ into the amniotic fluid.[122]

The presence of a fluid column in the fetal lung offers a large resistance to inspiration of the fetus in utero. This fluid must be removed early after breathing commences. Since the functional residual capacity of the infant rises to levels similar (by body weight) to those of the adult within 15 min after normal birth, it is probable that this fluid is rapidly removed, partly by drainage and swallowing, but also by evaporation and through the pulmonary capillary and lymphatic circulation.[10,49]

The movement of fluid into and out of the respiratory passages also depends on the characteristics of fetal respiratory movements during gestation. Since integrated and effective respiratory movements are vitally needed at the time of birth, their development in utero is of major interest. Recent work has shown that the fetus has active respiratory movements that indicate readiness to assume independent respiration.

2.2. Fetal Respiratory Movements

A major contribution to the understanding of fetal respiratory movements resulted from experiments stimulated by the review of Barcroft's and Barron's studies of fetal activity.[25] The experiments by Dawes and co-workers[90,95,96] and Merlet,[176] first with exteriorized fetal sheep, and later with chronic fetal sheep preparations, established the existence of several types of fetal respiratory activity. The presence of these movements in the human fetus was confirmed by Boddy and Dawes[46] and Boddy and Mantell[47] using ultrasonic recordings. Since monitoring of these movements may prove valuable in predicting fetal distress,[46] the movements are of great potential importance, and will be discussed in detail.

Dawes et al.[96] accomplished chronic implantation of a flow meter in the trachea and tracheal pressure cannulation in fetal sheep, which permitted continuous observations in the otherwise undisturbed fetal state. These workers noted episodic, spontaneous breathing movements with the characteristics shown in Table VIII.

The small back-and-forth flow of tracheal fluid with these breaths provides an explanation of why injections of radiocontrast material into the amniotic fluid have not resulted in filling of the respiratory

Table VIII. Fetal Respiratory Activity in Sheep[a]

Irregular rate (3–4 Hz) and depth (usually shallow, can reach 30 mm Hg pressure)

Increase in rate and depth from 80 days' gestation to term; may occur at 40 days

Back-and-forth flow of fluid in trachea usually 1 ml (insufficient to clear 8–10 ml tracheal dead space)

Movements noted in chest wall and respiratory muscles of fetus; not detectable on maternal abdomen

Occur in episodes, lasting for 1 min to 1 hr, which are present about 40% of time

Circadian rhythm with greatest flow (rate and depth increase) at 21:00 hours

Related to REM sleep, as documented by electrocortico-gram

[a] Based on information from Dawes.[90]

tree. These movements, not detectable on the ewe's abdomen, are apparently more readily noted in the human, as Preyer observed in 1885[214] and Ahfeld in 1905.[12] The relationship of this type of breathing in late gestation to rapid eye movement (REM) sleep with its characteristic electrocorticographic fast and low voltages has been confirmed readily in the exteriorized fetal lamb as it lies in a warm saline bath. Interestingly, the rapid spontaneous respiratory activity does appear earlier in gestation than electrocorticographic evidence of REM sleep.

In addition to this type of respiratory activity in sheep, periodic gasping and sighing efforts occur at 1–4/min for about 5% of the time and generate pressures as high as 20 mm Hg. These efforts are not associated with fetal blood gas changes or the electrocorticographic patterns of REM sleep. Also, asphyxial gasps that are related to blood gas alterations have been observed. Finally, the fetal sheep may be capable of panting at a rate of approximately 4 Hz if the amniotic temperature is elevated.[90]

The fetal respiratory motions associated with REM sleep occur when fetal blood gas tensions are normal. Decreasing fetal Pa_{O_2} diminishes this activity and results in electrocorticographic patterns indicative of quiet sleep with slow, large voltages. Increasing fetal Pa_{O_2} does not appear to increase the activity above its usual levels. On the other hand, hypercapnia causes a sustained increase in this type of fetal breathing, as shown in Fig. 12 in the exteriorized fetal lamb, with the effect primarily on the depth of breathing. Interestingly, we have noted that this effect occurs after bilateral peripheral chemodenervation with division of carotid sinus and vagal nerves.

Hypoxic fetal distress appears to suppress rapid fetal respiratory activity, as does hypoglycemia.[46,90] Anesthetic agents and sedatives reaching the fetus have a suppressive effect also, as does surgical trauma. The latter effect probably explains the failure in the past to be aware of these respiratory movements during a variety of acute experiments in which lambs were exteriorized. Also, a period of time must be permitted to elapse before observations are started when flow probes and cannulas have been placed in the fetal sheep for chronic studies. Table IX lists the conditions that have been shown to depress REM fetal respiratory activity in animals.

These conditions all represent factors known to be detrimental to the neonate at the time of birth.

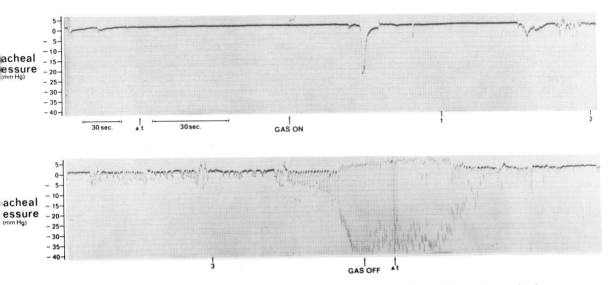

Fig. 12. Fetal respiratory response to hypercarbia. Rapid fetal respiratory activity, as shown by tracheal pressure changes (ordinate), is initiated approximately 2 min after the ewe has been breathing an 8% CO_2–15% O_2 mixture. Note the rhythmic quality and the vigorous breathing of this unanesthetized exteriorized term lamb, which persisted for a while after CO_2 was discontinued and while fetal P_{CO_2} remained elevated. Arousals after 30 sec of CO_2 administration and at 1 min 40 sec are noted, as are occasional isolated breaths.

Preservation of normal fetal respiratory activity should therefore be an important goal during normal gestation. Monitoring of this activity has been achieved by A scale ultrasonic recordings of the human fetus, but is quite difficult with present instrumentation. Proponents of this method believe that monitoring these respiratory patterns provides a much more sensitive indicator of fetal distress than the more established methods, such as monitoring fetal heartbeat.

A variety of neurophysiological studies have been performed to define the nature of fetal breathing.

Table XI. Conditions That Depress Fetal Respiratory Activity

Hypoxia
Hypoglycemia
Barbiturate therapy to mother—pentobarbitone
General anesthesia—chloralose
Surgical trauma
Maternal peritoneal infection
Maternal cigarette smoking[175]

Maloney et al.[174] recorded diaphragmatic electromyograms, which indicate efferent potential traffic to the muscles of respiration during this type of breathing. Bystrzycka et al.[65] recorded phrenic and intercostal neural activity, as well as medullary potentials, in exteriorized fetal sheep, and confirmed that the motor component of the respiratory reflex is mature in term lambs. About half their exteriorized lambs showed rapid, periodic spontaneous respiratory motions, and in these lambs, a few inspiratory and more expiratory units were detected in the region of the obex. The duration of inspiratory discharges relative to that of expiratory discharges was the same as detected later during normal breathing of newborn lambs. In striking contrast, there was marked prolongation of expiratory discharges when these discharges could be detected in the obex region during "gasping" respirations.

In the fetal lambs that were breathing, occlusion of the umbilical cord abolished inspiratory and expiratory activity as recorded in the medulla, except for short bursts of tonic activity in the medullary units.[65] Release of the cord resulted in return of the previous type of respiratory activity, which was also shown to be unaffected by chemoreceptor stimulation (injection of NaCN into the region of the carotid sinus) or by noise or light. Apnea between breathing periods did not appear to be related to respiratory depression, since discharge from medullary units was noted during these apneic intervals.

2.3. Functional Development of Peripheral Carotid Chemoreceptors

The chemical environment of the chemoreceptive areas of the fetus differs from the environment that will be present soon after birth. The carotid arterial blood that flows to the aortic, carotid, and central chemosensitive regions appears to have P_{CO_2} and pH levels quite similar to those of adults. In contrast, the P_{O_2} in carotid arterial blood is markedly below that of the adult. This low O_2 tension does not evoke respiration *in utero*, and one must conclude either that the peripheral glomera are not being subjected to critical hypoxic stimulation or that such chemoreceptive neural activity as is being produced by them provides an insufficient stimulus to evoke respiratory responses.

Varying the fetal carotid O_2 tension in the range of P_{O_2} from 10 to 200 mm Hg fails to elicit chemoreceptor responses as recorded off the carotid sinus nerve,[43] and injections of NaCN into the carotid artery likewise have not been shown to elicit a carotid chemoreceptive response.[26,43,224]

The failure to demonstrate marked tonic chemoreceptor activity in the undisturbed fetus, despite its very low carotid arterial Pa_{O_2}, contrasts strikingly with observations made in the adult animal. Von Euler *et al.*[256] detected chemopotentials in the carotid sinus nerve when the carotid arterial Pa_{O_2} was greater than 100 mm Hg, and Eyzaguirre and Lewin[110] suggested that chemopotentials may be present even in the adult anesthetized cat breathing 100% O_2. Also, Eyzaguirre and Lewin,[111] using an *in vitro* preparation of the carotid body with its attached carotid sinus nerve, found a low chemodischarge when the carotid body was bathed in saline exposed to 100% O_2, a maximum discharge in 20% O_2, and depression of discharge in a 5% solution, in which the P_{O_2} would be approximately 38 mm Hg.

The blood gas tensions remain quite constant in the undisturbed fetal sheep, as measured in the fetal inferior vena cava. Thus, alterations in fetal blood gases of the degree induced experimentally by Cross,[79] Harned *et al.*,[130] Avery *et al.*,[22] and Woodrum *et al.*[263] would not be expected to occur during normal gestation and would reflect abnormal states. Marked alteration of carotid O_2 tensions, either by administration of low O_2 gas mixtures to the ewes while maintaining constant Pa_{CO_2} and pH levels,[124] or by perfusion of the carotid artery with hypoxic blood,[130] does invoke fetal respiratory activity in the exteriorized lamb. Even with step change in the Pa_{O_2} of the perfusing blood, however, there is an unexplained time lag before the onset of breathing.[130,263] Reservations have been expressed about whether this respiratory activity is invoked through the mechanism of peripheral chemoreceptor activation or through an alternate mechanism related to fetal arousal.[124,212] Indeed, one group of investigators proposed that a central oxygen-sensing receptor mechanism is present in the fetus,[154] although such sensors have never been shown in the adult animal.

The exteriorized fetal sheep also breathes when the carotid arterial P_{CO_2} is changed rapidly[22,263] and when the ewe is given high CO_2 mixtures to inhale.[124] In these experiments, changes in P_{CO_2} would be expected to affect central as well as peripheral chemoreceptive regions. Interestingly, a combined stimulus of hypoxia and hypercarbia[201,263] or hypoxia and acidosis[130] appears to cause more active breathing than the stimulus of hypoxia alone.

2.4. Functional Development of Aortic Chemoreceptors

Tonic neural afferent activity has been demonstrated from the aortic group of chemoreceptors in the term fetal sheep.[205] These receptors are involved primarily in the control of circulation, and hypoxia has been shown to cause increased peripheral vasoconstriction and rise in systemic pressure through their increased activity.[94] Activation of these reflexes should result in vasodilatation of the cerebral blood vessels, as occurs in the adult,[71,206] so that vasodilatation is the major mechanism for the shifting pattern of fetal blood flow under hypoxic conditions; increased cerebral and myocardial flow with diversion to these areas of a greater portion of the relatively highly saturated umbilical venous blood may ensure survival of a threatened fetus. This increase, however, occurs at the expense of decreased renal, mesenteric, and pulmonary flow, setting up conditions that may predispose to postnatal clinical conditions such as renal failure, necrotizing enterocolitis, and respiratory distress syndrome.

The effect of hypoxia in increasing sympathetic activity generally in the fetus also results in an interplay between the aortic and carotid glomic functions. As is detailed in Section 3.3, increased cervical sympathetic activity is associated with increased carotid afferent discharge, perhaps by decreasing blood flow to the carotid body.[213] This interrelationship has not been proven in the fetus.

2.5. Development of the Fetal Pulmonary Circulation

The fetal lung must develop a rich blood supply to provide an intricate vascular network capable of sustaining gas exchange across the alveolar–capillary membrane immediately after birth. Development of this supply is accomplished even though the pulmonary arterial blood flow in the fetus comprises a relatively small fraction of the total fetal cardiac output.[16,97,159,232] The pulmonary arterial flow is determined primarily by the resistance in the smaller pulmonary arteries and varies considerably, depending on the state of the fetus. Temporary occlusion of the lamb's umbilical cord, for example, results in a major redistribution of blood flow, which favors vital areas of the fetus by increased perfusion of the brain and heart, but causes decreased perfusion of the lungs.[66] The small fetal pulmonary arteries appear to react as do the adult pulmonary arteries to alterations in gas tension; i.e., hypoxia and hypercarbia cause vasoconstriction. In fact, in the lower range of O_2 tensions present in fetal pulmonary arterial blood, a small decrease of P_{O_2} may produce a striking increase in pulmonary vasoconstriction.[233]

It has been proposed that pulmonary hypoperfusion that may have been initiated *in utero* may result in the respiratory distress syndrome of the neonate,[72] and that the biochemical alterations that cause diminished surfactant production may also result from decreased pulmonary perfusion (see Chapter 7). The clinical implications of this concept are great indeed and have focused investigative efforts on the relationships between pulmonary circulation and this disorder.

3. Initiation of Respiration at Birth

The complex neuromuscular mechanisms needed for the initiation and maintenance of independent respiration have been developed and are in readiness for birth. The fetal mammal normally makes rapid respiratory movements with occasional deeper motions, but otherwise survives quite passively in its warm, fluid intrauterine milieu, which has been likened for emphasis to the environment of the astronaut in space.[223] The lack of sensory stimulation at this time contrasts markedly with the barrage of sensory stimuli that will be provided during birth, including sensations of cold, touch, pain, light, sound, and gravity. In addition, chemical stimulation of peripheral and central chemoreceptor mechanisms will occur as a result of the asphyxia that takes place as placental gas exchange is compromised. Consideration of the physiologic roles of each of these stimuli in the initiation of respiration provides useful leads in understanding this complex process.

3.1. Chemoreceptor Stimulation

Multiple observations have revealed that the human[151,153,234] and other mammals undergo a degree of asphyxiation during normal birth. James and Adamsons[152] found that the infant at birth will show a fall in aortic arterial O_2 saturation to very low levels, with a rise in P_{CO_2} at a rate of approximately 10 mm Hg/min and a fall of 0.1 pH unit/min before breathing is initiated. The acidosis that develops has both respiratory and metabolic components, the latter resulting from fetal anaerobic glycolysis.[148,255]

Since the peripheral chemoreceptors appear to play a role in the breath-to-breath regulation of respiration of the adult and are especially involved in rapid reactions to hypoxia and hypercarbia, they might be expected to be important in initiating the first breaths. The central chemosensors of the adult are concerned more with maintenance of homeostatic relationships of CO_2 tension and acid–base states, and might be expected to be involved primarily in regulation of respiration once it has become established.

3.2. Peripheral Chemoreceptor Mechanisms and the Initiation of Respiration

In striking contrast to the difficulty in demonstrating increased chemoreceptor activity in

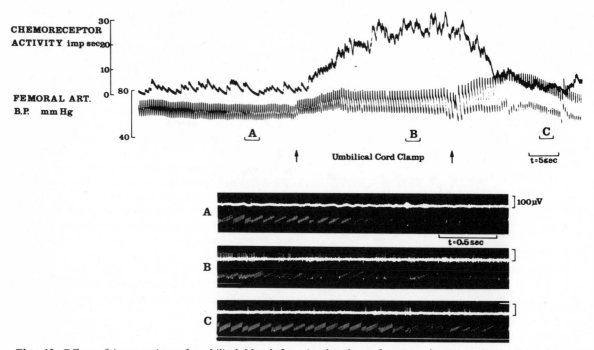

Fig. 13. Effect of interruption of umbilical blood flow in the sheep fetus on chemoreceptor activity. Top to bottom: Integrated chemoreceptor activity, femoral artery blood pressure, and three nerve recordings (A–C) taken at the points indicated. In each film strip, the upper trace is the nerve record, the lower is a millisecond resetting scale. The umbilical cord was occluded between the arrows. Reproduced from Biscoe *et al.*[43]

the carotid sinus nerve in the fetus subjected to hypoxia and hypercarbia, a marked increase in sinus neural activity is observed following cord occlusion of the term lamb at the time that it initiates breathing.[40,41,127,130,213]

Biscoe *et al.*[43] obtained recordings from chemoreceptor fibers of the lamb's carotid sinus nerve in a preparation in which the baroreceptors had been eliminated entirely. Figure 13 demonstrates the great increase in chemopotentials that occurs after umbilical cord occlusion. The temporal relationships shown in Fig. 13 are essentially the same as those in multifiber preparations,[130] and in both preparations, the activity is clearly not related to blood pressure.

3.3. Vasomotor Effects on Carotid Glomic Blood Flow

Biscoe *et al.*[42,43] studied the perinatal changes in neural activity as recorded simultaneously from the carotid sinus and cervical sympathetic nerves of

lambs. After occlusion of the umbilical cord, an almost immediate increase in sympathetic activity occurred, followed closely by a large increase in carotid sinus neural activity, presumably indicating more frequent transmittal of chemoreceptor potentials. Also, in the 135-day sheep fetus, stimulation of the postganglionic cervical sympathetic nerve caused an increase in chemoreceptor activity in the ipsilateral carotid sinus nerve (Fig. 14). Biscoe *et al.*[43] also showed that stimulation of the preganglionic and postganglionic sympathetic nerves of the fetal lamb altered the ipsilateral carotid body's capability of responding to carotid arterial infusion with NaCN. Under this combined stimulus, the carotid chemoreceptors responded actively, whereas identical infusions of NaCN without sympathetic stimulation evoked no significant chemoreceptor discharge. As a result of these experiments, these investigators proposed that the increase in sympathetic activity caused an increase in vasomotor tone in the afferent arterioles of the glomus and resulted in diminished blood flow to the carotid glomic cells to a critical level at which the mechanisms that initiate chemopotentials were strongly activated.[213]

In the adult cat, the cervical sympathetic nerves have been shown to have a vasoconstrictor effect on the carotid body blood flow over a wide range of blood gas tensions[211] and, with this effect, a fall in carotid body oxygen consumption. This fall appears to bear a closer relationship to chemoreceptor discharge than does the actual blood flow through the carotid body.[211] Arterial pressure changes appear to alter chemoreceptor activity minimally.[42]

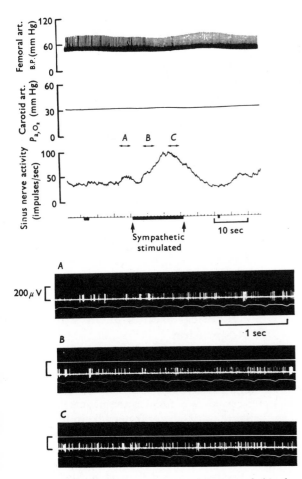

Fig. 14. Effect on chemoreceptor activity recorded in the sinus nerve of stimulating the postganglionic cervical sympathetic nerve. The filmed records of nerve activity were obtained before (A) and during (B, C) stimulation of the sympathetic nerve (10 V, 40/sec, 100-μsec-duration pulse), as indicated in the polygraph record. The time scales for polygraph and film records are as indicated. Reproduced from Biscoe and Purves.[41]

3.4. Chemical Effects on Carotid Glomic Blood Flow

Arteriovenous anastomoses bypassing the carotid body have been shown to influence the blood flow through the glomus.[118,238] The blood flow through these anastomotic channels appears to be altered by direct arterial chemical effects on them, since de Castro[100] showed that hypercarbia and hypoxemia increase such flow and concurrently decrease carotid glomic flow in the adult animal. Although there is no confirmation that this effect occurs in the perinatal period, it is reasonable to speculate that the combined arterial hypercarbia, hypoxia, and increase in H^+ ion concentration occurring at birth could promote shunting of arterial blood past the glomus.

3.5. Potentiation of Glomic Activity by Combined Hypercarbia and Hypoxia

The precise excitation mechanism for the carotid and aortic bodies[155] is not known, despite the intensive investigations that have been pursued since the discovery of the chemosensory function of the carotid body by de Castro,[99] Heymans and Neil,[140] and Heymans and Heymans.[141] Whatever the actual mechanisms involved, peripheral chemoreceptors that are subjected to lowered O_2 tension will generate markedly potentiated neural activity when the arterial blood reaching these receptors is made hypercarbic or acidic.[110,147,200] All these chemical stimuli of peripheral chemoreceptors occur during the asphyxia induced by cord occlusion or by the asphyxia during normal birth. These combined effects, which are more than just additive, could explain in part the greater carotid chemoreceptor activity observed with cord occlusion.

The question of the importance of carotid body chemoreceptors during experimental birth of the lamb has been approached by dividing the carotid sinus nerves bilaterally in the exteriorized fetus and comparing the breathing patterns of such lambs after cord occlusion with those of mock-operated animals.[126] In a small series of consecutively studied animals, a striking depression of respiratory activity was observed in the operated ones. In these experiments, all the animals of both groups began respiratory efforts at approximately the same time after cord occlusion. Within 3 min, however, it was apparent that the operated animals had been seriously compromised by elimination of their carotid chemoreceptor response to asphyxia.

On the other hand, later experiments showed that peripheral chemoreceptors are not essential in the initiation of effective breathing in the lamb. When the carotid sinus nerves had been divided bilaterally with the lamb still *in utero,* effective breathing developed shortly after delivery by hysterotomy and immediate cord occlusion. When the carotid sinus nerves and vagi had been divided to eliminate both the carotid and aortic body chemosensors, breathing that also started after umbilical cord clamping was less effective than that before vagal division.[138]

3.6. Central Chemosensor Mechanisms in the Initiation of Respiration

The CSF fluid bicarbonate and pH levels in the fetal lamb appear to be only slightly below those of the adult animal.[138] Soon after occlusion of the umbilical cord, CSF P_{CO_2} rises rapidly, and because this fluid lacks the intravascular buffers of hemoglobin and proteins to a large extent, pH falls dramatically.[138] As in the breathing animal, this fall would be expected to produce strong and persistent stimulation of central chemosensors until the shift of bicarbonate from blood to CSF occurs through active transport. Despite the potential importance of such a mechanism in initiating breathing, the evidence for activation of a central chemosensing mechanism at the time of birth is still fragmentary. Several experiments emphasize that this mechanism must be considered in an integrated hypothesis of the onset of breathing.

The experiments described above, in which bilateral division of the carotid sinus nerves and the cervical vagi produced an animal in which peripheral chemoreceptor input to the medulla had been eliminated, but that still initiated breathing following cord occlusion, offer some evidence in this regard. The respiration of such animals has been slow, as expected after vagotomy, but has become rhythmic and has sustained survival for as long as several hours.

Several additional experiments indicate that central chemoreceptors participate actively in regulation of breathing immediately after birth. Newborn lambs with bilaterally divided carotid sinus and vagus nerves respond to inhaled hypercarbic gas mixtures by hyperventilating even during the first few minutes after birth, when the lambs are still somewhat hypercarbic before the mixture is given.[125]

Also, division of both carotid sinus nerves of the newly born lamb, just after rhythmic breathing has been established, results in only a temporary depression of ventilation, and recovery to levels of ventilation as great as those before nerve section occurs after several minutes.[129] The recovery of respiration under such conditions strongly implies that central chemoreceptors are active at this time. Dawes[85] and Blatteis[44] likewise concluded that carotid chemoreceptors are not essential to the maintenance of respiration once respiration has become established.

More direct evidence of such activity of central chemosensing mechanisms should be detectable by determining the response of fetal animals to a perfusion of mock CSF in the region of the central medulla near the entry of the 7th and 8th cranial nerves, which has been described by Mitchell *et al.,*[190] Loeschke,[164] and Loeschke and Koepchen[165] as being responsive to alterations in $[H^+]$, P_{CO_2}, and $[HCO_3^-]$. These authors showed that solutions with high $[H^+]$ stimulate respiration of the adult animals, while solutions with low $[H^+]$ depress respiratory activity. In experiments on fetal and newborn lambs, technical difficulties have made the consistent demonstration of such an effect unreproducible as yet, but two newborn lambs showed the appropriate ventilatory responses to infusions of this area with mock CSF.[138] Introduction of NaCN directly onto the ventral surface of the medulla initiated fetal respiratory movements in the absence of peripheral chemoreceptors.[154]

3.7. Nonchemical Factors in the Initiation of Respiration

Fetal breathing associated with REM sleep occurs in the fetus under basal conditions unassociated with the blood gas changes described above. Some of the respiratory patterns present in the neonatal period may therefore simply be continued from those before birth independently of chemostimulation. In fact, on infrequent occasions, mature lambs delivered by hysterotomy will start breathing rhythmically while the cord is still intact and before the airways are open. Also, in normal delivery of infants, breathing often starts at a time when the umbilical circulation appears intact. On occasions, this breathing is very rapid and possibly might represent continued fetal breathing in a newborn in whom this breathing has not been depressed by perinatal trauma. Also, the initiation of breathing without

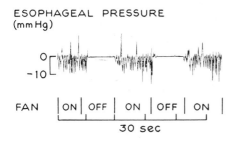

Fig. 15. Stimulation of respiration in the exteriorized fetal lamb by cooling with an electric fan. Reproduced from Dawes.[88]

alteration in fetal blood gas levels can be explained by other important stimuli or by factors releasing neural mechanisms that inhibit breathing.

3.8. Cold Stimulation

Tchobroutsky[250] showed that application of ice water to the snout region of the fetus still *in utero* initiates respiratory activity, and Dawes[88] showed the same effect when ice water was applied to the body of the exteriorized fetal lamb. Dawes[88] also showed that cooling of an exteriorized fetal lamb by intermittently turning on an electric fan can stimulate the lamb to breathe (Fig. 15). Active

breathing can be initiated invariably in the term fetal sheep delivered by hysterotomy into a pool of simulated amniotic fluid when the fluid temperature is decreased from 40°C to 29°C[123] (Fig. 16). Simultaneous monitoring of fetal carotid arterial P_{O_2}, P_{CO_2}, and pH and umbilical venous flow has revealed no significant changes during this induced breathing, which could also be stopped consistently by returning the simulated amniotic fluid temperature toward 40°C. Shivering was induced consistently in Dawes's lambs, but was not always observed in our experiments.[123] Most of the lambs we studied became aroused and more active. The breathing induced was rhythmic, never gasping, and usually slower than 40 breaths/min. The respiratory movements were obvious and appeared to involve the usual respiratory muscles, but were not very deep. The ease with which these respiratory efforts may be induced indicates that in the fetal sheep, at least, cold stimulation is a very important factor in the initiation of effective breathing.

3.9. Release from Immersion

Attention has been drawn to the interestingly parallel circulatory and metabolic changes of the newborn emerging from its water environment and

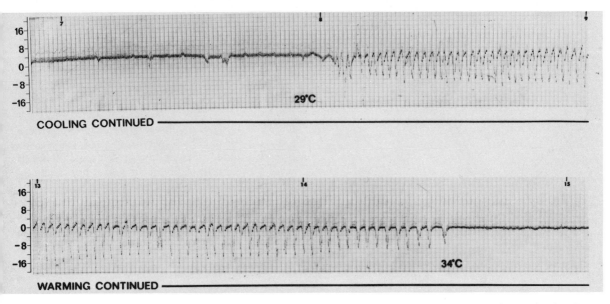

Fig. 17. Respiratory activity recorded by pressure change in the right atrium of an exteriorized term lamb. The temperature of the water bath in which the lamb was immersed was decreased from 40°C, and at 29°C, vigorous rhythmic breathing began (top tracing). With rewarming of the water (bottom tracing), breathing decreased in strength and rate before ceasing when the temperature reached 34°C.

those of the seal resurfacing after a dive.[151,237] The core circulation of each during immersion with the preferential blood flow to the brain and heart, the lower metabolic rate of the immersed animal, the capability of use of anaerobic metabolism during immersion and its attendant hypoxic state, and the washing out of acid metabolites by circulation to muscles and subcutaneous areas after the animal is released from submersion are evidences of this analogy.[236]

Efforts have been made to localize sensory regions involved in reflexes that inhibit breathing of the fetus and newborn. As in the adult, facial immersion of the newborn lamb results in a degree of respiratory inhibition even when the animal has been tracheotomized so that its airway is open (Fig. 17). This inhibition of respiration is not so severe as when the animal is totally immersed or when water is intro-

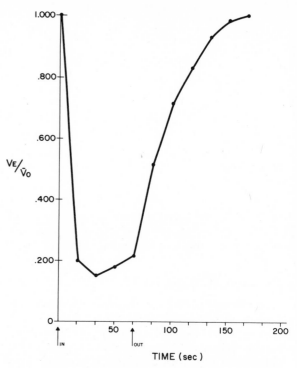

Fig. 18. Effect on ventilation, measured as described for Fig. 17, when warm water is introduced retrogradely into the trachea and nasopharynx. The suppressive effect is greater than that with facial immersion.

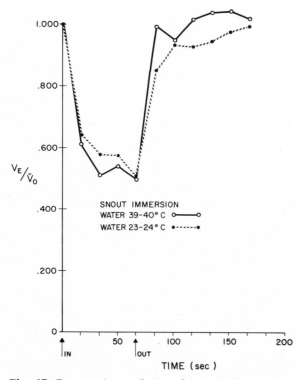

Fig. 17. Decrease in ventilation of a newly born term lamb with immersion of face and snout. The ratio V_E/V_0 on the ordinate represents ventilation determined by a Fleisch pneumotachometer during snout immersion (V_E) related to ventilation before immersion (V_0). The lamb was tracheotomized and was breathing air. No appreciable difference in ventilation was observed between immersion in cool and warm water.

duced into the laryngeal area (Fig. 18). There appears to be a marked inhibition of breathing of the newborn lamb when water is introduced into this region, to the extent that lambs delivered into a water bath will not sustain breathing after cord occlusion even when a tracheal airway has been provided (Fig. 19). In this latter experiment, the lamb's trachea was cannulated prior to delivery, and respiration was monitored by a pneumotachometer, the intake of which was exposed to atmospheric air. Gasps were initiated after cord occlusion, presumably from activation of chemoreceptors, and slow, rhythmic breathing developed for several minutes before death. Although no animal has been found to survive these conditions of delivery, lambs delivered into saline baths breathe much more actively and will survive.[157]

The region at the entrance of the larynx appears to be the critically sensitive area involved, and the newborn[157] and fetal[124] lamb is able to distinguish various types of fluid introduced into this region. When water is introduced, rapid reflex swallowing

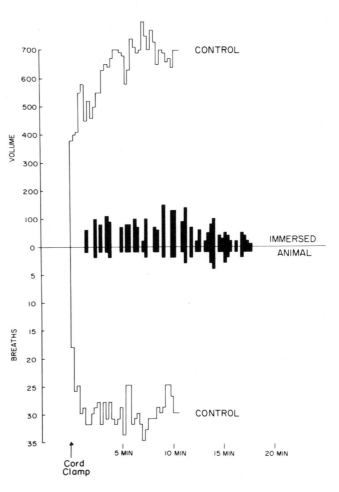

Fig. 19. Ventilation of a lamb immersed in water compared to that of a control animal in air when breathing has been initiated by cord clamping. The animals were tracheotomized and could breathe room air. The volume, recorded by a Fleisch pneumotachograph, and number of breaths are defined for approximately 15-sec time intervals. Control observations were discontinued after 10 min; the immersed lamb stopped breathing 18 min after cord clamping.

occurs, accompanied by a striking inhibition of breathing.[128,157] Other perfusing fluids have varying effects (Table X) in the newborn lamb. In the exteriorized fetal lamb that has been induced to breathe by being sprinkled with cold water, similar patterns have been noted, but inhibition of respiratory activity has been observed quite frequently when amniotic fluid is introduced into the laryngeal region. The effect of introducing even a very small amount of water may be very striking, and emphasizes the importance of clearing fluid from this region immediately after birth.

It has been proposed that the afferent limb of this reflex is initiated in taste receptors and transmitted via the superior laryngeal nerves.[157] Other receptors may be involved, including units sensitive to water, flow, and taste.[249] Bilateral division of the superior laryngeal nerves abolishes the reflex for the most part.[157] Other receptors in the naso-

pharyngeal regions may be involved in respiratory inhibition, but these receptors have not been delineated as clearly.

Important clinical correlations may be derived from these observations of an important region in the laryngeal area that permits selective detection of fluids and reflex apnea. Rapid clearance of fluid from this area at birth must either occur spontaneously or be effected by suctioning of the infant's laryngo-tracheal airway during resuscitation. Immature coordination of the extraordinarily complex processes of deglutition and breathing might be sought as a cause for the neonatal apneic episodes so common with feedings of the premature infant. These interrelationships may be important in the sudden infant death syndrome[105,157] (see also Chapter 33).

Thus, it is apparent that release from immersion has various components which are only beginning to be defined in the fetal and newborn animal. The

Table X. Effects of Fluids in the Laryngeal Area on Respiration and Swallowing[a]

Perfusing fluid	Hypopnea	Swallowing
Water	Marked	Active
Tracheal fluid		
Undiluted	Minimal or none	None
Diluted 1:4 in water	Moderate to marked	Occasional
Diluted 1:20 in water	Marked	Active
Saline		
0.9%	Minimal or none	None
0.45%	Moderate	Occasional
0.038%	Marked	Active
Amniotic fluid	Variable from minimal to marked	Variable
Glucose solutions	Marked	Active
Sucrose solution	Marked	Active

[a] From Harned and Ferreiro.[124]

effects of immersion and fluid in the respiratory tract in inhibiting effective perinatal respiration are probably the most important inhibitory influences identified thus far.

3.10. Pulmonary Respiratory Reflexes

The Hering–Breuer reflexes,[58,137] in which inflation of the lung inhibits inspiration, have been demonstrated to be present in the fetal and newborn lamb,[85] the newborn rabbit,[92] and the newborn infant.[82] Widdicombe[258,259] suggested that the receptors for the inflation reflex may be located in the intrapulmonary bronchi and bronchioles, and the afferents from these structures are known to exist as separate fibers in the vagus nerve.[9] Discharges from pulmonary stretch receptors, presumably inhibitory in nature, have been recorded from the vagus nerve of the fetal lamb.[212] If fluid is withdrawn from the trachea so that the lungs are deflated, these discharges decrease, and spontaneous respiration may start. Also, if spontaneous breathing is occurring, it can be reduced by inflating the lungs, a process associated with increased receptor discharge. Interestingly, temporary occlusion of the umbilical cord results in a striking fall in these potentials to near zero just before the first breath. This release of the strong inhibitory pulmonary stretch activity that occurs as fluid is drained from the lungs and cord occlusion occurs may be a very

important factor in the initiation of effective breathing. In vaginal delivery, removal of fluid from the respiratory passages during passage through the birth canal may cause release of the inhibitory activity of pulmonary stretch receptors.

3.11. Tactile and Painful Stimulation

Tactile, painful, and proprioceptive stimulation from passive movements of the joints may produce squirming of the fetal lamb and occasionally a short series of gasps. Sustained respirations could not be elicited, however, by such stimuli as clamping of the skin, dilatation of the rectum, movement of the distal leg joints, or certain operative procedures.[130] In fact, the fetal lamb with intact umbilical circulation, even when removed from the uterus, appears to be in a state resembling that of a very heavily sedated animal. Of considerable clinical importance is that such fetuses and even young newly born animals in their depressed state require only one-quarter to one-third the adult dose (by weight) of barbiturate and other anesthetics.[89]

3.12. Sound, Light, and Gravity

The roles that stimulation by sound, light, and gravity might play in the onset of effective breathing at birth have not been tested, but in the newborn infant, auditory stimulation increases respiratory rate.[241] Although fetal EEG responses to sound stimulation are less marked than those during the neonatal period,[239] it would appear that the fetus is capable of hearing (see Chapter 35), with noise from turbulent blood flow and muscle movement being the most prominent natural auditory stimuli.[257] Sound and light do not appear to have an important role in the initiation of respiration, since congenitally deaf and blind infants do not consistently have difficulty in breathing.

3.13. Release from an Obtunded State

As the infant is delivered either vaginally or by hysterotomy, one is often impressed by the obtunded state that persists until the first breath or thereafter. This state is also noted in the lamb, especially if it is immersed in a simulated amniotic fluid pool after removal from the uterus, as long as the umbilical cord is intact. There will be periodic general movements and, as described above, intermittent rapid respiratory movements, but the state of arousal is not dramatically altered until the umbilical cord is occluded. When occlusion is done, the lamb may writhe violently, stiffen, shake, and show marked improvement in muscle tone, often at the time of the first breath. The mechanism of this release from the obtunded state is not entirely known, but its patterns suggest massive sympathetic and catecholamine stimulation. Increased activation of the sympathetic nervous system has been related to cord occlusion,[41] and massive adrenal secretion of catecholamines has also been noted.[74] Changes in norepinephrine and epinephrine secretion that we have detected by sampling the left renal vein of the term lamb subjected to cord occlusion are shown in Table XI. The general arousal of the newly born at this time may thus be related more to elicitation of a form of "fight-or-flight" activity than to a more specific increase in the sensory modalities of the new environment.

Crehshaw et al.[78] suggested that the obtunded state that is seen after the 60th day of gestation in the sheep and disappears after delivery may be related to progesterone secretion by the placenta. He administered large amounts of progesterone intravenously to a newly born lamb that was breathing well. With the first dose of 6 mg/kg, the animal became less active and lost muscle tone; with the second similar dose, it developed irregular breathing; with a third dose, it stopped breathing. Since the sedative effects of large doses of progesterone

Table XI. Epinephrine and Norepinephrine Secretion in the Term Lamb before and after Cord Occlusion[a]

Before occlusion		After occlusion
Ep.	0.014	8.52
Norep.	0.011	4.25
Ep.	0.078	6.35
Norep.	0.083	3.84
Ep.	0.053	3.21
Norep.	0.045	3.54
Ep.	0.050	2.90
Norep.	0.052	2.70
Ep.	0.052	1.25
Norep.	0.070	0.85
Ep.	0.150	7.23
Norep.	0.180	4.15
Ep.	0.050	4.20
Norep.	0.060	3.42

[a] Data from Harned and Ferreiro.[124] The figures denote the secretion (in μg/ml per min) of epinephrine (Ep.) and norepinephrine (Norep.) as measured in the left renal vein blood before and for the first 2–7 min after occlusion of the umbilical cord of term sheep.

in the older animal are known, this effect might be essentially a pharmocological respiratory depression. It has been shown that the umbilical arterial blood contains enormously high levels of progesterone, which fall precipitously during the first day of life.[76] It has not been established whether these changes in progesterone level occur soon enough after occlusion of the umbilical cord to be vitally involved in the changing sensory state of the animal. Against ascribing a fundamental role for progesterone in the obtunded state is the observation, described previously, that reimmersion in warm water of a newly born lamb that has just established breathing appears to return it to its previous inhibited state, obviously without greatly altering progesterone levels.

3.14. Medullary Center Activity During Initiation of Respiration

The initial experiments by Bystrzycka et al.[65] revealed some of the patterns of medullary center activity during the transition from fetal to newborn life and opened up a new field of study of perinatal respiration. These studies indicated that temporary umbilical cord occlusion actually stops rapid fetal respiratory movements and concurrently abruptly abolishes medullary respiratory neural and electrocortical activities. The ensuing gasps may be important in reversing asphyxia if the fetus inflates the lungs with air and the preexisting medullary activity is reinitiated with reestablishment of rhythmic patterns. The role of general arousal, which occurs with perinatal asphyxia, in reversing medullary activity needs additional definition.

With such arousal of the newly born, the capability of voluntary respiratory response assumes increasing importance. This response may be involved in reactions during the fight-or-flight response and in reactions to the special sensory stimuli such as pain, sound, light, and taste. Thus, cortical and reticular activating systems are probably involved prominently in the process of initiating and sustaining breathing. The electrocorticographic association of fetal respiration with REM sleep indicates development of cortical respiratory pathways much earlier in fetal life than was formerly appreciated.

3.15. Other Reflexes That Influence Neonatal Respiration

Too little is known about some of the other reflexes that might be involved in the initiation of respiration to permit speculation, other than to point out possible areas for investigation.

For example, the profound *redistribution of blood flow* through the aorta, brain, lungs, liver, and heart and the associated *changes in arterial pressure* and character of pulsatile flows may activate reflexes that influence the respiratory centers. The complex relationships between chemoreceptor and baroceptor reflexes need further investigation. Although baroceptor stimulation of the carotid sinus area in the adult animal results in immediate decrease in ventilation,[139] the effects on respiration of stimulation of other areas in the circulation that are sensitive to stretch, including those in the atria, ventricles, great veins, pulmonary vessels, and coronary arteries, have not been studied extensively.

3.16. Conclusions

The multiplicity of factors involved in the initiation of effective breathing provides a margin of safety to the fetus undergoing this vital transition to an independent existence. One must be impressed

by the state of readiness of the fetus for this event. Fetal respiratory movements involving the motor apparatus occur rhythmically and with intermittent deeper breaths or sighs. The complex interrelationships of swallowing and breathing have been developed and their neuromuscular networks made ready. The fetus is capable of detecting different substances in the respiratory tract and pharynx. The pulmonary stretch receptors are functional, and medullary rhythmicity is established. Cortical activity is associated with fetal breathing.

During the actual birth process, the usual fetal respiratory movements may be suppressed by the trauma and asphyxiation occurring at a time when other mechanisms detailed above become operative. Various stimuli occur that activate excitatory neural pathways concurrent with the removal of important inhibitory mechanisms.

Burns[62] proposed that the degree of rhythmic activity of the respiratory centers is governed by input of potentials from a variety of nonspecific neurons, including both respiratory and nonrespiratory neurons. He believed that the initiation of breathing could occur when such an input achieved a threshold level sufficient to activate the efferent respiratory arcs. This hypothesis needs to be modified in view of the demonstration that medullary rhythmic activity exists in the fetus, especially during the rapid breathing episodes associated with rapid eye movements. The stimuli of asphyxiation actually appear to decrease medullary rhythmicity. Other nonspecific stimuli such as light, sound, touch, and pain do not seem to have much effect on the fetus, but are more important when independent respiration becomes established. The involvement of the cortex and reticular activating systems in perinatal breathing needs additional definition. It is apparent that as more is learned about the onset of breathing, more complex mechanisms are revealed and their relative importance redefined. Incorporation of the new knowledge relating to fetal respiratory movements is particularly important in understanding the onset of effective respiration at birth. With such knowledge, judicious use of resuscitative measures as needed will best assure safe passage of the infant through the "valley of the shadow of birth."

4. Maintenance of Breathing after Birth

The continuance of rhythmic respiration during the newborn period, like its initiation at birth, is a result of the interplay of many factors. There is considerable evidence indicating that the mechanisms that regulate respiration are similar to those of the adult, but important differences do exist.

There is strong evidence that the chemoregulatory mechanisms of the newborn are mature and capable of responding to changes in P_{O_2}, P_{CO_2}, and $[H^+]$ as in the adult. In the normal newborn, this capability is apparent from the reasonably consistent changes in P_{O_2}, P_{CO_2}, and $[H^+]$ that occur during and after the first few hours after birth that ensure a *milieu interieur* compatible with survival. Since the maintenance of this range of acid–base equilibrium and gas tensions must be due to regulation by peripheral or central chemoregulating mechanisms, or both, the evidence for activity of these mechanisms both in the human and in the experimental animal will be discussed.

4.1. Peripheral Chemoreceptors

Peripheral chemoreceptor function may be tested specifically by altering the systemic arterial O_2 tension, because central chemosensing mechanisms have not been shown to be responsive to such changes in P_{O_2}. Thus, both premature and term infants will show an almost immediate decrease in ventilation when given 100% O_2.[57,80] In contrast to older infants, who will sustain this response, the newborn infant will follow this period of hypoventilation with increased ventilation.

The opposite effect, that of invoking hypoxic stimulation of ventilation by giving the newborn low-O_2 mixtures to breathe, has been difficult to delineate because of the paradoxical responses elicited. Term infants during the first week of life and premature infants for the first 2 or 3 weeks of life show a short period of hyperventilation that is followed in 1 or 2 min by a more prolonged period of hypoventilation. Figure 20 shows the effects on term infants in carefully controlled studies performed in a thermoneutral environment in which 12% and 15% O_2 mixtures were administered. When the temperature of the infants' environment was lowered to 25–28°C, the initial hyperventilation was eliminated, and only decreased ventilation was observed.[69] On the other hand, infants over 6 days of age react similarly to adults by showing sustained hyperventilation throughout the hypoxic challenge. Also, the same infant, studied serially, will show an early response similar to that illustrated in Fig. 20 and then, after 6 days of age, will show the adult type of response. Slight environmental temperature changes do not appear to alter the response of the older infants.[69]

The causes of this disparate response to hypoxia of the young and older neonate have not been determined. Interestingly, in the newborn kitten, carotid sinus nerve activity continues to be very active throughout a hypoxic challenge even though ventilation may decrease, indicating that the paradoxical effect probably results from medullary depression. Several additional factors were considered by Brady and Ceruti,[54] including (1) decreased pulmonary blood flow, (2) decreased metabolism, and (3) hypoxic depression of medullary centers. Proposed mechanisms for production of

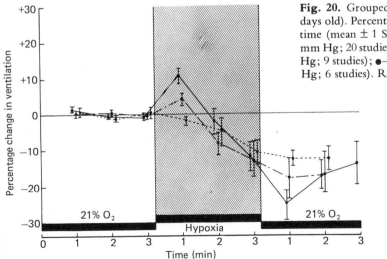

Fig. 20. Grouped data of 35 studies (infants less than 6 days old). Percentage change in heart rate plotted against time (mean ± 1 S.E.). ●———●, 12% O_2 (PA_{O_2} 55 ± 1 mm Hg; 20 studies); ●– · –●, 15% O_2 (PA_{O_2} 72 ± 2 mm Hg; 9 studies); ●– – – –●, 18% O_2 (PA_{O_2} 92 ± 2 mm Hg; 6 studies). Reproduced from Brady and Ceruti.[54]

decreased pulmonary blood flow early in the infant's life during hypoxia include (1) pulmonary arterial constriction associated with hypoxemia and (2) increase in right-to-left shunting through the foramen ovale or ductus arteriosus if these passages remain patent. Reduced pulmonary blood flow may result in turn in bronchoconstriction and reduced pulmonary compliance.[240] Support for this hypothesis that bronchoconstriction and reduced compliance might cause the fall in minute ventilation observed in the young neonate comes from the demonstration that two infants developed decreased pulmonary compliance during hypoxia.[54]

Decreased metabolism has not been documented to explain this phenomenon, which has such important clinical manifestations. Although medullary depression would appear to be the most probable reason for this unusual response of the newborn and premature infant to hypoxia, analogous animal studies have not clarified the situation, and have generally shown ventilatory responses to O_2 similar to those of the adult.

During the first few minutes after birth of unanesthetized lambs, bilateral carotid sinus nerve division will be followed immediately by a fall in ventilation, presumably from elimination of the input to the medulla of chemopotentials from the carotid glomera.[129] Within several minutes, ventilation returns to previous levels, which suggests that central chemoregulatory mechanisms are capable of compensating for this peripheral effect. During the first half hour of life, the newborn lamb is capable of responding to a hypoxic stimulus, even if the Pa_{O_2} level is low, and to a CO_2 stimulus, even if the Pa_{CO_2} level is high. Purves[210] showed in lambs anesthetized with pentobarbitone 40 min or more after birth that inhalation of 100% O_2 results in a fall of minute ventilation associated with a fall of chemopotentials in the carotid sinus nerve, and that inhalation of 10% O_2 causes a rise in ventilation and a rise in chemoactivity. Since both of these effects were abolished by bilateral division of the carotid sinus nerves, the peripheral chemoreceptors primarily responsible for this effect are the carotid bodies. In addition, when lambs were given 5% CO_2 to breathe with 20% O_2, a rapid rise in ventilation occurred and chemopotential activity was increased. Division of both carotid sinus nerves, before 5% CO_2 was given, resulted in a slower response. This finding indicates that the rapidly reacting carotid bodies are responsive to changes in Pa_{CO_2} at this time, but the more slowly reacting

central chemosensing mechanisms are also capable of responding when the carotid bodies have been denervated.

A fall in Pa_{O_2} of approximately 6 mm Hg is a sufficient stimulus for alteration of ventilation in the newborn anesthetized lamb.[210] This finding compares closely with the fall of 7 mm Hg found by Hornbein et al.[147] to provide an adequate stimulus to increased ventilation in the adult cat.

4.2. Central Chemosensing Mechanisms

Many investigators have shown that the newborn infant is also capable of increasing ventilation when breathing CO_2 gas mixtures; this response is immediate and is sustained.[56] The infant's sensitivity to this stimulus appears greater than that of the adult, with its CO_2 response curve shifted to the left of the adult,[21] and with resting Pa_{CO_2} lower than the adult. The infant increases minute ventilation approximately 0.045 liter/kg for each 1 mm Hg increase in Pa_{CO_2}, an effect similar in degree to that in the adult.[162]

The increased responsiveness of the infant to inspired CO_2 has not been explained. The $[H^+]$ of the CSF in the adult and newborn infant appears essentially identical (pH 7.33).[161,189] Low blood levels of bicarbonate persist for 2 years, whereas the CO_2 response becomes similar to the adult before then. Progesterone does not appear to increase the newborn's ventilation as it does the mother's. The response to CO_2 does not appear to be affected by environmental temperature.[69] Perhaps some of the variability in interpretations of the infant's sensitivity to CO_2 stimulation results from the fact that the CO_2 stimulus is in part central and in part peripheral.

The complex effects of CO_2 on the newborn's ventilatory response to hypoxia have been elucidated.[55] Figure 21 shows that when young term infants are given various CO_2 mixtures to breathe and are subsequently made hypoxic, the early hyperventilation induced is greater in the babies who received the higher concentrations of CO_2. Thus, hypercarbia augments the ventilatory increase from hypoxia. This response is transitory, and after 1 min of hypoxic challenge, ventilation begins to fall, reaching levels below the prehypoxic ones by the time the hypoxic challenge is discontinued.

The complex nature of the newborn's response to hypoxia and hypercarbia is in need of clearer definition because of important clinical applications in resuscitation and the care of the infant with respiratory distress. Significant hypoxia results in markedly shifting circulatory patterns, with diversion of blood flow to the brain and myocardium at the expense of flow to the lungs, kidneys, extremities, and mesenteric regions. Rapid development of metabolic acidosis, hypoglycemia with depletion of cardiac glycogen, hypocalcemia, hyperkalemia, and other incompletely defined derangements of cell function associated with hypoxia indicate that there must be rapid reversal of such effects for the newborn to survive. These changes, which are observed readily in extreme anoxia, perhaps indicate why it has been so difficult to define the physiologic effects of O_2 and CO_2 on neonatal breathing, because one is not simply altering the Pa_{O_2} or Pa_{CO_2} per se during the types of experiments described.

The responses of the newborn to hypoxia and hypercarbia also have important implications in the clinical condition of periodic breathing observed very frequently in premature infants.[225,226] Such babies appear to hypoventilate, and have a CO_2 response curve considerably to the right of their age-mates. They have an exaggerated decrease in early ventilation when given O_2. In addition, premature infants in general, when given low-O_2 mixtures to breathe, show more hypoventilation, more periodic breathing, and longer apneic intervals. The administration of higher-O_2 mixtures to such infants must obviously be carefully controlled to avoid O_2 toxicity, but this treatment is an important one for these babies. Improved aeration by periodic bag breathing and by use of constant positive airway pressure, often by nasal airway, has also proved valuable in the treatment of periodic breathing in the premature infant.

4.3. Maintenance of a Clear Airway

The inhibition of respiration by the presence of fluid in the deep respiratory tracts, which stimulates inhibitory stretch receptors, and of fluid in the laryngeal region, which inhibits respiration while stimulating deglutition, was stressed in the discussion of onset of breathing. In addition, Head's paradoxical reflex[134] appears to be actively present in the newborn. In this reflex, rapid inflation of the lung, either spontaneously or from forced insufflation, initiates a deep inspiration[79,82] or gasp. This reflex becomes far less active after the first 2 days of life, but may be important in early expansion of the lungs.

The coordination of respiration with swallowing must be in a highly developed state, for the term infant needs to be fed early. Deglutition is an extremely complicated process, involving multiple sensory regions of the mouth, tongue, and pharynx, and a motor apparatus of 25 muscles. In view of this complexity, it is not surprising that the newborn infant aspirates feedings quite easily, and that many apneic episodes, especially in the premature, are related to feeding. The nasal passages must also be clear to allow the infant to breathe effectively during feedings.

4.4. Stimuli from Light, Sound, Touch, and Gravity

As the infant leaves its inhibited or obtunded state, its general activity and breathing will be affected more and more by various stimuli from the external environment. Also, general activity and breathing will be related to gastric motility, hunger, micturition, defecation, postural position, and exercise. These factors must be taken into account during experimental observations of respiration and O_2 consumption in newborn infants, and comparable "resting" or "basal" states of the infants must be maintained.

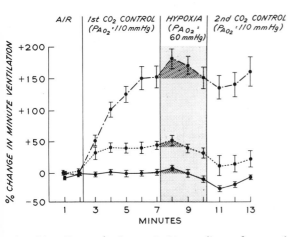

Fig. 21. Grouped data of 30 studies of normal newborn infants with percentage change in ventilation plotted against time (mean ± 1 S.E.M.) ●— — —● Low-CO_2 studies (10 experiments); ●------● medium-CO_2 studies (7 experiments); ●—·—● high-CO_2 studies (13 experiments). Shaded area represents extra increase in ventilation in response to hypoxia. Reproduced from Brady and Dunn.[55]

4.5. Cortical Respiratory Activity

Cortical influence on respiration would also be expected to become more important as the newborn infant is exposed to a wide variety of stimuli. Pleasurable sensations from contact with the mother as she holds, fondles, and feeds her baby, or from the taste and swallowing of food, and unpleasant sensations from wetness, hunger, and coldness all influence the rate and character of respiration. Crying is a particular respiratory act involving one of the infant's most primitive means of communicating. These modalities, involving cortical activity, also modify the basic respiratory regulation.

It is apparent that learning will occur early after birth, and will further augment the cortical phase of breathing. It has been suggested that failure of the infant to learn may result in an unstable respiratory control system that could contribute to apneic episodes and even death in the newly born.[212] Again, there is obvious need for research to define the mechanisms involved as cortical respiratory activity becomes more predominant.

4.6. Cold Stimulation

The effects of cold stimulation of the ambient air on the newborn as it starts its independent existence have been emphasized. The importance of these effects may give the implication that removal of the infant from a cold-air environment into a warm one might diminish breathing and impair the survival of the infant. Cold stimulation may prove useful in the initiation of breathing, but there are significant advantages in placing the baby in a reasonably warm environment immediately after such stimulation. It has been shown convincingly[8,198] that there is a thermoneutral environment (32–34°C for the human term infant) in which metabolism, as determined by O_2 consumption, is minimal, and cooler or warmer ambient environments increase this metabolism (see Chapter 21 for details).

4.7. Effects of Ambient Temperature on Respiration and Oxygen Consumption of the Newborn

Thus, after respiration has become established, an optimum environmental temperature that will favor survival of the infant should be maintained.[98] A direct relationship between O_2 consumption of the newborn and the volume of air breathed has been shown.[79] Since there is such a relationship, attention should be paid to the factors that influence the O_2 consumption of the neonate, because these factors will in turn modify ventilation.

In contrast to the nonhypoxic animal, the newborn hypoxic animal will decrease its O_2 consumption when exposed to cold.[6,91,144] Newborn infants exposed to less decreased O_2 atmospheres (15% O_2) have not shown this effect in carefully controlled experiments.[81] Brück et al.,[60] however, showed that infants with severe hypoxemia from congenital heart disease decrease their O_2 consumption during cold exposure (see also Chapter 21). Thus, it appears that the degree of hypoxia is important in determining this response of the neonate. The vulnerability of the severely cyanotic infant to cold stress, with resultant fall in cardiac output, poor peripheral blood flow, and severe metabolic acidosis, is well established. These conditions occur especially during deliveries in which the infant does not breathe immediately, and also in the infant with cyanotic congenital heart disease who has been exposed to cold.

4.8. Conclusions

After breathing has become established, the infant passes through a transitional period when its respiratory patterns differ in some respects from those expected several days later. The infant recovers from the hypoxic, hypercarbic, and acidotic stage associated with the process of labor and birth, and within hours adjusts its Pa_{O_2} to a level near that of the normal adult. Pa_{CO_2} adjusts to a level below that of the normal adult, and the metabolic acidosis present at birth is gradually resolved.

For up to 6 days, the infant responds to hypoxic challenge by hyperventilating for approximately 2 min, and then reduces its ventilation to below that preceding induction of hypoxia. After early infancy, the baby responds to hypoxic challenge by sustained hyperventilation, as does the adult. The decrease in ventilation of the newborn infant during inhalation of 100% O_2 indicates that peripheral chemoreceptors are involved in the regulation of breathing at this time. In addition, the response of newborn infants to inhalation of CO_2 appears quantitatively similar to that of adults, suggesting that the central chemosensing apparatus is also functioning, as in the adult.

In addition to this transitional period of chemoregulatory adjustment, the newborn infant passes through a period of thermoregulation in which its intrinsic thermogenic mechanisms differ from those to be acquired later. Environmental temperature has also been shown to be an important consideration in the evaluation of the ventilatory response of the neonate, as evidenced by the ability of the newborn to decrease metabolism when subjected to hypoxic challenge while in a cool environment.

Disorders of respiratory regulation are particularly important in the premature infant. Increased knowledge of the regulatory mechanisms during the fetal and perinatal periods should continue to have particular applications for these disadvantaged babies.

5. References

1. ACHESON, G. H., DAWES, G. S., AND MOTT, J. C., 1957, Oxygen consumption and the arterial oxygen saturation in foetal and new-born lambs, *J. Physiol.* **135**:623–642.
2. ADAMS, F. H., AND FUJIWARA, T., 1957, Surfactant in fetal lamb tracheal fluid, *J. Pediatr.* **63**:537–542.
3. ADAMS, F. H., DESILETS, D. T., AND TOWERS, B., 1967, Control of flow of fetal lung fluid at the laryngeal outlet, *Respir. Physiol.* **2**:302–309.
4. ADAMS, F. H., FUJIWARA, T., AND ROWSHAN, G., 1963, The nature and origin of the fluid in the fetal lamb lung, *J. Pediatr.* **63**:881–888.
5. ADAMS, F. H., MOSS, A. J., AND FAGAN, L., 1963, The tracheal fluid in the fetal lamb, *Biol. Neonat.* **5**:151–158.
6. ADAMSONS, K., JR., 1959, Breathing and the thermal environment in young rabbits, *J. Physiol.* **149**:144–153.
7. ADAMSONS, K., JR., 1965, Transport of organic substances and oxygen across the placenta, in: *Symposium on the Placenta,* Birth Defects Original Article Series, (D. Bergsma, ed.), Vol. I pp. 27–34, National Foundation March of Dimes, New York.
8. ADAMSONS, K., JR., GANDY, G. M., AND JAMES, L. S., 1965, The Influence of thermal factors upon oxygen consumption of the newborn human infant, *J. Pediatr.* **66**:495–508.
9. ADRIAN, E. D., 1933, Afferent impulses in the vagus and their effect on respiration, *J. Physiol.* **79**:332–358.
10. AHERNE, W., AND DAWKINS, M. J. R., 1964, The removal of fluid from the pulmonary airways after birth in the rabbit and the effect on this of prematurity and pre-natal hypoxia, *Biol. Neonat.* **7**:214–229.
11. AHERNE, W., AND DUNNILL, M. S., 1966, Morphometry of the human placenta, *Br. Med. Bull.* **22**:5–8.
12. AHFELD, F., 1905, Die intrauterine Tätigkeit der Thorax und Zwerchfellmuskulatur, intrauterine Atmung, *Monatsschr. Geburtshilfe Gynfiwkol.* **21**:143–163.
13. ANSELMINO, K. J., AND HOFFMAN, F., 1930, Die Ursachen des Icterus neonatorum, *Arch. Gynaekol.* **143**:477–499.
14. ASSALI, N. S., DASGUPTA, K., KOLIN, A., AND HOLMS, L., 1958, Measurement of uterine blood flow and uterine metabolism. V. Changes during spontaneous and induced labor in unanesthetized pregnant sheep and dogs, *Amer. J. Physiol.* **195**:614–620.
15. ASSALI, N. S., DOUGLASS, R. A., JR., BAIRD, W. W., NICHOLSON, D. B., AND SUYEMOTO, R., 1953, Measurement of uterine blood flow and uterine metabolism. IV. Results in normal pregnancy, *Amer. J. Obstet. Gynecol.* **66**:248–253.
16. ASSALI, N. S., MORRIS, J. A., AND BECK, R., 1965, Cardiovascular hemodynamics in the fetal lamb before and after lung expansion, *Amer. J. Physiol.* **208**:122–129.
17. ASSALI, N. S., RAURAMO, L., AND PELTONEN, T., 1960, Measurement of uterine blood flow and uterine metabolism. VIII. Uterine and fetal blood flow and oxygen consumption in early pregnancy, *Amer. J. Obstet. Gynecol.* **79**:86–98.
18. AVERY, M. E., 1964, *The Lung and Its Disorders in the Newborn Infant,* p. 6, W. B. Saunders Co., Philadelphia.
19. AVERY, M. E., 1972, Prevention of hyaline membrane disease, *Pediatrics* **50**:513, 514.
20. AVERY, M. E., AND MEAD, J., 1959, Surface properties in relation to atelectasis and hyaline membrane disease, *Amer. J. Dis. Child.* **97**:517–523.
21. AVERY, M. E., CHERNICK, V., DUTTON, R. E., AND PERMUTT, S., 1963, Ventilatory response to inspired carbon dioxide in infants and adults, *J. Appl. Physiol.* **18**:895–903.
22. AVERY, M. E., CHERNICK, V., AND YOUNG, M., 1965, Fetal respiratory movements in response to rapid changes of CO_2 in carotid artery, *J. Appl. Physiol.* **20**:225–227.
23. BAILLIE, P., DAWES, G. S., MERLET, C. L., AND RICHARDS, R., 1971, Maternal hyperventilation and foetal hypocapnia in sheep, *J. Physiol.* **218**:635–650.
24. BARCROFT, J., 1947, *Researches on Prenatal Life,* pp. 156–177, Charles C. Thomas, Springfield, Illinois.
25. BARCROFT, J., 1947, *Researches on Prenatal Life,* pp. 260–264, Charles C. Thomas, Springfield, Illinois.
26. BARCROFT, J., AND KARVONEN, M. J., 1948, The action of carbon dioxide and cyanide on foetal respiratory movements: The developments of chemoreflex function in sheep, *J. Physiol.* **107**:153–161.
27. BARCROFT, J., HERKEL, W., AND HILL, S., 1933, The rate of blood flow and gaseous metabolism of the uterus during pregnancy, *J. Physiol.* **77**:194–206.

28. BARRON, D. H., METCALFE, J., MESCHIA, G., HUCKABEE, W., HELLEGERS, A., AND PRYSTOWSKY, H., 1963, in: *Symposium on Physiological Effects of High Altitude* (W. H. Weihe, ed.), pp. 115–129, Pergamon Press, New York.

29. BARTELS, H., 1970, *Prenatal Respiration,* pp. 104 and 105, North-Holland Publishing Co., Amsterdam and London.

30. BARTELS, H., 1970, *Prenatal Respiration,* pp. 117–119, North-Holland Publishing Co., Amsterdam and London.

31. BARTELS, H., 1970, *Prenatal Respiration,* p. 138, North-Holland Publishing Co., Amsterdam and London.

32. BARTELS, H., MOLL, W., AND METCALFE, J., 1962, Physiology of gas exchange in the human placenta, *Amer. J. Obstet. Gynecol.* **84**:1714–1730.

33. BATTAGLIA, F. C., MESCHIA, G., MAKOWSKI, E. L., AND BOWES, W., 1968, The effect of maternal oxygen inhalation upon fetal oxygenation, *J. Clin. Invest.* **47**:548–555.

34. BAUER, C., LUDWIG, M., LUDWIG, I., AND BARTELS, H., 1969, Factors governing the oxygen affinity of human adult and foetal blood, *Respir. Physiol.* **7**:271–277.

35. BEATTY, C. H., BASINGER, G. M., AND BOCEK, R. M., 1968, Oxygen consumption and glycolysis in fetal, neonatal, and infant muscle of the rhesus monkey, *Pediatrics* **42**:5–16.

36. BEER, R., BARTELS, H., AND RACZKOWSKI, H. A., 1955, Die Sauerstoff-dissoziationskurve des fetalen Blutes und der Gasaustausch in der menschlichen Placenta, *Arch. Gesamte Physiol.* **260**:306–319.

37. BEHRMAN, R. E., LEES, M. H., PETERSON, E. N., DE LANNOY, C. W., AND SEEDS, A. E., 1970, Distribution of the circulation in the normal and asphyxiated fetal primate, *Amer. J. Obstet. Gynecol.* **108**:956–969.

38. BEHRMAN, R. E., PETERSON, E. N., AND DE LANNOY, C. W., 1969, The supply of O_2 to the primate fetus with two different O_2 tensions and anesthetics, *Respir. Physiol.* **6**:271–283.

39. BENESCH, R., AND BENESCH, R., 1967, The effect of organic phosphates from the human erythrocyte on all allosteric properties of hemoglobin, *Biochem. Biophys. Res. Commun.* **26**:162–167.

40. BISCOE, T. J., 1971, Carotid body: Structure and function, *Physiol. Rev.* **51**:437–495.

41. BISCOE, T. J., AND PURVES, M. J., 1965, Cervical sympathetic and chemoreceptor activity before and after the first breath of the new-born lamb, *J. Physiol.* **181**:70p, 71p.

42. BISCOE, T. J., BRADLEY, G. W., AND PURVES, M. J., 1970, The relation between carotid body chemo-receptor discharge, carotid sinus pressure and carotid body venous flow, *J. Physiol.* **208**:99–120.

43. BISCOE, T. J., PURVES, M. J., AND SAMPSON, S. R., 1969, Types of nervous activity which may be recorded from the carotid sinus nerve in the sheep foetus, *J. Physiol.* **202**:1–23.

44. BLATTEIS, C. M., 1964, Hypoxia and the metabolic response to cold in new-born rabbits, *J. Physiol.* **172**:358–368.

45. BLECHNER, J. N., COTTER, J. R., STENGER, V. G., HINKLEY, C. M., AND PRYSTOWSKY, H., 1968, Oxygen, carbon dioxide, and hydrogen ion concentrations in arterial blood during pregnancy, *Amer. J. Obstet. Gynecol.* **100**:1–6.

46. BODDY, K., AND DAWES, G. S., 1975, Fetal breathing, *Br. Med. Bull.* **31**:3–7.

47. BODDY, K., AND MANTELL, C. D., 1972, Observations of fetal breathing movements transmitted through the maternal abdominal wall, *Lancet* **2**:1219, 1220.

48. BOE, F., 1954, Vascular morphology of the human placenta, *Cold Spring Harbor Symp. Quant. Biol.* **19**:29–35.

49. BOSTON, R. W., HUMPHREYS, P. W., REYNOLDS, E. O. R., AND STRANG, L. B., 1965, Lymph flow and clearance of liquid from the lungs of the foetal lamb, *Lancet* **2**:473, 474.

50. BOYDEN, E. A., 1974, The mode of origin of pulmonary acini and respiratory bronchioles in the fetal lung, *Amer. J. Anat.* **141**:317–328.

51. BRADLEY, R. M., AND MISTRETTA, C. M., 1973, Swallowing in fetal sheep, *Science* **179**:1016, 1017.

52. BRADLEY, R. M., AND MISTRETTA, C. M., 1973, The sense of taste and swallowing activity in foetal sheep, in: *Foetal and Neonatal Physiology, Proceedings of the Sir J. Barcroft Centenary Symposium,* pp. 77–81, Cambridge University Press.

53. BRADLEY, R. M., AND MISTRETTA, C. M., 1973, The gustatory sense in foetal sheep during the last third of gestation, *J. Physiol.* **231**:271–282.

54. BRADY, J. P., AND CERUTI, E., 1966, Chemoreceptor reflexes in the newborn infant: Effects of varying degrees of hypoxia on heart rate and ventilation in a warm environment, *J. Physiol.* **184**:631–645.

55. BRADY, J. P., AND DUNN, P. M., 1970, Chemo-receptor reflexes in the newborn infant: Effect of CO_2 on the ventilatory response to hypoxia, *Pediatrics* **45**:206–215.

56. BRADY, J. P., AND TOOLEY, W. H., 1966, Cardiovascular and respiratory reflexes in the newborn, *Pediatr. Clin. North Amer.* **13**:801–821.

57. BRADY, J. P., COTTON, E. C., AND TOOLEY, W. H., 1964, Chemoreflexes in the newborn infant: Effects of 100% O_2 on heart rate and ventilation, *J. Physiol.* **172**:332–341.

58. BREUER, J., 1898, Die Selbststeuerung der Atmung durch den Nervus vagus, *Sitzungsber. Akad. Wiss. Wien Abt. II* **58**:909–937.

59. BROTANEK, V., HENDRICKS, C. H., AND YOSHIDA, T., 1969, Changes in uterine blood flow during uterine

contractions, *Amer. J. Obstet. Gynecol.* **103**:1108–1116.

60. Brück, K., Adams, F. H., and Brück, M., 1962, Temperature regulation in infants with chronic hypoxemia, *Pediatrics* **30**:352–360.

61. Bucher, U., and Reid, L., 1961, Development of the intrasegmental bronchial tree: The pattern of branching and development of cartilage at various stages of intrauterine life, *Thorax* **16**:207–218.

62. Burns, B. D., 1963, The central control of respiratory movements, *Br. Med. Bull.* **19**:7–9.

63. Burns, B., and Gurtner, G. H., 1973, A specific carrier for oxygen and carbon monoxide in the lung and placenta, *Drug Metab. Dispos.* **1**:374–379.

64. Burwell, C. S., and Metcalfe, J., 1958, *Heart Disease and Pregnancy: Physiology and Management,* Little, Brown and Co., Boston.

65. Bystrzycka, E., Nail, B. S., and Purves, M. J., 1975, Central and peripheral neural respiratory activity in the mature sheep foetus and newborn lamb, *Respir. Physiol.* **25**:199–215.

66. Campbell, A. G. M., Dawes, G. S., Fishman, A. P., and Hyman, A. I., 1967, Regional redistribution of blood flow in the mature fetal lamb, *Circ. Res.* **21**:229–235.

67. Campbell, A. G. M., Dawes, G. S., Fishman, A. P., Hyman, A. I., and James, G. B., 1966, The oxygen consumption of the placenta and foetal membranes in the sheep, *J. Physiol.* **182**:439–464.

68. Campiche, M., Jaccottet, M., and Juillard, E., 1962, La pneumonose à membranes hyalines, *Ann. Paediatr. (Basel)* **199**:74–88.

69. Ceruti, E., 1966, Chemoreceptor reflexes in the newborn infant: Effect of cooling on the response to hypoxia, *Pediatrics* **37**:556–564.

70. Chanutin, A., and Curnish, R., 1967, Effect of organic and inorganic phosphates on the oxygen equilibrium of human erythrocytes, *Arch. Biochem. Biophys.* **121**:96–102.

71. Chorobski, J., and Penfield, W., 1932, Cerebral vasodilator nerves and their pathway from the medulla oblongata, *Arch. Neurol. Psychiatry* **28**:1257–1289.

72. Chu, J., Clements, J. A., Cotton, E., Klaus, M. H., Sweet, A. Y., Thomas, M. A., and Tooley, W. H., 1965, The pulmonary hypoperfusion syndrome: A preliminary report, *Pediatrics* **35**:733–742.

73. Coleman, A. J., 1967, Absence of harmful effect of maternal hypocapnia in babies delivered at C-section, *Lancet* **1**:813, 814.

74. Comline, R. S., and Silver, M., 1966, Development of activity in the adrenal medulla of the foetus and new-born animal, *Br. Med. Bull.* **22**:16–20.

75. Comline, R. S., and Silver, M., 1975, Placental transfer of blood gases, *Br. Med. Bull.* **31**:25–31.

76. Conly, P., Morrison, W. T., Sandberg, D. H., and Cleveland, W. W., 1968, Plasma progesterone in the perinatal and neonatal period, *Pediatr. Res.* **2**:308.

77. Cotter, J. R., Blechner, J. N., and Prystowsky, H., 1969, Blood flow and oxygen consumption of pregnant goats, *Amer. J. Obstet. Gynecol.* **103**:1099–1101.

78. Crehshaw, M. C., Meschia, G., and Barron, D. H., 1966, Role of progesterone in inhibition of muscle tone and respiratory rhythm in foetal lambs, *Nature (London)* **212**:842, 843.

79. Cross, K. W., 1961, Respiration of the newborn baby, *Br. Med. Bull.* **17**:160–163.

80. Cross, K. W., and Warner, P., 1951, The effect of inhalation of high and low oxygen concentrations on the respiration of the newborn infant, *J. Physiol.* **114**:283–295.

81. Cross, K. W., Flynn, D. M., and Hill, J. R., 1966, Oxygen consumption in normal newborn infants during moderate hypoxia in warm and cool environments, *Pediatrics* **37**:565–576.

82. Cross, K. W., Klaus, M., Tooley, W. H., and Weisser, K., 1960, The response of the newborn baby to inflation of the lungs, *J. Physiol.* **151**:551–565.

83. Danesino, V., 1950, Dispositivi di blocco ed anatomosi arterovenose nei vasi fetali della placenta umana, *Arch. Ostet. Ginecol.* **55**:251–272.

84. Dawes, G. S., 1962, The umbilical circulation, *Amer. J. Obstet. Gynecol.* **84**:1634–1648.

85. Dawes, G. S., 1966, Transition to extrauterine life, in: *Neonatal Respiratory Adaptation* (T. K. Oliver, ed.), pp. 115 and 116, U.S. Public Health Service Publication 1432, Washington, D.C.

86. Dawes, G. S., 1967, Oxygen consumption of the placenta and foetal membranes in the sheep, in: *Development of the Lung—Ciba Foundation Symposium* (A. V. S. de Reuck and R. Porter, eds.), p. 306, Little, Brown, and Co., Boston.

87. Dawes, G. S., 1968, *Foetal and Neonatal Physiology: A Comparative Study of the Changes at Birth,* pp. 32 and 33, Year Book Medical Publishers, Chicago.

88. Dawes, G. S., 1968, *Foetal and Neonatal Physiology: A Comparative Study of the Changes at Birth,* p. 132, Year Book Medical Publishers, Chicago.

89. Dawes, G. S., 1968, *Foetal and Neonatal Physiology: A Comparative Study of the Changes at Birth,* p. 135, Year Book Medical Publishers, Chicago.

90. Dawes, G. S., 1973, Breathing and rapid eye movement sleep before birth, in: *Foetal and Neonatal Physiology, Proceedings of the Sir J. Barcroft Centenary Symposium,* pp. 49–62, Cambridge University Press.

91. Dawes, G. S., and Mott, J. C., 1959, The increase in oxygen consumption of the lamb after birth, *J. Physiol.* **146**:295–315.

92. Dawes, G. S., and Mott, J. C., 1959, Reflex respiratory activity in the new-born rabbit, *J. Physiol.* **145**:85–97.

93. Dawes, G. S., and Mott, J. C., 1964, Changes in

oxygen distribution and consumption in foetal lambs with variations in umbilical blood flow, *J. Physiol.* **170**:524–540.

94. DAWES, G. S., DUNCAN, S. L. B., LEWIS, B. V., MERLET, C. L., OWEN-THOMAS, J. B., AND REEVES, J. T., 1969, Hypoxaemia and aortic chemoreceptor function in foetal lambs, *J. Physiol.* **201**:105–116.

95. DAWES, G. S., FOX, H. E., LEDUC, B. M., LIGGINS, G. C., AND RICHARDS, R. T., 1970, Respiratory movements and paradoxical sleep in foetal lamb, *J. Physiol.* **210**:47p, 48p.

96. DAWES, G. S., FOX, H. E., LEDUC, B. M., LIGGINS, G. C., AND RICHARDS, R. T., 1972, Respiratory movements and rapid eye movement sleep in the foetal lamb, *J. Physiol.* **220**:119–143.

97. DAWES, G. S., MOTT, J. C., AND WIDDICOMBE, J. G., 1954, The foetal circulation in the lamb, *J. Physiol.* **126**:563–587.

98. DAY, R. L., CALIGUIRI, L., KAMENSKI, C., AND EHRICH, F., 1964, Body temperature and survival of premature infants, *Pediatrics* **34**:171–181.

99. DE CASTRO, F., 1928, Sur la structure et l'innervation du sinus carotidien de l'homme et des mammifères. Nouveau faits sur l'innervation et la fonction du glomus caroticum. Études anatomiques et physiologiques, *Trab. Inst. Cajal Invest. Biol.* **25**:331–380.

100. DE CASTRO, F., 1951, Sur la structure de la synapse dans les chemorecepteurs: Leur mécanisme d'excitation et rôle dans la circulation sanguine locale, *Acta Physiol. Scand.* **22**:14–43.

101. DEEDS-MATTINGLY, M., 1936, Absorptive area and volume of chorionic villi in circumvallate placentas, *Amer. J. Anat.* **59**:485–507.

102. DODDS, G. S., 1922, The area of the chorionic villi in the full term placenta, *Anat. Rec.* **24**:287–294.

103. DÖRING, G. K., AND LOESCHCKE, H. H., 1947, Atmung und Säure-Basengleichgewichte in der Schwangerschaft, *Arch. Gesamte Physiol.* **249**:437–451.

104. DÖRING, G. K., LOESCHCKE, H. H., AND OCHWADT, B., 1950, Weitere Untersuchungen über die Wirkung der Sexualhormone auf die Atmung, *Arch. Gesamte Physiol.* **252**:216–230.

105. DOWNING, S. E., AND LEE, J. C., 1975, Laryngeal chemosensitivity: A possible mechanism for sudden infant death, *Pediatrics* **55**:640–649.

106. EASTMAN, N. J., 1930, Foetal blood studies, *Bull. Johns Hopkins Hosp.* **47**:221–230.

107. EASTMAN, N. J., 1932, Foetal blood studies. III. The chemical nature of asphyxia neonatorum and its bearing on certain practical problems, *Bull. Johns Hopkins Hosp.* **50**:39–50.

108. ELLIOTT, F. M., 1964, The pulmonary artery system in normal and diseased lungs: Structure in relation to pattern of branching, Ph.D. thesis, University of London.

109. EMMANOUILIDES, G. C., HOBEL, C. J., YASHIRO, K.,

AND KLYMAN, G., 1972, Fetal responses to maternal exercise in the sheep, *Amer. J. Obstet. Gynecol.* **112**:130–137.

110. EYZAGUIRRE, C., AND LEWIN, J., 1961, Chemoreceptor activity of the carotid body of the cat, *J. Physiol.* **159**:222–237.

111. EYZAGUIRRE, C., AND LEWIN, J., 1961, Effect of different oxygen tensions on the carotid body *in vitro, J. Physiol.* **159**:238–250.

112. FABER, J. J., AND GREEN, T. J., 1972, Foetal placental blood flow in the lamb, *J. Physiol.* **223**:375–393.

113. FISCHER, W. M., VOGEL, H. R., AND THEWS, G., 1965, Der Säure–Basenstatus und die CO_2-Transportfunktion des mütterlichen und fetalen Blutes zum Zeitpunkt der Geburt, *Arch. Gesamte Physiol.* **286**:220–237.

114. FREDA, V. J., AND ADAMSONS, K., 1964, Exchange transfusion *in utero,* report of a case, *Amer. J. Obstet. Gynecol.* **89**:817–821.

115. FREESE, U. E., 1973, Morphological determinants in O_2 transfer across the human and rhesus hemochorial placenta, *Adv. Exp. Med. Biol.* **37**:1027–1039.

116. GARE, D. J., SHIME, J., PAUL, W. M., AND HOSKINS, M., 1969, Oxygen administration during labor, *Amer. J. Obstet. Gynecol.* **105**:954–961.

117. GOODLIN, R. C., AND KAISER, I. H., 1957, The effect of ammonium chloride induced maternal acidosis on the human fetus at term. I. pH, hemoglobin, blood gases, *Amer. J. Med. Sci.* **233**:662–673.

118. GOORMAGHTIGH, N., AND PANNIER, R., 1939, Les paraganglions du coeur et des zones vasosensibles carotidienne et cardio-aortique chez le chat adulte, *Arch. Biol. Paris* **50**:455–533.

119. GRAHN, D., AND KRUTCHMAN, J., 1963, Variation in neonatal death rate and birth weight in the United States and possible relations to environmental radiation, geology and altitude, *Amer. J. Hum. Genet.* **15**:329–352.

120. GURTNER, G. H., AND BURNS, B., 1972, Possible facilitated transport of oxygen across the placenta, *Nature (London)* **240**:473–475.

121. GURTNER, G. H., AND BURNS, B., 1973, The role of cytochrome P-450 of placenta in facilitated oxygen diffusion, *Drug Metab. Dispos.* **1**:368–373.

122. HAMILTON, L. A., AND BEHRMAN, R. E., 1972, Intra-amniotic infusion of bicarbonate in the treatment of human fetal acidosis, *Amer. J. Obstet. Gynecol.* **112**:834–847.

123. HARNED, H. S., JR., AND FERREIRO, J., 1973, Initiation of breathing by cold stimulation: Effects of change in ambient temperature on respiratory activity of the full-term fetal lamb, *J. Pediatr.* **83**:663–669.

124. HARNED, H. S., JR., AND FERREIRO, J., 1974, Unpublished observations.

125. HARNED, H. S., JR., AND HERRINGTON, R. T., 1968, Unpublished observations.

126. Harned, H. S., Jr., Griffin, C. A., Berryhill, W. S., Jr., MacKinney, L. G., and Sugioka, K., 1967, Role of carotid chemoreceptors in the initiation of effective breathing of the lamb at term, *Pediatrics* **39**:329–336.

127. Harned, H. S., Jr., Griffin, C. A., III, Berryhill, W. S., Jr., MacKinney, L. G., and Sugioka, K., 1968, Role of hypoxia and pH decrease in initiation of respiration, in: *Intrauterine Dangers to the Foetus, Proceedings of a Symposium,* Prague, Oct. 11–14, 1966, pp. 121–125, Excerpta Medica Foundation, Amsterdam.

128. Harned, H. S., Jr., Herrington, R. T., and Ferreiro, J., 1970, The effects of immersion and temperature on the respiration of newly born lambs, *Pediatrics* **45**:598–605.

129. Harned, H. S., Jr., Herrington, R. T., Griffin, C. A., III, Berryhill, W. S., Jr., and MacKinney, L. G., 1968, Respiratory effects of division of the carotid sinus nerve in the lamb soon after the initiation of breathing, *Pediatr. Res.* **2**:264–270.

130. Harned, H. S., Jr., MacKinney, L. G., Berryhill, W. S., and Holmes, C. K., 1966, Effects of hypoxia and acidity on the initiation of breathing in the fetal lamb at term, *Amer. J. Dis. Child.* **112**:334–342.

131. Harned, H. S., Jr., Rowshan, G., MacKinney, L. G., and Sugioka, K., 1964, Relationships of P_{O2}, P_{CO2} and pH to onset of breathing of the term lamb as studied by a flow-through cuvette electrode assembly, *Pediatrics* **33**:672–681.

132. Haselhorst, G., and Stromberger, K., 1931, Über den Gasgehalte des Nabelschnurblutes vor und nach der Geburt des Kindes und über den Gasaustausch in der Plazenta, *Z. Geburtshilfe Gynaekol.* **100**:48, 49.

133. Hasselbalch, K. A., 1912, Ein Beitrag zur Respirationsphysiologie der Gravidität, *Skand. Arch. Physiol.* **27**:1–12.

134. Head, H., 1889, On the regulation of respiration, *J. Physiol.* **10**:1–70.

135. Heese, H. de V., Davey, D. A., Rorke, M., and Molteno, C., 1973, Effect of maternal anesthesia on oxygenation and acid–base status of the newborn infant, *S. Afr. Med. J.* **47**:1991–1999.

136. Hendricks, C. H., 1957, Studies in lactic acid metabolism in pregnancy and labor, *Amer. J. Obstet. Gynecol.* **73**:492–506.

137. Hering, E., 1868, Die Selbststeuerung der Athmung durch den Nervus vagus, *Sitzungsber. Akad. Wiss. Wien Abt. II* **57**:672–677.

138. Herrington, R. T., Harned, H. S., Jr., Ferreiro, J., and Griffin, C. A., 1971, The role of the central nervous system in perinatal respiration. Studies of the chemoregulatory mechanisms in the term lamb, *Pediatrics* **47**:857–864.

139. Heymans, C., and Bouckoert, J. J., 1930, Sinus caroticus and respiratory reflexes: Cerebral blood flow and respiration; adrenaline apnoea, *J. Physiol.* **69**:254–266.

140. Heymans, C., and Neil, E., 1958, *Reflexogenic Areas of the Cardiovascular System,* pp. 131–136, Churchill, London.

141. Heymans, J. F., and Heymans, C., 1926, Stimulation et inhibition réflexes des mouvements respiratoires de la tete "isolée" du chien B dont le coeur-poumon "isole" est perfusé par un chien C., *C. R. Soc. Biol. (Paris)* **95**:1118–1121.

142. Hill, E. P., Power, G. G., and Longo, L. D., 1972, A mathematical model of placental O_2 transfer with consideration of hemoglobin reaction rates, *Amer. J. Physiol.* **222**:721–729.

143. Hill, E. P., Power, G. G., and Longo, L. D., 1973, A mathematical model of carbon dioxide transfer in the placenta and its interaction with oxygen, *Amer. J. Physiol.* **224**:283–299.

144. Hill, J. R., 1959, The oxygen consumption of newborn and adult mammals. Its dependence on the oxygen tension of the inspired air and on environmental temperature, *J. Physiol.* **149**:346–373.

145. Holland, R. A. B., 1973, Placental oxygen gradients due to diffusion and chemical reaction, *Adv. Exp. Med. Biol.* **37**:1055–1059.

146. Hörmann, G., 1953, Ein Beitrag zur funktionellen Morphologie der menschlichen Placenta, *Arch. Gynäkol.* **184**:109–123.

147. Hornbein, T. F., Griffo, Z. J., and Roos, A., 1961, Quantitation of the chemoreceptor activity: Interrelation of hypoxia and hypercapnia, *J. Neurophysiol.* **24**:561–568.

148. Huckabee, W. F., Metcalfe, J., Prystowsky, H., and Barron, D. H., 1962, Insufficiency of O_2 supply to pregnant uterus, *Amer. J. Physiol.* **202**:198–204.

149. Huggett, A. St. G., and Hammond, J., 1952, Physiology of the placenta, in: *Marshall's Physiology of Reproduction* (A. S. Parkes, ed.), Vol. 2, pp. 312–397, Longmans, Green and Co., London.

150. James, E. J., Raye, J. R., Gresham, E. L., Makowski, E. L., Meschia, G., and Battaglia, F. C., 1972, Fetal oxygen consumption, carbon dioxide production, and glucose uptake in a chronic sheep preparation, *Pediatrics* **50**:361–371.

151. James, L. S., 1960, Acidosis of the newborn and its relation to birth asphyxia, *Acta Paediatr.* **49**(*Suppl. 122*):17–28.

152. James, L. S., and Adamsons, K., 1964, Respiratory physiology of the fetus and newborn infant, *N. Engl. J. Med.* **271**:1352–1360.

153. James, L. S., Weisbrot, I. M., Prince, C. E., Holaday, D. A., and Apgar, V., 1958, The acid–base status of human infants in relation to birth asphyxia and the onset of respiration, *J. Pediatr.* **52**:379–394.

154. Jansen, A. H., and Chernick, V., 1974, Cardio-

respiratory response to central cyanide in fetal sheep, *J. Appl. Physiol.* **37**:18–21.

155. JOELS, N., AND NEIL, E., 1963, The excitation mechanism of the carotid body, *Br. Med. Bull.* **19**:21–24.

156. JOHNSON, G. H., BRINKMAN, C. R., III, AND ASSALI, N. S., 1972, Response of the hypoxic fetal and neonatal lamb to administration of base solution, *Amer. J. Obstet. Gynecol.* **114**:914–922.

157. JOHNSON, P., ROBINSON, J. S., AND SALISBURY, D., 1973, The onset and control of breathing after birth, in: *Foetal and Neonatal Physiology, Proceedings of the Sir J. Barcroft Centenary Symposium,* pp. 217–221, Cambridge University Press, Cambridge.

158. KAISER, I. H., CUMMINGS, J. N., REYNOLDS, S. R. M., AND MARBURGER, J. P., 1958, Acclimatization response of the pregnant ewe and fetal lamb to diminished ambient pressure, *J. Appl. Physiol.* **13**:171–177.

159. KAPLAN, S., AND ASSALI, N. S., 1972, Disorders of the fetal and neonatal circulation, in: *Pathophysiology of Gestation* (N. S. Assali, ed.), Vol. 3, pp. 1–86, Academic Press, New York.

160. KHAZIN, A. F., HON, E. H., AND HEHRE, F. W., 1971, Effects of maternal hyperoxia on the fetus. I. Oxygen tension, *Amer. J. Obstet. Gynecol.* **109**:628–637.

161. KRAUSS, A. N., THIBEAULT, D. W., AND AULD, P. A., 1972, Acid–base balance in cerebrospinal fluid of newborn infants, *Biol. Neonat.* **21**:25–34.

162. LAMBERTSEN, C., HALL, J. P., WOLLMAN, H., AND GOODMAN, M. W., 1963, Quantitative interactions of increased P_{O_2} and P_{CO_2} upon respiration in man, *Ann. N. Y. Acad. Sci.* **109**:731–742.

163. LIGGINS, G. C., AND HOWIE, R. N., 1972, A controlled trial of antepartum glucocorticoid treatment for prevention of the respiratory distress syndrome in premature infants, *Pediatrics* **50**:515–534.

164. LOESCHCKE, H. H., 1957, Intracranielle Chemorezeptoren mit Wirkung auf die Atmung, *Helv. Physiol. Pharmacol. Acta* **15**:25, 26.

165. LOESCHCKE, H. H., AND KOEPCHEN, H. P., 1958, Versuche zur Lokalisation des Angriffsortes der Atmungs- und Kreislaufwirkung von Novocain im Liquor cerebrospinalis, *Arch. Gesamte Physiol.* **266**:628–641.

166. LONGO, L. D., DELIVORIA-PAPADOPOULOS, M., AND FORSTER, R. E., II, 1974, Placental CO_2 transfer after fetal carbonic anhydrase inhibition, *Amer. J. Physiol.* **226**:703–710.

167. LONGO, L. D., HILL, E. P., AND POWER, G. G., 1972, Theoretic analysis of factors affecting placental O_2 transfer, *Amer. J. Physiol.* **222**:730–739.

168. LONGMUIR, I. S., 1971, in: *Microcirculatory Approaches to Current Therapeutic Problems,* Symposium, Sixth European Conference on Microcirculation, Aalborg, pp. 3–7, S. Karger, Basel.

169. LUMLEY, J., AND WOOD, C., 1973, Effect of changes in maternal oxygen and carbon dioxide tensions on the fetus, in: *Clinical Anesthiology,* Vol. 10, No. 2, *Parturition and Perinatology* (G. F. Marx, ed.), Chapter 9, pp. 122–137, F. A. Davis Co., Philadelphia.

170. MACKAY, R. B., 1957, Observations on the oxygenation of the foetus in normal and abnormal pregnancy, *J. Obstet. Gynaecol. Br. Emp.* **64**:185–197.

171. MACKINNEY, L. G., GOLDBERG, I. D., EHRLICH, F. E., AND FREYMANN, K. C., 1958, Chemical analyses of blood from the umbilical cord of the newborn: Relation to fetal maturity and perinatal distress, *Pediatrics* **21**:555–564.

172. MAKOWSKI, E. L., BATTAGLIA, F. C., MESCHIA, G., BEHRMAN, R. E., SCHRUEFER, J., SEEDS, A. E., AND BRUNS, P., 1968, Effect of maternal exposure to high altitude on fetal oxygenation, *Amer. J. Obstet. Gynecol.* **100**:852–861.

173. MAKOWSKI, E. L., MESCHIA, G., DROEQUMUELLER, W., AND BATTAGLIA, F. C., 1968, Distribution of uterine blood flow in the pregnant sheep, *Amer. J. Obstet. Gynecol.* **101**:409–412.

174. MALONEY, J. E., ADAMSON, T. M., BRODERECKY, V., CRANAGE, S., LAMBERT, T., AND RITCHIE, B. C., 1974, Respiratory activity in the foetal lamb, *Proc. Aust. Physiol. Pharmacol. Soc.,* May 22–24.

175. MANNING, F., WYN PUGH, E., AND BODDY, K., 1975, Effect of cigarette smoking on fetal breathing movements in normal pregnancies, *Br. Med. J.* **1**:552–553.

176. MERLET, C., HOERTER, J., DEVILLENEUVE, C., AND TCHOBROUTSKY, C., 1970, Mise en evidence de movements respiratoires chez le foetus d'agneau *in utero* au cours du dernier mois de la gestation, *C. R. Acad. Sci. Paris* **270**:2462–2464.

177. MESCHIA, G., COTTER, J. R., BREATHNACH, C. S., AND BARRON, D. H., 1965, The haemoglobin, oxygen, carbon dioxide, and hydrogen ion concentration in the umbilical bloods of sheep and goats as sampled via indwelling catheters, *Q. J. Exp. Physiol.* **50**:185–195.

178. MESCHIA, G., COTTER, J. R., BREATHNACH, C. S., AND BARRON, D. H., 1965, The diffusibility of oxygen across the sheep placenta, *Q. J. Exp. Physiol.* **50**:466–480.

179. MESCHIA, G., COTTER, J. R., MAKOWSKI, E. L., AND BARRON, D. H., 1967, Simultaneous measurements of uterine and umbilical blood flows and oxygen uptakes, *Q. J. Exp. Physiol.* **52**:1–18.

180. MESCHIA, G., HELLEGERS, A., PRYSTOWSKY, H., HUCKABEE, W., METCALFE, J., AND BARRON, D. H., 1961, Oxygen dissociation curves of the bloods of adult and fetal sheep at high altitude, *Q. J. Exp. Physiol.* **46**:156–160.

181. METCALFE, J., 1967, The oxygen supply of the fetus, in: *Development of the Lung—Ciba Found. Symp.* (A.

V. S. Reuck and R. Porter, eds.), pp. 258–271, Little, Brown and Co., Boston.

182. METCALFE, J., 1969, Uterine oxygen supply and fetal health, *Yale J. Biol. Med.* **42**:166–179.

183. METCALFE, J., BARTELS, H., AND MOLL, W., 1967, Gas exchange in the pregnant uterus, *Physiol. Rev.* **47**:782–838.

184. METCALFE, J., MESCHIA, G., HELLEGERS, A., PRYSTOWSKY, H., HUCKABEE, W., AND BARRON, D. H., 1962, Observations on the placental exchange of the respiratory gases in pregnant ewes at high altitude, *Q. J. Exp. Physiol.* **47**:74–92.

185. METCALFE, J., MESCHIA, G., HELLEGERS, A., PRYSTOWSKY, H., HUCKABEE, W., AND BARRON, D. H., 1962, Observations on the growth rates and organ weights of fetal sheep at altitude and sea level, *Q. J. Exp. Physiol.* **47**:305–313.

186. METCALFE, J., MOLL, W., BARTELS, H., HILPERT, P., AND PARER, J. T., 1965, Transfer of carbon monoxide and nitrous oxide in the artificially perfused sheep placenta, *Circ. Res.* **16**:95–101.

187. METCALFE, J., ROMNEY, S. L., RAMSEY, L. H., REID, D. E., AND BURWELL, C. S., 1955, Estimation of uterine blood flow in normal human pregnancy at term, *J. Clin. Invest.* **34**:1632–1638.

188. MINKOWSKI, A., AND SWIERCZEWSKI, E., 1959, in: *Oxygen Supply to the Human Foetus* (J. Walker and A. C. Turnbull, eds.), p. 237, Blackwell Scientific Publications, Oxford.

189. MITCHELL, R. A., 1965, The regulation of respiration in metabolic acidosis and alkalosis, in: *Cerebrospinal Fluid and Its Regulation of Ventilation* (C. M. Brooks, F. F. Kao, and B. B. Lloyd, eds.), pp. 109–131, F. A. Davis Co., Philadelphia.

190. MITCHELL, R. A., LOESCHCKE, H. H., SEVRINGHAUS, J. W., RICHARDSON, B. W., AND MASSION, W. H., 1963, Regions of respiratory chemosensitivity on the surface of the medulla, *Ann. N. Y. Acad. Sci.* **109**:661–681.

191. MOLL, W., 1973, Placental function and oxygenation in the fetus, *Adv. Exp. Med. Biol.* **37**:1017–1026.

192. MORISHIMA, H. O., DANIEL, S. S., ADAMSONS, K., AND JAMES, L. S., 1965, Effects of positive pressure ventilation of the mother upon the acid–base state of the fetus, *Amer. J. Obstet. Gynecol.* **93**:269–273.

193. MORISHIMA, H. O., MOYA, F., BOSSERS, A. C., AND DANIEL, S. S., 1964, Adverse effects of maternal hypocapnea on the newborn guinea pig, *Amer. J. Obstet. Gynecol.* **88**:524–529.

194. MOTOYAMA, E. K., RIVARD, G., ACHESON, F., AND COOK, C. D., 1966, Adverse effect of maternal hyperventilation on the foetus, *Lancet* **1**:286–288.

195. MOTT, J. C., 1961, The ability of young mammals to withstand total oxygen lack, *Br. Med. Bull.* **17**:144–148.

196. MOYA, F., MORISHIMA, H. O., SHNIDER, S. M., AND JAMES, L. S., 1965, Influence of maternal hyperventilation on the newborn infant, *Amer. J. Obstet. Gynecol.* **91**:76–84.

197. MYERS, R. E., 1973, Threshold values of oxygen deficiency leading to cardiovascular and brain pathologic changes in term monkey fetuses, *Adv. Exp. Med. Biol.* **37**:1047–1054.

198. OLIVER, T. K., JR. (ed.), 1964, Heat production, in: *Thermoregulation of the Newly Born* Supplement No. 2, Reports of Ross Conferences on Pediatric Research, Ross Laboratories, Columbus, Ohio.

199. ORZALEZI, M. M., AND HAY, W. W., 1971, The regulation of oxygen affinity of fetal blood. I. *In vitro* experiments and results in normal infants, *Pediatrics* **48**:857–864.

200. OTEY, E. S., AND BERNTHAL, T., 1960, Interaction of hypoxia and hypercapnia at the carotid bodies in chemoreflex stimulation of breathing, *Fed. Proc. Fed. Amer. Soc. Exp. Biol.* **19**:373.

201. PAGTAKHAN, R. D., FARIDY, E. E., AND CHERNICK, V., 1971, Interaction between arterial P_{O_2} and P_{CO_2} in the initiation of respiration of fetal sheep, *J. Appl. Physiol.* **30**:382–387.

202. PANIGEL, M., 1973, Experimental models for *in vivo* and *in vitro* investigations on placental hemodynamics and oxygen supply to the fetus, *Adv. Exp. Med. Biol.* **37**:1061–1065.

203. PARER, J. T., DE LANNOY, C. W., HOVERSLAND, A. S., AND METCALFE, J., 1968, Effect of decreased uterine blood flow on uterine oxygen consumption in pregnant macaques, *Amer. J. Obstet. Gynecol.* **100**:813–820.

204. PARMENTIER, R., 1962, L'aération néonatale du poumon. Contribution expérimentale et anatomo-clinique, *Rev. Belg. Pathol.* **29**:123–244.

205. PONTE, J., AND PURVES, M. J., 1973, Types of afferent nervous activity which may be measured in the vagus nerve of the sheep foetus, *J. Physiol.* **229**:51–76.

206. PONTE, J., AND PURVES, M. J., 1974, The role of the carotid body chemoreceptors and carotid sinus baroreceptors in the control of cerebral blood vessels, *J. Physiol.* **237**:315–340.

207. POWER, G. G., AND LONGO, L. D., 1973, Sluice flow in placenta: Maternal vascular pressure effects on fetal circulation, *Amer. J. Physiol.* **225**:1490–1496.

208. POWER, G. G., HILL, E. P., AND LONGO, L. D., 1972, Analysis of uneven distribution of diffusing capacity and blood flow in the placenta, *Amer. J. Physiol.* **222**:740–746.

209. POWER, G. G., LONGO, L. D., WAGNER, H. N., JR., KUHL, D. E., AND FORSTER, R. E., III, 1967, Uneven distribution of maternal and fetal placental blood flow, as demonstrated using macroaggregates, and its response to hypoxia, *J. Clin. Invest.* **46**:2053–2063.

210. PURVES, M. J., 1966, The effects of hypoxia in the new-born lamb before and after denervation of the carotid chemoreceptors, *J. Physiol.* **185**:60–77.

211. PURVES, M. J., 1970, The effect of hypoxia, hypercapnia, and hypotension upon carotid body blood flow and oxygen consumption in the cat, *J. Physiol.* **209**:395–416.

212. PURVES, M. J., 1974, Onset of respiration at birth, *Arch. Dis. Child.* **49**:333–343.

213. PURVES, M. J., AND BISCOE, T. J., 1966, Development of chemoreceptor activity, *Br. Med. Bull.* **22**:56–60.

214. PREYER, W., 1888, *Specielle Physiologie des Embryo: Untersuchungen über die Lebenscheingun vor der Geburt,* Grieben, Leipzig.

215. PRYSTOWSKY, H., 1957, Fetal blood studies. VII. The oxygen pressure gradient between the maternal and fetal bloods of the human in normal and abnormal pregnancy, *Bull. Johns Hopkins Hosp.* **101**:48–56.

216. PRYSTOWSKY, H., HELLEGERS, A., AND BRUNS, P., 1960, Fetal blood studies. XVIII. Supplementary observations on the oxygen pressure gradient between the maternal and fetal bloods of humans, *Surg. Gynecol. Obstet.* **110**:495, 496.

217. PRYSTOWSKY, H., HELLEGERS, A., MESCHIA, G., METCALFE, J., HUCKABEE, W., AND BARRON, D. H., 1960, The blood volume of fetuses carried by ewes at high altitude, *Q. J. Exp. Physiol.* **45**:292–298.

218. QUILLIGAN, E. J., AND CIBILS, L., 1964, Oxygen tension in the intervillous space, *Amer. J. Obstet. Gynecol.* **88**:572–577.

219. RAMSEY, E. M., 1962, Circulation in the intervillous space of the primate placenta, *Amer. J. Obstet. Gynecol.* **84**:1649–1663.

220. RAMSEY, E. M., 1965, Circulation of the placenta, in: *Symposium on the Placenta: Birth Defects* (D. Bergsma, ed.), Vol. I, pp. 5–12, Original Article Series, National Foundation—March of Dimes, New York.

221. RANKIN, J. H. G., 1973, Maternal alkalosis and fetal oxygenation, *Adv. Exp. Med. Biol.* **37**:1067–1074.

222. REID, L., 1967, The embryology of the lung, in: *Development of the Lung—Ciba Found. Symp.* (A. V. S. de Reuck and R. Porter, eds.), pp. 109–124, Little, Brown and Co., Boston.

223. REYNOLDS, S. R. M., 1961, Sensory deprivation, weightlessness, and antigravity mechanisms. The problem of fetal adaptation to a floating existence, *Aerospace Med.* **32**:1061–1067.

224. REYNOLDS, S. R. M., AND MACKIE, J. D., 1961, Development of chemoreceptor response sensitivity: Studies in fetuses, lambs and ewes, *Amer. J. Physiol.* **201**:239–250.

225. RIGATTO, H., AND BRADY, J. P., 1972, Periodic breathing and apnea in preterm infants. I. Evidence for hypoventilation possibly due to central respiratory depression, *Pediatrics* **50**:202–218.

226. RIGATTO, H., AND BRADY, J. P., 1972, Periodic breathing and apnea in preterm infants. II. Hypoxia as a primary event, *Pediatrics* **50**:219–228.

227. ROMNEY, S. L., REID, D. E., METCALFE, J., AND

BURWELL, C. S., 1955, Oxygen utilization by the human fetus *in utero, Amer. J. Obstet. Gynecol.* **70**:791–797.

228. ROOTH, G., 1963, Foetal respiration, *Acta Paediatr.* **52**:22–35.

229. ROOTH, G., 1964, Early detection and prevention of foetal acidosis, *Lancet* **2**:290–293.

230. ROOTH, G., AND SJÖSTEDT, S., 1962, The placental transfer of gases and fixed acids, *Arch. Dis. Child.* **37**:366–370.

231. ROOTH, G., SJÖSTEDT, S., AND CALIGARA, F., 1961, Hydrogen concentration, carbon dioxide tension and acid base balance in blood of human umbilical cord and intervillous space of placenta, *Arch. Dis. Child.* **36**:278–285.

232. RUDOLPH, A. M., AND HEYMANN, M. A., 1967, The circulation of the fetus *in utero.* Methods for studying distribution of blood flow, cardiac output and organ blood flow, *Circ. Res.* **21**:163–184.

233. RUDOLPH, A. M., AND YUAN, S., 1965, The pattern of pulmonary vascular response to hypoxia, *J. Pediatr.* **67**:929.

234. SALING, E., 1966, Amnioscopy and foetal blood sampling: Observations on foetal acidosis, *Arch. Dis. Child.* **41**:472–476.

235. SALING, E., 1968, *Foetal and Neonatal Hypoxia in Relation to Clinical Obstetric Practice,* Edward Arnold, London.

236. SCHOLANDER, P. F., 1959, Experimental studies on asphyxia in animals, in: *Oxygen Supply to the Human Foetus* (J. Walker and A. C. Turnbull, eds.), pp. 267–274, Blackwell Scientific Publications, Oxford.

237. SCHOLANDER, P. F., 1964, Animals in aquatic environments: Diving mammals and birds, in: *Handbook of Physiology. IV. Adaptation to the Environment* (D. B. Dill, ed.), Chapt. 45, pp. 729–739, American Physiological Society, Washington, D.C.

238. SCHUMACHER, S., 1938, Über die Bedeutung der arteriovenösen Anastomosen und der epitheloiden Muskelzellen (Quellzellen), *Z. Mikrosk-Anat. Forsch.* **43**:107–130.

239. SCIBETTA, J. J., ROSEN, M. G., HOCHBERG, C. J., AND CHIK, L., 1971, Human fetal brain response to sound during labor, *Amer. J. Obstet. Gynecol.* **109**:82–85.

240. SEVRINGHAUS, J. W., SWENSON, E. W., FINLEY, T. N., LATEGOLA, M. T., AND WILLIAMS, J., 1961, Unilateral hypoventilation produced in dogs by occluding one pulmonary artery, *J. Appl. Physiol.* **16**:53–60.

241. SOMEROFF, A. J., 1971, Respiration and sucking as components of the orienting reaction in newborns, *Psychophysiology* **7**:213–222.

242. SOROKIN, S., 1959, The development *in vitro* of mammalian lungs, *Anat. Rec.* **134**:642, 643.

243. SOROKIN, S., 1960, Histochemical events in developing human lungs, *Acta Anat. (Basel)* **40**:105–119.

244. STEMBERA, Z. K., HODR, J., AND JANDA, J., 1965, Umbilical blood flow in healthy newborn infants during the first minutes after birth, *Amer. J. Obstet. Gynecol.* **91**:568–574.

245. STEMBERA, Z. K., HODR, J., AND JANDA, J., 1968, Umbilical blood flow in newborn infants who suffered intrauterine hypoxia, *Amer. J. Obstet. Gynecol.* **101**:546–553.

246. STEMBERA, Z. K., HODR, J., KITTRICH, M., AND JANDA, J., 1972, Fetoplacental circulation in the umbilical cord when coiled around the fetal neck, *Biol. Neonat.* **20**:120–126.

247. STENGER, V. S., EITZMAN, D., ANDERSEN, T., COTTER, J., AND PRYSTOWSKY, H., 1965, A study of the oxygenation of the fetus and newborn and its relation to that of the mother, *Amer. J. Obstet. Gynecol.* **93**:376–385.

248. STIEVE, H., 1941, Die Entwicklung und der Bau der menschlichen Plazenta. 2. Zotten, Zottenraumgitter und Gefässe in der zweiten Hälfte der Schwangerschaft, *Z. Mikrosk.-Anat. Forsch.* **50**:1–120.

249. STOREY, A. T., AND JOHNSON, P., 1975, Laryngeal water receptors initiating apnea in the lamb, *Exp. Neurol.* **47**:42–55.

250. TCHOBROUTSKY, C., 1967, Personal communication.

251. THALME, B., 1967, Electrolyte and acid–base balance in fetal and maternal blood: An experimental and a clinical study, *Acta Obstet. Gynecol. Scand.* **45**(*Suppl. 8*):1–118.

252. THURLBECK, W. M., 1975, Postnatal growth and development of the lung, *Amer. Rev. Respir. Dis.* **111**:803–844.

253. TOMINAGA, T., AND PAGE, E. W., 1966, Accommodation of the human placenta to hypoxia, *Amer. J. Obstet. Gynecol.* **94**:679–691.

254. ULLRICH, J. R., AND ACKERMAN, B. D., 1972, Changes in umbilical artery blood gas values with the onset of respiration, *Biol. Neonat.* **20**:466–474.

255. VILLEE, C. A., 1958, *The Placenta and Fetal Membranes,* Williams and Wilkins Co., Baltimore.

256. VON EULER, U. S., LILIJESTRAND, G., AND ZOTTERMAN, V., 1939, The excitation mechanism of the chemoreceptors of the carotid body, *Skand. Arch. Physiol.* **83**:132–152.

257. WALKER, D., GRIMWADE, J., AND WOOD, C., 1971, Intrauterine noise: A component of the fetal environment, *Amer. J. Obstet. Gynecol.* **109**:91–95.

258. WIDDICOMBE, J. G., 1954, The site of pulmonary stretch receptors in the cat, *J. Physiol.* **125**:336–351.

259. WIDDICOMBE, J. G., 1963, Respiratory reflexes from the lungs, *Br. Med. Bull.* **19**:15–20.

260. WILKIN, P., AND BURSZTEIN, M., 1958, Etude quantitative de l'évolution, au cours de la grossesse, de la superficie de la membrane d'échange du placenta humain, in: *Le Placenta Humain* (Snoeck, ed.), Masson et Cie, Paris.

261. WILLIAMSON, C. S., 1916, Influence of age and sex on hemoglobin, *Arch. Intern. Med.* **18**:505–528.

262. WOLKOFF, A. S., BAWDEN, J. W., FLOWERS, C. E., AND McGEE, J. A., 1965, The effects of anesthesia on the unborn fetus, *Amer. J. Obstet. Gynecol.* **93**:311–320.

263. WOODRUM, D. E., PARER, J. T., WENNBERG, R. P., AND HODSON, W. A., 1972, Chemoreceptor response in initiation of breathing in the fetal lamb, *J. Appl. Physiol.* **33**:120–125.

264. WULF, H., 1959, Das Verhalten der Atemgase in den Nabelschnurgefässen nach der Geburt, *Z. Gesamte Exp. Med.* **132**:136–148.

265. WULF, H., 1962, Der Gasaustausch in der reifen Plazenta des Menschen, *Z. Geburtshilfe Gynaekol.* **158**:117–124.

266. WULF, H., 1964, The oxygen and carbon dioxide tension gradients in the human placenta at term, *Amer. J. Obstet. Gynecol.* **88**:33–44.

CHAPTER 7

Lung Maturity and Pulmonary Phospholipid Metabolism

T. Allen Merritt, Michael Obladen, and Louis Gluck

1. Introduction

The lung is composed of more than 40[1] different cell types, but no single type occupies the majority of lung mass. Although it has been reported that alveolar macrophages and Clara cells[7,84,96] can synthesize surface-active lecithin, most direct and indirect evidence suggests that the granular pneumatocyte (alveolar Type II cell) is responsible for the synthesis of surfactant, particularly the major surface-active phospholipid, dipalmityl phosphatidylcholine. The alveolar Type II cell is an attenuated cell, one of two cell types lining alveoli containing characteristic inclusion bodies. They appear to be extruded into alveolar spaces to provide surface-active material.[82] Radioactive labeled precursors of surfactant ([³H]acetate and [³H]palmitate) can be located by autoradiography in Type II cells

in the rabbit 30 min to several hours after intravenous injection.[37] Silver grains near but not over inclusion bodies suggest that these organelles may be sites of storage of surfactant, rather than the sites of synthesis of phospholipids that appear in the alveolar space.[18]

A close relationship exists between numbers of inclusion bodies and time of appearance of normal surfactant activity in fetal lamb lung at about 126 days' gestation.[74] Lipid-rich substances are secreted by granular pneumatocytes, but adverse conditions such as uncompensated acidosis alter the contents of lamellar bodies within the Type II cell.[10]

Histochemical analysis of inclusion bodies shows that they contain primarily phospholipids.[19] The 50-nm periodicity in lamellae of these osmiophilic inclusions is identical to the structure of synthetic dipalmityl phosphatidylcholine stained negatively with phosphotungstate[69]; that it is is substantiated by selective lipid-extraction techniques that preserve the inclusions.

Autoradiographic granules have also been found over lamellar inclusions and endoplasmic reticu-

T. Allen Merritt, Michael Obladen, and Louis Gluck · Department of Pediatrics, School of Medicine, University of California San Diego, La Jolla, California 92037

lum,[6,26] indicating that lamellae can incorporate palmitate into phospholipids. A specific precursor for phosphatidylcholine, [³H]choline, was incorporated into phospholipids solely by Type II alveolar cells, but not by Clara cells.[100] With a nonspecific precursor, [³H]acetate, findings also suggest that specific synthetic pathways are confined to the granular pneumatocyte.[7,96] Recently,[29] selective synthesis of phosphatidylcholine was reported in cultures of homogeneous Type II pneumocytes. Thus, strong evidence clearly implicates the Type II alveolar cell as the major site of synthesis of surface-active phospholipid in the lung.

2. Substrate Utilization in the Lung

Substrate utilization by the lung has been studied by a variety of techniques. Differences in species, tissue preparation (homogenized lung, lung slices, isolated perfused lung), and incubation procedures make meaningful comparisons of the various results difficult. The fetus is dependent on passage across the placenta of nutrients derived from the mother. Studies on the utilization of substrate in human fetal lung are limited; however, several pertinent studies in animals may help explain substrate utilization in the human. Selective uptake by Type II alveolar cells may differ from that of the lung as a whole, but those cells specifically involved in phospholipid synthesis can now be studied with newer cell culture techniques.[73]

Glucose uptake and utilization followed by incubating rabbit lung slices with radioactive label and determining the distribution of label in various metabolic products[36] showed that nearly one-third of the consumed glucose formed lactic acid, 20% CO_2, and 4% lipid, and that lesser amounts went into protein and nucleic acids. Lactate production is found even in the presence of optimal aerobic conditions with high P_{O_2}, but lactic acid levels in lung tissue exceed those in plasma.[133]

Although the metabolic demands for ATP in the early steps of lecithin synthesis may depend on the glycolytic pathway, oxidative phosphorylation serves as the primary energy source. An active hexose monophosphate shunt has been identified in lung tissue.[110,133] This pathway has an important role in protein synthesis in lung tissue,[85] and may serve to resist injury to lung tissue produced by oxidants similar to the role served by this pathway in erythrocytes.[126]

Glucose also serves the important function of providing the structural backbone—the glycerol moeity—for phospholipid synthesis. Radiolabel from glucose is catabolized directly into glycerol,[38,114] thus making glucose both an energy-providing source for lung metabolism and a structural component for phosphatidylcholine.

Active lipogenesis by fetal lung tissue is dependent on availability of precursors of lipids, such as acetyl-CoA, as well as on *de novo* synthesis of lipid from preformed fatty acids that reach the fetal lung from maternal serum across the placenta and fetal liver. Of the total amount of radioactive palmitate injected into the mother, 99% was found in the rat fetus within 5 min.[67] The rate of free fatty acid utilization depends on the concentrations of fatty acid and glucose presented to the lung as substrates. When radioactive palmitate was injected intravenously into the rat, about 2% appeared in the lung, and esterification was nearly complete within 30 min.[135] While the synthesis of surface-active compounds demonstrates the lipogenic capacity of the fetal and neonatal lung, no specific analysis has quantified the optimum amounts of precursor fatty acids and glucose required for peak rates of synthesis. The lung can readily oxidize fatty acids that may be derived from adipose tissues or hepatic sources.[127] Since carbohydrate stores in the fetal lung appear limited, the lipids supplied by placental transfer and from endogenous fetal stores may provide sufficient precursors in the fetus and neonate.

Fetal and neonatal lungs are exposed to vast alterations in blood flow that primarily shunts away from the lung in the fetal period and then rather quickly after birth receives the full cardiac output. As early as 1947, Barron *et al.*[8] found that oxygen consumption of lung tissue slices remained nearly constant for periods up to 5–6 hr when no substrate was added to the incubating medium. It was therefore reasoned that oxidative phosphorylation can be ongoing in the lung for some time without oxygen as a substrate.

In the fetus, oxygen reaches the parenchyma of the lung through the bronchial artery circulation. At birth, with the dynamic shifts in cardiopulmonary circulation, much of the lung tissue is within 50 μm of the alveolar surface—a distance that normally would permit adequate diffusion of oxygen from the air-filled alveolus into the cells that compose the alveolar wall. However, neither intact fetal nor neonatal lungs have been used in studies of oxygen consumption. Most investigators have used lung slices of varying thicknesses for the measurement of substrate utilization.[32,129] Differences in the application of this technique, however, have led to greatly differing conclusions. The oxygen consumption ($\dot{Q}_{O_2}$) of intact lungs has been reported to be lower than the $\dot{Q}_{O_2}$ of lung slices, thus making interpretation of data based on lung slice techniques difficult to place in physiological perspective. The condition of the intact lung must also be considered, since distending whole isolated lung increases the $\dot{Q}_{O_2}$ by nearly 50%.[8] These findings accentuate the lack of knowledge about both the nonventilated, fluid-filled fetal lung and the ventilated and perfused neonatal lung exposed to alveolar oxygen.

Protein synthesis in the growing lung depends on the generation of NADPH, primarily through the pentose monophosphate shunt, as mentioned in the discussion of glucose metabolism in the lung. Amino acid utilization occurs in the Type II cell[86]; autogradiographic techniques incubating [³H]leucine with lung slices localized the radiolabel to the rough endoplasmic reticulum. The later utilization of amino acids by the lung has not been studied adequately, nor has the contribution of amino acids to thne formation of the surfactant-associated apoprotein been adequately investigated.

Deficiencies in essential substrates and cofactors have been implicated in a decreased production of pulmonary surfactant. While fasting resulted in a decrease in pulmonary surfactant synthesis, no changes have been observed in hysteresis characteristics in adult rats subjected to short periods of fasting.[31a,102b,132b] Weanling rats deprived of chow for 60 hr showed a reduction in lung protein by one third; however, tissue phospholipid, and specifically phosphatidylcholine, was not reduced per gram of lung protein.[56a] The extent to which selective nutritional deprivation during gestation impairs fetal lung capabilities to synthesize surface-active phospholipids awaits further study.

3. Phospholipid Composition

Thannhauser et al.[122] first described the presence of dipalmityl lecithin in an ether extract obtained from 50 lb of adult beef lung. Later, Pattle and Thomas[99] found that beef lung effluent had an absorption spectrogram nearly identical to a mixture of 95% egg lecithin and 5% gelatin, and suggested that the bubble lining responsible for a reduction in surface tension was a lipoprotein. The major

lipid fractions of beef lung contain 74% phospholipids, 8% cholesterol, 10% triglycerides, and 8% fatty acids.[79] Only the phospholipid fraction reduced surface tension to 1–5 dynes·cm⁻¹ with a Wilhemy balance.

Sheep lung was found to contain fibrils composed of phospholipid and glycolipid, which likewise reduced surface tension.[17] In 1964, Brown[15] found the antiatelectasis factor of rabbit, dog, and human lung wash to be dipalmityl phosphatidylcholine. This observation was confirmed, and the surface-active material of both nonmammalian vertebrates and mammals was found to contain predominantly dipalmitic lecithin.[24] More than 93% of the lecithin was found to be sufficient for reducing surface tension to less than 12 dynes cm⁻¹/g in fresh lung tissue. The total amount of surface-active material correlated closely with the estimated alveolar surface area of the 11 animals studied (mouse, guinea pig, rat, rabbit, sea lion, chicken, dog, cow, frog, turtle) and man.

In each species, there was much more saturated phosphatidylcholine than that with ethylenic linkages. Clements et al.[24] suggested that the relative abundance of longer-chain unsaturated acyl groups in poikilothermic species met the need for lower "melting points" in the lipid structures exposed to wide variances in body temperature. Similar findings in several species were made by other workers. King and Clements[21,75–77] characterized the composition of surfactant from whole canine lung and alveolar wash by careful isolation of surface-active materials, using both differential and density gradient centrifugation. At each step of purification, the surface activity of the extracted material was determined at 25–37°C. Approximately 1–2.5 mg of surfactant was found per gram of whole lung tissue.

Phospholipids comprised more than 80% of the surface-active fraction, more than 50% of which is dipalmitoyl lecithin, with smaller amounts of phosphatidylglycerol, phosphatidylserine, phosphatidyglinositol, phosphatidylethanolamine, sphingomyelin, lysolecithin, free fatty acids, mono-, di-, and triglycerides, cholesterol, and cholesterol-esters.[9,21,39,42,63,109] The distribution of human amniotic fluid phospholipids approximates that found in human lung homogenates.[5,61,97,105] (see Table I). The fatty acid analysis of isolated phosphatidylcholine was as follows: palmitate (16:0), 71%; myristate (14:0), 6.1%; stearate (18.0), 3.6%; palmitoleate (16:1), 11%; oleate (18:1), 3.9%; and

Table I. Human Pulmonary Phospholipid Composition[a]

Author:	Harlan	Baxter	Arvidson	Hallman	Rooney	Rooney	Own observation
Material:	Total lung homogenate	Total lung homogenate	Amniotic fluid	Amniotic fluid	Lung fluid, fetus	Tracheal aspirate	Tracheal aspirate
Source:	Adult	Adult	At term	At term	At term	Adult	Newborn
Lysophosphatidylcholine	1.3	2.0	0.8				0.8
Phosphatidylcholine	50.9	47.5	67.6	76.2	56.7	57.4	69.4
Sphingomyelin	6.5	11.1	8.1	5.7			3.9
Phosphatidylserine	18.4	7.0	9.5[b]	2.1	12.0	12.4	5.1
Phosphatidylinositol		3.2		5.3			5.3
Phosphatidyl-ethanolamine		17.5	8.8	3.7	9.6	15.2	3.2
Phosphatidylglycerol	21.4[c]	2.5	5.1[d]	5.2	14.0	11.0	11.8
Phosphatidic acid		0.5					0.5
Lyso-bis-phosphatidic acid		1.5			7.6	4.1	

[a] Expressed as percentage of phospholipid-phosphorus.
[b] "Compound 3" as designated by the author.
[c] "PDME" as designated by the author.
[d] "Compound 1" as designated by the author.

3.6%, undefined. King and Clements[77] found that 46% of total lung lipid, or some 18% of whole lung tissue, was dipalmitoyl phosphatidylcholine. Some 13% of this lecithin, however, did not appear in the surfactant pool, a finding that had been suggested earlier.[63]

Scarpelli et al.[112] initially suggested the existence of a surfactant-associated lipoprotein. Dog and rabbit extracts, however, were assumed to be contaminated with serum proteins. Abrams[2] recovered a lipoprotein with a molecular weight of 2.4×10^5 daltons in homogenates from rabbit, sheep, horse, and human lungs that migrated with alpha globulin.

In adult lung, more than 9% of pulmonary surfactant is protein, while the proportion is 3.6% in fetal and 6.6% in neonatal dog lungs.[23,78] Three proteins were separated on polyacrylamide gel by electrophoresis, with molecular weights of 150,000, 68,000 (including IgG and albumin), and 1.07×10^4 daltons. The latter fraction comprised 50–75% of the protein appearing unique to lung, specifically reacting by immunoprecipitation to canine surface-active material. King et al.[78] reported a similar apoprotein in human surfactant, suggesting that immunoassay may permit identification of surfactant in amniotic and fetal pulmonary fluids. The precise role of this protein is not known, although it has been suggested to be a modifier of intracellular transport, cellular secretion, or surface properties within the alveolar lumen.

4. The Choline Pathway

The primary pathway for the synthesis of phosphatidylcholine (Fig. 1) is the choline-incorporation pathway described initially by Kennedy and Weiss[71] in 1956. By this pathway, choline is phosphorylated, then activated by conversion to cytidine diphosphate-(CDP-) choline, which is finally transferred to a diglyceride to form phosphatidylcholine:

(1) Choline + ATP $\xrightarrow[\text{Mg}^{2+}]{\text{choline kinase}}$ phosphorylcholine + ADP

(2) Phosphorylcholine + CTP $\xrightarrow{\text{cytidyltransferase}}$ CDP-choline + PPi

(3) CDP-choline + D-1,2-diglyceride $\xrightarrow[\text{Mg}^{2+}]{\text{choline phosphotransferase}}$ phosphatidylcholine + CMP

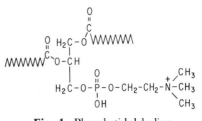

Fig. 1. Phosphatidylcholine.

Gluck et al.[53] first reported on the role of this pathway in the lung and its predominance in fetal life. In rabbit fetuses, a high rate of CDP-1,2-[^{14}C]-choline incorporation into phosphatidylcholine was found in the 21-day fetus in lung microsomes, mitochondria, and cell-free supernatant. The concentration of total lung phosphatidylcholine derived from the choline pathway peaked by the 28th day of gestation, and acetone-precipitable (surface-active) phosphatidylcholine peaked by day 29. These workers[45] found a 3- to 5-fold increase in total alveolar phosphatidylcholine in prematurely delivered rabbit fetuses after the initiation of breathing. Surface-active phosphatidylcholine, however, increased some 20- to 30-fold when incorporation was compared in breathing and nonbreathing prematurely delivered rabbits. By day 29, the choline-incorporation pathway was more active than the methylation pathway by some 16-fold, and some 90% of the acetone-precipitated surface-active phosphatidylcholine was produced by the choline pathway. Weinhold[130] observed a similar predominance of the choline pathway in the fetal rat. Of the total activity incorporated into phosphatidylcholine, 96–98% came from choline-methyl[^{14}C], while methionine methyl[^{14}C] incorporation accounted for a mere 4%. Using lung slices, Weinhold et al.[131] followed the incorporation of these substrates as gestation progressed, and found that the rate of incorporation peaked at the 19th day of a 21-day gestation period, with a slight decrease in total incorporation as the fetus reached term.

Farrell[33] reported on the predominance of the choline pathway in several species (Table II).

Human fetal lung tissue was found to possess the enzymes of the choline pathway.[133] The choline pathway predominates throughout gestation in the rhesus monkey in vitro using viable lung slices and in vivo using pathway-specific radioactive precursors,[29,138] and the choline-incorporation pathway is active in the lungs of human fetuses of 18 and 20 weeks' gestation.[49] This pathway was found to "surge" markedly at 35–36 weeks (90%) of gestation.

Table II. Relative Contribution to Phosphatidylcholine Synthesis

Species	Contribution by the choline pathway	Contribution by the methylation pathway
Fetal rat	97%	3%
Fetal rabbit	94%	6%
Fetal monkey	98%	2%
Human	95%	5%

From this period until term, dipalmatidyl phosphatidylcholine synthesis was found to be predominant.

Epstein and Farrell[29] found in the fetal rhesus three distinct phases of choline pathway activity. In early gestation (100–147 days), choline pathway activity was low; between 148 days and the choline surge at 153 days, this pathway exhibited an abrupt 2-fold increase peaking at 90% of term; finally, there was a steady decrease until birth. In air-breathing rhesus neonates, the pathway activity increased initially, but declined over the first 72 hr of life to levels found in adults of the same species. The surge in the choline pathway correlated closely with the increase in the lecithin/sphingomyelin ratio. This surge in choline incorporation also paralleled closely the time of rise in total and surface-active lung phosphatidylcholine in the fetal monkey lung.[72,92]

5. The Methylation Pathway

The synthesis of lecithin in the fetus by the methylation pathway was initially described by Bremer and Greenburg[14a] in rat liver. This synthesis involves phosphorylation, activation, and diglyceride linkage of ethanolamine to form phosphatidyl ethanolamine, which then undergoes three successive methylations from the methyl donor, S-adenosyl-L-methionine, forming mono- and dimethylethanolamine (PDME), intermediates of phosphatidylcholine.

Morgan et al.[93] initially reported the presence of PDME in dog lung, which they noted to contain acyl groups similar to those found in highly surface-active dipalmitoylphosphatidylcholine. Morgan et al.[93] further explored differences between methyltransferase of liver and that of lung. They found that the transferase system is probably composed of transferase(s), one of which methylates phosphatidylethanolamine, and others of which serve as isoenzymes for subsequent methylations.

Studies of the kinetics of the methylation pathway revealed that reaction rates were highest in the presence of saturated (specifically dipalmitoyl) acyl substrates, thus suggesting possible importance of this pathway in the synthesis of highly surface-active material. Methyltransferase activity was noted to be highly sensitive to oxygen, being facilitated by low ambient oxygen concentrations and specifically retarded by sulfhydryl oxidation. Methyltransferase activity was tentatively identified both in lung cell microsomes and in the lamellated inclusion bodies of the Type II pneumatocyte.

In fetal lambs, methyltransferase activity increased from very low levels at about 105 days' gestation, and tripled concomitant with the appearance of osmiophilic inclusion bodies.[90] Immediately prior to term, the activity of this enzyme decreased, generating the hypothesis that synthesis of phosphatidylcholine by the fetal lungs in the relatively hypoxic intrauterine environment was largely by the methylation synthetic route.

Conflicting studies by Spitzer et al.[118] assigned the methylation pathway a minor role in the lung, and suggested that phosphatidylcholine in lung is a heterogenous mixture of unsaturated phosphatidylcholine, which is synthesized via the methylation pathway, while surface-active highly saturated fatty acids are synthesized selectively by the CDP-choline pathway. The minor significance of the methylation pathway was also reported by DiAugustine,[28] who found no evidence of recycling of phosphatidylcholine methyl groups to PDME or vice versa in the rat lung. Gluck et al.[52] initially reported the minor contribution of the methylation pathway in fetal rabbit lung. The methylation pathway was found to have greatest activity on the 28th day of a 31-day gestation in the fetal rabbit. It was found to be pH-sensitive, with peak reaction rates at pH 7.8, while pH 7.0 or below was markedly deleterious to phosphatidylcholine synthesis. The finding of different carbon fatty acid composition in the biosynthetic intermediates of the methylation pathway[60] from those of CDP-choline incorporation suggested a possible means of determining relative contributions of total surface-active lecithins by each pathway. A possible technical error, however, leaves this work in question. This includes some studies on human fetal and neonatal lung phosphatidylcholine by Gluck and co-workers. These studies were based on previous studies in fetal rabbits. These investigations necessarily used indirect techniques utilizing tracheal effluents, pharyngeal aspirates, and lung tissue washes from expired fetuses and neonates. The methylation pathway was found to be active by 22–24 weeks of gestation. In prematurely born infants without clinical respiratory distress syndrome, presumed methylation pathway intermediates were detected by thin-layer TLC and gas chromotographic techniques and selective determination of the second carbon acyl groups. Infants with respiratory distress syndrome uniformly demonstrated a decrease in myristic acid on the second carbon in the phosphatidylcholine structure. Acidosis and perinatal asphyxia were found to selectively inhibit the appearance of methylation pathway intermediate in human neonates. Thus, it was hypothesized that from 22 to 24 weeks' gestation, the methylation pathway provided initial surface-active phosphatidylcholine the synthesis of which could be altered markedly be adverse conditions. At about 35 weeks' gestation, the major pathway for phosphatidylcholine synthesis, the choline pathway, achieved adequate synthetic rates for lecithin synthesis.

The contribution of this pathway to human fetal phosphatidylcholine synthesis has recently been disputed.[94] Early observations were based on detection of an intermediate in the pathway, phosphatidyldimethylethanolamine (PDME), which later could not be detected by several laboratories, including our own, when analytical two-dimensional TLC was used. Instead of phosphatidyldimethylethylethanolamine, a new compound, phosphatidylglycerol, was isolated using this methodology.

Other conflicting results were also reported by workers using the fetal rhesus monkey model.[30] This model shows striking similarities to the human fetal lung in respect to lung phospholipids, fatty acid composition, and amniotic fluid L/S ratios.[46]

Epstein et al.[29] studied fetal rhesus lung slices in vitro and used noninvasive catheter techniques in vivo for direct measurement of the pathways. These investigators found that the methylation pathway accounted for less than 4% of the incorporation of [14]choline for fetal newborn and adult rhesus monkey lungs. No gestational trends for the methylation pathway were found in the rhesus monkey fetus. Approximately 70% of phosphatidylcholine formed in the fetal and neonatal periods were synthesized de novo, as measured in vivo by [3H]choline and [14C]ethanolamine administration.

Thus, it may be concluded that methylation is a minor pathway for dipalmitoylphosphatidylcholine synthesis in lung. Previous observations relevant to this pathway were made using a presumed pathway intermediate, PDME, since identified as phosphatidylglycerol. This pathway may remain of some physiologic significance in the prematurely born human neonate prior to the onset of the CDP-choline incorporation surge for phosphatidylcholine production.

6. The Lysolecithin Pathway

An alternate route for continuous generation of disaturated lecithin is the lysophosphatidylcholine–phosphatidylcholine pathway.[80,81,104] Diacyl phosphatides undergo hydrolysis by phospholipases to form lysophosphatides. In the lung, phospholipases A and A_2 have been found responsible for this hydrolytic cleavage.[31,33]

The formation of phosphatidylcholine from the hydrolytic cleavage was identified by several workers:

(1) Lysophosphatidylcholine + acyl-CoA
$$\xrightarrow[\text{acyl-transferase}]{\text{acyl-CoA : lysophosphatidylcholine}}$$
phosphatidylcholine + CoA

(2) 2 Lysophosphatidylcholine $\xrightleftharpoons[\text{acyl-hydrolase}]{\text{acyl-transferase}}$
phosphatidylcholine + glycerophosphorylcholine

Using rat lung slices, Abe et al.[1] and Akino et al.[3] compared the ratio of ^{14}C and ^{3}H activities in phosphatidylcholine and lysophosphatidylcholine (Fig. 2) labeled with [3H]glycerol and [14C]-palmitate. The isotopic ratio of phosphatidylcholine was twice that of the substrates. This $^{14}C/^{3}H$ ratio suggests that reaction (2) above is the predominant pathway for the generation of disaturated (dipalmatoyl) phosphatidylcholine. Microsomal acyltransferase for the transport of palmitoyl-CoA and

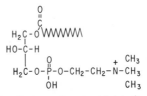

Fig. 2. Lysophosphatidylcholine.

archidonal CoA was not involved in phosphatidyl-choline synthesis in rat lung.[64] Acylation of lyso-phosphatidylcholine with acyl-CoA (reaction 1) is the predominant reaction in dog lung micro-somes.[42] No difference was found in the specific activity of 16:0-acylCoA with 1-lyso-2-acyl-phos-phatidylcholine as substrate, suggesting no preference in acylation in the C-1 or C-2 position.[43] Later, it was suggested that 16:0-acylCoA activity at either position on lysophosphatidylcholine would ensure sufficient palmitic acid for reacylation, thus forming a renewable pool.

Disaturated phosphatidylcholine may represent a continuously remodeled product,[59] initially syn-thesized via the choline-incorporation pathway and then "recycled" after phospholipase hydrolysis to return disaturated phosphatidylcholine. To date, however, the function of this pathway in the pre-natal developing human lung remains speculative.

7. Phosphatidylglycerol

Phosphatidylglycerol is the second most abundant phospholipid in pulmonary surface-active material in serveral adult species, including alveolar wash from human lung.[58,61,63,65,102] Earlier studies had demonstrated synthesis of phosphatidylglycerol in liver mitochondria, and in 1967, Body and Gray[14] used two-dimensional TLC to identify phosphatidyl-glycerol in whole swine lung. These workers observed that surfactant contained 10 times as much phosphatidylglycerol as did whole lung or exfoliated respiratory lining cells. They also found that surf-actant phosphatidylglycerol composed 10% of phospholipid phosphorous, while whole lung and free respiratory cells contained only 3 and 7%, respectively. Radioactive palmitic acid was found to be incorporated into phosphatidylglycerol at extraordinarily high rates[54]; in whole lung tissue, 68% of palmitic acid was incorporated into phos-phatidylglycerol, while the surfactant phosphatidyl-glycerol contained 79% palmitate, suggesting dif-ferential radioactive incorporation of fatty acids. Phosphatidylcholine, on the other hand, incorpo-rated 67% palmitate in whole lung tissue and 85% palmitate in surfactant fractions. This observation stressed the importance of differential incorporation into either whole lung or alveolar wash fractions. While there was equal incorporation of palmitate at C-1 and C-2 in phosphatidylcholine, the rate

at which palmitate was incorporated at the C-1 position was twice that of C-2.

Earlier reports failed to identify phosphatidyl-glycerol. Instead, great significance was placed on the detection of phosphatidyl N,-N-di-methyleth-anolamine (PDME), an intermediate in the methyl-ation pathway, as an important phospholipid in pulmonary surfactant. Pfleger and Thomas,[101] however, reported phosphatidylglycerol in surfac-tant using two-dimensional TLC and nuclear magnetic resonance techniques. They could not detect PDME in measurable quantities, leading to the conclusion that in the previous report of Morgan[90] and the later presumed verification by Gluck et al.,[51] they may have been measuring phosphatidylglycerol, rather than PDME as re-ported. Later, Hallman and Gluck[57] noted the similarities of migration of phosphatidylglycerol and PDME, but clearly differentiated these two fractions. Adult human, rabbit, and rhesus lung were found to contain amounts of phosphatidylglycerol similar to those found in beagle lung.

The synthesis of phosphatidylglycerol (Fig. 3) in the lung was localized in the microsomal fractions of the Type II cells of lung, according to the following pathways:

(1) CDP-diglyceride + sn-glycerol-3-P

$$\xrightarrow[\text{+ CMP phosphatidyl transferase}]{\text{L-glycerol 3-P: CMP}}$$

phosphatidylglycerol phosphate

(2) Phosphatidylglycerol phosphate

$$\xrightarrow[\text{phosphatase}]{\text{phosphatidylglycerol-P}}$$

phosphatidylglycerol + Pi

Fetal rabbit lungs contain small quantities of phosphatidylglycerol that increase 5-fold within 24 hr after delivery.[57] In developing rabbit lung, the correlation between the concentrations of phos-phatidylglycerol in surfactant and the activity of microsomal sn-glycerol-3-P:CMP phosphatidyl transferase was remarkable, indicating that this

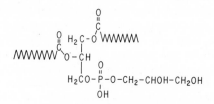

Fig. 3. Phosphatidylglycerol.

catalyst was rate-limiting. Interestingly, prematurely born rabbits with respiratory distress specifically lacked phosphatidylglycerol in their surfactant.

Simultaneously with the isolation of phosphatidylglycerol, a steric isomer, lyso-bis-phosphatidic acid, was isolated.[14,105] The significance of this compound in human surfactant has not been clarified.

Studies in the human fetus and neonate have been limited; however, phosphatidylglycerol has been reported in both amniotic and fetal lung fluid in humans. Prematurely born neonates (gestational ages from 28 weeks) without respiratory distress syndrome have had phosphatidylglycerol isolated from gastric, pharyngeal, and tracheal aspirates within 4 hr after birth. Infants with respiratory distress syndrome had no detectable phosphatidylglycerol in these aspirates, suggesting that deficiency of phosphatidylglycerol may play an important role in this disorder.[60]

Although the precise function of phosphatidylglycerol is speculative, Michaelson *et al.*[88] suggest that when phosphatidylcholine and phosphatidylglycerol are mixed in equimolar quantities, vesicles are formed, with phosphatidylglycerol stabilizing the outer surface of the lipoprotein complex. Present evidence suggests that phosphatidylglycerol is bound tightly to surfactant apoprotein, further suggesting a stabilizing role of this phospholipid species.

Analysis of human amniotic fluid for acidic phospholipids has demonstrated a stepwise appearance of phosphatidylglycerol and another minor phospholipid—phosphatidylinositol. The appearance of phosphatidylinositol closely paralleled the increase in the lecithin/sphingomyelin (L/S) ratio up to the point of maturity, thereafter falling as phosphatidylglycerol increased.[60a] At the present time, lung synthesis of phosphatidylinositol and modulation of the emergence of phosphatidylglycerol is a fruitful area for further research.

8. Enzymatic Regulation

Investigation of the mechanisms and timing of maturation of enzyme systems in the lung has lagged behind that of other organs, especially the liver, While the problems in studying the lung may be unusual due to cellular heterogenity, the sparsity of information may be more related to the fact that interest in the lung as a metabolic organ has developed only recently. Greengard[55]

illustrated in the liver the sequential development of patterns of enzyme accumulation.

Current investigations of rises and declines in precursor levels and neuroendocrine stimuli in fetal lung development, particularly in relation to enhancement of surfactant synthesis, have shown different effects of such hormones as glucocorticoids (presumably enzyme-mediated), which relate directly to fetal gestational age in cell culture preparations. In the rabbit fetus at 20–22 days' gestation, lung cell growth was enhanced by glucocorticoids; however, at 28 days' gestation, lung cellular differentiation and phosphatidylcholine synthesis were enhanced by these compounds. Smith and Torday[115] stressed the importance of specific gestational periods to enzyme-mediated effects on pathway synthesis of phosphatidylcholine by the choline pathway.

The major pathways contributing to synthesis of pulmonary phospholipids have been discussed previously. Figure 4 defines these synthetic pathways where enzymatic regulation presumably effects surfactant synthesis, and the following discussion illustrates possible mechanisms of enzymatic regulation of surfactant synthesis.

8.1. *De Novo* Palmitic Acid Synthesis: Fatty Acid Synthetase

Gross and Warshaw[56] studied fatty acid synthesis in the fetal rabbit lung. They demonstrated a constant rate of *de novo* fatty acid synthesis (primarily palmitic acid) via fatty acid synthetase from 23 days' gestation to the adult. These findings were strikingly different from the hepatic fatty acid synthesis in the same animal, in which high rates of enzymatic activity were noted during fetal life and declined by 50% during the suckling period. These results suggest differences in enzymatic patterns of organ development. In the lung, early maturation of fatty acid synthetase and fatty acid precursors occurs at a time of enhanced lung cell differentiation and surfactant synthesis.

8.2. Formation of 1,2-Diglyceride As a Common Precursor: Phosphatidic Acid Phosphohydrolase (PAPase)

Johnston *et al.*[68] identified the PAPase reaction, which catalyzes the hydrolytic cleavage of phosphatidic acid to form 1,2-diglyceride. This catalyst

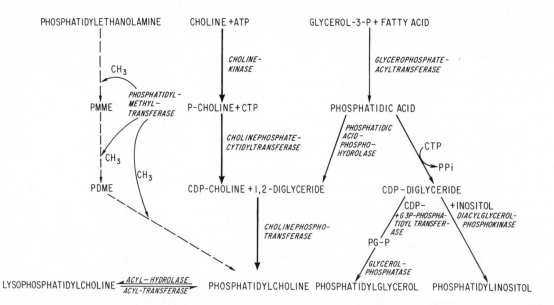

Fig. 4. Pulmonary surfactant phospholipid metabolism. The heavy arrows indicate the choline pathway, the major pathway for phosphatidylcholine synthesis. The light arrows indicate pathways for phosphatidylglycerol and phosphatidylinositol synthesis. Lysophosphatidylcholine pathway enzymes (acyl-hydrolase and acyl-transferase) may be identical in the reversible reaction from lysophosphatidylcholine to phosphatidylcholine. The broken arrows indicate the minor role of the methylation pathway in phosphatidylcholine synthesis.

plays an initial role in substrate regulation in phosphatidylcholine synthesis. Isolated lamellar bodies in fetal rabbit lung at 26 days' gestation had a 4- to 8-fold increase in PAPase activity.[119] This increase occurred 1 day before the first detectable accumulation of dipalmitylphosphatidyl choline. PAPase activity also precedes the rise in phosphatidylcholine synthesis in the human, as evidenced by a rise in the lecithin/sphingomyelin ratio.

8.3. The Choline-Incorporation Pathway: Choline Kinase (CK), Cytidyl Transferase (CyT), and Choline Phosphotransferase (CPT)

In the lung, the enzymes of the choline pathway have been studied in more detail than those of other pathways leading to lecithin synthesis. CK activity was found to be 2–3 fold higher in immature human neonates of 28 weeks' gestation than in those of 33–40 weeks.[136] CK[36] and CPT[130,132] were also studied in the fetal rat. In the early neonatal period, CK activity was found to fall at 24 hr of age in both rat and human

neonates. CyT activity in rat lung reached full activity at birth.[4] CyT activity in rat liver was enhanced by the presence of lysophosphatidylethanolamine and other unfractionated phospholipids.[41] Whether or not lung phospholipids or lysophosphatidylcholine concentrations provide positive feedback is currently under investigation. Thom and Zachman[123] characterized CyT in human neonatal lungs. The enzyme was stable after freezing, had a pH optimum of 6.0–6.5, and was not inhibited by oxygen. By comparing kinetic constants for CTP and phosphocholine, these workers speculated a possible allosteric effect of previous binding of CTP to CyT on the subsequent binding to phosphorylcholine.

CPT, the enzyme responsible for the final step of lecithin biosynthesis by the choline pathway, has been studied in fetal and human neonatal tissue.

In neonatal autopsy specimens of infants between 20 and 30 weeks' gestation, CPT activity was increased 2-fold over the activity in those born at term.[123] In newly born term rats and rabbits, lung CPT activity did not change from late fetal levels to that found at 24 hr of age. The pH optimum was found to be between 7.5 and 8.0 and the temperature optimum at 37°C for whole lung homogenate.[111] Magnesium was required as a cofactor for CPT activity, while calcium ion was found to inhibit CPT activity.

Markert and Ursprung[83] demonstrated that the first substrate in a synthetic pathway can induce the enzymes of the pathway. Thus, in the choline pathway, choline or phosphorylcholine levels could alter significantly the rate at which synthesis of lecithin occurs. This does not appear to be the case, however, in hepatic lecithin synthesis.[121,124] Human placental tissue contains CPT activity, and *de novo* placental synthesis of choline phosphoglycerides occurs.[70] CDP-choline was incorporated readily into lecithin in a reaction stimulated by exogenous diglyceride. In contrast, methylation pathway enzymes could not be isolated from placental tissue. Levels of fatty acids, choline, and other precursors have also been shown to be derived from transplacental sources.[107,108] As yet, the effect of limitations or excesses in maternal levels of these precursors of phospholipid on subsequent synthesis of pulmonary lecithin remains to be described quantitatively. Interestingly, Gluck et al.[50] emphasized the finding of acceleration of the appearance of mature phospholipid patterns in amniotic fluid in dysfunctional placenta syndromes, including those in which there is evidence of infection or chronic abruption. Whether or not availability, transport, and concentrations of substrates are regulatory for human type II pneumatocytes awaits further research.

8.4. The Methylation Pathway for *de Novo* Phosphatidylcholine Synthesis: Methionine-Activating Enzyme (MAE) and Phosphatidyl Methyltransferase (MT)

MAE and MT have been studied in human neonates, rats, and dogs. In 7 immature infants and infants dying of respiratory distress syndrome, no significant trend of enzyme activity was found in relation to gestational age.[137] Zachman[137] and Gluck et al.[49] found MT activity highest 3 days prior to birth in rat and rabbit fetuses. MAE was also found to be higher before birth than either immediately after birth or in the adult. Due to the small quantitative contribution of this pathway in fetal and neonatal lung lecithin synthesis, however, modulation of these enzymes appears insignificant when compared to those of the choline pathway.

Table III compares various properties of choline and methylation pathway enzymes in the human.

8.5. Transacylation of Phosphatidylcholine Fatty Acids into Dipalmitic Phosphatidylcholine: Lysophosphatidylcholine Acyltransferase and/or Lysophosphatidylcholine Acylhydrolase

Not all phosphatidylcholine is in the disaturated surface-active form. Hallman and Raivio[59] suggested a transacylation reaction from position 1 of

Table III. Enzymes of the Choline and Methylation Pathways in the Human Neonate

Properties	CK	CyT	CPT	MAE	MT
Locale of isolation	Supernatant, 3000g	Whole lung homogenate	Whole lung homogenate	Supernatant	Supernatant
Reaction time	Biphasic at 30 min and 1 hr	Biphasic at 20 min and 1 hr	Biphasic at 30 min and 1 hr	Biphasic at 15 min and 1 hr	Linear to 1 hr
Protein concentration	1–8 mg/g lung	1–12 mg/g lung	4–28 mg/g lung	2–10 mg/g lung	2–6 mg/g lung
Saturating conditions	ATP	CTP, P-choline	Diglyceride	ATP	S-Ad-Meth
Cofactor requirements	ATP, Mg^{2+}	Mg^{2+}, CTP	Mg^{2+}	Mg^{2+} ATP	
Temperature optimum	25–38°C	50°C	35–37°C	35–39°C	35–39°C
pH optimum	10.8	6–6.5	7.5	?	7.5

a 1-acyl-2-lysolecithin molecule to form disaturated lecithin.

The choline-incorporation pathway appears to combine with a lysophosphatidylcholine loop forming disaturated phosphatidylcholine. The same enzyme seems to be responsible for both acylhydrolase and acyltransferase activities. There are two different acyltransferases in rat lung microsomes[64]; the dienoic and monoenic phosphatidylcholine species are provided mainly by the pathway of *de novo* synthesis, while the saturated species and the polyenoic species are produced primarily by other than *de novo* synthesis.

8.6. Synthesis of Phosphatidylglycerol: Glycero-3-Phosphate: CMP-Phosphatidyltransferase

The rate of phosphatidylglycerol synthesis appears to be limited by microsomal glycero-3-phosphate: CMP-phosphatidyltransferase activity.[58]

The palmitate esterified to positions 1 and 2 of phosphatidylglycerol and phosphatidylcholine at different rates,[111] and seemed to be dependent on the source of precursor palmitate. Recently it has been shown that cortisol administration to 24-day fetal rabbits increases the activity of pulmonary glycerolphosphate phosphatidyltransferase activity.[105b]

8.7. Synthesis of Phosphatidylinositol: 1,2-Diacylglycerol Phosphokinase

The formation of phosphatidylinositol from CDP-diglyceride and inositol has been found in a large number of tissues. Enhanced synthesis may reflect increased tissue levels of cyclic inositol phosphate. Recently, an inverse relationship between phosphatidylinositol synthesis and phosphatidylglycerol was observed during human lung maturation. As the L/S ratio became mature and phosphatidylglycerol appeared in amniotic fluid, a fall in phosphatidylinositol was found. Obladen *et al.*[98] observed a rise in phosphatidylinositol in the early recovery phase of infants with severe respiratory distress syndrome; concomitantly, phosphatidylglycerol and phosphatidylcholine were reduced. The appearance of phosphatidylinositol can be explained by reduction of glycerol-3-phosphate: phosphatidyl transferase activity. The activity of 1,2-diacylglycerol phosphokinase in lung tissue has not yet been studied.

Key reactions in a metabolic sequence often serve

as metabolic regulators in the biosynthesis of compounds.[120,128] In the fetal rhesus monkey, Farrell[33] found CPT to be the rate-limiting enzyme. Besides being the last catalyst in the choline pathway, CPT also demonstrates the lowest specific activity of any enzyme of the choline pathway. This enzyme has uniformly been isolated from microsomal fractions of lung tissue, while both CK and CyT have been demonstrated in cytosol. Thus, at least three criteria associated with key reaction catalyst are met by CPT.

In the choline pathway, choline, phosphorylcholine, CDP-choline, diglyceride, CDP, and ATP serve as substrates in the formation of phosphatidylcholine. In early gestation, when lung phosphatidylcholine concentrations are small, the sequence of reactions remains relatively constant; in the last 10% of gestation, however, when phosphatidylcholine synthesis rises sharply, one or more of the reactions accelerates.

Expression of specific genes for protein synthesis and thus enzyme production was shown by Greengard[55] to play a great role in hepatic gluconeogenesis. Farrell[33] postulated that mRNA translation may be the level of one expression most likely affected by physiologic regulators, such as a rise in cortisol in the stimulation of CPT production.[34]

8.8. Adverse Factors That Affect Phospholipid Synthesis

Many investigators have studied the synthesis of pulmonary surfactant, especially its primary phospholipid, phosphatidylcholine, in adverse physiologic states. Unilateral pulmonary artery and main-stem bronchus ligation in dog lungs increase surface tension in lung extracts[40]; it was concluded that decreased blood flow altered the production of pulmonary surfactant. In atelectatic lungs, incorporation of [^{14}C]palmitate into phospholipids was diminished in proportion to the decrease in pulmonary blood flow.[95] Ligation of one main pulmonary artery was followed by incorporation of only one-tenth as much radioactive precursor into phospholipid as in sham-operated dogs. The concentrations of total phospholipid, phosphatidylcholine, phosphatidylethanolamine, and esterified palmitate were reduced significantly in the hemorrhagic areas of the ligated lung. Naimark[95] suggested that reduced phospholipid synthesis following pulmonary vasculature ligation could be explained by the interference in cellular metabolism of alveolar cells due to the interrupted blood supply. This view was substantiated by Chernick et al.,[20] who found that alterations in the deflation limb of the pressure–volume curve correlated closely with alterations in surfactant produced by the lung with inadequate circulation. In sheep fetuses of 128 days, lung stability in the upper lobes was lower on the side with pulmonary artery occlusion than in the lung that was not occluded.[66] In younger fetuses, this observation could not be documented, suggesting that fetal lung is vulnerable to the effects of hypoperfusion only during periods of relatively active metabolic development.

Interestingly, Morgan and Edmunds[91] reported the methylation pathway to be enhanced in the ischemic lung, with an increase in oxygen consumption and uptake of radioactive precursors in the ligated lung as compared with the lung receiving the total pulmonary blood flow. In guinea pigs, hypercarbia produced severe acidemia, atelectasis, edema, and hyaline membrane formation.[113] It caused a disappearance of inclusion bodies and a concomitant increase in surface tension, suggesting that acute uncompensated acidosis is deleterious to lung function.

Exposed fetuses of hypotensive ewes had significant reductions in pulmonary phosphatidylcholine synthesis.[16] Gluck et al.[49] found that hypothermia, acidosis, and hypercapnea adversely affect phosphatidylcholine synthesis, noting decreased phosphatidylcholine in tracheal and pharyngeal aspirates in term and prematurely born neonates. The methylation pathway in rabbits was sensitive to acidosis (pH less than 7.2). Infants resuscitated vigorously with normalization of pH recovered their phosphatidylcholine synthesis.[49] The choline and methylation pathways are adversely affected by low pH (6.9) in cultured fetal rabbit lung cells,[115] as indicated in Fig. 5. Merritt et al.,[87] however, found the choline-incorporation pathway to be affected by acidosis, while the methylation pathway was unaffected, in the newborn rat. The inhibition of phosphatidylcholine synthesis via choline incorporation was observed at pH 7.0–7.2, and was found to be rapidly reversible to peak levels with correction to pH 7.4. The influence of hydrogen ion concentration on phosphatidylcholine synthesis was attributed to specific effects on key enzymes in the choline pathway, namely, CK and CPT.

CyT activity was diminished at pH values greater than 7.5 in their in vitro preparation.[87] Similarly, lung phosphatidylcholine production in the fetal rhesus was significantly reduced by acidemia

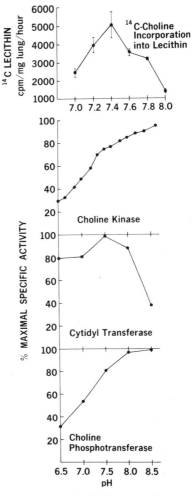

Fig. 5. Comparison of pH effects on phosphatidylcholine synthesis in vitro with pH profiles of choline pathway enzymes (top graph) and effect of pH on [¹⁴C]choline incorporation into phosphatidylcholine in vitro in term rats as compared with specific activities of choline pathway enzymes (bottom three graphs). Reproduced from Pediatrics by permission.

(umbilical venous pH < 7.20), suggesting that increased hydrogen ion concentration inhibits the choline pathway.[35a]

9. Clinical Considerations

In 1971, the quantitative assessment of pulmonary surfactant at various gestational ages in amniotic fluid was formulated into a clinically useful tool for determination of fetal pulmonary maturation by

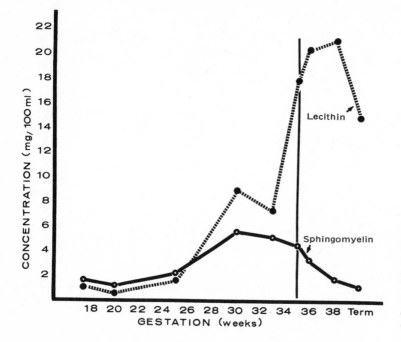

Fig. 6. Mean concentrations in amniotic fluid of sphingomyelin and lecithin during gestation in normal pregnancies. The acute rise in lecithin at 35 weeks marks pulmonary maturity. Reproduced from the *American Journal of Obstetrics and Gynecology* by permission.

Gluck et al.[48] (Fig. 6). However, since phospholipids are produced by fetal membranes in addition, these workers used the semiquantitative concentration of pulmonary surface-active phosphatidylcholine by precipitation with cold acetone, providing additional information by determining the percentage of precipitable compound. The concentrations of lecithin and sphingomyelin in amniotic fluid during gestation are very low until about the 25th or 26th week, when measurable amounts appear. Sphingomyelin concentrations are higher than those of lecithin until about the 31st or 32nd week, when the two become equal. After this time, lecithin concentrations increase rapidly, while sphingomyelin concentrations level off and actually decrease. Thus, by following the concentrations of these compounds in relation to each other and permitting sphingomyelin to be an internal standard, the L/S ratio was devised. Multiple investigations have centered about the synthesis of lecithin in various states; however, variations in sphingomyelin synthesis, alterations during complicated pregnancies, and alterations in sphingomyelin synthesis are less well understood.

Several methods that vary from that initially described make the critical end point of maturity for the L/S ratio highly dependent on methodology.[12] However, the basic principle in maturation

of the fetal lung is the same as initially described by Gluck in all pregnancies followed by serial amniocentesis and examination of the phospholipids, regardless of analytic expression. There is a progression during gestation from little lecithin and relatively more sphingomyelin (immature pattern) to equal lecithin/sphingomyelin or somewhat more lecithin (intermediate), and finally to significantly more lecithin than sphingomyelin (mature pattern). With the comparative reflectance densities or with spot area measurements of lecithin and sphingomyelin that are comparable, a ratio of less than 1.0 marks the immature lung; ratios of 1.0–2.0, the intermediate area; and ratios of 2.0 or greater, the point of maturation (Fig. 7). Determination of L/S by reflectance densitometry has had the greatest reproducibility; however, an alternate method based on spot area planimetry as devised by Borer is a valid clinical substitute.[47] Some 19 techniques or variations on the original measurement have been published; thus different end points for maturity have been seen with variations in methodology.[11,106] It is therefore important that each laboratory establish a numerical ratio indicative of maturity by using normal term and early gestation amniotic fluids and accompany these values with the stated experience of others using this method.

The significance of the acetone-precipitable frac-

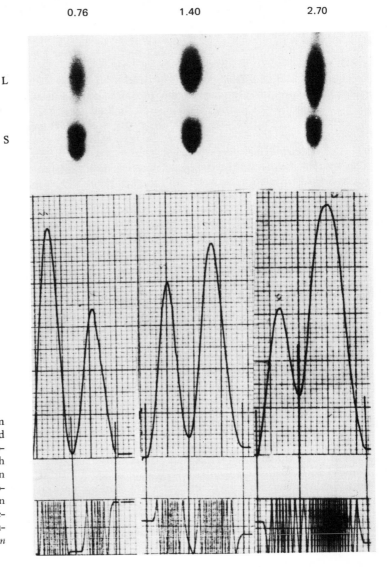

Fig. 7. Progression of L/S ratios from immature (0.76), to intermediate (1.40), and reaching the mature state (2.70). This progression is seen in all pregnancies, although the gestational age may vary depending on conditions affecting the fetus. The chromatographic (L and S) patterns are shown beneath the ratios, and densitometric integrations from which the ratios were calculated are shown. Reproduced from *Modern Perinatal Medicine* by permission.

tion is that maturity or very near maturity of fetal lung may be assumed when at least 45–50% of amniotic fluid lecithin is precipitable in cold acetone. Thus, fetal lung maturity can be predicted when an L/S ratio exceeds 2.0 and the precipitable fraction is 45–50% or more. In a certain number of fetuses with transitional L/S ratios and an acetone-precipitable fraction of lecithin of 45% or more, either respiratory distress syndrome does not occur or the newborn is mildly affected. The combination of L/S ratio and precipitable fraction has enhanced the predictive value of either value alone.

In 1972, Clements *et al.*[25] described a rapid, simple, inexpensive test that determines the amount of pulmonary surface-active material in amniotic fluid and thus is indicative of fetal lung maturity. Termed the *shake test* or *foam test*, this determination depends on pulmonary surfactant generating foam in the presence of ethanol. The rationale for assessing bubble stability is that of the relationship between a nonfoaming competitive surfactant—ethanol—and the surface-tension-reducing properties of pulmonary surfactant. Protein, bile salts, and salts of free fatty acids present in amniotic fluid form a highly stable surface film that can be eliminated by the addition of 47.5% ethanol; at this concentration, phosphatidylcholine generates a stable foam. Thus, if a mixture of equal volumes of amniotic fluid and 47.5% ethanol is shaken, the stable foam produced is due to the presence of pulmonary surfactant. Fetuses whose amniotic fluid gives a clearly positive test are at little risk for respiratory distress syndrome at birth. Bhagwanani et al.[11] found a high incidence of false negatives with the shake test; however, others have found close clinical correlation between both the L/S ratio and this test in *normal* pregnancies.

A number of fetal and maternal conditions affect the ratio. In Rh isoimmunization, the expected terminal rise in L/S may not occur. In one study,[63] 14 pregnancies complicated with Rh disease were followed with serial L/S determinations, and the L/S abruptly increased at 35½ weeks and decreased abruptly at 36½ weeks. The L/S decrease was due to an absolute decrease in lecithin, and there was no change in sphingomyelin. Infants of diabetic mothers often have an L/S of 2.0 with a low precipitable fraction, and these babies may develop respiratory distress syndrome. A group of disorders— mild diabetes, small nonparabiotic twins, and chronic nonhypertensive glomerulonephritis—have been associated with delayed pulmonary maturation. Another group of conditions, including severe prolonged toxemia, renal or cardiovascular hypertension, sickle cell disease, narcotic addiction, severe diabetes mellitus, maternal infections (choriamniotitis, urinary tract infection), smaller of parabiotic twins, and placental insufficiency, serve as potent stimuli for pulmonary acceleration.

One of the most interesting conditions associated with accelerated pulmonary maturation is prolonged rupture of membranes. Richardson et al.[103] found that even with initially very low L/S ratio (1.0), 3 or 4 days of ruptured membranes rapidly converted the ratio to a mature pattern. Glucocorticoids administered during pregnancy increase the L/S ratio.[117]

The effect of various maternal conditions on the L/S ratio is illustrated in Fig. 8.

If birth weight is plotted vs. the L/S, no specific relationship can be found. Indeed, infants as low as 650 g and estimated gestational ages of 26–28 weeks may have mature ratios. On the other hand, babies with gestational ages of 38 weeks have been found with low L/S, even with birth weights exceeding 3000 g. In both these extremes, no complication could be found that would accelerate or delay maturation. In an attempt to appreciate these differences more fully, minor phospholipids were investigated by Hallman et al.,[81] who followed phosphatidylinositol and phosphatidylglycerol sequentially throughout the last trimester of pregnancy. Phosphatidylinositol increased in parallel with the L/S ratio up to the value of 2.0, providing an additional index of maturity. Phosphatidylglycerol, on the other hand, appeared after 35 weeks' gestation and continued to rise beyond term. The presence of phosphatidylglycerol indicates lung maturity, and infants with this compound in the amniotic fluid or in the initial tracheal aspirate after birth have uniformly been free from respiratory distress syndrome.[61] Present evidence suggests that phosphatidylglycerol markedly improves the function of lung surfactant in stabilizing alveoli. An absence of phosphatidylglycerol therefore suggests that the surfactant may not be quite mature.

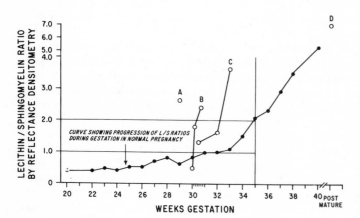

Fig. 8. Abnormal elevations of the L/S ratio compared with the ratios in normal pregnancies: (A) "Chronic stress" seen in retroplacental bleeding; (B) "acute stress" seen in rupture of membranes from 72 to 96 hr; (C) placental infarction; (D) value from a group of patients with postmaturity syndrome. Reproduced from the *American Journal of Obstetrics and Gynecology* by permission.

Additional investigations are needed to evaluate phosphatidylglycerol more fully as an index of maturity, as well as other factors that regulate its development.

Studies of the changes in the qualitative composition of surfactant both in normal infants and in premature infants with and without respiratory distress syndrome are presently under way.

Babies with respiratory distress syndrome often have an initially low L/S ratio in the tracheal aspirate of about 1.8 when measured within the first 12 hr of life, and a complete lack of phosphatidylglycerol.[13,61] Obladen et al.[98] made sequential phospholipid analyses by two-dimensional TLC in over 100 newborn and premature infants during the course of their disease (Fig. 9). After 12–24 hr of age, the infants who survived the respiratory distress syndrome showed a rise in L/S ratio in tracheal effluent. The most marked alteration, next to the rise in lecithin, was in the relative amount of phosphatidylinositol during the course of the disease. Parallel with clinical improvement in the babies and with decreasing F_{iO_2} requirements necessary to maintain adequate P_{O_2}, a rise in phosphatidylinositol was observed.

The understanding of the synthesis, metabolism, and function of phosphatidylinositol in lung is presently meager. However, these initial results add stimuli for further investigation of the minor phospholipids in the fetus and neonate.

10. Glucocorticosteroids and Fetal Lung Metabolism

Liggins[81a] initially demonstrated that intravenous administration of hydrocortisone to ewes stimulated premature delivery of lambs with pulmonary maturity unexpected for gestational age. Increasing evidence has come forth demonstrating that corticosteroids increase phosphatidylcholine production with the physiological effect of lowering surface tension characteristics of lung extracts in several species.[26a,102a]

Farrell and Zachman[34] showed a significant increase in phosphatidylcholine concentration and cholinephosphotransferase activity in the rabbit fetal lung after treatment with 9-fluoroprednisolone. Rooney et al.,[105a] however, failed to demonstrate induction of this enzyme with cortisol administration to 24-day rabbit fetuses, but rather glycerolphosphate phosphatidyltransferase for enhanced phosphatidyl-

glycerol synthesis. These authors, however, later reported that cortisol administration stimulated the activity of cholinephosphate cytidyltransferase and lysolecithin acyltransferase activity in lung lavage from 27-day rabbit fetuses treated for 2 days with intraamniotic cortisol.[105b]

In human gestations, cortisol levels have been correlated with L/S ratios in amniotic fluid, but amniotic fluid cortisol and palmitic acid levels have failed to predict lung maturation.[27, 114a, 114b]

Farrell and Kotas[35b] have reviewed the ongoing experience of applying these preliminary findings to "prevention" of respiratory distress syndrome in infants of women who have threatened premature labor.

While several ongoing studies are under way to evaluate the therapeutic potential of glucocorticoids for "prevention" of respiratory distress syndrome, many unanswered basic investigations are required to resolve the discrepancies cited earlier in this chapter.

While the use of steroids has been strongly advocated by some based upon limited, short-term experience in a highly select group of women, significant questions remain unresolved regarding the long-term outcome of infants exposed to enzyme manipulation *in utero*. Indeed, the medico-legal implications of this "therapeutic conundrum"[6a] require further discussion.

11. Questions and Perspectives

This review would be incomplete without some attention being given to numerous unanswered questions that still perplex the lipid chemist, enzymologist, and clinician. Newer analytic techniques, as well as the possibility of homogenous cell culture techniques, will answer many new questions. For example, what are the interrelationships of different surfactant lipids and their surface-tension-lowering abilities? Do excesses in one fraction potentiate or inactivate the contribution of the other phospholipids? Does the methylation pathway play any role in phosphatidylcholine synthesis, or have methodological differences confused methylation intermediates with phosphatidylglycerol? What are the developmental characteristics of phosphatidylglycerol, and does this phospholipid modify phosphatidylcholine function? What is the significance of phosphatidylglycerol deficiency in respiratory distress syndrome? What is the role of

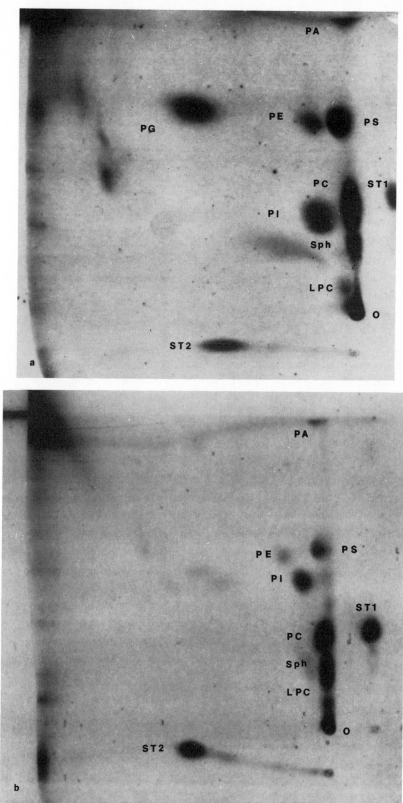

other minor phospholipids, especially phosphatidyl-inositol? Why does phosphatidylinositol increase in the premature infant?

Several workers have studied surfactant release from lamellar bodies. What regulates surfactant secretion and release from the Type II alveolar cell? Can this release be altered significantly by pharmacological means in the neonate without other adverse effects? In many species, surfactant composition is remarkably constant. What mechanism is responsible for this phylogenetic constancy? What is the function of the recently isolated apoprotein, and is this protein a regulator of phosphatidylcholine synthesis? Do naturally occurring antibodies to this protein exist. If they do, to what extent is immunologic reaction responsible for lung disease?

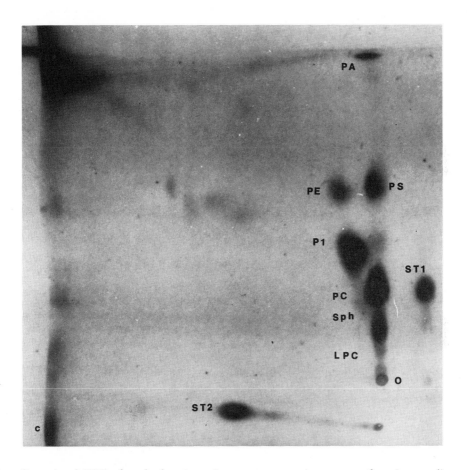

Fig. 9. Two–dimensional TLC of tracheal aspirates in neonates at various stages of respiratory distress syndrome compared with a term healthy newborn. (A) Mature healthy newborn– 3544-g infant delivered by cesarean section at 40 weeks' gestation. The L/S ratio is 3.62. The tracheal aspirate at birth shows normal phospholipid pattern. Note that phosphatidylglycerol is the second major surfactant phospholipid. (B) Premature infant—1580-g infant delivered vaginally. The L/S ratio is 1.45. The tracheal aspirate was taken at the first day of life when the infant was placed on the respirator at F_1O_2 50%. The phospholipid pattern demonstrates low phosphatidylcholine, high sphingomyelin, and low phosphatidylinositol. Note the absence of phosphatidylglycerol. (C) Recovery state of respiratory distress syndrome—same infant as in (B). The tracheal aspirate was taken at 5 days of age while the infant was still on the respirator with F_1O_2 25%. The L/S ratio is now 6.5. Note an increase in phosphatidylinositol, while phosphatidylglycerol is still absent. *Abbreviations:* (O) Origin; (LPC) lysophosphatidylcholine; (PA) phosphatidic acid; (PC) phosphatidylcholine; (PE) phosphatidylethanolamine; (PG) phosphatidylglycerol; (PI) phosphatidylinositol; (PS) phosphatidylserine; (Sph) spingomyelin standards: (ST1) phosphatidylcholine; (ST2) phosphatidylglycerol.

Several maternal conditions exist in which lung maturation is accelerated. What is the mechanism for such acceleration? If chronic fetal stress predisposes to enhanced maturation, is this via enzymatic induction, as demonstrated *in vitro* with cortisol, or does cortisol derepress other regulators of phosphatidylcholine synthesis? Do thyroxin, heroin, and Metabolite VIII of Bisolvon® stimulate pulmonary maturation by similar means, or do they interfere with enzyme sequencing?

How does the prematurely born infant with respiratory distress syndrome recover surfactant synthesis capabilities? What is the stimulus for increasing surfactant production after some days of life in the very immature infant who initially appears free from respiratory distress? What conditions inactive phosphatidylcholine synthesis *in vivo*, and how might these conditions be ameloriated?

Finally, in the biological sequence of maturation, two events appear to be inexorably related: the timing of fetal pulmonary maturation sufficient to withstand air breathing and the initiation of labor, which expels a fetus into the extrauterine world. Do the factors that control lung maturation also stimulate maternal labor, and how can alterations in these control mechanisms be modulated to provide for an optimal uterine environment of sufficient duration to permit the delivery of a mature neonate?

ACKNOWLEDGMENTS

This work was supported by the United States Public Health Service from the National Institute of Child Health and Human Development (HD-04380), the National Institute of Child Health and Human Development Fellowship (IF 32 HD05292), the National Heart and Lung Institute (SCOR HL-14169), the National Foundation—March of Dimes, and the German Forschungsgemeinschaft.

12. References

1. ABE, M., AKINO, T., AND OHNO, K., 1972, The formation of lecithin from lysolecithin in rat lung supernatant, *Biochim. Biophys. Acta* **280**:275.

2. ABRAMS, M. E., 1966, Isolation and quantitative estimation of pulmonary surface active lipoprotein, *J. Appl. Physiol.* **21**:718.

3. AKINO, T., ABE, T., AND ARAI, T., 1971, Studies on the biosynthetic pathways of molecular species of lecithin by rat lung slices, *Biochim. Biophys Acta* **248**:274.

4. ARTOM, C., 1968, Enzymes for the synthesis of lecithins from choline in tissues of developing rats, *Fed. Proc. Fed. Amer. Soc. Exp. Biol.* **27**:457.

5. ARVIDSON, G., EKELUND, H., AND ASTEDT, B., 1972, Phospholipid composition of human amniotic fluid during gestation and at term, *Acta Obstet. Gynecol. Scand.* **51**:71.

6. ASKIN, F. B., AND KUHN, C., 1971, The cellular origin of pulmonary surfactant, *J. Lab. Invest.* **25**:270.

6a. AVERY, M., AND CHERNICK, V., 1977, On decision making surrounding drug therapy: A continuing dilemma, *N. Engl. J. Med.* **296**:102.

7. AZZOPARDI, A., AND THURLBECK, W. M., 1969, The histochemistry of the non-edited bronchiolar epithelial cell, *Amer. Rev. Respir. Dis.* **99**:516.

8. BARRON, E. S. G., MILLER, Z. B., AND BARTLETT, G. R., 1947, Studies on biochemical oxidations. XXI. The metabolism of lung as determined by a study of slices and ground tissue, *J. Biol. Chem.* **171**:791.

9. BAXTER, C. F., ROUSER, G., AND SIMON, G., 1969, Variations among vertebrates of lung phospholipid class composition, *Lipids* **4**:243.

10. BENSCH, K., SCHAEFER, K., AND AVERY, M. E., 1964, Granular pneumocytes: Electron microscopic evidence of their exocrine function, *Science* **145**:1318.

11. BHAGWANANI, S. G., FAHMY, D., AND TURNBULL, A. C., 1972, Prediction of respiratory distress by estimation of amniotic fluid lecithin, *Lancet* **1**:159.

12. BLUMENFELD, T. A., 1975, Clinical laboratory tests for fetal lung maturity, in: *Pathology Annual 1975* (S. Sommers, ed.), p. 21, Appleton-Century-Crofts, New York.

13. BLUMENFELD, T. A., DRISCOL, J., AND JAMES, L. S., 1974, Lecithin/sphingomyelin ratios in tracheal and pharyngeal aspirates, *J. Pediatr.* **85**:403.

14. BODY, D. R., AND GRAY, G. M., 1967, The isolation and characterization of phosphatidylglycerol and a structural isomer from pig lung, *Chem. Phys. Lipids* **1**:254.

14a. BREMER, J., AND GREENBERG, D., 1961, Methyl transferring enzyme system of microsomes in the biosynthesis of lecithin (phosphatidylcholine), *Biochim. Biophys. Acta,* **46**:205–216.

15. BROWN, E. S., 1964, Isolation and assay of dipalmityl lecithin in lung extracts, *Amer. J. Physiol.* **207**:402.

16. BRUMLEY, G. W., 1971, Lung development and lecithin metabolism, *Arch. Intern. Med.* **127**:413.

17. BUCKINGHAM, S., 1961, Studies on the identification of an antiatelectasis factor in normal sheep lung, *Amer. J. Dis. Child.* **102**:521.

18. BUCKINGHAM, S., HEINGEMANN, H. O., SOMMERS, S. C., AND McNARY, W. F., 1966, Phospholipid synthesis in the large pulmonary alveolar cell: Its relation to lung surfactant, *Amer. J. Pathol.* **48**:1027.

19. CAMPICHE, M. A., 1960, Les inclusions lamellaires des cellules alveolaires dans le poumon du raton. Relations entre l'ultrasatructure et la fixation, *J. Ulstrastruct. Res.* **3**:302.

20. CHERNICK, V., HODSON, W. A., AND GREENFIELD, L. J., 1966, Effect of chronic pulmonary artery ligation on pulmonary mechanics and surfactant, *J. Appl. Physiol.* **21**:1315.

21. CLEMENTS, J. A., 1971, Comparative lipid chemistry of lungs, *Arch Intern. Med.* **127**:387.

22. CLEMENTS, J. A., 1973, Composition and properties of pulmonary surfactant, in: *Respiratory Distress Syndrome* (C. A. Villee, D. B. Villee, and J. Zuckerman, eds.), p. 77, Academic Press, New York.

23. CLEMENTS, J. A., AND KING, R. J., 1973, Pulmonary surfactant and its assay, in: *Foetal and Neonatal Physiology: Proceedings of the Sir Joseph Barcraft Centenary Symposium*, p. 618, Cambridge University Press, Oxford.

24. CLEMENTS, J. A., NELLENEEGEN, J., AND TRAHAN, H. J., 1970, Pulmonary surfactant and evolution of the lungs, *Science* **169**:603.

25. CLEMENTS, J. A., PLATZKER, A. C. G., TIERNEY, D. F., HOBEL, C. J., CREASY, R. K., MARJOLIS, A. J., THIBEAULT, D. W., TOOLEY, W. H., AND OH, W., 1972, Assessment of the risk of the respiratory-distress syndrome by a rapid test for surfactant in amniotic fluid, *N. Engl. J. Med.* **286**:1077.

26. DARRAH, H., AND HEDLEY-WHYTE, J., 1973, Rapid incorporation of palmitate into lung: Site and metabolic fate, *J. Appl. Physiol.* **34**:205.

26a. DE-LEMOS, R. A., SHERMETA, D. W., KNELSON, J., KOTAS, R., AND AVERY, J., 1970, Acceleration of appearance of pulmonary surfactant in the fetal lamb by administration of corticosteroids, *Am. Rev. Respir. Dis.* **102**:459.

27. DE FENCL, M., AND TULCHINSKY, D., 1975, Total cortisol in amniotic fluid and fetal lung maturation, *N. Engl. J. Med.* **292**:133.

28. DIAUGUSTINE, R. P., 1971, Lung phospholipids. 1. *In vivo* studies of the incorporation of ^{32}P, [methyl-^{14}C]choline, 1-^{14}C-palmitic acid and 1-^{14}C oleic acid into phosphatidylethanolamine, phosphatidyl-N,N-dimethylethanolamine and phosphatidylcholine, *Biochem. Biophys. Res. Commun.* **43**:29.

29. EPSTEIN, M. F., AND FARRELL, P. M., 1975, The choline incorporation pathway: Primary mechanism for *de novo* lecithin synthesis in fetal primate lung, *Pediatr. Res.* **9**:658.

30. EPSTEIN, M. F., FARRELL, P. M., AND WILLISON, J., 1975, Correlation of fetal lecithin synthesis and the amniotic fluid L/S ratio, *Pediatr. Res.* **9**:276.

31. ERBLAND, J. F., AND MARINETT, V. G., 1965, The enzymatic acylation and hydrolysis of lysolecithin, *Biochim. Biophys. Acta* **106**:128.

31a. Fariday, E. E., 1970 Effect of food and water deprivation on surface activity of lungs of rats, *J. Appl. Physiol.* **29**, 493–498.

32. FARIDY, E. E., AND NAIMARK, A., 1971, Effect of distension on metabolism of excised dog lung, *J. Appl. Physiol.* **31**:31.

33. FARRELL, P. M., 1973, Regulation of pulmonary lecithin synthesis, in: *Respiratory Distress Syndrome* (C. A. Villee, D. B. Villee, and J. Zucherman, eds.), p. 211, Academic Press, New York.

34. FARRELL, P. M., AND ZACHMAN, R. D., 1973, Induction of choline phosphotransferase and lecithin synthesis in the fetal lung by corticosteroids, *Science* **179**:297.

35. FARRELL, P. M., EPSTEIN, M. F., FLEISCHMAN, A. R., OAKES, G. K., AND KNIGHT, E., 1974, Lecithin synthesis in fetal primate tissues as measured *in vivo*, *Pediatr. Res.* **8**:446.

35a. FARRELL, P., EPSTEIN, M., FLEISCHMAN, A., OAKES, G. K., AND CHEZ, R., 1976, Lung lecithin biosynthesis in the nonhuman primate fetus: Determination of the primary pathway *in vivo*, *Biol. Neonate* **29**:238.

35b. FARRELL, P., AND KOTAS, R., 1976, The prevention of hyaline membrane disease: New concepts and approaches to therapy, in: *Advances in Pediatrics* (Barness, ed.), pp. 213–269, Yearbook Medical Publishers, Chicago.

36. FARRELL, P. M., LUNDGREN, D. W., AND ADAMS, A. H., 1974, Choline kinase and choline phosphotransferase in developing fetal rat lung, *Biochem. Biophys. Res. Commun.* **57**:696.

37. FAULKNER, C. S., 1969, The role of the granular pneumocyte in surfactant metabolism: An autoradiographic study, *Arch. Pathol. (Chicago)* **87**:521.

38. FELTS, J. M., 1964, Biochemistry of the lung, *Health Phys.* **10**:973.

39. FINLEY, T. N., PRATT, S. A., LADMAN, A. J., BREWER, L., AND MCKAY, M. G., 1968, Morphological and lipid analysis of the alveolar lining material in dog lung, *J. Lipid Res.* **9**:357.

40. FINLEY, T. N., TOOLEY, W. H., SWENSON, E. W., GARDNER, R. E., AND CLEMENTS, J. A., 1964, Pulmonary surface tension in experimental atelectasis, *Amer. Rev. Respir. Dis.* **89**:372.

41. FISCUS, W. G., AND SCHNEIDER, W. C., 1966, The role of phospholipids in stimulating phosphorylcholine cytidyltransferase activity, *J. Biol. Chem.* **241**:3324.

42. FROSOLONO, M. F., CHARMS, B. L., PAWLOWSKI, R., AND SLIRKA, S., 1970, Isolation, characterization, and surface chemistry of a surface-active fraction from dog lung, *J. Lipid Res.* **11**:439.

43. FROSOLONO, M. F., SLIRKA, S., AND CHARMS, B. L., 1971, Acyl transferase activities in dog lung microsomes, *J. Lipid Res.* **12**:96.

44. GALLAI-HATCHARD, J. J., AND THOMPSON, R. H. S., 1965, Phospholipase-A activity of mammalian tissue, *Biochim. Biophys. Acta* **98**:128.

45. GLUCK, L., 1972, Surfactant, *Pediatr. Clin. North Amer.* **19**:325.

46. GLUCK, L., CHEZ, R. A., KULOVICH, M. V., HUTCHINSON, D. L., AND NIEMANN, W. H., 1974, Comparison of phospholipid indicators of fetal lung

maturity in amniotic fluid of monkey (*Macaca mulatta*) and baboon *(Papio papio)*, *Amer. J. Obstet. Gynecol.* **230**:524.

47. GLUCK, L., KULOVICH, M. V., AND BORER, R., 1974, *Clin. Perinatol.* **1**:125.

48. GLUCK, L., KULOVICH, M. V., BORER, R. C., BRENNER, P. H., ANDERSON, G. G., AND SPELLACY, W. N., 1971, Diagnosis of the respiratory distress syndrome by amniocentesis, *Amer. J. Obstet. Gynecol.* **109**:440.

49. GLUCK, L., KULOVICH, M. V., EIDELMAN, A. L., CORDERO, L., AND KHATIN, A. F., 1972, Biochemical development of surface activity in mammalian lung. IV. Pulmonary lecithin synthesis in the human fetus and newborn and etiology of the respiratory distress syndrome, *Pediatr. Res.* **6**:81.

50. GLUCK, L., KULOVICH, M. V., AND KEIDEL, W. N., 1974, The interpretation and significance of the lecithin/sphingomyelin ratio in amniotic fluid, *Amer. J. Obstet. Gynecol.* **120**:142.

51. GLUCK, L., LANDOWNE, R. A., AND KULOVICH, M. V., 1970, Biochemical development of surface activity in mammalian lung. III. Structural changes in lung lecithin during development of the rabbit fetus and newborn, *Pediatr. Res.* **4**:352.

52. GLUCK, L., MOTOYAMA, E. K., SMITS, H. L., AND KULOVICH, M. V., 1967, The biochemical development of surface activity in mammalian lung. I. The surface active phospholipids; the separation and distribution of surface active lecithin in the lung of the developing fetus, *Pediatr. Res.* **1**:237.

53. GLUCK, L., SCRIBNEY, M., AND KULOVICH, M., 1967, The biochemical development of surface activity in mammalian lung. II. The biosynthesis of phospholipids in the lung of the developing rabbit fetus and newborn, *Pediatr. Res.* **1**:247.

54. GODINEZ, R. I., SANDERS, R. L., AND LONGMORE, W. J., 1975, Phosphatidylglycerol in rat lung. I. Identification as a metabolically active phospholipid in isolated perfused rat lung, *Biochemistry* **14**:830.

55. GREENGARD, O., 1973, The developmental formation of enzymes in rat liver, in *Biochemical Aspects of Hormones* (G. Litevack, ed.), p. 53–87, Academic Press, New York.

56. GROSS, I., AND WARSHAW, J. B., 1974, Enzyme activities related to fatty acid synthesis in developing mammalian lung, *Pediatr. Res.* **8**:193.

56a. GROSS, I., ILIC, I., WILSON, C., ROONEY, S., 1976, The influence of postnatal nutritional deprivation on the phospholipid content of developing rat lung, *Biochim. Biophys. Acta* **441**:412.

57. HALLMAN, M., AND GLUCK, L., 1974, Phosphatidyl glycerol in lung surfactant: I. Synthesis in rat lung microsomes, *Biochem. Biophys. Res. Commun.* **60**:1.

58. HALLMAN, M., AND GLUCK, L., 1975, The biosynthesis of phosphatidylglycerol in the lung of the developing rabbit, *Fed. Proc. Fed. Amer. Soc. Exp. Biol.* **34**:3.

59. HALLMAN, M., AND RAIVIO, K., 1974, Studies on the biosynthesis of disaturated lecithin of the lung: The importance of the lysolecithin pathway, *Pediatr. Res.* **8**:874.

60. HALLMAN, M., FELDMAN, B., AND GLUCK, L., 1975, RDS: The absence of phosphatidylglycerol in surfactant, *Pediatr. Res.* **9**:396.

60a. HALLMAN, M. KULOVICH, M., KIRKPATRICK, E., SUGARMAN, R., AND GLUCK, L., 1976, Phosphatidylinositol and phosphatidylglycerol in amniotic fluid: Indices of lung maturity, *Amer. J. Obstet. Gynecol.* **5**:613.

61. HALLMAN, M., KULOVICH, M., KIRKPATRICK, E., SUGARMAN, R., AND GLUCK, L., 1975, Phosphatidylinositol (PI) and phosphatidylglycerol (PG) in amniotic fluid: Indices of lung maturity, Paper presented at the 8th Annual Meeting of the Society for the Study of Reproduction, Ft. Collins, Colorado.

62. HARDING, P., POSSMAYER, F., AND MILNE, K., 1973, Amniotic fluid phospholipids and fetal maturity, *Amer. J. Obstet. Gynecol.* **115**:298.

63. HARLAN, W. R., MARGRAF, J. H., AND SAID, S. I., 1966, Pulmonary lipid composition of species with and without surfactant, *Amer. J. Physiol.* **211**:855.

64. HASEGAWA, S. H., AND OHNO, K., 1975, Acyltransferase activities in rat lung microsomes, *Biochim. Biophys. Acta* **380**:486.

65. HENDERSON, R. F., AND PFLEGER, R. C., 1972, Surface tension studies of phosphatidyl glycerol isolated from the lungs of beagle dogs, *Lipids* **7**:492.

66. HOWATT, W. F., AVERY, M. E., HUMPHREYS, P. W., NORMAND, I. C. S., REID, L., AND STRANGE, L. B., 1965, Factors affecting pulmonary surface properties in the foetal lamb, *Clin. Sci.* **29**:239.

67. HUMMEL, L., SCHIRRMEISTER, W., AND ZIMMERMANN, T., 1974, Origins of the fatty acid moiety of fetal serum phospholipids in rats, *Biol. Neonate* **24**:292.

68. JOHNSTON, J. M., SCHULTZ, F. M., JIMENEZ, J. M., AND MACDONALD, P. C., 1975, Phospholipid biosynthesis: The activity of phosphatidic acid phosphohydrolase in the developing lung and amniotic fluid, *Chest (Suppl.)* **67**:195.

69. KAIBARA, M., AND KIKKAWA, Y., 1971, Osmiophilia of the saturated phospholipid, dipalmitoyl lecithin, and its relationship to the alveolar lining layer of the mammalian lung, *Amer. J. Anat.* **132**:61.

70. KARP, W., SPRECHER, H., AND ROBERTSON, A., 1972, Human placental phospholipid synthesis, *Biol. Neonate* **22**:398.

71. KENNEDY, E. P., AND WEISS, S. B., 1956, The function of cytidine coenzymes in the biosynthesis of phospholipids, *J. Biol. Chem.* **22**:193.

72. KERR, G. R., AND HELMUTH, A. C., 1974, Growth and development of the fetal rhesus monkey. V. Fatty acids of phospholipids in fetal lung, *Biol. Neonate* **25**:10.

73. KIKKAWA, Y., AND YONEDA, K., 1974, The type II

epithelial cell of the lung. I. Method of isolation, *Lab. Invest.* **30**:76.

74. KIKKAWA, Y., MOTOYAMA, E. K., AND COOK, C. D., 1965, The ultrastructure of the lungs of lambs: The relation of osmiophilic inclusions and alveolar lining layer to fetal maturation and experimentally produced respiratory distress, *Amer. J. Pathol.* **47**:877.

75. KING, R. J., AND CLEMENTS, J. A., 1972, Surface active materials from dog lung. I. Method of isolation; *Amer. J. Physiol.* **223**:707.

76. KING, R. J., AND CLEMENTS, J. A., 1972, Surface active materials from dog lung. II. Composition and physiological correlations, *Amer. J. Physiol.* **223**:715.

77. KING, R. J., AND CLEMENTS, J. A., 1972, Surface active material from dog lung. III. Thermal analysis, *Amer. J. Physiol.* **223**:727.

78. KING, R. J., KLASS, D. J., GIKAS, E. G., AND CLEMENTS, J. A., 1973, Isolation of apoproteins from canine surface active material, *Amer. J. Physiol.* **224**:788.

79. KLAUS, M. H., CLEMENTS, J. A., AND HAVEL, R. J., 1961, Composition of surface-active material isolated from beef lung, *Natl. Acad. Sci. Proc.* **47**:1858.

80. KOKKE, R., HOOGHWINKEL, G. J. M., BOOIJ, H. L., VAN DEN BOSCH, H., ZELLES, L., MULDER, E., AND VAN DEENEN, L. L. M., 1963, Metabolism of lysolecithin and lecithin in a yeast supernatant, *Biochim. Biophys. Acta* **70**:351.

81. KOTAS, R. V., TRAINOR, E. J., MIMS, L. C., AND HARLOW, R. D., 1974, Discrepancies between the Brockenhoff and Gluck method of lung lecithin fatty acid analysis, *Amer. Rev. Respir. Dis.* **110**:669.

81a. LIGGINS, G. C., 1969, Premature delivery of foetal lambs infused with glucocorticoids, *J. Endocrinol.* **45**:515.

82. MACKLIN, C. C., 1954, The pulmonary alveolar mucoid film and the pneumonocytes, *Lancet* **1**:1099.

83. MARKERT, C. L., AND URSPRUNG, H., 1962, The ontogeny of isozyme patterns of lactate dehydrogenase in the mouse, *Dev. Biol.* **5**:363.

84. MASON, R. J., HUBER, G., AND VAUGHAN, M., 1972, Synthesis of dipalmitoyl lecithin by alveolar macrophages, *J. Clin. Invest.* **51**:68.

85. MASSARO, D., SIMON, M. R., AND STEINKAMP, H., 1971, Metabolic factors affecting protein synthesis by lung *in vitro, J. Appl. Physiol.* **30**:1.

86. MASSARO, G. D., AND MASSARO, D., 1972, Granular pneumocytes. Electron microscopic radioautographic evidence of intracellular protein transport, *Amer. Rev. Respir. Dis.* **105**:927.

87. MERRITT, A., AND FARRELL, P., 1976, Diminished pulmonary lecithin synthesis in acidosis: Experimental findings as related to the respiratory distress syndrome, *Pediatrics* **57**:32.

88. MICHAELSON, D. M., HORWITZ, A. F., AND KLEIN, M. P., 1973, Transbilayer asymmetry and surface homogeneity of mixed phospholipids in cosonicated vesicles, *Biochemistry* **12**:2637.

89. MORGAN, T. E., 1969, Isolation and characterization of lipid N-methyl-transferase from dog lung, *Biochim. Biophys. Acta* **178**:21.

90. MORGAN, T. E., 1971, Biosynthesis of pulmonary surface-active lipids, *Arch. Intern. Med.* **127**:401.

91. MORGAN, T. E., AND EDMUNDS, L. H., JR., 1967 Pulmonary artery occlusion. III. Biochemical alteration, *J. Appl. Physiol.* **22**:1012.

92. MORGAN, T. E., AND MORGAN, B. C., 1973, Surfactant synthesis, storage, and release by alveolar cells, in: *Respiratory Distress Syndrome* (C. A. Villee, B. P. Villee, J. Zuckerman, eds.), p. 117, Academic Press, New York.

93. MORGAN, T. E., FINLEY, T. N., AND FIALKOW, H., 1965, Comparison of the composition and surface activity of "alveolar" and whole lung lipids in the dog, *Biochim. Biophys. Acta* **106**:403.

94. MOTOYAMA, E. K., AND ROONEY, S. A., 1974, Does the methylation pathway contribute to the biosynthesis of surface active phosphatidylcholine in the lung, *Fed. Proc. Fed. Amer. Soc. Exp. Biol.* **33**:346.

95. NAIMARK, A., 1966, Pulmonary blood flow and the incorporation of palmitate-1-C^{14} by dog lung *in vivo, J. Appl. Physiol.* **21**:1292.

96. NIDEN, A. H., 1967, Bronchiolar and large alveolar cell in pulmonary metabolism, *Science* **158**:1323.

97. OBLADEN, M., AND MERRITT, A., 1975, Personal observations.

98. OBLADEN, M. W., MERRITT, T. A., AND GLUCK, L., 1976, Newborn tracheal phospholipid patterns during RDS, *Pediatr. Res.* **10**:465.

99. PATTLE, R. E., AND THOMAS, L. C., 1961, Lipoprotein composition of the firm lining the lung, *Nature (London)* **189**:844.

100. PETRIK, P., AND COLLET, A. J., 1974, Quantitative electron microscopic autoradiography of *in vivo* incorporation of ^{3}H-choline, ^{3}H-leucine, ^{3}H-acetate, and ^{3}H-galactose in non-ciliated bronchiolar (Clara) cells of mice: *Amer. J. Anat.* **139**:519.

101. PFLEGER, R. C., AND THOMAS, H. G., 1971, Beagle dog pulmonary surfactant lipids, *Arch. Intern. Med.* **127**:863.

102. PFLEGER, R. C., HENDERSON, R. F., AND WAIDE, J., 1972, Phosphatidylglycerol—A major component of pulmonary surfactant, *Chem. Phys. Lipids* **9**:51.

102a. PLATZKER, A., KITTERMAN, J., MESCHER, E., CLEMENTS, J., AND TOOLEY, W., 1975, Surfactant in the lung and tracheal fluid of the fetal lamb and acceleration of its appearance by dexamethasone, *Pediatrics* **56**:554.

102b. RHOADES, R. A., 1975, Influence of starvation on the lung: Effect on glucose and palmitate utilization, *J. Appl. Physiol.* **38**:513.

103. RICHARDSON, C. J., POMERANCE, J. J., CUNNINGHAM, M. D., AND GLUCK, L., 1974, Acceleration of fetal lung maturation following prolonged rupture of the membranes, *Amer. J. Obstet. Gynecol.* **118**:1115.

104. ROBERTSON, A. F., AND LANDS, W. E. M., 1962, Positional specificities in phospholipid hydrolysis, *Biochemistry* **1**:804.

105. ROONEY, S. A., CANAVAN, P. M., AND MOTOYAMA, E. K., 1974, The identification of phosphatidylglycerol in the rat, rabbit, monkey, and human lung, *Biochem. Biophys. Acta* **300**:56.

105a. ROONEY, S., GROSS, I., GASSENHEIMER, L., AND MOTOYAMA, E., 1975, Stimulation of glycerolphosphate phosphatidyltransferase activity in fetal rabbit lung by cortisol administration, *Biochim. Biophys. Acta* **398**:433.

105b. ROONEY, S., GOBRAN, L., GROSS, I., WAI-LEE, T., NARDONE, L., AND MOTOYAMA, E., 1976, Studies of pulmonary surfactant: Effects of cortisol administration to fetal rabbits on lung phospholipid content; composition and biosynthesis, *Biochim. Biophys. Acta* **450**:121.

106. ROSENTHAL, A. F., VARGAS, M. G., AND SCHIFF, S. V., 1974, Comparison of four indexes of fetal pulmonary maturity, *Clin. Chem.* **20**:486.

107. ROUX, J. F., AND MYERS, R. E., 1974, *In vitro* metabolism of palmitic acid and glucose in developing tissue of the rhesus monkey, *Amer. J. Obstet. Gynecol.* **118**:385.

108. ROUX, J. F., AND YOSHIOKO, T., 1972, *In vitro* metabolism of palmitic acid in human fetal tissue, *Pediatr. Res.* **6**:675.

109. SAID, S. I., HARLAN, W. R., BURKE, G. W., AND ELLIOTT, C. M., 1968, Surface tension, metabolic activity, and lipid composition of alveolar cells in washings from normal dog lungs and after pulmonary artery ligation; importance of a highly surface-active acellular layer, *J. Clin. Invest.* **47**:336.

110. SALISBURG-MURPHY, S., RUBINSTEIN, D., AND BECK, J. C., 1966, Lipid metabolism in lung slices, *Amer. J. Physiol.* **211**:989.

111. SANDERS, R. L., AND LONGMORE, W. J., 1975, Phosphatidylglycerol in rat lung. II. Comparison of occurrence, composition, and metabolism in surfactant and residual lung fractions, *Biochemistry* **14**:835.

112. SCARPELLI, E. M., CLUTARIO, B. C., AND TAYLOR, F. A., 1967, Preliminary identification of lung surfactant system, *J. Appl. Physiol.* **23**:880.

113. SCHAEFER, K. E., AVERY, M. E., AND BENSCH, H., 1964, Time course of changes in surface tension and morphology of alveolar epithelial cells in CO_2-induced hyaline membrane disease, *J. Clin. Invest.* **43**:2080.

114. SCHOLZ, R. W., AND RHOADES, R. A., 1971, Lipid metabolism by rat lung *in vitro*. Effect of starvation and re-feeding on utilization of $(U - {}^{14}C)$ glucose by lung slices, *Biochem. J.* **124**:257.

114a. SHARP-CAGEORGE, S., BLICHER, B., GORDON, E., AND MURPHY, B., 1977, Amniotic-fluid cortisol and human fetal lung maturation, *N. Engl. J. Med.* **296**:89.

114b. SIVAKUMARAN, T., DUNCAN, M., AND EFFER, S.,

1975, Relationship between cortisol and lecithin/sphingomyelin ratios in human amniotic fluid, *Am. J. Obstet. Gynecol.* **122**:291.

115. SMITH, B., AND TORDAY, J. S., 1974, Factors affecting lecithin synthesis by fetal lung cells in culture, *Pediatr. Res.* **8**:848.

116. SOROKIN, S. P., 1970, The cells of the lung, in: *Proceedings of the Biological Division,* Oak Ridge National Laboratory, Atomic Energy Commission, Series 21, Oak Ridge, Tennessee.

117. SPELLACY, W. N., BUHL, W. C., RIGGALL, E. C., AND HOLSINGER, K. L., 1973, Human amniotic fluid lecithin/sphingomyelin ratio changes with estrogen or glucocorticoid treatment, *Amer. J. Obstet. Gynecol.* **115**:216.

118. SPITZER, H. L., MORRISON, K., AND NORMAN, J. R., 1968, The incorporation of L-[Me-^{14}C]methionine and [Me-^{3}H]choline into lung phosphatides, *Biochim. Biophys. Acta* **152**:552.

119. SPITZER, H. L., RICE, J. M., MCDONALD, P. C., AND JOHNSON, J. M., 1975, Phospholipid biosynthesis in lung lamellar bodies, *Biochem. Biophys. Res. Commun.* **66**:17.

120. STADTMAN, E. T., 1970, Mechanisms of enzyme regulation in metabolism, in: *The Enzymes: Structure and Control* (P. D. Boyer, ed.), p. 397, Academic Press, New York.

121. STEIN, O., AND STEIN, Y., 1969, Lecithin synthesis, intracellular transport, and secretion in rat liver, *J. Cell. Biol.* **40**:161.

122. THANNHAUSER, S. J., BENOTTI, J., AND BONCODDO, N. F., 1946, Isolation and properties of hydrolecithin (dipalmitoyl lecithin) from lungs, its occurrence in the sphingomyelin fraction of the lung tissue, *J. Biol. Chem.* **155**:669.

123. THOM, M. L., AND ZACHMAN, R. D., 1975, The enzymes of lecithin biosynthesis in human neonatal lungs. IV. Phosphorylcholine cytidyltransferace, *Pediatr. Res.* **9**:201.

124. THOMPSON, W., MACDONALD, G., AND MOOKERJEA, X., 1969, Metabolism of phosphorylcholine and lecithin in normal and choline-deficient rats, *Biochim. Biophys. Acta* **176**:306.

125. TIERNEY, D. F., 1971, Lactate metabolism in rat lung tissue, *Arch. Intern. Med.* **127**:858.

126. TIERNEY, D. F., AYERS, L., HERZOG, S., AND YANG, J., 1973, Pentose pathway and NADPH production: A mechanism which may protect lung from oxidants, *Amer. Rev. Respir. Dis.* **108**:1348–1351.

127. WANG, M. C., AND MENG, H. C., 1972, Lipid synthesis by rat lung *in vitro, Lipids* **7**:207.

128. WEBER, G., 1963, Study and evaluation of regulation of enzyme activity and synthesis in mammalian liver, *Adv. Enzyme Regul.* **1**:1.

129. WEBER, K. C., AND VISSCHER, M. B., 1969, Metabolism of the isolated canine lung, *Amer. J. Physiol.* **217**:1044.

130. WEINHOLD, P. A., 1968, Biosynthesis of phosphatidyl-choline during prenatal development of the rat lung, *J. Lipid Res.* **9**:262.

131. WEINHOLD, P. A., SANDER, R., AND STERN, W., 1973, Regulation of choline phosphoglyceride synthesis during lung development in the rat, in: *Respiratory Distress Syndrome* (C. A. Villee, D. B. Villee, and J. Zuckerman, eds.), p. 29, Academic Press, New York.

132. WEINHOLD, P. A., SKINNER, R. S., AND SANDERS, R. D., 1973, Activity and some properties of choline kinase, choline phosphate cytidyltransferase and choline phosphotransferase during liver development in the rat, *Biochim. Biophys. Acta* **326**:43.

132a. WEISS, H. S., AND JURRUS, E., 1971, Starvation on compliance and surfactant of the rat lung, *Resp. Physiol.* **12**:123.

133. WOLFE, B M. J., ANHALT, B., BECK, J. C., AND RUBINSTEIN, D., 1970, Lipid metabolism in rabbit lungs, *Can. J. Biochem.* **48**:170.

134. YEAGER, H., JR., AND MASSARO, D., 1972, Glucose metabolism and glycoprotein synthesis by lung slices, *J. Appl. Physiol.* **32**:477.

135. YOUNG, S. L., AND TIERNEY, D. F., 1972, Dipalmitoyl lecithin secretion and metabolism by the rat lung, *Amer. J. Physiol.* **222**:1539.

136. ZACHMAN, R. D., 1971, The enzymes of lecithin biosynthesis in human newborn lungs. I. Choline kinase, *Biol. Neonate* **19**:211.

137. ZACHMAN, R. D., 1972, The enzymes of lecithin bio-synthesis in human newborn lungs. II. Methion-ine-activating enzyme and phosphatidyl methyl-transferase, *Biol. Neonate* **20**:448.

138. ZACHMAN, R. D., 1973, The enzymes of lecithin biosynthesis in human newborn lungs. III. Phos-phorylcholine glyceride transferase, *Pediatr. Res.* **7**:632.

CHAPTER 8

The Fetal Circulation and Its Alteration at Birth

S. Zoe Walsh and John Lind

1. Introduction

The great inaccessibility of the fetus and its placenta *in situ* has made it necessary to rely on animal experimentation. These studies have been invaluable in delineating many aspects of physiology and in pinpointing areas for future research in man. The conditions under which they have been performed however, have often not been physiologic. Development of the chronic fetal preparation has added a new dimension, but it is important to remember that "there is more variation throughout the mammalian order in reproductive physiology than in the physiology of any other body function."[118]

Until recently, the human fetus was regarded as a "placid, dependent, fragile vegetable who developed quietly in preparation for a life which started after birth."[118] Today, the view of the fetus has taken a *volte-face*, and far from being regarded as "an inert passenger in a pregnant mother," the fetus is now seen as in command of pregnancy. Thus, it is the fetus who guarantees the endocrine success of pregnancy, induces a number of changes in maternal physiology to make her a suitable host, is responsible for solving the homograft problem, and determines the duration of pregnancy. He does not live "in a state of total sensory deprivation but in a plastic, reactive structure which buffers and filters, perhaps distorts, but does not eliminate the outside world. Nor is the fetus himself inert and stuporous, but active and responsive .... When our cords are cut, we are not severed from our mothers but from our own organs—our placentae—which are appropriate to our old environment but unnecessary in our new one. We do not regard the fetal circulatory system, different as it is from the child's or adult's, as one big heap of congenital defects but as a system superbly adapted to his circumstances."[118]

Individual variation is undoubtedly as important in pre- as in postnatal life. The stresses of intrauterine life go largely unnoticed, but they certainly influence

S. Zoe Walsh and John Lind · Department of Pediatrics, Karolinska Hospital; and Wenner-Gren Research Laboratory Stockholm, Sweden

the rate of growth of both the fetus and its placenta.

The majority of infants appear to begin their extrauterine existence without much difficulty, although this transition requires elaborate and extensive preparation during fetal life. Birth itself is not uncommonly sudden and dramatic, but the transition from fetal to adult circulation is more gradual, with comparatively slow functional closure of fetal channels.

Any discussion of the fetal and neonatal circulation must take into account other systems, because adaptation during gestation and extrauterine life depends on integrated responses of these systems (Fig. 1).

2. Fetal Circulation

The fetal circulation is characterized by the following features:

1. The placenta, not the lung, is the organ of gas exchange.
2. The intrauterine environment is liquid, which presumably reduces sensory input and the need for some regulatory mechanisms and favors development of the lungs.
3. Six fetal vascular channels are present— umbilical vein, umbilical arteries, ductus venosus, foramen ovale, and ductus arteriosus—

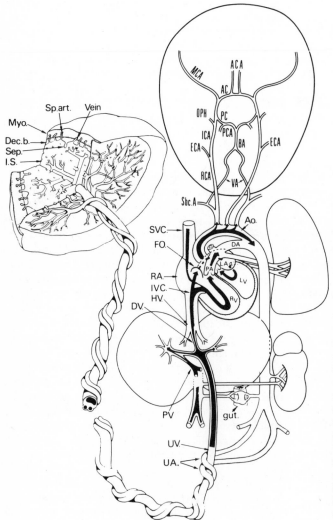

Fig. 1. Schematic diagram showing the course of the fetal circulation as well as the relatively large size of the brain and placenta and the considerable length of the umbilical cord. (ACA) anterior cerebral artery; (AC) anterior communicating artery; (MCA) middle cerebral artery; (PC) posterior communicating artery; (OPH) ophthalmic artery; (PCA) posterior cerebral artery; (ICA) internal carotid artery; (BA) basilar artery; (RCA) right carotid artery; (VA) vertebral artery; (ECA) external carotid artery; (Sbc. A)— subclavian artery; (SVC.) superior vena cava; (RA.) right atrium; (FO.) foramen ovale; (RV) right ventricle; (PA) pulmonary artery; (LA) left atrium; (LV) left ventricle; (DA) ductus arteriosus; (Ao.) aorta; (UV.) umbilical vein; (PV.) portal vein; (DV.) ductus venosus; (HV.) hepatic vein; (IVC.) inferior vena cava; (UA) umbilical artery; (Vein) uterine vein; (Sp. art.) spiral arteriole; (Myo.) myometrium; (Dec. b.) decidua basalis; (Sep.) septum; (I.S.) intervillous space. Reproduced from Walsh *et al.*[221] Courtesy of Charles C. Thomas, Publisher.

only one of which (the foramen ovale) may not normally obliterate after birth.

4. Both sides of the heart work partly in parallel to pump blood from the systemic veins to the aorta; i.e., blood from the inferior vena cava passes largely to the ascending aorta and arch via the foramen ovale, while blood from the superior vena cava is distributed to the descending aorta via the ductus arteriosus. Hence, the output of the right and left chambers may differ.

5. The pattern of circulation ensures somewhat better oxygenation of the heart and brain at the expense of the lower body.

6. Cardiac output is high and therefore provides a large blood flow to the placenta and fetal tissues.

7. The pulmonary circulation has a high vascular resistance and low blood flow, and is sensitive to changes in arterial P_{O_2} and P_{CO_2} and acidosis.

8. The lungs are solid organs secreting fluids into the respiratory passages. They extract oxygen from the blood instead of contributing to oxygenation of the blood.

9. The homeostatic mechanisms necessary for maintenance of the internal environment and those essential for the independent onset of respiration are established in ample time to permit fetal autonomy and survival after birth.[221]

2.1. The Placenta

The placenta is a fetal extracorporeal organ designed for rapid growth and disposal after a life span of 280 days. It is of dual origin and has two separate bloodstreams. Hence, satisfactory function of this organ depends on normal function of both the fetal and the maternal circulation.

The major portion of the placenta consists of fetal vessels (i.e., the chorionic villi system), their connective tissue supports, and coverings. The umbilical arteries and vein cross the fetal surface of the placenta beneath the amnion and give off branches that enter the main stem villus. Each main stem villus with its branches comprises a structural unit referred to as a *fetal cotyledon.* At term, the human placenta has an average of about 60 cotyledons, but the range is wide and the number disputed[30] (Fig. 2).

The placental floor has many projections (septa), which are formed by the maternal decidua (endometrium) and covered by a fetal layer. The septa divide the maternal surface of the placenta into about 20 lobes or *maternal cotyledons.* Each maternal cotyledon contains several fetal cotyledons. The septa act as baffles to maternal blood entering the communicating system of 50-μm wide cavities between the villi (intervillous space) via the spiral arterioles, which are continuations of the arcuate arteries.[162] These vessels tend to open at the bases of the septa or at the apices of low conical projections of decidua. At term, about 100 arteries supply the human placenta.[28] Maternal blood drains from the intervillous space by means of dilated endometrial veins, the orifices of which are distributed throughout the basal plate.

Some morphological changes bordering on the pathologic appear during pregnancy. Fibrin deposits are present on the surface and among the chorionic villi in the intervillous space (Fig. 2).

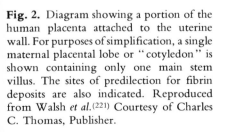

Fig. 2. Diagram showing a portion of the human placenta attached to the uterine wall. For purposes of simplification, a single maternal placental lobe or "cotyledon" is shown containing only one main stem villus. The sites of predilection for fibrin deposits are also indicated. Reproduced from Walsh *et al.*[221] Courtesy of Charles C. Thomas, Publisher.

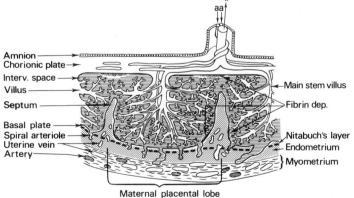

The amount increases during gestation, and at term, about 8% of all villi are covered by fibrin.[223] Large fibrin deposits and even localized thromboses are also common, as are infarcts, which are present in about 50% of all cases at birth, are usually confined to small areas, and probably have no functional significance. Wallenburg et al.,[206] for example, examined multiple serial histological sections of 536 well-defined infarcts from 1240 consecutively delivered placentas and found no significant changes in fetal stem vessels, whereas most of the uteroplacental vessels showed evidence of obstruction, and thrombosis was a frequent finding.

2.1.1. Maternal Side

The blood in the intervillous space is maternal, but outside the confines of the endothelium of the mother's vascular system and in direct contact with the fetal syncytium.

In a study of 23 women with normal term pregnancies, blood flow in the intervillous space was 65–120 ml/100 g per min, and fetal blood flow was 90–190 ml/100 g per min, as estimated after injection of ^{133}Xe.[47] According to the authors, there exists a relationship between blood flow in the intervillous space and fetal blood flow, since both seem to rise and fall in parallel independently of the duration of pregnancy and fetal body weight. Estimates of total volume are of doubtful accuracy because of the structural characteristics of this space. The most careful available studies suggest that the volume varies between 20 and 40% of total placental volume during the second and third trimesters.

The blood in the intervillous space enters in spurts via the spiral arterioles and spreads toward the chorionic plate. Since maternal blood pressure is considerably higher than in the intervillous space (where the pressure is about 10 mm Hg at rest in the supine position and resistance to flow is negligible in the relaxed uterus)[88,164] (Fig. 3), the entering arterial bloodstream moves toward the chorionic plate before lateral dispersion takes place, forcing the blood already present out through the endometrial veins, where the pressure is slightly lower (about 8 mm Hg). The veins are often of larger caliber than the arteries, though possibly less numerous.

The relative direction of flow is disputed, but present evidence favors "multivillous" flow; i.e.,

maternal blood flows past a series of fetal villi. With such a system, the fetal P_{O_2} has a value between that of the maternal arterial and venous P_{O_2}.[19]

The spiral arterioles represent the site of the greatest pressure drop in the maternal circuit. Although their number does not increase after the first few months of gestation, their lumens widen. Consequently, uterine vascular resistance falls and flow increases.

There is no nervous system in the placenta, but vascular smooth muscle extends into the villous stems to the precapillary arterioles and may be chemically activated. Thus, regulation of maternal flow in the intervillous space by contraction of villi is possible.[113]

Not all arterioles are patent at the same time, and flow may be increased in one segment and decreased in another. The exact mechanism for this intermittency of arterial flow is not known.

During labor, uterine blood flow slows by varying amounts in different segments during uterine contractions, which probably constitutes an extra margin of safety for the fetus. At the start of a contraction, uterine veins opening into the intervillous space are compressed, since they are thin-walled and pressure is lower. In the human midterm uterus, if intraamniotic pressure rises above 50 mm Hg during a contraction, all veins are compressed, whereas at pressures below this level, only 60% are compressed. At times, the myometrium may exert a sphincterlike action on the veins. The pressure in the intervillous space is about the same as that in the amniotic sac except at the height of a contraction, when the spiral arterioles may also be shut off.[162] The intraamniotic pressure increases from a value of 7–15 mm Hg during relaxation to 20–60 mm Hg during contraction. Thus, the amount of blood in the intervillous space is probably greater during contraction, which facilitates transfer of gaseous substances across the placenta. Indeed, judging from available evidence (in the cow and sheep), placental blood flow and fetal P_{O_2} are maintained until delivery of the fetus.

2.1.2. Fetal Side

Fetal blood enters the placenta via the umbilical artery in the cord and passes into the main stem villi. It then enters the capillary network of the villi and returns to the fetus via the umbilical vein. At term, there are about 50 million villous capillaries.[223] Most resistance to pulsatile blood

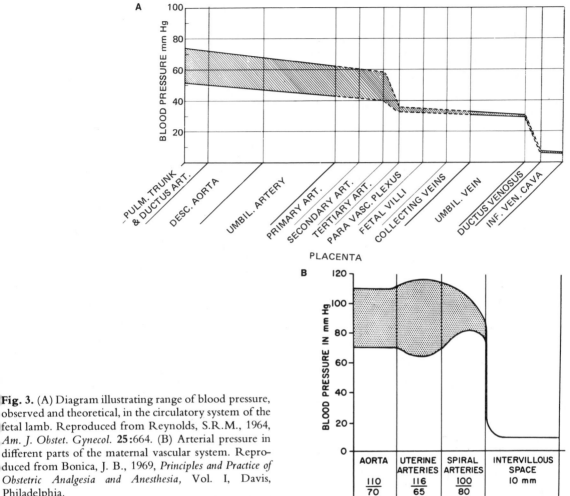

Fig. 3. (A) Diagram illustrating range of blood pressure, observed and theoretical, in the circulatory system of the fetal lamb. Reproduced from Reynolds, S.R.M., 1964, *Am. J. Obstet. Gynecol.* **25**:664. (B) Arterial pressure in different parts of the maternal vascular system. Reproduced from Bonica, J. B., 1969, *Principles and Practice of Obstetric Analgesia and Anesthesia,* Vol. I, Davis, Philadelphia.

flow occurs across this capillary bed (Fig. 3). Also present is an extensive paravascular network that communicates with the stem artery and vein and surrounds the smaller villous stem arteries. It may serve to divert blood away from the villous capillary plexus.

2.2. Umbilical Blood Flow

Umbilical blood flow increases with gestational age and weight, and is dependent on the vascular resistance and pressure gradient driving blood from the descending aorta through the placenta and back to the inferior vena cava. In the fetal lamb, the pressure gradient is about 65 mm Hg, and the greatest drop in pressure takes place across the

capillary bed of the fetal villi (about 35 mm Hg) (Fig. 3). In this species, the mean pressure in the umbilical artery slowly increases to 55 or 65 mm Hg, while at term, that in the umbilical vein remains about 10–12 mm Hg. The resistance in the ductus venosus and hepatic tributaries of the umbilical vein is responsible for the 4–5 mm Hg difference between the umbilical vein and the inferior vena cava. In the human infant, only a few values are available, and although the transition seems to be similar, umbilical venous pressure is higher, i.e., about 25 mm Hg at term.

The steady rise in fetal arterial pressure normally ensures an increase in umbilical flow almost in proportion to fetal growth, and thereby provides the means by which total O_2 consumption can increase in proportion to body weight. The gradual increase in systemic blood pressure is probably partly related to increasing activity of sympathetic vasoconstrictor tone in the systemic circulation, while the pressure in the umbilical vein depends on the amount of umbilical flow and the vascular resistance of the liver and the ductus venosus.

In the human fetus, mean umbilical blood flow, as determined with the cuff electromagnetic flow meter, is 110 ml/kg per min at 10–28 weeks' gestation[11] and 75 ml/kg per min as determined with local thermodilution between 35 and 42 weeks' gestation immediately after delivery.[193] The latter value seems low, however, and total flow may amount to 125 or even 150 ml/kg per min in the average human fetus at term.[53]

In previable human fetuses (75–650 g), fetal O_2 consumption is about 4 ml/min per kg,[11] and maternal O_2 inhalation does not increase this value unless the fetus is hypoxic.[18]

2.3. Regulation of Umbilical Blood Flow

It is difficult to reconcile the results of *in vivo* and *in vitro* studies concerning reactivity of umbilical blood vessels, the reason being partly that experiments have often not been done under physiologic conditions. *In vivo*, umbilical vessels show almost no direct local effect following large changes in blood gas tension in fetal arterial P_{O_2} from 15 to 65 mm Hg, although severe asphyxia produces vasoconstriction, presumably because of release of catecholamines from the fetal adrenals. No such effect has been produced in the immature fetal lamb, presumably because smaller amounts of catecholamines are liberated. According to Dawes,[53] umbilical blood flow can and does alter in response to small changes in arterial blood pressure, but umbilical vascular resistance is low and invariate.

In vitro, however, umbilical arteries react in response to many factors. Thus, vasoconstriction can be induced by high O_2 tension, tactile stimulation, and cold, while vasodilatation occurs in response to high CO_2 and low O_2 tensions.

The presence of neural elements in the *intra-abdominal part* of the umbilical vein has been clearly established.[191] Adrenergic nerves increase in number in the direction of the ductus venosus[61] and are most numerous at the site of origin of the ductus, where there is also an increased number of smooth muscle cells in the wall. Nerve fibers from the celiac plexus and anterior and posterior

vagal trunks are also present at the junction of the umbilical vein with the ductus venosus, but not in the wall of the duct. The function of these nerves in closure of the thicker and more muscular proximal end of the umbilical vein is not known.

The presence of neural elements in the *extra-abdominal part* of the cord is disputed. Spivack[191] reports that no such innervation is present. The illustrations in a paper by Zaitev[227] indicate, however, that such elements are present a distance of 10 cm beyond the umbilicus. Likewise, Nadkarni,[144] who carried out light- and electron-microscopic studies on human umbilical cords, found structures that he believed were myelinated nerves within the smooth muscle cells, but found no nerve fibers with the light microscope after silver staining. Ehinger *et al.*,[61] using histochemical techniques, were also unable to confirm these findings.

2.4. Uterine Blood Flow

Uterine blood flow and umbilical blood flow in the human seem to increase in a linear fashion throughout pregnancy. Uterine blood flow comes from the uterine and ovarian vessels at a rate that increases from about 50 ml/min at 3 months' gestation to 500 or 750 ml/min at term. When related to the weight of the uterus and conceptus, this volume amounts to 90 ml/kg per min in early gestation and 125–150 ml/kg per min in late gestation in man.[8,135] About 75% of total uterine blood flow perfuses the intervillous space,[19] and it may increase to as much as 90%.[127] When expressed per kilogram of fetus, however, the rate of uterine flow decreases substantially toward the end of pregnancy.

The high uterine blood flow is at least partly achieved by an increase in maternal cardiac output and fall in uterine vascular resistance. According to Power *et al.*,[159] one-fourth of the total placental weight receives less than one-twentieth of the total flow. The authors noted a remarkably small degree of uneven perfusion down to the level of 1 g placental slices (in the sheep).

The regulatory mechanisms involved in uterine blood flow are still not understood. Experimental studies in animals show that blood P_{O_2} and P_{CO_2} have no direct influence on flow, as assessed by acute changes of blood P_{O_2} and P_{CO_2} induced by maternal hyperoxia and hypoxia.[134] Some data suggest that maternal blood flow is primarily under hormonal control, i.e., that estrogen produces vasodilatation and progesterone vasoconstriction. Thus, Caton et al.[44] noted a fall in uterine blood flow at the same time as plasma levels of progesterone started to rise. Other substances also affect uterine blood vessels; e.g., histamine and acetylcholine produce vasodilatation, while various drugs, such as adrenaline and norepinephrine, produce vasoconstriction. Angiotensin, which is produced by placental renin, may also influence placental flow.[73] Flow is doubled in the case of twins,[135] and diminished in preeclampsia, diabetes, chronic hypertension, and maternal hemorrhage.[83]

Small-for-gestational-age infants produced by mothers with acquired or congenital heart disease may have normal saturation of arterial blood. In women with cyanotic congenital heart disease, there is a direct relationship between the degree of unsaturation in arterial blood (as assessed by the level of the hemoglobin or hematocrit) and fetal weight. These patients also have significant decreases in urinary pregnanediol excretion and sometimes in estriol excretion. Since injections of estrogens increase uterine blood flow, maternal O_2 deficiency may affect her endocrine function as well as fetal growth. The latter effect presumably results from an inability to increase cardiac output sufficiently during pregnancy, and thereby leads to inadequate uterine blood flow.

2.5. Maternal Factors and Adjustments to Pregnancy

Pregnancy is accompanied by a 15% increase in basal O_2 uptake. Pulmonary ventilation increases throughout pregnancy by about 40%, and since the increase in ventilation is greater than the increase in O_2 uptake, the pregnant woman hyperventilates at rest primarily by means of an increased tidal volume. This situation results in a lower P_{CO_2} in arterial blood and alveolar air. Maternal arterial pH influences the P_{O_2} in the umbilical vein, and thus significantly affects the O_2 supply to the fetus. Maternal alkalosis, for example, from maternal hyperventilation, causes a decrease, while respiratory acidosis causes an increase, in P_{O_2} in the umbilical vein. In sheep, acute production of maternal hypoxemia does not result in increased uterine blood flow, but leads to increased arterial pressure and increased umbilical flow, at least initially, while chronic maternal hypoxemia causes increased uterine blood flow and increased placental permeability to O_2.

The total blood volume increases from about 4.0 to 5.5 liters. This increase is due primarily to an increase in plasma volume, which rises from about 2.6 liters at the end of the first trimester to about 4.0 liters near term, as estimated by dye dilution and isotope studies. Hemoglobin also increases in pregnancy, though to a lesser degree than plasma volume. The change in hemoglobin, however, depends on the use of routine iron supplements in pregnancy.[104]

Cardiac output also increases from about 4.5 liters/min during the first trimester to about 6 liters/min at the end of the second trimester, i.e., about 30%. A further small increase may occur near term. The increase in cardiac output is achieved by increases in both heart rate (from about 70 to 80 beats/min) and stroke volume (from about 64 to 71 ml).[104]

Although estimates of the distribution of the increase in cardiac output during pregnancy cannot be regarded as accurate, about one-third of the increase in cardiac output is accounted for by the increase in uterine blood flow, one-third by the increase in skin blood flow, one-fifth by the increase in kidney blood flow, and the remainder by increases in flow to the mammary glands, intestines, and other areas.

During each uterine contraction, cardiac output rises by about 20%, and mean systemic arterial pressure increases by about 20%. Hence, cardiac work increases considerably. The pressures in the right atrium and pulmonary artery also rise. When the patient assumes a lateral position, however, the changes in cardiac output are significantly less.[201] The positional difference is caused by compression of pelvic vessels by the pregnant uterus.

Systolic blood pressure falls initially and then returns to prepregnancy values near term; diastolic blood pressure falls comparatively more, and pulse pressure therefore widens. However, no significant change in mean arterial pressure occurs. Since cardiac output increases, these findings indicate that peripheral vascular resistance decreases during pregnancy. Central venous pressure, in contrast, falls throughout pregnancy.[48]

2.6. Development of the Fetal Circulation

The cardiovascular system is the first organ system to become functional in the fetus, because the embryo is unable to grow more than a few millimeters without a functional circulation for transport of O_2, nutritive substances, and metabolites. In the chick embryo, development of the primitive endothelial network may be genetically determined, while development of the larger vessels may require presence of a circulation. In the human, by the age of 6 weeks, the size of the heart relative to the body of the embryo is about 9 times that in the adult,[7] and it has the same external shape and markings of adult life, but is located higher. At 8 weeks, partition of the heart and its major arterial trunks is complete, apart from persistence of an interatrial foramen and not completely functional atrioventricular cusps. At birth, the relative weight of the heart is 0.7% of total body weight, as compared with 0.4–0.5% in the adult.[82]

2.7. Course of the Fetal Circulation

Knowledge of the course of the circulation, relative size of the vessels, and distribution of blood in the fetus is based to a considerable extent on cineangiographic and microsphere studies in the fetal lamb and human fetus.[14,15,119,170] These studies show that at midterm, arterial blood from the placenta enters the ·inferior vena cava from the umbilical vein, which is larger in diameter than the descending aorta, either by perfusing the liver and entering the hepatic veins or by entering the ductus venosus, a low-resistance bypass around the liver. The actual amount passing through the ductus venosus is not known, but it seems likely that it is about 50%. Both streams reunite and enter the inferior vena cava, which now carries "highly oxygenated" blood from the ductus venosus, "somewhat less saturated" blood from the liver, and "venous" blood from the abdominal viscera and lower half of the body.

On entering the heart, the blood is divided into two streams by the *crista dividens*, a projection of the anterior edge of the foramen ovale extending posteriorly almost to the limits of the atrial cavity (Fig. 4). In the lamb fetus at term, about one-third of the comparatively well-oxygenated blood enters the left atrium directly where the inferior vena cava ends, i.e., via the foramen ovale, and thus bypasses the lungs.[90] In the left atrium, the O_2 content of the blood is lowered by mixing with a small amount of pulmonary venous blood and a tiny stream from the right atrium (about 3% of the superior vena caval flow). The latter amount increases markedly in experimental studies involving production of fetal hypoxemia or asphyxia, which

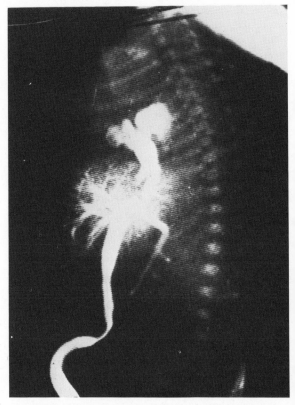

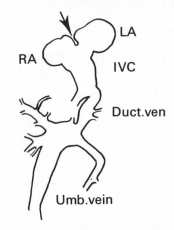

Fig. 4. Angiographic demonstration of the crista dividens. Injection of contrast medium in umbilical vein. The liver vasculature and the portal vein are visualized, as are the ductus venosus (Duct. ven) and inferior vena cava (IVC). On entry into the heart, the contrast medium is split into two streams by the crista dividens (arrow). (RA) Right atrium; (LA) left atrium. LAO-fetus of about 14 weeks' gestation. Reproduced from Walsh et al.[221] Courtesy of Charles C. Thomas, Publisher.

are accompanied by a fall in heart rate. A decrease in umbilical flow results in a decrease in inferior vena caval blood returning to the heart and a relative increase in superior vena caval flow. According to Rudolph and Heymann,[171] superior vena caval flow across the foramen ovale may increase by more than 50%, at term, when the fetal arterial [H+] rises and the P_{O_2} falls markedly.

Blood from the left heart is distributed mainly to the left myocardium (about 3% of total cardiac output), the proportionally large head (about 15% of total output), and the upper body via vessels arising from the aortic arch.

The path taken by the stream from the inferior vena cava through the foramen ovale and to the upper part of the body is known as the *via sinistra* (Figs. 5 and 6).

The remaining two-thirds of the comparatively well-oxygenated blood from the inferior vena cava continues to the right atrium, where some mixing occurs with poorly oxygenated blood returning via the coronary sinus and superior vena cava. The blood from the right atrium enters the right ventricle and pulmonary trunk. Since the pulmonary vascular bed offers considerable resistance to blood flow, particularly at the arteriolar level, and pulmonary arterial pressure is higher than systemic arterial pressure, the blood largely bypasses the lungs by entering the widely patent ductus arteriosus, which represents a continuation of the main pulmonary artery. It then passes down the descending aorta, where it joins the small residue from the left ventricle that has not gone to the head. Thus, little blood enters the aortic isthmus— i.e., the aortic segment between the origin of the left subclavian artery and the entry of the ductus arteriosus—which is therefore of relatively small caliber[154] (see Section 3.9). In the *human* previable fetus weighing 50–300 g,[203] about 40% of the combined ventricular output (vs. 50–60% in the fetal lamb) is returned for oxygenation to the low-vascular-resistant placenta via the descending aorta, common and internal iliac arteries, and the umbilical arteries, which are at least three times as long as the aorta. A smaller portion supplies the abdominal viscera, lower trunk, and legs, and drains into the inferior vena cava.

The path taken by the stream from the right atrium through the ductus arteriosus and down the descending aorta is referred to as the *via dextra*.

During growth, the proportion of blood flow to various organs and to the placenta changes.

Studies[173] performed by injection of radionuclide-labeled 15-μm microspheres in the fetal lamb *in utero* (a minimum of 3–5 days after surgery) show that *near term*, the major portion of right ventricular output enters the ductus arteriosus (60% of the combined output), whereas one-third of left ventricular output (10% of the combined output) traverses the aortic isthmus. Only about one-third of the blood from the inferior vena cava (26% of the combined output) passes via the foramen ovale and the left atrium. These authors also note that 70% of the combined output passes down the descending aorta, 20% passes to the brachiocephalic vessels, 7% to the lungs, and 3% to the coronary arteries. The data are of particular interest because of the greater accuracy of the methods used. The findings are at variance with previous estimates in the anesthetized exteriorized fetal lamb, which showed similar outputs for both ventricles.[9,56,124]

Although blood in the left heart should be better oxygenated than that in the right, the difference is usually small, at least in the lamb. The findings therefore suggest that the work load of the right heart should become greater than that of the left during fetal life, because arterial pressure is increasing, and much of the flow to the lower part of the body and through the very long umbilical arteries to the placenta comes mainly from right ventricular output. This concept accords with electrocardiographic studies showing a totally upright R wave in V_1 present from early gestation onward (Fig. 7A) and autopsy studies showing equal thickness of the right and left ventricular myocardium until the middle of the second trimester and relatively increased thickness of the right ventricular myocardium in the latter half of gestation.[64,102,163]

2.8. Regulation of the Fetal Circulation

In the human fetus, anatomic pathways of the parasympathetic and sympathetic system are laid down early. Vagal fibers in the A-V bundle have been reported as early as at 6 weeks of gestation,[28] and well-developed chemoreceptor areas around the great vessels are present at about 8 weeks of gestation. Large stores of catecholamines have also been found in the human fetal adrenal medulla and in the organs of Zucherkandl.[29] The presence of anatomic pathways for cardiovascular reflexes, however, is no indication of the age at which they become functional. Likewise, the presence of even large stores of catecholamines provides no information

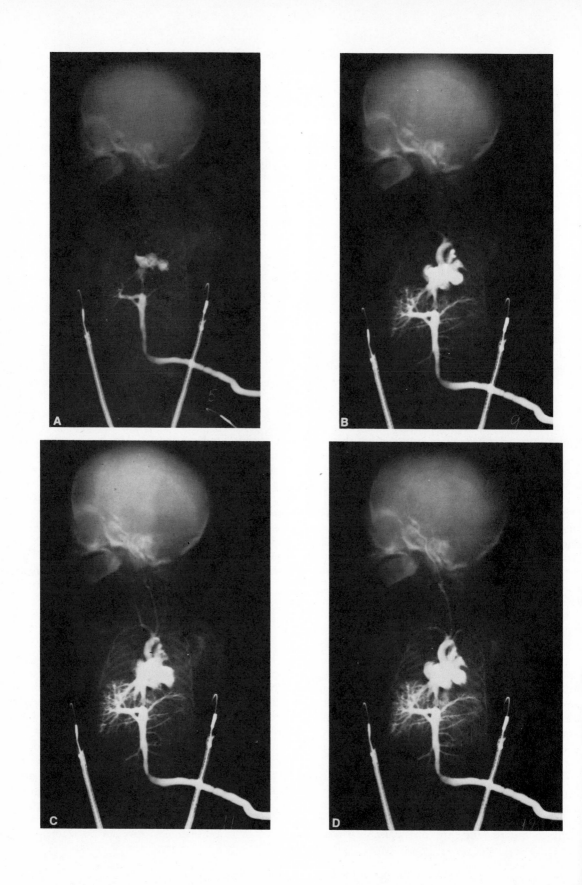

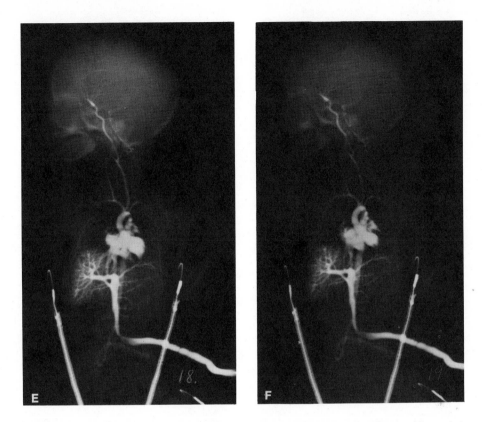

Fig. 5. Course of circulation in the fetus (weight, 70 g; gestational age, 15 weeks). (A) Contrast medium is injected into the umbilical vein, which is well opacified as are the main branches of the liver vessels. The ductus venosus and heart chambers are clearly seen. The distribution of the medium indicates that more contrast bypasses the liver by way of the ductus venosus than passes through the hepatic vascular bed. (B) Contrast medium has passed through the liver sinusoids, and the hepatic veins are now visualized. All heart chambers are well opacified in ventricular systole, as is the ascending aorta and its branches up to the level of insertion of the ductus arteriosus. The descending aorta, however, is not seen at all. In the aortic window, the main stem of the pulmonary artery and ductus arteriosus can be distinguished, but there is no filling of the pulmonary branches. (C) In the following ventricular diastole, the ventricular chambers have increased considerably in size, and the vessels to the head are well seen. During the coinciding atrial systole, the liver veins increase in caliber. (D) In the following ventricular systole, the descending aorta is becoming faintly opacified, while the pulmonary branches are still not seen. The atria are increased in size, and their appendages are well outlined. (E) The descending aorta and umbilical arteries are seen, but the concentration of contrast medium is now much less than in the ascending aorta. There is still no opacification of the pulmonary arteries. (F) The cyclical changes in shape and size of the heart chambers are again evident.

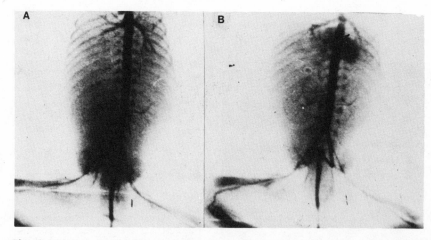

Fig. 6. (A) Retrograde filling of aorta descendents. The right and left pulmonary arteries are well visualized. They are relatively small. (B) Slight opacification of left atrium and left ventricle. The pulmonary circulation time is 2 sec.

concerning the rate of turnover, which is more important for assessment of function.

Experimental studies in animals suggest that parasympathetic and α-sympathetic regulations develop considerably earlier in fetal life than β-sympathetic regulation, which seems to mature later and continues to develop after birth. In accordance with these findings, sympathetic inner-

vation to the heart is incomplete in the fetus and develops after birth.

Baroreceptor and chemoreceptor activity have been demonstrated in fetuses of various species.[24,55,183] The baroreceptor response is present in the fetal lamb at midgestation, and its sensitivity increases during gestation. In some instances, no difference in response can be shown before and after birth.

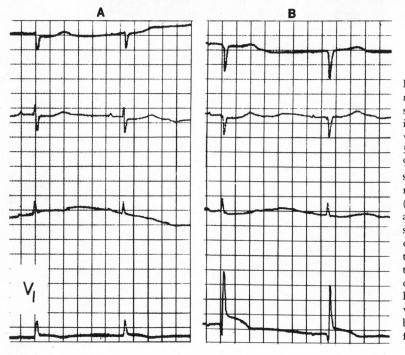

Fig. 7. Effect of clamping cord *in utero*. Simultaneous recording of standard bipolar leads and lead V_1 in a 260-g fetus (gestation age ∼ 16 weeks) still *in utero*. Paper speed 50 mm/sec; 2 cm = 1 mV; heart rate, 97 beats/min. (A) Initial tracing shows right axis deviation and relatively good voltage T waves. (B) Tracing recorded immediately after clamping the cord shows a striking alteration in the amplitude of the QRS complex, elevation of the S–T segment, and some shift in the direction of the T vector. These changes are particularly evident in lead V_1, in which a prominent Q wave is also seen. Heart rate, 81 beats/min. Reproduced (with modifications) from Stern *et al.*[195]

Aortic chemoreceptors are very sensitive to small changes in P_{O_2} and are important for fetal survival during hypoxemia. On the other hand, carotid chemoreceptors show little tonic activity until immediately after initiation of ventilation and clamping of the umbilical cord.[161] Dawes[54] suggested that only the aortic chemoreceptors may be important in fetal life, because they are involved principally in control of the circulation, whereas the carotid chemoreceptors are involved principally in control of respiration.

In the human fetus, the activity of various reflexes is assumed on the basis of studies in various other species, studies on the isolated human fetal heart, and studies of reflexes in premature infants after birth and in term infants during labor and delivery. The data indicate that some degree of autonomic nervous control is established early in gestation before the fetus becomes viable, and that the heart of the mature fetus is under autonomic nervous control. Chemoreceptor and baroreceptor reflexes are well developed at birth. The fetal bradycardia response to maternal hypoxia, umbilical cord occlusion, and fetal head compression is believed to be reflexly induced, and may be associated with selective constriction in the lung vessels and other vascular beds. Bradycardia in this situation may serve to reduce cardiac work and expenditure of cardiac carbohydrate stores, and thus maintain the circulation during hypoxic episodes. It is not certain, however, whether nervous control of the fetal circulation is in fact necessary for survival during fetal life and after birth. In human infants, gross abnormalities of the brainstem and cord are compatible with survival until term. The local mechanisms that regulate heart rate, force of contraction, and peripheral vasomotor tone appear to be sufficient to ensure survival without central control.[53]

Reflex control of the circulation becomes particularly important in the event of an acute reduction in O_2 supply or an increase in demand or both. In this situation, the fetus is able to maintain preferential perfusion of the heart, brain, adrenal, and placenta by a variety of mechanisms, including a high cardiac output, the distinctive pattern of the fetal circulation, increasing control of the autonomic nervous system, and active cardiovascular reflexes. As hypoxemia increases (in the fetal lamb near term), the combined ventricular output falls,[20] largely because of a decrease in heart rate. The decrease in rate can be abolished by atropine.

However, although neither acidemia nor hypoxia alone impairs left ventricular function in newborn lambs, together they cause marked deterioration of myocardial performance.

The effects of this selective "circulatory ischemia" on other organs in the human fetus are not known. Recent data suggest that hypoxemia may cause degeneration of the intramural ganglion cells in the distal colon and thereby result in Hirschsprung's disease.[188,198] These studies are of particular interest, since they indicate that a systemic stress *in utero* may alter neurogenic function *without* producing other evidence of tissue injury.

Anoxic survival also appears to depend on the amount of glycogen in the heart, though not on the amount in the liver. Myocardial cells contain large amounts of glycogen throughout gestation (30–40 mg/g in the cardiac ventricles of most species, including man). That they do would suggest that the enzymes necessary for glycogen synthesis appear very early. These stores increase at term.[182] Presumably for this reason, heart muscle can function without oxygen for relatively longer periods than later in life.

2.9. Fetal Cardiac Output

Several methods have been used to measure cardiac output in the fetal lamb, and reported values range from 235 to 525 ml/kg fetal wt. per min.[9,56,89,124,173] These values are similar to those reported in 11 previable human fetuses weighing 65–225 g after delivery by hysterotomy with the placenta *in situ*, i.e., 360 ml/kg fetal wt.[175] Judging from available information, the combined cardiac output in various species when related to fetal weight is 2–4 times that in the adult. It is possible that this increased cardiac output represents an important form of adaptation by the fetus to the low fetal arterial saturation *in utero*. Moreover, cardiac output appears to increase with fetal growth. Studies by Rudolph and Heymann[173] suggest that changes in cardiac output in the fetal lamb are induced almost solely by alterations in heart rate. When heart rate decreases, the fetal ventricles seem unable to increase stroke volume, and cardiac output falls. An increase in stroke volume can be induced by rapid volume loading (which might be regarded as the equivalent of firmly milking the cord toward the infant, as practiced by a number of obstetricians at the time of delivery) and by isoproterenol infusion. When heart rate is increased above the resting level (i.e., to almost 300 beats/min), the cardiac output continues to increase because the fetus is able to maintain its stroke volume.

According to others,[108] in the fetal lamb near term, as in the adult, a decrease in fetal heart rate of as much as 50% of control values is accompanied by a compensatory increase in stroke volume, provided heart rate remains regular. Stroke volume, blood pressure, and blood flow fall only when the bradycardia is accompanied by a dysrhythmia.

2.10. Fetal Pulmonary Circulation

Before birth, the lung is not an organ of gas exchange. It contributes to the formation of amniotic fluid, and it is uncertain what other functions it may have. The fetal lungs extract an average of 1.6 ml O_2 per 100 ml of blood. The high metabolism of the lungs is due not only to their needs for growth, but also to secretion of fluid into the respiratory tract.[1] Since vascular resistance is higher in the pulmonary than in the systemic circulation, most of the output of the right ventricle flows from right to left around the lungs by way of the ductus arteriosus to the descending aorta. In the fetal lamb near term, the volume of blood flow to the lungs is probably less than 10% of total cardiac output. The resistance offered to flow by the pulmonary vascular bed is sufficient to completely impede contrast filling when the injection is made in the umbilical vein or jugular vein, because hypoxia is inevitably present in fetal studies, and causes more complete shutdown of the constricted pulmonary vessels and disturbed flow patterns. The pulmonary vessels can be easily visualized on retrograde aortograms, however, because the procedure raises intraaortic pressure. The pulmonary vascular bed is then seen to be large even at midterm, although the vessels themselves are narrow (see Fig. 6). At times, the peripheral parts of the lungs also become outlined.[221]

The high resistance of the fetal pulmonary vascular bed is believed to be localized to precapillary muscular arterioles, which develop a thick muscular coat during the latter part of gestation. This smooth muscle mass permits them to function as sphincters controlling the volume of flow to the lungs,[153] and regresses by about 40% at 2 weeks of age.[145] It is uncertain whether this smooth muscle mass develops in response to high pulmonary arterial pressures and hypoxic vasoconstriction or vice versa, but pulmonary vessels of the fetal lamb at mid-gestation are highly reactive, even though pulmonary arterial pressures are still comparatively low.

The high pulmonary vascular resistance of the fetal lung is the resultant of several factors probably acting on it locally. The most important of these factors are the low O_2 tension (20–25 mm Hg, as compared with postnatal values of 80–100 mm Hg), and relatively high CO_2 tension (about 40 mm Hg), with accompanying increase in the $[H^+]$ of blood normally perfusing the lung (in lambs).[43,51] This response of fetal pulmonary vessels to reduced O_2 tension is very similar to that of the adult.[53,172] Reflex pulmonary vasoconstriction from stimulation of aortic or cardiac chemoreceptors also occurs when arterial P_{O_2} falls or $[H^+]$ rises.[49]

2.11. Regulation of Fetal Pulmonary Circulation

The action of various drugs and rhythmical ventilation with gases on the pulmonary circulation has been studied extensively in fetal animals. Pulmonary vasodilatation is produced by a rise in arterial or alveolar P_{O_2} and fall in arterial or alveolar P_{CO_2}. Above a narrow range, however, the effects on pulmonary vascular resistance are no longer linear. Ventilation with air, O_2, or N_2, but not expansion of the lung with warm saline, also causes vasodilatation.[43,114] This vasodilatation occurs within the parenchyma by local action, and is independent of fetal blood gas composition. Histamine, isoprenaline, acetylcholine, and especially bradykinin have a vasodilator action. Their effects are much reduced after ventilation, possibly because of the considerable increase in flow and vasodilatation that follow aeration of the lungs. Heymann et al.[91] suggested that bradykinin is the mediator for the profound fall in pulmonary vascular resistance consequent to ventilation of fetal animals. Other studies in the adult dog, however, have been interpreted as indicating that the arteries upstream to the veins are passively distended in response to an increase in cardiac output.[103] In the normal human adult breathing air, bradykinin also has little effect, but if the subject is first made hypoxic (by breathing a low-O_2 mixture), bradykinin causes pulmonary vasodilatation, a response that has also been noted for acetylcholine.[179]

Unlike the situation with the adult lung, small doses of adrenaline and norepinephrine produce pulmonary vasoconstriction, a response that can be blocked by dibenamine, which blocks the vasocontrictor action of norepinephrine and adrenaline. Similarly, stimulation of sympathetic nerves before the lamb is viable or the lungs can be expanded with gas causes a 75% decrease in pulmonary blood flow. In both mature and immature lambs, asphyxia also produces pulmonary vasoconstriction, which can be abolished by dibenamine.

2.12. Fetal Ductus Arteriosus

The ductus arteriosus develops from the distal portion of the sixth left aortic arch and becomes the main outlet of the right ventricle by about the 5th week of gestation. It connects the main pulmonary trunk to the medial aspect of the aorta just distal to the origin of the left subclavian artery. The duct constitutes a direct continuation of the pulmonary trunk, and there is no visible demarcation between the two vessels. Anatomic and angiographic studies in the human fetus suggest that the internal diameter of the duct is slightly less than that of both great vessels. Its microscopic structure differs from that of the two great vessels it joins in that its media consists primarily of muscular cells, while that of the pulmonary artery and aorta consists primarily of elastic tissue. The differences in structure presumably depend on factors related to embryonic differentiation and function, since the vessels are subject to similar pressures and flow during fetal life.

The amount of the right ventricular output carried by the ductus is about 60% of the combined output, but there appear to be wide individual variations that depend on the various resistances in this hemodynamic system. Although the duct is assumed to be a passive structure, its muscular wall permits it to contract and thereby oblige more blood to enter the pulmonary vascular bed, augment right ventricular work, and possibly even cause an increase in the smooth muscle mass of the pulmonary arterioles.

Animal studies *in vivo* and *in vitro* show a linear correlation between P_{O_2} and flow; i.e., when the blood P_{O_2} reaches 50–60 mm Hg, ductus blood flow begins to decrease.[10] It is not clear whether in the normal fetal arterial P_{O_2} range of about 20 mm Hg, small physiologic changes in P_{O_2} have any effect. The influence of variations in O_2 concentration on the isolated ductus arteriosus is independent of changes in pH and CO_2 within wide limits, and is not abolished by high concentrations of cyanide. The effect of O_2 appears to be exerted on the smooth muscle cells themselves, rather than on some intermediate cell type.[70,112] Extreme asphyxia also causes ductal constriction by release of sympathetic amines.[26] Judging from the marked vasoactivity of the duct, it seems likely that disturbed intrauterine conditions may also affect its size, but probably not until some time · after midterm, because changes in O_2 tension at constant pH have no effect on the human ductus prior to this time.[129]

In vitro experiments on the human fetal ductus arteriosus show that prompt ductal contraction follows the administration of noradrenaline and acetylcholine in a dose-dependent fashion. According to Boréus et al.,[25] the adrenergic nerve terminals of the duct resemble those of the adult, which would suggest earlier maturation of these fibers and a possible role in postnatal closure of the duct. Since the concentration needed for the same response does not increase during the second trimester, observed increases in response of the smooth muscle during development must be due to increased strength of the effector system, rather than to changes in the characteristics of the drug–receptor interaction.

2.13. Fetal Foramen Ovale

The foramen ovale is an obliquely elongated opening between the inferior vena cava and the left atrium. It constitutes the end of the inferior vena cava, which is divided at its termination by the interatrial septum, i.e., a protruding fold of endocardial tissue known as the *crista dividens* (Figs. 4 and 8). It forms at about 6 weeks of gestation when the ostium primum is closing. It is quite large in early gestation, but does not grow to the same extent as the septum subsequently.

Throughout fetal life, the cross-sectional area of the foramen is less than that of the inferior vena cava, measuring one-half the area of the inferior vena cava in infants of low birth weight and slightly more than one-third at term.[155] This relationship would suggest that the volume load on the right heart increases as more blood enters the right atrium, a view that accords with anatomic studies showing that the right atrium surpasses the left atrium in weight and size.[133,143]

The foramen ovale is the main route for relatively direct passage of blood from the placenta to the brain. Estimates of the amount of blood flowing through this opening in the fetal lamb vary.

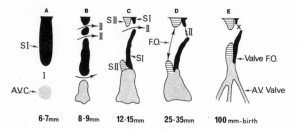

Fig. 8. Developmental stages in formation of the septum primum, septum secundum, and foramen ovale. (A) The septum primum (SI) grows down toward the atrioventricular canal (A.V.C.), the later site of the A.V.C. cushion, to close the ostium primum (I). (B) Before the septum primum reaches the ostium primum, a new opening forms in the septum primum, the ostium secundum (II), which is also known as the foramen ovale (F.O.). (C–E) While the septum secundum (SII) develops and the ostium primum closes, blood continues to pass from right to left through this opening, which gradually becomes smaller and the functional outlet size of which is indicated (X). After birth, pressure in the left atrium rises and exceeds that in the right atrium. The valve of the foramen ovale (or SI) then shuts off return flow. Later, it closes structurally when fibrous adhesions form. Based on drawings by Patten (1968). Reproduced from Walsh et al.[221] Courtesy of Charles C. Thomas, Publisher.

According to a recent report, only about one-third of the inferior vena caval return (26% of the combined ventricular output of 500 ml/kg per min) crosses the foramen into the left atrium.[90] Since pulmonary venous return is comparatively small, and only about 3% of superior vena caval blood crosses the foramen,[171] normal development of the left heart depends on patency of the foramen during fetal life.

2.14. Fetal Heart Rate

The human heart is believed to set blood in motion at the end of the 3rd or the beginning of the 4th week when the embryo is about 2 mm long. Contraction is a purely muscular phenomenon, since nerves apparently first invade the heart several weeks later. In the 15-mm embryo, the heart rate is about 65 beats/min. It increases to 125 beats/min at 45 days, reaches a peak of 175 beats/min at 9 weeks, and then gradually decreases to a value of about 145 beats/min at 15 weeks.[167] From midgestation to term, the human fetal heart rate usually ranges from 135 to 155 beats/min, and probably slows slightly toward term. The individual fetus

tends to maintain a constant rate of ±5–10 beats/min from day to day, with some beat-to-beat variation in successive R–R intervals, a characteristic that persists after birth.[95,202]

The degree of variability of heart rate shown in fetal life persists into adult life; i.e., a labile heart rate *in utero* tends to be labile at 20 years of age, while a stable heart rate remains stable.[190] Moreover, the slower the resting heart rate, the faster the poststimulus rate, a trait that is also clearly evident after birth.[220] Some studies show that the human fetus has varying states of arousal, as evidenced by heart rate response to an extra- or intrauterine stimulus (e.g., external pressure, sound, light, tilt table, percussion).[81] Disappearance of fetal heart rate variability or alternation of a fixed rate with a sinusoidal rhythm is often of serious prognostic significance.[125]

The relatively narrow range of fetal heart rate is attested to by the findings of Sureau, who found that only 2% of 500 consecutive recordings obtained from 18 to 40 weeks' gestation showed a rate of 130 beats/min or less.[196] In Hon's opinion, a persistent fetal heart rate of less than 120 or more than 160 beats/min with or without irregularity is probably abnormal.[96] There appears to be general agreement that fetal tachycardia between contractions is an early sign of fetal distress and is accompanied by biochemical and clinical evidence of asphyxia at birth.[32] This opinion is not shared by Wood,[224] who found no obvious risk for the fetus with heart rates between 160 and 200 beats/min and between 100 and 120 beats/min when unrelated to uterine contractions. Persistent bradycardia for more than 30 min before delivery is a more ominous sign, and is associated with an increased incidence of perinatal mortality.

2.15. Types of Bradycardia During Labor

Alterations of fetal heart rate occur frequently during labor, and have been studied by continuous monitoring of fetal heart rate in combination with intrauterine pressure measurements. Caldeyro-Barcia et al.[42] devised a classification of bradycardia into type I and type II dips based on the time lag between peak uterine contraction and the slowest recorded fetal heart rate (or dips) during simultaneous recordings of intraamniotic fluid pressure and fetal heart rate. Type I dips are brief and have a mean time lag of about 3 sec between peak intrauterine pressure and nadir of heart rate, and 95% of values range from −14 to +20 sec, with return to basal levels before the contraction ends. This pattern corresponds to the "early decelerations" described by Hon and Quilligan,[99] and is often seen toward the end of the first stage of labor when the membranes are ruptured and the head is entering the pelvis. Manual compression of the head has the same effect, while atropine administered to mother or fetus abolishes it.[131,168]

This suggests that the effect may be vagal in origin and due to strong compression and deformation of the head. Baroreceptor stimulation from increasing fetal arterial blood pressure during a contraction might also result in reflex bradycardia. This type of pattern is not associated with depression of the newborn infant.

Type II dips are of longer duration and have a mean time lag of about 40 sec between peak intrauterine pressure and nadir of heart rate, and 95% of values range from 20 to 60 sec (Fig. 9). The pattern corresponds to the "U-shaped bradycardia" or "late deceleration" described by Hon.[97] This type of dip is not abolished by atropine, is found in a significantly greater number of newborns with low Apgar scores, and is believed to be induced by fetal hypoxia and acidosis. The amplitude and duration of these dips provide a good indication of the severity of fetal asphyxia. The incidence is greater in nuchal cord, maternal toxemia, and hypotension. If more than 20 such dips occur before delivery, the newborn infant will probably be depressed[42]; if more than 2 of 20 uterine contractions are accompanied by type II dips, the fetus is not in normal condition.[132]

A third pattern has been described by Hon[98]— "variable deceleration." This type of pattern characteristically shows variability in duration (from 10 sec to several minutes) and nadir of dips (as low as 50–60 beats/min) from contraction to contraction. It is usually not associated with fetal acidosis, is probably due to umbilical cord occlusion, and can be greatly altered by the administration of atropine.

Continuous simultaneous monitoring of fetal heart rate and uterine contractions is still used mainly in high-risk pregnancy labors, since the systems are for the most part expensive and elaborate. This is chiefly because of the difficulty of separating fetal cardiac electric activity from such interferences as maternal cardiac and abdominal electric activity (which is a stronger electric signal). Direct application of electrodes, such as the spiral electrode of Paul and Hon,[156] to the scalp, after rupture of the membranes, results in better recordings.

2.16. Fetal Electrocardiography

The ECG has been recorded from the human heart at 7 weeks' gestation with direct leads. At 9½ weeks, deflections and intervals are not so unlike those encountered in infants of low birth weight, if one discounts the difference in amplitude and relatively longer duration of intervals. Immediately after exteriorization, however, intervals lengthen,

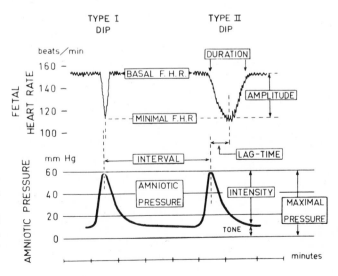

Fig. 9. Diagram of fetal type I and type II dips in fetal heart rate (F.H.R.), caused by "normal" uterine contractions, showing relationship to amniotic fluid pressure tracing as well as parameters for making measurements. Modified by Althabe, O., Jr., *et al.* 1967, Effects on fetal heart rate and fetal P$_{O_2}$ of oxygen administration to the mother, *Amer. J. Obstet. Gynecol.* **98**:858, from Méndez-Bauer.[131]

deflections decrease, and rhythm disturbances ensue. In 12–34 cm human fetuses, such changes are temporarily reversed by injection of a small amount of oxygenated heparinized blood.[222] Healthy full-size infants show somewhat similar changes immediately after birth.[209,210] At midterm, the tracing may be largely indistinguishable from that of a preterm infant of 5 times the weight (see Figs. 7 and 19). It is noteworthy that if the fetus remains *in utero*, clamping of the umbilical cord may induce an immediate change in electrical axis in the frontal plane, a deep Q wave, high-amplitude R wave, and elevation of the S–T segment (Fig. 7B). Thus, increased amplitude of the R wave in V_1 is not solely the result of relatively greater dominance of the right ventricle consequent to hypertrophy.

With indirect electrodes, utilizing various combinations of leads, e.g., abdominal, vaginal, rectal, and endouterine, fetal electrocardiography permits accurate determination of variations in heart rate as well as of amplitude and duration of electrical events. It is primarily used for diagnosis of fetal life (more accurate after midgestation), fetal death (although electric activity may persist for some hours), fetal presentation (discordant maternal and fetal complexes denote cephalic; concordant maternal and fetal complexes denote breech), multiple pregnancy, and recognition of disorders of heart rhythm.

2.17. Fetal Ductus Venosus

The ductus venosus arises from the umbilical recess, which is the direct continuation of the umbilical vein with the left branch of the portal vein. It is not easily accessible to experimental investigations because it lies on the dorsal surface of the liver and is usually covered by a thin layer of connective tissue or by the liver parenchyma. In fetal life, it is about half the size of the umbilical vein and, unlike the umbilical and portal veins (the latter are of similar caliber), does not give off branches to the substance of the liver (Fig. 10). It drains into either the left hepatic vein or the left side of the middle hepatic vein, and then into the inferior vena cava. It therefore constitutes a direct connection between the umbilical vein and the inferior vena cava.

Cineangiographic studies in lambs[14,158] and humans[119] show that contrast medium injected into the umbilical vein enters the umbilical recess, ductus venosus, and inferior vena cava, and also passes into the left branch of the portal vein, the portal

trunk, and the right branch of the portal vein. The amount estimated to pass through the ductus venosus ranges from one-third to two-thirds of placental venous return in the human fetus (see Fig. 5).

Amoroso *et al.*[2] found in lambs that the O_2 content of blood in the ductus venosus and umbilical vein is identical and considerably greater than that in the portal vein, which indicates that blood in this vessel does not usually enter the ductus venosus.

Available studies suggest that the duct functions as a low-resistance bypass to the heart, and is unresponsive to changes in blood gas or acid–base equilibrium. Thus, when umbilical flow and pressure decrease, ductal flow decreases, whereas when umbilical flow and pressure increase, ductal flow increases.[171] Such an increase in umbilical flow and pressure is observed during experimental asphyxia in the lamb.

Although intermittent contractions of the ductus venosus have been observed on angiograms in fetal lambs[16,17,74] and in human fetuses,[119] little smooth muscle is present in the wall of the human ductus venosus, nor does there appear to be a muscular sphincter at the origin of the duct.[136] Small bundles of nerve fibers from the celiac plexus and from the anterior and posterior vagal trunks (with ganglion cells along their course) have been traced to the junction of the umbilical vein with the ductus venosus.[157] Histochemical and pharmacological studies also support the theory of an adrenergic sphincter mechanism at this bypass in the human fetus at the age of 20–24 weeks.[61]

Patency of the ductus venosus in early fetal life may be important for normal development in the human, since complete absence of the duct has been associated with portal hypertension,[123] ascites, enlargement of the placenta,[152] and various malformations. Species differences undoubtedly exist, as evidenced by the early disappearance of the ductus venosus in the fetal horse and pig. It does not appear to be necessary for survival of the human fetus shortly before birth, since Emery[63] reports almost complete closure in 1 of 30 newborn infants without evidence of liver damage.

2.18. Fetal Portal Circulation

The portal venous system consists of two capillary beds, one in the gastrointestinal organs, pancreas, and spleen, the other in the liver connected by the portal vein and its tributaries. By $5\frac{1}{2}$ weeks' gestation, the portal sinus, major portal and hepatic veins, and

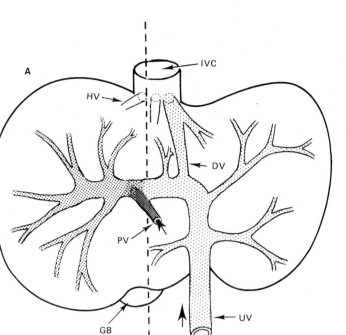

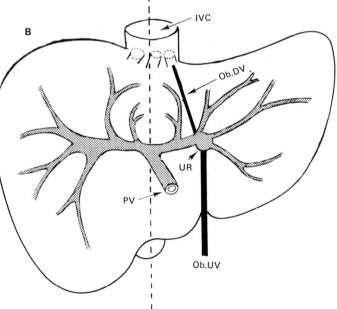

Fig. 10. (A) Distribution of the umbilical and portal blood flow in the fetal liver. The left "half" of the liver, i.e., the part supplied by the umbilical recess and the left part of the portal sinus (up to the opening of the trunk of the portal vein), receives only oxygenated umbilical blood (stippled). The right "half" of the liver is supplied by the umbilical vein as well as the portal vein (solid gray). (B) In the adult liver, all the portal branches are supplied exclusively by the venous blood of the portal vein. Note the difference in the shape of the fetal and adult liver, caused by the relative diminution of the left "half" of the liver after birth. (HV) Hepatic vein; (GB) gallbladder; (DV) ductus venosus; (IVC) inferior vena cava; (Ob.) obliterated; interrupted black line—line of functional division along the vena cava gallbladder plane; (UV) umbilical vein. Reproduced from Walsh *et al.*[(221)] Courtesy of Charles C. Thomas, Publisher.

ductus venosus are clearly defined. In the fetus, portal venous return passes through either the liver parenchyma or the ductus venosus until the ductus closes. It is then obliged to pass through the liver sinusoids to the inferior vena cava. Hence, the fetal liver has three sources of blood supply: the umbilical vein, the portal vein, and the hepatic artery. The artery arises from the celiac axis and has an intra-arterial pressure equal to the systemic blood pressure and somewhat less saturated blood than the ductus venosus. Hepatic arterial blood empties into the same sinusoids as the portal (and umbilical venous blood), but the small size of the human hepatic artery on angiograms and at autopsy suggests that it contributes little to hepatic blood supply during fetal life.

The pressure in the portal vein (and ductus venosus) in fetal life is not known, but is similar to that in the umbilical vein; hence, it is considerably higher than after birth. Since the portal trunk prior to birth is considerably narrower than its main branches and the gut is inactive, it is assumed that the fetal liver is supplied by blood primarily from the umbilical vein, rather than from the portal vein. However, the left main branch of the portal vein, i.e., the direct lateral continuation of the terminal segment of the umbilical vein (otherwise known as the umbilical recess), presumably carries only oxygenated blood from the placenta, whereas the right main branch of the portal vein presumably receives not only oxygenated blood from the placenta, but also "venous" blood from the portal venous trunk, since it is a direct continuation of this vessel. Various anatomic observations by Emery[62] support this view, as evidenced by a larger left than right liver "lobe" during fetal life, presumably because of preferential flow of "oxygenated" blood from the placenta via the umbilical vein to the left "lobe" and more hemopoietic tissue and vacuolation in the right "lobe," a sign of prolonged intrauterine placental insufficiency because of preferential flow of "poorly oxygenated" blood from the portal vein to the right "lobe." Studies of the distribution of blood flow in fetal lambs *in utero* show no such preferential distribution in the liver.[170]

3. Neonatal Circulation

The circulation of the newborn infant differs from that of the fetus and adult in several ways. The main features include:

1. Loss of the low-resistance placental circulation, with simultaneous increase in pulmonary blood flow.
2. Transformation of the heart from two pumps that have been functioning partly in parallel to two pumps performing in series.
3. Closure of the major fetal vascular channels (umbilical vessels, ductus venosus, ductus arteriosus, and foramen ovale). Their different closure rates permit smooth alterations in size and direction of shunts, should the delicate balance of pressure and resistance become upset.
4. A highly responsive pulmonary vascular bed capable of vigorous constriction in response to a decrease in O_2 or to acidosis.
5. High though declining pulmonary vascular resistance and pressure, with increasing pulmonary blood flow.
6. Rising systemic vascular resistance and pressure.
7. Higher cardiac output than in the adult, in combination with a high O_2 consumption (4.6 ml/kg per min in a neutral thermal environment).
8. Thicker right than left ventricular wall.
9. Multiple hemodynamic effects if significant changes in blood volume occur at birth.[221]

3.1. Aeration at Birth

The first breath of air must overcome the counterforces of surface tension, viscosity of fluid in the airway, and tissue resistance. During vaginal delivery with cephalic presentation, the thorax is subjected to pressures up to 95 cm H_2O. On crowning, some fluid is probably expressed from the lungs. There is then an elastic recoil of the thorax that results in aeration of at least the upper part of the respiratory tract. This passive process results in replacement of the expressed fluid by 7–42 ml of air. Active inspiration of 30–70 ml is achieved by diaphragmatic contraction, and most of this first inspired air remains to form part of the residual volume of the lungs, which amounts to 20–30 ml of the first expiration. This volume increases with subsequent breaths, and the functional residual capacity is 17 ml/kg body weight at 10 min, about twice this 20 min later, and shows no further increase during the week.[78,109]

Judging by cineroentgenograms before and after the first breath, little change seems to occur in the size or shape of the thoracic cage and diaphragm,[121] and the lungs appear well aerated one-third of a second after introduction of air.[69] These findings accord with the view that initial aeration consists largely of replacement of lung fluid by air.

In the healthy term newborn rabbit, wet weight determinations of the lungs show that resorption of pulmonary fluid begins 15 min postpartum and is largely complete during the first 4 hr of extra-uterine life. Moreover, roentgenograms of the chest (in this species) suggest that the position of the ribs shifts within the first 10 sec after onset of breathing, as though the lungs were hyperexpanded by a mixture of air and unresorbed fetal pulmonary fluid.[85] Histological studies likewise indicate progressive alveolar expansion, which is not complete even at 24 hr of age.[84]

In the human infant, postnatal respiratory adaptation may follow a similar course, since thoracic gas volume is high shortly after birth, and there is a discrepancy between thoracic gas volume and functional residual capacity, which disappears more rapidly in term than in preterm infants. This discrepancy is ascribed to an initial phase of hyperexpansion of the lungs with air-trapping, and may result from collapse of small respiratory bronchioles or formation of stable bubbles in terminal air spaces.[12,146,197]

3.2. Respiration and Pulmonary Circulation

When breathing begins after birth, pulmonary blood flow in the lamb increases from about 35 to about 160 ml/kg per min because of a 5- to 10-fold reduction in pulmonary vascular resistance, i.e., from a prenatal level of about 1.6 to about 0.3 mm Hg/ml per kg.[57] The pulmonary circulation must then accept the entire right ventricular output, whereas prior to birth, it has received as little as 10% of total cardiac output. The greater part of the reduction in pulmonary vascular resistance is achieved by dilatation of thick-walled, small, muscular pulmonary arteries and arterioles consequent to the rise in P_{O_2} and fall in P_{CO_2} on ventilation with air. Thus, the effect of O_2 on the pulmonary vasculature is opposite to that on the ductus arteriosus and other vessels. Staub[192] showed with a rapid freezing technique that O_2 can diffuse from surrounding alveoli directly into the small pulmonary arterioles, but locally produced chemical mediators are also important, since a cuff of pulmonary parenchyma surrounding the arteriole is necessary for demonstration of the O_2 effect.[122]

It is uncertain as yet whether the mediator is bradykinin, but there is circumstantial evidence suggesting that it may be. In lambs, bradykinin produces dilatation of pulmonary vessels and constriction of the ductus arteriosus and umbilical vessels. Moreover, cord blood of the human newborn infant contains higher levels of bradykinin than the adult, as well as inactive kinin precursor and kinin-releasing enzyme.[130] Furthermore, high levels of bradykinin are found in left atrial blood samples of the fetal lamb when the lungs are inflated with O_2, but not with N_2, which would suggest that bradykinin is formed in the lungs.[91] Lauweryns and Peuskens[115] suggested that the argyrophil or Kultschitsky cell of the airway epithelium may be the site of production of kinins in the human infant.

Other factors also contribute to the reduction in pulmonary vascular resistance and increase in pulmonary flow on ventilation with air. For example, the production of a liquid–gas interface following replacement of liquid by air may produce vasodilatation and thereby reduce pulmonary vascular resistance, because vessels exposed to alveolar pressure may be pulled open by the surface tension of the alveolar lining layer. Some increase in pulmonary flow has also been shown to accompany the mechanical effect of ventilating the lung with gas and the normal expression of lung fluid during delivery.[84,107]

3.3. Placental Circulation

Numerous studies indicate that unless the umbilical cord is clamped immediately after birth, at which time the placenta contains about 125 ml of blood or 33% of the total blood volume, the placental circulation continues at a rapidly declining rate until the placenta separates, about 2–4 min after delivery (Fig. 11). Štembera et al.,[193] using thermodilution, found that about 75 ml/kg per min of blood is transferred to the infant during the first 30 sec after delivery. This volume amounts to transfer of about 15 ml of O_2 to the infant, at a time when O_2 consumption is about 20–30 ml/min, which may be needed prior to satisfactory establishment of pulmonary gas exchange. Likewise, in blood samples taken from the umbilical vein during the first 2–4 min after birth, O_2 saturation, O_2 tension, CO_2 tension, pH, and base excess remain largely unchanged despite simultaneous onset of respiration until there are clinical signs of placental separa-

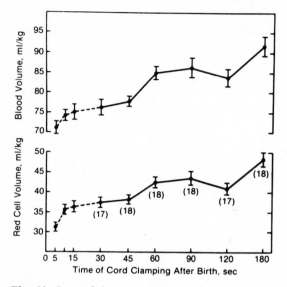

Fig. 11. Rate of placental transfusion in 106 healthy full-size infants delivered spontaneously with the cord clamped at different times after birth (means ± S.E.M.) The figures in parentheses are the numbers of infants in each group. Reproduced from Yao *et al.*[225]

tion.[67,126] This stability of blood gas and acid–base balance is interpreted by the authors as evidence of persistence of placental gas exchange.

Anatomic studies of umbilical vessels during the first 3 min after delivery with double clamping of the cord, a technique that largely reduces the artifact of postmortal contraction, have shown that the umbilical vein is still patent at 3 min, even if localized contractions appear earlier. They are more numerous and the degree of occlusion is greater in the arteries than in the vein.[140] The vascular contractions may have been accelerated, since all the mothers received methergine intravenously at the time of delivery.

Placental separation normally occurs at different times, depending on such factors as maternal analgesia, anesthesia, oxytocics, and mode of delivery. In one study, separation appeared to be impeded by immediate clamping of the cord,[212] since 5 mothers (9%) required manual removal of placental secundines, while no mother whose infant had late clamping developed this complication. Since the completeness with which the placenta is separated is determined both by how much of the subplacental area of the uterine wall is reduced and by the speed with which this reduction is accomplished, it is not surprising that the larger residue of blood in the placenta following early clamping should have this

effect. Similar findings have since been independently noted by Botha.[27]

Closure of umbilical vessels is achieved by multiple localized contractions to one side, which first take the form of slight indentations involving the surface of the cord. They rapidly deepen to form folds, but ultimate occlusion seems to depend primarily on diminution of blood flow[221] (Fig. 12). The exact mechanism of closure remains to be elucidated, but mechanical, thermal, and chemical stimuli, e.g. catecholamines acting directly on the cord vessels themselves, may be involved. Constriction of human cord vessels has also been noted in response to bradykinin and angiotension, trauma, adrenaline, histamine, and prostaglandins. Parasympathetic stimulants have no effect, while hypoxia results in prolonged pulsation of the cord, presumably because of low P_{O_2}, high P_{CO_2}, and low pH.[59] The role played by release of substances from the wall of the umbilical vessels or alterations in the complex mucoproteins in Wharton's jelly has yet to be determined.

Single umbilical artery occurs in about 1% of single and slightly more of multiple births. An atrophic remnant of the vessel is often present in the abdominal portion, and occasionally the entire iliac bed of the involved side is hypoplastic.[180]

Accessory vessels, which are probably remnants of vitelline vessels, though less commonly of the right umbilical vein, occur in about 5% of cords from normal singleton deliveries.[138] The vessel is usually paired, and both vessels, each measuring about 0.5 mm in diameter, lie close together between both arteries, occasionally near the surface of the cord. No significant anomalies have been detected in 16 infants (from a series of 310 consecutive deliveries) after a 2-year follow-up.

3.4. Foramen Ovale

At term, the foramen ovale measures 8 mm in diameter. On the left atrial side, it is loosely covered by the lower portion of the unresorbed septum primum, which acts as a one-way valve (valvula foraminis ovalis) permitting flow only from right to left (see Fig. 8). With the first breath, pulmonary vascular resistance decreases, and pulmonary venous flow to the left atrium increases. At the same time, umbilical blood flow ceases, inferior vena caval pressure falls, and the inferior vena caval–left atrial pressure difference is reversed. This pressure change is observed even if ventilation

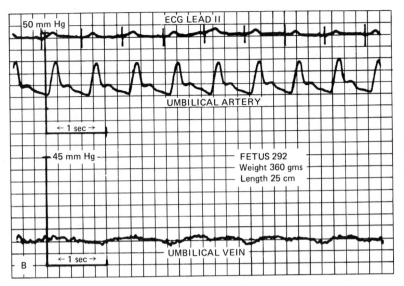

Fig. 12. (A) Angiographic demonstration of contractions in the umbilical vein of the human midterm fetus. (B) Pressure recordings in the umbilical vein and artery of a fetus weighing 360 g obtained with the fetus still *in utero* and the placenta *in situ*. Courtesy of Drs. T. Mohr and J. Lind. Reproduced from Walsh *et al.*[221] Courtesy of Charles C. Thomas, Publisher.

does not occur.[56] The valve then shuts, though incompletely, thereby balancing atrial intake and helping to accomplish a smooth transition from prenatal to postnatal life. All blood from the inferior vena cava and superior vena cava now enters the right atrium, right ventricle, and pulmonary artery, and pulmonary venous return increases.

Right-to-left shunting may normally persist during the first days of life,[92,119] and can be induced by any condition that causes an increase in pulmonary vascular resistance or interferes with pulmonary ventilation.

Left-to-right shunting through a stretched flap is sometimes seen in asphyxiated infants at birth,[106] and at times can be detected for several months after birth. Significant left-to-right shunts through the foramen ovale (with pulmonary/systemic flow ratios of as much as 2:1) occur in healthy infants, but their frequency is not known. This finding is not surprising, since in about 1 of every 5 fetuses and newborns, the edge of the septum secundum does not completely overlap the rather large ostium secundum that has developed in the septum primum.[142] This condition tends to become corrected during infancy.

3.5. Atrial Pressures

Before delivery, the mean pressure in the right atrium (of the lamb) is about 1 mm higher than in the left (right atrium 3.5 mm Hg, left atrium 2.5 mm Hg); after birth, the relationship reverses, and the pressure difference (in the human infant) may also be only about 1 mm Hg during the first minutes of life.[39] After the first 30 min of life, the pressure in the left atrium is always greater than in the right atrium. This is true of the mean pressures and the amplitude of the components; i.e., the gradient remains about 4 mm Hg between 30 min and 14 hr of age (the same as in the adult), but falls to

Table I. Atrial Pressures in 93 Normal Full-Size Infants Between 30 Minutes and 14 Hours of Age with Early and Late Clamping of the Cord[a]

Age group	Cord-clamping[b]	Hematocrit (mean ± S.E.)	Right atrial pressure (mm Hg)			Left atrial pressure (mm Hg)		
			Number of subjects	Mean ± S.E.	Range	Number of subjects	Mean ± S.E.	Range
<1 hour	Early	48.3 ± 2.0	8	0 ± 0.52	−2.0–2.0	6	4.2 ± 0.89	1.5– 7.0
	Late	54.3 ± 1.95	13	4.8 ± 0.73	−1.0–8.0	13	9.7 ± 0.71	7.0–12.0
1–3 hours	Early	49.4 ± 0.90	15	0.2 ± 1.2	−2.0–3.0	10	4.3 ± 0.42	2.0– 6.0
	Late	57.7 ± 1.88	11	1.0 ± 0.68	−2.0–5.0	10	5.7 ± 0.63	3.0– 9.0
3–6 hours	Early	48.3 ± 3.2	5	0 ± 0.27	−1.0–1.0	3	3.5 ± 1.43	1.0– 6.0
	Late	58.7 ± 1.27	16	1.8 ± 0.50	−1.0–6.5	11	5.0 ± 0.66	1.5– 9.0
>6 hours	Early	47.3 ± 4.6	5	−0.8 ± 0.25	−1.0–0	3	3.0 ± 1.14	1.0– 5.0
	Late	58.3 ± 1.11	19	0.2 ± 0.38	−1.5–4.0	16	4.6 ± 0.39	2.0– 8.0

[a] Modified from Arcilla et al.[4]

[b] Atrial pressures are higher in late-clamped infants, but the differences are statistically significant ($P < 0.001$) only during the first hour of life.

2 mm Hg at 24 hr of age. The difference in pressure gradient is not affected by the size of the placental transfusion, though the level of the pressures is. Thus, infants with stripped cords or late-clamped cords have high atrial pressures between 30 and 60 min of age (mean pressures: left atrium, 9.5 mm Hg; right atrium, 5 mm Hg), while those with early-clamped cords have comparatively low pressures (mean pressures: left atrium, 4 mm Hg; right atrium, 0 mm Hg)[4] (Table I). In both groups of infants, the configuration of the left atrial curve is characterized by tall v waves with rapid ascending and descending limbs and comparatively high x levels, while right atrial curves show low v waves and x levels (Fig. 13). The appearance of the curve permits recognition of the location of the catheter and suggests mitral regurgitation, but the majority of healthy newborn infants do not have an apical systolic murmur, though Burnard[37] has occasionally heard one. It has been suggested that the tall v wave may be due to the lower compliance of the left atrial chamber, which has to accommodate the large increase in pulmonary venous return.[4] The decline in mean atrial pressures after the first hour of life presumably indicates adaptation of the low-pressure reservoir to sudden functional expansion of the cardiovascular bed in combination with various readjustments, e.g., plasma shift to the extravascular tissues and regional redistribution of blood.

Although functional closure is a rapid process that may even occur with the first vigorous cry,[120] anatomic closure is a slow process that is only exceptionally complete at 3 months, and usually takes a year or more and often longer. Probe patency is seen in 50% of children up to 5 years of age, and in about 10–25% of adults.

3.6. Ductus Arteriosus

At term, the duct has an external diameter of 0.5–0.6 cm, a mean length of 1.25 cm,[34] and a mean internal circumference of about 1.1 cm.[58] Closure of the duct occurs in two stages: rapid constriction after birth, followed by anatomic obliteration over a period of weeks or months. Numerous studies have demonstrated that the duct constricts in response to a variety of stimuli, including normal breathing on delivery, inflation of the lungs with a gas mixture containing O_2, infusion of sympathetic amines in the presence of a constant arterial saturation, bradykinin, hemorrhage, and asphyxia (possibly by release of catecholamines), to name a few. But most workers agree that the duct constricts at birth primarily in response to a high P_{O_2}. Some *in vitro* evidence has been presented that the oxygen response may be mediated by acetylcholine and blocked by atropine.[149] Others have concluded from studies in the guinea pig that oxygen triggers constriction of ductal smooth muscle

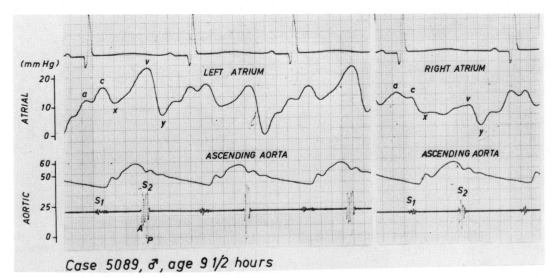

Case 5089, ♂, age 9 1/2 hours

Fig. 13. Relationship of phonocardiogram and ECG to atrial and aortic pressures. 100 mm/sec. Courtesy of Drs. R. A. Arcilla and J. Lind.

by increasing the rate of oxidative phosphorylation consequent to a direct effect on a terminal cytochrome component.[71] In the fetal lamb ductus, the oxygen response is not dependent on the presence of extrinsic nerves. In this species, the duct is rich in sympathetic nerve supply, and substantial amounts of norepinephrine exist in increasing concentration from its aortic to its pulmonary end.[105,185]

Constriction of adjacent vessels does not occur because they show a preponderance of elastic tissue in the media. Some ductal muscle may be incorporated into the wall of the aorta, however, and this tissue, at least in laboratory animals, responds in the same way as the duct to high P_{O_2}.

In experimental studies on newborn rats and rabbits *in vivo*, using the whole-body freezing technique, administration of prostaglandins effectively reopens the closing duct, whereas administration of prostaglandin synthetase inhibitor (indomethacin) contracts the duct. The mechanism is not understood,[181] and there is no such evidence

in the human. It is well known, however, that the constricted duct reopens in the human, and the "fetal pattern of circulation" may be reestablished if pulmonary vascular resistance increases as a result of hypoxia or hypercapnia. A variety of other conditions associated with hypoxemia, such as the respiratory distress syndrome, pulmonary atelectasis, birth and residence at high altitude, and premature delivery, are associated with delayed closure of the duct. Conversely, administration of 100% O_2 during the first 8 hr of life eliminates a left-to-right shunt.

Shunting of blood through the duct may be bidirectional during the first hours of life[106,177] (Figs. 14A, B), but is then usually left-to-right until the age of 15 hr, when flow ceases or is no longer physiologically significant. If pulmonary vascular resistance increases (cry, hypoxia), transient reversal of the shunt may ensue. The ability to tolerate a left-to-right shunt in infancy, judging by studies in dogs, may depend on the presence of normal sympathetic nervous system activity and of cate-

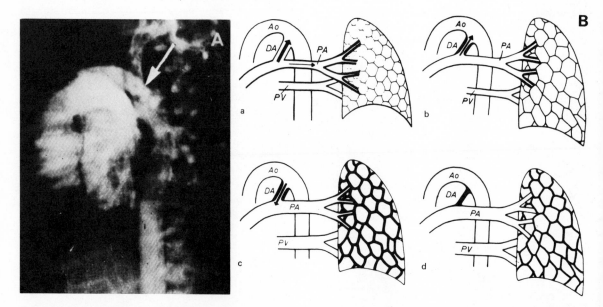

Fig. 14. (A) Transient right-to-left shunt through the ductus arteriosus in a healthy 6-hour-old infant with cyanotic lower extremities. Contrast medium is injected into the cubital vein, and the heart is seen in the right anterior oblique projection. The right atrium is opacified in diastole and the right ventricle in systole. The ductus arteriosus shunts contrast medium into the descending aorta from the trunk of the pulmonary artery. The ascending aorta is not visualized. Note the wide lumen of the duct (arrow). Only a small amount of medium is directed into the pulmonary arterial tree. Reproduced from Lind *et al.*[120] Courtesy of Charles C. Thomas, Publisher. (B) Schematic diagram showing how the size and direction of a shunt through the ductus arteriosus influence the pulmonary circulation. (a) Large right-to-left shunt, minimal pulmonary blood flow (PBF); (b) small right-to-left shunt, more PBF; (c) left-to-right shunt, large PBF; (d) duct closed, average PBF. Reproduced from Tähti *et al.*, 1968, *Ann. Paediatr. Fenn.* **14**:94.

cholamine release. Normal catecholamine levels improve ventricular contractility, lower left ventricular end-diastolic pressure, and favor normal pulmonary vessel maturation; low levels of catecholamines or inadequate myocardial response will have the opposite effects.[176]

In small animals (pig, guinea pig, rabbit, rat, and mouse), rapid whole-body freezing techniques show that complete occlusion of the duct is achieved not by intimal proliferation, but by central displacement of the tunica intima and the inner part of the tunica media.[100] In the human infant, however, closure is effected by a series of changes, including constriction of muscular elements of the media, dissociation of the intimal–medial junction, formation of cystlike accumulations of ground substance, whorl-like muscular nodules, and intimal folds,[137] followed by secondary changes, such as tears in the intima and necrosis, possibly because of interference with nutritional supply.[72] Thrombosis seldom occurs, and anatomic closure is entirely a process of growth by fibrous tissue.[60]

In various congenital lesions of the heart, survival depends on persistent patency of the ductus arteriosus. In pulmonary and tricuspid atresia, for instance, there is no pulmonary outflow from the right ventricle, and blood flows largely from the venae cavae into the right atrium and from there via the foramen ovale into the left atrium, left ventricle, and out into the aorta. Thus, the pulmonary circulation is supplied by blood flowing from left to right from the descending aorta through the ductus arteriosus. The diameter of the duct is probably markedly reduced in this condition because in fetal life it conducts only about 10% of the combined ventricular output, rather than the 50–60% it normally transports. In pulmonary and tricuspid atresia, however, death is often caused by constriction of the duct even when arterial tension is low, possibly because of release of circulating vasoactive substances in the severely hypoxemic infant or greater facility of the smaller diameter duct to occlude. Such infants may derive benefit from infiltration of a buffered formalin solution into the wall of the duct, which inhibits closure.[174] Infusion of prostaglandin E_1 directly into the aorta adjacent to the ductus arteriosis has also been reported to be of value.[89a]

In aortic atresia, there is no normal escape of blood from the left side of the heart, and the valve of the foramen ovale is usually herniated into the right atrium. Hence, a channel develops that permits passage of blood from the left to the right atrium.

Since the opening is often small, pulmonary venous obstruction tends to develop. In aortic atresia, the diameter of the duct may enlarge during fetal life because it carries a larger flow. Following birth, the duct may not close completely, possibly because of reduced sensitivity of the smooth muscle to oxygen tension or inability of a larger diameter duct to occlude completely.

3.7. Pulmonary Artery

At term birth, the main pulmonary artery is a relatively short, wide vessel with a length of about 1 cm and a mean internal diameter of about 6.7 mm that divides into two branches of almost equal size (mean internal diameter: left branch, 3.7 mm; right branch, 3.9 mm).[154] During the first months of life, the diameter of the trunk shows only a small increase in size, whereas the diameter of both branches enlarges, so that each is about three-fourths that of the main trunk. The discrepancy in size presumably arises during fetal life, because the entire right ventricular output enters the pulmonary trunk, but only a relatively small portion of it continues into the pulmonary branches, while the remainder bypasses the lungs by entering the ductus arteriosus. In some infants, a small pressure difference of 8–15 mm Hg has been detected between the main pulmonary trunk and its branches, which may give rise to a systolic murmur, suggesting the presence of peripheral stenosis of the pulmonary artery branches.

At birth, the wall of the pulmonary trunk and its main branches consists of concentrically arranged overlapping sheets of elastic membranes (lamellae) that alternate with thin layers of smooth musculature. Unlike the wall of the aorta, the membranes are fewer and less regular on cross section. During infancy, the membranes spread apart. On tangential sections, they are seen to have a starlike form.[137] Thus, the preformed elastic tissue does not become fragmented, an impression derived from cross sections that show sticklike elastic fibrils, but rather the initial tight lamellar structure assumes a looser structural pattern, a change that may be the counterpart of the postnatal rearrangement of the musculature in the heart with slower growth of the right ventricle.[106]

The trunk of the pulmonary artery with its main branches is regarded as an elastic artery, but it also contains a considerable amount of muscle, which is capable of producing a significant reduction in the intraarterial diameter, a response that has been elicited by hypoxia in the newborn piglet.[169]

After midgestation, the elastic structure of the pulmonary artery extends to the same level within the lung as in the adult. In contrast, the change from muscular to partially muscular and non-muscular arteries of the pulmonary arterial bed occurs more proximally in the fetus and term infant than in the adult. Thus, in the fetus, there is no muscle within pulmonary arterial walls beyond the level of the terminal bronchiolus, whereas in the adult, muscle extends to the level of the alveolus. In the opinion of Hislop and Reid,[94] children may respond less to hypoxia because they may have fewer muscle cells in direct contact with alveoli.

3.8. Pulmonary Pressures

Although the decrease in pulmonary vascular resistance following aeration is immediate and probably due to the combined effects of increased arterial P_{O_2} and release of bradykinin,[130] the fall in pulmonary arterial pressures is not. The major decline in pressure occurs during the first 2 or 3 days of life, but during the first 60 min, pulmonary arterial pressures equal or exceed those in the aorta in about 50% of subjects.[177] Between 2 and 4 hr of age, pulmonary arterial pressures begin to diverge from systemic values. During the first day, the rate of decline is influenced to a considerable extent by both the amount of the placental transfusion and the left–to–right shunt through the ductus arteriosus, factors that seem to be partly interrelated, since infants who receive a small placental transfusion probably have earlier closure of the duct.[213] Thus, infants with immediate clamping of the cord may have pulmonary arterial pressures as low as 70% of aortic pressures at 2 hr of age and 50% at 4 hr, while infants with late clamping have pulmonary pressures of about 90% of aortic during the first 9 hr.[5] In the presence of elevated pulmonary vascular resistance and pressure, an increased hematocrit in itself may produce a further rise in pressure.[151]

Human infants living at sea level often attain adult levels of mean pulmonary arterial pressure of about 15 mm Hg by 6 weeks of age. This subsequent more gradual decline shows considerable individual variation and appears to parallel the involutionary changes taking place in the walls of the small pulmonary arteries and arterioles. Either hypoxemia or acidosis alone elevates pressures in the pulmonary artery by causing vasoconstriction; together, the effects are greatly enhanced. The responsiveness of pulmonary vessels decreases after birth with regression of the muscular layer.

Infants born at high altitude show an amount of smooth muscle in their pulmonary arterioles similar to that in infants born at sea level. The reason is probably that the human fetus at high altitude has an internal environment in which the oxygen pressure is not very different from that of the fetus at sea level (P_{O_2} 19 mm Hg vs. 22 mm Hg).[189] The fetus at high altitude subsequently tends to retain some degree of pulmonary hypertension and increased pulmonary vascular resistance, presumably because the dramatic decrease in pulmonary vascular resistance after birth is principally due to the local vasodilator action of an increased P_{O_2}, and any condition that interferes with normal oxygenation, such as a low environmental O_2 consequent to high altitude, will delay the normal decrease in pulmonary vascular resistance and regression of smooth muscle in these vessels. If the infant is brought down to sea level, pulmonary vascular resistance falls within a week or two. Residence at high altitude at the time of birth in combination with a persistent left–to–right shunt causes an additional delay in regression of the smooth muscle. Hence, infants with these lesions who reside at high altitude have higher pulmonary vascular resistance and pulmonary arterial pressures than those with comparable lesions who reside at sea level.

At times, pulmonary vascular resistance remains elevated after birth in the presence of comparatively increased thickness for age of the smooth muscle layer of the pulmonary arterioles. Right-to-left shunts through the foramen ovale and ductus arteriosus then persist, and relief may be obtained by administration of O_2 and correction of metabolic acidosis with intravenous buffers. Such findings have been noted in infants with the atypical respiratory distress syndrome, hyperviscosity, and hypoglycemia. An idiopathic type has also been noted, and has usually been associated with perinatal stress accompanied by hypoxia.[41,76,117,184]

3.9. Aorta

At birth, the aorta is about 12.5 cm long, as measured on angiograms from the summit of the aortic arch to the bifurcation,[221] and has a mean internal diameter of 6.0 mm at the aortic outlet,

5.75 mm in the descending aorta, and 4.3 mm in the isthmus, which is located about 1 cm distal to the origin of the left subclavian artery.[154] The isthmus may take about 4 months to acquire the same diameter as the thoracic aorta.

The discrepancy in size of the isthmus is due to the comparatively small amount of blood entering this segment during fetal life.

At birth, the histological appearance of the wall of the aorta resembles that of the pulmonary trunk, but it is somewhat thicker because of a greater number of longer, more regularly disposed, concentrically arranged, overlapping sheets of elastic membranes (lamellae) that alternate with interlamellar zones. The interlamellar zones contain ground substance rich in mucopolysaccharides, elastic fibers, muscle cells, and some fine collagenous fibers interlinked in a three-dimensional network. During the first months of life, the aortic wall, unlike the pulmonary arterial wall, increases markedly in thickness while retaining its structural pattern. The histological resemblance between the two vessels at birth diminishes successively as a result of characteristic changes in the pulmonary artery (see Section 3.7).

3.10. Systemic Pressures

At birth, systemic arterial pressure does not change significantly after the first breath despite the sudden increase in pulmonary circulation. After about 10–15 min, systemic pressure gradually decreases over the next few hours from a mean of about 80 mm Hg (in late-clamped term infants) to a mean of about 65 mm Hg; it then gradually increases during the rest of the first week of life to the same or even higher values (Fig. 15). Early-clamped infants show lower initial values, i.e., about 60–65 mm Hg during the first 3 hr of life, followed by a similar rise during the week. Term infants delivered by cesarean section show about the same pattern as early-clamped infants, since their cords are also clamped early. Infants of lower birth weight have lower pressure. Mild hypoxemia has a variable effect on blood pressure, while severe hypoxia induces a decrease.

Systemic blood flow is low on the first day of life (1.96 liters/min per M²) and increases on the second or third day (3.54 liters/min per M²), primarily because of closure of the ductus arteriosus. Mean systemic vascular resistance is 30 P.R.U. (1 P.R.U. = 80 dynes sec · cm⁻⁵) on the first day, which is higher than that reported for normal

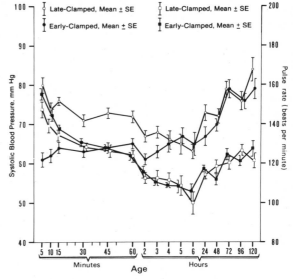

Fig. 15. Serial determination of heart rate (lower curves) and blood pressure in 25 early-clamped and 25 late-clamped full-size infants during the first 5 days of life. The heart rate falls rapidly during the first 6 hours of life, and then gradually rises again to somewhat lower values than initially. Blood pressure shows a similar fall in late-clamped infants, followed by a gradual rise. Reproduced (with modifications) from Oh *et al.*, 1966, The circulatory and respiratory adaptation to early and late cord clamping in newborn infants, *Acta Paediatr. Scand.* **55**:17.

children, and declines to a mean of 20 P.R.U. on the second day, consequent to the comparatively greater increase in systemic flow than in systemic arterial pressure[6] (Fig. 16).

Celander[45] reported studies of peripheral blood flow in newborns, using occlusion plethysmography. He found that blood flow in the extremities is greater and resistance to flow less in the newborn than in adults. This difference is even more evident in infants of low birth weight. Both the asphyxiated newborn and the healthy newborn exposed to hypoxia, however, have increased peripheral resistance, while reactive hyperemia results in a considerable increase in resting blood flow. The peripheral blood flow for the foot and calf normally ranges from 5 to 10 ml/min per 100 g tissue.[45,166] Experimental production of hypovolemia corresponding to a 15% reduction of total blood volume causes a 2-fold increase in resistance to blood flow in the calf.[207] Thus, peripheral vasomotor tone adequately controls systemic blood pressure by decreasing perfusion of the vascular compartments

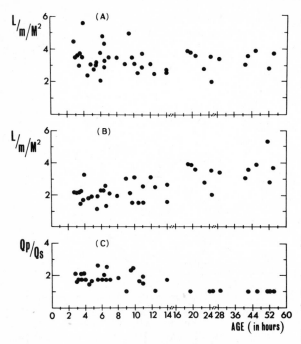

Fig. 16. Scattergram of (A) pulmonary blood flow index, (B) systemic blood flow index, and (C) pulmonary flow ratio according to age. Note the tendency of the systemic blood flow to increase. After Arcilla *et al.*[6]

in the calf muscle and is not accompanied by any change in cutaneous blood flow. The ensuing rapid decrease in arterial hematocrit represents an effort to restore plasma volume.

During the first feeding at 30 min of age, however, calf perfusion falls to an average of about 50% of control values, and at about 1½–3 hr after the meal, it rises to about 50% above control values. The initial fall in perfusion is due solely to increased regional vascular resistance, since blood pressure is not affected.[226] Postprandial vasoconstriction in the lower limb appears to be unique to the newborn, since it has not been reported in adult man or in other species. The early circulatory demand provoked by feeding may be relatively greater in the newborn than in the adult, and seems to be achieved partly at the expense of lower limb perfusion.

These studies of hypovolemia and other studies of regional blood flow in the newborn have shown that cutaneous perfusion[35] and limb perfusion[46] are subject to vasomotor control and respond, for the most part, in a manner similar to that in the adult.

3.11. Cardiac Output

Scanty information is available on cardiac output in the human newborn. Available measurements may also not be accurate because of the presence of shunts through the foramen ovale, ductus arteriosus, and bronchial vessels, and various factors associated with delivery (maternal analgesia or anesthesia, mode of delivery, amount of placental transfusion, and body temperature). Nevertheless, all estimates indicate that cardiac output is 2–3 times greater per unit body weight than in the adult. In the newborn infant, this difference may be partly due to the high metabolic rate in the postnatal period (Table II).

3.12. Heart Size

Toward the latter part of gestation, the right ventricle starts to grow faster than the left, and at term its mass equals or exceeds that of the left ventricle by as much as 25%.[64,101]

This view was recently challenged by Hislop and Reid,[93] who found, using the method of dissection of Fulton *et al.*,[75] that right ventricular weight never exceeds that of the left.

After birth, left ventricular weight increases rapidly, while right ventricular weight does not. The increase in *left* ventricular weight during the first months of life is accompanied by doubling of the muscle fiber nuclei, a 50% increase in myocardial blood flow, and a rise in RNA concentration (equivalent to new tissue formation). The rapid increase in left ventricular weight, among other changes, presumably occurs in response to the rising systemic vascular resistance and pressure.

In contrast, right ventricular weight after birth may actually decrease by as much as 20% (about 1 g) during the first month of life because of the fall in right ventricular and pulmonary arterial pressure, the fall in pulmonary vascular resistance, and closure of the ductus arteriosus. The decrease in right ventricular weight is accompanied by a decrease in fiber diameter without evidence of degeneration, no rise in RNA concentration, a decrease in myocardial blood flow, and doubling of the right ventricular cavity size during the first month. By 6 months but not later than 10 months of age, adult ventricular weight relationships are attained.

3.13. Heart Volume

Heart volume normally increases between 15 and 30 min of life and then decreases from a mean of 48

Table II. Cardiac Output in 110 Healthy Infants from 0 to 2 Days of Age[a]

References	No.	Age (hr)	LVO[b] (liters/min per m²)	RVO[b] (liters/min per m²)	Notes
Prec and Cassels[160]	10	2–26	2.500 ± .825	2.500 ± .825 (S.D.)	Indicator injection (Evans blue) in umbilical vein and recording through earpiece oximeter.
Gessner et al.[77]	14	0–2	3.900 ± .746	2.500 ± .410 (S.D.)	Indicator injection (Cardiogreen) in left atrium and sampling from aorta ($K^c = 0.34$).
Burnard et al.[40]	18	1–28	5.700 ± .700	3.830 ± .720 (S.D.)	Thermodilution. Oxygen consumption values increased.
Arcilla et al.[6]	45	2–54	3.350 ± .267	2.450 ± .251 (S.E.)	Indicator injection (Cardiogreen) in left atrium and sampling from aorta ($K^c = 0.25$).
Emmanouilides et al.[65]	23	6–35	4.070 ± .268	3.100 ± .175 (S.E.)	Indicator injection (Cardiogreen) in left atrium and sampling from aorta ($K^c = 0.34$).

[a] Modified from Emmanouilides et al.[65]
[b] LVO: Left ventricular output; RVO: right ventricular output.
[c] K: Factor relating forward triangle portion of primary curve to its total area.

ml to 37 ml at the end of the first week.[39,110,119] This decrease corresponds to a mean reduction of about 25%. These differences presumably reflect alterations in expansion of the cavities of the heart. With cessation of the placental circulation, there occurs an immediate decrease in blood volume corresponding to the amount left in the placenta. A further reduction occurs during the first hours of life consequent to hemoconcentration. Since heart volume varies directly with blood volume and body weight, higher values are noted in infants with late clamping or stripping of the cord and in the plethoric twin in the parabiotic syndrome, while lower values are noted in infants of low birth weight and with early clamping, e.g., after cesarean section. The heart size of infants with pulmonary atelectasis and asphyxia also tends to be greater than that of the healthy neonate during the first days of life,[39,128] presumably because of cardiac dilatation.

3.14. Baroreceptor and Chemoreceptor Reflexes

There is considerable evidence that the sinoaortic baroreceptor and chemoreceptor reflexes (peripheral and central) are active in the newborn infant.

The *baroreceptors* are located in the adventitia of the aortic arch and the carotid bifurcations. They are stimulated by acute changes of blood pressure induced by abrupt changes in blood volume (hypo-, hypervolemia), intrathoracic pressure (onset of respiration, crying, Valsalva), posture (head-up tilting), and carotid sinus massage, and therefore play a role in regulation of the cerebral circulation. The receptors inhibit activity of the cardioaccelerator and vasoconstrictor centers and allow unopposed action of the cardioinhibitor centers. This effect results in peripheral vasodilatation and a fall in heart rate and blood pressure (Table III).

The *chemoreceptors* are located below the aortic arch between the aorta and pulmonary trunk (*aortic bodies*), at the bifurcation of each common carotid artery (*carotid bodies*), and close to the origins of the ninth and tenth cranial nerves in the ventrolateral medulla (*central* chemoreceptors). The peripheral chemoreceptors (aortic and carotid bodies) are stimulated by decreases in arterial P_{O_2} or blood flow and increases in arterial P_{O_2} and $[H^+]$. They therefore serve to reduce the effects of anoxia and may cause the first gasp. They are active at least from 28 weeks' gestation, and are probably not important in triggering periodic breathing or apnea in preterm infants.[165] The central chemoreceptors are discussed in detail in Chapter 6.

Table III. Summary of Baroceptor, Chemoreceptor, and Other Reflexes[a]

Reflex	Site of receptors	Afferent nerve supply	Stimulus	Response	Maturity at birth
Baroreceptors	*Carotid sinus:* carotid bifurcation	Sinus branch of glosso-pharyngeal			
	Aortic: aortic arch	Aortic nerve branch of vagus	Increased stretch (pressure)	Bradycardia; hypotension; apnea	Mature
	Common carotid: between subclavian and superior thyroid artery	Aortic nerve branch of vagus			
Chemoreceptors Peripheral	*Carotid body:* bifurcation between internal and external carotid arteries	Sinus nerve branch of glosso-pharyngeal	Anoxia; hypercapnia; increased $[H+]$; decreased blood flow	Increased ventilation; bradycardia; peripheral vasoconstriction; increased bronchiolar tone; increased pulmonary vascular resistance; increased activity of adrenal medulla and of motor cortex	Mature
	Aortic body: aortic arch	Aortic nerve branch of vagus		Increased ventilation; tachycardia; peripheral vasoconstriction and hypertension; increased pulmonary vascular resistance	
Central	Ventrolateral medulla	?	Increased CO_2; increased $[H+]$	Increased ventilation	Mature
Other reflexes Cough	Larynx and trachea	Vagus	Irritation	Cough; bronchoconstriction	Mature
Vascular	Right and left atrium "A"	Vagus	Increased pressure		?
	Right and left atrium "B" (close to great veins)	Vagus	Increased volume	Bradycardia; hypotension	?
	Pulmonary artery: main pulmonary artery	Vagus	Increased pressure		?

[a] Modified from Brady and Tooley.[31]

Table III. Continued

Reflex	Site of receptors	Afferent nerve supply	Stimulus	Response	Maturity at birth
	Small pulmonary artery	Vagus	?	?	?
	Ventricular: wall of right and left ventricles	Vagus	Increased pressure	Bradycardia; hypotension	?
	Coronary: main coronary arteries	Vagus	Increased mean pressure	Bradycardia; hypotension	?

8.15. Electrocardiogram of the Full-Size Infant

Although ECGs have been recorded in infants since 1908, most studies have either not been serial or not been carried out immediately after birth, or else the data have not been evaluated statistically or the effects of some of the multiple factors involved in delivery have not been considered. Other parameters that might help in the interpretation of the ECG have also not been recorded. Partly for these reasons, the assessment of a single tracing, particularly in the newborn period, often provides little information, and the range of normal variation appears wide. It is true that in no equally brief span of existence do such profound alterations and adjustments occur as in the weeks, days, or hours following birth, but if such variables as maternal analgesia and anesthesia, type of delivery, blood volume, and time and type of feedings are controlled, normal variation may be reduced, and more meaningful baseline values should become available.

It has been appreciated only recently that a placental transfusion significantly augments the blood volume of the neonate and affects hemodynamic adaptation to extrauterine life.[187,203] Recent serial longitudinal studies in a group of optimally healthy infants show that placental transfusion is indeed an important variable for understanding early electrocardiographic changes.[216-218]

8.15.1. Findings in Late-Clamped Infants

In late-clamped (LC) infants (about 3–5 min after delivery), a continuing series of electrocardiographic changes is seen during the first week of life. These changes occur at different rates, but most intervals and deflections appear to be affected. The most striking changes are transient, being present primarily during the first 30–60 min of life.

The heart rate increases on crowning, if the mother receives minimal analgesia or anesthesia or both, and then starts to decrease. Some beat-to-beat variation is normally present. Electrocardiographic intervals are prolonged, e.g., P wave duration, QRS, S–T segment, and Q–T intervals (Fig. 17). The amplitude of QRS deflections is increased, especially in leads reflecting right ventricular potential, while the incidence of Q waves in left precordial leads is low (Fig. 17). T waves are positive and of good amplitude in *all* precordial leads.

After a few hours, the heart rate decreases and shows only a small increase after a cry. Intervals are considerably shorter (P duration, P–R interval, QRS). The amplitude of QRS deflections has decreased in most precordial leads. The incidence of Q waves in left precordial leads has increased. T waves are now more positive in right and isoelectric or inverted in left precordial leads.

On the 2nd and 3rd days of life, the heart rate slowly increases again. The amplitudes of QRS deflections may increase in midprecordial leads. T waves now become positive in left precordial leads (usually on the 2nd day) and negative in right precordial leads (the majority on the 3rd day).

At the end of the week, the mean heart rate has increased slightly, and shows a much larger increase after a cry (Fig. 18). Intervals have further decreased in duration (P duration, P–R, S–T, Q–T, Q–Tc). The amplitude of QRS deflections in *left* precordial leads has increased, and in most other leads has decreased. The incidence of Q waves in left

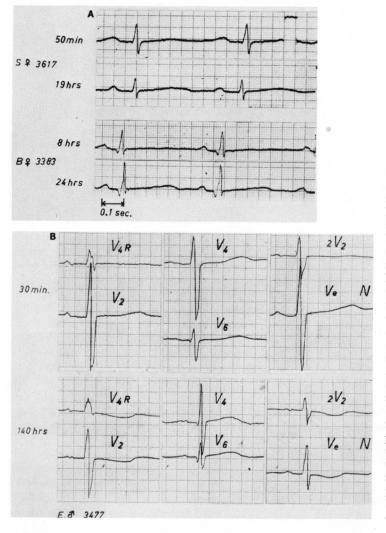

Fig. 17 (A) Top: Lead II recorded at 5 min and at 19 hr after birth in a healthy infant with a birth weight of 3350 g. The heart rate has increased only slightly, but the P wave duration and PR interval have both decreased with age. Bottom: Lead II recorded at 8 hr and at 24 hr in a healthy infant with a birth weight of 3030 g. The heart rate has increased only slightly, and the P wave duration and PR interval have remained unchanged. In other words, both the P wave duration and the PR interval are prolonged in infants less than 1 hr of age. Paper speed 100 mm/sec. (Numbers in figure refer to infants' hospital numbers. After Walsh.[210]) (B) Tracings recorded at 30 min and at 140 hr after birth. Note the initial tiny Q and dominant S in lead V_6 comparatively high amplitude QRS deflections, and positive T waves in 4 of the precordial leads are inverted. Birth weight the QRS deflections are lower, the amplitude of the Q in V_6 is deeper, the R wave in V_6 is now dominant, and T waves in right precordial leads are inverted. Birth weight 3650 g. Paper speed 100 mm/sec. Reproduced from Walsh.[210]

precordial leads has increased further (Fig. 17 and Table IV).

In the case of the P and P–R intervals, the decreases in duration are independent of changes in heart rate except during the first hour of life. In the case of the S–T segment and Q–T interval, further decreases during the week are related to the heart rate, but the relationship to the rate alters; i.e., the slope of the regression line flattens. Hence, at the end of the week, a faster rate is needed to obtain the same duration interval as on the first day.

3.15.2. Findings in Early-Clamped Infants

In early-clamped infants (EC), those with clamping

within 4 sec of delivery of the feet, the ECG also shows a continuous series of changes, but the pattern of change differs somewhat from that encountered in LC infants. EC infants have a somewhat slower and narrower range of heart rate during the first few hours of life and a greater increase in rate after a cry than LC infants, regardless of the prestimulus level. They also have shorter intervals (P duration, P–R segment, P–R interval, QRS duration, Q–Tc), lower deflections (PII, QV_6, RV_6, SV_6, TV_1), earlier inversion of the T wave in V_1, and a higher T wave in V_6 on the first day of life. The T wave differences are still significant on the 2nd day of life, and the P wave differences are significant even at the end of the week. As in LC infants, the rate response

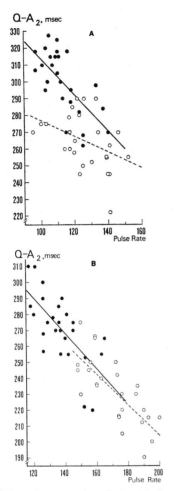

Fig. 18. Effect of cry on the relationship between heart rate and the Q–A$_2$ interval in the same healthy full-size infants examined between 1 and 4 hr of age (○) and again at the end of the week (●). (A) With infants half asleep, the slope of the regression line is seen to be considerably flatter at the end of the week (●) than during the first hours of life (○). (B) After a cry, the slopes of the regression lines are almost identical on both examinations. Reproduced from Walsh and Gyulai.[220]

to a cry increases during the week, and no significant difference is present at the end of the week (Table V).[213,216,220]

3.15.3. Findings in Stripped-Cord Infants

If the transfusion is hastened by firmly milking the cord toward the infant, the pattern of change in electrocardiographic findings during the week resembles that seen in LC infants,[214] because blood

volume is not further increased.[203] Thus, infants with stripped cords have longer intervals (P, P–R, Q–Tc); higher amplitude P waves in lead II; lower R/S ratios in V$_1$ and V$_6$, because of lower amplitude R waves; and delayed inversion of the T wave in V$_1$ (Fig. 19). The infant may briefly show some ill effects from the accelerated transfer of blood, however, such as cyanosis, irritability, and tachypnea.

3.16. Electrocardiogram of the Healthy Low-Birth-Weight Infant During the First Year of Life

3.16.1. ECG Features During the First Week of Life

During the first week of life, the ECG of the healthy low-birth-weight infant is characterized by the following features: a fast, labile heart rate that rises to 200 beats/min or more, with minor stimuli, falls to 100 beats/min, or less, during sleep, and shows an inverse correlation with the Q–T interval, but no correlation with the P, P–R, or QRS intervals; short P, P–R, and QRS intervals; depressed S–T junction, particularly in leads Ve,★ V$_1$, and V$_2$; short S–T segment; relatively long Q–T interval, especially in infants weighing less than 1500 g at birth; short or absent T–P segment; a very wide range of QRS axis deviation in the frontal plane (from −82° to 210°), and less right-axis deviation than in full-term infants; peaked P waves, especially in leads Ve and V$_2$ (Fig. 20); a lower incidence of Q waves in leads Ve and V$_4$R than in full-size infants; lower amplitude P, Q, R, S, and T waves in most leads than in full-size infants (Fig. 20); and bizarre, scooped-out T waves, a characteristic that shows no correlation with serum K and Na levels (Tables VI–VIII).[218]

Comment: Some of these characteristics are apparent on inspection of tracings and on comparison of measurements with those of full-term infants.

3.16.2. Significant ECG Changes from 1–4 Weeks to 6–12 Months

Subsequent changes during the first year of life may be summarized as follows: the heart rate continues to be labile during the first 2 months of life; P wave duration more than doubles during the first year, so that most infants have values between

★ Recorded from the tip of the sternal xyphoid process.

Table IV. Electrocardiographic Intervals in Healthy Infants on the First and on the Fifth or Sixth Days of Life[a]

Interval	Day	Group[b]	No.	Milliseconds Mean ± S.D.	S.E.	Range
PII duration	1	A	38	68 ± 10	1.62	45–90
		B	30	59 ± 13	2.45	25–100
		A	38	51 ± 7	1.14	40–65
	5–6	B	30	49 ± 8	1.48	30–65
P–RII segment	1	A	38	50 ± 15	2.43	20–90
		B	30	47 ± 14	2.57	25–105
		A	38	48 ± 9	1.52	25–70
	5–6	B	30	49 ± 13	2.33	30–70
P–RII interval	1	A	38	119 ± 19	3.06	90–160
		B	30	107 ± 12	2.21	85–150
	5–6	A	38	96 ± 29	4.68	80–130
		B	30	99 ± 18	3.35	70–140
QRS(V) interval[c]	1	A	38	55 ± 5	0.83	45–70
		B	29	52 ± 6	1.17	40–65
	5–6	A	38	52 ± 5	0.81	40–60
		B	30	53 ± 6	1.08	40–60
$Q–RV_1$ interval	1	A + B	67	20 ± 5	0.59	10–35
	5–6	A + B	68	20.5 ± 5	0.63	10–35
$Q–RV_6$ interval	1	A + B	67	21 ± 6.5	0.82	10–30
	5–6	A + B	68	21 ± 5	0.61	5–30
Q–TII interval	1	A + B	66	290 ± 33	4.06	210–380
	5–6	A + B	68	270 ± 19	2.30	220–310
Q–TcII interval	1	A + B	66	450 ± 45	5.54	340–540
	5–6	A + B	68	430 ± 25	3.03	370–490

[a] From Walsh.[213a]

[b] Group A: infants initially examined at 1 hr or less; Group B: infants initially examined at more than 1 hr.

[c] Differences significant only when findings in infants less than 30 min of age are compared with those in infants more than $4\frac{1}{4}$ hr of age.

45 and 65 msec at the end of the year; the P–R interval shows a small increase in duration, and most infants have values between 95 and 120 msec at the end of the year; the QRS interval increases in duration, and 95% of infants have values between 45 and 65 msec at the end of the year; the Q–R interval in lead V_6 increases to a maximum of 30 msec and in V_6R to a maximum of 40 msec at the end of the year; the Q–T interval shows no increase in median or range from the age of 2 days to the end of the year, when the median is 260 msec (range 230–310 msec), presumably because the interval is prolonged out of proportion to heart rate until the age of 3 months; and the percentage of infants with

a normal QRS axis in the frontal plane increases from 25% at 1–4 weeks to 85% at 6–12 months. P wave amplitude does not increase in any lead. Q wave amplitude increases in leads III, V_6, and V_6R to a maximum of 1.1 mV in lead III. Values of 0.6–0.8 mV are not uncommon. Such amplitudes are often seen with large-amplitude R and T waves. Q waves with an amplitude greater than 25% of the R wave in lead III, i.e., a finding that occurs in a substantial proportion of patients with clinical or pathologic evidence of myocardial infarction, are present in two-thirds of infants during the first 18 months of life. The incidence of this finding increases during the year. R wave amplitude increases

Table V. Comparison of Electrocardiographic Changes During the First Week in Healthy Early- and Late-Clamped Infants[a]

Parameter	Early-clamped infants	Late-clamped infants
Heart rate	Decreases immediately after birth; increases slowly during the week.	Decreases immediately after birth to a slightly faster rate; increases slowly during the week
	Range narrower first few hours after birth in EC infants. Cry stimulus causes greater increase on day 1 in EC infants.	
P duration	Decreases during the week.	Decreases during the week.
	Shorter on day 1 in EC infants.	
P–R segment	Increases during the week.	Shows no change in ≈75%; decreases in ≈25%.
	Shorter on day 1 in EC infants.	
P–R interval	Shows no change.	Decreases during the week.
	Shorter on day 1 in EC infants.	
QRS interval	Shows no change.	Decreases during first hours.
	Shorter on day 1 in EC infants.	
Q–Tc interval	Decreases during the week.	Decreases during the week.
	Shorter on day 1 in EC infants.	
QRS axis (F[b])	Shows no change.	Shows no change.
	No significant difference.	
P amplitude	Decreases during the week.	Shows slight increase during the week.
	Lower throughout the week in EC infants.	
RV_1	Decreases during the week.	Decreases during the week.
	No significant difference.	
SV_1	Decreases after 3 hr.	Decreases during the week.
	No significant difference.	
TV_1	Inverts usually after 24 hr.	Inverts usually after 48 hr.
	More negative on day 2 in EC infants.	
QV_6	Increases during the week.	Increases during the week.
	Lower on day 1 in EC infants.	
RV_6	Increases during the week.	Increases during the week.
	Lower on day 1 in EC infants.	
SV_6	Shows no change.	Decreases during the week.
	Lower on day 1 in EC infants.	
TV_6	Increases during the week.	Increases during the week.
	More positive on day 2 in EC infants.	

[a] From Walsh.[217]
[b] (F) Frontal plane.

significantly in all leads other than aVR, V_1, Ve, $2V_1$ and $2V_2$ (the latter two leads are recorded from the second intercostal space at the right and left sternal border). V_4R is the only lead in which a significant decrease in amplitude has been observed. S wave amplitude increases significantly in aVR and right precordial leads V_4R, V_6R, $2V_1$, and $2V_2$; decreases in leads V_8 and Ve; and shows no change in lead V_1. A dominant S wave in V_6 or V_8 or both is very uncommon after the age of 1 month (Table VIII). T wave amplitude increases in all leads except III, V_8, Ve, V_4R, and V_6R. Some very high ampli-

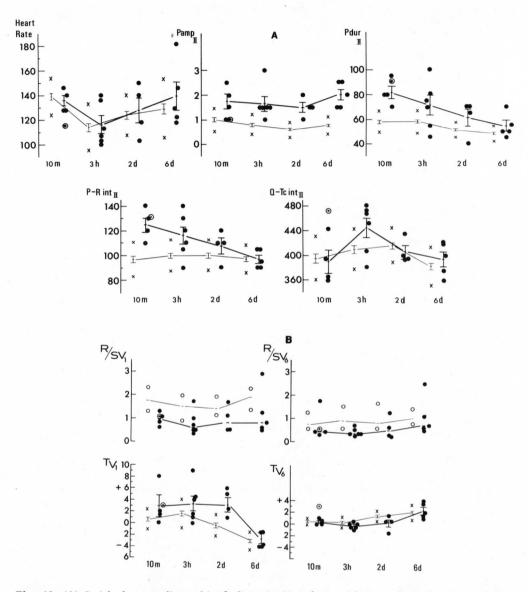

Fig. 19. (A) Serial electrocardiographic findings in 31 infants with immediate clamping of the cord (light lines) and in 6 infants with vigorous stripping of the cord (heavy lines) during the first week of life. Means ±S.E. (vertical brackets) and S.D. (X) are shown. Note the higher P amplitude (Pamp) and longer P–R and Q–Tc intervals, particularly on the first day of life, in infants with cord-stripping. ⊙ Individual values in infants with cord-stripping; a 45-min-old infant is not included in the mean. (All the infants had all the examinations.) Reproduced from Walsh.[214] (B) R/S and T in leads V_1 and V_6 in 31 infants with immediate clamping of the cord (light lines) and in 6 infants with stripping of the cord (heavy lines) during the first week of life. The median (lines) and quartiles (○) are shown in early-clamped infants and the median (lines) and individual values (●) in stripped-cord infants for the R/S; the mean, S.E., and S.D. are shown for the T wave. Note the lower R/S ratios and delayed inversion of T_{V_1} in infants with cord-stripping. Reproduced from Walsh.[214]

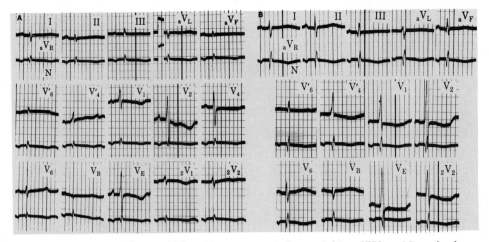

Fig. 20. (A) Tracing from a 13-hr-old premature infant weighing 1750 g. Note the low-amplitude Q, R, S, and T deflections in most leads, peaked P wave in leads V_2 and V_E, depressed S–T junction in V_2 with artifact in S–T segment, and slurred, notched R wave in V_{4R} (V'_4). Reproduced from Walsh, 1963, *Acta Paediatr. Scand. Suppl.,* 145. (B) Tracing from a 6-day-old premature infant weighing 1920 g. The P waves are notched in various right precordial leads, as is the R wave in V_{4R}. The S–T junction is depressed, particularly in leads V_1 and V_E. Note the absence of the S–T segment and the scooped-out T waves in the right precordial leads. Reproduced from Walsh, 1963, *Acta Paediatr. Scand. Suppl.,* 145.

Table VI. ECG Differences Between Infants with a Birth Weight of Less Than 1500 g and Infants with a Birth Weight of 1500–2000 g

1. Faster heart rate at 1–3 months
2. Longer P duration for heart rate at 1–3 months
3. Slightly shorter P–R interval during the first year (borderline significance)
4. Increase in duration of the Q–R interval in lead V_{6R} during the first year
5. Delayed shift in QRS axis F[b] from 60–90° to 30–60° at 6–12 months
6. Higher incidence of S–T junction displacement in lead V_2 during the first week
7. Prolonged Q–T interval for heart rate and longer interval at 2–6 days
8. Prolonged Q–T interval for heart rate but shorter interval at 1–3 months
9. Slightly higher incidence of dominant S in V_1 during the first year (25 vs. 5–10%)

[a] From Walsh.[218] The differences listed apply to infants with a birth weight of less than 1500 g. Some differences ascribable to weight are still present at the end of the year.
[b] F: Frontal axis.

tudes are seen transiently—such as 0.8 mV in right precordial leads—on one or more examinations.[218]

Comment: These characteristics of the ECG of the low-birth-weight infant after the age of 2 weeks are less striking than those seen shortly after birth, and may be missed on casual inspection. Intervals are short, however, and deflections may be even greater than in the adult. Some differences between tracings of infants of different birth weight persist during the first year of life (Table VI). This should be borne in mind when interpreting the tracings of very low birth weight infants.

In the *early* neonatal period, the large circulatory adjustment after birth, larger heart size in relation to the body than in the adult (0.8 vs. 0.4–0.5%) or full-term infant (0.7%), larger or smaller placental transfusion depending on the time the cord is clamped than in the full-term infant, altered electrolyte balance, tendency to pulmonary atelectasis and hypoxemia, little or no interposed lung tissue, and thin chest wall with equal transverse and A-P diameter are among the possible causes of the findings.

In the *later* neonatal period, the complex processes accompanying growth and development of the heart, lungs, and chest, such as the descent of the heart into the chest, greater increase of the transverse

Table VII. Incidence of a Dominant R (=RV) and Dominant S (=LV) in Lead V_1 in Infants of Low Birth Weight During the First Year of Life[a]

	≤ 48 hr	48 hr to 6 days	7 days to 1 month	1–3 months	3–6 months	6–12 months
RV	63%	90%	83%	89%	80%	62%
LV	20%	10%	12%	7%	17.5%	34%
n	30	41	65	65	40	50

[a] From Walsh.[218]

diameter than of the A-P diameter of the chest, and the smaller increase in the size of the heart than of the body (100 vs. 200%) offer an explanation that is convenient and sufficiently vague to cover large lacunae in knowledge.

In the healthy infant of very low birth weight, the pattern type changes little in right precordial leads, but changes considerably in left precordial leads, during the first year. This transition appears to mirror underlying structural changes in the heart, and may be of value in early detection of congenital heart disease, particularly that associated with hypertrophy of the right side of the heart.

3.17. Phonocardiogram of the Full-Size Infant

The phonocardiogram is a simple yet useful means for studying heart sounds and murmurs and their relationship to other parameters. Multiple recordings during the first weeks of life show a pattern of change that appears to reflect the physiologic alterations occurring after birth.

3.17.1. Heart Sounds

The *first sound* is loud at birth, best heard over the lower precordial area, and of lower amplitude than the second sound during the first 2 days of life. Subsequently, both sounds are of about equal intensity, although there is considerable variation. The first component occurs at about 35–45 msec (Q–S_1 interval) and the second component at about 70 msec after the Q wave of the ECG.[169,219] A third component is not infrequently noted about 30–40 msec after the first component. It is usually prominent on the first day of life, when it simulates the early ejection click seen in stenosis or dilatation of the pulmonary or aortic valves. Although no agreement exists regarding derivation of the various components of the first sound, the first high-frequency component is often ascribed to mitral valve closure. Even those who dispute this origin report that the Q–S_1 interval is prolonged with increased left ventricular overload. This prolongation is presumably due to increased left atrial pressure. In newborns, the interval remains constant during the first week even during acute experimental increments

Table VIII. Incidence of a Dominant S (=RV) and qR(s) (=LV) in Leads V_6 and/or V_8 in Infants of Low Birth Weight During the First Year of Life[a]

	≤ 48 hr	48 hr to 6 days	7 days to 1 month	1–3 months	3–6 months	6–12 months
RV	32%	9%	10%	1.5%	0	0
LV	13%	20%	10%	40%	70%	74%
n	31	44	66	64	37	52

[a] From Walsh.[218]

nd decrements of blood volume (mean 10%)[86] nd despite initial elevation of left atrial pressure fter birth.

The *second sound* is loudest at the upper left ternal border and of greater intensity than the first ound at this site throughout the neonatal period. The first high-frequency component is usually due o aortic closure, while the second high-frequency component is usually due to pulmonary closure, except during the first 12 hr of life, when the ductus arteriosus is still physiologically significant.[87] In this condition, as in various heart lesions, the heart sounds may become paradoxically split; i.e., the aortic component of the second sound may follow the pulmonary component to produce splitting in expiration because of increased stroke volume of the left ventricle. The first component occurs at about 270 msec after the Q wave of the ECG (Q–A$_2$ interval).[219] This interval is assumed to reflect the duration of left ventricular systole. In adults, the interval is prolonged in either systolic or diastolic overload or failure; in newborns, its duration increases and decreases with experimentally induced acute hyper- and hypovolemia, respectively,[86] and it is transiently prolonged after birth while the shunt through the ductus arteriosus is significant and there is left ventricular diastolic overload.[219] The duration of the Q–A$_2$ interval varies inversely with heart rate. It is prolonged out of proportion to heart rate during the first hours of life, especially in LC infants. The inverse relationship between duration of the interval and heart rate at rest alters during the first week, so that the same increment in rate produces a smaller decrease in duration of the Q–A$_2$ interval than on the first day of life. An increase in rate induced by a cry at the end of the week, however, immediately restores the relationship to that seen during the first hours of life[220] (see Fig. 18).

The pulmonary closure component is of comparatively higher amplitude than the aortic closure component during the first 2 days of life while pulmonary arterial pressures are high; the relationship then reverses. The second sound is more widely split at birth than in the following 3 hr. Detectable splitting (15 msec or more) varying little with quiet respiration occurs in about 50% of infants during the first 3 hr, in 75% during the first 3 days, and in 85% during the first 2 weeks of life, when it mainly ranges from 15 to 25 msec (Fig. 21). EC infants often have slightly wider splitting than LC infants on the first day, because they have an earlier fall in pulmonary arterial pressure. Support for this

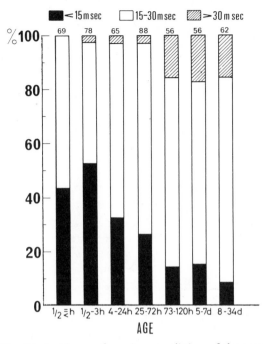

Fig. 21. Incidence of maximum splitting of the second heart sound during the first month of life in 59 healthy full-size infants. During the first 3 hr of life, little or no splitting can be detected in about 50% of infants. The degree of splitting then increases, but shows little change after the third day of life. The figures shown above each column correspond to the number of observations in each age group. Based on data from Arcilla and Lind.[3]

view is also provided by studies in newborns during the first week of life that show that acute experimental increments and decrements in blood volume (of a mean of 10%) cause immediate increases and decreases, respectively, in the duration of splitting of the second heart sound, as well as alterations in the intensity of the pulmonary component of the second heart sound[86] (Fig. 22).

3.17.2. Other Sounds

A *third sound* is not present in the healthy newborn. If it is present, it suggests volume overloading of the heart or myocardial failure. Variable low-frequency disturbances thought to represent auricular sounds have been noted in many tracings by Walsh,[215] but neither Braudo and Rowe[33] nor Arcilla and Lind[3] have heard or recorded a *fourth sound*. The difference may well be one of interpretation.

Inconstant high-pitched sounds occurring irregularly during systole and diastole appear to have no clinical significance, and may be of extracardiac origin.

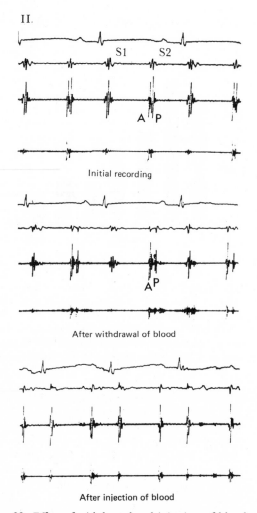

Fig. 22. Effect of withdrawal and injection of blood on the second heart sound in a 5-day-old infant weighing 2030 g at birth. Immediately after withdrawal of 10% of total blood volume, the heart rate increases from 118 to 125 beats/min, and the $Q-A_2$ interval shortens more than the $Q-P_2$ interval. These changes result in wide splitting of the second heart sound. Immediately after injection of double the amount of blood withdrawn, the heart rate increases to 140 beats/min, and the $Q-A_2$ interval increases relatively more than the $Q-P_2$ interval. These changes result in an almost single second sound. Top trace: ECG lead II. Bottom traces: PCG at frequencies of 25, 100, and 400 Hz. Paper speed 100 mm/sec. Reproduced from Gyulai and Walsh.[101]

3.17.3. Murmurs

The incidence of murmurs in the newborn is low ($\approx 2\%$) in studies based on large series of cases examined by different physicians without prior agreement as to criteria and high (50–90%) in studies based on relatively small series with frequent and careful follow-up examinations. Other factors are also involved. Warming, for example, increases the incidence of all types of murmurs,[37] while hypoxia, for example, as a result of birth asphyxia or respiratory distress syndrome, is accompanied by high pulmonary vascular resistance and decrease in ductal tone, with consequent alteration in auscultatory findings. Infants with a low blood volume, for example, after early clamping of the cord, also have a higher incidence of murmurs during the first weeks of life.

(a) Systolic Murmurs. The systolic murmur heard on the first day may differ from that at the end of the week, although subjective impressions are unreliable. On the first day, the murmur more often is louder in the pulmonic area, grade I or II (on a scale of VI), short and early with midsystolic accentuation, usually maximal at the upper left sternal border. Its peak incidence is between $1\frac{1}{2}$ and 8 hr when it has been recorded in 70% of 59 subjects. It then disappears. The systolic murmur heard at the end of the week seems to have a different, more vibratory quality, and may be maximal either somewhat lower down the left sternal border or may extend over a larger precordial area, both down the sternal border and out toward the apex.

A crescendo *late* systolic murmur is not common,[3,33] although Burnard[36] encountered it in one-third of 100 healthy infants. This murmur is best heard near the sternum at the fourth left interspace, more frequent at 5 or 6 hr of age, occasionally extends beyond the second sound, and may be conducted beyond the apex. It occurs in mature infants and premature infants with dyspnea and cardiac enlargement, and is more common in infants of heavily sedated mothers.

The genesis of some of these murmurs is disputed. The murmur heard on the first day of life tends to be ascribed to flow through the patent duct, while that heard late is variously ascribed to flow at either the pulmonary or the aortic valves or flow into a dilated vessel beyond a normal valve. In one instance, a late systolic murmur was studied by intracardiac phonocardiography, and the findings suggested regurgitation through the mitral valve,[36] but the infant had an Apgar score of 1 at 1 min after delivery by cesarean section.

(b) Diastolic Murmurs. The true incidence of an isolated diastolic murmur in the newborn is not known, because it is not only difficult to hear and record but also transient. To date, it has been reported by only two investigators,[36,211] which presumably reflects a low incidence or infrequent careful auscultation of the newborn or continued reluctant acceptance of phonocardiography as a routine procedure in confirmation of auscultatory findings in many institutions.

The *isolated diastolic murmur* starts immediately after the second sound, extends up to and even slightly beyond the first sound, tends to middiastolic accentuation, varies in duration and intensity with respiration, is best seen in the high frequency ranges, and is usually localized to the left first and second intercostal spaces. In one series of serially longitudinally examined healthy infants, it was detected in 4 of 73 EC infants between 2 and 4 hr of age, but in none of 127 LC infants.[211]

The genesis of this murmur is likewise disputed. Burnard[38] attributes the murmur to a venous hum. A venous hum, however, is usually continuous, though maximum in diastole; best heard in the *right* supraclavicular region, but may be transmitted below the clavicles in some cases; and tends to disappear or diminish when the subject lies down (the usual position for auscultation of an infant) or when the head is turned toward the same side as the murmur or by compression of the internal jugular vein just lateral to the thyroid cartilage.

A venous hum is also more common in anemia, and might therefore be expected to occur more frequently in infants with early clamping of the cord. On the other hand, it is difficult to explain why a diastolic murmur should be heard only on the *left* side between 2 and 4 hr of age unless, in fact, it is due to flow through the ductus itself.

Pulmonary diastolic pressure decreases at a comparably faster rate than does pulmonary systolic pressure,[66] and not uncommonly, a diastolic pressure difference is present with nearly equivalent systolic pressures in the pulmonary artery and descending aorta. Indeed, these authors note that pulmonary diastolic pressure is uniformly lower than systemic diastolic pressure during the first 10 hr of age; in other words, there is a hemodynamic situation that would produce an isolated diastolic murmur.

Studies by Arcilla *et al.*[5] show that the diastolic pressure difference occurs earlier in EC than in LC infants, i.e., at the age when a diastolic murmur occurs in EC infants.

Furthermore, when the murmur appears, serial ECGs show increased amplitude of the Q, R, and S waves and greater inversion of the T wave in V_6, which has been adduced as additional evidence in favor of a ductal origin.[211]

(c) Continuous Murmur. A continuous murmur in the pulmonary area was heard in 11 of 84 infants (14%) of normal birth weight, usually around 5 or 6 hr of age.[33] Of these 11, 4 later developed a crescendo murmur. A crescendo systolic murmur with or without a diminuendo in early diastole was found in 37 of 100 healthy infants. Of 21 infants in the series who had apnea for 3 min or more after birth, 15 (71%) had such a murmur.[36] In contrast, neither Craige and Harned[52] nor Arcilla and Lind[3] observed a truly continuous murmur, while Walsh[215] heard it in 2 of 100 healthy LC infants, the majority of whom were examined a minimum of four times each during the first week of life.

Since all infants have a patent duct, it is generally assumed that such a murmur should be audible at some time between $\frac{1}{2}$ and 15 hr of age, while hemodynamic conditions are such as to favor production of this murmur. Although a continuous murmur is usually ascribed to flow from the aorta to the pulmonary artery because of an aorto-pulmonary pressure gradient throughout most of systole and diastole, in newborn piglets, the gradient may be present but the murmur not detectable.[68] These studies also show that a continuous murmur may be present in the pulmonary artery, but not audible on the chest. The authors conclude that continuous crescendo systolic and short early systolic murmurs are all related to closure of the ductus arteriosus.

3.18. Ductus Venosus

In premature and full-term newborns, the duct has a length of 1.2–2 cm and a diameter about half that of the umbilical vein.[141] It is narrowest at the inlet and widest at the outlet where it empties into the very short terminal portion of the left hepatic vein. Judging by indicator dilution and angiographic studies, the channel is usually partly constricted on the first day and still patent at about 2 weeks of age in infants of normal birth weight.[92] In the 3- to 6-day-old lamb, injections of acetylcholine, adrenaline, and norepinephrine into the umbilical or jugular veins reopen the duct.[158] Persistent functional patency may modify liver function by virtue of a reduction in the amount of blood perfusing the liver.

Functional closure of the duct appears to be the consequence of the postnatal decrease in flow and pressure in the umbilical recess following cessation of the placental circulation. Retraction and narrowing of the origin of the duct then occurs, and is probably accompanied by active contraction of the smooth muscle in the adjacent walls of the left branch of the portal vein and the umbilical recess. In the ductus venosus itself at term, there is little smooth muscle and no muscular sphincter.[136]

Anatomic closure of the ductus venosus is achieved by proliferation of connective tissue that protrudes into the inlet of the duct, i.e., at its junction with the left branch of the portal vein. This connective tissue subsequently becomes overlaid by a wide layer of young loose connective tissue rich in cells and poor in fibers. Final adhesion is probably aided by superficial fibrin deposition on the surface of the proliferating connective tissue, but without formation of thromboses. This process is usually complete by 2, 3, or more (up to 8) weeks.[136,178]

3.19. Portal Vein

At birth, the trunk of the portal vein is a contracted, thick-walled vessel with a lumen that is considerably narrower than its main branches. Its small size is assumed to reflect transport of only a small amount of blood from the relatively inactive gut, a view that is supported by cineangiographic studies in the human fetus. Within a few days, the infant starts to ingest daily a quantity of milk equivalent to about one-eighth of its weight. By 2 weeks of age, the quantity has increased to $\frac{1}{2}$ or even 1 liter. In terms of body surface area, this amount corresponds to an intake of 10–20 liters of milk by an adult. Over the same period, the infant's systemic blood pressure gradually rises, and flow through the ductus venosus decreases. Blood flow through the portal vein and hepatic artery, and hence through the liver sinusoids, must therefore increase during the first days of life. To what extent the loss of oxygenated umbilical blood flow is compensated for by the increase in hepatic arterial flow and what consequences, if any, result from the sudden drop in blood pressure in the branches of the portal vein are not known.

By 3 weeks of age, the diameter of the trunk has increased by 1–2$\frac{1}{2}$ times, and it is gradually becoming wider than its two main branches. The increase in diameter is achieved primarily by unfolding of the longitudinal smooth muscle bundles in the dorsal and lateral portions of the wall because of greater distensibility of the dorsal than of the ventral wall. This change is at least partly related to the absence of anatomic structures to oppose distension of the dorsal wall, whereas the ventral wall is more firmly fixed to adjacent tissues. Changes in the elastic network also contribute to structural adaptation of the venous wall. In the newborn, the subendothelial elastic layer of the portal vein is very thin and consists only of fine elastic networks; it therefore cannot offer much resistance to widening of the lumen.[136]

3.20. Portal Pressures

Immediately after delivery, the pressure in the umbilical vein (and in the portal venous branches) falls from a range of 15–50 mm Hg at 10 sec to 20 mm Hg at 100 sec, and then to a range of 2–10 mm Hg during the first 14 hr of life.[4,148,208] There is a slight decline in mean portal pressure from about 7.5 mm Hg during the first hour to about 6.0 mm Hg thereafter. As far as can be determined from the limited data available, the level of the pressure on the first day of life is not influenced by the amount of the placental transfusion, as judged by the time the cord is clamped after delivery.[4] Thus, portal pressure after birth immediately falls to values similar to those encountered in the adult without liver disease. Pressure in the inferior vena cava likewise falls, and the direction of blood flow in the left main branch of the portal vein reverses from left-to-right (from the umbilical vein) to right-to-left (from the portal trunk). This reversal in direction involves a reduction in the level of oxygenation of the blood if not in the amount of blood supplied to the left "lobe" of the liver, because the trunk of the portal vein now becomes its chief source of blood supply, and the opening of the trunk is initially not only directed somewhat toward the right, but also the left branch of the portal vein arises from the trunk at a sharp angle (see Fig. 10). The pressure in the portal vein is higher than that in the inferior vena cava. The pressure difference, an important determinant of liver blood flow, since most of the liver's blood supply comes from the portal vein, is likewise similar to that encountered in the adult. Thus, the hemodynamic adaptation of the liver circulation appears to be very rapidly achieved after birth. Disturbances in this adaptive process no doubt go unrecognized.

4. Conclusion

At birth, every organ starts a new mode of life, and multiple circulatory adjustments are necessary to ensure a smooth transition from the fetal to the adult type of circulation. This transition is partly effected by three mechanisms that together permit alterations in size and direction of shunts when the delicate balance of pressure and resistance is upset: (1) anatomic patency of fetal channels (ductus venosus, ductus arteriosus, foramen ovale); (2) declining pulmonary vascular resistance; and (3) increased and more pronounced response of the pulmonary vasculature to such stimuli as changes in O_2 tension and pH.

A host of other mechanisms are also involved, all of which require that preparatory structural changes have progressed sufficiently in advance of birth to permit cardiovascular adaptation of the newborn infant to extrauterine life. The success with which these changes are accomplished even in the very premature infant attests to the remarkable integration of these processes.

5. References

1. ADAMS, F. H., 1966, Functional development of the fetal lung, *J. Pediatr.* **68**:794.
2. AMOROSO, E. C., DAWES, G. S., MOTT, J. C., AND RENNICK, B. R., 1955, Occlusion of the ductus venosus in the mature foetal lamb, *J. Physiol.* **128**:64.
3. ARCILLA, R. A., AND LIND, J., 1965, Serial phono-cardiography during the neonatal period: A comparative study on infants born with early and late clamping of the cord, *Z. Kinderheilkd.* **93**:354.
4. ARCILLA, R. A., OH, W., LIND, J., AND BLANKENSHIP, W., 1966, Portal and atrial pressures in the newborn period, *Acta Paediatr. Scand.* **55**:615.
5. ARCILLA, R. A., OH, W., LIND, J., AND GESSNER, I. H., 1966, Pulmonary arterial pressures of newborn infants with early and late clamping of the cord, *Acta Paediatr. Scand.* **55**:305.
6. ARCILLA, R. H., OH, W., WALLGREN, G., HANSON, J. S., GESSNER, I. H., AND LIND, J., 1967, Quantitative studies of the human neonatal circulation. II. Hemo-dynamic findings in early and late clamping of the umbilical cord, *Acta Paediatr. Scand. Suppl.* **179**:25.
7. AREY, L. B., 1965, Developmental anatomy, in: *A Textbook and Laboratory Manual of Embryology* (7th Ed.), p. 380, W. B. Saunders, Philadelphia.
8. ASSALI, N. S., DOUGLASS, R. A., BAIRD, W. W., NICHOLSON, D. B., AND SUYEMOTO, R., 1953, Measurement of uterine blood flow and uterine metabolism, *Amer. J. Obstet. Gynecol.* **66**:248.
9. ASSALI, N. S., MORRIS, J. A., AND BECK, R., 1965, Cardiovascular hemodynamics in the fetal lamb before and after lung expansion, *Amer. J. Physiol.* **208**:122.
10. ASSALI, N. S., MORRIS, J. A., SMITH, R. W., AND MANSON, W. A., 1963, Studies on ductus arteriosus circulation, *Circ. Res.* **13**:478.
11. ASSALI, N. S., RAURAMO, L., AND PELTONEN, T., 1960, Measurement of uterine blood flow and uterine metabolism. VIII. Uterine and fetal blood flow and oxygen consumption in early pregnancy, *Amer. J. Obstet. Gynecol.* **79**:86.
12. AULD, P. A. M., NELSON, N. M., CHERRY, R. B., RUDOLPH, A. J., AND SMITH, C. A., 1963, measurement of thoracic gas volume in the newborn infant, *J. Clin. Invest.* **42**:476.
13. AVERY, M. E., FRANK, N. R., AND GRIBETZ, I., 1959, The inflationary force produced by pulmonary vascular distention in excised lungs: the possible relation of this force to that needed to inflate the lungs at birth, *J. Clin. Invest.* **38**:456.
14. BARCLAY, A. E., FRANKLIN, K. J., AND PRICHARD, M. M. L., 1944, *The Foetal Circulation and Cardiovascular System and the Changes That They Undergo at Birth*, pp. 74–75, 160–161, 219, Blackwell Scientific Publications, Oxford.
15. BARCLAY, J., BARRON, D. H., AND FRANKLIN, K. J., 1939, A radiographic demonstration of the circulation through the heart in the adult and in the fetus and the identification of the ductus arteriosus, *Br. J. Radiol.* **18**:505.
16. BARCROFT, J., 1946, *Researches on Prenatal Life*, Blackwell Scientific Publications, Oxford.
17. BARRON, D. H., 1942, The sphincter of the ductus venosus, *Anat. Rec.* **82**:398.
18. BARTELS, H. W., 1970, Prenatal respiration, *Front. Biol.* **17**:148.
19. BARTELS, H., AND MOLL, W., 1964, Passage of inert substances and oxygen in the human placenta, *Pfluegers Arch.* **290**:165.
20. BEHRMAN, R. E., LEES, M. H., PETERSON, E. N., DE LANNOY, C. W., AND SEEDS, A. E., 1970, Distribution of the circulation in the normal and asphyxiated fetal primate, *Amer J. Obstet. Gynecol.* **108**:956.
21. BERG, D., AND DÖRFLER, J., 1971, Das Verhalten des Säure-Basen-Haushalt von normalen Neugeborenen am ersten Lebenstag, *Z. Geburtshilfe Gynaekol.* **175**:1.
22. BERGQVIST, G., 1974, Rheologic studies in the newborn infant, Medical thesis, Karolinska Institute, Stockholm, Sweden.

23. BEUTNAGEL, H., GAUCH, D., AND FABEL, H., 1971, Blutgase and Säure-Basen-Haushalt von normalen Neugeborenen am ersten Lebenstag, *Z. Geburtshilfe Gynaekol.* **175**:1.

24. BISCOE, T. J., PURVES, M. J., AND SAMPSON, S. R., 1969, Types of nervous activity which may be recorded from the carotid sinus nerve in the sheep foetus, *J. Physiol. (London)* **202**:1.

25. BORÉUS, L. O., MALMFORS, T., McMURPHY, D. M., AND OLSON, L., 1969, Demonstration of adrenergic receptor function and innervation in the ductus arteriosus of the human fetus, *Acta Physiol. Scand.* **77**:316.

26. BORN, G. V. R., DAWES, G. S., AND MOTT, J. C., 1956, The constriction of the ductus arteriosus caused by oxygen and by asphyxia in newborn lambs, *J. Physiol. (London)* **132**:304.

27. BOTHA, M. C., 1968, The management of the umbilical cord in labor, *S. Afr. J. Obstet. Gynaecol. Suppl.* (August).

28. BOYD, J. D., 1937, Development of the human carotid body, *Carnegie Inst. Washington, Contrib. Embryol.* **26**:1.

29. BOYD, J. D., 1960, Origin, development and distribution of chromaffin cells, in: *Ciba Foundation Symposium on Adrenergic Mechanisms* (J. R. Vane, G. E. W. Wolstenholme, and M. O'Conner, eds.), p. 63, Churchill, London.

30. BOYD, J. D., AND HAMILTON, W. I., 1970, *The Human Placenta*, W. Heffer and Sons, Cambridge.

31. BRADY, J. P., AND TOOLEY, W., 1966, Cardiovascular and respiratory reflexes in the newborn infant, *Pediatr. Clin. North Amer.* **13**:801.

32. BRADY, J. P., JAMES, L. S., AND BAKER, M. A., 1963, Fetal electrocardiographic studies. Tachycardia as sign of fetal distress, *Amer. J. Obstet. Gynecol.* **86**:785.

33. BRAUDO, M., AND ROWE, R. D., 1961, Auscultation of the heart—early neonatal period, *Amer. J. Dis. Child.* **101**:67.

34. BRUCE, J., WALMSLEY, R., AND ROSS, J. A., 1964, *Manual of Surgical Anatomy*, E & S Livingstone, Edinburgh.

35. BRÜCK, K., BRÜCK, M., AND LEMTIS, H., 1957, Hautdurchblutung und Thermoregulation bei neugeborenen Kindern, *Pfluegers Arch. Gesamte Physiol. Menschen Tiere* **264**:55.

36. BURNARD, E. D., 1958, A murmur from the ductus arteriosus in the healthy newborn baby, *Br. Med. J.* **1**:806.

37. BURNARD, E. D., 1959, A murmur from the ductus arteriosus in the newborn baby, *Br. Med. J.* **1**:1495.

38. BURNARD, E. D., 1966, Influence of delivery on the circulation, in: *The Heart and Circulation in the Newborn and Infant* (D. E. Cassels, ed.), p. 92, Grune & Stratton, New York.

39. BURNARD, E. D., AND JAMES, L. S., 1961, Radiographic heart size in apparently healthy newborn

40. infants: Clinical and biochemical correlations, *Pediatrics* **27**:726.

40. BURNARD, E. D., GRAUAUG, A., AND GRAY, R. E. 1966, Cardiac output in the newborn infant, *Clin. Sci.* **31**:121.

41. BURNELL, R. H., JOSEPH, M. C., AND LEES, M. H. 1972, Progressive pulmonary hypertension in newborn infants, *Amer. J. Dis. Child.* **123**:167.

42. CALDEYRO-BARCIA, R., MÉNDEZ-BAUER, C., POSEIRO J. J., ESCARCENA, L. A., POSE, S. V., BIENARZ, J. ARNT, I., GULIN, L., AND ALTHABE, O., 1966, Control of human fetal heart rate during labor, in: *The Heart and Circulation in the Newborn and Infant* (D. E. Cassels, ed.), p. 7, Grune & Stratton, New York.

43. CASSIN, S., DAWES, G. S., MOTT, J. C., ROSS, B. B. AND STRANG, L. B., 1964, The vascular resistance of the foetal and newly ventilated lung of the lamb, *J. Physiol.* **171**:61.

44. CATON, D., ABRAMS, R. M., LACKORE, L. K., JAMES G. B., AND BARRON, D. H., 1973, Effects of progesterone administration on the rate of uterine blood flow of early pregnant sheep, in: *Foetal and Neonatal Physiology* (K. S. Comline, K. W. Cross, G. S. Dawes, and D. W. Nathanielsz, eds.), pp. 28 and 287, *Proceedings of the Sir Joseph Barcroft Centenary Symposium*, Cambridge University Press, Cambridge.

45. Celander, O., 1966, Studies of the peripheral circulation, in: *The Heart and Circulation in the Newborn and Infant* (D. E. Cassels, ed.), p. 98, Grune & Stratton, New York.

46. CELANDER, O., AND MÅRILD, K., 1962, Reactive hyperemia in the foot and calf of the newborn infant *Acta Paediatr. Scand.* **51**:385.

47. CLAVERO, J. A., NEGUERUELA, J., ORTIZ, L., DE LOS HEROS, J. A., AND SEVERINO, P., 1973, Blood flow in the intervillous space and fetal blood flow, *Amer. J. Obstet. Gynec.* **116**:340.

48. COLDITZ, R. B., AND JOSEY, W. E., 1970, Central venous pressure in supine position during normal pregnancy. Comparative determinations during first, second and third trimesters, *Obstet. Gynecol.* **36**:769.

49. COLEBATCH, H. J. H., DAWES, G. S., GOODWIN, J. W. AND NADEAU, R. A., 1965, The nervous control of the circulation in the foetal and newly expanded lungs of the lamb, *J. Physiol.* **178**:544.

50. COMLINE, R. S., AND SILVER, M., 1974, in: *Recent Advances in Physiology* (R. J. Linden, ed.), No. 9 pp. 406–454, Churchill, Livingstone, Edinburgh.

51. COOK, C. D., DRINKER, P. A., JACOBSON, N. H. LEVISON, H., AND STRANG, L. B., 1963, Control of pulmonary blood flow in the foetal and newly born lamb, *J. Physiol.* **169**:10.

52. CRAIGE, E., AND HARNED, H. S., 1963, Phonocardiographic and electrocardiographic studies in normal newborn infants, *Amer. Heart. J.* **65**:180.

53. DAWES, G. S., 1968, *Foetal and Neonatal Physiology*

A Comparative Study of the Changes at Birth, p. 167, Year Book Medical Publishers, Chicago.

54. DAWES, G. S., 1969, in: *Ciba Foundation Symp.: Foetal Autonomy* (G. E. W. Wolstenholme and M. O. O'Connor, eds.), Churchill, London.

55. DAWES, G. S., MOTT, J. C., AND RENNICK, B. R., 1956, Some effects of adrenaline, noradrenaline and acetylcholine on the foetal circulation in the lamb, *J. Physiol. (London)* 34:139.

56. DAWES, G. S., MOTT, J. C., AND WIDDICOMBE, J. G., 1954, The foetal circulation in the lamb, *J. Physiol.* 126:563.

57. DAWES, G. S., MOTT, J. C., WIDDICOMBE, J. G., AND WYATT, D. G., 1953, Changes in the lungs of the newborn lamb, *J. Physiol. (London)* 121:141.

58. DESLIGNÈRES, S., AND LARROCHE, J. C., 1970, Ductus arteriosus. I. Anatomical and histological study of its development during the second half of gestation and its closure after birth. II. Histological study of a few cases of patent ductus arteriosus in infancy, *Biol. Neonate* 16:278.

59. DESMOND, M. M., KAY, J. L., AND MEGARITY, A. L., 1959, The phases of "transitional distress" occurring in neonates in association with prolonged postnatal umbilical cord pulsations, *J. Pediatr.* 55:131.

60. EDWARDS, J., 1966, in: *The Heart and Circulation in the Newborn Infant* (D. E. Cassels, ed.), p. 133, Grune & Stratton, New York.

61. EHINGER, B., GENNSER, G., OWMAN, C., PERSSON, H., AND SJÖBERG, N. O., 1968, Histochemical and pharmacological studies on amine mechanisms in the umbilical cord, umbilical vein and ductus venosus of the human fetus, *Acta Physiol. Scand.* 72:15.

62. EMERY, J. L., 1953, Involution of the left liver in the newborn and its relationship to physiological icterus, *Arch. Dis. Child.* 28:463.

63. EMERY, J. L., 1963, Functional asymmetry of the liver, *Ann. N. Y. Acad. Sci.* III:37.

64. EMERY, J. L., AND MacDONALD, M. S., 1960, The weight of the ventricles in the later weeks of intrauterine life, *Br. Heart J.* 22:563.

65. EMMANOUILIDES, G. C., MOSS, A. J., MONSET-COUCHARD, M., MARCANO, B. A., AND RZEZNIC, B., 1969, Cardiac output in newborn infants, *Biol. Neonate* 15:186.

66. EMMANOUILIDES, G. C., MOSS, A. J., DUFFIE, E. R., JR., AND ADAMS, F. H., 1964, Pulmonary arterial pressure changes in human newborn infants from birth to three days of age, *J. Pediatr.* 63:327.

67. ENGSTRÖM, L., KARLBERG, P., ROOTH, G., AND TUNELL, R., 1966, The onset of respiration, in: *A Study of Respiration and Changes in Blood Gases and Acid–Base Balance,* Association for the Aid of Crippled Children, New York.

68. EVANS, J. R., DOWNIE, R. D., AND ROWSELL, H. C., 1963, Murmurs arising from ductus arteriosus in normal newborn swine, *Circ. Res.* 12:85.

69. FAWCITT, J., LIND, J., AND WEGELIUS, C., 1960, The first breath, *Acta Paediatr. Scand.* 49(*Suppl. 23*):5.

70. FAY, F. S., 1971, Guinea pig ductus arteriosus. I. Cellular and metabolic basis for oxygen sensitivity. *Amer. J. Physiol.* 221:470.

71. FAY, F. S., 1973, Biochemical basis for response of ductus arteriosus to oxygen, in: *Foetal and Neonatal Physiology* (K. S. Comline, K. W. Cross, G. S. Dawes, and D. W. Nathanielz, eds.), *Proceedings of the Sir Joseph Barcroft Centenary Symposium,* Cambridge University Press, Cambridge.

72. FAY, F. S., AND COOKE, P. H., 1972, Guinea pig ductus arteriosus. II. Irreversible closure after birth, *Amer. J. Physiol.* 222:841.

73. FERRIS, T. R., STEIN, J. H., AND KAUFFMAN, J., 1972, Uterine blood flow and uterine renin secretion, *J. Clin. Invest.* 51:2827.

74. FRANKLIN, K. J., BARCLAY, A. E., AND PRICHARD, M. M. L., 1947, *The Circulation in the Foetus,* Blackwell Scientific Publications, Oxford.

75. FULTON, R. M., HUTCHINSON, E. C., AND TORES, A. M., 1952, Ventricular weight in cardiac hypertrophy, *Br. Heart J.* 14:413.

76. GERSONY, W. M., DUC, G. V., AND SINCLAIR, J. C., 1969, "PFC" syndrome (persistence of the fetal circulation), *Circulation* 40(*Suppl. 3*):87.

77. GESSNER, I. H., KROVETZ, L. I., BENSON, R. W., PRYSTOWSKY, H., STENGER, V., AND EITZMAN, D. V., 1965, Hemodynamic adaptations in the newborn infant, *Pediatrics* 36:752.

78. GEUBELLE, F., KARLBERG, P., KOCH, G., LIND, J., AND WEGELIUS, C., 1959, The aeration of the lung in the newborn infant, *Biol. Neonate* 1:169.

79. GILBERT, R. P., HINSHAS, L. B., KUIDA, H., AND VISSCHER, M. B., 1958, Effects of histamine, 5-hydroxytryptamine and epinephrine on pulmonary hemodynamics with particular reference to arterial and venous segment resistances, *Amer. J. Physiol.* 194:165.

80. GOLDBERG, S. J., LEVY, R. A., SIASSI, B., AND BETTEN, J., 1971, The effects of maternal hypoxia and hyperoxia upon the neonatal pulmonary vasculature, *Pediatrics* 48:528.

81. GOODLIN, R. C., AND SCHMIDT, W., 1972, Human fetal arousal levels as indicated by heart rate recordings, *Amer. J. Obst. Gynecol.* 114:613.

82. GOULD, S. E., 1960, *Pathology of the Heart* (2nd Ed.), p. 95, Charles C. Thomas, Springfield.

83. GREISS, F. C., 1965, Uterine vascular responses to hemorrhage during ovine pregnancy, *Amer. J. Obstet. Gynecol.* 97:962.

84. GROSSMAN, G., 1974, Lung expansion in the newborn rabbit, Medical thesis, Karolinska Institute, Stockholm.

85. GROSSMAN, G., LAMKE, B., AND ROBERTSSON, B., 1974, Lung aeration in the full-term newborn rabbit.

Roentgenologic and histologic investigations, *Acta Radiol., Diagn.* **15**:423.

86. GYULAI, F., AND WALSH, S. Z., 1971, Phono-cardiographic studies during experimental hypo- and hypervolemia in newborns, *J. Electrocardiol.* **4**:158.

87. HEINTZEN, P., 1961, The genesis of the normally split first heart sound, *Amer. Heart J.* **62**:332.

88. HENDRICKS, C. H., 1964, Patterns of fetal and placental growth: The second half of normal pregnancy, *Obstet. Gynecol.* **24**:357.

89. HEYMANN, M. A., AND RUDOLPH, A. M., 1972, Effects of congenital heart disease on fetal and neonatal circulation, *Prog. Cardiovasc. Dis.* **15**:115.

89a. HEYMANN, M. A., AND RUDOLPH, A. M., 1977, Ductus arteriosus dilatation by prostaglandin E_1 in infants with pulmonary atresia, *Pediatrics* **59**:325.

90. HEYMANN, M. A., CREASY, R. K., AND RUDOLPH, A. M., 1973, Quantitation of blood flow patterns in the foetal lamb *in utero*, in: *Foetal and Neonatal Physiology* (K. S. Comline, K. W. Cross, G. S. Dawes, and W. Nathanielsz, eds.), pp. 129–135, *Proceedings of the Sir Joseph Barcroft Centenary Symposium,* Cambridge University Press, Cambridge.

91. HEYMANN, M. A., RUDOLPH, A. M., NIES, A. S., AND MELMON, K. L., 1969, Bradykinin production associated with oxygenation of the fetal lamb, *Circ. Res.* **25**:521.

92. HIRVONEN, L., PELTONEN, T., AND RUOKOLA, M., 1961, Angiocardiography of the newborn with contrast injected into the umbilical vein, *Ann. Paediatr. Fenn.* **7**:124.

93. HISLOP, A., AND REID, L., 1972, Weight of the left and right ventricles of the heart during fetal life, *J. Clin. Pathol.* **25**:534.

94. HISLOP, A., AND REID, L., 1974, Growth and development of the respiratory system—anatomical development, in: *Scientific Foundations of Pediatrics* (J. A. Davis and J. Dobbins, eds.), p. 214, William Heinemann Medical Books, London.

95. HON, E. H., 1960, The diagnosis of fetal distress, *Clin. Obstet. Gynecol.* **3**:860.

96. HON, E. H., 1963, Instrumentation of fetal heart rate and fetal electrocardiography. II. A vaginal electrode, *Amer. J. Obstet. Gynecol.* **86**:772.

97. HON, E. H., 1967, *Proceedings of the Fifth World Congress of Gynecology and Obstetrics,* Australia, p. 58, Butterworth & Co., London.

98. HON, E. H., 1969, *An Atlas of Fetal Heart Rate Patterns,* Harty Press, New Haven, Connecticut.

99. HON, E. H., AND QUILLIGAN, E. J., 1967, The classification of fetal heart rate. II. A reviewed working classification, *Conn. Med.* **31**:779.

100. HÖRNBLAD, P. Y., 1967, Studies on closure of the ductus arteriosus. III. Species differences in closure rate and morphology, *Cardiologia (Basel)* **51**:26.

101. HORT, W., 1955, Morphologische Untersuchungen an Herzen vor, während und nach der postnatalen

Kreislaufumschaltung, *Virchows Arch. Pathol. Anat.* **326**:458.

102. HORT, W., 1966, The normal heart of the fetus and its metamorphosis in the transition period, in: *The Heart and Circulation in the Newborn and Infant* (D. E. Cassels, ed.), p. 210, Grune & Stratton, New York.

103. HYMAN, A. L., 1969, The direct effects of vasoactive agents on pulmonary veins. Studies of responses to acetylcholine, serotonin, histamine and isoproterenol in intact dogs, *J. Pharmacol. Exp. Ther.* **168**:96.

104. HYTTEN, F. E., AND LEITCH, I., 1971, *The Physiology of Human Pregnancy,* Blackwell Scientific Publications, Oxford.

105. IKEDA, M., SONNENSCHEIN, R. R., AND MASUOKA, D. T., 1972, Catecholamine content and uptake of the ductus arteriosus of the fetal lamb, *Experientia* **28**:914.

106. JAMES, L. S., 1959, *Adaptation to Extrauterine Life,* 31st Ross Conference on Pediatric Research, p. 28, Ross Laboratories, Columbus, Ohio.

107. JÄYKÄÄ, S., 1957, Capillary erection and lung expansion, *Acta Paediatr. Scand.* **46**(Suppl. 112).

108. KAPLAN, S., AND ASSALI, N. S., 1972, Disorders of circulation, in: *Pathophysiology of Gestation* (N. S. Assali and C. R. B. Brinkman, eds.), Academic Press, New York.

109. KARLBERG, P., CHERRY, R. B., ESCARDÓ, F. E., AND KOCH, G., 1962, Respiratory studies in newborn infants. II. Pulmonary ventilation and mechanics of breathing in the first minutes of life, including the onset of respiration, *Acta Paediatr. Scand.* **51**:121.

110. KJELLBERG, S. R., RUDHE, U., AND ZETTERSTRÖM, R., 1954, Heart volume variations in neonatal period. I. Normal infants, *Acta Radiol. (Stockholm)* **42**:173.

111. KOCH, G., AND WENDEL, H., 1968, Adjustment of arterial blood gases and acid–base balance in the normal newborn infant during the first week of life, *Biol. Neonate* **12**:136.

112. KOVALČIK, V., 1963, The response of the isolated ductus arteriosus to oxygen and anoxia, *J. Physiol. (London)* **169**:185.

113. KRANTZ, K. E., AND PARKER, J. C., 1963, Contractile properties of the smooth muscle on the human placenta, *Clin. Obstet. Gynecol.* **6**:26.

114. LAUER, R. M., EVANS, J. A., AOKI, H., AND KITTLE, C. F., 1965, Factors controlling pulmonary vascular resistance in fetal lambs, *J. Pediatr.* **67**:568.

115. LAUWERYNS, J. M., AND PEUSKENS, J. C., 1969, Argyrophil (kinin and amine-producing?) cells in human infant airway epithelium, *Life Sci.* **8**:577.

116. LEES, M. H., HILL, J. D., OCHSNER, A. J., THOMAS, C. L., AND NOVY, M. J., 1971, Maternal placental and myometrial blood flow of the rhesus monkey during uterine contractions, *Amer. J. Obstet. Gynecol.* **110**:68.

117. LEVIN, D. L., CATES, L., NEWFELD, E. A., MUSTER,

A. J., AND PAUL, M. H., 1975, Persistence of the fetal cardiopulmonary pathway: Survival of an infant after a prolonged course, *Pediatrics* **56**:58.

118. LILEY, A. W., 1972, The fetus as a personality, *Aust. N. Z. J. Psychiatry* **6**:99.

119. LIND, J., AND WEGELIUS, C. E., 1954, Human fetal circulation: Changes in the cardiovascular system at birth and disturbances in postnatal closure of the foramen ovale and ductus arteriosus, *Cold Spring Harbor Symp. Quant. Biol.* **19**:109.

120. LIND, J., STERN, L., AND WEGELIUS, C. E., 1964, *Human Fetal and Neonatal Circulation,* Charles C. Thomas, Springfield, Illinois.

121. LIND, J., TÄHTI, E., AND HIRVENSALA, M., 1966, Roentgenologic studies of the size of the lungs of the newborn baby before and after aeration, *Ann. Paediatr. Fenn.* **12**:20. ,

122. LLOYD, T. C., JR., 1968, Hypoxic pulmonary vasoconstriction: Role of perivascular tissue, *J. Appl. Physiol.* **25**:560.

123. MACMAHON, H. E., 1960, The congenital absence of the ductus venosus: Report of a case, *Lab. Invest.* **9**:128.

124. MAHON, W. A., GOODWIN, J. W., AND PAUL, W. M., 1966, Measurements of individual ventricular outputs in the fetal lamb by an indicator dilution technique, *Circ. Res.* **19**:191.

125. MANSEAU, P., VAQUIER, J., CHAVINIÉ, J., AND SUREAU, C., 1972, Le rhythme cardiaque foetal "sinusoidal." Aspect évocateur de souffrance foetale au cours de la grossesse, *J. Gynecol. Obstet. Biol. Reprod. (Paris)* **1**:343.

126. MARQUIS, L., AND ACKERMAN, B. D., 1973, Placental respiration in the immediate neonatal period, *Amer. J. Obstet. Gynecol.* **117**:358.

127. MARTIN, C. B., 1968, The anatomy and circulation of the placenta, in: *Intra-Uterine Development* (A. C. Barnes, ed.), p. 35, Lea & Febiger, Philadelphia.

128. MARTIN, J. F., AND FRIEDELL, H. L., 1952, The roentgen findings in atelectasis of the newborn, *Amer. J. Roentgenol.* **67**:905.

129. MCMURPHY, D. M., AND BORÉUS, L. O., 1971, Studies on the pharmacology of the perfused human fetal ductus arteriosus, *Amer. J. Obstet. Gynecol.* **109**:937.

130. MELMON, K. M. L., CLINE, H. J., HUGHES, T., AND NIES, A. S., 1968, Kinins, possible mediators of neonatal circulatory changes in man, *J. Clin. Invest.* **47**:1295.

131. MÉNDEZ-BAUER, C., 1963, Effects of atropine on the heart rate of the human fetus during labor, *Amer. J. Obstet. Gynecol.* **85**:1033.

132. MÉNDEZ-BAUER, C., GUEVARA-RUBIO, G., MONLÉON, J., CARILLO-ANDRADE, A., YABO, R., AND CALDEYRO-BARCIA, R., 1970, A practical approach for evaluating fetal condition during labor by the fetal heart rate, in: *Fetal Growth and Development*

(H. A. Waisman and G. Kerr, eds.), McGraw-Hill, New York.

133. MERKEL, H., AND WITT, H., 1955, Die Massenverhältnisse des foetalen Herzens, *Beitr. Pathol. Anat.* **115**:178.

134. MESCHIA, G., AND BATTAGLIA, F. C., 1973, Acute changes of oxygen pressure and the regulation of uterine blood flow, in: *Foetal and Neonatal Physiology* (K. S. Comline, K. W. Cross, G. S. Dawes, and D. W. Nathanielsz, eds.), pp. 272–278, *Proceedings of the Sir Joseph Barcroft Centenary Symposium,* Cambridge University Press, Cambridge.

135. METCALFE, J., ROMNEY, S. L., RAMSEY, L. D., REID, D. E., AND BURWELL, C. S., 1955, Estimation of uterine blood flow in normal human pregnancy at term, *J. Clin. Invest.* **34**:1632.

136. MEYER, W. W., AND LIND, J., 1966, The ductus venosus and the mechanism of its closure, *Arch. Dis. Child.* **41**:597.

137. MEYER, W. W., AND SIMON, E., 1960, Die präparatorische Angiomalacie des Ductus Arteriosus Botalli als Voraussetzung seiner Engstellung und als Vorbild krankhafter Arterienveränderungen, *Virchows Arch. Pathol. Anat.* **333**:119.

138. MEYER, W. W., MOINIAN, M., AND LIND, J., 1969, An accessory fourth vessel of the cord, *Amer. J. Obstet. Gynecol.* **105**:1067.

139. MODANLOU, H., YEH, S., HON, E. H., AND FORSYTHE, A., 1973, Fetal and neonatal biochemistry and Apgar scores, *Amer. J. Obstet. Gynecol.* **117**:942.

140. MOINIAN, M., MEYER, W. W., AND LIND, J., 1969, Diameters of umbilical cord vessels and the weight of the cord in relation to clamping time, *Amer. J. Obstet. Gynecol.* **105**:604.

141. MONTAGNANI, C. A., 1963, Intrahepatic vascular pattern in the newborn infant, *Ann. N. Y. Acad. Sci.* **111**:121.

142. MORISON, J. E., 1952, *Foetal and Neonatal Pathology,* p. 156, Butterworth & Co., London.

143. MÜLLER, W., 1883, Die Massenverhältnisse des menschlichen Herzens, L. Voss, Hamburg and Leipzig.

144. NADKARNI, B. B., 1970, Innervation of the human umbilical artery. An electron microscope study, *Amer. J. Obstet. Gynecol.* **107**:303.

145. NAEYE, R. L., 1961, Arterial changes during the perinatal period, *Arch. Pathol. (Chicago)* **71**:121.

146. NELSON, N. M., PROD'HOM, L. S., CHERRY, R. B., AND SMITH, C. A., 1963, Pulmonary function in the newborn infant. V. Trapped gas in the normal infant's lung, *J. Clin. Invest.* **42**:1850.

147. NORMAN, I. C. S., OLIVER, R. E., REYNOLDS, E. D. R., STRANG, L. B., AND WELCH, K., 1971, Permeability of lung capillaries and alveoli to non-electrolytes in the foetal lamb, *J. Physiol.* **219**:303.

148. NYBERG, R., AND WESTIN, B., 1958, On the influence of uterine contractions on the blood pressure in the

umbilical vein at birth, *Acta Pediatr. Scand.* **47**:350.

149. OBERHANSLI-WEISS, I., HEYMANN, M. A., RUDOLPH, A. M., AND MELMON, K. L., 1972, The pattern and mechanisms of response to oxygen by the ductus arteriosus and umbilical artery, *Pediatr. Res.* **6**:693.

150. OLIVER, T. K., JR., DEMIS, J. A., AND BATES, G. D., 1970, Serial blood gas tensions and acid–base balance during the first hour of life in human infants, *Acta Paediatr. Scand. (Suppl. 207).*

151. PALMER, W. H., AND AGARWAL, J. B., 1970, The effects of red blood cell concentration on pulmonary blood flow, *Prog. Respir. Res.* **5**:84.

152. PALTAUF, R., 1888, Einfall von Mangel des Ductus venosus Arantii, *Wien. Klin. Wochenschr.* **1**:165.

153. PARMENTIER, R., 1962, L'aeration néonatale du poumon. Contribution expérimentale et anatomo-clinique, *Rev. Belg. Pathol.* **29**:121.

154. PATTEN, B. M., 1953, *Human Embryology* (2nd Ed.), p. 698, Blakiston Co., New York.

155. Patten, B. M., SOMMERFIELD, W. A., AND PAFF, G. H., 1929–1930, Functional limitations of the foramen ovale in the human foetal heart, *Anat. Rec.* **44**:165.

156. PAUL, R. H., AND HON, E. H., 1973, Clinical fetal monitoring. IV. Experience with a spiral electrode, *Obstet. Gynecol.* **41**:777.

157. PEARSON, A. A., AND SAUTER, R. W., 1969, The innervation of the umbilical vein in human embryos and fetuses, *Amer. J. Anat.* **125**:345.

158. PELTONEN, T., AND HIRVONEN, L., 1965, Experimental studies on fetal and neonatal circulation, *Acta Paediatr. Scand. Suppl. 161.*

159. POWER, G. C., LONGO, L. D., WAGNER, H. N., KUHL, D. E., AND FORSTER, R. E., 1966, Distribution of blood flow to the maternal and fetal portions of the sheep placenta using macro-aggregates, *J. Clin. Invest.* **45**:1058.

160. PREC. K. J., AND CASSELS, D. E., 1955, Dye dilution curves and cardiac output in newborn infants, *Circulation* **11**:789.

161. PURVES, M. J., AND BISCOE, T. J., 1966, Development of chemoreceptor activity, *Br. Med. Bull.* **22**:56.

162. RAMSEY, E. M., 1968, Uteroplacental circulation during labor, *Clin. Obstet. Gynecol.* **11**:78.

163. RECAVARREN, S., AND ARIAS-STELLA, J. G., 1964, Growth and development of the ventricular myocardium from birth to adult life, *Br. Heart J.* **26**:187.

164. REYNOLDS, S. R. M., FREESE, U. E., BIENARZ, J., CALDEYRO-BARCIA, R., MÉNDEZ-BAUER, C., AND ESCARCENA, L., 1968, Multiple simultaneous intervillous space pressures recorded in several regions of the hemochorial placenta in relation to functional anatomy of the fetal cotyledon, *Amer. J. Obstet. Gynecol.* **102**:1128.

165. RIGATTO, H., BRADY, J. P., AND DE LA TORRE VERDUZCO, R., 1975, Chemoreceptor reflexes in preterm infants: 1. The effect of gestational and post-natal age on the ventilatory response to inhalation of 100% and 15% oxygen, *Pediatrics* **55**:604.

166. RILEY, I. D., 1954, Hand and forearm flow in full term and premature infants, *Clin. Sci.* **13**:317.

167. ROBINSON, H. P., AND SHAW-DUNN, J., 1973, Fetal heart rates as determined by sonar in early pregnancy, *J. Obstet. Gynaecol. Br. Commonw.* **80**:805.

168. ROMNEY, S. L., 1966, Fetal hypoxic stress in the human, in: *The Heart and Circulation in the Newborn and Infant* (D. E. Cassels, ed.), pp. 53–64, Grune & Stratton, New York.

169. ROWE, R. D., AND MEHRIZI, A., 1968, *The Neonate with Congenital Heart Disease*, p. 57, W. B. Saunders, Philadelphia.

170. RUDOLPH, A. M., 1969, The course and distribution of the foetal circulation, in: *Foetal Autonomy* (G. E. W. Walstenholme and M. O. O'Connor, eds.), p. 147, J. & A. Churchill, London.

171. RUDOLPH, A. M., AND HEYMANN, M. A., 1967, The circulation of the fetus in utero: Methods for studying distribution of blood flow, cardiac output and organ blood flow, *Circ. Res.* **21**:163.

172. RUDOLPH, A. M., AND HEYMANN, M. A., 1968, The fetal circulation, *Ann. Rev. Med.* **19**:195.

173. RUDOLPH, A. M., AND HEYMANN, M. A., 1970, Circulatory changes during growth in the fetal lamb, *Circ. Res.* **26**:289.

174. RUDOLPH, A. M., HEYMANN, M. A., FISHMAN, N., AND LAKIER, J. B., 1975, Formalin infiltration of the ductus arteriosus. A method for palliation of infants with selected congenital cardiac lesions, *N. Engl. J. Med.* **292**:1263.

175. RUDOLPH, A. M., HEYMANN, M. A., TERAMO, K. A. W., BARRET, C. T., AND RAIHÄ, N. C. R., 1971, Studies on the circulation of the previable human fetus, *Pediatr. Res.* **5**:452.

176. RUDOLPH, A. M., MESEL, E., AND LEVY, J. V., 1963, Epinephrine in the treatment of cardiac failure due to shunts, *Circulation* **28**:3.

177. SALING, E., 1960, Neue Untersuchungsergebnisse über den Kreislauf des Kindes unmittelbar nach der Geburt, *Arch. Gynaekol.* **194**:287.

178. SCAMMON, R. E., AND NORRIS, E. H., 1918–1919, A statistical summary of the data on the time of obliteration of the foramen ovale, ductus arteriosus and ductus venosus in man, *Anat. Rec.* **15**:165.

179. SEGEL, N., STANĚK, V., JOSHI, R., AND SINGHAL, S., 1970, The influence of bradykinin on the pulmonary hypoxic response in normal man, *Prog. Respir. Res.* **5**:119.

180. SEKI, M., AND STRAUSS, L., 1964, Absence of one umbilical artery, *Arch. Pathol.* **78**:446.

181. SHARPE, G. L., AND LARSSON, K. S., 1975, Studies on closure of the ductus arteriosus. X. *In vivo* effect of prostaglandin, *Prostaglandins* **9**:703.

182. SHELLEY, H. J., 1961, Glycogen reserves and their changes at birth, *Br. Med. Bull.* **17**:137.

183. SHINEBOURNE, E. A., VAPAAVUORI, E. K., WILLIAMS, R. L., HEYMANN, M. A., AND RUDOLPH, A. M., 1972, Development of baroreflex activity in unanesthetized fetal and neonatal lambs, *Clin. Res.* **31**:710.

184. SIASSI, B., GOLDBERG, S. J., EMMANOUILIDES, G. C., HIGASHINO, S. M., AND LEWIS, E., 1971, Persistent pulmonary vascular obstruction in newborn infants, *J. Pediatr.* **78**:78.

185. SILVA, D. G., AND IKEDA, M., 1971, Ultrastructural and acetylcholinesterase studies on the innervation of the ductus arteriosus, pulmonary trunk and aorta of the fetal lamb, *J. Ultrastruct. Res.* **34**:358.

86. SILVER, M., STEVEN, D. H., AND COMLINE, R. S., 1973, Placental exchange and morphology in ruminants and the mare, in: *Foetal and Neonatal Physiology* (K. S. Comline, K. W. Cross, G. S. Dawes, and D. W. Nathanielsz, eds.), pp. 245–271, *Proceedings of the Sir Joseph Barcroft Centenary Symposium,* Cambridge University Press, Cambridge.

187. SISSON, T. R. C., AND WHALEN, L. E., 1960, The blood volume of infants. III. Alterations in the first hours after birth, *J. Pediatr.* **56**:43.

188. SMITH, B., 1968, Pre- and postnatal development of the ganglion cells of the rectum and its surgical implications, *J. Pediatr. Surg.* **3**:386.

189. SOBREVILLA, L. A., CASSINELLI, M. T., CARCELEN, A., AND MALAGA, J., 1971, Tension de oxigeno y equilibrio acido–base de madre y feto durante el parto en la altura, *Ginecol. Obstet.* **17**:45.

190. SONTAG, L. W., 1966, Implications of fetal behavior and environment for adult personalities, *Ann. N. Y. Acad. Sci.* **134**:2, 782.

191. SPIVACK, M., 1943, On presence or absence of nerves in umbilical blood vessels of man and guinea pig, *Anat. Rec.* **85**:85.

192. STAUB, N. C., 1963, Site of action of hypoxia on the pulmonary vasculature, *Fed. Proc. Fed. Amer. Soc. Exp. Biol.* **22**:453.

193. ŠTEMBERA, Z. K., HODR, J., AND JANDA, J., 1965, Umbilical blood flow in healthy newborn infants during the first minutes after birth, *Amer. J. Obstet. Gynecol.* **91**:568–574.

194. STEPHENSON, J. M., DU, J. N., AND OLIVER, T. K., JR., 1970, The effect of cooling on blood gas tension in newborn infants, *J. Pediatr.* **76**:848.

195. STERN, L., LIND, J., AND KAPLAN, B., 1961, Direct human foetal electrocardiography (with studies of the effects of adrenalin, atropine, clamping of the umbilical cord and placental separation on the foetal ECG), *Biol. Neonate* **3**:49.

196. SUREAU, C., 1960, Electrocardiographic foetale humaine normale, *Bull. Soc. Roy. Belge Gynecol. Obstet.* **30**:123.

197. THIBEAULT, D. W., WONG, M. M., AND AULD, P. A. M., 1967, Thoracic gas volume changes in premature infants, *Pediatrics* **40**:403.

198. TOULOUKIAN, R. J., AND DUNCAN, R., 1975, Acquired aganglionic megacolon in a premature infant: Report of a case, *Pediatrics* **56**:459.

199. TUNELL, R., 1975, The influence of different environmental temperatures on pulmonary gas exchange and blood gas changes after birth, *Acta Paediatr. Scand.* **64**:57.

200. TUNELL, R., COPHER, D., AND PERSSON, B., 1975, The pulmonary gas exchange and blood gas changes in connection to birth, in: *Current Concepts of Neonatal Intensive Care* (J. B. Stetson and P. Swyer, eds.), Warren H. Green, St. Louis.

201. UELAND, K., HANSEN, J., ENG, M., KALAPPA, R., AND PARER, J. T., 1970, Maternal cardiovascular dynamics. V. Cesarean section under thiopental, nitrous oxide, and succinylcholine anesthesia, *Amer. J. Obstet. Gynecol.* **108**:615.

202. URBACH, J. R., PHUVICHIT, B., ZWEITIG, H., MILLICAN, E., CARRINGTON, E. R., LOVELAND, M., WILLIAMS, J. M., LAMBERT, R. L., DUNCAN, A. M., FARRELL, S. L., SIMONS, P. O., AND SPURGEON, I. L., 1965, Instantaneous heart rate patterns in newborn infants, *Amer. J. Obstet. Gynecol.* **93**:965.

203. USHER, R., SHEPARD, M., AND LIND, J., 1963, The blood volume of the newborn infant and placental transfusion, *Acta Paediatr. Scand.* **52**:497.

204. VAN LEEUWEN, G., BEHRINGER, B., AND GLENN, L., 1967, Single umbilical artery, *J. Pediatr.* **71**:103.

205. VLIETINCK, R. F., THIERY, M., ORYE, E., DE CLERCQ, A., AND VAN VAERENBERGH, P., 1972, Significance of the single umbilical artery: A clinical, radiological, chromosomal, and dermatoglyphic study, *Arch. Dis. Child.* **47**:639.

206. WALLENBURG, H. C., STOLTE, L. A., AND JANSSENS, J., 1973, The pathogenesis of placental infarction. I. A morphologic study in the human placenta, *Amer. J. Obstet. Gynecol.* **116**:835.

207. WALLGREN, G., AND LIND, J., 1967, Quantitative studies of the human neonatal circulation. IV. Observations on the newborn infant's peripheral circulation and plasma expansion during moderate hypovolemia, *Acta Paediatr. Scand. (Suppl. 179)* **55**:68.

208. WALLGREN, G., KARLBERG, P., AND LIND, J., 1960, Studies of the circulatory adaptation immediately after birth, *Acta Paediatr. Scand.* **49**:843.

209. WALSH, S. Z., 1963, Electrocardiographic intervals during the first week of life, *Amer. Heart J.* **66**:36.

210. WALSH, S. Z., 1963, The electrocardiogram during the first week of life, *Br. Heart J.* **25**:784.

211. WALSH, S. Z., 1968, A diastolic murmur in the healthy newborn infant, *Amer. Heart J.* **75**:582.

212. WALSH, S. Z., 1968, Maternal effects of early and late clamping of the umbilical cord, *Lancet* **1**:996.

213. WALSH, S. Z., 1968, Early versus late clamping of the cord: A comparative study of the ECG in the neonatal period, *Biol. Neonate* **12**:343.

213a. WALSH, S. Z., 1968, ECG in infants and children,

in : *Paediatric Cardiology* (H. Watson, ed.), pp. 115–159, Lloyd-Luke, London.

214. WALSH, S. Z., 1969, Early clamping versus stripping of the cord: A comparative study of the electro-cardiogram in the neonatal period, *Br. Heart J.* **31**:122.

215. WALSH, S. Z., 1970, Phonocardiographic studies in the newborn (unpublished observations).

216. WALSH, S. Z., 1974, The electrocardiogram in healthy full term and premature infants, Medical thesis, Karolinska Institute, Stockholm.

217. WALSH, S. Z., 1975, ECG changes during the first 5–6 days after birth. Some factors that may be involved, *Praxis (Rev. Suisse Med.)* **64**:747.

218. WALSH, S. Z., 1975, Characteristic features of the ECG of premature infants during the first year of life. With a comment on a large Q in lead III and the incidence of pattern types in right and left precordial leads, *Praxis* **64**:754.

219. WALSH, S. Z., AND GYULAI, F., 1970, Electro-mechanical intervals in the healthy newborn, *J. Electrocardiol.* **3**:259.

220. WALSH, S. Z., AND GYULAI, F., 1973, The effect of cry on heart rate and the Q–A$_2$ interval in early and late clamped infants, *Biol. Neonate* **23**:193.

221. WALSH, S. Z., MEYER, W. W., AND LIND, J., 1974 *The Human Fetal and Neonatal Circulation: Function and Structure,* pp. 32, 38–46, 152–159, 172–199 Charles C. Thomas, Springfield, Illinois.

222. WESTIN, B., AND ENHÖRNING, G., 1955, An experimental study of the human fetus with special reference to asphyxia neonatorum, *Acta Paediatr. Scand.* **44**:79.

223. WILKIN, P., AND BURZSTEIN, M., 1958, *Le Placenta Humain* (J. Snoeck, ed.), Masson, Paris.

224. WOOD, C., 1968, Use of fetal blood sampling and fetal heart rate monitoring, in : *Diagnosis and Treatment of Fetal Disorders* (K. Adamsons, ed.), Springer-Verlag, Berlin.

225. YAO, A. C., HIRVENSALO, M., AND LIND, J., 1968, The rate of placental transfusion in normal full-term infants, *Lancet* **1**:380.

226. YAO, A. C., WALLGREN, G. C., SINHA, S. N., AND LIND, J., 1971, Peripheral circulatory response to feeding in the newborn infant, *Pediatrics* **47**:378.

227. ZAITEV, N. D., 1959, Development of neural elements in the umbilical cord, *Arkh. Anat. Gistol. Embriol.* **37**:81.

CHAPTER 9

Blood Volume

Thomas R. C. Sisson

1. Introduction

The development of the fetal circulation is an orderly process, predesigned as is the development of other systems toward a moment when the human organism must survive independently. It is subject, of course, not only to genetic direction, but also to environmental effects of pervasive influence: maternal nutrition and health, deleterious chemicals and drugs, radiation, viral invasion of placental and fetal structures, age and parity of the mother, social and economic status, and so on. Of more immediate concern at birth, it is affected by the character and management of delivery.

The competence of the fetus to adapt to independent life is significantly affected by the hemodynamic state of the mother at birth. At the same time, circulation in the placenta and its growth and functional adequacy are influenced as well. Various methods of obstetric delivery are known to bear on the responses of the fetus to extrauterine life, most particularly on the function of respiratory and circulatory systems. The function of these systems in turn most profoundly influences perinatal metabolic function, acid–base balance, and the character of cellular respiration.

Thomas R. C. Sisson · Department of Pediatrics, Obstetrics and Gynecology (Perinatology), Temple University School of Medicine, Philadelphia, Pennsylvania 19140

2. Blood Volume in the Pregnant Woman

The total blood volume of the pregnant woman increases in roughly linear fashion from the second month of gestation on, but the ratios of plasma volume to red cell mass may be altered by anemia, dietary intake, and systemic complications of pregnancy such as toxemia, diabetes, and heart disease. In the first 6 weeks of pregnancy, the plasma, red cell, and total circulating blood volumes are comparable to those of the normal, healthy, nonpregnant woman. Beyond the midpoint of the second month of gestation, however, the plasma volume increases steadily, an increment of 21% being attained by the 20th week of gestation. Up to this period, the red cell volume does not increase to any appreciable degree, but tends to remain constant at the level of nonpregnant women, i.e., 26–27 ml/kg.[33,34] In effect, this 20-week period is a time of relative hemodilution, even though the total red cell volume has increased to a degree.

It should be noted that although there is a considerable variation of volumes among women from the 8th week of gestation on, there is a rather good constancy of values for the individual, as shown by serial plasma volume measurements. The maintenance of an almost uniform red cell volume, on the basis of body weight, illustrates the ease with which the maternal marrow responds to pregnancy

Table I. Mean Circulating Maternal Plasma, Red Cell, and Total Blood Volumes During Pregnancy[a]

Week of gestation	Plasma		Red cells		Blood	
	ml	ml/kg	ml	ml/kg	ml	ml/kg
Nonpregnant	2800	50	1550	27	4350	77
6	2900	52	1500	26–27	4400	79
12	3100	54	1575	27	4675	81
16	3400	57	1625	27	5025	84
20	3800	63	1650	27	5450	90
24	4400	68	1775	27	6175	95
28	4400	66	1800	27	6200	93
32	4600	67	1825	27	6425	94
36	4700	70	1875	27	6575	97
40	4700	72	1975	27	6675	99

[a] After Lund and Donovan.[33]

demands, because the total red cell mass, in order to sustain an average 26–27 ml/kg mass, rises steadily throughout gestation.

After the 24th week of pregnancy, the maternal plasma volume holds to a plateau at about 67 ml/kg. This average level is a stable one through the rest of pregnancy. The red cell volume, too, remains constant at 27 ml/kg, with a nearly linear total increment as gestation proceeds. Total plasma volume increases about 50%, and total red cell mass about 20%, in the 40 weeks of normal gestation (Table I).

There are women who seem to have, for them, a marked deviation from average volumes; they may be termed *hypervolemic* or *hypovolemic*. They too exhibit a constancy of volume state, not only throughout gestation, but also through repeated pregnancies. There is no adequate explanation for the finding of markedly elevated or constricted blood volumes in these women; certainly it seems not to affect pregnancy itself. It was shown by Prichard and co-workers[54,55] that the presence of a conceptus is not, indeed, necessary, since they found hypervolemia of the pregnancy type in association with hydatidiform mole.

Maintenance of an adequate red cell volume is also influenced by iron intake during pregnancy. It is possible, in fact, to force an elevation of red cell volume by adding therapeutic iron preparations to the diet of the pregnant woman. Whether an increased red cell mass in the mother is of benefit not only to her but also to her unborn infant is somewhat in question. The common feeling that a little is good, a lot is a lot better, may really not apply. Too small a mass, implying anemia, is obviously a detriment, but too large a mass, by altering placental flow or rates of flow, may also be detrimental. The oxygen-carrying capacity of the blood of the mother bears little real relationship to that of the fetus late in pregnancy, when this capacity is considered a function of volume, for the volumes are independent of one another in the two bodies, and the factors of hemoglobin type and thus oxygen dissociation are more relevant. Exceptions to this independence may occur, as in fetomaternal transfusion or where uterine blood flow is seriously compromised, but as a general rule, maternal–fetal blood volume ratios do not seem to influence fetal oxygen capacity, as was stated by Barcroft[5] 30 years ago.

The changes in plasma and red cell volume that occur during pregnancy are the result of adaptive processes that seem to be necessary to give an environment suitable for proper perfusion of the placenta and for growth and protection of the fetus.

It is now generally agreed that amniotic fluid is derived only in part from fetal urine, and that much of its volume and substance are from secretory or perfusant action of the chorioamnion itself. The similarity of amniotic fluid to the constituents of plasma, and far less to fetal urine, especially in the early months of gestation, supports this view. The presence in amniotic fluid of the phospholipids found in tracheal secretions indicates another source for its composition. At this time, no correlation between maternal plasma volume and volume of amniotic fluid has been reported, although such information would be of interest and perhaps of importance.

The anemia of pregnancy, although of more immediate and pervasive effect on the mother than on the fetus, has been shown to influence the newborn in that if the mother suffers from iron deficiency and anemia, as evidenced by a low hemoglobin mass and red cell volume and a low serum iron with elevated total iron-binding capacity of the serum, the infant will tend to share these lower-than-normal values.[34,61] Reduced iron stores and the early appearance (during the first year of life) of iron deficiency anemia in such infants do occur despite the notorious ability of the fetus to extract a sufficiency of nutritional elements from its mother. In this index, as in almost any other index of fetal outcome, the fetus cannot be considered a perfect parasite.

The outstanding influence of maternal iron deficiency is on the red cell volume and hemoglobin mass of her infant, with some effect on the iron stores. Mothers with adequate depot iron or effective treatment with iron compounds give birth to infants with a superior erythrocyte and hemoglobin mass. Conversely, infants of mothers who are severely anemic reflect this anemia in having a comparatively lower red cell volume and hemoglobin mass.[40]

The serum iron of infants newly born to women with severe anemia is lower than that of infants born to women treated with iron preparations during pregnancy. One may infer that the serum iron of the neonate reflects maternal iron supply in most instances, although administration of iron to the mother may not always ensure passage of this element across the placenta. The demands for iron by the fetus are not entirely met at the expense of the mother if she is anemic, for she will satisfy, at least in part, her own needs for an enlarging red cell volume and for hemoglobinization of her red cells.

3. Circulatory Alterations in the Placenta

Maternal blood flow to the placenta is mediated by so many factors of pressure, rate, posture, general physiologic adaptability, state of health, and others, that it is difficult to pick one from this tangle of interrelated mechanisms and treat its effect as if it operated alone. Ultimately, though, the flow of maternal blood depends on the volume available in the space of the uterine vascular compartment. Changes in the rate of flow of a given volume at any particular time in gestation depend on other factors, and changes in volume may be compensated for under usual circumstances.

The greater blood volume in the circulation of the pregnant woman appears to be manifest about the sixth week of pregnancy, before the placenta is of appreciable size and before the uterine mass has added seriously to the total vascular bed of the body. Clearly, an important physiologic adaptation of a somewhat preparative nature has begun. The increase in the total blood volume, albeit greater in the plasma compartment, thus ensures a readily available circulatory mass for uterine and placental flow without need for increased cardiac work or compromising increases in rate of flow.

The oxygen-carrying capacity of maternal blood reaching the placenta and exposed in the intervillous spaces to the oxygen gradient at the fetal side is quite labile. Its lability is the result of alterations in blood volume and a number of indirect factors that are not well understood, including hormonal effects. The integrity of the uterine and maternal–placental circulation may be compromised not only by toxemia of pregnancy, but by drug-induced circulatory changes, blood loss from the mother either at the placental attachment (abruptio placenta, placenta praevia, infarcted placenta) or elsewhere, by high altitude, and by profound alterations in health or nutritional state, as found in pneumonia, starvation, or hyperemesis gravidarum. Although a good deal is known about the effects of changes in uterine blood flow on the fetus during labor, less information is available on the effects earlier in pregnancy. We give the outcome a name—placental dysfunction—yet precise mechanisms are unclear.

The placenta and fetus seem to resist damaging fluctuations in maternal blood volume or blood flow in part because the processes fostering transfer of oxygen from mother to fetus appear to work so advantageously in that direction. The oxygen-carrying capacity of the fetus rises rapidly in the early weeks of gestation and more slowly in the last trimester, but throughout it remains higher than in the mother, more emphatically in the last trimester, when the hemoglobin mass of the fetus is greater than the mother's on the basis of body weight. For this knowledge, we are again indebted to the basic studies of Barcroft[5] on the sheep, and to those of Wintrobe and Shumacker[76] in other species.

Oxygen dissociation curves of fetal hemoglobin differ from those of the mother, due, it is now thought,[53] to differences in electrolyte or total base content, or perhaps to carbonic anhydrase activity, rather than to differences in molecular construction of the hemoglobins alone. In any event, the greater dissociation is, in times of stress, at least temporarily protective of the fetus, and is for the most part designed to facilitate transfer (see also Chapter 12). That the oxygen dissociation of fetal hemoglobin is to the right of adult hemoglobin carried to the intervillous spaces by maternal blood (see Chapter 6, Figs. 2 and 4) demonstrates the greater ease with which oxygen will leave the maternal circulation and be accepted by the blood of the fetal–placental circulation.

It should be pointed out that the work of Power et al.[53] and others[71] has indicated that maternal blood flow is of uneven distribution among the cotyledons, as is fetal blood flow. Furthermore, these investigators found that the *relationship* of maternal and fetal placental blood flow is remarkably uneven. More uniform maternal and fetal flows and relationship of flows ensue, however, when the mother is hypoxic. If this greater uniformity is true for the human, it means that normally, at any given time, the placental tissue does not have an equally efficient exchange of oxygen throughout, but that if the placental circulation is reduced in oxygen content, then these flows become more uniform, and the efficiency of placental oxygen exchange is promoted. This is an undoubtedly important advance in our knowledge of hemodynamics in this organ.

The placenta itself, as a functioning as well as a functional organ, has a considerable oxygen consumption that decreases in the last half of gestation.[28] Its high rate of consumption may explain why a marked rise in maternal oxygen tension is not matched by an equal increase in fetal P_{O_2}, and also why maternal hypoxemia is reflected to only a certain degree by a fall in fetal oxygen tension. In other words, the placenta dampens the fluctuations in maternal blood oxygen tension under conditions of stress, anesthesia, and so on.

That the oxygen tensions of fetal and fetal–placental blood are low compared with the maternal is not a point of concern. It is quite obviously a physiologically desirable state if blood volume is adequate, if the oxygen–carrying capacity of maternal and fetal bloods is unimpaired, and if flow is not too seriously embarrassed. There is, indeed, a modest margin of safety most of the time.

Despite the ability of the placenta and fetus to resist deleterious effects of maternal change, and despite the margin of safety, these protective mechanisms may be overcome. The fetus, especially at term and most particularly during labor, has been shown[28] to reflect a fall in maternal blood pH, and to demonstrate asphyxia with consequent depression from serious changes in maternal blood pressure and myometrial blood flow. A reduction of maternal uterine and placental blood flow is well known in preeclampsia, and this reduction may become a distinct hazard to the fetus.

Uterine contractions will cause a decrease in arterial flow to the intervillous spaces, but a simultaneous arrest of venous outflow permits a slower, more prolonged gas exchange in the placental pool of blood. The common use of oxytocic drugs to promote labor causes a reduction of uterine blood flow by increasing uterine activity. Of itself, this reduction is seldom troublesome to the oxygen demands of the fetus, but if for other reasons the competence of fetal–maternal gas exchange and metabolic activity is reduced, fetal distress will inevitably result.

The complications of labor increase, on the one hand, with newer obstetric techniques that are poorly managed, and decrease, on the other, as older methods of management are abandoned. We become increasingly sophisticated in knowledge of the physiology of labor and fetal dependence, and directional control of the progress of labor has improved as better methods of monitoring fetal reactions are introduced. It was shown by Wilcox et al.[75] as early as 1959 that in normal labor, there is a progressive fall in fetal scalp (capillary) P_{O_2} and pH, while there is a simultaneous rise in P_{CO_2}. These changes are usually within limits of variance that the fetus can tolerate and for which it can compensate. These alterations of biochemical behavior may be accelerated and exaggerated, however, by abnormal circumstances: excessive maternal hyperventilation, acidosis, deficiencies of maternal blood flow or oxygen supply (as in general anesthesia, spinal anesthesia, or paracervical block), hypotension, premature separation of the placenta, caesarean section, prolapse of the cord, and feto-fetal transfusion in the case of twinning.

The type of delivery of the fetus is known to have certain effects that place the fetus in danger, although the precise reasons for fetal distress may be either obscure or multiple. Caesarean section increases neonatal morbidity compared with vaginal delivery, and respiratory distress is then not uncommon. This distress is due, in great measure, not so much to the method of delivery as to the complication that led to this choice for extraction of the infant. Caesarean section may as easily be said to reduce morbidity in many instances by preventing the inappropriate delivery *per vaginum* of a fetus that would be otherwise placed at risk by prolonged labor, blood loss, poorly controlled diabetes in the mother, and so on. When a fetus is delivered vaginally, but with breech or footling presentation, neonatal morbidity is increased. Delay in delivery of the head will cause hypoxia. Compression of the chest wall, then release with passage beyond the introitus, may cause an inspiratory gasp while the head is still encased. Some aspiration may then occur, which must be corrected by prompt measures, particularly should the amniotic fluid contain much meconium. The most pronounced effect, however, is the greater degree of hypoxia that supervenes in this type of delivery and the more frequent finding of respiratory depression compared with head presentations. These complications may be due partly to the prolongation of labor in many breech deliveries. Such infants are subjected to periods of partial asphyxia that have a cumulative effect that leads to acidemia, lowered tissue oxygen tensions, and increased blood carbon dioxide tensions.

It is difficult to determine with any degree of accuracy the amount of blood lost by a woman during labor and delivery. Many estimates are given for all types of delivery, and it is unfortunate that this subject has received so little study, for the blood loss by the mother has a direct and profound effect on uterine blood flow and on the circulatory responses of the fetus and neonate. Blood loss during normal vaginal delivery is variously estimated at 150–600 ml. Higher estimates are made in complicated vaginal delivery. It has become almost a dictum among many experienced obstetricians that the usual estimate recorded by obstetrical house officers and those with limited obstetrical practice is often close to 50% of actual blood loss. In caesarean sections, the average loss of blood has been calculated to be 1028 ml,[41] with a range of 274–3180 ml. Whether the loss is much or little, the uterine arterial pressure is reduced with blood loss, and in consequence, the flow of blood through the myometrium is decreased, placental flow on the maternal side is reduced, and tissue hypoxia is enhanced in both placenta and fetus. With speedy performance of the operative delivery, the effect on the fetus is minimal (except as it alters fetal blood volume), but oxygenation may be impaired. If the maternal blood loss is considerable, and in about 50% it exceeds 1 liter,[41] a further complication of hypotension occurs, compromising maternal–fetal gas exchange. One mechanism helps to preserve the P_{O_2} of the fetus in this situation: as the uterine arterial blood flow is reduced and as uterine contractility is decreased or obliterated, venous outflow from the maternal placental pool is also reduced, and the blood therein remains for a longer period of time, permitting more complete gas exchange. In this instance, then, oxygen transfer to the fetal circulation in the placenta is prolonged. This prolongation tends to protect the fetus from hypoxia of maternal derivation, although the tech-

nique of delivery of the infant may act against such a transfer by reducing the fetal blood volume and thus oxygen-carrying capacity.

Monitoring of the fetus during labor by the use of sophisticated electronic devices that show the fetal ECG simultaneously with uterine activity, and by fetal scalp blood-sampling to measure pH and gas tensions, has aided remarkably in the correct management of delivery and the increase of fetal salvage. Interpretation of the fetal ECG in relation to uterine contractions assists in identifying the fetus in jeopardy. Some misinterpretations are still possible in this relatively new aspect of perinatology, however, notably the effect of partial cord compression. This contingency may yield tracings that mimic other, more serious intrauterine events. In such a complication of labor, the umbilical vein, having a low pressure, is more easily occluded by compression than the umbilical arteries. Consequently, unless all three vessels are occluded, arterial blood is sent to the placenta, but little or none can return to the fetus. The net result is a significant diversion of blood volume from the body of the fetus to its placenta. If delivered under these circumstances, the infant will be hypovolemic and the placenta unduly engorged. There will be not only hypovolemia, but also such a restriction of red cell mass that the infant may be actually anemic and its oxygen-carrying capacity reduced. Although this difficulty has not been documented in the human, one may speculate that infants with lowered blood pressure immediately after birth may have suffered just such a sequence of events. Late decelerations without loss of beat-to-beat variability in fetal ECG tracings may suggest this occurrence.

It is certain that the foregoing consequences of partial (venous) cord occlusion have also followed transplacental hemorrhage. A recent study[50] showed that fetomaternal hemorrhage may result in fetal death, neonatal anemia, or the birth of clinically normal infants, depending on the time in pregnancy and the amount of bleeding into the maternal circulation. If hemorrhage occurs days or weeks before birth, fetal erythropoiesis may correct the loss, and the infant may be born with an essentially normal blood volume. If it occurs late in pregnancy or at birth, the hemorrhage will result in hypovolemia. Correction of the constricted blood volume will be by expansion of the plasma compartment; there will be no time for reconstitution of the red cell mass. The end result will be a low erythrocyte volume and true anemia. These authors suggest that the maternal blood should be examined for the presence of fetal red cells within a few hours of birth whenever an infant is born anemic in the absence of obvious blood loss or maternal–fetal blood group incompatibility. In this way, a transplacental hemorrhage of recent origin can be easily demonstrated.

Hemorrhage occurring shortly before delivery can be clinically misleading. The hypovolemia and shocklike state that may ensue can be confused with central depression, intrauterine hypoxia from other causes, and poor ventilatory perfusion. Efforts may be misdirected toward purely pulmonary resuscitative measures when expansion of the volume is a more critical choice of treatment.

It is only good medical practice to follow, *seriatim,* the hematocrit values of infants suspected of transplacental hemorrhage, blood loss from placenta praevia, or partial cord occlusion. This monitoring is a simple means of determining anemia of blood loss, which may not be otherwise too readily identifiable. Peripheral, usually heelstick, hematocrits are not reliable in the first hours or day after birth, for there are significant alterations in blood volume in that time until an equilibrium between red cell and plasma volumes has been reached. Furthermore, the distal extremities are the sites of chilling, vasodilatation, sluggish capillary flow, and often falsely high hematocrit values. A determination of the packed red cell volume of blood sampled from large peripheral vessels or centrally is far more reliable. If an infant in such suspect condition exhibits pallor, the blood pressure should be determined to assist in the diagnosis of severe hypovolemia and shock. It should be recalled that the evidence may not be clearly manifest for as long as 24 hr after delivery, so that the serial determination of blood pressure and hematocrit ought to be followed for at least one full day.

It has been recognized for many years that women who have high weight gain in normal pregnancy tend to have larger babies than those with low weight gain, although for years it was the practice to limit such gain. Studies in Aberdeen[21] of 53 normal pregnancies in which plasma volume, total body water, and plasma protein concentrations were measured showed that those women with high plasma volume, large weight gain, edema, and elevated intravascular protein mass produced larger babies than mothers with lower plasma volume and weight gain, and less edema. This is not to say that larger babies are better babies, but rather it illustrates again the point that the infant reflects in fundamental ways the mother's physiologic condition.

3.1. Placental Separation

In normal vaginal delivery, the placenta separates from the uterine wall almost as the fetus is expelled. The circulation in the placental tissues quickly halts, and the umbilical vessels lose much of their intralumenal pressure. The umbilical arteries may continue to pulsate for several minutes or may cease pulsation shortly after exposure to air and manipulation, since they are quite sensitive to external stimuli and will constrict forcefully, as Reynolds[59] showed. The umbilical vein, having no muscular coat, collapses from lack of sufficient pressure and flow. Fetal, or more properly neonatal, blood loss does not ordinarily occur, since the placental circulation diminishes so rapidly and the cord is usually clamped with dispatch. By deliberate manipulation, however, the neonatal blood volume may be augmented or reduced.

Abnormal separation of the placenta, completely or partially covering the os, occurring in the last trimester, and occasioning a significant amount of painless bleeding, is considered *placenta praevia.* The incidence of this condition was reported to be 0.6% of pregnancies in a collaborative study from 13 institutions.[26] Whether the condition is mild, moderate, or severe, the fetus is at great risk of blood loss, although this loss may be gradual. With partial separation of the placenta, blood flow from the mother is impaired; some of the cotyledonous structure is no longer exposed to liquid, but rather to clotted, blood. This lack alone need not deprive the fetus of an adequate placental exchange, but should the fetal side of the placenta be torn, however slightly, appreciable loss of blood volume may occur. The fetus will then suffer anemia, which will trigger erythropoiesis and eventual recovery of red cell mass while the fetus is *in utero,* or, if the anemia is severe enough, will lead to hemorrhagic shock and intrauterine demise.[50]

Abruptio placenta is a most serious obstetric complication, accounting for nearly 15% of perinatal deaths.[26] In this condition, which is potentially disastrous to the fetus, the acute and inordinate loss of blood causes a precipitous fall of central venous pressure in the mother, a sudden loss of blood volume, and quite naturally then, a reduction in placental blood flow in intact portions. Oxygen exchange in the fetus is thus abruptly compromised, and a state of severe tissue hypoxia supervenes. Should the fetal structures of the placenta be damaged, as they most commonly are, acute fetal blood loss will take place, magnifying the consequences. About one-third of mothers with this complication lose their infants *in utero*.[8,26] If the infant is born alive, survival is over 85%, provided, of course, that anemia and shock are promptly recognized and adequate oxygen is provided. The degree of anoxia suffered by the fetus in this disorder is substantial. Neonatal depression, aside from the deranged circulation, is pronounced, especially in the premature. The chance of neurologic deficit at 1 year of age was found to be as much as 1 in 4 if the infant was premature, 1 in 10 if it was mature.[26]

It may be stated that placenta praevia and abruptio placentae, most particularly the latter, may cause a reduction in the blood volume of the fetus, even to the point of shock and death. Loss of blood volume that does not cause intrauterine death may lead to functionally damaging anoxia and neonatal anemia so profound that adaptation to circulatory changes may be delayed.

3.2. Anomalous Circulatory Patterns

Unusual patterns in the development of placental vessels do not necessarily produce maldevelopment of the fetus, although maldevelopment is a frequent result. Vascular anomalies may present, however, a great risk of hemorrhage and consequent drop in the volume of circulating blood in the fetus. If not actually fatal, it is at least potentially life-threatening.

Velamentous insertion of the cord, wherein the umbilical vessels divide in the chorion laeve before the marginal insertion of the membranes, is associated with fetal maldevelopment. This type of insertion is found in about 1% of single pregnancies.[8] The membranous vessels, especially if they pass across the internal cervical os, are easily torn or ruptured in delivery, and this damage may result in fetal exsanguination. The vessels are frequently subject to thrombosis. In twin pregnancies, the vessels may cross over dividing membranes, making the chance of exsanguination of both infants greater. Support for the umbilical vessels and their immediate branches is fragile, increasing the risk of hemorrhage from injury to the tissues involved if the cord is short or wound about a presenting part.

Absence of one umbilical artery is also observed in about 1% of deliveries, sometimes in association with velamentous insertion. Benirschke[7] found an incidence of 7.2% in twin placentas, which may well be evidence of disturbed placental growth. It is known that a wide variety of malformations are found with this anomaly, and there are frequent chromosomal disturbances. The condition is more frequent in twin birth, where it may occur in either one or both infants. The relationship of single umbilical artery to differences in blood volume of twins has not been studied, but the finding of other cardiovascular abnormalities in association with it would presuppose a relationship.

Vascular communications in the placentas of twins are common in the monochorial type, and may be arterial, venous, or capillary, or a combination of these. *Fetofetal transfusion*, or the twin transfusion syndrome, may result from such communications. The most frequent anastamosis is between arteries, the least frequent between veins, and arteriovenous somewhere in the middle. Artery-to-vein and vein-to-artery communication may be small. Regardless of which vessels communicate and which multiplicity of anastomotic combinations is found, there may be a variety of discordant abnormalities from which but one twin will suffer.

With respect to fetal hemodynamics, the twin transfusion syndrome is most important to consider, for it is more and more frequently recognized: though not common, it is vividly impressive. In this condition, one twin of a pair with monochorial placenta will transfuse the other. There will be a marked disparity of hemoglobin values at least 5 g/dl, as suggested by Rausen *et al.*,[56] and an increased number of normoblasts will be found in the donor twin. Hydramnios of the sac of the recipient is common. Besides the fact that even on cursory inspection, one twin is plethoric, the other pale, it may be observed that the placenta of the anemic twin is also pale, soft, and bulky, while that of the plethoric twin is dark red and turgid. Often, the anemic twin is significantly smaller, not only in general body size, but also in organ size. The heart of the recipient may be twice again as large in mass as that of the donor. The transfused twin may have a hematocrit of 70% or more, and may be a greater problem in the nursery than the donor, who, though anemic, has adapted fairly well to his chronic blood loss. The recipient twin, on the other hand, may have difficulty in circulatory adaptations after birth, may suffer the consequences of multiple microthrombi because of excessive erythrocyte volume, and will at the very least develop hyperbilirubinemia.

Strong and Corney[69] reported that the chorionic villi of the anemic infant are bulky, pleomorphic, and edematous, and 2 or 3 times as great in volume as those of the plethoric infant, with double the surface area. The capillaries tend to be longer and more narrow, and are often filled with nucleated erythrocytes. These differences are due to edema, and the capillaries of narrow caliber in the donor twin imply greater vascular resistance and slower blood flow. Physiologically, these differences seem appropriate, given the lesser body mass of the anemic twin.

It is possible that some factor other than simple anastamotic shunt over a long period of time could account for some of the findings in this syndrome. The studies of Reissman[58] in parabiotic rats, in which one rat was kept in a normal atmosphere and the other in a state of chronic hypoxia, demonstrated a similar stimulation of marrow erythropoiesis in both animals. Reissman concluded that the stimulus was not hypoxemia alone, since hypoxemia did not exist in one, but rather that a humoral factor, probably erythropoietin, produced in the hypoxic rat was transferred to the other. The possibility that this same mechanism causes part of the excessive red cell volume in the plethoric human twin has not been proved, but is an intriguing hypothesis.

Vascular communication between fused dichorionic placentas is infrequent, occurring possibly once in 1000 births.[69] The mixing of blood between dissimilar twins is unusual. It may result in red cell chimerism, a situation of great rarity in the human, although common enough in cattle.

4. Placental Transfusion

Transfusion of the newly born infant with blood from the placenta is still considered of questionable value by many investigators, at least in a number of circumstances. Indeed, it is thought by some to be less than a physiologic necessity. Arguments for and against it are at best tentative after more than 20 years of controversy and spasmodic research. The supposed benefits of placental transfusion are

engaging, but not as yet confirmed, and its possible hazards are as alarming as the benefits are attractive.

If one considers that the volume of blood in the placenta is an amount sufficient to accomplish the filling of the entire vascular bed of the organ beyond the amount provided by the fetus for its own circulatory capacity, one may quite properly wonder why there should be any physiologic need for the placental blood to augment the infant's own presumably adequate supply—at least it was adequate *in utero*. This position is perhaps further strengthened when it is recalled that the placenta is an organ of impermanence, meant to be amputated at birth. It may be questioned whether the blood it contains, which is useful before birth as a vehicle of transport and respiration, is of any more value to the delivered infant than its other tissues.

Under some circumstances, placental transfusion must be useful. Severe fetal blood loss from premature separation of the placenta or other causes could be reversed, with careful manipulation, by transfer of residual placental blood. In fetofetal transfusion, some relief of the donor twin's anemia might be contrived, but this relief is likely to be minimal, and might too drastically disturb the infant's hemodynamic state, which is usually well compensated, volumetrically, because of the chronicity of the transfusion. The infant of a severely anemic mother might be helped to some extent by such a transfusion of the placental residual if her condition were known in advance.

The argument has been offered that placental transfusion will give a readily available supply of hemoglobin iron to fortify the infant's accumulated reserves. A reasonable transfusion of 60 ml would increase the iron pool by close to 32 mg, which is not a spectacular amount, but is serviceable.

Unquestionably, placental transfusion alters the blood volume of the neonate. The ability of the infant to cope with added volume is affected at a time when he must adapt to a changing pattern of respiration and circulation. In the premature infant, this ability may be compromised by too great a load on the heart; in any infant, too large an added volume may increase a left-to-right shunt and further complicate a dysfunctional cardiopulmonary system.

The hemodynamic state of the newborn is so complex and changes so rapidly in the minutes and hours after birth that the effect of placental transfusion cannot be judged without taking into account several vitally important factors of equal gravity: uterine activity before birth, manipulation of the cord and uterus, administration of drugs and anesthetics to the mother, presentation of the fetus, whether the infant once delivered is held above or below the level of the placenta, the method of delivery, vigor of the infant, degree of oxygenation, distress *in utero*, the time of establishment of respiration, and chilling of the infant. In many situations in which the fetus has been distressed *in utero*, is greatly depressed on delivery, or for any reason needs immediate resuscitation, attempts to ensure a placental transfusion are misplaced and the priorities for intervention misguided.

4.1. Clamping of the Cord

A placental transfusion cannot be accomplished without some delay in clamping of the cord after delivery of the infant. The many reports of the effect of delayed clamping are difficult to reconcile because of the variety of intervals in time between delivery and cord ligation. Actually, the opposite technique of immediate clamping is rarely duplicated in all the reported investigations. Small wonder, then, that there is such a disparity of data and points of view.

It is clear, however, that besides delay in clamping of the cord, such a transfusion requires the enlistment of at least one other of several features: (1) gravity, (2) external mechanical force, and (3) uterine contraction.

The effect of gravity can be exerted by holding the infant well below the level of the uterus, although even a slight distance below the introitus will suffice if enough time is allowed, while the placenta is still within, or by holding the expelled placenta above the infant as blood drains. Reverse flow will take place, however, if the infant is held above the level of the placenta.

External mechanical force may be applied to the intact cord, stripping or milking it repeatedly toward the infant.

The pressures exerted by uterine contractions are themselves sufficient to propel blood to the infant, although not if he is held above the mother's abdomen.[74] Placental transfusion may be accelerated if the mother is given methylergotamine within 30 sec after delivery of the infant.[78] In this study by Yao and her associates, it was reported that the transfusion could be nearly completed after 1 min with the injection of a uterine stimulant.

The timing of cord clamp may be influenced by the onset of respirations. If the cord is clamped before respiratory effort has begun, it is possible that only a partial placental transfusion could take place. It was shown in one study[57] that a smaller residual volume of blood remained in the placenta if clamping of the cord took place after the first breath. It should be remarked, however, that the time of onset of respiration is greatly variable, and that waiting for this event in itself causes a delay; therefore, the interpretation of this type of data is still open to some question. It was estimated[67] that about 10% of an infant's blood volume will be contained in the pulmonary vascular bed when the lungs are fully expanded after birth. This volume may amount to a diversion of about 30 ml of blood on the average, and may be significant. In the premature infant, the amount will be less in proportion to the total blood volume of an infant of that size. Whether the blood needed to fill the expanding circulatory network in the lungs of the newborn should come entirely from the placental reservoir or not is undecided. That it should has been advocated by some,[20,57] because they found clinical improvement in those with delayed clamping. Such a causal relationship rests on the shakiest ground, mainly statistical, ignoring the many other factors that determine perinatal morbidity and general extrauterine adaptability. Reynolds[59] spoke of the reservoir of blood in the liver that permits the fetus to adjust to its new environment. Could this not be an adequate reserve of blood on which the pulmonary vascular bed might draw as it expands?

The many comparisons of blood volume produced or occasioned by early vs. late cord-clamping have two things in common: the lack of definition of "early" and "late" (seldom the same in two studies) and the wide range of values determined. The latter is not to be condemned, because it is probably true in this as in most other human biological measurements that great variation exists, and it must be accepted. Delay in cord-clamping may mean a wait of 1[60] to 5 or more minutes, until the placenta is drained,[31,42,57] until the cord stops pulsating,[72] until respirations are established (first or second breath),[12] or only until after the placenta has separated. With respect to this last criterion, it is very difficult to determine the time of placental separation from the uterine wall, and so this measure of delay is hard to interpret. Needless to say, as the wait for separation is kept, uterine contractions occur and produce their pressure effect.

Early clamping of the cord has been subject to several constructions. It has meant any time from the delivery of the buttocks to something less than 30 sec after delivery of the whole infant to as much as a minute after delivery. The most reliable technique should be to clamp the cord as soon as it is exposed on expulsion of the fetus.

It was suggested by Moss and Monset-Couchard[38] that early clamping of the cord should be defined as "within 15 seconds after birth, and before the first breath occurs," and that delayed clamping be defined as "after two or more breaths occur and at least 5 minutes after birth." These defined limits are eminently suitable, the first allowing a simulation of fetal blood volume, but one other definition should be added: that the infant's position should be no higher than the level of, or even below the level of, the placenta if a delay is called for. If a transfusion is to occur, the effect of gravity should be enlisted, not resisted. In practical terms, it is not always possible, or even obstetrically permissible, to wait 5 min before clamping the cord and completing the delivery, so any variation from this limit should be precisely recorded.

4.2. Effects on Blood Volume

Though it is difficult enough to interpret the comparative results of early and late cord-clamping, it is even more difficult to reconcile the reported plasma and blood volume determinations made in the hours and days subsequent to delivery.

It has been recognized for many years that the hematocrit changes as the newborn adapts to extrauterine life.[25,37] Serial blood volume measurements have confirmed this view repeatedly, but with the timing of cord clamp, the amount of blood transferred from the placenta has varied, as has the effect. Furthermore, amounts that profoundly affect the premature may not so affect the full-term infant.

Still another difficulty is met when considering the data derived from volume determinations made at different times after birth. The apparent lack of significant volume differences between the early and late cord-clamped infants of vaginally delivered infants reported by Whipple et al.[74] is now seen to have been due to the fact that measurements were made 1 and 3 days after delivery, by which time plasma and blood volume alterations had already taken place, and a rather steady state, after hemodynamic adjustment, had been achieved. It

should be stated again that hematocrit values of blood sampled from heel-prick or puncture of other peripheral sites are imprecise in the first hours of life, and that samples from large peripheral vessels or central loci such as the inferior vena cava are much more reliable. The studies of blood volume performed serially during the hours immediately after birth[38,60,63,68,72] have been more informative, since they have demonstrated that alterations do indeed take place with rapidity regardless of the type of cord-clamping, and have shown more distinctly the differences resulting from delayed clamping.

There is no question that if the proper conditions are met, a placental transfusion can be accomplished successfully. Such a transfusion will increase both plasma and red cell volumes, and thus the total blood volume, by as much as 100 ml. The increase in blood volume will be even greater if the cord is vigorously stripped. Within minutes, probably no more than half an hour, some alteration of the red cell/plasma ratio will take place, decreasing as plasma shifts from intravascular to extravascular compartments.[16,25,43] These shifts continue for at least 12 hr in one direction or another (but largely to the extravascular space), with less and less rapidity as the infant stabilizes with his environment and cardiopulmonary function becomes established in its extrauterine pattern.

Delivery by *cesarean section* creates a special condition in regard to placental transfusion. The usual obstetric practice is to clamp the cord either immediately or shortly after the infant is extracted from the noncontracting uterus and placed on the mother's abdomen. This practice results not only in no placental transfusion, but also often a loss of fetal blood by drainage back to the placenta. Yao et al.[80] reported that infants delivered in this way for various maternal indications and with the cord clamped *in utero* had low blood volumes (determined between 30 and 180 min after birth), averaging 66.4 ml/kg; a mean plasma volume of 35.0 ml/kg; and a red cell volume of 31.2 ml/kg. Another group of infants with fetal distress, with cords also clamped *in utero*, had significantly higher volumes (blood volume 90.2 ml/kg, plasma volume 45.8 ml/kg, and red cell volume 44.4 ml/kg), comparable to those of infants born vaginally and with cord-clamping delayed.

In another study, Sisson et al.[64] found that at 3.5–4.0 hr of age, the volumes of cesarean section infants without fetal distress were significantly lower if the cord was clamped within 10 sec after delivery to the mother's abdomen than the volumes of infants held below the level of the placenta with cord-clamping delayed for 120–180 sec. The immediately clamped group had a mean blood volume of 79.0 ml/kg, a plasma volume of 45.4 ml/kg, and a red cell volume of 33.4 ml/kg. Infants whose cords were clamped only after 180 sec and while held below the placental level had a mean blood volume of 97.9 ml/kg, a plasma volume of 55.5 ml/kg, and a red cell volume of 42.4 ml/kg. It is possible that some difficulties reported in the past with the management of infants born by cesarean section were in part the result of injudicious malpositioning of the infants above the placenta before ligation of the cord, resulting in a reduction of blood volume sufficient to compromise the infants.

Secher and Karlberg[60] reported their ability to induce a placental transfusion in cesarean section infants by drainage of blood from the placenta suspended above the infant. This method produces a blood volume similar to that of the infant delivered *per vaginum*.

Though it has not been demonstrated that a placental transfusion is necessary for infants born by section, the chances are that if there is no fetal distress, the blood volume will be low unless an effort is made to transfer some amount of blood from the placenta. The finding of Yao et al.[80] that distressed infants delivered by section already have at birth a large blood volume would seem to caution against attempting a placental transfusion, since a state of hypervolemia would be produced. This hypervolemia could seriously disrupt the infant's hemodynamic adjustments.

That a placental transfusion of 24–60% of the original blood volume can be accomplished within 1–3 min after birth has been very well documented. The effects are profound and involve the most fundamental systemic adaptations of the infant.

4.3. Effects on Circulation and Circulatory Adaptation

Once disconnected from the maternal circulation and the placenta, the vascular pathways of the infant change radically. Whereas in the fetus the largest volume of blood flows to the caudal end of the body and to the placenta, at birth the pattern is altered, and the expanding lungs may receive 10%[67] or as much as 20%[73] of the blood volume. Diversion of this amount of the blood flow to the cephalic end of the body is accelerated. This diversion assures the maintenance of gas exchange in the pulmonary circulation, and guarantees adequate oxygenation of the brain.

There is a transudation of plasma, up to onehalf the original volume during the first 8–15 min and continuing during the first 4–6 hr after delivery.[32,35] This loss of plasma from intra- to extravascular spaces has not been found to occur in infants deprived of a placental transfusion.[32,52,63] As plasma transudation appears to take place mainly in those infants whose blood volume has been augmented, it is perhaps useful to question the wisdom of a deliberate expansion of the vascular content or mass. The infant who has only the blood volume with which he is endowed at birth (equivalent to the fetal blood volume excluding the placenta) need not accommodate an extra supply by capillary engorgement, stroke volume, transudation of plasma, tachycardia, tachypnea, or any other compensatory physiologic mechanism to which he may be thus driven.

In effect, then, if an infant must adjust to an expanded blood volume in addition to other adaptive responses, it is possible that the additional adjustment is either unnecessary, unphysiologic, or both. James[28] considered the quantity of blood contained in the fetus and placenta to be physiologically distributed between them, and the blood in the placenta not to be regarded as on loan by the fetus, to be returned at birth.

The normally changing circulatory patterns of the newborn are also influenced by varying amounts of placental blood. Central and portal venous pressures during the first hours of life in infants receiving large transfusions average 5.7 mm Hg, whereas those receiving smaller transfusions have a mean pressure of 1.7 mm Hg, although pressures distal to the ductus venosus, averaging 7.7 mm Hg, seem unaffected by differences in blood volume.[29] These values illustrate the significant effect of large amounts of placental blood on the heart of the newly born and the magnitude of the compensatory forces the infant must employ to accommodate to the augmented volume.[70]

The effect of increased blood volume on arterial pressure is likewise quickly apparent. Compared with infants who have had no placental transfusion, the systolic blood pressure of late-clamped infants is higher at birth, declining in the first 6 hr, a decline that is reversed thereafter. Early-clamped infants, on the contrary, have been shown to maintain a fairly steady systolic pressure during the first day of life, with a subsequent increase similar to that of placentally transfused infants, although this increase occurs several hours later.[44] Adjustments in the pulmonary circulation differ between early- and late-clamped infants, as was reported by Arcilla et al.[4] The pulmonary arterial pressures are 90% of aortic pressures by 9 hr of age in those infants receiving a placental transfusion, but in contrast, the pulmonary artery pressures in immediately clamped infants are but 70% of aortic pressures by 2 hr of age and even less by 4 hr. It is possible that these marked disparities in pulmonary arterial pressure are caused by vasoconstriction as the result of capillary–venous overfilling from the increased blood volume of the late-clamped infants. It is certain that increased pulmonary artery pressure in the infant with respiratory distress is an added burden that may encourage shunting.

The pulse rates of newborns with early or immediate cord-clamping have not been observed to differ from those of infants with large placental transfusions. That they have not demonstrates the lack of known relationship between cardiac output and blood volume and the poverty of information that may be gained from pulse rate observations alone. The experience of the author and of many other pediatricians has shown the danger to the very small preterm infant of an excessive placental transfusion. The most conspicuous result of cord-stripping to transfuse such infants is the rapid onset of cardiac failure and, shortly thereafter, death.

4.4. Effects on Respiration and Respiratory Adaptation

It has been established that infants whose umbilical cords are clamped immediately after delivery breathe sooner than late-clamped infants.[12] The respiratory rates of both are similar (51–60/min) for the first 30 min of life when body temperature is kept stable in a neutral thermal environment. In the succeeding 3 hr, however, those infants with delayed clamping have a faster rate of respiration. The difference in rate persists for the first 2 days of life.[28]

During the initial 6 hr after delivery, placentally transfused newborns appear to have a lower lung compliance with a smaller functional residual capacity.[44,46]

Respiratory distress has been reported to occur in infants with high blood hematocrit and viscosity.[17,24,77] States of hypercoagulability may also occur if the hematocrit is excessively elevated. Therefore, since the hematocrit tends to rise after placental transfusion[63] or without a transfusion,[16,25] moderation in this maneuver should probably be practiced. An opposite view was expressed by Bound et al.[9] in relation to low-birth-weight infants, and Usher et al.[72] found no respiratory distress in full-term infants whether or not a placental transfusion had occurred.

It is theoretically possible that these differing respiratory and other adaptive responses, occurring at a time when placental transfusion has caused an increased blood volume, are the result of a larger heart volume and greater pulmonary venous–capillary filling, a situation demonstrated by Oh et al.[46] In the opinion of these authors, these vascular differences produce contrasting respiratory performances from plasma transudation in the pulmonary capillary bed—perhaps a degree of pulmonary edema and consequent increase in respiratory rate. Gairdner et al.[25] suggested that plasma transudation would occur most particularly where markedly changing hemodynamics take place following birth. Rerouting of the bloodstream pattern when the fetal circulation ends and extrauterine life begins is no greater or more significant than in the lungs, so that if edema occurs anywhere, it should be in these organs. Clark and Gairdner[16] examined the postnatal plasma shift in premature infants and concluded that a major transudation does indeed take place there, but were unable to verify a causal relationship between hyaline membrane disease and pulmonary edema from the plasma transudate. It is nonetheless an attractive hypothesis that if not proved, has not been disproved.

The higher lung compliance and greater functional residual capacity that Oh et al.[46] determined in immediately clamped infants may be caused by the stimulus of a more rapid fall in blood oxygen tension and a rise in carbon dioxide tension. These changes do not explain the persistent decline in the respiratory rate of such infants, which, viewed in one way, should be elevated if blood oxygen tension is to increase and if the smaller oxygen-carrying capacity of the reduced red cell volume is to be compensated. Further investigation in this area would be helpful.

4.5. Effects on Renal Function

Total blood volume, hematocrit, systemic arterial pressure, atrial and central venous pressures, and pulmonary vascular filling are all lower in infants having either none or only a small quantity of placental blood transferred at birth. Measurements in the early neonatal hours have shown the marked influence of placental transfusion on renal function of term infants.[45]

Urine flow is significantly higher in transfused newborns, and renal blood flow is also higher during the initial 12 hr after birth. In this same period, the glomerular filtration rate is also greater. Between the 2nd and 5th days, these differences are erased. The rate and quality of renal function of immediately clamped infants improves to match the performance of infants with initially greater blood volume.

The functional adaptation of the newborn kidney is related to blood volume through compensatory mechanisms not called on by the infant deprived of placental blood (see Chapter 27). Infants who receive a placental transfusion have a greater percentage of tubular sodium reabsorption and a lower urinary sodium excretion, indicating retention of sodium despite a higher urinary output. This retention is thought to be due to the redistribution of plasma and body fluid in the infants with higher blood volume. These data have not been duplicated by comparable studies, and do not reconcile with the implications of the studies of Gairdner et al.[25] who found no change in plasma sodium concentrations despite measurable plasma shifts. The conclusions drawn from these data may be disputed, then, but the results are consistent with other physiologic alterations known to follow placental transfusion, and cannot be contested.

5. Blood Volume in Newly Born Infants

There have appeared to be irreconcilable discrepancies among the several studies of blood volume in the newborn. These disparate values were thought to be due in large measure to the different techniques of blood volume determination employed. It is now clear that the differences in reported blood volume are due rather to varied timing of ligation of the cord, weight and gestational age of the infants studied, and the different times after delivery that volume determinations have been made. If performed with scrupulous attention to detail and to the mechanics of the method used, any technique of blood volume measurement should be reproducible with only small but acceptable error. No one method has meaningful superiority over another, whether it be a determination by dye-dilution, radioactive tracer in plasma, tagged erythrocytes, or whatever. Comparative studies have been made to show that this is so.[1,19,30] It is well established that there are rather considerable variations of blood volume among infants of similar age and condition, and that average values represent wide ranges of individual observations. There are volumetric differences between premature and term infants and those born small for gestational age, between those with early and late clamping of the cord, and between infants born vaginally as compared with those delivered by cesarean section.

It should be remembered in considering these values that measurement of blood volume is actually derived from plasma or red cell volume and the hematocrit. Most important, it should be remarked that such values represent what we know to be the *circulating* blood volume, and that blood sequestered in the liver, spleen, or splanchnic bed may not enter completely into the determination. This quantity is not known, although it has been measured in animals,[2,23] and it probably changes from hour to hour in response to vascular and homeostatic changes, as the blood pressure is known to do in the newborn following postural changes.[39] It can therefore be said with fair certainty that the true total blood volume is an incompletely defined entity, and that we work with but a reasonably accurate estimate.

5.1. Term Infant

The total blood volume lies between 85 and 100 ml/kg during the first hour of life,[65] depending on the extent of or absence of a placental transfusion. The plasma volume at this time is between 45 and 50 ml/kg (Table II).

At 4 hr of age, plasma and blood volumes decrease by as much as 20% and 10%, respectively, if there has been late clamping of the cord. On the other hand, if the cord has been clamped immediately after birth, there is no appreciable change in plasma volume, but the total blood volume may decrease 2–5%, perhaps through sequestration.

By 24 hr of age, there have occurred redistributions of plasma and body fluids, the establishment of a stable environment, alimentation, a stable temperature, and so on. Both plasma and total blood volumes return nearly to or even slightly above the 30-min values.

Table II. Range of Mean Circulating Plasma, Red Cell, and Blood Volumes in the Term Neonate

Age (hr)	Plasma volume (ml/kg)	Red cell volume (ml/kg)	Blood volume (ml/kg)
0–1	45–50	40–50	85–100
3–4	40	50	80–95
24	45–54	44–51	86–100
72	44–51	41–49	82–99

Red cell volumes tend to remain at one level throughout the first day of life, regardless of the initial total blood volume or method of handling the cord. The hematocrit tends to vary, which may lead to some confusion. Often, this variation is due to sampling of blood from heel-prick in a cool limb with rather sluggish circulation. A central venous sample is more reliable, though the site is not always appropriate.

On the third day of life, the blood, plasma, and red cell volumes are virtually unchanged from the first day, stability apparently having been achieved.

5.2. Premature Infant

In general, the premature infant has a greater blood volume on the basis of body weight than does the term infant during the first 3 days after delivery. The plasma volume is higher, but the red cell volume is approximately the same.[66]

On the first day of life, the blood volume is between 100 and 110 ml/kg, but it is perhaps 10–25% higher if cord ligation is delayed, a procedure seldom employed in these infants. The plasma volume is close to 60 ml/kg, but is subject to wide variation, and because of the many environmental factors involved, both intra- and extrauterine, the measurement is unreliable as a representative volume for this entire class of infants. The premature is subject to so many adaptive stresses and changes, and is so exquisitely sensitive to the environment, that we must consider present data as estimates.

By the third day of life, the blood, plasma, and red cell volumes of the premature infant have changed very little from the first day unless respiratory distress, sepsis, or other systemic derangement occurs. This apparent uniformity may indicate only the greater length of time the premature requires to adjust to extrauterine existence, and perhaps also the greater care with which he is managed.

The few studies of the blood volume of premature infants with respiratory distress syndrome (RDS)[27,47,62,72] indicate low blood volume, high hematocrit, and constricted plasma volume at 12–15 hr of age. These early studies did not differentiate infants with Type I and Type II RDS as did a later study[11] that showed that infants with Type I RDS had significantly lower blood volumes than those with Type II, due largely to a smaller red cell volume. In both types of RDS, however, the plasma volume was smaller than in the normal neonate of low birth weight. These data suggest that a transudation of plasma takes place as in the infant with placental transfusion. These circumstances may signify the operation of a compensatory mechanism that possibly causes as much disturbance as it is meant to relieve, shifting a vascular load to inadequately ventilated lung tissue.

6. Special Clinical Considerations

It has long been known that the plethoric infant is peculiarly susceptible to the development of hyperbilirubinemia. It would seem unwise to produce a deliberate large placental transfusion in the prematurely born, who must cope with so many other adaptive changes. Of special concern in such infants is the high incidence of respiratory distress, in particular, hyaline membrane disease. The respiratory and metabolic acidosis accompanying this condition cause a weakening of albumin–bilirubin binding, with consequent release in the plasma of free bilirubin. It is incontrovertible that bilirubin encephalopathy is the unhappy consequence of neonatal hyperbilirubinemia with the circulation of free pigment in the plasma. Any circumstance promoting an increase of plasma bilirubin concentration is therefore to be condemned.

The small-for-gestational-age (SGA) infant has a characteristically high blood volume, affecting both plasma and red cell compartments, and like the infant born by caesarean section, also has an enlarged extracellular water compartment.[14,15] The explanation for this state is obscure, but for the SGA infant, prolonged relative intrauterine hypoxia from a dysfunctional placenta may amplify red cell production.

The infant of the diabetic mother (either overt

or gestational) has a blood volume greater than that of the normal infant and an elevated hematocrit, and is notoriously prone to develop hyperbilirubinemia. It is believed that the large blood volume and significant expansion of red cell mass lead to an exaggerated heme breakdown and consequent increase of bilirubin production. The infant's normal, and in other respects adequate, capacity to conjugate and excrete the pigment is outstripped—thus, jaundice.

In any newborn with elevated blood volume, such as the recipient twin of fetofetal transfusion, the infant of induced placental transfusion, the dehydrated and hemoconcentrated infant, the newborn with placental dysfunction or other cause for chronic fetal hypoxia—in any clinical situation of high red cell volume, the physician should be alert to the development of hyperbilirubinemia, for which appropriate corrective measures must be taken.

The immature infant with respiratory distress has been shown to have a smaller blood volume than normal.[11,13,22,27,62] It has also been demonstrated[79] that normal term infants with late cord-clamping, presumed to have received a placental transfusion, tend to develop expiratory grunting. This grunting is thought to serve as a compensatory mechanism to improve respiratory adaptation at birth in the presence of an overdistended circulatory system.

In the face of such evidence, a cautious approach to placental transfusion in infants predisposed to respiratory distress is clearly justified, since it would appear that even the normal newborn may exhibit difficulty in respiratory adaptation if the circulation is overloaded.

Infants with hemolytic disease of the newborn have been variously described as hypervolemic,[18,36,49] normo- to hypovolemic,[51] and hypovolemic.[10] This confusion of opinion is not surprising in view of the diverse groups studied, but it is possible to reconcile these disparate conclusions by careful interpretation of the data.

Nonhydropic infants with Rh or ABO hemolytic disease severe enough to require exchange transfusion are hypovolemic if mature, and hypo- or normovolemic if premature (depending on one's definition of "normovolemia"). In most respects, one can consider both mature and premature infants in this condition to be hypovolemic. Hydropic infants are generally normovolemic, though they may not be anemic. When hydropic infants *are* anemic, the constricted red cell volume is countered by an expanded plasma volume, so that the total blood volume is within normal range.

In short, we no longer feel that the infant with hemolytic disease of the newborn has an elevated blood volume; rather, we feel that he is usually hypovolemic, and if only mildly hydropic, normovolemic despite a lowered red cell mass. It is therefore not recommended that such infants be phlebotomized or denied an adequate replacement transfusion.

It has been suggested from the work of Aranda et al.[3] and Bard et al.[6] that infants who have received significant volumes of transfused blood or undergone exchange transfusion in the neonatal period should be considered at risk for retrolental fibroplasia. The reason is thought to be that high partial pressures of oxygen in retinal tissues are promoted by the substitution of blood with high oxygen affinity (HbF) by blood of low oxygen affinity (HbA). No attempt has been made to correlate these findings with altered red cell volume (usually increased by transfusion) or hemoglobin type, though these may well be significant additive factors.

The effect of intrauterine anemia on the oxygen affinity of fetal blood and on the concentration of 2,3-diphosphoglycerate(2,3-DPG) in red cells was studied by Orzalesi and Hay.[48] They determined that the lower the hemoglobin concentration in the fetus, the higher is the oxygen affinity of the blood and the higher also is the content of 2,3-DPG. These findings mimic those in older anemic children and adults.

Thus, the correction of anemia in neonates, while mandatory in some circumstances, may have two serious drawbacks: (1) the sudden overload of the cardiovascular system and the imposition of shunting by zealous transfusion, and (2) the possibility of exposing such infants to retinal damage unless arterial oxygen tensions are carefully monitored.

7. Conclusions

The pregnant woman adapts to her pregnancy by an increase of blood volume starting in the 6th week of gestation. This increase demonstrates a remarkably efficient preparative mechanism for the nurture of the fetus. Increasing size and function of the placenta are encouraged by alterations of plasma and red cell volume during pregnancy. Normally, the red cell mass enlarges to a degree that guarantees adequate gas exchange and transfer of iron to the infant *in utero*. If the woman is anemic, however, her ability to maintain sufficient iron levels for her fetus may be lessened, and her anemic state may be reflected to some extent in the infant at birth.

The competence of the circulation in the placenta is easily disturbed by systemic disease in the mother, by multiple pregnancy, drugs, anesthetics, anomalous circulatory patterns, and by abnormal placental separation. The effects on the fetus are rapid and often profound: development of fetal acidosis, hypoxia, or anoxia, and even circulatory collapse from blood loss may occur. It is vital that the deleterious effects from embarrassment of placental circulation be understood so that conditions potentially harmful to the fetus, a silent partner in pregnancy, may be handled to the advantage of the fetus.

Two things can be said for placental transfusion: (1) that it may be useful, at least in the full-term infant; and (2) that its consequences deserve far more evaluation. Increasing the total blood volume may help to assure rapid filling of the pulmonary vascular bed in the newborn and thus assist the onset of respiration, promote ventilatory perfusion, and aid the establishment of stable respiratory function. On the other hand, it may be disadvantageous to the premature infant, who has less resilience in accommodating to an augmented blood volume.

If placental transfusion is too generous, extreme plethora of the infant will occur. This condition is not only unphysiologic, but may be harmful. In the prematurely born, circulatory adaptation may be badly disturbed, sufficiently so that heart failure may ensue. In some infants, right-to-left shunt will be unduly prolonged. Pulmonary vascular resistance, rather than diminishing with adequate capillary filling, may actually increase from overfilling; thus, respiratory adaptation may be impaired. Hyperbilirubinemia, especially in the immature and SGA infant, can result from excessive red cell mass. Last, hemostasis may be seriously altered and a state of hypercoagulability fostered.

The blood volume of newly born infants alters during the first hours after birth, but reaches a state of relative equilibrium by the second day. The full-term infant has a total blood volume of between 80 and 100 ml/kg at birth, and averages 85–87 ml/kg within 12 hr, partly as a result of a decrease in plasma volume. Shifts of plasma from intra- to extravascular spaces account for the principal quantitative changes in blood volume.

The total circulating blood volume of the premature tends to be higher than that of the full-term, averaging 110 ml/kg at birth. Plasma shifts also occur in these infants, and it has been suggested that plasma transudate into the lungs may further the appearance of respiratory distress. Premature infants with RDS have a lower blood volume than comparable infants without RDS, averaging 85 ml/kg.

Further studies of blood volume alteration in the neonate would be valuable, not only in a predictive sense in regard to pulmonary and circulatory adaptation, but also in better management of labor and delivery as they affect the infant's neonatal course.

8. References

1. ADAMS, R., WOODWARD, I. C., CRANE, M. G., AND HOLLOWAY, J. E., 1958, The simultaneous determination of Cr^{51} and I^{131} activities in doubly labeled blood, *J. Lab. Clin. Med.* **52**:754.
2. ALLEN, T. H., AND REEVE, E. B., 1953, Distribution of "extra plasma" in blood of some tissues in the dog as measured by P^{32} and T1824, *Amer. J. Physiol.* **175**:218.
3. ARANDA, J. V., CLARK, T. E., MANIELLO, R., AND OUTERBRIDGE, E. W., 1975, Blood transfusion: Possible potentiating risk factor in RLF, *Pediatr. Res.* **9**:362.
4. ARCILLA, R. A., OH, W., LIND, J., AND GESSNER, I. H., 1966, Pulmonary arterial pressures of newborn infants born with early and late clamping of the cord, *Acta Paediatr. Scand.* **55**:305.
5. BARCROFT, SIR J., 1946, *Researches in Pre-Natal Life,* p. 153, Charles C. Thomas, Springfield, Illinois.
6. BARD, H., CORNET, A., ORQUIN, J., AND DORAY, B. H., 1975, Retrolental fibroplasia and exchange transfusion, *Pediatr. Res.* **9**:362.
7. BENIRSCHKE, K., 1965, Twin placenta and perinatal mortality, *N.Y. Med. J.* **61**:1499.
8. BENIRSCHKE, K., AND DRISCOLL, S. G., 1967, *The Pathology of the Human Placenta,* p. 20, Springer-Verlag, New York.
9. BOUND, T. P., HARVEY, P. W., AND BAGSHAW, H. B., 1962, Prevention of pulmonary syndrome of the newborn, *Lancet* **1**:1200.
10. BRANS, Y. W., MILSTEAD, R. R., BAILEY, P. E., AND CASSADY, G., 1974, Blood volume estimates in Coombs-test-positive infants, *N. Engl. J. Med.* **290**:1450.
11. BROWN, E. G., KROUSKOP, R. W., McDONNELL, B. S., AND SWEET, A. Y., 1975, Blood volume and pressure in infants with respiratory distress, *J. Pediatr.* **87**:1133.
12. BROWN, R. J. K., 1965, Relation of the onset of respiration to placental transfusion, *Lancet* **1**:550.

13. CASSADY, G., 1966, Plasma volume studies in low birth weight infants, *Pediatrics* **38**:1020.
14. CASSADY, G., 1970, Body composition in intrauterine growth retardation, *Pediatr. Clin. North Amer.* **17**:79.
15. CASSADY, G., 1971, Effect of cesarean section on neonatal body water, *N. Engl. J. Med.* **285**:887.
16. CLARK, A. C. L., AND GAIRDNER, D., 1960, Postnatal plasma shift in premature infants, *Arch. Dis. Child.* **35**:352.
17. DANKS, D. M., AND STEVENS, L. H., 1964, Neonatal respiratory distress associated with a high haematocrit reading, *Lancet* **2**:498.
18. DAVID, G., 1969, Emergency treatment of the hydropic newborn infant, in *Perinatal Medicine—First European Congress, Berlin* (P. J. Huntingford, H. A. Hüter, and E. Saling, eds.), p. 66 and 67, Academic Press, New York.
19. DONOVAN, J. C., LUND, C. J., AND WHALEN, L., 1964, Simultaneous determinations of blood volumes using Evans blue and sodium radiochromate, *Surg. Gynecol. Obstet.* **119**:1031.
20. DUCKMAN, S., MERK, H., LEHMAN, W. X., AND REGAN, E., 1953, The importance of gravity in delayed ligation of the umbilical cord, *Amer. J. Obstet. Gynecol.* **66**:1214.
21. DUFFUS, G. M., MacGILLIVRAY, I., AND DENNIS, K. J., 1971, The relationship between body weight and changes in maternal weight, total body water, plasma volume, electrolytes and proteins and urinary oestriol excretion, *J. Obstet. Gynecol. Brit. Commonw.* **78**:97.
22. FAXELIUS, G., RAYE, J. R., GUTHERLET, R. L., SWANSTROM, S., DYER, N., BRILL, A., AND STAHLMAN, M. T., 1970, Comparison of red cell volumes in infants with hyaline membrane disease and other forms of respiratory distress, *Proc. Soc. Pediatr. Res.,* p. 237.
23. FUDENBERG, H., BALDINI, M., MOHONEY, J. P., AND DAMESHEK, W., 1961, The body hematocrit/venous hematocrit ratio and the "splenic reservoir," *Blood* **17**:71.
24. FRANK, D. J., AND GABRIEL, M., 1967, Timing of cord ligation and newborn respiratory distress, *Amer. J. Obstet. Gynecol.* **97**:1142.
25. GAIRDNER, D., MARKS, J., ROSCOE, J. D., AND BRETTELL, R. O., 1958, The fluid shift from the vascular compartment immediately after birth, *Arch. Dis. Child.* **33**:489.
26. HAYNES, D. M., 1966, Premature separation of the placenta, ten years experience, *Amer. J. Obstet. Gynecol.* **96**:660.
27. INALL, J. A., BLUHM, M. M., KERR, M. M., DOUGLAS, T. A., HOPE, C. S., AND HUTCHINSON, J. H., 1965, Blood volume and hematocrit studies in respiratory distress syndrome of the newborn, *Arch. Dis. Child.* **40**:480.
28. JAMES, L. S., 1966, Onset of breathing and resuscitation, *Pediatr. Clin. North Amer.* **13**:621.
29. JEGIER, W. BLANKENSHIP, W., AND LIND, J., 1963, Venous pressure in the first hour of life and its relation to placental transfusion, *Acta Paediatr. Scand.* **52**:485.
30. JEGIER, W., McLAURIN, J., BLANKENSHIP, W., AND LIND, J., 1964, Comparative study of blood volume estimation in the newborn infant using I[131] labeled human serum albumin (IHSA) and T1824, *Scand. J. Clin. Lab. Invest.* **16**:125.
31. LANDAU, D. B., GOODRICH, H. B., FRANCKA, W. F., AND BURNS, F. R., 1950, Death of caesarean infants: A theory as to its cause and a method of prevention, *J. Pediatr.* **36**:421.
32. LIND, J., 1968, Placental transfusion and cardiorespiratory adaptation of the newborn infant, *Acta Paediatr. Fenn.* **14**:1.
33. LUND, C. J., AND DONOVAN, J. C., 1967, Blood volume during pregnancy: Significance of plasma and red cell volumes, *Amer. J. Obstet. Gynecol.* **98**:393.
34. LUND, C. J., AND SISSON, T. R. C., 1958, Blood volume and anemia of mother and baby, *Amer. J. Obstet. Gynecol.* **76**:1013.
35. McCUE, C. M., GARNER, F. B., HURT, W. G., SCHELIN, E. C., AND SHARPE, A. R., JR., 1968, Placental transfusion, *J. Pediatr.* **72**:15.
36. MOLLISON, P. L., AND CUTBUSH, M., 1949, Haemolytic disease of the newborn: Criteria of severity, *Br. Med. J.* **1**:128.
37. MOLLISON, P. L., VEALL, N., AND CUTBUSH, M., 1950, Red cell volume and plasma volume in newborn infants, *Arch. Dis. Child.* **25**:242.
38. MOSS, A. J., AND MONSET-COUCHARD, M., 1967, Placental transfusion: Early versus late clamping of the umbilical cord, *Pediatrics* **40**:109.
39. MOSS, A. J., EMMANOUILIDES, G. C., MONSET-COUCHARD, M., AND MARCANO, B., 1968, Vascular responses to postural changes in normal newborn infants, *Pediatrics* **42**:250.
40. NECHTMAN, C. M., AND HUISMAN, T. H. J., 1964, Comparative studies of oxygen equilibria of the human adult and cord blood, red cell hemolysates and suspensions, *Clin. Chim. Acta* **10**:165.
41. NISWANDER, K. R., FRIEDMAN, E. A., HOOVER, D. B., PIETROWSKI, H., AND WESTPHAL, M. C., 1966, Fetal morbidity following potentially anoxygenic obstetric conditions: II. Placenta praevia, *Amer. J. Obstet. Gynecol.* **95**:846.
42. NYBERG, R., AND WESTIN, B., 1958, Residual blood volume of the placenta after delayed clamping of the cord, *Nord. Med.* **59**:441.
43. OH, W., AND LIND, J., 1966, Venous and capillary hematocrit in newborn infants and placental transfusion, *Acta Paediatr. Scand.* **55**:38.
44. OH, W., LIND, J., AND GESSNER, I. H., 1966, The circulatory and respiratory adaptation to early and late cord clamping in newborn infants, *Acta Paediatr. Scand.* **55**:17.
45. OH, W., OH, M. A., AND LIND, J., 1966, Renal

function and blood volume in newborn infants related to placental transfusion, *Acta Paediatr. Scand.* **55**:197.

46. OH, W., WALLGREN, G., HANSON, J. S., AND LIND, J., 1967, The effects of placental transfusion on respiratory mechanics of normal term newborn infants, *Pediatrics* **40**:6.

47. O'RIORDAN, A., 1964, Personal communication.

48. ORZALESI, M., AND HAY, W. W., 1975, The effect of intrauterine anemia on the oxygen affinity of fetal blood, *Pediatr. Res.* **9**:369.

49. OSKI, F. A., AND NAIMAN, J. L., 1966, *Hematologic Problems in the Newborn*, p. 161, W. B. Saunders, Philadelphia.

50. PAI, M. K., BEDRITUS, I., AND ZIPURSKI, A., 1975, Massive transplacental haemorrhage: Clinical manifestations in the newborn, *Can. Med. J.* **112**:585.

51. PHIBBS, R. H., JOHNSON, P., AND TOOLEY, W. H., 1974, Cardiorespiratory status of erythroblastotic newborn infants: II. Blood volume, hematocrit, and serum albumin concentration in relation to hydrops fetalis, *Pediatrics* **53**:13.

52. PIETRA, G. G., D'AMODIO, M. D., LEVENTHAL, M. M., OH, W., AND BRANDO, J. L., 1968, Electron microscopy of cutaneous capillaries of newborn infants: Effects of placental transfusion, *Pediatrics* **42**:678.

53. POWER, G. G., LONGO, L. D., WAGNER, H. N., JR., KUHL, D. E., AND FORSTER, R. E., II, 1967, Uneven distribution of maternal and fetal placental blood flow, as demonstrated using macroaggregates, and its response to hypoxia, *J. Clin. Invest.* **46**:2053.

54. PRITCHARD, J. A., AND ROWLAND, R. C., 1964, Blood volume changes in pregnancy and the puerperium, *Amer. J. Obstet. Gynecol.* **88**:391.

55. PRITCHARD, J. A., WIGGINS, K. M., AND DICKEY, J. C., 1960, Blood volume changes in pregnancy and the puerperium: I. Does sequestration of red blood cells accompany parturition?, *Amer. J. Obstet. Gynecol.* **80**:956.

56. RAUSEN, A. R., SEKI, M., AND STRAUSS, L., 1965, Twin transfusion syndrome, *J. Pediatr.* **66**:613.

57. REDMOND, A., ISANA, S., AND INGALL, D., 1965, Relation of onset of respiration to placental transfusion, *Lancet* **1**:283.

58. REISSMAN, K. R., 1950, Studies of the mechanism of erythropoietic stimulation in parabiotic rats during hypoxia, *Blood* **5**:372.

59. REYNOLDS, S. R. M., 1955, Circulatory adaptations to birth and their clinical application, *Amer. J. Obstet. Gynecol.* **70**:148.

60. SECHER, O., AND KARLBERG, P., 1962, Placental blood transfusion for newborns delivered by caesarean section, *Lancet* **1**:1203.

61. SISSON, T. R. C., AND LUND, C. J., 1958, Influences of maternal iron deficiency on the newborn, *Amer. J. Clin. Nutr.* **6**:376.

62. SISSON, T. R. C., AND WHALEN, L. E., 1959, Unpublished data.

63. SISSON, T. R. C., AND WHALEN, L. E., 1960, The

blood volume of infants: III. Alterations in the first hours after birth, *J. Pediatr.* **56**:43.

64. SISSON, T. R. C., KNUTSON, S., AND KENDALL, N., 1973, The blood volume of infants: IV. Infants born by caesarean section, *Amer. J. Obstet. Gynecol.* **117**:351.

65. SISSON, T. R. C., LUND, C. J., WHALEN, L. E., AND TELEK, A., 1959, The blood volume of infants: I. The full-term infant in the first year of life, *J. Pediatr.* **55**:163.

66. SISSON, T. R. C., LUND, C. J., WHALEN, L. E., AND TELEK, A., 1959, The blood volume of infants: II. The premature infant in the first year of life, *J. Pediatr.* **55**:430.

67. SMITH, C. A., 1959, *The Physiology of the Newborn Infant*, 3rd Ed., pp. 69–108, Charles C. Thomas, Springfield, Illinois.

68. STEELE, M. W., 1962, Plasma volume changes in the neonate, *Amer. J. Dis. Child.* **103**:42.

69. STRONG, S. J., AND CORNEY, G., 1967, *The Placenta in Twin Pregnancy*, pp. 71 and 72, Pergamon Press, London.

70. TAYLOR, P. M., EGAN, T. J., BIRCHARD, E. L., BRIGHT, N. H., AND WOLFSON, J. H., 1961, Venous hypertension in the newborn infant associated with delayed clamping of the umbilical cord, *Acta Paediatr.* **50**:149.

71. TREMBLAY, J. C., SYBULSKI, S., AND MANGHAN, G. B., 1965, Role of the placenta in fetal malnutrition, *Amer. J. Obstet. Gynecol.* **91**:597.

72. USHER, R., SHEPPARD, M., AND LIND, J., 1963, The blood volume of the newborn infant and placental transfusion, *Acta Paediatr. Scand.* **52**:497.

73. WALLGREN, G., KARLBERG, P., AND LIND, J., 1960, Studies of the circulatory adaptation immediately after birth, *Acta Paediatr. Scand.* **49**:843.

74. WHIPPLE, G. A., SISSON, T. R. C., AND LUND, C. J., 1957, Delayed ligation of the umbilical cord, *Obstet. Gynecol.* **10**:603.

75. WILCOX, C. F., III, HUNT, A. B., AND OWEN, C. A., JR., 1959, The measurement of blood lost during caesarean-section, *Amer. J. Obstet. Gynecol.* **77**:772.

76. WINTROBE, H. M., AND SHUMACKER, H. B., JR., 1936, Erythrocyte studies in mammalian fetus and newborn: Erythrocyte counts, Hb content, and proportion of immature red cells in blood of fetus and newborn of pig, rabbit, rats, cat and man, *Amer. J. Anat.* **58**:313.

77. WOOD, J. L., 1959, Plethora in the newborn infant associated with cyanosis and convulsions, *J. Pediatr.* **54**:143.

78. YAO, A. C., HIRVENSALO, M., AND LIND, J., 1968, The rate of placental transfusion in normal full term infants, *Lancet* **1**:380.

79. YAO, A. C., LIND, J., AND VUORENKOSKI, M. A., 1971, Expiratory grunting in the late clamped normal neonate, *Pediatrics* **48**:865.

80. YAO, A. C., WIST, A., AND LIND, J., 1967, The blood volume of the newly born infant by caesarean section, *Acta Paediatr. Scand.* **56**:585.

CHAPTER 10

Formed Elements of Human Blood

Ronald G. Strauss and Alvin M. Mauer

1. Introduction

The formed elements present in the blood of the human fetus and newborn differ in many respects from those found in older children and adults. Differences have been reported in the metabolism, functions, and cell concentrations in the bone marrow and circulating blood. Obviously, adult values cannot be used for reference when studying fetal and neonatal cells. Thus, these age-related variations in normal values must be appreciated to define the physiology of the perinatal period and to recognize disease. In this chapter, a brief review of the development of the formed elements during fetal life will be given, followed by a description of the characteristics of the erythrocytes, leukocytes, and platelets present during perinatal life.

2. Development of Blood Cells in the Fetus

Hematopoiesis begins in mesenchymal tissue present in the yolk sac as early as 2 weeks after conception.[35] The predominant cells recognized

during this early period are erythrocytes. A few undifferentiated mononuclear cells, which are probably monocyte precursors, are also present, but distinct varieties of leukocytes cannot be clearly identified. The primitive erythrocytes are large, nucleated cells with low hemoglobin concentrations. They retain their nuclei even as they circulate and contain the embryonic hemoglobin types Gower I, Gower II, and Portland (see Chapter 11). These early erythrocytes are produced for only a brief period of time. By the 4th month of gestation, nearly all the circulating, nucleated erythrocytes have been replaced by smaller cells devoid of nuclei. These cells contain mostly hemoglobin F, but 5–10% is hemoglobin A.

Hematopoiesis in the yolk sac diminishes sharply by 9 weeks of gestation. The liver is the major site of production during the second and third month of gestation, and all the major elements, including erythrocytes, megakaryocytes, and various types of leukocytes, are present.[36] Cells with peroxidase activity, which presumably represent granulocytes or in some instances monocytes, appear at 2 months and increase rapidly in number. Lymphocytes are seen in the blood at this stage of gestation and increase in number to 10,000 cells/μl by 5 months of gestation. Production of all cell lines occurs

Ronald G. Strauss and Alvin M. Mauer · St. Jude Children's Research Hospital, Memphis, Tennessee 38101

transiently in the spleen during the 3rd and 4th months, but only lymphopoiesis persists at this site under normal circumstances. A brief period of hematopoiesis has been identified even in the thymus. The bone marrow becomes the major site of production after the 4th month of gestation, and all extramedullary hematopoiesis ceases within the first postnatal week in healthy infants.

The development of the bone marrow was described recently in vertebrae from human fetuses.[6] The marrow at this site is encased in cartilage, rather than bone, and it could be prepared for study with minimum distortion of the architecture. Since the bone marrow appears in the vertebrae at a later gestational age than the long bones, it was possible to study even the earliest phases of marrow development in relatively mature fetuses. The marrow cavity began to form near the center of the vertebral body at approximately 13 weeks of gestation. The development is reported as follows: The primary bone marrow is composed of blood vessels occupying cartilage lacunae and contains a few extravascular mesenchymal and mononuclear cells. Hematopoietic cells appear in the extravascular space about 1 week later and are quite plentiful by 17 weeks of gestation. The endothelial cells of the sinuses are thin and are indented by the blood cells developing in the extraluminal sites. The endothelial cells form a continuous wall. Blood cells are permitted to pass through it. The extravascular space is compartmentalized by reticular cell processes. The hematopoietic cells are confined within these compartments, and are in close apposition to the reticular cells. Factors that control the production and release of cells from the hematopoietic compartment into the vascular sinuses and subsequently into the circulating blood will be discussed in each of the following sections.

3. Erythrocytes

In the perinatal period, there are consistent and striking alterations of the erythrocytes both in number and in metabolic activity. Also apparent are a number of significant differences from the normal erythrocytes of later life that must be acknowledged. The following discussion will consider these differences and will focus primarily on characteristics that are unique to perinatal erythrocytes.

3.1. Normal Values

Erythrocytes are the first blood cells produced by the fetus. The earliest erythrocytes are megaloblastic

and circulate as nucleated cells. Normoblastic erythropoiesis begins at about the 6th gestational week. The erythrocyte count at 10–12 weeks of gestation is approximately 1,000,000/μl, with 80% reticulocytes. By 34 weeks, the count will increase to approximately 4,500,000/μl. During this time interval, the mean corpuscular volume decreases from 180 μm^3 to 118 μm^3, and the mean corpuscular hemoglobin drops accordingly from 60 pg to 38 pg. The mean corpuscular Hb concentration, however, remains rather steady between 31 and 34%. The Hb concentration of whole blood is between 8 and 10 g/dl at 12 weeks of gestation, and averages 14.0 g/dl at 24 weeks and 15.0 g/dl at 34 weeks.

The production rate of erythrocytes during early fetal life has not been reported. When assessed by techniques employing radioiron kinetics, the rate in the final 2 months of gestation and at birth was 3–5 times greater than in adults.[11] Infants at birth produce approximately 4% of their circulating red cell volume each day. The factors that initiate and regulate erythropoiesis in very young fetuses are unknown. This process during the third trimester is controlled by erythropoietin that is produced endogenously by the fetus.[19] Increased concentrations of this hormone can be demonstrated in the blood or urine of both preterm and term infants at birth, and they are capable of increasing its concentration in response to anemia or hypoxia. The importance of fetal erythropoietin as a regulator of erythropoiesis in mammalian fetuses was confirmed by several animal studies in which techniques of hypertransfusion or the administration of exogenous erythropoietin and antierythropoietin antibodies were employed.[41] Another important regulatory mechanism in erythrocyte production is the one that controls the synthesis of the various types of hemoglobins during fetal and perinatal life. This mechanism is discussed in Chapter 11.

Normal hematologic values vary greatly at birth. The mean values with one standard deviation for the erythrocytes in the cord blood samples of 59 term infants studied by Guest et al.[13] were as follows: red blood cell count, 4.638 ± 0.495 million/μl; volume of packed red cells, $52.3 \pm 5.3\%$; hemoglobin 17.1 ± 1.78 g/dl. No apparent relationship was demonstrated in these term infants between cord blood erythrocyte values and birth weight, maturity, maternal age, or parity and sex of the infant. The erythrocytes of the cord blood were large, with an average volume of 113 μm^3. The average corpuscular Hb was 36.9 pg, and the average corpuscular

Hb concentration was 32.6%. The reticulocyte counts in particular were variable, but generally averaged between 3 and 6%. Nucleated erythrocytes were found in the blood of nearly all term infants during the first day of life. This value was variable when expressed as the number of nucleated erythrocytes per 100 leukocytes because of the wide range of leukocyte counts present in the blood at this age. It was generally 4–10/100 WBC. When expressed as the percentage of erythrocyte count, as done for reticulocytes, it was about 0.1%. Unfortunately, it is not common practice to express data in this form. Nucleated erythrocytes disappeared rapidly and were not seen after the 4th day of life.

The hematologic values in the cord blood of premature infants vary somewhat with the degree of immaturity. Erythrocyte concentration is similar to that found in term infants except in very small (<1200 g) babies, in whom it is slightly lower. The reticulocyte count in cord blood of premature infants is greater than that of full-term infants, usually in the range of 5–10%, although counts as high as 20% may be found in infants under 30 weeks of gestation. In addition, a correlation exists between gestational age and the number of nucleated red blood cells in the cord blood. The usual range in premature infants is 2–20/100 WBC, with two-thirds of the infants having a value greater than 10. Greater numbers may be found in infants under 24 weeks of gestational age. For example, 6- to 8-week-old fetuses have 200–300 nucleated red blood cells/100 WBC.

It is important to note factors that may influence erythrocyte numerical values at birth. In one study, determinations of the Hb concentration in capillary and venous blood samples obtained simultaneously within an hour of birth resulted in values that averaged 3.6 g/dl greater in the capillary samples.[27] In this same study, at 5 days of age, this difference was 2.2 g/dl, and at 3 weeks of age, the mean difference was 1.1 g/dl. Thus, shortly after birth, the venous blood erythrocyte concentration was about 80% of the result obtained from a capillary sample, but for practical purposes, by 3 weeks of age, the two values had become nearly identical. Obviously, this relationship can be influenced greatly by the status of the circulatory system. It is important, to be aware, however, that capillary values may not accurately reflect the circulating red cell mass during the immediate perinatal period.

Another factor that may affect erythrocyte concentration in the neonatal period is the practice of cord-clamping. Hemoglobin concentrations 1–3 days after birth in infants who have had immediate ligation of the cord are from 2 to 4 g/dl lower than the values obtained in infants in whom the cord has been allowed to stop pulsating before ligation. In one study, infants held above the placenta continued to bleed into it, whereas those held 40 cm below the mother's introitus received the placental blood within 30 secs.[40] The relationship of placental transfusion to blood volume is discussed in Chapter 9.

An increase in erythrocyte concentration occurs in the blood of infants immediately after birth because of a decrease in plasma volume. This increase reaches the maximum of 9–12% greater than cord blood values at 2–6 hr of age. Thereafter, the concentration decreases, and the values have usually returned to the cord blood level by about 1 week of age.

3.2. Physiologic Anemia

After the first week of life, the erythrocyte concentration of the blood begins a gradual decline that progresses to a nadir between 6 and 12 weeks of age.[26] The Hb concentration decreases to about 10 g/dl in term infants, and to levels as low as 7–8 g/dl in prematures (directly related to the birth weight).[33] This process is generally referred to as the *physiologic anemia of the newborn*, because it occurs naturally in the majority of infants and is without apparent ill effects. Under normal circumstances, this fall in erythrocyte concentration cannot be prevented by the administration of hematinics. During this period, there is a cessation of erythropoiesis, as indicated by reticulocytopenia and erythroid hypoplasia in the bone marrow.

This process is best explained by decreased erythropoietin production. During this period of time, the infant is in a physiologic state in which a hypoxic stimulus does not exist for the production of this hormone. It is well established that during the third trimester of pregnancy, erythropoiesis is primarily controlled by erythropoietin produced in the fetus. In the somewhat hypoxic (45% arterial oxygen saturation) intrauterine environment, erythropoietin levels are high, erythropoiesis is brisk, and the infant is born polycythemic. At birth, the arterial oxygen saturation rises rapidly to 95%, and in a teleological sense, there is no need for the high Hb concentration. Erythropoiesis ceases and is not reinitiated until the Hb falls to approximately 10 g/dl.

The corresponding Hb concentration at the nadir in premature infants is often lower, for reasons that are not completely defined. Although controversial, it has been reported that values for oxygen consumption and heat production per unit of body weight are lower in premature than in full-term infants. Thus, it is postulated that the quantity of oxygen required for tissue oxygenation is less, and that erythropoiesis is not stimulated until the Hb falls to a lower concentration. This concept has been criticized because the metabolic rate, though low in premature infants during the first 2 weeks of life, actually exceeds that of term infants by 6 weeks of age, the nadir of the anemia. It is important to remember that increased rates of erythropoietin-mediated erythropoiesis can occur during this period at times of hypoxic stress, e.g., cyanotic heart disease and respiratory insufficiency. Nutritional factors that are important in the late anemia of prematurity (after 3 months of age) have no pathogenic role in "physiologic anemia," and the prophylactic administration of these agents will not prevent the decline of the Hb.[26,33]

Other factors are involved in physiologic anemia of the newborn, but are not so important as the decrease in erythropoiesis. There is an increase in blood volume accompanying the rapid weight gain that characterizes the first few months of life. This hemodilution, in itself, cannot explain the fall in Hb. In addition, the survival of neonatal erythrocytes is shorter than cells from older children and adults.[31] This shorter survival is particularly true for prematures; however, the fall in Hb cannot be explained without invoking diminished erythropoiesis as well.

Studies of erythrocyte survival by the chromium-labeling method have been done in full-term and premature infants during the first week of life. Generally, normal survival times with half-lives of radioactivity greater than 24 days were found in full-term infants, but shortened survival times were found in the premature infants, who had half-lives of erythrocyte radioactivity averaging 22 days, with some as short as 8 days. Concern has been expressed that there may be excessive elution of chromium from fetal Hb, resulting in falsely shortened survival times, but studies of elution from intact fetal red cells have demonstrated that the rate is the same as for adult cells.[15,16] Studies of Hb catabolism as measured by carbon monoxide production have also indicated a slightly increased rate of erythrocyte destruction in the neonatal period.

During the period from 15 to 60 days after birth, studies of erythrocyte survival with radioactive chromium indicate shortened half-lives in both full-term and premature infants. It must be remembered,

however, that most of the infants' erythrocytes a[t] this time were produced during the months befor[e] birth, resulting in a relatively large proportion o[f] aged cells in the blood. In addition, it is durin[g] this time that production of new erythrocytes begin[s] again in the bone marrow to compensate for th[e] expanding blood volume with growth of the infan[t]. The labeled erythrocytes will thus be rapidly dilute[d] by the influx of unlabeled cells from the marrow[.] It has been shown that erythrocytes produced durin[g] the first week of life have a normal or near-norma[l] life-span.

3.3. Metabolism

The erythrocyte can be divided metabolically int[o] three interrelated units: the plasma membrane, th[e] hemoglobin, and the cytosol. Many importan[t] enzyme systems with their substrates and cofacto[rs] are contained in the cytosol. These enzyme system[s] are designed to produce energy, to provide reducin[g] materials that protect the Hb and plasma membran[e] from oxidative injury, and to modulate the role o[f] Hb in oxygen transport. Many differences betwee[n] the erythrocytes from the newborn infant and th[e] adult have been described (reviewed in reference 29[). Several are outlined in Table I. It is importan[t], when interpreting metabolic studies, to realize tha[t] the infant erythrocyte cell population is quite heter[o]geneous. The rate of erythropoiesis is great durin[g] the final weeks of gestation, and as a consequenc[e] a large proportion of the cells are young. Thu[s], before features are considered to be unique t[o] neonatal cells, they must be distinguished fro[m] features that are merely characteristic of youn[g] erythrocytes (reticulocyte-rich fractions) taken fro[m] any subject.[29]

The metabolism of glucose by anaerobic glycolys[is] provides the main energy source for the red cel[l]. Glycogen cannot be stored by erythrocytes; there[-]fore, glucose must be continuously available in th[e] environment. The end product of glycolysis in th[e] red cells is lactate. Mature erythrocytes do not con[-]tain mitochondria, and subsequently lack the trica[r]boxylic acid cycle of Krebs. Fructose, mannose, an[d] galactose can serve as substrates for the glycolyt[ic] pathway.

One of the important functions of glycolysis [is] the generation of ATP. ATP is generated in ery[-]throcytes by the reactions in the glycolytic pathwa[y] catalyzed by phosphoglycerate kinase and pyruvat[e] kinase. Several enzymes of the glycolytic pathwa[y]

Table I. Metabolic Characteristics of the Erythrocytes of the Newborn[a]

Carbohydrate metabolism
  Glucose consumption is increased.
  Galactose is more completely utilized as substrate both under normal circumstances and for methemoglobin reduction.[b]
  Decreased activity of sorbitol pathway.[b]
  Decreased triokinase activity.[b]
Glycolytic enzymes
  Increased activity of hexokinase, phosphoglucose isomerase,[b] aldolase, glyceraldehyde-3-phosphate dehydrogenase,[b] phosphoglycerate kinase,[b] phosphoglycerate mutase, enolase,[b] pyruvate kinase, lactic dehydrogenase, glucose-6-phosphate dehydrogenase, 6-phosphogluconic dehydrogenase, galactokinase, and galactose-1-phosphate uridyltransferase.
  Decreased activity of phosphofructokinase.[b]
  Distribution of hexokinase isoenzymes differs from that of adults.[b]
Nonglycolytic enzymes
  Increased activity of glutamic-oxaloacetic transaminase and glutathione reductase.
  Decreased activity of NADP-dependent methemoglobin reductase,[b] catalase,[b] glutathione peroxidase, carbonic anhydrase,[b] adenylate kinase,[b] and glutathione synthetase.[b]
ATP and phosphate metabolism
  Decreased phosphate uptake,[b] slower incorporation into ATP and 2,3-diphosphoglycerate.[b]
  Accelerated decline of 2,3-diphosphoglycerate on red cell incubation.[b]
  Increased ATP levels
  Accelerated decline of ATP during brief incubation
Storage characteristics
  Increased potassium efflux and greater degrees of hemolysis during short periods of storage.[b]
  More rapid assumption of altered morphological forms on storage or incubation.[b]
Membrane
  Decreased ouabain-sensitive ATPase.[b]
  Decreased potassium influx.[b]
  Decreased permeability to glycerol and thiourea.[b]
  Decreased membrane deformability.[b]
  Increased sphingomyelin, decreased lecithin content of stromal phospholipids.
  Decreased content of linoleic acid.[b]
  Increase in lipid phosphorus and cholesterol per cell.
  Greater affinity for glucose.[b]
Other
  Increased methemoglobin content.[b]
  Increased affinity of hemoglobin for oxygen.[b]
  Glutathione instability.[b]
  Increased tendency for Heinz body formation in the presence of oxidant compounds.[b]

[a] This table is reproduced with the permission of the authors, Oski and Komazawa.[29]
[b] This characteristic appears to be unique to the newborn's erythrocytes, and not merely a function of the presence of young red cells.

including phosphoglycerate kinase, exhibit genuinely increased activity in neonatal cells. Glucose consumption by neonatal erythrocytes is greater than that observed in cells from normal adults. When the cells from infants are compared with adult cells of a similarly young age (reticulocyte-rich fractions), however, their rate of glucose consumption is actually smaller than expected. The diminished glycolytic metabolism is due largely to the decreased activity of phosphofructokinase, one of the rate-limiting enzymes of the glycolytic pathway.[29]

Another factor that influences the activity of the

glycolytic pathway is the intracellular concentration of 2,3-diphosphoglycerate (2,3-DPG).[28] This substance inhibits several critical glycolytic enzymes, including hexokinase and phosphofructokinase, the two rate-limiting enzymes, and phosphoglycerate kinase and pyruvate kinase, the two enzymes that catalyze the ATP-generating steps. During incubation, the concentration of 2,3-DPG declines more rapidly in erythrocytes from infants than in those from adults. This more rapid decline is primarily the result of accelerated catabolism, although the precise biochemical events have not been defined.[28]

2,3-DPG can bind to reduced Hb and reduce its affinity for oxygen. This drop in oxygen affinity serves as a compensatory mechanism that facilitates the release of oxygen to the tissues during hypoxic states. The binding constant (affinity) of 2,3-DPG for fetal Hb is considerably less than that for adult Hb; consequently, the effect of this substance on the delivery of oxygen to tissues by neonatal erythrocytes is diminished when compared with its effect in adult cells. This lesser effect explains the previous observation that although intact neonatal erythrocytes possess a higher affinity for oxygen than do the cells of adults, the oxygen affinity is identical when estimated in solutions of fetal or adult Hb that have been dialyzed to remove other cellular materials (2,3-DPG).

The "P_{50}" is a convenient method of describing the affinity of Hb for oxygen. P_{50} is defined as the partial pressure of oxygen at which the Hb is 50% saturated with oxygen under standard conditions. The P_{50} value at birth is lower than that of an adult, and is even less in a premature infant; i.e., the Hb in premature erythrocytes is 50% saturated with oxygen at a lower partial pressure of oxygen than the Hb of cells from infants or adults. The P_{50} value approximates that of the adult by 4–6 months of age. The low P_{50} *in utero* would promote the transfer of oxygen from mother to fetus. The fetal erythrocytes with their increased affinity for oxygen would accept oxygen at a partial pressure low enough to promote oxygen release from the maternal cells.[28,29] Additional information on fetal hemoglobin will be found in Chapter 11 and on gas transport in Chapter 12.

Another important function of erythrocyte metabolism is to produce the reduced adenine nucleotides, NADH and NADPH. NADPH is generated by the hexose monophosphate shunt. The proportion of glucose traversing this pathway in newborn erythrocytes is as great as or greater than that found in adult cells. NADPH provided by the hexose monophosphate pathway is, in turn, used to reduce glutathione in a reaction catalyzed by the enzyme glutathione reductase and to reduce methemoglobin to Hb. Despite these metabolic pathways, neonatal erythrocytes are more susceptible to oxidative injury, which likely contributes to shortened survival. This injury is characterized by Heinz body formation, glutathione instability, and methemoglobinemia. There is no satisfactory explanation for this process, although the activities of two enzymes that act to prevent the intracellular accumulation of H_2O_2, catalase and glutathione peroxidase, are decreased in cord blood.

The formation of NADH is controlled by the interaction of the glycolytic enzymes glyceraldehyde-3-phosphate dehydrogenase and lactic dehydrogenase. Both enzymes have increased activities in newborn erythrocytes.[29] An important use for NADH is in the reduction of methemoglobin by the diaphorase system related to the enzyme methemoglobin reductase. The concentration of methemoglobin in erythrocytes of newborn premature and full-term infants is increased, and the activity of the diaphorase system is decreased during this period. It is not known whether the reduction of activity occurs because of decreased amounts of enzyme or because NADH is less available.[4]

Thus, the erythrocyte is not simply an enucleated carrier of oxygen. It is a metabolically active cell. Several aspects of erythrocyte physiology are unique to the fetal and neonatal period. Many of these features have been related to clinical observations and seem to have logical purposes. Others remain unexplained.

4. Leukocytes

There are three basic types of leukocytes found in blood: granulocytes, monocytes, and lymphocytes. The granulocytic leukocytes are subdivided into three types based on the staining characteristics of the cytoplasmic granules and their function: eosinophilic, basophilic, and neutrophilic granulocytes. Functional differences also exist among lymphocytes, and they are divided into two broad groups designated as T and B cells. The functions of monocytes vary greatly during maturation or with environmental (tissue) influences, but it is not currently possible to divide them into distinct subgroups. Although these cells are generally regarded

Table II. Range of Normal Blood Leukocyte Concentrations During Childhood[a]

Age (yr)	Total white blood count	Neutrophils	Eosinophils	Basophils	Lymphocytes	Monocytes
Birth	4–40	2.1–20.3	0–1.3	0–0.3	0.8–9.4	0–1.5
½	5–24	0.5–9.5	0–2.7	0–0.4	1.4–22	0–2.4
2	6–13	Counts for individual cell types are not available for this age.				
4–7	5–15	1.5–7.5	0–0.8	0–0.2	1.5–8.5	0–0.8
8–18	4–13	1.5–6.5	0–0.6	0–0.2	1.5–6.5	0–0.8
Adult	4–11	1.5–7.5	0–0.4	0–0.2	1.0–4.5	0–0.8

[a] Absolute number $\times 10^3/\mu l$.

to be blood cells, in actuality, each of the cell types uses the blood merely as a means of transport from sites of production to sites of function. Production sites are extravascular, and for the most part, the sites of function are likewise extravascular.

4.1. Normal Values

The variation in blood leukocyte concentration is greater in the perinatal period than at any other time. To evaluate white blood counts properly, particularly as they may reflect a response to disease, the normally occurring variations must be appreciated. The ranges of blood leukocyte counts at varying ages are given in Table II. There is no difference in normal values related to sex in children; in adults, however, the total leukocyte count is greater in women than in men due to a significantly higher neutrophil count.[2] The mean total leukocyte count in black children greater than 1 year of age is lower than in whites because of a significantly decreased neutrophil count. There are no racial differences in lymphocyte, monocyte, eosinophil, or basophil counts. Information regarding sex and race differences in neonatal leukocyte counts is not available.

A wide range of leukocyte counts exists at birth, and the neutrophil is the predominant cell.[39] Significant changes in the proportion of the various types of leukocytes (differential white blood cell count) occur during the first few days of life, as illustrated Fig. 1.[39] The mean total leukocyte count during the first 10 days of life is 15,200/μl. In term infants, the mean neutrophil count at birth is 8000/μl. The count rises rapidly to a mean value of 13,000/μl at 12 hr of age, but drops to a mean of 4000/μl by 72 hr. There is a continued decrease in the neutro-

phil count over the next 2–3 weeks, so that the lymphocyte becomes the predominant cell. Neutrophil counts in premature infants are somewhat lower than those in term infants, but the change in counts as related to time intervals after birth is similar. During the first 2–3 days of life, varying numbers of immature neutrophils, such as myelocytes and metamyelocytes, can be identified in the blood, particularly in premature infants. The diurnal variation in neutrophil counts observed in adults is not present in infants. The absolute number of lymphocytes decreases during the first 3 days of life. It then rises to a value of approximately 5000/μl on the 10th day, after which it remains constant throughout childhood. The monocyte concentration during the first month of life may transiently exceed that observed in adults.

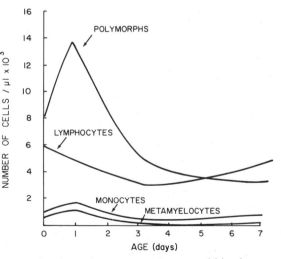

Fig. 1. Leukocyte count in neonatal blood.

Table III. Changes in Cellular Composition of the Bone Marrow During the First 2 Months of Life[a]

Age	Nucleated marrow cells (%)		
	Erythroid	Myeloid	Lymphoid
Birth	40.0	46.4	12.1
1 week	15.3	60.6	22.9
2 weeks	8.0	50.0	37.3
4 weeks	6.8	31.1	55.6
8 weeks	14.8	36.6	48.5

[a] Reproduced (with modifications) from Glaser, K., Limarzi, L. R., and Poncher, H. G., 1950, Cellular composition of the bone marrow in normal infants and children, *Pediatrics* **6**:789.

Leukocytes are formed in the bone marrow for release into the blood. During the first 2 months of life, there are changes in marrow cell composition, as shown in Table III. These changes are characterized by a decrease in erythroid elements, which is maximum at about 1 month of life, and an increase in lymphoid cells, which reaches a peak between the first and fourth months of life. Plasma cells are not present in the bone marrow at birth, but begin to appear between the fourth and sixth weeks of life. The concentration of plasma cells in older children is the same as that in adults.

4.2. Production and Kinetics

The studies that have contributed information to this area have been performed in animals and adult subjects because of the need for adequate sampling of blood and bone marrow, and because of the reluctance to subject normal infants to investigational procedures procedures employing radioactive materials. The following information deals with neutrophils unless otherwise specified.

All hematopoietic cells arise from a common self-sustaining pool of pluri-potent stem cells that are able to differentiate into several cell lines. These primitive cells have not been morphologically identified, but eventually they are committed into precursor cells of one of the recognizable cell lines. Committed granulocytic stem cells are present in increased numbers in cord blood.[17] The factors that control the entry of pluripotential stem cells into the neutrophil pathway of differentiation *in vivo* are unknown, but the clonal growth of committed

granulocytic stem cells *in vitro* is dependent on colony-stimulating factors (CSF). This material originally described as a glycoprotein with a molecular weight of 45,000, may be composed of at least three components.[32] CSF is produced by adherent mononuclear cells (presumably monocytes) by antigen-stimulated lymphocytes. It is found in the blood and urine of normal individuals in increased amount when there is an increased demand for neutrophils and it may function most importantly in amplification, i.e., to increase the proliferation of previously committed cells, in a manner analogous to that of erythropoietin in erythrocyte production.

In a preliminary report, the colony-stimulating activity of blood and urine was increased in sample collected during the immediate neonatal period.[3 Many factors undoubtedly influence neutrophil production in the bone marrow, but their interrelationships and biological importance in man are presently undefined.

Once committed to the neutrophil cell line, the precursors progress in an orderly manner through stages of cell division (myeloblast, promyelocyte and myelocyte) and maturation (metamyelocyte and polymorphonuclear leukocyte). This development takes approximately 10–12 days under normal steady-state conditions, following which the mature polymorphonuclear neutrophils are stored in the marrow or released into the circulating blood. Once in the bloodstream, they are equally divided into the marginating and circulating pools, between which there is a constant exchange of cells. The marginating pool can be mobilized into the circulating one by epinephrine. Cells leave the blood in a random fashion after a circulating half-life of about 7 hr, and do not reenter the blood from the tissues.

4. 3. Microbial Functions

Neutrophils must perform a series of coordinated complex maneuvers to function as efficient phagocytes (reviewed in reference 34). Sufficient number of cells must be delivered from the bloodstream to the area of infection. After opsonization, the organisms are engulfed by the neutrophils, and phagolysosomes are formed. A series of metabolic event accompanies phagocytosis, and a variety of mechanisms become available to kill the pathogens. Normal leukocyte functions will be briefly summarized in the following discussion. Studies that have employed neutrophils from infants will be specifically acknowledged.

Chemotaxis is the vectorial movement of neutrophils that permits their accumulation at inflammatory sites. The relationship of this type of directed movement to that of random motility is undefined. The chemotactic response *in vitro* is gradient-dependent, with migration toward the highest concentration of the chemotaxin. A variety of substances derived from inflammatory or immune responses act as chemotaxins (attractants), including products of bacterial growth and tissue injury, antigen–antibody complexes, and materials released from platelets, neutrophils, and antigen-stimulated lymphocytes. Although some of these possess intrinsic chemotactic activity, many interact enzymatically with components of the complement and coagulation systems to generate kallikrein, $C\overline{567}$, and small-molecular-weight fragments of C3 and C5. These biologically active peptides then mediate chemotactic activity. Apparently all chemotaxins are recognized by the neutrophil through activation of a common serine proesterase on the cell membrane. Movement is dependent on ATP production by glycolysis, requires both magnesium ions and calcium ions, and is inhibited by agents that greatly increase intracellular concentrations of cyclic adenosine monophosphate, stabilize lysosomal membranes, block activation of serine esterase sites, or interfere with functions of either microfilaments or microtubules. Antagonists are present in normal plasma, and are produced by the inflammatory reaction, including at least one that is released by neutrophils. These inhibitors can interact directly with the cell membrane, rendering it unresponsive to chemotaxins, or they can inactivate the chemotactic factors in the fluid phase and render them incapable of reacting with the neutrophil cell membrane. Cell movement is determined by the interrelationships of the chemotaxins, the antagonists, and the ability of the neutrophil to respond.

Abnormalities of both the humoral and cellular components of the chemotactic response have been reported in neonatal infants.[21] Infants 3–5 days old and weighing at least 2500 g were studied. (The number of infants sampled was not reported.) The number of neonatal leukocytes that migrated through the filter in an *in vitro* chemotaxis apparatus was significantly less than that of adult cells. In addition, neonatal serum yielded lesser amounts of chemotactic activity than adult serum. Studies were not performed that would detect inhibitors. *In vivo* studies, such as the Rebuck skin window, were not done, and the relationship of these *in vitro* studies to cell migration as it occurs *in vivo* has not been established. Certain complement proteins are deficient in neonatal blood, and it is likely that this deficiency is the explanation for the impaired production of chemotactic activity by infant sera.[25] Random migration of neonatal neutrophils is normal when assessed by *in vitro* methods. The plasma membrane is rigid and poorly deformable when compared with that of adult neutrophils.[22] This lack of flexibility may be related to the diminished mobility of neonatal neutrophils.

The phagocytic process is complex and involves the opsonization and ingestion of microorganisms, the formation of phagolysosomes, and a series of biochemical events (reviewed in reference 34). The process can be assessed by bactericidal assays and by determining the activity of various metabolic pathways. Information in this area is conflicting and incomplete in regard to the newborn. In many studies, engulfment of pathogenic bacteria is reported to be inefficient. These organisms, unlike the inert and unphysiologic particles used in other studies, require opsonization by serum proteins for engulfment. Most heat-labile opsonins are immunoglobulins with specificity for an antigen on the surface of a particular organism. The heat-stable opsonins of infant sera are variable. The IgM antibodies in infant blood must be synthesized by the newborn in response to antigenic stimulation. On the other hand, IgG antibodies are acquired transplacentally, and the spectrum of opsonins that is present depends on the mother's immunity. Heat-labile opsonins are derived from the complement system. The concentration of serum complement components varies among newborns, but the concentrations of several components are decreased in prematures.[25] Sufficient quantities of these components are available for certain complement-mediated functions, but in most reports, phagocytosis of particles requiring opsonization is inefficient in neonatal serum. Opsonization by the alternative pathway of complement activation, which does not require specific antibody, was found to be impaired in a small number of newborns with moderately low serum concentrations of the C3 proactivator protein. Because infants may lack the specific antibodies required for heat-stable opsonization and activation of the complement system through the classical pathway, this relatively nonspecific method of opsonization is an important body defense. A phagocytic abnormality, intrinsic to the neutrophil, that is of sufficient severity to account for defective bactericidal function has not been described.

The attachment of opsonized particles to the neutrophil is a surface phenomenon and does not expend energy. The ingestion that follows requires ATP. It is inhibited by substances that block glycolysis (iodoacetate and sodium fluoride), but not by anaerobiosis, inhibition of mitochondrial respiration (cyanide), or interference with ATP production at the mitochondrial membrane, i.e., uncoupling of oxidative phosphorylation (2,4-dinitrophenol). Thus, in normal cells, the necessary ATP is generated by substrate phosphorylation during anaerobic glycolysis; however, mitochondrial oxidative phosphorylation can serve as an auxiliary source of energy. Inhibition of either RNA or protein synthesis by actinomycin D or puromycin, respectively, does not interfere with engulfment. Ingestion is an evagination process with pseudopodia extending out and around the particle in a cuplike fashion until they fuse on the distal side. Thus, the particle is within a phagocytic vesicle, the limiting membrane of which is the inverted neutrophil plasma membrane. When lectin-binding or transport carrier sites are used as markers for specific areas of the cell membrane, it is apparent that only certain portions of this structure are internalized during phagocytosis. The composition of the membrane at these sites and the role of the cell membrane in mediating the intracellular events that follow ingestion are unknown. Increased turnover and biosynthesis of lipids and RNA accompany phagocytosis, but there is no evidence for effective membrane renewal in neutrophils.

Ingestion is a process of cell movement and, like chemotaxis, requires divalent cations. It is inhibited by substances that greatly increase intracellular concentration of cyclic AMP; by cytochalasin B, which alters microfilament function and blocks glucose transport; and by certain concentrations of colchicine that disrupt microtubules.

Even before ingestion is completed, cytoplasmic granules approach the phagocytic vesicle, fuse with it, and discharge their contents into it, forming a phagolysosome. The molecular biology of degranulation *in vivo* is unknown, but the process in neonatal neutrophils was reported to be normal when assessed by fairly simple techniques.[8]

A burst of oxidative metabolism accompanies the phagocytosis of particles *in vitro*. It is characterized by increases in oxygen consumption and hexose monophosphate shunt activity, the production of reactive forms of oxygen, including hydrogen peroxide and superoxide anion, and by chemiluminescence. The last has been attributed to energy emitted by singlet oxygen as it reverts to its more stable ground state. This increase in oxidative metabolism is accompanied by the reduction of nitroblue tetrazolium (NBT) dye to formazan precipitate, a process that is mediated in part by superoxide anion. This increase in oxidative metabolism occurs spontaneously in neutrophils taken from the blood of patients with untreated bacterial infections when assessed by NBT dye reduction. Neutrophils from these patients reduce NBT *in vitro* in the absence of exogenous particles.

Oxidative metabolism in neutrophils from the blood of newborn infants (within the first month of life) is similar in some respects to that described for cells from infected patients. Although a few dissenting reports exist, most investigators have found that NBT dye is reduced spontaneously, and that the basal level of oxygen consumption and hexose monophosphate shunt activity is increased in neutrophils from term and premature babies when compared with that in cells from older children and adults. A further increase in oxidative metabolism occurs *in vitro* as a response to the phagocytosis of particles. However, the postphagocytic increase may be blunted in neutrophils from infected infants.[1] The activity of leukocyte alkaline phosphatase is also increased when studied by histochemical techniques.

The characteristics of the enzyme systems involved in the oxidative burst must include insensitivity to cyanide and the ability to produce H_2O_2. Neutrophilic enzymes that are then capable of initiating the oxidative burst are the oxidases for NADH and NADPH, and the amino acid oxidases.[9] Considerable controversy exists as to the enzyme responsible for this process.

All the metabolic events that compose the postphagocytic oxidative burst could be explained by activation of NADH oxidase, with the sequence of events as follows:

1. NADH is provided by the increase in anaerobic glycolysis accompanying ingestion.
2. NADH combines with molecular oxygen in a reaction catalyzed by NADH oxidase. Oxygen is reduced in the process to form superoxide anion and H_2O_2.
3. H_2O_2 is used in microbicidal activity and to oxidize reduced glutathione in a reaction that can occur independently of glutathione peroxidase.

4. The glutathione that is generated can act as an electron acceptor for NADPH with the subsequent generation of NADP. This reaction occurs in the presence of glutathione reductase, but can proceed without enzyme catalysis.

5. The increase in the NADP : NADPH ratio activates glucose-6-phosphate dehydrogenase, permitting entry of glucose-6-phosphate into the hexose monophosphate shunt. (NADP serves a structural function by linking together halves of the active dimer of the enzyme, and the increase in the NADP : NADPH ratio releases the inhibition of this enzyme normally mediated by the relatively high intracellular concentration of NADPH.)

6. NADPH is generated by the hexose monophosphate shunt, and additional H_2O_2 is produced in a reaction catalyzed by NADPH oxidase present in the primary granules.

On the other hand, several investigators favor activation of NADPH oxidase as the most important event in triggering the oxidative burst. In this series of reactions, NADPH is oxidized by granule-bound NADPH oxidase to form superoxide anion and H_2O_2. NADPH is converted to NADP by this reaction, with the subsequent activation of glucose-6-phosphate dehydrogenase and increase in hexose monophosphate shunt activity. The reactive forms of oxygen that are generated are then employed by the cell for bactericidal activities. This metabolic sequence is particularly attractive because the entire oxidative burst can be explained by a single reaction, and there is no need to recruit other enzyme systems (anaerobic glycolysis as a source of NADH, glutathione system), as is necessary for the NADH oxidase pathway. In addition, the K_m of NADPH oxidase in phagocytic cells is 8-fold lower than in resting cells, so that the intracellular concentrations of NADPH are in the range required for maximum enzyme activity. Further evidence favoring this pathway over that of the NADH oxidase is the 3-fold increase in the NADP:NADPH ratio accompanying phagocytosis, whereas the NAD : NADH ratio is unchanged. Furthermore, the increase in NADPH oxidase activity demonstrated in normal phagocytic cells could not be elicited in phagocytic cells from patients with chronic granulomatous disease—a disorder characterized by the inability to produce the postphagocytic oxidative burst.

It is to be emphasized that neither of these enzymes (NADH or NADPH oxidase) has received universal support (reviewed in reference 9). Although the basal rate of oxidative metabolism is increased in nonphagocytic neonatal neutrophils, there is no evidence at present to suggest that the response to phagocytosis is mediated by metabolic pathways that are unique to neonatal cells.

Neonatal neutrophils perform normally in bactericidal assays *if* satisfactory amounts of opsonins are provided. In 1910, Tunnicliff,[37] using a variety of bacteria as test organisms, concluded that the phagocytic activity of the leukocyte was normal at birth, but declined during the first few months of life and did not reach the adult level until about 2 years of age. Opsonic factors were found to follow the same pattern of decline after birth, followed by gradual return to an adult level of function. Matoth[18] reported that phagocytosis of starch granules was less efficient in leukocytes of the newborn than in those of the adult, and that the phagocytosis-promoting power of serum from the newborn was less than that of adult serum. Gluck and Silverman[12] reported the results of studies of phagocytosis of carbon particles in 54 premature infants and 15 full-term infants. They defined effective phagocytes as those containing 10 or more carbon particles, and reported that there was no significant difference in effective phagocytosis between adult leukocytes and those of infants over 2000 g. The number of effective phagocytes was smaller in premature infants, and tended to approach normal with increasing birth weight. Improved phagocytic function occurred when serum from a normal adult was added to the test system of the premature. Miyamoto,[23] using killed streptococci, reported that phagocytic activity for both the premature and full-term infants was decreased during the neonatal period as compared with studies at 1 month of age. Cocchi and Marianelli[7] reported that the blood of premature infants had a higher phagocytic rate than that of normal adult blood, but that this higher rate was associated with decreased killing of the bacteria. *Pseudomonas aeruginosa* was the test organism, and neonatal neutrophils disintegrated following phagocytosis. These authors suggested a defect in the intracellular killing capacity of these cells due to cell injury that was unrelated to serum factors. Miller[20] reported that heparinized plasma from newborn infants had diminished opsonizing activity toward yeast when compared with plasma from adults. The differences were statistically significant, however, only when the plasma was considerably diluted. In a similar manner, neutrophils from neonates ingested yeast less efficiently than adult cells in the presence of highly diluted plasma. The biological importance of this observation remains undefined.

Forman and Stiehm[10] found that serum from low-birth-weight neonates provided inadequate opsonins, but that neutrophils from healthy neonates of varying birth weights functioned normally in the presence of adult serum. Infants who were sick with a variety of illnesses, however, had impaired neutrophil function even in the presence of adult serum. These infants were not studied in a serial manner, and it was impossible to determine whether this impairment was merely a transient one due to the illness. Coen et al.[8] found phagocytic and bactericidal activity to be normal in neutrophils taken from infants greater than 24 hr of age. A proportion of newborns, however, had defective intracellular killing of bacteria during the first day of life. In addition, an abnormality in postphagocytic oxidative metabolism was detected. It seemed very likely, by the evidence presented, that the bacterial defect was of a transient nature, and that the abnormality of oxidative metabolism was causally related to the impaired bacterial killing. Serial studies were not performed to document the transient nature of the defect, however, and data were not given that permitted one to relate infants with the bactericidal defect to those possessing the metabolic one. Wright et al.[38] confirmed the earlier suspicions of Forman and Stiehm that neutrophil bactericidal activity decreases transiently during periods of stress. This situation, however, is not unique to neonatal cells.

In summary, the neutrophils from healthy, normal neonates possess normal phagocytic and bactericidal functions in the presence of adult serum. These functions may be transiently abnormal at times of stress, such as immediately after birth or during episodes of infection. It is clear that neonatal serum is a poor source of opsonins for most microorganisms. This deficiency is particularly true for the heat-labile (complement-dependent) opsonin system.

4.4. Other Leukocytes

Little information is available regarding monocyte function in the fetus and newborn. Mononuclear phagocytes are components of the reticuloendothelial system (reviewed in reference 34). These fixed and motile cells are derived from monocyte precursors in the bone marrow and share physiologic properties, including adhesion to glass, membrane ruffling, and the avid ingestion of colloidal or particulate material.

Although present as clearly recognized monocytes in the $4\frac{1}{2}$-month human fetus, these cells have variable function. This variability is probably related to the availability of opsonins and not to cellular defects. Reticuloendothelial cells clear the blood of both exogenous and endogenous materials such as microorganisms, endotoxin, tissue debris, fibrin, hemoglobin, steroids, proteins, and drugs. In addition, these cells produce proteolytic enzymes, peroxidase, lysozyme, interferon, at least three serum complement components (C4, C2, and C3), and possibly the clotting factor VIII (antihemophilic globulin). They participate in the afferent phase of the immune response by the engulfment and processing of antigens, but not by the synthesis of immunoglobulins. In addition, they contribute to the inflammatory process in the efferent phase of the immune response.

The mononuclear phagocytes are viewed as a series of cells originating from a common precursor, but with varying characteristics and function. Many of these changes accompany maturation or are induced by the tissue environment. The development of the cell line can be divided into a proliferative phase in the bone marrow, a circulating phase of nondividing monocytes in the blood, and a phase of accumulation in the tissues with differentiation into tissue phagocytes (macrophages). After the cells enter the tissues, they avidly engulf material and differentiate into macrophages through a series of structural and physiologic changes that are greatly influenced by the environment. The most prominent of these changes are increases in cell size, in the numbers of mitochondria and lipid droplets, in the number and size of lysosomes, and in lysosomal enzyme activities. Considerable heterogeneity exists in the morphology and metabolism of these cells, depending on their anatomic location and the stimuli to which they are exposed. For example, pulmonary alveolar macrophages, which function in an aerobic environment, have increased numbers of mitochondria and rely primarily on mitochondrial oxidative metabolism for energy, while cells in other parts of the body, where oxygen tension may be less, have fewer mitochondria and derive energy from anaerobic glycolysis. The cell membrane is ruffled by pseudopodia, the undulating movements of which probably increase the efficiency of engulfment. The extensive Golgi complex is rimmed by mitochondria, and the cytoplasm contains a variety of vacuoles and peroxidase-negative granules. Giant cells are produced by extensive engulfment of large particles. Tissue mononuclear phagocytes (macrophages) are divided into those with basophilic cytoplasm and loose nuclear chromatin and those with acidophilic cytoplasm and dense chromatin. The former cells retain proliferative activity, but the latter are terminal, nonreplicating cells. They can survive in the tissues for months, and only rarely reenter the circulation.

Three major factors are important for the satisfactory removal of material from the blood by mononuclear phagocytes. Normal blood flow through the sinusoids of the reticuloendothelial organs is required to deliver particles to the cells, and sufficient quantities of both plasma proteins (opsonins) and recognition sites on the cell membrane (receptors) must be available to enhance ingestion. Reticuloendothelial blockade exists when there is impaired clearance of material by this system. This state is usually due to insufficient quantities of humoral opsonins, but it can also exist if all phagocytic membrane receptors are occupied, as during administration of excessive numbers of particles. This state is a temporary one that reverts to normal when opsonins again become available or when the membrane receptors are renewed.

Although mononuclear phagocytes are particularly important in the defense against intracellular organisms, they are relatively ineffective as phagocytes when compared with neutrophils. They ingest organisms slowly and kill them less efficiently. They do have an important role in the immune response. There is no information to suggest that monocyte function in neonatal infants is abnormal as compared with that in adults, although the question has not been adequately studied.

Lymphocytes are discussed in great detail in Chapter 14, and only a brief introduction will be presented here. These cells in neonates can be divided into two broad classes, designated as the *thymus-derived (T) cells* and *bone-marrow-derived (B) cells* (reviewed in reference 34).

The B lymphocyte arises in the bone marrow and is the progenitor of antibody-forming plasma cells. It is recognized by the presence of surface immunoglobulins, a receptor for the Fc portion of aggregated immunoglobulins, and receptors for the C3b and C3d fragments of complement. Reports indicating the percentage of B lymphocytes in the blood vary depending on the precautions taken to remove the mononuclear phagocytes, but 10–30% of these cells possess at least one B-cell marker. Each B cell makes only a single class of immunoglobulin and

light chain with specificity to one antigen; therefore, these molecules are considered to function as antigen receptors. Normal cord-blood lymphocytes and cells from patients with chronic lymphocytic leukemia are exceptions, and more than one immunoglobulin type can be identified on the cell surface. Precautions must always be taken in such instances to exclude the possibility that the multiple labeling was due simply to the absorption of plasma proteins. Cells with IgM surface immunoglobulins predominate in young children, but decrease in number with age, while the IgG-labeling cells increase, a fact of obvious importance when considering normal values.[14]

The T lymphocytes are identified by the lack of B-cell markers, their ability to form rosettes with unsensitized sheep erythrocytes in the absence of complement, and their interaction with monospecific anti-T-lymphocyte antiserums. Although the percentage of cells forming T-cell rosettes varies greatly depending on the methods used, 70–80% of circulating blood lymphocytes can be identified as T lymphocytes when several methods of detection are used. The percentage of lymphocytes in cord blood identified as T-cells is lower than in adult blood; the absolute number, however, is the same.

B and T lymphocytes cannot be distinguished by simply examining stained blood smears. In addition to the specific markers discussed above, several studies aid in their identification. The lectins concanavalin A, phytohemagglutinin, and staphylococcal enterotoxin B preferentially stimulate T lymphocytes to proliferate. Pokeweed mitogen stimulates both T and B cells, while the lipid moiety in endotoxin stimulates B lymphocytes. On scanning electron microscopy, the surfaces of T lymphocytes are relatively smooth; B lymphocyte surfaces, however, have a complex villous surface architecture. This method is not very satisfactory for differentiating cell types, since there is considerable overlap, and the appearance can change with antigenic or mitogenic stimulation. When lymphocyte suspensions are subjected to electrophoresis, the T cells migrate more rapidly toward the anode than the B cells.

5. Platelets

5.1. Normal Values

Megakaryocytes can be located in the hematopoietic tissues of the liver and spleen at 10 weeks of gestation. At about the same time, platelets appear in the blood. They are present in clumps at 12–15 weeks, suggesting that they are capable of adhering to each other. Platelet counts in term infants are equal to those in adults. These counts may be lower in premature babies, but generally are not below 100,000/μl in healthy infants.[5]

5.2. Functions

Information about the functions of platelets from human fetuses is sparse. Decreased aggregation was demonstrated in platelets from 5 fetuses between 19 and 24 weeks of gestation.[30] The platelets did respond to ADP, although less vigorously than platelets from adults, but failed to aggregate in response to adrenalin and collagen.

Platelet functions are mildly impaired after birth for a period of 1–2 weeks.[5] In both term and premature infants, aggregation in response to ADP, collagen, and thrombin is decreased. In addition, clot retraction is poor, and platelet factor 3 availability is diminished in neonatal platelets as compared with adults. The bleeding time is generally normal, however, except in small premature infants.

6. References

1. ANDERSON, D. C., PICKERING, L. K., AND FEIGIN, R. D., 1974, Leukocyte function in normal and infected neonates, *J. Pediatr.* **85**:420.
2. BAIN, B. J., AND ENGLAND, J. M., 1975, Normal haematological values: Sex difference in neutrophil count, *Br. Med. J.* **1**:307.
3. BARAK, Y., BLASCHAR, Y., FRIEDMAN, R., AND LEVIN, S., 1976, Granulopoiesis in the newborn infant: Appraisal by an assay of urinary and serum granulocytic colony stimulating factor (CSF), Paper presented at the Fifth Meeting of the European Society for Paediatric Hematology and Immunology, Caesarea, Israel.
4. BARTOS, H. R., AND DESFORGES, J. F., 1966, Erythrocyte DPNH dependent diaphorase levels in infants, *Pediatrics* **37**:991.
5. BLEYER, W. A., HAKAMI, N., AND SHEPARD, T. H., 1971, The development of hemostasis in the human fetus and newborn infant, *J. Pediatr.* **79**:838.
6. CHEN, L. T., AND WEISS, L., 1975, The development of vertebral bone marrow of human fetuses, *Blood* **46**:389.
7. COCCHI, P., AND MARIANELLI, L., 1967, Phagocytosis and intracellular killing of *Pseudomonas aeruginosa* in premature infants, *Helv. Paediatr. Acta* **22**:110.
8. COEN, R., GRUSH, O., AND KAUDER, E., 1969, Studies of bactericidal activity and metabolism of the leukocyte in full-term neonates, *J. Pediatr.* **75**:400.
9. DE CHATELET, L. R., 1975, Oxidative bactericidal mechanisms of polymorphonuclear leukocytes, *J. Infect. Dis.* **131**:295.
10. FORMAN, M. L., AND STIEHM, E. R., 1969, Impaired opsonic activity but normal phagocytosis in low-birth-weight infants, *N. Engl. J. Med.* **281**:926.
11. GARBY, L., SJOLIN, S., AND VUILLE, J. C., 1964, Studies on erythro-kinetics in infancy. V. Estimation of the life span of red cells in the newborn, *Acta Paediatr.* **53**:165.
12. GLUCK, L., AND SILVERMAN, W. A., 1957, Phagocytosis in premature infants, *Pediatrics* **20**:951.
13. GUEST, G. M., BROWN, E. W., AND LAHEY, M. E., 1957, Normal blood values in infancy and childhood, *Pediatr. Clin. North Amer.* **4**:357.
14. JAMES, K. K., HURBUBISE, P. E., MACPHERSON, G. R., AND MURPHY, S. G., 1974, Human lymphocyte membrane immunoglobulin as a reflection of maturation, *J. Immunol.* **113**:698.
15. KAPLAN, E., 1959, Studies of red cell survival in early infancy, *Amer. J. Dis. Child.* **98**:603.
16. KAPLAN, E., AND HSU, K. S., 1961, Determination of erythrocyte survival in newborn infants by means of Cr^{51}-labeled erythrocytes, *Pediatrics* **27**:354.
17. KNDTZON, S., 1974, *In vitro* growth of granulocytic colonies from circulating cells in human cord blood, *Blood* **43**:357.
18. MATOTH, Y., 1952, Phagocytic and ameboid activities of the leukocytes in the newborn infant, *Pediatrics* **9**:748.
19. McINTOSH, S., 1975, Erythropoietin excretion in the premature infant, *J. Pediatr.* **86**:202.
20. MILLER, M. E., 1969, Phagocytosis in the newborn infant: Humoral and cellular factors, *J. Pediatr.* **74**:255.
21. MILLER, M. E., 1971, Chemotactic function in the human neonate: Humoral and cellular aspects, *Pediatr. Res.* **5**:487.
22. MILLER, M. E., 1975, Pathology of chemotaxis and random mobility, *Semin. Hematol.* **12**:59.
23. MIYAMOTO, K., 1965, Phagocytic activity of leukocytes in premature infants. II. Correlation of the plasma components and phagocytic activities of leukocytes in premature and full-term infants, *Hiroshima J. Med. Sci.* **14**:19.
24. MOSS, A. J., AND MONSET-COUCHARD, M., 1967, Placental transfusion: Early versus late clamping of the umbilical cord, *Pediatrics* **40**:109.
25. NORMAN, M. E., GALL, E. P., TAYLOR, A., LASTER, L., AND NILSSON, W. R., 1975, Serum complement profiles in infants and children, *J. Pediatr.* **87**:912.
26. O'BRIEN, R. T., AND PEARSON, H. A., Physiologic anemia of the newborn infant, *J. Pediatr.* **79**:132.
27. OETTINGER, L., JR., AND MILLS, W. B., 1949, Simultaneous capillary and venous hemoglobin determinations in the newborn infant, *J. Pediatr.* **35**:362.

28. OSKI, F. A., 1973, The unique fetal red cell and its function, *Pediatrics* **51**:494.

29. OSKI, F. A., AND KOMAZAWA, M., 1975, Metabolism of the erythrocytes of the newborn infant, *Semin. Hematol.* **12**:209.

30. PANDOLFI, M., ASTEDT, B., CRONBERG, L., AND NILSSON, I. M., 1972, Failure of fetal platelets to aggregate in response to adrenalin and collagen, *Proc. Soc. Exp. Biol. Med.* **141**:1081.

31. PEARSON, J. A., 1967, Life-span of the fetal red blood cells, *J. Pediatr.* **70**:166.

32. PRICE, G. B., SENN, J. S., MCCULLOCH, E. A., AND TILL, J. E., 1975, The isolation and properties of granulocytic colony-stimulating activities from activities from medium conditioned by human peripheral leukocytes, *Biochem. J.* **148**:209.

33. STOCKMAN, J. A., III, 1975, Anemia of prematurity, *Semin. Hematol.* **12**:163.

34. STRAUSS, R. G., AND MAUER, A. M., 1975, Leukocyte physiology and response to infection, in: *Brennemann–Kelley, Practice of Pediatrics* (V. C. Kelley, ed.), Chapter 65A, pp. 507–529, Harper and Row, Hagerstown, Maryland.

35. THOMAS, D. B., AND YOFFEY, J. M., 1962, Human fetal haematopoiesis, I. The cellular composition of foetal blood, *Br. J. Haematol.* **8**:290.

36. THOMAS, D. B., AND YOFFEY, J. M., 1964, Human fetal haematopoiesis. II. Hepatic haematopoiesis in the human feotus, *Br. J. Haematol.* **10**:193.

37. TUNNICLIFF, R., 1910, Observation on the anti-infectious power of the blood of infants, *J. Infect. Dis.* **7**:698.

38. WRIGHT, W. C., JR., ANK, B. J., HERBERT, J., AND STIEHM, R., 1975, Decreased bactericidal activity of leukocytes of stressed newborn infants, *Pediatrics* **56**:579.

39. XANTHOU, M., 1970, Leukocyte blood picture in healthy full-term and premature babies during neonatal period, *Arch. Dis. Child.* **45**:242.

40. YAO, A. C., MOINIAN, M., AND LIND, J., 1969, Distribution of blood between infant and placenta after birth, *Lancet* **2**:871.

41. ZANJANI, E. D., MANN, L. I., BURLINGTON, H., GORDON, A. S., AND WASSERMAN, L. R., 1974, Evidence for a physiologic role of erythropoietin in fetal erythropoiesis, *Blood* **44**:285.

CHAPTER 11

The Hemoglobins

Enno Kleihauer

1. Introduction

The permanent change in the morphological, biochemical, and functional characteristics of the red cell during development is a physiologic event the significance of which is not precisely known. The changes in different erythrocyte properties are not strongly correlated with each other or limited to the production processes of cells in the various hematopoietic sites. Among the criteria used to differentiate between fetal and adult erythrocytes, the shorter life span and the high susceptibility to oxidation stress do not imply that these cells are of inferior value. No data exist to suggest functional immaturity of fetal red cells under normal developmental conditions.

The properties that characterize fetal red cells are important for questions related to the physiology of the perinatal period, as well as for antenatal diagnosis of hemoglobinopathies. In addition, exploration of the reappearance of fetal hemoglobin synthesis and other fetal red cell characteristics beyond infancy in certain malignant diseases may become significant for the understanding of the molecular basis of malignant transformation. Another related problem is the protective effect of fetal hemoglobin on red cell survival, which has implications for the therapeutic approach to the treatment of sickle cell anemia and homozygous β thalassemia.

Little is known about factors that affect the changes in red cell production and hemoglobin synthesis in different erythropoietic sites. Much more is known about the structure and amounts of hemoglobin types present during gestation and the perinatal period. Considerable information has been accumulated in recent years concerning the genetic control of different polypeptide chains, except for ε-chains and ζ-chains, which constitute the majority of the embryonic hemoglobins.

2. Hematopoiesis in the Human Embryo and Fetus

During human development, the production of morphologically different erythrocytes and various hemoglobin types is connected with a continuous change in blood-forming sites. The first red cell production begins 14 days postconception. This generation of cells (Fig. 1), the primitive erythroblasts or megaloblasts,[28,63,116,195] originates and is produced in the primitive mesenchyme of the yolk sac during the *mesoblastic period of hematopoiesis*. These red cells are gradually replaced in the circulation between the 2nd and 3rd months of gestation by mostly nonnucleated macrocytes derived from the *hepatic period of hematopoiesis*. The liver remains

Enno Kleihauer · Department of Pediatrics, University of Ulm, D79 Ulm (Donau), West Germany

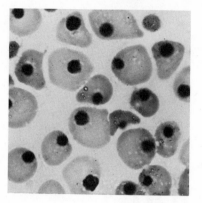

Fig. 1. Red cell morphology in a 14–mm human embryo.

the major site of erythropoiesis for the entire fetal period, whereas the spleen remains an active site of erythropoiesis for only a few months. Final blood formation in the bone marrow, which constitutes the *myeloid period of hematopoiesis,* begins at approximately 12 weeks, and the marrow becomes the major site of erythropoiesis at approximately the 8th month of gestation. Extramedullary hematopoiesis normally disappears shortly after birth.

The most impressive feature of fetal erythropoiesis *in utero* is the coordinated series of changes in blood-forming sites (yolk sac → liver/spleen → bone marrow), red cell morphology (megaloblast → megalocyte → macrocyte → normocyte), and hemoglobin types (embryonic → fetal → adult hemoglobin). The same developmental characteristics are found in mammals other than man, modified only by a shorter or longer gestation time. This subject was reviewed by Kitchen and Brett[106] and Kleihauer.[110]

Some evidence exists that circulating stem cells of the yolk sac colonize the hepatic anlage and the bone marrow. The alternative to this hypothesis of colonization is that the mesenchymal tissue differentiates to new stem cell lines in fetal liver and bone marrow (for reviews, see Wood[191] and Yoffey[195]). Investigations of the regulatory effect of environmental factors on the change of red cell characteristics during development are promising.[138,146] Erythropoiesis has been reviewed by Finne and Halvorsen.[57]

3. Hemoglobin—Quantitative and Qualitative Aspects

Normal human hemoglobin has a tetrameric structure of two unlike pairs of chains: one pair of

identical α-chains, and one pair of non-α-chains (β-, γ-, δ-, or ε-chains); non-α-chains thus characterize the various hemoglobin types. One exception to the composition of unlike pairs of chains is the naturally occurring Hb Bart's (γ_4). The α-chains contain 141 amino acid residues, and the non-α-chains consist of 145 or 146 amino acids. The molecular weight is calculated as 68.458.[50,158] There is evidence for the existence of an embryonic α-chain called the ζ-*chain.*[37] Except for the ζ- and the ε-chains, the amino acid sequence of the polypeptide chains of human hemoglobin is known. The γ-chain of fetal hemoglobin ($\alpha_2\gamma_2$) is very similar to the β-chain of adult hemoglobin ($\alpha_2\beta_2$). The two chains differ in primary structure only at 39 positions.[167] A heme group is attached to each polypeptide chain by links between the iron and the imidazole side chains of the proximal histidine residues. The heme group is located in a deep pocket composed of amino acid residues with nonpolar side chains. This nonaqueous environment allows reversible binding of oxygen and protects iron from oxidation.

A basic principle for the function of the tetrameric molecule is the structural arrangement of segments of α helices with nonhelical regions and the extensive areas of contact between unlike chains and heme groups. Amino acids with nonpolar side chains are located, in general, within the interior of the molecule, while polar side chains are directed to the outer surface, and are in contact with aqueous surroundings. The main function of the hemoglobin tetramer is to transport oxygen from the lungs to the tissues and to facilitate the return transport of carbon dioxide. Oxygen affinity and the ability to unload oxygen are dependent not only on the bonds between subunits, but also on a variety of factors such as heme–heme interactions, the Bohr effect, the Haldane effect (reversed Bohr effect), and the allosteric effect of 2,3-diphosphoglycerate (2,3-DPG) and other phosphates. All these interactions are known as the *cooperative effects* of hemoglobin.

The relationship between structure and function is the subject of several reviews.[8,79,104,128,147,152,160]

4. Hemoglobin Types in Man

During human development, the change in the production of morphologically different erythrocytes in different blood forming sites is coordinated with a change in the constitution of hemoglobin (Fig. 2). The production of embryonic hemo-

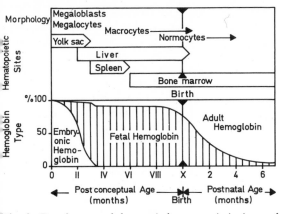

Fig. 2. Developmental changes in hematopoietic sites, red cell morphology, and hemoglobin types.

globins (Gower hemoglobins $\zeta_2\varepsilon_2$ or ε_4 and $\alpha_2\varepsilon_2$; Hb Portland $\zeta_2\gamma_2$) is followed by synthesis of fetal hemoglobin ($\alpha_2\gamma_2$), which is finally replaced by adult hemoglobin types ($\alpha_2\beta_2$ and $\alpha_2\delta_2$).

4.1. Adult Hemoglobin

Adult hemoglobin (HbA) consists of two well-defined types: the major component HbA$_1$ ($\alpha_2\beta_2$) and the minor component HbA$_2$ ($\alpha_2\delta_2$). The amount of HbA$_2$ is generally about 2–3% of total hemoglobin. Furthermore, in adult life, 0.4–0.8% of the total hemoglobin is found to be HbF, and less than 0.1% of Hb Gower ($\alpha_2\varepsilon_2$) is synthesized.

Among other nongenetically determined minor types, HbA$_{Ic}$ is believed to have prognostic significance for diabetic patients.[59,117] HbA$_{Ic}$, in which one or more hexoses are bound to the β-chains, comprises 5–7% of the hemoglobin of normal persons, while it is increased to 6–12% of the total hemoglobin in diabetic patients. Hemoglobin A$_3$ is supposed to be an acetylated modification of both α- and β-chains of HbA (Kohne and Kleihauer[118]; Table I). In addition, these studies showed that while there is little or no acetylation *in vivo*, it does occur during storage of hemolysates. Both HbA$_{Ic}$ and HbA$_3$ exhibit high oxygen affinity.[34]

4.2. Fetal Hemoglobin

Fetal hemoglobin (HbF) was first described in 1866 by Körber[122] and published in his M.D. thesis, the title page of which is shown in Fig 3. The title of the thesis is "On the Differences in Hemoglobin," and the inscription reads: "This thesis is

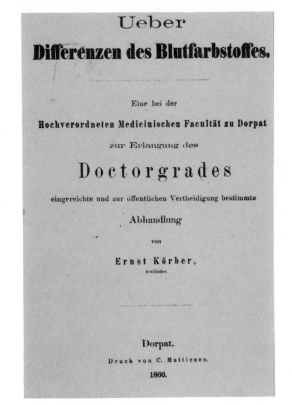

Fig. 3. Title page of the M.D. thesis submitted in 1866 by Ernst Körber.[122] (See the text for a translation.)

submitted by Ernst Körber, native of Estonia, to the highly esteemed medical faculty of Dorpat to obtain the Doctoral Degree, and is intended for public discussion."

HbF is the predominant blood pigment in fetuses and newborn infants. By chromatography (Fig. 4) and electrophoretic procedures,[91] two components can be separated: HbF$_{II}$ ($\alpha_2\gamma_2$) and HbF$_I$. The structure of HbF$_I$ is contestable. It is assumed that the γ-chains have acetic acid attached to the N-terminal glycine residue, i.e., $\alpha_2\gamma\gamma^{N\text{-acetyl}}$[162] or $\alpha_2\gamma_2^{N\text{-acetyl}}$.[171] Furthermore, it has been questioned whether HbF$_I$ contains γF chains at all.[80] The ratio of the major component HbF$_{II}$ to the minor component HbF$_I$ is rather constant at 85:15 in the pre- and postnatal period.[134] The high oxygen affinity of HbF$_I$ is in accordance with the finding that HbF$_I$ does not interact at all with 2,3-DPG.[35] The α-chains from HbFs and HbAs are identical.[87,166]

The different properties of HbA and HbF[20,109,187] stem mainly from structural differences between β- and γ-chains (Table II). The

Table I. Normal Variants of Human Hemoglobins Produced During Development

Hemoglobin variants	Structural formulas	Genetically determined?	Amount present during development (%)[a]		
			Embryo (≈45 days)	Newborn infant	Adult
Adult					
HbA$_1$	$\alpha_2\beta_2$	Yes	0	25–45	96–97
HbA$_2$	$\alpha_2\delta_2$	Yes	0	0.2–0.6	1.5–3.0
HbA$_3$	Not known		0	ND[b]	5
HbA$_{Ia, b, c}$	Not known	No	0	ND	1–2
HbA$_{Ic}$	$\alpha2\,\beta2^{\text{N-glycosyl}}$		0	ND	5
Fetal					
HbF$_I$	$\alpha_2\gamma_2^{\text{N-acetyl}}$	No	ND	6–8	
HbF$_{II}$	$\alpha_2^{\text{G}}\gamma_2$				<1
	$\alpha_2^{\text{A}}\gamma_2$	Yes	50	55–75	
	$\alpha_2^{\text{Thr}}\gamma_2$				
Embryonic					
Hb Gower 1	$\zeta_2\varepsilon_2(\varepsilon_4\,?)$	Yes	25	0	0
Hb Gower 2	$\alpha_2\varepsilon_2$	Yes	15	Traces (?)	0
Hb Portland	$\zeta_2\gamma_2$	Yes	10	0	0

[a] Approximate values.
[b] Not done.

tyrosine in position 130 of the β-chain (β 130), which is substituted by tryptophan in the γ-chains, gives HbF the characteristic ultraviolet spectrum. Three additional important substitutions (β 51 proline→γ alanine, β 112 cysteine→γ threonine, and β 116 histidine→γ isoleucine) at contacts between $\alpha_1\beta_1$ interfaces may account for the reduced tendency of HbF to dissociate into mono-mers, and for the increased resistance to alkali denaturation.[147] The substitution of histidine β 143 by serine in the γ-chain is responsible for the lesser capacity of HbF for binding 2,3-DPG. Consequently, the oxygen affinity of HbF is not reduced by 2,3-DPG to the same extent as is that of HbA, and this difference explains in part the higher oxygen affinity of HbF.[15] Sources to which the reader

Table II. Difference in Structure Between β- and γ-Chains[a]

Location in the molecule	Number of substitutions
Internal sites	7
Heme contacts	2
$\alpha_1\beta_1$ contact	4
Central cavity	2
2,3-DPG-binding site	2
External sites	22
TOTAL:	39

[a] Data from Lorkin.[131]

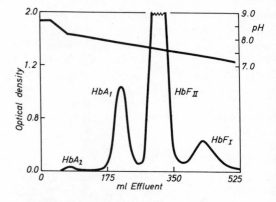

Fig. 4. Chromatographic separation[49] of cord blood hemoglobin on DEAE–Sephadex.

Table III. Differences Between Fetal and Adult Hemoglobin

Properties	Differences/Methods of determining differences	References
Protein structure[a]	γ-Chain/β-chain	Schroeder[167]
Resistance	Alkali[a]	Betke et al.[26]
	Acid	Kleihauer[107]
	Heat	Betke and Greinacher[22]
Solubility	Phosphate buffer	Roche and Derrien[154]
	Acid elution[a]	Kleihauer et al.[114]
Electrophoretic[a]	Various techniques	Jonxis and Huisman[91]
Chromatographic[a]	Various techniques	Jonxis and Huisman[91]
Spectral	Tryptophan fine structure band	Beaven et al.,[16] Jope[92]
Oxidation	Methemoglobin formation	Betke,[20] Betke et al.[25]
Oxygen affinity	Hb solution	Allen et al.[6]
	Whole blood	Darling et al.[46]
Immunologic characteristics[a]	Various techniques	Bhattacharya et al.,[27] Boyer et al.,[29] Wood et al.[193]

[a] Denotes that methods used for determination or identification are described in the reference(s) cited.

may refer for discussions of further differences between HbF and HbA are presented in Table III.

The chemical heterogeneity of HbF is now well established. Schroeder and Huisman and colleagues[84,85,159,164] discovered that HbF in man contains a mixture of two γ-chains differing in the presence of glycine or alanine at position 136 of the polypeptide chain.[164] The γ-chains ($^{G}\gamma$- and $^{A}\gamma$-chains) are the products of distinct loci (Section 5.8.2). During the transition from HbF to HbA production, the ratio of the two HbFs, $\alpha_2\gamma^{136\,Gly}$: $\alpha_2\gamma^{136\,Ala}$, changes from approximately 7:3 in cord blood to about 2:3 (in the trace amounts of HbF) in healthy adults.

4.3. Embryonic Hemoglobin

The existence of an embryonic hemoglobin in human development was first suggested by Drescher and Künzer,[51] and was later confirmed.[36,78,81–83,95] Earlier reports from other investigators[51,65,66,133] need careful interpretation in the light of present knowledge.

Embryonic hemoglobins consisting of Hb Gower 1, Hb Gower 2, and Hb Portland are regularly found in human embryos and fetuses with a crown–rump (CR) length of less than 85 mm. However, trace amounts of Hb Gower 2 and Hb Portland have been found in normal cord blood,[68,182] and ε-chain synthesis persists into adulthood.[118]

Hb Gower 1 migrates on starch gel (pH 8.6–7.7) more slowly than HbA$_2$. On the basis of hybridization studies, it was initially believed that the tetramer consists only of ε-chains (ε_4). However, the finding that heme–heme interactions of embryonic red cells are normal is a strong argument against the ε_4 structure and favors the suggestion that Hb Gower 1 consists of ζ-chains combined with ε-chains: $\zeta_2\varepsilon_2$.[78,96]

Hb Gower 2 migrates on starch gel between Hbα^A and HbC/G. The tryptophan fine structure band is resolved at a wavelength of 289.9 nm, slightly less pronounced than HbF. The rate of alkali denaturation is intermediate between the rates of HbA and HbF. Fingerprint analyses as well as hybridization experiments strongly indicate a tetrameric structure composed of α- and ε-chains, i.e., $\alpha_2\varepsilon_2$.[81]

Hb Portland is the third embryonic hemoglobin type[95] that migrates electrophoretically at alkaline pH between HbA and Hb Bart's. It has also been

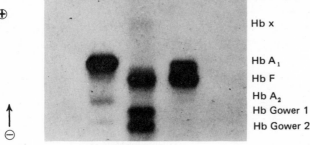

Hb x

Hb A$_1$
Hb F
Hb A$_2$
Hb Gower 1
Hb Gower 2

Fig. 5. Electrophoretic separation of human hemoglobin types of starch gel. Adult (left): HbA$_1$ and HbA$_2$; the faint band below HbA$_2$ is carbonic anhydrase. Fetus (middle), 38 mm CR length: HbX, HbF, Hb Gower 1, and Hb Gower 2. Newborn (right): HbA$_1$, HbF, and traces of HbA$_2$.

described in a newborn infant with multiple congenital malformations and complex autosomal chromosomal mosaicism,[36] in newborn infants with D$_1$ trisomy,[69] in hemoglobin hydrops fetalis syndrome, and in trace amounts in normal newborn infants.[182] Hb Portland has a unique structure composed of γ-chains plus a pair of new polypeptide chains denoted ζ-*chains*; thus, the structure is written $\zeta_2\gamma_2$.[37] It has been suggested that the ζ-chain is an embryonic α-chain.[78,96,175] ζ-Chains may combine with β-chains ($\zeta_2\beta_2$), as they have been found to do in homozygous α thalassemia.[173] An additional, but not further characterized, fast-moving minor component with electrophoretic characteristics similar to those of Hb Bart's (Fig. 5) and present in young fetuses has been described.[81,109]

5. Ontogeny of Human Hemoglobin

There is evidence that embryos *sensu strictu* contain predominantly embryonic hemoglobin, which is replaced during fetal life by HbF and finally by HbA. When the amounts of hemoglobins present at different developmental stages were evaluated, it was found that the replacement of one type by the other occurs gradually because of different life spans and increasing production of red cells during different periods of hematopoiesis. In evaluations of the rate of synthesis, the transition from one hemoglobin type to the other seems to be a more abrupt process, as was demonstrated for the postnatal switch from HbF to HbA.

The quantitative changes of developmental hemoglobin in man have been thoroughly investigated. Enough information is available for a continuing discussion about the relationship between synthesis of various hemoglobin types and blood-forming

sites. Since proper and sufficient human material is difficult to obtain, animal studies are suitable models for evaluating factors and mechanisms involved in the change from HbF to HbA. For future work, more knowledge about these mechanisms is needed to provide us with tools to manipulate hemoglobin synthesis for the benefit of genetic diseases resulting from defective globin synthesis. This subject and other aspects of hemoglobin synthesis during human development were reviewed by several authors.[101,110,131,180,183,191]

5.1. Hemoglobins in the Human Embryo and Fetus Through the Second Fetal Stage

The available data on the amounts of hemoglobin types present in embryos and young fetuses are based primarily on electrophoretic determinations. The same is true of data on the relative amounts of the polypeptide chains (Figs. 6 and 7), which have been calculated from the corresponding hemoglobin types.

For early human developmental stages, the exact determination of polypeptide chain synthesis will remain inaccurate as long as the onset of HbA production, i.e., β-chain synthesis, is not precisely known. Difficulties arise especially from the similar electrophoretic behavior of HbA, Hb Portland,[95] and HbF Koelliker. The latter hemoglobin type is an artifact characterized by the absence of the C-terminal arginine of the α-chains: α_2 minus 141 Arg γ_2. It is produced *in vitro* from a digestion of HbF by carboxypeptidase B during storage of hemolysates prepared from macerated fetuses.[120] However, both Hb Portland and HbF Koelliker can be distinguished from HbA on citrate agar gels.[118,145] Contamination of fetal blood samples with maternal

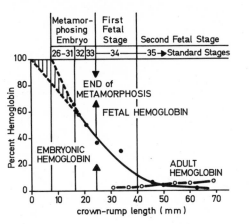

Fig. 6. Relationship between hemoglobin types and developmental stages in early human life. Dashed lines and hatched area indicate expected development.

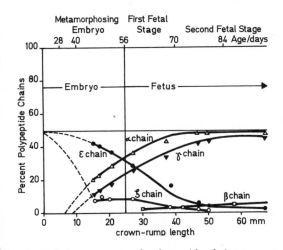

Fig. 7. Relative amounts of polypeptide chains present in early developmental stages. The calculated data for ε-, ζ-, γ-, and α-chains are corrected with regard to supposed concentrations of Hb Portland, and to the structure of Hb Gower 1, which is assumed to be $\zeta_2\varepsilon_2$. Dashed lines indicate expected development.

blood can be detected easily by the absence or presence of HbA cells using the acid elution test.

5.1.1. Synthesis of Embryonic Hemoglobin

In very early developmental stages, Hb Gower 1 and Hb Gower 2 are predominant among the embryonic hemoglobins[70] until the end of the metamorphosis corresponding to the standard stages 31–33 of Witschi,[190] or to a CR length of 16–21

mm. Since the structure of Hb Gower 1 is now supposed to be $\zeta_2\varepsilon_2$ and not ε_4, the assumption of a relative α-chain deficiency during this period of development[68] is no longer tenable. This problem is considered further in Section 5.2.4. Until the end of the first fetal stage (Fig. 6), the embryonic hemoglobins decrease to 10% of the total pigment. Hb Gower 1 is always present in greater amounts than Hb Gower 2.

Only a few data on the amounts of Hb Portland are available, and the exact timing of appearance and disappearance of this third embryonic hemoglobin remains unsolved. Provided the HbA-like component described by Hecht et al.[68] and Huehns et al.[82] is identical to Hb Portland, it amounts to roughly 15% in the metamorphosing embryo, decreasing rapidly during the first fetal stage. This assumption is compatible with data on the onset of HbA synthesis.[72,145] Whether Hb Portland is produced in larger amounts in earlier developmental stages depends primarily on the onset of γ-chain synthesis. The amounts of ζ-chains produced in the early embryo, as determined by theoretical considerations, are shown in Fig. 7.

5.1.2. Synthesis of Fetal Hemoglobin

In the smallest human embryo (16 mm CR length) sampled to date, 34% HbF was found.[68] At the end of the first fetal stage (40 mm CR length), HbF comprises approximately 90% of total hemoglobin, the rest being HbA; from then on, HbF remains constant until about the 36th week of gestation.

5.1.3. Synthesis of Adult Hemoglobin

The relative amount of HbA in embryos with a CR length between 16.3 and 21.3 mm was estimated as 13–16%[68]; another investigator failed to detect HbA in a 34-mm fetus,[83] and it was reported by another to be regularly present in small fetuses.[82] From recent studies, it was judged that HbA production starts between the 7th and 11th weeks of gestation.[102,145] These contradictory results demonstrate the difficulty in reliably identifying HbA by electrophoretic or chromatographic procedures alone. Direct measurements of globin-chain synthesis by the incorporation of radiolabeled amino acids show that the onset of β-chain production is as early as at 6 weeks of fetal life, i.e., at the end of the first fetal stage.[13,72,97,102,192]

5.1.4. Conclusion

Despite the lack of data on some polypeptide chain synthesis, calculation of relative amounts from the hemoglobin types provides enough information to survey the general developmental changes as summarized in Figs. 6 and 7. The rapid decline in ε-chains is caused by several factors, such as the short life span of megaloblasts and megalocytes, decreasing ε-chain synthesis, and excessive production of red cells containing mainly HbF. Virtually nothing is known about the onset of and the correlation between ζ-chain and α-chain synthesis. However, the prevalence of Hb Gower 1 ($\zeta_2\varepsilon_2$) until the end of metamorphosis indicates that ζ-chain synthesis precedes α-chain synthesis. Furthermore, from the supposed structure of Hb Gower 1, it can be predicted that the onset of ζ-chain synthesis is strongly correlated with the onset of ε-chain synthesis. The genes for synthesis of β-chains are turned on at the very end of the first fetal stage, which coincides with the disappearance of ε- and ζ-chain production or with the beginning of liver hematopoiesis. At least two switch mechanisms are operative in this very early period of development: one is the switch from ζ- to α-chains; the other is the switch from ε- to γ-chains. In addition, the initiation of β-chain synthesis occurs toward the end of the first fetal stage.

5.2. Hemoglobin in Older Fetuses and Newborn Infants

5.2.1. Fetal Hemoglobin

The HbF concentration remains relatively consistent until the 34th–36th week of gestation. From then on, there is a decline in HbF, due primarily to an increase in HbA synthesis rather than to a decrease in HbF synthesis.[110] This decline is demonstrated by the increasing number of HbA-containing reticulocytes and erythrocytes, and by the increasing HbA concentration (Fig. 8).[23,58,109,169,197]

The postnatal decline of HbF is variable, and depends on a variety of factors (see Section 5.9.1). In general, HbF is almost fully replaced by the HbAs HbA₁ and HbA₂ approximately 6 months after birth.[17,20,109,168] Adult distribution of HbF levels, however, is not achieved before puberty.[21] That the pattern of HbF disappearance after birth is complex was stated in 1954 by Betke,[20] and was recently rediscovered.[43] It is affected by gestational age, postnatal erythropoietic activity,

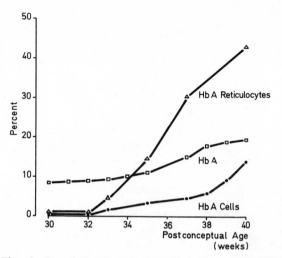

Fig. 8. Correlation between gestational age and HbA synthesis. The relative HbA production in cord blood is represented by HbA₁, HbA cells, and HbA reticulocytes. The curves demonstrate the lag in time between the rise in HbA reticulocytes and the other HbA values. The number of HbA reticulocytes is expressed as the percentage of the total number of reticulocytes.

and the life span of fetal erythrocytes. It is characterized by three periods[11,20,43]:

1. HbF remains constant after birth for a limited time of about 15 days in full-term infants. This early period is highly dependent on the lack in erythropoiesis.
2. The following linear decrease ends approximately 3–4 months after birth.
3. A slower rate of disappearance leads to the adjustment to HbF levels in childhood.

This development is very similar in full-term and preterm infants, differing only in the length of the initial plateau.[43]

Analyses[11] of the pre- and postnatal decline of HbF by synthesis studies in full-term infants show that the period of rapid transition is between 30 and 52 weeks postconception, followed by a gradual decline from approximately 7% by 16 weeks of age to 1–2% in later life. A faster rate of decline in HbF synthesis, from 47% at term to 20% at 4 weeks and to 5% at 6 weeks, was reported when the data were calculated from the number of HbA reticulocytes (Fig. 9) present at the respective ages.[108] These data were confirmed by measuring the amounts of radioactive iron incorporated into HbF and HbA respectively.[61] The explanation for the

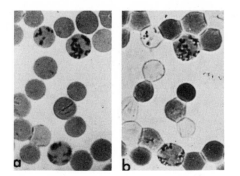

Fig. 9. Demonstration of HbA- and HbF-containing reticulocytes in cord blood. (A) Brilliant cresyl blue preparation before acid elution; (B) the same cells after acid elution.

difference from the aforementioned results[11] remains obscure. It is self-evident that the lag between estimated amounts of HbF being synthesized and those present in identical blood samples is explained by the survival time of fetal cells.[62,112]

The rate of decline in HbF synthesis during the perinatal period is correlated with the infant's gestational age.[12,52,61,74,105,109] Birth *per se* and intrauterine transfusion[9,12,20] do not influence HbF or HbA synthesis. It is reported, however, to be altered by a variety of conditions, such as intrauterine growth retardation,[10] pregnancies complicated by maternal toxemia and chronic hypoxia,[33,61] chromosomal abnormalities, and hereditary defects of hemoglobin synthesis. These circumstances and others that modify HbF levels during the perinatal period will be considered in Section 5.9.1. HbF values in infants with intrauterine growth retardation are an appropriate subject for further discussion, especially in view of the significance of HbF and HbA as an index of maturity.[110]

From *in vitro* studies, it is evident that environmental factors may influence the rate of HbF synthesis.[5,60,67,137,172] The reported results of these experimental studies with cell cultures have not been fully confirmed.[183,194] The ratio of the two γ-chains, $^G\gamma:^A\gamma$, remains constant at 7:3 throughout gestation.[139] The change in the proportion to the adult ratio of 2:3 occurs postnatally.[163]

5.2.2. Adult Hemoglobin

Increasing data are now available on β-chain synthesis in fetuses, since the antenatal diagnosis of

hemoglobinopathies has become an important goal for research. Alter *et al.*[7] and Nathan *et al.*[136] have provided excellent summaries of this subject. With the use of radioactive methods,[72] the earliest β-chain synthesis was found to occur in fetuses as small as 32 mm CR length, or 60 days of gestation (see Fig. 7). Synthesis of HbA in fetuses from 32 to 250 mm CR length (fetal age between 8 and 21 weeks) accounted for 4.3–13% of total hemoglobin synthesis, and varied with fetal size.[102] These data are in agreement with results obtained by other investigators.[13,72,97,192] The $\beta:\gamma$ synthesis ratio is significantly correlated with fetal CR length and with gestational age.[42,103] After 20 weeks of gestation, the amount of HbA remains constant on the order of 5–10% of total hemoglobin[12,118] until the switch begins at 36 weeks of fetal life (see Fig. 8).

5.2.3. Minor Components

(a) Hemoglobin A_2. Normal values for HbA_2 ($\alpha_2\delta_2$) in newborn infants are significantly lower than those in adults. In newborns, however, the reported data differ considerably, depending on the methods used for quantitation of the minor component (Table IV). Synthesis of HbA_2, i.e., δ-chain production, starts between the 34th and 35th weeks of gestation (Fig. 10). The amount at this stage of development, as estimated by column chromatography,[118] varies between 0.12 and 0.24% of total hemoglobin. At term, the mean value for HbA_2 is 0.35% (0.19–0.60%). The normal range for adults is reported to be reached 3–5 months after birth,[53,188] while our data (Fig. 10) indicate that adult values are not found before the end of the first year of life.[118] In 6-month-old infants, HbA_2 varies between 1.6 and 2.4%, and in children and adults, the range is between 2.08 and 3.17%.

The $\delta:\beta$ synthesis ratio in adults is approximately 1:40,[189] while in cord blood it is roughly estimated to be 1:80. No correlations have been found between the amounts of HbA_2 and HbA_1 or HbF.[135]

(b) Hemoglobin Bart's. Hb Bart's (γ_4) is a tetramer composed of four normal γ-chains.[1,88] It differs significantly from HbF ($\alpha_2\gamma_2$) in electrophoretic mobility (it is the "fast hemoglobin" of Fessas and Papaspyrou[56]). The rate of alkali denaturation is intermediate between the rates of HbA and HbF,[45] and the tryptophan fine structure band

Table IV. Percentage of Hemoglobin A$_2$ in Newborn Infants

References	Method	Mean value	Range
Horton *et al.*[75]	Chromatography	0.20	0.1 –0.4
Minnich *et al.*[135]	Starch block	0.60	0–1.8
Wilson *et al.*[188]	Chromatography	0.20	0.03–0.58
Karaklis and Fessas[100]	Starch block	0.23	0–0.3
Jonxis and Huisman[91]	Chromatography	0.22	0.05–0.45

is more resolved at 289.6 nm than that of HbF. Analogous to HbH, Hb Bart's has a very high oxygen affinity and is lacking heme–heme interaction and the Bohr effect.[75] Since Hb Bart's is virtually unable to release oxygen to the tissues, it is physiologically inactive. Red cells containing high proportions of Hb Bart's exhibit sickling properties.[149]

A surplus of γ-chains in the red cells of normal cord blood (less than 0.5%) is thought to be due to a slightly imbalanced α-chain synthesis.[178] The alternative explanation for the occurrence of the γ_4 product is the higher affinity of α-chains for β-chains than for γ-chains.[77] Except in α thalassemic states, elevated amounts of Hb Bart's are also found in newborns with the D$_1$ trisomy syndrome.[81,126]

(c) Embryonic Hemoglobin. Persistence of Hb Gower 2 synthesis into later fetal life of healthy subjects was reported in a 7.5-month-old premature,[75] and there is good evidence that trace amounts of Hb Gower 2 occur regularly at least until birth.[118] The failure to demonstrate Hb Gower 2 in all cases of trisomy D$_1$ syndrome in-

vestigated until recently may be explained by the marked instability of ε-chain-containing hemoglobins, especially during cold storage.[19,113] The persistence of embryonic hemoglobins in newborns with chromosomal abnormalities is discussed in Section 5.7.1.

(d) Hemoglobin Alexandra Type. This minor component with characteristics similar to the abnormal γ-chain variant Hb Alexandra[132] was inconsistently detected in trace amounts of hemolysates of infants during the first weeks of life.[133] It was found in 10% of the newborns investigated and in 31% of infants up to 4 weeks of age. The existence of this Hb Alexandra-type hemoglobin as a normally occurring hemoglobin during the switchover period is not in accordance with this author's data.[110]

5.2.4. Imbalance of α-Chain Synthesis

The occurrence of tetrameric structures composed of four identical non-α-chains (Hb Bart's = γ_4; HbH = β_4; Hbδ_4) is considered to be the result of an imbalanced α-chain synthesis. A well-known

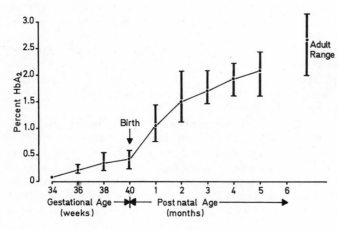

Fig. 10. Development of HbA$_2$ values in relation to gestational age and postnatal age. HbA$_2$ was estimated by column chromatography.[49] The vertical brackets denote maximum and minimum values; the curve was plotted from median values.

condition in which such tetramers are produced is α thalassemia.

It was earlier supposed that imbalanced α-chain synthesis occurs twice during normal development: (1) during early embryonic life, on the assumption that the predominant Hb Gower 1 consists of ε-chains only[70,82]; and (2) during the neonatal period, because of the occurrence of Hb Bart's in normal cord blood.[178] Since the structure of Hb Gower 1 is not ε_4, but is most likely $\zeta_2\varepsilon_2$, and since the ζ-chain has α-chain characteristics,[78,96,175] the assumption of an impaired α-chain synthesis in embryonic life has become baseless. Furthermore, the supposed deficit of α-chains in the perinatal period is not generally accepted.[118] By chromatographic methods, trace amounts of free α-chains are demonstrable in fetal blood, ranging between 0.1 and 0.3% of total hemoglobin.[118] Synthesis studies confirmed that the surplus of α-chains is due to higher production, the rate depending on the gestational age. Of total chains synthesized, 58% are α-chains, in a 20-week-old fetus, 53% after 28 weeks of gestation, and 51% at term. Transitory imbalance with a higher rate of α-chain synthesis was also reported in a newborn with trisomy 13.[90]

5.3. Intracellular Distribution of Hemoglobin

Cytochemical and immunologic methods have been successfully applied in demonstrating the presence of normal hemoglobin types in individual red cells. The acid elution test[114] and immunologic techniques[29,44,76,174] have been developed. Because of its simple technical procedure, the acid elution test is especially useful in distinguishing among the various conditions associated with elevated HbF levels (equal and unequal distribution) as well as for recognizing fetal–maternal and maternal–fetal transfusion. In addition, the test is applicable to a variety of other clinical and theoretical problems.[111] Furthermore, some basic information related to the immunologic prevention of Rh hemolytic disease of the newborn has been elaborated by use of the acid elution test. The cytochemical technique is based on the differential resistance of HbF and HbA to elution under acid conditions. After HbA elution, HbF remains in the cells, and these HbA cells appear as "ghosts" after hematoxylin–eosin staining. Other elution techniques have been developed for the visualization of

HbA[94] and embryonic hemoglobin,[115] while HbA$_2$ can be demonstrated only by immunofluorescent methods.[71]

5.3.1. Embryonic Hemoglobin

The presence of embryonic hemoglobin in red cells is based on indirect evidence.[115] With a modified elution procedure, HbFs and HbAs are eluted from red cells, while under identical conditions, hemoglobin is retained in a number of nucleated and nonnucleated erythrocytes from embryos and young fetuses. From comparison of the cytochemical results with the hemoglobin pattern present in the investigated embryos and fetuses, it was concluded that the nonelutable pigment is identical to embryonic hemoglobin; consequently, the elutable pigment is either HbF or HbA. Under these conditions, the results of the elution pattern indicate that embryonic hemoglobin is unevenly distributed among red cells from embryos and young fetuses. Therefore, megaloblasts derived from the mesoblastic period of hematopoiesis seem to synthesize embryonic hemoglobin as well as HbF in different amounts, depending on the stage of development (Fig. 11). Furthermore, our available data indicate that a small population of erythroblasts derived from liver hematopoietic tissue is capable of synthesizing embryonic hemoglobin.

The suggestion that yolk sac megaloblasts contain HbF is not in accordance with data mentioned by Wood,[191] who found no or little HbF in yolk sac cells by using a fluorescent anti-HbF antibody.

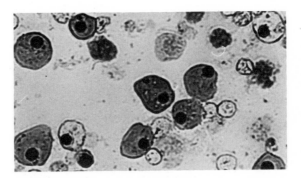

Fig. 11. Demonstration of embryonic hemoglobin and HbF in megaloblasts from a 25-mm human embryo. Densely stained cells presumably contain predominantly embryonic hemoglobin; ghost cells are presumably HbF-containing cells.

5.3.2. Fetal and Adult Hemoglobin

The elution of HbA and HbF from red cells is dependent on the concentration and temperature of ethanol used for fixation and on the pH of the elution medium. The pH-dependent sensitivity offers the possibility of adapting the method, within limits, to special requirements.[111] In addition, the immunologic techniques[27,29,140,193] further supplement the battery of methods to cover all problems related to intracellular distribution of HbF.

Throughout development, fetal and nonfetal hemoglobin are unevenly distributed among red cells.[23,58,109,115,169] The first HbA-containing cells and intermediate cells are found, although not consistently, in fetuses at approximately 30 weeks of gestation[58,110,118] (see Fig. 8). A reported earlier appearance of HbA cells[196] was most probably due to contamination with maternal blood. At term, the mean value of HbA cells is about 5%, ranging between 1 and 8%. As a practical procedure, values above 10% are considered to be elevated. The number of intermediate cells containing both HbA and HbF, as determined by photodensitometric methods, is 2% of total red cell mass at 34 weeks of gestation, and reaches 20% at term.[109,169]

Postnatal development is characterized by a rapid increase of HbA cells. Data concerning the number of intermediate cells differ widely.[44,81,109,169] In infancy and in normal adults, the number of HbA cells and the percentage of HbF are closely related.[29,193]

5.3.3. Minor Component HbA$_2$

Immunofluorescent studies have shown that HbA$_2$ is uniformly distributed among red cells of normal adult subjects,[193] whereas the distribution is irregular in cord blood cells and erythrocytes of young infants.[71,76,193] Even cells containing high proportions of HbF exhibit slight fluorescence with anti-HbA$_2$ antibodies, indicating that single red cell precursors are capable of synthesizing β-, γ-, and δ-chains during the switchover period.

5.4. Relationship Between Red Cell Diameter and Fetal Hemoglobin

During the perinatal period, the mean red cell diameter decreases from 8.2 μm to 7.4 μm.[184] There are three different theories concerning the relation-

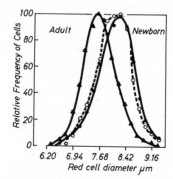

Fig. 12. Comparison of diameters of HbA cells and HbF cells in a 14-day-old infant. (●) HbF cells (newborn); (○) HbA cells (newborn); (▲) HbA cells (adult). See the text for technical details.

ship between red cell size and type of hemoglobin: (1) HbF-containing erythrocytes are larger than HbA cells[32]; (2) the mean diameter of HbF cells is significantly smaller[30]; and (3) erythrocytes containing HbF and HbA are identical in diameter (Fig. 12).[24,110] Recently, this problem was reinvestigated and discussed,[121] but without consideration being given to earlier results.[24,32] Komazawa et al.[121] found that in newborn infants investigated during the first 24 hs of life, the small erythrocytes contain significantly greater proportions of HbF than do the larger erythrocytes. The conclusion that the youngest and largest erythrocytes synthesize less HbF at the time of birth is correct. The result was to be expected. The crucial point, however, and it should be emphasized, is whether there is a close relationship between the two characteristics of a fetal cell, i.e., cell size and type of hemoglobin, irrespective of the age of the individual red cell. Questions dealing with this subject, including technical problems, are discussed in detail elsewhere.[24,110]

5.5. Relationship Between Hemoglobin Synthesis and Hematopoietic Sites

During intrauterine development, there is a correspondence in timing of the changeover among erythropoietic sites, red cell morphology, and hemoglobin types (see Fig. 2). This correspondence does not mean, however, that synthesis of the various hemoglobin types is restricted to specific sites of erythropoiesis.[109]

5.5.1. Yolk Sac

The question whether megaloblasts of yolk sac erythropoiesis are able to synthesize only embryonic hemoglobin remains unanswered. On the basis of cytochemical results, it was suggested[115] that megaloblasts contain either predominantly embryonic hemoglobin or HbF or both hemoglobins in different amounts (see Fig. 11), while data obtained by a fluorescent antibody technique cast some doubt on this suggestion.[191]

5.5.2. Liver

There is no doubt that liver erythroid cells synthesize HbF as well as HbA. The finding[110] that a small proportion of embryonic hemoglobin is produced in red cell precursors derived from the very beginning of liver erythropoiesis needs to be confirmed. The high proportion of HbA present in red cells obtained from macerated liver as compared with peripheral erythrocytes of the same fetus[155] can now be explained by an artifact product, identified as HbF Koelliker.[120]

5.5.3. Bone Marrow

Bone marrow is capable of synthesizing both HbF and HbA. Synthesis of large amounts of HbF beyond infancy occurs under pathologic conditions, such as β thalassemia and hereditary persistence of HbF. Embryonic hemoglobin (Hb Gower 2, Hb Portland) is synthesized in bone marrow red cell precursors in cases of α thalassemia and chromosomal abnormalities (see Section 5.7.1); under normal conditions, minute amounts of Hb Gower 2 are also produced beyond infancy.[118]

5.5.4. Conclusion

From these data, it can be concluded that in general, synthesis of normally occurring developmental hemoglobins is not organ-specific. One exception might be the restriction of embryonic hemoglobin production to yolk sac erythropoiesis, considering the suggestion that both liver and bone marrow are capable of synthesizing ε-chains. Finally, it was shown[192] that the relative proportions of HbA and HbF produced appear to be equal throughout all erythropoietic sites (liver, spleen, bone marrow) during the corresponding time of fetal development. This is a strong argument that the switch from HbF to HbA is synchronized and not under control of a local tissue environment.

5.6. Function of Developmental Hemoglobins

The presence of a developmental hemoglobin is considered to be advantageous to the fetus and his physiology. However, fetal survival is not comprised either in the absence of HbF (intrauterine exchange transfusion) or in the presence of maternal blood exhibiting a higher oxygen affinity than fetal blood. Conversely, infants and adults with high levels of HbF are neither hypoxic nor grossly polycythemic.[41,153]

The cooperative oxygen-binding function of the hemoglobin molecule requires two pairs of unlike chains, i.e., α-chains and non-α-chains. In addition, oxygen transport to the tissues is influenced by the interaction of several factors.[143] In the fetus, HbF plays an important role, since 2,3-DPG has a minor effect on its oxygen affinity.[15] Mechanisms that regulate gas transport in the fetus are discussed in Chapter 12.

5.6.1. Embryonic Hemoglobin

The structure formerly claimed for Hb Gower 1 (ε_4) made it difficult to understand oxygen transport in young embryos,[110] since the noncooperative effect of the ε_4 tetramer could be predicted from the high oxygen affinity of Hb Bart's (γ_4) and HbH (β_4).[18,75] Recent investigations,[78] however, showed that the heme–heme interactions are the same in embryonic red cells as in fetal or adult erythrocytes. That they are is an indication that Hb Gower 1 is composed of ε-chains and non-ε-chains. As mentioned above, the structure is most likely $\zeta_2\varepsilon_2$.[96] Moreover, these data demonstrate that the binding and unloading of oxygen is essentially identical in all normal human hemoglobin types. This also applies to Hb Portland, which shows cooperative function.[175] Compared with HbA, the oxygen affinity is higher and the alkaline Bohr effect is diminished. These functional properties of hemoglobin Portland have some bearing on the fetus's surviving the condition of homozygous α thalassemia.[96]

5.6.2. Fetal Blood

Blood from the fetus and the newborn infant is known to have a significantly greater oxygen

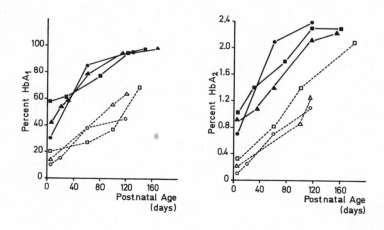

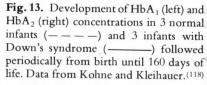

Fig. 13. Development of HbA$_1$ (left) and HbA$_2$ (right) concentrations in 3 normal infants (— — — —) and 3 infants with Down's syndrome (————) followed periodically from birth until 160 days of life. Data from Kohne and Kleihauer.[118]

affinity than adult blood. This subject was reviewed in detail by several authors.[14,47,143] The reason for the different properties is that HbF binds less strongly to 2,3-DPG than does HbA at comparable intracellular 2,3-DPG concentrations.[15,48] While the minor component HbF$_I$ shows absolutely no decrease in oxygen affinity after addition of 2,3-DPG, the major component HbF$_{II}$ reacts with a 20% decrease when compared with HbA under identical conditions.[34] These effects are explained by the differences in structure between β-chains and γ-chains. The binding site of 2,3-DPG is histidine in position 143 of the β-chain, which is replaced in the γ-chain by serine. Furthermore, the N-terminal amino group is involved in the binding of 2,3-DPG, which is blocked in HbF$_I$ as well as in HbA$_{Ic}$.[35,73]

5.7. Abnormal Hemoglobin Synthesis During Development

5.7.1. Abnormal Hemoglobin Patterns in Chromosomal Abnormalities

Synthesis of abnormal patterns of developmental hemoglobins has been observed most frequently in chromosomal abnormalities. Newborn infants with D$_1$ trisomy (chromosome 13), however, have been inconsistently reported[54,176,188] to have Hb Gower 2, Hb Portland, and Hb Bart's.[37,69,81] The imbalanced polypeptide chain synthesis[90] was discussed in Section 5.2.4. The higher level of HbF in this syndrome, compared with that in the cord blood of normal controls, is subsequently followed by a delayed decline during the postnatal period.[176,188]

The reported low levels of HbA$_2$ at term[126,150,176] have not been confirmed.[188] The reverse situation, an accelerated switch from HbF to HbA, was observed in an infant with C/D translocation,[186] and persistence of Hb Gower 2 has been reported to occur in D/D translocation.[19] These observations support the thesis that a locus on the D group chromosome is involved in the regulation of synthesis of developmental hemoglobins. It must be taken into consideration, however, that the alteration of the hemoglobin pattern may also reflect the overall retardation of infants with D$_1$ trisomy syndrome. Moreover, changes in hemoglobin composition similar to those observed in D/D translocation have been documented in non-D-chromosome abnormalities, such as E trisomy and C trisomy.[119] In this connection, it should be mentioned that trisomy 21 (Down's syndrome) is associated at term with low HbF and elevated HbA$_2$ levels[119,188] (Fig. 13), while the hemoglobin pattern is normal later in infancy.[39,185] An observation that is probably related is that infants with Down's syndrome are polycythemic at birth, and it has therefore been suggested that the altered hemoglobin pattern is not due exclusively to the chromosomal abnormality, but is also influenced by the increased red cell production.[119]

5.7.2. Thalassemia Syndromes

Thalassemia is generally defined as a genetically determined, quantitatively defective synthesis of one or more polypeptide chains. The defect results in hypochromia and an excess of nonaffected polypeptide chains. The severity of hematologic symptoms is in general highly dependent on the severity of the genetic defect. The first manifestation of symptoms is closely correlated with the developmental change in globin synthesis (see below). The thalassemias were reviewed in detail by Weatherall and Clegg,[181] Fessas and Loukopoulos,[55] and Wasi et al.[177]

(a) α Thalassemia. The defect of α-chain synthesis shows full expression with the onset of α-chain production. Homozygous α thalassemia, i.e., Hb Bart's hydrops fetalis syndrome, is not compatible with postnatal survival. In the absence of any α-chain synthesis, the hemoglobin consists only of Hb Bart's (γ_4), Hb Portland ($\zeta_2\gamma_2$), and HbH (β_4). Most likely, the oxygen-unloading capacity of Hb Portland allows the fetus to survive in utero,[149] since HbH and Hb Bart's show no cooperative effects. In HbH disease, the α-chain deficiency is less severe, resulting in a hemoglobin pattern consisting of 25% Hb Bart's and minute amounts of HbH, the rest being HbA and HbF. Hb Bart's is gradually replaced by HbA during the first year of life. In α thalassemia 2-trait, the amount of Hb Bart's is 1–2%, and it is 5–6% in α thalassemia 1-trait. This difference indicates that the level of Hb Bart's in cord blood is a sensitive indicator for α thalassemia.[178]

(b) β Thalassemia. Depending on the severity of impaired β-chain synthesis, homozygous β thalassemia is characterized in the newborn period only by low HbA levels, while clinical symptoms usually develop at around 6 months of life. Heterozygous β thalassemia is generally asymptomatic, except that a hypochromic anemia becomes apparent at the end of the first year of life. For problems related to antenatal diagnosis, the reader is referred to the review by Nathan et al.[136]

(c) γ Thalassemia. A defect of γ-chain synthesis causes symptoms only as long as HbF is synthesized. This type of thalassemia has been hypothesized[170] and most probably diagnosed in a newborn in combination with β thalassemia (γβ thalassemia)[99]; the clinical and hematologic symptoms resemble those of thalassemia intermedia.

5.7.3. Hemoglobinopathies

(a) Non-γ-Chain Variants. Among the common hemoglobinopathies, the α-chain variants produce the forms corresponding to HbA_1 ($\alpha_2\beta_2$), HbF ($\alpha_2\gamma_2$), and HbA_2 ($\alpha_2\delta_2$), i.e., $\alpha_2{}^x\beta_2$, $\alpha_2{}^x\gamma_2$, and $\alpha_2{}^x\delta_2$. After birth, the α-abnormal fetal variant ($\alpha_2{}^x\gamma_2$) decreases at the same time and at the same

rate as normal HbF is replaced by HbA. Conversely, β-chain variants ($\alpha_2\beta_2{}^x$) develop symptoms with increasing β-chain synthesis.

(b) γ-Chain Variants. Abnormal hemoglobins resulting from an abnormal γ-chain are extremely rare. They are detectable over only a limited period of time as long as γ-chains are present. Except for HbF Poole,[127] which is an unstable variant causing a hemolytic Heinz body anemia in the newborn, none of the others is associated with any clinical or hematologic symptoms. That they are not is the reason why γ-chain variants for the most part are detected only incidently. Hb Kenya[86] is a γβ-fusion product in which the non-α-chain is composed partly of a normal γ-chain and partly of a normal β-chain. This fusion most likely results from an unequal crossing over during meiosis.

The γ-chain variants are of great theoretical interest, since they have lent support to the concept of multiple structural γ genes as it was developed by Schroeder et al.[164] This topic will be discussed in Section 5.8.2. Among the γ-chain variants listed in Table V, HbF Koelliker is an artifact.

5.8. Genetic Control of Fetal Hemoglobin Production

5.8.1. Chemical Heterogeneity of the γ-Chain

Careful chemical analyses of a cyanogen bromide-cleaved tridecapeptide from the C-terminal portion of the γ-chain have shown the existence of two types of γ-chain, one with glycine and one with alanine at position 136.[164] The two chains are termed $^G\gamma$ and $^A\gamma$, respectively. The ratio of the mixture of $\alpha_2\gamma_2{}^{136\,Gly}$ and $\alpha_2\gamma_2{}^{136\,Ala}$ molecules changes during postnatal replacement of HbF by HbA, and it differs under various pathologic conditions.[85]

5.8.2. Number and Arrangement of Genes

There is evidence that the production of the three structurally different γ-chains, i.e., $^A\gamma$, $^G\gamma$, and $^T\gamma$, is under the control of separate gene loci. The nonallelic genes for $^A\gamma$- and $^G\gamma$-chains are distributed worldwide in the human race.[165] Data on the $^T\gamma$-chain are insufficient for a discussion on possible genetic control of γ-chain synthesis. The actual number of the structural γ-chain loci has been discussed[84,85,164] with reference to the postnatal change

Table V. Fetal Hemoglobin Mutants with Substitutions in the γ-Chain

Name	Substitution			γ 136	References
Malaysia	1	(NA | 1)	Gly→Cys	Gly	Lie-Injo et al.[129]
Texas I	5	(A | 2)	Glu→Lys	Ala	Jenkins et al.[89]
						Ahern et al.[4]
Texas II	6	(A | 3)	Glu→Lys	?	Larkin et al.[125]
Auckland	7	(A | 4)	Asp→Asn	Gly	Carrell et al.[38]
Alexandra	12	(A | 9)	Thr→Lys	?	Loukopoulos et al.[132]
Kuala Lumpur	22	(B | 4)	Asp→Gly	Ala	Lie-Injo et al.[130]
Jamaica	61	(E | 5)	Lys→Glu	Ala	Ahern et al.[3]
Sardinia	75	(E | 19)	Ileu→Thr	Gly	Grifoni et al.[64]
Victoria Jubilee	80	(EF | 4)	Asp→Tyr	Ala	Ahern et al.[2]
Dickinson	97	(FG | 4)	His→Arg	Ala	Schneider et al.[157]
Malta I	117	(G | 19)	His→Arg	Gly	Cauchi et al.[40]
Hull	121	(GH | 4)	Glu→Lys	Ala	Sacker et al.[156]
Port Royal	125	(H | 3)	Glu→Ala	Gly	Brimhall et al.[31]
Poole	130	(H | 8)	Trp→Gly	Gly	Lee-Potter et al.[127]
Koelliker[a] α_2	145 minus Arg γ_2					Kohne et al.[120]

[a] HbF Koelliker is not a gene product.

in the $^{G}\gamma$:$^{A}\gamma$ ratio, and to the amounts of $^{G}\gamma$ and $^{A}\gamma$ mutants synthesized relative to total HbF (Table VI). The $^{G}\gamma$-chain variants contribute either about one-fourth or one-eighth to total HbF production in the heterozygote, whereas the $^{A}\gamma$-chain variant contributes either one-eighth or one-sixteenth of total HbF. On the assumption that the amount of gene product is directly related to the number and activity of genes, the existence of four γ-chain loci, pairs of $^{G}\gamma$ genes and pairs of $^{A}\gamma$ genes, has been postulated. The genes are designated by subscripts according to their activity: m = more activity;

l = less activity. It is suggested that the $^{G}_{ml}\gamma$ locus is completely suppressed during the switch from HbF to HbA (Table VII).

The ratio of $^{G}\gamma$- to $^{A}\gamma$-chains in the fetus and newborn averages 7:3,[139,161] whereas the ratio approaches a value of about 2:3 by 5 months of age.[163] This ratio is also characteristic of HbF isolated from normal adults. Among the structural variants of the γ-chain (see Table V), 50% have alanine alone in position 136 and 50% have glycine. No variant has been observed to have a mixture of both alanine and glycine as in normal HbF. These

Table VI. Characteristics of Some γ-Chain Mutants: Basis for Genetic Control of γ-Chain Synthesis

Variant	Fraction of total HbF	Mutant chain	Relative production	Gene designation
HbF Malta I HbF Malaysia	20% ($\frac{1}{4}$)	$^{G}\gamma$	4	$^{G}_{m}\gamma$ ("more" active)
HbF X HbF Auckland	13% ($\frac{1}{8}$)	$^{G}\gamma$	2	$^{G}_{l}\gamma$ ("less" active)
HbF Jamaica	13% ($\frac{1}{8}$)	$^{A}\gamma$	2	$^{A}_{m}\gamma$ ("more" active)
HbF Malta II	5% ($\frac{1}{16}$)	$^{A}\gamma$	1	$^{A}_{l}\gamma$ ("less" active)

Table VII. Genetic Control of γ-Chain Synthesis During Development

γ-Gene activity		Ratio
$^G_m\gamma : ^G_l\gamma : ^A_m\gamma : ^A_l\gamma$		$^G\gamma : ^A\gamma$
Newborn	$4 : 2 : 2 : 1$	$7:3$
Adult	$0 : 2 : 2 : 1$	$2:3$

results indicate that there must be at least two non-allelic structural genes, one gene for the $^G\gamma$-chain and one gene for the $^A\gamma$-chain.

Recently, Ricco *et al.*[151] found a new type of HbF with the isoleucine residue at position 75 substituted by a threonine ($\gamma^{75 \text{ Thr}}$) that is present not only in the HbF of most patients with β thalassemia, but also in the HbF of 40% of normal newborns and premature infants, and of one 14-week-old fetus investigated. The amount of this γ-chain ($^T\gamma$-chain) varies between traces and 40% of total HbF. The same amino acid replacement ($\gamma^{75 \text{ Thr}}$) was described[64] in the γ-chain mutant HbF Sardinia (see Table V). The frequent occurrence of this substitution favors the assumption that it is not an abnormal variant, but a new type of normal HbF.[151]

The weak point in this model is that in such a complex system of protein synthesis, it is difficult to predict the number of genes directly from the protein ratios synthesized (see the following paragraph). On the other hand, the amounts of γ-chain mutants present in heterozygotes vary considerably, as has been shown particularly for HbF Malta I.[85,183] Furthermore, it is obvious that the British type of hereditary persistence of HbF is not completely compatible with this concept.[179]

Recently developed hybridization techniques have made it possible to assay directly the number of genes.[124] The results from these studies confirm[98,144] the presence of two α-chain genes per haploid genome, of one β-chain gene, and of one δ-chain gene. For the γ-chain, however, only two or at most three genes have been detected.[141] These results are an indication that the different ratios for $^G\gamma$- and $^A\gamma$-chains obtained in the various conditions mentioned above are not a result of the gene dosage, but rather are due to transcriptional or translational discriminations.

Regarding the arrangement of genes, evidence exists from studies on Hb Kenya (a $\gamma\beta$-fusion product) and Hb Lepore (a $\beta\delta$-fusion product) that the loci for γ-, δ-, and β-chains are closely linked.[86] Thus, the order of the non-α-chain genes on the chromosome is assumed to be γ–δ–β. The order of the loci for the $^G\gamma$-, $^A\gamma$-, and $^T\gamma$-chains awaits clarification in the light of recent data on the actual number of γ-chain genes. Nothing is known about the number and linkage of ε and ζ genes.

5.9. Switch from Fetal to Adult Hemoglobin

During human development, there occur two switches in hemoglobin types: The first takes place during the first fetal stage, when the embryonic hemoglobins are replaced by HbF. On the level of the polypeptide chains, this switch means that synthesis of ε- and ζ-chains is replaced by production of γ- and α-chains. In addition, synthesis of β-chains starts at this time (see Fig. 7). The second switch occurs at about 34–36 weeks of gestation and is characterized primarily by quantitative changes; i.e., γ-chain synthesis declines while β-chain synthesis increases.[103] Qualitative changes occur with the uneven suppression of $^G\gamma$- and $^A\gamma$-chain synthesis.[161]

Virtually nothing is known about the biological basis of these switches. Several hypotheses[93,94,101,159] have been proposed to understand the mechanisms responsible or involved at both the molecular and cellular levels. Many *in vivo* and *in vitro* experiments have been performed to find tools or factors that might enhance or reverse the switches, or that might reveal the secret of the functional rules of a supposed internal clock.

5.9.1. Relationship to Gestational Age and Other Factors

The switch from HbF to HbA is related primarily to gestational age, and is independent of the process of birth *per se*. The quantitative changes and the pattern of HbF disappearance have been thoroughly investigated.[9,11,12,20,43] However, the following problems need further discussion: (1) the postnatal decline of HbF in premature infants: (2) HbF concentrations in small-for-gestational-age infants; and (3) polycythemia and HbF values at term.

(a) Postnatal Decline of Fetal Hemoglobin in Premature Infants. At corresponding postconceptional ages, the HbF values are identical in term and preterm infants until approximately 40 weeks. That they are is generally accepted,[9,20,43] but only

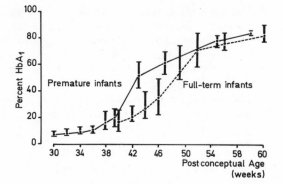

Fig. 14. Follow-up studies on the development of HbA$_1$ values in peripheral blood from premature and full-term infants until 60 weeks postconception. The vertical brackets denote maximum and minimum values of 12–15 infants; the curves were plotted from median values. See the text for details. Data from Kohne and Kleihauer.[118]

limited information is available[43] from follow-up studies on the disappearance of HbF in prematures during the first months after birth. We[118] therefore estimated HbF and HbA by column chromatography in a group of 12 premature and 15 term infants at 2-week intervals over a period of 30 weeks, beginning at the 30th week of gestation (Fig. 14). In both groups, the follow-up measurements showed identical values for HbA at 40 weeks postconception. Thereafter, the transition to HbA was significantly faster in the group of premature infants than in the group of term infants. Most probably, the enhanced HbA production in premature infants is influenced by environmental factors, which may be related to the characteristics of postnatal red cell destruction and production.

(b) Fetal Hemoglobin Concentrations in Small-for-Gestational-Age Infants. An exception to the close correlation between HbA synthesis and gestational age seems to be the group of small-for-gestational-age (SGA) infants. It was reported that infants with intrauterine growth retardation exhibit significantly higher HbF values than normal newborn infants at term.[10] Other data, however, indicate that the maturity-dependent hemoglobin synthesis also applies to SGA infants.[11] The preliminary results of our continuing investigations of this problem[118] can be summarized as follows:

1. In a group of SGA infants characterized by appropriate length but low birth weight in relation to gestational age, HbA values re-

semble those of normal term infants. That they do means that HbA synthesis in this group of SGA infants is strongly correlated with gestational age.

2. In a group of SGA infants characterized by low measurements for both birth weight and length in relation to gestational age, the HbA values more closely resemble those of premature infants of corresponding weight.

(c) Polycythemia and Fetal Hemoglobin Values at Term. As already mentioned, a variety of inborn and acquired conditions, such as chromosomal abnormalities, maternal hypoxia, and hemolytic anemias,[109,142] are associated with an altered pattern of developmental hemoglobins. In Down's syndrome and in two cases of E and C trisomy, the precocious synthesis of HbA was reported to occur together with polycythemia.[119] In approximately 50% of a group of otherwise healthy newborn infants with unexplained polycythemia—maternal–fetal transfusion was excluded—we found HbA levels significantly higher (31.1 ± 6.2%) than in normal newborns (17.7 ± 4.5%). Synthesis studies in these polycythemic infants revealed that 60% of synthesized hemoglobin was HbA, whereas the ratio in normal newborn infants is approximately 35% HbA.

The enhanced HbA production in combination with polycythemia in apparently healthy newborns presumably occurs in response to functional requirements. The capacity to transport oxygen can be increased by raising the hemoglobin concentration. The oxygen-unloading capacity, however, can be substantially improved in newborns by an increase in HbA synthesis. The need for such an improvement is a possible explanation for the simultaneous occurrence of high HbA levels and polycythemia. Further investigations are necessary to prove this hypothesis.

6. Future Outlook

Developmental hemoglobins were recognized years ago as a special blood pigment having some physiologic significance for the developing fetus. Later, HbF became of interest to hematologists because of its diagnostic relevance for inherited and acquired conditions, such as β thalassemia, hereditary persistence of fetal hemoglobin, Fanconi anemia, and malignant diseases. Since it has been shown that HbF is beneficial in the survival of red cells in β thalassemia and sickle cell anemia, research in this field is focused on switch mechanisms occurring during the perinatal period or on the occasion of reactivation of HbF synthesis. A fuller understanding of how these mechanisms operate— activation of HbA synthesis and reactivation of HbF synthesis may be basically different—would provide a basis for manipulation of γ-chain synthesis. Another aspect is the continuous development of methods for antenatal diagnosis. All these efforts, which are initiated primarily by a considerable practical need, will also be of benefit for the understanding of human development and differentiation.

ACKNOWLEDGMENTS

The author is indebted to Mrs. R. Gerhard and Mrs. E. Köhler for help in preparing the manuscript, and to Mrs. M. Krause for preparing the drawings. Mrs. Dozent Dr. E. Kohne has supported this review by discussions and unpublished data.

7. References

1. AGER, J. A. M., AND LEHMANN, H., 1958, Observations on some "fast" haemoglobins: K, J, N, and Bart's, *Br. Med. J.* **1**:929.
2. AHERN, E., HOLDER, W., AHERN, V., SERJEANT, G. R., SERJEANT, B. E., FORBES, M., BRIMHALL, B., AND JONES, R. T., 1975, Haemoglobin F Victoria Jubilee ($\alpha 2 A\gamma 2$ 80 Asp→Tyr), *Biochim. Biophys. Acta* **393**:188.
3. AHERN, E. J., JONES, R. T., BRIMHALL, B., AND GRAY, R. H., 1970, Haemoglobin F Jamaica ($\alpha_2\gamma_2$ 61 Lys→Glu; 136 Ala), *Br. J. Haematol.* **18**:369.
4. AHERN, E. J., WILTSHIRE, B. G., AND LEHMANN, H., 1972, Further characterization of haemoglobin F Texas I $\gamma 5$ glutamic acid→lysine; γ 136 alanine, *Biochim. Biophys. Acta* **271**:61.
5. ALLEN, D., AND JANDL, J., 1960, Factors influencing relative rates of synthesis of adult and fetal hemoglobin *in vitro*, *J. Clin. Invest.* **39**:1107.
6. ALLEN, D. W., WYMAN, J., JR., AND SMITH, C. A., 1953, The oxygen equilibrium of fetal and adult hemoglobin, *J. Biol. Chem.* **203**:81.
7. ALTER, P. A., KAN, Y. W., FRIGOLETTO, F. D., AND NATHAN, D. G., 1974, The antenatal diagnosis of the haemoglobinopathies, *Clin. Haematol.* **3**:509.
8. BALDWIN, J. M., 1976, A model of co-operative oxygen binding to haemoglobin, *Br. Med. Bull.* **32**:213.
9. BARD, H., 1973, Postnatal fetal and adult hemoglobin synthesis in early preterm newborn infants, *J. Clin. Invest.* **52**:1789.
10. BARD, H., 1974, The effect of placental insufficiency on fetal and adult hemoglobin synthesis, *Amer. J. Obstet. Gynecol.* **120**:67.
11. BARD, H., 1975, The postnatal decline of hemoglobin F synthesis in normal full-term infants, *J. Clin. Invest.* **55**:395.
12. BARD, H., MAKOWSKI, E. L., MESCHIA, G., AND BATTAGLIA, F. C., 1970, The relative rates of synthesis of hemoglobin A and F in immature red cells of newborn infants, *Pediatrics* **45**:766.
13. BASCH, R. S., 1972, Hemoglobin synthesis in short-term cultures of human fetal hemopoietic tissues, *Blood* **39**:530.
14. BAUER, C., 1974, On the respiratory function of hemoglobin, *Rev. Physiol. Biochem. Pharmacol.* **70**:1.
15. BAUER, C., LUDWIG, I., AND LUDWIG, M., 1968, Different effects of 2,3-diphosphoglycerate and adenosine triphosphate on the oxygen affinity of adult and foetal human haemoglobin, *Life Sci.* **7**:1339.
16. BEAVEN, G. H., ELLIS, M. J., AND WHITE, J. C., 1960, Studies on human foetal haemoglobin. I. Detection and estimation, *Br. J. Haematol.* **6**:1.
17. BEAVEN, G. H., HOCH, M., AND HOLIDAY, E. R., 1951, The haemoglobins of the human foetus and infant, *Biochem. J.* **49**:374.
18. BENESCH, R., AND BENESCH, R. E., 1964, Properties of haemoglobin H and their significance in relation to function of haemoglobin, *Nature (London)* **202**:773.
19. BETHLENFALVAY, N. C., LOURO, J. M., AND GREER, H. A., 1972, Translocation trisomy D syndrome 46, XX, D-, t (Dq Dq) +: Report of a case with a note on the cold-instability of Hb Gower 2, *Pediatrics* **50**:928.
20. BETKE, K., 1954, *Der menschliche rote Blutfarbstoff bei Fetus und reifem Organismus,* Springer-Verlag, Berlin.
21. BETKE, K., 1958, Hämatologie der ersten Lebenszeit, *Ergebn. Inn. Med. Kinderheilkd.* **9**:437.
22. BETKE, K., AND GREINACHER, I., 1954, Hitzedenaturierung und Hitzecoagulation bei fetalem und bleibendem Hämoglobin des Menschen, *Z. Kinderheilkd.* **75**:235.
23. BETKE, K., AND KLEIHAUER, E., 1958, Fetaler und bleibender Blutfarbstoff in Erythrozyten und Erythroblasten von menschlichen Feten und Neugeborenen, *Blut* **4**:241.
24. BETKE, K., KLEIHAUER, E., BRAKEBUSCH, E., AND NIERHAUS, K., 1965, Zytologische Untersuchungen zur perinatalen Ablösung von HbF durch HbA und ihre Beziehungen zur Makrozytose des Neugeborenen, *Paediatr. Paedol.* **1**:17.
25. BETKE, K., KLEIHAUER, E., AND LIPPS, M., 1956, Vergleichende Untersuchungen über die Spontanoxydation von Nabelschnur- und Erwachsenenhämoglobin, *Z. Kinderheilkd.* **77**:549.

26. BETKE, K., MARTI, H. R., AND SCHLICHT, I., 1959, Estimation of small percentages of fetal hemoglobin, *Nature (London)* **184**:1877.

27. BHATTACHARYA, S. P., ANYAIBE, S. I., AND HEADINGS, V. E., 1976, Biological variation in the heterogeneous distribution of haemoglobin F among erythrocytes, *Br. J. Haematol.* **33**:401.

28. BLOOM, W., AND BARTELMEZ, G. W., 1940, Hematopoiesis in young human embryos, *Amer. J. Anat.* **67**:21.

29. BOYER, S. H., BELDING, T. K., MARGOLET, L., AND NOYES, A. N., 1975, Fetal hemoglobin restriction to a few erythrocytes (F cells) in normal human adults, *Science* **188**:361.

30. BREATHNACH, C. S., 1962, Red cell diameters in human cord and neonatal blood, *Q. J. Exp. Physiol.* **47**:148.

31. BRIMHALL, B., VEDVICK, T. S., JONES, R. T., AHERN, E., PALOMINO, E., AND AHERN, V., 1973, Haemoglobin F Port Royal ($\alpha 2 G\gamma$ 125 Glu → Ala), *Br. J. Haematol.* **27**:313.

32. BRODY, S., AND ENGSTRÖM, L., 1960, Foetal and adult haemoglobin in newborn infants with erythroblastosis foetalis, *Acta Paediatr. Scand.* **49**:868.

33. BROMBERG, Y. M., ABRAHAMOV, A., AND SALZBERGER, M., 1956, The effect of maternal anoxaemia on foetal haemoglobin of the newborn, *J. Obstet. Gynaecol. Br. Commonul.* **63**:875.

34. BUNN, H. F., AND BRIEHL, R. W., 1970, The interaction of 2,3-diphosphoglycerate with various human hemoglobins, *J. Clin. Invest.* **49**:1088.

35. BUNN, H. F., AND JANDL, J. H., 1970, Control of hemoglobin function within the red cell, *N. Engl. J. Med.* **282**:1414.

36. CAPP, G. L., RIGAS, D. A., AND JONES, R. T., 1967, Hemoglobin Portland 1: A new human hemoglobin unique in structure, *Science* **157**:65.

37. CAPP, G. L., RIGAS, D. A., AND JONES, R. T., 1970, Evidence for a new haemoglobin chain (ζ-chain), *Nature (London)* **228**:278.

38. CARRELL, R. W., OWEN, M. C., ANDERSON, R., AND BERRY, E., 1974, Haemoglobin F Auckland Gγ7 Asp→Asn—further evidence for multiple genes for the gamma chain, *Biochim. Biophys. Acta* **365**:323.

39. CARVER, M. J., 1948, Basic studies in mongolism. II. Hemoglobin, *J. Nerv. Ment. Dis.* **127**:374.

40. CAUCHI, M. N., CLEGG, J. B., AND WEATHERALL, D. J., 1969, Haemoglobin F (Malta): A new foetal haemoglobin variant with a high incidence in Maltese infants, *Nature (London)* **223**:311.

41. CHARACHE, S., SCHRUEFER, J. J., AND BIAS, W. B., 1968, Hereditary persistence of fetal red cells, *J. Clin. Invest.* **47**:17A.

42. CIVIDALLI, G., NATHAN, D. G., KAN, Y. W., SANTAMARINA, B., AND FRIGOLETTO, F., 1974, Relation of beta to gamma synthesis during the first trimester: An approach to prenatal diagnosis of thalassemia, *Pediatr. Res.* **8**:553.

43. COLOMBO, B., KIM, B., PEREZ ATENCIO, R., MOLINA, C., AND TERRENATO, L., 1976, The pattern of fetal haemoglobin disappearance after birth, *Br. J. Haematol.* **32**:79.

44. DAN, M., AND HAGIWARA, A., 1967, Detection of two types of hemoglobin (HbA and HbF) in single erythrocytes by fluorescent antibody technique, *Exp. Cell. Res.* **46**:596.

45. DANCE, N., HUEHNS, E. R., AND BEAVEN, G. H., 1963, The abnormal haemoglobins in haemoglobin H-disease, *Biochem. J.* **87**:240.

46. DARLING, R. C., SMITH, C. A., ASMUSSEN, E., AND COHEN, F. M., 1941, Some properties of human fetal and maternal blood, *J. Clin. Invest.* **20**:739.

47. DAWES, G. S., 1967, New views on O_2 transfer across the placenta, in: *The Scientific Basis of Medicine,* Annual Reviews, British Postgraduate Medical Federation, pp. 74–89, Ashlone Press, London.

48. DE VERDIER, C. H., AND GARBY, L., 1969, Low binding of 2,3-diphosphoglycerate to haemoglobin F: A contribution to the knowledge of the binding site and an explanation for high affinity of foetal blood, *Scand. J. Clin. Lab. Invest.* **23**:149.

49. DOZY, A. M., KLEIHAUER, E. F., AND HUISMAN, T. H. J., 1968, Studies on the heterogeneity of hemoglobin. XIII. Chromatography of various human and animal hemoglobin types on DEAE-Sephadex, *J. Chromatogr.* **32**:723.

50. DRABKIN, D. L., 1965, The molecular weight of haemoglobin, its iron and nitrogen content and optical properties—Their relevance in the problem of a reference standard for haemoglobin measurement, in: *Standardization, Documentation and Normal Values in Haematology* (C. G. de Boroviczény, ed.), *Bibl. Haematol. (Basel)* **21**:33.

51. DRESCHER, H., AND KÜNZER, W., 1954, Der Blutfarbstoff der menschlichen Feten, *Klin. Wochenschr.* **32**:92.

52. DREYFUS, J. C., SCHAPIRA, G., AND HARARI, M., 1954, Incorporation du fer radioactif *in vitro* dans les globules rouges du nouveau-né (hémoglobine foetale et hémoglobine adulte), *C. R. Soc. Biol. (Paris)* **148**:1798.

53. ERDEM, S., AND AKSOY, M., 1969, The increase of hemoglobin A_2 to its adult level, *Isr. J. Med. Sci.* **5**:427.

54. ERKMAN, B., BASUS, V. R., AND CONEN, P. E., 1965, D/D translocation "D" syndrome, *J. Pediatr.* **67**:270.

55. FESSAS, P., AND LOUKOPOULOS, D., 1974, The β-thalassaemias, *Clin. Haematol.* **3**:411.

56. FESSAS, P., AND PAPASPYROU, A., 1957, A new fast hemoglobin associated with thalassemia, *Science* **126**:1119.

57. FINNE, P. H., AND HALVORSEN, S., 1972, Regulation of erythropoiesis in the fetus and newborn, *Arch. Dis. Child.* **47**:683.

58. FRASER, I. D., AND RAPER, A. B., 1962, Observations

on the change from foetal to adult erythropoiesis, *Arch. Dis. Child.* **37**:289.

59. GABBAY, K. H., 1976, Glycosylated hemoglobin and diabetic control (editorial), *N. Engl. J. Med.* **295**:443.

60. GABUZDA, T. G., SILVER, R. K., CHUI, L. C., AND LEWIS, H. B., 1970, The formation of foetal and adult haemoglobin in cell cultures of neonatal calf marrow, *Br. J. Haematol.* **19**:621.

61. GARBY, L., SJÖLIN, S., AND VUILLE, J. C., 1962, Studies of erythrokinetics in infancy. II. The relative rate of synthesis of haemoglobin F and haemoglobin A during the first months of life, *Acta Paediatr. Scand.* **51**:245.

62. GARBY, L., SJÖLIN, S., AND VUILLE, J., 1964, Studies on erythrokinetics in infancy. V. Estimations of the life span of red cells in the newborn, *Acta Paediatr. Scand.* **53**:165.

63. GILMOUR, J. R., 1941, Normal hematopoiesis in intrauterine and neonatal life, *J. Pathol. Bacteriol.* **52**:25.

64. GRIFONI, V., KAMUZORA, H., LEHMANN, H., AND CHARLESWORTH, D., 1975, A new Hb Variant: HbF Sardinia γ75 (E19) isoleucine $\rightarrow$ threonine found in a family with Hb G Philadelphia, β-chain deficiency and a Lepore-like haemoglobin indistinguishable from HbA$_2$, *Acta Haematol.* **53**:347.

65. HALBRECHT, I., AND KLIBANSKI, C., 1956, Identification of a new normal embryonic haemoglobin, *Nature (London)* **178**:794.

66. HALBRECHT, I., KLIBANSKI, C., AND BAR ILAN, F., 1959, Co-existence of the embryonic (third normal) haemoglobin fraction with erythroblastosis in the blood of two full-term newborn babies with multiple malformations, *Nature (London)* **183**:327.

67. HALL, J., AND MOTULSKY, A., 1968, Production of fetal hemoglobin in marrow cultures of human adults, *Nature (London)* **217**:569.

68. HECHT, F., JONES, R. T., AND KOLER, R. D., 1967, Newborn infants with Hb Portland 1, an indicator of α chain deficiency, *Ann. Hum. Genet.* **31**:215.

69. HECHT, F., KEIL, J. V., AND MOTULSKY, A. G., 1964, Developmental hemoglobin anomalies in a chromosomal triplication: D$_1$ trisomy syndrome, *Proc. Natl. Acad. Sci. U.S.A.* **51**:89.

70. HECHT, F., MOTULSKY, A. G., LEMIRE, R. J., AND SHEPARD, T. E., 1966, Predominance of hemoglobin Gower 1 in early human embryonic development, *Science* **152**:91.

71. HELLER, P., AND YAKULIS, V., 1969, The distribution of hemoglobin A$_2$, *Ann. N. Y. Acad. Sci.* **165**:54.

72. HOLLENBERG, M. D., KABACK, M. M., AND KAZAZIAN, H. H., 1971, Adult hemoglobin synthesis by reticulocytes from the human fetus at midtrimester, *Science* **174**:698.

73. HOLMQUIST, W. R., AND SCHROEDER, W. A., 1966, A new N-terminal blocking group involving a Schiff base in hemoglobin A$_{IC}$, *Biochemistry* **5**:2489.

74. HONIG, G. R., 1967, Inhibition of synthesis of fetal hemoglobin by an isoleucine analogue, *J. Clin. Invest.* **46**:1778.

75. HORTON, B. F., THOMPSON, R. B., DOZY, A. M., NECHTMANN, C., NICHOLS, E., AND HUISMAN, T. H. J., 1962, Inhomogeneity of hemoglobin. VI. The minor hemoglobin components of cord blood, *Blood* **20**:302.

76. HOSOI, T., 1968, Fluorescent antibody technique utilized for studies on cellular distribution of erythrocytic antigens, *Acta Haematol. Jpn.* **31**:138.

77. HUEHNS, E. R., AND BEAVEN, G. H., 1962, The reaction of haemoglobin α^4 with haemoglobin H and haemoglobin Bart's, *Biochem. J.* **83**:40.

78. HUEHNS, E. R., AND FAROOQUI, A. M., 1975, Oxygen dissociation properties of human embryonic red cells, *Nature (London)* **254**:335.

79. HUEHNS, E. R., AND SHOOTER, E. M., 1965, Human haemoglobins, *J. Med. Genet.* **2**:48.

80. HUEHNS, E. R., AND SHOOTER, E. M., 1966, The properties and reactions of haemoglobin F$_I$ and their bearing on the dissociation equilibrium of haemoglobin, *Biochem. J.* **101**:852.

81. HUEHNS, E. R., DANCE, N., BEAVEN, G. H., HECHT, F., AND MOTULSKY, A. G., 1964, Human embryonic hemoglobins, *Cold Spring Harbor Symp. Quant. Biol.* **24**:327.

82. HUEHNS, E. R., DANCE, N., BEAVEN, G. H., KEIL, J. V., HECHT, F., AND MOTULSKY, A. G., 1964, Human embryonic haemoglobins, *Nature (London)* **201**:1095.

83. HUEHNS, E. R., FLYNN, F. V., BUTLER, E. A., AND BEAVEN, G. H., 1961, Two new haemoglobin variants in a very young human embryo, *Nature (London)* **189**:496.

84. HUISMAN, T. H. J., AND SCHROEDER, W. A., 1970, New aspects of the structure, function, and synthesis of hemoglobins, *Crit. Rev. Clin. Lab. Sci.* **1**:471.

85. HUISMAN, T. H. J., SCHROEDER, W. A., BANNISTER, W. H., AND GRECH, J. L., 1972, Evidence for four nonallelic structural genes for the γ chain of human fetal hemoglobin, *Biochem. Genet.* **7**:131.

86. HUISMAN, T. H. J., WRIGHTSTONE, R. N., WILSON, J. B., SCHROEDER, W. A., AND KENDALL, A. G., 1972, Hemoglobin Kenya, the product of fusion of γ and β polypeptide chains, *Arch. Biochem. Biophys.* **153**:850.

87. HUNT, J. A., 1959, Identity of α-chains of adult and fetal haemoglobin, *Nature (London)* **183**:1373.

88. HUNT, J. A., AND LEHMANN, H., 1959, Haemoglobin "Bart's": A foetal haemoglobin without α chains, *Nature (London)* **184**:872.

89. JENKINS, G. C., BEALE, D., BLACK, A. J., HUNTSMAN, G. R., AND LEHMANN, H., 1967, Haemoglobin F Texas I (α2 γ2 5 Glu$\rightarrow$Lys): A variant of haemoglobin F, *Br. J. Haematol.* **13**:252.

90. JENSEN, M., AND MURKEN, D. J., 1976, Hemoglobin chain synthesis in two children with trisomy 13. Evidence for temporary imbalance during switch

from gamma to beta chain synthesis, *Eur. J. Pediatr.* **122**:151.

91. JONXIS, J. H. P., AND HUISMAN, T. H. J., 1968, *A Laboratory Manual on Abnormal Haemoglobins,* 2d Ed., Blackwell Scientific Publications, Edinburgh and Oxford.

92. JOPE, E. M., 1949, The ultra-violet spectral absorption of haemoglobin inside and outside of the red blood cell, in: *Haemoglobin* (F. J. W. Roughton and J. C. Kendrew, eds.), pp. 205–219, Butterworths, London.

93. KABAT, D., 1972, Gene selection in hemoglobin and in antibody-synthesizing cells, *Science* **175**:134.

94. KABAT, D., 1974, The switch from fetal to adult hemoglobin in humans: Evidence suggesting a role for γ–β gene linkage, *Ann. N. Y. Acad. Sci.* **241**:119.

95. KALTSOYA, A., FESSAS, P., AND STAVROPOULOS, A., 1966, Hemoglobins of early human embryonic development, *Science* **153**:1417.

96. KAMUZORA, H., AND LEHMANN, H., 1975, Human embryonic haemoglobins including a comparison by homology of the human ζ and α chains, *Nature (London)* **256**:511.

97. KAN, Y. W., DOZY, A. M., ALTER, B. P., FRIGOLETTO, F. D., AND NATHAN, D. G., 1972, Detection of the sickle gene in the human fetus: Potential for intrauterine diagnosis of sickle-cell anemia, *N. Engl. J. Med.* **287**:1.

98. KAN, Y. W., DOZY, A., VARMUS, H. E., TAYLOR, J. M., HOLLAND, J. P., LIE-INJO, L. E., GANESAN, J., AND TODD, D., 1975, Deletion of α-globin genes in haemoglobin H disease demonstrates multiple α-globulin structural loci, *Nature (London)* **255**:255.

99. KAN, Y. W., FORGET, B. G., AND NATHAN, D. G., 1972, Gamma-beta-thalassemia. A cause of hemolytic disease of the newborn, *N. Engl. J. Med.* **286**:129.

100. KARAKLIS, A., AND FESSAS, P., 1963, The normal minor components of human foetal haemoglobin, *Acta Haematol. (Basel)* **29**:267.

101. KAZAZIAN, H. H., 1974, Regulation of fetal hemoglobin production, *Semin. Hematol.* **11**:525.

102. KAZAZIAN, H. H., AND WOODHEAD, A. P., 1974, Adult hemoglobin synthesis in the human fetus, *Ann. N. Y. Acad. Sci.* **241**:691.

103. KAZAZIAN, H. H., SILVERSTEIN, A., SNYDER, P. G., AND VAN BENEDEN, R. J., 1976, Increasing haemoglobin β-chain synthesis in foetal development is associated with a declining γ- to α-mRNA ratio, *Nature (London)* **260**:67.

104. KILMARTIN, J. V., 1976, Interaction of haemoglobin with protons, CO_2 and 2,3-diphosphoglycerate, *Br. Med. Bull.* **32**:209.

105. KIRSCHBAUM, T. H., 1962, Fetal hemoglobin content of cord blood determined by column chromatography, *Amer. J. Obstet. Gynecol.* **84**:1375.

106. KITCHEN, H., AND BRETT, I., 1974, Embryonic and fetal hemoglobin in animals, *Ann. N. Y. Acad. Sci.* **241**:653.

107. KLEIHAUER, E., 1957, Denaturierung von fetalem und bleibendem Hämoglobin durch Salzsäure, *Naturwissenschaften* **44**:308.

108. KLEIHAUER, E., 1960, Beitrag zur postnatalen HbF-Bildung. III. Internationales Erythrozyten-Symposium, Berlin, *Folia Haematol. (Leipzig)* **78**:69.

109. KLEIHAUER, E., 1966, Fetales Hämoglobin und fetale Erythrozyten, *Arch. Kinderheilkd. Suppl.* 53.

110. KLEIHAUER, E., 1970, The hemoglobins, in: *Physiology of the Perinatal Period* (U. Stave, ed.), pp. 255–297, Appleton-Century-Crofts, New York.

111. KLEIHAUER, E., 1974, Determination of fetal hemoglobin: Elution technique, in: *The Detection of Hemoglobinopathies* (R. M. Schmidt, T. H. J. Huisman, and H. Lehmann, eds.), pp. 20–22, CRC Press, Cleveland Ohio.

112. KLEIHAUER, E., AND BRANDT, G., 1964, Überlebenszeit fetaler Erythrozyten im mütterlichen Kreislauf, *Klin. Wochenschr.* **42**:458.

113. KLEIHAUER, E., BETKE, K., AND KÖNIG, P. A., 1965, Embryonale Hämoglobine, *Klin. Wochenschr.* **43**:435.

114. KLEIHAUER, E., BRAUN, H., AND BETKE, K., 1957, Demonstration von fetalem Hämoglobin in Erythrozyten eines Blutausstriches, *Klin. Wochenschr.* **35**:637.

115. KLEIHAUER, E., TANG, D., AND BETKE, K., 1967, Die intrazelluläre Verteilung von embryonalem Hämoglobin in roten Blutzellen menschlicher Embryonen, *Acta Haematol. (Basel)* **38**:264.

116. KNOLL, W., 1949, Der Gang der Erythropoese beim menschlichen Embryo, *Acta Haematol. (Basel)* **2**:369.

117. KOENIG, R. J., PETERSON, C. M., JONES, R. L., SAUDEK, C., LEHRMAN, M., AND CERAMI, A., 1976 Correlation of glucose regulation and hemoglobin A_{Ic} in diabetes mellitus, *N. Engl. J. Med.* **295**:417.

118. KOHNE, E., AND KLEIHAUER, E., 1974–1976, Unpublished data.

119. KOHNE, E., AND KLEIHAUER, E., 1975, Beziehungen zwischen Polyglobulie und Hämoglobinmuster bei Neugeborenen mit G Trisomie, *Klin. Wochenschr* **53**:111.

120. KOHNE, E., KRAUSE, M., LEUPOLD, D., AND KLEIHAUER, E., 1977, Hemoglobin F Koelliker (α_2 minus 141 [HC 3] Arg γ_2)—A modification of fetal hemoglobin, *Hemoglobin* **1**:257.

121. KOMAZAWA, M., GARCIA, A. M., AND OSKI, F. A., 1974, The relation of red cell size to fetal hemoglobin concentration in the term infant, *J. Pediatr* **85**:114.

122. KÖRBER, E., 1866, Über Differenzen des Blutfarbstoffes, M. D. Thesis, University of Dorpat.

123. KÜNZER, W., 1957, Human embryo haemoglobins *Nature (London)* **179**:477.

124. LANYON, W. G., OTTOLENGHI, S., AND WILLIAMSON, R., 1975, Human globin gene expression and linkage in bone marrow and fetal liver, *Proc. Natl. Acad Sci. U.S.A.* **72**:258.

125. LARKIN, I. L. M., BAKER, T., LORKIN, P. A. LEHMANN, H., BLACK, A. J., AND HUNTSMAN, R. G.

1968, Haemoglobin F Texas II ($\alpha2\gamma2$ 6 Glu→Lys), the second of the haemoglobin F Texas variants, *Br. J. Haematol.* **14**:233.

26. LEE, C. S. N., BOYER, S. H., BOWEN, P., WEATHERALL, D. J., ROSENBLUM, H., CLARK, D. B., DUKE, J. R., LIBORO, C., BIAS, W., AND BORGAONKAR, D. S., 1966, The D_1 trisomy syndrome: The subjects with unequally advancing development, *Bull. Johns Hopkins Hosp.* **118**:374.

27. LEE-POTTER, J. P., DEACON-SMITH, R. A., SIMPKISS, M. J., KAMUZORA, H., AND LEHMANN, H., 1975, A new cause of haemolytic anaemia in the newborn. A description of an unstable fetal haemoglobin: F Poole, $\alpha2G\gamma2$ 130 tryptophan→glycine, *J. Clin. Pathol.* **28**:317.

28. LEHMANN, H., AND HUNTSMAN, R. G., 1974, An introduction to the structure and function of haemoglobin, *Clin. Haematol.* **3**:217.

29. LIE-INJO, L. E., KAMUZORA, H., AND LEHMANN, H., 1974, Haemoglobin F Malaysia: $\alpha2\gamma2$ 1 (NA1) glycine→cysteine; 136 glycine, *J. Med. Genet.* **11**:25.

30. LIE-INJO, L. E., WILTSHIRE, B. G., AND LEHMANN, H., 1973, Structural identification of haemoglobin F Kuala Lumpur ($\alpha2\gamma2$ 22 (B4) Asp→Gly: 136 Ala), *Biochim. Biophys. Acta* **322**:224.

31. LORKIN, P. A., 1973, Fetal and embryonic haemoglobins, *J. Med. Genet.* **10**:50.

32. LOUKOPOULOS, D., KALTSOYA, A., AND FESSAS, P., 1969, On the chemical abnormality of Hb "Alexandra," a fetal hemoglobin variant, *Blood* **333**:114.

33. MARTI, H. R., 1964, Hämoglobin vom "Alexandra-Typus" im ersten Lebensjahr, *Experientia* **20**:138.

34. MATSUDA, G., SCHROEDER, W. A., JONES, R. T., AND WELIKY, N., 1960, Is there an "embryonic" or "primitive" human hemoglobin?, *Blood* **16**:984.

35. MINNICH, V., CORDONNIER, J. K., WILLIAMS, W. J., AND MOORE, G. V., 1962, Alpha, beta and gamma hemoglobin polypeptide chains during the neonatal period with a description of the fetal form of hemoglobin D (St. Louis), *Blood* **19**:137.

36. NATHAN, D. G., ALTER, B. P., AND FRIGOLETTO, F. D., 1975, Antenatal diagnosis of hemoglobinopathies: Social and technical considerations, *Semin. Hematol.* **12**:305.

37. NECHELES, T., SHEEHAN, R., AND MEYER, H., 1965, Effect of erythropoietin and oxygen tension on *in vitro* synthesis of hemoglobin A and F by adult human bone marrow, *Proc. Soc. Exp. Biol. (N. Y.)* **119**:207.

38. NIENHUIS, A. W., BAKKER, J. E., DEISSEROTH, A., AND ANDERSON, W. F., 1976, Regulation of globine gene expression, in: *Congenital Disorders of Erythropoiesis, Ciba Found. Symp. 37*, pp. 329–345, Elsevier, Excerpta Medica, North-Holland, Amsterdam, Oxford, New York.

39. NUTE, P. E., PATARYAS, H. A., AND STAMATOYANNOPOULOS, G., 1973, The $^{G}\gamma$ and $^{A}\gamma$ hemoglobin chains during human fetal development, *Amer. J. Hum. Genet.* **25**:271.

140. NUTE, P. E., WOOD, W. G., STAMATOYANNOPOULOS, G., OLWENY, C., AND FAILKOW, P. J., 1976, The Kenya form of hereditary persistence of fetal haemoglobin: Structural studies and evidence for homogeneous distribution of haemoglobin F using fluorescent anti-haemoglobin F antibodies, *Br. J. Haematol.* **32**:55.

141. OLD, J., CLEGG, J. B., WEATHERALL, D. J., OTTOLENGHI, S., COMI, P., GIGLIONI, B., MITCHELL, J., TOLSTOSHEV, P., AND WILLIAMSON, R., 1976, A direct estimate of the number of human γ-globin genes, *Cell* **8**:13.

142. OPPÉ, T. E., AND FRASER, I. D., 1961, Foetal haemoglobin in haemolytic disease of the newborn, *Arch. Dis. Child.* **36**:507.

143. OSKI, F. A., 1972, Fetal hemoglobin, the neonatal red cell, and 2,3-diphosphoglycerate, *Pediatr. Clin. North Amer.* **19**:907.

144. OTTOLENGHI, S., LANYON, W. G., WILLIAMS, R., WEATHERALL, D. J., CLEGG, J. B., AND PITCHER, C. S., 1975, Human globin gene analysis for a case of $\beta^{o}/\delta\beta^{o}$ thalassaemia, *Proc. Natl. Acad. Sci. U.S.A.* **72**:2294.

145. PATARYAS, H. A., AND STAMATOYANNOPOULOS, G., 1972, Hemoglobins in human fetuses: Evidence for adult hemoglobin production after 11th gestational week, *Blood* **39**:688.

146. PAUL, J., 1976, Haemoglobin synthesis and cell differentiation, *Br. Med. Bull.* **32**:277.

147. PERUTZ, M. F., 1974, Mechanism of denaturation of haemoglobin by alkali, *Nature (London)* **247**:341.

148. PERUTZ, M. F., 1976, Structure and mechanism of haemoglobin, *Br. Med. Bull.* **32**:195.

149. POOTRAKUL, S., WASI, P., AND NA-NAKORN, S., 1967, Haemoglobin Bart's hydrops foetalis in Thailand, *Ann. Hum. Genet.* **30**:293.

150. POWARS, D., ROHDE, R., AND GROVES, D., 1964, Foetal haemoglobin and neutrophil anomaly in D_1-trisomy syndrome, *Lancet* **1**:1363.

151. RICCO, G., MAZZA, U., TURI, R. M., PICK, P. G., CAMASCHELLA, C., SAGLIO, G., AND BERNINI, L. F., 1976, Significance of a new type of human foetal hemoglobin carrying a replacement isoleucine→threonine at position 75 (E19) of the γ-chain, *Hum. Genet.* **32**:305.

152. RIGGS, A., 1965, Functional properties of hemoglobins, *Physiol. Rev.* **45**:619.

153. RINGELHANN, B., KONOTEY-AHULY, F. I. D., LEHMANN, H., AND LORKIN, P. A., 1970, A Ghanasian adult homozygous for hereditary persistence of foetal haemoglobin and heterozygous for elliptocytosis, *Acta Haematol. (Basel)* **43**:100.

154. ROCHE, J., AND DERRIEN, Y., 1953, Les hémoglobines humaines et les modifications physiologiques et pathologiques de leur caractères, *Sang* **24**:97.

155. ROSENBERG, M., 1969, Fetal hematopoiesis: Case report, *Blood* **33**:66.

156. SACKER, L. S., BEALE, D., BLACK, A. J., HUNTSMAN, R. G., LEHMANN, H., AND LORKIN, P. A., 1967, Haemoglobin F Hull (γ 121 glutamic acid→lysine), homologous with haemoglobins O Arab and O Indonesia, *Br. Med. J.* **3**:531.

157. SCHNEIDER, R. G., HAGGARD, M. E., GUSTAVSON, L. P., BRIMHALL, B., AND JONES, R. T., 1974, Genetic haemoglobin abnormalities in about 9000 black and 7000 white newborns; haemoglobin F Dickinson (A 97 His→Arg), a new variant, *Br. J. Haematol.* **28**:515.

158. SCHROEDER, W. A., 1965, Factors in the difference between the calculated and determined molecular weight of human haemoglobin, in: *Standardization, Documentation and Normal Values in Haematology* (C. G. de Boroviczény, ed.), *Bibl. Haematol. (Basel)* **21**:50.

159. SCHROEDER, W. A., 1974, Multiple cistrons for fetal hemoglobin in man, *Ann. N. Y. Acad. Sci.* **241**:70.

160. SCHROEDER, W. A., AND JONES, R. T., 1965, Some aspects of the chemistry and function of human and animal hemoglobin, *Fortschr. Chem. Org. Naturst.* **23**:113.

161. SCHROEDER, W. A., BANNISTER, W. H., GRECH, J. L., BROWN, A. K., WRIGHTSTONE, R. N., AND HUISMAN, T. H. J., 1973, Non-synchronized suppression of postnatal activity in non-allelic genes which synthesize $^G\gamma$ chain in human foetal haemoglobin, *Nature (London)* **244**:89.

162. SCHROEDER, W. A., CUA, J. T., MATSUDA, G., AND FENNINGER, W. D., 1962, Hemoglobin F₁, an acetyl-containing hemoglobin, *Biochim. Biophys. Acta* **65**:532.

163. SCHROEDER, W. A., HUISMAN, T. H. J., BROWN, A. K., UY, R., BOUVER, N. G., LERCH, P. O., SHELTON, J. R., SHELTON, J. B., AND APPELL, G., 1971, Postnatal change in the chemical heterogeneity of human fetal hemoglobin, *Pediatr. Res.* **5**:493.

164. SCHROEDER, W. A., HUISMAN, T. H. J., SHELTON, J. R., SHELTON, J. B., KLEIHAUER, E. F., DOZY, A. M., AND ROBBERSON, B., 1968, Evidence for multiple structural genes for the γ-chain of human fetal hemoglobin, *Proc. Natl. Acad. Sci. U.S.A.* **60**:537.

165. SCHROEDER, W. A., SHELTON, J. R., SHELTON, J. B., APPELL, G., HUISMAN, T. H. J., AND BOUVER, N. G., 1972, World-wide occurrence of nonallelic genes for the γ-chain of human foetal hemoglobin in newborns, *Nature (London) New Biol.* **240**:273.

166. SCHROEDER, W. A., SHELTON, J. R., SHELTON, J. B., AND CORMICK, J., 1963, The amino acid sequence of the α-chain of human fetal hemoglobin, *Biochemistry* **2**:1353.

167. SCHROEDER, W. A., SHELTON, J. R., SHELTON, J. B., CORMICK, J., AND JONES, R. T., 1963, The amino acid sequence of the γ-chain of human fetal hemoglobin, *Biochemistry* **2**:992.

168. SCHULMAN, I., SMITH, C. H., AND STERN, G. S., 1954, Studies on the anemia of prematurity. I. Fetal and adult hemoglobin in premature infants, *Amer. J. Dis. Child.* **88**:567.

169. SHEPARD, M. K., WEATHERALL, D. J., AND CONLEY, C. L., 1962, Semi-quantitative estimation of distribution of fetal hemoglobin in red cell population, *Bull. Johns Hopkins Hosp.* **110**:293.

170. STAMATOYANNOPOULOS, G., 1971, Gamma-thalassaemia, *Lancet* **2**:192.

171. STEGINK, L. D., MEYER, P. D., AND BRUMMEL, M. C., 1971, Human fetal hemoglobin F₁. Acetylation status, *J. Biol. Chem.* **246**:3001.

172. THOMAS, E. D., LOCHTE, H. L., JR., GREENOUGH, W. B., AND WALES, M., 1960, *In vitro* synthesis of foetal and adult haemoglobin by foetal haematopoietic tissues, *Nature (London)* **185**:396.

173. TODD, D., LAI, M. C. S., WHITE, G. H., AND HUEHNS, E. R., 1970, The abnormal hemoglobins in homozygous α-thalassemia, *Br. J. Med.* **19**:27.

174. TOMADA, Y., 1964, Demonstration of foetal erythrocytes by immunofluorescent staining, *Nature (London)* **202**:910.

175. TUCHINDA, S., NAGAI, K., AND LEHMANN, H., 1975, Oxygen dissociation curve of haemoglobin Portland, *FEBS Lett.* **49**:390.

176. WALZER, S., GERALD, P. S., O'NEILL, R., AND DIAMOND, K., 1966, Hematologic changes in D₁ trisomy syndrome, *Pediatrics* **38**:419.

177. WASI, P., NA-NAKORN, S., AND POOTRAKUL, S. N., 1974, The α-thalassaemias, *Clin. Haematol.* **3**:383.

178. WEATHERALL, D. J., 1963, Abnormal haemoglobins in the neonatal period and their relationship to thalassaemia, *Br. J. Haematol.* **9**:265.

179. WEATHERALL, D. J., 1975, Hereditary persistence of fetal hemoglobin, *Br. J. Haematol.* **29**:191.

180. WEATHERALL, D. J., 1976, Fetal haemoglobin synthesis, in: *Congenital Disorders of Erythropoiesis, Ciba Found. Symp. 37*, pp. 307–328, Elsevier, Excerpta Medica, North-Holland, Amsterdam, Oxford, New York.

181. WEATHERALL, D. J., AND CLEGG, J. B., 1972, *The Thalassaemia Syndromes,* 2nd Ed., Blackwell Scientific Publications, Oxford.

182. WEATHERALL, D. J., CLEGG, J. B., AND BOON, W. H., 1970, The haemoglobin constitution of infants with the haemoglobin Bart's hydrops foetalis syndrome, *Br. J. Haematol.* **18**:357.

183. WEATHERALL, D. J., PEMBREY, M. E., AND PRITCHARD, J., 1974, Fetal haemoglobin, *Clin. Haematol.* **3**:467.

184. WEICKER, H., WAGNER, I., GUTTMANN, A. B., KRIEGER, F., LOHREY, H. F., AND VON ZIMMERMANN, H., 1953, Der Erythrozytendurchmesser des Kindes, *Acta Haematol. (Basel)* **10**:50.

185. WEINSTEIN, E., RUCKNAGEL, D. L., AND SHAW, M. W., 1965, Quantitative studies on A₂, sickle cell, and fetal haemoglobins in Negros with mongolism, with observations on translocation mongolism in Negros, *Amer. J. Hum. Genet.* **17**:443.

186. WELLER, S. D. V., APLEY, J., AND RAPER, A. B., 1966, Malformations associated with precocious synthesis of adult hemoglobin—a new chromosomal anomaly syndrome, *Lancet* **1**:777.

187. WHITE, J. C., AND BEAVEN, G. H., 1959, Foetal haemoglobin, *Br. Med. Bull.* **15**:33.

188. WILSON, M. G., SCHROEDER, W. A., GRAVES, D. A., AND KACH, V. D., 1967, Hemoglobin variations in D-trisomy syndrome, *N. Engl. J. Med.* **277**:953.

189. WINSLOW, R. M., AND INGRAM, V. M., 1966, Peptide chain synthesis of human hemoglobin A and A₂, *J. Biol. Chem.* **241**:1144.

190. WITSCHI, E., 1956, *Development of Vertebrates,* W. B. Saunders Co., Philadelphia.

191. WOOD, W. G., 1976, Haemoglobin synthesis during human fetal development, *Br. Med. Bull.* **32**:282.

192. WOOD, W. G., AND WEATHERALL, D. J., 1973, Haemoglobin synthesis during human development, *Nature (London)* **244**:162.

193. WOOD, W. G., STAMATOYANNOPOULOS, G., LIM, G., AND NUTE, P., 1975, F-cells in the adult: Normal values and levels in individuals with hereditary and acquired elevations of HbF, *Blood* **46**:671.

194. WOOD, W. G., WHITTACKER, J. H., CLEGG, J. B., AND WEATHERALL, D. J., 1972, Haemoglobin synthesis in human bone marrow culture, *Biochim. Biophys. Acta* **277**:413.

195. YOFFEY, J. M., 1971, The stem cell problem in the fetus, *Isr. J. Med. Sci.* **7**:825.

196. ZILLIACUS, H., VARITIAINEN, E., AND OTTELIN, A. M., 1962, Adult haemoglobin in the blood of very young human embryos, *Nature (London)* **193**:386.

197. ZIPURSKY, A., NEELANDS, P. J., POLLOCK, J., CHOWN, B., AND ISRAELS, L. G., 1962, The distribution of fetal hemoglobin in the blood of normal children and adults, *Pediatrics* **30**:262.

CHAPTER 12

Respiratory Gas Transport Characteristics of Blood and Hemoglobin

Klaus P. Riegel and Hans T. Versmold

1. Introduction

Hemoglobin is needed to supply the tissues with oxygen and to facilitate carbon dioxide transport in exchange; in addition, it acts as an important buffer in the extracellular compartment. Close interaction exists between oxygen and carbon dioxide binding and the buffering capacity. In this chapter, age-dependent differences and their physiological relevance will be discussed. Also, some clinical data will be used to put physiological data in perspective with perinatology. Chapters 6 and 11 provide supplemental information.

In the past decade, numerous studies have considerably increased the knowledge of red blood cell (RBC) biochemistry and physiology. In particular, the interdependence of structure and function in

RBCs and hemoglobin has become much better understood. [6,18,54,66,72,114]

2. Oxygen Transport

The oxygen transport characteristics of blood are defined by its oxygen capacity and hemoglobin–oxygen affinity.

2.1. Oxygen Capacity

The oxygen capacity corresponds to the amount of "active" hemoglobin (Hb) present. Since 1 mol Hb binds 4 mol O_2, according to the known molecular weight of 64,450[28,119] for human adult hemoglobin (HbA) and fetal hemoglobin (HbF), 1 g Hb is able to bind 1.39 ml O_2. Recent studies with appropriate methods[35,137] confirmed this figure. For practical purposes, it is justified to use a binding

Klaus P. Riegel and Hans T. Versmold · University Children's Hospital, Munich, Germany coefficient of 1.35 ml O_2/g Hb. In whole blood, less oxygen is bound maximally per gram of Hb, particularly in the RBCs of newborn infants. This reduced binding is due to increased levels of inactivated Hb, mainly methemoglobin and carbon monoxide hemoglobin (CO–Hb).

In cord blood, the mean methemoglobin concentration is approximately 0.5% of total Hb,[68] and increases up to 4% postnatally. The higher values are found in smaller infants.[25,70] The normal adult values are between 0.1 and 1.4%.[68]

In healthy newborn infants, mean cord blood CO–Hb concentrations are about 1%.[51] These values decrease *postpartum*. Higher values are found in hemolysis[37,50]; in Rh disease of the newborn, values up to 5.8% have been reported.[76]

In Vivo Data: A progressive increase of blood Hb concentration during intrauterine development has been described[24] up to an O_2 capacity of approximately 22 ml O_2/dl blood at term.[14] This level may be reached as early as 32 weeks of gestation,[5,142,147] probably only in male fetuses.[30] Near term, the normal distribution ranges from 19 to 28 ml O_2/dl blood.[97] It is to be suspected that the normal range is considerably smaller, since in previous studies, all possible interfering factors leading to a maldistribution of blood have not been considered systematically. Higher values, for instance, occur in infants with growth retardation[30] due to activated erythropoiesis[52] and in acute subpartal hypoxia due to an increased blood shift from placenta to fetus.[53]

Changes of blood O_2 capacity after birth and the implications of early or late clamping of the umbilical cord are well studied. Blood volume and related phenomena are discussed in Chapter 9.

With regard to O_2 capacity, late clamping of the cord results in an average gain of 3–5 ml O_2/dl, irrespective of birth weight and gestational age.[147] According to data from the literature, the O_2 capacity of blood in normal infants 1–2 days of age is between 19 and 31 ml O_2/dl. After the first week, blood O_2 capacity begins to decrease in the well-known manner, as shown in Fig. 1.

2.2. Oxygen Equilibrium

If the O_2 tension falls below the P_{O_2} of ambient air, Hb becomes only partially oxygenated. The relationship between O_2 tension and the rate of chemical combination with Hb can be demonstrated by the O_2 equilibrium curve (Fig. 2). The higher

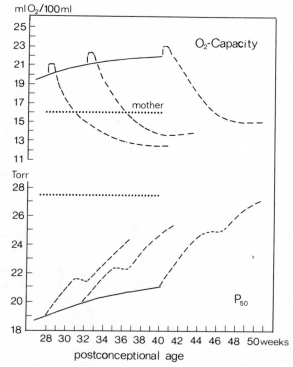

Fig. 1. Changes of blood O_2 capacity (top) and blood O_2 affinity as defined by the standard P_{50} value (bottom) in the fetus (————) and newborn infant (— — — —). The curves are smoothed curves according to the literature.[24,30,40,109,124,140] For comparison, mean values for pregnant women[14] (······) are shown.

the amount of O_2 bound at a given O_2 tension, the higher is the affinity of Hb for O_2. The most interesting properties of Hb are the cooperativity of O_2 binding ("heme–heme interaction") and certain influences of some factors in the Hb and red cell environment. Comprehension of these properties is based on the fact that Hb undergoes structural transition when O_2 or other ligands, e.g., CO_2, are bound or removed.[101,102] Considering relevant factors such as Hb types and concentrations, organic phosphates, CO_2 and protons, temperature, and electrolytes, O_2 equilibrium between 20 and 80% Hb O_2 saturation can be expressed mathematically by the following equation (modified from reference 60):

$$\log P_{O_2} = k_1 + k_2 + k_3(\text{pH } 7.4) + k_4(\text{BT } 37°\text{C}) + k_5 \log(S/100 - S) \quad (1)$$

These influences and the respective k values will be described in the following sections.

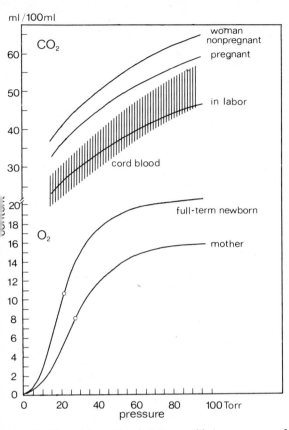

Fig. 2. Top: Mean blood CO_2 equilibrium curves of nonpregnant and pregnant women and during labor. The shaded area denotes the range of blood CO_2 equilibrium of newborn infants.[107] Standard conditions: 37°C, fully O_2-saturated. Bottom: Mean blood O_2 equilibrium curves of full-term newborn infants and pregnant women.[107] (O) P_{50} values. Standard conditions: pH 7.4, 37°C.

2.2.1. P_{50} Values of HbA and HbF in the Absence of Organic Phosphates

The position of the O_2 equilibrium curve is defined by the O_2 tension at 50% oxygen saturation, i.e., the P_{50} value. At basic *in vivo* conditions (37°C, RBC Hb concentration 5 mM, pH 7.15, appropriate electrolytes), but in the absence of organic phosphates, the P_{50} of human HbA is approximately 12.6 torr, and that of HbF is approximately 13.2 torr.[137] Thus, in equation (1), the constant k_1 of HbA is log 12.6 = 1.10, and that of HbF is log 13.2 = 1.12.

Evidently, the basic O_2 affinity of "stripped" HbF and HbA is almost equal, and that of HbF is slightly lower than that of HbA. This observation confirms earlier findings.[4,78] On the other hand, it is a long-established fact[148] that the O_2 affinity of fetal blood is higher than that of adult blood. This discrepancy is caused by varying concentrations of organic phosphates.

The P_{50} values of both HbA and HbF are markedly reduced in the presence of methemoglobin[137] and CO-Hb.[116]

2.2.2. Influence of Organic Phosphates

2,3-Diphosphoglycerate (2,3-DPG) is a well-known intermediate of the glycolytic pathway in RBCs[105] (Fig. 3). Its importance as a regulator of Hb–O_2 affinity, however, was discovered only about ten years ago.[23,32] 2,3-DPG stabilizes the deoxyconformation of the Hb tetramer, thereby decreasing its O_2 affinity. Erythrocytes contain about equimolar concentrations of Hb and 2,3-DPG. 2,3-DPG is preferentially bound to the β-subunits of deoxyhemoglobin.[92,135] The allosteric effect of 2,3-DPG with regard to the P_{50} of HbA ($\alpha_2\beta_2$) is therefore approximately 2.5 times greater than with regard to the P_{50} of HbF ($\alpha_2\gamma_2$).[20,29,42,43,87,88,90,91,130,140] In equation (1), the factor k_2 ($\Delta \log P_{50}/ \Delta$ 2,3-DPG) is 0.065 × 2,3-DPG (mM/liter RBCs) for HbA_1 and 0.026 × 2,3-DPG for HbF.[140]

It becomes apparent that the changing HbF/HbA pattern in the perinatal period affects P_{50} only via different 2,3-DPG-binding characteristics of the hemoglobins involved. The factors that control RBC 2,3-DPG levels are therefore of special interest.

2,3-DPG is synthesized in RBCs from 1,3-DPG by the enzyme diphosphoglycerate mutase (Fig. 3). Its breakdown occurs via 2,3-DPG phosphatase, yielding 3-phosphoglycerate and inorganic phosphate. These reactions are controlled by pH. Increasing pH leads to increasing 2,3-DPG levels; decreasing pH causes 2,3-DPG to decrease.[10] In the physiologic range, a linear relationship exists between RBC pH and 2,3-DPG.[31,112,137] Normal RBC enzyme activities are a prerequisite.[41]

Variations in the degree of Hb oxygenation are accompanied by changes in RBC pH: decreasing Hb O_2 saturation leads to increasing pH, which in turn enhances synthesis of 2,3-DPG. Any significant constant increase of deoxyhemoglobin in circulation is therefore transmitted via RBC pH to the system that determines the respiratory properties of blood. The RBC pH, of course, also depends on plasma

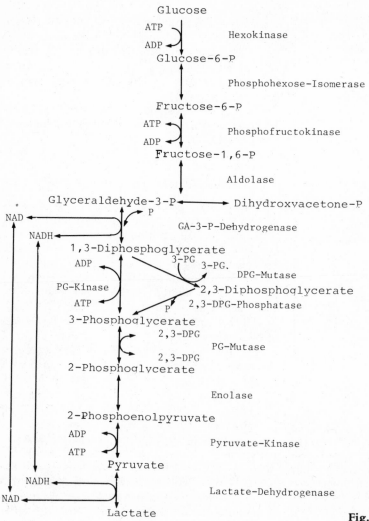

Fig. 3. The red cell glycolytic pathway.

pH and, in addition, on the phosphate ester 2,3-DPG itself.[16,22,45]

There is some positive correlation between RBC 2,3-DPG and plasma inorganic phosphate concentration.[33] Hypophosphatemia, for example, during intravenous hyperalimentation,[128] should therefore be avoided.

It is unclear yet whether other substances such as thyroid and growth hormones[82,111,122] or androgen[56,99] influence RBC 2,3-DPG production independent of pH. In the newborn infant, there is a simultaneous rise of RBC 2,3-DPG and plasma thyroxine.[138]

RBC 2,3-DPG synthesis is also influenced by RBC age. Young cells contain more and produce more on hypoxic stimulation than old cells.[48,58]

2.2.3. Influence of Protons and Carbon Dioxide

In 1904, Bohr et al.[27] discovered that CO_2 greatly decreases blood O_2 affinity. Barcroft[12] attributed this (alkaline) Bohr effect (below pH 6.5 it is reversed and called acid Bohr effect) entirely to an increase of proton concentration. In fact, in Hb solutions containing no chemicals other than buffers, a strict thermodynamic relationship between O_2 affinity and proton activity has been demonstrated.[7,146] The *in vivo* situation, however, is more complex. Independent of pH, CO_2 specifically decreases Hb–O_2 affinity,[71,110] and both CO_2 and 2,3-DPG influence the Bohr effect itself.[55,121,145]

The Bohr effect in fetal and adult blood differs only slightly,[107] though significantly.[9] In clinical routine, it is justified to use the same Bohr coefficient [$(\Delta \log P_{50}/\Delta \text{pH}) - 0.50$] for both newborn and adult blood. This figure is constant k_3 in equation (1).

2.2.4. Influence of Temperature

Hb–O_2 affinity decreases with increasing temperature. The higher the temperature, the higher is the P_{50}. The respective coefficient (k_4) for this relationship ($\Delta \log P_{50}/\Delta$ body temp., °C) is 0.024.[11] Clinically, this influence must be considered in hyper- and hypothermia.

2.2.5. Shape of the Hemoglobin–Oxygen Equilibrium Curve: Heme–Heme Interaction

Unlike the monomeric myoglobin, the tetrameric Hb binds O_2 cooperatively: O_2 binding to certain sites in Hb increases the O_2 affinity of the remaining ones, this effect being called *heme–heme interaction*.[146] A quantitative estimate for cooperativity is given by the exponent n in Hill's equation.[61] This exponent represents the minimum estimate of the number of heme groups that interact on ligand binding. At neutral pH in an O_2 saturation range between 20 and 80%, n is found to be between 2.5 and 3.0 for all normal tetrameric Hb's.[18] An average figure for human fetal and adult blood is 2.7.[107] On the basis of this figure, the P_{50} of a venous blood sample can be estimated from P_{O_2}, S_{O_2} (and pH) according to the equation

$$\log P_{50} = \frac{2.7 \log P_{O_2} - \log [S_{O_2}\%/(100 - S_{O_2}\%)]}{2.7} \tag{2}$$

In equation (1), factor k_5 is the reciprocal of Hill's n, i.e., 0.37.

Lower n values are observed when Hb subunits are fixed in their conformational state, e.g., if Hb is partially ligated with CO or partially oxidized to methemoglobin. No significant differences exist between HbA and HbF.[137] Heme–heme interaction is practically absent ($n = 1$) if there is no allosteric transition on ligand binding as in Hb Bart's (γ_4) and HbH (β_4).[127] Such compounds behave like myoglobin, the O_2 equilibrium curve of which is hyperbolic.

2.2.6. Normal P_{50} Data

For comparative reasons, it is customary to describe the O_2 equilibrium curve and its P_{50} values at standard plasma or RBC pH, and a standard temperature. Standard P_{50} values reported for the perinatal period until 1967 were reviewed previously[107]; new values are presented in Table I. Smoothed curves are demonstrated in Fig. 1. There is a small but steady increase of P_{50} during the last 3 months of fetal life from approximately 19 to 21 torr. At 20 weeks of gestation, a P_{50} of 14.5 torr was found.[38] The normal range ($\bar{x} \pm 2$ S.D.) is about ± 3 torr. Independent of gestational age, birth promotes an increase of standard P_{50} of about 1 torr/week during the first month, which under these conditions depends on the enhanced change of the HbA/HbF ratio and on a significant rapid increase of RBC 2,3-DPG concentration immediately after birth.[42,63,87,109,140]

This normal perinatal course is modified in several clinical states. In hyperbilirubinemia, decreased RBC 2,3-DPG[103] and blood P_{50} values have been observed.[104] Other clinically more important disorders will be discussed in the following section.

2.3. Clinical Aspects of Changes in Hemoglobin–Oxygen Affinity and Capacity

2.3.1. Hemoglobin–Oxygen Affinity and Tissue Oxygenation

A decrease in Hb–O_2 affinity should facilitate O_2 unloading from blood to the tissues. As derived from O_2 equilibrium curves, at a given P_{O_2}, the amount of O_2 that can be given off to tissues increases with a shift to the right, i.e., with an increased P_{50}. The validity of this interpretation is supported by clinical and experimental observations.[18,28] Versmold and Brauser,[136] employing the spectra of cytochrome oxidase in a perfused liver preparation, were able to demonstrate directly a marked shift of O_2 from Hb to tissue on addition of 2,3-DPG in anemic hypoxia. Evidently, P_{50} changes observed in response to alterations of blood

Table I. Oxygen-Carrying Parameters of Blood—Normal Mean Values

Infants	Number	Age (days)	O_2 cap.[a] (ml/100 ml)	P_{50}[b] (torr)	RBC 2,3-DPG (μmol/ml)	HbF (%)	References
Full-term	19	1	24.7	19.4	5.43	77	Delivoria-Papadopoulos
	18	5	22.6	20.6	6.58	77	et al.[42]
	14	21	16.7	22.7	5.38	70	
	10	<1	23.6	21.5	3.94	59	Versmold et al.[140]
	7	2–4	24.7	21.2	3.93	54	
	9	5–10	22.6	22.9	4.93	54	
	10	11–20	21.3	23.6	4.80	50	
(Adults:	10		19.1	25.9	4.11	—)	
	10	1	26.5		3.73	62	Schettini et al.[118]
	10	2	27.6		6.41	—	
	10	3	25.7		6.07	51	
	10	4	24.7		5.74	41	
	10	5	25.7		4.85	45	
	10	6	24.3		5.15	51	
(Adults:	11		19.9		3.87	<1.8)	
Preterm							
1001–1500 g		1–2	21.0	18.0	4.12	87	Delivoria-Papadopoulos
		5–8	18.7	18.9	4.50	84	et al.[42]
		14–21	15.9	21.2	5.72	83	
1501–2000 g		1–2	22.4	19.3	4.48	87	
		5–8	25.3	19.8	5.49	89	
		14–21	18.8	21.3	6.00	81	
30–36 weeks GA	7	<1	22.4	20.0	4.36	75	Riegel and Versmold[109]
	7	2–5	20.9	20.3	5.56	75	
	7	6–14	19.5	21.9	5.46	67	
1200–2840 g	19	0–2	25.0	19.6	5.95		Manzke and Dörner[77]

[a] O_2 capacity, partially calculated from Hb concentration.
[b] P_{50} value at plasma pH 7.4, 37°C.

oxygenation are of physiologic relevance, as are changes of Hb O_2 capacity or cardiac output, including blood flow distribution.[28] All three variables show close interrelationships.[85,120,123,126] However, the beneficial effect of a right shift of the Hb–O_2 equilibrium curve on tissue oxygenation holds true only as long as the arterial O_2 saturation is high, i.e., is located on the upper flat part of the curve.[109,129,143]

(a) Oxygen Exchange in the Placenta. It is generally assumed that the fetus is in a situation of arterial hypoxemia,[75] and the objections just made must be valid. In arterial hypoxemia, O_2-unloading capacity and O_2-unloading tension depend on the magnitude of the blood O_2 capacity. Hb–O_2 affinity is of minor importance. Thus, low blood

P_{50} values of the fetus do not impair his tissue O_2 supply. In general, the same principle applies to the O_2 uptake on the fetal side of the placenta, where the O_2-loading tensions depend on the P_{O_2} and O_2 content in arterial blood of the mother and on the special blood-matching conditions in the placenta.[75] The higher fetal than maternal blood O_2 affinity present in all mammals studied thus far, excepting the cat,[84] when compared at standard conditions, is nearly abolished in vivo. Due to gestational alkalosis in arterial blood of the mother and (probably) fetal acidosis, the fetal and maternal O_2 equilibrium curves are found to be considerably narrowed.[67,73,74] In the human (and many mammals),[75,107] this situation requires a higher fetal than maternal blood O_2 capacity for appropriate

O_2 supply to the fetus. Clinical observations on hemoglobinopathies[98] and on the effect of intra-uterine transfusions[15,86] have demonstrated that a higher fetal than maternal blood O_2 affinity is not a prerequisite for intrauterine existence. To this observation we must add: provided blood O_2 capacity is high enough. The finding that reticulo-cytosis was seen 6–10 days after intrauterine ex-change transfusion[15] can be interpreted in this sense.

Since maternal blood passing through the placenta becomes acid and fetal blood alkaline, the Bohr effect works twofold.[13] This effect accounts for about 8% of the O_2 transferred from the mother to the fetus.[62]

(b) Hemoglobin–Oxygen Affinity and Ery-thropoiesis. It has become clear that the blood O_2 affinity is one of the regulating factors of erythropoiesis when the erythroid generating tissue is functioning.[2,81,85,98,113,141] There is evidence that the postnatal depression of erythropoiesis is initiated by the surplus of circulating O_2 after birth.[106] Later on, with the increasing HbA/HbF ratio, the P_{50} becomes elevated, allowing for a sustained restric-tion of erythrogenesis during the first 6 weeks *postpartum*. At this age, a population of red cells with a high mean age is predominating. These cells contain less 2,3-DPG.[57,140] It is suggested that the resulting drop of P_{50} (see Fig. 1) might trigger the onset of erythropoiesis via the reduced O_2 unloading from Hb,[140] since even lower Hb concentrations are tolerated transitorily without an erythropoietic response after exchange transfusion.[141]

(c) Anemic Hypoxia and Hemoglobin–Oxygen Affinity. A lowered circulating Hb mass in anemia is answered quite effectively after 1–2 days' duration by an increase in RBC 2,3-DPG and P_{50},[21] provided pH is normal. A compensatory P_{50} in-crease is less pronounced in states in which an appreciable amount of HbF is present, because of the low binding of 2,3-DPG to HbF (see Section 2.2.2). Nevertheless, (increased) P_{50} values were significantly correlated with (lowered) cord blood Hb concentrations in Rh incompatibility,[89] in another study after intrauterine transfusions.[86] In anemic newborn infants, blood P_{50} values were found to be considerably elevated.[108]

The restricted adaptation in the presence of HbF via Hb–O_2 affinity is the reason why blood O_2 capac-ity in newborn infants should not fall below 16 ml O_2/dl (equivalent to 12 g Hb/dl, or 35% hema-tocrit) during the first days after birth; higher Hb concentrations may be necessary in hypoxic hypoxemia.

(d) Hemoglobin–Oxygen Affinity in Cardio-respiratory Disorders and the Effect of Acid–Base Abnormalities. High blood P_{50} values have been demonstrated in newborn infants,[44] child-ren,[115,139] and adults[49,80,144] suffering from cyano-tic heart disease or low output failure. As already mentioned, this change depends on normal acid-base equilibrium. The priority of blood O_2 capacity with respect to tissue O_2 supply in such states has also been mentioned.

Severe arterial hypoxemia is frequently ac-companied by acidosis. In many instances, there-fore, normal or decreased RBC 2,3-DPG levels and thus standard P_{50} values will be ob-served.[42,47,91] This is the case most often in infants suffering from respiratory distress syndrome. Relevant data are presented in Table II.

These standard P_{50} values do not reflect *in vivo* conditions. The actual P_{50} values of persons with grossly impaired cardiorespiratory functions are in-creased only slightly above normal, since pH ex-erts an opposite effect on P_{50} via the Bohr effect. It appears that in acid–base abnormalities, the 2,3-DPG mechanism tends to counterbalance changes in the O_2 affinity of Hb that would occur if the Bohr effect were unopposed.[22,126,139,143]

2.3.2. Therapeutic Alterations of Hemoglobin–Oxygen Affinity

In vitro experiments with cord blood show that exposure to blue light increases the P_{50} value con-siderably.[96] Drugs have been used more or less effectively to decrease blood O_2 affinity in patients who might benefit from such treatment. Pro-pranolol[3,93,100] and, with some limitations, Dia-mox[81] and dipyridamol[46] should be mentioned. We do not know of any relevant study in new-born infants.

(a) Blood Storage and Conservation of Functional Properties. Valtis and Kennedy[134] first reported that the P_{50} of blood stored in acid citrate dextrose (ACD) decreases markedly. Both the duration of storage and the kind of preservative greatly affect the O_2-carrying characteristics of donor blood, and thus of blood in the recipient following transfusion.[26,132,133] Attempts have been made to preserve normal, or to produce increased, RBC 2,3-DPG concentrations and thus P_{50} values in stored blood by adding phosphates, inosine,

Table II. Oxygen-Carrying Parameters of Blood in Cardiorespiratory Disorders

Source/disease	Number	Age	O_2 cap.[a] (ml/100 ml)	P_{50}[b] (torr)	RBC 2,3-DPG (μmol/ml)	HbF (%)	References
Cord blood	25			19.0			Joly et al.[64]
RDS[c]	8	0–6 hr		17.5			
	6	7–12 hr		16.9			
	7	13–18 hr		18.2			
	6	19–24 hr		18.7			
	15	25–48 hr		18.3			
RDS	12			16.5	2.64	87	Delivoria-Papadopoulis et al.[42]
RDS	18	0–2 days	21.7	21.6	4.96		Manzke and Dörner[77]
RDS	11	0–2 days	20.9	19.5	2.79	70	Riegel and Versmold[109]
	5	3–5 days	20.3	20.7	4.96	—	
	9	6–18 days	19.4	22.8	5.18	58	
RDS	10			23.5	0.72 (mol/mol Hb)		Duc and Engel[44]
Cardiac malformation: R–L shunt	8			29.4	1.32 (mol/mol Hb)		

[a] O_2 capacity, partially calculated from Hb concentration.
[b] P_{50} value at pH 7.4, 37°C.
[c] Respiratory distress syndrome.

adenine, buffer solutions, and so on.[94,95,125,133] For massive transfusions, it is reasonable to use fresh blood with unimpaired functional properties.

(b) Effect of Blood Exchange Transfusions. Abrahamov and Smith first described in newborn infants a decreased blood O_2 affinity induced by exchange transfusion with adult blood. Their findings were later confirmed.[31,40,64,141] The examples shown in Table III demonstrate the O_2-carrying parameters of the blood of infants before and after exchange transfusion as compared with the characteristics of banked blood. These examples should indicate that (1) blood P_{50} can be manipulated in vitro in both directions; and (2) the properties of stored blood are to be taken into account, since they have considerable effect on the O_2-transportation parameters of infants.

Blood exchange transfusions have been recommended as a treatment for severely hypoxemic newborn infants for a replacement of HbF by the "better functioning HbA," and favorable results have been reported.[39] As already stated, the O_2-unloading capacity of blood depends on the magnitude of the O_2 capacity, when the arterial O_2 saturation decreases below 75%.[129,143] The question remains whether the beneficial effect of such treatment is due to the altered P_{50}. Unquestionably, though, many of these immature babies need supplemental Hb for missing RBCs.[117,131]

3. Carbon Dioxide Transport

CO_2 is carried in the blood as bicarbonate and carbamate, and in the dissolved form.[116] The hydration reaction of CO_2 that takes place in the blood yields bicarbonate ions and protons. In the red cell, this reaction is accelerated by the enzyme carbonic anhydrase. In the placenta and lung, a dehydration reaction occurs that leads to the re-formation of molecular CO_2 again. It is the interaction between the binding of O_2, protons, and CO_2 to Hb that is of particular interest for the understanding of CO_2 transport in blood.

3.1. Carbon Dioxide Carrying Capacity

The CO_2-carrying capacity is exceedingly high in vitro. Under physiologic conditions in vivo, however, it is regulated within narrow limits by acid–base (H^+ and CO_2) homoeostasis. This clinically important aspect is discussed in Chapter 6.

3.2. Carbon Dioxide Equilibrium in Blood

The steady-state relationship between CO_2 tension and concentration in blood can be demonstrated as a CO_2 equilibrium curve (see Fig. 2). For practical purposes, the curve is based on standard conditions such as fully oxygenated Hb at 37°C. The position of the curve is determined by the concentration of CO_2 that can be extracted from blood at given CO_2 tensions. For comparison, the position of the curve is described by the CO_2 content at a P_{CO_2} of 40 torr. In clinical routine, standard bicarbonate has replaced this C_{40} value.

The slope of the curve is determined mainly by the blood Hb concentration, and to some extent by the Hb buffering capacity. Consequently, the CO_2 equilibrium curve of the blood of newborns is steeper than that of their mothers due to their higher blood O_2 capacity.

At normal acid–base conditions, the apparent metabolic buffer value is slightly higher in fetal than in adult blood (32 vs. 28 mEq H^+/liter·pH·mM Hb),[9] but lower in acidemia.[8] The apparent respiratory buffer value is not significantly different in fetal and adult blood.[8,107]

3.2.1. Binding of Carbon Dioxide to Hemoglobin

The terminal α-amino groups of Hb are capable of forming carbamate ($HbCO_2$). This reaction depends on several variables (pH, HbO_2 saturation, organic phosphates).[18] At a given pH value (in the normal range), deoxygenated fetal RBCs contain more $HbCO_2$ than adult RBCs.[19] On oxygenation (at constant pH), $HbCO_2$ drops in both types of erythrocytes. The fraction of "oxilabile carbamate" ($\Delta HbCO_2/\Delta HbO_2$) is approximately 50% higher

Table III. Oxygen-Carrying Parameters of Stored Blood and of the Blood of Infants Before and After Blood Exchange Transfusion—Mean Values

Subjects/sources	Number	Hb (g/100 ml)	P_{50}^{b} (torr)	pH	RBC 2,3-DPG	References
					(mol/mol Hb$_4$)	
Stored ACD blood	5	13.5	16.2	6.85	0.31	Bursaux et al.[31]
Infants						
Before ET^{a} (bilirubin (21.1 mg/100 ml)	5	13.5	20.8	7.30	0.78	
Immediately after ET	5	13.2	19.5	7.29	0.39	
20–22 hr after ET	5	12.6	24.5	7.41	0.90	
Stored CPD blood	5	13.5	20.5	7.06	0.61	
Infants						
Before ET (bilirubin 20.1 mg/100 ml)	5	16.3	22.0	7.27	0.77	
Immediately after ET	5	13.0	23.3	7.31	0.64	
20–22 hr after ET	5	13.2	26.5	7.39	0.81	
					(μmol/ml)	
Stored ACD blood	16	12.4	16.9	6.75	1.6	Versmold et al.[141]
ACD blood + THAM	5	11.6	22.0	7.36	2.8	
Infants						
Before ET	22	12.3	21.5	7.32	3.6	
Immediately after ET	22	11.5	21.8	7.30	2.7	
1–2 days after ET	16	11.5	25.0	7.41	4.7	
7–14 days after ET	15	9.8	27.5	7.34	4.4	

^{a} Exchange transfusion.
^{b} P_{50} value at pH 7.4, 37°C.

in fetal than in adult red cells.[18] The contribution of carbamino compounds of Hb to the amount of CO_2 that is exchanged during the respiratory cycle was calculated to be 10.5% in adult and 19% in fetal blood under physiologic conditions.[20] An antagonism between carbamate formation and 2,3-DPG binding has been established in adult erythrocytes,[17,83] which, however, should not be relevant quantitatively for CO_2 transport.

3.3. Physiological Aspects of Carbon Dioxide Transport in Blood

The liberation of CO_2 from blood on oxygenation is known as the Christiansen–Douglas–Haldane[34] effect (CDH effect), and it must be considered as important as the Bohr effect. In normal adult blood, it amounts to 0.28 mol CO_2/mol O_2,[59,65] and in cord blood, to 0.43 mol CO_2/mol O_2.[107] At a normal respiratory exchange ratio of 0.85 (mol CO_2/mol O_2), the CDH effect contributes 50% to the CO_2 exchange in the placenta and in newborn's lung, compared with 33% in the pulmonary capillaries of the adult. One-third of the CDH effect originates from $HbCO_2$ in both fetal and adult blood. It appears, therefore, that the low blood carbonic anhydrase activity of prematures (584 EU/ml) and full-term newborns (1100 EU/ml) with respect to adult blood (4429 EU/ml)[69] is no serious disadvantage.

4. References

1. ABRAHAMOV, A., AND SMITH, C. A., 1959, Oxygen capacity and affinity of blood from erythroblastotic newborns, *Amer. J. Dis. Child.* **97**:375–379.
2. ADAMSON, J. W., PARER, J. T., AND STAMATOYAN-NOPOULOS, G., 1969, Erythrocytosis associated with hemoglobin Rainier: Oxygen equilibria and marrow regulation, *J. Clin. Invest.* **48**:1376–1386.
3. AGOSTONI, A., BERFASCONI, C., GERLI, G. C., LUZZANO, M., AND ROSSI-BERNARDI, L., 1973, Oxygen affinity and electrolyte distribution of human blood: Changes induced by propranolol, *Science* **182**:300–301.
4. ALLEN, D. W., WYMANN, J., AND SMITH, C. A., 1953, The oxygen equilibrium of fetal and adult hemoglobin, *J. Biol. Chem.* **203**:81–87.
5. ALVAREZ, P. A., AND MATEU, V. S., 1974, Hemoglobin level in the human fetus and its relation to the acid–base status and other fetal–material parameters, *Z. Geburtshilfe Perinatol.* **178**:285–296.
6. ANTONINI, E., AND BRUNORI, M., 1971, Hemoglobin and myoglobin in their reactions with ligands, North-Holland Publishing, Amsterdam and Oxford.
7. ANTONINI, E., WYMAN, J., BRUNORI, M., BUCCI, E., FRONTICELLI, C., AND ROSSI-FANELLI, A., 1963, Studies on the relations between molecular and functional properties of hemoglobin. IV. The Bohr effect in human hemoglobin measured by proton binding, *J. Biol. Chem.* **238**:2950–2957.
8. ARCZYNSKA, W., 1973, A further study of the metabolic buffer value and the Bohr effect in human fetal whole blood, *Pediatr. Res.* **7**:996–1000.
9. ARCZYNSKA, W., AND PROD'HOM, L. S., 1973, The buffer values and the Bohr effect of human fetal and adult whole blood *in vitro* in an acid range, *Pediatr. Res.* **7**:126–131.
10. ASAKURA, T., SATO, Y., MINAKAMI, S., AND YOSHI-KAWA, H., 1966, pH dependency of 2,3-diphosphoglycerate in red blood cells, *Clin. Chim. Acta* **14**:840–841.
11. ASTRUP, P., ENGEL, K., SEVERINGHAUS, J. W., AND MUNSON, E., 1965, The influence of temperature and pH on the dissociation curve of oxyhemoglobin of human blood, *Scand. J. Clin. Lab. Invest.* **17**:515–523.
12. BARCROFT, J., 1928, *The Respiratory Function of the Blood, Part II: Haemoglobin,* Cambridge University Press, Oxford.
13. BARTELS, H., 1959, Chemical factors affecting oxygen carriage and transfer from maternal to foetal blood, in: *Oxygen Supply to the Human Foetus,* Blackwell, Scientific Publications, Oxford.
14. BARTELS, H., AND WULF, H., 1965, Physiologie des Gasaustausches in der Placenta des Menschen, in: *Fortschritte der Pädologie* (F. Linneweh, ed.), pp. 124–146, Springer-Verlag, Berlin–Heidelberg–New York.
15. BATTAGLIA, F. C., BOWES, W., McGAUGHEY, H. R. MAKOWSKI, E. L., AND MESCHIA, G., 1969, The effect of fetal exchange transfusions with adult blood upon fetal oxygenation, *Pediatr. Res.* **3**:60–65.
16. BATTAGLIA, F. C., McGAUGHEY, H., MAKOWSKI, E. L., AND MESCHIA, G., 1970, Postnatal changes in oxygen affinity of sheep red cells: A dual role of diphosphoglyceric acid, *Amer. J. Physiol.* **219**:217–221.
17. BAUER, C., 1969, Antagonistic influence of CO_2 and 2,3-diphosphoglycerate on the Bohr effect of human haemoglobin, *Life Sci.* **8**:1041–1046.
18. BAUER, C., 1974, On the respiratory function of haemoglobin, *Rev. Physiol. Biochem. Pharmacol.* **70**:1–31.
19. BAUER, C., AND SCHRÖDER, E., 1972, Carbamino compounds of haemoglobin in human adult and foetal blood, *J. Physiol. (London)* **227**:457–471.
20. BAUER, C., LUDWIG, M., LUDWIG, I., AND BARTELS, H., 1969, Factors governing the oxygen affinity of

human adult and foetal blood, *Respir. Physiol.* **7**:271–277.

21. BELLINGHAM, A. J., 1974, The red cell in adaptation to anaemic hypoxia, *Clin. Haematol.* **3**:577–594.

22. BELLINGHAM, A. J., DETTER, J. C., AND LENFANT, C., 1971, Regulatory mechanisms of hemoglobin oxygen affinity in acidosis and alkalosis, *J. Clin. Invest.* **50**:700–706.

23. BENESCH, R., AND BENESCH, R. E., 1967, The effect of organic phosphates from the human erythrocyte on the allosteric properties of hemoglobin, *Biochem. Biophys. Res. Commun.* **26**:162–167.

24. BETKE, K., 1958, Hämatologie der ersten Lebenszeit, *Ergebn. Inn. Med. Kinderheilkd. N.F.* **9**:437–509.

25. BETKE, K., AND RAU, H., 1952, Zur Frage der Neigung junger Säuglinge an Methämoglobinämie zu erkranken, *Arch. Kinderheilkd.* **145**:195–202.

29. BEUTLER, E., AND WOOD, L., 1969, The *in vivo* regeneration of red cell 2,3-diphosphoglyceric acid (DPG) after transfusion of stored blood, *J. Lab. Clin. Med.* **74**:300–304.

27. BOHR, C., HASSELBALCH, K., AND KROGH, A., 1904, Über einen in biologischer Beziehung wichtigen Einfluss, den die Kohlensäurespannung des Blutes auf dessen Sauerstoffbindung übt, *Scand. Arch. Physiol.* **16**:402–412.

28. BRAUNITZER, G., HILSE, K., RUDLOFF, V., AND HILSCHMANN, N., 1964, The hemoglobins, *Adv. Protein Chem.* **19**:1–71.

29. BUNN, F. H., AND BRIEHL, R. W., 1970, The interaction of 2,3-diphosphoglycerate with various human hemoglobins, *J. Clin. Invest.* **49**:1088–1095.

30. BURMAN, D., AND MORRIS, A. F., 1974, Cord haemoglobin in low birthweight infants, *Arch. Dis. Child.* **49**:382–385.

31. BURSAUX, E., FREMINET, A., BROSSARD, Y., AND POYART, C. F., 1973, Exchange transfusion in the neonate with ACD or CPD stored blood, *Biol. Neonate* **23**:123–132.

32. CHANUTIN, A., AND CURNISH, R. R., 1967, Effect of organic and inorganic phosphate on the oxygen equilibrium of human erythrocytes, *Arch. Biochem. Biophys.* **121**:96–102.

33. CHILLAR, R. K., AND DESFORGES, J. F., 1974, Red-cell organic phosphates in patients with chronic renal failure on maintenance haemodialysis, *Brit. J. Haematol.* **26**:549–556.

34. CHRISTIANSEN, J., DOUGLAS, C. G., AND HALDINE, J. S., 1914, The absorption and dissociation of carbon dioxide by human blood, *J. Physiol. (London)* **48**:244–271.

35. CLAUVEL, M., AND SCHWARTZ, K., 1968, Blood oxygen capacity, *Clin. Chem.* **14**:253–261.

36. COBURN, R. F., FORSTER, R. E., AND KANE, P. B., 1965, Considerations of the physiological variables that determine the blood carboxyhemoglobin concentration in man, *J. Clin. Invest.* **44**:1899–1910.

37. COBURN, R. F., WILLIAMS, W. J., AND KAHN, S. B., 1966, Endogenous carbon monoxide production in patients with hemolytic anemia, *J. Clin. Invest.* **45**:460–468.

38. CORNET, A., AND BARD, H., 1975, Changes in hemoglobin oxygen affinity in relation to gestational age, *Pediatr. Res.* **9**:276.

39. DELIVORIA-PAPADOPOULOS, M., MILLER, L. D., TUNNESSEN, W. W., AND OSKI, F. A., 1972, The effect of exchange transfusion on altering mortality in infants weighing less than 1300 gm at birth and its role in the management of severe respiratory distress syndrome, *Proc. Soc. Pediatr. Res.* **6**:82.

40. DELIVORIA-PAPADOPOULOS, M., MORROW, G., AND OSKI, F. A., 1971, Exchange transfusion in the newborn infant with fresh and "old" blood: The role of storage on 2,3-diphosphoglycerate, hemoglobin–oxygen affinity, and oxygen release, *J. Pediatr.* **79**:898–903.

41. DELIVORIA-PAPADOPOULOS, M., OSKI, F. A., AND GOTTLIEB, A. J., 1969, Oxygen–hemoglobin dissociation curves: Effect of inherited enzyme defects of the red cell, *Science* **165**:601–602.

42. DELIVORIA-PAPADOPOULOS, M., RONCEVIC, N. P., AND OSKI, F. A., 1971, Postnatal changes on oxygen transport of term, preterm, and sick infants: The role of red cell 2,3-diphosphoglycerate and adult hemoglobin, *Pediatr. Res.* **5**:235–245.

43. DUC, G., AND ENGEL, K., 1969, Effect of 2,3-DPG concentration on hemoglobin–oxygen affinity of whole blood, *Scand. J. Clin. Lab. Invest.* **24**:405–412.

44. DUC, G., AND ENGEL, K., 1971, Hemoglobin–oxygen affinity and erythrocyte 2,3-diphosphoglycerate content in hyaline-membrane disease and cardiac malformations, in: *Perinatal Medicine* (P. J. Huntingford, R. W. Beard, F. E. Hytten, and J. W. Scopes, eds.), pp. 266–268, S. Karger, Basel–München–Paris–London–New York–Sydney.

45. DUHM, J., 1971, Effects of 2,3-diphosphoglycerate and other organic phosphate compounds on oxygen affinity and intracellular pH of human erythrocytes, *Pfluegers Arch.* **326**:341–356.

46. DUHM, J., DEUTICKE, B., AND GERLACH, E., 1969, Abhängigkeit der 2,3-Diphosphoglyzerinsäure-Synthese in Menschen-Erythrozyten von der ADP-Konzentration, *Pfluegers Arch.* **306**:329–335.

47. EDWARDS, M. J., AND CANON, B., 1972, Normal levels of 2,3-diphosphoglycerate in red cells despite severe hypoxemia of chronic lung disease, *Chest* **61**:25s.

48. EDWARDS, M. J., CANON, B., ALBERTSON, J., AND BIGHLEY, R. H., 1971, Decreased blood O_2 affinity because of young red cells, *Clin. Res.* **19**:179.

49. EDWARDS, M. J., NOVY, M. J., WALTERS, C. L., AND METCALF, J., 1968, Improved oxygen release: An adaptation of mature red cells to hypoxia, *J. Clin. Invest.* **47**:1851–1857.

50. ENGEL, R. R., RODKEY, F. L., AND KRILL, C. E., 1971, Carboxyhemoglobin levels as an index of hemolysis, Pediatrics 47:723–730.

51. FÄLLSTRÖM, S. P., 1968, On the Endogenous Formation of Carbon Monoxide in Full-Term Newborn Infants, Elanders Boktr. Akt., Göteborg.

52. FINNE, P. H., AND HALVORSEN, S., 1972, Regulation of erythropoiesis in the fetus and newborn, Arch. Dis. Child. 47:683–687.

53. FLOD, N. E., AND ACKERMAN, B. D., 1971, Perinatal asphyxia and residual placental blood volume, Acta Paediatr. Scand. 60:433–436.

54. GARBY, L. (ed.), 1974, Anaemia and hypoxia, Clin. Haematol. 3(3).

55. GARBY, L., ROBERT, M., AND ZAAR, B., 1972, Proton- and carbamino-linked oxygen affinity of normal human blood, Acta Physiol. Scand. 84:482–492.

56. GORSHEIN, D., DELIVORIA-PAPADOPOULOS, M., OSKI, F. A., AND GARDNER, F. H., 1972, The effect of androgen administration on erythrocyte 2,3-diphosphoglycerate level and hemoglobin oxygen affinity in primates, Clin. Res. 20:487.

57. GRAUEL, E., 1973, Zur Reifung und Alterung von Erythrozyten im I. Trimenon nach der Gubert, Habilitationsschrift, Berlin.

58. HAIDAS, S., LABIE, D., AND KAPLAN, J. C., 1971, 2,3-Diphosphoglycerate content and oxygen affinity as a function of red cell age in normal individuals, Blood 38:201–207.

59. HARMS, H., AND BARTELS, H., 1961, CO_2-Dissoziationskurven des menschlichen Blutes bei Temperaturen von 5–37°C bei unterschiedlicher O_2-Sättigung, Pfluegers Arch. 272:384–392.

60. HELLEGERS, A. E., MESCHIA, G., PRYSTOWSKY, H., WOKOFF, A. S., AND BARRON, D. H., 1959, A comparison of the oxygen dissociation curves of the blood of maternal and fetal goats at various pHs, Q. J. Exp. Physiol. 44:215–221.

61. HILL, A. V., 1910, The possible effects of the aggregation of the molecules of haemoglobin on its dissociation curves, J. Physiol. (London) 40:IV–VII.

62. HILL, E. P., POWER, G. G., AND LONGO, L. D., 1973, A mathematical model of carbon dioxide transfer in the placenta and its interaction with oxygen, Amer. J. Physiol. 224:283–299.

63. HJELM, H., 1969, The content of 2,3-diphosphoglycerate and some other phosphocompounds in human erythrocytes during the neonatal period, Försvarsmedicin 5:195–198.

64. JOLY, J. B., BLAYO, M. C., AND GAUDEBOUT, C., 1972, Intérêt séméiologique et prognostique de la P_{50} chez les nouveaunés de moins de 48 heures en détresses vitale, Bull. Physio-Pathol. Respir. 8:1323–1338.

65. KEYS, A. F., HALL, G., AND GUZMAN BARRON, E. S., 1936, The position of the oxygen dissociation curve of human blood at high altitude, Amer. J. Physiol. 115:292–307.

66. KILMARTIN, J. V., AND ROSSI-BERNARDI, L., 1973, The interaction of hemoglobin with hydrogen ions, carbon dioxide, and organic phosphates, Physiol. Rev. 53:836–922.

67. KIRSCHBAUM, T. H., DeHAVEN, J. C., SHAPIRO, N., AND ASSALI, N. S., 1966, Oxyhemoglobin dissociation characteristics of human and sheep maternal and fetal blood, Amer. J. Obstet. Gynecol. 96:741–759.

68. KLEIHAUER, E., 1966, Fetales Hämoglobin und fetale Erythrocyten, F. Enke, Stuttgart.

69. KLEINMAN, L. I., PETERING, H. G., AND SUTHERLAND, J. M., 1967, Blood carbonic anhydrase activity and zinc concentration in infants with respiratory-distress syndrome, N. Engl. J. Med. 277:1157–1161.

70. KRAVITZ, H., ELEGANT, L. D., KAISER, E., AND KAGAN, B. M., 1956, Methemoglobin values in premature and mature infants and children, Amer. J. Dis. Child.. 91:1–5.

71. KREUZER, F., ROUGHTON, F. J. W., ROSSI-BERNARDI, L., AND KERNOHAN, J. C., 1972, Specific effect of CO_2 and bicarbonate on the affinity of hemoglobin for oxygen, in: Oxygen Affinity of Hemoglobin and Red Cell Acid–Base Status (M. Rørth and P. Astrup, eds.), pp. 208–218, Munksgaard, Copenhagen.

72. LEHMANN, H., AND HUNTSMAN, R. G., 1974, Man's Haemoglobins, 3rd Ed., North-Holland Publ. Co., Amsterdam and Oxford.

73. LEHMANN, V., 1969, Individuelle Sauerstoff-Bindungskurven und Säure–Basen-Status des mütterlichen und fetalen Blutes zum Zeitpunkt der Geburt, Z. Gebhilfe Gynaekol. 170:14–21.

74. LEHMANN, V., 1970, Die O_2-Affinität des fetalen Blutes zu Beginn der Eröffnungsperiode, Arch. Gynaekol. 209:215–221.

75. LONGO, L. D., AND BARTELS, H. (eds.), 1972, Respiratory Gas Exchange and Blood Flow in the Placenta, U.S. Department of Health, Education and Welfare, Bethesda, Maryland.

76. MAISELS, M. J., PATHAK, A., NELSON, N. M., NATHAN, D. G., AND SMITH, C. A., 1971, Endogenous production of carbon monoxide in normal and erythroblastotic newborn infants, J. Clin. Invest. 50:1–8.

77. MANZKE, H., AND DÖRNER, K., 1973, Bohr effect, 2,3-DPG and ATP concentrations in the blood of premature infants with RDS, Biol. Neonate 22:141–154.

78. McCARTHY, E. F., 1943, The oxygen affinity of human maternal and foetal haemoglobin, J. Physiol. (London) 102:55–61.

79. MELDON, J. H., AND GARBY, L., 1975, The blood oxygen transport system, Acta Med. Scand. Suppl. 578:19–29.

80. METCALFE, J., DHINDSA, D. S., EDWARDS, M. J., AND MOURDJINIS, A., 1969, Decreased affinity of

blood for oxygen in patients with low-output heart failure, *Circ. Res.* **25**:47–56.

81. MILLER, M. F., RØRTH, M., PARVING, H. H., HOWARD, D., REDDINGTON, I., VALERI, C. R., AND STOHLMAN, F., 1973, pH Effect on erythropoietin response to hypoxia, *N. Engl. J. Med.* **288**:706–710.

82. MILLER, W. W., DELIVORIA-PAPADOPOULOS, M., MILLER, L. D., AND OSKI, F., 1970, Increased release of oxygen from hemoglobin in hyperthyroidism. Control by red cell 2,3-diphosphoglycerate, *J. Amer. Med. Assoc.* **211**:1824.

83. MORROW, J. S., KEIM, P., VISSCHER, R. B., MARSHALL, R. C., AND GURD, F. R. N., 1973, Interaction of $^{13}CO_2$ and bicarbonate with human hemoglobin preparations, *Proc. Natl. Acad. Sci. U.S.A.* **70**:1414–1418.

84. NOVY, M. J., AND PARER, J. T., 1969, Absence of high blood oxygen affinity in the fetal cat, *Respir. Physiol.* **6**:144–150.

85. NOVY, M. J., EDWARDS, M. J., AND METCALF, J., 1967, Hemoglobin Yakima. II. High blood oxygen affinity associated with compensatory erythrocytosis and normal hemodynamics, *J. Clin. Invest.* **46**:1848–1854.

86. NOVY, M. J., FRIGOLETTO, F. D., EASTERDAY, C. L., UMANSKY, I., AND NELSON, N. M., 1971, Changes in umbilical-cord blood oxygen affinity after intrauterine transfusions for erythroblastosis, *N. Engl. J. Med.* **285**:589–595.

87. ORZALESI, M. M., AND HAY, W. W., 1971, The regulation of oxygen affinity of fetal blood. I. *In vitro* experiments and results in normal infants, *Pediatrics* **48**:857–864.

88. ORZALESI, M. M., AND HAY, W. W., 1972, The relative effect of 2,3-diphosphoglycerate on the oxygen affinity of fetal and adult hemoglobin in whole blood, *Experientia* **28**:1480, 1481.

89. ORZALESI, M. M., AND HAY, W. W., 1975, The effect of intrauterine anemia on the oxygen affinity of fetal blood, *Pediatr. Res.* **9**:369.

90. OSKI, F. A., 1972, Fetal hemoglobin, the neonatal red cell, and 2,3-diphosphoglycerate, *Pediatr. Clin. North Amer.* **19**:907–917.

91. OSKI, F. A., AND DELIVORIA-PAPADOPOULOS, M., 1970, The red cell, 2,3-diphosphoglycerate, and tissue oxygen release, *J. Pediatr.* **77**:941–956.

92. OSKI, F. A., GOTTLIEB, A. J., MILLER, W. W., AND DELIVORIA-PAPADOPOULOS, M., 1970, The effect of deoxygenation of adult and fetal hemoglobin on the synthesis of red cell 2,3-DPG and its *in vivo* consequences, *J. Clin. Invest.* **49**:400–407.

93. OSKI, F. A., MILLER, L. D., DELIVORIA-PAPADO-POULOS, M., MANCHESTER, J. H., AND SHELBURNE, J. C., 1972, Oxygen affinity in red cells: Changes induced *in vivo* by propranolol, *Science* **175**:1372–1374.

94. OSKI, F. A., SUGERMAN, H. D., AND MILLER, L. D.,

1972, Experimentally induced alterations in the affinity of hemoglobin for oxygen. I. *In vitro* restoration of erythrocyte 2,3-diphosphoglycerate and its relationship to erythrocyte purine nucleoside phosphorylase activity in a variety of species, *Blood* **39**:522–525.

95. OSKI, F. A., TRAVIS, S. F., MILLER, L. D., DELIVORIA-PAPADOPOULOS, M., AND CANNON, E., 1971, The *in vitro* restoration of red cell 2,3-diphosphoglycerate levels in banked blood, *Blood* **37**:52–57.

96. OSTREA, E. M., AND ODELL, G. B., 1974, Photosensitized shift in the O_2 dissociation curve of fetal blood, *Acta Paediatr. Scand.* **63**:341–346.

97. PANTLITSCHKO, M., ROBERG, E., WEIPPL, G., AND BAUER, P., 1970, Normalwerte und Verteilung von Hämoglobin beim Neugeborenen, *Wien. Klin. Wochenschr.* **82**:785–787.

98. PARER, J. T., 1970, Oxygen transport in human subjects with hemoglobin variants having altered oxygen affinity, *Respir. Physiol.* **9**:43–49.

99. PARKER, J. P., BEIRNE, G. J., DESAI, J. N., RAICH, P. C., AND SHAHIDI, N. T., 1972, Androgen induced increase in red cell 2,3-diphosphoglycerate, *N. Engl. J. Med.* **287**:381–383.

100. PENDLETON, R. G., NEWMAN, D.-J., SHERMAN, S. S., BRANN, E. G., AND MAYA, W. E., 1972, Effect of propranolol upon the hemoglobin–oxygen dissociation curve, *J. Pharmacol. Exp. Ther.* **180**:647–651.

101. PERUTZ, M. F., 1970, Stereochemistry of cooperative effects in haemoglobin, *Nature (London)* **228**:726–739.

102. PERUTZ, M. F., 1972, Nature of haem–haem interaction, *Nature (London)* **237**:495–499.

103. PETRICH, C., GEMPP-FRIEDRICH, W., AND GÖBEL, U., 1973, Comparative measurements of enzyme activities and 2,3-diphosphoglycerate in the erythrocytes of newborns with and without transitory hyperbilirubinaemia, *Acta Paediatr. Scand.* **62**:596–600.

104. PETRICH, C., GÖBEL, U., AND BLANKE, H., 1974, Position of the oxygen dissociation curve in newborns with transitory hyperbilirubinaemia, *Biol. Neonate* **24**:89–93.

105. RAPOPORT, S., AND GUEST, G. M., 1941, Distribution of acid-soluble phosphorus in the blood cells of various vertebrates, *J. Biol. Chem.* **138**:269–282.

106. RIEGEL, K., 1965, Die Atemgas-Transportgrößen des Blutes im Kindesalter, in: *Fortschritte der Pädologie* (F. Linneweh, ed.), pp. 147–154, Springer-Verlag, Berlin—Heidelberg—New York.

107. RIEGEL, K. P., 1970, Respiratory gas transport characteristics of blood and hemoglobin, in: *Physiology of the Neonatal Period* (U. Stave, ed.), pp. 299–321, Appleton-Century-Crofts, New York.

108. RIEGEL, K., 1977, unpublished data.

109. RIEGEL, K. P., AND VERSMOLD, H., 1973, Postnatal blood oxygen transport, with special respect to idiopathic respiratory distress syndrome, *Bull. Physio-Pathol. Respir.* **9**:1533–1548.

110. RIGGS, A., 1965, Functional properties of hemoglobin, *Physiol. Rev.* **45**:619–673.

111. RODRIGUEZ, J. M., AND SHAHIDI, N. T., 1971, Erythrocyte 2,3-DPG in adaptive red-cell-volume deficiency, *N. Engl. J. Med.* **285**:479–482.

112. RÖRTH, M., 1970, Dependency on acid–base status of blood of oxyhemoglobin dissociation and 2,3-DPG level in human erythrocytes. I. *In vitro* studies on reduced and oxygenated blood, *Scand. J. Clin. Lab. Invest.* **26**:43–46.

113. RØRTH, M., 1974, Hypoxia, red cell oxygen affinity and erythropoietin production, *Clin. Haematol.* **3**:595–607.

114. RØRTH, M., AND ASTRUP, P. (eds.), 1972, Oxygen affinity of hemoglobin and red cell acid base status, Munksgaard, Copenhagen, and Academic Press, New York.

115. ROSENTHAL, A., MENTZER, W. C., EISENSTEIN, E. B., NATHAN, D. G., NELSON, N. M., AND NADAS, A. S., 1971, The role of red cell organic phosphates in adaptation to congenital heart disease, *Pediatrics* **47**:537–543.

116. ROUGHTON, F. J. W., 1964, Transport of oxygen and carbon dioxide, in: *Handbook of Physiology*, Section 3, *Respiration I* (W. O. Fenn and H. Rahn, eds.), pp. 767–826, American Physiological Society, Washington, D.C.

117. RUBENSTEIN, S. D., STARK, A. R., AND DELIVORIA-PAPADOPOULOS, M., 1975, Effect of exchange transfusion with fresh "settled" red blood cells on tissue oxygen transport of low birth weight infants, *Pediatr. Res.* **9**:326.

118. SCHETTINI, F., MAUTONE, A., AND DELUCA, I., 1975, 2,3-Diphosphoglycerate and hydrogen-ion concentration in erythrocytes from full-term newborn infants, *Riv. Ital. Pediatr. (I.J.P.)* **1**:11–16.

119. SCHROEDER, W. A., 1963, The hemoglobins, *Annu. Rev. Biochem.* **32**:301–320.

120. SHAPPELL, S. D., AND LENFANT, C. J. M., 1972, Adaptive, genetic, and iatrogenic alterations of the oxyhemoglobin-dissociation curve, *Anesthesiology* **37**:127–139.

121. SIGGAARD-ANDERSEN, O., SALLING, N., NÖRGAARD, B., AND RØRTH, M., 1972, Oxygen-linked hydrogen binding of human hemoglobin. Effects of carbon dioxide and 2,3-diphosphoglycerate. III. Comparison of the Bohr effect and the Haldane effect, *Scand. J. Clin. Invest.* **29**:185–193.

122. SNYDER, L. M., AND REDDY, W. J., 1970, Mechanism of action of thyroid hormones on erythrocyte 2,3-diphosphoglyceric acid synthesis, *J. Clin. Invest.* **49**:1993–1998.

123. STAMATOYANNOPOULOS, G., PARER, J. T., AND FINCH, C. A., 1969, Implications of a hemoglobin with decreased oxygen affinity, *N. Engl. J. Med.* **281**:915–919.

124. STOCKMAN, J. A., 1975, Anemia of prematurity, *Semin. Hematol.* **12**:163–173.

125. STRUMIA, M. M., AND STRUMIA, P. V., 1972, Conditions affecting the maintenance of adenosine triphosphate, 2,3-diphosphoglycerate and oxygen dissociation by addition of adenine and inosine to blood stored at 1°C, *Transfusion* **12**:68–74.

126. THOMAS, H. M., LEFRAK, S. S., IRWIN, R. 'S., FRITTS, H. W., AND CALDWELL, P. R. B., 1974, The oxyhemoglobin dissociation curve in health and disease, *Amer. J. Med.* **57**:331–348.

127. THOMPSON, R. B., WARRINGTON, R. L., AND BELL, W. N., 1965, Physiologic differences in hemoglobin variants, *Amer. J. Physiol.* **208**:198–202.

128. TRAVIS, S. F., SUGERMAN, H. J., RUBERG, R. L., DUDRICK, S. J., DELIVORIA-PAPADOPOULOS, M., MILLER, L. D., AND OSKI, F. A., 1971, Alterations of red cell glycolytic intermediates and oxygen transport as a consequence of hypophosphatemia in patients receiving intravenous hyperalimentation, *N. Engl. J. Med.* **285**:763–768.

129. TUREK, Z., KREUZER, F., AND HOOFD, L. J. C., 1973, Advantage or disadvantage of a decrease of blood oxygen affinity for tissue oxygen supply at hypoxia, *Pfluegers Arch.* **342**:185–208.

130. TYUMA, I., AND SHIMIZU, K., 1970, Effect of organic phosphates on the difference in oxygen affinity between fetal and adult human hemoglobin, *Fed. Proc. Fed. Amer. Soc. Exp. Biol.* **29**:1112–1114.

131. USHER, R. H., SAIGAL, S., O'NEILL, A., SURAINDER, Y., AND CHUA, L.-B., 1975, Estimation of red blood cell volume in premature infants with and without respiratory distress syndrome, *Biol. Neonate* **26**:241–248.

132. VALERI, C. R., 1971, Viability and function of preserved red cells, *N. Engl. J. Med.* **284**:81–88.

133. VALERI, C. R., 1974, Oxygen transport function of preserved red cells, *Clin. Haematol.* **3**:649–688.

134. VALTIS, D. J., AND KENNEDY, A. C., 1953, The causes and prevention of defective function of stored red blood cells after transfusion, *Glasgow Med. J.* **34**:521–543.

135. VERDIER, C. H. DE, AND GARBY, L., 1969, Low binding of 2,3-diphosphoglycerate to haemoglobin F. A contribution to the knowledge of the binding site and an explanation for the high oxygen affinity of foetal blood, *Scand. Clin. Lab. Invest.* **23**:149–151.

136. VERSMOLD, H., AND BRAUSER, B., 1973, Improved cellular oxygenation by 2,3-diphosphoglycerate: Quantitative measurement of tissue hypoxia by registration of absorption spectra of cytochrome a and hemoglobin in the intact organ, in: *Metabolism and Membrane Permeability of Erythrocytes, Thrombocytes and Leukocytes* (E. Gerlach, K. Moser, W. Wilmanns, and E. Deutsch, eds.), pp. 170 and 171, Georg Thieme, Stuttgart.

137. VERSMOLD, H. T., FÜRST, K., AND RIEGEL, K. P., 1974, Influence of 2,3-diphosphoglycerate on the oxygen affinity of partially autoxidized hemoglobins A_1 and F, *Pediatr. Res.* **8**:140 (abstract).

138. VERSMOLD, H., HORN, K., WINDTHORST, H., AND RIEGEL, K. P., 1973, The rapid postnatal increase of red cell 2,3-diphosphoglycerate: Its relation to plasma thyroxine, *Respir. Physiol.* **18**:26–33.

139. VERSMOLD, H. T., LINDERKAMP, O., DÖHLEMANN, C., AND RIEGEL, K. P., 1976, Oxygen transport in congenital heart disease: Influence of fetal hemoglobin, red cell pH and 2,3-DPG, *Pediatr. Res.* **10**:566–570.

140. VERSMOLD, H., SEIFERT, G., AND RIEGEL, K. P., 1973, Blood oxygen affinity in infancy: The interaction of fetal and adult hemoglobin, oxygen capacity, and red cell hydrogen ion and 2,3-diphosphoglycerate concentration, *Respir. Physiol.* **18**:14–25.

141. VERSMOLD, H., WENNER, J., AND RIEGEL, K., 1972, Changes of blood oxygen affinity and capacity and red cell 2,3-diphosphoglycerate evoked by exchange transfusions with ACD preserved blood in newborn infants: Their interrelationship and influences on oxygen supply of tissues and erythropoiesis, *Z. Kinderheilkd.* **113**:1–18.

142. WALKER, J., AND TURNBULL, E. P. N., 1953, Haemoglobin and red cells in the human foetus and their relation to the oxygen content of the blood in the vessels of the umbilical cord, *Lancet* **2**:312–318.

143. WOODSON, R. D., 1974, Red cell adaptation in cardiorespiratory disease, *Clin. Haematol.* **3**:627–648.

144. WOODSON, R. D., TORRANCE, J. D., SHAPPELL, S. D., AND LENFANT, C., 1970, The effect of cardiac disease on hemoglobin oxygen binding, *J. Clin. Invest.* **49**:1349–1356.

145. WRANNE, B., WOODSON, R. D., AND DETTER, J. C., 1972, Bohr effect: Interaction between H^+, CO_2, and 2,3-DPG in fresh and stored blood, *J. Appl. Physiol.* **32**:749–754.

146. WYMAN, J., 1948, Heme proteins, *Adv. Protein Chem.* **4**:407–531.

147. YAO, A. C., LIND, J., TIISALA, R., AND MICHELSSON, K., 1969, Placental transfusion in the premature infant with observation on clinical course and outcome, *Acta Paediatr. Scand.* **58**:561–566.

148. YLPPÖ, A., 1916, Neugeborenen-, Hunger- und Intoxikations-acidosis in ihren Beziehungen zueinander, *Z. Kinderheilkd.* **14**:268–448.

CHAPTER 13

Blood Coagulation Factors and Fibrinolysis

Leonard E. Reisman

1. Introduction

This chapter will review the features of blood coagulation and fibrinolysis in the prenatal period, the coverage being confined to the involvement of the plasma clotting factors.

Certainly, in the past, the evaluation of hemostasis in the newborn has been especially difficult because of a lack of understanding of the normal hemostatic mechanisms in the adult, as well as in infancy. It is obvious that quantitatively, as well as qualitatively, hemostasis in the prenate differs from that in the older person. It is important, however, that the pathophysiology of the "normal" clotting mechanism be fully understood. This review will therefore begin with a discussion of the various plasma factors involved in clotting and an effort to familiarize the reader with the current state of knowledge about the blood-clotting mechanism. There will be a sum-

Leonard E. Reisman · Departments of Pathology and Pediatrics, Jefferson Medical College, Philadelphia, Pennsylvania 19107

mary of the outstanding features of blood coagulation in the fetus and neonate and the alterations in hemostasis, followed by an evaluation of transitory hemorrhagic and fibrinolytic disorders resulting from the special circumstances of perinatal coagulation physiology.

Although our knowledge of the normal (and abnormal) coagulation mechanisms in the perinatal period admittedly remains incomplete, sufficient data are available to allow comprehension of many of the hemorrhagic and thrombotic phenomena in the newborn.

2. Current Concepts of the Mechanism of Hemostasis

For adequate comprehension of the subject of the plasma coagulation and fibrinolytic factors of the perinatal period, it is reasonable to discuss first the current concepts of the hemostatic mechanism. This mechanism has been defined as the sum total of

Table I. Nomenclature and Synonyms for the Blood Coagulation Factors

Factor	Synonyms and abbreviations
I	Fibrinogen
II	Prothrombin, prethrombin
III	Tissue factor, tissue thromboplastin
IV	Calcium
V	Proaccelerin, labile factor, Ac globulin
(VI)	Not assigned
VII	Procon vertin, SPCA, stable factor, autoprothrombin I
VIII	Antihemophilic globulin (AHG), antihemophilic factor (AHF), antihemophilic factor A, platelet cofactor I
IX	Plasma thromboplastin component (PTC), Christmas factor, antihemophilic factor B, autoprothrombin II, platelet cofactor II
X	Stuart–Prower factor, Stuart factor, autoprothrombin III, thrombokinase
XI	Plasma thromboplastin antecedent (PTA), antihemophilic factor C
XII	Hageman factor
XIII	Fibrin stabilizing factor, fibrinase, Laki–Lorand factor, plasma transglutaminase

those forces that control the formation and disposition of blood clots. Along with the other primary components of the hemostatic process (platelets and blood vessels), the plasma factors interact to ensure orderly coagulation and fibrinolysis. Table I lists the plasma coagulation factors, including the numerical nomenclature and synonyms utilized in the past.

The substance and strength of the blood clot lie in the physical nature of the fibrin polymer that is formed as the end product of the intricate and complex series of sequential reactions by these factors.[12,19] Each of the clotting factors acts as a specific amplifying enzyme directed at the final conversion of soluble fibrinogen to an insoluble, gelatinous coagulum of fibrin. The classic cascade or waterfall hypothesis of blood coagulation envisions clotting as occurring physiologically via one of two convergent pathways, with each of the clotting factors existing in an inactive (proenzyme or procoagulant) and an activated state (Fig. 1). The activated form of one factor specifically activates the next in a sequential series—with progressive amplification—culminating in the formation of a fibrin clot. This bimodal pathway of interacting circulating enzymes can be interrupted by a deficiency or depletion of one of the sequential blood factors, or it can be inhibited by antibodies or anticoagulant substances.

It might be worthwhile to review briefly the cascade scheme and the succession of enzymatic events that take place.

2.1. The Coagulation Mechanism

The intrinsic pathway of thrombus formation—referring to clotting inside the vascular system—is relatively slow in comparison with the extrinsic pathway because of the lack of tissue thromboplastin in this sequence of events. This slowness is reflected in the relatively long clotting time of blood.

The first phase involves the surface activation of factor XII (Hageman factor) when plasma, depleted of cells, comes into contact with a foreign surface, such as glass, bentonite, or kaolin. Activated XII brings about, successively, the activation of factors XI and IX. Activated IX, or potent procoagulant, participates with factor VIII to form a complex (along with platelet phospholipid and calcium ions).

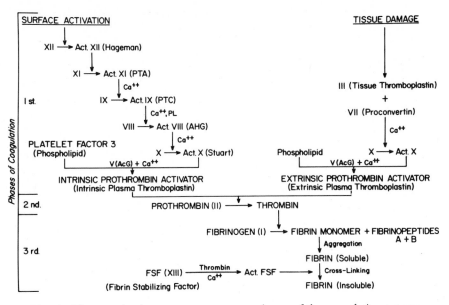

Fig. 1. The cascade phenomenon: a current scheme of the coagulation process. Reproduced from Oski and Naiman.[24]

This "factor VIII complex" is aided by the presence of small quantities of thrombin, and itself generates an agent that transforms factor X (Stuart factor) to an activated form. The interaction of activated X with factor V, phospholipids, and calcium ions forms a "prothrombinase" that releases thrombin from prothrombin.

The formation of extrinsic activator follows a more rapid pathway, generating thrombin in a matter of seconds. This extrinsic pathway—referring to clotting outside the vascular system—is the sequence believed to occur when plasma comes into contact with tissue thromboplastin. The initial contact phases of the intrinsic pathway are bypassed, since tissue thromboplastin (factor III) and factor VII interact to form a complex that converts factor X directly to its activated form. From this point, the final common pathway of both sequences is identical, converting prothrombin to thrombin.

Once the active enzyme, prothrombin, is released, it cleaves fibrinogen into fibrinopeptides and fibrin monomers, and so changes factor XIII that it can bind adjacent fibrin strands together by strong cross-linking chemical bonds. The fibrin monome and fibrinopeptides are polymerized to insoluble fibrin, a process that is certainly the essence of blood-clotting. Thrombin also apparently engages in a "positive feedback" by increasing platelet aggrega-

tion and aiding in the formation of the factor VIII complex.

It is important to recognize that there appear to be plasma inhibitors for each activation stage in the clotting mechanism that has been outlined. The most clearly identified of these naturally occurring inhibitors are the antithrombins.

2.2. Fibrinolysis

The fibrinolytic system provides a means whereby fibrin clots can be removed from the vascular system. The significance of fibrinolysis in the prevention of thrombosis is obvious. The normal fibrinolytic system is diagrammed schematically in Fig. 2.

Plasminogen is the inactive precursor of plasma that is normally found in plasma. It is activated to plasmin by the action of certain factors that are found in plasma, urine, and tissue. Plasmin, once formed, is a proteolytic enzyme, capable of hydrolyzing other substances, lysing fibrin clots by splitting arginine and lysine bonds. Plasma can also attack fibrinogen and factors V and VIII.

Just as previously mentioned in the discussion of the coagulation mechanism, the fibrinolytic system is also held in check by a series of natural inhibitors—in this case, inhibitors of plasminogen

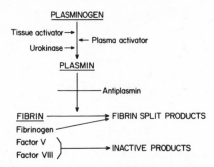

Fig. 2. Activation mechanism of the fibrinolytic system. Reproduced from Oski and Naiman.[24]

activators and of plasma. Thus, both the coagulation mechanism and the fibrinolytic system—in adults as well as in neonates—are normally held in a state of dynamic equilibrium.

3. Coagulation Factors and Fibrinolysis in the Fetus

The clotting factors are generally of high molecular weight (32,000–1,200,000) and have low diffusion constants. Evidence strongly indicates a failure of transport of the clotting factors across the placenta. There is no correlation between fetal and maternal clotting factor activities, except possibly for factors IX and XIII.[8] For example, despite marked factor deficiency in the perinate in the hereditary defects hemophilia and afibrinogenemia, substantial factor activity is always present in the mother. In the absence of placental transport, when clotting factor activity can be demonstrated in the fetus, it must reflect fetal synthesis.

Bleyer *et al.*[6] traced the development of hemostasis in the human fetus during intrauterine development (Fig. 3). Blood from embryos and fetuses less than 60–70 mm in crown–rump length (10–11 weeks' gestational age) does not clot.[32] For this time, the whole blood clotting time promptly decreases to adult value during the remainder of fetal life. Fetuses up to 22 weeks of age have factor VIII and IX levels of less than 1%.[13] Fibrinogen, which is synthesized by the liver, is evident as early as 5 weeks' gestation, and reaches substantial levels (100–200 mg/dl) by 15 weeks.[10,31] Factor V reaches adult levels by the same gestational age.[6,23]

Fibrinolytic activity is detectable at 10 or 11 weeks of gestation, and remains active from then on. Studies indicate that the rate of fibrinolysis is linearly proportional to the rate of clotting. Thus, at the time when blood begins to clot, fibrinolysis becomes evident, and then both phases of the hemostatic mechanism apparently parallel each other in future development.[30]

4. Coagulation Factors and Fibrinolysis in the Premature Infant

Investigations of the hemostatic mechanism in preterm infants often show contradictions. These contradictions may be due partly to failure to distinguish between preterm infants and those low-birth-weight infants who are small for gestational age. The results of investigations may also be influenced by such variables as maternal medication, perinatal asphyxia, and type of feeding in the newborn.

"Sick" premature infants, primarily those with respiratory distress syndrome, have lower levels of clotting factors, particularly fibrinogen and factor V. Despite the decreased levels of most clotting factors (with the exception of fibrinogen[8] and factor XIII[4]), the whole blood clotting time in premature infants is accelerated, as measured by the Lee–White clotting time.[6]

The plasma contains low levels of clotting factor activity: factors XI (5–20%),[23] IX (10–25%),[6,22] X (10–45%),[8,22] VII (20–45%),[8] II (20–80%),[8,22] VII (20–80%),[8] and V (65–80%).[15]

Plasminogen levels gradually increase as the preterm infant reaches term. Antiplasmin and activator activities are at full-term levels throughout the later part of gestation.[11] Fibrin degradation products are not normally found in the serum of premature infants.[30]

5. Coagulation Factors and Fibrinolysis in the Full-Term Newborn

5.1. Coagulation Factors

Again, as for "normal" premature infants in comparison with adults, the whole blood clotting time in the full-term newborn is normal or accelerated (leaving some investigators to describe blood from full-term infants as being "hypercoagulable"). Many clotting factors continue to have low activity in the perinatal period, however, and especially during the first few hours and days of

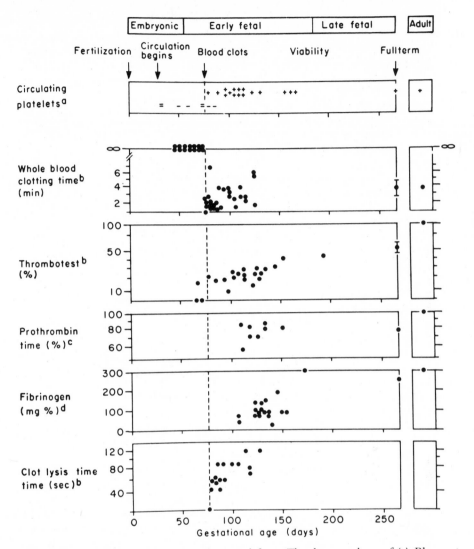

Fig. 3. Hemostasis in the human embryo and fetus. The data are those of (a) Bleyer *et al.,*[6] (b) Zilliacus *et al.,*[32] (c) Vahlquist *et al.,*[31] and (d) Ekelund *et al.*[11] Reproduced from Bleyer *et al.*[6]

life, significant alterations in the coagulation mechanism take place—specifically, the decreases in the vitamin-K-dependent factors.

Factors V and VIII attain adult levels prior to the end of gestation, and are present in the normal adult range in term infants. At birth, the fibrinogen concentration is only slightly less than adult levels (210–250 mg/dl).[6] Despite the almost normal levels of fibrinogen, however, the *in vitro* thrombin time is prolonged (delayed clotting with addition of excess thrombin) in the newborn. The abnormal

thrombin time, which measures the conversion of fibrinogen to fibrin, and is not associated with any clinical coagulation defect, has been attributed to an increased heparin activity during this period, an increased antithrombin activity in neonates, and the existence of a special "fetal" fibrinogen.[14]

In addition to the prolonged thrombin time, newborn fibrinogen apparently differs qualitatively from adult fibrinogen. The fibrin clot formed is characterized by decreased tensile strength, decreased optical density, diminished compressibility, and a higher resistance to fibrinolysis. Even though newborn and adult fibrinogen have the same molecular weight, size, shape, and immunologic properties, column chromatography demonstrates a difference in electrical charge.

The most widely publicized defect of the newborn is the alteration of the prothrombin time, which measures the activity of factors V, VII, and X, as well as that of prothrombin. In general, cord blood values of prothrombin activity are normal, although the prothrombin concentration is consistently low. The cord levels of factors IX, VII, and X are low, and they become increasingly abnormal, along with the prothrombin time, during the first few days of life.[2,6,9,14] The levels of prothrombin and factors VII and X reach minimum values between the second and fourth day; then they begin to rise, approaching normal adult values some time between 2 and 12 months of age. Factor X may fall to from 55 to 45% of normal adult levels, while factor VII falls to 20% by the third day of life (the cord level being 40–70%). Factor IX activity is also decreased in the cord blood and in the newborn.[18]

Brinkhous et al.[7] were the first to describe a decrease in true prothrombin in the neonate (and relate it to hemorrhagic disease). Other workers later demonstrated the connection between this hypoprothrombinemia and vitamin K deficiency.[1,2,28] It is now understood that vitamin K is required for synthesis in the liver of not only prothrombin, but also factors VII, IX, and X (which make up the "prothrombin complex").

As a result of the deficiency of factors IX (20–60%) and X (20–55%), the serum factors involved in the generation of thromboplastic activity (as measured by thromboplastin generation time), a derangement in the first stage of coagulation is evidenced.

The levels of factors XI[17] and XII are also diminished in the newborn, and their low activity may accentuate the abnormal thromboplastin generation. Factor XII attains normal adult levels within 10–14 days after birth, but factor XI reaches these levels at 1–2 months of age.

Almost all studies conclude that factor XIII reaches 100% of its activity in the newborn. However, using a fluorescent method based on the ability of the thrombin and calcium-activated factor XIII to incorporate dansyl cadaverine into casein, some workers found a mean value immediately after birth of about 50% of that found in adults.[16]

5.2. Fibrinolysis

Plasminogen levels in the full-term infant are approximately half those in adults, but antiplasmin levels are usually within normal limits. In the first few hours of life, there is increased fibrinolytic activity, as demonstrated by the short euglobulin clot lysis time. This increased lysis is a reflection of increased plasminogen activator activity. Reports of the levels of fibrin degradation products in the blood of full-term infants vary according to the methodology used.

Utilizing a tanned red cell hemagglutination inhibition immuno-assay, Uttley et al.[30] found raised levels of fibrin degradation products in early infancy; another group of workers, however, using a modified version of the assay, found a low titer in only 5% of blood samples from healthy infants.[10] Methodology utilizing immunoelectrophoresis also showed either very little or no evidence of fibrin degradation products in cord serum and on follow-up at 24 hr.

6. Transitory Deficiencies of the Coagulation Factors in the Newborn

6.1. "Classic" Hemorrhagic Disease of the Newborn

In 1894, when Townsend[29] originally coined the term *hemorrhagic disease of the newborn*, it was used to distinguish a type of generalized bleeding that was observed during the newborn period. There was no attempt (indeed, inadequate understanding of the coagulation mechanism and the unsophisticated laboratory methodology made it very difficult) to distinguish bleeding disorders of varying etiologies. Properly, hemorrhagic disease of the newborn should be reserved to describe the hemorrhagic disorder of the first few days of life—most commonly the second to fourth day—caused by a deficiency of vitamin K and the vitamin-K-dependent blood clotting factors, II, VII, IX, and X. The deficiencies of these factors produce a defect in the intrinsic clotting system as well.

The hemorrhagic tendency manifests itself most often in GI tract bleeding, bleeding from the umbilicus and circumcision site, and occasional widespread bleeding into the skin and internal organs. It is characterized by a gross prolongation of the prothrombin time, a defect that shows a dramatic and rapid clinical response to the administration of vitamin K.

When hemorrhagic disease is thus strictly defined, estimates of the incidence in newborn infants not receiving vitamin K range from 1 in 119 to 1 in 2500 births. That this incidence is far below what one would expect from examining the levels of the blood coagulation factors encountered in the newborn suggests that as yet unknown factors play a role.

Vitamin K has a narrowly specific role in conferring on parenchymal liver cells the capability of synthesizing the factors of the prothrombin complex. The exact manner in which vitamin K performs this selective function is as yet unsolved. The normal newborn infant has decreased concentrations of the vitamin-K-dependent factors because of the immaturity of the liver, as well as the very limited stores of vitamin K at birth. It is now generally agreed that administration of vitamin K to the newborn infant prevents the previously described decrease in prothrombin activity (and laboratory-determined prolongation of the prothrombin time) that is commonly observed during the first few days of life.

Aballi and De Lamerens[2] reported, however, that in the premature infant, whose prothrombin levels are frequently more depressed than those of full-term infants, the response to vitamin K is not so predictable. The inadequate response to vitamin K in the preterm infant may reflect the greater hepatic immaturity and inability to synthesize factor VII and other coagulation factors, despite adequate amounts of vitamin K.

The diet of the young infant also exerts a strong effect on the transitory coagulation factor deficiency. If additional vitamin K is not given by prophylactic administration, one can demonstrate improvement in prothrombin levels—and a reduction in the incidence of hemorrhagic disease—in infants given supplemental feedings, beginning at 4 hr of age. Breast milk is a poor source of vitamin K (1.5 mg/dl), but cow's milk contains significant amounts (6 mg/dl).[24] Sutherland et al.[28] showed that bleeding associated with hypoprothrombinemia was confined to breast-fed infants who had not received vitamin K. Twice as many episodes of hemorrhagic disease occurred among the breast-fed infants who received no vitamin K as among infants who received vitamin K or a cow's milk preparation, or both.

It has been found that a single dose of 1 mg vitamin K is entirely sufficient to prevent hemorrhagic disease of the newborn. Aballi and De Lamerens[2] found that 25 mg vitamin K would protect infants from a prolonged prothrombin time and the typical postnatal drop in plasma coagulation factors.

6.2. Disseminated Intravascular Coagulation

Aballi and De Lamerens[2] distinguished between two different forms of hemorrhagic disease of the newborn infant: the "classic" form discussed above and the "secondary" type. This secondary type was characterized by a hemorrhagic diathesis not responsive, or only partially responsive, to vitamin K, and primarily attributable to developmental immaturity or some disease of the liver. This secondary hemorrhagic disease of the newborn was thus more commonly evidenced in premature infants and those full-term infants suffering from anoxia or septicemia.

This entity is now recognized as disseminated intravascular coagulation (DIC). DIC, which is frequently fatal but often self-limited, is now defined as a pathophysiologic mechanism that is triggered by some underlying process and is characterized by the intravascular consumption of platelets, plasma clotting factors II, V, and VIII, and fibrinogen. The stimuli may come from a host of sources and be related to a myriad of conditions, such as intravascular hemolysis; transplacental passage of thromboplastin material from the eclamptic mother; bacterial endotoxins, especially gram-negative organisms; circulating antigen–antibody complexes; acidosis; respiratory distress syndrome; rubella; and cytomegalovirus infections, among the many etiologies.[3,15]

The intravascular coagulation results from uncontrolled generation and deposition of fibrin thrombi throughout the microcirculation, along with the associated consumption of the coagulation factors. There are progressive deficiencies of the platelets and factors, so that widespread hemorrhage occurs.[14]

The fibrinolytic system is rapidly activated and attempts to play a protective role, due to the declining levels of plasmin substrate (factors I, V, and VIII) and the inhibitory effects of fibrinogen and fibrin "split products" on thrombin and fibrin polymer formation. Thus, there arises the "paradox" that hypercoagulability leads to hemorrhage.[14,21] This hypercoagulability—or shortening of the clotting time of whole blood—is especially prominent in those infants with respiratory distress syndrome. In light of the deficiencies of blood-clotting factors noted previously, this paradoxical finding may also be related to deficiencies of naturally occurring anticoagulants. Three such anticoagulants have been characterized: antithrombin III, anti-Xa, and antiactivated factor XI. Low activities of antithrombin III have been described in the cord blood of infants who developed the respiratory distress syndrome. Antithrombin III is a proteinase inhibitor, capable of inactivating both thrombin and activated factor X.[20]

A familial deficiency (transmitted as an autosomal dominant), involving a defect in this protein and a clinical picture of recurrent thrombosis, has been described. As in the case of coagulation factors, however, the fibrinolytic factors may also be depleted by the DIC process. This process is thus characterized by thrombocytopenia, specific deficiencies of factors I, II, V, and VIII, and the presence of the effects of fibrinolysis.

7. Hereditary Deficiencies of the Coagulation Factors

Hemophilia A and hemophilia B are hereditary, sex-linked deficiencies (or the production of nonfunctional variants, as has been recently suggested) of factors VIII (AHF) and IX (PTC), respectively. The disorders, which are clinically undistinguishable and can be differentiated only by laboratory test, account for 90% of all the hereditary only by account for 90% of all the hereditary disorders of the coagulation factors.[24,25] Hemophilia A occurs with a frequency of 1 per 10,000 while PTC deficiency is estimated as occurring once in 50,000 births.

There is good evidence now to support the concept that in hemophilia A (and possibly in hemophilia B), the molecular basis of the defect lies in the production of a structurally abnormal and functionally inept variant of the supposedly missing clotting protein.[33] Almost all patients with hemophilia A (and some with hemophilia B) have antiserum-neutralizing activity equal to that of plasma from normal individuals. It is expected that with improvements in methodology (including immunochemical studies), many of the other functional hereditary deficiencies of clotting factors to be discussed will also eventually be related to defective synthesis, rather than lack of the coagulation factors

per se. One important result of the recognition of functional and immunochemical factors VIII and IX will be the ability to identify heterozygous carriers because of the distinction between the two levels as compared with normal individuals.[33]

The clinical picture of AHF (factor VIII) and PTC (factor IX) deficiencies in the newborn is apparently determined to a great extent by the concentration of antihemophilic factor. From infancy, one can generalize that if the concentration is less than 1–2%, the disease will be severe; between 2 and 5%, moderate; and above 5%, mild. The "mild hemophilic" will almost always have a normal blood-clotting time.[26]

Schulman[26] observd that 11 of 25 children with severe factor VIII or IX deficiencies had hemorrhagic manifestations during the first week of life; on the other hand, only 3 of 22 infants with mild hemophilia had a bleeding diathesis. In 1965, Strauss[27] reported that of 16 newborns with mild or moderate hemophilia, only 2 had some mild bleeding; in contrast, in a group of 20 infants with severe hemophilia (factor VIII and IX levels under 2%), 10 had mild bleeding and 4 had severe and prolonged bleeding from the circumcision site. Other studies reveal that the most common hemorrhagic manifestation is that following circumcision, followed in incidence by bleeding into the scalp, intracranial hemorrhagic, and umbilical bleeding. Baehner and Strauss[5] reviewed the records of 192 patients with hemophilia A or B, and found that only 9 had bleeding unrelated to circumcision during the first week of life; even following circumcision, only 26 of 61 of the "severe" type of hemophiliac had serious bleeding.

Since, as has been previously noted, there is virtually no transplacental passage of factors VIII or IX, or other coagulation factors, old wives' tales referable to the protection of the newborn hemophiliac by maternal factors are no longer tenable. As of now, it is not possible to explain why the incidence of serious hemorrhage—even in severe hemophiliacs—is relatively low in the newborn hemophiliac.

Von Willebrand's disease is inherited as an autosomal dominant. In addition to the disorder of factor VIII, there is an associated defect of platelet adhesion to injured blood vessels. Thus, the bleeding time is prolonged.

Other hereditary deficiencies of plasma coagulation factors are relatively uncommon, and it is therefore not within the scope of this chapter to discuss them.

8. References

1. ABALLI, A. J., 1965, The action of vitamin K in the neonatal period, *South. Med. J* **58**:48.
2. ABALLI, A. J., AND DE LAMERENS, S., 1962, Coagulation changes in the neonatal period and in early infancy, *Pediatr. Clin. North Amer.* **9**:785.
3. ABILDGAARD, C. F., 1969, Recognition and treatment of intravascular coagulation, *J. Pediatr.* **74**:163.
4. AMBRUS, C. M., AMBRUS, J. L., NISWANDER, K. R., WEINTRAUB, D. H., BROSS, I. D. J., AND CASSMAN, H. B., 1970, Change in fibrin-stabilizing factor levels in relation to maternal hemorrhage and neonatal disease, *Pediatr. Res.* **4**:82.
5. BAEHNER, R. L., AND STRAUSS, H. S., 1966, Hemophiliacs in the first year of life, *N. Engl. J. Med.* **275**:524.
6. BLEYER, W. A., HAKUM, I. H., AND SHEPARD, T. H., 1971, The development of hemostasis in the human fetus and newborn infant, *J. Pediatr.* **79**:838.
7. BRINKHOUS, K. M., SMITH, H. P., AND WARNER, E. D., 1937, Plasma prothrombin level in normal infancy and in hemorrhagic disease of the newborn, *Amer. J. Med. Sci.* **193**:475.
8. CADE, J. F., HIRSH, J., AND MARTIN, M., 1969, Placental barrier to coagulation factors: Its relevance to the coagulation defect at birth and to haemorrhage in the newborn, *Br. Med. J.* **2**:281.
9. DYGGVE, H., 1958, Prothrombin and proconvertin in the newborn and during the first year of life, *Acta Paediatr.* **47**:251.
10. EKELUND, H., HEDNER, U., AND ASTEDT, B., 1970, Fibrinolysis in human foetuses, *Acta Paediatr. Scand.* **59**:369.
11. EKELUND, H., HEDNER, U., AND NILSSON, I. M., 1970, Fibrinolysis in newborns, *Acta Paediatr. Scand.* **59**:33.
12. ERSLEV, A. J., AND GABUZDA, T. G., 1975, *Pathophysiology of Blood*, W. B. Saunders Co., Philadelphia.
13. FORTUNE, W. A., AND COX, J. R., 1973, Fetal factor VIII and IX levels in early pregnancy and their significance in prenatal diagnosis, *Acta Haematol.* **49**:314.
14. HATHAWAY, W. E., 1970, Coagulation problems in the newborn infant, *Pediatr. Clin. North Amer.* **79**:838.
15. HATHAWAY, W. E., MULL, M. M., AND PECHET, G. S., 1969, Disseminated intravascular coagulation in the newborn, *Pediatrics* **43**:233.
16. HENRIKSSON, P., HEDNER, U., NILSSON, I. M., BOEHM, J., ROBERTSON, B., AND LORAND, L., 1974, Fibrin-stabilizing factor (factor XIII) in the fetus and the newborn infant, *Pediatr. Res.* **8**:789.
17. HILTGARTNER, M. W., AND SMITH, C. H., 1965, Plasma thromboplastin antecedant (factor XI) in the neonate, *J. Pediatr.* **66**:747.
18. JENSEN, A. H.-B., JOSSO, F., ZAMET, P., COUCHARD-MONSET, M., AND MINKOWSKI, A., 1973, Evolution of blood clotting factor levels in premature infants during the first 10 days of life: A study of 96 cases with comparison between clinical status and blood clotting factor levels, *Pediatr. Res.* **7**:638.
19. KAZAL, L. A., 1967, Congenital disorders of hemostasis and blood coagulation in infancy, in: *The Clinical Pathology of Infancy* (F. W. Sunderman and F. W. Sunderman, Jr., eds.), pp. 103–117, Charles C. Thomas, Springfield, Illinois.
20. MAHASANDANA, C., AND HATHAWAY, W. E., 1973, Circulating anticoagulants in the newborn: Relation to hypercoagulability and the idiopathic respiratory distress syndrome, *Pediatr. Res.* **7**:670.
21. MARKARIAN, M., GITHENS, J. H., JACKSON, J. J., BANNON, A. E., LINDLEY, A., ROSENBLÜT, F., MARTORELL, R., AND LUBCHENCO, L. O., 1967, Fibrinolytic activity in premature infants, *Amer. J. Dis. Child.* **113**:312.
22. MARKARIAN, M., LINDLEY, A., JACKSON, J. J., AND BANNON, A. E., 1967, Coagulation factors in pregnant women and premature infants with and without respiratory distress syndrome, *Thromb. Diath. Haemorrh.* **17**:587.
23. NOSSEL, M. L., LANZKOWSKY, P., LEVY, S., MIBASHAN, R. S., AND HANSEN, J. D. L., 1966, A study of coagulation factor levels in women during labor and in their newborn infants, *Thromb. Diath. Haemorrh.* **16**:185.
24. OSKI, F. A., AND NAIMAN, J. L., 1972, *Hematologic Problems in the Newborn,* W. B. Saunders Co., Philadelphia.
25. PRENTICE, C. R. M., AND RATNOFF, O. D., 1967, Genetic disorders of blood coagulation, *Semin. Hematol.* **4**:93.
26. SCHULMAN, I., 1962, Pediatric aspects of the mild hemophilias, *Med. Clin. North Amer.* **46**:93.
27. STRAUSS, H., 1965, Clinical pathological conference, *J. Pediatr.* **66**:443.
28. SUTHERLAND, J. M., GLUECK, H. I., AND GLESER, G., 1967, Hemorrhagic disease of the newborn, *Amer. J. Dis. Child.* **113**:524.
29. TOWNSEND, C. W., 1894, The hemorrhagic disease of the newborn, *Arch. Pediatr.* **11**:559.
30. UTTLEY, W. S., ALLAN, A. G. E., AND CASH, J. D., 1969, Fibrin/fibrinogen degradation products in sera of normal infants and children, *Arch. Dis. Child.* **44**:761.
31. VAHLQUIST, B., WESTBERG, V., AND DELAS HEGAS, M., 1953, Prothrombin and fibrinogen values in the young human fetus, *Acta Soc. Med. Ups.* **58**:281.
32. ZILLIACUS, M., OTTELIN, A. M., AND MATTISON, T., 1966, Blood clotting and fibrinolysis in human foetuses, *Biol. Neonat.* **10**:108.
33. ZIMMERMAN, T. S., RATNOFF, O. D., AND LITTELL, A. S., 1971, Detection of carriers of classic hemophilia using an immunologic assay for antihemophilic factor (factor VIII), *J. Clin. Invest.* **50**:255.

CHAPTER 14

Maturation of Cellular and Humoral Immunity

Gaspard de Muralt

1. Introduction: Antibody-Mediated Immunity and Cell-Mediated Immunity

In mammals, immunologic responses can be divided into those mediated by humoral antibodies (antibody-mediated immunity) and by cells (cell-mediated immunity). Both depend on the activity of small lymphocytes that are themselves ultimately derived from bone marrow precursors.[226] The stem cells, which originate in the early embryonic stage in the yolk sac and in later stages of development in the liver, and in adults in the bone marrow, differentiate to form two distinct lymphocyte populations, one thymus-derived (*T lymphocytes*), the other bone-marrow-derived (*B lymphocytes*).[77,167] The life span of lymphocytes is not uniform. One can distinguish two populations of lymphocytes: a short-lived population of small, medium, and large lymphocytes with a life span of 1–10 days, and a long-lived population of small lymphocytes with a life span of some 100 days[275]; some of these small lymphocytes have a life span

of 10 years and more.[192] For many years, there has been a tendency to equate long-lived lymphocytes with T cells and short-lived lymphocytes with B cells. Recent studies suggest, however, that B- and T-cell populations contain similar proportions of long- and short-lived lymphocytes.[91] T and B cells differ in their distribution.

1.1. T Lymphocytes

The T lymphocytes amount to 65–85% of the lymphocytes present in the thoracic duct, blood, and lymph nodes. They are found mainly in the deep cortical areas of lymph nodes.[144] The long-lived lymphocytes represent the major portion of the thoracic duct cells (90%), whereas the short-lived lymphocytes are located mainly in the thymus, spleen, and bone marrow.[112] A large proportion of the long-lived T lymphocytes recirculate between blood and lymph through specialized endothelial cells lining the postcapillary venules and lymph organs.[91] Their mobility is superior to that of red blood cells.[192]

The major functions of T cells have been elucidated. T cells are effector cells in delayed sensitivity reactions and in elimination of foreign

Gaspard de Muralt · Department of Perinatology, University Women's Hospital, Bern, Switzerland

tissues. They also play an important role in the expression of some humoral immune responses (Fig. 1). On stimulation with specific or non-specific mitogens, the T cells can release a variety of nonspecific chemical mediators called *lymphokines*. A certain number of lymphokines have been identified,[91,132] among which are the following:

1. *Interferon*, which is active on viruses.
2. *Transfer factor* (TF), which can induce delayed hypersensitivity *in vivo* in nonsensitive recipients.[132]
3. *Mitogenic factor* (MF), which induces transformation and proliferation of other lymphocytes.
4. *Migration inhibition factor* (MIF), which is capable of inducing the lymphocytes of a sensitized animal to secrete a substance that inhibits the migration of macrophages.
5. *Cytotoxic and growth inhibitory factors,* which, after injection, can evoke inflammatory lesions in the skin, including typical delayed hypersensitivity responses, though their significance and their relationship to other lymphocyte products are still uncertain.
6. *Lymph node permeability factor,* which can be extracted from sensitized lymph nodes and increases the permeability of the vascular endothelium.

1.2. B Lymphocytes

In birds, the B lymphocytes originate in the bursa fabricii, in mammals, mainly in the bone marrow,[279] and possibly in the gut-associated lymphoid tissues, including the appendix and Peyer's patches.[144] In this connection, a peculiar cell type—the tuft cell—should be mentioned. Tuft cells have been encountered in the epithelium of the GI tract of several mammals, including man. Their cytoplasm contains numerous phagosomes and lysosomes and a well-developed Golgi apparatus. The function of these tuft cells seems to be the selective absorption of macromolecular antigenic substances.[118]

The cells of the B system[226] seem to be more sessile than those of the T-cell population. They are found primarily in the peripheral lymphoid organs, in lymph nodes, and in the thymic-independent follicular areas around germinal centers.[91] They are also present, although in small amounts (10–25%), in the peripheral blood. They seem to be short-lived (about 1 week),[54] and do not recirculate in greater amounts. The B cells

differentiate in plasma cells, which are ultimately responsible for the synthesis and secretion of all forms of antibody and all circulating immunoglobulins. The turnover of plasma cells is very fast; their life span averages 0.5–2 days.[275]

1.3. Cooperation of T and B Lymphocytes

Although each type of lymphocyte is independent, the regulation of the immune response in both positive directions (induction of humoral antibody production and of antigen-sensitive T lymphocytes) and negative directions (induction of immunologic tolerance) appears to involve some cooperative interactions between B and T cells (Fig. 1), as has been shown in numerous experiments in animals.[144,226] This collaboration between B and T cells requires the presence of macrophages. The macrophages bind the T-cell products with the antigen on their surfaces, thus preparing these complexes to stimulate the B cells.[69]

1.4. Immunologic Memory

As a rule, primary immunization is not followed by antibody production, but causes the development of immunologic memory.[306] Immunologic memory is carried by both T cells (memory T cells) and B cells (memory B cells).[91,306] Two distinct cell populations are of importance in the development, expression, and maintenance of immunologic memory (Fig. 1). One is localized primarily in the germinal centers (memory B cells). The second is made up of small, long-lived lymphocytes (memory T cells); some memory T cells are sessile in the lymphoid tissues, whereas others recirculate between blood and lymph.[91,171,306]

The morphology and functions of T and B lymphocytes and macrophages are summarized in Table I.

2. Identification of T and B Lymphocytes

Although T and B cells appear identical in routine light microscopy, they can be differentiated by three methods: (1) markers for different membrane-surface antigens and receptors, (2) response to various mitogens, and (3) scanning electron microscopy.

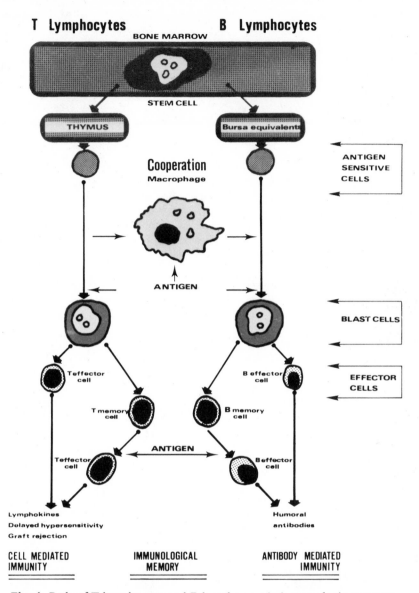

Fig. 1. Role of T lymphocytes and B lymphocytes in immunologic responses.

2.1. Markers for Different Membrane-Surface Antigens and Receptors

The markers of human mononuclear cells are summarized in Table II.

B cells are distinguished primarily by the presence of immunoglobulins tightly bound to the cell surface.[36,77–79,81,207–209,219,224a] They also have receptors for the Fc fragment of IgG,[20,297] the third component of complement, C3,[127,297] aggre-gated IgG,[36,297] and Epstein–Barr virus.[297] It is not quite certain that the cell populations characterized by these markers are identical; there is a considerable amount of overlapping. Fc receptors, for instance, have also been described on T lymphocytes.[127] On the other hand, B cells do not form rosettes with sheep cells, as do T lymphocytes.[36,91,127,297]

In most, but not in all,[103] normal B lymphocytes, membrane-bound immunoglobulin (Ig) is

Table I. Morphology and Functions of T and B Lymphocytes and of Macrophages[a]

Characteristic	T lymphocytes	B lymphocytes	Macrophages
Origin	Bone marrow, thymus	Bone marrow, bursa equivalents	Bone marrow
Life span	Long (years)		Long (years): tissues
	Short (a few days): corticosteroid-sensitive	Short ($\sim$1 week)	Short: blood
Main localizations		Germinal centers of whole lymphoid tissue	Blood: monocytes
	Lymph nodes: deep cortex, perifollicular zones	Lymph nodes: subcapsular rim, centers of primary follicles, medullary cords	Lymph nodes: germinal centers, medullary cords
	Spleen: periarteriolar sheaths of white pulp	Spleen: diffuse interfollicular area	Spleen: white pulp, cords of Billroth
			Tissues: histiocytes
Mobility	+++ (blood, lymph)	++	++ (blood monocytes)
Recirculation	Yes	Weak ($\sim$5%)	None
Sensitivity to X rays	+++	++++	0
Sensitivity to antigens and blast transformation	Nonspecific: +++ Specific: +++	Nonspecific: 0 Specific: ++ (plasmo-cytes)	0
Immunity			
Cell-mediated	+++ (production of lymphokines)		Phagocytosis: antigenic concentration
Antibody-mediated	0	+++ (production of Ig)	Superantigen (?)
Immunologic memory	+++	+	?
Membrane-bound Ig	± (IgM, γ chain)	+++	+ (cytophilic antibodies)

[a] Data from Greaves et al.[91] and Nezelof and Diebold.[192]

restricted to one Ig class, one IgG subclass, and one Gm allotype.[80] IgM and IgD are present, however, on the same lymphocytes; they are a product of the cell to which they are attached.[219] A switch from IgM to IgG in the same cell can occur,[199] however, as shown by the presence of IgM and IgG on the surfaces of some B lymphocytes at different stages of their development.[135] Lymphocytes with surface-bound Ig were found in all the healthy adults studied. The average percentages of surface-immunoglobulin-positive lymphocytes in adults found in various laboratories[79,297] are summarized in Table III.

In cord blood, even if the titers of serum Ig are low, lymphocytes with surface-bound Ig can easily be detected. The mean percentages found were the following: total Ig-positive lymphocytes, 14% (range, 5–32%); IgM-positive, 9% (range, 4–14%);

IgG-positive, 5–17% (range, 0–22%); IgA-positive <1–5% (range, 0–5%)[77–79,145]; IgD-positive, 14.5% (range, 7–24%).[235] IgD was the most frequently detectable membrane-bound Ig, even though IgD is usually undetectable or present only in very low levels (see Section 7.1) in newborn serum.[235] The significance of this finding is still obscure. Lymphocytes carrying surface-bound IgG and IgM are found in cord blood in percentages comparable to those found for adults. For three of the four IgG subclasses, the following percentages have been found: IgG_1, 1–2%; IgG_2, 2–5%; IgG_3, 1–2%. In newborns, these values were slightly higher. The fourth subclass, IgG_4, was found in only a few individuals on 1% of the lymphocytes.[78–81]

T cells are able to form rosettes with erythrocytes incubated at room temperature with washed red

Table II. Markers of Human Mononuclear Cells

Technique	B lymphocytes	T lymphocytes	Thymus lymphocytes	Monocytes	Reference numbers
Surface-membrane immunoglobulin	+	−	−	−	35, 36, 77, 78, 79, 81 91, 127, 207–209
Rosette formation with sheep erythrocytes	−	+	+	−	13, 36, 91, 127, 208, 300
Brain antigens	−	+	+		35, 36
Heat-aggregated human immunoglobulins	+	−	−	+	36, 208
Receptors for activated C3	+	−	±	+	127, 208
Receptors of Epstein–Barr virus	+	−		−	127, 208
Receptors for Fc fragment of IgG	+	+	+	+	127, 208
T- or B-lymphocyte-specific antigen	+	+			21, 127

cells (either untreated sheep red blood cells or neuraminidase-treated human red cells).[13,35,36,91, 127,297]

In washed whole blood of adult donors, about 80% were found to be T cells and 15% B cells, and the remainder did not react with the four markers used.[35]

As shown by Table II, some markers are not exclusive to lymphocytes; monocytes may have receptors for C3 or the Fc fragment of IgG and bind aggregated immunoglobulins. Most monocytes can be readily distinguished from B and T lymphocytes, however, by their general morphology, by phagocytic activity, and by endogeneous enzymatic activity.[297]

Table III. Surface-Immunoglobulin-Positive Cells as Average Percentages of Total Peripheral Blood Lymphocytes of Healthy Adults[a]

Immunoglobulin	Average of means of all laboratories	Range of means
Total Ig	21	16 –28
IgG	7.1	4.0–12.7
IgA	2.2	1.0– 4.3
IgM	8.9	6.7–13.0
IgD	6.2	5.2– 8.2

[a] Data from WHO.[297]

2.2. Response to Various Mitogens

Mitogens are nonspecific activating agents that induce proliferation of lymphocytes *in vitro*, similar to the activation of cells by antigens *in vivo*. The best-known mitogens are phytohemagglutinin (PHA), concanavalin A (Con A), and the pokeweed mitogen (PWM).[250,291]

T lymphocytes respond to the mitogenic stimulus of PHA, whereas B lymphocytes are unresponsive.[192,228]

2.3. Scanning Electron Microscopy

Routine light- and electron-microscopic studies do not permit morphological distinction between B and T lymphocytes. Scanning electron microscopy of critical point dried specimens shows that normal B and T lymphocytes have very different surface architecture. B lymphocytes have an irregular surface with an average of 150 microvilli ("villous" cells). The surface of T lymphocytes is generally smooth and slightly irregular, with or without a moderate number of surface digitations ("smooth" cells).[214] With the use of immunologic methods, 20–30% of normal peripheral blood lymphocytes were identified as B cells and 69–82% as T cells. Scanning electron microscopy gave 20% villous cells (equal to B cells) and approximately 80% smooth cells (equal to T cells).[214]

3. Development of T and B Lymphocytes in the Fetus

A general scheme of the development of T and B lymphocytes in the fetus is presented in Fig. 2. This development is discussed in detail in this section.

3.1. Development of T Lymphocytes

In the human thymus, lymphocytes are first seen in the 9th week of gestation. From the 14th week on, a cortical zone rich in mitotically active lymphocytes and precursor cells of lymphocytes appears, reaching its maximum thickness at 20 weeks.[205] Lymphocytes capable of responding to PHA are present in human fetal thymus tissue by 12 weeks of gestation.[6] The human fetal thymus at 20–22 weeks of gestation contains cells capable of binding bacterial flagellar antigens in far greater numbers than does the postnatal thymus. There are also more antigen-binding lymphocytes in fetal thymus than in the corresponding fetal spleen and blood, but the reverse holds true for the adult thymus.[57]

In the spleen, the first lymphocytes are detectable from the 15th week of gestation[230]; they can also be stimulated by mitogens (PHA). Establishment of the PHA response is associated with the appearance of small lymphocytes in cuffs surrounding central arterioles.[12]

From the 12th week of gestation, the lymphoid cells of the bone marrow comprise about 25% of the total nucleated cells.[305] This percentage increases with gestation, and in the 4th week of postnatal life, lymphocytes form about 40–50% of all nucleated marrow cells.[85,131]

In fetal human blood, the first lymphocytes are detectable at about 8–10 weeks of gestation.[212,269] Their number increases rapidly, and reaches a plateau of 2500–3000 lymphocytes/mm³ at the 25th week of gestation. This number remains constant until birth. Since active lymphocytopoiesis continues during the entire gestation, this plateau results from a dynamic equilibrium between production and removal of lymphocytes from the blood.[212,269] At birth, peripheral blood contains 3000–5000 lymphocytes/mm³ in full-term infants,[269,301] and somewhat lower levels in premature babies.[301]

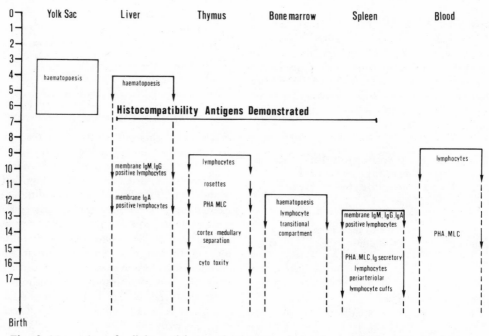

Fig. 2. Maturation of cellular and humoral immunity during human embryonic development. Redrawn from Prindull[215] with permission.

Lymphocytes capable of responding to PHA were used to map T cells, and where initially seen in the fetal human thymus at 10–12 weeks, in spleen at 13–15 weeks, and in peripheral blood at 14 weeks of gestation.[12,264] Virtually no responses to PHA were detected in bone marrow or hepatic cells. Mixed lymphocyte reaction reactivity was first detected in the thymus as early as the 12th to 14th week of gestation, and somewhat later in peripheral blood, but never in the bone marrow.[263] The lymphocytes reacting in these mixed lymphocyte cultures were able to evoke a graft-vs.-host reaction.[211] Lymphocytes from thymuses of human fetuses of 16 weeks of gestation[103] and from cord blood[264] are capable of causing damage to erythrocytes of another species (chicken erythrocytes) when cultured in the presence of PHA.

Rosette-forming cells are found in the human fetal thymus as early as 11 weeks' gestational age. The percentage of these cells increases to 65% around the 15th to 16th week of gestation,[103,264,300] and decrease slightly afterward. At the same time, rosette-forming cells appear outside the thymus in small amounts in liver, spleen, and peripheral blood, suggesting a migration from the thymus.[264,300] The presence of histocompatibility antigens on cells from human organs (brain, thymus, lung, spleen, stomach, gut, adrenal gland, kidney, skin, testis) has been demonstrated from 6 weeks' gestation to birth.[9,246]

The percentage and absolute number of T cells are slightly[135a] or markedly decreased in children suffering from severe protein–caloric malnutrition (17%, compared with 60% in normal children and Caucasian adults, $P < 0.001$)[70] and moderately reduced in small-for-gestational-age newborns (50%, compared with 65% in appropriate-for-gestational age newborns, $P < 0.001$).[70] When compared to their function in normal adults, the function of T cells is depressed in nonjaundiced infants aged 3 days and even more depressed in jaundiced infants (average bilirubin level = 15 mg/dl) of the same gestational age and the same birth weight.[236a]

3.2. Development of B Lymphocytes

Lymphocytes bearing membrane-bound Ig are first found in the liver of human fetuses at 10 weeks and in the spleen at 12 weeks of gestation. The order of appearance of cells bearing different immunoglobulins is as follows: IgM, IgG, IgA.[145] B lymphocytes are more numerous in fetal human spleen than in thymus.[103] From the 14th week of gestation onward, the percentage of cells in spleen and peripheral blood that stains for each class of Ig is within the range found in blood from normal infants, children, and adults.[145] The temporal consistency of appearance of these cells suggests that their development is an event of normal differentiation, rather than one dependent on random antigenic stimulation.[145]

The sum of percentages for the Ig classes roughly equals that found for the total Ig with a polyspecific antiserum [anti-F(ab')$_2$]; likewise, the sum of percentages for the IgG subclasses in most experiments equals that found for total IgG.[78] The percentage of lymphocytes in peripheral blood that bears IgG-subclass determinants is higher in the newborn child than in his mother. This difference is particularly striking for IgG$_2$, but it is also seen in several cases of IgG$_1$ and IgG$_3$, but not in IgG$_4$, which is very rare.[78]

B lymphocytes containing secreted cytoplasmic Ig are found in the spleen by 15½ weeks of gestation. At 23 weeks, cells containing IgM, IgG, and IgA can be found in spleen and thymus. IgM-positive cells occur most frequently, followed by IgG and IgA. However, only small numbers of these cells exist before birth.[145] These findings show that the development of the B lymphocytes starts at about the same time as that of the T lymphocytes. The concentrations of the different immunoglobulin classes are described in Section 4.2.

After birth, the percentage of B lymphocytes in peripheral blood remains constant until adult life (14–18%). Depending on changes in the number of circulating lymphocytes, however, the number of B lymphocytes per cubic millimeter increases rapidly after birth to a peak level at age 3–4 months, followed by a slow decrease from the second year of life until adult levels are reached.[277] The percentages of lymphocytes bearing IgG, IgA, and IgM in infancy and childhood, as revealed by monospecific immunosera, are shown in Fig. 3. A lower percentage of IgG- and IgM-bearing cells has been reported in pregnant women as compared to normal adults, suggesting humoral immunodepression in women during pregnancy.[42a,79]

4. Human Immunoglobulins

4.1. Nomenclature

Immunoglobulins (Ig) are serum globulins the main property of which is their antibody activity.

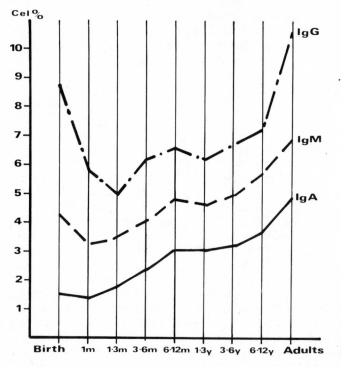

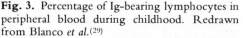

Fig. 3. Percentage of Ig-bearing lymphocytes in peripheral blood during childhood. Redrawn from Blanco *et al.*[29]

Electrophoretically, the Ig migrate in the α_2, β, and γ regions. By the use of very sensitive immunochemical methods and according to the international nomenclature, five classes of Ig, designated IgG, IgM, IgA, IgD, and IgE,[221,297] have been identified in normal adult serum. The molecule of Ig has a symmetrical structure, consisting of two long and two short polypeptide chains held together by a few disulfide bonds (Fig. 4). The heavy chains (H-chains) make up about 74% of the molecule. The H-chains have a molecular weight of 50,000, and for each class of Ig, they are distinctive in

structure, amino acid sequence, and biological function. The notations IgG, IgA, IgM, IgD, and IgE distinguish Ig according to their H-chains. The H-chains themselves are designated as γ, α, μ, δ, and ε, respectively, to correspond to the capital Roman letter suffixes designating the Ig classes.

The light chains (L-chains) account for 25% of the molecule. The L-chains have a molecular weight of 20,000, and they can be found in each of the Ig classes. They occur in two forms, the κ- and λ-chains; these chains are antigenetically distinct and present on different molecules; about 70% of these

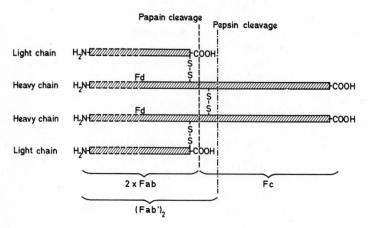

Fig. 4. Immunoglobulin structure. Diagram of proposed four-chain structure after Porter. Data from Holborow.[111]

Table IV. The 10 Immunoglobulin Classes[a]

Immunoglobulin class		Subunits	
		Light chain	Heavy chain
IgG	$(\kappa\gamma)_2$	κ	γ
	$(\lambda\gamma)_2$	λ	
IgA	$(\kappa\alpha)_2$	κ	α
	$(\lambda\alpha)_2$	λ	
IgM	$(\kappa\mu)_2$	κ	μ
	$(\lambda\mu)_2$	λ	
IgD	$(\kappa\delta)_2$	κ	δ
	$(\lambda\delta)_2$	λ	
IgE	$(\kappa\varepsilon)_2$	κ	ε
	$(\lambda\varepsilon)_2$	λ	

[a] Nomenclature of WHO.[296]

molecules contain κ- and 30% λ-chains. A normal serum therefore contains at least ten distinct kinds of antibody molecules (Table IV); each type presumably has the same function—to interact with a given antigen.[82]

The intact molecule of IgG can be split by proteolytic enzymes, papain and pepsin. Fragmentation by papain gives two Fab fragments and one Fc fragment. The Fab fragments contain the L-chains and one fraction of the H-chains designated as Fd. The Fc fragment contains only H-chains. The molecular weight of the Fab fragments is about 42,000; that of the Fc fragment, about 48,000. The Fab (*antigen-binding*) fragments carry the antibody activity. The Fc (*crystallizable*) fragment carries no anti-body activity, but it plays an important role in non-specific functions of the Ig, such as binding of complement, binding to cells and tissues, catabolism, and passage through biological membranes. In some instances, it has been crystallized. Digestion of the molecule of IgG with pepsin at pH 5 leaves a fragment, F(ab′)2, and a few residual fragments. F(ab′)2 has a molecular weight of about 91,000, and contains the entire antibody activity of the molecule. The biological half-life of the Fc fragment is of the order of magnitude of that of the intact IgG molecule, whereas the half-lives of Fab and F(ab′)2 are only a few hours.[173]

4.2. Physicochemical, Metabolic, Biological, and Immunologic Properties

In the adult human, the total serum Ig level (sum of the major classes IgG, IgA, IgM, IgD, and IgE), as measured by quantitative immunochemical techniques,[114] averages about 1700 mg/dl, or 1.7 g/dl.[67] The total Ig therefore comprise about 25% of the total serum proteins. All values given for Ig in this review will refer to values obtained by immunochemical methods, unless stated otherwise.

The properties of the major classes of Ig, and their levels in normal adults, are summarized in Tables V–IX.

4.2.1. IgG Globulins

The IgG globulins account for 70–80% of all Ig of the adult serum. They are synthesized in plasma cells that are located primarily in the red pulp of

Table V. Physicochemical Properties of Immunoglobulins[a]

Property	IgG	IgA	IgM	IgD	IgE
Molecular weight	150,000	150,000–400,000	900,000	180,000	200,000
Sedimentation rate	6.7 S	7–11 S	19 S	7 S	8 S
Sensitivity to mercaptans	0	+	+	?	?
Chains					
Heavy (H)	γ	α	μ	δ	ε
Light (L)	$\kappa\lambda$	$\kappa\lambda$	$\kappa\lambda$	$\kappa\lambda$	$\kappa\lambda$
Genetic factors	Gm				
	Inv	Inv	Inv	Inv	Inv
		Am			
Number of subclasses	4	2	2	1	1

[a] Data from de Muralt,[181] completed with data from Stiehm,[260] Waldmann *et al.*,[288] and Wang *et al.*[290]

Table VI. Metabolic Properties of Immunoglobulins[a]

Property	IgG	IgA	IgM	IgD	IgE
Primary distribution (% intravascular)	40–50	40	80	75	50
Biological half-life, $T_{1/2}$ (days)	23	6	5	2.8	2.4
Rate of synthesis (mg/kg per day)	35	25	7	0.4	0.02
Fractional catabolic rate (% of body content catabolized per day)	3	12	14	35	89
Total body pool (mg/kg)	150	230	49	1.5	0.04
Placental transfer	+	−	−	−	−
Mature levels (mg/dl)[b]	1200	100–400	50–200	3	0.03
Percentage of total Ig	70–80	10–15	5–10	<1	<0.01

[a] Data from de Muralt,[181] completed with data from Stiehm,[260] Waldmann et al.,[288] and Wang et al.[290]

[b] Determined by immunochemical methods.

the spleen, the medulla of lymph nodes, and the lamina propria of the intestine.[66,162] In contrast, 80% of the plasma cells of the intestinal mucosa are IgA-containing cells.[47] As a general rule, one single cell produces antibody to one antigen.[194–196] Only a small portion of cells can be shown to be synthesizing two different antibodies.[295] It has been shown that single guinea pig plasma cells are synthesizing antibodies to Fc and Fab fragments of human gammaglobulin, and these findings suggested that a single cell may be able to produce antibodies to different specificities of a single antigen.[107]

In the human newborn, plasma cells are absent

Table VII. Biological Properties of Immunoglobulins[a]

Property	IgG	IgA	Secretory IgA	IgM	IgD	IgE
First detectable antibody	0	0	0	+	0	0
Major part of secretory response	+	0	0	0	0	0
Complement binding	+	0	0	+	0	0
Agglutination	+	0	0	++	0	0
Opsonization	+	0	0	++	0	0
Hemolysis	+	0	0	++	0	0
Virus neutralization	+	0	+	+	0	0
Anaphylactic activity	0	0	0	0	0	+
Presence in body secretions	+	+	++	0	0	+
Antibody function	+	+	Major antibody in secretions	+	No unique antibody activity	Reagins

[a] Data from de Muralt,[181] completed with data from Stiehm[260] and Waldmann et al.[288]

Table VIII. Immunologic Properties of Immunoglobulins[a]

Stimulus	Antibody specificity				Note
	IgG	IgA	IgM	IgE	
Diphtheria	+++	++	+		IgG that probably
Tetanus	++	+	−		modified the primary
Typhoid (H antigen)	++	+	++++		structure:
Typhoid (O antigen)	+	−	++++		LE factor
Paratyphoid B	++	−	+++		Rheumatoid factor
Escherichia coli			++		CRP (C-reactive
Dysenteria			++		protein)
Pertussis	++	++	++		
Poliomyelitis					
(Types I–III)	+++	++	+		
Antistreptolysin O	++	+	−		
Anti-A and anti-B					
antibodies					
Complete	+	+	+++		
Incomplete	+++	+	+		
Anti-Rh antibodies					
Complete			+++		
Incomplete	+++				
Measles	+++				
Influenza	+++				
Herpes simplex	+++				
Vaccinia	+++				
Cold agglutinins			++		
Reagins				++	
Syphilis antibodies			++		
Forsman hemolysin					
(rabbit)			++		
Waaler–Rose factor			++		
Anti-insulin antibodies		+			
Anti-*HLA* antibodies[b]	++		+		
Anti-Gm antibodies[c]	++		+		

[a] Data from de Muralt.[181]
[b] Data from Ahrons and Glavind-Kristensen.[6]
[c] Data from Nathenson et al.[189]

from the bone marrow and the lamina propria of ileum and appendix; they appear only between the 4th and 6th weeks of extrauterine life.[34] No secondary follicles or plasma cells could be found in fetal human lymph nodes.[28] The fetal spleen, however, has been shown to be able to synthesize IgG and IgM, but no IgA or IgD, from the 20th week of gestation.[84] These results explain why IgG is normally produced only in trace amounts prenatally, and why full synthesis begins at 3–4 weeks after birth. Following immunization, IgG usually appears in the serum of normal adults immediately after IgM antibody, but it may be very delayed or not appear at all in the newborn infant similarly stimulated by an immunization.[255] IgG is distributed throughout the extracellular fluid, including the blood. Its particular function is the neutralization of toxins, such as diphtheria toxin, and of viruses. It is unique in being the only class that is actively transferred in significant amounts

Table IX. Levels of Immunoglobulins in Serum and Secretions from Normal Adults (mg/dl)[a]

Serum/secretion	IgG	IgA	IgM
Serum	1230	328	132
Colostrum	10	1234	61
Unstimulated whole saliva	5	30	0.5
Jejunal secretion	34	28	ND[b]
Colonic secretion	86	83	ND[b]

[a] Data from Hanson and Brandtzaeg.[98]
[b] Not determined.

through the placenta from mother to fetus. The Fc fragment of the IgG H-chain has a special molecular site that permits an active transfer through the placenta. Small amounts have also been shown to cross the placenta from the fetus to the mother.[65,68,83,159,189] It has the longest half-life of all Ig—about 33 days in the newborn, about 22 days in the child, and about 17 days in the adult.[16] The half-life of IgG decreases with increasing concentration.[31] The normal level of IgG in adult blood is 1200 mg/dl.

(a) IgG Globulin Subclasses. The IgG class is not homogeneous; four subclasses have been recognized. They are defined by antigenic differences of the IgG H-chains,[76] and are designated IgG_1, IgG_2, IgG_3, and IgG_4.[173,267] These subclasses vary in electrophoretic mobility and in biological functions.[173,266] Their principal metabolic properties are summarized in Table X.

The IgG_3 subclass is readily digested with papain; IgG_2 and IgG_4 are relatively resistant to papain, and IgG_1 molecules are intermediate. In contrast, IgG_3 and IgG_4 are sensitive to pepsin digestion, whereas IgG_1 and IgG_4 are resistant. These differences are caused by variations in the number and location of the disulfide bonds.[173]

Antibody activity differs among the IgG subclasses. Incomplete Rh antibodies are usually of the IgG_1 and IgG_3 subclasses, occasionally of the IgG_4, but never of the IgG_2 subclass.[173] Coagulation factor VIII (antihemophilic globulin) antibodies are limited to the IgG_4 subclass, and the antibodies against thrombocytes in idiopathic thrombocytic purpura to the IgG_3 subclass, whereas the antibodies against thrombocytes in the blood of cases with lupus erythematosus or after repeated platelet transfusions belong to all four subclasses (complete references in reference 173).

4.2.2. IgA Globulins

The IgA globulins comprise about 10–15% of the Ig in normal adult, and they are the principal secretory form of antibody.[272] This class is also produced by elements of the plasma-cell series.[47,48,162] A high proportion is secreted actively into the colostrum and milk,[93,96] tears,[42,271] respiratory system,[10,223] and GI tract[47,105] by acinar or epithelial cells of the mucosal surfaces. The so-called "coproantibodies" present in the secretions of the intestine are probably largely of the IgA class.[42,152,245] The structure and some properties of

Table X. Metabolic Properties of the Four IgG Subclasses[a]

Property	IgG_1	IgG_2	IgG_3	IgG_4
Biological half-life, $T_{1/2}$ (days)	21	20	7	21
Fractional catabolic rate (% of body content catabolized per day)	8	7	17	7
Primary distribution (% intravascular)	50	54	65	55
Rate of synthesis (mg/kg per day)	25	9	3.5	1.3
Intravascular pool (mg/kg)	300	135	20	20
Serum concentration (mg/dl)	700	300	50	50

[a] Data from Morell et al.[173]

the IgA molecule differ, depending on whether it is derived from secretions (secretory IgA) or the serum (serum IgA). Serum IgA is mainly a monomer of 7S consisting of two H- and two L-chains. Only about 10% appear as molecule aggregates.[272] In the secretory IgA, on the other hand, 7S IgA constitute only a minor fraction (10–20%); polymeric forms predominate in the secretory IgA. These forms consist of two apparently identical monomeric IgA molecules coupled by a unique peptide synthesized in epithelial cells which is termed *transport* or *secretory piece*.[271, 272] The serum IgA has a sedimentation constant of 7 S and a molecular weight of 170,000. The secretory IgA has a sedimentation constant of 11 S and a molecular weight of about 390,000. The molecular weight of the transport piece is reported as being 50,000–80,000, depending on the method of estimation.

In normal adults, the IgA-producing plasma cells, or less often the lymphoid cells, are most abundant in the basal part of the lamina propria of the intestine, where they outnumber the IgG- and IgM-producing cells by a factor of 4 to 1.[47,105] There is a preponderance of IgA-producing cells adjacent to glandular structures throughout the body. In the nasal mucosa, the normal ratio of IgA-/IgG-producing cells averages 3:1.[33] The local IgA immunocytes, which may derive from circulating lymphocytes,[95] apparently develop earlier than those of lymphoid organs, since IgA may be detected in the saliva of newborns a few days earlier than in the serum.[101] The serum IgA does not pass from the serum to the exocrine glands.[272] A large proportion of the serum IgA, however, may be produced in the plasma cells of the exocrine glands; instead of being excreted as secretory IgA, it enters the circulation. Thus, the serum IgA will have the antibody specificities of the secretory IgA molecule, which is the chief antibody providing antiviral and antibacterial activity to mucous surfaces.

IgA is not produced by the normal human fetus.[84] If it does pass the placenta from mother to child, it may pass only in small amounts.[87] The serum of the conceptus may contain low concentrations of IgA, probably of maternal origin,[87] from the 7th week of gestation onward. No IgA, or only a small amount, is present in cord blood. IgA synthesis begins 2[4] to 4[293] weeks after birth. The half-life of IgA is 6 days,[106] and is independent of the serum concentration.[31] The normal level of IgA in adults is about 300–400 mg/dl.

(a) IgA Globulin Subclasses. There are two subclasses of IgA, termed IgA_1 and IgA_2 (complete references in reference 82). About 90% of the serum IgA is IgA_1 and 10% is IgA_2; in contrast, secretory IgA may contain up to 45% of the IgA_2 subclass. IgA_2 differs from IgA_1 in lacking disulfide bonds between the L- and H-chains.[260]

4.2.3. IgM Globulins

IgM globulins comprise between 5 and 10% of the total serum Ig. In contrast to the IgG globulins, the intact IgM globulins remain primarily (80%) confined to the circulation and do not migrate into extravascular spaces.[44] They are synthesized in lymphocytoid plasma cells and reticular cells of the spleen[39] and the lymph nodes.[39] The origin of these cells may be phylogenetically older in terms of the evolution of the immune system, just as IgM globulin appears to have preceded other Ig in the evolutionary schema.[154] The lymphoid spleen cells of the human fetus begin to synthesize IgM approximately after the 20th week of gestation.[84] Under normal conditions, the fetal production of IgG and IgM by the fetus is low, but in comparison with the adult, the fetal spleen synthesizes relatively more IgM than IgG.[84] The IgM class is the first to appear in the circulation after initial immunization[253] and is the predominant class produced by infants in the neonatal period.[255] At birth, the human infant has a plasma level of IgM that is about one-twentieth the normal adult level, with most if not all this immunoglobulin being of fetal origin. Within 2–5 days after birth, the rate of IgM synthesis increases rapidly.[293] In some cases, IgM globulins have several hundred times the capacity of IgG molecules against the same antigen to promote phagocytosis or to lyse bacteria.[224] IgM does not cross the human placenta. The half-life of IgM is 5 days, and is independent of the serum concentration.[31] The normal adult serum contains 100–200 mg/dl IgM.

(a) IgM Globulin Subclasses. It appears that at least two subclasses of IgM molecules exist,[82] but the biological properties of these subclasses have not yet been defined.[260]

4.2.4. IgD Globulins

Recently, IgD globulin was described as the fourth class of Ig, which accounts, on the average, for less than 1% of the normal serum Ig of the adult.[233] Only a few of its properties have been studied as yet. In immunoelectrophoresis, it migrates in the fast γ region,[234] and it has a sedimentation rate of 7.04S.[233] The estimated molecular weight is about 180,000. Most of it (75%) is found in the intravascular compartment.[225] Even with very sensitive immunofluorescence techniques, no evidence of IgD synthesis during fetal life could be found.[84] When IgD is present in cord blood, the mean level is 0.03 mg/dl. IgD can be detected consistently in the blood only at the end of the first year of life.[124] It was only recently that IgD was shown to have antibody activity.[260] It does not seem to cross the placenta. Only traces of IgD are present in external secretions. No structural and quantitative data are available.[98] The half-life of IgD is shorter than that of other Ig (2.8 days according to Rogentine et al.[225]). Normal adult serum contains 3 mg IgD/dl.[225]

4.2.5. IgE Globulins

Only a few properties of IgE are known to date. In immunoelectrophoresis, it migrates in the fast γ region, and it has a sedimentation rate of 8.0S. The estimated molecular weight is 200,000.[117] It seems to be of importance in atopic allergy.[117] In patients suffering from asthma and hay fever, the mean concentration of IgE in blood is about 6 times higher than in the blood of nonallergic healthy individuals.[123,125] Antibodies of the IgE class fulfill all the criteria for reaginic or skin-sensitizing antibodies, and it is primarily but not exclusively responsible for such antibody activity.[117] IgE efficiently liberates histamine and other substances responsible for the clinical manifestations of allergic reactions. The histamine-releasing ability of IgE is related to its affinity to tissue mast cells and blood basophils, the cells that contain most of the body's histamine. Extremely high levels have been found in Ethiopian preschool children infected with *Ascaris lumbricoides*.[126] These findings support the hypothesis that parasitic infections are also important factors in stimulating IgE production. IgE globulin passes the placenta in small amounts and is present in the secretions. In cord serum, a mean level of 0.0036 mg/dl (which is about 15% of the average adult level) has been found.[122] There is no correlation between the IgE concentration in the serum of newborns and their mothers.[122] The average half-life is about 2.3 days.[117] The mean level of IgE in the plasma of normal adults is 0.03–0.07 mg/dl.[122,126]

4.3. Genetic Factors

The sera of frequently transfused individuals may contain antibodies specific for genetically controlled antigen determinants of the Ig molecule. These determinants constitute the allotypes of the human Ig molecule. To date, three groups of genetic factors are known in human beings: the Gm factors present on the γ H-chain of IgG, and thus limited to IgG classes; the Am factor present on the α H-chain of IgA; and the Inv factors present on the κ L-chain, and thus characteristic of all three classes of immunoglobulins.[260] These factors are inherited according to simple Mendelian laws.[82]

The Gm groups are numbered Gm(1) through Gm(25) according to the WHO nomenclature.[221] Some populations have a high incidence of one or another genetic factor that is absent in other populations. For example, Gm(4) is present in 90% of Caucasians, but absent in Negroes, whereas Gm(6) is present in 25–50% of Negroes, but in fewer than 1% of Caucasians.[82] Most of the Gm factors are present in the papain-Fc fragment of the IgG molecule. The Gm factors are distributed within the different IgG subclasses (complete references in reference 173).

Three Inv antigens differing in amino acid composition exist: Inv(1), Inv(2), and Inv(3).

Recently, a genetic marker on the α H-chain of the IgA$_2$ subclass termed Am(1) was described. The Am(1) factor is found in 98% of Caucasians and 51% of Negroes. No relationship between the Am allotype and the Gm or Inv allotype exists.[260]

5. Immunoglobulins in Pregnant Women

5.1. General Electrophoretic and Immunoelectrophoretic Pattern

In the human species at least, the profound changes occurring in the plasma-protein pattern during pregnancy do not appear to be related to any transfer of significant amounts of protein from the conceptus (fetus, placenta, and amnion) to the mother. Rather, they seem to reflect the response of the mother's organism to a complex set of stimuli, among which one may recognize components of the inflammatory syndrome, of as yet ill-defined endocrine influences, and of some degree of immunologic stimulation.[245]

In pregnant women, the level of 6.5–7.5 g total plasma proteins/dl is at the lower limit of normal values of healthy adults. Because of the simultaneously increased plasma volume, however, the total pool of serum proteins in the blood of pregnant women is 22–49% higher than in normal, nonpregnant women (references in reference 181). Expressed in absolute figures, the blood pool of pregnant women contains up to 50 g more plasma proteins than the blood of nonpregnant women. Analyzed by electrophoresis, the albumin fraction is especially decreased, whereas the α_1-, α_2-, and β_1-globulins show a slight but statistically significant increase, and the β_2- and γ-globulins remain unchanged, as compared with normal adults (references in reference 181). The changes described hold true for white women living in the temperate zone. Well-nourished African, Hindu, and Bantu women, living in their own countries, may even show an increased level of |7.2–8.0 g total protein/dl toward the end of pregnancy. As in white women, the hypoalbuminemia is also pronounced, 2.4–3 g/dl, but the IgG globulin is always high, 1.4–1.9 g/dl (complete references in reference 181). The level of 3 g/dl albumin in maternal sera has since been confirmed by immunologic methods.[46]

Immunoelectrophoretic analysis of the serum proteins of pregnant women has not revealed any changes in the beginning of pregnancy as compared with nonpregnant women, but toward the end of pregnancy, an increase of α_2-macroglobulin, α_2- and β-lipoprotein, and transferrin was observed.[181] In white pregnant women, the serum levels of IgG remain constant between 1000 and 1400 mg/dl, and those of IgA and IgM between 100 and 200 mg/dl, from the 16th week of gestation until birth.[46,94] The serum levels of IgA and IgG of healthy white Swedish mothers and of mothers of a very low socioeconomic group living in a developing country are similar. But the serum IgM level of the latter group is usually high, presumably due to a higher frequency of infection.[39b]

5.2. Presence of Antibodies Against Fetal Antigens in Maternal Blood

Studying their own family, Fudenberg and Fudenberg[83] found that an agglutinating antibody against the Gm(a) factor appeared in the mother's serum during the third trimester of the fourth pregnancy. The mother was Gm(a−), A Rh+; the father, Gm(a+), B Rh+; the male newborn, Gm(a+), AB Rh+. Evidence for maternal immunization by components of fetal blood was provided by the increase in the titer of anti-B agglutinins in the maternal blood from 1:32 to 1:256 and by a simultaneous increase of the anti-Gm(a) titer from 0 to 1:8.

After multiple pregnancies, maternal antibodies to their infants' (paternally derived) IgG are not so rare.[155,277] In two larger series, they have been detected in the sera of 4–6% of the women tested,[65,159,283] and the frequency of this antibody seems to be slightly higher after the fourth pregnancy than after the second.[65] Antibodies specific for the genetic factors Gm(1), Gm(2), and Gm(5)[68,159,282] have been detected in the sera of pregnant women. Some of these antibodies are of the 11S type or of an intermediate size, and are not able to cross the placenta.[159] Most of the anti-Gm-antibodies, however, are of the 7S type,[83,155,159] and are therefore able to pass the placenta from the mother to the fetus. They have been detected in the blood of the newborn,[155,159,282] and it has been suggested[83] that certain cases of transient hypogammaglobulinemia in male and female infants might be caused by maternal isoimmunization; the transplacental passage of maternal antibodies against the genetic determinants of the infant's IgG produces a suppression or abnormally rapid disappearance of IgG that has been synthesized by the infant. Rosen and Janeway,[229] however, were unable to find anti-Gm antibodies in 4 mothers of infants with transient hypogammaglobulinemia. Nathenson et al.,[189] on the other hand, found antibodies against Gm(a), Gm(b), and Gm(f) factors in the blood of 1.6% of 1763 normal pregnant women. Four infants with Gm factor incompatibilities were followed over 2 years. These maternal antibodies (even if they are of the IgG type and can cross the placenta) do not suppress the IgG production in the infants, in contrast to what has been observed in mice[120,121,150] and rabbits.[153] The etiology of transient hypogammaglobulinemia remains to be explained.

In certain cases, small amounts of fetal IgA can also cross the placenta, enter the maternal circulation, and induce the production of maternal antibodies against the fetal IgA. These antibodies have been found in the blood of 15% of recently delivered mothers.[286] When they are of the IgG type, these antibodies can cross the placenta.[286] On transfusion with IgA-incompatible blood or plasma, they can cause anaphylactoid reactions.[287]

Similarly, precipitating anti-β-lipoprotein antibodies have also been detected in the sera of women after multiple deliveries.[56,282] No woman with anti-Gm, anti-IgA, or anti-β-lipoprotein antibodies had ever received a blood transfusion. The physiologic role of the anti-β-lipoprotein antibodies is as yet unknown.

6. Immunoglobulins in Fetal Blood

6.1. Time Sequence of Appearance

A considerable amount of data has been gathered by zone and boundary electrophoresis on the progressive development of the protein pattern in human fetal serum (complete references in references 8, 180, 181, and 245). The total serum protein increases from 1.5 g/dl in the 3rd fetal month to an average of 5.8 g/dl at birth. During the same time, the albumin fraction increases from 2 g/dl to near-adult values at term, i.e., 3.5–4 g/dl (absolute concentration). The α_1- and β-globulins decrease in proportion to the total proteins. The α_2-globulins do not change, whereas the γ-globulins rise steadily, in both absolute and relative amounts, from an average of 0.1 g/dl in the 4th fetal month to values at birth that are similar to those in the mother (see Section 6.3.1).

Pioneering work on the antigenic analysis of fetal proteins was done by Swiss authors (complete references are in reference 181). Immunoelectrophoresis of sera from 8-week-old fetuses enabled these workers to obtain five precipitation lines that correspond to tryptophan-rich prealbumin, albumin, transferrin, and two unidentified α-globulins, presumably α_1-antitrypsin and α_2-macroglobulin. From the 11th week of gestation, IgG, and from the 14th[185] to the 20th week,[84] IgM could be detected in fetal plasma, whereas traces of IgA were found in only a few[184] of the fetuses studied.[84]

When the Ouchterlony test was performed between the 11th week of gestation and birth, the fetal antigens always corresponded with those of the mother; this correspondence was found for albumin, α_2-macroglobulin, β-lipoprotein, transferrin, IgM, and IgG.[185] It was suggested that neither fetal development (for protein fractions synthesized by the fetus himself, such as albumin or IgM) nor

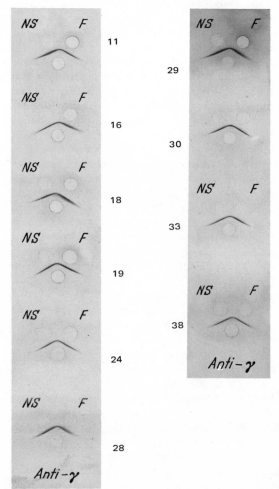

Number of weeks:

Fig. 5. Ouchterlony test—reaction of identity between fetal and maternal IgG. In each triplet of holes: left: maternal serum; right: fetal serum; bottom: anti-IgG serum. Data from de Muralt.[180]

transplacental passage (for the maternal IgG transferred from mother to fetus) produces significant changes of the physicochemical structure of these proteins. IgG is used as an example in Fig. 5; Fig. 6 shows the concentrations of Ig in fetal and neonatal blood.

6.1.1. IgG Globulins

The blood level of IgG increases from about 20 mg/dl[25] in the 13th week of gestation to

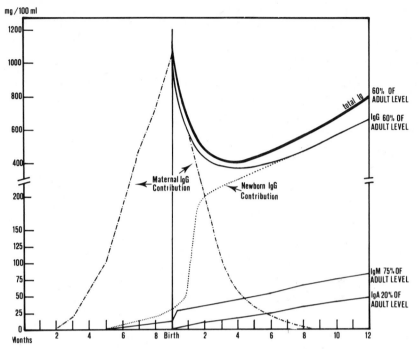

Fig. 6. Total Ig and IgG, IgA, and IgM levels in the human fetus and human infant. Drawn with data from Allansmith *et al.*,[4] Johansson and Berg,[124] Sidiropoulos,[247] and Stiehm.[260]

200[46] to 1400 mg/dl[25] in the 40th week. Fetal IgG serum concentrations equal the maternal values by the 34th week of gestation.[94]

5.1.2. IgM Globulins

This Ig is found only in small amounts in the blood of normal fetuses. At 14–16 weeks of gestation, fetal blood contains about 4 mg/dl,[25] and at the time of birth, 10[25,46,128] to 20 mg/dl.[247]

5.1.3. IgA, IgD, and IgE Globulins

These Ig are not found, or are present only in very small amounts, in fetal blood. The mean cord level of IgA is 3 mg/dl[94,113,260]; of IgD, 0.03 mg/dl (adult mean, 3 mg/dl); and of IgE, 0.003 mg/dl (adult mean, 0.03 mg/dl).[260]

6.2. Origin

6.2.1. Synthesis by the Fetus

For a long time, it was customary to regard the human fetus as well as other mammalian fetuses as immunologically incompetent and incapable of synthesizing their own immunoglobulins. This concept was derived from the repeatedly demonstrated very poor response of newborns to various vaccines (diphtheria, pertussis, tetanus) and other antigens.[63] The concept also gained credence from the reported absence of plasma cells in the normal human fetus[28] and newborns,[34] as well as from the repeated observations that children from agammaglobulinemic mothers are born with a very low IgG blood level.[34] In the latter cases, plasma cells were found after the 3rd month of life, and shortly thereafter, Ig appeared in the blood.[34]

In recent years, it has been necessary to revise this concept of an immunologically inactive fetus and newborn. A few plasma cells have been found in lymphoid organs and bone marrow.[143] Even in the absence of exogenous stimulation such as infections or vaccinations, the spleen of the human fetus is able to synthesize IgG and IgM from the 20th week of gestation, but no IgA or IgD.[84] According to Epstein *et al.*,[62] the human fetus seems to be more prone to produce IgM antibodies of the L type than of the K type. The presence of antibodies against fetal genetic factors of IgG in the mother's blood (see Section 5.2) is taken as further proof that the fetus is capable of synthesizing at least small amounts of IgG. About 0.1–5% of the total IgG globulin present at birth is of fetal origin.[83,155]

6.2.2. Synthesis by the Placenta

The possibility of placental synthesis of Ig was often claimed in the past on the basis of not very convincing cytochemical, electrophoretic, immunochemical, and clinical findings.[181] This controversial question was clarified by the work of Dancis et al.[51] and Bardawil et al.[18] By incubating tissue slices with glycine-2 C^{14}, the former authors[51] were able to show that the normal human placenta was able to synthesize some α- and β-globulins in vitro, but no albumin and no γ-globulins. By using the fluorescent antibody technique, Bardawil et al.[18] found that in the human placenta near or at term, albumin and γ-globulins were present only in extracellular spaces, with very small amounts localized in the trophoblastic cytoplasm. These findings do not support the thesis that these two protein fractions are synthesized in the placenta.

Normally, the placenta contains no plasma cells. The presence of plasma cells in a human placenta at the 22nd week of pregnancy[23] must be considered the result of a chronic infection. Good et al.[89] described a unique case of a mother with severe hypogammaglobulinemia (10–13 mg/dl) who acquired temporarily the ability to produce antityphoid and antiparatyphoid antibodies during the last trimester of pregnancy. This antibody production was not present in the first and second trimesters of her pregnancy, and it disappeared after delivery of the child, who was not able to produce antibodies.[89] For these reasons, the placenta must be considered a potential but rarely active source of Ig.[245]

6.2.3. Synthesis by the Amniotic Membrane

The synthesis of plasma protein in the amniotic membrane is still a controversial issue. The origin of specific components in human amniotic fluid[140,141] certainly resides in the amniotic epithelium.[239] In the rhesus and cynomologous monkey (*Macaca irus*), the major serum proteins in the liquor amnii are derived from, and return to, the maternal circulation. With the exception of traces of albumin derived from fetal urine, the fetus contributes little to these proteins.[15] In man, the origin of the proteins in the liquor amnii is less clear than in monkeys. The results obtained by comparison of the electrophoretic pattern of human liquor amnii and fetal and maternal serum,[1,17] and the results of experiments with ^{131}I-labeled albumin[52] and ^{131}I-labeled γ-globulin,[52,88] seem to be indicative of a maternal origin of the liquor proteins.

To explain all observed facts dealing with the origin of the liquor proteins, however, the roles of placenta,[298] of the amniotic epithelium, and of the fetus itself[164] must be considered. Brzezinski et al.[37] described a double albumin peak in the amniotic fluid of a bisalbuminemic child who was born in the 6th month of gestation to a normoalbuminemic mother. The controversy could be settled by comparing the phenotypes of amniotic, fetal, and maternal proteins, but to our knowledge, no such study has been published. The IgG level in human amniotic fluid increases during pregnancy from 10 mg/dl in the 8th–12th weeks to 20–50 mg/dl at term.[88,180] At term, IgA, secretory IgA, and IgM are also present in very low concentrations.

It is certain that in the rhesus monkey[38,149] and in the human,[181] proteins from the amniotic fluid normally reach the gut of the fetus, but their contribution to the mass of circulating fetal proteins appears to be very small. The specific "liquor α-globulin" has not been found in fetal monkey serum.[15] In the human, the faster of the two amnion-specific proteins was identified in only 3 of 20 samples of cord blood,[141] but the amnion-specific protein of the rabbit was always present in the serum of the newborn, from which it disappeared within 20 days.[142] Dancis et al.[52] injected ^{131}I-labeled γ-globulin directly into the amniotic fluid of two women in the 3rd month of pregnancy and observed a transfer of only small amounts into the fetal, but not into the maternal blood. Recently, it was also shown that virtually no IgA is absorbed by the human fetus from amniotic fluid at or near term.[87] Human infants with esophageal atresia were born with normal serum levels of IgG, and their levels of diphtheria antibodies corresponded to the serum levels in their mother's blood.[181] The intestine of the fetal rhesus monkey has the capacity to take up macromolecular protein (mol.wt. ≈ 40,000) from swallowed amniotic fluid; this capability is acquired well before term.[149] Only traces of labeled γ-globulins, however, have been observed to be transferred from the amniotic fluid into the fetal blood in this species.[14]

6.3. Transfer of Immunoglobulins from Mother to Fetus in Humans

6.3.1. Comparison of the IgG Globulin Serum Levels in Maternal and Cord Blood at Birth

Since the introduction of electrophoresis, numerous authors have compared the γ-globulin levels in cord and maternal blood at delivery. From the literature available, we have reviewed the papers in which the levels in maternal and cord blood were examined at the same time and with the same method. From these 58 papers with 2173 mother and newborn pairs (references in references 181 and 183), it is obvious that maternal and fetal values of electrophoretically determined γ-globulins are very similar with respect to absolute concentrations (g/dl). Due to the physiologic hypoproteinemia of the newborn, the proportion of γ-globulins in the total protein is distinctly higher in cord serum than in maternal serum.

The correlation between the absolute concentrations of γ-globulins in the mother and her offspring is especially evident if the γ-globulin level in the maternal serum is abnormally high or low. High levels were found in Senegalese, Congolese,[181] Gambian,[236] Nigerian,[158] and Papuan women,[181] and in a mother with liver cirrhosis,[251] and mothers and newborns had γ-globulin levels of 1800–1900 mg/dl. Abnormally low levels are exemplified by the classic observation of the absence of γ-globulin in the cord blood of children born to agammaglobulinemic mothers.[181]

More recently, the IgG levels in maternal and newborn sera have been studied by immunochemical methods (Table XI). In healthy term newborns, the levels of IgG in the cord blood roughly equal those in maternal blood, and amount to 900–1300 mg/dl in white children and 1700–1900 mg/dl in African children. In certain cases, the level of IgG in the cord blood rises above that in the corresponding maternal serum, but the differences reported are barely significant. Four possible explanations have been offered as to how the cord blood levels have increased: (1) active carrier or enzymatic placenta transport mechanism against a concentration gradient,[87,136] which is directly or indirectly inhibited

Table XI. Immunochemical Comparison of IgG Levels in Maternal and Newborn Sera

Number of mother–child pairs	Maternal blood (g/dl)	Cord blood (g/dl)	References
31	0.97	1.08	Zak and Good[305a]
20	No difference		de Muralt and Gugler[183a]
16	1.09	1.25	Hitzig[108a]
	0.97	1.13	Heimlich et al.[105a]
133	1.75	1.56	Gitlin et al.[88]
38[a]	1.99	1.73	Michaux[165a]
10	1.1	1.2	Allansmith et al.[6a]
46	1.26	1.51	Kohler and Farr[136]
18	0.81	0.76	Fulginiti et al.[83a]
79	1.30	1.56	Thom et al.[268]
45[b]	2.7	2.5	McFarlane and Udeozo[158]
38	1.28	1.1	Connon[45]
23	0.96	1.26	Corrodi and Hitzig[46]
30[c]	140%	103%	Iyengar and Selvaraj[119]

[a] Africans (Kinshasa).
[b] Africans (Ibadan).
[c] Expressed as percentage of reference serum (WHO Batch No. 67/97).

by high maternal serum IgG levels[87]; (2) synthesis of IgG by the fetus (see Section 6.2.1); (3) the longer half-life of IgG in newborns than in adults (see Section 4.2.1); and (4) synthesis of IgG by the placenta (see Section 6.2.2). Unfortunately, in none of the papers reviewed in Table XI was the mode of delivery mentioned. The IgG cord blood levels as well as the albumin cord blood levels in infants delivered *per vaginam* are significantly higher than those of their mothers.[43,130,163] In infants delivered by elective cesarean section (i.e., before the onset of labor), the concentrations of IgG and albumin in cord blood correspond to the concentrations in their mothers' blood (Table XII). In infants delivered by cesarean section following various periods of labor, on the other hand, the levels of IgG in the cord blood are higher than the levels in maternal blood.[43] Fetuses delivered by elective cesarean section are not submitted to the high intraamniotic pressure existing during contractions. During labor, the intraamniotic pressure rises from 8–15 mm Hg during relaxation to 20–60 mm Hg during contraction.[289]

It has been suggested that the higher concentrations of IgG and albumin in the newborn are due to ultrafiltration of these proteins into the fetal venous system. This ultrafiltration is caused by uterine contractions during vaginal delivery.[206] This mechanism does not refer to IgA and IgM, which are not transferred across the placenta.[163,302] The duration of labor does not influence the levels of Ig in cord blood.[108] The mode of delivery has no effect on the blood concentrations of IgG, IgA, or IgM in mothers.[302]

6.3.2. Placental Transfer of IgG Globulin Subclasses

In recent years, the placental transfer of the IgG subclasses has been studied by numerous authors (references in reference 173). Placental transfer from mother to fetus occurs for all four subclasses (Fig. 7). From the 13th to the 16th week of gestation, the serum levels of the subclasses are low in early fetal sera. At this early time, their relative concentrations reflect the subclass distribution in normal sera, i.e., $IgG_1 > IgG_2 > IgG_3 > IgG_4$. Later, fetal serum concentrations of all IgG subclasses rise rapidly. Fetal IgG_1 reaches a concentration corresponding to maternal concentration in approximately the 30th week of gestation, the other three subclasses in about the 33rd week of gestation. From then on, the fetal/maternal ratios of the four subclasses are 1.0.[175]

The finding during routine testing of a monoclonal IgG_2 protein in the serum of a healthy woman in her 6th month of pregnancy provided the opportunity to study the placental transfer of this IgG subclass and to calculate the half-lives for IgG (45 days) and IgG_2 (60 days).[284] These half-lives were unexpectedly long, considering the reported half-lives in adults for total IgG and the subclasses IgG_1, IgG_2, and IgG_4 (about 21 days), and for IgG_3 (7 days).[173] The concentrations of the four subclasses

Table XII. Fetal IgA, IgM, and IgG Serum Levels at Term vs. Mode of Delivery

	Vaginal delivery		Elective cesarean section		
Ig class	Maternal blood	Cord blood	Maternal blood	Cord blood	References
IgG (g/dl)	0.91	1.23	0.72	0.76	Jones and Payne[130]
	1.42	1.59	1.87	1.48	Mendenhall[163]
	1.23	1.30	1.20	1.10	Yang *et al.*[302]
	1.18	1.46	1.05	1.07	Cochran[43]
	1.38	1.52	1.24	1.39	Turmero[274]
IgA (mg/dl)	247	7	223	6	Yang *et al.*[302]
	152	0	155	0	Cochran[43]
IgM (mg/dl)	124	9	107	8	Mendenhall[163]
	159	13	147	13	Yang *et al.*[302]
	131	16	133	13	Cochran[43]

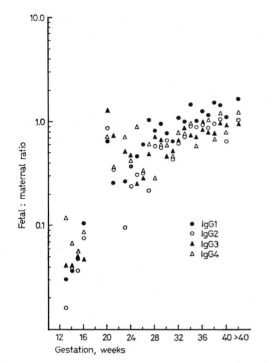

Fig. 7. Ratios of the means of fetal and maternal serum IgG subclass concentrations. The points plotted are the means of all fetal concentrations divided by the means of all maternal concentrations for each gestation week. Reproduced from Morell *et al.*[175] with permission.

Table XIII. Blood Levels of IgG Subclasses in 58 Mother–Child Pairs at Term (mg/dl)[a]

IgG sub-class	Maternal blood		Cord blood	
	Mean	Range	Mean	Range
IgG$_1$	514	300–850	559	210–910
IgG$_2$	270	170–500	269	100–470
IgG$_3$	48	12–114	51	10–145
IgG$_4$	19	5–56	20	4–76

Data from Morell *et al.*[174]

in cord blood and in the corresponding maternal blood are shown in Table XIII.

6.3.3. Mechanism of the Placental Transfer of Immunoglobulins

Since the human fetus is able to synthesize only small amounts of IgG, he has to rely on maternal

IgG for his humoral antiinfectious defense. The following observations and experiments have led to the conclusion that the bulk of IgG present at birth is of maternal origin:

1. The serum IgG concentrations are almost equal on the maternal and fetal side of the placenta, and the quantitative equilibration is particularly evident in mother–child pairs with hyper- or hypogammaglobulinemia.

2. In the majority of cases, the Gm phenotype of the newborn's IgG at birth is the same as that of its mother, irrespective of the child's own phenotype. The child's own phenotype is not detectable until a few weeks after birth, when the IgG produced by the child itself has reached a sufficient level.[181]

3. Contrary to the IgA and IgM levels, which increase after birth, the serum IgG level in the newborn decreases at an exponential rate that leads to the suggestion of an insufficient synthesis in the presence of continuous destruction; the half-life of the "borrowed" IgG is 20–30 days.[181]

4. ^{131}I-labeled γ-globulin injected intravenously into pregnant women shortly before delivery is directly transferred via the placenta into the fetal circulation.[181]

The placental transfer of Ig is selective. IgA, IgM, IgD, and IgE do not cross the placenta, or do so only in traces under certain conditions.[88] Leakage of blood from mother to fetus (maternofetal transfusions) seems to be as common as fetomaternal transfusion.[27] The amount of transfused maternal blood is usually 0.1–0.3 ml,[27] but can reach 7% of the child's blood volume in certain cases.[183] The leakage of blood from mother to fetus is responsible for about 5–10% of instances of elevated IgM in cord blood,[260] and can be suspected if the level of cord blood IgA is also increased. Leakage can be confirmed by repeated assay of infant IgM and IgA levels; maternally derived IgM and IgA will decrease after 6 days because of their short half-lives. In contrast, IgM and IgA synthesized by the newborn will be maintained, or may even increase. In a study of Gm and Inv phenotypes in maternal and cord blood, the cord blood lacked, in 22% of the cases, a factor that is present in the mother, thus suggesting a selective permeability also for some IgG molecules.[227]

The selectivity of the placental transfer is not due to simple diffusion, but to an active transport process across the trophoblastic cells of the placenta. From studies in mice, it appears that the maternofetal transfer of IgG is mediated by two mechanisms. One has first-order kinetics, in that the amount of IgG transported to the fetus by this mechanism is proportional to the maternal IgG concentration (diffusion). This mechanism continues to operate at very high maternal IgG levels, levels at which the second mechanism is entirely inhibited. The second mechanism is a carrier or enzymatic process that is specific for IgG. It is an active process: at low maternal serum IgG concentrations, proportionally more IgG is transferred from mother to fetus than at higher maternal IgG levels; as maternal IgG levels increase further, the amount of IgG transferred to the fetus decreases, until at very high maternal IgG concentrations, little or no IgG is transported by this second mechanism.[87] It is not yet known whether the placental transfer of IgG in humans can also be inhibited by high maternal serum IgG concentration. But it must be noted from Table XI that infants born to mothers with low serum IgG concentrations (under 1700 mg/dl) tend to have somewhat higher cord blood levels of IgG than those of their mothers, whereas the infants born to mothers with high serum IgG levels (over 1700 mg/dl) tend to have cord blood levels of IgG that are lower than those of their mothers.

The selective permeability of the placenta is mediated by certain transmission sites[111] that are present only in the Fc fragment of the IgG H-chain. This hypothesis was suggested by the results of experiments with labeled IgG globulin fractions administered to pregnant women. The relative plasma concentrations obtained in the fetus were highest for the Fc fragment, followed by the Fab fragment, and both fragments had a higher relative plasma concentration than the intact IgG molecule.[88]

The experiments described above may lead to the conclusion that the placenta is a rare example of a nonentodermal membrane with a selective permeability for proteins.[14] It seems that IgG is taken up by pyknocytosis in the human syncytial trophoblast,[202] and that it escapes to the opposite side into the intervillous space of the placental villi.

6.3.4. Antibody Transfer Across the Human Placenta

The findings with labeled γ-globulin mentioned in the preceding paragraph confirm what has been observed for a long time with biologically labeled immunoglobulins. As early as 1904, Polano[213] observed for the first time the passage of passively acquired diphtheria antitoxins from the mother to the child. Since this first observation, a large number of authors have been working on the transplacental passage of antibodies in the human (Table XIV), which depends on the pattern of maternal antibodies, on the variations in placental permeability for different types of antibody, and on the degree of placental maturity.[281] Antibodies against a considerable number of infectious diseases are completely lacking in adult blood. This lack may be due either to an extremely low incidence for such exotic diseases as plague, cholera, and so on, or to the short-lived persistence of antibodies in blood after recovery. In regard to widespread and highly contagious diseases such as measles, varicella, and mumps, it can be assumed that antibodies exist in practically all adults. If the antibody is of a type that can cross the placenta, the offspring can be assumed to be protected against this particular disease for the first months of life. At one time, it was suggested that a similar situation existed for diphtheria, but since this disease became so rare, a "sterile" population has grown up lacking diphtheria antitoxins, and thus the newborn infant is susceptible to infection.[281] In the future, situations like this will also occur for other diseases.

The problem that some antibodies (e.g., incomplete Rh) are able to pass easily across the placenta and others (e.g., complete Rh) are not was resolved by the grouping of antibody activity over three classes of immunoglobulins. Antibodies of the IgG class usually attain the same levels on both sides of the placenta, whereas antibodies belonging mainly or exclusively to the IgA or IgM class are either absent or considerably less concentrated in cord blood than in maternal blood. In certain cases, higher levels in fetal than in maternal blood have been reported for antistaphylococcal antitoxins, antidiphtheria antitoxins, antistaphylolysins, antistreptolysins, antibodies to cow's milk protein (especially to β-lactoglobulin) and to gluten, and occasional antibodies against vaccinia and smallpox (references in reference 181). However, this evidence cannot be accepted as proof for antibody production by the fetus without further discussion (see Section 6.2.1).

Table XIV summarizes only data obtained at or near term, but during gestation, the placenta undergoes marked structural changes.[2] With aging of the placenta, the thickness of the trophoblast decreases, whereas the surface of villi and the number of fetal capillaries increase. The total area of the placental membrane increases from about 1 m² at 100 days to 10–14 m² at term; during the same time, the proportion of that area that is occluded by fibrinoid degeneration gradually increases from 1.3 to about 8% of the total surface. The layer of Langhans' cells disappears at the 3rd to 4th month of pregnancy. In consequence of these structural changes, the permeability of the placenta increases. Per unit of placental weight, the rate of sodium transfer increases by 70 times from the 9th to the 36th week of gestation.[75] A similar but less pronounced progressive increase in the placental transfer of antibodies during the course of gestation has been found for antistreptolysins, antistaphylolysins, and diphtheria antitoxins (references in reference 181). This rise in the fetal antibody level roughly parallels the increase in the fetal IgG level (see Section 6.1.1). Antibodies of maternal origin can also be found in the CSF of newborns, as was recently shown for diphtheria and tetanus antitoxins.[270] After birth, the concentration of passively acquired maternal antibodies, as with IgG, decreases exponentially, with a half-life that has been variously estimated as being between 18 and 42 days.[63]

Maternal antibodies may be detected in the child as long as 6–9 months after birth, but detection depends on the initial concentration and on the sensitivity of the method of testing.[63]

6.3.5. Antibody Transfer from Mother to Offspring in Animals

The transplacental route of antibody transfer from mother to child described above applies only to the human (Fig. 8). In rabbits and in guinea pigs, the transfer of antibodies from mother to fetus occurs not only before birth, but also by a route other than via the placenta (references in reference 181). The yolk sac or vitelline membrane is the main site of protein and antibody transfer from mother to fetus in the rabbit[30] and in guinea pigs[19] (Fig. 8). The Fc fragment of the IgG molecule is responsible for antibody transmission across the fetal yolk sac.[31] In these species, no transfer of antibodies occurs by the maternal colostrum and milk.

In contrast to the foregoing species, the newborn of cows, goats, sheep, pigs, and horses (references in references 180 and 181) are born without electrophoretically detectable γ-globulins and without antibodies, but immediately after birth, these substances

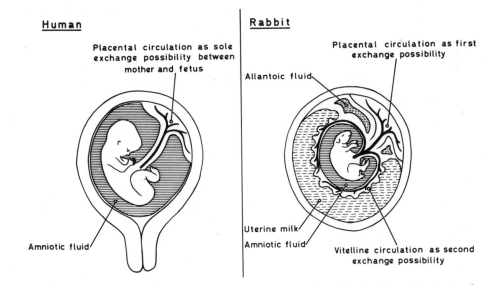

Human

Placental circulation as sole exchange possibility between mother and fetus

Amniotic fluid

Rabbit

Placental circulation as first exchange possibility

Allantoic fluid

Uterine milk

Amniotic fluid

Vitelline circulation as second exchange possibility

Fig. 8. Fetal–maternal relationship in the human and in the rabbit. In the rabbit, most of the protein transmitted from mother to fetus is absorbed by way of the inner wall of the yolk sac (the homologue of intestinal epithelium), which is exposed to the secretions of the uterine wall (uterine milk). In the human, the yolk sac constitutes a rudimentary, nonfunctional formation that is soon withdrawn into the umbilical stalk as embryonic development proceeds.

Table XIV. Antibody Transfer Across the Human Placenta[a]

Types of antibodies (with indication of predominant immunoglobulin class)	Comparative levels in mother and child		
	Approximately equal	Lower levels in cord blood	Absent in newborn
A. Antibodies against human constituents			
1. Antierythrocyte antibodies			
Isoagglutinins anti-A and anti-B			
Complete IgM (and IgA)		+	
Incomplete IgG	+		
Anti-M, anti-S, anti-Fy[a], anti-Kell, anti-Le[a], anti-Le[b]	+		
Anti-Rh antibodies			
Complete IgM (and IgA)			+
Incomplete IgG	+		
Anti-M, anti-S, anti-Fy[a], anti-Kell, anti-Le[a], anti-Le[b]	+		
Incomplete autoagglutinins	+		
2. Antileukocyte antibodies[b]			
Agglutinins	+		
Anti-*HLA* antibodies		(+)	+
3. Genetic factors of Ig			
Anti-Gm antibodies[c]	+		
Anti-IgA[d]	+		
4. Antiplatelet antibodies		+	
5. Antinuclear antibodies IgG, IgM (IgA?)		+	
6. Miscellaneous			
Antithyroid antibodies IgM			+
Rheumatoid factor IgM			+
Antiintrinsic factor	+		
C-reactive protein			+
B. Antibodies against infective agents			
1. Neutralizing antibodies			
Antidiphtheria antitoxin	+		
Anti-scarlet fever antitoxin	+		
Antitetanus antitoxin	+		
Antistreptolysins	+		
Antistaphylolysins	+		
Antihyaluronidase	+		
2. Antibacterial agglutinins IgG, IgM, IgA			
Hemophilus pertussis	+		
Hemophilus influenzae		+	
Shigella dysenteriae		+	+
Salmonella typhi (H antigen)	+		
(O antigen)		+	
Escherichia coli			+
3. Antibacterial bactericidins			
Salmonella typhi IgG	+		
IgM			+
Escherichia coli IgG	+		
IgM			+

Table XIV (continued)

Types of antibodies (with indication of predominant immunoglobulin class)	Comparative levels in mother and child		
	Approximately equal	Lower levels in cord blood	Absent in newborn
4. Antiviral antibodies IgG			
Protective			
Measles	+		
Herpes simplex	+		
Poliomyelitis	+		
Japanese B encephalitis	+		
Vaccinia	+		
Coxsackie	+		
Varicella zoster	+		
Rubella	+		
Complement-binding			
Influenza	+		
Mumps	+		
APC virus	+		
Rickettsien	+		
5. Antibodies against larger microorganisms			
Syphilis IgG, IgA, IgM		+	
Toxoplasmosis	+		
Histoplasmosis	+		
Coccidiodomycosis	+		
C. Antibodies against allergens			
Skin-sensitizing reagins IgE			+
Blocking antibodies IgG	+		
D. Miscellaneous antibodies			
Anti-cow milk precipitins IgG	+		
Anti-sheep erythrocyte agglutinins IgG, IgA, IgM		+	

[a] Data from de Muralt.[181]
[b] Data from Ahrons,[5] Bertrams et al.,[26] and Overweg and Engelfried.[200]
[c] Data from Nathenson et al.[189]
[d] Data from Vyas et al.[286]

are transmitted to the newborn via colostrum and milk; 36 hr after birth, this resorption is no longer possible. The rat, the mouse, the dog, and the cat (references in references 179 and 181) occupy an intermediate position: the transmission of antibodies from mother to offspring takes place before as well as after birth. The resorption of colostrum and milk antibodies through the gut proceeds, however, for a longer time than in other animals: up to 10 days in the dog and cat, to about 16 days in the mouse,

and 20 days in the rat (references in reference 181). At least in rats, the amount of antibody present in the infant seems to be in direct relationship to the duration of suckling.[218] One part of the antibodies is transferred to the fetus through the yolk sac splanchnopleure,[32] and another part through the placenta.[217]

For a long time, these differences in the transmission of antibodies from mother to offspring were attributed to differences in the placental barrier.[139]

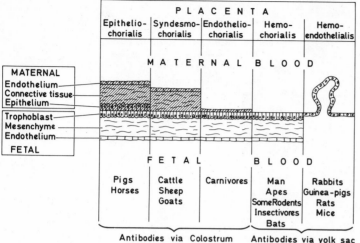

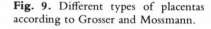

Fig. 9. Different types of placentas according to Grosser and Mossmann.

Traditionally, the chorioallantoic placentas of eutherian mammals have been classified into five groups, according to Grosser and Mossmann (Fig. 9) (references in reference 181). More recent studies by electron microscopy[7,299] have shown, however, that we must now consider only three main types of placentas: (1) the epitheliochorial placenta, as found in mares, sows, cows, goats, and ewes; (2) the endotheliochorial placenta, as found in dogs and cats; and (3) the hemochorial placenta, as found in primates (including man), as well as in rabbits, rats, mice, and guinea pigs. As shown in Table XV, the disappearance of the uterine epithelium (Ep) from the placental formation makes the organ permeable to maternal IgG. This does not hold true for other transmitted substances. For electrolytes, for instance, the disappearance of the uterine endothelium (En) increases the rate of transfer through the placenta roughly 10 times.[74]

7. Development of the Postnatal Immunoglobulin Pattern

7.1. General Immunoglobulin Pattern in Newborns

Since the introduction of electrophoresis as an analytic tool, a large number of studies on the development of the postnatal plasma-protein pattern have been published (references in references 180 and 245). At birth, the newborn has a total protein level of 5.5–6.0 g/dl, which is lower than the maternal level. This relative hypoproteinemia is due to lowered α_1-, α_2-, and β-globulins levels, and to a lesser extent, to hypoalbuminemia. After birth, an accelerated increase in the concentrations of α- and β-globulins and to some extent of albumin occurs. The most impressive change is the fast decline of the electrophoretically measured γ-globulin level during the first 3 months. At birth, the newborn has a γ-globulin concentration corresponding to that of its mother (i.e., 1100–1300 mg/dl for Caucasians and 1800–1900 mg/dl for black babies); between the 6th and 8th weeks, this concentration usually reaches a minimum of about 400 mg/dl.

At least three factors contribute to this decline of the γ-globulin level in the young infant: (1) The catabolism of γ-globulins that were received from the mother. In the neonate, IgG is degraded in the reticuloendothelial system[245] at a rate of approximately 2.3% of the total body IgG per day,[87] which is equivalent to a half-life of about 30 days. In addition, some loss of IgG occurs by secretion into the intestinal tract (references are in reference 181). The amount of this loss into the intestine is still unknown. (2) The neonate synthesizes sufficient IgG to replace only a small fraction of the IgG catabolized.[87] (3) There is a dilution of the mass of the transmittted IgG in an expanding volume of plasma and tissue fluids.[276] Consequently, the IgG level falls in the infant until the amount synthesized by the infant equals that being degraded, an event that normally occurs between 1 and 3 months of life. After the 3rd month, the

Table XV. Modes of Transfer of Proteins and Antibodies from Mother to Child

Type of placenta	Maternal layers[b]	Development of yolk sac	Transmission — Before birth		Transmission — After birth (Transfer by colostrum and milk)		
			Amount	Type[c]	Amount	Duration	Type
Epitheliochorial	En, C, Ep						
Cow, sheep, goat		Rudimentary	0	−	++++	24–36 hr	Nonselective
Pig		Rudimentary	0	−	++++	24–36 hr	Nonselective
Horse		Rudimentary	0	−	++++	24–36 hr	−
Endotheliochorial	En, 0, 0						
Dog, cat (Carnivora)		Rudimentary (+ in early stages)	++	?	++	10 days	?
Hemochorial	0, 0, 0						
Rat, mouse		++++	++	Full	++	16–20 days	Selective
Guinea pig		++++	++++	Full	−	−	−
Rabbit		++++	++++	Full	−	−	−
Man, apes, monkeys (primates)		Rudimentary	++++	IgG	0 (traces)	?	(Nonselective?)

[a] Adapted from Schultze and Heremans,(245) by courtesy of Elsevier Publishing Company.

[b] The layers interposed between the maternal blood and the fetal trophoblast are named in the order of their disposition: endothelium (En), connective tissue (C), and uterine epithelium (Ep). Absence of a layer is denoted by 0.

[c] Full: Full transmitters (many different proteins, besides Ig, are transferred, although preference is given to homologous IgG); −: nontransmitters (no transference of plasma proteins from mother to child); IgG: IgG transmitters (homologous IgG is virtually the only protein transferred from mother to child).

IgG level increases again, but it is not before age 12–18 months that near-adult values of IgG globulins are obtained.[180,245] In infants born before term, the hypoproteinemia increases with lower gestational age. The IgG levels in the cord blood of these infants are lower than the levels in infants born at or near term, and the fall of the IgG levels at 3 months of age is more pronounced (references are in reference 180).

The introduction of immunologic methods for quantitation of various serum protein fractions has greatly promoted a better understanding of these changes. At present, single radial immunodiffusion with monospecific antisera is the best available method for determining Ig.[259] This method has a precision of 5%,[124,261] and it can easily detect levels of 1 mg/dl.[124,261]

The *total IgG* level of 1000–1200 mg/dl in the cord blood of healthy Caucasian newborns approaches normal adult levels (see Fig. 6) because of the placental passage of this Ig. It drops gradually and reaches a minimum of 400–500 mg/dl between 4 and 6 months. Thereafter, it remains low during the second half of the first year (500–600 mg/dl). The adult level is reached again very late, between 6[4] and 16 years of age.[261] As can be seen in Fig. 10, the concentrations of the four IgG subclasses throughout the first 2 years of life show considerable heterogeneity, leading to the conclusion that for each subgroup, there is a different age of onset and speed of synthesis; within 1 month after birth, IgG_3 values rise to considerable levels, and after 3 months to adult levels. IgG_1 synthesis begins before 3 months of age, and concentrations are close to adult values at 8 months, whereas IgG_2 and IgG_1 synthesis is still far from maturity at age 2 years.[174]

The *IgA concentration* at birth is very low, averaging 3 mg/dl.[260] It might be undetectable[124] in cord blood, but at 6 weeks, it is always detectable, and thereafter it increases slowly to reach 20[124] to 40 mg/dl[4] at 1 year of age. Adult levels are attained by 12[4] to 16 years of age.[261]

The *IgM concentration* at birth is about 10[124,260] to 20,[4,247] and then it rises very rapidly during the first weeks of life, reaching about 30 mg/dl at 8 days,[247] and about half the adult level (45 mg/dl) at 3[124] to 6 months.[261]

There is no marked difference in levels of IgG, IgA, and IgM between male and female infants during the first year of life.[4,161,261] Normal black infants tend toward higher IgG values than normal white

infants; conversely, white infants tend to have higher levels of IgM than normal black infants.[161]

With very sensitive immunochemical methods, *IgD* has been found in 4.5–8% of the samples of cord blood tested.[148] The measured levels amounted to 0.03 mg/dl.[148,260] At 1 year, it was detectable in about one-fifth of the infants examined (average, 0.6 mg/dl), and at 5 years, in 61% of the 13 cases tested (average, 2.4 mg/dl). In adults, IgD was found in 79% of the 89 cases studied (average, 11.7 mg/dl).[124]

IgE is present in small amounts in cord blood (average, 0.003 mg/dl). It increases gradually during childhood to an average level of 0.03 mg/dl in adults.[122]

7.2. Factors That Influence the Postnatal Immunoglobulin Pattern

7.2.1. Length of Pregnancy

In infants of low birth weight, the electrophoretically defined γ-globulin level is decreased at birth in proportion to the degree of immaturity; the postnatal decline is steeper and the recovery is more protracted than in full-size infants (references in references 180 and 245). This pattern has also been confirmed by immunologic methods. The IgG concentration in cord blood rises steeply with increasing birth weight,[41,102,232,268,292] an increase of 500 g in birth weight being associated with a rise in IgG of about 200 mg/dl.[268] Nevertheless, the IgG levels in cord blood are correlated with gestational age even better than with birth weight.[24,64,94,109,129,203,304] The postnatal decline in newborns of low gestational age occurs earlier[24] and results in much lower IgG values around 9–13 weeks than is the case in babies born at term (Fig. 11). After the age of 9–13 weeks, however, more than 80% of newborns born before term rapidly increase their IgG concentration, thus equaling that of the full-term babies.[210]

Small-for-date newborn babies have significantly lower IgG levels than do normal babies of the same gestational age. After term, the serum IgG level declines; infants born after a gestation of 42 weeks or longer also have significantly lower IgG levels than full-term normal infants. In both cases, this decrease seems to be related to impaired placental function.[129,304]

Conflicting evidence has been published concerning the relationship between birth weight and

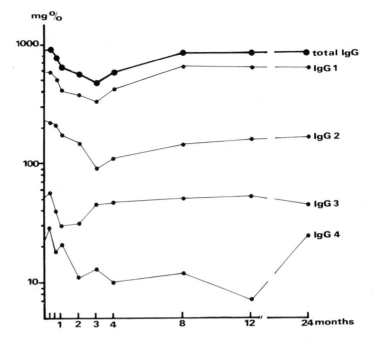

Fig. 10. Development of the IgG subclasses during the first 2 years of life. Reproduced from Morell *et al.*[174] with permission.

the concentration of IgA and IgM at birth. Some authors[49,129,204,231,242,292] have found lower levels of IgA and IgM at birth in infants of low birth weight than in full-size babies, and this difference was still present at 6 months of age.[49] The analysis of over 5000 cord-blood levels and their correlation with birth weight showed an increase in the 97th percentile of about 0.5 mg/dl with every 200 g increase of birth weight above the 1800-g level.[303] Other authors found no correlation

between cord-blood IgA and/or IgM levels and birth weight[41,64,102,232,268] or length of pregnancy.[24,64,210] When IgM was absent at birth, its postnatal appearance was more delayed in the 1500- to 2000-g birth-weight group than in the 2000- to 2500-g birth-weight group.[242] This delay was even more pronounced in infants with a birth weight of less than 1500 g.[292] At 24 hr of life, small-for-date newborns have an IgM blood level lower than the level corresponding to their gesta-

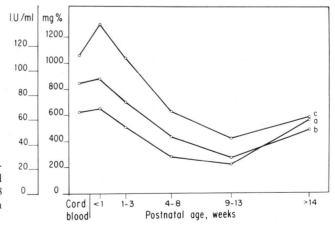

Fig. 11. IgG concentrations in infants' serum during the first weeks of life in relation to gestational age: (a) 30–33 weeks; (b) 34–37 weeks; (c) > 38 weeks. Reproduced from Pilgrim *et al.*[210] with permission.

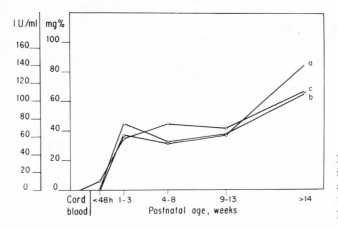

Fig. 12. IgM concentrations in infants' serum during the first weeks of life in relation to gestational age: (a) 30–33 weeks; (b) 34–37 weeks; (c) > 38 weeks. Reproduced from Pilgrim *et al.*[210] with permission.

tional age.[204] Figure 12 shows the postnatal development of IgM concentrations in three groups of infants of different gestational ages. Three phases may be distinguished: a steep rise within the first few days,[24,124,210,220] then a leveling off for several weeks,[124,210] followed by another rise less sharp than the initial one.[210,220]

Birth weight is also related to the amount of passively transmitted maternal antibodies (see Section 6.3.4). For example, for diphtheria antitoxin, the ratio of the mother/child concentrations is 2.5 in babies of less than 1000 g, 2.0 in babies between 1000 and 1500 g, 1.5 in babies between 1500 and 2000 g, and 1.0 in babies weighing more than 2000 g.[50]

7.2.2. Nutritional State

There is a positive correlation between the dietary protein intake and Ig production in infants and children. In malnourished children without evidence or a recent history of concurrent infection, there is a significant decrease of the serum IgG level and a tendency to lowered IgA and IgM levels.[40] In contrast, in undernourished children with infection, the serum IgG level is doubled, and the IgA and IgM levels are significantly increased.[40,256] In older children, a daily supplement of 25 g of dietary protein produced a significant increase of IgG synthesis and antibody production after primary immunization with flagellin from *Salmonella adelaide* as compared with children receiving the usual daily intake of about 10 g protein.[156] It thus appears that even among ostensibly healthy children, a low intake of dietary protein is associated with a reduced capacity for production of immunoglobulins.

7.2.3. Naturally Occurring Infections in Humans

Normally, the human fetus is well protected by the placenta and the fetal membranes; i.e., it is kept essentially antigen-free, and it is not submitted to any immunologic stress.[11] Although the absence of plasma cells in the normal fetus has been observed,[28,34] it should not be taken as indicative of an immunologic null state, but rather as freedom from antigenic stimuli provided by the normal function of the placenta. Should the placenta fail in this protective function by permitting a fetal infection with a highly antigenic pathogen, then an immunologic response might ensue, with production of plasma cells and antibodies. In fact, appearance of plasma cells and production of IgM have been observed in human fetuses with congenital syphilis and toxoplasmosis from the 28th week of gestation.[60,249] At birth and in the following days, their IgA and IgM levels are significantly higher than in normal controls.[222,262] These observations give more credit to earlier reports that human newborns with congenital syphilis occasionally show higher Wassermann titers than their mothers, and even positive Wassermann titers despite negative maternal serology (complete references in reference 181). Elevated levels of IgM in cord blood have also been reported in cases of congenital herpes simplex infection,[248] in congenital coxsackie infection,[261] in congenital cytomegalic inclusion disease,[157] in congenital rubella syndrome,[3,261,304] and in some infants who were suffering from a threatened abortion during the early months of gestation.[160] In infants born after premature rupture of the fetal membranes or suffering from neonatal sepsis, the vels of IgM in cord blood can be normal, and may not be increased in the infant's blood until 6 ays after birth.[147]

The determination of IgG, IgM, and IgA levels the blood of newborns is now being widely sed in the early detection of chronic inapparent erinatal infections, such as congenital toxoplasnosis, cytomegalovirus infection, rubella synrome, and syphilis. The question was recently viewed,[3,182] and can be summarized as follows: ie host response to the chronicity of inapparent ongenital infections appears to be predominantly ne of overreaction as regards Ig production.

IgM development is excessively rapid beginning *utero* and continuing through the early months f life. The average levels reached in cord blood vere 35 mg/dl (normal controls, <20 mg/dl); at ge 10 days, 45 mg/dl (normal controls, 25–30 1g/dl); and at age 6 months, 100 mg/dl (normal ontrols, 60 mg/dl).

IgG development, which is apparently normal utero, is significantly stimulated shortly after irth, resulting in a foreshortened catabolic phase or maternally derived IgG and persistently elevated vels of this Ig throughout infancy. The levels eached in cord blood do not differ from the levels f normal, noninfected children; at age 3 months, ie levels in infected infants average 700 mg/dl normal controls, 500 mg/dl); at age 6 months, 00 mg/dl (normal controls, 600 mg/dl); and at ge 9 months, 1250 mg/dl (normal controls, 800 1g/dl). At 1 year of age, there is no difference etween the blood levels of IgG in infected and oninfected infants.

It is not unusual to find low or absent production f IgA in congenital rubella, and occasionally after ytomegalovirus infection, herpes simplex virus inection, or syphilis. In addition, aberrant or absent esponses to foreign antigens, e.g., DPT immunizaion, and deficiencies in cellular immune response nay also occur. Congenital toxoplasmosis may also etard or ablate IgA synthesis for months.

Infection with *Pneumocystis carinii* produces a ignificant rise of the IgM levels in affected inants.[137] Antibody production after infections with enteropathogenic types of *Escherichia coli* that vere acquired shortly after birth has been decribed.[265] In an epidemic of *Salmonella* (type Newport),[90] antibody to the somatic antigen was lemonstrated in the sera of 11 1- to 2-month-old nfants of low birth weight. The type of antibody n all the infected infants was found to be IgM.

No IgG was detected as late as 60 days after the onset of symptoms. This finding is in accordance with earlier observations showing that in infants of low birth weight who were suffering from various infections, the postnatal decline of the electrophoretic γ-globulin levels is less marked than in healthy infants of the same weight, and that IgA and IgM also appear in the blood of the infected infants of low birth weight at an earlier time than in healthy ones (references in reference 181).

7.2.4. Inoculations with Various Antigens in Humans

(a) Active Antibody Production. Immunization of infants of low birth weight and of full-size newborn infants with *Salmonella* vaccines,[72,255] with bacteriophage θ 174,[278] with diphtheria toxoid,[53] or with attenuated polio virus[201] has shown that even very small babies of less than 1000 g were able to respond to this antigenic stimulus by antibody formation. In many instances, the titers were comparable to those obtained in adults.

(b) Timing and Sequence of Antibody Production. Antibody production in the adult and the infant is quantitatively similar, but differs in the timing of its appearance. In full-size infants as well as in infants of low birth weight, the immunizations with *Salmonella* vaccines and with bacteriophage result in the formation of IgM 10–20 days after immunization; the production of IgG starts about 6–10 weeks after immunization.[72,255] Booster doses always result in the production of IgG.[72] The long interval between the appearance of IgM and IgG antibodies is consistent with the overall pattern of Ig synthesis (see Section 4.2). The same sequence of appearance has been observed in animals (references in reference 181). In adults, the IgM synthesis starts 4 to 5 days after immunization, followed 3 or 4 days later by the appearance of IgG.[255]

(c) Immunosuppressive Effect of Maternal Antibodies. Infants with maternal antibodies in their circulation do not respond to antigen as well as infants without maternal antibodies. The maternal antibodies can reach the infant either by the placental route (antibodies of the IgG type) or by the colostral route (antibodies of the secretory IgA type). Table XVI shows the maternal antibodies that have been studied in newborn blood and the type of antigenic stimuli with which the antibody

Table XVI. Immunosuppressive Effect of Maternal Antibodies on the Immune Response of the Newborn[a]

Passively acquired maternal antibodies	Immunization
Transplacentally transferred antibodies	
Diphtheria	Diphtheria toxoid
Typhoid agglutinins	Typhoid vaccine
Paratyphoid agglutinins	Paratyphoid vaccine
Poliomyelitis antibodies	Attenuated polio vaccine (Sabin)
	Killed polio vaccine (Salk)
Measles antibodies	Attenuated measles vaccine
Pertussis	Pertussis vaccine
Colostral antibodies	
Poliomyelitis antibodies	Attenuated polio vaccine (Sabin)

[a] Data from de Muralt.[182]

production has been evoked in the organism of the newborn. The inhibition of antibody production by the newborn is related to the levels of maternal antibodies at the time of immunization, as shown by the antibody responses of the human newborn to *Salmonella* flagellar (H) and somatic (O) antigens.[255] Only newborn infants who had high levels of passively acquired maternal antibodies to H antigen (titers of 1 : 40 or more) did not respond to *Salmonella* vaccine with a significant H agglutinin response.

All the antibodies transferred across the placenta belong to the IgG type. The immunosuppressive effect of IgG on IgM antibody synthesis[73,238] is more pronounced than that of IgM.[172] IgM antibody that was acquired during exchange transfusion did not inhibit active antibody formation, whereas passively received IgG antibody inhibited active antibody formation completely and for as long as 6 months after antigen administration.[71]

The *immunosuppression* induced by maternal antibodies can generally be overcome by the administration of sufficient antigen.[58,280] The final titer obtained after a booster dose seems to be satisfactory whether passive antibodies are present or not.[240] After intrauterine transfusion, Hobbs *et al.*[110] observed elevated serum levels of IgA and IgM, but normal levels of IgG, in the newborn.

At 1 year of age, most of these babies had subnormal IgA and IgM levels compared with those found in controls matched for prematurity and severity of hemolytic disease of the newborn. The most likely explanation is that the fetus was stimulated atigenically by the donor blood, but the possibility of transfer of globulins or the inadvertent inclusion of viable lymphocytes in the donor plasma (either of which might lead to delayed emergence of the infant's own Ig) cannot be ruled out.

(d) Other Immunosuppressive Factors. Other factors present in the newborn, such as bilirubin, might exert a suppressive effect on active antibody production. A group of 12 infants with hyperbilirubinemia (>15 mg/dl) who had no exchange transfusion showed significantly less antibodies against pertussis, diphtheria, tetanus, and *E. coli* after immunization than the control group of normal infants.[191] Infants given repeated intramuscular injections of preparations of standard γ-globulin produce significantly less antibodies after immunization against diphtheria, whooping-cough, and tetanus than do infants without injections of γ-globulin.[190]

7.2.5. Response to Antigenic Stimuli in Animals

(a) Fetal and Neonatal Response to Immunization with Various Antigens. In animals the antibody formation following immunization has been studied in embryos, fetuses, and newborn of many species (references in references 181 and 257). Three facts emerge from these studies: (1) the importance of the lymphoid tissues and the small lymphocyte in antibody production; (2) achievement of immunologic competence may not be equally and simultaneously effected toward all antigens; and (3) the strong immunosuppressive effect of passively administered IgM antibody.

The capacity to react immunologically can be demonstrated as soon as small lymphocytes appear in the circulation. As in humans, plasma cells appear in fetuses after intrauterine infection at a stage which they are still absent in normal, noninfected fetuses. The sequence of appearance of the Ig in animals is the same as in humans: the first antibodies to appear in the circulation belong to the IgM class. Depending on the species studied, IgG appears 20–40 days later.

(b) Appearance of Immunoglobulins in Germ-Free Animals. The importance of antigenic stimuli for the production of Ig is underlined by the work with germ-free animals (complete references in references 181 and 257). Germ-free animals have greatly reduced levels of serum γ-globulins compared with conventional animals. This reduction is due to a 2–5 times lower rate of synthesis of γ-globulins. Synthesis of IgA and IgM is more affected by a germ-free environment than IgG synthesis; total proteins and albumin remain unchanged when compared with normal animals. Germ-free-raised animals cannot replace the transmitted maternal γ-globulins by a sufficient endogenous production of γ-globulins. The number of blast cells and immature and mature plasma cells in germ-free animals is about 10 times lower than in normal animals. In colostrum-deprived and sterilely raised animals, no "natural" antibody is produced. Two weeks after introduction of a normal bacterial flora into the gut of germ-free animals, the number of lymphocytes and plasmocytes in the intestinal wall normalizes, followed by a rise of α_2- and β-globulins; however, the γ-globulin level does not increase earlier than 4 weeks after the first contact with microorganisms, and then slowly reaches normal adult levels. These experiments demonstrate clearly that the ability of germ-free animals to actively produce antibody is not impaired, and that a normal flora of microorganisms is a strong antigenic stimulus accelerating immunologic maturation.

Situations that may be compared with these experiments in animals have been observed in man. The intestinal tracts of breast-fed and artificially fed full-term and premature newborn infants were colonized with a nonpathogenic E. coli serotype O 83, which remained predominant for several months. The hemagglutinating antibody against E. coli O 83 appeared in the sera and stools of colonized infants within 2 weeks after the beginning of the colonization with E. coli O 83, and the titer was significantly higher than in controls. The premature infants developed a titer of O 83 antibody lower than the full-term ones, but higher than the average titer against other E. coli types that naturally colonized the intestinal tract. Concentrations of IgA and IgM were higher in the sera of colonized infants than in the sera of controls; there was no difference in the level of IgG. In stool extracts, IgG was absent, IgM was present in trace quantities in most of the colonized infants, and IgA was detected in the first 3 weeks in artificially fed colonized infants and after 5 weeks in controls. IgA, probably of colostral origin, was present in the stools of breast-fed infants soon after birth.[152] Keller et al.[133] demonstrated the development of poliovirus-IgA-neutralizing coproantibodies in newborn infants following a single immunization with a living polio virus vaccine administered orally or parenterally. Oral immunization resulted in the production of coproantibodies before serum antibodies were produced. This coproantibody production in breast-fed infants is correlated with the level of antibodies in mother's milk, thus suggesting passive transfer from the milk.[134]

These results are in agreement with those obtained by Schneegans et al.,[241,242] who observed enhanced IgM antibody synthesis in premature infants kept in a normal environment as compared with the IgM production in babies raised in semisterile conditions.

7.2.6. Absorption of Immunoglobulins from Colostrum and Milk by the Human Newborn

Many authors have studied the question of how much the Ig from colostrum and milk contribute to the antibody pool of the young infant. The proteins of human milk have been extensively analyzed by electrophoretic and immunologic methods. Several reviews of these studies have been published.[99,186,285] Human colostrum and milk represent an abundant source of IgM, and still more of secretory IgA (Table XVII and Fig. 13).

The *secretory IgA* is the predominant Ig in human colostrum and milk. Early colostrum contains as mush as 2000–4000 mg IgA/dl. After the first 2–4 days, these values drop to about 100 mg/dl, but the increase in milk production may then compensate for the fall in Ig concentration.[100] Over a 4-month period, there is essentially no drop in the quantity of IgA that the breast-fed infant consumes.[22] The infant ingests a sufficient amount of milk antibodies to permit their detection in the stools.[86,134,165] A correlation between the titer of such coproantibodies and a reduction in the number of coliform bacteria in the stool could be shown.[165] On the 4th day of life, IgA and the "secretory piece" were recovered in the stools of all but one of a group of infants breast-fed since birth. IgM was found in the stools of only half these infants. The presence or absence of IgA in

Table XVII. Serum Proteins Detected in Human Colostrum and Milk[a]

Serum protein	Colostrum[b]	Milk[b]
Prealbumin	(+)	(+)
Albumin	++	+
Acid seromucoid	(+)	(+)
α_1-Antitrypsin (3.5 S)	(+)	(+)
α_2-Lipoprotein	(+)	((+))
β-Lipoprotein	(+)	((+))
Ceruloplasmin	(+)	((+))
Haptoglobin	(+)	(+)
Transferrin	(+)	(+)
β_{1A}-Globulin (C3)	+	+
Fibrinogen	(+)	−
IgA	+	++
IgM	++	+
IgG	+	+
IgD	+	+
IgE	(+)	(+)
Properdin	+	+
C1	+	+
C2	+	+
C3	+	+

[a] Data from de Muralt,[181] completed with data from Hanson and Johansson.[99]

[b] ++ denotes larger amounts; + denotes distinct amounts; (+) denotes traces; ((+)) denotes smallest traces [detectable only by the enrichment procedure (comparative immunoelectrophoresis after Wadsworth, Hanson, and Ossermann)].

the stools did not correlate with the IgA levels in blood serum. IgA found in the stools was immunologically identical to the IgA found in colostrum. No IgA, no secretory piece, and no IgM could be found in the stools of control infants fed with cow's milk only.[92]

The secretory IgA molecule is more resistant to pH changes and proteolytic enzymes than are serum IgA or other Ig that may enable the secretory IgA antibodies of milk to function in the variable milieu of the gut. A certain amount of the secretory IgA present in colostrum and milk is produced by glandular secretion in the human mammary tissue.[98] Some amount of this secretory IgA is also synthesized by the cells present in human colostrum. Human colostrum contains as many as 1000–7000

leukocytes/mm³.[170,252] The median concentration of lymphocytes in human colostrum is about 200/mm³,[55] and that of macrophages is 2000/mm³.[252] Of the colostral lymphocytes, 50% are T cells[22,55] and 20–50% B cells.[22,55] Colostral leukocytes are able to synthesize IgA, β_{1C},[22,187,188] and a protein specific to colostrum.[22] Most of the IgA produced is of the secretory type.[88a] IgA secretion and presumably synthesis are not affected by the transition from colostrum to milk.[115] Breast milk from Guatemalan and North American mothers contains the same amount of secretory IgA.[264a]

The *IgG* concentration amounts to about 40–80 mg/dl in early colostrum and drops to about 4–12 mg/dl after the 4th day. The IgG present in colostrum and milk is actively and specifically transported from blood into milk.[115] No evidence for the formation of IgG by colostral cells has been found.[22,188]

The *IgM* concentration is 125–160 mg/dl in early colostrum and 10–30 mg/dl in 4th-day colostrum. IgM is transmitted through glandular epithelium.[9]

As for IgG, no evidence for the formation of IgM by colostral cells has been found.[22,188] Small traces of *IgD* and *IgE* are also present in colostrum.

No difference in IgA, IgG, and IgM content has been found between the milk from the right and the left mammary gland, and no variations were registered during the individual breast feeding, nor for the 24-hr period as a whole.[206a]

Human colostrum contains antibodies against bacteria (especially against the most important bacterial pathogen of the neonate, i.e., *E. coli*), viruses, and blood group substances (A, B, Rh) (Table XVIII). Antibody activity against staphylococci, pneumococci, *E. coli*, polio virus, and blood group substances seem to be associated primarily with the secretory IgA fraction of human milk.[98,9] For *E. coli* O antibodies, it has been shown that the ratio milk antibody/serum antibody is very high for IgA, suggesting a local production; the ratios for IgG are under 1, suggesting a restricted transfer from serum into milk; ratios of about 1 for IgM do not exclude some local production.[39b] The IgA *E. coli* O antibodies are present in similar concentrations in milk from mothers of a very low socioeconomic group and in milk from healthy Swedish mothers.[39a] Breast milk from Guatemalan and North American mothers has the same antitoxin activity against *E. coli* and *V. cholerae* entero

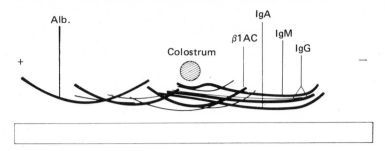

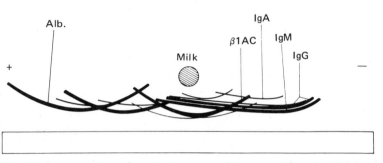

Fig. 13. Immunoelectrophoretic diagrams of human milk and colostrum developed with horse immune serum against human serum. Data from de Muralt.[180]

oxins[264a]; this antitoxic activity is correlated with the IgA content of the milk.[264a] The titers of these antibodies present in colostrum and milk fall rapidly to undetectable levels within 5–10 days after birth, as has been shown, for instance, for antistreptolysin,[193] typhoid agglutinins,[244] Rh antibodies,[237], and *E. coli* O antibodies.[39b] The maternal *E. coli* O antibodies given to the infant

in milk do not prevent intestinal colonization by *E. coli*.[89a]

An overwhelming body of evidence indicates that virtually none or only traces of this large supply of Ig are absorbed and enter the infant's circulation. This is already evident from the fact that the two predominant Ig from colostrum and milk, i.e., IgA and IgM, are precisely those that

Table XVIII. Antibodies Detected in Human Colostrum and Milk*a*

Antibacterial antibodies	Antiviral antibodies
Diphtheria	Influenza
Tetanus	Poliomyelitis
Pertussis	Coxsackie
Typhoid (H antigen)	Mumps
Typhoid (O antigen)	Vaccinia
Dysenteria	Trachom
Escherichia coli (pathogenic strains)	Antierythrocyte antibodies
Pneumococci*b*	Anti-A and anti-B antibodies
Antistreptolysins	Anti-Rh antibodies
Antistaphylolysins	

a Data from de Muralt.[182]
b Data from Hanson and Johansson.[99]

are poorly represented in the serum of the normal newborn. In a large number of full-size infants, the observed increases of the IgA and IgM levels in the serum proceeded at the same rate whether the infant was breast-fed or fed with cow's milk since birth (complete references in reference 181). Concerning the time when IgA and IgM appear in the sera of artificially fed infants, the observation is of interest that infants of low birth weight did not differ significantly from infants of the same birth weight who were fed colostrum. It was recently shown in a small series of 18 infants, however, that on the 5th day of life, the levels of IgG, IgA, and IgM were significantly higher in the sera of infants who received only colostrum in the first 3 days of life than in the sera of those infants who did not receive colostrum.[119] Many unsuccessful attempts to detect oral transfer of antibodies present in colostrum and milk have been published (references in reference 181). No concrete evidence for intestinal absorption has been disclosed with the aid of ^{131}I-labeled human γ-globulin (references in reference 181).

Despite all these negative results, we have some reason to believe that Ig from milk and colostrum can be absorbed by the infant's digestive tract, but only in very small amounts. According to some authors (references in reference 181), a transfer of minute amounts of antibodies to diphtheria antitoxin, tetanus toxoid, *Salmonella* antigens, and blood group substance A occurs by this route.

The results cited above lead to the conclusion that a very small portion of the colostrum antibodies reaches the infant's circulation, and that better resistance of breast-fed infants against many bacterial and viral infections[97,100,243] cannot result from transmission of maternal antibodies of milk to the fetal blood. With the appreciation of secretory IgA as the main Ig in breast milk, and also as an important immune factor for epithelial surface, a new situation has developed. Recently reported studies[116] suggest that secretory antibodies in human milk could provide local passive immunity during the first days of the neonatal period, when local antibodies are low or absent from intestinal secretions. Since antibodies ingested in milk are not absorbed from the intestine into the serum in appreciable quantities, the high concentrations of IgA and bacterial and viral antibodies in human milk most probably function in the intestine to protect the epithelial surface against bacterial invasion and antigen uptake.

7.2.7. Absorption of Immunoglobulins from Colostrum and Milk by Animal Newborns

Whereas the intestinal tract plays no role or only a negligible role in the transfer of Ig from mother to child in human newborns, the situation is quite different in a large number of mammals. As early as 1892, Ehrlich[59] reported in his classic paper "Über Immunität durch Vererbung und Säugung," that antibodies from maternal colostrum and milk were transmitted to suckling mice by intestinal absorption. The same route of transfer was later demonstrated to occur in other species in which a part of the antibody transfer takes place during fetal life (see Section 6.3.5), e.g., the rat, dog, and cat. In rabbits and guinea pigs, the antibody transfer takes place only during fetal life, and no antibody transfer occurs after birth (references in reference 180). In the newborn calf, lamb, kid, and piglet,[180] no antenatal transfer of antibody is possible (see Section 6.3.5); the entire transfer of Ig from the colostrum into the neonatal circulation occurs immediately after birth (Figs. 14 and 15), and is accompanied, at least in the newborn calf, by proteinuria due largely to β-lactoglobulin.

In certain species, this intestinal absorption seems to be selective; the young mouse[177,178] and the newborn colostrum-deprived piglet[151] have been shown to absorb IgG antibodies but no IgM antibodies from a mixture of orally administered antibodies. Ig from one species can interfere with the intestinal absorption of Ig from another species, as shown in rats and mice.[31,176] The Fy fragment is responsible for this interference.[178] This fragment is absorbed about 11 times less easily than the whole molecule, but it proves to be a very effective blocking agent, presumably because it remains attached to the receptors of the intestinal cell.[197] The intestinal absorption of Ig is limited to a certain time after birth (see above).

As shown by the work of Krähenbühl and Campiche,[138] the functional differences of the jejunal absorptive cells correspond to these various modes of antibody absorption from the gut. These authors studied the jejunal absorption of IgG antibodies injected directly into the jejunal lumen in the newborn of three species: (1) rabbits, in which the transfer of passive antibodies occurs, as in humans, only through the placenta; (2) pigs, in which passive immunity is transmitted only by intestinal absorption of antibodies from colostrum

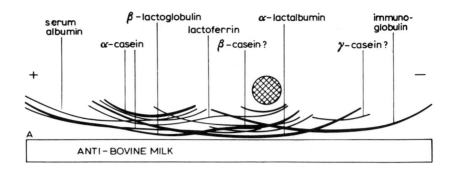

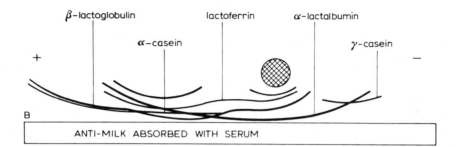

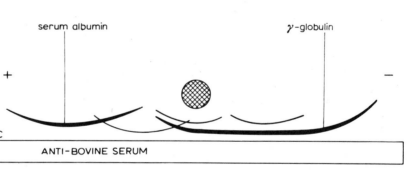

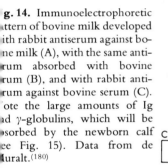

Fig. 14. Immunoelectrophoretic pattern of bovine milk developed with rabbit antiserum against bovine milk (A), with the same antiserum absorbed with bovine serum (B), and with rabbit antiserum against bovine serum (C). Note the large amounts of Ig and γ-globulins, which will be absorbed by the newborn calf (see Fig. 15). Data from de Muralt.[(180)]

nd milk; and (3) rats, in which antibodies are transmitted both across the placenta and by intestinal absorption after birth (see above). Intact antibodies were transferred into the circulation of the pig and the rat, but not into that of the rabbit. In the three species, the jejunal absorptive cells took up antibodies by endocytosis. In the pig, the intact IgG molecules were then transported across the epithelial cells in vacuoles, whereas in the rabbit, all absorbed IgG molecules were trapped in lysosomes; in this latter case, endocytosis of proteins triggered the release of lysosomal enzymes, including increased proteolytic activity. In the rat, both situations were found; there was no evidence of transfer of antibody fragments into the circulation.

It therefore seems likely that lysosomal activity is the means by which the jejunal cells of the newborn rabbit prevent the absorption of antibodies into the blood. The presence of a similar mechanism in the human intestine has not yet been studied.

8. Immunoparalysis and Immune Tolerance

Originally, it was thought that immune tolerance could be induced only in immunologically immature animals. It is now known, however, that chronological age is not the all-important factor in

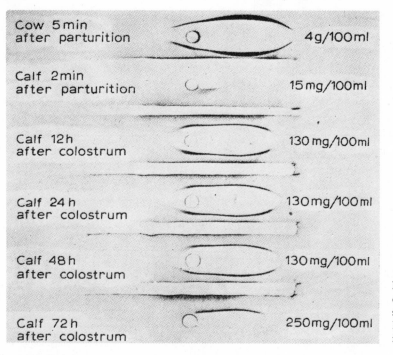

Cow 5 min after parturition	4g/100ml
Calf 2 min after parturition	15 mg/100ml
Calf 12 h after colostrum	130 mg/100ml
Calf 24 h after colostrum	130 mg/100ml
Calf 48 h after colostrum	130 mg/100ml
Calf 72 h after colostrum	250 mg/100ml

Fig. 15. Appearance of Ig in newborn calf's serum after birth. Virtually absent from the calf's serum at birth, the Ig appear rapidly as soon as colostrum is given. Data from de Muralt.[180]

determining whether an antigen will induce tolerance or immunity[166]; factors such as the type and relative dose of antigen, the efficiency of the reticuloendothelial system for adequate processing of the antigen,[198] and the existence of immunologically competent cells seem to determine the final outcome—tolerance or immunity. Antigen can drive a responsive lymphocyte in one of two basic directions, i.e., toward activation and clonal expansion or toward the tolerant state, which means temporary or permanent incapacity to react to antigen. A very low dose of antigen can produce a specific unresponsiveness that affects primarily T cells, while very high doses of antigen can produce immunologic tolerance in both B and T cells.[146] At present, only the early phase of tolerance induction in mature B cells is understood; in this phase, it appears that an overly close saturation of receptor sites on the membranes of B lymphocytes with antigenic determinants linked to each other, through a carrier or through antibody, can initiate tolerance even when only a very restricted portion of the cell's surface is affected.[197] Thus, tolerance can be induced in immunologically mature animals by low-dosage methods.[169] Immunity can be induced in most neonatal animals by the administration of an appropriate dose of antigen [see

Section 7.2.5(a)]. *Immunologic paralysis* implies that (1) a larger dose of antigen is needed to induce paralysis than tolerance, and (2) the maintenance of paralysis depends on the presence of antigen in the body (which is not required for tolerance).[168]

In humans, antibodies to maternal IgG were found in 3–10% of the infants examined who possessed an IgG factor different from that of their mothers.[258,294] The frequency of these antibodies declined with increasing age, and in adults, they were found in only 3 per 1000 of the cases.[258] Infants displaying this phenomenon are considered to have prenatally acquired immunologic paralysis to their mothers' IgG that was transplacentally transmitted. As soon as the maternal IgG fall below a certain level in the newborn, the infant loses this immunologic paralysis and becomes able to produce antibodies against the small amount of foreign IgG left in his circulation. Since the passively acquired IgG can remain in the infant's circulation for a variable time (see Section 6.3.4), this production of antibodies can occur as early as age 7 weeks,[294] or at 6 months.[258] These anti-IgG antibodies are not a source of transfusion reactions.[260]

A few cases have been described in which antibodies to maternal IgA were present in cord lood.[286] These antibodies belonged to the IgM or IgG class. Anti-IgA antibodies may cause ana-hylactic transfusion reactions.[287]

Immunologic paralysis against pertussis antigen as also been induced in newborn infants by a vigorous immunization schedule started within 24 hr after birth.[216] The immune response continued to be suppressed in 75% of the infants up to 5 months of age, but the same children were capable of responding normally to tetanus and to diphtheria toxoids. Although numerous investigators have reported that paralysis is highly selective for specific antigenic determinants, the induction of paralysis to one component of an antigen (while an immune response was induced to another component of the same antigen in the same animal) has also been described.[216] Evidence suggesting a failure of the immune response analogous to immune tolerance has been found in newborn infants[61,254] and in newborn chimpanzees.[61] The data reported may lead to the conclusion that newborn primates may react immunologically to foreign proteins either by antibody production or by immune tolerance. We still do not know all the factors involved, however, such as exact dosage; the importance of attaining certain stages of maturity; the function of B cells, T cells, and phagocytes; and the role of antigen-antibody complexes containing an excess of antigen. All these factors are decisive for producing immunologic tolerance.

9. References

1. ABBAS, T. M. AND TOVEY, J. E., 1960, Proteins of the liquor amnii, *Br. Med. J.* **1**:476.
2. AHERNE, W., AND DUNNILL, M. S., 1966, Morphometry of the human placenta, *Br. Med. Bull.* **22**:5.
3. ALFORD, C. A., REYNOLDS, D. W., AND STAGNO, S., 1974, Current concepts of chronic perinatal infections, in: *Modern Perinatal Medicine* (Gluck, ed.), p. 285, Year Book Medical Publishers, Chicago.
4. ALLANSMITH, M., McCLELLAN, B. H., BUTTERWORTH, M., AND MALONEY, J. R., 1968, The development of immunoglobulin levels in man, *J. Pediatr.* **72**:276.
5. AHRONS, S., 1971, *HL-A*-antibodies. Influence on the human foetus, *Tissue Antigens* **1**:129.
6. AHRONS, S., AND GLAVIND-KRISTENSEN, 1971, Cytotoxic *HL-A* antibodies. Immunoglobulin classification, *Tissue Antigens* **1**:121.
6a. ALLANSMITH, M., MALONEY, J., AND WYMER, B., 1966, Change in immunoglobulin levels in the same babies from birth to age 6 months, *Fed. Proc.* **25**:489.

7. AMOROSO, E. C., 1961, Histology of the placenta, *Br. Med. Bull.* **17**:81.
8. ANDREOLI, M., AND ROBBINS, J., 1962, Serum proteins and thyroxine–protein interaction in early human fetuses, *J. Clin. Invest.* **41**:1070.
9. ANDRES, G. A., MATTIUZ, P. L., AND CEPPELINI, R., 1970, Ontogenesi degli antigeni della istoincompatibilità, 54e Congr. Naz. Soc. Ital. Ost. Ginecol., Milano.
10. ARTENSTEIN, M. S., BELLANTI, J. A., AND BUESCHER, E. L., 1964, Identification of the antiviral substances in nasal secretions, *Proc. Soc. Exp. Biol. Med.* **117**:558.
11. ATKINS, H. J. B., 1958, A study in the transmission of maternal antibodies, *Br. Med. J.* **1**:187.
12. AUGUST, C. S., BERKEL, A. J., DRISCOLL, S., AND MERLER, E., 1971, Onset of lymphocyte function in the developing human fetus, *Pediatr. Res* **5**:539.
13. BACH, J. F., 1973, Evaluation of T-cells and thymic serum factors in man using the rosette technique, *Transplant. Rev.* **16**:196.
14. BANGHAM, D. R., 1960, The transmission of homologous serum proteins to the foetus and to the amniotic fluid in the rhesus monkey, *J. Physiol.* **153**:265.
15. BANGHAM, D. R., HOBBS, K. R., AND TEE, D. E. H., 1961, The origin and nature of proteins of the liquor amnii in the rhesus monkey; a new protein with some unusual properties, *J. Physiol.* **158**:207.
16. BARANDUN, S., STAMPFLI, K., SPENGLER, G. H., AND RIVA, G., 1959, Die Klinik des Antikörpermangel-syndroms (AMS), *Helv. Med. Acta* **26**:163.
17. BARBANTI, A., 1956, Il quadro proteico del liquido amniotico valuto elettroforeticamente e suoi rapporti col siero materno e quello fetale, *Minerva Ginecol.* **8**:780.
18. BARDAWIL, W. A., TOY, B. L., AND HERTIG, A. T., 1958, Localization of homologous plasma proteins in the human placenta by fluorescent antibody, *Amer. J. Obstet. Gynecol.* **75**:708.
19. BARNES, J. M., 1959, Antitoxin transfer from mother to fetus in the guinea pig, *J. Pathol. Bacteriol.* **77**:371.
20. BASTEN, A., MILLER, J. F. A. P., SPRENT, J., AND PYE, J., 1972, Receptor for antigen–antibody complexes used to separate T cells from B cells, *Nature (London)* **235**:178.
21. BASTEN, A., SPRENT, J., AND MILLER, J. F. A. P., 1972, A receptor for antibody–antigen complexes on B cells: Its value in separating T cells from the lymphocyte population, *Nature (London) New Biol.* **235**:178.
22. BEER, A. E., 1975, The cellular component of milk and its significance, *Report of the 68th Ross Conference on Pediatric Research*, p. 49, Ross Laboratories, Columbus, Ohio.
23. BENIRSCHKE, K., AND BOURNE, G. L., 1958, Plasma cells in an immature human placenta, *Obstet. Gynecol.* **12**:495.

24. Berg, T., 1968, Immunoglobulin levels in infants with low birth weights, *Acta Paediatr. Scand.* **57**:369.

25. Berg, T., and Nilsson, B. O., 1969, The foetal development of serum levels of IgG and IgM, *Acta Paediatr. Scand.* **58**:577.

26. Bertrams, J., Kuwert, E., and Lohmeyer, H. H., 1971, Die Spezifität von Leukozytenisoantikörpern zur Histokompatibilitätsbestimmung im Serum von Primi- und Multiparae, *Bibl. Haematol. (Basel)* **37**:98.

27. Betke, K., 1972, Maternofetal transfusion; its incidence and clinical significance, Clinical conferences, XIVth International Congress of Haematology, Sao Paulo.

28. Black, M. M., and Speer, F. D., 1959, Lymph node reactivity. II. Fetal lymph nodes, *Blood* **14**:848.

29. Blanco, S., Blanco, A., and Sanchez Villares, E., 1973, B lymphocytes during childhood, *Lancet* **2**:384.

30. Brambell, F. W. R., 1958, The passive immunity of the young mammal, *Biol. Rev.* **33**:488.

31. Brambell, F. W. R., 1966, The transmission of immunity from mother to young and the catabolism of immunoglobulins, *Lancet* **2**:1087.

32. Brambell, F. W. R., and Halliday, R., 1956, The route by which passive immunity is transmitted from mother to foetus in the rat, *Proc. R. Soc. Med.* **145B**:170.

33. Brandtzaeg, P., Fjellanger, J., and Gjeruldsen, S. T., 1967, Localization of immunoglobulins in human nasal mucosa, *Immunochemistry* **4**:57.

34. Bridges, R. A., Condie, R. M., Zak, S. J., and Good, R. A., 1959, The morphologic basis of antibody formation development during the neonatal period, *J. Lab. Clin. Med.* **53**:331.

35. Brown, G., and Greaves, M. F., 1974, Enumeration of absolute numbers of T and B lymphocytes in human blood, *Scand. J. Immunol.* **3**:161.

36. Brown, G., and Greaves, M. F., 1974, Cell surface markers for human T and B lymphocytes, *Eur. J. Immunol.* **4**:302.

37. Brzezinski, A., Sadovsky, E., and Shafrir, E., 1964, Protein composition of early amniotic fluid and fetal serum with a case of bis-albuminemia, *Amer. J. Obstet. Gynecol.* **89**:488.

38. Burtin, P., 1964, The immune sera and their utilization, in: *Immunoelectrophoretic Analysis* (P. Grabar and P. Burtin, eds.), p. 82, Elsevier Publishing Co., Amsterdam—London—New York.

39. Burtin, P., Guilbert, B., and Ternynck, T., 1960, A study of serum proteins related to immunity and their cellular origin, in: *Ciba Found. Symp.: Cellular Aspects of Immunity* (G. E. W. Wostenholme and M. O'Connor, eds.), p. 213, Churchill, London.

39a. Carlsson, B., Ahlstedt, S., Hanson, L. Å., Lidin-Janson, G., Lindblad, B. S., and Sultana, R., 1976, *Escherichia coli* O antibody content in milk from healthy Swedish mothers and mothers from a very low socio-economic group of a developing country, *Acta Paediatr. Scand.* **65**:417.

39b. Carlsson, B., Gothefors, L., Ahlstedt, S. Hanson, L. Å., and Winberg, J., 1976, Studies of *Escherichia coli* O antigen specific antibodies in human milk, maternal serum and cord blood, *Acta Paediatr. Scand.* **65**:216.

40. Chandra, R. K., 1972, Immunocompetence in undernutrition, *J. Pediatr.* **81**:1194.

41. Chandra, R. K., Guha, D. K., and Ghai, O. P., 1970, Serum immunoglobulins in the newborn, *Indian J. Pediatr.* **37**:361.

42. Chodirker, W. B., and Tomasi, T. B., Jr., 1963, Gammaglobulins: Quantitative relationship in human serum and nonvascular fluids, *Science* **142**:1080.

42a. Christiansen, J. S., Osther, K., Peitersen, B., and Bach-Mortensen, N., 1976, B, T and null lymphocytes in newborn infants and their mothers, *Acta Paediatr. Scand.* **65**:425.

43. Cochran, T. E., 1972, Fetal and maternal immunoglobulin concentrations at delivery and postpartum, *J. Obstet. Gynaecol. Br. Commonw.* **79**:238.

44. Cohen, A., and Freeman, T., 1961, Metabolism of human γ-globulins, in: *Protides of the Biological Fluids* (H. Peeters, ed.), 8th Colloquium, Bruges, 1960, Elsevier Publishing Co., Amsterdam.

45. Connon, A. F., 1970, Immunoglobulin levels for maternal and foetal serum, amniotic fluid and foetal gastric juice in normal pregnancy, *Aust. J. Exp. Biol. Med. Sci.* **48**:691.

46. Corrodi, U., and Hitzig, W. H., 1973, Die pränatale Entwicklung det Immunglobuline, *Monatsschr. Kinderheilkd.* **121**:1.

47. Crabbé, P. A., Carbonara, A. O., and Heremans, J. F., 1963, The normal human intestinal mucosa as a major source of plasma cells containing γA-immunoglobulins, *Lab. Invest.* **14**:235.

48. Cruchaud, A., Rosen, F. S., Craig, J. M., and Janeway, C. A., 1962, Site of synthesis of 19 S-γ-globulins in dysgammaglobulinemia, *J. Exp. Med.* **115**:1141.

49. Csorba, S., 1968, Some facts on the problem of the appearance and quantitative relationship of the β_2 immune globulins, *Helv. Paediatr. Acta* **23**:395.

50. Dancis, J., 1952, Diphtheria antitoxin in mother and child in premature delivery, cited by Vahlquist, B., 1952, Placental transfer of antibodies in human beings, *Etud. Néo-Natales* **1**:31.

51. Dancis, J., Braverman, N., and Lind, J., 1957, Plasma protein synthesis in the human fetus and in placenta, *J. Clin. Invest.* **36**:398.

52. Dancis, J., Lind, J., and Vara, P., 1960, Transfer of proteins across the human placenta, in: *The Placenta and Fetal Membranes* (C. A. Villee, ed.), p. 185, Williams and Wilkins, Baltimore.

53. Dancis, J., Osborne, J. J., and Kunz, H. W., 1953,

Studies of the immunology of the newborn infant, *Pediatrics* **12**:151.

54. DAVIES, A. J. S., 1969, The thymus and the cellular basis of immunity, *Transplant. Rev.* **1**:43.

55. DIAZ-JOUANEN, E. P., AND WILLIAM, R. C., JR., 1974, T and B cells in human colostrum, *Clin. Res.* **22**:416A.

56. DÜRWALD, W., LEOPOLD, D., AND KRÄMER, K.-H., 1965, The formation of precipitating antibodies after multiple pregnancies, *Vox Sang.* **10**:94.

57. DWYER, J. M., AND MACKAY, I. R., 1970, Antigen-binding lymphocytes in human fetal thymus, *Lancet* **1**:1199.

58. EDSALL, G., 1956, Active and passive immunity of the infant, *Ann. N. Y. Acad. Sci.* **66**:32.

59. EHRLICH, P., 1892, Über Immunität durch Vererbung und Säugung, *Z. Hyg. Infektions-kr.* **12**:183.

60. EICHENWALD, H. F., AND SHINEFIELD, H. R., 1963, Antibody production by the human fetus, *J. Pediatr.* **63**:870.

61. EITZMAN, D. V., 1964, Fate of defined antigens in the newborn chimpanzee, *Pediatrics* **34**:787.

62. EPSTEIN, W. V., FONG, S. W., AND TAN, M., 1966, Naturally occurring macroglobulin antibody of foetal origin in the normal human newborn, *Immunology* **10**:259.

63. EVANS, D. G., AND SMITH, J. W. G., 1963, Response of the young infant to active immunization, *Br. Med. Bull.* **19**:225.

64. EVANS, H. E., AKPATA, S. O., AND GLASS, L., 1971, Serum immunoglobulin levels in premature and full-term infants, *Amer. J. Clin. Pathol.* **56**:416.

65. EYQUEM, A., KRIEG, H., AND PODLIACHOUK, L., 1966, Anti-Gm and antiglobulinic antibodies after multiple pregnancies, *Vox Sang.* **11**:623.

66. FAGRAEUS, A., 1948, Antibody production in relation to the development of plasma cells, *Acta Med. Scand. Suppl. 204* **130**:3.

67. FAHEY, J. L., AND LAWRENCE, M. E., 1963, Quantitative determination of 6,6 S γ-globulins, β_{2A}-globulins and γ_1-macroglobulins in human serum, *J. Immunol.* **91**:597.

68. FAULK, W. P., VAN LOGHEM, E., AND STICKLER, G. B., 1974, Maternal antibody to fetal light chain (Inv) antigens, *Amer. J. Med.* **56**:393.

69. FELDMANN, M., 1972, Cell interactions in the immune response *in vitro*. II. The requirement for macrophages in lymphoid cell collaboration, *J. Exp. Med.* **135**:1049.

70. FERGUSON, A. C., LAWLOR, G. J., AND OH, W., 1974, Decreased rosette-forming lymphocytes in malnutrition and intrauterine growth retardation, *J. Pediatr.* **85**:717.

71. FINK, C. W., AND LOSPALLUTO, J., 1964, Effect of prior administration of 7 S and 19 S antibody on active antibody formation, *J. Pediatr.* **65**:1083.

72. FINK, C. W., MILLER, W. E., DORWARD, B., AND LOSPALLUTO, J., 1962, The formation of macro-globulin antibodies. II. Studies on neonatal infants and older children, *J. Clin. Invest.* **41**:1422.

73. FINKELSTEIN, M. S., AND UHR, J. W., 1964, Specific inhibition of antibody formation by passively administered 19 S and 7 S antibody, *Science* **146**:67.

74. FLEXNER, L. B., AND GELLHORN, A., 1942, The comparative physiology of placental transfer, *Amer. J. Obstet. Gynecol.* **43**:965.

75. FLEXNER, L. B., COWIE, D. B., HELLMAN, L. M., WILDE, W. S., AND VOSBURGH, G. J., 1948, The permeability of the human placenta to sodium in normal and abnormal pregnancies and the supply of sodium to the human fetus as determined with radioactive sodium, *Amer. J. Obstet. Gynecol.* **55**:469.

76. FRANGIONE, B., MILSTEIN, C., AND PINK, J. R. L., 1969, Structural studies of immunoglobulin G, *Nature (London)* **221**:145.

77. FRÖLAND, S. S., AND NATVIG, J. B., 1971, Classes and subclasses of surface-bound immunoglobulins on peripheral blood lymphocytes in man, in: *Progress in Immunology* (B. Amos, ed.), p. 107 Academic Press, New York.

78. FRÖLAND, S. S., AND NATVIG, J. B., 1972, Lymphocytes with membrane-bound immunoglobulin (B-lymphocytes) in newborn babies, *Clin. Exp. Immunol.* **11**:495.

79. FRÖLAND, S. S., AND NATVIG, J. B., 1972, Surface-bound immunoglobulin on lymphocytes from normal and immunodeficient humans, *Scand. J. Immunol.* **1**:1.

80. FRÖLAND, S. S., AND NATVIG, J. B., 1972, Class, subclass and allelic exclusion of membrane-bound Ig of human B lymphocytes, *J. Exp. Med.* **136**:409.

81. FRÖLAND, S. S., NATVIG, J. B., AND BERDAL, P., 1971, Surface-bound immunoglobulin as a marker of B lymphocytes in man, *Nature (London) New Biol.* **234**:251.

82. FUDENBERG, H. H., 1971, Immunoglobulins: Structure, function and genetic control, in: *Immunologic Incompetence* (B. M. Kagan and R. E. Stiehm, eds.), p. 17, Year Book Medical Publishers, Chicago.

83. FUDENBERG, H. H., AND FUDENBERG, B. ROOF, 1964, Antibody to hereditary human gammaglobulin (Gm). Factor resulting from maternal–fetal incompatibility, *Science* **145**:170.

83a. FULGINITI, V. A., SIEBER, O. F., CLAMAN, H. N., AND MERRILL, D., 1966, Serum immunoglobulin measurement during the first year of life and in immunoglobulin-deficiency states, *J. Pediatr.* **68**:723.

84. VAN FURTH, R., SCHUIT, H. R. E., AND HIJMANS, W., 1965, The immunological development of the human fetus, *J. Exp. Med.* **122**:1173.

85. GAIRDNER, D., MARKS, J., AND ROSCOE, J. D., 1952, Blood formation in infancy, *Arch. Dis. Child.* **27**:128.

86. GINDRAT, J. J., GOTHEFORS, L., HANSON, L. Å., AND WINBERG, J., 1972, Antibodies in human milk against

E. coli of the serogroups most commonly found in neonatal infections, *Acta Paediatr. Scand.* **61**:587.

87. GITLIN, D., 1971, Development and metabolism of the immune globulins, in: *Immunologic Incompetence* (B. M. Kagan and R. E. Stiehm, eds.), p. 3, Year Book Medical Publishers, Chicago.

88. GITLIN, D., KUMATE, J., URRUSTI, J., AND MORALES, C., 1964, The selectivity of the human placenta in the transfer of plasma proteins from mother to fetus, *J. Clin. Invest.* **43**:1938.

88a. GOLDBLUM, R. M., AHLSTEDT, S., CARLSSON, B., AND HANSON, L. Å., 1975, Antibody production by human colostrum cells, *Pediatr. Res.* **9**:330.

89. GOOD, R. A., VARCO, R. L., AUST, J. B., AND ZAK, S. J., 1957, Transplantation studies in patients with agammaglobulinemia, *Ann. N. Y. Acad. Sci.* **64**:882.

89a. GOTHEFORS, L., CARLSSON, B., AHLSTEDT, S., HANSON, L. Å., AND WINDBERG, J., 1976, Influence of maternal gut flora and colostral and cord serum antibodies on presence of *Escherichia coli* in faeces of the newborn infant, *Acta Paediatr. Scand.* **65**:225.

90. GOTOFF, S. P., AND COCHRANE, W. D., 1968, Antibody response to the somatic antigens of *Salmonella* Newport in pemature infants, *Pediatrics* **37**:610.

91. GREAVES, M. F., OWEN, J. J. T., AND RAFF, M. C., 1974, *T and B Lymphocytes: Origins, Properties and Roles in Immune Responses,* Exerpta Medica, Amsterdam, and American Elsevier Publishing Co., New York.

92. GUGLER, E., 1970, *Das exokrine IgA-System beim Menschen,* Habilitationsschrift, Bern.

93. GUGLER, E., BOKELMANN, G., DÄTTWYLER, A., AND VON MURALT, G., 1958, Über immunoelektrophoretische Untersuchungen an Frauenmilchproteinen, *Schweiz. Med. Wochenschr.* **88**:1264.

94. GUDSON, J. P., 1969, Fetal and maternal immunoglobulin levels during pregnancy, *Amer. J. Obstet. Gynecol.* **103**:895.

95. HALL, J. G., AND SMITH, M. E., 1970, Homing of lymph-borne immunoblasts to the gut, *Nature (London)* **226**:262.

96. HANSON, L. Å., 1959, Immunological analysis of human milk, *Int. Arch. Allergy* **15**:245.

97. HANSON, L. Å., 1973, Zur immunologischen Bedeutung der Frauenmilch, *Pädiatr. Fortbildungskurse Praxis* **37**:1.

98. HANSON, L. Å., AND BRANDTZAEG, P., 1973, Secretory antibody-system, in: *Immunologic Disorders in Infants and Children* (E. R. Stiehm and V. A. Fulginiti, eds.), p. 107, W. B. Saunders Co., Philadelphia—London—Toronto.

99. HANSON, L. Å., AND JOHANSSON, B. G., 1970, Immunological studies of milk, in: *Milk Proteins. Chemistry and Molecular Biology* (H. A. McKenzie, ed.), Vol. I, p. 45, Academic Press, New York and London.

100. HANSON, L. Å., AND WINBERG, J., 1972, Breast milk and defense against infection in the newborn, *Arch. Dis. Child.* **47**:845.

101. HAWORTH, J. C., AND DILLING, L., 1966, Concentration of IgA-globulin in serum, saliva and nasopharyngeal secretions of infants and children, *J. Lab. Clin. Med.* **67**:922.

102. HAWORTH, J. C., NORRIS, M., AND DILLING, L., 1965, A study of the immunoglobulins in premature infants, *Arch. Dis. Child.* **40**:243.

103. HAYWARD, A. R., AND EZER, G., 1974, Development of lymphocyte populations in the human foetal thymus and spleen, *Clin. Exp. Immunol.* **17**:169.

104. HAYWARD, A. R., AND SOOTHILL, J. E., 1972, Reaction to antigen by human foetal thymus lymphocytes, in: *Ciba Found. Symp.: Ontogeny of Acquired Immunity* (R. Porter and J. Knight, eds.), p. 261, Elsevier—Excerpta Medica—North-Holland.

105. HAZENBERG, B. P., 1968, Gastrointestinal excretion of serum proteins. An investigation on the excretion of serum proteins in the gastrointestinal tract and the production of immunoglobulins in the jejunal wall, Thesis, Groningen.

105a. HEIMLICH, E. M., BENIS, M., AND BUSSER, R. J., 1964, Immunoglobulin levels of maternal-cord blood pairs. Quoted in V. A. Fulginiti, O. F. Sieber, H. N. Claman, and D. Merrill, 1966, Serum immunoglobulin measurement during the first year of life and in immunoglobulin deficiency states, *J. Pediatr.* **68**:723.

106. HEREMANS, J. F., AND VAERMAN, J. P., 1971, Biological significance of IgA antibodies in serum and secretions, in: *Progress in Immunology* (B. Amos, ed.), p. 875, Academic Press, New York.

107. HIRAMOTO, R. N., AND HAMLIN, M., 1965, Detection of two antibodies in single plasma cells by paired fluorescence technique, *J. Immunol.* **95**:214.

108. HIRVONEN, T., ROSSI, T., AND TOIVANEN, P., 1969, Cord IgG and duration of labour, *Lancet* **1**:315.

108a. HITZIG, W. H., 1960, Praktische und theoretische Ergebnisse neuerer Bluteiweissuntersuchungen, *Schweiz. Med. Wochenschr.* **90**:1449.

109. HOBBS, J. R., AND DAVIS, J. A., 1967, Serum γG-globulin levels and gestational age in premature babies, *Lancet* **1**:757.

110. HOBBS, J. R., HUGHES, M. J., AND WALKER, W., 1968, Immunoglobulin levels in infants after intrauterine transfusion, *Lancet* **1**:1400.

111. HOLBOROW, E. J., 1967, An ABC of modern immunology, *Lancet* **1**:829ff.

112. HONG, R., AND AMMANN, A. J., Lymphocytes and delayed hypersensitivity, in: *Immunologic Disorders in Infants and Children* (E. R. Stiehm and V. A. Fulginiti, eds.), p. 16, W. B. Saunders Co., Philadelphia—London—Toronto.

113. HOŠKOVÁ, A., ROZPRIMOVÁ, L., HLAVOŇ, J., AND PÁTKOVÁ, P., 1975, Perinatal immunoglobulin levels

in premature and small-for-date infants, *Z. Kinderheilkd.* **119**:217.

114. HUMPHEREY, J. H., AND BATTY, I., 1974, International reference preparation for human Serum IgG, IgA, IgM, *Clin. Exp. Immunol.* **17**:708.

115. HYSLOP, N. F., AND KERN, K., 1973, Physiology of human breast function: Regulation of immunoglobulin secretion into colostrum and breast milk, *Fed. Proc. Fed. Amer. Soc. Exp. Biol.* **32**:1035.

116. HYSLOP, N., AND WALKER, A., 1975, Importance of nursing in passive intestinal immunity, *Report of the 68th Ross Conference on Pediatric Research,* p. 44, Ross Laboratories, Columbus, Ohio.

117. ISHIZAKA, K., AND ISHIZAKA, T., 1971, Immunoglobulin E and homocytotropic properties, in: *Progress in Immunology* (B. Amos, ed.), p. 859, Academic Press, New York.

118. ISOMÄKI, A. M., 1973, A new cell type (tuft cell) in the gastro-intestinal mucosa of the rat, *Acta Pathol. Microbiol. Scand. Sect. A Suppl. 240.*

119. IYENGAR, L., AND SELVARAJ, R. J., 1972, Intestinal absorption of immunoglobulins by newborn infants, *Arch. Dis. Child.* **47**:411.

120. JACOBSON, E. B., AND HERZENBERG, L. A., 1972, Active suppression of immunoglobulin allotype synthesis. I. Chronic suppression after perinatal exposure to maternal antibody to paternal allotype in mice, *J. Exp. Med.* **135**:1151.

121. JACOBSON, E. B., HERZENBERG, A. L., RIBLET, R., AND HERZENBERG, L. A., 1972, Active suppression of immunoglobulin allotype synthesis. II. Transfer with spleen cells, *J. Exp. Med.* **135**:1163.

122. JOHANSSON, S. G. O., 1968, Serum IgND levels in healthy children and adults, *Int. Arch. Allergy* **34**:1.

123. JOHANSSON, S. G. O., AND BENNICH, H., 1967, Studies on a new class of human immunoglobulins. I. Immunological properties, *Nobel Symp.* **3**:193.

124. JOHANSSON, S. G. O., AND BERG, T., 1967, Immunoglobulin levels in healthy children, *Acta Paediatr. Scand.* **56**:572.

125. JOHANSSON, S. G. O., BENNICH, H., AND WIDE, L., 1968, A new class of immunoglobulin in human serum, *Immunology* **14**:265.

126. JOHANSSON, S. G. O., MELLBIN, T., AND VAHLQUIST, B., 1968, Immunoglobulin levels in Ethiopian preschool children with special reference to high concentrations of immunoglobulin E (IgND), *Lancet* **1**:1118.

127. JONDAL, M., WIGZELL, H., AND AIUTI, F., 1973, Human lymphocyte subpopulations: Classification according to surface markers and/or functional characteristics, *Transplant. Rev.* **16**:163.

128. JONES, W. R., 1969, Immunoglobulins in fetal serum, *J. Obstet. Gynaecol. Br. Commonw.* **76**:41.

129. JONES, W. R., 1972, Cord serum immunoglobulin levels in "small-for-dates" babies, *Aust. Paediatr. J.* **8**:30.

130. JONES, W. R., AND PAYNE, R. B., 1967, Effect of mode of delivery on immunoglobulin G concentration in the newborn, *Amer. J. Obstet. Gynecol.* **99**:1160.

131. JOPPICH, G., AND LISSENS, P., 1937, Knochenmarksuntersuchungen beim lebenden Säugling, *Monatsschr. Kinderheilkd.* **71**:382.

132. KAY, H. E. M., 1971, Lymphocyte function. Annotation, *Br. J. Haematol,* **20**:139.

133. KELLER, R., DWYER, J. E., WILLIAM, O. H., AND D'AMODIO, M., 1969, Intestinal IgA neutralizing antibodies in newborn infants following poliovirus immunization, *Pediatrics* **43**:330.

134. KENNY, J. F., BOESMAN, M. J., AND MICHAELS, R. H., 1967, Bacterial and viral coproantibodies in breast-fed infants, *Pediatrics* **39**:202.

135. KINKADE, P. W., AND COOPER, M. D., 1971, Development and distribution of immunoglobulin-containing cells in the chicken, *J. Immunol.* **106**:371.

135a. KHADRAOUI, S., LOPEZ, V., HAMZA, B., AND SMITH, N. J., 1977, L'immunité cellulaire au cours de la malnutrition protéino-calorique, *Arch. Franç. Péd.* **34**:143.

136. KOHLER, F., AND FARR, R. S., 1966, Elevation of cord maternal IgG immunoglobulin: Evidence for an active placental IgG transport, *Nature (London)* **210**:1070.

137. KOLTAY, M., AND JLLYÉS, M., 1966, A study of immunoglobulins in the blood serum of infants with interstitial plasma cellular pneumonia, *Acta Paediatr. Scand.* **55**:489.

138. KRÄHENBÜHL, J. P., AND CAMPICHE, M. A., 1969, Early stages of intestinal absorption of specific antibodies in the newborn. An ultrastructural, cytochemical and immunological study in the pig, rat and rabbit, *J. Cell. Biol.* **42**:345.

139. KUTTNER, A., AND RATNER, B., 1923, The importance of colostrum to the newborn infant, *Amer. J. Dis. Child.* **25**:413.

140. LAMBOTTE, R., AND SALMON, J., 1962, Etude immuno-électrophorétique du liquide amniotique humain, *C. R. Séances Soc. Biol. Paris* **156**:530.

141. LAMBOTTE, R., AND SALMON, J., 1962, Passage du liquide amniotique dans la circulation maternelle lors de l'accouchement, *C. R. Séances Soc. Biol. Paris* **156**:1187.

142. LAMBOTTE, R., AND SALMON, J., 1963, Etude immuno-électrophorétique du liquide amniotique du lapin, *C. R. Séances Soc. Biol. Paris* **157**:1849.

143. LAMY, M., NEZELOF, C., SELIGMAN, M., AND GRISCELLI, C., 1966, L'acquisition de l'immunité chez l'enfant, *Minerva Pediatr.* **18**:1579.

144. LAWTON, A. R., AND COOPER, M. D., 1973, Development of immunity: Phylogeny and ontogeny, in: *Immunologic Disorders in Infants and Children* (E. R. Stiehm and V. A. Fulginiti, eds.), p. 28, W. B. Saunders Co., Philadelphia—London—Toronto.

145. Lawton, A. R., Self, K. S., Royal, S. A., and Cooper, M. D., 1972, Ontogeny of B-lymphocytes in the human fetus, *Clin. Immunol. Immunopathol.* **1**:84.

146. Leading article, 1975, Immunological tolerance, *Lancet* **1**:555.

147. De Lemos, L., and Gautier, E., 1972, Influence de la rupture prolongée des membranes et des infections de la période néonatale sur les IgM sériques du nouveau-né, *Schweiz. Med. Wochenschr.* **102**:505.

148. Leslie, G. A., and Swate, T. E., 1972, Structure and biologic functions of human IgD. I. The presence of immunoglobulin D in human cord sera, *J. Immunol.* **109**:47.

149. Lev, R., and Orlic, D., 1973, Uptake of protein in swallowed amniotic fluid by monkey fetal intestine *in utero*, *Gastroenterology* **65**:60.

150. Liebermann, R., and Dray, S., 1964, Maternal–fetal mortality in mice with isoantibodies to paternal γ-globulin allotypes, *Proc. Soc. Exp. Biol. Med.* **116**:1069.

151. Locke, R. F., Segre, D., and Myers, W. L., 1964, The immunologic behavior of baby pigs. IV. Intestinal absorption and persistence of 6,6 S and 18 S antibodies of ovine origin and their role in immunologic competence of baby pigs, *J. Immunol.* **93**:576.

152. Lodinova, R., and Wagner, V., 1971, Immunoglobulins and coproantibodies after oral colonization (*E. coli*), in: *Immunologic Incompetence* (B. M. Kagan and E. R. Stiehm, eds.), p. 61, Year Book Medical Publishers, Chicago.

153. Mage, R., and Dray, S., 1965, Persistent altered phenotypic expression of allelic γG-immunoglobulin allotypes in heterozygous rabbits exposed to isoantibodies in fetal and neonatal life, *J. Immunol.* **95**:525.

154. Marchalonis, J., and Edelman, G. M., 1965, Phylogenetic origins of antibody structure. I. Multichain structure of immunoglobulins in the smooth dogfish (*Mustelus canis*), *J. Exp. Med.* **122**:601.

155. Mårtensson, L., and Fudenberg, H. H., 1965, Gm genes and γG-globulin synthesis in the human fetus, *J. Immunol.* **94**:514.

156. Mathews, J. D., McKay, I. R., Whittingham, S., and Malcolm, L. A., 1972, Protein supplementation and enhanced antibody-producing capacity in New Guinean school-children, *Lancet* **2**:675.

157. McCracken, G. H., and Shinefield, H. R., 1965, Immunoglobulin concentration in newborn infants with congenital cytomegalic inclusion disease, *Pediatrics* **36**:933.

158. McFarlane, H., and Udeozo, J. O. K., 1968, Immunochemical estimation of some proteins in Nigerian paired maternal and fetal blood, *Arch. Dis. Child.* **43**:42.

159. McKay, E., and Thom, H., 1971, Antibodies to gamma globulin in pregnant women: Incidence, aetiology and size, *J. Obstet. Gynaecol. Br. Commonw.* **78**:345.

160. McKay, E., Thom, H., and Gray, D., 1967, Immunoglobulins in umbilical cord plasma. II. Congenital deformities, other abnormalities and multiple pregnancies, *Arch. Dis. Child.* **42**:264.

161. Mellits, E. D., 1971, Relationship between cord serum immunoglobulin levels and later abnormalities. Is neonatal screening for IgM a worth-while procedure?, *Johns Hopkins Med. J.* **128**:306.

162. Mellors, R. C., and Korngold, L., 1963, The cellular origin of human immunoglobulins (γ_2, γ_{1M}, γ_{1A}), *J. Exp. Med.* **118**:387.

163. Mendenhall, H. W., 1970, Serum protein concentrations in pregnancy. III. Analysis of maternal–cord serum pairs, *Amer. J. Obstet. Gynecol.* **106**:718.

164. Mentasti, P., 1960, Valutazione elettroforetica delle proteine della membrana amniotica. Considerazioni sulla genesi dei protidi del liquido amniotico, *Minerva Ginecol.* **12**:276.

165. Michael, J. G., Ringenback, R., and Hottenstein, S., 1971, The antimicrobial activity of human colostral antibody in the newborn, *J. Infect. Dis.* **124**:445.

165a. Michaux, J. L., 1966, Les immunoglobulines des Bantoux à l'état normal et pathologique, *Ann. Soc. Belg. Méd. Trop.* **46**:491.

166. Miller, J. F. A. P., 1966, Immunity in the foetus and the newborn, *Br. Med. Bull.* **22**:21.

167. Mitchell, G. F., Mishel, R. J., and Herzenberg, L. A., 1971, Studies on the influence of T-cells in antibody production, in: *Progress in Immunology*, First International Congress of Immunology, Academic Press, New York.

168. Mitchison, N. A., 1961, Immunological tolerance and immunological paralysis, *Br. Med. Bull.* **17**:102.

169. Mitchison, N. A., 1964, Induction of immunological paralysis in two zones of dosage, *Proc. R. Soc. London Ser. B* **161**:275.

170. Mohr, J. A., Leu, R., and Mabry, W., 1970, Colostral leucocytes, *J. Surg. Oncol.* **2**:163.

171. Mohr, R., 1975, Über Funktionen von B- und T-Zellen, in: *Lymphozyt und klinische Immunologie* (H. Theml and H. Begemann, eds.), p. 27, Springer-Verlag, Berlin—Heidelberg—New York.

172. Möller, G., and Wigzell, H., 1965, Antibody synthesis at the cellular level: Antibody-induced suppression of 19 S and 7 S antibody response, *J. Exp. Med.* **121**:969.

173. Morell, A., Skvaril, F., and Barandun, S., 1975, *IgG-Subklassen der menschlichen Immunglobuline. Immunochemische, genetische, biologische und klinische Aspekte*, S. Karger, Basel—Munich—Paris—London—New York—Sydney.

174. Morell, A., Skvaril, F., Hitzig, W. H., and Barandun, S., 1972, IgG subclasses: Development

of the serum concentrations in "normal" infants and children, *J. Pediatr.* **80**:960.

175. MORELL, A., SKVARIL, F., VAN LOGHEM, E., AND KLEEMOLA, M., 1971, Human IgG subclasses in maternal and fetal serum, *Vox Sang.* **21**:481.

176. MORRIS, J. G., 1958, The effects of heterologous sera on the uptake of rabbit antibody from the gut of young mice, *Proc. R. Soc. London Ser. B* **148**: 84.

177. MORRIS, J. G., 1963, Transmission of anti-*Brucella abortus* agglutinins across the gut in young mice, *Nature (London)* **197**:813.

178. MORRIS, J. G., 1963, Interference with the uptake of guinea pig agglutinins in mice due to fractions of papain hydrolyzed rabbit γ-globulin, *Proc. R. Soc. London Ser. B* **157**:160.

179. MORRIS, J. G., 1964, The transmission of antibodies and normal γ-globulins across the young mouse gut, *Proc. R. Soc. London Ser. B* **160**:276.

180. DE MURALT, G., 1962, *La Maturation de l'Immunité Humorale chez l' Homme*, Benno Schwabe & Co., Basel and Stuttgart.

181. DE MURALT, G., 1970, Immunoglobulins in the human fetus and newborn, in: *Physiology of the Perinatal Period* (U. Stave, ed.), Vol. I, p. 323, Appleton-Century-Crofts, New York.

182. DE MURALT, G., 1972, Die klinische Bedeutung der immunologischen Wechselbeziehungen zwischen Mutter und Kind, *Paediatr. Fortbildungskurse Praxis* **35**:24.

183. DE MURALT, G., 1975, Immunologische Beziehungen zwischen Mutter und Kind. Eine Übersicht, *Geburtshilfe Frauenheilkd.* **35**:583.

183a. DE MURALT, G., AND GUGLER, E., 1959, Die Reifung der Immunglobuline, *Helv. Med. Acta* **26**:410.

184. DE MURALT, G., AND ROULET, D. L. A., 1961, Etude immunologique des protéines sériques foetales humaines, *Helv. Paediatr. Acta* **16**:517.

185. DE MURALT, G., AND ROULET, D. L. A., 1962, Recherches immunologiques sur les protéines foetales, en particulier sur une globuline spécifique du foetus humain, in: *Protides of the Biological Fluids* (H. Peeters, ed.), 9th Colloquium, Bruges, 1961, Elsevier Publishing Co., Amsterdam.

186. DE MURALT, G., GUGLER, E., AND ROULET, D. L. A., 1964, Immuno-electrophoretic studies of the proteins of human milk and colostrum, in: *Immunoelectrophoretic Analysis* (P. Grabar and P. Burtin, eds.), p. 261, Elsevier Publishing Co., Amsterdam—London—New York.

187. MURILLO, G. J., 1971, Synthesis of secretory IgA by human colostral cells, *South. Med. J.* **64**:1333.

188. MURILLO, G. J., AND GOLDMAN, A. S., 1970, The cells of human colostrum. II. Synthesis of IgA and β_{1C}, *Pediatr. Res.* **4**:71.

189. NATHENSON, G., SCHORR, J. B., AND LITWIN, S. D., 1971, Gm factor fetomaternal gamma globulin incompatibility, *Pediatr. Res.* **5**:2.

190. NEJEDLÁ, A., 1967, Über den Einfluss wiederholter Gaben von γ-globulin auf die Antikörperbildung bei Säuglingen, *Monatsschr. Kinderheilkd.* **115**:333.

191. NEJEDLÁ, A., 1970, The development of immunological factors in infants with hyperbilirubinemia, *Pediatrics* **45**:102.

192. NEZELOF, G., AND DIEBOLD, J., 1975, Le tissu lymphatique, in: *Encyclopédie Médico-Chirurgicale*, Vol. I, *Sang et Organes Hématopoïétiques*, Editions Techniques, Paris.

193. NORDBRING, F., 1957, The appearance of antistreptolysin and antistaphylolysin in human colostrum, *Acta Paediatr. Scand.* **46**:481.

194. NOSSAL, G. J. V., 1958, Antibody production by single cells, *Br. J. Exp. Pathol.* **39**:544.

195. NOSSAL, G. J. V., 1959, Antibody production by single cells. II. The difference between primary and secondary response, *Br. J. Exp. Pathol.* **40**:118.

196. NOSSAL, G. J. V., 1960, Antibody production by single cells. IV. Further studies on multiply immunized animals, *Br. J. Exp. Pathol.* **41**:89.

197. NOSSAL, G. J. V., 1971, Recent advances in immunological tolerance, in: *Progress in Immunology* (B. Amos, ed.), p. 665, Academic Press, New York.

198. NOSSAL, G. J. V., AND MITCHELL, J. M., 1966, The thymus in relation to immunological tolerance, in: *Ciba Foundation Symposium on the Thymus: Experimental and Clinical Studies* (G. E. W. Wostenholme and R. Porter, eds.), p. 105, Churchill, London.

199. NOSSAL, G. J. V., SZENBERG, A., ADA, G. L., AND AUSTIN, C. M., 1964, Single cell studies on 19 S antibody production, *J. Exp. Med.* **119**:485.

200. OVERWEG, J., AND ENGELFRIED, C. P., 1969, Cytotoxic leucocyte isoantibodies formed during the first pregnancy, *Vox Sang.* **16**:97.

201. PAGANO, J. S., PLOTKIN, S. A., AND CORNELY, D., 1964, The response of premature infants to infection with type 3 attenuated poliovirus, *J. Pediatr.* **65**:165.

202. PAGE, E. W., 1957, Transfer of materials across the human placenta, *Amer. J. Obstet. Gynecol.* **74**:705.

203. PAPADATOS, C., PAPAEVANGELOU, G., ALEXIOU, D., AND MENDRIS, J., 1969, Immunoglobulin levels and gestational age, *Biol. Neonate* **14**:365.

204. PAPAEVANGELOU, G., ALEXIOU, D., AND PAPADATOS, C., 1973, Les immunoglobulines M et A chez le nouveau-né normal et dysmature (small-for-date), *Ann. Pediatr.* **20**:187.

205. PAPIERNIK, M., 1970, Correlation of lymphocyte transformation and morphology in the human fetal thymus, *Blood* **36**:470.

206. PAYNE, R. B., 1969, Cord IgG and duration of labour, *Lancet* **1**:372.

206a. PEITERSEN, B., BOHN, L., AND ANDERSEN, H., 1975, Quantitative determination of immunoglobulins, lysozyme, and certain electrolytes in breast milk during the entire period of lactation, during a 24-hour period and in milk from the individual mammary gland, *Acta Paediatr. Scand.* **64**:709.

207. PERNIS, B., FERRARINI, M., FORNI, L., AND AMANTE, L., 1971, Immunoglobulins on lymphocyte membranes, *First International Congress of Immunology 1971*, p. 95, Academic Press, New York.

208. PERNIS, B., FORNI, L., AND AMANTE, L., 1971, Immunoglobulins as cell receptors, *Ann. N. Y. Acad. Sci.* **190**:420.

209. PIESSENS, W. F., SCHUR, P. H., MILONEY, W. C., AND CHURCHILL, W. H., 1973, Lymphocyte surface immunoglobulins. Distribution and frequency in lymphoproliferative diseases, *N. Engl. J. Med.* **288**:176.

210. PILGRIM, U., FONTANELLAZ, H. P., EVERS, G., AND HITZIG, W. H., 1975, Normal values of immunoglobulins in premature and full-term infants, calculated in percentiles, *Helv. Paediatr. Acta* **30**:121.

211. PIROFSKY, B., DAVIES, G. H., RAMIREZ-MATEOS, J. C., AND NEWTON, B. W., 1973, Cellular immune competence in the human fetus, *Cell. Immunol.* **6**:324.

212. PLAYFAIR, J. H. L., WOLFENDALE, M. R., AND KAY, H. E. M., 1963, The leucocytes of the peripheral blood in the human foetus, *Br. J. Haematol.* **9**:336.

213. POLANO, O., 1904, Der Antitoxinübergang von der Mutter auf das Kind, *Z. Geburtshilfe Gynaekol.* **53**:456.

214. POLLIACK, A., LAMPEN, N., CLARKSON, B. D., AND DE HARVEN, E., 1973, Identification of human B and T lymphocytes by scanning electron microscopy, *J. Exp. Med.* **138**:607.

215. PRINDULL, G., 1974, Maturation of cellular and humoral immunity during human embryonic development, *Acta Paediatr. Scand.* **63**:607.

216. PROVENZANO, R. W., WETTERLOW, L. H., AND SULLIVAN, C. L., 1965, Immunization and antibody response in the newborn infant. 1. Pertussis inoculation within twenty-four hours of birth, *N. Engl. J. Med.* **273**:959.

217. QUINLIVAN, L. G., 1964, Transplacental passage of gamma-globulin-I[131] in the rat, *Amer. J. Physiol.* **207**:782.

218. QUINLIVAN, L. G., 1964, Antepartum and postpartum transfer of gamma globulin I[131] in the rat, *Amer. J. Physiol.* **207**:787.

219. RABELLINO, E., COLON, S., GREA, H. M., AND UNANUE, E. R., 1971, Immunoglobulins on the surface of lymphocytes. I. Distribution and quantitation, *J. Exp. Med.* **133**:156.

220. RAUER, U., AND FREUND, R., 1969, Normalwerte von Immunglobulinen im Kindesalter, *Monatsschr. Kinderheilkd.* **117**:559.

221. RECOMMENDATIONS FOR THE NOMENCLATURE OF HUMAN IMMUNOGLOBULINS (editorial), 1972, *J. Immunol.* **108**:1733.

222. REMINGTON, J. S., MILLER, M. J., AND BROWNLEE, J., 1968, IgM antibodies in acute toxoplasmosis. I. Diagnostic significance in congenital cases and a method for their rapid demonstration, *Pediatrics* **41**:1082.

223. REMINGTON, J. S., VOSTI, K. L., LIETZE, A., AND ZIMMERMAN, A. L., 1964, Serum proteins and antibody activity in human nasal secretions, *J. Clin. Invest.* **43**:1613.

224. ROBBINS, J. B., KENNY, K., AND SUTER, E., 1965, Isolation and biological activities of rabbit γM- and γG-anti-*Salmonella typhimurium* antibodies, *J. Exp. Med.* **122**:385.

224a. ROELANTS, G., FORNI, L., AND PERNIS, B., 1973, Blocking and redistribution ("capping") of antigen receptors on T and B lymphocytes by anti-immunoglobulin antibody, *J. Exp. Med.* **137**:1060.

225. ROGENTINE, G. N., ROWE, D. S., BRADLEY, J., WALDMANN, T. A., AND FAHEY, J. L., 1966, Metabolism of human immunoglobulin D (IgD) *J. Clin. Invest.* **45**:1467.

226. ROITT, I. M., GREAVES, M. F., TORRIGIANI, G., BROSTOFF, J., AND PLAYFAIR, J. H. L., 1969, The cellular basis of immunological responses, *Lancet* **2**:367.

227. ROPARTZ, C., RIVAT, L., AND ROUSSEAU, P. Y., 1965, La transmission des facteurs Gm et Inv de la mère à l'enfant nouveau-né, *Ann. Génét.* **8**:39.

228. ROSEN, F. S., 1974, Immunity in the fetus and newborn, in: *Modern Perinatal Medicine* (Gluck, ed.), p. 273, Year Book Medical Publishers, Chicago.

229. ROSEN, F. S., AND JANEWAY, C. A., 1966, The gamma globulins. III. The antibody deficiency syndromes, *N. Engl. J. Med.* **275**:709.

230. ROSENBERG, M., 1969, Fetal hematopoiesis. Case report, *Blood* **33**:66.

231. ROTH, N., 1962, Zur semiquantitativen Erfassung der beiden Serum-Immunglobuline Beta$_{2A}$ und Beta$_{2M}$ im Neugeborenen und Kindesalter, *Ann. Paediatr. (Basel)* **199**:548.

232. ROTHBERG, R. M., 1969, Immunoglobulin and specific antibody synthesis during the first weeks of life of premature infants, *J. Pediatr.* **75**:391.

233. ROWE, D. S., AND FAHEY, J. L., 1965, A new class of human immunoglobulins. I. A unique myeloma protein, *J. Exp. Med.* **121**:171.

234. ROWE, D. S., AND FAHEY, J. L., 1965, New class of human immunoglobulins. II. Normal serum IgD, *J. Exp. Med.* **121**:185.

235. ROWE, D. S., HUG, K., AND FAULK, W. P., 1973, IgD on the surface of peripheral blood lymphocytes on the human newborn, *Nature (London) New Biol.* **242**:155.

236. ROWE, D. S., McGREGOR, I. A., SMITH, S. J., HALL, P., AND WILLIAMS, K., 1968, Plasma immunoglobulin concentrations in a West African (Gambian) community and in a group of healthy British adults, *Clin. Exp. Immunol.* **3**:63.

236a. Rubaltelli, F. F., Piovesan, A. L., Semenzato, G. P., Barbato, A., and Ongaro, G., 1977, Immune competence assessment in hyperbilirubinemic newborns before and after phototherapy, *Helv. Paediatr. Acta* **32**:129.

237. Ruckstuhl, J., 1970, Titerverlauf und hämolytische Späteffekte der Rhesusantikörper bei Austauschtransfusion bei Neugeborenen mit rhesusbedingter hämolytischer Anämie, *Helv. Paediatr. Acta* **25**:258.

238. Sahiar, K., and Schwartz, R. S., 1965, The immunoglobulin sequence. 1. Arrest by 6-mercaptopurine and restitution by antibody, antigen or splenectomy, *J. Immunol.* **95**:345.

239. Salmon, J., Lambotte, R., and Smoliar, V., 1962, Etude par immunofluorescence de la sécrétion du liquide amniotique humain, *Arch. Int. Physiol. Biochim.* **70**:731.

240. di Sant'Agnese, P. A., 1949, Combined immunization against diphtheria, tetanus and pertussis in newborn infants; duration of antibody levels; antibody titers after booster dose; effect of passive immunity to diphtheria on active immunization with diphtheria toxoid, *Pediatrics* **3**:181.

241. Schneegans, E., Heumann, G., de Muralt, G., Bütler, R., and Geisert, J., 1968, Etude comparée des immunoglobulines des prématurés élevés en service semi-stérile et en service normal, *Ann. Pédiatr.* **15**:642.

242. Schneegans, E., de Muralt, G., Bütler, R., Heumann, G., and Geisert, J., 1966, Immunologische Probleme beim Frühgeborenen, *Acta Paediatr. Acad. Sci. Hung.* **7**:213.

243. Schneegans, E., Rohmer, A., de Muralt, G., Heumann, G., Haarscher, A., Cohen, A., and Cronmuller, G., 1969, Alimentation des prématurés au lait de femme et au colostrum, Rapport 22e Congrès Assoc. Pédiatres langue française, Strasbourg 1969 (Expansion scientifique française Paris 1969), p. 173.

244. Schubert, J., and Grünberg, A., 1949, Zur Frage der Übertragung von Immunantikörpern von der Mutter auf das Kind, *Schweiz. Med. Wochenschr.* **79**:1007.

245. Schultze, H. E., and Heremans, J. F., 1966, *Molecular Biology of Human Proteins,* Vol. 1, Elsevier Publishing Co., Amsterdam—London—New York.

246. Seigler, H. F., and Metzgar, R. S., 1970, Embryonic development of human transplantation antigens, *Transplantation* **9**:478.

247. Sidiropoulos, D., 1975, Personal communication.

248. Sieber, O. F., Jr., Fulginiti, V. A., Brazie, J., and Umlauf, H. J., 1966, *In utero* infection of fetus by herpes simplex virus, *J. Pediatr.* **69**:30.

249. Silverstein, A. M., 1962, Congenital syphilis and the timing of immunogenesis in the human foetus, *Nature (London)* **194**:196.

250. Skoog, V. T., Weber, T. H., and Richter, W., 1974, Studies on the interaction between mitogens and human lymphocytes *in vitro*, *Exp. Cell Res.* **85**:339.

251. Slater, R. J., 1954, Investigation of an infant born of a mother suffering from cirrhosis of the liver, *Pediatrics* **13**:308.

252. Smith, C. W., and Goldman, A. S., 1968, The cells of human colostrum. I. *In vitro* studies of morphology and functions, *Pediatr. Res.* **2**:103.

253. Smith, R. T., 1960, Response to active immunization of human infants during the neonatal period, in: *Ciba Foundation Symposium on Cellular Aspects of Immunity* (G. E. W. Wostenholme and M. O'Connor, eds.), p. 348, Churchill, London.

254. Smith, R. T., 1964, Immunologic tolerance: Developmental phenomenon, *Pediatrics* **34**:14.

255. Smith, R. T., Eitzman, D. V., Catlin, M. E., Wirtz, E. O., and Miller, B. E., 1964, The development of the immune response. Characterization of the response of the human infant and adult to immunization with *Salmonella* vaccines, *Pediatrics* **33**:163.

256. Smythe, P. M., Brereton-Stiles, G. G., Grace, H. J., Mafoyane, A., Schonland, M., Coovadia, H. M., Loening, W. E. K., Parent, M. A., and Vos, G. H., 1971, Thymolymphatic deficiency and depression of cell-mediated immunity in protein-calorie malnutrition, *Lancet* **2**:939.

257. Solomon, J. B., 1971, *Foetal and Neonatal Immunology,* North-Holland Publishing Co., Amsterdam and London.

258. Speiser, P., 1963, Über Antikörperbildung von Säuglingen und Kleinkindern gegen mütterliches γ_2-globulin. Ein bisher unbekanntes, dem Erythroblastenmechanismus konträres Phänomen mit anscheinend immunogenetisch obligatem Charakter, *Wien. Med. Wochenschr.* **113**:966.

259. Stege, N., and Gugler, E., 1968, Die quantitative Bestimmung der Immunglobulinreifung mit Hilfe einer einfachen radialen Immunodiffusionsmethode, *Helv. Paediatr. Acta* **22**:242.

260. Stiehm, E. R., 1973, Immunoglobulins and antibodies, in: *Immunologic Disorders in Infants and Children* (E. R. Stiehm and V. A. Fulginiti, eds.), p. 42, W. B. Saunders Co., Philadelphia—London—Toronto.

261. Stiehm, E. R., and Fudenberg, H. H., 1966, Serum levels of immune globulins in health and diseases. A survey, *Pediatrics* **37**:715.

262. Stiehm, E. R., Ammann, A. J., and Cherry, J. D., 1966, Elevated cord macroglobulins in the diagnosis of intrauterine infections, *N. Engl. J. Med.* **275**:971.

263. Stites, D. P., Carr, M. C., and Fudenberg, H. H., 1974, Ontogeny of cellular immunity in the human fetus. Development of responses to phytohemagglutinin and to allogenic cells, *Cell. Immunol.* **11**:257.

264. Stites, D. P., Wybran, J., Carr, M. C., and

FUDENBERG, H. H., 1972, Development of cellular immunocompetence in man, in: *Ciba Found. Symp.: Ontogeny of Acquired Immunity* (R. Porter and J. Knight, eds.), p. 113, Elsevier–Excerpta Medica–North-Holland.

264a. STOLIAR, O. A., PELLEY, R. P., KANIECKI-GREEN, E., KLAUS, M. H., AND CARPENTER, C. L. J., 1976, Secretory IgA against enterotoxins in breast-milk, *Lancet* **1**:1258.

265. STULBERG, C. S., ZUELZER, W. W., AND PAGE, R. H., 1956, *Escherichia coli* 0 127:B 8, a serotype causing infantile diarrhea. III. The antibody response of infants, *J. Immunol.* **76**:281.

266. TERRY, W. D., 1965, Skin-sensitizing activity related to γ-polypeptide chain characteristics of human IgG, *J. Immunol.* **95**:1041.

267. TERRY, W. D., AND FAHEY, J. L., 1964, Subclasses of human γ_2-globulin based on differences in heavy polypeptide chains, *Science* **146**:400.

268. THOM, E., MCKAY, E., AND GRAY, D., 1967, Immunoglobulins in umbilical cord plasma. I. Healthy infants, *Arch. Dis. Child.* **42**:259.

269. THOMAS, D. B., AND YOFFEY, J. M., 1962, Human foetal haematopoiesis. I. The cellular composition of fetal blood, *Br. J. Haematol.* **8**:290.

270. THORLEY, J. D., HOLMES, R. K., KAPLAN, J. M., MCCRACKEN, G. H., AND SANFORD, J. P., 1975, Passive transfer of antibodies of maternal origin from blood to cerebrospinal fluid in infants, *Lancet* **1**:651.

271. TOMASI, T. B., JR., AND ZIGELBAUM, S., 1963, Selective occurrence of γ1A-globulins in certain body fluids, *J. Clin. Invest.* **42**:1552.

272. TOMASI, T. B., TAN, E. M., SOLOMON, A., AND PRENDERGAST, R. A., 1965, Characteristics of immune system common to certain external secretions, *J. Exp. Med.* **121**:101.

273. TONGIO, M. M., AND MAYER, S., 1963, Immunisation foeto-maternelle anti-*HL-A*. Passage des anticorps anti-*HL-A* de la mère à l'enfant, *Nouv. Rev. Fr. Hématol.* **13**:181.

274. TURMERO, J. A., 1974, Antibody transfer during labor, *Amer. J. Obstet. Gynecol.* **119**:486.

275. TREPEL, F., 1975, Kinetik lymphatischer Zellen, in: *Lymphozyt und klinische Immunologie* (H. Theml and H. Begemann, eds.), p. 16, Springer-Verlag, Berlin–Heidelberg–New York.

276. TREVORROW, V. E., 1959, Concentration of gamma-globulin in the serum of infants during the first 3 months of life, *Pediatrics* **24**:746.

277. UGAZIO, A. G., MARCIONI, A. F., ASTALDI, A. J., AND BURGIO, G. R., 1974, Peripheral blood B lymphocytes in infancy and childhood, *Acta Paediatr. Scand.* **63**:205.

278. UHR, J. W., DANCIS, J., FRANKLIN, E. C., FINKELSTEIN, M. S., AND LEWIS, E. W., 1962, The antibody response to bacteriophage θX 174 in newborn premature infants, *J. Clin. Invest.* **41**:1509.

279. UNANUE, E. R., GREY, H. M., RABELLINO, E., CAMPBELL, P., AND SCHMIDTKE, J., 1971, Immunoglobulins on the surface of lymphocytes. II. The bone marrow as the main source of lymphocytes with detectable surface-bound immunoglobulin, *J. Exp. Med.* **133**:1188.

280. UNGAR, J., 1956, Les anticorps chez l'enfant, *Sem. Hop. Paris (Pathol. Biol)* **5**:1105.

281. VAHLQUIST, B., 1958, The transfer of antibodies from mother to offspring, *Adv. Pediatr.* **10**:305.

282. VIERUCCI, A., PEDONE, S., AND MORGESE, G., 1967, L'isoimmunizzazione materno-fetale verso fattori ereditari plasmatici, in: *Proceedings of Symposium on Problems of Fetal Distress,* Siena, 16–18 Sept. 1966 (A. Centaro and F. Ragazzini, eds.), p. 713, Piccin Edition, Padova.

283. VIERUCCI, A., VARONE, D., AND INGIULLA, A., 1964, La sintesi delle immunoglobuline del tipo lgG (7 S) nel periodo feto-neonatale studiata mediante l'impegio dei marcatori genetici Gm, *Riv. Clin. Pediatr.* **74**:505.

284. VIRELLA, G., DE PASCHLE, A., AND LIPPI, U., 1971, Placenta transfer of human IgG_2 macroclonal protein, *Experientia* **27**:324.

285. VORHERR, H., 1974, *The Breast: Morphology, Physiology and Lactation,* Academic Press, New York–San Francisco–London.

286. VYAS, G. N., LEVIN, A. S., AND FUDENBERG, H. H., 1970, Intrauterine isoimmunization caused by maternal IgA crossing the placenta, *Nature (London)* **225**:275.

287. VYAS, G. N., PERKINS, H. A., AND FUDENBERG, H. H., 1968, Anaphylactoid transfusion reactions associated with anti-IgA, *Lancet* **2**:312.

288. WALDMANN, T. A., STROBER, W., AND BLAESE, R. M., 1971, Metabolism of immunoglobulins, in: *Progress in Immunology* (B. Amos, ed.), p. 891, Academic Press, New York.

289. WALSH, S. Z., AND LIND, J., 1970, The dynamics of the foetal heart and circulation and its alteration at birth, in: *Physiology of the Perinatal Period* (U. Stave, ed.), Vol. I, p. 161, Appleton-Century-Crofts, New York.

290. WANG, A. C., FAULK, W. P., STUCKEY, M. A., AND FUDENBERG, H. H., 1970, Chemical differences of adult, fetal and hypogammaglobulinemic IgG immunoglobulins, *Immunochemistry* **7**:703.

291. WEBER, T. H., SKOOG, V. T., MATTSSON, A., AND LINDAHL-KIESSLING, K., 1974, Kinetics of lymphocyte stimulation *in vitro* by non-specific mitogens, *Exp. Cell Res.* **85**:351.

292. WERDER-KIND, H., 1963, Das Serumeiweissbild beim Frühgeborenen, *Helv. Paediatr. Acta* **18**:450.

293. WEST, C. D., HONG, R., AND HOLLAND, N. H., 1962, Immunoglobulin levels from the newborn period to adulthood and in immunoglobulin deficiency states, *J. Clin. Invest.* **41**:2054.

294. WILSON, J. A., AND STEINBERG, A., 1965, Antibodies to gamma globulin in the serum of children and adults, *Transfusion (Philadelphia)* **5**:516.

295. WHITE, R. G., 1958, Antibody production by single cells, *Nature (London)* **182**:1383.

296. WHO, 1964, Nomenclature for human immunoglobulins, *Bull. WHO* **30**:447.

297. WHO, 1974, Identification, enumeration and isolation of B and T lymphocytes from human peripheral blood, Report of a WHO/IARC-Sponsored workshop on human B and T cells, London, 15–17 July 1974, *Scand. J. Immunol.* **3**:521.

298. WIRTSCHAFTER, Z. T., 1958, Free amino acids in human amniotic fluid, fetal and maternal serum, *Amer. J. Obstet. Gynecol.* **76**:1219.

299. WISLOCKI, G. B., 1955, Comparative anatomy and histology of the placental barrier, in: *Gestation* (L. B. Flexner, ed.), Transactions of the 1st conference, p. 219, Josiah Macy Foundation, New York.

300. WYBRAND, J., CARR, M. C., AND FUDENBERG, H. H., 1972, The human rosette-forming cell as a marker of a population of thymus-derived cells, *J. Clin. Invest.* **51**:2537.

301. XANTHOU, M., 1970, Leucocyte blood picture in healthy full-term and premature babies during neonatal period, *Arch. Dis. Child.* **45**:242.

302. YANG, S. L., KLEINMANN, A. M., AND WEI, P. Y., 1971, The effect of labor and mode of delivery on immunoglobulin concentrations in the neonate, *Amer. J. Obstet. Gynecol.* **109**:78.

303. YEAGER, A. S., 1973, Variation of cord IgM level with birth weight, *Pediatrics* **51**:616.

304. YEUNG, C. Y., AND HOBBS, J. R., 1968, Serum γG-globulin levels in normal, premature, postmature and "small-for-dates" newborn babies, *Lancet* **1**:1167.

305. YOFFEY, J. M., AND THOMAS, D. B., 1964, The development of bone marrow in the human foetus, *J. Anat.* **98**:463.

305a. ZAK, S. J., AND GOOD, R. A., 1959, Immunochemical studies of human serum gamma globulins, *J. Clin. Invest.* **38**:579.

306. ZIMMERMANN, A., BRUN DES RE, G., BÜRKI, H., KELLER, H.-U., HESS, M. W., AND COTTIER, H., 1975, Lymphozytenformen—Morphologische und funktionelle Charakterisierungsmöglichkeiten, Herkunft und Entwicklung, in: *Lymphozyt und klinische Immunologie* (H. Theml and H. Begemann, eds.), p. 2, Springer-Verlag, Berlin—Heidelberg—New York.

CHAPTER 15

Digestion and Absorption

Otakar Koldovský

1. Introduction

In this chapter, data on human material only are reviewed, since it is not possible to describe animal studies due to limitations in the scope of this volume. Only where there is a lack of human data have I briefly discussed animal experiments in that particular area. Space restrictions have forced me to omit from the finished review some of the text and some references. As a result, some comparative aspects have disappeared, and the priority of the researchers is not always apparent. The originators of an approach are then only cited in the listed work by their followers. I therefore apologize to the authors in question and to the reader for this incompleteness.

The interested reader is referred to my previous reviews on this subject,[161–163] in which factors that influence the development of digestion (diet, hormones) are extensively discussed. Recent studies on experimental animals, published after completion of the cited reviews, have both expanded comparative aspects, studying development in various animal species, and further analyzed the role of the adrenals in the regulation of the development of intestinal functions,[58,87,88,165,166] and have furthermore shown the involvement of the thyroid in the perinatal period.[58,165,315]

2. Structural Development of the Digestive Tract

2.1. Pharynx and Esophagus

The distance from the anterior margin of the upper jaw to the esophageal opening is about 6.5 cm at birth, 10 cm at 2 years, and 11 cm at 10 years. The length of the esophagus is about 10 cm at birth and increases about 0.6–0.7 cm every year.[304] The intraabdominal segment of the esophagus is very short, practically nonexistent at birth. This segment lengthens with increasing age, and within several years measures between 0.5 and 1.5 cm.[42]

2.2. Stomach

2.2.1. Inner Structure

During the 5th week of intrauterine life, the primitive stomach appears as a dilatation in the foregut, caudal to the lung buds. By about 8 weeks, the epithelial lining becomes studded with numerous tiny depressions, around which the cells are arranged

Otakar Koldovský · Joseph Stokes' Research Institute, Children's Hospital of Philadelphia, and Department of Pediatrics, University of Pennsylvania, Philadelphia, Pennsylvania 19104

radially. Gastric pits appear between the 6th and 9th weeks.[211,243] First, they appear on the small curvature; later, in the pyloric region; and finally, in the cardiac region. Glandular epithelial cells are found in the 11th week.[211,243] At this time, a high activity of succindehydrogenase typical for parietal cells is found, even before the appearance of morphologically distinct pariental cells.[235] Chief cells appear in embryos at age 12 weeks. Their number increases during embryonal development. Typical pepsinogen granules can be demonstrated only in newborn full-term infants, but the intensity of staining of these granules is still lower in newborns than in adults.[243] Newborns weighing less than 2500 g do not have these granules. Only in infants heavier than 3000 g do these granules appear in the basal part of the main gastric glands, while in adults, they are found at up to three-fourths of the height of the gastric glands.[303] Mucous neck cells (staining distinctly with PAS) are detected at 3 months of gestation.

Salenius[243] showed that the gastric pits appeared later in the antral region (at 10 weeks of age) than in the fundus.

The fundus cannot be defined in 7-week-old embryos. It appears during the 3rd to 4th month of gestation. The glands of the pylorus differentiate between the 11th and 13th weeks. In both the cardiac and pyloric regions, intestinal cells (goblet cells and epithelial cells with microvilli) are found; their number decreases during fetal life, and they virtually disappear before birth.[243] No information is yet available on the development of gastrin-secreting cells (G cells) in the fetus or the infant. Falck et al.[73] found enterochromaffinlike cells (possibly of this variety) present in fetuses (11–33 cm total length). In mature newborns, the parietal cell mass (per unit area) is about 2 or 3 times that of adults.[125,303] Both the mucosa and the entire stomach wall are much thinner than in adults.[185,143]

A greater amount of parietal cells correlates with the relative hypersecretion in term infants during the first 10 days [see Section 5.1.1(b)(1)].[233,234] Muscularis mucosae differentiates first at the cardiac end of the 40-mm (crown–rump) stage, then extends to the body of the stomach at the 120-mm stage, and to the pylorus at the 135-mm stage.[144]

2.2.2. Muscular Coat

The circular muscular coat extends throughout the stomach in 13- to 14-mm-long fetuses, and the longitudinal muscle coat is to be found throughout the organ when the fetus has reached a length of 30 mm.[144]

2.3. Small and Large Intestine

2.3.1. General Characteristics

(a) Length and Width. The length of the small intestine increases during prenatal development; postnatally, it decreases (Fig. 1). The width of the wall of the small intestine increases after birth, this increase being caused by the thickening of the muscular layer.[108] In the newborn, the ratio of mucosa to muscle is approximately 1 : 1, whereas in the adult, the ratio approaches 1 : 1.5.

(b) Color of the Small Intestine. As in other infant mammals, the ileum is colored differently from the jejunum at a certain period of development. After the 13th to 14th week of embryonal life, the distal part of the small intestine begins to be filled with meconium, which is evidently absorbed by the mucosa and gives it its characteristic dark brownish-green coloring. The intensity of this coloring increases with age up to the 25th week, according to Parat[220] and our own observations on numerous fetuses.

2.3.2. Villi, Crypts, and Paneth's and Enterochromaffin Cells

(a) Prenatal Period. Jirásek et al.,[141] who had access to fresh, healthy fetuses from legal abortions, showed that the wall of the small intestine of embryos of the XIIth–XIIIth horizon, according to Streeter (26th–28th postconceptional days), is composed of one layer of cylindrical epithelium, a mesenchymal layer, and a high mesodermal cylindrical epithelium of the splanchopleura. Germ cells are found in all layers. Primitive intestinal epithelium contains a large amount of glycogen. In embryos of the XIVth horizon, the epithelium is cylindrical and pseudostratified. Germinative cells are found mainly in the region of the mesenterium. In the stage of the XVth horizon, the lumen is relatively narrow, and the epithelial cells contain a large amount of glycogen. In the XVIth horizon, proliferation of the duodenal epithelium occurs, and the lumen disappears temporarily, due to the epithelial cells. Smooth muscle cells are found in the external layers of the mesenchyme in embryos of the XXth horizon.

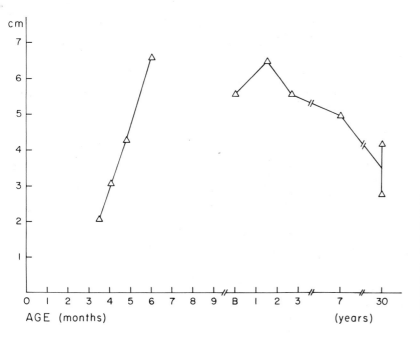

Fig. 1. Length of the small intestine of human fetuses, children, and adults. *Ordinate:* Length of small intestine (cm) per centimeter of C–H length. *Abscissa:* Age in months before birth (B) and in years after. The data for fetuses were recalculated from Lindberg[188]; for newborn and older, from Beneke.[24]

The number of villi increases during the embryonic period. Various authors report the first appearance of villi in fetuses 18–38 mm long[221]; in 80-mm-long fetuses, villi were found in the whole small intestine except for the distal parts.[141] Villi appear first as prolonged invaginations that grow and break up. Fully developed villi and young villi exist next to each other.

Many vessels grow into the growing villi, and connective tissue accumulates in the propria. The epithelium, which is pseudostratified and cylindrical at the tops of the villi, changes and becomes unilayered. It differentiates from the tips of the villi toward their base. Among villi, the epithelium remains pseudostratified and cylindrical, containing a large amount of glycogen.[26,141]

In the large intestine of human fetuses, villi can be seen during the 3rd month[182,188,221]; later, they cannot be found.[48]

Crypts of Lieberkühn were observed from the 12th week after conception.[141]

Paneth's cells were found in fetuses up to a length of 132 mm.[221] Mucinar cells (goblet cells) appear between the 66th and 70th days of postconceptional life in the small intestine[141,183]; in the large intestine, they appear several weeks later.[183]

Enterochromaffin cells (E cells) of Kulczicki appear after the second embryonic month.[141,160] The number of E cells rises considerably during the fetal period.[160] In 5-month-old fetuses, the relative proportions of three different types of cells (EC, EG, and S) are similar to those found in adults; these ratios are different in younger fetuses.

(b) Postnatal Period. Gerlovin[91] reported that the multilayered epithelium is flat in newborns and has 4 or 5 cell layers. The cells of the middle and superficial layers divide amitotically. The border of the connective tissue and the epithelium is regular. With age, the number of layers increases, and connective tissue enters the epithelium. In 4- to 11-month-old infants, ten layers were found. Mitotic divisions were observed throughout. Amitotic divisions also occurred in the superficial layer.

In adults, 25–30 layers of epithelial cells were found. Banza *et al.*[18] found a morphological and histochemical picture similar to adults in 3- to 9-year-old infants.

The rate of enterocyte renewal was not studied in human development. In suckling rats, the enterocyte migration rate was approximately 2–3 times lower than in adult rats[167]; there are similar later findings in other animal species.

2.3.3. Microscopic Studies of Enterocytes

Inclusions are found in small intestinal enterocytes from the 14th week, primarily in the ileum. At the end of the 6th month, they fill the whole of the ileal cells. Toward the end of gestation, inclusions become less frequent, and are found only at the tips of the villi. They are absent from the crypts.

Since these particles have some characteristics in common with the meconium, they have been termed *meconial particles*. A more detailed study[5] using electron microscopy and histochemistry characterizes these particles as lysosomes.

The nature of the deposited substance(s) is not clear, and recently, this subject was approached again by Ruebner *et al.*,[240] studying specimens from human and other primates.

2.3.4. Vascular Supply of the Small Intestine (*in Vivo*)

India ink injected into the umbilical vein of living fetuses does not reach some organs (lungs, kidney, intestine), while in other organs, it can be demonstrated macroscopically.[140] There are turgid epitheloid cells in the arteriovenous anastomoses of such fetuses. Jaykka[140] believes that they block blood flow through the capillaries of these organs in embryonal life.

2.3.5. Lymphatic Tissue

The presence of Payer's plaques was reported in embryos 4–5 months old,[48,141] but they were not found in younger fetuses.[53,145] The size and number of Payer's plaques increase from the fetal period up to the time of puberty[53]; later, their number decreases again.

2.3.6. Muscularis Mucosae

The muscularis mucosae was found in fetuses of 160- to 170-mm crown–rump length.[141,145] In the large intestine, it develops craniocaudally. First, it is visible in the anorectal region of fetuses of 97-mm length, and it reaches the cecum when the fetal length is 160 mm.[146] Muscularis submucosae develops about the time of birth.[159]

2.3.7. Muscular Coat of the Intestinal Wall

The circular layer appears in the upper part of the duodenum in 10-mm-long (head–rump) fetuses. In fetuses of 21-mm length, this muscular layer is found along the whole length of the small intestine. The longitudinal layer begins to differentiate in fetuses of 21-mm length, and reaches the ileum in fetuses of 30 mm. The circular layer in the wall

of the large intestine appears first in 21-mm fetuses, the longitudinal layer in 38-mm fetuses. Differentiation begins from the caudal end and reaches the proximal part of the colon when the fetus is 47 mm long. Jit also studied the development of striated muscle in the esophagus[147] and anal canal.[148]

2.4. Exocrine Pancreas

Liu and Potter[191] showed that in 15-mm-long human fetuses, the pancreas consists of a conglomerate of primitive tubules. In the 4th month, a lobular arrangement appears, and in the 8th month of gestation, the pancreatic tissue is compact. Differentiation of the exocrine part could be detected by an increase of nonspecific esterase activity in cells of the primitive tubules. Significant numbers of mature zymogen granules appear in the 5th month.[173]

3. Motility of the Digestive Tract

3.1. Sucking and Swallowing

A fetus starts to swallow amniotic fluid between the 3rd and 5th months.[199] Contrast material injected into the amniotic sac appears sooner in the stomachs of older fetuses than in those of younger ones. As prenatal development progresses, the rate of gastric emptying increases, and the material moves more rapidly along the small intestine. Thus, certain constituents of amniotic fluid might be broken down and absorbed from the fetal GI tract (see Section 4.3.1). The amount could be considerable. On the basis of his study of 5 full-term fetuses, Pritchard[227] calculated that a fetus swallows about 50% of the amniotic fluid (5 ml/kg per hr) daily; similar values were found for one 6-month-old fetus. A detailed description of swallowing in babies is given in reports of Ardran *et al.*[10] and Colley and Cramer[51] where the differences between breast and bottle feeding are also discussed.

The sucking reflex was observed in fetuses after 6 months of gestational age. Gryboski[104,105] defined three developmental stages: the mouthing (initial) stage is followed consecutively by immature suck–swallow, which then develops into a mature type of suck–swallow pattern. The mature pattern is acquired in full-term infants within the first 2 days of life, but in prematures, the first stage may last a month or more, and in very small immatures, the third stage may not appear before the 3rd month. In infants younger than 3 months, solid food placed in the mouth is forced by the tongue against the palate and is either swallowed or forced out through the mouth. Older infants recognizing solid food transfer it selectively to the back of the pharynx and then swallow.

3.2. Movement of the Esophagus

The average transit time for a semisolid bolus to travel from the cricopharyngeal area to the stomach increases with age.[256] This increase could be related to the increase of esophageal length (see Section 2.1), since it was shown that the speed of progression of the primary esophageal peristaltic wave did not differ after 1 week of age. In full-term infants under 12 hr of age and in prematures less than 1 week old, esophageal peristaltis was faster than in older and more mature infants.[104,105] Progression of the primary peristaltic wave into the fundus occurs in children younger than 2 years, but not in older subjects. This phenomenon is interpreted as a protection that reduces the risk of reflux. The tone of the gastroesophageal sphincter is low during the first 2 weeks of life and increases after the first week in the full-term infant and after several weeks in the premature. It reaches adult values at about 1 or 2 months of life.[104–106,308]

3.3. Gastric Emptying

In recent years, using new radioisotopic methods, it has been found that gastric emptying follows an exponential pattern. The "half-life" of emptying was 87 min; no correlation was found between "half-life" and age of infants (1–10 weeks; mean, 25 days).[258] Emptying time in adults—measured by the same method but after a meal of a different consistency (porridge, eggs and bread)—was 65 min.[102] Gastric peristalsis is absent during the first few days of life; characteristics of the peristaltic waves change during the first half-year.[106] Yu,[317] measuring the disappearance of a marker (phenol red) after 30 min, did not observe differences in the gastric emptying rate in 2-week-old full-term, preterm, and small-for-date infants; others, in an X-ray study,[245] found no correlation of gastric emptying time with either postnatal age (3–33 days) or weight at the time of the study (1–2.6 kg). Comparing their own data with studies performed by others on full-term infants, Schell et al.[245] concluded that a faster emptying time is indicated in prematures than in full-term infants. Similar conclusions were reported later.[213]

Breast milk empties earlier than cow's-milk mixture. Milk formula empties later than glucose solution or water.[245] Emptying of glucose from the stomach is controlled by osmoreceptors present in the duodenum. These osmoreceptors are already functional in babies during the first few days of life, since a solution containing a higher glucose concentration (10%) leaves the stomach more slowly than a 5% solution.[132] Since polysaccharides are poorly digested by infants, a 10% starch solution leaves the stomach more rapidly than a 10% glucose solution. By contrast, in adults, these isocaloric solutions empty at the same rate.[133] Yu[317] confirmed older data showing that the stomach empties more rapidly in the prone and right lateral positions than in the supine and left lateral positions.

3.4. Intestinal Motility

3.4.1. Prenatal Period

Spontaneous rhythmic activity of the small intestine was observed in human fetuses as early as in the 6th to 7th weeks.[169] This activity also correlates with the appearance of Auerbach's plexus. Neuroblasts of the myenteric plexus originate in the vagal trunks about the 5th week and migrate in a proximal-to-distal direction, normally reaching the rectum around the 12th week.[216] At birth, the ganglion cells of the enteric plexuses are not fully morphologically mature, especially in the ileum; maturation continues after birth.[263] Rhythmic activity increases with age.[169] Peristaltic movements are described in 3- to 5-month-old human fetuses, and may gradually appear in the more distal portion of the bowel.[286]

Acetylcholine causes a prompt contraction of human fetal ileum *in vitro*.[39] Epinephrine, isoprenoline, or norepinephrine relaxed this contraction, and the effects of these drugs did not change in fetuses between 11 and 23 weeks of age.[201] Adrenoreceptors in fetal intestine were found in an 11-week-old fetus.[116] Both the small and the large intestine of 14- to 26-week-old fetuses react *in vitro* to prostaglandin E_2 and $F_2\alpha$ by contraction.[115] Motility, as studied by means of X rays using contrast substances injected into the amniotic fluid of 24- to 40-week-old fetuses, increases with age.[199]

3.4.2. Postnatal Period

Postnatally, there is a change in motility of the digestive tract. In newborn infants, food passes through the small intestine during a longer period than in adults (3–6 hr, compared with 2.5 hr).[264] On the other hand, passage to the large intestine decelerates with age; emptying of the large intestine was most rapid in prematures, less rapid in full-term infants, and slowest in older infants.[153,295] With the use of carmine red markers, the complete intestinal transit time was determined to be 13.4 ± 4.4 hr in the normal newborn.[238]

This value is in agreement with data published by Fomon[81] on 1½- to 6-month-old infants, fed human milk (fresh from the breast or by bottle). In those fed processed human milk, cow's milk, or a formula with protein from cow's milk and fat supplied as a mixture of corn and coconut oils, the passage time was 30–50% shorter. The passage time reacts immediately to a change in diet, suggesting that alteration in intestinal flora is probably not an important determinant of passage time. The significance of the diet-dependent difference is not known. In some newborns, especially prematures, delayed maturation of the colonic rectal expulsive reflex was described.[70]

A wide range of functional abnormalities in the colon of newborn infants was described and related to a functional immaturity of the neural plexus of the bowel, involving predominantly the distal colon, as it matures progressively in a proximal-to-distal direction.[181] The disordered colonic peristaltis is reflected in the narrowed, poorly functioning distal colon. The length of this segment is said to increase with decreasing gestational age.

4. Digestion and Absorption of Carbohydrates

4.1. Digestion of Polysaccharides

4.1.1. Prenatal Period

Salivary amylase is detectable in the second half of gestation or even later.[264] Pancreatic amylase activity was found in 22-week-old fetuses[79]; it had

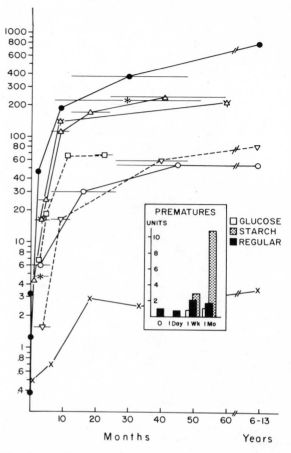

Fig. 2. Amylase activity in the duodenal fluid of infants of different ages. *Ordinate:* Units of activity. Open symbols denote concentration; solid symbols denote output per 50 min/kg body weight (logarithmic scale). *Abscissa:* Age in months/years. The horizontal lines on the curves denote the age ranges of the groups studied (not given if the range was smaller than the size of the symbol). *Inset:* Changes in output of amylase (per 50 min/kg body weight) in prematures on different diets during the first months of life.[319] *Symbols and references:* Δ[4]; □[14]; ○[61]; ⋈[74]; ▽[93]; ●[109,319]; ✳[136]; ×.[157] All samples were collected from fasted subjects. The data reported by Klumpp and Neale[157] are from subjects after test meal also. Stimulation by secretin was used[93]; the data without secretin gave a similar pattern. Pancreozymin–secretin stimulation was used by others.[61,109,319] Test meal stimulation was also used by Auricchio *et al.*[14] The reports in references (109) and (319) were originated by the same research group. The authors in references (4) and (74) used the identical method. No changes in amylase activity during the first 3 weeks of life in full-term infants were reported.[287] Others[288] did not find different activity in children 11 months to 2 years old as compared with children 8–11 years old.

increased in 27-week-old fetuses, but was still only 30% of the activity found in newborns. Amylase of both salivary and pancreatic origin was found in the amniotic fluid and shown electrophoretically as early as in the 16th–18th week of pregnancy.[309] The concentration of amylase in amniotic fluid increased between weeks 16–24 and weeks 36–40 approximately 3–4 times.

Small intestinal homogenate from a 3-month-old fetus was reported to possess amylase activity.[15,79]

4.1.2. Postnatal Period

1. *Amylase activity in the duodenal content* increases postnatally (Fig. 2). Electrophoretic studies on the duodenal juice of 3- to 15-day-old newborns after feeding indicated that the amylase is of salivary origin only.[213]

2. *The digestion of starch* in newborns was studied both by carbohydrate-tolerance-type studies and by balance studies.

Gastric administration of starch solution causes a slow and small increase of blood glucose in newborns; an equicaloric amount of glucose solutions administered to the same children evoked higher and earlier increase, with an earlier return to starting values within 120 min[133] (see also Section 3.3).

Whereas amylopectin is very rapidly hydrolyzed into glucose, maltose, maltotriose, and branched dextrins in 1-year-old children, in infants younger than 6 months, amylopectin hydrolysis was incomplete (with large amounts of dextrins containing more than 30 glucose units. Although the digestion of starch in infants is considerable, the tolerance of young infants to very large quantities is limited.[62] This limit may vary in individual infants. Thus, early administration of starch to a child with "a physiologic deficiency" of pancreatic amylase may evoke iatrogenic diarrhea.[187] Early administration of a small amount of starch to premature babies during one month increased the activity of α-amylase in the duodenal juice obtained after pancreozymin–secretin stimulation (feeding glucose instead of starch did not evoke the amylase activity increase).[319]

4.2. Digestion of Disaccharides

Two approaches were used to evaluate the digestion of the disaccharides: (1) direct determination of disaccharide activity in intestinal mucosa and (2) changes of blood sugar levels after a peroral load.

4.2.1. Prenatal Period

Data from different laboratories on changes of sucrase and lactase activity in the jejunum are summarized in Figs. 3 and 4. Data for changes of other α-glycosidases (maltase, isomaltase, and palatinase) show a similarity to sucrase changes, while data for changes of cellobiase are similar to those for lactase. The activity of sucrase and lactase is lower in young fetuses than in specimens from the small intestinal mucosa of adults. Sucrase increases earlier than lactase, as was pointed out as far back as 1910[134,135] (Fig. 3). It should also be mentioned that in lower mammals, lactase develops (prenatally and postnatally) earlier than α-glycosidases.[161,163]

Figure 4 demonstrates the development of sucrase activity in different parts of the intestinal canal. In the jejunum and ileum, the activity increases between the 10th and 14th fetal weeks. There is no jejunoileal difference. Later, the activity in the jejunum increases further, but not in the ileum. In agreement with previous reports,[55,69,79] sucrase activity was found in the colon, indicating that during this period, as far as sucrase is concerned, the colon resembles the small intestine. During the latter part of gestation, sucrase disappears from the colon.

The total maltase activity (which is, in the adult, a sum of several maltase activities) in fetuses is represented only by maltase Ta and Tb (nomenclature of Dahlqvist), which are already very active in 3-month-old fetuses. Maltase II and maltase III develop during the last part of intrauterine life (maltase III does not develop fully until after birth).[55] Premature infants surviving longer than 24 hr show higher values of lactase and cellobiase than those succumbing within the first day. No such change was shown in the α-glycosidases.[15]

4.2.2. Postnatal Period

(a) **Lactose Digestion.** Digestion of this saccharide has attracted the attention of many research groups, both because of its nutritional importance (approximately 40% calories in breast milk) and because of clinical problems related to malabsorption of lactose. Our knowledge in this area has increased substantially, especially in the last decade, but many questions (especially genetic) remained undecided. Before summarizing this problem from the point of view of developmental physiology, I would like to cite several reviews

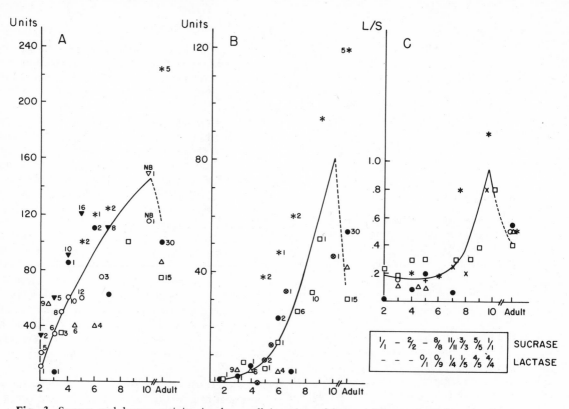

Fig. 3. Sucrase and lactase activity in the small intestine of human fetuses. *Symbols and references:* □(15); △(55); ✳(69); ▼(79); ⊗(118); ○(143); ●.(255) The small figures at the symbols denote the number of fetuses studied. (A, B) Data for sucrase and lactase (mean values from individual papers) are expressed as micromoles per minute per gram protein (□, ✳, △, ○, ●) or in arbitrary units per gram wet weight (⊗, ▼). (C) Lactase/sucrase ratio as calculated from corresponding data. The legend in the lower right-hand corner was compiled from the data of Ibrahim(134) and Ibrahim and Kaumheimer.(135) The age corresponds to that in (C); denominator: number of fetuses tested; numerator: number of fetuses with a positive test for the disaccharidase.

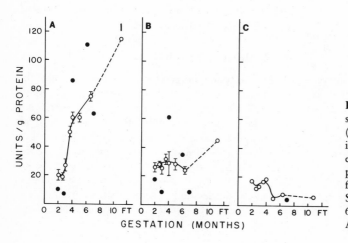

Fig. 4. Comparison of the development of sucrase in the jejunum (A), ileum (B), and colon (C) of human fetuses and newborn. *Abscissa:* Age in gestational months; (FT) one full-term-born exencephalus. *Ordinate:* Micromoles sucrose split per minute per gram protein. (○) Total of 44 fetuses studied; vertical brackets represent 2 S.E.M. Data from Jirsová *et al.*(142,143) (●) Total of 6 fetuses studied. Data from Sheehy and Anderson.(255)

(or comments) in which the interested reader can find more information.[11,23,36,100,170,241,260,261]

Two types of studies were performed: (1) direct determination of lactase activity in mucosal specimens and (2) "lactose tolerance" tests (changes in blood sugar after a peroral load of lactose).

1. *Direct determination of lactase activity*[11] has been standardized on the basis of an assay introduced by Dahlqvist in 1964.[11] There are several factors that can influence the results. It is obvious that a specimen from surgery of a normal gut is the ideal but not always accessible sample. Specimens taken at different times after death undergo both premortem and postmortem changes (differing degrees of autolysis). If the luminal contents are rinsed, the digested upper parts of the villi (usually showing the highest enzyme specific activity) can be lost. This effect of washing could also be seen with biopsy specimens, where a simple rinsing in saline causes approximately 50% loss of protein and lactase, sucrase, maltase, and palatinase.[8] The results of enzyme activity determination in rinsed samples were lower when expressed per wet weight than in unrinsed samples (results expressed per protein were not affected).

Since Asp and Dahlqvist[11] have developed specific assays for determining three β-galactosidases—i.e., microvillar lactase (so-called "true lactase"), lysosomal acid β-galactosidase, and cytosol hetero-β-galactosidase—present in the human small intestine, we can discuss further conditions more specifically. The localization of the mucosal specimen is also important. Microvillar lactase is high in the jejunum and about 50% lower in the duodenum and ileum. Its activity was found exclusively in jejunal villi enterocytes, with a maximum in their middle to apical parts, and none in crypt cells. This type of distribution along the length of the small intestine and along the height of the mucosa was found both in adults with high and in adults with low lactase.[11] (Acid β-galactosidase and hetero-β-galactosidase had a different distribution pattern.) Furthermore, because lactase showed a more apical localization than sucrase, the lactase/sucrase ratio varied along the height of the villus (the ratio was approximately 2 times higher in the lower portion of the villus than in the apex). Finally, we must bear in mind that determination of lactase using lactose as a substrate gives accurate values of microvillar lactase only if the lactase activity is high; if the activity of lactase is low, the acid β-galactosidase at pH 6.015 can represent from 15 to as much as 90% of the total lactase activity.

There are various speculations in the literature about the possible existence of "infant" and "adult" type lactase and, furthermore, about the possibility that hetero-β-galactosidase might be the precursor of lactase. Both possibilities are at the present time not supported by sufficient evidence. The chromatographic and kinetic properties of lactase partially isolated from infants and from adult subjects with low or high lactase showed no difference.[12,179] An unpublished study by Alpers and co-workers indicates the possibility of qualitative differences in isolated lactase from low- and high-lactase-activity subjects.

2. The *lactose tolerance test* evaluates the digestion and absorption of lactose by the changes in blood sugar level after a peroral application of lactose. In some studies, the rise of blood sugar above 20–25 mg/dl is judged as an indication of efficient lactose digestion, and the subject studied is listed as a "lactose absorber," or the blood sugar value is given directly as a quantitative value. In some studies summarized in our figure, another criterion for lactose nondigestion was used: the presence of abdominal complaints (distention, abdominal discomfort, cramps, pain, diarrhea, loose stools, abdominal bloating, "gas" and flatulence).

In earlier years, the expression *lactase deficiency* was used. During the last decade, some 40 to 50 papers have appeared proving that the high activity of lactase in adulthood is the exception rather than the norm; in other words, a postnatal decrease occurs generally in man, as in other mammals.[163] The persistence of high intestinal lactase activity in some populations as a whole seems to be a product of natural selection in areas in which milking and consumption of milk has occurred for tens of centuries.[200,260,261] High incidence of lactose intolerance (which is equivalent to low lactase activity) in adulthood is reported in African and American Negroes (with the exception of the Fulani people, who are pastoral),[171] North and South American Indians, Eskimos, Orientals, Pakistanis, Indians, Australian aborigines, New Guinea natives, Jews, Greek Cypriots, Southern Italians, and Arabs. Only · people of Caucasian extraction living in (or coming from), e.g., Denmark, Finland, Germany, Poland, Czechoslovakia, Sweden, Australia, and the United States have a low incidence of lactose intolerance in adulthood (1–20%). We therefore prefer (in accordance with some other authors) to use the expression lactose *absorbers* or *digesters* (and lactose *nonabsorbers* or

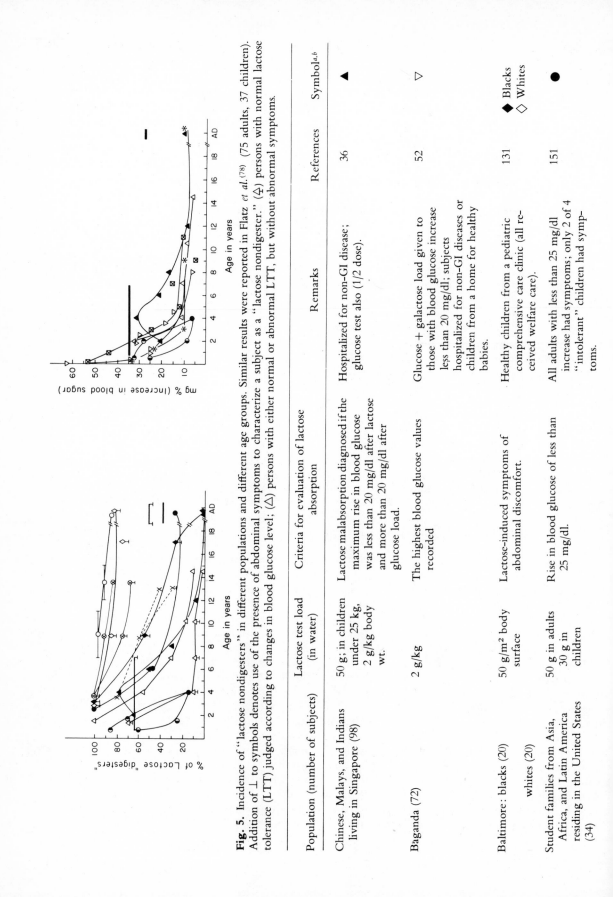

Fig. 5. Incidence of "lactose nondigesters" in different populations and different age groups. Similar results were reported in Flatz et al.[78] (75 adults, 37 children). Addition of ⊥ to symbols denotes use of the presence of abdominal symptoms to characterize a subject as a "lactose nondigester." (⟂) persons with normal lactose tolerance (LTT) judged according to changes in blood glucose level; (△) persons with either normal or abnormal LTT, but without abnormal symptoms.

Population (number of subjects)	Lactose test load (in water)	Criteria for evaluation of lactose absorption	Remarks	References	Symbol[a,b]
Chinese, Malays, and Indians living in Singapore (98)	50 g; in children under 25 kg, 2 g/kg body wt.	Lactose malabsorption diagnosed if the maximum rise in blood glucose was less than 20 mg/dl after lactose and more than 20 mg/dl after glucose load.	Hospitalized for non-GI disease; glucose test also (1/2 dose).	36	▲
Baganda (72)	2 g/kg	The highest blood glucose values recorded	Glucose + galactose load given to those with blood glucose increase less than 20 mg/dl; subjects hospitalized for non-GI diseases or children from a home for healthy babies.	52	▽
Baltimore: blacks (20) whites (20)	50 g/m² body surface	Lactose-induced symptoms of abdominal discomfort.	Healthy children from a pediatric comprehensive care clinic (all received welfare care).	131	◆ Blacks ◇ Whites
Student families from Asia, Africa, and Latin America residing in the United States (34)	50 g in adults 30 g in children	Rise in blood glucose of less than 25 mg/dl.	All adults with less than 25 mg/dl increase had symptoms; only 2 of 4 "intolerant" children had symptoms.	151	●

Population	Dose	Criteria	Comments	Ref.	◐ Living with parents ◑ Living in orphanage
Thai (172)	2 g/kg	Rise of blood glucose by 20 mg/dl or more considered as "tolerance."	Sucrose and glucose tolerance also studied; data for American and Thai adults included.	156	✳
Nigeria: Yoruba (90)	2 g/kg (maximum 100 g)	Only the highest increase of blood glucose was recorded.	Healthy subjects; also sucrose tolerance; unweaned and weaned.	171	⊠
Nigeria: Yoruba (89)	2 g/kg in children under 25 kg; in heavier, only 1 g/kg	Same	In weaned children, also glucose–galactose test.	217	
Peru: Mestizo population (90)	50 g/m²	(1) Maximum increase in blood sugar less than 25 mg/dl. (2) Also presence of symptoms.	Children originally admitted for marasmus or kwashiorkor and their siblings.	219	△
Hyderabad, India (27)	**2 g/kg**	Same	Healthy adults.	228	▬
Finnish village (129 children, 158 adults)	1 g/kg (maximum 50 g)	Values above 25 mg/dl increase judged normal; 20–24 mg/dl repeated with double dose; above 20 mg/dl then judged normal.	Volunteers from a random sample.	242	⊕
Mexican-American children (MA) (282) and Anglo-American children (AA) (51) of Northern European descent	2 g/kg	(1) Lower sucrase than 25 mg/dl judged as malabsorption of lactase. (2) Presence of GI symptoms recorded.	Both parents of Mexican-Americans had Spanish surnames.	313	X (MA) ⊗ (AA)
Japanese children	3.5 g/kg (max 50 g)	Lactose "malabsorption" was diagnosed if maximum rise of blood glucose was less than 20 mg/dl.	Additional data (not plotted in the figure). Maximum blood glucose increases (in mg/dl) in low-birth-weight infants were 39.4 ± 16.4 (S.D.) before feeding; 49.5 ± 6.2 at one week old; 93.5 ± 16.2 at 3 weeks old; in full term infants (0–11 months old) an increase of 59.8 ± 0.7 was observed. The percentages of lactose digesters were: (under one year) 100%; (1–2.9 years) 67%; (3–7.9 years) 46%; (8–15.9 years and adults) 0%.	257	Not plotted

nondigesters) as opposed to "deficiency," which indicates something not normal, even pathologic.

After this rather lengthy introduction, which I felt necessary, I would like to discuss Fig. 5, which demonstrates the postnatal development of lactose-digestion capacity in man. Determinations of lactase activity performed in various laboratories support the conclusions that can be drawn from Fig. 5.

Newborns and young children digest lactose quite efficiently (for some exceptions, depending mainly on the stage of maturity, see below); later, as the children grow older, the incidence of lactose nondigesters increases. Not all races show the same rate of decreased lactose-digestion capacity. People from Finnish villages and white Americans showed a small and slow decrease. Thai orphans showed the fastest decrease; as early as 2 years of age, the incidence of lactose nondigesters was on a level of that reported in Thai adults. A slower rate of decrease was observed in Singapore. In American Negroes and Asian, African, and Latin Americans residing in the United States, the adult values were found after the first decade. In other groups, adult values were achieved at about 4–5 years of age.

Several studies have followed the changes in the first weeks of life in more detail. Both term and premature healthy newborn infants have a limited capacity to absorb lactose (Fig. 6). In term infants, the absorption capacity increases already after the first day of life.[52] In prematures, it increases later—after 2 to 3 weeks[35,76,139]; in some prematures, it may take 2 months.[1] Premature babies handle well doses of lactose that are within the limited functional capacity of their GI tract.[186]

Boellner *et al.*[35] reported that in both term and premature infants (0–3 days old), duodenal administration of lactase (a Sigma Chemical Co. product, not further specified) 1–36 hr prior to the lactose tolerance test increased the absorption of lactose, as judged by blood glucose elevation.

In infants, transient lactose intolerance may follow various pathologic states (gastroenteritis, neonatal surgery, cystic fibrosis, gluten enteropathy, immune deficiency disorders[21] and various forms of malnutrition).[138,226] Small-for-date term infants severely underweight for their gestational age (birth weight below 1500 g) also show decreased capacity to absorb lactose; glucose/galactose tolerance curves were identical with other weight groups that had higher lactose-absorption capacity.[76]

Jarrett and Holman[139] attempted to influence the lactose-absorption capacity postnatally in premature infants, feeding them in the first 2 weeks one of two formulas differing in lactose content (one containing lactose as the only disaccharide, the other sucrose as the principal disaccharide). At the age of 13–17 days, both groups exhibited identical lactose (and sucrose) tolerance tests.

Paige *et al.*,[219] comparing well-nourished Peruvian children with their previously malnourished siblings, found no difference in their handling of lactose. Keusch *et al.*[156] reported that the decrease in lactose-absorption capacity occurred earlier in Thai infants living in an orphanage than in Thai infants living in villages with their parents. This difference might be a result of environmental factors (institutionalized infants had recurrent acute diarrhea, presumably infectious). In Oriental children in Singapore, intolerance to lactose appeared at a later age in milk-drinkers than in non–milk-drinkers.[36]

(b) Digestion of α-Disaccharides. Data from various laboratories show no substantial effect of age or race on activity of sucrase, total maltase, isomaltase, or trehalase.

Absorption of sucrose and maltose from a peroral load (as judged from blood glucose curves) proceeded similarly if 2-week-old premature infants were fed diets in which the carbohydrate was either only lactose or predominantly sucrose.[139]

4.3. Absorption of Monosaccharides

4.3.1. Prenatal Period

Active transport of hexoses was demonstrated using the "everted sac" *in vitro* technique in freshly obtained, healthy human fetuses (Fig. 7). Transport increases between the 10th and 18th weeks of gestation only in the jejunum, leading to a jejunoileal difference known in adults. The potential difference evoked by glucose transfer shows parallel changes (Fig. 7). "Apparent" K_m values for the glucose transfer potential difference (GTPD) in all used sacs of the jejunum were fairly close, indicating that the affinity of glucose for the locus forming the potential difference did not change. This finding suggests that the increase of GTPD during gestation is a quantitative change.

Further studies have shown that the GTPD was immediately abolished by the addition of phlorizin to the mucosal fluid; α-methylglucoside and 3-methyl-O-glucose also evoked an increase in the

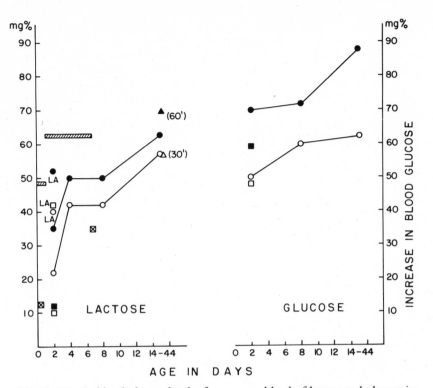

Fig. 6. Rise in blood glucose levels after a peroral load of lactose and glucose in infants during the first 6 weeks of life. Values 30 min (△,○) and 60 min (▲,●) after sugar load in premature infants; 30 min (□) and 60 min (■) after sugar load in full-term infants; (LA) in children who received lactase duodenally. *Symbols and references:* ○, □, ●, ■ [35]; △, ▲ [139]; ▨▨▨ [52]; ⊠ [9] A postnatal lactose-connected rise in blood sugar was found to be highly significant. [35] Due to the large scatter, the data of Cook [52] did not differ significantly between the two age groups. Infants were fasted 4 hr [35,139] or 6 hr [52] before being fed with lactose (1.75/kg body weight; Cook [52] used 2 g/kg body weight). Boellner *et al.* [35] studied 49 infants of undisclosed race; Cook's subjects were Bagandas; Jarrett and Holman [139] studied 16 American Negroes and 4 American Caucasians. Blood glucose was determined using the glucose-oxidase method [9,35,52] or the "true glucose" technique (Technical Bulletin No. 6073C, Spinco). [139]

potential difference. Figure 7 shows that in contrast to conditions known in adulthood, active glucose transport also proceeds *in vitro* under anaerobic conditions, similarly as it was reported in experimental animals before or shortly after birth. [163]

What does the existence of active transport of hexoses and amino acids (see Section 5.2.3) in the fetal small intestine mean? Two main explanations are possible: (1) it has no functional significance, being only the first appearance of a mechanism that will become important at the beginning of oral nutrition; (2) it might both have a nutritional signi-

ficance and play a role in the mechanisms of regulation of the composition and volume of amniotic fluid, since the fetus swallows amniotic fluid.

Finally, it is theoretically and practically interesting and significant that active transport can also function anaerobically, which is not possible in adults. That it can is important not only from the aspect of the physiology of the small intestine, but also from the aspect of the more general question of the physiology of the fetus. Some other functions may also occur under anaerobic conditions, thus decreasing the risk of hypoxic situations.

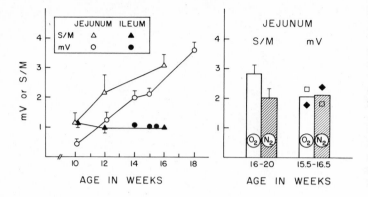

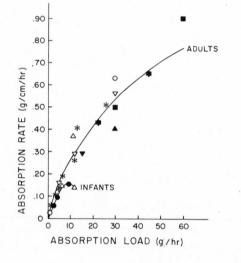

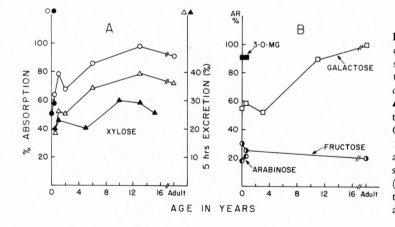

Fig. 7. Development of active glucose transport in human fetuses. *Left:* Prenatal development of glucose transport as studied *in vitro* (technique of everted sacs) in an oxygen atmosphere. *Abscissa:* Age in postconception weeks. *Ordinate:* (S/M) Ratio of concentration of glucose in serosal fluid to glucose in mucosal fluid at the end of a 60-min incubation period or (mV) potential difference of glucose transfer. Vertical brackets represent S.E.M. *Right:* Comparison of transport in an oxygen and nitrogen atmosphere. Vertical brackets represent S.E.M. (□, ♦): Individual values. Data from Jirsová et al.[142,143] and Levin et al.[18]

Fig. 8. Rate of glucose absorption from the perfused jejunum in infants and adults. *Symbols and references:* Infants: (△) 2–4 months old[283]; (●) 7–21 months old[138]; (○) 3 weeks to 6 months old.[192] Adults: (■) [54]; (▼)[85]; (○)[86]; (✱)[101]; (▽)[126]; (★)[244]; (△)[276]; (▲)[289] The concentration of the glucose solution administered to infants varied between 0.15 and 16%; to adults, between 0.12 and 10%. Data for infants compiled by Younoszai[316]; for adults, by Fordtran and Ingelfinger.[84]

Fig. 9. Postnatal changes in absorption of monosaccharides in children. (A) Absorption of xylose. *Left ordinate:* Absorption of xylose (%): ○,[175] ●[27]; *right ordinate:* 5-hr excretion (%): △[175] and ▲.[202] (B) Absorption of galactose, fructose, arabinose, and 3-O-methylglucose. *Ordinate:* AR% = (SA p.o./SA i.v.) × 100. SA denotes the surface area under a curve depicting the changes in given sugar levels in blood after peroral load (p.o.) and after intravenous administration (i.v.) of an identical dose between 60 and 120 min. Data from Beyreiss.[27]

.3.2. Postnatal Period

Several types of data are available to evaluate the bsorption rate of monosaccharides during postnatal development.

Various laboratories have published data on hanges in blood glucose levels after a peroral load f glucose in infants of various ages.[35,224] Infants ounger than 38 days reached the maximum blood lucose level after 60 min, whereas in older infants, he peak value was attained (as in adults) after 30 min. The rate of decrease to starting blood glucose values vas also slower in younger children. The interpreta-ion of these differences (as far as the rate of glucose bsorption is concerned) is not simple. They can be udged to indicate a slower rate of glucose absorption ut also a slower rate of glucose utilization in infants. The "diabetic-type" oral glucose tolerance curve in he newborn infant correlates with the slow dis-ppearance rate of glucose administered intraven-usly in these infants.[224]

Two other techniques that yield data for more ccurate evaluation of absorption of glucose have lso been used:

1. The rate of absorption after intubation under teady conditions was determined in some institu-ions in adults; infants were studied by other groups ater. We have plotted the data as compiled by Younoszai[316] for infants and by Fordtran and ngelfinger[84] for adults in Fig. 8. These data ndicate that glucose absorption in infants is less fficient than in adults. In infants, the maximum ate of absorption (plateau) was achieved with a load f 6–10 g/hr, whereas in adults, this plateau value is bout 10 times higher.

2. Beyreiss[27] determined the absorption rate by comparing the changes in blood glucose after peroral application of 3-O-methylglucose (a nonmetabol-zed, actively transported analogue of glucose) with he changes after intravenous administration (see the Fig. 9 caption). He did not find any difference petween 3- to 6-day-old full-term newborn and 4-to 9-month-old healthy infants.

Data for absorption of galactose studied by means of the two last-mentioned techniques indicate a ower absorption of galactose in infants than in dults. Beyreiss et al.[30] showed the postnatal in-crease of galactose absorption rate (Fig. 9); adult values are achieved between 4 and 8 years. The reason for this might be a relative "immaturity" of the galactose metabolism in the liver and/or the small intestine of children.

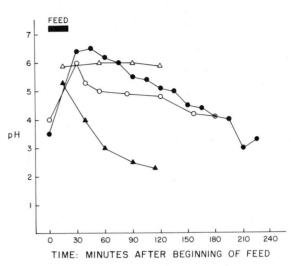

Fig. 10. Effect of feeding on pH values of the stomach contents of infants of different ages. (○) 10 premature babies, 3–13 days old[114]; (●) 25 full-term newborn infants[198]; (△) infants 1–2 months old[312]; (▲) children 3–13 years old.[312]

Meeuwisse and Dano[202] reviewed older data on xylose absorption in infancy and presented a detailed discussion of the interpretation and significance of a xylose absorption test in infants. Figure 9 demon-strates the postnatal increase of xylose absorption. Data of Hawkins[117] also show a slower absorption of xylose in infants, up to 6 months old, as com-pared with the other three age groups studied ($\frac{1}{2}$–1, 1–4, and 4–10 years of age). Further data[27–30] on arabinose and fructose absorption rates are also depicted in Fig. 9. The absorption rate of xylose in children was found to be inhibited by glucose.[31] Fructose conversion to glucose (based on determina-tion of fructose and glucose concentrations in portal and arterial blood during fructose absorption) already occurs in the small intestine of premature newborns (32 gestational weeks).

Malnourishment decreases the absorption capacity for glucose in children,[138] as does acute diar-rhea.[192] .

5. Digestion and Absorption of Protein

5.1. Digestion of Protein

Proteolytic enzymes are found in the stomach, pancreas, and small intestine.

5.1.1. Proteolysis in the Stomach

(a) Prenatal Period. Proteolytic activity has been described in fetuses older than 16 weeks.[155,292] Pepsinogen excreted by the kidneys into the amniotic fluid appears between the 7th and 8th months of gestation.[292]

The fluid found in the stomach of fetuses may be derived either from gastric secretion or from amniotic fluid (see Section 3.1). The amniotic fluid decreases the acidity of the contents. The first traces of gastric acidity appear in fetuses aged 4–5 months.[155]

(b) Postnatal Period. *(1) Gastric Acidity.* The pH of gastric fluid in newborns is usually neutral or slightly acid, and the acidity increases shortly after birth (within several hours).[311,312]

The actual pH of the stomach contents in infants depends strongly on food intake. The entry of milk into the infant's stomach causes a sharp increase in the pH of the gastric contents (Fig. 10). These findings not only stress the importance of defining the time after feeding when pH is determined, but also show that the gastric acidity of the newborn is unsuitable for optimum pepsin action, but might be favorable for action of other enzymes [see Sections 5.1.1(b)(2) and 6.1.1(b)(1,2)]. Some controversy exists in the literature as to whether newborns have achlorhydria in the early hours after birth and whether its presence depends on the birth weight or not. Such a condition might be a result of real immaturity of the HCl-producing parietal cells or an

effect of the presence of alkaline amniotic fluid[16,114] in different amounts immediately after the delivery. Later, the effect of the presence of milk must also be considered as the cause of the "apparent achlorhydria."

HCl secretion was found to be much lower in prematures than in full-term infants.[205] The concentration and output of titratable acid following histamine stimulation are very low in newborns; the values increase until the 3rd week of life.[3] Output values show a short decline in the 3rd to 4th week, and a second sustained rise continuing into the 2nd and 3rd months of life. Whereas the concentration data for 2- to 3-month-old infants and adults do not overlap, output data (per body weight) show some overlap (Fig. 11). The increase of stimulated acid output occurs between the first and second year of life (a similar increase is observed for the basal output).[231]

According to several studies, gastric acidity reaches a peak within 24 hr after birth. This increase has been related to transfer of some hormonal substances from the mother[206]; the effect disappears within a few days as the acidity again decreases. Recently, Rogers *et al.*[233,234] approached this problem by determining perinatal changes of gastrin, glucagon, and secretin levels. Table I was compiled from their data. Various interesting aspects arise from their study; we can discuss only a few of them. Their study does not exclude the possibility of transfer of gastrin from mother to baby during spontaneous labor. Similarly, maternal and placental

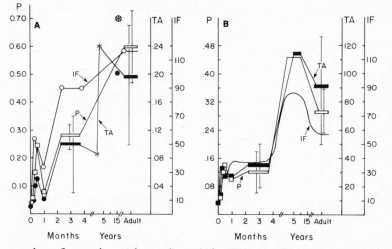

Fig. 11. Postnatal development of secretion of pepsin, titratable acid, and intrinsic factor in infants. *Left:* Output per kilogram body weight and hour. (P) Pepsin: □; (TA) titratable acid: ■; (IF) intrinsic factor: ○ (data of Agunod *et al.*[3]). Further TA data ●[92]; ✳[231]; ✴[232] (assuming a mean adult weight of 70 kg). *Right:* Same data as left panel, expressed as concentration. The lengths of the horizontal rectangles denote the extent of the age groups; vertical brackets denote ranges of values (used only in the 2- to 3-month-old and adult groups). *Ordinates:* (P) Pepsin (*left ordinates*): left panel—ng/hr per kg; *right panel*—mg/ml; (TA) titratable acid (*inside right ordinates*): left panel—meq/hr per kg; *right panel*—meq/liter; (IF) intrinsic factor (*outside right ordinates*): left panel—ng B₁₂/hr per kg; *right panel*—ng B₁₂/ml.

Table I. Levels of Gastrin, Glucagon, and Secretin in Venous Plasma of Infants[a]

Plasma source		Gastrin		Glucagon		Secretin
		Oxytocin[b]	No oxytocin[b']	C-terminal (pancreatic)	N-terminal	
Maternal plasma ⎫ at birth		52 ± 14.7	29.5 ± 6.9	57 ± 8	62 ± 5	12.5 ± 3.6
Cord plasma ⎭		59 ± 15	89.0 ± 20.9	432 ± 54^{b} $227 \pm 26^{b'}$		
Cord plasma						
(Groups b and b' combined)		64 ± 12.5		336 ± 42	17 ± 12	92.8 ± 23.9
4-Day-old infants		151 ± 15.8		891 ± 239	1318 ± 264	299 ± 58

Compiled from data of Rogers et al.[233,234] Values are means ± S.E.M. (groups were comprised of 11, 19, or 22 subjects).
Indicates only whether oxytocin was ([b]) or was not ([b']) used during delivery; otherwise, both groups were combined.

transfer of C-glucagon and of secretin is possible. They conclude further that the newborn baby secretes gastrin C- and N-glucagon independently. The raised glucagon and secretin levels occurring on day 4 may inhibit the gastric secretory effect of the raised gastrin levels at the same time.

(2) Proteolytic Activity. The peptic activity of newborn infants is very low and in proportion to the degree of maturity[303]; e.g., in newborns weighing 4000 g, it is about 3–4 times higher than in prematures weighing 1000 g; it increases in the fundus by about 4 times after food intake on the 2nd day of postnatal life.[292] Figure 11 shows that low concentration and output (per body weight) of pepsin in newborns increase until the 3rd week of life. Output values show a transient decline in the 3rd and 4th weeks, and a second rise continuing into the 2nd and 3rd months of life. The range of values found in the 2nd and 3rd months is below the range of adult values.

The transient high production of pepsin (as well as HCl) in the first 3 weeks of life may also be related to the transplacental transfer of maternal gastrin to the infant; its effect might be both direct on parietal cell secretion and also stimulatory on growth and development of fundic glands.

Controversy exists concerning the occurrence of rennin (a peptidyl peptide hydrolase) in the stomach. This enzyme coagulates milk at pH values between 5.0 and 6.5. Thus, if the pH of the gastric content is increased by a large amount of milk (see Fig. 10), rennin may become effective.[264] Malpress,[197] however, did not find rennin in the neonatal stomach. The process leading to precipitation of protein in the stomach of newborns is not clear; nevertheless, it is very effective. Precipitated breast milk caseinogen was found as early as within 30 min of feeding.[198]

No substantial digestion of protein was found in specimens of gastric contents taken from 5- to 8-day-old infants.[198] A most probable explanation for this finding is that the pepsin (which is low at that time) is almost completely inactivated at the high levels of pH that were found in the newborn stomach at various intervals after feeding (compare Fig. 10). In older infants (mean, 23 days; range, 13–44 days of age), traces of hydrolyzed protein were found in stomach contents, cow's milk protein being hydrolyzed to a greater degree than the proteins of human milk.[25]

5.1.2. Pancreatic Proteolytic Enzymes

(a) Prenatal Period. Pancreatic enzymes begin to form about the 3rd fetal month.[155] Pancreatic secretion starts at the beginning of the 5th month.[168]

The presence of trypsinogen and chymotrypsinogen was demonstrated in fetuses weighing as little as 500 g.[185] The enterokinase-activated activity did not change up to a weight of 3000 g. Only in fetuses weighing 350–500 g were measured values low. These results are in contrast to those of Werner,[303] who found both histologically and biochemically low proteolytic activity (activated by enterokinase) in the pancreas of infants with low birth weight. In infants up to a weight of 1000 g, no granules were found; between birth weights of 1000 and 2000 g, they appeared on rare occasions; above 3000 g, they were numerous. Proteolytic activity in newborn infants weighing 4000 g was about 6 times higher than that in infants weighing 1000 g; in full-term infants,

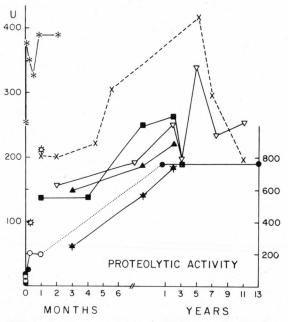

Fig. 12. Postnatal changes in proteolytic activity in th[e] duodenal juice. Note: Methods are dated; in recent year[s] the definition of trypsin activity as opposed to othe[r] protease activities (see the text) has specifically narrowe[d] The reader is advised to check original papers for detailed description of method and substrates. Earli[e] papers determined, for example, changes in the viscosity o[f] gelatin[4,74,157]; later, casein[288] and hemoglobin[93] wer[e] used as substrates. *Left ordinate:* Concentration of enzym[e] activity: (▽) Samples obtained after fasting and after tes[t] meal[157]; (■ [4] and × [74]) same assay method used on sam[ples] from a fasting subject; ✳ stimulation with Doryl[287] (▲) pancreozymin–secretin stimulation[61]; (✦) chymo[ ]trypsin from the same study.[61] *Right ordinate:* Outpu[t] of trypsin (μg/kg body weight) 50 min after pan[ ]creozymin–secretin stimulation[319]: (☼) Prematures o[n] a high-protein diet; (●) full-term babies and (○) prema[ ]tures on a regular diet. Whereas the data of Andersen[ ] do not show any statistically significant differences amon[g] age groups (even with the considerable number of subject[s] studied: 54), the data of Zoppi et al.[319] show bot[h] significant postnatal increase and significant effect of th[e] high-protein diet in the early postnatal period. Previou[s] data from the same laboratory[109] in a smaller group o[f] children did not show statistical differences among various age groups (0–½, ½–1, 1–5, and 5–13 years old). In addition t[o] these data, mean trypsin values (fasting and after test meal) in 42 children 1–6 years of age (mean 2½ years) wer[e] published.[136] The mean concentration and output of trypsin per body weight were reported to be 50% higher in infants 1–11 months of age (mean, 7 months) that in 6 children (2–11 years; mean, 5¼ years).[93] An extensive study[288] found no difference in trypsin activity in children 1–2 years old as compared with that in children 8–1[3] years old; the values in the intermediate age group were similar, but with an unexplained 30% lower activity i[n] 2- to 3-year-old children. No postnatal change was found in α-chymotrypsin and carboxy peptidase activity in 2[ ] infants and children from 6 weeks to 13 years of age.[109] Results of the same group[319] with trypsin, wher[e] previous reports also indicated no postnatal changes, suggest that these findings should be judged as preliminary.

the histological appearance almost resembles that of adults.

Proteolytic activity in meconium was found to be present in similar amounts in fetuses weighing 500 g or more.[185]

Fomina[79] found that peptone-splitting activity is present from the 2nd month of pregnancy, and that it increases about 2 times by the end of the 7th month (the same activity was found in stillborns). Enterokinase was absent until the 7th month of pregnancy; in 40-week-olds, it was about 4% of the activity found in adults. Activation of trypsinogen by the pancreatic tissue occurs only in fetuses weighing more than 1500 g.[185]

Some discrepancies and contradictions in the reports described above are obviously based on the use of different analytic techniques and differences in the material that was obtained from stillborn infants.

(b) Postnatal Period (Fig. 12). Various reports show no significant difference in the concentration of trypsin collected either after simple fasting during food digestion[4,41,60,74,93,136,189,288] or after pancre[ ]ozymin–secretin stimulation[61,109] during postnata[l] development. Similarly, no difference was observe[d] in premature babies between the ages of 2 days an[d] 7 weeks.[74,195]

Levels of trypsin concentration encountere[d] during the first 2 years of life are already reache[d] at the age of 3 months.[107,287] During the foo[d] intake, the concentration of trypsin did not increas[e] in one group of children.[40] On the contrar[y] Norman et al.,[213] who also measured chymo[ ]trypsin, and Lindberg,[189] who measured tota[l] proteolytic activity (sum of trypsin, chymotrypsin[,] carboxypeptidase, and elastase), observed a decreas[e] that was not seen in adults.

From birth, the concentration of chymotrypsi[n] (after pancreozymin–secretin stimulation) increase[s] approximately 3 times, and reaches adult levels i[n] 3-year-old children. The activity of chymotrypsi[n] in pancreatic homogenates of infants who died a[t] various periods after birth was found to be higher i[n] infants surviving 1–4 months than in those survivin[g] ss than 1 month of postnatal life.[185] Comparison f output of trypsin per unit weight shows some ontroversy. Whereas Gibbs[93] found that trypsin utput (after secretin stimulation) was higher by)% in infants 1–11 months of age (mean, 7 months) han in children 26–132 months old (mean, $5\frac{3}{4}$ years), thers[74,319,320] clearly show an increase of output uring development. An increase of trypsin activity as observed in pancreatic homogenates of infants irviving longer after birth.[185]

Feeding a high-protein diet to prematures evoked substantial increase of trypsin at the ages of both week and 1 month, as compared with values ound in children on a diet with a lower protein ontent.[319]

.1.3. Proteolytic and Peptidase Activity in the Small Intestinal Mucosa

(a) Prenatal Period. Protease activity in the :junum did not change markedly between the 8th nd 17th weeks of gestation, but in the ileum, a ronounced increase was measured. In younger etuses, no difference was found in the activity of oth parts of the intestine, but in older fetuses, the ctivity was significantly higher in the ileum than in he jejunum.[122] Enzyme activity breaking down eptone is present in the small intestine of 7- to 0-week-old fetuses, and rises slightly after the 14th veek.[79]

Aminopeptidase activity does not change in the junum between the 8th and 17th weeks after onception, but it increases in the ileum. In the ldest fetuses, the activity is significantly higher in ie ileum than in the jejunum, while in the ounger ones, the activity is the same in both parts f the intestine.[122] Tripeptidase activity changes nly slightly in the same period. No significant ifference was found between the jejunum and ileum 1 any of the age groups.[122] Dipeptidase (glycyl-lycine) is present in the small intestine of 2-month-ld fetuses, and it increases in the 3rd month of estation.[34,188] This and other dipeptidases (sub-trates: alanyl-glutamic acid, alanyl-proline, glycyl-:ucine and glycyl-valine) were present in the small ntestine of fetuses aged 11–23 weeks, without any ronounced developmental changes. Dipeptidase ctivities were slightly higher in the proximal than n the distal part of the intestine; practically the same ate of breakdown of substrates was observed in the arge intestine.[188] Dipeptidase activity toward -glutaminyl-L-proline and glycylproline is present fter the 16th week of age, at levels comparable vith those of adults.[239] Whereas some biochemical

properties of glycyl-L-proline dipeptidase did not change during the age period studied, the other peptidase showed some changes. γ-Glutamyl-trans-peptidase (an enzyme implicated in both hydroly-sis of peptides and transport of amino acids across cell membranes) did not show any change in specific activity with age, in fetuses 13–24 weeks old, but exceeded approximately 8 times the activity found in surgical biopsies from adults' jejunum.[13]

Nevertheless, the extent to which all the changes in peptidase activity in fetuses described above are related to developmental changes in the ability to deal with peptides in the small intestine from absorbed proteins, or the extent to which they are related to the development of intracellular protein metabolism in the small intestine, cannot be deter-mined at present.

(b) Postnatal Period. Dahlqvist et al.[56] re-ported values for (eight) dipeptidases in infants and children with gastrointestinal symptoms, but with histologically normal mucosa obtained on biopsy. They did not find any difference between activities in 12 2-month- to 14-year-old children and 37 adult subjects.

5.2. Absorption of Protein

This problem will be reviewed in two parts: the first deals with the absorption of unchanged (intact) protein; the second, with the absorption of products of protein digestion.

5.2.1. Absorption of Proteins Without Change or With Minimal Changes

This subject is dealt with in Chapter 18; therefore, we will review it only briefly here. Various aspects of this problem have been reviewed quite exten-sively.[44,161–163,209,293]

Two main groups of protein have been studied: those that can act as *antigens* (mainly food protein, e.g., cow's milk proteins, egg proteins), and *anti-bodies.*

(a) Prenatal Period. Proteins are present in the amniotic fluid. About 50% of its volume is swallowed by the fetus daily[94]; thus, the protein amount obtainable at or near term from the amniotic fluid is about one-fifth of the daily protein gain of the fetus. A fairly wide spectrum of protein is transferred to the fetus by this process (human serum albumin, IgG, IgA, chorionic gonadotropin, and growth hormone.[94]

Reports that the mean birth weight of infants with duodenal or esophageal atresia is lower than that of normal infants were interpreted by some authors as a support for the theory of nutritional significance of this paraplacental route of protein delivery to the fetus.[94] Others,[57,172] however, were unable to prove the passage into the fetal circulation of the tetanus antibody of bovine serum albumin introduced into the amniotic cavity.

Various morphological studies on the so-called meconium corpuscles later identified as lysosomes also indicate absorption of protein molecules through the fetal small intestine. These studies[5,141] do not unequivocally solve the question of the origin of the protein; it might merely be the protein of desquamated gastrointestinal cells, since Tobeck[281] observed a similar histological picture indicating protein absorption in the intestinal epithelium, distal to an atresia.

(b) Postnatal Period. Various studies indicate the permeability for intact *food proteins* of the small intestine during the neonatal period,[6,190,294] but passage of proteins was also demonstrated in older children and even in adults.[103] The serum of infants contains a higher percentage of antibodies to food antigens than does the serum of adults,[236] which suggests that food proteins are absorbed intact in sufficient quantities for immunologic response. The mechanism of this phenomenon is not clear; one contributing factor may be that the digestion proceeds to a lesser extent in younger infants than later in life. Insulin administered orally to newborn infants within 20 min of birth has a hypoglycemic effect, while later it has no effect.[318] This might be related to the increase in gastric acidity [see Section 5.1.1(b)(1)]. Rh antibodies are not destroyed when incubated with the gastric juice of 1-week-old infants.[45] Also, the trypsin inhibitors present in the colostrum and milk may protect the proteins from digestion.[176] In the last 50 years, numerous studies have been published proving or disproving absorption of immunologically active proteins from the intestinal lumen of newborn infants. Two reports make a strong case for the absorption of immunologically active proteins in the early postnatal period. Leissring et al.[180] fed newborn infants with antityphoid–tetanus immune serum. The titers of the infant's sera, sampled 15 hr after the first feeding, were between $\frac{1}{2}$ and $\frac{1}{64}$ of the titers of the immune serum administered. According to Morris,[209] the procedure used by Leissring et al.[180] for detection does not differentiate between the intact and degraded antibodies. Thus, the relationship between the titers (of infants' sera and immune sera) remains obscure; nevertheless, Leissring's experiments show penetration of large molecules. Iyengar and Selvaraj[137]

evaluated the absorption of colostral immuno globulins by measuring the concentration of IgA IgG, and IgM in cord blood and following the changes in the infant sera on the 5th day after birth. Levels of all three Ig's were significantly higher in the sera of colostrum-fed infants than in the sera of those who did not receive colostrum.

5.2.2. Absorption of Food Protein

Information about digestion and absorption o protein in infants was obtained using three differen methodological approaches: (1) balance studies, (2 analysis of intestinal contents during absorption o test meal, and (3) observation of changes of variou nitrogen metabolites in blood during absorption The last-mentioned approach will not be reviewed here because of possible ambiguity.

(a) Balance Studies. Various reports[75,80,97,110 194,237,253,269,305,321] show that about 85% of the foo nitrogen in infants is absorbed from the gu independently of age (0–150 days), type of diet, o maturity. A detailed description of nitrogen retentior (in which losses of protein via the urine are taker into account, and thus the infants' overall metabolism of protein is evaluated) would exceed the framework of this chapter (see Chapter 18).

(b) Analysis of Intestinal Contents During Absorption of Test Meal. Borgstrom et al.[40,41 fed radioiodinated human serum albumin in a test meal containing cow's milk protein and observed the rate of disappearance by collecting samples of contents via tube from the lower duodenum and upper jejunum. They found the absorption of protein at the duodenal level to be about the same in 1- to 2-week-old full-term and 1- to 4-week-old prematures, although the 1-week-old prematures had lower trypsin values.

Hirata et al.[124] introduced a tube into the ileocecal region and analyzed quantitatively and qualitatively the protein of its contents during digestion in infants fed breast milk or whole cow's milk. The protein nitrogen concentration in the ileocecal contents of 4- to 5-month-old infants fed whole cow's milk formula was more than 3 times higher than that found in breast-fed infants. When the protein concentration in cow's milk formula was reduced, there ceased to be a difference between these data and data for breast milk. Furthermore, the authors found unsplit casein in the ileal contents of infants fed 3.3% cow's milk protein, but not in breast milk or 1.3% protein cow's-milk-fed infants. Using this technique, they determined the maximum digestibility of cow's milk casein in infants of different ages (for their criteria, see the Fig. 13 caption).

Figure 13 shows clearly that digestion and absorption of cow's milk casein increases with age. In agreement with this finding, Lindberg[189] calculated that adults can digest about 1.6 g of casein per kilogram body weight per hour, whereas in children, the corresponding value was 1.0 g.

The studies described above show that whereas the digestion and absorption of protein evaluated by rather gross balance studies does not show substantial difference among various age groups and also does not indicate any difference between handling of homologous and heterologous proteins (cow's vs. human milk), the study of the group from Kobe[179] shows age dependency in protein digestion, which could be related to developing enzymatic equipment of the GI tract [see Section 5.1.2(b)].

5.2.3. Absorption of Amino Acids

Active transport of amino acids is connected with an increase of potential differences between the mucosal and serosal sides of the intestinal wall *in vitro*; therefore, this *in vitro* approach was used to provide evidence of active transport in human fetal small intestine. According to these experiments, L-alanine

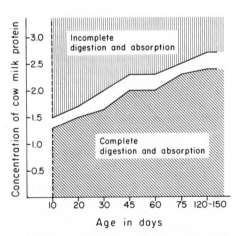

Fig. 13. Change of digestion and absorption of cow's milk protein in infants during the first 4 postnatal months of life. Digestion and absorption were considered "complete" when analysis of ileal contents showed absence of undigested casein and both the nitrogen protein concentration and the nitrogen protein/total nitrogen ratio was the same as in infants of corresponding age fed breast milk. Reproduced from Hirata *et al.*[124]

is actively transported in human 12- to 18-week-old fetuses.[184] This transport was found to be specific; D-alanine was not transported.

6. Digestion and Absorption of Lipids

6.1. Luminal Phase

6.1.1. Lipase Activity of the GI Tract

(a) Prenatal Period. Only a few studies have been reported in the literature. Tachibana[274] found lipase (using tributyrin as the substrate) in the stomachs of fetuses in the 4th fetal month; its activity increased with subsequent development. *Pancreatic* homogenates contain lipase (tributyrin); its activity increases up to the 7th month.[155,273]

Small intestinal homogenates split tributyrin in 3-month-old fetuses; this activity increases considerably in the 4th month.[275] Fomina[79] detected tributyrin-splitting activity in the small and large intestine of 4 fetuses (14, 18, 22, and 27 weeks old); no substantial difference of activity was observed with age and between the large and small intestine. Nonspecific esterase activity (using β-naphthylacetate) did not change between the 8th and 22nd weeks of fetal life.[222]

(b) Postnatal Period: *(1) Milk Lipases.* Milk contains lipase(s)[47] with activity several times higher in human than in cow's milk.[123,279] In addition to the serum-activated lipase (lipoprotein lipase), milk contains another active lipolytic system.[152] The latter system has several interesting biochemical characteristics, such as activation by bile salts and relative stability at pH as low as 3.5. Interestingly, maximum activation occurs in a 1–2 mM solution of bile salts, which is the critical micellar concentration under the conditions similar to those in the intestinal lumen, and is equal to the concentration of bile salts in the duodenum of newborn infants fed on human milk[259] (see Sections 6.1.2(b) and 6.1.3). This human milk lipase is completely inactivated at 55°C.[152] Milk lipase may participate in the digestion of fat by a newborn infant if the infant is fed a milk containing active lipase, i.e., preferably fresh human milk.

(2) Lipase in Stomach Contents. Lipolytic activity was reported in newborns.[50,274] This lipase [in contrast to the lipase(s) in duodenal aspirates] was stable at pH 2, had a lower pH optimum, and had limited activity against long-chain triglycerides, but

was active against short-chain triglycerides.[50] Thus, it may play a role in the digestion of medium-chain triglycerides (milk is rich in MCT).[43] The existence of gastric lipase independently of milk lipase and duodenal regurgitation in gastric contents was described in 3 (3- to 12-week-old) infants with pyloric stenosis.[218] Studies in adult subjects indicate that this enzyme is of lingual origin[112] (lingual lipase is present in both suckling and adult rats).[111]

(3) Pancreatic Lipases. In adults, pancreatic juice contains two enzymes that are active against neutral lipids. The so-called "pancreatic lipase" is more active against insoluble, emulsified substrates than against soluble ones. The second lipase (also called *pancreatic carboxyl esterase*) is more active against micellar or soluble substrates than against insoluble, emulsified substrates. In contrast to the first lipase, it is strongly stimulated by bile salts. Colipase removes the inhibiting effect of bile salts on lipase. The studies summarized below (Fig. 14) usually do not differentiate these lipases. Generally, the

data show the lowest values after birth. The increase toward adult values occurs within the first 6 months of life, which is earlier than in the case of amylase (see Fig. 2). Prematures and very-low-birth-weight infants have lower values than full-term neonates.[67,154,319] Furthermore, data of Zoppi et al.[319] indicate that during the first week of life, lipase activity increases about 4 times in prematures whereas it does not in full-term infants. The findings concerning the effect of diet (Fig. 14) on prematures are intriguing, but require further studies. Infants on a high-fat diet (49%) did not have higher lipase activity than infants on low-fat diets (less than 2%). Infants on diets C and D (Fig. 14), which contained 31–37 cal% of protein, had higher lipase activities than infants on diet A, which contained 9 cal%. Diet B did not evoke an increase of lipase, although it too contained 31 cal% protein, but differed from diets C and D in that it contained starch (this diet increases amylase; see Section 4.1.2 and Fig. 14). One possible explanation for this discrepancy might be

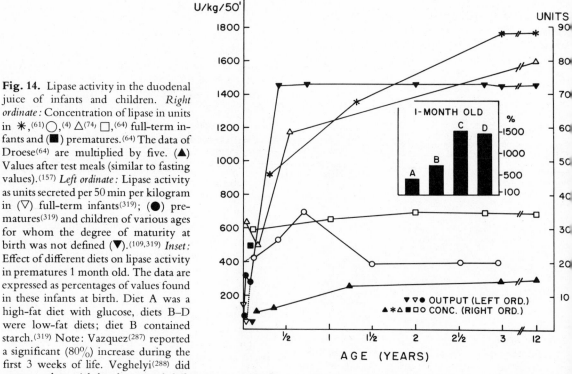

Fig. 14. Lipase activity in the duodenal juice of infants and children. *Right ordinate:* Concentration of lipase in units in ✳,[61] ○,[4] △[74] □,[64] full-term infants and (■) prematures.[64] The data of Droese[64] are multiplied by five. (▲) Values after test meals (similar to fasting values).[157] *Left ordinate:* Lipase activity as units secreted per 50 min per kilogram in (▽) full-term infants[319]; (●) prematures[319] and children of various ages for whom the degree of maturity at birth was not defined (▼).[109,319] *Inset:* Effect of different diets on lipase activity in prematures 1 month old. The data are expressed as percentages of values found in these infants at birth. Diet A was a high-fat diet with glucose, diets B–D were low-fat diets; diet B contained starch.[319] Note: Vazquez[287] reported a significant (80%) increase during the first 3 weeks of life. Veghelyi[288] did not see substantial developmental differences in multiple determinations on 47 children from 1 to 11 years of age. Samples were obtained: (1) without stimulation[4,74]; (2) after magnesium sulfate stimulation[64]; (3) after pancreozymin-secretin stimulation[61,109,319]; and (4) after test meal.[157]

he small number of infants studied. Alternately, this
might be a biological difference, and might indicate
that the exocrine pancrease of a premature infant
responding to one stimulus (starch) is not able to
respond simultaneously to the high-protein content
of the diet.

5.1.2. Bile Acids

(a) **Prenatal Period.** Fetal gallbladder bile contains cholic and chenodeoxycholic acid; the latter
seems to predominate. No secondary bile acids were
detected.[225,254] (The amount of total conjugated
bile acids in the gallbladder is low: 2.3 meq g/liter;
compare Fig. 15.) Taurine conjugates predominate
in fetal samples over glycine conjugates[225,254]
(T:C = 0.09). This finding is in agreement with
higher taurine content of the fetal liver as compared
with adult liver. No free bile acids were found.
Secondary bile acids present in the meconium are
probably maternal in origin (transplacental passage),
because they are absent in the stools of infants after
the passage of the meconium.[254]

Enterohepatic circulation, while it has not been
studied in human fetuses, has been shown to
exist in dog fetuses (perfusion of the fetus *in vivo*).[262]

The fetal dog liver is quite mature in the handling
of bile salt, but the fetal intestine does not show an
adult pattern of absorption[262]; furthermore, no
ileum specialization (as known in adults) was found.

Back and Ross[17] confirmed previously published
data,[254] and showed that in addition to the four
common bile acids, the meconium of premature and
full-term infants may also contain ursodeoxycholic
and 3-β-hydroxy-5-cholenoic acids, the former also
found in the bile of 1- to 5-year-old children.[254,290]
Both deoxycholic and 3-β-hydroxy-5-cholenoic acid
are present in higher proportions in the meconium
from prematures than from full-term infants.[17]

(b) **Postnatal Period.** The results of several
studies on postnatal changes in concentration of bile
salts are summarized in Fig. 15. These results show
clearly that infants during the first days of life have
a lower concentration of bile acids in the duodenum,
if samples are collected during feedings. Low-birth-
weight infants[178] have lower duodenal bile salt
levels than do older and large infants. After birth,
several qualitative differences in the bile salt composition were observed (Fig. 16). The cholic/
chenodeoxycholic ratio is higher postnatally and
decreases later. Deoxycholic acid appears after the
first year of life.[37,71,72,225] Watkins *et al.*[297]
reported the appearance of deoxycholate in 4
premature infants already on day 7 postnatally
(forming 14.7% of the total bile salts present in the
intestinal lumen). The ratio of glycine to taurine
conjugates changes substantially after birth (Fig. 16).
In a similar change observed in sheep, the effect of
changing diet was implicated.[223] Watkins *et al.*[297]
measured the size of the cholate pool and its rate

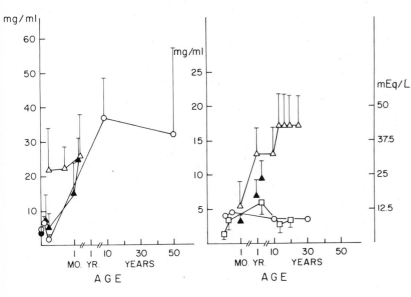

Fig. 15. *Left:* Bile acid concentration in gallbladder bile in infants and adults (postmortem
samples). *Symbols and references:*
(○) full-term[37]; (●) prematures[37]; (△) full-term[63]; (▲)
prematures.[63] The vertical
brackets denote 1 S.D. *Right:* Bile
acid concentration in duodenal
contents. *Symbols and references:*
(□)[225]; (○)[72]; (△) full-term[63];
(▲) prematures.[63] In two studies,[72,225] samples were obtained
after a 6- to 8-hr fast, and the
data are expressed as meq/liter;
the last study[63] used samples obtained after magnesium sulfate
stimulation, and expressed the
data as mg/ml. The vertical
brackets denote 1 S.D.

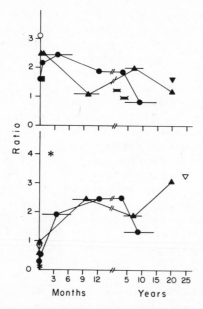

Fig. 16. Postnatal changes in composition of bile acids in duodenal juice. *Top:* Cholic : chenodeoxycholic acid ratio. *Bottom:* glycine : taurine conjugate ratio. *Symbols and references:* ▲[71,72]; ●[225]; ▼[204]; ■[213]; ○[297]; ✳[154]; ▽[46]; ▬[290] The horizontal lines denote age ranges.

of synthesis in full-term normal newborns by isotope dilution (using nonradioactive-deuterium-labeled bile salts). When they expressed their data per square meter of body surface area, and the data for adults from the literature were recalculated in the same way, the infants' values were 50% of those found in adults. When data were expressed per body weight, however, they did not differ at all from values found in adults.[298] In premature infants, these values were reported to be lower than in full-term infants[299]: 50% if expressed per body weight, 30% if expressed per body surface.

The deficiency of bile salts in the prematures may be aggravated by increased fecal loss; prematures[259] had increased excretion when compared with values for older children. Prematures fed cow's milk excreted more bile acids than those fed human milk.[259] Cholate and deoxycholate daily synthesis in prematures (4–11 days of age) equaled roughly 40% of pool size (twice the normal adult value) and resembled synthesis in normal ful-term infants.

Since only very small amounts of bile acids are found in the urine of normal infants,[212] and serum bile acid values do not differ substantially from those

in normal adults, we may at present conclude that the pool of bile acid in the normal neonate is confined to the enterohepatic circulation. Von Bergman *et al.*[290] studied the composition of biliary lipids in children after pancreozymin–secretin stimulation. The children showed lower cholesterol and phospholipid values, but higher bile acids, than adults.[2] None of the children had supersaturated bile; the mean cholesterol concentration was 51%, with a range of 32–73%. There was no correlation between these parameters and the age or weight of the children.

6.1.3. Studies on Fat Absorption (Retention)

Histochemical studies indicate the possibility of fat absorption (from the amniotic fluid) in the small[249] and large intestine[89] of 3- to 5-month-old fetuses.

There exist a large number of studies evaluating absorption of fat in *infants and children,* the first of which was published a century ago.[284] The reason for this interest is clear. Let us just mention the most obvious questions: Could some other food substitute for human milk? (If so, which food?) What is the natural food for a premature child? It is clear that such questions are not restricted to the problem of the quality and quantity of fat consumed. Furthermore, absorption studies alone cannot provide the ultimate answers; other criteria (general health) must be applied, but discussion of these subjects is beyond the scope of this review (see Chapters 16 and 19).

The methods employed for fat absorption studies are generally alike. The infant is fed a known amount of fat-containing food; at given times, a marker is added to the food to space the period of stool collection. Fat absorption (retention) is then defined as the difference between the intake and the output in the feces. There is some fat excretion "background," but this value seems to induce a significant error only when diets with very low fat content are used.

Results of fat absorption (retention) studies are most commonly expressed as percentage of fat intake, both in studies dealing with total fat absorption and in studies dealing with a specified lipid fraction (e.g., unsaturated vs. saturated, individual fatty acids). The studies summarized in Fig. 17 show that (independently for each type of fat and for each group) fat absorption is proportional to the amount of fat fed (within the range 2–11 g/kg body weight per day and within the age range

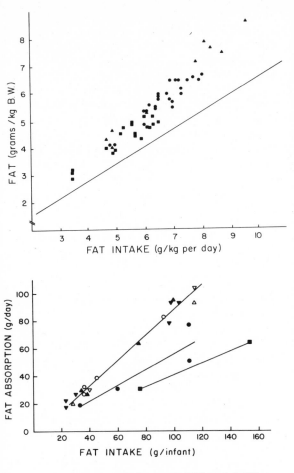

Fig. 17. Fat retention in infants and children fed different doses of fat. *Top:* Fat intake and retention expressed per kilogram body weight. (●, ■, ▲) A group of 55 full-term infants, 1 week of age, fed four adapted formulas or breast milk.[307] Regression line taken from Morales *et al.*[208] (24 determinations on 8 3-week-old prematures fed skimmed milk and butterfat). *Bottom:* Retention of fat in celiac children. Each child was studied at different levels of fat intake. Each symbol denotes a different subject: (○) 20-month-old; (●) 8-month-old; (■) 7½-year-old; (▼, ▲, △, ▽) 4 other subjects. Data taken from Tables IV–VII in Holt.[127]

studied). The data follow a linear relationship between fat intake and fat retention (intake/excretion). Similarly, a linear dependency between fat absorption and fat intake (in a range between approximately 0.5 and 5 g fat/day per kg body weight) was described in adults.[310]

Only Southgate *et al.*[271] give values for a correlation coefficient between fecal fat (plotted on a logarithmic scale) and fat intake (plotted on a linear scale) and suggest that the infant's capacity to absorb fat is limited, and that as the intake is increased, proportionally less fat is absorbed. Unfortunately, they did not give results of linear regression calculations of their data. Recalculation of their figures (based on values taken from the published chart) shows that their data also follow a linear relationship reasonably well. In other words, their dissenting voice is important, but at present—especially against the background of data from other studies—more determinations are needed to solidify their conclusions.

We can thus still accept the validity of comparing different fat absorption studies in infants and children, using the fat absorption coefficient. At the same time, the existence of a linear relationship between fat intake (determined up to 11 g/kg per day) and fat absorption suggests that the mechanisms of fat absorption in infants are not saturated, and that we actually do not know the maximum absorption capacity of infants as compared with adults.

Let us now turn our attention to studies on absorption of fat *during the postnatal period* in man, as followed in various laboratories during the last century.

Figure 18 summarizes data on absorption of fat from *breast milk.* Absorption increases slightly during the first month in full-term babies, achieving values close to 95%. In prematures (Fig. 19), several studies after 1950 show a similar picture: absorption values are close to those found in full-term babies.[65,214, 268,321] On the other hand, some older studies reported several low absorption coefficient values in prematures 1 month old and younger, significantly lower than other studies. The reason for this discrepancy is not clear.

Fat absorption from *cow's milk* in full-term babies also increases postnatally (Fig. 18), but values are somewhat lower than those given for breast milk in corresponding age groups; the difference disappears around 6 months.[285,301] In prematures (Fig. 19), absorption during the first weeks of life is substantially lower and reaches the 80% value around 10 weeks of postnatal life.

The conclusion that prematures absorb less fat than full-term infants during the first months of life is supported by comparing data from various laboratories (Figs. 18 and 19) and by studies performed in one laboratory concurrently on prematures and full-term infants. In studies on absorption of butterfat or olive oil or both, lower absorption in prematures

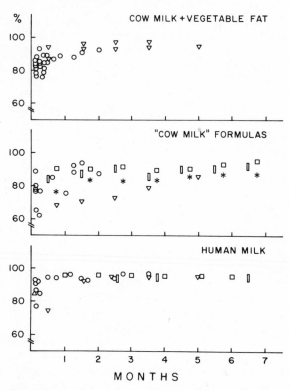

Fig. 18. Fat absorption in full-term infants (expressed as percentage of intake). The symbols used for studies in which several age periods were compared are ▽,[83] ▯,[129] ▢,[301] and ✳[65]; (○) used immediately for all other studies. Additional references—*top, middle, and bottom sections*: 269, 271, 285, and 305; *top and middle sections only*: 63, 96, 97, 194; *bottom section only*: 16, 113, 128, 307.

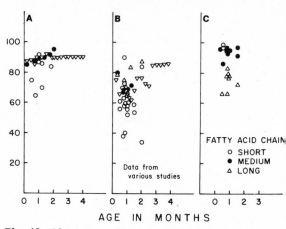

Fig. 19. Absorption of human-milk (A) and cow's-milk (B) fat and comparison of retention of triglycerides of various fatty-acid chain lengths (C) in prematures (expressed as percentage of fat intake). *Symbols and references*— (A) ▽[65,66]; ● [268]; ○[6,97,214,259,321]; (B) ▽[66]; △[154]; ● [268]; ○[19,59,96,97,207,208,214,253,267,280]; (C) references 237, 266, 267, 278, and 314.

was found in 2-month-old infants[129,280] and in 5-week-old infants.[96] In studies using various cow's-milk-base formulas, the lower absorption rate in prematures was observed up to 2½ months of age.[65,66]

One study[259] already mentioned in the section describing bile salts [see Section 6.1.2(b)] shows an interesting aspect important for the comparison of fat absorption from human milk and from cow's milk. In 2-week-old prematures fed breast milk, no correlation between bile acid levels in the duodenal juice and fat absorption was found, whereas in those fed on cow's milk, a correlation existed between the degree of fat absorption and the mean bile acid concentration during the first 60 min after the test meal. The human-milk-fed prematures have lower bile acid concentrations, both in the "fasting" state and after the meal, than those fed with cow's milk

formula. Despite this lower bile acid concentration (coinciding with their lower gestational age of 2 weeks), human-milk-fed prematures absorbed fat better (Fig. 20). These results show that the absorption of human milk fat is less dependent on bile acids than is the absorption of cow's milk.

Higher absorption of fat from breast milk than from simple cow's-milk-based formulas is proved again in the results of comparison tests set up between laboratories and within laboratories. Such studies were reported on infants of undefined degree of maturity[128,284,285,301]; premature infants 1–2 months of age[96,97,214,268,321]; and in full-term infants: 1 week old,[113,271,305] 2 weeks old,[269] and of different ages (4–6 months).[63–65,83,259,285,301]

Figure 18 summarizes the developmental pattern of fat absorption in *full-term* infants from formulas in which some cow's-milk fat was replaced by vegetable fat (see also below); absorption values are closer to those reported from breast-milk fat. Figure 19 depicts absorption of long-chain fatty acid triglycerides (LCT), corn oil, linolein, medium-chain fatty acid triglycerides (MCT), and short-chain fatty acid triglycerides (SCT) (tributyrin, triacetin) in prematures, as studied in various laboratories. Whereas absorption of LCT is lower during the first 6 weeks of life, MCT and SCT are already absorbed quite efficiently in prematures soon after birth.

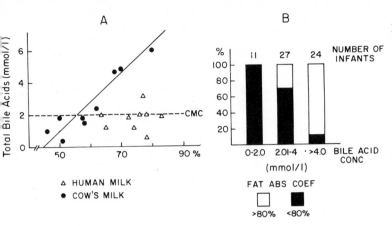

Fig. 20. Relationship between fat absorption and bile acid concentration in infants. (A) *Abscissa:* Fat absorption in percentage of fat intake: (△) human-milk fat; (●) cow's-milk fat. Infants 11–14 days of age from gestations lasting 35–37 weeks. (CMC) Critical micellar concentration. Data from Signer *et al.*[259] (B) *Ordinate:* Percentage of infants with fat absorption higher than 80% (white portions of bars) or lower than 80% (black portions). Data from Lavy[177] and Lavy *et al.*[178]

Emulsification (by homogenization) increases the low absorption of butterfat in prematures[208]; the same procedure did not affect the higher absorption in full-term infants.[129] Addition of surface-active agents (Tween) also increases the absorption of butterfat in prematures with a low absorption rate,[266] but not in prematures of undisclosed age with a higher absorption rate.[150] Relatively high absorption of corn oil in prematures (78.1%) was also not influenced by addition of Tween.[266]

In Fig. 21, I have summarized data on retention of fatty acids of different chain length and saturation as studied in prematures and full-term infants. Some authors have fed only one type of fat: pure olein or linolein[129,280]; triacetin and tributyrin[267]; or stearic acid, oleic acid, or linoleic acid.[193] Other authors have fed a complete diet (breast milk or other formulas). In recent studies, the retention of individual fatty acids was determined by gas–liquid chromatography. The limitations of the latter determination are obvious: the composition of fatty acids in the stool is influenced by bacterial metabolism in the gut.[95,300] Thus, for example, the apparent low retention of stearic acid in some studies might be partially a result of hydrogenation of nonabsorbed oleic acid.[32,33] Nevertheless, we can conclude that unsaturated fatty acids are better absorbed than saturated ones of a corresponding chain. Further-

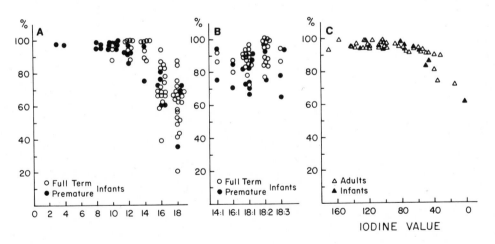

Fig. 21. Absorption of various fats classified according to (A) fatty-acid chain length, (B) unsaturated bonds, and (C) iodine value (expressed as percentage of fat intake). (A, B) Data taken from references 20, 77, 113, 129, 193, 237, 246, 267, 278, 280, 296, 302, 307, and 314. (C) Data from Holt *et al.*,[129] who originated the data for infants and compiled the data of Langworthy[174] for adults.

more, saturated fatty acids of C8–C14 chain length (even C3–C4[267]) are retained to a greater extent than those with longer chains.

A correlation between bile acid concentration in duodenal juice and absorption of fat from formulas containing unsaturated fat in low- and very-low-birth-weight infants is demonstrated in Fig. 20. Medium-chain triglycerides derived from coconut oil were used in so-called "MCT formulas" for the feeding of prematures. Retention is high (>95%) even in the 2nd week of life. The studies[237,278,314] also confirmed the lower absorption of long-chain triglycerides in the same age group (see Fig. 19). The higher retention of MCT is explained by the relative independence of MCT absorption mechanisms of bile salt and pancreatic lipase [see Section 6.1.1(b)(2)]. It is interesting (and not explained) that in the presence of MCT, the absorption of the saturated long-chain fatty acids increased significantly.[278] Although the absorption of MCT is very efficient in prematures, the possible relationship between the high osmolality of MCT formulas and necrotizing enterocolitis (and unknown long-term effects on infants) stresses the necessity for further tests.[38]

Another approach to understanding the mechanism of fat absorption and digestion is the analysis of characteristics of fecal fat. Unfortunately, interpretation of such analytical data is hampered by the effect of bacteria, both *in vivo* and later during collection and storage. Holt *et al.*[129] were one of the first to employ this approach; they showed, among other things, that infants on a butterfat diet excrete more fat in the form of soap than those fed breast milk. Recently, Watkins *et al.*[296] partitioned the fecal fat of full-term infants (fed Similac) aged 3–11 days and 23–72 days. The total fat retention in these infants was about 90%. Neutral fat represented about half the fecal fat (glycerides about one-eighth of total fat), calcium soaps (primarily of long-chain fatty acids) about one-fourth, and ionized fatty acids and bound lipids the rest. Demonstration of higher amounts of glycerides (tri-, di-, and mono-) indicates a "defect" in lipolysis in the GI tracts of infants, and is in agreement with findings reviewed in Section 6.1.1(b)(2) concerning the low lipolytic activity of the GI tract in newborn infants.

There is only one study on the composition of the oil and micellar phases during fat digestion in infants (1–6 years old; 6 subjects),[229] in which a correlation was found between the degree of hydrolysis and the percentage of lipids solubilized, and preferential solubilization and faster rate of absorption of monoglycerides.

6.2. Mucosal Phase

No data on human material are available, although some speculation about a possible "defect" of this phase in children has been mentioned.[296] The only available data concerning the process during postnatal development pertain to rats, and various aspects of this question were discussed in a recent paper from our laboratory.[130] Suckling rats have a high fat intake and, at the same time, a very low lipolytic activity in the lumen of the GI tract. Their intestinal mucosa contains amounts of fatty-acid-binding protein (FABP) equivalent to those found in adult rats, and a high capacity for fatty acid esterification (as indicated both by activity determination of microsomal oleoyl-CoA synthetase and acyl-CoA monoglyceride aceyltransferase and by the esterification of oleic acid in jejunal slices *in vitro*). This apparent paradox between low lipolytic activity and relatively high esterification capacity suggests that the fatty acid esterification process in the small intestine of the suckling rat may be involved with aspects of lipid metabolism other than that of fatty acid absorption. Extrapolating these observations on experimental animals to the human neonate, we suggested as a working hypothesis that inefficient fat absorption in human neonates need not necessarily be attributed to diminished mucosal epithelial cell function.

6.3. Transport Phase

It is known from studies in adults that fat is transported from the GI tract via two main routes: the lymphatic system and the portal vein. No investigation exists on the difference between the two transport routes in newborn mammals.

The transport of lipids is reflected by changing blood levels of various lipids and metabolites. This method was applied in adults as well as in children for an evaluation of fat absorption.[264] Choremis *et al.*[49] did not observe any difference in the lipemic curves (turbidimetric determination) in children up to 3 years and 3–14 years of age. The age-dependent difference is apparent earlier, as can be seen from the data summarized in Fig. 22, which depicts changes of lipids after fat loads in infants and children.[203]

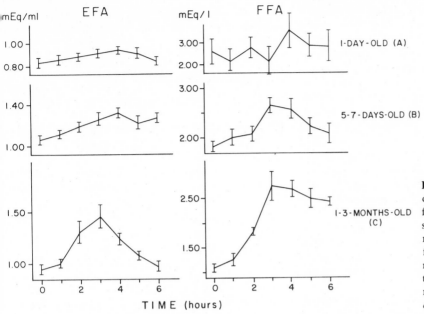

Fig. 22. Changes in the levels of esterified fatty acids (EFA) and free fatty acids (FFA) in blood serum during absorption of breast milk in premature infants (6 infants in each group). Similar results were obtained on full-term infants. Reproduced (with modifications) from Melichar *et al.*[203]

Nonesterified fatty acid serum levels rise after a fat load in all age groups, particularly in younger infants (with maximum levels at 3–4 hr). Esterified fatty acid serum levels follow the same time course of rise in all age groups, with the exception of 1-day-old infants, in whom no rise occurs with cream or free fatty acids; after olive oil, a small rise was observed after 6 hr. Serum from newborn infants never appeared opalescent, and chylomicrons were not observed in infants younger than 4 days. After 4 days, they gradually increased in both size and number. Premature infants showed the same kind of development; thus, the moment of birth and the subsequent supply of food seem to be more important than the chronological age. The absence of a rise of esterified fatty acids in newborns is corroborated by similar findings in newborn dogs and rats.[161,164] Similar observations (using nephelometry) on premature newborns were reported by Murano and Di Toro.[210] These findings[203,210] lead to two conclusions: First, the analysis of esterified fatty acids (or chylomicrons) would easily mislead in studies of lipid absorption in newborns. Second, the higher rate of disappearance of esterified fatty acids from the blood in the newborns seems to be indicative of a higher turnover rate of lipids or an extensive deposit of lipids in certain tissues. This problem is discussed in Chapter 19; for a discussion of fat lipid uptake after parenteral administration in newborns, see Anonymous.[7]

7. Absorption of Minerals and Vitamins

In Sections 4–6, we have discussed the digestion and absorption of caloric components of food. In this brief section, we discuss another important group of food components: minerals. A detailed description from a developmental point of view would involve not only discussion of absorption data, but also—to prevent the creation of a distorted picture—a thorough discussion of *retention* studies. Such extensive discussion, however, exceeds the scope of this chapter. The interested reader is referred to an extensive review of this subject from a pediatric nutrition point of view,[81] or can find further references in papers cited below and in Chapter 20.

Of most interest is the absorption of *calcium*. Comparison of data from various laboratories shows substantial variations among values published in different studies. Some obviously depend on the composition of the food: (1) breast milk vs. cow's milk preparation[305]; (2) source (type) and amount of fat,[20,22,67,68,82,113,194,271,272,277,307] although recent studies question the relevance of this consideration because of the lack of relationship between fat and calcium absorption in premature infants[19] (see also the discussions in Southgate and Widdowson[270] and Wadsworth[291]; or (3) content of lactose.[158]

The effect of age has been clearly demonstrated.[305] A substantial increase of calcium absorption from cow's milk formula was shown in full-term babies during the first 4–6 weeks of life, whereas no substantial change was observed when breast milk was fed. Similarly, data of Baltrop and Oppé[19] indicate a postnatal increase in premature infants.

The regulatory mechanisms involved in absorption of calcium during development have yet to be elucidated; we judge it interesting that increased dietary phosphate decreases the absorption of calcium from the gut in adults,[265] whereas in 1-week-old neonates, the absorption of calcium was increased.[306] Absorption of other minerals, as determined by balance studies, was also reported in some of the recent papers cited above (*magnesium*,[158,159,277,305] *phosphorus*,[20,113,305,307] *potassium*,[305] and *sodium*[305]). Torres-Pinedo *et al.*[282,283] reported changes in composition of saline solutions perfused through a segment of jejunum or instilled into the colon of infants.

Absorption of *iron* in infants and children was studied by various authors.[90,98,,99,119–121,215,248,250,251] In 4-month-old infants, iron absorption was found to be $2\frac{1}{2}$ times higher than in 1- to 3-month-old infants,[196] which is related to the postnatal depletion of the body iron reserves (see Chapter 20).

The only data available on the absorption of *vitamins* are those pertaining to processes related to vitamin B_{12} absorption. *Intrinsic factor* (IF) has been demonstrated in fetal gastric mucosa from the 11th week of gestation.[252] It is present in the gastric juice of premature and newborn babies.[247] It is not detectable during the first 24 hr. Output increases during the first 4 months of life, and at 2 months of age, the total output of IF per kilogram body weight was within 80% of the adult values.[230–232] In children (mean age 24 months), IF output expressed per kilogram body weight was similar to, or even higher than, that found in adults.[3,230–232]

ACKNOWLEDGMENTS

The work on this chapter was supported in part by NIH Grant AM 14531.

I am grateful to Eva Koldovský for editorial help.

8. References

1. ABDO-BASSOLS, F., LIFSHITZ, F., DIAZ DEL CASTILLO, E., AND MARTINEZ-GARZA, V., 1971, Transient lactose intolerance in premature infants, *Pediatrics* **48**:816.

2. ADLER, R. D., BENNION, L. J., DUANE, W. C., AND GRUNDY, S. M., 1975, Effects of low dose of chenodeoxycholic acid feeding on biliary lipid metabolism, *Gastroenterology* **68**:326.

3. AGUNOD, M., YAMAGUCHI, N., LOPEZ, R., LUHBY, A. L., AND GLASS, G. B., 1969, Correlative study of hydrochloric acid, pepsin, and intrinsic factor secretion in newborns and infants, *Amer. J. Dig. Dis.* **14**:400.

4. ANDERSEN, D. H., 1942, Pancreatic enzymes in the duodenal juice in the celiac syndrome, *Amer. J. Dis. Child.* **63**:643.

5. ANDERSEN, H., BIERRING, F., MATTHIESSEN, M., EGEBERG, J., AND BRO-RASMUSSEN, F., 1964, On the nature of the meconium corpuscles in human foetal intestinal epithelium. 2. A cytochemical study, *Acta Pathol. Microbiol. Scand.* **61**:377.

6. ANDERSON, A., SCHLOSS, O. M., AND MEYERS, E., 1925, Intestinal absorption of antigenic proteins by normal infant, *Proc. Soc. Exp. Biol. Med.* **23**:180.

7. ANONYMOUS, 1974, Intravenous nutrition of newborn infants with lipid, *Nutr. Rev.* **32**:298.

8. ANTONOWICZ, I., ISHIDA, S., KHAW, K. T., AND SHWACHMAN, H., 1970, Effect of tissue preparation on determinations of disaccharidase activities in intestinal mucosa, *Pediatrics* **45**:104.

9. ANYON, C. P., AND CLARKSON, K. G., 1965, Lactose absorption in the neonate, *N. Z. Med. J.* **64**:694.

10. ARDRAN, G. M., KEMP, F. H., AND LIND, J., 1958, A cineradiographic study of breast feeding, *Br. J. Radiol.* **31**:156.

11. ASP, N.-G., AND DAHLQVIST, A., 1974, Intestinal β-galactosidases in adult low lactase activity and in congenital lactase deficiency, *Enzyme* **17**:84.

12. ASP, N.-G., BERG, N. O., DAHLQVIST, A., JUSSILA, J., AND SALMI, H., 1971, The activity of three different small-intestinal β-galactosidases in adults with and without lactase deficiency, *Scand. J. Gastroenterol.* **6**:755.

13. AURRICCHIO, S., CICCIMARRA, F., VEGNENTE, A., ANDRIA, G., AND VETRELLA, M., 1973, Enzymatic activity hydrolyzing γ-glutamyl-β-naphthylamide in human intestine during adult and fetal life, *Pediatr. Res.* **7**:95.

14. AURICCHIO, S., DELLA PIETRA, D., AND VEGNENTE, A., 1967, Studies on intestinal digestion of starch in man. II. Intestinal hydrolysis of amylopectin in infants and children, *Pediatrics* **39**:853.

15. AURICCHIO, S., RUBINO, A., AND MURSET, G., 1965, Intestinal glycosidase activities in the human embryo, fetus, and newborn, *Pediatrics* **35**:944.

16. AVERY, G. B., RANDOLPH, J. G., AND WEAVER, T., 1966, Gastric acidity in first day of life, *Pediatrics* **37**:1005.

17. BACK, P., AND ROSS, K., 1973, Identification of 3β-hydroxy-5-cholenoic acid in human meconium, *Hoppe-Seyler's Z. Physiol. Chem.* **354**:83.

18. BANZA, C. A., REID, A., AND BRUNSER, O., 1962, A morphologic and histochemical study of the normal small intestinal epithelium in the child. *Acta Pediatr. (Uppsala)* **79**:328.

19. BARLTROP, D., AND OPPÉ, T. E., 1973, Absorption of fat and calcium by low birthweight infants from milks containing butterfat and olive oil, *Arch. Dis. Child.* **48**:496.

20. BARNES, L. A., MORROW, G., SILVERIO, J., FINNEGAN, L. P., AND HEITMAN, S. E., 1974, Calcium and fat absorption from infant formulas with different fat blends, *Pediatrics* **54**:217.

21. BARTROP, R. W., AND HULL, D., 1973, Transient lactose intolerance in infancy, *Arch. Dis. Child.* **48**:963.

22. BAUM, D., COOPER, L., AND DAVIES, P. A., 1968, Hypocalcaemic fits in neonates, *Lancet* **1**:599.

23. BAYLESS, T. M., ROTHFELD, B., MASSA, C., WISE, L., PAIGE, D., AND BEDINE, M. S., 1975, *N. Engl. J. Med.* **292**:1156.

24. BENEKE (DR.), 1880, Über die Länge des Darmkanals bei Kindern, sowie über die Capacität des Magens Neugeborener, *Dtsch. Med. Wochenschr.* **32**:433, 448.

25. BERFENSTAM, R., JAGENBURG, R., AND MELLANDER, O., 1955, Protein hydrolysis in the stomachs of premature and full-term infants, *Acta Paediatr.* **44**:348.

26. BERRY, J. M., 1900, On the development of the villi of the human intestine, *Anat. Anz.* **17**:242.

27. BEYREISS, K., 1971, Resorption von 3-O-Methylglukose, D-Xylose und L-Arabinose. I. Untersuchungen bei stoffwechselgesunden Neugeborenen und Säuglingen, *Paediatr. Grenzgebiete* **10**:151.

28. BEYREISS, K., 1972, Resorption und Umsatz von Fruktose bei Neugeborenen und Säuglingen, *Acta Biol. Med. Ger.* **29**:409.

29. BEYREISS, K., AND HOEPFFNER, W., 1971, Resorption von 3-O-Methylglukose, D-Xylose und L-Arabinose. II. Vergleichende Untersuchungen bei Säuglingen und Kleinkindern mit Malabsorptionssyndromen, *Paediatr. Grenzgebiete* **10**:235.

30. BEYREISS, K., RAUTENBACH, M., WILLGERODT, H., SCHÖNE, S., AND AL-REBATE, I., 1972, Besonderheiten der Resorption und des Stoffwechsels von Kohlenhydraten bei Früh- und Neugeborenen, *Wiss. Z. Friedrich-Schiller Univ., Jena, Math.-Naturwiss. Reihe* **21**:683.

31. BEYREISS, K., THEILE, H., AND WILLGERODT, H., 1968, Active absorption of D-xylose in children, *Ger. Med. Monthly* **13**:544.

32. BLOMSTRAND, R., AND LINDQVIST, B., 1955, Intestinal absorption of carbon-labeled oleic acid in normal infant and in congenital bile duct atresia, *Acta Paediatr. Helv.* **10**:627, 640.

33. BLOMSTRAND, R., LINDQVIST, B., AND PAABO, K., 1955, Intestinal absorption of carbon-labeled oleic acid and palmitic acid in normal infant and in cystic fibrosis of pancreas, *Acta Paediatr. Helv.* **10**:640.

34. BLUM, E., YARMOSCHKEWITSCH, A. I., AND YAKOROTSCHUK, A. I., 1936, Die proteolytischen Fermente menschlicher Embryonen in den verschiedenen Stadien der Entwicklung, *Bull. Biol. Med. Exp. USSR* **1**:113.

35. BOELLNER, S. W., BEARD, A. G., AND PANOS, T. C., 1965, Impairment of intestinal hydrolysis of lactose in newborn infants, *Pediatrics* **36**:542.

36. BOLIN, T. D., DAVIS, A. E., SEAH, C. S., CHUA, K. L., YOH, V., KHO, K. M., SIAK, C. L., AND JACOB, E., 1970, Lactose intolerance in Singapore, *Gastroenterology* **59**:76.

37. BONGIOVANNI, A. M., 1965, Bile acid content of gallbladder of infants, children and adults, *J. Clin. Endocrinol.* **25**:678.

38. BOOK, L. S., HERBST, J. J., ATHERTON, S. O., AND JUNG, A. L., 1975, Necrotizing enterocolitis in low-birth-weight infants fed an elemental formula, *J. Pediatr.* **87**:602.

39. BOREUS, L. O., 1968, Demonstration of a receptor reserve for acetylcholine in the human fetus, *Acta Physiol. Scand.* **72**:194.

40. BORGSTRÖM, B., LINDQVIST, B., AND LUNDH, G., 1960, Enzyme concentration and absorption of protein and glucose in duodenum of premature infants, *Amer. J. Dis. Child.* **99**:338.

41. BORGSTRÖM, B., LINDQVIST, B., AND LUNDH, G., 1961, Digestive studies in children, *Amer. J. Dis. Child.* **101**:454.

42. BOTHA, G. S. M., 1958, The gastro-oesophageal region in infants, *Arch. Dis. Child.* **33**:78.

43. BRACCO, V., 1973, Human milk lipids and problems related to their replacement, in: *Dietary Lipids and Postnatal Development* (C. Galli, G. Jacini, and A. Pecile, eds.), pp. 23–39, Raven Press, New York.

44. BRAMBELL, F. W. R., 1970, *The Transition of Passive Immunity from Mother to Young,* North Holland-American Elsevier, Amsterdam and New York.

45. CATHIE, I. A. B., 1947, Breast feeding in erythroblastosis foetalis, *Br. Med. J.* **2**:650.

46. CHALLACOMBE, D. N., EDKINS, S., AND BROWN, G. A., 1975, Duodenal bile acids in infancy, cited from: *Pediatric Gastroenterology* (C. M. Anderson and R. Burke, eds.), Fig. 4.14, p. 142, Blackwell Scientific Publications, Oxford.

47. CHANDRAN, R. C., PARRY, R. M., AND SHAHANI, K. M., 1968, Lysozyme, lipase and ribonuclease in milk of various species, *J. Dairy Sci.* **51**:606.

48. CHO, D., 1931, Histological investigation of the digestive tract of the human fetus. II. Development of small intestines, *Jpn. J. Obstet. Gynecol.* **14**:324.

49. CHOREMIS, K., KYRIAKIDES, B., NESTORIDES, M., AND ZOUMBOULAKIS, D., 1956, La courbe lipemique chez l'enfant normal et l'enfant dystrophique, *Sem. Hôp.* **32**:1440.

50. COHEN, M., MORGAN, R. G. H., AND HOFMANN, A. F., 1971, Lipolytic activity of human gastric and

duodenal juice against medium and long chain triglycerides, *Gastroenterology* **60**:1.

51. COLLEY, J. R. T., AND CRAMER, B., 1958, Sucking and swallowing in infants, *Br. Med. J.* **2**:422.

52. COOK, G. C., 1967, Lactase activity in newborn and infant Baganda, *Br. Med. J.* **1**:527.

53. CORNES, J. S., 1965, Number, size and distribution of Peyer's patches in the human small intestine. I. The development of Peyer's patches; II. The effect of age on Peyer's patches, *Gut* **6**:225, 229.

54. CUMMINS, A. J., AND JUSSILA, R., 1955, Comparison of glucose absorption rates in the upper and lower human small intestine, *Gastroenterology* **29**:982.

55. DAHLQVIST, A., AND LINDBERG, T., 1966, Development of the intestinal disaccharidase and alkaline phosphatase activities in the human foetus, *Clin. Sci.* **30**:517.

56. DAHLQVIST, A., LINDBERG, T., MEEUWISSE, G., AND AKERMAN, M., 1970, Intestinal dipeptidases and disaccharidases in children with malabsorption, *Acta Paediatr. Scand.* **59**:621.

57. DANCIS, J., LIND, J., ORATZ, M., SMOLENS, J., AND VARA, P., 1961, Placental transfer of proteins in human gestation, *Amer. J. Obstet. Gynecol.* **82**:167.

58. DANIELS, V. G., HARDY, R. N., AND MALINOWSKA, K. W., 1973, The effect of adrenalectomy or pharmacological inhibition of adrenocortical function on macromolecule uptake by the new-born rat intestine, *J. Physiol.* **229**:697.

59. DAVIDSON, M., AND BAUER, C. H., 1960, Patterns of fat excretion in feces of premature infants fed various preparations of milk, *Pediatrics* **25**:375.

60. DAVISON, W. C., 1925, The duodenal contents of infants in health and during and following diarrhea, *Amer. J. Dis. Child.* **29**:743.

61. DELACHAUME-SALEM, E., AND SARLES, H., 1970, Normal human pancreatic secretion in relation to age, *Biol. Gastro-Enterol.* **2**:135, Suppl. 2; *Arch. Fr. Mal. Appareil Digestif* **59**:10, 11.

62. DEVIZIA, B., CICCIMARRA, F., DECICCO, N., AND AURICCHIO, S., 1975, Digestibility of starches in infants and children, *J. Pediatr.* **86**:50.

63. DROESE, W., 1952, Über die Fettoleranz der Säuglinge. Klinisch-experimentelle Untersuchung des Gallensäuren- und Lipasengehaltes im Duodenalsaft, *Ann. Paediatr.* **178**:121, 238.

64. DROESE, W., 1952, Untersuchungen über den Gallensäuren- und Lipasengehalt im Duodenalsaft von Säuglingen, *Monatsschr. Kinderheilkd.* **100**:233.

65. DROESE, W., AND STOLLEY, H., 1960, Probleme des Fettstoffwechsels in der Säuglingsernährung, *Fette, Seifen, Anstrichm.* **62**:281.

66. DROESE, W., AND STOLLEY, H., 1961, Kuhmilchfett und pflanzliches Fett in der Ernährung des jungen, gesunden Säuglings, *Dtsch. Med. Wochenschr.* **17**:855.

67. DROESE, W., AND STOLLEY, H., 1967, Zur Frage der Calcium-Ausnützung gesunder Säuglinge bei Ernäh-rung mit Kuhmilchmischungen mit unterschiedlichem Fettgehalt, *Monatsschr. Kinderheilkd.* **115**:238.

68. EADES, S., 1968, Hypocalcemic fits in neonates, *Lancet* **1**:644.

69. EGGERMONT, E., 1966, Enzymic activities in meconium from human foetuses and newborns, *Biol. Neonate* **10**:266.

70. ELLIS, D. G., AND CLATWORTHY, H. W., 1966, The meconium plug syndrome revisited, *J. Pediatr. Surg.* **1**:54.

71. ENCRANTZ, J.-C., AND SJÖVALL, J., 1957, Bile acids in newborn and adult humans, *Acta Chem. Scand.* **11**:1093.

72. ENCRANTZ, J.-C., AND SJÖVALL, J., 1959, On the bile acids in duodenal contents of infants and children, *Clin. Chim. Acta* **4**:793.

73. FALCK, B., HAKANSON, R., OWMAN, C., AND SJÖBERG, N.-O., 1967, Monoamine-storing cells of the enterochromaffin type in gastrointestinal tract of human fetus, *Acta Physiol. Scand.* **71**:403.

74. FARBER, S., SHWACHMAN, H., AND MADDOCK, C. L., 1943, Pancreatic function and disease in early life. 1. Pancreatic enzyme activity and the celiac syndrome, *J. Clin. Invest.* **22**:827.

75. FEINSTEIN, M. S., AND SMITH, C. A., 1951, Digestion of protein by premature infants, *Pediatrics* **7**:19.

76. FEKETE, M., GALFI, I., SOLTESZ, G., AND MESTYAN, J., 1969, Lactose absorption in growth retarded newborn infants, *Acta Paediatr. Acad. Sci. Hung.* **10**:303.

77. FILER, L. J., MATTSON, F. H., AND FOMON, S. J., 1969, Triglyceride configuration and fat absorption by the human infant, *J. Nutr.* **99**:293.

78. FLATZ, G., SAENGUDOM, C., AND SANGUANBHOKHAI, T., 1969, Lactose intolerance in Thailand, *Nature (London)* **221**:758.

79. FOMINA, L. S., 1960, Soderzhanije nekotorikh fermentov v kishechnikje i drugikh organakh ploda chelovjeka, *Vopr. Med. Chim.* **6**(2):176.

80. FOMON, S. J., 1961, Nitrogen balance studies with normal full-term infants receiving high intakes of protein, *Pediatrics* **28**:347.

81. FOMON, S. J., 1974, *Infant Nutrition,* 2nd Ed., W. B. Saunders Co., Philadelphia.

82. FOMON, S. J., OWEN, G. M., JENSEN, R. L., AND THOMAS, L. N., 1963, Calcium and phosphorous balance studies with normal full-term infants fed pooled human milk or various formulas, *Amer. J. Clin. Nutr.* **12**:346.

83. FOMON, S. J., ZIEGLER, E. E., THOMAS, L. N., JENSEN, R. L., AND FILER, L. J., 1970, Excretion of fat by normal full-term infants fed various milks and formulas, *Amer. J. Clin. Nutr.* **23**:1299.

84. FORDTRAN, J. S., AND INGELFINGER, F. J., 1968, Absorption of water, electrolytes, and sugars from the human gut, in: *Handbook of Physiology,* Sec. 6, *Alimentary Canal,* Vol. III. *Intestinal Absorption* (C. F.

Code, ed.), pp. 1457–1490, American Physiological Society, Washington.

85. FORDTRAN, J. S., CLODI, P. H., SOERGEL, K. H., AND INGELFINGER, F. J., 1962, Sugar absorption tests, with special reference to 3-O-methyl-D-glucose and D-xylose, *Ann. Intern. Med.* **57**:883.

86. FORDTRAN, J. S., LEVITAN, R., BIKERMAN, V., BARROWS, B. A., AND INGELFINGER, F. J., 1961, The kinetics of water absorption in the human intestine, *Trans. Assoc. Amer. Physicians* **74**:195.

87. FURIHATA, C., KAWACHI, T., AND SUGIMURA, T., 1972, Premature induction of pepsinogen in developing rat gastric mucosa by hormones, *Biochem. Biophys. Res. Commun.* **47**:705.

88. GALAND, G., AND FORSTNER, G. G., 1974, Isolation of microvillus plasma membranes from suckling-rat intestine, *Biochem. J.* **144**:293.

89. GARBARSCH, C., AND VON BULOW, F. A., 1969, Histochemical and electron microscopical studies on the epithelium of the fetal colon with special reference to the occurrence of lipids, *Histochemie* **20**:201.

90. GARBY, L., AND SJÖLIN, S., 1959, Absorption of labelled iron in infants less than three months of age, *Acta Paediatr. (Uppsala)* **48**:24.

91. GERLOVIN, E. M., 1963, Structure of the gastro-intestinal mucosa of children of different ages, in: *Proceedings of the Sixth Scientific Conference on Problems of Developmental Morphology, Physiology and Bio-chemistry,* p. 41, University Press, Charkov.

92. GHAI, O. P., SINGH, M., WALIA, B. N. S., AND GADEKAR, N. G., 1965, An assessment of gastric acid secretory response with maximal augmented hist-amine stimulation in children with peptic ulcer, *Arch. Dis. Child.* **40**:77.

93. GIBBS, G. E., 1950, Secretin test with bilumen gastro-duodenal drainage in infants and children, *Pediatrics* **5**:941.

94. GITLIN, D., KUMATE, J., MORALES, C., NORIEGA, L., AND AREVALO, N., 1972, The turnover of amniotic fluid protein in the human conceptus, *Amer. J. Obstet. Gynecol.* **113**:632.

95. GOMPERTZ, S. M., AND SAMMONS, H. G., 1963, The origin of faecal lipids, *Clin. Chim. Acta* **8**:591.

96. GORDON, H. H., AND McNAMARA, H., 1941, Fat excretion of premature infants, I. Effect on fecal fat of decreasing fat intake, *Amer. J. Dis. Child.* **62**:328.

97. GORDON, H. H., LEVINE, S. Z., WHEATLEY, M. A., AND MARPLES, E., 1937, Respiratory metabolism in infancy and in childhood, *Amer. J. Dis. Child.* **54**:1030.

98. GORTEN, M. K., 1965, Iron metabolism in premature infants, *Amer. J. Clin. Nutr.* **17**:322.

99. GÖTZE, C., SCHÄFER, K. H., HEINRICH, H. C., AND BARTELS, H., 1970, Eisenstoffwechselstudien an Früh-geborenen und gesunden Reifgeborenen während des ersten Lebensjahres mit dem Ganzkörperzähler und anderen Methoden, *Monatsschr. Kinderheilkd.* **118**:210.

100. GRACEY, M., AND BURKE, V., 1973, Sugar-induced diarrhoea in children, *Arch. Dis. Child.* **48**:331.

101. GRAY, G. M., AND INGELFINGER, F. J., 1966, Intestinal absorption of sucrose in man: Interrelation of hydrolysis and monosaccharide product absorption *J. Clin. Invest.* **45**:388.

102. GRIFFITH, G. H., OWEN, G. M., CAMPBELL, H., AND SHIELDS, R., 1968, Gastric emptying in health and in gastroduodenal disease, *Gastroenterology* **54**:1.

103. GRUSKAY, F. L., AND COOKE, R. E., 1955, The gastrointestinal absorption of unaltered protein in normal infants and in infants recovering from diarrhea, *Pediatrics* **16**:763.

104. GRYBOSKI, J. D., 1965, The swallowing mechanism of the neonate. I. Esophageal and gastric motility, *Pediatrics* **35**:455.

105. GRYBOSKI, J. D., 1969, Suck and swallow in the premature infant, *Pediatrics* **43**:96.

106. GRYBOSKI, J. D., THAYER, W. R., JR., AND SPIRO, H. M., 1963, Esophageal motility in infants and children, *Pediatrics* **31**:382.

107. GUILBERT, P. W., AND BARBERO, G. J., 1954, The importance of trypsin in infancy and childhood. II. Clinical considerations, *Amer. J. Med. Sci.* **227**:672.

108. GUNDOBIN, N., 1892, Über den Bau des Darmkanals bei Kindern, *Jahrb. Kinderheilkd.* **33**:439.

109. HADORN, B., ZOPPI, G., SHMERLING, D. H., PRADER, A., McINTYRE, I., AND ANDERSON, C. M., 1968, Quantitative assessment of exocrine pancreatic func-tion in infants and children, *J. Pediatr.* **73**:39.

110. HAMILTON, B., 1922–1923, The calcium and phos-phorus metabolism of prematurely born infants, *Acta Paediatr.* **2**:1.

111. HAMOSH, M., AND SCOW, R. O., 1973, Lingual lipase and its role in the digestion of dietary fat, *J. Clin. Invest.* **52**:88.

112. HAMOSH, M., KLAEVEMAN, H. L., WOLF, R. O., AND SCOW, R. O., 1975, Pharyngeal lipase and digestion of dietary triglyceride in man, *J. Clin. Invest.* **55**:908.

113. HANNA, F. M., NAVARRETE, D. A., AND HSU, F. A., 1970, Calcium–fatty acid absorption in term infants fed human milk and prepared formulas simulating human milk, *Pediatrics* **45**:216.

114. HARRIES, J. T., AND FRASER, A. J., 1968, The acidity of the gastric contents of premature babies during the first fourteen days of life, *Biol. Neonate* **12**:186.

115. HART, S. L., 1974, The actions of prostaglandins E_2 and $F_2\alpha$ on human foetal intestine, *Br. J. Pharmacol.* **50**:159.

116. HART, S. L., AND MIR, M. S., 1971, Adrenoceptors in the human foetal small intestine, *Br. J. Pharmacol.* **41**:54.

117. HAWKINS, K. I., 1970, Pediatric xylose absorption test: Measurements in blood preferable to measurements in urine, *Clin. Chem.* **16**:749.

118. HEILSKOV, N. S. C., 1951, Studies on animal lactase. II. Distribution in some of the glands of the digestive tract, *Acta Physiol. Scand.* **24**:84.

119. HEINRICH, H. C., AND BARTELS, H., 1967, Bestimmungsmethoden und Normalbereiche der intestinalen Eisenresorption beim Menschen, *Klin. Wochenschr.* **45**:553.

120. HEINRICH, H. C., BARTELS, H., GÖTZE, C., AND SCHÄFER, K. H., 1969, Normalbereich der intestinalen Eisenresorption bei Neugeborenen und Säuglingen, *Klin. Wochenschr.* **47**:984.

121. Heinrich, H. C., GABBE, E. E., WHANG, D. H., BENDER-GÖTZE, C., AND SCHÄFER, K. H., 1975, Ferrous and hemoglobin-⁵⁹Fe absorption from supplemented cow milk in infants with normal and depleted iron stores, *Z. Kinderheilkd.* **120**:251.

122. HERINGOVÁ, A., KOLDOVSKÝ, O., JIRSOVÁ, V., UHER, J., NOACK, R., FRIEDRICH, H., AND SCHENK, G., 1966, Proteolytic and peptidase activities of the small intestine of human fetuses, *Gastroenterology* **51**:1023.

123. HEYNDRICKX, G. V., 1962, Investigations on the enzymes in human milk, *Ann. Pediatr. (Basel)* **198**:356.

124. HIRATA, Y., MATSUO, T., AND KOKUBU, H., 1965, Digestion and absorption of milk protein in infants' intestine, *Kobe J. Med. Sci.* **11**:103.

125. HIRSCHOWITZ, B. I., 1955, Pepsinogen in the blood, *J. Lab. Clin. Med.* **46**:568.

126. HOLDSWORTH, C. D., AND DAWSON, A. M., 1964, The absorption of monosaccharides in man, *Clin. Sci.* **27**:371.

127. HOLT, E. L., JR., 1955, Celiac disease—What is it?, *J. Pediatr.* **46**:369.

128. HOLT, L. E., COURTNEY, A. M., AND FALES, H. L., 1919, Fat metabolism of infants and young children. I. Fat in the stools of breast fed infants; II. Fat in the stools of infants fed on modifications of cow's milk, *Amer. J. Dis. Child.* **17**:241, 423.

129. HOLT, L. E., TIDWELL, H. C., KIRK, C. M., CROSS, D. M., AND NEALE, S., 1935, Studies in fat metabolism. I. Fat absorption in normal infants, *J. Pediatr.* **6**:427.

130. HOLTZAPPLE, P. G., SMITH, G., AND KOLDOVSKÝ, O., 1975, Uptake, activation, and esterification of fatty acids in the small intestine of the suckling rat, *Pediatr. Res.* **9**:786.

131. HUANG, S. S., AND BAYLESS, T. M., 1967, Lactose intolerance in healthy children, *N. Engl. J. Med.* **276**:1283.

132. HUSBAND, J., AND HUSBAND, P., 1969, Gastric emptying of water and glucose solutions in the newborn, *Lancet* **2**:409.

133. HUSBAND, J., HUSBAND, P., AND MALLINSON, C. N., 1970, Gastric emptying of starch meals in the newborn, *Lancet* **2**:290.

134. IBRAHIM, J., 1910, Die Doppelzuckerfermente (Lactase, Maltase, Invertin) beim menschlichen Neugeborenen und Embryo, I. Mitteilung, *Hoppe-Seyler's Z. Physiol. Chem.* **66**:19.

135. IBRAHIM, J., AND KAUMHEIMER, L., 1910, Die Doppelzuckerfermente (Lactase, Maltase, Invertin) beim menschlichen Neugeborenen und Embryo, II. Mitteilung, *Hoppe-Seyler's Z. Physiol. Chem.* **66**:37.

136. INGOMAR, C. J., AND TERSLEV, E., 1967, Chronic diarrhoeas in infancy and childhood. II. Enzyme content of duodenal juice, *Arch. Dis. Child.* **42**:289.

137. IYENGAR, L., AND SELVARAJ, R. J., 1972, Intestinal absorption of immunoglobulins by newborn infants, *Arch. Dis. Child.* **47**:411.

138. JAMES, W. P. T., 1970, Sugar absorption and intestinal motility in children when malnourished and after treatment, *Clin. Sci.* **39**:305.

139. JARRETT, E. C., AND HOLMAN, G. H., 1966, Lactose absorption in the premature infant, *Arch. Dis. Child.* **41**:525.

140. JAYKKA, S., 1961, The problem of dormant fetal organs: The kidneys, lung, and the gut, *Biol. Neonate* **3**:343.

141. JIRÁSEK, J. E., UHER, J., AND KOLDOVSKÝ, O., 1965, A histochemical analysis of the development of the small intestine of human fetuses, *Acta Histochem. (Jena)* **22**:33.

142. JIRSOVÁ, V., KOLDOVSKÝ, O., HERINGOVÁ, A., HOŠKOVÁ, J., JIRÁSEK, J., AND UHER, S., 1966, The development of the functions of the small intestine of the human fetus, *Biol. Neonate* **9**:44.

143. JIRSOVÁ, V., KOLDOVSKÝ, O., HERINGOVÁ, A., UHER, J., AND JODL, J., 1968, Development of invertase activity in the intestines of human fetuses, appearance of jejunoileal differences, *Biol. Neonate* **13**:143.

144. JIT, A., 1956, The development of the muscular coats in the human oesophagus, stomach and small intestine, *J. Anat. Soc. India* **5**:1.

145. JIT, A., 1957, The development of the muscularis mucosae in the human gastrointestinal tract, *J. Anat. Soc. India* **6**:83.

146. JIT, A., 1958, Development of the muscularis coats of the large intestine, *J. Anat. Soc. India* **7**:9.

147. JIT, I., 1974, Development of striated muscle fibres in the human oesophagus, *Indian J. Med. Res.* **62**:838.

148. JIT, I., 1974, Prenatal and postnatal structure of the anal canal and development of its sphincters, *J. Anat. Soc. India* **23**:37.

149. JIT, I., 1974, Muscularis submucosae ani and its development, *J. Anat.* **118**:11.

150. JOHNSON, A. L., SCOTT, R. B., AND NEWMAN, L. H., 1950, "Tween 20" and fecal fat in premature infants, *Amer. J. Dis. Child.* **80**:545.

151. JONES, D. V., AND LATHAM, M. C., 1974, Lactose intolerance in young children and their parents, *Amer. J. Clin. Nutr.* **27**:547.

152. JUBELIN, J., AND BOYER, J., 1972, The lipolytic activity of human milk, *Eur. J. Clin. Invest.* **2**:417.

153. KAHN, W., 1922, Weitere Mitteilungen über die Dauer der Darmpassage im Säuglingsalter, *Z. Kinderheilkd.* **33**:48.

154. Katz, L., and Hamilton, J. R., 1974, Fat absorption in infants of birth-weight less than 1,300 gm, *J. Pediatr.* **85**:608.

155. Keene, M. F. L., and Hewer, E. E., 1929, Digestive enzymes of the human foetus, *Lancet* **1**:767.

156. Keusch, G. T., Troncale, F. J., Miller, L. H., Promadhat, V., and Anderson, P. R., 1969, Acquired lactose malabsorption in Thai children, *Pediatrics* **43**:540.

157. Klumpp, T. G., and Neale, A. V., 1930, The gastric and duodenal contents of normal infants and children, *Amer. J. Dis. Child.* **40**:1215.

158. Kobayashi, A., Kawai, S., Ohbe, Y., and Nagashima, Y., 1975, Effects of dietary lactose and a lactase preparation on the intestinal absorption of calcium and magnesium in normal infants, *Amer. J. Clin. Nutr.* **28**:681.

159. Kobayashi, A., Utsunomiya, T., Ohbe, Y., and Nagashima, Y., 1974, Intestinal absorption of calcium and magnesium in hepatobiliary disease in infancy, *Arch. Dis. Child.* **49**:90.

160. Kojecký, Z., and Malinský, J., 1974, Differentiation of E cells in human intestinal mucosa during prenatal period, Abstract, Proceedings of the International Nutrition Congress—Mexico, p. 266.

161. Koldovský, O., 1969, *Development of the Functions of the Small Intestine in Mammals and Man*, S. Karger, Basel and New York.

162. Koldovský, O., 1970, Digestion and absorption during development, in: *Physiology of the Perinatal Period* (U. Stave, ed.), Appleton-Century-Crofts, New York.

163. Koldovský, O., 1972, Hormonal and dietary factors in the development of digestion and absorption, in: *Nutrition and Development* (M. Winick, ed.), John Wiley & Sons, New York.

164. Koldovský, O., Hahn, P., Melichar, V., Novák, M., Procházka, P., Rokos, J., and Vacek, Z., 1963, Absorption and transport of lipids from the small intestine of infant rats, in: *Biochemical Problems of Lipids, Biochem. Biophys. Acta Library,* Vol. I, pp. 161–169, Elsevier, New York.

165. Koldovský, O., Jumawan, J., and Palmieri, M., 1975, Effect of thyroidectomy on the activity of α-glucosidases and acid hydrolases in the small intestine of rats during weaning, *J. Endocrinol.* **66**:31.

166. Koldovský, O., Palmieri, M., and Jumawan, J., 1972, Inhibition of the cortisone-evoked increase of intestinal sucrase by actinomycin D[1], *Proc. Soc. Exp. Biol. Med.* **140**:1108.

167. Koldovský, O., Sunshine, P., and Kretchmer, N., 1966, Cellular migration of intestinal epithelia in suckling and weaned rats, *Nature (London)* **212**:1389.

168. Koshtoyants, C. S., 1931, Beitrag zur Physiologie des Embryos (Embryosecretin), *Pfluegers Arch. Gesamte Physiol.* **227**:359.

169. Koshtoyants, C. S., and Mitropolitanskaya, R. D., 1934, 1935, *Fiziol. Zh. USSR* **17**:309 (1934) and **19**:687 (1935); cited by Moratchevskaya, E. V., 1953, Characteristics of motor activity of the gut in different age periods, *Fiziol. Zh. USSR* **39**:437.

170. Kretchmer, N., 1972, Lactose and lactase, *Sci. Amer.* **227**:71.

171. Kretchmer, N., Ransome-Kuti, O., Hurwitz, R., Dungy, C., and Alakija, W., 1971, Intestinal absorption of lactose in Nigerian ethnic groups, *Lancet* **2**:392.

172. Kulangara, A. C., Menon, M. K. K., and Willmott, M., 1965, Passage of bovine serum albumin from the uterine lumen into the human foetus, *Nature (London)* **206**:1259.

173. Laitio, M., Lev, R., and Orlic, D., 1974, The developing human fetal pancreas: An ultrastructural and histochemical study with special reference to exocrine cells, *J. Anat.* **117**:619.

174. Langworthy, C. F., 1923, The digestibility of fats, *Ind. Eng. Chem.* **15**:276; cited according to Holt et al.[129]

175. Lanzkowsky, P., Madenlioglu, M., Wilson, J. F., and Lahey, M. E., 1963, Oral d-xylose test in healthy infants and children, *N. Engl. J. Med.* **268**:1441.

176. Laskowski, M., Jr., and Laskowski, M., 1951, Crystalline trypsin inhibitor from colostrum, *J. Biol. Chem.* **190**:563.

177. Lavy, U., 1974, personal communication; cited according to Watkins, J. B., 1974, Bile acid metabolism and fat absorption in newborn infants, *Pediatr. Clin. North Amer.* **21**:501.

178. Lavy, U., Silverberg, M., and Davidson, M., 1971, Role of bile acids in fat absorption in low birth weight infants, *Pediatr. Res.* **5**:387.

179. Lebenthal, E., Sunshine, P., and Kretchmer, N., 1973, Characterization of human intestinal lactase and β-galactosidase in infants and adults, *Gastroenterology* **177**:863.

180. Leissring, J. C., Anderson, J. W., and Smith, D. W., 1962, Uptake of antibodies by the intestine of the newborn infant, *Amer. J. Dis. Child.* **103**:160.

181. Le Quesne, G. W., and Reilly, B. J., 1975, Functional immaturity of the large bowel in the newborn infant, *Radiol. Clin. North Amer.* **13**:331.

182. Lev, R., and Orlic, D., 1974, Histochemical and radioautographic studies of normal human fetal colon, *Histochemistry* **39**:301.

183. Lev, R., Siegel, H. I., and Bartman, J., 1972, Histochemical studies of developing human fetal small intestine, *Histochemie* **29**:103.

184. Levin, R., Koldovský, O., Hošková, J., and Jirsová, V., 1968, Electrical activity across human foetal small intestine associated with absorption processes, *Gut* **9**:206.

185. Lieberman, J., 1966, Proteolytic enzyme activity in

fetal pancreas and meconium, *Gastroenterology* **50**:183.

186. LIFSHITZ, F., DIAZ-BENSUSSEN, S., MARTINEZ-GARZA, V., ABDO-BASSOLS, F., AND DEL CASTILLO, E. D., 1971, Influence of disaccharides on the development of systemic acidosis in the premature infant, *Pediatr. Res.* **5**:213.

187. LILIBRIDGE, C. B., AND TOWNES, P. L., 1973, Physiologic deficiency of pancreatic amylase in infancy: A factor in iatrogenic diarrhea, *J. Pediatr.* **82**:279.

188. LINDBERG, T., 1966, Intestinal dipeptdases: Characterization, development and distribution of intestinal dipeptidases of the human foetus, *Clin. Sci.* **30**:505.

189. LINDBERG, T., 1974, Proteolytic activity in duodenal juice in infants, children, and adults, *Acta Paediatr. Scand.* **63**:805.

190. LIPPARD, V. W., SCHLOSS, O. M., AND JOHNSON, P. A., 1936, Immune reactions induced in infants by intestinal absorption of incompletely digested cow's milk protein, *Amer. J. Dis. Child.* **51**:562.

191. LIU, H. M., AND POTTER, E. L., 1962, Development of the human pancreas, *Arch. Patol.* **74**:439.

192. LUGO-DE-RIVERA, C., RODRIGUEZ, H., AND TORRES-PINEDO, R., 1972, Studies on the mechanism of sugar malabsorption in infantile infectious diarrhea, *Amer. J. Clin. Nutr.* **25**:1248.

193. LUTHER, G., AND SCHREIER, K., 1963, Untersuchungen zur Resorption einzelner Fettsäuren an Säuglingen, *Klin. Wochenschr.* **41**:189.

194. MACLAURIN, J. C., MURPHY, W., WATSON, J., AND STEWART, M. E., 1975, Fat, calcium and nitrogen balance in full-term infants, *Postgrad. Med. J.* **51**:45.

195. MADEY, S., AND DANCIS, J., 1949, Proteolytic enzymes of the premature infant, *Pediatrics* **4**:177.

196. MAHDI, S., AND HEINE, W., 1974, Die intestinale Eisenresorption aus eisenangereicherter Säuglingsnahrung bei 1 bis 4 Monate alten Säuglingen, *Kindeaerztl. Prax.* **42**:505.

197. MALPRESS, F. H., 1967, Rennin and the gastric secretion of normal infants, *Nature (London)* **215**:855.

198. MASON, S., 1962, Some aspects of gastric function in the newborn, *Arch. Dis. Child.* **37**:387.

199. MCCLAIN, C. R., 1963, Amniography studies of the gastrointestinal activity of the human fetus, *Amer. J. Obstet. Gynecol.* **86**:1079.

200. MCCRACKEN, R. D., 1971, Lactose intolerance and dietary evolution, *Curr. Anthropol.* **12**:479.

201. MCMURPHY, D. M., AND BOREUS, L. O., 1968, Pharmacology of the human fetus: Adrenergic receptor function in the small intestine, *Biol. Neonate* **13**:325.

202. MEEUWISSE, G. W., AND DANO, G., 1965, The xylose absorption test in infancy, *Acta Paediatr. Scand.* **54**:33.

203. MELICHAR, V., NOVÁK, M., HAHN, P., KOLDOVSKÝ, O., AND ZEMAN, L., 1962, Changes in the blood levels of lipid metabolites and glucose following a fatty meal in infants, *Acta Paediatr.* **51**:481.

204. MIETTINEN, T. A., AND SIURALA, M., 1971, Bile salts, sterols, sterol esters, glycerides and fatty acids in micellar and oil phases of intestinal contents during fat digestion in man, *Z. Klin. Chem. Klin. Biochem.* **9**:47.

205. MIGNONE, F., AND CASTELLO, D., 1961, Ricerche sulla secrezione gastrica di acido cloridrico nell'immaturo, *Minerva Pediat.* **13**:1098.

206. MILLER, R. A., 1941, Observations on the gastric acidity during the first month of life, *Arch. Dis. Child.* **16**:22.

207. MILNER, R. D. G., DEODHAR, V., CHARD, C. R., AND GROUT, R. M., 1975, Fat absorption by small babies fed two filled milk formulae, *Arch. Dis. Child.* **50**:654.

208. MORALES, S., CHUNG, A. W., LEWIS, J. M., MESSINA, A., AND HOLT, L. E., JR., 1950, Absorption of fat and vitamin A in premature infants. I. Effect of different levels of fat intake on the retention of fat and vitamin A; II. Effect of particle size on the absorption of these substances, *Pediatrics* **6**:86, 644.

209. MORRIS, J. G., 1968, Gamma globulin absorption in the newborn, in: *Handbook of Physiology, Sect. VI. Alimentary Canal,* Vol. III, *Intestinal Absorption* (C. Code, ed.), p. 1491, American Physiological Society, Washington, D.C.

210. MURANO, G., AND DI TORO, R., 1970, I lipidi nella alimentazione dell'immaturo nelle prime epoche della vita, *Pediatria* **5**:781.

211. NOMURA, Y., 1966, On the submicroscopic morphogenesis of parietal cell in the gastric gland of the human fetus, *Z. Anat. Entwicklungsgesch.* **125**:316.

212. NORMAN, A., AND STRANDVIK, B., 1973, Bile acid excretion after disappearance of jaundice in intrahepatic cholestasis of infancy, *Acta Pediatr. Scand.* **62**:264.

213. NORMAN, A., STRANVIK, B., AND OJAMAE, O., 1972, Bile acids and pancreatic enzymes during absorption in the newborn, *Acta Paediatr. Scand.* **61**:571.

214. OCKLITZ, H. W., AND REINMUTH, B., 1959, Fettbilanzstudien bei Frühgeborenen, *Z. Kinderheilkd.* **82**:321.

215. OETTINGER, L., MILLS, W. B., AND HAHN, P. F., 1954, Iron absorption in premature and full term infants, *J. Pediatr.* **45**:302.

216. OKAMOTO, E., AND UEDA, T., 1967, Embryogenesis of intramural ganglia of the gut and its relation to Hirschsprung disease, *J. Pediatr. Surg.* **2**:437.

217. OLANTUNBOSUN, D. A., AND ADADEVOH, B. K., 1972, Lactose intolerance in Nigerian children, *Acta Paediatr. Scand.* **61**:715.

218. OLIVECRONA, T., BILLSTROM, A., FREDRIKZON, B., JOHNSON, O., AND SAMUELSON, G., 1973, Gastric lipolysis of human milk lipids in infants with pyloric stenosis, *Acta Paediatr. Scand.* **62**:520.

219. PAIGE, D. M., LEONARDO, E., CORDANO, A., NAKASHIMA, J., ADRIANZEN, T. B., AND GRAHAM, G. G., 1972, Lactose intolerance in Peruvian children:

Effect of age and early nutrition, *Amer. J. Clin. Nutr.* **25**:297.

220. PARAT, M., 1924, Histophysiology of digestive organs in embryo, *C. R. Soc. Biol.* **90**:1023.

221. PATZELT, B. M., 1931, Die feinere Ausbildung des menschlichen Darmes von der fünften Woche bis zur Geburt, *Z. Mikrosk.-Anat. Forsch.* **27**:269.

222. PELICHOVÁ, H., KOLDOVSKÝ, O., UHER, J., KRAML, J., HERINGOVÁ, A., AND JIRSOVÁ, V., 1966, Fetal development of nonspecific esterase and alkaline phosphatase activities in the small intestine of man, *Biol. Neonate* **10**:281.

223. PERIC-GOLIA, L., AND SOCIC, H., 1968, Biliary bile acids and cholesterol in developing sheep, *Amer. J. Physiol.* **215**:1284.

224. PILDES, R. S., HART, R. J., WARRNER, R., AND CORNBLATH, M., 1969, Plasma insulin response during oral glucose tolerance tests in newborns of normal and gestational diabetic mothers, *Pediatrics* **44**:76.

225. POLEY, J. R., DOWER, J. C., OWEN, C. A., JR., AND STICKLER, G. B., 1964, Bile acids in infants and children, *J. Lab. Clin. Med.* **63**:838.

226. PRINSLOO, J. G., WITTMANN, W., KRUGER, H., AND FREIER, E., 1971, Lactose absorption and mucosal disaccharidases in convalescent pellagra and Kwashiorkor children, *Arch. Dis. Child.* **46**:474.

227. PRITCHARD, J. A., 1965, Deglutition by normal and anencephalic fetuses, *Obstet. Gynecol.* **25**:289.

228. REDDY, V., AND PERSHAD, J., 1972, Lactase deficiency in Indians, *Amer. J. Clin. Nutr.* **25**:114.

229. RICOUR, C., AND REY, J., 1970, Study of the oil and micellar phases during fat digestion in the normal child, *Rev. Eur. Etud. Clin. Biol.* **15**:287.

230. RODBRO, P., AND CHRISTIANSEN, P. M., 1967, Quantitative determination of gastric intrinsic factor after large histamine doses in healthy persons, *Scand. J. Clin. Lab. Invest.* **19**:186.

231. RODBRO, P., KRASILNIKOFF, P. A., AND BITSCH, V., 1967, Gastric secretion of pepsin in early childhood, *Scand. J. Gastroenterol.* **2**:257.

232. RODBRO, P., KRASILNIKOFF, P. A., AND CHRISTIANSEN, P. M., 1967, Parietal cell secretory function in early childhood, *Scand. J. Gastroenterol.* **2**:209.

233. ROGERS, I. M., DAVIDSON, D. C., LAWRENCE, J., ARDILL, J., AND BUCHANAN, K. D., 1974, Neonatal secretion of gastrin and glucagon, *Arch. Dis. Child.* **49**:796.

234. ROGERS, I. M., DAVIDSON, D. C., LAWRENCE, J., AND BUCHANAN, K. D., 1975, Neonatal secretion of secretin, *Arch. Dis. Child.* **50**:120.

235. ROSSI, F., PESCETTO, G., AND REALE, E., 1957, Enzymatic activities in human ontogenesis: First synoptic tables of histochemical research, *J. Histochem. Cytochem.* **5**:221.

236. ROTHBERG, R. M., 1969, Immunoglobulin and specific antibody synthesis during the first weeks of life of premature infants, *J. Paediatr.* **75**:391.

237. ROY, C. C., STE-MARIE, M., CHARTRAND, L., WEBER, A., BARD, H., AND DORAY, B., 1975, Correction of the malabsorption of the preterm infant with a medium-chain triglyceride formula, *J. Pediatr.* **86**:446.

238. RUBALTELLI, F., AND LARGAJOLLI, G., 1973, Effect of light exposure on gut transit time in jaundiced newborns, *Acta Pediatr. Scand.* **62**:146.

239. RUBINO, A., PIERRO, M., LA TORRETTA, G., VETRELLA, M., DI MARTINO, D., AND AURICCHIO, S., 1969, Studies on intestinal hydrolysis of peptides. II. Dipeptidase activity toward L-glutaminyl-L-proline and glycyl-L-proline in the small intestine of the human fetus, *Pediatr. Res.* **3**:313.

240. RUEBNER, B. H., KANAYAMA, R., BRONSON, R. T., AND BLUMENTHAL, S., 1974, Meconium corpuscles in intestinal epithelium of fetal and newborn primates, *Arch. Pathol.* **98**:396.

241. SAHI, T., 1974, The inheritance of selective adult-type lactose malabsorption, *Scand. J. Gastroenterol.* **9**(Suppl. 30):1.

242. SAHI, T., ISOKOSKI, M., JUSSILA, J., AND LAUNIALA, K., 1972, Lactose malabsorption in Finnish children of school age, *Acta Paediatr. Scand.* **61**:11.

243. SALENIUS, P., 1962, On the ontogenesis of the human gastric epithelial cells, *Acta Anat.* **50**(Suppl. 46):7.

244. SCHEDL, H. P., AND CLIFTON, J. A., 1963, Kinetics of intestinal absorption in man: Normals and patients with sprue, in: *Proceedings of the Second World Congress of Gastroenterology,* Munich, 1962, Vol. II, p. 728, S. Karger, Basel.

245. SCHELL, N. B., KARELITZ, S., AND EPSTEIN, B. S., 1963, Radiographic study of gastric emptying in premature infants, *J. Pediatr.* **62**:342.

246. SCHEPPE, K. J., ZEISEL, H., ALLETAG, U., HABETH, E., AND HECKER, H., 1965, Fettadaptierte Milchfertig-nährung im Kinderkrankenhaus, *Med. Ernähr.* **6**:80.

247. SCHIPPERIJN, A. J. M., 1965, *Een Bepaling von Castle's Intrinsic Factor in menselijk Maagsap in vitro,* Denderen, Groningen; cited according to Rodbro et al.[232]

248. SCHMIDT, J., AND SCHREIER, K., 1965, Über die Eisenresorption aus Spinat bei jungen Säuglingen, *Z. Kinderheilkd.* **94**:304.

249. SCHMIDT, W., 1967, Über den paraplacentaren, fruchtwassergebunden Stofftransport beim Menschen, *Z. Anat. Entwicklungsgesch.* **126**:276.

250. SCHULZ, J., AND SMITH, N. J., 1958, A quantitative study of the absorption of food iron in infants and children, *Amer. J. Dis. Child.* **95**:109.

251. SCHULZ, J., AND SMITH, N. J., 1958, Quantitative study of the absorption of iron salt in infants and children, *Amer. J. Dis. Child.* **95**:120.

252. SCHWARTZ, J., 1967, Unpublished observation; cited according to Rodbro et al.[232]

253. SENTERRE, J., AND LAMBRECHTS, A., 1972, Nitrogen, fat and mineral balances in premature infants fed acidified or nonacidified half-skimmed cow milk, *Biol. Neonate* **20**:107.

254. SHARP, H. L., PELLER, J. CAREY, J. B., AND KRIVIT, W., 1971, Primary and secondary bile acids in meconium, *Pediatr. Res.* **5**:274.

255. SHEEHY, T. W., AND ANDERSON, P. R., 1971, Fetal disaccharidases, *Amer. J. Dis. Child.* **121**:464.

256. SHEPARD, R., FENN, S., AND SIEBER, W. K., 1966, Evaluation of esophageal function in postoperative esophageal atresia and tracheoesophageal fistula, *Surgery* **59**:608.

257. SHIBUYA, S., 1970, A study on lactose intolerance in infancy and childhood, *J. Kurume Med. Assoc.* **33**:1440.

258. SIGNER, E., AND FRIDRICH, R., 1975, Gastric emptying in newborns and young infants, *Acta Paediatr. Scand.* **64**:525.

259. SIGNER, E., MURPHY, G. M., EDKINS, S., AND ANDERSON, C. M., 1974, Role of bile salts in fat malabsorption of premature infants, *Arch. Dis. Child.* **49**:174.

260. SIMMONS, F. J., 1969, Primary adult lactose intolerance and the milking habit: A problem in biological and cultural interrelation. I. Review of the medical research, *Amer. J. Dig. Dis.* **14**:819.

261. SIMMONS, F. J., 1970, Primary adult lactose intolerance and the milking habit: II. Culture historical hypothesis, *Amer. J. Dig. Dis.* **15**:695.

262. SMALLWOOD, R. A., LESTER, R., PIASECKI, G. J., KLEIN, P. D., GRECO, R., AND JACKSON, B. T., 1972, Fetal bile salt metabolism II. Hepatic excretion of endogenous bile salt and of a taurocholate load, *J. Clin. Invest.* **51**:1388.

263. SMITH, B., 1968, Pre- and postnatal development of the ganglion cells of the rectum and its surgical implications, *J. Pediatr. Surg.* **3**:386.

264. SMITH, C. A., 1959, *The Physiology of the Newborn Infant*, pp. 279–286, Charles C. Thomas, Springfield, Illinois.

265. SMITH, D. A., AND NORDIN, B. E. C., 1964, The effect of a high phosphorus intake on total and ultrafiltrable plasma calcium and on phosphate clearance, *Clin. Sci.* **26**:479.

266. SNYDERMAN, S. E., MORALES, S., CHUNG, A. W., LEWIS, J. M., MESSINA, A., AND HOLT, L. E., 1953, Absorption of fat and vitamin A in premature infants. III. Effect of surface active agents on the absorption of these substances, *Pediatrics* **12**:158.

267. SNYDERMAN, S. E., MORALES, S., AND HOLT, L. E., 1955, The absorption of short-chain fats by premature infants, *Arch. Dis. Child.* **30**:83.

268. SÖDERHJELM, L., 1952, Fat absorption studies in children. I. Influence of heat treatment of milk on fat retention by premature infants, *Acta Paediatr.* **41**:207.

269. SOUTHGATE, D. A. T., AND BARETT, I. M., 1966, The intake and excretion of calorific constituents of milk by babies, *Br. J. Nutr.* **20**:363.

270. SOUTHGATE, D. A. T., AND WIDDOWSON, E. M., 1969,

271. SOUTHGATE, D. A. T., WIDDOWSON, E. M., SMITS, B. J., COOKE, W. T., WALKER, C. H. M., AND MATHERS, N. P., 1969, Absorption and excretion of calcium and fat by young infants, *Lancet* **1**:487.

272. STOLLEY, H., AND DRESE, W., 1967, Die Ausnützung von Gesamtfettsäuren und Calcium von gesunden Säuglingen im I. Lebensvierteljahr in Abhängigheit vom Fettsäurengehalt und von der Fettsäuren-Zusammensetzung in Milchmischungen, *Fette, Seifen, Anstrichm.* **69**:291.

273. TACHIBANA, T., 1928, Lipase in pancreas, *Jpn. J. Obstet.* **11**:92.

274. TACHIBANA, T., 1929, Fetus. I. Enzymes in the digestive tract. Trypsinogen in the pancreas; II. A peptone-splitting enzyme in the intestinal canal; III. Lipase in the stomach, *Chem. Abstr.* **23**:5222.

275. TACHIBANA, T., 1930, Lung lipase in the human fetus and the newborn child. Supplement: Other intestine lipases, *Chem. Abstr.* **25**:5454.

276. TALLEY, R. B., SCHEDL, H. P., AND CLIFTON, J. A., 1964, Small intestinal glucose, electolyte, and water absorption in cirrhosis, *Gastroenterology* **47**:382.

277. TANTIBHEDHYANGKUL, P., AND HASHIM, S. A., 1971, Enhanced calcium and magnesium absorption in premature infants by feeding formulas containing medium chain triglyceride, *Pediatr. Res.* **5**:387.

278. TANTIBHEDHYANGKUL, P., AND HASHIM, S. A., 1975, Medium-chain triglyceride feeding in premature infants: Effects on fat and nitrogen absorption, *Pediatrics* **55**:359.

279. TARASSUK, N. P., NICKERSON, T. A., AND YAGUCHI, M., 1964, Lipase action in human milk, *Nature (London)* **201**:298.

280. TIDWELL, H. C., HOLT, L. E., FARROW, H. L., AND NEALE, S., 1935, Studies in fat metabolism, *J. Pediatr.* **6**:481.

281. TOBECK, A., 1925, Über angeborene Verschlusse (Atresien) des Darmrohres (gleichzeitig ein Beitrag zur Frage der Enstehung der Meconium Körperchen), *Virchows Arch. Pathol. Anat.* **265**:330.

282. TORRES-PINEDO, R., CONDE, E., ROBILLARD, G., AND MALDONADEO, M., 1968, Studies on infant diarrhea. III. Changes in composition of saline and glucose-saline solutions instilled into the colon, *Pediatrics* **42**:303.

283. TORRES-PINEDO, R., RIVERA, C. L., AND FERNANDEZ, S., 1966, Studies on infant diarrhea. II. Absorption of glucose and net fluxes of water and sodium chloride in a segment of the jejunum, *J. Clin. Invest.* **45**:1916.

284. UFFELMAN, J., 1881, Über den Fettgehalt der Faeces von Säuglingen, *Arch. Kinderheilkd.* **2**:1.

285. VAN DE KAMER, J. H., AND WEIJERS, H. A., 1961, Malabsorption syndrome, *Fed. Proc. Fed. Amer. Soc. Exp. Biol.* **7**:333.

Neonatal metabolism of calcium and fat (a reply), *Lancet* **1**:1319.

286. VANHOUTTE, J. J., AND KATZMAN, P., 1973, Roentgenographic manifestation of immaturity of the intestinal neural plexus in premature infants, *Radiology* **106**:363.

287. VAZQUEZ, C., 1951, La funcion pancreatica del recien nacido, *Rev. Esp. Pediatr.* **7**:75.

288. VEGHELYI, P. V., 1949, Pancreatic enzymes: Normal output and comparison of different methods of assay, *Pediatrics* **3**:749.

289. VINNIK, I. E., KERN, F., JR., AND SUSSMAN, K. E., 1965, The effect of diabetes mellitus and insulin on glucose absorption by the small intestine in man, *J. Lab. Clin. Med.* **66**:131.

290. VON BERGMANN, J., VON BERGMANN, K., HADORN, B., AND PAUMGARTNER, G., 1975, Biliary lipid composition in early childhood, *Clin. Chim. Acta* **64**:241.

291. WADSWORTH, G. R., 1969, Neonatal metabolism of calcium and fat, *Lancet* **1**:1319.

292. WAGNER, H., 1961, The development to full functional maturity of the gastric mucosa and the kidneys in the fetus and newborn, *Biol. Neonate* **3**:257.

293. WALKER, W. A., AND ISSELBACHER, K. J., 1974, Uptake and transport of macromolecules by the intestine, *Gastroenterology* **67**:531.

294. WALZER, M., 1927, Studies on absorption of undigested proteins in human beings. I. A simple direct method of studying the absorption of undigested proteins, *J. Immunol.* **14**:143.

295. WASSON, W. W., 1941, Study of gastrointestinal tract of children and its relation to adult, *Radiology* **37**:277.

296. WATKINS, J. B., BLISS, M., DONALDSON, R. M., AND LESTER, R., 1974, Characterization of newborn fecal lipid, *Pediatrics* **53**:511.

297. WATKINS, J. B., INGALL, D., SZCZEPANIK, P., KLEIN, P. D., AND LESTER, R., 1973, Bile-salt metabolism in the newborn: Measurement of pool size and synthesis by stable isotope technic, *N. Engl. J. Med.* **288**:431.

298. WATKINS, J. B., KLEIN, P. D., INGALL, D., AND LESTER, R., 1972, Bile-salt metabolism in newborn infants, *Pediatr. Res.* **6**:432.

299. WATKINS, J. B., SZCZEPANIK, P., GOULD, J., KLEIN, P. D., AND LESTER, R., 1973, Bile-salt kinetics in premature infants: An explanation for inefficient lipid absorption, *Gastroenterology* **64**:817.

300. WATSON, W. C., 1965, Intestinal hydrogenation of dietary fatty acids, *Clin. Chim. Acta* **12**:340.

301. WEIJERS, H. A., DRION, E. F., AND VAN DE KAMER, J. H., 1960, Analysis and interpretation of the fat-absorption coefficient, *Acta Paediatr.* **49**:615.

302. WELSCH, H., HEINZ, F., LAGALLY, G., AND STUHLFAUTH, K., 1965, Fettresorption aus Frauenmilch beim Neugeborenen, *Klin. Wochenschr.* **43**:902.

303. WERNER, B., 1948, Peptic and tryptic activity of the digestive glands in newborns. A comparison between premature and full-term infants, *Acta Paediatr. (Suppl. 6)* **35**:65.

304. WHITBY, J. D., AND DUNKIN, L. J., 1970, Oesophageal temperature differences in children, *Br. J. Anaesth.* **42**:1013.

305. WIDDOWSON, E. M., 1965, Absorption and excretion of fat, nitrogen, and minerals from "filled" milks by babies one week old, *Lancet* **2**:1099.

306. WIDDOWSON, E. M., McCANCE, R. A., HARRISON, G. E., AND SUTTON, A., 1963, Effect of giving phosphate supplements to breast fed babies on absorption and excretion of calcium, strontium, magnesium and phosphates, *Lancet* **2**:1250.

307. WILLIAMS, M. L., ROSE, C. S., MORROW, G., SLOAN, S. E., AND BARNESS, L. A., 1970, Calcium and fat absorption in neonatal period, *Amer. J. Clin. Nutr.* **23**:1322.

308. WILLICH, E., 1973, Insufficiency of the cardia in infancy—manometric and cineradiographic studies, *Ann. Radiol.* **16**:137.

309. WOLF, R. O., AND TAUSSIG, L. M., 1973, Human amniotic fluid isoamylases. Functional development of fetal pancreas and salivary glands, *Obstet. Gynecol.* **41**:337.

310. WOLLAEGER, E. E., COMFORT, M. W., AND OSTERBERG, A. E., 1947, Total solids, fat and nitrogen in the feces: III. A study of normal persons taking a test diet containing a moderate amount of fat: Comparison with results obtained with normal persons taking a test diet containing a large amount of fat, *Gastroenterology* **9**:272.

311. WOLMAN, I. J., 1943, Gastric digestive secretions in infancy and childhood: A review, *Amer. J. Med. Sci.* **206**:770.

312. WOLMAN, I. J., 1946, Gastric phase of milk digestion in childhood, *Amer. J. Dis. Child.* **71**:394.

313. WOTEKI, C. E., WESER, E., AND YOUNG, E. A., 1976, Lactose malabsorption in Mexican-American children, *Amer. J. Clin. Nutr.* **29**:19.

314. YAMASHITA, F., SHIBUYA, S., FUNATSU, I., KUNO, T., AND IDE, H., 1969, Absorption of medium chain triglyceride in the low birth weight infant and evaluation of MCT milk formula for low birth weight infant nutrition using the Latin square technique, *Kurume Med. J.* **16**:191.

315. YEH, K. Y., AND MOOG, F., 1975, Development of the small intestine in the hypophysectomized rat. II. Influence of cortisone, thyroxine, growth hormone, and prolactin, *Dev. Biol.* **47**:173.

316. YOUNOSZAI, M. K., 1974, Jejunal absorption of hexose in infants and adults, *J. Pediatr.* **85**:446.

317. YU, V. Y. H., 1975, Effect of body position on gastric emptying in the neonate, *Arch. Dis. Child.* **50**:500.

318. ZNAMENACEK, K., AND PŘIBYLOVÁ, H., 1963, The effect of glucose and insulin administration on the

blood glucose levels of the newborn, *Cesk. Pediatr. (Prague)* **18**:104.

319. Zoppi, G., Andreotti, G., Pajno-Ferrara, F., Njai, D. M., and Gaburro, D., 1972, Exocrine pancreas function in premature and full-term neonates, *Pediatr. Res.* **6**:880.

320. Zoppi, G., Shmerling, D. H., Gaburro, D., and Prader, A., 1970, The electrolyte and protein contents and outputs in duodenal juice after pancreozymin and secretin stimulation in normal children and in patients with cystic fibrosis, *Acta Paediatr. Scand.* **59**:692.

321. Zoula, J., Melichar, V., Novák, M., Hahn, P., and Koldovský, O., 1966, Nitrogen and fat retention in premature infants fed breast milk, "humanized" cow's milk or half skimmed cow's milk, *Acta Paediatr. Scand.* **55**:26.

CHAPTER 16

Nutrition of the Newborn

Peter Hahn

1. Fetal Nutrition

The fetus is not a parasite. It consumes what it is given. It can be underfed or overnourished. Fetal nutrition is directly dependent on maternal nutrition. Frequently, a few more grams of protein and calories a day may prevent the delivery of premature or small-for-date infants.[32]

It must be admitted, however, that we still know very little about the factors that control transport of nutrients from mother to fetus, particularly during the early part of gestation. The majority of data in man come from measurements made during labor. Additional data are available from ovine pregnancies, usually between 90 and 150 days of gestation. Experiments in sheep, rats, and other mammals indicate that maternal undernutrition during the first part of gestation has fewer deleterious effects than an inadequate food supply during the second half of pregnancy. Overnutrition, as exemplified by fetuses from diabetic mothers, also appears to have its greatest effect during the last part of pregnancy, when adipose tissue has developed.

Essentially, there are three undesirable nutritional states: undernutrition, overnutrition, and malnutrition. The first and second terms refer to a dearth or

excess of calories; the third, to an imbalance of essential nutrients, e.g., protein or a trace metal or vitamin.

It is difficult to distinguish between malnutrition and undernutrition, since they often go hand in hand. Good examples of specific malnutrition are zinc or riboflavin deficiency in the maternal diet.[7] General undernutrition has been studied extensively in recent years. It has been shown that undernutrition of the pregnant rat leads to reduced growth of her fetuses. The number of cells in different fetal organs is reduced. This reduction is particularly striking in the cerebellum, which is last to mature and hence presumably more easily affected by lack of calories during late pre- and early postnatal life (for a review, see Brasel[6]). It has been shown that a similar reduction in the final number of brain cells can also occur in man.[6,8] We would stress, however, that both in the rat and in man, undernutrition was very severe, not more than one-third of the usually required calories being supplied.

The caloric requirements of the fetus and its mother have been worked out in some detail, and tables of recommended allowances have been prepared. There is no doubt that during the last 50 years or so, birth weights of infants have increased, particularly in countries such as Japan, where nutritional requirements have been covered more and more adequately.

In view of these data, it is somewhat surprising that for quite some time, obstetricians carefully

Peter Hahn · Centre for Developmental Medicine, Department of Obstetrics and Gynaecology and Department of Paediatrics, Faculty of Medicine, University of British Columbia, Vancouver, British Columbia, Canada

357

watched the weight gain of their pregnant patients and drew an arbitrary line beyond which maternal weight should not be permitted to rise. The rationale of this "treatment" was apparently a belief that delivery would be less smooth if more than the recommended daily ration were consumed, and toxemia of pregnancy would be prevented. Now, a more rational approach prevails.[32]

1.1. Maternal Diet

Nutritionists suggest "well-balanced" diets for pregnant women. Well-balanced (presumably) means not too much and not too little and the *right proportions of different nutrients in a final symphony of adequate calories.*

Perhaps it is best, however, to examine the fetal "diet" first, and from that extrapolate requirements.

1.2. Fetal Diet

Three main components of the diet must be considered: (1) calories, (2) proteins, and (3) minerals and vitamins.

1.2.1. Calories

Most of the calories, i.e., the energy necessary for growth and differentiation, are supplied to the fetus in the form of glucose. Even though calculations in the ovine fetus have shown that other substances (probably amino acids; see also Section 3) also contribute to the energy supply, the staple calorie of the fetus is glucose. Other substances that have been considered repeatedly are fatty acids. It is unlikely, however, that they contribute to any very large degree to the *energy* needs of the fetus, although probably those that do cross from mother to fetus are used to build up adipose tissue and to contribute to the ever-increasing need for phospholipid molecules.[11] On the other hand, evidence is accumulating that ketone bodies may serve as a good source of energy under special conditions (see Chapter 19).

The point of importance in this area appears to be the control of blood glucose levels in both mother and fetus, which seems to differ from that of other metabolites, e.g., ketones. Thus, a consistently high level of maternal blood glucose occurs only if diabetes is present in the mother, i.e., impaired regulation in the mother. This higher blood level leads to higher blood glucose levels in the fetus, to premature maturation of the fetal insulin response,

and thus to excessive fat formation and other changes.

Nothing is known about the effect of periodic loading with sucrose, which occurs if the future mother has a sweet tooth. A scenario could be written as follows: Sucrose (sweets) is ingested by the mother, a high blood sugar results, excess insulin is released, reactive hypoglycemia occurs (see Blazquez et al.[5]). All these changes are reflected in the fetus, and the foundations for future problems may be laid. Undernutrition (lack of calories) of the mother, of course, results in somewhat lower blood sugar levels, and also in elevated levels of fatty acids and ketones. (The tendency toward ketosis during food deprivation is much more pronounced during pregnancy.) This lower maternal level of blood sugar and perhaps also the elevated ketones are reflected in similar changes in the fetus, perhaps causing a decreased rate of insulin secretion, which in turn may help to retard growth.[9] Of course, the main cause of stunted prenatal growth is lack of nutrient supply from the mother, be it due to maternal undernutrition or to an insufficient rate of transfer of nutrients from mother to fetus (e.g., placental insufficiency, compression of umbilical cord). In addition, it appears that high maternal blood ketone levels may induce enzymes of ketone metabolism already in the fetal brain, when usually these enzymes show enhanced activity only postnatally.[9]

1.2.2. Amino Acids

Amino acids (with a few exceptions) seem to be transported well and rapidly to the fetus, and their levels in fetal blood are usually higher than those in maternal blood (see Chapter 18). It appears that no definite effect of protein deficiency in the mother on the fetus has as yet been demonstrated in man. In the rat, however, a low-protein diet during pregnancy can lead to stunting of the fetuses and to reabsorption (for a review of the literature, see *Nutritional Reports International*[31]).

The importance of the nutritional state of the mother for fetal development has been underlined only recently. Our knowledge in this field is meager, and much needs to be done. The two main, apparently conflicting, data are:

1. Even severe maternal undernutrition (such as the Dutch famine during 1944) has only a slight effect on the human fetus, who is, however, slightly smaller and shorter at birth. Nutri-

tional problems in the newborn really commence only when babies are weaned (see Section 3).

2. Numerous animal experiments and some data from human populations indicate that severe intrauterine undernutrition may have lasting effects on brain function and composition.[6]

How far we should extrapolate from rat and even monkey experiments to man is difficult to decide at the moment. The nature-against-nurture argument, however, is still wide open, e.g., in the case of I.Q. There are good indications that early nutrition is important, but more data are required. In the rat, reduction of protein intake during pregnancy (so that only 5% of total calories are derived from protein) results in stunted growth, with a bad postnatal prognosis. Restricting the blood supply to the fetus toward the end of pregnancy causes a small-for-date newborn with a large head and little alteration in brain development. Such animals are relatively easy to rehabilitate.[39] Thus, apparently not only the degree of undernutrition but also its duration and the type of food given the mother decide the outcome of such pregnancies.

1.2.3. Minerals and Vitamins

Again, animal experiments have demonstrated the importance of certain trace substances for normal development. Zinc seems to be such a substance (see Chapter 20). Similarly, vitamin deficiencies during rat pregnancies have deleterious and often lethal effects on the fetus.

1.2.4. Drugs

Finally, even though drugs are not nutrients in the normal way, it should be mentioned that many drugs cross the placental barrier and can, in the fetus, alter some metabolic functions, particularly in liver microsomes. The consequences of such effects are only now being examined.

2. Experimental Intrauterine Growth Retardation

This approach deserves special mention, since in recent years, tremendous efforts have been made to come up with an animal model that would mirror the human situation. Usually, the blood supply to the fetus is restricted. This restriction results in stunted growth and other changes which, for mammals, have been reviewed by Minkowski *et al.*[28] and by Widdowson.[38] Recently, IUR has also been produced in monkeys.[16] The most striking conclusion to be drawn from these experiments is that except for the obvious retardation of growth, there are very few obvious biochemical changes that could be used to assess future development. Thus, in rats, except for the first postnatal day, no differences are found for gluconeogenic enzyme activities, hormone levels (including cortisone, glucagon, insulin), or liver glycogen. Only blood glucose levels are slightly lower than in control animals, and they attain normal levels by day 10 postnatally. These data may be contrasted with the well-known late effects of prenatal and postnatal malnutrition on brain development.

3. Neonatal Nutrition

A normal, full-term infant born to a normal mother requires nothing but breast milk; however, he should be fed soon after birth.[37] The widespread practice of feeding glucose as the first meal is based on the same rationale as blood-letting some 100 years ago, i.e., an impression and belief that it might help.

Normal delivery stresses the infant, deprives him suddenly of a steady food supply, and thus requires him to initiate new reactions, particularly to release glucagon, to decrease insulin secretion, and to release catecholamines. In other words, he is suddenly aroused to produce a large amount of cyclic AMP, thus initiating glycolysis, gluconeogenesis, and lipolysis, and suppressing glycogen synthesis. All these processes are suppressed if glucose is given for any length of time. This has been demonstrated in the newborn rat, but not in man. In fact, the islets of Langerhans of the newborn seem to be less responsive to glucose than those of older infants. Nevertheless, they do react very soon after birth, and it has even been suggested that perhaps the neonatal relative insensitivity to glucose is an artifact. Thus, to feed a newborn full-term infant glucose lacks rationale.

More and more mothers, particularly in North America, breast-feed their babies for a very short time only or not at all. Confusion is well exemplified by the fact that several workers discuss the effect of adding solids to the milk diet of the newborn without specifying the type of milk fed. Many

Table I. Composition of Human Breast Milk and Commercial Milk Preparations

Substance	Breast milk	Commercial milk
Fat	Human triglycerides, etc. Composition depends to some extent on diet.	Soya lipids or cow's milk with lipids
Proteins	Homologous	Usually cow's milk
Antibodies	Yes	No
Enzymes	Several, e.g., lipase, phosphatase	No
Hormones	?	?
Minerals	Low Na	Special care has to be taken to maintain low Na.

milk preparations are on the market, most of them apparently perfectly adequate and meeting all the requirements of the baby. They are not human breast milk, however, and they differ from it, even in the most favorable instances, as shown in Table I.

In addition, of course, most of the milk preparations can be given either diluted or concentrated, depending on the recommendations of the physician or the manufacturer, or the whims of the mother. The four most usual deviations from optimum nutrition when using milk preparations are: (1) too much protein, (2) too much salt, (3) too little fat, and (4) too much sugar.

1. Too much protein: Even though artificial feeding of newborns was first made possible by the introduction of sufficient protein into their diet, there is a persistent tendency to overdose babies with protein. The protein content of breast milk averages 1.2%, and any excess protein is used for energy purposes; i.e., amino acids are deaminated and changed into glucose and fat, urea production is enhanced, and amino acids are excreted as such (see for example, Zoula et al.[40]).

Of particular interest here are the data of Räihä,[34] who showed that in premature babies, excess protein feeding leads to very high tyrosine blood levels, which may, presumably, be harmful to the brain. In this connection, the data of Lindblad[24] are of interest. The blood level of tyrosine in newborn infants rises considerably as soon as they are weaned.

2. Excess salt: That contained, for instance, in cow's milk causes water retention (the kidney of the newborn cannot rid the body of the salt load efficiently enough) and thus apparent good growth curves. This phenomenon is so well established that hardly any pediatrician will use undiluted cow's milk to feed newborn babies.

3. Too little fat: The mistaken belief that the newborn cannot absorb fat has led to the conclusion that it is better to reduce the fat content of milk. It may be stressed here that the amount of fat absorbed is usually not less than 80% of the amount fed, and that this figure gradually rises to over 90% as the baby grows. Hence, even at the lowest rate of fat absorption, only 20% is lost. Again, it is best to take breast milk as the reference point. It should also be pointed out here that the blood cholesterol level of newborns fed breast milk is *higher* than for any other milk.[10] This we consider to be another argument *for* breast milk (see Hahn and Koldovský,[15] Reíser and Sidelman,[35] Section 4). Furthermore, it contains 2–4% fat and is well tolerated.

If an artificial milk that contains no fat is fed, the metabolic development of the newborn differs from that of a breast-fed one. Instead of utilizing fat for energy purposes and for lipid synthesis (e.g., myelin, cell walls), the newborn must *make* his own fat from the carbohydrates and proteins he receives. He also produces fewer ketones in his liver, and thus perhaps deprives the brain of its usual lipid precursors (see Chapter 19). Depending on the type of fat contained in the milk, the infant may require extra vitamin E (soybean-based formulas have highly unsaturated fatty acids), or, alternatively, he may lack essential fatty acids (if fed cow's milk fat).

4. Too much sugar: A consequence of the lower fat content of many milk preparations is a relative excess of sugar. In addition, sugar or carbohydrates constitute a large part of the extra "solids" fed to very young babies. The possible deleterious consequences of excess sugar consumption are discussed in more detail in Section 4. Again, it should be borne in mind that the glycid added to milk preparations can be anything from lactose to sucrose, dextrose, or other sugars.[10]

In this connection, it may also be mentioned that a jar of a popular brand of "strained" bananas lists water, bananas, sugar, food starch, concentrated orange juice, citric acid, and vitamin C. Less than 30% of the total solids consist of actual bananas.[10] Thus, any canned solid food is not only more expensive than breast milk or even homemade solid food, but also probably contains considerably more sugar than is required by the baby. Note that we are not even mentioning added preservatives.

4. Late Effects of Early Nutrition

There is no doubt that early undernutrition of the fetus and newborn has permanent effects on cell numbers, e.g., in the brain (see Section 1.2.2). It has also been known for many years[26,27] that caloric undernutrition of weaned animals for the rest of their lives prolongs life and decreases the incidence of disease. That it does has been confirmed more recently.[4,36] It has also been demonstrated that hormonal imbalances induced at particular moments of development have permanent effects, probably by affecting the maturation of the hypothalamus (testosterone given to newborn female rats, thyroid hormone; see, for example, Bakke et al.[2]). In recent years, an old finding[33] has been analyzed in great detail: neonatal overnutrition. Overnutrition is easily produced in rats[17,19,20,25,38] and mice[23] by reducing litter sizes from the normal 8 or 9 to 3 or 4. Undernutrition, on the other hand, is evoked by leaving 14–20 young with one mother. In overnourished rodents, body weight increases more rapidly than in the controls or underfed ones, and the two never meet; i.e., the body weight of the animals from small litters is always greater than that of animals from large litters. Knittle and Hirsch[20] showed that this increased weight is due to an increase both in the number and in the size of fat cells in the fat depots.

In other words, these animals contain more fat in their body, and that fat is contained in more cells that are larger than normal. On the other hand, overfeeding of weaned rats (usually by offering a high-fat diet[3]) leads to an increase in fat cell size only; their number remains unchanged. Thus, it appears that only during a certain period of development can the final cell number be altered.

It is still not certain whether the same applies to man (cf. Appelbaum[1]). Candidates for increased fat cell numbers would be infants of diabetic mothers who are born heavy and with large fat depots and children who started to become obese very early after birth, e.g., in the 6th month (see Hahn and Novak[13]). Such children and those who are, for example, 6–48 months old consume a large part of their calories as carbohydrate, especially refined sugar. This habit in itself may well lead to a predisposition toward diabetes and obesity later in life, as indicated by some experiments with rats.[29] Rats fed a high-sucrose diet for 50 days after weaning were fatter and had higher levels of both blood cholesterol and insulin than those fed a high-starch diet. It was not possible to reverse this trend by changing the diets after 50 days. It has also been shown that repeated injections of insulin to fetal and newborn rats lead to obesity later in life.[18] Thus, it appears that early nutrition in man also determines the adult state, particularly with regard to the so-called degenerative diseases, e.g., atherosclerosis and obesity.

Attempts have been made to obtain more information on these relationships in rats. It was first suggested[21] that early weaning of rats may have deleterious effects, since among other things, the animals are suddenly forced to regulate food and water intake separately, whereas no such choice was necessary while they were breast-feeding. In addition, the data of Barboriak et al.[3] indicated that obesity is best produced in rats weaned early. A more systematic analysis showed that rats normally commence to nibble at solid food between the 14th and 18th postnatal days, and are completely weaned on day 30 (see, for example, Hahn and Koldovský[14]). One of the consequences of prematurely weaning a rat (on day 16–18) is that it is suddenly deprived of its high fat intake (milk is a relatively high-fat diet; rat milk contains 7–10% fat, and hence is a very high-fat diet). The scheme adopted for subsequent experiments was to wean rats on day 18, feed them different diets between days 18 and 30, and then feed them the normal laboratory diet and compare them with rats normally weaned on day 30. One of the most striking findings was the deleterious effect of premature weaning to the laboratory diet or a high-carbohydrate diet on spermiogenesis in 6- and 12-month-old rats.[22] This effect could be prevented by feeding a high-fat diet between days 18 and 30, suggesting that either fat itself or some factor(s) in the fat was essential for normal testicular function to be maintained up to 6 months or more. In the same experiment using 500 rats, it was shown that prematurely weaned animals are also "less intelligent," as judged by the speed with which a conditioned reflex could be elaborated and recalled in 8-month-old animals.[30] A very striking finding was the high level of blood cholesterol in 12-month-old prematurely weaned female rats fed an atherogenic diet for the last 2 months.[22] It was later confirmed that premature weaning led to significantly higher blood cholesterol levels in 7-month-old male rats fed normally (Purina Chow).[12] Reiser and Sidelman[35] showed that in male rats, there was an inverse relationship between the blood level of cholesterol in suckling male rats and the blood level 100 days later; i.e., the higher the level in the suckling period, the lower in adults. Finally, Hahn and Koldovský[15] confirmed that early weaning to a high-carbohydrate diet led to higher blood cholesterol levels 10 months later than weaning to a high-fat diet or normal weaning, and that, again, there was an inverse relationship between blood cholesterol levels during the weaning period and those found much later in life.

In conclusion, it seems well established today, in particular for the rat, that the quality and quantity of nutrition *in utero* and during the suckling and weaning periods has permanent effects. It may be said that they "set" feedback mechanisms for life. It seems clear that the type of food that appears most beneficial in one period of life need not necessarily be of benefit in another one. Thus, a high-fat diet is the norm in the suckling period and appears to be the most advantageous, but this is not true after weaning. On the other hand, other components of the diet, such as sucrose, seem to be of little value at any time of life, and may have a detrimental effect whenever fed. This effect is more pronounced, however, early in life.[29]

Finally, two points should be stressed:

1. The data are obtained mostly in experimental animals. How far they apply to man is not known.

2. This ignorance does not imply that we should wean babies early to a high-sugar diet or any other diet. On the contrary, the experimental data suggest that we should be very cautious in changing from breast milk to any other form of food during the first few months of life (see Fomon[10]).

5. References

1. APPELBAUM, M., BRIGANT, L., AND DURET, F., 1974, Relationship between the age of appearance of obesity and adipocyte diameter in 256 obese and 57 non-obese women, in: *The Regulation of the Adipose Tissue Mass* (J. Vague and J. Boyer, eds.), pp. 215–218, Excerpta Medica, Amsterdam.
2. BAKKE, J. L., LAWRENCE, L. L., BENNET, J., AND ROBINSON, S., 1975, Late effects of neonatal undernutrition and overnutrition on pituitary–thyroidal and gonadal function, *Biol. Neonate* **27**:259–270.
3. BARBORIAK, J. J., KREHL, W. A., AND COWGILL, G. R., 1958, Influence of high fat diets on growth and development of obesity in the albino rat, *J. Nutr.* **64**:241–250.
4. BERG, B. N., AND SIMMS, H. S., 1960, Nutrition and longevity in the rat, *J. Nutr.* **71**:255–265.
5. BLAZQUEZ, E., LIPSHAW, L. A., BLAZQUEZ, M., AND FOA, P. P., 1975, The synthesis and release of insulin in fetal, nursing and young adult rats: Studies *in vivo* and *in vitro*, *Pediatr. Res.* **9**:17–25.
6. BRASEL, J. A., 1974, Cellular changes in intrauterine malnutrition, in: *Nutrition and Fetal Development* (M. Winick, ed.), Vol. 2, pp. 13–26, John Wiley & Sons, New York.
7. CALDWELL, D. F., OBERLEAS, D., AND PRASAD, A. S., 1973, Reproductive performance on chronic mildly zinc deficient rats and the effect on behaviour of their offspring, *Nutr. Rep. Int.* **7**:309–320.
8. DAVIES, P. A., AND RUSSEL, H., 1968, Later progress of 100 infants weighing 1000–2000 g at birth fed immediately with breast milk, *Devel. Med. Child Neurol.* **10**:725–735.
9. DIERCKS-VENTLING, C., AND CONE, A. L., 1971. Acetoacetyl-CoA thiolase in brain, liver and kidney during maturation of the rat, *Science*, **172**:380–383.
10. FOMON, S. J., 1974, *Infant Nutrition*, W. B. Saunders Co., Philadelphia.
11. HAHN, P., 1972, Lipid metabolism in nutrition in the prenatal and perinatal periods, in: *Nutrition and Development* (M. Winick, ed.), pp. 99–134, John Wiley & Sons, New York.
12. HAHN, P., AND KIRBY, L., 1973, Immediate and late effects of premature weaning and of feeding a high fat or high carbohydrate diet to weanling rats, *J. Nutr.* **103**:690–696.

3. HAHN, P., AND NOVAK, M., 1975, The development of brown and white adipose tissue, *J. Lipid Res.* **16**:79–91.

4. HAHN, P., AND KOLDOVSKÝ, O. (eds.), 1966, *Utilization of Nutrition During Postnatal Development,* Pergamon Press, Oxford.

15. HAHN, P., AND KOLDOVSKÝ, O., 1976, Late effects of premature weaning on blood cholesterol levels in adult rats, *Nutr. Rep. Int.* **13**:87–91.

16. HILL, D. E., 1974, Experimental growth retardation in rhesus monkeys, in: *Size at Birth, Ciba Found. Symp.* **27**:99–126, Excerpta Medica, Amsterdam.

17. HIRSCH, J., AND HAN, P. W., 1969, Cellularity of rat adipose tissue: Effect of growth, starvation and obesity, *J. Lipid Res.* **10**:77–82.

18. KAZDOVA, L., AND FABRY, P., 1974, Adipose tissue hyperplasia induced by small doses of insulin, in: *The Regulation of the Adipose Tissue Mass* (J. Vague and J. Boyer, eds.), pp. 215–218, Excerpta Medica, Amsterdam.

19. KENNEDY, G. C., 1957, The development with age of hypothalmic restraint upon the appetite of the rat, *J. Endocrinol,* **16**:9–15.

20. KNITTLE, J. L. AND HIRSCH, J., 1968, Effect of early nutrition on the development of rat epididymal fat pads: Cellularity and metabolism, *J. Clin. Invest.* **47**:2091–2098.

21. KRECEK, J., 1963, Premature weaning in the rat, *Cesk. Fysiol.* **12**:347.

22. KUBAT, K., cited in Hahn and Koldovský.[14]

23. LEMONNIER, D., AND ALEXIU, A., 1974, Nutritional, genetic and hormonal aspects of adipose tissue cellularity, in: *The Regulation of the Adipose Tissue Mass* (J. Vague and J. Boyer, eds.), pp. 158–173, Excerpta Medica, Amsterdam.

24. LINDBLAD, B. S., 1970, Free amino acid levels in venous plasma of the nonpregnant woman, of the mother and cord during delivery and of the full term and early born neonate, in: *Metabolism of the Newborn* (G. Joppich and H. Wolf, eds.), pp. 106–114, Hippokrates Verlag, Stuttgart.

25. McCANCE, P. A., 1962, Food, growth and time, *Lancet* **2**:621–622.

26. McCAY, C. M., MAYNARD, L. A., SPERLING, G., AND BARNES, L. L., 1939, Retarded growth, life span, ultimate body size and age changes in the albino rat after feeding diets restricted only from weaning, *J. Nutr.* **18**:1–14.

27. McCAY, C. M., SPERLING, G., AND BARNES, L. L., 1939, Growth, ageing, chronic disease and life span in rats, *Arch. Biochem.* **2**:469–479.

28. MINKOWSKI, A., ROUX, J., AND TORDET-CARIDROIT, C., 1974, Pathophysiological changes in intrauterine malnutrition, in: *Nutrition and Fetal Development* (M. Winick, ed.), Vol. 2, pp. 45–78, John Wiley & Sons, New York.

29. MOSER, P. B., AND BERDANIER, C. D., 1974, Effect of early sucrose feeding on the metabolic pattern of mature rats, *J. Nutr.* **104**:687–694.

30. NOVAKOVA, V., FALTIN, J., FLANDERA, J., HAHN, P., AND KOLDOVSKÝ, O., 1962, Effect of early and late weaning on learning in adult rats, *Nature (London)* **193**:280.

31. *Nutritional Reports International,* 1973, **7**(5).

32. O'BRIEN, D., 1975, Nutrition education of the prenatal mother, in: *Nutrition and Development. Modern Problems of Paediatrics,* Vol. 14 (C. A. Canosa, ed.), pp. 264–272, S. Karger, Basel.

33. PARKES, A. S., 1926, The growth of young mice according to the size of litter, *Ann. Appl. Biol.* **13**:374–376.

34. RÄIHÄ, N. C., 1973, Biochemical basis for nutritional management of preterm infants, *Pediatrics* **53**:147–156.

35. REISER, R., AND SIDELMAN, Z., 1972, Control of serum cholesterol homeostasis by cholesterol in the milk of the suckling rat, *J. Nutr.* **102**:1009–1012.

36. ROSS, M. H., 1972, Length of life and caloric intake, *Amer. J. Clin. Nutr.* **25**:834.

37. ROSSI, E., 1975, Early feeding, hypoglycemia and development, in: *Nutrition and Development. Modern Problems of Paediatrics,* Vol. 14 (C. A. Canosa, ed.), pp. 134–139, S. Karger, Basel.

38. WIDDOWSON, E. M., 1974, Immediate and long-term consequences of being large or small at birth: A comparative approach, in: *Size at Birth, Ciba Found. Symp.* (G. Wolstenholme, ed.), **27**:65–81, Elsevier—North-Holland.

39. WINNICK, M., 1975, Maternal nutrition and intrauterine growth failure, in: *Nutrition and Development. Modern Problems of Paediatrics,* Vol. 14 (C. A. Canosa, ed.), pp. 48–56, S. Karger, Basel.

40. ZOULA, J., MELICHAR, V., NOVAK, M., HAHN, P., AND KOLDOVSKÝ, O., 1966, Nitrogen and fat retention in premature infants fed breast milk, "humanized" cow's milk or half skimmed cow's milk, *Acta Paediatr. (Upsalla)* **55**:26–36.

CHAPTER 17

Carbohydrate Metabolism and the Regulation of Blood Glucose

F. John Ballard

. Introduction

Many differences in carbohydrate metabolism in the fetus, newborn, and adult are related to the changing nutritional environment of the various ges. The fetus is characterized by having a constant nd plentiful supply of glucose, which, except in ungulates, is not normally accompanied by other hexoses. The newborn, on the other hand, obtains only small amounts of glucose due to the low carbohydrate content of milk. There is therefore a changeover at birth from a high-carbohydrate to a high-fat diet, and many of the alterations in metabolic pathways can be interpreted in this context. I would also like to emphasize that although the relative importance of carbohydrate as a nutrient for adults will differ among herbivorous, carnivorous, and omnivorous mammals, and will be apparent from measurements of pathway activities, only minor nutritional differences are seen when interspecies comparisons are made between fetuses or neonates. Accordingly, the observations made on

fetal and newborn experimental animals can often be extrapolated to the human infant. Where differences have been noted, attention will be drawn to them.

The central role of the liver in the regulation of blood sugar is well established. For this reason, the greater part of this review will be directed to a report of the developmental changes in carbohydrate metabolism as they occur in the liver. Wherever possible, I shall include pertinent information on the factors responsible for the initiation of metabolic changes, and I shall stress the role of hormones in these alterations. However, I shall avoid discussing the mechanisms of action of the various hormones as well as the maturation of endocrine function. These subjects are covered in Chapter 39.

One general problem should be emphasized. Although an understanding of the changing developmental role of a metabolic pathway is sought by researchers, the actual measurements are usually of enzyme activities. It is far preferable, however, to determine the *rate* or *flux* through the pathway under the actual physiologic conditions in the tissue at the time in question. This determination can be

. **John Ballard** · CSIRO, Division of Human Nutrition, Adelaide, South Australia 5000, Australia

made only by *in vivo* experimentation, and since radioactive isotopes are usually needed, there have been very few studies made in humans. While enzyme activity measurements give some clue to the potential maximum activity of a pathway, they give no information on the actual metabolic flux. Indeed, even a large increase or decrease in an enzyme activity may not reflect a change in flux. For this reason, I shall stress those studies in which flux measurements have been attempted.

2. Development of Metabolic Pathways

2.1. Glycogen Synthesis and Degradation

It has been more than a hundred years since Claude Bernard[11] described the accumulation of glycogen in fetal liver, and it is now clearly established that glycogen can account for up to 10% of the liver wet weight at term.[68] Indeed, electron-microscopic analysis of 21-day fetal rat liver shows hepatocytes in which essentially all the cytoplasm is occupied by glycogen granules.[28] When allowance is made for the numbers of hemopoietic cells in fetal liver, it is apparent that the glycogen content of hepatocytes at term is about 15% by weight. Although these high values in rat liver are rather extreme, livers of all mammalian species that have been investigated have large glycogen reserves at the end of gestation.[68] While many fetal tissues contain glycogen, only liver has the capability to degrade glycogen to glucose for the replenishment of blood glucose, a process known to occur by the first day after birth. I shall discuss these changes in hepatic glycogen content not only for the purpose of describing the causative effects, but also as a basis for an understanding of the various abnormalities in the regulation of blood glucose levels.

Some species, such as the lamb, monkey, and human, have detectable liver glycogen before the last quarter of gestation, while other and usually smaller mammals, such as the rat and guinea pig, have no glycogen until near term.[68] An understanding of the changes responsible for the initiation of glycogen deposition can best be obtained from a study of the latter group, since one can measure the levels and activities of potential regulators before, as well as during, the glycogen–accumulation period. Since the fetus is supplied with glucose via the maternal circulation at all developmental stages, some factor other than precursor availability must

trigger glycogen deposition. Activity measurements of the enzymes in fetal rat liver that catalyze reactions from glucose to glycogen, viz., hexokinase, phosphoglucomutase, UDPG pyrophosphorylase, UDPG glycogen synthetase, and branching enzyme, show that hexokinase is present throughout gestation, while the activities of the other enzymes parallel the increase in glycogen[7,25] (Fig. 1). Phosphorylase activity also increases over the same period, but since phosphorylase and UDPG glycogen synthetase catalyze opposing reactions (Fig. 2), a coordinate increase in the two enzymes cannot explain glycogen accumulation.

UDPG glycogen synthetase occurs as an active form (synthetase *a*) and an inactive form (synthetase *b*).[40] Synthetase *a* is derived from synthetase *b* by a dephosphorylation reaction that is catalyzed by synthetase phosphatase[40] (Fig. 2). Measurements in fetal rat liver show that synthetase phosphatase can first be detected at day 17 of gestation, a situation leading to the initial formation of synthetase *a* and hence glycogen deposition[25] (Fig. 1). Devos and Hers[25] point out, however, that the activity of synthetase *a* is just sufficient to account for the rate of glycogen accumulation. The low activity must therefore reflect an extremely low activity of phosphorylase *a* (the active form), notwithstanding the considerable total phosphorylase activity present in fetal liver. Although measurements of phosphorylase *a* and *b* activities show a considerable amount of the active form in fetal rat liver, elegant isotope incorporation experiments eliminate the possibility of substantial glycogen breakdown.[25] Apparently, the observed phosphorylase *a* activity is an artifact caused by the extremely rapid formation of this enzyme after anesthesia of the mother or excision of fetal liver samples. To summarize, glycogen accumulation occurs in late fetal liver, even though the opposing synthetase and phosphorylase are both increasing in activity, since the synthetase is in the active (*a*) form, while the phosphorylase is present as the inactive (*b*) form.

What hormonal or other factors contribute to the activation of synthetase, the inactivation of phosphorylase, and the resultant accumulation of glycogen in fetal liver? The interrelationships between the two series of cascade reactions leading to the formation of synthetase *a* and phosphorylase *a* eliminate a simple answer to this question, although some information can be obtained from the individual actions of pertinent hormones (see Table I).

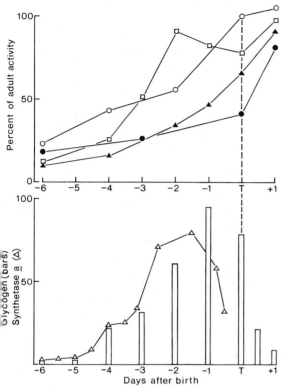

Fig. 1. Glycogen accumulation and enzymes of glycogen metabolism in fetal rat liver. Phosphoglucomutase[7] (○), phosphorylase $a + b$[7] (▲), UDPG pyrophosphorylase[7] (●), and glycogen synthetase $a + b$[7] (□) activities are expressed as percentages of the activities in adult liver; glycogen synthetase a[25] activity is in milliunits per gram liver (△); glycogen content[25] (bars) is given in milligrams per gram liver.

Table I. Hormonal Effects on Glycogen Metabolism in Fetal and Neonatal Liver

Hormone	Observed action[a]	
Glucocorticoids[27,78]	Synthetase $a + b$	↑
	Phosphorylase a	↓
Insulin[27,40,65]	cAMP	↓?
	Synthetase a	↑
	Phosphorylase a	↓?
Glucagon[35,40,56]	cAMP	↑
	Phosphorylase a	↑
	Synthetase a	↓
	Glucose-6-phosphatase	↑

[a] Symbols: (↑) increase; (↓) decrease; (?) some doubt.

Glucocorticoids. Corticosterone increases in rat blood at about the time of initial glycogen accumulation.[41] This and other glucocorticoids act to increase the amount of total synthetase ($a + b$) present, and will restore glycogen accumulation in adrenalectomized rat fetuses.[78] Studies with fetal liver explants suggest that the increase in synthetase activity following glucocorticoid administration is not mediated by an increase in the proportion of synthetase a present.[27]

Insulin. This hormone would be expected to act to counteract a glucagon-induced increase in cyclic AMP.[40] Insulin has been shown to increase the fraction of synthetase present in the a form.[27,65]

Glucagon. cAMP concentrations increase in fetal liver toward the end of gestation,[56] and would be expected to activate phosphorylase and inactivate synthetase a.[40] Glucagon is the presumed mediator of the cAMP increase, and has been shown to induce glucose-6-phosphatase.[35]

Notwithstanding the changes in cAMP levels, it is apparent from the careful studies of Devos and Hers[25] that the high concentrations of glucocorticoids and insulin have an overriding effect and lead to glycogen accumulation.

What are the factors that control hepatic glycogen breakdown at birth? The most relevant change in enzyme content at this stage is the appearance of glucose-6-phosphatase. This enzyme, which is essential for glucose formation and thus release of glucose from hepatic parenchymal cells, has been the subject of extensive investigation. Glucose-6-phosphatase activity is very low in the liver of the fetal rat, guinea pig, lamb, mouse, and rabbit, and increases to above adult levels within a day or two

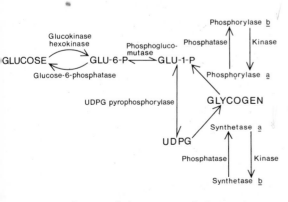

Fig. 2. Pathways of glycogen metabolism in liver.

after birth.[24] In monkey and also human fetuses, considerable glucose-6-phosphatase has been found early in gestation, but there is still a postnatal increase in activity.[24] The mechanism of the increase in activity appears to be related to the birth process itself, rather than to a particular stage in development, since premature delivery of rat fetuses is accompanied by a rapid rise in glucose-6-phosphatase activity.[24] Similarly, if birth is delayed, so is the appearance of the enzyme.[24] The importance of glucose-6-phosphatase development to the newborn is discussed in Section 3.

In the rat and human, birth is associated with an increase in blood glucagon and a decrease in blood insulin levels, presumably a consequence of neonatal hypoglycemia.[17,33,71] These hormonal changes would be expected to lead to the conversion of glycogen synthetase from the *a* form to the inactive *b* form and a concomitant increase in the active form of phosphorylase (the *a* form). Such a situation is opposite to that existing in fetal liver, and will result in net glycogen breakdown. When glycogen degradation is coupled with the increase in glucose-6-phosphatase activity, the glucose-6-phosphate that is derived from glycogen can be released from the liver. The sequence of events related to these hormonal and enzyme changes in postnatal liver is described in Table II.

2.2. Glycolysis and the Pentose Pathway

Although it is often assumed that the rate of glycolysis is higher in fetal tissues than in tissues from the newborn or adult, actual experimental data do not show such a simple picture. Villee and co-workers[79,81] found little variation in aerobic glycolysis during liver development, but if liver slices were incubated in the absence of oxygen, glycolytic rates were higher, especially in fetal liver. The stimulation of glycolysis when oxygen availability is low (the Pasteur effect) would permit fetal tissues to obtain energy by an acceleration of glycolysis. While this concept is attractive because the availability of glucose to the fetus is limited only by the mother's ability to maintain her blood sugar levels, there is only scanty evidence that a condition of "relative hypoxia" (as compared with the newborn) really does exist in the fetus, except under pathologic situations or during prolonged labor.

Age differences are not usually found when glycolytic rates are measured in liver homogenates.[23]

Table II. Sequence of Events After Birth b Which Blood Glucose Levels Are Restored b Mobilization of Liver Glycogen

1.	Birth.
2.	Maternal glucose supply stops.
3.	Blood glucose falls in the newborn.
4.	Pancreas responds by increasing glucagon releas and decreasing insulin release.
5.	Hepatic cAMP rises.
6.	Glycogen synthetase *a* activity falls; phosphorylas *a* activity increases.
7.	Glycogen synthesis depressed; glycogen breakdown accelerated.
8.	Glucose released from the liver.
9.	Blood glucose concentration restored.

The activities of enzymes involved in liver glycolysi may be higher in the fetus than the newborn, a is found with hexokinase, phosphofructokinase pyruvate kinase, and aldolase; they may be lowe (phosphoglucoseisomerase and lactate dehydrogen ase); or they may be unchanged.[15] Recent studie by D. G. Walker and his co-workers have clarified some of the discrepancies noted earlier. Thus, Le and Walker[49] showed only minor differences with age in lactate production by liver supernatant frac tions incubated with either glucose-6-phosphate o fructose diphosphate, but if homogenates were used there was a marked depression of glycolysis afte birth. This finding is interpreted as reflecting th appearance of glucose-6-phosphatase, an enzym that is present in microsomes and competes witl glycolysis for glucose-6-phosphate as well as being essential for glucose release from the liver. Accord ingly, the developing ability of the liver to ac as a glucose reserve and maintain blood glucos will in effect reduce hepatic glycolysis. Snell anc Walker[70] measured rates of glucose and lactat turnover in intact newborn rats delivered b cesarean section. The experiments show that the hig rate of glucose utilization at delivery falls to les than 20% by 2 hr after birth. By 2 days afte birth glucose utilization has increased to approxi mately 50% of the rate at delivery. The author make no definitive conclusions about the mecha nisms responsible for these dramatic changes i glucose metabolism, but draw attention to th rapid mobilization of liver and muscle glycogen i the first day after birth. Perhaps glucose utilizatio is spared in the 2-hr-old rat by the utilization o glycogen reserves and the oxidation of the substantial lactate pool.

A further factor that modulates glycolysis from glucose is the changing activity pattern of liver hexokinase and glucokinase. Although these two enzymes catalyze the same reaction, the liver-specific glucokinase has a high Michaelis constant for glucose, and will show an increased activity with increases in the blood glucose (and therefore hepatic glucose) levels. Glucokinase is not present in fetal liver of any species tested, whereas hexokinase activity with a low Michaelis constant for glucose is active.[8,82] Hexokinase will catalyze glucose phosphorylation to a maximum extent at all physiologic glucose concentrations, and since the activity of the enzyme is sufficiently low to limit glycolysis from glucose in liver, any change in hexokinase activity will be reflected in a corresponding change in glycolysis. Hexokinase activity falls in rat liver during development,[82] and with it the potential rate of glycolysis from glucose is also reduced.

In addition to glucokinase, phosphofructokinase and pyruvate kinase have been implicated as regulatory enzymes in glycolysis. The liver pyruvate kinase normally functions at a low catalytic rate, because its affinity for phosphoenolpyruvate is low.[73] However, an increased flux through the initial reactions of glycolysis (such as would be produced by a rapid increase in glucose availability) will lead to an increase in fructose diphosphate concentration. This intermediate acts as a feedforward activator of liver pyruvate kinase and increases the affinity of the enzyme for phosphoenolpyruvate. The net result will be an increased flux through the entire glycolytic sequence. This rather neat regulatory system permits the liver to channel glucose carbon via glycolysis toward lipid synthesis, so that the large increases in portal glucose concentrations following a carbohydrate meal will result in hepatic lipid synthesis. Of course, the high-Michaelis-constant glucokinase is also important in this role, and the presence of glucokinase and liver-type pyruvate kinase is most important for liver lipogenesis from glucose.

Fetal blood glucose does not reflect the large changes occurring in the maternal portal vein, and the fetus is not faced with marked alterations in glucose availability. Accordingly, it is not surprising to find low activities of the liver-type pyruvate kinase activity[52] and the absence of glucokinase in fetal liver.[82] Fetal liver contains a pyruvate kinase of the muscle type that is active

at much lower levels of phosphoenolpyruvate and is not subject to activation by fructose diphosphate.[52,73] Glucokinase and the liver-type pyruvate kinase remain absent or low, respectively, throughout the postnatal suckling period, and increase only at weaning.[52,82]

Changes in glycolytic enzymes should be considered in the context of the nutritional status of the growing infant, with transitions from a high and constant carbohydrate diet in the fetus to a high-fat diet during suckling, and finally after weaning to a high-carbohydrate diet in man and many other mammalian species. It is only in this last situation that lipid synthesis is required to provide an energy source for fasting, and it is only at this stage that there is an appearance of the glucokinase and pyruvate kinase typical of adult liver cells.

The hormonal mechanisms responsible for the increases in pyruvate kinase and glucokinase activities have not been completely resolved. Glucocorticoids may induce the enzymes prematurely so long as the young animals are given additional glucose,[43] although this point has been disputed.[58] Thyroxine levels increase in rat blood immediately prior to the increases in enzyme activities, and this hormone will initiate glucokinase synthesis as early as 2 days after birth.[58]

Analysis of enzyme changes in developing liver is plagued by the diverse cell population of the tissue, especially the large proportion of hemopoietic cells in fetal liver. Hemopoietic cells have a high glycolytic activity, and may contribute to the hexokinase and non-liver-type pyruvate kinase activities found in fetal liver.

The hexose monophosphate shunt, a series of reactions by which glucose-6-phosphate is oxidized first to 6-phosphogluconate and then to ribulose-5-phosphate, results in the reduction of NADP to NADPH. The NADPH is required for the synthesis of triglycerides and steriods, and accordingly, the pathway is present at a high activity in lipogenic tissues. Since the hexose monophosphate shunt catalyzes the removal of carbon-1 of glucose as CO_2, experiments with glucose specifically labeled in carbons-1 and -6 have been used to evaluate the fraction of glucose that is metabolized via the shunt. Although there are some criticisms of the quantitative validity of this experimental approach,[47] the method has been widely used. Results show a high activity of the hexose monophosphate shunt in fetal liver, in confirmation of the lipogenic capacity of the tissue at this time.[2,80] Likewise, the two key dehydrogenases of the shunt, glucose-6-phosphate dehydrogenase and 6-phosphogluconate dehydrogenase, are present at high activities in fetal liver.[15]

2.3. Gluconeogenesis

Gluconeogenesis, the process by which glucose is synthesized from lactate, glycerol, propionate, and certain amino acids, is a most important function of the liver, so much so that if it has been calculated to account for up to half the energy utilization of the tissue.[85] Although the pathway is found in kidney and possibly intestinal mucosa as well as in the liver, it is well established that the majority of *de novo* glucose synthesis occurs in the liver.[66]

The sequence of gluconeogenesis is essentially the reversal of glycolysis, but with specific enzyme-catalyzed reactions overcoming energetic barriers in glycolysis. Thus, glucose-6-phosphatase, fructose diphosphatase, phosphoenolpyruvate carboxykinase, and pyruvate carboxylase are essentially irreversible enzymes in the gluconeogenic pathway that compete with the glycolytic enzymes hexokinase (or glucokinase), phosphofructokinase, and pyruvate kinase.[66] Gluconeogenesis from lactate, pyruvate, or alanine requires 6 mol nucleotide triphosphate to provide the energy for the synthesis of 1 mol glucose. Because of this large energy expenditure, it would be expected that a situation with a constant supply of glucose, i.e., the fetus, would be accompanied by a low activity of gluconeogenesis. Numerous studies with developing rat liver have confirmed the initial finding[7] that gluconeogenesis is absent in the fetus and develops within a few hours after birth. Many substrates have been tested with liver slices, but with the possible exception of compounds that enter the gluconeogenic sequence above phosphoenolpyruvate, essentially no glucose synthesis is detectable. Investigations of the activities of the four key gluconeogenic enzymes in rat liver during the period between 1 day before birth and 1 day after birth (Table III) show 2- to 4-fold increases in glucose-6-phosphatase, fructose diphosphatase, and pyruvate carboxylase, while phosphoenolpyruvate carboxykinase increases by about 50-fold over the 2 days.[9]

Three aspects of this increase in phosphoenolpyruvate carboxykinase have been investigated in recent years: (1) whether the enzyme is truly rate-limiting, so that there is a concomitant increase in pathway activity with the increase in enzyme

Table III. Changes in Gluconeogenic Flux, Key Enzymes, and Metabolites in Developing Rat Liver[a]

Measurement	1 day before birth	1 day after birth
Gluconeogenic flux[7]	0.02	0.63
Glucose-6-phosphatase[7]	6.5	17
Fructose diphosphatase[7]	0.6	2
Pyruvate carboxylase[9]	4.0	12.7
Phosphoenolpyruvate carboxykinase[9,38]	0.05	2.6
Lactate[6,9]	5.25	0.55
ATP/ADP[6,9]	1.77	6.20

[a] Rates are expressed as micromoles per minute per gram liver; lactate, as micromoles per gram liver.

activity; (2) whether factors other than phosphoenolpyruvate carboxykinase may be important in the initiation of pathway activity; and (3) what the situation is in other species, especially the neonatal human.

Phosphoenolpyruvate carboxykinase can be induced *in utero* by the injection of either glucagon or cAMP directly into the fetus.[38,87] Shortly after these treatments, there is an increase in the synthesis rate of the enzyme, and within a few hours, activity may be increased by up to 10-fold.[38] When liver slices are prepared from these fetuses and incubated with a gluconeogenic precursor such as lactate, it is found that the overall rate of glucose synthesis increases to about the same extent as the change in enzyme activity.[9] Other experiments have established that net protein synthesis is required for the increase in enzyme activity,[38,87] whereas the occurrence of significant amounts of an inactive enzyme precursor has been eliminated.[60]

Since gluconeogenesis cannot occur without appropriate substrates or without large amounts of nucleotide triphosphate, regardless of the activities of phosphoenolpyruvate carboxykinase or other key enzymes, it is possible that factors other than enzyme availability may limit glucose synthesis. Fetal blood levels of lactate and amino acids are about the same as found in the maternal blood, while lactate concentrations markedly increase during the birth process in the rat.[7,70] The situation in the human is less clear, although blood lactate in the newborn is higher than found later in life.[57,61] A deficiency of nucleotide triphosphates may indeed occur in fetal rat liver or in the liver of the neonate during the first half hour after birth,[9] resulting from a lower degree of phosphorylation of the adenine nucleotide pool. Thus, the ATP/ADP ratio is about 4 in liver from adult rats and 7 in day-old newborns, but only 1.5–2.0 in fetal liver or in newborn rats prior to breathing.[6,9] We have tried to assess the significance of these lowered ATP/ADP ratios by comparing the rate of gluconeogenesis in the intact fetal rat to that found in the suckling animal.[59] Not surprisingly, since phosphoenolpyruvate carboxykinase is absent, we found no gluconeogenesis in the intact fetus.[9,59] What was surprising, however, was the complete lack of glucose synthesis from pyruvate and other precursors in fetuses that had been injected with glucagon some hours previously.[9,59] As mentioned above, these fetuses had high activities of phosphoenolpyruvate carboxykinase and the other gluconeogenic enzymes, and liver slices had the capacity to convert lactate to glucose.[9,59] Obviously, the pathway of gluconeogenesis was present, but it was not active (Table IV). We reasoned that a relative hypoxic situation *in vivo* was likely to be responsible for the inactive pathway, and we were able to create a similar situation in suckling rats by exposing them to hypoxic conditions. Gluconeogenesis was diminished in these animals during rather mild hypoxia.[9]

Unfortunately, the experiments with fetal rats were acute studies and necessitated the use of anesthesia. The absence of fetal gluconeogenesis could have been the result of anesthesia difficulties, and need not reflect the true situation in the fetus. This interpretation seems especially possible, since Snell and Walker[70] found substantial gluconeogenic rates in the newborn rat within an hour after birth. To overcome any difficulty associated with anesthesia, we measured rates of glucose synthesis in fetal sheep that had been cannulated some days previously[84]. The pregnant ewes were conscious and active and the fetuses healthy. Several fetuses with femoral cannulae were subsequently born either naturally or by cesarean section and were quite normal. No gluconeogenesis could be detected in any fetal sheep, even though phosphoenolpyruvate carboxykinase and the other gluconeogenic enzymes were present at activities comparable to those found in the adult. If, however, the radioactive gluconeogenic precursor was injected into the

Table IV. Premature Induction of Phosphoenolpyruvate Carboxykinase in Rat Liver and Effects on Gluconeogenesis *in Vitro* and *in Vivo*[a]

Measurement	Control fetus[b]	Glucagon-treated fetus[b]
Phosphoenolpyruvate carboxykinase	2.2	43
Gluconeogenesis		
liver slices	4.3	51
in vivo	0.2	0.2

[a] Data from Ballard and Philippidis[9] and Philippidis and Ballard.[59]
[b] Values are expressed as percentages of those found in 1-day newborn rats.

young lamb as early as 3 min after birth, a substantial rate of glucose synthesis could be measured. On the other hand, lambs that were premature and had breathing difficulties (with the concomitant problems of hypoxia) showed no glucose synthesis during the hypoxic period. We therefore consider that gluconeogenesis does not occur in fetuses, even though some may have the full complement of gluconeogenic enzymes.

The ability of the sheep fetus to initiate glucose formation immediately after birth is not shared by the rat, which must first synthesize phosphoenolpyruvate carboxykinase, a process that takes several hours. Clearly, the newborn rat is more dependent on carbohydrate stores (glycogen) and on exogenous food than sheep. It appears that most species tested are more similar in this regard to the sheep than to the rat. Accordingly, guinea pigs,[32] pigs,[75] cattle,[32] and human infants[62] have substantial phosphoenolpyruvate carboxykinase activities *in utero* and all should be capable of gluconeogenesis within a few minutes after birth. Further aspects of the regulation of blood glucose and the role of gluconeogenesis are discussed in Section 3.

2.4. Interconversion of Hexoses

Galactose and fructose are present in human diets at various gestational ages. These sugars are phosphorylated in the liver by specific phosphotransferases at the carbon-1 position to form galactose-1-phosphate and fructose-1-phosphate, respectively. Although intestinal mucosa and other extrahepatic tissues may metabolize these hexoses for the production of energy within the tissues, glucose cannot be formed unless glucose-6-phosphatase is present. Since this enzyme is localized primarily in the liver and kidney, it can be inferred that glucose formed from either galactose or fructose has been derived from liver or kidney. Of course, the non-glucose hexoses may be glycolysed to lactate and the lactate released from cells as a transmitted nutrient. Some isotopic evidence suggests that a process of this latter type may occur during absorption of galactose or fructose in the intestinal mucosa, but the high concentrations of the hexoses in portal blood argues strongly in favor of the direct transmission of these sugars to the blood.

Galactose is formed from lactose by lactase in the intestine, and is absorbed and passed to the liver for phosphorylation by galactokinase. This enzyme has both a high affinity for galactose and a high activity, at least during the suckling stage.[5,22] Experiments with rats show maximum activities of galactose uptake, galactokinase, and galactose-1-phosphate uridyl transferase, and the overall conversion of galactose to glycogen in liver tissue shortly after birth.[10,22,67] Accordingly, the suckling infant is well adapted to a diet in which the carbohydrate may be up to 50% galactose.

Although direct measurements of the relevant enzymes and the rates of galactose metabolism by the liver of human infants have apparently not been made, quantitative studies on the overall turnover of galactose in humans reveal a situation in which high concentrations of infused galactose are metabolized in newborns at 2–4 times the rate in adults.[12] This metabolism is reflected in a higher increment in glucose concentration in newborns after galactose ingestion.[26] It is not implied that adults are unable to utilize galactose for glucose production; instead, the newborn has a capacity to use very large amounts of the sugar. The age-dependent decrease in glucose production from galactose is accompanied by an increase rather than a decrease in the galactose removal rate from blood, so long as the measurements are carried out at low galactose concentrations.[26] This more rapid galactose clearance rate from blood in adults cannot be explained by a higher galactose uptake and utilization by erythrocytes, since these cells have a lower capacity to convert [1-^{14}C]galactose to $^{14}CO_2$ in adults than in newborn infants.[26] Indeed, the relative importance of erythrocytes in galactose utilization may be very slight as compared to either gut

or liver,[18] although no quantitative physiological comparisons have been made. Certainly, the initial enzyme in galactose metabolism, galactokinase, has an activity in liver some 100 times greater than found in erythrocytes,[22,26] so that low concentrations of galactose are cleared by a single passage through the liver.[77]

Fructose, like galactose, is efficiently extracted by the liver. A major difference between the two sugars is the ability of the nonspecific hexokinase of muscle and other tissues to phosphorylate fructose.[21] Galactose is not a substrate of any mammalian hexokinase.[21] The difference is somewhat theoretical, however, because fructose phosphorylation by hexokinase occurs only at high fructose concentrations,[37] and is inhibited competitively and powerfully by glucose,[21] a situation that precludes fructose metabolism by muscle unless the sugar is present at extremely high concentrations.

There is one physiologic example of high fructose levels in blood. Fetal whales and ungulates[34] have blood fructose concentrations of approximately 100 mg/dl at developmental stages in which the glucose concentration is 20 mg/dl or less. Although these results have been known for many years, there is no convincing evidence for a role of fructose during the fetal development of such species. For example, fructose can be used only at a very slow rate by fetal sheep, a limitation caused by the negligible activity of hepatic fructokinase.[8] What is even more puzzling is the postnatal fate of fructose in ungulates. Fructose is not metabolized to any extent by the newborn,[3] but instead is excreted in the urine. Fructokinase activity certainly develops in the neonate, but only after 2–5 days,[8] well after the blood fructose concentrations have been depleted. It is possible that the fructose in fetal ungulates may act as a carbohydrate reserve in an analogous way to glycogen, but the fact that it is excreted rather than metabolized seems to argue against such a hypothesis; alternatively, fructose may have an osmotic effect. No definitive conclusions can be made at present.

The simultaneous occurrence of fructose and sorbitol in fetal ungulates led to the suggestion that fructose might be formed from glucose via sorbitol.[39] The enzymes involved, aldose reductase and sorbitol dehydrogenase, are present in placenta and fetal sheep liver, respectively, and it seems most probable that glucose obtained from the mother is reduced to sorbitol in the placenta, transmitted to the fetal liver, and there oxidized to fructose. Other vidence argues for both reactions occurring in placental tissue. The sorbitol pathway does not occur in the placenta/fetal liver of nonungulates, ut it is present in the testes of adult mammals and accounts for the formation of fructose in seminal uid.[39]

Fructose utilization in other mammalian species s similar to that described above for newborn sheep. Thus, fructokinase activity is essentially absent in etal liver and develops shortly after birth.[83] There s a parallel appearance of fructose-1-phosphate aldolase as well as triokinase at about the same levelopmental stage.[83] Of these enzymes, it appears hat the specific aldolase limits the overall metabolism of fructose, a situation resulting in the massive accumulation of fructose-1-phosphate under conditions of fructose loading.[83] Fetal animals liffer from the newborn, since *both* fructokinase and he aldolase are deficient.[83]

Because fructose metabolism is not finely regulated by insulin, the sugar has been infused into human infants as a nutritional alternative to glucose. This procedure can be valuable, especially in diabetics or during liver disease, but it can be counterproductive if larger amounts of fructose are infused han can be metabolized by the liver.[14] In such cases, there is an accumulation of fructose-1-phosphate and a concomitant decrease in hepatic ATP and inorganic phosphate.[14,86] A result of these changes is an acceleration of glycolysis, with a resultant lactic acidosis and hypoglycemia.[14]

Careful measurements in human infants showed an effective fructose utilization rate of 1 g fructose/kg body weight per hour in 4- to 6-day-old infants, and a value about twice as great in 6-month-old babies.[13] Less than 10% of this fructose was excreted. Nevertheless, premature newborns appeared to form less glucose from infused fructose than full-term infants. By 10–12 days after birth, the premature babies gave a hyperglycemic response to fructose infusion, implying the attainment of normal fructose metabolism.[13]

3. Regulation of Blood Glucose Levels

3.1. Normal Transition from Fetus to Newborn

In adult mammals, the liver has the capacity to remove glucose from the blood in times of glucose excess and return it to the blood during periods of

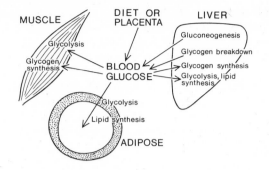

Fig. 3. Schematic representation of the major reactions responsible for producing or utilizing glucose from the blood pool.

glucose insufficiency.[55] Other tissues contribute to the removal of glucose from the blood. Thus adipose tissue and muscle take up the sugar and convert it to triglyceride and glycogen, respectively. Alterations in the rate of glucose uptake by these tissues will certainly affect blood glucose levels (see Fig. 3) but since they do not contain glucose-6-phosphatase they cannot release glucose into the blood (Fig. 3). Gluconeogenesis is active in kidney cortex, and can result in glucose release. The precise metabolic function of gluconeogenesis in kidney is not established, although it seems to be related to the regulation of the acid–base status. I shall not consider the development of kidney gluconeogenesis, since it is unlikely that the pathway plays a major role in the overall glucose balance of the infant.

The factors that contribute to the regulation of blood glucose by the liver are listed in Table V and will be considered separately. Liver cells are freely permeable to glucose, a property that facilitates both glucose uptake and release. The presence of a glucokinase with a Michaelis constant of 10 mM for glucose enables the hepatocyte to phosphorylate more glucose as the blood levels increase in the range 3–10 mM.[82] Metabolism of glucose by liver can be considered as occurring by a reversible pathway toward glycogen and an irreversible pathway toward oxidation or storage as triglyceride. Of course, triglyceride is not an inert product, but lipolysis and fatty acid oxidation cannot produce significant amounts of glucogenic substrates. Glycogen synthesis, on the other hand, can be reversed and glucose produced as required. The amount of glucose that can be stored as glycogen is limited, however, by the relatively small size of the liver. Accordingly, glycogen serves as only a transient source, and can replenish blood glucose for only a

Table V. Assessment of Factors That Contribute to Glucose Uptake or Output by the Liver During Development[a]

	Uptake			Output			
	Glucokinase	Glycogen synthesis	Glycolysis	Glucose-6-phosphatase	Glycogen breakdown	Gluconeogenic enzymes	Gluconeogenic flux
Rat							
Midterm fetus	−	−	+	−	−	−	−
Term fetus	−	+	+	±	−	−	−
Immediate newborn	−	−	+	+	+	−	−
1-day young	−	±	+	+	±	+	+
Weaning	±	+	+	+	+	+	+
Adult	+	+	+	+	+	+	+
Human							
Midterm fetus	−?	+	+	+	±?	±	−?
Term fetus	−?	+	+	+	±?	+	−?
Immediate newborn	−?	−	+	+	+	+	+
1-day young	−?	±	+	+	±	+	+
Weaning	±?	+	+	+	+	+	+
Adult	+	+	+	+	+	+	+

[a] Symbols: (−) absent; (±) low capability or activity; (+) active; (?) no reliable data.

limited time. Gluconeogenesis, on the other hand, utilizes amino acids, which in turn may be obtained from the body's protein reserves. So long as the gluconeogenic pathway is active, glucose can be synthesized even during prolonged starvation.

Some of the developmental changes pertinent to the regulation of blood glucose have already been considered. Fetal liver does not contain glucokinase,[8,22] and is not capable of finely regulated glucose uptake. Glycogen is present in fetal liver, and can be mobilized to some extent, particularly toward the end of gestation. Thus, maternal starvation, hypoxia, insulin insufficiency, glucagon, or adrenalin treatment will depress glycogen levels in sheep and probably human fetuses.[1,35,46] Since sheep and human fetal liver contain appreciable amounts of glucose-6-phosphatase,[24] any glycogenolytic stimulus can result in hepatic glucose production. This response cannot occur to any extent in fetal rats due to the lack of glucose-6-phosphatase until the last few days of gestation.[24] Moreover, rat liver does not contain glycogen until the last quarter of gestation.[68]

Although the liver of the human fetus may have the capacity to convert glycogen to glucose, it is doubtful whether the pathway occurs under normal physiologic conditions. Instead, the mother regulates fetal glucose levels indirectly, through maintenance of her own blood levels.[1] This arrangement obviates the necessity of the fetus controlling its own blood glucose concentrations, and it would seem that breakdown of fetal glycogen would be undesirable during continual fetal growth.

The situation regarding gluconeogenesis has been discussed in a previous section. Suffice it to say that although fetal liver may have the enzymes required for the pathway, there is no evidence in favor of gluconeogenesis in the intact fetus.[9,59,84] If these suppositions regarding glycogenolysis and gluconeogenesis are valid, then the fetal liver plays a very passive role with respect to the regulation of blood glucose.

Mention should be made here of the overall importance of glucose in fetal nutrition. Although large amounts of amino acids are passed to the fetus,[1,36] these are used primarily for the synthesis of fetal proteins, rather than as an energy source. Nevertheless, amino acids can account for about 25% of the oxidative energy in fetal sheep.[1,36] Lipids, on the other hand, do not seem to be important metabolic fuels for the fetus.[1,44] This result was predicted by early experiments in which a fetal respiratory quotient of about 1 was reported, and was confirmed by more recent studies in which radioactive fatty acids were infused into the mother.[1] Estimates of the quantitative importance of glucose as a metabolic fuel in fetuses range from nearly 100% to less than 50%.[1,76] Whatever the true value is under any particular pregnancy state, glucose is certainly the most important fuel for fetal metabolism.

Birth forces the newborn infant to regulate its own glucose levels. Fluctuations in blood glucose concentrations in the neonate occur to a much greater extent than is found in adults,[1] and are caused by the different times of appearance of the various metabolic sequences, enzymes, and hormonal responses. There are also major interspecies differences with respect to the ability of the liver in the newborn to carry out these processes. In full-term human infants, the cessation of maternal glucose supply is first noted as a fall in the blood glucose from approximately 70 to 50 mg/dl.[1,71] This change occurs within the first hour or so after birth, and is accompanied by an increase in blood glucagon and perhaps a fall in blood insulin.[71] The observed change in the glucagon/insulin ratio is most likely caused by a direct recognition of the falling blood glucose by pancreatic receptors, although clear evidence of a cause-and-effect relationship has not been obtained. These hormone changes may be accompanied by an increase in blood catecholamines. A catecholamine response can be predicted as a direct consequence of trauma associated with birth, but again, no measurements have been recorded. Nevertheless, the effect of a catecholamine increase on blood glucose levels will be similar to that caused by the glucagon and insulin changes, and is also mediated by an increase in hepatic cAMP.[25,55] This nucleotide will activate phosphorylase, reduce the activity of glycogen synthetase, and thus produce a coordinate glycogenolytic response.[25] Since glucose-6-phosphatase is present at a high level in full-term human infants,[62] glycogen breakdown will lead to glucose release.

At the same time or even before glycogenolysis is stimulated, gluconeogenesis may be activated. As mentioned previously, newborn sheep commence gluconeogenesis within 3 min of birth,[84] and perhaps a similar activation occurs in human infants. The actual processes involved in the rapid onset of gluconeogenesis are not understood, al-though they are delayed until breathing commences and the tissues are further oxygenated. There are indirect experiments suggesting that the gluconeogenic pathway may not be as active in the newborn human as is found a few days later. Thus, the utilization of lactate[16] and alanine is low in the newborn.

The premature human infant can perhaps be compared with the newborn rat in its gluconeogenic ability. Rat liver does not contain the full complement of gluconeogenic enzymes at birth, with phosphoenolpyruvate carboxykinase present at an activity less than 5% of that found in the adult.[9] Since this enzyme is induced by cAMP and repressed by insulin,[38] the observed postnatal changes in the glucagon/insulin ratio[33] will initiate the synthesis of phosphoenolpyruvate carboxykinase. By 48 hr after birth in the rat, gluconeogenic capacity is high, and phosphoenolpyruvate carboxykinase activity has increased to that found in the starved adult.[6,9] The activity of this enzyme is quite low in the livers of preterm human infants, and there is a postnatal enzyme increase.[62]

If neonatal hypoglycemia is treated by glucose infusion or feeding, the blood glucose may be raised but the gluconeogenic capacity of the newborn retarded. This effect results from the ability of glucose and various other hexoses to repress the increase in phosphoenolpyruvate carboxykinase activity, at least in rats.[87]

3.2. Disorders of Blood Glucose Regulation in Human Infants

This section is perhaps not appropriate for a chapter on carbohydrate metabolism during normal development. However, I have stressed the difficulties that must be overcome before a researcher can obtain valid measurements of metabolic flux in normal human infants, and I consider that much of the useful information on the relative importance of individual reactions or metabolic sequences has been derived from human conditions in which a particular reaction pathway is absent. To put it simply, we learn of the normal by investigating the abnormal.

Abnormalities in the control of blood glucose will rarely cause difficulties for the fetus, since, as discussed in the preceding section, the maintenance of fetal glucose levels is a function carried out by the maternal liver. After birth, this control ceases. A transient hypoglycemia in the first few hours after birth should be considered as a nor-

Table VI. Disorders of Blood Glucose Regulation—Possible Changes in Reaction Rates that Contribute to the Observed Hypoglycemia[a]

Disorder	Reaction and possible rate change			
	Glycogen synthesis, liver	Glycolysis, liver and peripheral tissues	Glycogen breakdown, liver	Gluconeogenesis, liver
Transient hypoglycemia in low-birth-weight infants	0	0	↓	↓
Children of diabetic mothers (insulin excess)	↑	↑	↓	↓
"Glycogen storage diseases"				
Phosphorylase or debranching enzyme deficiencies	0	0	↓↓	0 to ↑
Synthetase or branching enzyme deficiencies	↓↓	0	↓↓	0
Glucose-6-phosphatase deficiency	0	0	↓↓	↓↓
Gluconeogenesis defects				
Specific enzyme deficiencies	0	0	0	↓↓
Biotin, riboflavin, pyridoxal deficiencies	0	0	0	↓ to ↓↓
Hereditary fructose intolerance (effects following a fructose meal)	0	↑↑	↓	↓
Galactosemia				
(effects following a galactose meal)	0	↑ to ↑	↓	0
Hypoxia	↓	↑↑	↑	↓

[a] Symbols: (0), no effect; (↑, ↓) slight increase or decrease; (↑, ↓) moderate increase or decrease; (↑↑, ↓↓) severe increase or decrease.

mal physiologic event,[1] but more prolonged hypoglycemia or symtomatic hypoglycemia can occur as a result of a variety of defects that in some instances can be traced to maternal or placental abnormalities. In other cases, they may be caused by genetic defects in the newborn. I do not propose to discuss all the known abnormalities at length; instead, I shall illustrate the similarities and differences among the various groups. The possible sites of action for each condition are given in Table VI. It should be stressed that the effects have been predicted after consideration of known changes, and are not always based on direct measurements.

3.2.1. Transient Symptomatic Hypoglycemia in Full-Term, Low-Birth-Weight Infants

Hypoglycemia in infants with low birth weights has been described on numerous occasions. Cornblath and Schwartz[20] list a birth weight below the 10th percentile, the smaller member of twins, and

toxemia or placental insufficiency as factors that predispose the infant to hypoglycemia. In all cases, the failure to grow in utero can be attributed to inadequate nutrition of the fetus. Such fetuses would be expected to have reduced hepatic glycogen levels, although postnatal glucagon administration usually produces a glycemic response.[1] Since no information on gluconeogenesis in these fetuses is available, a clear distinction cannot be made between inadequate glycogenolysis and a reduced gluconeogenic rate as a prime cause of the neonatal hypoglycemia. However, liver glycogen levels were very low in low-birth-weight term infants dying within the first few days after birth.[69] There are no indications of an accelerated rate of glucose utilization that could account for the hypoglycemia in these full-term infants.

3.2.2. Hypoglycemia in Children of Diabetic Mothers

Development in utero of children whose mothers are insulin-dependent is characterized by high fetal blood glucose and the presence of insulin antibodies.[1] Except for a propensity to obesity, growth is usually normal. After birth, on the other hand, there may be a sharp drop in blood glucose,[50] presumably caused by the large amount of insulin secreted as a result of β-cell hyperplasia.[72] Yet direct evidence of an elevated insulin level in infants of diabetic mothers dependent on exogenous insulin is not available because of the insulin antibodies present in fetal blood.[1,30] An insulin excess could produce hypoglycemia by a variety of means, such as reduction in phosphorylase activation, maintenance of glycogen synthetase in the active form, inhibition of phosphoenolpyruvate carboxykinase induction, or an increased rate of glucose utilization by extrahepatic tissues. The magnitude of these effects would be determined by the severity of the hyperinsulinemia and the efficacy of compensating hormonal responses. Although glucose infusion will reverse the hypoglycemic symptoms, it may also delay the compensating hormonal changes, especially if the gluconeogenic pathway is not fully developed. Since glucagon or adrenalin will counteract the effects of high insulin levels as well as induce phosphoenolpyruvate carboxykinase, the administration of one of these hormones together with glucose may be a more appropriate treatment than glucose infusion alone.

3.2.3. Inability to Utilize Liver Glycogen Stores

Hypoglycemia may result from those glycogen storage diseases characterized by the inability to mobilize glycogen. Thus, infants with a deficiency of debranching enzyme, phosphorylase, or phosphorylase b kinase in liver are characterized by a poor or absent glycemic response to glucagon.[54] Hypoglycemia will accompany fasting unless there is a compensatory increase in gluconeogenesis. A similar lack of glucagon response and a fasting hypoglycemia will also occur in branching enzyme deficiency or glycogen synthetase deficiency, but in these two glycogen storage diseases, the lack of a glycogenolytic effect is due to the absence of glycogen rather than an inability to degrade it. Actually, a polysaccharide storage product is present in branching enzyme deficiency, but the abnormal "glycogen" formed is less accessible to phosphorylase action.[51] A detailed discussion of these diseases, the muscle-specific glycogen storage diseases, and

their diagnosis and control is given in the review by Moses and Gutman.[54]

3.2.4. Gluconeogenic Defects

Fasting hypoglycemia accompanied by lactic acidosis and hyperalaninemia will occur if any of the four key gluconeogenic enzymes are absent or below a critical activity. Indeed, deficiencies of each of the enzymes have been noted in human infants: glucose-6-phosphatase[19,54] (von Gierke's disease), fructose diphosphatase,[4,29] phosphoenolpyruvate carboxykinase,[48] and pyruvate carboxylase[42] (Leigh's encephalomyelopathy). Of course, an absence of glucose-6-phosphatase will prevent glycogenolysis as well as gluconeogenesis. In each of these deficiency states, an accumulation of lactate (and pyruvate) will accompany exercise, whereas net protein degradation in muscle will result in alanine and glutamine release from that tissue. Both amino acids would be expected to increase, although I have not seen any reports of hyperglutaminemia accompanying hypoglycemia.

Because amino acids are the major substrates for gluconeogenesis except during severe exercise, a reduced activity or the absence of transaminases will restrict gluconeogenesis. Some transaminase deficiencies have been noted,[63] but since pyridoxal phosphate is an obligatory cofactor for the transaminases, a restriction in vitamin B_6 availability will have a more general effect. Deficiencies of biotin or thiamine may lead to an inhibition of gluconeogenesis, since these vitamins are cofactors for pyruvate carboxylase and pyruvate dehydrogenase, respectively.

3.2.5. Disorders of Fructose and Galactose Metabolism

Genetic deficiency states in which either galactokinase[18,53] or fructokinase[64] is absent lead to an inability to metabolize these sugars. Hypoglycemia is not usually found. If, on the other hand, the sugars can be phosphorylated to form galactose-1-phosphate or fructose-1-phosphate, a block in the subsequent metabolism of the sugar phosphates will influence overall carbohydrate metabolism. An accumulation of fructose-1-phosphate in infants lacking the liver-specific fructose-1-phosphate aldolase will occur after fructose ingestion.[31] Not only is fructose-1-phosphate a powerful inhibitor of phosphorylase,[74] but the enormous increase in this sugar phosphate after a fructose-containing meal will deplete inorganic phosphate and ATP. Accordingly, glycogenolysis is lowered both by phosphorylase inhibition and by a reduction in inorganic phosphate availability, while the change in adenine nucleotide proportions will accelerate glycolysis and inhibit gluconeogenesis.[74] The resultant hypoglycemia may be very severe.

Galactose-1-phosphate accumulates in galactosemic infants lacking galactose-1-phosphate uridyl transferase.[26] Hypoglycemia occurs to some extent in these infants, but since the more deleterious consequences of galactosemia do not seem to be related to hypoglycemia, a discussion of them would be out of place in this review.

An inability to hydrolyze lactose in the intestine occurs in all adult mammals with the exception of some human populations,[45] and is caused by the absence of intestinal lactase. Lactase activity is present in suckling infants, however, and lactose intolerance is rare at this age.[45]

3.2.6. Neonatal Hypoxia

Some discussion of neonatal hypoxia is appropriate in a section on disorders of blood glucose regulation. Large amounts of oxygen are required to generate the ATP needed for gluconeogenesis, and it has been argued that fetal oxygenation is not adequate to support gluconeogenesis.[84] The increase in oxygen concentration between the fetus and neonate in human development is probably minimal, and is not accompanied by the large changes in adenine nucleotide proportions that occur in rat liver at the same stage. Nevertheless, the liver can apparently restrict ATP utilization to processes that are essential to the hepatocyte,[6,9] at the expense of gluconeogenesis and other processes that are of benefit to extrahepatic tissues. Accordingly, a slightly lower rate of ATP generation in fetal liver or during neonatal hypoxia could markedly reduce gluconeogenesis. The mechanism of this putative regulatory control by which ATP is diverted away from gluconeogenesis toward "essential" processes in the cell is completely unknown. Yet an investigation into the effect may help explain how gluconeogenesis is inhibited in fetal animals and in newborns exposed to moderate hypoxia.[6,59,61,84]

4. Summary and Conclusions

Fetuses obtain most of their nutrient energy as glucose but have a very restricted ability to regulate their blood glucose levels, a function that is carried out by the mother. Immediately after birth, the neonate must develop the capacity to regulate its own blood sugar, and it must be able to do this at a time when the diet changes from high-carbohydrate to high-fat. Even the small amount of carbohydrate present in milk is there as lactose, so that the infant must be able to hydrolyze this sugar to glucose and galactose and then utilize the galactose formed. Clearly, these capacities are present in the neonate.

The regulation of blood glucose appears in three postnatal stages, two of which are combined in man and some other species. First, there is an activation of glycogenolysis and an inhibition of glycogen synthesis. This combined effect is caused primarily by an increase in the cAMP concentration, and results from alterations in glucagon, adrenalin, and insulin levels. The second stage is the development of gluconeogenesis, probably via a derepression of the gene coding for phosphoenolpyruvate carboxykinase. The same hormonal changes mentioned above are the causative agents, although the synthesis of phosphoenolpyruvate carboxykinase is much slower than the glycogenolytic response. In human infants, it is likely that some gluconeogenic capacity is present immediately after birth, since phosphoenolpyruvate carboxykinase occurs in fetal liver. The third stage in the maturation of glucose regulation does not take place until weaning, at least in the rat. This stage is associated with the initial appearance of the high-K_m hepatic glucokinase. The kinetic properties of glucokinase permit the liver to instantly increase or decrease the glucose uptake with increases or decreases in portal blood glucose concentrations. Neither hormonal changes nor enzyme synthesis is required. Once glucokinase activity appears, the liver can carry out blood glucose regulation with an ability equivalent to that found in adult tissue.

In the past few years, many genetic defects of liver carbohydrate metabolism have been discovered. Further investigation of these rare conditions will facilitate a more complete understanding of the importance of the various metabolic pathways. If a study of genetic defects is accompanied by measurements of overall flux in the discrete pathways that make up carbohydrate metabolism, we will be in a much better position to both recognize human abnormalities and treat them in the most satisfactory manner. A restriction on the use of radioactive substrates will limit our measurements of pathway flux in human infants, but a growing appreciation of the uses of stable isotopes and the more widespread availability of the appropriate measuring techniques should lead to important advances in this area.

5. References

1. ADAM, P. A. J., 1971, Control of glucose metabolism in the human fetus and newborn infant, *Adv. Metab. Disord.* **5**:183.
2. AGRANOFF, B. W., BRADY, R. O., AND COLODZIN, M., 1954, Differential conversion of specifically labelled glucose to $C^{14}O_2$, *J. Biol. Chem.* **211**:773.
3. ANDREWS, W. H. H., BRITTON, H. G., HUGGETT, A. St. G., AND NIXON, D. A., 1960, Fructose metabolism in the isolated perfused liver of the foetal and newborn sheep, *J. Physiol.* **153**:199.
4. BAKER, L., AND WINEGRAD, A., 1970, Fasting hypoglycemia and metabolic acidosis associated with deficiency of hepatic fructose-1,6-diphosphatase activity, *Lancet* **2**:13.
5. BALLARD, F. J., 1966, Kinetic studies with liver galactokinase, *Biochem. J.* **101**:70.
6. BALLARD, F. J., 1971, The development of gluconeogenesis in rat liver. Controlling factors in the newborn, *Biochem. J.* **124**:265.
7. BALLARD, F. J., AND OLIVER, I. T., 1963, Glycogen metabolism in embryonic chick and neonatal rat liver, *Biochim. Biophys. Acta* **71**:578.
8. BALLARD, F. J., AND OLIVER, I. T., 1965, Carbohydrate metabolism in liver from fetal and neonatal sheep, *Biochem. J.* **95**:191.
9. BALLARD, F. J., AND PHILIPPIDIS, H., 1971, The development of gluconeogenic function in rat liver, in: *Regulation of Gluconeogenesis* (H.-D. Soling and B. Williams, eds.), pp. 66–81, Georg Thieme Verlag, Stuttgart.
10. BERTOLI, D., AND SEGAL, D., 1966, Developmental aspects and some characteristics of mammalian galactose 1-phosphate uridyltransferase, *J. Biol. Chem.* **241**:4023.
11. BERNARD, C., 1859, De la matière glycogène considérée comme condition du développement de certain tissus, chez le foetus, avant l'apparition de la fonction glycogénique du foie, *C. R. Acad. Sci.* **48**:673.
12. BEYREISS, K., 1971, Untersuchungen über den Umsatz von Galaktose Neugeborener, Säuglinge und Erwachsener bei intravenöser Galaktose-infusion, *Acta Biol. Med. Ger.* **27**:125.
13. BEYREISS, K., AND RAUTENBACH, M., 1974, Utilization and turnover rate of fructose during continuous infusion in pre-term and term newborns in dependence on age, *Biol. Neonate* **24**:330.
14. BODE, J. C., BODE, C., RUMPELT, H. J., AND ZELDER, O., 1974, Loss of hepatic adenosine phosphates and metabolic consequences following fructose or sorbitol administration in man and in the rat, in: *Regulation of Hepatic Metabolism* (F. Lundquist and N. Tygstrup, eds.), pp. 267–281, Munksgaard, Copenhagen.
15. BURCH, H. B., LOWRY, O. H., KUHLMAN, A. M., SKERJANCE, J., DIAMANT, E. J., LOWRY, S. R., AND VON DIPPE, P., 1963, Changes in patterns of enzymes of carbohydrate metabolism in the developing rat liver, *J. Biol. Chem.* **238**:2267.
16. CIAMPOLINI, M., AND FRANCHINI, F., 1966, Modifications of lactate metabolism in the first month of life: Intravenous loading tests of DL-lactate in premature newborn infants, *Ann. Paediatr.* **207**:335.
17. COHEN, N. M., AND TURNER, R. C., 1972, Plasma insulin in the foetal rat, *Biol. Neonate* **21**:107.
18. COHN, R. M., AND SEGAL, S., 1973, Galactose metabolism and regulation, *Metabolism* **22**:627.
19. CORI, G. T., AND SCHULMAN, J. L., 1954, Glycogen storage disease of the liver. II. Enzymic studies, *Pediatrics* **14**:646.
20. CORNBLATH, M., AND SCHWARTZ, R., 1966, *Disorders of Carbohydrate Metabolism in Infancy*, W. B. Saunders, Philadelphia.
21. CRANE, R. K., AND SOLS, A., 1955, Animal tissue hexokinases, *Methods Enzymol.* **1**:277.
22. CUATRECASAS, P., AND SEGAL, S., 1965, Mammalian galactokinase: Developmental and adaptive characteristics in the rat liver, *J. Biol. Chem.* **240**:2382.
23. DAWKINS, M. J. R., 1959, Respiratory enzymes in the liver of the newborn rat, *Proc. R. Soc. London Ser. B* **150**:284.
24. DAWKINS, M. J. R., 1966, Biochemical aspects of developing function in newborn mammalian liver, *Br. Med. Bull.* **22**:27.
25. DEVOS, P., AND HERS, H. G., 1974, Glycogen metabolism in the liver of the foetal rat, *Biochem. J.* **140**:331.
26. DONNELL, G. N., NG, W. G., HODGMAN, J. E., AND BERGREN, W. R., 1967, Galactose metabolism in the newborn infant, *Pediatrics* **39**:829.
27. EISEN, H. J., GOLDFINE, I. D., AND GLINSMANN, W. H., 1973, Regulation of hepatic glycogen synthesis during fetal development: Roles of hydrocortisone, insulin, and insulin receptors, *Proc. Natl. Acad. Sci. U.S.A.* **70**:3454.
28. FAVARD, P., AND JOST, A., 1966, Différenciation et charge en glycogène de l'hépatocyte du foetus de rat normal ou décapité, *Arch. Anat. Microsc. Morphol. Exp.* **55**:603.

29. Fernandes, J., and Blom, W., 1974, The intravenous L-alanine tolerance test as a means for investigating gluconeogenesis, *Metabolism* **23**:1149.

30. François, R., Picaud, J. J., Ruitton-Ugliengo, A., David, L., Cartal, M. J., and Bauer, D., 1974, The newborn of diabetic mothers, observations on 154 cases, 1958–1972, *Biol. Neonate* **24**:1.

31. Froesch, E. R., Wolf, N. P., Baitsch, N. Prader, A., and Labhart, A., 1963, Hereditary fructose intolerance. An inborn defect of fructose-1-phosphate splitting aldolase, *Amer. J. Med.* **34**:151.

32. Garber, A. J., and Ballard, F. J., Unpublished experiments.

33. Girard, J., Bal, D., and Assan, R., 1972, Glucagon secretion during the early postnatal period in the rat, *Horm. Metab. Res.* **4**:168.

34. Goodwin, R. F. W., 1956, Division of the common mammals into two groups according to the concentration of fructose in the blood of the foetus, *J. Physiol.* **132**:146.

35. Greengard, D., and Dewey, H. K., 1970, The premature deposition or lysis of glycogen in livers of fetal rats injected with hydrocortisone or glucagon, *Dev. Biol.* **21**:452.

36. Gresham, E. L., James, E. J., Raye, J. R., Battaglia, F. C., Makowski, E. L., and Meschia, G., 1972, Production and excretion of urea by the fetal lamb, *Pediatrics* **50**:372.

37. Grossbard, L., and Schimke, R. T., 1966, Multiple hexokinases of rat tissues. Purification and comparison of soluble forms, *J. Biol. Chem.* **241**:3546.

38. Hanson, R. W., Fisher, L., Ballard, F. J., and Reshef, L., 1973, The regulation of phosphoenolpyruvate carboxykinase in fetal rat liver, *Enzyme* **15**:97.

39. Hers, H. G., 1960, Le mecanisme de la formation du fructose seminal et du fructose foetal, *Biochim. Biophys. Acta* **37**:127.

40. Hers, H. G., De Wulf, H., and Stalmans, W., 1970, The control of glycogen metabolism in the liver, *FEBS Lett.* **12**:73.

41. Holt, P. G., and Oliver, I. T., 1968, Plasma corticosterone concentrations in the perinatal rat, *Biochem. J.* **108**:339.

42. Hommes, F. A., Polman, H. A., and Reerink, J. D., 1968, Leigh's encephalomyelopathy: An inborn error of gluconeogenesis, *Arch. Dis. Child.* **43**:423.

43. Jamdar, S. C., and Greengard, O., 1970, Premature formation of glucokinase in developing rat liver, *J. Biol. Chem.* **245**:2779.

44. James, E., Meschia, G., and Battaglia, F. C., 1971, A–V differences of free fatty acids and glycerol in the ovine umbilical circulation, *Proc. Soc. Exp. Biol. Med.* **138**:823.

45. Johnson, J. D., Kretchmar, N., and Simoons, F. J., 1974, Lactose malabsorption. Its biology and history *Adv. Pediatr.* **21**:197.

46. Jost, A., and Picon, L., 1970, Hormonal control of fetal development and metabolism, *Adv. Metab. Disord.* **4**:123.

47. Katz, J., Landau, B. R., and Bartson, G. E., 1966, The pentose cycle, triosephosphate, isomerization and lipogenesis in rat adipose tissue, *J. Biol. Chem.* **241**:727.

48. Lardy, H. A., Personal communication.

49. Lea, M. A., and Walker, D. G., 1965, Factors affecting hepatic glycolysis and some changes that occur during development, *Biochem. J.* **94**:655.

50. McCann, M. L., Chen, C. H., Katigbak, E. B., Kotchen, J. M., Likly, B. F., and Schwartz, R., 1966, Effects of fructose on hypoglucosemia in infants of diabetic mothers, *N. Engl. J. Med.* **275**:1.

51. Mercier, C., and Whelan, W. J., 1973, Further characterization of glycogen from type-IV glycogen-storage disease, *Eur. J. Biochem.* **40**:221.

52. Middleton, M. C., and Walker, D. G., 1972, Comparison of the properties of two forms of pyruvate kinase in rat liver and determination of their separate activities during development, *Biochem. J.* **127**:721.

53. Monteleone, J. A., Beutler, E., Monteleone, P. L., Utz, C. L. L., and Casey, E. C., 1971, Cataracts, galactosuria and hypergalactosemia due to galactokinase deficiency in a child. Studies of a kindred, *Amer. J. Med.* **50**:403.

54. Moses, S. W., and Gutman, A., 1972, Inborn errors of glucose metabolism, *Adv. Pediatr.* **19**:95.

55. Newsholme, E. A., and Start, C., 1973, *Regulation in Metabolism*, pp. 247–292, John Wiley, London.

56. Novák, E., Drummond, G. I., Skála, J., and Hahn, P., 1972, Developmental changes in cyclic AMP, protein kinase, phosphorylase kinase, and phosphorylase in liver, heart, and skeletal muscle of the rat, *Arch. Biochem. Biophys.* **150**:511.

57. Otey, E., Stenger, V., Eitzman, D., and Prystowsky, H., 1967, Further observations on the relationships of pyruvate and lactate in human pregnancy, *Amer. J. Obstet. Gynecol.* **97**:1076.

58. Partridge, N. C., Hoh, C. H., Weaver, P. K., and Oliver, I. T., 1975, Premature induction of glucokinase in the neonatal rat by thyroid hormone, *Eur. J. Biochem.* **51**:49.

59. Philippidis, H., and Ballard, F. J., 1970, The development of gluconeogenesis in rat liver. Effects of glucagon and ether, *Biochem. J.* **120**:385.

60. Philippidis, H., Hanson, R. W., Reshef, L., Hopgood, M. F., and Ballard, F. J., 1972, The initial synthesis of proteins during development. Phosphoenolpyruvate carboxykinase in rat liver at birth, *Biochem. J.* **126**:1127.

61. Přibylová, H., and Novák, L., 1970, Influence of environmental temperature on the energetic and glycide metabolism of pathological newborns during the first three hours of life, *Biol. Neonate* **15**:315.

62. Räihä, N. C. R., and Lindros, K. O. 1969, De-

velopment of some enzymes involved in gluconeogenesis in human liver, *Ann. Med. Exp. Biol. Fenn.* **47**:146.

63. RAIVIO, K. O., AND SEEGMILLER, J. E., 1972, Genetic diseases of metabolism, *Annu. Rev. Biochem.* **41**:543.

64. SCHAPIRA, F., NORDMAN, Y., AND GREGORI, C., 1972, Hereditary alterations of fructose metabolizing enzymes. Studies on essential fructosuria and on hereditary fructose intolerance, *Acta Med. Scand. Suppl.* **542**:77.

65. SCHWARTZ, A. L., AND RALL, T. W., 1973, Hormonal regulation of glycogen metabolism in neonatal rat liver, *Biochem. J.* **134**:985.

66. SCRUTTON, M. C., AND UTTER, M. F., 1968, The regulation of glycolysis and gluconeogenesis in animal tissues, *Annu. Rev. Biochem.* **37**:249.

67. SEGAL, S., ROTH, H., AND BERTOLI, D., 1963, Galactose metabolism by rat liver tissue: Influence of age, *Science* **142**:1311.

68. SHELLEY, H. J., 1961, Glycogen reserves and their changes at birth and in anoxia, *Br. Med. Bull.* **17**:137.

69. SHELLEY, H. J., AND NELIGAN, G. A., 1966, Neonatal hypoglycaemia, *Br. Med. Bull.* **22**:34.

70. SNELL, K., AND WALKER, D. G., 1973, Glucose metabolism in the newborn rat. Temporal studies *in vivo*, *Biochem. J.* **132**:739.

71. SPERLING, M. A., DeLAMATER, P. V., PHELPS, D., FISER, R. H., OH, W., AND FISHER, D. A., 1974, Spontaneous and amino acid-stimulated glucagon secretion in the immediate postnatal period, relation to glucose and insulin, *J. Clin. Invest.* **53**:1159.

72. STEINKE, J., AND DRISCOLL, S. G., 1966, The extractable insulin contents of pancreas from fetuses and infants of diabetic and control mothers, *Diabetes* **14**:573.

73. TANAKA, T., HARANO, Y., MORIMURA, H., AND MORI, R., 1965, Evidence for the presence of two types of pyruvate kinase in rat liver, *Biochem. Biophys. Res. Commun.* **21**:55.

74. THURSTON, J. H., JONES, E. M., AND HAUHART, R. E., 1974, Decrease and inhibition of liver glycogen phosphorylase after fructose. An experimental model for the study of hereditary fructose intolerance, *Diabetes* **23**:597.

75. TILDON, J. T., SWIATEK, K. R., AND CORNBLATH, M.,

76. TSOULOS, N. G., COLWILL, J. R., BATTAGLIA, F. C., MAKOWSKI, E. L., AND MESCHIA, G., 1971, Comparison of glucose, fructose and O_2 uptakes by fetuses of fed and starved ewes, *Amer. J. Physiol.* **221**:234.

77. TYGSTRUP, N., AND WINKLER, K., 1958, Galactose blood clearance as a measure of hepatic blood flow, *Clin. Sci.* **17**:1.

78. VAILLANT, R., AND JOST, A., 1971, Influence des corticostéroides sur le glycogène particulaire du foie foetal de rat, *Biochimie* **53**:797.

79. VILLEE, C. A., AND HAGERMAN, D. D., 1958, Effect of oxygen deprivation on the metabolism of fetal and adult tissues, *Amer. J. Physiol.* **194**:457.

80. VILLEE, C. A., AND LORING, J. M., 1961, Alternative pathways of carbohydrate metabolism in foetal and adult tissues, *Biochem. J.* **81**:488.

81. VILLEE, C. A., HAGERMAN, D. D., HOLMBERG, N., LIND, J., AND VILLEE, D. B., 1958, The effects of anoxia on the metabolism of fetal tissues, *Pediatrics* **22**:953.

82. WALKER, D. G., 1963, On the presence of two soluble glucose-phosphorylating enzymes in adult liver and the development of one of these after birth, *Biochim. Biophys. Acta.* **77**:209.

83. WALKER, D. G., 1968, Development of carbohydrate metabolism, in: *Carbohydrate Metabolism and Its Disorders*, Vol. 1 (F. Dickens, P. J. Randle and W. J. Whelan, eds.), pp. 465–496, Academic Press, London.

84. WARNES, D. M., SEAMARK, R. F., AND BALLARD, F. J., 1977, The appearance of gluconeogenesis at birth in sheep. Activation of the pathway associated with blood oxygenation, *Biochem. J.* **162**:627.

85. WILLIAMSON, J. R., AND BROWNING, E. T., 1969, Control mechanisms of gluconeogenesis and ketogenesis. 2. Interactions between fatty acid oxidation and the citric acid cycle in perfused rat liver, *J. Biol. Chem.* **244**:4617.

86. WOODS, H. F., EGGLESTON, L. V., AND KREBS, M. A., 1970, The cause of hepatic accumulation of fructose 1-phosphate on fructose loading, *Biochem. J.* **119**:501.

87. YEUNG, D., AND OLIVER, I. T., 1968, Factors affecting the premature induction of phosphopyruvate carboxylase in neonatal rat liver, *Biochem. J.* **108**:325.

CHAPTER 18

Protein and Amino Acid Metabolism

Selma E. Snyderman

1. Introduction

The deposition of nitrogen during the perinatal period occurs at a rate greater than that at any other period of life. Although there are few quantitative data in the human, the magnitude of protein synthesis can be appreciated from the following analyses of the nitrogen content of the human fetus: at 6 weeks of age, the total body protein is 0.4 mg; at 20 weeks, the fetus contains 15 g protein[90]; at term, the content is 500 g.[16] This increase occurs not only as a result of growth of the fetus, but also because of the change in body composition, which results in a reduction in the water content and an increase in nitrogen.[51] This maturation of body composition does not stop at birth, but continues at a similar rate for the first months of life, then becomes slower and virtually ceases by the age of 4 years.

The synthesis of protein is a complex multistep process that results in the formation of a macromolecule from 20 individual amino acids in a specified sequence under genetic control. Although precise knowledge of this process dates back to the 1950's, a number of facets are still under investigation. Amino acids are first activated in the cytoplasm by an amino-acyl-tRNA synthetase that is highly specific for the amino acid and its corresponding tRNA; the amino acid is esterified to its corresponding tRNA at the expense of ATP energy. In the second phase, initiation, mRNA and the aminoacyl-tRNA are bound to the surface of the ribosome (particles of ribonucleoprotein). Three specific initiation factors as well as GTP and magnesium are required for this step. Elongation is the process by which the chain is lengthened by the sequential addition of aminoacyl residues transferred enzymatically from aminoacyl-tRNA esters, each of which is bound to the ribosomes in response to a specific codon (base triplet) in the mRNA. Two elongation factors are required for the lengthening of the chain. After the formation of each new peptide bond, the ribosome moves along the mRNA to bring the next codon in position for alignment of the next aminoacyl-tRNA. The energy for this step is also provided by GTP. The final step is termination; when appropriate signals in the mRNA are reached, the product is released from the ribosome.

All cellular constituents are continuously being degraded and replaced by newly synthesized com-

Selma E. Snyderman · Department of Pediatrics, New York University Medical School, New York, New York 10016

ponents[67]; this is also true, of course, of protein turnover in the perinatal period. Since there is marked accumulation of protein at this time, synthetic processes must exceed those of degradation, but there is little information as to whether this accumulation is the result of increased synthesis or of decreased degradation, or a combination of both. In fact, the mechanisms that control protein synthesis and degradation in general are still largely unknown. Protein synthesizing systems do rely on an ample supply of amino acids,[94] which are required for the maintenance of polysome integrity, and hence the efficiency of utilization of mRNA.[20,70] The regulation of protein degradation is even less well understood. However, high amino acid levels have been shown to reduce protein degradation.[30] The effect of amino acid concentration on both the stimulation of synthesis and the inhibition of degradation is of particular interest in view of the elevated amino acid levels during fetal life. The continuous degradation of protein may serve functions of particular significance during fetal life, such as the removal of abnormal proteins, and a greater adaptability to environmental changes, such as the availability of nutrients or the supply of key enzymes such as insulin.

2. The Fetus

The increased deposition of protein that takes place during fetal life occurs at different rates in the various organs at different stages of gestation. These differences are due in part to different growth rates of individual organs. Thus, at 72 days' gestation (half the gestation time), the liver of the sheep fetus is twice as heavy as the GI tract, but at term, the gut is heavier; at the same stage of gestation, muscle weighs twice as much as bone, but is of equal weight at term.[8] This different growth rate of individual organs with different protein content suggests the possibility that the requirements for individual amino acids may vary at different stages in development.

Not only are there differences in the development of whole organs, but also there are both structural and chemical differences in the organ components. Thus, the histological appearance of fetal muscle differs from that of both the newborn and the adult.[89] The nuclei of fetal muscle are large, while the fibers are small and widely separated by extracellular material; this structure is in contrast to that of adult muscle, which contains large fibers and nuclei that are small and fewer in number. Changes in sarcoplasmic, fibrillar, and extracellular nitrogen reflect this microanatomic development; fibrillar protein increases at a more rapid rate during fetal life than do the other protein fractions. These changes in proportion and concentration of the nitrogen-containing tissues imply that the amounts of the individual amino acids laid down in tissue vary at different times. A study of mouse embryos by Singer et al.[72] revealed that the ratio of lysine to leucine and to tryptophan varied with age, and Jakobsen[34] was able to demonstrate that the amino acid composition of a fetal calf at 20 weeks was different from that at 40 weeks.

Although there is different protein synthetic activity in various organs, there is a similar sequence of events. Initially, there is an increase in DNA synthesis; this increase represents an increase in cell number. After a varying time interval, there is an acceleration of RNA synthesis, which is a manifestation of hypertrophic growth. Protein synthesis occurs as a concomitant of RNA accumulation; simultaneously, there is an increased concentration of free amino acids, which presumably is the initiation factor in protein synthesis. A number of analyses of free amino acid content of fetal tissue have been performed; these include analyses of human liver, monkey liver, and brain, and rabbit liver, muscle, and kidney. These tissues all demonstrated higher levels than those of adult tissues. The differences were greatest in muscle in the rabbit.[88] The concentration of the free amino acids of monkey brain did not change greatly during fetal development, but there was a tendency for an increase in glutamic, aspartic, and β-aminoisobutyric acids and glutamine, and some decrease in the proline and threonine levels.[22] There was, however, no correlation between the brain and liver levels. The only human study, that of liver at 22–24 weeks of gestational age, revealed that fetal levels of a number of amino acids were 2–4 times higher than mature levels, with one exception, valine, which was present in significantly higher amounts in adult liver.[64]

The processes of protein formation have been extensively studied in the sea urchin.[32] In this primitive organism, protein synthesis is accelerated immediately after fertilization, with an increased concentration of DNA, and the first signs of biochemical differentiation are apparent at the initiation of gastrulation.[33,56] Similar differentiation has also been observed at this stage of development in the amphibian embryo.[44] This acceleration of protein formation has been demonstrated by a study of the nucleic acid concentration in the rat liver; the concentration is much higher in fetal liver than in the adult.[23,54] Study of the incorporation of ^{14}C-labeled amino acids into protein of the rat liver has also confirmed this rapid rate of synthesis in the fetus, which accelerates as the fetus matures.[6,57] A similar study in the rabbit using ^{35}S-methionine also demonstrated this rapid rate and showed that the rate of protein synthesis was paralleled by the RNA concentration.[50]

There is very little of this type of information about the human fetus, but a study of minced human placenta demonstrated that the efficiency of protein synthesis paralleled the RNA concentration and was greatest at the 3rd month of gestation.[49] Winick et al.[93] found that the human placenta and its protein content increased until term, but there was no further increase in DNA content after the 35th week of gestation, indicating that cell division stopped before total growth and protein deposition. This continuation of protein deposition in the absence of cell division was also found in a study of the development of the human brain.[92] There was a linear increase in brain weight, protein, and RNA content within the span of time studied (the gestational age of 13 weeks to 13 months postpartum), but the increase in DNA content started falling off at birth and reached its maximum at 5 months of age.

A longitudinal study[36] of RNA, DNA, and protein concentration of human liver, brain, heart, lung, and kidney from the 6th to the 20th weeks of gestation also suggests the existence of characteristic changes for individual organs. The RNA/DNA ratio for a particular organ did not vary much with the stage of pregnancy, while the protein/DNA ratio showed the most marked increase with advancing pregnancy in the liver, brain, and heart.

An increased rate of protein degradation as well as synthesis is suggested by the increased urea production that has been found in both the sheep and the human fetus. Urea excretion via the placenta was approximately 3 times greater than that of the adult sheep.[28] The plasma urea concentration of the human fetus is higher than that of maternal plasma, and in addition, urea production is greater: an estimated production of 540 mg/kg per day, which exceeds by a significant margin that of adults, which ranges from 200 to 400 mg/kg per day.[29]

The need for increased quantities of amino acids for protein synthesis is satisfied by placental transport. This is an active process against a concentration gradient that is dependent on placental blood flow and, to a lesser degree, on the concentration of amino acids in the maternal plasma.[31] A number of studies have demonstrated both increased total amino nitrogen and elevated levels of individual amino acids in cord blood.[11,12,26] The data on the human are still quite sparse, but there does seem to be a tendency for the concentration of amino acids in cord blood to decrease as pregnancy progresses.[4,7,24,41–43] Tyrosine, threonine, and taurine are exceptions, however, in that their levels remain fairly stationary. The levels at term are within the upper range of normal for other periods of life, with the exception of taurine, which is significantly higher at this time. There is no explanation of this elevation, but this finding is of interest in that the taurine content of fetal brain is higher than that of mature brain.[53,63]

A number of analyses of the amino acid content of amniotic fluid have been made at various times after gestation.[41] The content also shows a tendency to fall as pregnancy advances. This decline is not uniform, but occurs at different rates for individual amino acids.[15,68,69] The use of amino acid levels, or several different ratios of them, has been proposed as an indicator of fetal age; although the data are suggestive, there are still not enough to warrant their use for this purpose. These analyses might also be useful in the prenatal diagnosis of inborn errors of metabolism; however, there has not as yet been any instance of a diagnosis confirmed by this means.

Under certain circumstances, the active transport of amino acids across the placenta may work to the detriment of the fetus. Thus, when pregnant monkeys are fed excess phenylalanine, the plasma phenylalanine levels may rise to 10–20 times normal[37]; the concentration on the fetal side takes place in the usual fashion, and the resultant fetal levels are extremely high. This finding offers an explanation for the poor growth and mental retardation of the nonphenylketonuric infants of phenylketonuric mothers.[95]

The presently available information about cord blood amino acid levels is listed in Table I.

Other organic nitrogeneous compounds, including urea, uric acid, and creatinine, are present in similar concentrations in amniotic fluid and maternal and fetal blood in early pregnancy. These compounds increase gradually in the amniotic fluid to become significantly higher than levels in the maternal or fetal blood. A sharp rise in the creatinine

Table I. Free Amino Acids of Cord Blood (mg/dl)

Amino acid	16–22 weeks[a]	19–25 weeks[b]	33–37 weeks[c]	Full term[b]	Full term[d]	Full term[e]	Full term[f]
Alanine	7.79	3.66	3.79	2.55	3.92	3.01	3.78
Arginine	0.68	2.63	1.23	1.84	1.13	1.84	0.90
Aspartic acid	1.33	0.35	0.24	0.28	0.13		0.22
Citrulline	1.13	0.15	0.16	0.38	0.16	0.23	
Cystine	0.71	1.39		0.79	0.46		1.69
Glutamic acid	7.12	1.89	1.35	1.33	1.00	3.98	2.20
Glutamine	4.04	8.14		11.81	8.03	5.38	
Glycine	3.54	1.99	1.51	1.72	1.79	2.1	1.73
Histidine	1.40	1.83	1.95	1.82	1.74	1.94	1.17
Isoleucine	0.80	0.81	0.72	0.73	0.81	0.75	0.93
Leucine	1.93	1.58	1.42	1.28	1.54	1.61	1.49
Lysine	4.98	7.07	5.50	5.75	4.64	5.23	4.35
Methionine	0.22	0.35	0.51	0.29	0.27	0.42	0.30
Ornithine	2.12	1.74	1.08	1.18	1.17	2.24	1.04
Phenylalanine	1.3	1.19	1.18	0.92	1.10	1.42	1.28
Proline	2.25	1.94	1.7	1.47	1.84	2.42	1.68
Serine	2.16	1.71	1.31	1.50	1.37	2.46	1.54
Taurine	4.43	2.15	2.48	2.04	2.39	1.91	2.29
Threonine	4.01	3.89	3.14	3.67	2.78	3.58	3.22
Tyrosine	1.1	0.92	1.17	1.16	1.10	1.03	1.01
Valine	2.94	3.27	2.82	2.25	2.62	2.29	2.38
α-Aminobutryic acid	0.23	0.39		0.40	0.25	0.28	

[a] Recalculated from A'zary et al.[4]
[b] Ghadimi and Pecora.[24]
[c] Lindblad and Zetterstrom.[43]
[d] Lindblad and Baldesten.[42]
[e] Recalculated from Levy and Montag.[41]
[f] Butterfield and O'Brien.[7]

level occurs at about the 37th week of gestation to one that is 2–3 times higher than that of normal serum.[59]

3. The Premature Infant

The process of birth seems to interrupt temporarily the high rate of protein synthesis that has been occurring in the fetus; this interruption occurs regardless of the maturity of the fetus.[66] The reappearance of the high synthetic rate varies in different organs; in addition, there seem to be two peaks of activity in certain organs, one around the 3rd to the 5th day of life, and a second one at approximately the 19th day.[13,14,48] The depressed synthetic rate is most likely the result of the shift from the constant nutrient supply of the placenta to the inadequate and sporadic intake of the first days of life. The first peak would seem to coincide with the onset of adequate oral intake, while the second peak occurs at the time of weaning. Similar information is not available for the human infant, but a reduced or even negative nitrogen balance is a well-known occurrence during the first days of life.

GI protein digestion and absorption of the released amino acids is well developed even in the smallest premature baby, and there is no evidence that whole protein is less efficiently handled by the premature than by more mature individuals.[45] When protein of good quality is fed, the total stool nitrogen does not exceed 15% of the intake; this value is similar to that obtained at other periods of life. Nitrogen is retained with avidity, and as with the more mature infant, the amount retained is directly proportional to the intake. High-protein intake is accompanied by high nitrogen retention for prolonged periods of time; this situation is different from that in older individuals, in whom such an effect is only temporary. The avidity of the premature for protein is even greater than that of the mature infant; similar intakes of protein will result in higher nitrogen retention in the premature infant. For example, a moderate and commonly used protein intake of 3 g/kg per day is accompanied by a nitrogen retention in the range of 200 mg/kg per day in the full-term infant, and over 300 mg/kg per day in the premature infant.[78]

The GI tract of the premature infant is apparently more permeable to protein than that of older infants.[9] After intravenous administration of ^{131}I-labeled polyvinylpyrrolidine, a higher concentration of this polymer was found in the stools of 10 premature infants than in the stools of full-term babies. Although this permeability had decreased by 1 month of age, it still exceeded that of the full-term infant; it involved both albumin and γ-globulin.

Plasma proteins of premature infants determined on the first day of life and before initiation of feeding reveal that both the total protein and its electrophoretically separable components are lower than those of the full-term baby.[65] The smaller the infant, the more depressed are the values. An average total protein of 4.2 g/dl with 2.5 g albumin and 1.7 g globulin was found in infants with a birth weight of less than 1500 g. Restudy on the 21st day of life revealed that the total protein and each of its components were lower than at birth.[58] There does not seem to be any systematic study of how long these values continue to be depressed.

There have been few determinations of the plasma amino acid levels of premature infants before the initiation of feeding. These levels do reflect the same changes noted in the cord blood levels; taurine, tyrosine, and lysine are the only amino acids that are elevated.[1,17] These levels then tend to be in the low normal range until food intake is adequate. Free hydroxyproline is present in readily measurable amounts; this amino acid is also present in the plasma of the full-term infant. Moderate elevation of the proline and threonine levels is seen on occasion, but these elevated levels cannot be considered to be characteristic of the majority of premature infants. The protein intake greatly affects the plasma amino acid levels. Plasma amino acid levels of premature infants fed adequate but not excessive intakes of protein (3 g/kg per day) at different ages are summarized in Table II.

The plasma amino acid levels at a given time represent the net balance between a number of different processes: the amount available from the diet, that being used for tissue repair and growth, that used for specific purposes, that excreted in the urine, and the excess remaining, which must be metabolized. Since there is every indication that new tissue growth in the premature is proceeding at a rapid pace, and there is a greater loss of amino acids in the urine than at other periods of life, it must follow that some defect in enzyme activity must account for any elevation in amino acid levels in the plasma of the premature. The moderate-to-great elevation of the plasma tyrosine level that occurs in at least 10% of all premature infants is the result of such a deficit in enzyme activity.

This anomaly of tyrosine metabolism, which was first described in 1941 by Levine et al.,[39] came to be known as *tyrosyluria* because of the presence of derivatives of tyrosine (*p*-hydroxyphenylpyruvic, *p*-hydroxyphenyllactic, and *p*-hydroxyphenylacetic acids) in the urine. They observed its occurrence in premature infants on high-protein diets and its cure by the administration of vitamin C.[40] Subsequently, the presence of increased levels of tyrosine was noted in the plasma; all these findings have been related to an immaturity of the *p*-hydroxyphenylpyruvic acid oxidizing system. The enzyme is inhibited by its substrate, and thus the biochemical abnormalities can be reversed by reducing the increased level of the substrate (caused by a high-protein intake with resulting elevated amounts of tyrosine); it may also be reversed by the use of a reducing agent such as ascorbic acid. The majority of instances of tyrosinemia may be completely reversed by the administration of vitamin C. Levels of tyrosine as high as 40–60 mg/dl have returned to normal after 48 hr of this therapy. A small number of cases of tyrosinemia do not respond to this therapy, and cases are on record that have persisted for as long as 1 year.[5] The etiology of the latter cases has not been clarified.

The relationship of this transient tyrosinemia to

Table II. Plasma Amino Acid Levels in the Premature Infant (mg/dl)[a,b]

Amino acid	3–6 days n = 5	6–9 days n = 9	10–18 days n = 11	20–30 days n = 5	30–45 days n = 4
Alamine	1.63	2.72	2.24	2.31	2.46
α-Aminobutyric acid	0.10	0.10	0.10	0.15	0.13
Arginine	0.69	0.80	1.0	1.12	1.36
Aspartic acid	0.06	0.11	0.10	0.05	0.06
Asparagine	0.51	0.34	0.41	0.43	0.45
Citrulline	0.17	0.24	0.28	0.59	0.54
Cystine	0.65	0.62	0.61	0.62	0.45
Glycine	1.59	1.65	1.77	1.83	1.12
Histidine	1.01	1.18	1.10	1.12	1.09
Homocitrulline	Trace	Trace	0.06	0.02	0.02
Hydroxyproline	0.11	0.21	0.28	0.27	0.30
Isoleucine	0.41	0.67	0.51	0.53	0.50
Leucine	0.87	1.39	1.06	1.08	0.91
Lysine	1.26	1.68	1.71	1.51	0.78
Methionine	0.28	0.34	0.27	0.26	0.33
Ornithine	0.85	1.47	1.73	1.48	1.30
Phosphoethanolamine	Trace	0	0	0	0
Phenylalanine	0.66	0.89	0.60	0.62	0.59
Proline	1.90	3.07	2.08	1.87	1.76
Serine	1.28	1.50	1.50	1.43	1.31
Taurine	0.55	0.62	0.63	0.51	0.21
Threonine	1.51	2.14	2.13	1.59	1.36
Tyrosine	3.49	2.51[c]	1.84	1.39	1.24
Valine	1.31	2.00	1.64	1.83	1.29

[a] Data from Snyderman et al.[82]

[b] All infants were fed cow's milk formulas providing 3–4 g protein/kg per day. Birth weights were 1500–2000 g.

[c] After vitamin C supplementation.

such sequelae as neurological symptoms and mental retardation is not clear. It has been the opinion of most investigators[3,55] that it is probably a benign condition. In a recent follow-up study[47] of such children at 7 and 8 years of age, however, data were obtained that demonstrated long-term sequelae of tyrosinemia in a group of infants who weighed over 2000 g at birth. These sequelae included lower intelligence quotients and an increased incidence of visual–perceptual problems. A similar correlation could not be found for the smaller premature infant. A concomitant finding in many cases of tyrosinemia is an elevation of plasma phenylalanine level to a degree sufficient to give a positive result in the routine screening of newborn infants for phenylketonuria.

High-protein intakes, similar to those used in many areas for the feeding of premature infants, result in elevated levels of other amino acids as well as of tyrosine and phenylalanine.[80] The level of methionine in particular is affected, and values 10–20 times normal have been recorded. Elevated plasma proline levels may also be a manifestation of high-protein intake. When blood samples are drawn too early in the postprandial period, these amino acids as well as the branched-chain amino acids—leucine, isoleucine, and valine—are elevated above the normal range. These high levels may cause considerable confusion in the diagnosis of the inherited diseases of amino acid metabolism.

It is of interest to speculate that these elevations of plasma amino acids are the reflection of imperfectly developed enzyme activity in the catabolic pathways of these amino acids. They may reflect developmental defects in the same enzyme systems that are involved in the inherited diseases of amino acid metabolism. For example, the inactivity of the phenylalanine hydroxylating system in the premature is the counterpart of phenylketonuria, and the tyrosyluria of the premature is a developmental expression of tyrosinemia. The existence of other similar relationships may be demonstrated in the future.

The well-known renal immaturity of the newborn, especially that involving tubular function, is responsible for certain peculiarities in the amino acid content of the urine of the premature. It has been known since the beginning of this century that the total α-amino nitrogen excretion is elevated in the premature.[10,71] This elevation is true regardless of the mode of expression, whether as the total excretion per 24 hr or in relation to the creatinine or to the total nitrogen excretion. Both qualitative and quantitative difference are noted when the urine is assayed for individual amino acids. All the amino acids found in the urine in later life are present in excess. In addition, significant quantities of hydroxyproline, an amino acid not excreted by the mature individual, are present.[19] The presence of measurable quantities of this amino acid in the plasma at the same time suggests that its origin in the urine may be both metabolic and renal. The appearance of free hydroxyproline in the urine is to be differentiated from the combined or peptide form of hydroxyproline, which is a normal constituent of all urine and reflects collagen turnover. The presence of unusual quantities of taurine, phosphoethanolamine, and homocitrulline (this component appears in the plasma only when heat-processed milk is fed) are all related to the increased plasma levels at this stage of life.

The protein requirement of the premature infant has been the subject of a great deal of study, but it is still not possible to state with any degree of assurance just what the minimum or the optimum intake should be. Human milk, which contains a relatively low protein content and provides on the average 2 g protein/kg per day, was the feeding of choice until the studies of Gordon et al.[27] demonstrated that premature infants gained more weight when fed cow's-milk formulas of higher protein content than human milk. These studies were followed by widespread use of high-protein formulas, and intakes in the range of 5–6 g/kg per day were

used. However, the demonstration that much of this added weight gain was due to water retention, which occurred as a result of the high electrolyte content of cow's milk[35] and the consequences of an additional renal solute load imposed on an immature kidney, had led, more recently, to the use of more moderate protein intakes, slightly higher than that provided by human milk.

Our own experience, as well as that of others, has been that the majority of premature infants do well and gain weight normally on intakes varying between 2 and 9 g protein/kg per day as long as the caloric and fluid intakes are adequate.[75] At the lower intake, less nitrogen is retained, and certain of the plasma amino acids tend to be in the low normal range, but other biochemical parameters and the growth rate, with certain exceptions, are normal. The exceptions are small premature infants with birth weights of less than 1100 g. At the other extreme, the infant receiving 9 g/kg does not grow any faster. He does, however, have a much higher nitrogen retention, and plasma nonprotein nitrogen and blood urea nitrogen levels may be strikingly elevated, while the concentration of a number of the plasma amino acids may be increased. Some degree of elevation of the blood urea nitrogen has been observed with all protein intakes over 3.5 g/kg per day.[91] The rate of weight gain of infants fed both these extremes of intake is very similar to that of infants receiving more moderate intakes. That the increasing amount of nitrogen retained with increasing intake is accompanied by similar rates of weight gain leads to the conclusion that these infants are attaining a much more mature body composition at an earlier age. Such an acceleration of the usual maturation process has been demonstrated in animals.[18] Whether this earlier attainment of a more mature body composition has any physiologic advantages or possible disadvantages for the premature infant must await further study.

A systematic study of the essential amino acid requirements of the premature infant has not yet been completed.[82] The figures obtained thus far do demonstrate that these requirements are higher than those of the full-term infant. In Table III, these figures are compared with the amino acid content of 170 ml of human milk, which was found to be adequate for the normal growth of premature infants,[61] and with the amounts provided by 2 g cow's milk/kg.

In addition to the requirement for larger amounts

Table III. Essential Amino Acid Requirements of the Premature Infant (mg/kg/day)

Amino acid	Requirement studies[a]	Human milk (170 mg/kg per day)[b]	Cow's milk (2 g protein/kg per day)[b]
Histidine	Not available	39	48
Isoleucine	150 (120 < 150)	146	128
Leucine	200 (150 < 200)	272	216
Lysine	200 (150 < 200)	133	156
Methionine[c]	60 (45 < 60)	39	52
Phenylalanine[d]	120 (90 < 120)	108	104
Threonine	120 (90 < 120)	105	92
Tryptophan	Not available	37	30
Valine	150 (120 < 150)	153	138

[a] The first figure is the highest figure obtained. The figures in parentheses denote the variation in requirement obtained; the higher requirement for each amino acid is qualified by the symbol "less than" because the minimum figure must be between that which is adequate and a lower figure that was shown to be inadequate.
[b] Comparative essential amino acid content of two milks that premature infants do well on.
[c] In the presence of adequate cystine.
[d] In the presence of adequate tyrosine.

of essential amino acids, certain other amino acids not regarded as essential for the more mature individual are dietary requirements for the premature infant.[73,82] These requirements are a consequence of imperfectly developed enzyme systems. Cystine and tyrosine are included in this group, and proline may be partially essential for the very small premature infant.

4. The Full-Term Infant

All the peculiarities of amino acid and nitrogen metabolism noted for the premature infant also occur in the full-term baby, although to a lesser degree. The full-term infant also retains nitrogen with great avidity, but at similar intakes of protein, the retention is somewhat less than in the premature. Another expression of this tendency to retain nitrogen is seen in the defense of body protein from catabolism for energy. Thus, McCance and Strangeways[46] found that when 6 newborn infants were starved for 2 days, they derived approximately 4% of their basal calories from protein breakdown, while adults derived 10% of their basal calories from this source when subjected to similar food deprivation.

The total serum protein values of full-term babies are significantly lower than the maternal values, and rise slowly after birth.[52] Albumin, however, is higher in newborn than in maternal blood, and values for this component approach the adult level at about 3 months. The concentration of globulin falls for the first 3 months and then starts to rise, reaching adult values before the end of the first year of life, usually between 7 and 11 months. Values for nonprotein nitrogen and blood urea nitrogen exhibit special patterns during the first months of life; the nonprotein nitrogen is comparatively high at birth, while the blood urea nitrogen is low.[21] During the first 10 days, the nonprotein nitrogen falls to values corresponding to the blood urea nitrogen, and then both start to rise until adult values are reached between 3 and 6 months. The level of the blood urea nitrogen is always higher in babies fed high-protein intakes than in those on lower intakes, but the rise with age is apparent in both groups. Blood uric acid is elevated at birth, falls rapidly during the first days of life, and reaches adult values by the end of the first month.[38]

The plasma aminogram of the full-term newborn is very similar to that of the premature. In particular, taurine, hydroxyproline, and ornithine are higher than at later periods of life. Dickinson et al.[17] called attention to the presence of ethanolamine in the plasma during the first 16 hr of life and to

Table IV. Plasma Amino Acid Values of the Full-Term Infant (mg/dl)

Amino acid	Less than 6 hr[a]	4–17 hr[b]	Less than 17 hr[c]	48 hr[d]	12–48 hr[e]	2–13 days[e]	2–4 wk[e]	1–2 mo[e]	2–3 mo[e]	3–5 mo[e]	Adult[e]
Alanine	3.4	3.16	2.94	2.75	2.57	2.46	2.84	2.24	2.65	2.74	2.67
α-Aminobutyric atid		0.15	0.22	0.17	0.17	0.13	0.18	0.17	0.20	0.16	
Arginine	0.97	0.89	0.94	1.20	0.62	0.71	0.97	0.91	0.71	0.98	1.20
Aspartic acid			0.11	0.25	0.03	0.05	0.07	0.06	0.04	0.09	0.04
Asparagine			0.60		0.49	0.46	0.47	0.47	0.43	0.67	0.54
Citrulline	0.12		0.28	0.47	0.19	0.26	0.40	0.37	0.36	0.35	0.39
Cystine		1.39	1.47	1.15	0.80	0.62	0.68	0.62	0.68	0.55	0.95
Glycine	2.3	2.35	2.58	2.40	1.77	1.61	1.45	1.18	1.21	1.00	1.51
Histidine	1.12	1.32	1.19	1.41	1.01	0.98	1.07	0.91	0.97	1.20	1.14
Hydroxyproline			0.42		0.05	0.05	0.14	0.12	0.10	0.11	Trace
Isoleucine	0.74	0.43	0.52	0.63	0.45	0.59	0.80	0.77	0.80	0.93	0.77
Leucine	1.02	0.81	0.95	0.99	0.95	1.30	1.53	1.44	1.26	1.64	1.42
Lysine	2.59	2.82	2.93	3.23	1.71	1.65	1.85	1.60	1.39	1.76	2.18
Methionine	0.40	0.45	0.44	0.36	0.30	0.34	0.34	0.33	0.31	0.35	0.27
Ornithine	0.92	0.84	1.21	1.89		1.22	1.21	0.95	0.96	1.03	0.97
Phosphoethanolamine			0.32	0.17	Trace	0	0	0	0	0	0
Phenylalanine	1.12	1.07	1.30	0.89	1.0	0.94	0.99	0.76	0.91	0.90	0.78
Proline	1.73	2.08	2.13	2.69	2.19	2.44	2.77	2.26	2.39	2.86	2.24
Serine	1.48	1.86	1.72	1.93	1.16	1.16	1.31	1.16	1.26	1.52	1.03
Taurine		1.63	1.76	1.71	0.63	0.74	0.56	0.32	0.30	0.32	0.54
Threonine	2.42	2.03	2.59	1.82	1.31	1.15	1.52	1.60	1.90	1.55	1.73
Tryptophan	0.45		0.65								0.79
Tyrosine	1.29	1.0	1.26	2.5	1.27	1.68	1.76	1.54	1.44	1.55	0.84
Valine	1.82	1.36	1.60	1.54	1.35	1.77	2.47	2.26	2.30	2.62	2.43

[a] Data recalculated from Arbetbal et al.[1]
[b] Data recalculated from Reisner et al.[62]
[c] Data from Dickinson et al.[17]
[d] Data from Ghadimi and Pecora.[25]
[e] Data from Snyderman et al.[82]

the virtual disappearance of this amino acid from the blood by the 3rd day. Table IV summarizes data on the plasma levels during the first days of life from the study of Dickinson et al.,[17] that of Ghadimi and Pecora,[25] and from the author's laboratory for various ages during the first year. The same peculiarities of urinary amino acid excretion noted for the premature infant also occur in the full term infant: the presence of free hydroxyproline and homocitrulline and of larger quantities of taurine and ethanolamine.[2] The increased excretion of this group of amino acids is a reflection of the increased plasma levels. In addition, there is increased excretion of all the usual amino acid constitutents of urine, which is again a manifestation of relative renal tubular immaturity. The quantities are smaller than in the premature, however, and do not persist as long.

The exact protein requirement of the newborn infant has not been firmly established. It would seem, however, that the amount provided by human milk is certainly sufficient. How far above minimum requirement this amount may be cannot be stated with certainty at present. There is no reason to believe that the protein requirement is higher with artificial feeding than with breast feeding, since the amino acid content of human milk and cow's milk, as determined with modern techniques, is quite similar. Differences in performance on these two feedings reported in the past were probably due to extraneous factors, such as sterility and the curd tension, factors that are no longer of importance with modern feeding practices. Both human milk and cow's milk in the various forms in which it is usually fed meet the individual requirements for all the essential amino acids as determined by Snyderman and co-workers[60,74,76,77,81,83-87] for infants 2–4 months of age. These studies utilized a completely synthetic diet, the nitrogen moiety of which was a mixture of 18 L-amino acids in the proportions in which they occur in human milk. After a control period in which the complete mixture was fed, the amino acid under study was completely withdrawn from the diet and reintroduced in a stepwise fashion until weight gain and nitrogen retention were equivalent to that of the control period. These studies gave quantitative data concerning the requirements of the amino acids that are known to be essential to man. In addition, they demonstrated that histidine, which is not considered to be an essential amino acid for the human adult, is required by the infant. The withdrawal of each of the individual essential amino acids had the same effect: a fall in the rate of weight gain, a reduction in the amount of nitrogen retained, anorexia, and lassitude. The withdrawal of histidine was unique in that it was accompanied by a specific symptom: the appearance of a rash that was very similar to that of ordinary infantile eczema, except that it did not ooze and was not accompanied by itching. It also had a number of histological similarities to eczema. This rash did not appear in infants over the age of 6 months, although other evidence that histidine is still essential at that age was obtained by the rate of weight gain and the quantity of nitrogen retained. The age at which histidine is no longer a dietary essential has not yet been ascertained.

These values for amino acid requirements obtained with a synthetic diet approximate those obtained with a more natural diet. In a series of studies, the intake of cow's-milk protein was gradually reduced until weight gain was depressed and nitrogen retention was impaired.[79] Supplementation of the diet at this point with unessential nitrogen in the form of either glycine or urea allowed immediate resumption of normal weight gain and nitrogen retention. In addition to the demonstration that the infant can utilize these simple forms of nitrogen for growth, these studies also add to the information on the amino acid requirements of

Table V. Amino Acid Requirements of the Full-Term Infant (mg/kg/day)

Amino acid	Requirement studies[a]	Provided by 1.3 g cow's milk protein/kg
Histidine	34 (16 < 34)	31
Isoleucine	100 (80 < 100)	84
Leucine[b]	150 (76 < 229)	141
Lysine	130 (88 < 103)	101
Methionine[c]	45 (33 < 45)	34
Phenylalanine[d]	90 (47 < 90)	68
Threonine	87 (45 < 87)	60
Tryptophan	22 (15 < 22)	20
Valine	105 (85 < 105)	90

[a] The first figure is the highest value obtained. The figures in parentheses denote the variation in value obtained; the higher requirement for each amino acid is qualified by the symbol "less than" because the minimum requirement must be somewhere between that which is adequate and a lower figure that was shown to be inadequate.

[b] With one exception, the leucine requirement did not exceed 150 mg/kg per day; the subject who required 229 mg/kg per day may have represented an anomaly.

[c] In the presence of adequate cystine.

[d] In the presence of adequate tyrosine.

infants. All the infants studied in this manner did well on an intake of 1.3 g milk protein/kg. Calculation of the amino acid content of this protein gives intakes very similar to those obtained with the synthetic diets. These two sets of values are compared in Table V. It should be noted that these requirements are valid only when all other dietary essentials are provided, when caloric intake is adequate, and when sufficient unessential nitrogen is available.

There are a number of inherited disorders of amino acid metabolism that may be manifest from earliest infancy. Although a detailed discussion of these disorders is beyond the scope of this chapter, the following diseases have been observed from the first days of life: phenylketonuria, tyrosinemia, histidinemia, branched chain ketoacidemia, isovaleric acidemia, β-hydroxyisovalericacidemia, β-methyl,β-hydroxybutyricacidemia, propionicacidemia, methylmalonicacidemia, nonketotic glycinemia, and the various urea cycle syndromes. Diagnosis before birth has also been possible in a number of these entities by means of amniocentesis, tissue culture, and specific assay for enzyme activity.

The feasibility of this approach is now well established.

5. References

1. ARBETBAL, C. L., FELDMAN, D. B., AHMANN, P., AND RUDMAN, D., 1975, Plasma amino acid patterns during supplemental intravenous nutrition of low birth weight infants, *J. Pediatr.* **86**:766.
2. ARMSTRONG, M. D., YATES, K. N., AND CONNELLY, D., 1964, Amino acid excretion of newborn infants during the first 24 hours of life, *Pediatrics* **33**:975.
3. AVERY, M. E., CLOWE, C. L., MENKES, J. H., RAMOS, A., SCRIVER, C. R., STERN, C., AND WASSERMAN, B. P., 1967, Transient tyrosinemia of the newborn. Dietary and clinical aspects, *Pediatrics* **39**:378.
4. A'ZARY, E., SOIFER, A., AND SCHNECK, L., 1973, The free amino acids in maternal and fetal extracellular fluids collected during early pregnancy, *Amer. J. Obstet. Gynecol.* **116**:854.
5. BLOXAM, H. R., DAY, M. G., GIBBS, N. K., AND WOOLF, L. I., 1960, An inborn defect in the metabolism of tyrosine and infants on a normal diet, *Biochem. J.* **77**:320.
6. BURRASTON, J., AND POLLOCK, J. K., 1961, Amino acid incorporation into embryonic rat liver, *Exp. Cell Res.* **25**:687.
7. BUTTERFIELD, L. J., AND O'BRIEN, D., 1963, The effect of maternal toxaemia and diabetes on transplacental gradients of free amino acids, *Arch. Dis. Child.* **38**:326.
8. CARLYLE, A., 1945, The weights of certain tissues of the sheep fetus during gestation relative to body weight, *J. Physiol. (London)* **104**:34p.
9. CEVINE, G., 1964, Intestinal permeability to I^{131} labelled polyvinylpyrrolidone in premature infants, *Biol. Neonate* **7**:290.
10. CHILDS, B., 1952, Urinary excretion of free alpha-amino acid nitrogen by normal infants and children, *Proc. Soc. Exp. Biol. Med.* **81**:225.
11. CHRISTENSEN, H. N., AND STREICHER, J. A., 1948, Association between rapid growth and elevated cell concentration of amino acids, *J. Biol. Chem.* **175**:95.
12. CLEMETSON, C. A. B., AND CHURCHMAN, J., 1954, The placental transfer of amino acids in normal and toxemic pregnancy, *J. Obstet. Gynaecol. Br. Emp.* **61**:364.
13. CZAJKA, D. M., MILLER, S. A., AND BROWNING, A. B., 1968, Protein synthesis in neonatal rat pups maintained artificially on a low protein diet, *Biol. Neonate.* **13**:291.
14. CZAJKA, D. M., MILLER, S. A., AND BROWNING, A. B., 1970, Hepatic protein metabolism in the infant rat, *J. Nutr.* **100**:309.
15. DALLAIRE, L., POTIER, M., MELANCON, S. B., AND PATRICK, J., 1974, Feto-maternal amino acid metabolism, *J. Obstet. Gynaecol. Br. Commonw.* **81**:761.
16. DICKERSON, J. W., AND WIDDOWSON, E. M., 1970, Chemical changes in skeletal muscle during development, *Biochem. J.* **74**:247.
17. DICKINSON, J. C., ROSENBLUM, H., AND HAMILTON, P. B., 1965, Ion exchange chromatography of the free amino acids in the plasma of the newborn infant, *Pediatrics* **36**:2.
18. FILER, L., JR., AND CHURELLA, H., 1963, Relation of body composition, chemical composition, homeostasis and diet in the newborn animal, *Ann. N. Y. Acad. Sci.* **110**:380.
19. FOWLER, D. I., NORTON, P. M., CHEUNG, M. W., AND PRATT, E. L., 1957, Observations on the urinary amino acid excretion in man: The influence of age and diet, *Arch. Biochem.* **68**:452.
20. FULKS, R. M., LI, J. B., AND GOLDBERG, A. L., 1975, Effects of insulin, glucose and amino acids on protein turnover in rat diaphragm, *J. Biol. Chem.* **250**:290.
21. FURST, P., AND JOSEPHSON, B., 1967, Non-protein serum nitrogen in infancy, *Amer. J. Dis. Child.* **113**:345.
22. GERRITSEN, T., AND WAISMAN, H. A., 1968, The free amino acids of brain and liver during fetal life of macaca mulatta, *Proc. Soc. Exp. Biol. Med.* **129**:542.
23. GESCHWIND, I., AND LI, C. H., 1949, Nucleic acid content of fetal rat liver, *J. Biol. Chem.* **180**:467.
24. GHADIMI, H., AND PECORA, P., 1964, Free amino acids of cord plasma as compared with maternal plasma during pregnancy, *Pediatrics* **33**:500.
25. GHADIMI, H., AND PECORA, P., 1964, Plasma amino acids after birth, *Pediatrics* **34**:182.
26. GLENDENING, M. B., MARGOLIS, A. J., AND PAGE, E. W., 1961, Amino acid concentration in fetal and maternal plasma, *Amer. J. Obstet. Gynecol.* **81**:591.
27. GORDON, H. H., LEVINE, S. Z., AND MCNAMARA, H., 1947, Feeding of premature infants: A comparison of human and cow's milk, *Amer. J. Dis. Child.* **73**:442.
28. GRESHAM, E. L., JAMES, E. J., RAYE, J. R., BATTAGLIA, F. C., MAKOWSKI, E. L., AND MESCHIA, G., 1972, Production and excretion of urea by the fetal lamb, *Pediatrics* **50**:372.
29. GRESHAM, E. L., SIMONS, P. S., AND BATTAGLIA, F. C., 1971, Maternal–fetal urea concentration differences in man, *J. Pediatr.* **79**:809.
30. HAIDER, M., AND SEGAL, H. L., 1972, Some characteristics of the alanine aminotransferase- and arginine-inactivating system of lysosomes, *Arch. Biochem. Biophys.* **148**:228.
31. HILL, P. M. M., AND YOUNG, M., 1973, Net placental transfer of free amino acids against varying concentrations, *J. Physiol.* **235**:409.
32. HULTIN, T., AND BERGSTRAND, 1960, Incorporation of C^{14} leucine into protein by cell-free systems from sea urchin embryos at different stages of development, *Dev. Biol.* **2**:61.
33. IMMERS, J., 1961, Comparative study of the localization of incorporated C^{14} labelled amino acids $^{35}SO_4$ in the

sea urchin ovary, egg, and embryo, *Exp. Cell. Res.* **24**:356.

34. JAKOBSEN, P. E., 1957, 299de Beretng, Kobenhaun, Forsøgslab.

35. KAGAN, B. M., FELLIX, N., AND MOLANDER, C. W., 1963, Body water changes in relation to nutrition of premature infants, *Ann. N. Y. Acad. Sci.* **110**:830.

36. KAPELLER-ADLER, R., AND HAMMAD, W. A., 1972, A biochemical study on nucleic acids and protein synthesis in the human fetus and its correlation with relevant embryological data, *J. Obstet. Gynaecol. Br. Commonw.* **79**:924.

37. KERR, G. M., CHAMOVE, A. S., HARLOW, H. F., AND WAISMAN, H. A., 1968, "Fetal PKU": The effect of maternal hyperphenylalaninemia during pregnancy in the Rhesus monkey *(Macaca mulatta), Pediatrics* **42**:27.

38. LEONE, A., CHIAPPI, F., AND TOCCO, A., 1966, Sui ricambeo dell acido urico in soggetti prematuri e immaturi, *Ann. Ital. Pediatr.* **19**:241.

39. LEVINE, S. Z., GORDON, H. H., AND MARPLES, E., 1941, Defect in the metabolism of tyrosine and phenylalanine in premature infants. II. Spontaneous occurrence and eradication by vitamin C, *J. Clin. Invest.* **20**:209.

40. LEVINE, S. Z., MARPLES, E., AND GORDON, H. H., 1941, Defect in the metabolism of tyrosine and phenylalanine in premature infants: Identification and assay of intermediate products, *J. Clin. Invest.* **20**:199.

41. LEVY, H. L., AND MONTAG, P. P., 1969, Free amino acids in human amniotic fluid. A quantitative study by ion-exchange chromatography, *Pediatr. Res.* **3**:113.

42. LINBLAD, B. S., AND BALDESTEN, A., 1967, The normal venous plasma free amino acid levels of non-pregnant women and of mother and child during delivery, *Acta Paediatr. Scand.* **56**:37.

43. LINDBLAD, B. S., AND ZETTERSTROM, R., 1968, The venous plasma free amino acid levels of mother and child during delivery. II. After short gestation and gestation complicated by hypertension with special reference to the "small for dates" syndrome, *Acta Paediatr. Scand.* **57**:195.

44. LØUTRUP, S., AND WERDINIUS, B., 1957, Metabolic phases during amphibian embryogenesis, *J. Exp. Zool.* **135**:203.

45. MADEY, S., AND DANCIS, J., 1949, Proteolytic enzymes of the premature infant, *Pediatrics* **4**:177.

46. McCANCE, R. A., AND STRANGEWAYS, W. M. B., 1954, Protein catabolism and oxygen consumption during starvation in infants, young adults, and old men, *Br. J. Nutr.* **8**:21.

47. MENKES, J. H., WELCHER, D. W., LEVI, H. S., DALLAS, J., AND GRETSKY, N. E., 1972, Relationship of elevated blood tyrosine to the ultimate intellectual performance of premature infants, *Pediatrics* **49**:218.

48. MILLER, S. A., LOPEZ, A. S., MORI, Y., AND WOO, A. F., 1970, Hepatic protein metabolism in the infant rat, *J. Nutr.* **100**:309.

49. MORI, M., 1965, Study of protein biosynthesis in fetus and placenta. I. Incorporation of C^{14} amino acids into the human placenta, *Amer. J. Obstet. Gynecol.* **19**:1164.

50. MORI, M., AND ISO, H., 1965, Study of protein biosynthesis in fetus and placenta. II. Transfer of S^{35} methionine across the placenta and mechanism of protein biosynthesis in the fetus, *Amer. J. Obstet. Gynecol.* **93**:1172.

51. MOULTON, C. R., 1923, Age and chemical development in mammals, *J. Biol. Chem.* **57**:79.

52. OBERMAN, J. W., *et al.,* 1952, Electrophoretic analysis of serum proteins in infants and children, *N. Engl. J. Med.* **255**:743.

53. OJA, S. S., AND PIHA, R. S., 1966, Changes in the concentration of free amino acids in the rat brain during postnatal development, *Life Sci.* **5**:865.

54. OLIVER, I. T., BALLARD, F. J., SHIELD, S., AND BENTLEY, P. J., 1962, Liver growth in early postpartum rat, *Dev. Biol.* **4**:108.

55. PARTINGTON, M. W., AND MATHEWS, J., 1966, The relation of plasma tyrosine level to weight gain of premature infants, *J. Pediatr.* **68**:749.

56. PEARLMANN, P., AND GUSTOFSON, T., 1948, Antigens in the egg and early developmental stages of the sea urchin, *Experimentia* **4**:481.

57. PIHA, R. S., AND UNSITALO, A. J., 1964, Incorporation of C^{14}-labeled amino acids into proteins of organs, tissues, and body fluids in foetal and newborn rats, *Ann. Med. Intern. Fenn.* **53**:167.

58. PINCUS, J. B., GITTLEMAN, I. F., SCHMERZLER, E., AND BRUNETTI, N., 1962, Protein levels in serum of premature infants fed diets varying in protein concentrations, *Pediatrics* **30**:622.

59. PITKIN, R. M., AND ZWIREK, S. J., 1967, Amniotic fluid creatinine, *Amer. J. Obstet. Gynecol.* **98**:1135.

60. PRATT, E. L., SNYDERMAN, S. E., CHEUNG, M. W., NORTON, P., AND HOLT, L. E. JR., 1955, The threonine requirement of the normal infant, *J. Nutr.* **56**:231.

61. RÄIHÄ, N. C. R., HEINONEN, K., RASSIN, D. K., AND GAULL, G. E., 1976, Milk protein quantity and quality in low-birth weight infants. 1. Metabolic responses and effects on growth, *Pediatrics* **57**:659.

62. REISNER, S. H., ARANDA, J. V., COLLE, E., PAPAGEORGIO, A., SCHIFF, D., SCRIVER, C. R., AND STERN, L., 1973, The effect of intravenous glucagon on plasma amino acids in the newborn, *Pediatr. Res.* **7**:184.

63. ROBERTS, E., FRANKEL, S., AND HARMON, P. J., 1950, Amino acids of nervous tissue, *Proc. Soc. Exp. Biol. Med.* **74**:383.

64. RYAN, W. C., AND CARVER, M. J., 1966, Free amino acids of human foetal and adult liver, *Nature (London)* **212**:292.

65. SAITO, M., GITTLEMAN, I. F., PINCUS, J. B., AND SOBEL, H. E., 1956, Plasma protein patterns in premature infants of varying weights on the first day of life, *Pediatrics* **17**:657.

66. SCHAIN, R. J., CARVER, M. J., COPENHAVER, J. H. AND UNDERDAHL, N. R., 1967, Protein metabolism

and the developing brain: Influence of birth and gestational age, *Science* **156**:984.

67. SCHOENHEIMER, R., 1942, *Dynamic State of Body Constituents,* Harvard University Press, Cambridge.

68. SCHULMAN, J. D., QUEENAN, J. T., AND DOORES, L., 1972, Gas chromatographic analysis of concentrations of amino acids in amniotic fluid from early, middle and late periods of human gestation, *Amer. J. Obstet. Gynecol.* **114**:243.

69. SCOTT, R. C., TENG, C. C., SAGERSON, R. N., AND NELSON, T., 1962, Amino acids in amniotic fluid; changes in concentrations during the first half of pregnancy, *Pediatr. Res.* **6**:659.

70. SIDRANSKY, H., SARMA, D. S. R., BONGIORO, M., AND VERNEY, E., 1968, Effect of dietary tryptophan on hepatic polyribosomes and protein synthesis in fasted mice. *J. Biol. Chem.* **243**:1123.

71. SIMON, S., 1911, Zur Stickstoffverteilung im Urin des Neugeborenen, *Z. Kinderheilkd.* **2**:1.

72. SINGER, E. J., HOCHSTRASSER, H., AND CERECEDI, C. R., 1956, The tryptophan, leucine and lysine content of the chick and mouse embryo during development, *Growth* **20**:229.

73. SNYDERMAN, S. E., 1971, The protein and amino acid requirements of the premature infant, in *Metabolic Processes in the Foetus and Newborn Infant* (E. S. Kroese, ed.), Leiden, Holland.

74. SNYDERMAN, S. E., BOYER, A., AND HOLT, L. E., JR., 1959, The arginine requirement of the infant, *Amer. J. Dis. Child.* **97**:192.

75. SNYDERMAN, S. E., BOYER, A., KOGUT, M. D., AND HOLT, L. E., JR., 1969, The protein requirement of the premature infant. I. The effect of protein intake on the retention of nitrogen, *J. Pediatr.* **74**:872.

76. SNYDERMAN, S. E., BOYER, A., PHANSALKAR, S. V., AND HOLT, L. E., JR., 1961, Essential amino acid requirements of infants: Tryptophan, *Amer. J. Dis. Child.* **102**:163.

77. SNYDERMAN, S. E., BOYER, A., ROITMAN, E., HOLT, L. E., JR., AND PROSE, P. H., 1963, The histidine requirement of the infant, *Pediatrics* **31**:786.

77. SNYDERMAN, S. E., HOLT, L. E., JR., AND BOYER, A., 1968, Unpublished data.

79. SNYDERMAN, S. E., HOLT, L. E., JR., DANCIS, J., ROITMAN, E., BOYER, A., AND BALIS, M. E., 1962, "Unessential" nitrogen: A limiting factor in human growth, *J. Nutr.* **78**:75.

80. SNYDERMAN, S. E., HOLT, L. E., JR., NORTON, P. M., AND PHANSALKAR, S. V., 1970, Protein requirements of the premature infant. II. Influence of the protein

intake on the free amino acid content of the plasma and the red blood cells, *Amer. J. Clin. Nutr.* **23**:890.

81. SNYDERMAN, S. E., HOLT, L. E., JR., SMELLIE, F., BOYER, A., AND WESTALL, R. G., 1959, The essential amino acid requirements of infants: Valine, *Amer. J. Dis. Child.* **97**:186.

82. SNYDERMAN, S. E., NORTON, P. M., AND BOYER, A., 1968, Unpublished data.

83. SNYDERMAN, S. E., NORTON, P. M., FOWLER, D. I., AND HOLT, L. E., JR., 1959, The essential amino acid requirements of infants: Lysine, *Amer. J. Dis. Child.* **97**:175.

84. SNYDERMAN, S. E., NORTON, P. M., ROITMAN, E., AND HOLT, L. E., JR., 1964, The essential amino acid requirements of infants. IX. Isoleucine, *J. Clin. Nutr.* **15**:313.

85. SNYDERMAN, S. E., NORTON, P. M., ROITMAN, E., AND HOLT, L. E., JR., 1964, The essential amino acid requirements of infants. X. Methionine, *J. Clin. Nutr.* **15**:322.

86. SNYDERMAN, S. E., PRATT, E. L., CHEUNG, M. W., NORTON, P. M., HOLT, L. E., JR., HANSEN, A. E., AND PANOS, T. C., 1955, The phenylalanine requirement of the normal infant, *J. Nutr.* **56**:253.

87. SNYDERMAN, S. E., ROITMAN, E. BOYER, A., AND HOLT, L. E., JR., 1961, Essential amino acid requirements of infants: Leucine, *Amer. J. Dis. Child.* **102**:157.

88. STAVE, U., AND ARMSTRONG, M. D., 1973, Tissue free amino acid concentrations in perinatal rabbits, *Biol. Neonate* **22**:374.

89. WIDDOWSON, E. M., AND DICKERSON, J. W., 1960, The effect of growth and function on the chemical composition of soft tissues, *Biochem. J.* **77**:30.

90. WIDDOWSON, E. M., AND SPRAY, C. M., 1951, Chemical development *in utero, Arch. Dis. Child.* **26**:205.

91. WILLIAMS, C. M., 1963, Effect of different feedings on blood urea levels in prematurity, *Med. J. Aust.* **2**:698.

92. WINNICK, M., 1968, Changes in nucleic acid and protein content of human brain during growth, *Pediatr. Res.* **2**:352.

93. WINICK, M., COSCIA, A., AND NOBLE, A. 1967, Cellular growth in the human placenta. I. Normal placental growth, *Pediatrics* **39**:248.

94. WOODSIDE, K. H., AND MORTIMORE, G. E., 1972, Suppression of protein turnover by amino acids in perfused rat liver, *J. Biol. Chem.* **247**:6474.

95. YU, J. S., AND O'HALLORAN, M. T., 1970, Children of mothers with phenylketonuria, *Lancet* **1**:210.

CHAPTER 19

Lipids

Peter Hahn

1. Introduction

The term *lipids* covers a heterogeneous group of substances that can be extracted from tissues by nonpolar solvents. The main lipid classes are: (1) fatty acids; (2) neutral fat (triglycerides or triacylglycerols); (3) phospholipids (phosphatides), including: (a) derivatives of glycerol-3-phosphate and (b) derivatives of sphingosine or related compounds; (4) glycolipids, including derivatives of glycerol; (5) aliphatic alcohols and waxes, (6) terpenes; and (7) steroids. Only some of these lipids will be discussed in this chapter; those that do not occur in mammals and those about which too little is known during development will be omitted. The steroids, excepting cholesterol, are dealt with in Chapter 37.

In the living animal, lipids serve three main functions: insulation, supply of energy, and structure.

The insulating fat (subcutaneous and other) consists mainly of triglycerides, which, when hydrolyzed into fatty acids and glycerol, serve as a ready source of energy. Phosphatides (phospho-lipids), together with cholesterol, are an important part of all cellular and intracellular membranes.

In most mammalian species, the fat content increases during development, prenatally in some and postnatally in others, depending on the degree of maturity at birth and ecological factors (Fig. 1). This perinatally accumulated fat apparently serves mainly as a store of energy that can be mobilized and utilized at and after birth.

Immediately after birth, when glycogen stores are exhausted, lipids serve as the main source of energy (see Section 2). In man, this was first shown by Babák,[4] who observed a pronounced fall of the respiratory quotient within the first few days after birth. The guinea pig, although it gains weight during the first 7 postnatal days, actually loses calories in the form of fat during that same period, evidently because the energy supply from the milk is insufficient.[49,50] The rat, in contrast, gains fat during that same period, since the fat supply in the milk is high.

2. Fatty Acids

In the adult, the blood level of fatty acids is relatively low (0.5–2.0 meq/liter) in comparison with glucose (about 5 mM/liter), but since the turnover rate of fatty acids is higher than that of

Peter Hahn · Centre for Developmental Medicine, Department of Obstetrics and Gynaecology and Department of Paediatrics, Faculty of Medicine, University of British Columbia, Vancouver, British Columbia, Canada

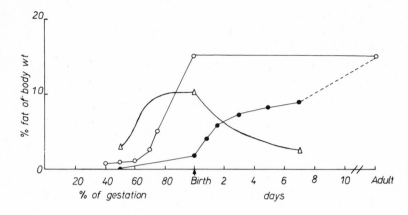

Fig. 1. Fat content in fetuses and newborns of different species. (△) Guinea pig; (●) rat; (○) man.

glucose, both contribute to energy production at about the same rate. In extreme situations, such as starvation, fatty acid oxidation can become the main source of energy.

The transport of fatty acids across cell membranes appears to be a passive process, since it depends mainly on concentration gradients. This seems to be true for adipose tissue and liver, but not for the placenta. In most species, the fatty acid concentration in the fetal blood is much lower than in the mother, and variations in the maternal fatty acid level are not reflected in the blood of the fetus. The placental transport of fatty acids still needs further investigation, but it does undoubtedly occur,[111,85] as shown in rabbits, sheep, and guinea pigs.[59] This transport may be of particular importance for the supply of essential fatty acids to the fetus. In general, however, the mammalian fetus obtains most of its energy from utilizing carbohydrates, and fatty acid synthesis predominates well over fatty acid oxidation. Recently, it was shown that the rate of transport of fatty acids across the isolated human placenta depends on chain length. Palmitic acid is transported only very slowly, while octanoic acid crosses much more rapidly.[21]

The rabbit and the guinea pig differ from most of the other species in that the level of TG but not fatty acids in the blood of the fetus is higher than that in the mother, at least toward the end of gestation. In general, however, the blood levels of fatty acid and TG is low during gestation.[33] It increases soon after birth, usually up to values that are higher than those found in well-fed adults (Table I and Fig. 2). This postnatal increase is due to the beginning of milk feeding in rats (colostrum has an especially high fat content) and to the release of fatty acids from adipose tissues. The latter cause seems to be mediated by the release of noradrenaline from sympathetic nerve endings in adipose tissues. The relative importance of these two factors differs according to species. In man and animals that have large fat deposits at birth, such as guinea pigs, the initial postnatal rise in blood fatty-acid concentration is undoubtedly related to an increased release of

Table I. Blood Level of Free Fatty Acids in Different Species (meq/liter)

Mother	Fetus	Newborn	1	3	12	24	Species	References
			— Hours after birth					
1.22	0.42	0.73	1.37		1.5	1.2	Man	Keele and Kay[67]
1.2	0.4	0.4	1.2			1.9	Man	Roux and Romney[90]
1.3		0.4	0.8			1.2	Man	Hahn and Koldovský[50]
0.65	0.51					1.7	Rabbit	Van Duyne et al.[112] and Roux[89]
1.0	0.1		0.6	0.6			Sheep	Van Duyne et al.[112]
0.8	0.2	0.2		0.3	0.5	0.5	Rat	Hahn and Koldovský[50]

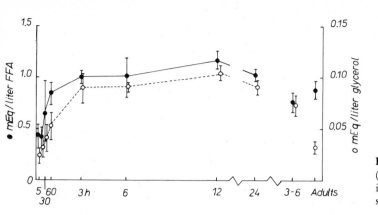

Fig. 2. Blood levels of free fatty acids (FFA) and glycerol in full-term newborn infants. Data from Hahn and Koldovský.[50]

fatty acids from adipose tissues. Later, i.e., after 1 week in human infants, nutritional factors become more important. In animals born with small fat deposits, e.g., the rat, the effect of a high-fat diet appears much sooner, probably as soon as the animal is first nursed. This early effect was recently shown by Girard.[38] The level of free fatty acids (FFA) in the blood of *unfed* newborn rats increases only transiently if they are not fed, and normal high postnatal levels are obtained only after suckling.[38] The high level of fatty acids in the blood of most suckling animals (including rabbits) indicates that fatty acid utilization must be higher during that time than before birth and after weaning.

The fatty acid content of liver, adipose tissue, and lungs (nothing is known of other tissues) is also greater in the suckling period than before birth and after weaning, at least in the rat. No such data are available for the human baby. In the suckling rat, the level of fatty acids in lungs and blood decreases during starvation.[50] From these results, we concluded that most of the fatty acids were derived from food and not from endogenous sources, as is known to occur in adults. In adults, on the other hand, starvation leads to an increase of the blood level of fatty acids; the same was also found in rabbits.[89] This rise in adults is due to a release of fatty acids from adipose tissue triglycerides by a hormone-sensitive lipase[87]; in the rat, the activity of this enzyme is low in the suckling period.[41]

Ignoring fatty acid utilization for the moment, the level of fatty acids in the blood is determined by the supply of fat in the diet and the release of fatty acids from adipose tissues. In most suckling mammals, the diet is the decisive factor. In adult animals, the regulation of fatty acid release from adipose tissue is far more important.

2.1. Synthesis

In considering this complex process, it is important to remember that two different pathways exist for fatty acid synthesis, one via malonyl-CoA, the other via a reversal of β-oxidation. Very little is known about the prenatal and postnatal development of these pathways in different tissues. The rate of mitochondrial elongation of fatty acids in the rat heart is highest in suckling animals.[116] It was shown by Villee and Hagerman[113] and by others that fatty acid synthesis from various precursors is higher in human and other mammalian fetuses than in their mothers, and that the rate of this synthesis decreases rapidly after birth, particularly in the liver. In the rat, this decrease after birth is evidently due to the high fat content in milk, since fatty acid synthesis in the liver increases again only after weaning, provided the animals are fed the usual high-carbohydrate diet.[14] The work of Roux *et al.*[92] is of particular importance, since young fetuses have rarely been examined. These authors showed that in human fetuses, the liver supernatant fraction to which microsomes were added did not synthesize fatty acids from acetate or citrate before the 28th week of gestation; hence, they postulated that before that time, fetal fatty acids were derived from the mother via the placenta. In the human brain, fatty acid synthesis begins during the 16th week of gestation. In the fetal rat, fatty acid synthesis is greater on day 20 than on day 16 of gestation.[33] Since so little is known about the metabolism in young fetuses, we would like to suggest that during early fetal development, tissues other than liver can synthesize fatty acids. Until more is known in this field, conclusions will have to remain equivocal.

The importance of examining not only different

species but also different organs in the same species is emphasized by the fact that changes found in the liver need not reflect changes in other tissues. For instance, fatty acid synthesis in the brain is higher in suckling rats than in adult animals.[93,114] Recent work in this area has shown that the enzyme complex called *fatty acid synthetase* (FAS) is synthesized at a more rapid rate in the brains of suckling than those of fetal rats. The opposite holds for the liver enzyme.[114] Acetyl-CoA carboxylase activity is also decreased after birth in both liver and adipose tissue.[43] In the brain, however, it reaches a peak on about the 10th postnatal day[43] This finding suggests, of course, that in liver and adipose tissue, the rate of fatty acid synthesis depends on the diet, while this relationship is not true for the brain. The experiments of Smith and Abraham[105] bear this hypothesis out. It appears that essential fatty acids control the rate of fatty acid synthesis, at least in the mouse. If the mother animal is fed a diet devoid of essential fatty acids, then fatty acid synthesis in her suckling young is not suppressed, as is usually the case.

It has been postulated that the initial steps of fatty acid synthesis involve a transfer of citrate from the mitochondrial into the cytoplasmic compartment, where this metabolite is broken down into oxaloacetate and acetyl-CoA by citrate cleavage enzyme. The acetyl-CoA is then used for fatty acid synthesis. The activity of citrate cleavage enzyme is very low in both liver and adipose tissue of suckling rats, lower than before birth and after weaning.[43] This situation would agree with changes in the rate of fatty acid synthesis. It is possible, however, that the pathways of fatty acid synthesis differ in different tissues. The existence of such tissue difference is supported by Roux et al.,[92] who found that fatty acid synthesis is much less from acetate than from citrate in human fetal liver, but observed no such difference in human fetal brain. Probably the most important advance in recent years is the possibility of studying actual rates of synthesis and breakdown of enzymes. In the case of FAS, which is a complex of several enzymes, it has nevertheless been possible to purify the enzyme, inject it into rabbits to produce antibodies, and then precipitate previously labeled enzyme with antibody. Such studies have shown that changes in FAS activity are usually due to changes in enzyme amount.[114] Changes in the rate of fatty acid synthesis occur much faster, however, than changes in the rate of FAS synthesis (the half-life of FAS is about 50 hr; the change in

the rate of fatty acid synthesis can occur within minutes). Hence, it is quite obvious that there are both short-term and long-term regulatory factors at work. Thus, immediately after birth, fatty acid synthesis in the liver is suppressed very rapidly, probably because of the accumulation of some metabolites (glycerol, fatty acids, acyl-CoA) and the rise in the rate of gluconeogenesis, which will decrease the availability of citrate. It should also be mentioned that the half-life of PEPK carboxykinase is only about 3–6 hr, and its sudden appearance after birth could thus lead to more oxaloacetate being pulled toward PEP and less toward citrate, long before FAS synthetase is suppressed. Fatty acid synthesis, however, would be effectively inhibited.

2.2. Oxidation

In contrast to the passive, gradient-dependent transport of fatty acids through cell membranes, the transport from the cytoplasm into the mitochondrion, where fatty acid oxidation occurs, is a complex process that has been worked out by Fritz.[35] Apparently, fatty acids can reach their site of oxidation in the mitochondria only by being transported in the form of acylcarnitine.[35] They are then reassembled into acyl-CoA compounds, which can be oxidized.

$$\text{fatty acids} + \text{CoA} \longrightarrow \text{acyl-CoA}$$

$$\text{acyl-CoA} + \text{carnitine} \longrightarrow \text{acylcarnitine} + \text{CoA}$$

$$\text{acylcarnitine} + \text{CoA} \longrightarrow \text{carnitine} + \text{acyl-CoA}$$

The oxidation of fatty acids requires more oxygen than does the oxidation of carbohydrates, or more correctly, the former requires more hydrogen acceptors. This requirement is important in neonatal physiology, since the tolerance to hypoxia and anoxia is usually greater in newborn and suckling animals than later in life, although suckling animals utilize more fatty acids for energy supply. This paradoxical finding remains to be explored.

There is no doubt that the oxidation of fatty acids is greatly enhanced after birth in all mammalian species examined so far.[50] But again, this enhancement is not necessarily true for all organs. In this regard, the results of Wittels and Bressler[122] are a very important contribution to the analysis of the development of fatty acid oxidation. These author examined heart muscle homogenates of rats during postnatal development. In newborn rats, the oxidation of labeled palmitic acid to CO_2, and similarly of labeled palmityl CoA, is about 10 times lower than that in adult animals. This low rate of fatty acid oxidation in the newborn heart is due, first, to the low activity of long-chain fatty acyl-CoA-carnitine transferase, the enzyme that is responsible for transferring fatty acids from acyl-CoA to carnitine and vice versa, and, second, to the low level of carnitine in the heart muscle of newborn rats. The authors speculate that "since the capacity of the heart of nursing infant rats to oxidize palmitic acid increases to approximately 50% of the adult rate by 5 days of age and is not significantly different from adults 10 days after birth, an induction period during which plasma free fatty acid levels are higher than they are during fetal life may be necessary for long-chain fatty acid oxidation." In puppies, fatty acids are also not utilized by heart muscle.[12] β-Hydroxyacyl-CoA dehydrogenase activity in various organs of the rabbit was found highest perinatally, again indicating preferential utilization of fat in the neonatal period.[108]

A similar situation prevails in brown adipose tissue,[31] since its mitochondria always oxidize fatty acids at a high rate, and this oxidation is completely dependent on the presence of carnitine and ATP. In addition, acetate oxidation also appears to be carnitine-dependent. Although the oxidation of fatty acids in brown adipose tissue proceeds at a high rate in fetal rats, there is an increase soon after birth. In recent years, considerable progress has been made in this field. Acyl carnitine transferases (at least four are known: acetyl, octanoyl, and two · palmitoylcarnitine transferases) predominantly situated in the mitochondria increase in activity soon after birth in liver,[3,47] brown adipose tissue,[51,52] and heart.[52,115] The carnitine content of the tissues also rises postnatally. Carnitine is also required for optimum ketone production by liver mitochondria. It has been demonstrated that lysine is a precursor of carnitine, and hence it may be assumed that in situations such as kwashiorkor, when little protein is consumed, there may also be a carnitine deficiency due to insufficient intake of both carnitine and lysine, which may be one of the causes of fatty liver in infants on a low-protein/high-carbohydrate diet.

2.3. Ketone Bodies

The liver has a special position in fatty acid oxidation, since it lacks the enzyme necessary for

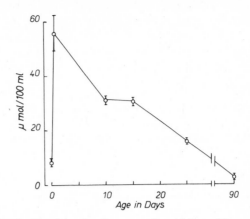

Fig. 3. Blood levels of acetoacetic acid in suckling rats. Data from Drahota et al.[29]

transfer of CoA from succinyl-CoA to acetoacetate. Hence, the final products of fatty acid oxidation in the liver are the ketone bodies, which are acetoacetic acid, β-hydroxybutyric acid, and acetone.

The rate at which ketone bodies are produced by the liver seems to depend mainly on the supply of fatty acids to the liver, which is high in starving and diabetic adults. In suckling mammals, the liver is also supplied with a large amount of fatty acids; hence, it is not surprising to find a rapidly increasing blood level of ketone bodies in the human infant and the rat after birth (Figs. 3 and 4). This increase is more pronounced in rats, and is due mainly to the sudden and high supply of fat from the milk. In the human infant, fatty acid mobilization is mainly responsible for the postnatal increase in ketone bodies in the blood.

In the rat, this postnatal rise in the blood level of ketone bodies is actually due to overproduction, not to low utilization by the periphery. As soon as 12 hr after birth, the rate of formation of acetoacetate by rat liver slices is much greater than before birth, when it is undetectably low, and than later, after weaning (Fig. 5). The mechanism of this phenomenon has not been completely elucidated. The concentration of fatty acids in the liver seems to be very important, since in vitro, the addition of relatively large amounts of fatty acids to liver slices increases ketone body formation. This increase was observed in preparations from all ages, but the age differences were still preserved. Other, probably regulatory mechanisms are

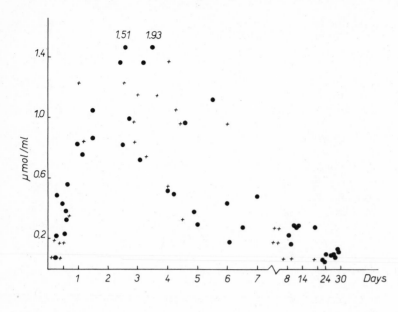

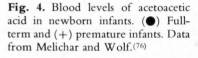

Fig. 4. Blood levels of acetoacetic acid in newborn infants. (●) Full-term and (+) premature infants. Data from Melichar and Wolf.[76]

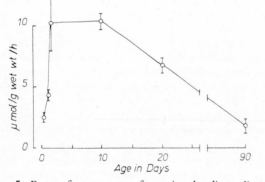

Fig. 5. Rate of acetoacetate formation by liver slices from suckling rats.

Table II. Fatty Acid Content of Liver Mitochondria from Suckling and Adult Rats[a]

Age[b]	FFA (μmol/g mitochondrial protein)
90 days ($n = 6$)	27.3 ± 3.6
7–9 days ($n = 5$)	61.5 ± 14.9

[a] Data from Drahota et al.[28]

[b] n = Number of determinations; 8–10 suckling rats were used for one determination.

evidently involved.[62] The basic mechanism, however, seems to depend on the fatty acid concentration, probably within the mitochondria (Table II and Fig. 6).

In the human fetus, the liver is capable of producing ketone bodies from acetate and octanoate at the earliest age examined, which was the 10th week of gestation.[53] The rate of production was low, and probably lower than in the newborn, but the latter age group was not examined.

In contrast to fatty acids, ketone bodies pass easily through the placenta in humans[84] and in rats.[95] During gestation, the mothers in both species are more prone to ketosis, so that the further fate of ketones in the fetus would be of interest. However, the utilization of ketone bodies by fetal and suckling humans and animals has rarely been examined. In adult heart muscle, for instance, ketones are utilized in preference to glucose,[121] and in the brains of suckling rats, acetoacetate utilization is greater than later in life.[30] The study on heart muscle also indicated that more ketone bodies were utilized in suckling rats than in adult animals, but this result needs to be confirmed. In recent years, ketone body utilization by newborn and fetal brains was examined in more detail.[43] It was shown that the brains of suckling rats utilize ketones to a larger extent than glucose,[30] that the enzymes of ketone formation (β-hydroxybutyrate dehydro-

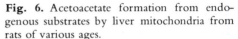

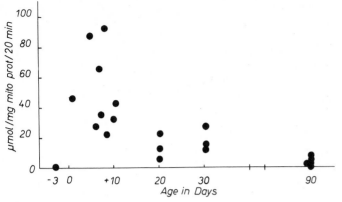

Fig. 6. Acetoacetate formation from endogenous substrates by liver mitochondria from rats of various ages.

genase, acetoacetyl-CoA deacylase) in the rat brain increase in activity to a peak soon after birth and later decline again,[120] that they can be induced before birth by feeding a high-fat diet to the mother rat,[23] and that very similar developmental changes are likely to occur in the human brain. In fact, the human fetal brain utilizes ketone bodies more than it does glucose.[1] Very recent experiments with labeled β-OH butyrate injected into pregnant rats indicate rapid transport of the acid into the fetus and its rapid utilization for fatty acid synthesis. In liver and brown fat, most of the label was found in triglycerides, elsewhere in phospholipids (Seccombe, personal communication). It was also shown that the oxidation of fatty acids to ketone bodies by rat liver is low prenatally and increases rapidly after birth,[29] together with the activities of mitochondrial hydroxymethylglutaryl-CoA lyase and synthetase and acetoacetyl-CoA thiolase.[7] Finally, it was recently shown that ketones, particularly β-hydroxybutyric acid, are utilized for fatty acid and sterol synthesis in the nervous tissue and skin of suckling rats.[32]

Figure 7 summarizes the fate of fatty acids in suckling mammals and probably also in the human baby during the first week of life. Fatty acids enter the liver in large amounts. Immediately after birth, they are derived mainly from adipose tissue, and later from exogenous sources such as milk. In the liver, fatty acids are broken down to ketone bodies, which are transported to other tissues and organs, where they serve as a source of energy. If this scheme is correct, it would explain: (1) the low utilization of long-chain fatty acids by heart muscle and probably other organs in very young suckling animals; (2) the high rate of ketone body formation; (3) the greater resistance of newborn mammals to hypoglycemia; and (4) the relatively low rate of glucose utilization in newborn infants, as compared with that in older infants.

3. Neutral Fat (Triglycerides or Triacylglycerols)

The level of triglycerides in the blood is dependent on fat absorption from the gut, on the release of triglycerides from the liver, and on the removal of triglycerides from the blood. In contrast to fatty acids, triglycerides cannot serve as an immediate source of energy, since they must first be hydrolyzed into fatty acid and glycerol.

In the blood, triglycerides are transported as lipoproteins. In humans and rats, chylomicrons appear in the blood 1–3 days after birth.[50] Before that time, a denser form of lipoprotein predominates. Triglycerides are removed from the circulation by many tissues, but very little is known about the mechanism involved.

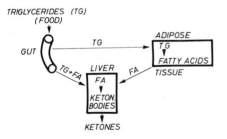

Fig. 7. Diagram of fat transport and utilization.

Table III. Serum Lipid Values of Control and Alloxan Diabetic Rabbits and Their Fetuses at 28 Days of Gestation (Means ±S.D.)[a]

Rabbits	No.	Phospholipid (mg/dl)	Triglyceride (meq/liter)	Cholesterol Ester (mg/dl)	Cholesterol Free (mg/dl)
Mothers					
Control	12	1.2 ± 0.7	1.7 ± 1.8	11.8 ± 12.7	3.6 ± 8.9
Alloxan diabetic	16	1.4 ± 0.7	2.4 ± 0.9	8.9 ± 5.3	3.5 ± 3.3
Fetuses					
Control	12	4.9 ± 1.1	2.8 ± 1.6	33.7 ± 7.9	28.2 ± 11.1
Alloxan diabetic	16	4.5 ± 1.2	2.5 ± 1.4	35.9 ± 13.2	19.3 ± 7.1

[a] From Sisson and Plotz.[98]

In most species, the blood level of triglycerides is low before birth and increases after birth. The rabbit and guinea pig, however, are exceptions. In these two species, the triglyceride level in the blood is higher in the older fetus than in the newborn and mother (Table III).

In the mammalian fetus, the triglyceride content of most organs is very low, the liver and the adrenal glands containing the largest amounts. Fat appears in the fetal liver earlier, however, than does glycogen[119]—on the 24th day of gestation in the guinea pig and on the 19th day in the rabbit.[71] In the rabbit and guinea pig fetus, the triglyceride content of the liver is higher than in the doe. In guinea pigs (Fig. 8), and similarly in the rabbit, the triglyceride content of the liver increases at birth, while in the rat, this increase occurs after birth.[50] In all species studied, the blood level of triglycerides increases after birth, and is higher in newborns than in adults. Triglycerides cannot pass through the placenta, but in sheep, monoglycerides and perhaps diglycerides seem to be transferred transplacentally to a limited extent.[96] In the rat and in other species that are born at an immature stage of development, the fat content of the body increases rapidly after birth, from about 1–2% at birth to 10% 10 days later. Most of this fat is accumulated as triglycerides, whereas most of fetal lipids are phospholipids. This composition is in contrast to that in the human infant, who is born with fully developed adipose tissues and a total fat content of approximately 15% of body weight.

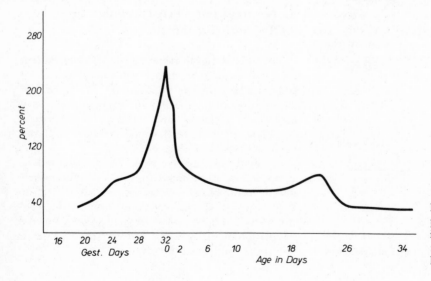

Fig. 8. Fat content of liver in percentage of fat-free dry weight in guinea pigs during development. Data from Logothetopoulos et al.[71]

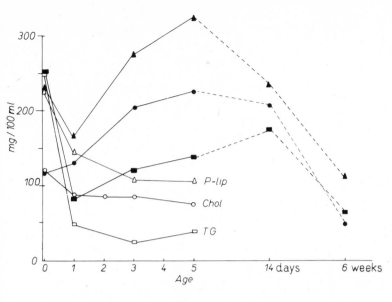

Fig. 9. Levels of cholesterol (Chol), triglycerides (TG), and phospholipids (P-lip) in the blood of suckling rabbits fed normal rabbit milk (solid symbols) or a fat-free milk (open symbols). Data from Friedman and Byers.[34]

In human infants, the postnatal rise of blood triglycerides and apparently the increase of lipids in other organs, too, is closely related to food intake,[50] and this relationship seems to hold true for other species, including the rabbit.[34] If fat is omitted from the diet (fat-free milk), the triglyceride content of the blood decreases in rabbits (Fig. 9).

Starvation or feeding of a protein-free diet to pregnant rats at the end of gestation causes an accumulation of triglycerides in the fetal liver. These triglycerides are probably not derived from the mother. Linoleic and palmitic acids pass through the placenta in guinea pigs,[59] and they might well be incorporated into liver triglycerides.

3.1. Lipogenesis

The formation of triglycerides from fatty acids occurs as follows:

$$\text{fatty acid} + \text{CoA} \longrightarrow \text{acyl-CoA}$$

$$3\text{ acyl-CoA} + \text{glycerol-3-phosphate} \longrightarrow \text{triglyceride}$$

As shown by the formulas, the fatty acid and the glycerol moiety must first be activated. Acyl-CoA formation must occur before birth in man and, if not before birth, then immediately after birth in all mammalian species; however, this requirement has not been determined directly. Since the initial steps of phospholipid formation also involve acyl-CoA

formation, and since phospholipids are present in all cells, it is quite evident that acyl-CoA is formed at all developmental ages. Glycerol-3-phosphate is discussed below.

3.2. Lipolysis

The breakdown of triglyceride is not a reversal of triglyceride formation, since

$$\text{triglyceride} \xrightarrow{\text{lipase}} \text{fatty acids} + \text{glycerol}$$

Lipolysis is known to occur in many tissues, but seems to be most pronounced, at least under certain conditions, in adipose tissue. The enzyme responsible for the hydrolysis of triglycerides is called *lipase* (EC 3.1.1.3), but at present, it is still uncertain how many lipases actually exist. In adipose tissue, at least three types have been described, together with more than ten isoenzymes of esterase, some of which might be identical with lipases. The two main enzymes are the hormone-sensitive lipase and the lipoprotein lipase. In addition, adipose tissues contain a monoglyceride lipase. Pancreatic lipase is evidently a different enzyme (see Chapter 15).

Hormone-sensitive lipase has been studied mainly in adipose tissue, and it is not certain how much of this enzyme activity is present in other organs. In adipose tissue, it is responsible for the breakdown of triglycerides *within* the fat cell. It is activated by various hormones and starvation. Thus, this enzyme serves to supply the rest of the body with nutrients

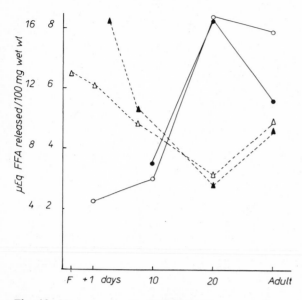

Fig. 10. Hormone-sensitive (○,●) and lipoprotein lipase (△,▲) activities in white (●,▲) and brown (○,△) adipose tissue of suckling rats. (F) Fetus. Data from Hahn[41] and Hahn and Drahota.[44]

stored in fat depots. It therefore appears logical that in the suckling period, when exogenous food supply is abundant and when, in the rat at least, fat is being deposited, the activity of hormone-sensitive lipase is low in adipose tissue, and that it increases with age (Fig. 10). Nothing is known about its development in other species.

Lipoprotein lipase seems to be more ubiquitously distributed than the hormone-sensitive lipase. In addition to being present in adipose tissue, it has been found in heart muscle and blood, and is probably present in the lungs.[80] It is called *lipoprotein lipase* because it hydrolyzes lipoproteins. It is activated by heparin, which apparently also causes its release from the walls of blood vessels into the blood. In adipose tissue, it serves to break down triglycerides (chylomicrons) when they enter the tissue from the blood, and thus this enzyme provides a mechanism that channels triglycerides into the fat cells by splitting the neutral fat into fatty acids and glycerol, which can both enter the cell. Triglyceride as such cannot pass through the cell wall to any considerable extent. As can be expected, lipoprotein lipase activity is highest in rat adipose tissue of the newborn and decreases with age (Fig. 10).

Another lipase activity has been determined histochemically and biochemically, and it was found to

increase with age in the heart, lungs, and liver of the rat, and in the heart muscle of the chick.[37] It is not clear, however, what type of lipase was actually measured in those experiments. In addition, mitochondria seem to have a lipase of their own, the activity of which in heart and brain mitochondria increases with age in the rat. In the heart, this might well be a lipoprotein lipase that, in this organ, serves to supply lipids when they are required for energy purposes, as indicated by the fact that the activity of lipoprotein lipase in this organ increases during starvation, while it decreases in adipose tissue of adult rats. In the human, lipoprotein lipase increases with age after birth.[103]

Glycerol-3-phosphate arises by the phosphorylation of glycerol by glycerol kinase. Glycerol-3-phosphate can also be formed during glycolysis or gluconeogenesis. The final step in both is

$$\text{dihydroxyacetone phosphate} + \text{NADH} + \text{H}^+$$
$$\longrightarrow \text{glycerol-3-phosphate} + \text{NAD}^+$$

The enzyme that catalyzes this reaction is glycerol-3-phosphate dehydrogenase (EC 1.1.1.8).

Glycerol-3-phosphate is an important factor in lipogenesis, since obviously no triglycerides can be formed if no glycerol-3-phosphate is available. Glycerol is released from adipose tissue during lipolysis, but it can serve as a source of energy only after being phosphorylated.

It has been suggested that the rate of fatty acid synthesis depends on a sufficient supply of glycerol-3-phosphate, since the fatty acids will be removed after esterification with this compound. If esterification does not occur, fatty acids accumulate, and finally the excess of acyl-CoA inhibits further fatty acid synthesis and also glycolytic reactions.

Glycerol kinase activity is low in the liver of suckling rats[46,110] (Fig. 11), and in the liver of newborn rabbits, the activity of glycerol-3-phosphate dehydrogenase was found to be only 40% of the adult level.[107] Since the rate of glycolysis is low in the immediate postnatal period, the only other source of glycerol-3-phosphate is gluconeogenesis, which at that time is high (see Chapter 17). What happens to the glycerol that enters the blood from adipose tissues and from the gut? In adipose tissues of suckling rats and of newborn infants, glycerol kinase activity is higher than in adults,[45] as shown by the higher rate of incorporation of labeled glycerol into triglyceride. Hence, glycerol might be reutilized for triglyceride synthesis in adipose tissue. Glycerol kinase activity might also be

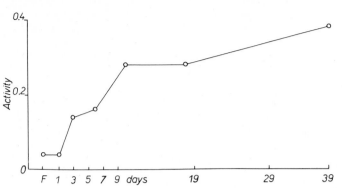

Fig. 11. Glycerol kinase activity of the liver of suckling rats (μmol/mg protein per 20 min). (F) Fetus. Data from Hahn and Greenberg.[45]

high in other tissues at that time, and glycerol might serve there as a source of energy to a greater extent in newborn than adult mammals. In newborn human infants, glycerol is rapidly utilized, as shown by its disappearance from the blood after loading tests.[123] Lipids that contain glycerol are intensively synthesized in rat brain during the 2nd and 3rd postnatal weeks, but the activity of glycerol-3-phosphate dehydrogenase in brain is low in the newborn rat[69] (see Chapter 29). Glycerol kinase activity has not been detected in the brains of newborn rabbits (Stave, personal communication).

3.3. Fatty Acid Composition of Triglycerides

In most mammalian species, the fatty acid composition of triglycerides in the fetus differs from that in the mother animal, the main difference being a smaller amount of unsaturated fatty acids and a larger amount of palmitic acid in the former.[70]

Table IV. Fatty Acid Composition of Adipose Tissue of Newborn Infants and Adults[a]

Fatty acid	Newborn (%)	Adult (%)
14:0	3.0	3.3
16:0	40.2	19.5
16:1	14.6	6.9
18:0	5.1	4.2
18:1	25.2	46.7
18:2	1.3	11.4

[a] Data from Hirsch.[60]

This difference has been taken to indicate that most of the fatty acids in the fetus are synthesized *de novo*, and that the transport of fatty acid from the mother to the fetus is limited (Table IV). After birth, the fatty acid composition of the newborn changes, and it becomes apparently more related to the fatty acid composition of the milk, as shown in man[60] and the rat.[27]

Jahn *et al.*[65] examined the fatty acid composition of triglycerides, phospholipids, and cholesterolesters of fetal and maternal rat liver and of the placenta. They found certain variations in these three organs during the last 3 days of gestation; e.g., the linoleic acid content of the maternal liver increased, that of the fetal liver decreased, and in the placenta, it remained unchanged; the arachidonic acid content of the placenta increased.

4. Phospholipids

The term *phospholipid* is used for any lipid that contains a radical derived from phosphoric acid. *Phosphoglycerides* are derivatives of glycerophosphoric acid; *sphingolipids* are lipids containing a long-chain base. If both remaining hydroxyl groups of glycerol are esterified with fatty acids, of which usually one is a saturated (R') and one an unsaturated (R) fatty acid, then we are dealing with phosphatidic acid (Fig. 12). Commonly, choline, ethanolamine, or serine is attached to the phosphate group, e.g., phosphatidylcholine (Fig. 12).

The level of phospholipids in the blood is low in the fetus and rises after birth (Fig. 13). In the rabbit and guinea pig, we find again an exception, since the blood level is higher in the fetus than in the dam, but still a postnatal increase is observed (see Fig. 9).

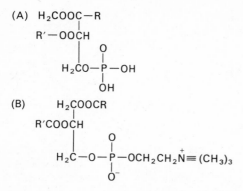

Fig. 12. Structural formulas of (A) phosphatidic acid and (B) phosphatidylcholine (lecithin) (right). (R) an unsaturated fatty acid; (R') a saturated fatty acid.

The reason for and significance of this finding are unknown.

Phospholipids are an important part of cell walls and cell particle membranes, such as mitochondria. Other and special phospholipids are part of the myelin sheaths of nerves. Apparently phospholipids play a very important role in the transport mechanisms of substances across cell walls.

In the early human fetus and in rat fetuses, most of the fatty acids are bound in phospholipids, except in the liver and the adrenal gland.[82] Since they are of vital importance, it is very likely that they are already present in the fertilized cell. They are synthesized by the fetus and do not pass the placental barrier; however, such a passage has been considered to occur in sheep.[96] The placenta synthesizes phospholipids.[88]

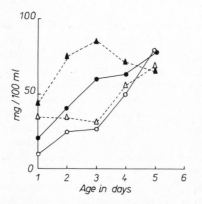

Fig. 13. Blood levels of cholesterol (○,●) and phospholipids (△,▲) in newborn infants fed breast milk (●,▲) or tea with sugar (○,△) for 3–5 days. Data from Kohn et al.[68]

4.1. Synthesis

The initial steps of phospholipid and triglyceride synthesis are the same. In both cases, glycerol-3-phosphate and acyl–CoA are required to form phosphatidic acid (see Fig. 12). The phosphatidic acid then either combines with two more molecules of acyl–CoA to form a triacylglycerol or forms a phospholipid via cytidine diphosphate diglyceride (CDP). Lecithin is formed from diglyceride and CDP choline, but there exist other possible mechanisms.

Phospholipid synthesis in fetuses and newborns has been examined only sporadically and in no detail. Most work deals with the rate of incorporation of a labeled fatty acid or phosphate into phospholipids of different tissues. In the rat, the rate of incorporation into both lung and liver phospholipids is at its highest immediately after birth,[26] while in the brain, conditions are more complex, mainly because this organ contains so many different types of phospholipids, some being related to the myelin sheath, others to cell structure.[118]

There are two pathways of phosphatidylcholine and phosphatidylethanolamine synthesis in the liver, lung, and brown adipose tissue of fetal, newborn, and adult rats.[25] The pathway of phospholipid synthesis that requires ATP and CoA matures postnatally, while the other pathway does not require these cofactors (as examined in the high-speed supernatant) and is already developed prenatally. This seems to be the only study on phospholipid breakdown during development, and evidently, much more work is required in this field. The physiologic, biochemical, and physicochemical roles of phospholipids as such have also to be elucidated to a larger extent. Some of our knowledge in the field of phospholipid classes is summarized in Table V.

4.2. Fatty Acid Composition

The composition of fatty acids in phospholipids changes considerably with age and is different in different organs.[27] In contrast to triglycerides, the fatty acid composition of phospholipids is less dependent on dietary changes, and it appears that age–dependent changes are conditioned by other, as yet unknown factors. The fatty acid composition of lecithin of human maternal and cord blood is shown in Table VI. Differences in the content of unsaturated fatty acids are apparent.

Phospholipids definitely play a special role in the lungs, where the alveoli are lined with a film that

Table V. Lipid Composition of Developing Rat Brain[a]

Lipid	Concentration (μmol/g wet weight)							
	3 days	6 days	12 days	18 days	24 days	42 days	180 days	330 days
Phosphoglycerides								
Phosphatidylcholine	14.72	14.82	20.38	24.38	24.79	24.95	24.65	24.89
Phosphatidylethanolamine	5.25	5.66	7.96	9.37	11.00	10.89	10.72	10.49
Phosphatidylglycerol	0.12	0.20	0.16	0.20	0.29	0.27	0.28	0.29
Phosphatidylinositol	1.21	1.38	1.59	1.86	2.04	2.17	2.20	2.30
Phosphatidylserine	2.91	3.56	4.51	6.10	7.04	8.25	8.50	8.97
Phosphatidylglycerol phosphate	0.10	0.13	0.20	0.16	0.16	0.17	0.06	0.04
Phosphatidic acid	0.14	0.21	0.26	0.39	0.70	1.03	1.31	1.36
Diphosphatidylglycerol	0.19	0.21	0.34	0.52	0.57	0.68	0.60	0.55
Diphosphoinositide	0.01	0.05	0.05	0.16	0.15	0.19	0.21	0.20
Triphosphoinositide	0.03	0.04	0.05	0.14	0.17	0.24	0.41	0.39
Choline plasmalogen	0.04	0.06	0.07	0.09	0.16	0.22	0.35	0.34
Ethanolamine plasmalogen	2.19	2.75	4.73	7.02	11.3	13.5	13.0	13.2
Inositol plasmalogen	0	0	0.05	0.08	0.13	0.13	0.13	0.11
Plasmalogenic acid	0.02	0.05	0.15	0.17	0.18	0.15	0.20	0.12
Ethanolamine phosphoglycerol ether	0.18	0.23	0.38	0.69	1.02	1.06	1.04	1.13
Sphingolipids								
Sphingomyelin	0.23	0.26	1.04	2.15	3.19	3.62	3.70	4.10
Cerebroside	0	0	2.3	5.8	10.3	18.6	21.8	22.5
Sulfatide	0.14	0.32	0.79	1.28	2.04	3.22	4.22	4.48
Gangliosides								
Hexosamine	0.31	0.73	0.84	0.96	1.01	1.06	1.15	1.13
Sialic acid	0.51	1.27	1.45	1.74	1.97	2.08	2.18	2.07
Others								
Cholesterol	10.7	12.6	22.6	32.2	38.3	39.5	40.2	40.6
Galactosyldiglyceride	0.05	0.06	0.31	0.86	1.29	1.46	1.5	1.62
Brain weight (g)	0.40	0.61	1.11	1.34	1.55	1.63	1.85	1.86
Percentage recovery of phosphorus in combined fractions	97.0	96.5	98.0	98.5	97.0	97.0	98.0	98.0

[a] From Wells and Dittmer.[18] Courtesy of American Chemical Society.

consists of protein and lecithin (Tables VII and VIII). The biochemistry and function of this lipid are fully discussed in Chapter 7.

Phospholipids are also a very important constituent of nervous tissue (see also Chapter 29). In the rat brain, four periods of development have been distinguished and have been shown to be associated with changes in the composition of different phospholipids in the brain. Wells and Dittmer[118] studied these changes in detail; however, the prenatal period was not studied. In the second period, lasting from birth to day 10, the brain increases in size and axons and dendrites grow. During this period, the sterol ester content of the brain decreases, and the ganglioside content increases considerably. The third period lasts from day 10 to day 20, when myelinization begins and is most intensive. At this time, the concentration of lipids in the myelin sheaths increases 2- to 3-fold. The lipids consist of cerebrosides, sphingomyelin, triphosphoinositide, phosphatidic acid, galactosidyl diglyceride, and inositol plasmalogen. In the fourth period, this increase is considerably slower. The content of other phospholipids, such as lecithin, phosphatidylethanolamine, and some

Table VI. Fatty Acid Distribution in Percentage of Total Fatty Acids in Cord and Maternal Serum Lecithin (Means ±S.D.)[a]

Source	Palmitate 16:0	Palmitoleate 16:1	Stearate 18:0	Oleate 18:1	Linoleate 18:2	Arachidonate 20:4
Cord	40.0 ± 1.3	12.6 ± 4.9	12.2 ± 1.4	15.5 ± 1.4	8.2 ± 2.0	11.4 ± 4.5
Mother	42.9 ± 3.3	6.8 ± 1.7	9.3 ± 1.4	15.1 ± 1.2	20.2 ± 3.0	5.9 ± 1.9

[a] From Zee.[125]

others, continues to increase from the second period through the fourth. The authors studied a total of 24 classes of brain lipids. Unfortunately, very little is yet known about the functional significance of these changes. Undoubtedly, however, such knowledge may contribute to defining critical periods of development more exactly (see Section 8). The biochemical development of the human fetal brain was studied by Svennerholm.[109]

5. Cholesterol

Cholesterol occurs in the free and esterified form. The latter is an ester of cholesterol and fatty acid. Both forms are found in the blood and most tissues.

The blood level of cholesterol is low before birth (except in the rabbit and guinea pig) and rises after birth in all mammalian species (Table IX). The cholesterol blood level is actually so high after birth that atherosclerotic plaques have been described in human babies and suckling rabbits.[11,50] They disappear after weaning.

The postnatal increase of the blood cholesterol level depends to some extent on the diet (see Figs. 9 and 13) in both man and rabbit, the only two species

in which this increase has been studied. It has still not been determined whether or not cholesterol passes through the placenta from the mother to the fetus. Connor and Lin[17] concluded that a considerable amount of the cholesterol content of newborn guinea pigs and rabbits originates from the maternal blood.

5.1. Synthesis

In newborn rats, cholesterol is synthesized not only in the liver, but also in the brain. The rate of synthesis in the liver is higher before than after birth, similar to the rate of fatty acid synthesis.[14] The decreased rate of the cholesterol synthesis seen after birth in the rat is probably due to inhibition by dietary cholesterol acting on the rate-limiting enzyme β-hydroxy-β-methylglutaryl-CoA reductase. The activity of this microsomal enzyme is very low during the suckling period, and rises at the time animals are weaned to the usual high-carbohydrate laboratory diet.[75]

Cholesterol is rapidly synthesized from labeled acetate in the brains of suckling rats, where it is also part of the myelin sheath. It is never deposited from external supplies.[79] In the newborn rat, desmosterol

Table VII. Phospholipid Content of Lung Tissue from Newborn Infants[a]

Infant weight (g)	Microscopic finding	Total phospholipids (mg/g wet weight)	Lecithin (%)
400	Immature lung	12	50
1275	Atelectasis	20	43
1725	Hyaline membrane	9	33
3235	Stillborn	22	55

[a] Data from Adams et al.[2]

Table VIII. Incorporation of [1-¹⁴C]Acetate into Lung Phospholipids of Lung Slices from Fetal and Newborn Lambs after 3 hr of Incubation[a]

Age	Activity (cpm/10 mg protein)
105[b]	1,119
110[b]	2,061
135[b]	4,788
1[c]	6,091
3[c]	10,168
5[c]	34,619
Adult	700

[a] From Chida and Adams.[16]
[b] Fetal age, days of gestation.
[c] Postnatal age, days.

is the main product of synthesis, indicating that the final step of synthesis is not fully active at this time.[61] In addition to the brain, skin is the only other tissue that synthesizes desmosterol in the rat. In man, it was also found in the fetal brain. Myelinization of the brain is most rapid between days 10 and 20. After that time, hardly any turnover of cholesterol can be demonstrated in the brain, and radioactively labeled cholesterol and phospholipids that are deposited in infancy are found unaltered in the brain months later.

Postnatally, the cholesterol content of rat brain increases considerably from about 5 μmol/g wet weight on day 5 to 10 μmol/g on day 30, and to 18 μmol/g in adult animals. About 70% of the cholesterol is found in myelin.[20] It has been sug-

gested that the turnover of cholesterol esters in the blood is somehow related to the ease with which atherosclerosis can be induced. The activity of the enzyme lecithin cholesterolacyltransferase (LCAT) is apparently inversely proportional to the occurrence of atherosclerosis in a given species. Thus, rats, in which it is very difficult to induce atherosclerosis, have high levels of LCAT in their blood. The activity increases with age,[36] as it does in humans.

Another very important recent development in this area is the discovery of an apparent inborn error of metabolism in hypercholesterolemic infants. Fibroblasts cultured from such individuals do not react in the usual way to low-density proteins in the medium. Normal fibroblasts cease cholesterol synthesis after such an addition (the activity of β-hydroxy, β-methyl glutaryl CoA reductase is suppressed) and increase the rate of formation of cholesterol esters within the cell.[13] These reactions are absent from defective fibroblasts, apparently because these fibroblasts lack a membrane receptor for low-density lipoproteins.

6. Adipose Tissue

Triglycerides predominate in adipose tissue, although in newborn rats, it contains a relatively large amount of phospholipids. The amount of triglycerides in adipose tissue depends on the nutritional state of the animal.

Two types of adipose tissue have been described: brown adipose tissue (BAT) and white adipose tissue (WAT). There is still some discussion as to whether the latter originates from the former, but it seems more reasonable to consider them as distinct

Table IX. Levels of Cholesterol in Blood of Various Species (mg/dl)

Mother	Fetus	Days after birth						Species	References
		0	1	3	6	12	35		
23	102	121	162	222	258	372	51	Rabbit	Friedman and Byers[34]
13.1	93.6							Rabbit	Sisson and Plotz[98]
57		115						Guinea pig	Connor and Lin[17]
50		80		90	120	120	40	Rat	Hahn and Koldovský[50]
180		10		28	85			Man	Hahn and Koldovský[50]
264		95		140				Man	Kaplan and Lee[66]

Table X. Differences between White and Brown Adipose Tissue

	Brown	White
Occurrence	Newborn mammals; hibernators; cold-exposed rats	In adults of most mammalian species; in newborn mammals only if born in mature state
Sites	Between shoulder blades, around aorta, perirenally, and elsewhere	Subcutaneous, abdominal, etc.
Morphology	Irregularly shaped cells, multilocular fat globules, numerous mitochondria with dense cristae	Spherical cells, one large fat globule, few mitochondria
Oxygen consumption *in vitro*	Very high (very high cytochrome content)	Low
Function	Heat production	Storage and release of fat; insulation

entities. The development of both tissues was recently reviewed.[51]

BAT is much more abundant in fetal and newborn animals, including man, than in adults of the same species. The morphological development of adipose tissues has been described repeatedly.[9,117] In recent years, much attention has been paid to both tissues, and today it is possible to summarize the differences between them fairly accurately (Table X). Figure 14 summarizes our knowledge of enzyme development in BAT.

This tissue appears in man around the 6th month of gestation. In rats, it begins to develop very rapidly after birth. In rats and in man, subcutaneous fat develops earlier than does abdominal fat tissue, and even on day 30 after birth, very little fat is found within the abdominal cavity (perirenal, omental,

mesenteric). A special organ in male rats is the epididymal fat pad, which has been extensively used for *in vitro* metabolic studies. Yet almost nothing is known about its postnatal development. Adipose tissues from different sites have different metabolic characteristics, but nothing is known about developmental differences. The most obvious morphological finding is the increasing size of adipose tissue cells throughout life. The importance of adipose tissue in the newborn is well demonstrated by the data shown in Table XI. In the human newborn, 12% of the total body protein is found in adipose tissue; in the adult, only 3.3% is located there. Hence, the relative importance of WAT is about 3 times greater in the newborn than in the adult. Table XII summarizes our knowledge of metabolic development in human adipose tissue. It should be noted that, for example,

Table XI. Parameters of White Adipose Tissue in Man[a]

Age	Fat in body (%)	Adipose tissue (% body wt)	Protein in fat (%)	Protein (g/kg body wt)	Protein (% of total body protein, approx.)	Fat cells/kg body wt	O_2 μeq/ total fat per kg body wt)	O_2 (μmol/cells in 1 kg adipose tissue)
Newborn	15	33	6.2	20	12	89×10^8	45×10^3	3888
6 Months	26	36	3.41	12.3	5	49×10^8	130×10^3	
Adult	25	33	2.17	7.16	3.3	16×10^8	45×10^3	1112

[a] Data recalculated from Baker.[6]

Table XII. Metabolic Characteristics of Human White Adipose Tissue[a]

Substance, unit	Newborn	120 hr	Adult
Glycogen, mg/g wet wt	1.0	0.3 (1.0 = IDM)	0.25
ATP, mg/g wet wt	0.2	0.2	
HAD (homogenate), U/g prot.	124	220	
MDH (mitochondria), μmol/g prot. (premature)	350	600 (300)	
CAT, nmol/mg prot. (mitochon.)	91.8		56.2
PCT, nmol/mg prot. (mitochon.)	75.5		20.0
PFK, nmol/mg prot. per min	299	201	45
PK, μmol/mg prot. per min	0.108	0.081	0.075
Glyc. PDH, μmol/mg prot. per min	0.7	0.4	0.3
Gluc.-6-PDH, nmol/mg prot. per min	20	20	0
			3.6
			11.9
Phosphorylase, μmol gluc.-6-P/g prot. per 60 min	1500	600	
PEPK, nmol/mg prot. per min	30	30	30
CCE, nmol/mg prot. per min	14	14.8	2.4
ME, nmol/mg prot. per min	69	32	5.0
Adenylcyclase, nmol/g prot. per min	12	18	

[a] Data from Hahn and Novak.[51]

an activity of PEPK of 30 nmol/min per mg protein in newborn and adult tissue implies that per kilogram body weight, adipose tissue PEPK activity is more than 3-fold greater in the newborn than in the adult.

6.1. White Adipose Tissue

In newborn babies immediately after birth, WAT is already capable of reacting to stimuli, as mentioned in Section 2. Fatty acids and glycerol are released into the circulation, and triglyceride formation is suppressed for some time after birth (Fig. 15). These occurrences can also be demonstrated *in vitro* (Fig. 16). The WAT of newborn rats differs metabolically from that of weaned animals. First, it metabolizes more actively per unit of weight, probably because of the smaller cell size in younger animals. Second, it is less sensitive to the presence of glucose than later in life. Thus, glucose enhances acetate incorporation into lipids to a much lesser extent in suckling than in adult rats.[55] This finding has been confirmed for human adipose tissue (Fig. 17). The reason for this age-dependent difference might be the more pro-

nounced glycerol-3-phosphate formation from gluconeogenesis and from glycerol in newborns. In adipose tissue, the rate of fatty acid oxidation is low in all age groups, but fatty acid synthesis proceeds at a high rate, depending on age, cell size (?), and diet. Thus, the rate of fatty acid synthesis per unit wet weight is greater in suckling than in adult rats.[55] Table XII summarizes the data on WAT development in man. Table XI underlines the large metabolic role played by WAT in the newborn.

6.2. Brown Adipose Tissue

The role of this tissue is to produce heat. This role was discovered by Smith and Horwitz[104] in hibernators and rats adapted to cold, and by Dawkins and Hull[22] in newborn rabbits and human babies. The blood supply to WAT is extensive, but that to BAT is even greater. In newborns of most species, BAT is located between the shoulder blades, in the axilla, and in the thorax surrounding the aorta. The biochemistry of heat production and the function of BAT in newborns are discussed in Chapter 21. Its development was recently reviewed[43,51]

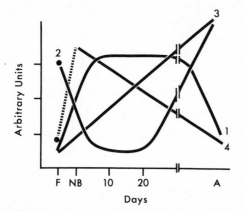

Fig. 14. Schematic representation of enzyme development in brown adipose tissue of the rat. (F) Late fetus; (NB) newborn; (A) adult. *Curve 1:* Phosphoenolpyruvatekinase, phosphorylasekinase, activated protein kinase, activation of adenylcyclase by NE, pyruvatekinase, phosphofructokinase, carnitine acyl and acetyltransferase, and carnitine content, number of mitochondria and electrontransfer, pyruvatedehydrogenase. *Curve 2:* Citrate cleavage enzyme, acetyl-CoA carboxylase, acetyl-CoA synthetase, FAS. The same development (except for the high fetal values) for the same enzymes is also seen in WAT of the pig. *Curve 3:* Fat content, P/O ratio (pyr → mal, guinea pig), hormone sensitive lipase, malic enzyme, adenylcyclase. *Curve 4:* Glycerolphosphate dehydrogenase, glyceraldehyde-phosphate dehydrogenase, glucose-6-phosphate dehydrogenase, protein content, glycerol kinase, phosphorylase, glycogen, cyclic AMP, DNA and RNA content. See Hahn[43] and Hahn and Novak.[51]

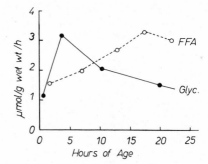

Fig. 16. Release of fatty acids (FFA) and glycerol (Glyc) from adipose tissue from newborn human infants. Data from Hahn and Koldovský.[50]

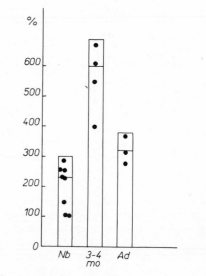

Fig. 17. Increase in the rate of incorporation of labeled palmitate into triglycerides of human adipose tissue due to addition of 100 mg glucose/dl to the incubation medium. Ordinate: Percentage increase over rate of incorporation without glucose. (Nb) Newborns; (Ad) adults. Data from Hahn et al.[56]

7. Regulatory Factors

7.1. Hormones

Adipose tissue is very sensitive to the action of various hormones. In fact, the deposition and release of fatty acids and glyceride glycerol in adipose tissue are regulated, to a large extent, by hormones. Most important are adrenaline and noradrenaline. Both stimulate lipolysis, i.e., the hydrolysis of triglycerides into fatty acids and glycerol. Noradrenaline appears

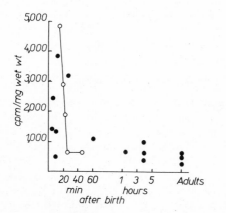

Fig. 15. Rate of incorporation of labeled palmitate into triglycerides of human adipose tissue in newborn infants. Data from Hahn et al.[56]

to be the mediator, and is released by sympathetic nerve endings so that lipolysis can occur in response to various stresses. Adrenaline and noradrenaline are thought to act by inducing the formation of cyclic adenosine-3′,5′-monophosphate (cAMP) by the enzyme adenyl cyclase; cAMP, in turn, seems to activate the protein kinase system:

$$ATP \xrightarrow{\text{adenyl cyclase}} cAMP \xrightarrow{\text{phosphodiesterase}} AMP$$

Very little is known about developmental changes in the reactivity of the organism or adipose tissue to adrenaline and noradrenaline. In newborn infants, the blood levels of fatty acids and glycerol increase in response to noradrenaline administration as early as on the first day of life, but in rats, this rise is not observed in the suckling period. *In vitro*, however, the WAT of man and rats reacts with fatty acid and glycerol release at all ages, although the response is slightly different in intensity (Table XIII). BAT, however, releases more glycerol than fatty acids in response to these hormones *in vitro*, presumably because fatty acids are rapidly oxidized in this tissue.

In suckling rats, cyclase activity in adipose tissue seems to be lower than later in life, while postnatally, the activity of phosphodiesterase, which inactivates cAMP, is high. In the BAT of the rat, the development of adenylcyclase, proteinkinase, and cAMP content has been studied.[28,100,102] Adenylcyclase is already NaF- and hormone-sensitive prenatally. An interesting point is the presence of a protein kinase inhibitor,[101] the content of which is highest in the neonatal period. In man, Novak's group has demonstrated the presence of fluoride-stimulated adenylcyclase in newborn subcutaneous adipose tissue,[124] and it appears that all the mechanisms necessary for lipolysis to occur are already present in both types of adipose tissue in both man and rat in late gestation.

A number of *other hormones* have been shown to have a lipolytic effect *in vitro* and *in vivo*. Most studies have been performed with ACTH and glucagon. Nothing is known about the effect of ACTH during development, but glucagon has been studied in newborn infants. Administration of glucagon to newborn infants results in an increase of the blood level of glucose and in a decrease of the level of fatty acids.[77] The dominant effect of glucagon is thought to be on the liver; consequently, the decrease of blood fatty acids is secondary to the increase of the blood glucose level. It has been shown that glucose inhibits the release of fatty acids from adipose tissue, and the same seems to occur in newborn infants, even though to a lesser extent than in adults.

Insulin and lipolytic hormones have opposite effects. Insulin promotes lipogenesis. The action of insulin is similar in many respects to that of glucose, and many of the *in vitro* effects of insulin are not seen if glucose is omitted from the incubation medium. It has been postulated, but without sufficient experimental proof, that insulin stimulates phosphodiesterase activity and consequently the breakdown of cAMP.[94] The main effect of insulin, however, is to facilitate glucose transport across cell

Table XIII. Release of Free Fatty Acids by Adipose Tissue in Rats of Difference Weights[a,b]

Release[b]	Group 1 Age: 15–40 days Weight: 100 g	Group 2 Age: 80–120 days Weight: 180–300 g	Group 3 Age: 140 days Weight: 280–500 g
FFA release (μeq/g per hr)	24.76 ± 3.63[c] ($n = 20$)	4.77 ± 0.57 ($n = 12$)	6.5 ± 0.91 ($n = 18$)
FFA release after epinephrine (μeq/g per hr)	45.59 ± 7.68 ($n = 14$)	10.54 ± 0.98 ($n = 6$)	20.81 ± 2.38 ($n = 17$)

[a] Data from Spitzer.[106] Means $\pm$ S.E.
[b] From epididymal fat pad.

membranes, particularly in muscle and adipose tissues. Little is known about the effect of insulin on lipid metabolism during development. Evidently, at least in human fetuses, insulin acts as in adults, since a large accumulation of lipids occurs in fetal adipose tissues if the mother is suffering from diabetes. These fetuses produce abnormally high amounts of insulin, the secretion of this hormone by the fetal pancreas presumably being stimulated by the high blood glucose level. In rats Bacon,[5] found that CO_2 production from [1-^{14}C]glucose by WAT (*in vitro*) in the presence of insulin is smaller in very young animals than later in life, but this single report has not been confirmed as yet.

In adult animals, the *thyroid* gland is known to influence the levels of lipids in the blood. This influence has also been shown to be true for the fetal rabbit, in which thyroidectomy on the 29th day of gestation leads to an increase in blood cholesterol from 71 to 118 mg/dl.[10] Cuarón et al.[19] showed that feeding the doe with methylthiouracil, which produced hypothyroidism, also led to a slower turnover in brain phospholipids of newborn rabbits. Otherwise, however, the thyroid does not seem to play an important role in brain phospholipid metabolism after birth.[81]

In fetal rats, decapitation on the 20th day of gestation (a method considered equal to hypophysectomy) caused fat accumulation in the fetal liver, and the same effect was achieved by adrenalectomy, but not by thyroidectomy.[78] Administration of cortisone reverses these changes to some extent. The role of *adrenal cortical hormones* in fat metabolism is still not fully explored. In suckling rats, cortisone administration doubles the weight of BAT.[42] The significance of this finding remains uncertain, but has been attributed to a decrease in the rate of fatty acid utilization by impaired mitochondria.[99]

7.2. Nervous Factors

As mentioned in Section 7.1, noradrenaline is released at sympathetic nerve endings and causes lipolysis in adipose tissue. This is evidently the mechanism by which the level of fatty acids and glycerol is increased after birth in newborn infants and lambs,[111] since the administration of sympatholytic drugs could prevent this increase. Heat production in BAT is also dependent on the sympathetic nervous system in newborn rabbits. Administration of pronethanol or propanalol prevents the rise of oxygen

consumption in newborn rabbits after noradrenaline treatment,[58,64] and denervation of BAT prevents the loss of lipids from this organ on cold exposure of newborn rabbits.[63]

7.3. Metabolic Factors

For a developmental physiologist, it is intriguing to ask to what extent age-dependent changes are genetically predetermined and to what extent they are directly or indirectly due to environmental effects.

In recent years, many feedback controls of metabolic processes have been discovered, particularly in the metabolism of carbohydrates and lipids. It has been shown that the metabolism of glucose and FFA is closely and manifoldly related,[86] and that several control points exist at which it is decided whether glucose or fatty acids are predominantly synthesized or oxidized. In general, glucose synthesis is promoted by fatty acid oxidation, and vice versa. Consequently, a high-fat diet enhances gluconeogenesis and fatty acid oxidation, and it causes a decrease of lipid synthesis, at least in the liver. In this respect, the effects of a high-fat diet are very similar to those of starvation, but the difference is that fatty acids are derived from the diet in one case and from adipose tissue in the other.

If we now inquire whether the high-fat diet (milk) has a similar effect in the suckling mammal, we find that it undoubtedly does, and the reader will have noted repeated reference to this fact. Moreover, the newborn human infant first goes through a period of starvation and then receives milk; this sequence is not so drastic as it might seem to be, since both starvation and milk-feeding lead to a rise in the level of fatty acids in the blood. On the other hand, fetal nutrition is high in carbohydrates, and fetal metabolism and enzyme patterns are in accord with this circumstance.

Thus, the large supply of fatty acids to the newborn mammal may be held to be responsible for several metabolic changes: (1) a decrease in the rate of glycolysis in liver and brain, as indicated by the fall in pyruvate kinase and phosphofructokinase activities immediately after birth; (2) an increase in the rate of fatty acid oxidation in the liver, as evidenced by the rapid increase in the rate of acetoacetate formation; (3) a decrease in the rate of fatty acid and cholesterol synthesis in the liver; and (4) a postnatal increase in the rate of gluconeogenesis, as indicated by the increase of phosphoenol pyruvate carboxykinase activity in the liver (see Chapter 22).

Some of these changes are of such a nature that the processes that are suddenly altered after birth have been shown to be already present before birth. In other words, enzyme activities were high before birth and decreased immediately after birth, e.g., citrate cleavage enzyme, fatty acid synthetase, or pyruvate kinase. As far as these enzyme activities are concerned, it can be considered that the change at birth is due to changes in substrate concentrations due to nutrition or fatty acid release from adipose tissue. Other changes are characterized by the fact that metabolic pathways that perform efficiently after birth are not found before birth (gluconeogenesis and, to a certain extent, acetoacetate formation). Here, birth and the beginning of oral nutrition seem to be less decisive. Such problems can be investigated by using species that differ in the degree of maturity at birth. This approach has been taken in the case of glucose-6-phosphatase (see Chapter 17). Another approach is to delay parturition, which can be done in the rabbit. Roux[89] studied the effect of delayed parturition on triglyceride and fatty acid content in the liver and of acetate incorporation into liver lipids in the rabbit. It was shown that as far as lipid synthesis is concerned, the moment of birth is decisive, since the rate of synthesis dropped more than 10 times in the newborn, but was equally high in term and postmature fetuses. Liver triglyceride content, on the other hand, was decreased in the postmature rabbit to values nearly equal to the newborn, indicating a utilization of this fat by the postmature fetus. Similarly, lipid synthesis from labeled pyruvate is much greater in the postmature fetus than in the newborn or 4-day-old rabbit.[91] In recent years, it has become increasingly clear that neonatal metabolic changes are controlled to a large extent by hormones, particularly insulin, glucagon, the catecholamines and glucocorticoids, and perhaps also growth hormone and others. This control obtains, of course, at any time of life. Numerous data indicate, for instance, that the effects of a high-fat or a high-carbohydrate diet depend, to a large extent, on the hormonal balance of the individual. It is possible, for instance, to prevent the normal metabolic changes that occur on a high-carbohydrate diet (a fall in gluconeogenesis, a rise in fatty acid synthesis) by injecting rats with glucagon or epinephrine.[48] The perinatal period is unique, however, insofar as many changes occur for the first time in the individual's life, at a moment when not every function has as yet matured and when hormonal equilibria differ from those found later in life.

In both man and rat, the blood level of glucagon rises and that of insulin decreases within a few hours after birth. There is also a transient rise in glucocorticoid levels.[39] It is assumed that the rise in the glucagon/insulin ratio is responsible for the sudden postnatal rise in the rate of gluconeogenesis and the fall in fatty acid synthesis. Evidence for the former is much firmer than for the latter. Fatty acid oxidation and ketone body formation both rise after birth, and these increases are probably ascribable to a large extent to sympathetic stimulation of lipolysis in adipose tissue, and the resulting increased fatty acid delivery to the liver.

7.4. Environmental Factors

The most important environmental factor in development is nutrition. Not only the level of nutrition but also the qualitative composition of the food consumed are of prime importance. During gestation, nutrition of the mother is important, as has been discussed by Barcroft.[8] Several studies have been performed on the effect of the fat composition of the mother's diet on the fatty acid composition of her fetus. Essential fatty acids were usually tested. In most cases, they were transferred from the mother and appeared in the fetal fat.[74] In rats, starvation of the pregnant animal or feeding of a protein-free diet resulted in fat accumulation not only in the maternal but also in the fetal liver and placenta.[73] This increase was most pronounced on the 22nd day of gestation, and it was due mainly to triglycerides in which linoleic acid accumulated. This latter essential fatty acid is considered to be derived from the mother animal. Unsaturated essential fatty acids seem to have a special position in transplacental passage. Postnatally, the content of essential fatty acids (as related also to vitamin E content) is of considerable importance.[57] Lack of essential fatty acids in the diet (e.g., fat-free milk) can lead to pronounced skin and other tissue disorders, particularly in the early postnatal period.

The effect of the lipid content of the diet in the prenatal and the early postnatal period has been studied in rabbits and to some extent in man. Popják[85] found that supplementing the diet of pregnant rabbits with 1 g cholesterol, which raised the blood level of all lipids in the doe, had no effect on the lipid composition of the fetal plasma. Sisson and Plotz[97] fed rabbits with a diet high in cholesterol and other lipids, and found that the fatty acid composition of FFA, triglycerides, and cholesterol esters was altered not only in the blood of the mother rabbit, but also in the fetal blood (Table XIV). Friedman and Byers[34] performed a similar experiment, but continued to study the young rabbits after birth. They found no effect of the maternal diet on the amount of triglycerides, phospholipids, and cholesterol in fetal blood. After birth, the usual increase in the levels of all three lipid groups could be prevented by feeding a milk diet with very low-fat content (see Fig. 9), and this decrease in blood lipid levels could be achieved in normally breast-fed rabbits by sudden weaning on the 14th postnatal day to this low-fat diet. This finding is direct evidence for the effect of milk on the blood level of lipids in suckling mammals. In man, the postnatal rise of the blood cholesterol level can be delayed by feeding newborn infants tea with glucose for the first 5 days (see Fig. 13). In this connection, it is of interest to note that the blood cholesterol level of the newborn is smaller on an artificial milk mixture than during breast-feeding.[72] The type of fat in conditioned cow's milk and its amount of protein are also important for the blood level of cholesterol.[40]

Undernutrition in early life has been shown to have some effect on lipid metabolism. Chase *et al.*[15] showed that sulfatide synthesis in the rat brain (sulfatide is a component of the myelin sheath) is permanently decreased in animals that were undernourished at the time of onset of myelin synthesis but were later refed. The cholesterol content of brains of young rats (cholesterol is another component of the myelin sheath) is also low in undernourished animals up to the 21st postnatal day, but later these animals have normal values.[24] These data underline the importance of adequate nutrition during critical periods of development, i.e., in periods when some part of the body differentiates.

8. Perspectives

In recent years, evidence has been accumulating that early unfavorable environmental effects on metabolic processes may be involved in late adult disturbances. Protein malnutrition in infancy, e.g., kwashiorkor, has received great attention, but it appears that in some instances, lipid malnutrition and fat metabolism are equally important. This was discussed in some detail by Hahn and Koldovský.[50] In this chapter, some important data related to lipid metabolism have been intentionally omitted, since they are not yet established enough to justify their discussion, e.g., the development of reduced and oxidized NAD and NADP concentrations in the liver, the content of acetyl-CoA, and some other values. Nevertheless, it is quite possible that these data and additional information on carbohydrate metabolism will turn out to be of great importance.

As an example, the activity of pyruvate kinase in rat brain is high in the fetus, decreases after birth,

Table XIV. Mean Plasma Lipid Values of Rabbits Fed a Normal Diet and a Fat Cholesterol-Enriched Diet and of Their Fetuses at 28 Days of Gestation[a]

Rabbits	Phospholipids (mg/dl)	Triglycerides (meq/liter)	Cholesterol Ester (mg/dl)	Cholesterol Free (mg/dl)
Mothers				
Normal diet	1.1	2.0	8.9	4.2
Cholesterol	2.2	1.9	38.7	10.9
Fetuses				
Normal diet	5.7	4.5	55.8	37.8
Cholesterol	6.1	4.2	71.0	39.5

[a] Data from Sisson and Plotz.[97]

nd rises again after weaning. In the perinatal period, he blood level of acetoacetic acid undergoes changes hat are just the reverse. In the suckling period, the rain utilizes acetoacetate more intensively than efore birth and after weaning. It may thus be peculated that glucose in the brain is saved for ynthetic processes in the suckling period, and that his saving is achieved by a large supply of acetoace- ate. Hence, any change of this normal course of development that can be induced, for example, by feeding a high-carbohydrate diet or by undernutri- tion, may cause irreparable brain alterations by lead- ng to or suppressing the synthesis of some substances that normally would occur later in life. This is still considered to be a hypothesis. Nevertheless, it has been shown that feeding a high-carbohydrate diet prematurely to weaning rats does impair their ability to form conditioned reflexes when they are adult, and furthermore that this deficiency can be pre- vented by feeding a high-fat diet for the crucial period before weaning.[50]

The seemingly useless work of identifying the ndividual fatty acids in phospholipids may one day turn out to be of prime importance, since phospho- lipids are known to be essential for membrane transport. Hence, their fatty acid composition may prove to be highly significant for many metabolic cell functions.

9. Conclusions

An attempt has been made to indicate the important aspects of lipid metabolism during devel- opment. It appears that prenatally, lipid synthesis predominates considerably over lipid breakdown. As yet, there are hardly any data that would indicate fatty acid oxidation to any significant extent pre- natally. After birth, fatty acid oxidation proceeds at an increased rate, and at the same time, fat supply to the newborn is increased (milk). Thus, many of the changes at and after birth, as far as lipid meta- bolism is concerned, may be ascribed to the sudden increase in lipid supply.

As yet, we know very little about lipid metabol- ism and supply during early fetal life. There are some indications that perhaps more lipids are transferred to the fetus soon after conception than later during fetal development. Here, the role of the placenta in lipid metabolism and lipid transfer from mother to fetus and vice versa must be examined much more thoroughly.[88]

Finally, much remains to be investigated in the field of endocrine and nervous control of lipid metabolism during pre- and postnatal life.

10. References

1. ADAM, P. A. J., RAIHA, N., RAHIALA, E. L., AND KEKOMAKI, M., 1975, Oxidation of glucose and D-B-OH-butyrate by the early human fetal brain, *Acta Paediatr. Scand.* **64**:17–24.
2. ADAMS, T. H., FUJIWARA, T., EMMANOUILIDES, G., AND SCUDDER, A., 1965, Surface properties and lipids from lungs of infants with hyaline membrane disease, *J. Pediatr.* **66**:357–364.
3. AUGENFELD, J., AND FRITZ, I. B., 1970, Carnitine palmitoyl transferase activity and fatty acid oxidation by livers from fetal and neonatal rats, *Can. J. Biochem.* **48**:288–294.
4. BABAK, E., 1900, Respirometrische und calori- metrische Untersuchungen bei Kindern mit supra- normaler und subnormaler Körpertemperatur, *Bull. Int. Acad. Sci. Boheme*, pp. 27–40.
5. BACON, G. E., 1967, Effect of insulin on carbon dioxide production in adipose tissue from immature rats, *Experimentia* **23**:72–75.
6. BAKER, G. L., 1969, Human adipose tissue composi- tion and age, *Amer. J. Clin. Nutr.* **22**:829–835.
7. BAILEY, E., AND LOCKWOOD, E. A., 1973, Some aspects of fatty acid oxidation and ketone body formation and utilization during development, *Enzyme* **15**:239–253.
8. BARCROFT, J., 1946, *Researches on Prenatal Life*, Black- well Scientific Publications, Oxford.
9. BARNARD, T., AND SKALA, J., 1970, The develop- ment of brown adipose tissue, in: *Brown Adipose Tissue*, (O. Lindberg, ed.), Elsevier, New York.
10. BEARN, J. G., AND PILKINGTON, T. R. E., 1963, Hormonal control of the metabolism of cholesterol in the rabbit foetus, *Nature (London)* **198**:1005, 1006.
11. BRAGDON, J. H., 1952, Spontaneous atherosclerosis in the rabbit, *Circulation* **5**:641–648.
12. BREUER, E., BARTA, E., ZLATOS, L., AND PAPPOVA, E., 1968, Developmental changes of myocardial meta- bolism. II. Myocardial metabolism of fatty acids in the early postnatal period in dogs, *Biol. Neonatl.* **12**:54–64.
13. BROWN, M. S., FAUST, J. R., AND GOLDSTEIN, J. L., 1975, Role of low density lipoprotein receptor in regulating the content of free and sterified cholesterol in human fibroblasts, *J. Clin. Invest.* **55**:783–793.
14. CARROL, K. K., 1964, Acetate incorporation into cholesterol and fatty acids by livers of fetal, suckling and weaned rats, *Can. J. Biochem.* **42**:79–86.
15. CHASE, H. P., DORSEY, J., AND MCKHANN, G. M., 1967, The effect of malnutrition on the synthesis of a myelin lipid, *Pediatrics* **40**:551–559.

16. Chida, N., and Adams, F. H., 1966, Incorporation of acetate into fatty acids and lecithin by lung slices from fetal and newborn lambs, *J. Lipid Res.* **8**:335–341.

17. Connor, W. E., and Lin, D. S., 1967, Placental transfer of cholesterol-4-^{14}C into rabbit and guinea-pig fetus, *J. Lipid Res.* **8**:558–564.

18. Counis, R., and Raulin, J., 1970, Activate adenyl-cyclase au cours du developement foetal et neonatal du tissue adipeux brun, *Bull. Soc. Chim. Biol.* **52**:1393–1405.

19. Caurón, A., Gamble, J., Myant, N. B., and Osorio, C., 1963, The effect of thyroid deficiency on the growth of the brain and on the deposition of brain phospholipids in foetal and newborn rabbits, *J. Physiol. (London)* **168**:613–630.

20. Cuzner, M. L., and Davison, A. N., 1968, The lipid composition of rat brain myelin and subcellular fractions during development, *Biochem. J.* **106**:29–34.

21. Dancis, J., Jansen, V., Kayden, H. J., Bjornson, L., and Levitz, M., 1974, Transfer across human placenta. III. Effect of chain length on transfer of free fatty acids, *Pediatr. Res.* **8**:796–799.

22. Dawkins, M. J. R., and Hull, D., 1964, Brown adipose tissue and the response of the newborn rabbit to cold, *J. Physiol. (London)* **172**:216–238.

23. Dierks-Ventling, C., and Cone, A. L., 1971, Acetoacetyl-CoA thiolase in brain, liver and kidney during maturation of the rat, *Science,* **172**:380–382.

24. Dobbing, J., 1964, The effect of early nutrition on the development and myelination of the brain, *Proc. R. Soc. (Biol.)* **15g**:503–509.

25. Dobiasova, M., and Hahn, P., 1968, Lysophospholipid metabolism in lung, liver and brown adipose tissue of the rat during development, *Physiol. Bohemoslov,* **17**:26–35.

26. Dobiasova, M., Hahn, P., Drahota, Z., and Dominas, H., 1966, The metabolism of ^{14}C-palmitate in the lungs and liver of rats during development, *Biol. Neonate.* **10**:200–206.

27. Dobiasova, M., Hahn, P., and Koldovský, O., 1964, Fatty acid composition in developing rats, *Biochim. Biophys. Acta* **84**:538–545.

28. Drahota, Z., Hahn, P., Honova, E., and Novak, V., 1967, Acetoacetate formation by liver mitochondria from infant and adult rats, *Physiol. Bohemoslov.* **16**:104–110.

29. Drahota, Z., Hahn, P., Kleinzeller, A., and Kostolanska, A., 1964, Acetoacetate formation by liver slices from adult and infant rats, *Biochem. J.* **93**:61–68.

30. Drahota, Z., Hahn, P., Mourek, J., and Trojanova, M., 1965, Effect of acetoacetate on oxygen consumption of brain slices from infant and adult rats, *Physiol. Bohemoslov.* **14**:134–136.

31. Drahota, Z., Honova, E., and Hahn, P., 1968, The effect of ATP and carnitine on the endogenous respiration of mitochondria from brown adipose tissue, *Experientia* **24**:431–432.

32. Edmund, J., 1974, Ketone bodies as precursors of sterols and fatty acids in the developing brain, *J. Biol. Chem.* **249**:72–80.

33. Fain, J. N., and Scow, R. O., 1966, Fatty acid synthesis *in vivo* in maternal and fetal tissue in the rat, *Amer. J. Physiol.* **210**:19–25.

34. Friedman, M., and Byers, S. O., 1961, Effects of diet on serum lipids of fetal, neonatal and pregnant rats, *Amer. J. Physiol.* **201**:611–616.

35. Fritz, I. B., 1959, Action of carnitine on long chain fatty acid oxidation by liver, *Amer. J. Physiol.* **197**:297–302.

36. Frolich, J., Bernstein, V., and Bernstein, M., 1975, Lecithin : cholesterol acyltransferase. Initial fractional rates of esterification in human and rat serum during development, *Clin. Chin. Acta* **65**:79–82.

37. George, J. C., and Iype, P. T., 1959, A study of the lipase activity in the developing chick heart, *J. Exp. Zool.* **141**:291–297.

38. Girard, J., 1975, Regulation du metabolisme energetique pendant la periode perinatale chez le rat, Thesis, Faculty of Sciences, Paris University, Paris V1.

39. Girard, J. R., Cuendet, G. S., Marliss, E. B., Kervran, A., Rientort, M., and Assan, R., 1973, Fuels, hormones and liver metabolism at term and during the early postnatal period in the rat, *J. Clin. Invest.* **52**:3190–3200.

40. Gyorgy, P., Rose, C. S., and Chu, E. H., 1963, Serum cholesterol and lipoprotein in premature infants, *Amer. J. Dis. Child.* **106**:165–169.

41. Hahn, P., 1965, Adipose tissue hormone sensitive lipase during development of the rat, *Experientia* **21**:634–637.

42. Hahn, P., 1969, The effect of cortisone on brown adipose tissue of young rats, *Can. J. Physiol. Pharmacol.* **47**:975–980.

43. Hahn, P., 1972, Lipid metabolism and nutrition in the prenatal and postnatal period, in: *Nutrition and Development* (M. Winick, ed.), pp. 99–134, John Wiley & Sons, New York.

44. Hahn, P., and Drahota, Z., 1966, The activities of citrate cleavage enzyme, acetyl-CoA synthetase and lipoprotein lipase in white and brown adipose tissue of the rat during development, *Experientia* **22**:706–709.

45. Hahn, P., and Greenberg, R., 1968, Incorporation of 1,3-C^{14}-glycerol into triglycerides of adipose tissue from suckling rats, *Life Sci.* **7**:187–190.

46. Hahn, P., and Greenberg, R., 1968, The development of pyruvate kinase, glycerol kinase and phosphoenolpyruvate carboxykinase activities in liver and adipose tissue of the rat, *Experientia* **24**:428.

47. Hahn, P., and Kirby, L., 1973, Immediate and

late effects of premature weaning and of feeding a high fat or high carbohydrate diet to weaning rats, *J. Nutr.* **103**:690–696.

48. HAHN, P., AND KIRBY, L., 1974, The effects of catecholamines, glucagon and diet on enzyme activities in brown fat and liver of the rat, *Can. J. Biochem.* **52**:739–743.

49. HAHN, P., AND KOLDOVSKÝ, O., 1960, The effect of complete starvation on body composition and energy losses in rats of different ages, *Physiol. Bohemoslov.* **9**:172–185.

50. HAHN, P., AND KOLDOVSKÝ, O., 1966, *Utilization of Nutrients During Postnatal Development*, Pergamon Press, Oxford.

51. HAHN, P., AND NOVAK, M., 1975, The development of brown and white adipose tissue, *J. Lipid Res.* **16**:79–97.

52. HAHN, P., AND SKALA, J., 1972, Carnitine and brown adipose tissue metabolism in the rat during development, *Biochem. J.* **127**:107–111.

53. HAHN, P., AND VAROUSKOVA, E., 1964, Acetoacetate formation by livers from human fetuses aged 8–17 weeks, *Biol. Neonate* **7**:348–352.

54. HAHN, P., DRAHOTA, Z., AND NOVAK, M., 1966, Triglyceride and fatty acid synthesis in liver and adipose tissue of suckling rats, *Biol. Neonate* **9**:82–92.

55. HAHN, P., GREENBERG, R., DOBIASOVA, M., AND DRAHOTA, Z., 1968, Triglyceride synthesis from various precursors in adipose tissue of the rat during development, *Can. J. Biochem.* **46**:735.

56. HAHN, P., NOVAK, M., AND MELICHAR, V., 1966, Incorporation of 1-^{14}C-palmitic acid into the lipids of human adipose tissue during postnatal development, *Physiol. Bohemoslov.* **15**:493–497.

57. HANSEN, A. E., STEWART, R. A., HUGHES, G., AND SODERHJELM, L., 1962, The relation of linoleic acid to infant feeding, *Acta Paediatr.* **51**(*Suppl. 137*).

58. HEIM, T., AND HULL, D., 1966, The effect of propranalol on the calorigenic response in brown adipose tissue of newborn rabbits to catecholamines, glucagon, corticotrophin and cold exposure, *J. Physiol. (London)* **187**:271–283.

59. HERSHFIELD, M. S., AND NEMETH, A. M., 1968, Placental transport of free palmitic and linoleic acids in the guinea pig, *J. Lipid Res.* **9**:460–468.

60. HIRSCH, J., 1965, Fatty acid patterns in human adipose tissue, in: *Handbook of Physiology* (A. E. Renold and G. F. Cahill, Jr., eds.), Vol. 5, pp. 181–190, Waverly Press, Baltimore.

61. HOLSTEIN, T. J., FISH, W. A., AND STOKES, W. M., 1966, Pathways of cholesterol biosynthesis in the brain of the neonatal rat, *J. Lipid Res.* **7**:634–638.

62. HONOVA, E., DRAHOTA, Z., AND HAHN, P., 1966, Factors regulating the formation of acetoacetate by liver slices during development of the rat, *Physiol. Bohemoslov.* **15**:415–419.

63. HULL, D., AND SEGAL, M. M., 1965, The

contribution of brown adipose tissue to heat production in the new-born rabbit, *J. Physiol. (London)* **181**:449–457.

64. HULL, D., AND SEGAL, M. M., 1965, Sympathetic nervous control of brown adipose tissue and heat production in the new-born rabbit, *J. Physiol. (London)* **181**:458–467.

65. JAHN, A., JOPPE, U., WINKLER, L., AND GOETZE, E., 1967, Die Fettsäurezusammensetzung individueller Lipidfraktionen der fetalen und mutterlichen Rattenleber sowie der Plazenta und deren Veränderungen am Ende der Gravidität, *Acta Biol. Med. Ger.* **19**:231–239.

66. KAPLAN, A., AND LEE, F. V., 1965, Serum lipid levels in infants and mothers at parturition, *Clin. Chim. Acta* **12**:258–263.

67. KEELE, D. K., AND KAY, J. L., 1966, Plasma free fatty acid levels in newborn infants and their mothers, *Pediatrics* **37**:597–604.

68. KOHN, R., NOVAK, M., MELICHAR, V., AND HAVLOVA, M., 1961, Zmeny cholesterolemie a hladiny fosfolipidu sera v neonatalnim obdobi pri menene vyzive, *Cesk. Pediatr.* **16**:979–983.

69. LAATSCH, R. H., 1962, Glycerol phosphate dehydrogenase activity of developing rat central nervous system, *J. Neurochem.* **9**:487–492.

70. LEAT, W. M. F., Fatty acid composition of the plasma lipids of newborn and maternal ruminants, *Biochem. J.* **98**:598–603.

71. LOGOTHETOPOULOS, J., RIDOUT, J. H., AND LUKAS, C. C., 1966, Fatty livers in fetal and newborn rabbits, *Can. J. Physiol. Pharmacol.* **44**:173–175.

72. LOHR, H., AND WOLF, H., 1962, Anstieg des Cholesterins im Serum von Säuglingen bei Ernährung mit Frauenmilch, *Klin. Wochenschr.* **40**:648–651.

73. MALBERG, K., AND WINKLER, L., 1966, Der Einfluss von Hunger und proteinfreier Diat auf die foetalen Leberlipide sowie die Lipide von Plazenta und mutterlicher Leber, *Acta Biol. Med. Ger.* **17**:567–577.

74. McCONNEL, R. P., AND SINCLAIR, R. G., 1937, Passage of elaidic acid through the placenta and also into the milk of the rat, *J. Biol. Chem.* **118**:123–128.

75. McNAMARA, D. J., QUACKENBUSH, F. W., AND RODBELL, V. W., 1972, Regulation of hepatic 3-hydroxy-3-methyl-glutaryl CoA reductase. Developmental patterns, *J. Biol. Chem.* **247**:5805–5810.

76. MELICHAR, V., AND WOLF, H., 1967, Ketone bodies in the blood of full term newborns, premature and dysmature infants and infants of diabetic mothers, *Biol. Neonate* **11**:23–28.

77. MILNER, R. D. G., AND WRIGHT, A. D., 1967, Plasma glucose, nonesterified fatty acids, insulin and growth hormone response to glucagon in the newborn, *Clin. Sci.* **32**:249–255.

78. MORIKAWA, Y., AND EGUCHI, Y., 1966, Fat content

of the liver in fetal rats: Observations in decapitated adrenalectomized or thyroidectomized fetal rats, *Endocrinol. Jpn.* **13**:355–357.

79. MORRIS, M. D., AND CHAIKOFF, I. L., 1961, Concerning incorporation of labelled cholesterol fed to the mother into the brain cholesterol of 20-day-old suckling rats, *J. Neurochem.* **8**:226–229.

80. MOSINGER, B., PECHAR, J., AND SEGOVA, N., 1964, Some characteristics of lipolytic activity of rat and human lungs, *Physiol. Bohemoslov.* **13**:300–305.

81. MYANT, N. B., 1966, On the possible role of the thyroid in the control of the development of the mammalian brain, *Biol. Neonate* **9**:148–161.

82. NOVAK, M., 1968, Personal communication.

83. NOVAK, M., AND MONKUS, E., 1973, Metabolism of subcutaneous adipose tissue in the immediate post-natal period of human newborns. III. Role of fetal glycogen in lipolysis and fatty acid esterification in the first hours of life, *Pediatr. Res.* **9**:769–777.

84. PATERSON, P., SHEATH, J., TAFT, P., AND WOOD, C., 1967, Maternal and foetal ketone concentrations in plasma and urine, *Lancet* **1**:862–865.

85. POPJÁK, G., 1954, The origin of fetal lipids, *Cold Spring Harbor Symp. Quant. Biol.* **19**:200–208.

86. RANDLE, P. J., GARLAND, P. B., HALES, C. N., AND NEWSHOLM, E. A., 1963, The glucose fatty acid cycle, *Lancet* **1**:785–789.

87. RIZACK, M. A., 1965, Hormone sensitive lipolytic activity of adipose tissue, in: *Handbook of Physiology* (A. E. Renold and G. F. Cahill, Jr., eds.), Vol. 5, pp. 309–312, Waverly Press, Baltimore.

88. ROBERTSON, A. F., AND SPRECHER, H., 1967, Human placental lipid metabolism and transport, *Acta Paediatr. Scand. Suppl. 183.*

89. ROUX, J., 1966, Lipid metabolism in the fetal and neonatal rabbit, *Metabolism* **15**:856–864.

90. ROUX, J., AND ROMNEY, S. L., 1967, Plasma free fatty acid and glucose concentration in the human fetus and newborn exposed to various environmental conditions, *Amer. J. Obstet. Gynecol.* **97**:268–278.

91. ROUX, J., DINNERSTEIN, A., AND ROMNEY, S. L., 1962, Ageing and environmental manifestations in pyruvate metabolism of rabbit foetal and neonatal liver, *Nature (London)* **194**:875.

92. ROUX, J., GRIGORIAN, A., AND TAKEDA, Y., 1967, *In vitro* "lipid" metabolism in the developing human fetus, *Nature (London)* **216**:819, 820.

93. SCHNELL, W., SCHREIER, K., WIEDERHOLT, I., AND HARTMANN, W., 1961, Untersuchungen zur Entwicklungsphysiologie der Lipidsynthese, *Clin. Chim. Acta* **6**:229–232.

94. SCHULTZ, G., SENFT, G., AND MUNSKE, K., 1966, Die Wirkung von Insulin auf Phosphodiesterase, *Naturwissenschaften* **53**:529.

95. SCOW, R. O., CHERNICK, S. S., AND BRINLEY, M. S., 1964, Hyperlipemia and ketosis in the pregnant rat, *Amer. J. Physiol.* **206**:796–804.

96. SHORLAND, F. B., BODY, D. R., AND GLASS, J. P., 1966, The foetal and maternal lipids of Romney sheep, *Biochim. Biophys. Acta* **125**:207–225.

97. SISSON, J. A., AND PLOTZ, E. J., 1967, Plasma lipids in maternal and fetal rabbits fed stock and pea-nut oil cholesterol diets, *J. Nutr.* **92**:435–442.

98. SISSON, J. A., AND PLOTZ, E. J., 1967, Effect of alloxan diabetes on maternal and fetal serum lipids in the rabbit, *Exp. Mol. Pathol.* **6**:274–281.

99. SKALA, J., AND HAHN, P., 1971, Effect of single cortisone injections on brown adipose tissue of developing rats, *Can. J. Physiol. Pharmacol.* **49**:501–507.

100. SKALA, J., HAHN, P., AND BRAUN, T., 1970, Adenyl cyclase activity in brown adipose tissue of young rats, *Life Sci.* **9**(I):1201–1212.

101. SKALA, J., HAHN, P., AND DRUMMOND, G. I., 1974, A protein kinase inhibitor in brown adipose tissue of developing rats, *Biochem. J.* **138**:195–199.

102. SKALA, J., NOVAK, E., HAHN, P., AND DRUMMOND G. I., 1972, Changes in interscapular brown adipose tissue of the rat during perinatal and early postnatal development and after cold acclimation. V. Adenyl cyclase, cyclic AMP, protein kinase, phosphorylase phosphorylase kinase and glycogen, *Int. J. Biochem.* **3**:229–242.

103. SMIGURA, F. C., BRYAN, H., AND ANGEL, A., 1974, Post heparin lipase activity in newborn infants, in *The Role of Fat in Intravenous Feeding of the Newborn Proceedings of a Conference* (P. Hahn, S. Segal, and S. Israels, eds.), pp. 129–139, Pharmacia, Dorval, Quebec.

104. SMITH, R. E., AND HORWITZ, B. A., 1969, Brown fat and thermogenesis, *Physiol. Rev.* **49**:330–425.

105. SMITH, S., AND ABRAHAM, S., 1970, Fatty acid synthesis in developing mouse liver, *Arch. Biochem. Biophys.* **136**:112–121.

106. SPITZER, J., 1962, in: *Adipose Tissue as an Organ* (L. W. Kinsell, ed.), p. 250, Charles C. Thomas, Springfield, Illinois.

107. STAVE, U., 1964, Age-dependent changes of metabolism. I. Studies of enzyme patterns of rabbit organs, *Biol. Neonate* **6**:128–147.

108. STAVE, U., 1975, Perinatal changes of interorgan differences in cell metabolism, *Biol. Neonate* **26**:318–332.

109. SVENNERHOLM, L., 1964, The distribution of lipids in the human nervous system, *J. Neurochem.* **11**:839–853.

110. THIEL, S., 1966, Die Aktivität der Glycerokinase in Placenta, mütterlicher und foetaler Leber bei Ratten, *Naturwissenschaften* **53**:436, 437.

111. VAN DUYNE, C. M., HAVEL, R. J., AND FELTS, J. M., 1962, Placental transfer of palmitic acid 1-^{14}C in the rabbit, *Amer. J. Obstet. Gynecol.* **84**:1069–1074.

112. VAN DUYNE, C. M., PARKER, H. R., HAVEL, R. J., AND HOLM, L. W., 1960, Free fatty acid metabolism

in fetal and newborn sheep. *Amer. J. Physiol.* **199**:987–990.

113. VILLEE, C. A., AND HAGERMAN, D. D., 1958, Effect of oxygen deprivation on the metabolism of fetal and adult tissue, *Amer. J. Physiol.* **194**:457–464.

114. VOLPE, J. J., AND KIHIMOTO, Y., 1972, Fatty acid synthetase of brain: Development, influence of nutritional and hormonal factors and comparison with liver enzyme, *J. Neurochem.* **19**:737–753.

115. WARSAW, J. B., 1972, Cellular energy metabolism during fetal development. IV. Fatty acid activation, acyl transfer and fatty acid oxidation during development of the chick and rat, *Dev. Biol.* **28**:537–544.

116. WARSAW, J. B., AND KIMURA, R. E., 1973, Cellular energy metabolism during fetal development. V. Fatty acid synthesis by the developing rat, *Dev. Biol.* **33**:224–228.

117. WASSERMANN, F., 1965, The development of adipose tissue, in: *Handbook of Physiology* (A. E. Renold and G. F. Cahill, Jr., eds.), Vol. 5, pp. 87–100, Waverly Press, Baltimore.

118. WELLS, M. A., AND DITTMER, J. C., 1967, A comprehensive study of the postnatal changes in the concentration of the lipids of developing rat brain, *Biochemistry* **6**:3169–3175.

119. WILDI, F., 1948, Appearance of glycogen and fat in liver of guinea-pig embryos, *Schweiz. Med. Wochenschr.* **78**:446–450.

120. WILLIAMSON, D. H., AND BUCKLEY, B. M., 1973, The role of ketone bodies in brain development, in: *Inborn Errors of Metabolism,* pp. 80–96, Academic Press, New York.

121. WILLIAMSON, J. R., AND KREBS, H. A., 1961, Acetoacetate as fuel of respiration in the perfused heart, *Biochem. J.* **85**:540–547.

122. WITTELS, B., AND BRESSLER, R., 1965, Lipid metabolism in the newborn heart, *J. Clin. Invest.* **44**:1639–1646.

123. WOLF, H., MELICHAR, V., AND MICHAELIS, R., 1968, Elimination of intravenously administered glycerol from the blood of newborns, *Biol. Neonate* **12**:162–169.

124. WOLF, H., STAVE, U., NOVAK, M., AND MONKUS, E., 1974, Recent investigations on neonatal fat metabolism, *J. Perinat. Med.* **2**:75–87.

125. ZEE, P., 1967, Lipid metabolism in the newborn. I. Phospholipids in cord and maternal sera, *Pediatrics* **39**:82–87.

CHAPTER 20

Functions and Metabolism of Trace Elements

Maria C. Linder

1. Introduction and Background

1.1. Essential and Nonessential Trace Elements

The human and animal body contains most, if not all, of the elements in the periodic table (Fig. 1). Some of these elements are found in larger amounts, and their main functions have been quite well elucidated. Others are present only in trace quantities, and their functions (if indeed they have any) are not understood at all. The presence of an element in larger or smaller amounts in the body cannot be taken as an indication of its greater or lesser importance for the organism. Cobalt, for example, is found only in the tiniest quantities and has only a few enzyme-linked functions in the mammalian body, but it is an "essential" element, meaning that it is crucial for life, health, and reproduction. Elements for which essentiality has not been established are

often more important quantitatively than some trace elements known to be essential (Table I). These elements include the so-called "heavy metals" lead, mercury, and cadmium, which have become more prevalent in our environment because of industrialization. Because of our preoccupation with the toxic aspects of their actions, we have largely ignored the possibility that these elements might also be "essential." Two cases in point are selenium and tin, both of which are known for their damaging effects, yet were only recently shown to be also essential in trace amounts for the animal organism. It is very possible that all elements may thus eventually be found essential in very small amounts, and even the most benign will be found toxic if administered in sufficient quantity.

Traditionally, the "trace" elements have been defined as those present in the human and animal organism in quantities equal to or less than the quantities in which iron is present. Iron is thus the most abundant trace element. Many other elements are present in similar or lesser amounts (Table I). These elements may be subcategorized into essential and nonessential (or "other"), based on the experi-

Maria C. Linder · Physiological Chemistry Laboratories, Department of Nutrition and Food Science, Massachusetts Institute of Technology, Cambridge, Massachusetts

425

Table I. Content, Absorption, and Distribution of Trace Elements in the Normal Adult Human[a]

Element (*essential)	Content in adult body (mg)[b]	Ease of absorption from diet (%)[b]	Blood distribution and plasma binding (*most in red cells)	Blood concentration (μg/dl)	Main organ of accumulation or storage (*airborne source)	Main route of excretion
*Iron (Fe)	4000–5000	5–15	*Transferrin	50,000	Liver	Bile
*Fluorine (F)	2600–4000	40–100	Mainly albumin bound[c]	10–20	Bone	Urine
*Zinc (Zn)	1600–2300	31–51	*α_2-Globulin; also α_1-globulin, albumin	100	Skin, bone	Pancreatic secretions, bile
*Silicon (Si)	(1100)[d]	(1–4)	Monosilicic acid	500	Skin	
Zirconium (Zr)	250–420	0.01	Like V?		Fat? (*Lung)	Bile
Strontium (Sr)	340	<20	Half loosely bound to protein / Half small chelates		Bone	
Rubidium (Rb)	320	90	*Free (like K+)		None	
Bromine (Br)	200	99	Free (like Cl−)	300	None	
Lead (Pb)	122	5	*Protein-bound (?)	15–40	Bone	Bile
Aluminum (Al)	50–150	0.1	?	13–17	(*Lung)	Urine
Copper (Cu)	72–100	30–60	Ceruloplasmin; also albumin, a.a.s.	100	Liver	Bile
Boron (B)	48	99	?		Bone	Urine
*Tin (Sn)	(42)[e]	2	?		Lung? Liver?	Urine
Cadmium (Cd)	30–38	25	Protein-bound (?) (like Cu^{2+}, Zn^{2+}?)	0.5–0.7	Kidney	Urine
Barium (Ba)	22	1–15	?	2–10	Skin?	Urine
*Selenium (Se)	21	35–85	Firmly to 2 proteins, loosely to LDLs and vLDLs[f]	10–30	Kidney?	Urine (bile, exhalation)
Germanium (Ge)	(20)	Easy	?		Spleen	Urine
*Iodine (I)	10–20	100	Almost all as PBI (thyroid hormones)	2–4	Thyroid	Urine
Arsenic (As)	8–20	(5)	*	10–64	Skin? Hair?	Urine (organic), bile (inorganic)
*Manganese (Mn)	12–16	3–4	Transferrin (?)[g]	1–2	Liver, bone	Bile
*Molybdenum (Mo)	9–16	40–100	Protein-bound	1	Liver?	Urine (bile?)
Mercury (Hg)	13	5–10	As natural complex absorbed from diet?	0.5–1	Kidney	
Vanadium (V)	10	0.1–1	Transferrin (little in cells)[h]	0.5–23	Fat?	Urine
Titanium (Ti)	9	1–2	Like Z_I?		(*Lung)	Urine
*Nickel (Ni)	5–10	3–6	Most albumin-bound; some free	2–4	Skin, liver, muscle?	Urine
Tellurium (Te)	7	20–50	Like Se?		Bone	
Antimony (Sb)	6	Poor	Like As?		Spleen, liver, kidney	
*Chromium (Cr)	1–5	1	Transferrin[g]; also globulins	1–6	Spleen, heart	Urine
*Cobalt (Co)	1.1–1.5	63–97	Albumin (little as vitamin B_{12})	0.007–6	Liver, fat	Urine

[a] This table is based on information from many sources extrapolated to the 70-kg adult, notably Underwood,[123] Schroeder,[97] Schwarz,[102] Nielson and Ollerich,[78] Hopkins and Mohr,[50] Carlisle,[19] Linder and Munro,[62] and Tipton and Cook.[121]
[b] Values in parentheses are tentative or controversial.   [c] Taves.[119]   [d] Based on concentrations found for blood (7%), skin (10%), and other tissues (70% of body weight).   [e] Based on an overall concentration of 0.6 μg/g.   [f] Burk et al.[15]   [g] Guenther et al.[37] and Hopkins and Schwarz[51] (for chromium).   [h] Hopkins.[49]

mental evidence available at this time. For those presently classified as essential, a requirement for normal life and growth, and deficiency symptoms that respond to treatment with the element, have been established at least for animals (mammals). The assumption that the elements that are essential for mammals are also essential for man appears to be entirely valid. That they are has been the overwhelming experience with those elements for which deficiency symptoms in man have been observed and treated. Indeed, it is unlikely that overt deficiency of many of the remaining "nonessential" trace elements will be shown in man, since such demonstrations in animals have depended on highly purified food and an uncontaminated environment,[102] which would be undesirable to impose on human beings.

Through the use of such highly refined environments, and primarily through the efforts of one laboratory, there has been a renaissance of discoveries of essential trace elements in the last five years. Following the determinations in 1928–1935 that copper, manganese, zinc, and cobalt are essential, and the interim demonstration of essentialness for molybdenum, selenium, and chromium in the 1950s, five new elements (tin, vanadium, fluorine, silicon,

and nickel) have been added since 1970. According to Klaus Schwarz (the power behind most of these discoveries), these additions should continue. He feels that most elements, including silver, gold, mercury, and arsenic, will eventually be included in the "essential" list. Henry Schroeder, who also spent a lifetime working with trace elements, did not agree, but he agreed that the present list will certainly be extended based on his considerations of (1) the relative distribution and abundance of the remaining trace elements in body organs of man and other species; (2) changes in the concentrations of these elements from birth to adulthood; and (3) their relative occurrence in Western vs. nonindustrialized man.[97]

Figure 1 shows the periodic table of elements and the positions and relative abundance of essential and other trace elements in the hypothetical 70-kg adult human. It can be seen that the essential elements derive mainly from the upper tiers, which are associated with smaller atomic sizes. The five most abundant essential trace elements are iron, fluorine, zinc, silicon, and copper, fluorine and silicon having been added only in 1972. It is notable that many other trace elements that may not be essential, e.g., zirconium, rubidium, bromine, and aluminum, are

1	2	3	4	5	6	7	8	9	10	11	12	13	14	15	16	17	18
H																**H**	He
(2.2) Li	(36) Be											(48) B	**C**	**N**	**O**	(3300) F* 1972	Ne
Na	**Mg**											(100) Al	(1100) Si* 1972	**P**	**S**	**Cl**	Ar
K	**Ca**	Sc	(9) Ti	(10) V* 1971	(3) Cr* 1959	(14) Mn* 1931	(4500) Fe* 17thC	(1.3) Co* 1935	(8) Ni* 1973	(87) Cu* 1928	(2000) Zn* 1934	Ga	(20) Ge	(14) As	(21) Se* 1957	(200) Br	Kr
(320) Rb	(340) Sr	Y	(340) Zr	(120) Nb	(13) Mo* 1953	Tc	Ru	Rh	Pd	(0.8) Ag	(34) Cd	In	(42) Sn* 1970	(6) Sb	(7) Te	(15) I* 1850	Xe
(1.4) Cs	(22) Ba	La	Hf	Ta	W	Re	Os	Ir	Pt	Au	(13) Hg	(7) Tl	(122) Pb	(0.2) Bi	Po	At	Rn
Fr	Ra	Ac															

Fig. 1. Periodic table of elements showing the relative positions of essential and nonessential elements. (The lanthanoid and actinoid series have been omitted.) The symbols for essential elements present in greater than trace quantities are in large letters; those for trace elements presently recognized as essential are in medium-size letters followed by asterisks and with the years in which their essentialness was discovered. Those for trace elements not presently known as essential are shown in the smallest letters. Quantities (mg) of the trace elements found in the average 70-kg human are given in parentheses (averaged from values in Table I).

present in considerable quantities, and in this case in quantities equal to, or exceeding, those of copper. The relative abundance of strontium is to us less surprising because of its similarity to calcium in metabolism. From the positions of vanadium, chromium, and nickel in the periodic table, it is perhaps not unexpected that they should have been found essential. Similarly, a potential usefulness for boron, aluminum, bromine, arsenic, germanium, strontium, rubidium, cadmium, silver, and perhaps others does not seem out of question. Biological roles for some of these have already been demonstrated in nonanimal systems, e.g., the need for boron in plants.

1.2. Metabolism and Functions of the Trace Elements

1.2.1. Absorption, Retention, and Excretion

Table I summarizes the relative abundance of the essential and other trace elements in the bodies of adult Americans. The data are derived from many sources, and there is considerable variation among individuals, which has been glossed over due to the necessity of presenting easily comprehensive, mean values. The mean retention of trace elements within the body does not correspond precisely to their relative content in the average American diet (see Table V), although there is some general similarity. The lack of correspondence may be attributed in part to differences in the absorbability of these elements from the diet. The low absorption of aluminum, silicon, manganese, and vanadium, for example, contributes to their lower retention within the body. Retention, however, is determined not only by absorption but also by the ease with which an element is stored or excreted. Lead, cadmium, and mercury, for instance, are absorbed fairly readily, and yet their relative abundance is greater within the body than in the diet, suggesting a limitation of the capacity for excretion. Indeed, along with germanium, tin, antimony, and tellurium, these elements accumulate with age in the human.[97]

A variety of factors, endogenous and exogenous, affect the rates of absorption and excretion of elements in the body. Inherent factors include permeability of the intestinal mucosa; the presence or absence of special uptake and carrier mechanism therein, such as calcium-binding protein for calcium the capacity to eliminate an element from the body once it has entered (iron, for instance, is eliminated very poorly, whereas zinc, copper, and manganese exit more readily); and finally, the capacity to sequester quantities of an element in innocuous form somewhere within the tissues, e.g., iron as ferritin in the liver and fluorine and manganese in bone hydroxylapatite.

Exogenous factors exert their effects primarily at the level of absorption by influencing the chemical form in which trace elements are offered to the intestine. Since it appears that many elements are absorbed best in the water-soluble, ionic, or chelated state, dietary factors that form insoluble compounds render them less available for absorption, while others that promote chelation may make them more available. As an illustration, iron is absorbed in the ferrous or ferric form (perhaps as a chelate or as part of the heme group of hemoglobin or myoglobin in meat). The presence of phytate, carbonate, or oxalate in the diet reduces the absorbability of the nonheme forms through the formation of insoluble salts, while fructose, ascorbate, citrate, and some amino acids enhance absorption by forming chelates. Additional dietary influences may be the presence of trace elements that compete for absorption. Thus, copper, cobalt, manganese, cadmium, and zinc may inhibit iron absorption or the absorption of each other, depending on the relative quantities of each present. The exact mechanism of this competition is at present not understood, but it implies a common route of entry into the body for groups of trace elements, and suggests a shared membrane carrier.

For many elements, homeostatic control of body content may be exerted by regulating rate of entry at the level of the intestine, or rate of elimination once the element has entered the body. In the case of iron, it appears that regulation is exerted at entry, the degree of absorption showing an inverse relationship to the size of body iron stores and the rate of erythropoiesis, and there is little variation in the rate of excretion (through the bile). In the case of zinc, copper, and manganese, the situation is reversed, and control is exerted at the level of excretion, so that the degree of uptake from the diet remains about the same, but the amount eliminated (via the bile) is responsive to the size of the body burden. It is greater when exces s present and less when stores are depleted. (This form of regulation may be peculiar to trace elements other than iron eliminated through the bile.) Most other trace elements are eliminated through the urine (Table I), and homeostatic control of their elimination has not been established.

The capacity of an element to bind firmly to body constituents, either within cells or as part of connective tissue and skeleton, also influences the ease with which it is eliminated. Rubidium, bromine, boron, and iodine, for example, which enter the body almost quantitatively from the diet, are also very easily eliminated and do not accumulate. This ease of elimination is not difficult to understand, since their close cousins in the same periodic groups (potassium and chlorine, respectively) are present in completely ionized form, floating within the intra- and extracellular fluids of the body, unattached to larger molecules that would prevent their exit from cells and tissues. Evidence suggests that is true for rubidium (Rb+)[123] and bromine (Br−)[43]; it may also be true for excess iodine (I−), although in this case, the thyroid produces thyroglobulin, which tightly binds and retains a certain quantity of the element. This process allows iodine to be stored and to provide thyroid hormone despite fluctuations in dietary supply. Many other trace elements also have strong affinities for intra- and extracellular proteins (or other macromolecules) within the body, and this affinity promotes their retention. Zinc, copper, and cadmium, for example, are sequestered by a group of small cysteine-containing proteins, including metallothionein, in liver and kidney, and most trace elements are associated with proteins while traveling in the blood plasma (Table I). In addition, the hydroxylapatite of bone offers a depot for a variety of trace elements (Table I), including fluorine, strontium, lead, boron, manganese, and tellurium.

1.2.2. Functions

Much is known about the functions and effects of trace elements within the human and animal body, but even more remains to be discovered. At present, four kinds of roles may be distinguished: (1) roles as cofactors in enzyme reactions (in analogy to the roles of many vitamins); (2) roles in oxygen binding and diffusion; (3) structural roles as integral constituents of nonenzymic macromolecules; and (4) roles as ionic constituents of body fluids, affecting the osmolarity of the internal and external cellular environment, membrane potential, membrane charge, and so on. With regard to the first role, there are numerous enzymes in all areas of metabolism that depend for their activity on the presence of one or two trace elements. Usually, just a few atoms per molecule are required to provide full catalytic activity, and this limited requirement explains the effectiveness of trace amounts. The role in enzyme function also explains how these elements are linked to the basic life processes of the organism. Some trace elements are known associates of *many* enzyme reactions, while others have associations with only one, or a few. Zinc, for example, is presently considered a cofactor in the reaction of more than 15 enzymes within the mammalian body, whereas selenium has been connected with just one, glutathione peroxidase.[48] (The lack of selenium nevertheless has severe and life-threatening effects, as discussed in Section 3.9.)

With regard to oxygen binding, diffusion, and respiration, the roles of iron (porphyrin) and copper in mitochondrial electron transport are well known.

As regards structural roles of the trace elements, some interesting examples have begun to emerge, including the mucopolysaccharides and collagen of connective tissue, bone, and vitreous humor[125] shown to contain silicon. It is thought that this silicon may be part of the C–O cross linkages for these macromolecules.[102] Tin may play a similar role, since it, like carbon, is capable of forming truly covalent linkages and could be integrated into the basic structure of organic biological molecules[102] (whether this occurs is not known). In contrast, the trace elements fluorine and strontium are integrated into the inorganic matrix of bone, the hydroxylapatite, probably by replacing some carbonate[123] and calcium, respectively.

Other roles of trace elements, such as in electrolyte balance and perhaps also in the regulation of hormone release, are of interest, but have been less well studied. It is likely that bromine and rubidium ions mimic the actions and fates of, respectively, chloride and potassium ions—which are involved in electrolyte balance—as strontium is thought to mimic calcium. Several recent reports on the actions of cobalt (not involving vitamin B_{12}) suggest a role in the release of renal hormones, erythropoietin, and bradykinin.[114] This would explain its stimulatory effect on erythropoiesis, and also suggests a role for cobalt in blood pressure control. Other evidence[42] suggests that mercury, cadmium, barium, and zinc may stimulate the release of catecholamines from the adrenal gland, though it is difficult to say whether this evidence is of physiological significance, the experiments having been done with isolated, perfused adrenal glands.

2. Perinatal Metabolism of Trace Elements

Because of the important functions of the trace elements, it is not suprising that provision is made for their maternofetal transfer during gestation, that some elements are indeed stored up for use during the postnatal period when milk is the main food, and that overall, large, and crucial changes in the uptake and distribution of trace elements accompany growth and development before and after birth. It will be the main task of this chapter to review what is known about these changes, and how they are related to the metabolism of the fetus and infant.

2.1. Maternofetal Transfer

2.1.1. Evidence of Transfer and Screening

From the finding that an element is essential for life and health, it would be expected that a mechanism had been developed by the organism for its transfer from mother to fetus through the blood circulation. Such a mechanism has indeed been verified for most of the essential and some of the other trace elements by establishing their presence in tissues or blood of the fetus or newborn infant (Tables II and III) and animal. As regards the exceptions, the early report of Schroeder et al.[99] that tin is absent in the newborn human infant has now been confirmed for the animal by Schwarz,[103] despite some problems associated with the analysis.[106] Methodological problems[123] may, however, explain the lack of detection of cadmium in some newborn samples. Nickel has not been studied, but the transfer of some potentially toxic heavy metals such as lead,[7] mercury,[80] and arsenic[97] has been well documented. Indeed, it appears that most trace elements

are transferred to the fetus, since reports of nondetection are generally lacking.

Transfer across the placenta is nevertheless not indiscriminate, and some screening of elements does occur. Thus, for example, relatively little cadmium appears in the fetus.[86] (This element is not known to be essential and may have toxic effects.) As a bearer of radioactivity, strontium is a potential hazard; it is transferred one-eighth as well as calcium.[3] Some barrier also exists to the transfer of all but trace quantities of fluorine.[123] The existence of this barrier may be significant, since fluorine is, with selenium, one of the few essential trace elements for which amounts required by the body and those resulting in toxicity are not widely separated.[123]

Comparative values for whole-body concentrations of trace elements in term fetuses and normal adults illustrate their relative abilities to cross the placental barriers (Tables II and III). Three groups of trace elements may be distinguished: (1) those that show a higher concentration in the fetus, suggesting rapid transfer and storage, including iron, copper, chromium, and perhaps zinc (the latter based on a comparison of liver values); (2) those present in equal concentrations, suggesting a kind of equilibration with the mother (including silicon, selenium, manganese, and perhaps boron); and (3) those that show distinctly lower concentrations in the fetus, suggesting limitation of transfer across the maternofetal barrier; trace elements in this group would be fluorine and strontium (already mentioned), barium and iodine, probably tin, molybdenum, rubidium, and cobalt, as well as cadmium and several other nonessential elements (Table III). Data are not available for some of the trace elements.

Further evidence on ease of placental transfer comes from Baglan et al.,[6] who determined concentrations of several trace elements (including potentially toxic ones) in whole blood milked from the placenta, and corresponding maternal blood, at the time of birth (Table IV). The results (for more than 500 pairs) show that lead and cadmium are present in significantly lower amounts in fetal blood, further supporting a screening of these elements. Zinc is also lower, but this may be accounted for by the low level of carbonic anhydrase in the fetal red blood cells.[133] The majority of the trace elements examined did show, however, a close correspondence between the concentrations in maternal and fetal blood, both on the basis of average values (Table IV) and on the basis of individual pairs.[6]

Table II. Trace Elements in the Human Body at Birth and in Adulthood[a]

Trace elements	Total amount in the adult body (mg)	Overall concentration (µg)		Primary storage organ[b]			Maternofetal transfer	Fetal accumulations[c]
		Adult	Term fetus	Organ	Concentration (µg/g) Adult	Term fetus		
Confirmed essential								
Iron (Fe)	4000–5000	64	94–100	Liver	50–200	550	+	+ (Liver)
Fluorine (F)	2600–4000	47	0–0.3 (Rat)	Bone	100–600[d]	50–150[d]	+ (Low)	−
Zinc (Zn)	1600–2300	28	24	Skin, bone, liver	200 / 55–70	116	+	−
Silicon (Si)	(1100)[e]	16	16	Skin	100		+	
Copper (Cu)	72–100	1.2	4.7–5.0	Liver	7	63	+	+(Liver)
Tin (Sn)	(42)	(0.60)	≈0	Lung? / Liver?	0.43[f] / 0.34[f]	0 / 0	− / −	− / −
Selenium (Se)	21	0.30	0.30 (Infant)	Muscle[g] liver	0.39	0.34	+(Some forms)	
Iodine (I)	10–20	0.21	Less	Thyroid	270–1300	12–60	+	−(?)
Manganese (Mn)	12–16	0.20	Less/similar	Liver (bone not mobilizable)	1.7	1.7	+	−(Liver)
Molybdenum (Mo)	9–16	0.18	Less	Liver?	0.8–13.6	0.18	+	−(Liver)
Vanadium (V)	10	0.14		Fat?	1.62		+	+(?)
Nickel (Ni)	10	0.14		Skin?	0.15–0.82		?	
Chromium (Cr)	1–5	0.043	More	Spleen[g] / Heart[g]	0.02 / 0.05	0.29 / 0.90	+	+(Spleen, heart)
Cobalt (Co)	1.1–1.5	0.019	Less[g]	Liver / Fat?	0.04–0.20 / 0.24	?	?	−(Liver)
Possible essential								
Strontium (Sr)	340	4.9	0.01–0.10	Bone	(2400)[d]	1600[d]	+	−
Rubidium (Rb)	320	4.6	Less	None			+(?)	−(?)
Bromine (Br)	200	2.9		None	2.9–3.7 (blood)		?	−
Boron (B)	48	0.69		Bone	43–90[d]	(48–88[d] (Infants))	+(?)	+(?)
Barium (Ba)	22	0.31	(0 in bones)	Skin?	0.04–0.17	?	?	

[a] Values are estimates of actual figures for the adult (70-kg) body or term fetus (3.4 kg) based on a large number of literature reports of trace-element contents of human tissues (see Table I). Literature values for concentration per gram dry weight were converted on the basis of factors calculated from Tipton and Cook.[121]
[b] Based on the sensitivity of organ concentration to dietary excess.
[c] Accumulation of higher-than-adult levels in tissues during fetal life.
[d] Values per gram ash.
[e] Based on reported concentrations in blood, skin, and soft tissues.
[f] Values are underestimates due to methodological problems.
[g] Schroeder.[97]

Table III. Whole-Body Concentrations (μg/g) of Nonessential Trace Elements in U.S. and Non-U.S. Adults and Fetuses[a]

Element	U.S. adult	U.S. term fetus	Nonindustrialized man (adult)
Strontium (Sr)[c]	4.9	Similar	4.6
Zirconium (Zr)[c]	4.8	(9.5 rat)	6.0
Rubidium (Rb)[c]	4.6	Less	4.6
Bromine (Br)[c]	2.9	0.46 (excluding bone)	1.0
Lead (Pb)	1.7	Much less	0.01
Aluminum (Al)[c]	1.4[b]	Much less	0.4
Boron (B)[c]	0.69	Same (bone)	0.3
Cadmium (Cd)	0.49[b]	Very low	0.001
Barium (Ba)[c]	0.31		0.3
Germanium (Ge)	0.29[b]	Less (0.18 rat)	Less
Arsenic (As)	0.20[b]	Less	0.05
Mercury (Hg)	0.19	Similar (liver, kidney, brain)	<0.001
Titanium (Ti)[c]	0.13	Less	0.4
Tellurium (Te)	0.10[b]	Less	0.001
Antimony (Sb)	0.08[b]	Less	<0.001

[a] Mainly based on, or calculated from, Schroeder[97] and Underwood.[123]
[b] Accumulation with age in adults.
[c] Relatively nontoxic.

In this study, it was also noted that with the exception of cadmium and iron, the concentration of an element in placental tissue was 0.6- to 6-fold greater than in either maternal or fetal blood. This relationship was especially true for lead, cobalt, and zinc, and suggested that the placenta may have a storage function. When one compares the concentration of iron in the placenta with that in serum, rather than in whole blood (see Table IV) (thus excluding the iron contribution from red cells), the same suggestion holds for iron, and there is other evidence from animal experiments to support this view. Mansour et al.[67] found that in rats, iron still accumulated in placentas and was removed from the maternal plasma, *after* fetuses had been surgically excised.

The relative concentrations of trace elements in serum from term fetuses and nonpregnant adults have also been compared (see Table IV). The comparison shows, again, a great similarity between fetus and adult. For the elements shown, the few exceptions are strontium and copper, with considerably lower values for the fetus, and iron and lead, with much higher values. The values for lead are of interest when compared to those for whole blood (see Table IV), since in adults, most of the lead is sequestered in the red cells, rather than in the serum, and the results here suggest that the reverse is true for the fetus. The lower fetal values for strontium and copper are also interesting. They support other experiments with strontium showing a depression of maternofetal transfer,[3] and for copper, it is well known that the amount circulating as ceruloplasmin in the plasma of the fetus and neonate is very low.[62] Ceruloplasmin is not a copper-transport protein in the manner of transferrin. The concentrations of cobalt also deserve comment, since they suggest an enormous variability in individual concentrations, and a low transfer to the fetus. Methodological problems may be involved, however.[123] The proportion of cobalt present in the body in the form of vitamin

Table IV. Blood and Serum Trace-Element Concentrations in Term Fetuses, Mothers, and Normal Adults

Trace element[a]	Blood concentration (μg/dl)[b]			Serum concentration (μg/dl)[b]	
	Term fetus	Mother	Normal adult	Term fetus	Normal adult
Fe	27,500	23,100	50,000	238	143
Zn	149[c]	365	100	115(83)[d]	134
Sr				1.8	4.2
Rb	178	154			
Pb	5.8[c]	9.1	15–40	6.5	2.4
Al			13–17	38	51
Cu	(60)	(150)	100	32(29)[d]	108
Cd	0.73[c]	0.93	0.5–0.7	31	38
Ba				20	19
Se	10.4	11.0	10–30		
Mn			1–2	3.4	2.8
Mo			1	3.1	2.1
Hg	0.54	0.48	0.5–1		
Cr			1–6	16	13
Co			0.07–6	0–2.6	0–94
Ag				3.4	2.9

[a] In decreasing order of occurrence in the adult body (Table I).
[b] Except for copper, blood concentrations for term fetuses and mothers were calculated from values of Baglan et al.[6] (μg/g dry weight), assuming a blood dry weight of 10%; other values from Table I. Serum concentrations are from Butt et al.[18] Except for the newborn sera (7 samples), both reports are for large numbers of samples (250–600+ per group).
[c] Fetal blood not equilibrated with that of the mother ($P < 0.05$).
[d] From Henkin[44]; for serum, 27/33 and 32/48 μg zinc/dl were ultrafilterable for fetus and mother, respectively; similarly, for copper, 5/29 and 18/221 μg/dl were filterable.

B_{12} (the only form known to be essential) is uncertain; at least in adults, however, relatively little of the cobalt of plasma is in the vitamin.[123]

2.1.2. Mechanism of Maternofetal Transfer

Little is known about the forms in which the various trace elements are transferred to the fetus, although it is likely that this transfer may occur through diffusion or active uptake of the soluble ions across the placental barrier.[44,133] On this basis, trace-element ions would arrive at the placental barrier in the same manner and form in which they are carried in the circulation to other tissues of the maternal organism, from there to be absorbed into the fetal plasma and carried (probably in similar fashion) to the fetal organs in which they may be deposited. This mechanism appears to be the case for iron,[62] which is carried to the placenta by transferrin and transferred to the fetus, the maternal (now empty) transferrin remaining behind in the mother's circulation. (Perhaps because of a lower transferrin concentration, less iron appears to be transferred to fetuses of protein-deficient mothers.[66]) Table I summarizes what is known about the forms in which trace elements occur in adult plasma and how they are bound for transport between various organs. Several general conclusions may be drawn. First, many of the trace elements are associated with proteins. The bulk of the iron, zinc, copper, selenium, manganese, and chromium is bound to α_2- and β-globulins. Second, smaller quantities of trace elements may be bound to chelating agents such as citrate (calcium, iron) and amino acids (copper, zinc), or loosely bound to albumin (copper, zinc, nickel). Third, the trace elements not associated with proteins within the plasma belong to groups I, IIA, and VIIA of the periodic table, or to groups that form highly ionized compounds, explaining this behavior.

Finally, those plasma proteins that have trace elements attached may or may not be carriers designed for delivery of the elements to the various tissues. For example, transferrin, which binds most of the iron and probably most of the chromium,[37,51] manganese,[37] and vanadium[49] in the serum, is a true carrier protein involved in the delivery of not just iron, but of all three of these elements, to tissues (and probably also the placenta). On the other hand, copper-containing ceruloplasmin, the major zinc-containing α_2-globulin,[52] and the two major selenium-containing proteins of plasma[15,23] do not have this kind of function. The metal ions are incorporated into the proteins when they are made within the liver, and free metal ions do not attach or equilibrate when incubated with the plasma proteins. The main functions of these proteins in plasma may be enzymatic. Ceruloplasmin, for one, is an oxidase with activity toward a number of endogenous and synthetic substrates (including ferrous ion, ascorbate, and catecholamines).[62] Special transport functions for these proteins (such as delivery of an element to a specific organ) should not, however, be excluded. In experiments with rats using ceruloplasmin labeled with ^{67}Cu, it was found that radioactivity appeared in the heart, lung, and testicles within a few hours of intravenous infusion.[84] It is not known whether the radioactive copper within these organs is still attached to ceruloplasmin, but the results suggest a dual function for this protein, namely, as an enzyme active in the mobilization of iron and as a carrier of copper to certain organs and for biliary excretion (see Section 3.2).

Those metal ions that are *transported* by plasma proteins (excepting transferrin) are generally more loosely bound than those serving an enzymatic function, and may be dialyzed away. This is true for zinc, copper, selenium, nickel, and cobalt not bound to enzyme, and is probably also true for others such as lead. As a consequence of this relatively loose binding to protein, a larger proportion of the trace element in plasma remains in small-molecular-weight form, either as the free ion or chelated with other small molecules. A significant fraction (perhaps 5%) of the total copper in plasma,

for example, will be in the form of amino acid chelates, notably with histidine,[62] and other evidence suggests that an even larger proportion of plasma zinc is in relatively free form.[44] For copper and zinc, the relative proportions of free and bound ions have been measured in term fetuses and their respective mothers at the time of birth.[44] The results, which are given in footnote *e* to Table IV, show that while there is a greater total concentration of zinc in the plasma of the fetus than in the mother, the concentration of free zinc (as determined by ultrafiltration) is similar in the two, perhaps with a slight concentration gradient from mother to fetus. For copper, a different situation pertains, and the mother has both a much larger total concentration in the plasma (due to a high level of ceruloplasmin) and a high level of "free copper," so that there is a larger concentration gradient between mother and fetus.

From the data, it seems likely that the concentration of "free copper" in the maternal plasma determines the rate of transfer to fetus, but it cannot at this time be excluded that ceruloplasmin is not also, or even solely, involved. Two kinds of evidence favor this idea. First, along with transferrin, ceruloplasmin is elevated during pregnancy, and we also know that copper from ceruloplasmin is taken up by certain tissues.[84] Second, there is a recent Russian report[30] that administration of estrone to pregnant rats increases the concentration of copper in the placenta and uterus. Since estrogens are well-known inducers of ceruloplasmin, this finding suggests that ceruloplasmin has deposited extra copper in the placenta for eventual transfer to the fetus.

2.2. Patterns of Accumulation of Trace Elements During Gestation and After Birth

2.2.1. Prenatal Changes

During gestation, the embryo and then the fetus initially grow almost exponentially, but this growth rate gradually diminishes as gestation progresses. In contrast, the total accumulation of several trace elements in the fetal body continues exponentially and does not abate during the last trimester. This continued exponential accumulation is known to be the case for iron, copper, zinc,[133] iodine,[132] and lead,[7] and is probably true for some others as well,

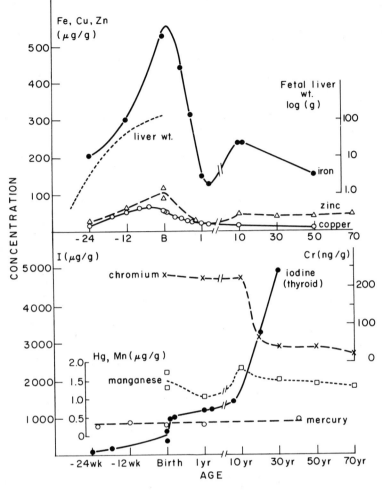

Fig. 2. Concentrations of various trace elements in human liver before and after birth. *Top:* Changes in liver iron (●—●), zinc (△---△), and copper (○——○) concentrations (μg/g). The data for iron and copper are taken from Linder and Munro[62] and Widdowson *et al.*[133]; those for zinc are from Widdowson and Spray,[132] Widdowson *et al.*,[133] and Schroeder *et al.*[101] Values for log liver weight are included to indicate the rate of liver growth during gestation.[7] *Bottom:* Changes in liver mercury (○---○), manganese (□---□), and chromium (×---×), and in thyroid iodine (●——●). Values for mercury and manganese (μg/g) are from Nishimura *et al.*[80] and Schroeder *et al.*,[96] those for chromium are from Schroeder *et al.*[98] (ng/g), and those for iodine (μg/g) are from Widdowson and Spray.[142]

such as chromium.[88] For iron, copper, and chromium, it is reflected in an overall greater body concentration in the fetus as compared with the adult (see Table II), and for all, it indicates that the major, quantitative, gestational uptake occurs during the very last period of pregnancy. Widdowson *et al.*[133] summarized the evidence on iron, copper, and zinc for the human, and their data show that 15–20% of amounts present at full term are delivered to the fetus in the last 2 weeks before birth. Infants delivered prematurely will thus have lower body stores, with consequences such as anemia during postnatal life. Trace-element deficiency in the mother will of course cause the same problem even if infants are not premature. Large fractions of these three elements (iron, zinc, and copper) are deposited in the fetal liver—about 15% of the iron, 25% of the

zinc, and 50% of the copper—and accumulations in these organs follows the exponential rate of accumulation observed for the body as a whole.[133] At birth, therefore, these elements are present in liver at concentrations exceeding those in the adult (see Table II). These patterns of uptake into fetal liver, and log changes in fetal liver weight, are summarized in Fig. 2 (top), along with changes in concentrations that occur postnatally. Iodine in the thyroid gland appears to follow the same prenatal pattern of accumulation as iron, zinc, and copper, although the major uptake occurs after birth and later in life (Fig. 2).

While all evidence suggests a great capacity for transfer of iron from mother to fetus, there is nevertheless a limit. In the rat, it has been demonstrated that the quantity of iron lost from the maternal liver closely corresponds to the total amount deposited in the fetuses, thus pointing to liver stores as the source of the iron transferred.[77] In the absence of adequate stores, the iron appears to come more directly from the maternal diet.[62] However, the total amount of iron transferred to the livers of a total litter for storage was found always to be the same (about 500 μg), irrespective of litter size, and was only marginally increased by preloading the mothers with an excess of iron.[64] This finding implies an upper limit to the amount that may be transferred during pregnancy, and also suggests that for human twins or triplets, iron stores should be lower at birth.

The majority of the trace elements probably do not follow this pattern of accumulation. Manganese, selenium, silicon, and boron (in bone) are present in the same overall concentrations in term fetuses and adults (Table II). More detailed work on manganese shows a constancy of concentration values throughout gestation in the liver (considered the storage organ) as well as other tissues.[123] This constancy persists during postnatal growth, perhaps with a slight dip in the first year (Fig. 2). Recent results suggest this pattern is also the case for mercury in the liver, kidney, and brain,[80] which have similar concentrations throughout gestation and into adulthood.

The third and largest group of trace elements shows its primary accumulation in the body after birth and less maternofetal transfer. This group includes fluorine, tin, iodine, molybdenum, and cobalt (see Table II), as well as potentially toxic elements (see Table III).

2.2.2. Trace-Element Storage Forms

For many, but not all, of these trace elements (see Tables I and II), the liver is quantitatively the main site for deposition of mobilizable stores. That it is is demonstrated by injecting larger quantities of an element into animals to see which organs it deposits in, and also by determining which organ gives up the element most readily when animals are placed on a diet deficient in the element. As in the blood and plasma, most trace elements are associated with proteins within cells, and excess quantities of trace elements may actually stimulate formation of binding or storage proteins within the tissues. A well-studied example of this phenomenon is the iron stimulation of ferritin synthesis, ferritin being a large spherical protein capable of sequestering up to 5000 atoms of iron per molecule in nontoxic form.[62] It has no known enzymic function, and is considered the main storage site for iron in mammalian cells. When iron is administered, there is a stimulation of ferritin synthesis, and its concentration increases. On a deficient diet, this iron is mobilized, and the concentration of ferritin diminishes. Another example of adaptive storage involves metallothionein and related proteins of molecular weights of 6000–11,000 that are found especially in the liver and kidney. Metallothionein accumulates in the liver and kidney in response to zinc[11] and cadmium,[53] respectively. A similar response to mercury has recently been reported for the kidney, but not the liver,[95] and a different liver protein that also binds zinc and has many chemical similarities to metallothionein appears to be induced by copper in the adult rat[28] and ruminant.[91] The isolated rat protein has a lower cysteine content than metallothionein and holds 6 or 7 atoms of metal ions per molecule, including zinc and some copper.[28,53] Under normal conditions in the adult, metallothioneinlike proteins probably bind 20% of the zinc in the liver[10,12] (with little cadmium) and a similar percentage of the cadmium in the kidney (with little zinc), as well as some copper (perhaps 10%) in these two organs.[53] The amount of zinc bound in the liver varies with the total liver zinc concentration,[12] supporting the view of metallothionein as a storage (or at least detoxifying) protein. Superoxide dismutase, on the other hand, long known as erythro-, cerebro-, or hepatocuprein,[62] also binds substantial amounts of copper and zinc in the liver, brain, and erythrocytes, but it is probably not a storage protein, since it has an important enzymatic function that depends on the presence of both trace elements.[8] (Cadmium, mercury, and cobalt can, however, at least in vitro, replace the zinc.[8]) This enzyme prevents the accumulation of superoxide anions, which have damaging effects on red cell membranes,[8] and probably other factors.

For most species, the liver concentration of iron increases dramatically during the last stages of gestation,[62] and for the rat, this increase has been shown to be in ferritin. It has also been determined recently that the concentration of metallothionein is high in the fetal liver, but low in the fetal kidney.[95] This finding would correlate with observations of increased storage of zinc in the liver before birth, but relatively little maternofetal transfer of cadmium stored in the kidney (see Table II).

Metallothionein appears to be less important in copper storage, since the major copper accumulation in the fetal liver of man or rat is in the mitochondria attached to a protein with high cysteine content, christened *neonatal mitochondrocuprein*.[62] This protein is not found in adult liver, and gradually disappears during the suckling period in the rat and probably during the first year of human life. This disappearance correlates with the increasing appearance of ceruloplasmin in the plasma. Indeed, ceruloplasmin may represent another copper storage site, since it accounts for about 5% of body copper and its copper content is very responsive to deficiency, diminishing more readily and earlier than tissue copper concentrations.[62] Storage of copper and zinc in adults is in any case not as critical for survival as is storage of iron, since the copper and zinc are absorbed much more readily and are generally more available in the diet (see Tables I and II). Moreover, iron is required in much larger quantities for hemoglobin.

2.2.3. Changes in Trace Elements After Birth

In contrast to iron, zinc, and copper, much less is known about the transfer and storage of other trace elements, especially in the perinatal period. Nevertheless, as already noted, the majority do not accumulate in appreciable quantities until well after birth, judging from the difference in overall concentrations between adults and fetuses at term (see Tables II and III). This pattern is true for fluorine, strontium, rubidium, molybdenum, and cobalt, and probably for tin and barium, as well as for concentrations of many of the potentially toxic, "nonessential" elements. That the accumulation of some of these elements between birth and maturity may not be natural but imposed by our industrialized environment is borne out by data from Schroeder.[97] These data show whole-body concentrations of lead, cadmium, boron, aluminum, bromine, germanium, arsenic, mercury, tellurium, and antimony to be substantially less in nonindustrialized man. The mechanism of maternofetal transfer thus filters out substantial amounts of the same elements that accumulate due to our industrial environment, implying a built-in protection for the developing fetus.

2.2.4. Trace Elements in Milk

Many of the same essential and nonessential trace elements filtered during transfer from mother to fetus appear to be filtered during production of milk, the main food of the newborn infant. This filtration is true for strontium, fluorine, and cobalt, as illustrated by the data in Table V. As can be seen, the concentrations of most trace elements (except zinc, iodine, molybdenum, chromium, boron, rubidium, and germanium) are lower in milk than in the average American diet. Concentrations of the more toxic nonessential elements lead, cadmium, and arsenic, however, are especially low, in part because of their relatively low absorption from the maternal diet (see Table I). Aluminum is also very low because of exceedingly poor absorption. It is worth noting that the concentrations of most if not all of these trace elements (including some potentially toxic ones) is increased in colostrum. This increase provides an especially rich diet for the infant immediately after birth, and is obtained only by breast-feeding. Also, the concentrations of trace elements in milk are substantially the same for the cow and the human. In addition and from feeding experiments mainly with cows, it has been shown that the milk content of most trace elements is related to dietary intake, and may be raised above normal levels by supplementation (Table V). The exceptions are silicon, iron, and copper, the milk concentrations of which are relatively unresponsive to maternal dietary excess.

In comparison with the normal diet, milk concentrations of iron and copper are especially low. These low concentrations are compensated by the massive storage of these elements in the fetal liver before birth. Their accumulation during gestation thus anticipates and provides for the crucial period after birth, when the diet of the infant is primarily or exclusively milk. Other substances such as glycogen are also stored in apparent readiness for the birth event.[34] These prenatal stores are partly or fully utilized at birth (glycogen) and during the suckling period (iron and copper) as the infant grows and increases its blood volume and body mass. During the postnatal suckling period, many enzymes with trace metal cofactors also appear and increase, such as zinc-containing erythrocyte carbonic anhydrase,[133] δ-amino levulinate dehydratase,[29] and copper-containing plasma ceruloplasmin,[62] as is discussed in greater detail in Section 3.

A low concentration of the trace elements in milk need not imply that these elements are absorbed in the same manner and at the same rate in infants as in adults. For many species, absorption of intact proteins, including immunoglobulins, from the gut

Table V. Trace Elements in the Adult American Diet in Comparison with Milk[a]

Trace element	Adult American diet concentration (ng/g)[b]	Milk concentration (ng/ml) Cow's	Milk concentration (ng/ml) Human	Milk variation with diet[c]
Essential				
Silicon (Si)	?	1400[d,g]		−
Zinc (Zn)	5300–7900	3000–5000[e]	3500–4000[e]	+
Fluorine (F)	2100–7400	100–200		(+)
Iron (Fe)	2600–5300	300–600[g]	300–600[g]	−
Manganese (Mn)	1100–4700	20–190[e]	7–20	+
Copper (Cu)	1100–2600	50–600[g]	150–600[f]	−
Tin (Sn)	2100?	190		
Vanadium (V)	1100	0.07–10		
Nickel (Ni)	150–300	30[d]		
Iodine (I)	110	20–140[f]	40–80[e]	+
Molybdenum (Mo)	50–150	20–120[g]		+
Cobalt (Co)	3–200	0.4–1.1[f]		+
Selenium (Se)	80 (44)	5–67	13–53	+
Chromium (Cr)	60	10–80[g]	10–13[e]	
Other				
Aluminum (Al)	9500–22100	150–1000[g]		
Bromine (Br)	3900	5–2600		+
Zirconium (Zr)	1800–2200	800–960		
Strontium (Sr)	740–1100	200–400		
Rubidium (Rb)	790+	570–3400		
Germanium (Ge)	790	1510		
Boron (B)	680	500–1000		
Barium (Ba)	390–790	?		
Arsenic (As)	530 (3)	30–60		+
Titanium (Ti)	190–440	?		
Lead (Pb)	210 (18)	20–80[g]		+
Cadmium (Cd)	110–260 (0.4)	Trace–15		(+)
Antimony (Sb)	80	?		
Tellurium (Te)	60	?		
Mercury (Hg)	3–11 (0.9)			

[a] Values taken from many sources, including Underwood[123] and his references and Schroeder[97] and several of his references, as well as from abstracts of two recent Soviet publications[2,36]. Some values were calculated on the basis of average daily intake divided by 1900 g of diet.

[b] Values in parentheses from Compliance Program Evaluation, Total Diet Studies: FY 1973, Bureau of Foods, National Institure of Health, Bethseda, Maryland.

[c] Symbols: − : little variation with diet; reduced in deficiency; + : variation with dietary intake; (+): very little transferred to milk.

[d] Value may be too high.[103]

[e] Elevated 3- to 5-fold in colostrum.

[f] Elevated 4- to 10-fold in colostrum.

[g] Elevated in colostrum.[1,36]

occurs in the period directly after birth,[58] and in the milk, iron, copper, and molybdenum, for example, are present in protein-bound form, probably mainly as lactoferrin,[13,68] ceruloplasmin,[31] and xanthine oxidase.[59] Controversy still exists over whether substantial absorption of intact proteins also occurs in the human infant, although the weight of the evidence is against the idea.[9] On the other hand, for the rat, which is less mature at birth, most, or all, of the iron in the diet is absorbed during the suckling period[62] until the time when full maturation of the intestine occurs, a maturation that may be precociously evoked by administration of glucocorticosteroids.[62] In the case of the newborn pig, where intact proteins are also absorbed, a recent report suggests that copper may be transferred in the form of intact ceruloplasmin from the mother's milk.[31] This possibility is intriguing, and warrants further study. If so, it would have implications for the feeding of milk to infants across species.

Studies on the absorption of trace elements from milk by normal or premature infants have begun only recently under the leadership of Widdowson,[133] and the initial results do not bear out the idea of enhanced absorption in the human infant during the early suckling period. Full-term infants were found to absorb substantial amounts of copper and zinc but very little iron from human milk. On fortification, uptake of iron was 20–25%, which is not unusual for food iron as a whole, given to adults. An earlier report indicated that 10% of milk iron was absorbed by infants 3 months of age.[133] Premature infants, who would have been more likely to absorb whole proteins, absorbed much lower amounts of zinc and copper as well as low amounts of iron from either cow's milk or formula, suggesting that their capacity for intestinal absorption was less than that of the full-term baby and adult. Another explanation, though a less probable one, for the differences in absorption observed between premature and full-term infants involves the type of milk fed. Premature infants received cow's milk or formula, whereas term infants received mother's milk, so that it is possible the human milk provided zinc and copper in a form more available for the human infant. The most important implication of these experiments, however, is that even with fortification, the premature infant will not gain as much iron, copper, and zinc (especially iron and copper) from milk or formula as it would if it were still connected to the mother, *in utero*.

Some balance studies on absorption and retention of iron, zinc, copper, manganese, and cadmium in newborns, done by the same group, are also interesting in the light of what we know about storage of these elements in the perinatal period. The results are surprising, since they show newborn infants to be in substantial *negative* balance for iron and manganese, and also initially for zinc.[133] As summarized in Table VI, babies 1 week of age were found to be excreting an average of 3.6 mg more iron, 0.8 mg more zinc, and 3.1 mg more manganese per day than they were taking in from the diet, a daily loss of 1–4% of the total in the body. Widdowson et al.[133] suggest that for iron and manganese, this finding may reflect an immaturity of the digestive system, so that the forms of these elements secreted in the bile are not broken down and reabsorbed. The negative balance for zinc appeared to be more transient, and infants were soon in positive balance. A strong positive balance also soon occurred for copper.

2.2.5. Changes During the Suckling Period

Liver stores of iron, copper, and zinc fall during the suckling period, in part from fecal losses. This fall continues through the first year of life (see Fig. 2) as the stored elements are used for the needs of the rapidly gowing infant. The fall in liver concentration is particularly dramatic in the case of iron, which, although it shows a transient increase directly after birth (probably in connection with reduced erythropoiesis), falls about 6-fold by the end of the first year. In the rat, it has been shown that even when derived from iron-loaded mothers, pups have lost almost all liver ferritin by the end of suckling.[62] Zinc and copper continue to fall very slowly into adulthood, whereas iron stores are on the average partly replenished as the infant grows and matures (Fig. 2). Individual variations in body iron stores throughout are nevertheless enormous.[115] Liver concentrations of all three trace elements thus never return to the values observed for the term fetus (Fig. 2).

Concentrations of some other elements, notably chromium (Fig. 2), also decline with growth and development. The decline of chromium occurs much later, however, beginning in the second decade of life.[98] Its higher concentration in organs at birth thus does not indicate a storage of the element in preparation for the suckling period, when chromium is less available from the diet. Instead, Schroeder[97]

Table VI. Balance Studies of Trace Elements in 1-Week-Old Babies[a]

Trace element	Total in body (mg)	Intake (6–8 days of age) (mg/day)	Net loss from body	
			(mg/day)	(% body content)
Iron	320	0.35	3.6	1.1
Zinc	53	2.3	0.80	4.3
Copper	13.7	0.35	0.04	0.3
Manganese	0.70[b]	0.007	0.031	1.0
Cadmium	Very low	0.013	−0.003	?

[a] Summarized from Widdowson.[131]
[b] 0.20 μg/g (Table II) × 3.5 kg.

proposes that the decline reflects a deficiency of chromium in the refined diet of Americans, and would not occur with more natural, unrefined food. Chromium is associated with sugar in sugar cane and with the germ of wheat and in brown rice, but it is largely removed during production of white sugar, flour, and rice,[97] all staples of the American diet. In support of the view that this removal contributes to a dietary chromium deficiency, Schroeder[97] found 7-fold higher chromium levels in tissues of humans from nonindustrialized countries and also much higher concentrations in wild animal tissues. Chromium plays an important role in glucose tolerance (see Section 3.6), and impaired glucose tolerance is common in our society. In many cases, administration of supplemental chromium has been beneficial in reversing these effects.[72] Manganese may also fall into this category, since its concentration is 2-fold or more higher in the tissues of nonindustrialized man and wild animals.[97]

In contrast to those elements that fall in concentration after birth are those that either stay quite constant [such as manganese (see Fig. 2) and silicon and selenium (see Table II)], and those that increase. As already mentioned, the latter group includes potentially toxic elements (cadmium, lead, germanium, arsenic, titanium, tellurium, and antimony) (see Table III), some of which deposit increasingly in the lungs from dust inhalation. It also includes many known essential elements (fluorine, tin, iodine, molybdenum, and cobalt) (Table II). However, the main increases in concentration occur well after the postnatal period, as the organism gradually increases in size, fully develops its enzymatic capacities, and

deposits a maturing skeleton. For some trace elements at least, this increase is accompanied by redistributions among the various tissues, although for most, details are not presently available. The accumulation and redistribution of the essential trace elements with age are related to the changing metabolism and changing needs of the organism as it passes through the various phases of development. This relationship becomes more obvious when one studies the various metabolic functions of the trace elements in the body, as is discussed below.

3. Functions of Individual Essential Trace Elements with Special Reference to the Perinatal Period

It is not within the scope of this chapter to cover the full range of functions of the trace elements. Nevertheless, the highlights will be given, with emphasis on aspects relating to the perinatal period. Major recent reviews on functions of individual trace elements are cited so that the reader may inform himself in greater depth.

3.1. Iron

Some two-thirds of the iron in the body is sequestered in red blood cell hemoglobin, 5–10% as myoglobin in muscle, 20% is stored in the form of ferritin and hemosiderin, and the remaining 1–2% in iron-containing enzymes and enzyme cofactors. These latter include the ubiquitous cytochromes, catalase, liver tryptophan oxygenase, leukocyte myeloperoxidase, and the mitochondrial enzyme cofactor, adrenodoxin, involved in steroid biosynthesis. (A review of iron metabolism, with special reference to the perinatal period, is provided by Linder and Munro.[62]) The functions of hemoglobin and myoglobin in oxygen diffusion and transport are well known, as is the dependence of all cells on the cytochromes for respiration and formation of ATP. Ferritin, the primary storage place for iron in the body and present within most cells, has been the focus of recurrent interest as a possible regulator of iron-involved functions. Already in the 1940s, Hahn et al.[39] and Granick[33] proposed that ferritin functions as a "mucosal block" in the regulation of iron absorption, since accumulation of ferritin in the intestine correlates with decreased uptake of iron into the body proper. Later evidence has not supported this idea,[63] and it is now thought that accumulation of ferritin in the intestinal mucosa is a *consequence* of iron accumulation in these cells, transfer of iron from mucosal cells into the blood being more stringently regulated than uptake of iron into mucosal cells from the gut. The primary site of regulation of iron uptake into the body is thus at the serosal surface.[129]

The finding of distinctive isomeric forms of ferritin in different tissues, and particularly the presence of two unusual forms within the cardiac and skeletal muscle of rats[126] and humans,[76] also prompted speculation that ferritins have functions additional to those of passive iron storage, such as a direct role in myoglobin formation. Interest in ferritin has also recently been aroused by the finding of small amounts circulating in the plasma, the concentrations of which show, in the absence of disease, a relationship to body iron stores.[65] In newborn infants, serum ferritin concentrations are high (>200 ng/ml as compared with values of 27–88 ng/ml for normal adult donors), and turnover is very rapid (half-lives of 2–6 min).[111] The origin and function of this serum ferritin is still unclear, but preliminary evidence suggests that it derives at least partly from reticuloendothelial digestion of erythrocytes on its way to liver parenchymal cells for storage.[110] This view agrees with kinetic experiments in rats showing that iron in the form of damaged erythrocytes enters the Kupffer cells of the liver (in preference to the hepatocytes) and is released again within minutes, eventually ending up in ferritin of the hepatocytes.[45] In contrast to iron in red blood cells, iron in any other form enters the hepatocytes, not the reticuloendothelial cells. In the newborn infant, iron is lost in the bile in amounts comparable to those involved in daily turnover of hemoglobin.[131] Since bile is the main route for normal iron excretion, it is tempting to think that this iron comes directly from ferritin released into plasma by the reticuloendothelial cells, taken up by the liver, and partially or completely degraded there en route to the bile.

Because of the vast quantity of iron employed in oxygen transport, iron deficiency has its first and most dramatic effects on blood hemoglobin concentrations. In comparison with hemoglobin, such minute quantities of iron are required for the iron-containing enzymes, and the iron in these enzymes is so tightly bound, that it is virtually impossible for them to become deficient in iron unless the anemia is extremely severe. The suggestion has been made that the increased susceptibility of anemic persons to infection may be the result of decreased iron-dependent myeloperoxidase in leukocytes, which would diminish the capacity of these cells to destroy invading bacteria and other agents.[5] While evidence from animals is not incompatible with this idea, myeloperoxidase activity being decreased and susceptibility to infection increased in severe iron deficiency, it is difficult to assess whether the latter is indeed a consequence of the former or due to a generalized weakness of the organism from oxygen insufficiency. Indeed, a decrease in plasma iron, as normally occurs in infection,[135] appears to be of benefit in fighting bacteria, probably because it deprives them of iron-dependent factors needed for growth and proliferation.[13,127] Similarly, the presence of unsaturated lactoferrin in human and animal milk is probably of benefit in preventing gastroenteritis in infants.[12] (It is noteworthy that this benefit is lost by fortifying milk with iron.[13])

As regards the perinatal period, we have already stressed the importance of iron stores deposited in the fetus for growth and development after birth, a period when new tissue is laid down, blood volume is increased, and a large quantity of iron must be provided for production of additional red cells, with smaller amounts for more myoglobin and cytochromes. Tryptophan oxygenase of liver[35] and leukocyte myeloperoxidase[5] are both present but relatively low at birth in the human and rat, respectively, and gradually rise to adult levels during the suckling period (which is approximately equivalent to the first postnatal human year). Iron deficiency anemia is a common occurrence in infancy, and indeed even with adequate iron stores, a slight anemia may be a normal event. With full-term infants, iron deficiency anemia is not likely to occur before the 6th to the 9th month, although in prematures, it may occur as early as 3 months of age. The appearance of anemia is in the majority of cases a signal that fetal iron stores have been used up and the content of available iron in the diet is inadequate to provide for daily needs. This deficiency is quite easily remedied through iron supplementation. For neither the adult nor the infant is there evidence at present that *transient* iron deficiency has permanent consequences for health or for development.

3.2. Copper

Copper is distributed fairly evenly in organs of the adult with the exception of the hair (which has very high concentrations) and liver and brain in the human, which have concentrations 2- to 3-fold higher than other organs. For a review of copper distribution and metabolism in general and in growth and development, see Evans[26] and Linder and Munro.[62] Because of its mass, muscle is also a major copper depot, and blood and plasma contain substantial quantities as well. Among the copper components isolated that have known functions are a number of enzymes with oxidation–reduction reactions. These enzymes include the cytochromes (in which half as much copper as iron is present); superoxide dismutase, the function of which in red cells was mentioned in Section 2.2.2 (it is probably found in most other cells as well[120]); plasma ceruloplasmin, which may function as an oxidase for ferrous ions, catecholamines, and some other endogenous and exogenous amino substrates; and amine oxidase, which is also an important interstitial fluid enzyme responsible for the cross-linking of elastin and thus the integrity of blood vessels. The reason for the high concentration of copper in the brain is not understood at this time, although its involvement with superoxide dismutase, DOPA decarboxylase, and the cytochromes may be factors. Copper may also be involved in collagen synthesis.[62]

Within most cells, a large proportion of the copper is present in the cytosol fraction, where it is attached to proteins of two sizes, probably superoxide dismutase (mol. wt. 33,000), and metallothionein[120] or similar small proteins (mol. wt.

6000–11,000).[11,28,91] The latter are presumed to have some copper-storage function, while the function of the former (as already mentioned) is to inactivate superoxide anions produced in various reactions such as the microsomal hydroxylations of drugs or steroids. These anions could have harmful effects on cell membranes and other cellular components. Dopamine-β-hydroxylase and monoamine oxidase are both particulate enzymes (both of mol. wt. 290,000) concerned with the synthesis and catabolism of catecholamines, and account for some of the copper present in the adrenal medulla, brain, and other nervous tissue. The former, which is associated with chromaffin granules, is a mixed-function oxidase that catalyzes the conversion of DOPAmine to norepinephrine, while the latter is a mitochondrial flavoprotein concerned with the oxidative deamination of DOPAmine and the catecholamines in many tissues, including the liver. Copper is involved in an additional conversion of aromatic amino acids, namely, the catabolism of tyrosine via *p*-hydroxyphenyl pyruvate oxidase, which is present primarily in the liver.

Ceruloplasmin, the copper-containing α_2-glycoprotein of plasma made by liver that accounts for most of the copper in blood fluid, has already been mentioned in connection with pregnancy and fetal development. This protein is of interest, since it may have several roles. These roles include an enzymatic one related to iron metabolism, as well as nonenzymatic roles in copper excretion and in copper donation to certain specialized tissues. It is of further interest for its responsiveness to diseases, being elevated in cancer, acute infection,[135] and myocardial infarction,[124] and reduced in Wilson's disease[134] and nephrosis.[134] Ceruloplasmin appears to be the enzyme most sensitive to copper depletion, oxidase activity falling off soon after removal of copper from the diet (see Linder and Munro[62]). The oxidase activity of ceruloplasmin is very low at birth, and increases slowly during the suckling period in apparent relation to release of copper from liver neonatal stores (it is stored in the mitochondrocuprein of mitochondria, as already mentioned). Prenatal stores of copper may not be sufficient to provide for the suckling period either if the mother has been deficient during gestation or if the infant is born prematurely. Indeed, there are several reports of copper deficiency occurring in infants born prematurely or maintained on total parenteral nutrition or both.[2,4,54]

With regard to the function of ceruloplasmin in

iron metabolism, the current theory holds that it functions in mobilizing liver iron stores for red blood cell production. To leave intracellular storage sites within ferritin, iron is reduced from the ferric to the ferrous form, and this reduced iron is thought to be oxidized by ceruloplasm in the plasma, thus allowing attachment to transferrin for transport. In support of this idea, it is well known that copper deficiency (associated with a reduction in plasma ceruloplasmin oxidase activity) results in an anemia similar to that of iron deficiency. This anemia is not caused by a reduction in the capacity for hemoglobin synthesis,[61] but rather by a reduction in the flow of iron from liver to plasma. Intravenous administration of active ceruloplasmin to deficient animals (or livers thereof) immediately results in efflux of iron from liver stores (and perhaps also from other tissues). Nevertheless, efflux of iron is impaired only when ceruloplasmin is at very low levels[94] (5% of normal), such as occurs in extreme deficiency. Whether the relative lack of ceruloplasmin oxidase activity in newborn infants (20% of adult) has a similar effect on iron flow and thus contributes to anemia or reduced erythropoiesis is not known. The relationship of copper to erythropoiesis is undoubtedly more complex, however, since copper also plays an important role in the red cell *per se*, as part of superoxide dismutase and some other proteins.[62]

Ceruloplasmin oxidase activity is low in the plasma of newborns of many species, but it appears that this low activity may reflect a relative lack of copper bound to the apoprotein, not a lack of the protein itself. In the human infant, it has been reported that immunoreactive ceruloplasmin is present in the same concentrations as in adults,[109] although oxidase activity is low and there is little copper bound firmly to protein. While this finding bears repeating, it suggests that the capacity of the liver to attach copper to ceruloplasmin is relatively lacking, and that this capacity enjoys its major increase in the first year of life, when active ceruloplasmin appears in plasma in increasing quantities.

Additional roles for ceruloplasmin in excretion and transport of copper are inferred from (1) observations in Wilson's disease patients that a reduced capacity to form this protein is coupled with accumulation of copper in liver (and brain); (2) observations that increased ceruloplasmin in plasma accompanies reduced copper excretion in the bile, as observed in adrenalectomy[27]; and (3) the finding

that a few tissues (notably the heart, lung, and testes) take up copper derived from ceruloplasmin in preference to "free" plasma copper.[84]

3.3. Molybdenum

Molybdenum is notable in the body for reasons of its important interactions with iron and copper. In relation to iron, it has been found associated with two (possibly three) soluble flavorprotein enzymes that also contain iron and are present in the liver, spleen, kidney, and other tissues of animals and man. These enzymes are principally xanthine oxidase (which is also present in milk), which is concerned with the degradation of purines (from dietary or endogenous sources); aldehyde oxidase (in liver), which catalyzes the formation of acetic acid from acetyl CoA; and xanthine dehydrogenase (detected in chicken liver), which is also concerned with purine metabolism.[130] (The presence of copper xanthine oxidase in milk has also recently been reported.[59]) In these enzymes, molybdenum functions as an electron carrier in oxidation or reduction. In relation to copper, molybdenum has been implicated in producing copper deficiency, particularly in grazing sheep, through mechanisms that operate both at the site of absorption and more directly through formation of an inactive copper–molybdate molecule. The primary explanation for copper deficiency in animals on high-molybdenum diets is that the latter antagonizes or competes with uptake of copper from the gut. (Molybdenum also antagonizes absorption of iron, as already mentioned, but this action has not been of nearly as much concern.[107]) The effects of excess molybdenum on copper metabolism may thus be reversed through injection of copper, as has been demonstrated by Suttle[117] in recent years. Alternatively, or in addition to the possibility of direct competition at the intestinal muscosal level, is the possibility of formation of a compound such as cupric–molybdate in the gut prior to absorption (see Suttle[118]). Such a compound forms *in vitro* at neutral pH in solutions containing the two elements, and though absorbed into the body, is unavailable for ceruloplasmin synthesis. In nonruminants, it is more likely that the interaction of copper with molybdenum causes a relative deficiency of the latter rather than the former, since the human diet contains an excess of copper relative to molybdenum.[107] Suttle,[118] however, feels that dietary sulfate may be more important in determining molybdenum availability because of its marked competition for uptake by intestinal mucosal cells.

Xanthine oxidase is important for the catabolism of purines in normal turnover of endogenous nucleic acids and nucleotides within the body or after their absorption from a diet high in nucleic acid content (e.g., liver and thymus). This enzyme is low or absent at least in rat liver at birth,[69] and, like ceruloplasmin, appears during the suckling period. Although xanthine oxidase may be present in normal amounts in other tissues of the neonate (it is present in adult concentrations in the intestine in rats[69]), its relative absence in the liver correlates with a decreased overall body concentration in the term fetus as compared with the adult (see Table II) and with reports of limited maternofetal transfer in pigs.[108]

Because of the coincidence in the rise of xanthine oxidase and depletion of liver iron stores, and because of *in vitro* findings that xanthine oxidase plus xanthine or hypoxanthine can release iron from ferritin, Mazur and Carleton[69] postulated that this enzyme plays a role in iron mobilization. Indeed, it has been shown that the anemia of pregnancy and also of the neonate is alleviated more readily by iron supplementation if molybdenum is also given (see Suttle[118]). However, the rise of this enzyme associated with increased utilization of liver iron stores may be coincidental, since the coenzyme involved in the oxidation–reduction reaction ($FADH_2$) and other small reducing molecules in cells (ascorbate, glutathione, and especially $FMNH_2$) can directly release iron from ferritin.[112]

3.4. Zinc

Zinc is a truly multifunctional trace element, being directly and indirectly involved in a great many areas of metabolism. A number of enzymes in animal tissues (mainly dehydrogenases) associated with glycolysis, energy production, gluconeogenesis, and protein degradation have been shown to be zinc-dependent (for a partial review, see Parisi and Vallee[85]). These enzymes are remarkably resistant to deficiency, however, and decreased activity in the liver (the organ most readily depleted) is difficult to demonstrate.[14]

Zinc enzymes involved in energy metabolism include glyceraldehyde-3-phosphate, lactate, malate, and glutamate dehydrogenases in various tissues,

but zinc has also been implicated from another angle. Some aspects of the finding are still controversial, but two of three investigators have shown a decrease in glucose tolerance in zinc deficiency (see Halstead et al.[40]). The association of zinc with pancreatic islet cells and insulin *per se* has long been known, although its attachment to insulin was shown to be unimportant for its activity. (Reviews of zinc metabolism and nutriture are provided by Halstead et al.[40] and Underwood.[123]) Coupled with the finding that zinc-deficient rats are more resistant to insulin coma and that this resistance occurs independently of changes in blood glucose levels,[90] these findings stress the complex involvement of zinc in energy metabolism.

The recent report of Burch et al.[14] may offer a clue to this complexity, since it suggests mediation of the zinc effects through other metal ions. These ions include copper, which is increasingly retained in the liver in zinc deficiency (and is perhaps held increasingly by metallothionein as zinc is withdrawn; indeed, the amount of zinc lost per gram of liver corresponds to the amount of copper gained), and selenium, manganese, and magnesium, which are significantly reduced in the liver and also the heart in zinc deficiency. Further support for zinc effects through changes in the metal ions comes from the observations that in rats, hypercholesterolemia results from an increased ratio of zinc to copper in the diet irrespective of whether the absolute concentration of either is kept the same.[55] Since the diets of many Americans have zinc/copper ratios that exceed values that cause hypercholesterolemia in rats, these high ratios have been postulated as an underlying cause of atherosclerosis.[56,57] Others had previously reported increasing blood levels of cholesterol with added zinc in the diet, but also partial success in reducing atherosclerotic plaques in humans using supplemental zinc.[123] These discrepancies may have been introduced by variations in dietary copper content.

In addition to its roles in energy metabolism, zinc has been shown to have stimulatory effects on protein synthesis, and has also been implicated in its catabolism through leucine aminopeptidases of liver[32] and intestinal mucosa, and through pancreatic carboxypeptidase, all zinc-requiring enzymes. In zinc deficiency, decreased synthesis of protein has been shown for the skin,[70] and in the liver, there is decreased production of retinol-binding protein.[113] The effect of zinc on protein synthesis in the skin is of special interest, since several studies have reported beneficial effects of zinc supplements (50 mg $ZnSO_4$, 3 times daily) on the rate of closure of postoperative wounds,[123] implying a role for this trace element in the synthesis of connective tissue protein. The finding of a decreased production of retinol-binding protein by liver would explain the implied involvement of this element in vitamin A metabolism, since this protein is responsible for release and distribution of the vitamin stored in the liver when it is needed elsewhere in the body.

An involvement of zinc in nucleic acid synthesis and cell proliferation, though not presently understood, may be even more fundamental though less specific than effects on protein metabolism. That it is was recently suggested by Chesters[21] from work with lymphocytes and other nonmalignant cells in tissue culture. Chesters showed inhibition of DNA synthesis on addition of EDTA, and reversal of the effect with zinc. However, inhibition of DNA synthesis has also been shown in the absence of iron, removed by EDTA.[92]

As already discussed in relation to the blood, zinc is an important component of carbonic anhydrase in red cells, which is necessary for transport of carbon dioxide and acid–base balance, and of an α_2-glycoprotein of unknown function present in plasma. Both these proteins are low in the fetus and at birth, increasing in the postnatal period. This increase is especially rapid for the glycoprotein, which reaches adult levels (3- to 4-fold greater than in the fetus) 1–2 weeks postpartum.[52] δ-Amino levulinate dehydrase of erythrocytes (involved in porphyrin biosynthesis) has also recently been implicated as a zinc-dependent enzyme.[29]

Because of these wide-ranging effects and the dearth of specific enzyme data for the perinatal period, we can only say that the roles of zinc in fetal development and after birth must be multifaceted and complex. Zinc deficiency appears not to be a common problem in either the newborn or the adult, but the incidence may be significant for older infants and preschool children.[41] Its beneficial effects for adults in special circumstances (such as after surgery) also cannot be dismissed, and suggest that there are occasions when additional zinc may be required. Indeed, Quarterman[89] pointed out that zinc is *not* present in excess in the North American diet, contrary to common assumptions.

3.5. Manganese

As with zinc, the involvements of manganese in metabolism cover a very broad spectrum. In soft tissues, manganese is especially concentrated in the mitochondria, in part, at least, attached to enzymes of the tricarboxylic acid cycle, fatty acid synthesis, and gluconeogenesis: isocitrate dehydrogenase, acetyl CoA carboxylase, and pyruvate carboxylase. It is also associated with some enzymes of the cytosol, including arginase, which is important for urea formation; serine hydroxymethyltransferase; glucokinase; and enzymes of the pentose phosphate pathway. Perhaps its most important and specific association is with the membrane-bound glycosyl transferases, which transfer sugars in the synthesis of mucopolysaccharides, glycoproteins, and lipopolysaccharides (gangliosides). Synthesis of the important membrane phospholipid phosphatidyl inositol is also manganese-dependent. In bone, apart from the cells, manganese is attached to the mineral portion (the hydroxylapatite). This form of manganese does not appear to be a storage form, since it is not readily available to the soft tissues of the body (for reviews, see Leach[60] and Underwood[123]).

Many or most of the enzyme reactions with which manganese ions have been associated are able to function with magnesium ions as a substitute, and thus its physiologic importance in these reactions may be questioned. Pyruvate carboxylase, for example, appears to function normally in manganese deficiency by substituting the more ubiquitous magnesium ions,[60] and for the adult human, cases of actual deficiency have not been reported.[122] However, the glycosyl transferase reactions, which are involved in mucopolysaccharide, glycoprotein, and glycolipid production, more clearly prefer manganese as a cofactor, and indeed, deficiency of manganese in the diet of animals has many serious effects. It produces skeletal malformations in the newborn and young, probably from inadequate formation of cartilage mucopolysaccharides. Impairment of glucose tolerance, decreased general growth, and defective reproduction also occur, effects that may well relate to decreased activities of other manganese-associated enzymes. Because of the broadness of its metabolic involvements, and particularly its role in cartilage and skeleton production, the importance of this element in the perinatal period must be underscored. The remarkable constancy of manganese concentrations in the body, which begins in fetal life, further supports these contentions.

3.6. Chromium

Chromium is one of the newer essential trace elements and is present in tissues at concentrations 3 orders of magnitude less than zinc (see Table II). In similarity with zinc and some other metal ions (manganese, nickel), it has a tendency to associate with nucleic acids, but more importantly (like zinc and manganese), it too plays a role in glucose tolerance. In similarity to manganese and iron, it is transported in the blood by transferrin (see Table I). Its association with a small, rather labile protein, glucose tolerance factor (GTF), is the only known physiologic function of this element in the human and animal body, and may explain all the symptoms associated with chromium deficiency. This factor is not a substitute for, but rather enhances, insulin action by reducing peripheral insulin resistance (for a review, see Mertz[72]).

In monkeys and rats, in which it has been studied, impaired glucose tolerance is the first sign of chromium deficiency, occurring when deficiency is only marginal. In humans with impaired glucose tolerance, administration of chromium as inorganic salts often results in improvement, and in malnourished children with similar impairment, improvement is consistent. As already mentioned in Section 2.2.5, the American diet usually contains much less chromium than diets of less developed countries, most likely because of the refining of sugar, rice, and wheat flour, and it is postulated that this lack contributes to the prevalence of glucose intolerance in our society.[97]

The form in which chromium is provided may also determine its effectiveness. While simple chromium salts may enhance glucose tolerance, they are not always active in man, and indeed, it appears that they do not provide a form of chromium that is readily transferred from mother to fetus (at least for the rat, in which this problem has been studied[73]). In contrast, chromium provided in the diet after incorporation into Brewer's yeast is transferred, implying that transfer occurs with chromium in the form of some natural complex.[73] Perhaps in relation to this transfer, or in relation to impairment of glucose tolerance, blood levels of chromium are depressed in pregnancy.[17]

In addition to its glucose tolerance role, chromium has been implicated in regulation of cholesterol synthesis. The evidence is difficult to interpret at this time, however, since depending on its concentration, stimulation or depression of synthesis has been shown in experimental animals.[123]

3.7. Vanadium

Another element that may play a role in cholesterol metabolism is vanadium, which was added to the list of essential elements only recently (for reviews, see Curran and Burch,[22] Underwood,[123] Schwarz,[102] Hopkins,[49] and Hopkins and Mohr[50]). Studies on young adult rats showed that vanadium suppresses hepatic cholesterol synthesis both *in vivo* and *in vitro*,[22] and in humans, it lowers plasma cholesterol.[123] In older rats, however, and in older humans with or without hypercholesterolemia or ischemic heart disease, vanadium does not have this effect. Curran[22] attributed these age differences to inhibition and stimulation, respectively, of two enzymes, squalene synthetase (on the pathway of cholesterol synthesis) and acetoacetyl CoA deacylase (which would remove acetoacetyl CoA from the cholesterol precursor pool). The former enzyme is especially strongly inhibited by vanadium in younger rats, and the latter is stimulated only in the older animals.

The bases of the other general effects of vanadium on growth and metabolism are completely unknown. It appears to influence the levels of plasma triglyceride (in the same direction as cholesterol), and may be important in the growth of teeth, bone, and cartilage. (Rapid uptake of radiovanadium by mineralizing zones has been reported for adult mice and their fetuses.[50])

3.8. Iodine and Cobalt

Both these elements appear to exert their actions through inclusion in single forms of molecules. The action of iodine in the body occurs through attachment to tri- and tetraiodothyronine (thyroid hormones), whereas cobalt acts through its inclusion in vitamin B_{12}. No need for cobalt other than in the vitamin has ever been demonstrated, although it is likely that much more cobalt in the body occurs in forms other than the vitamin (blood levels of cobalt, for example, are very much higher than levels of B_{12}). Recently, there has also been interest in the possibility that nonvitamin cobalt is a direct stimulator for release of kidney hormones. These hormones include bradykinin,[114] a hypotensive agent, and erythropoietin, which stimulates erythropoiesis (cobalt has long been used to enhance red cell production). Erythropoietic doses of $CoCl_2$ also stimulate production of kidney cyclic GMP prior to release of lysosomal enzymes from the kidney to the plasma. It is postulated that these enzymes may be involved in activation of the kidney hormones.[93]

As a component of vitamin B_{12}, cobalt is central to two kinds of enzyme reactions, methylations and mutases. The former involve it directly in methionine and cysteine metabolism, and indirectly in methylations of nucleic acid and proteins. The latter is important in conversion of methylmalonyl CoA to succinyl CoA, a last step in the utilization of fatty acids with odd numbers of carbons and the breakdown of branched-chain amino acids, both for energy. Methylation reactions, e.g., for nucleic acid and protein synthesis, are especially active in the growing organism.

Through the methylmalonyl CoA reaction, cobalt is involved in adaptations of the body to fasting and starvation and to meals high in fat and protein. Either way, fats and amino acids are degraded to provide energy, or for conversion to energy-storage forms (glycogen) for later utilization. The capacity for gluconeogenesis is already developed late in gestation, and is first used in conjunction with the birth event when the child is separated from the mother. At birth, energy stored as glycogen (and perhaps also some protein) is quickly broken down (this event is associated with the appearance of some amino-acid-metabolizing enzymes[34,35]). It is likely, though unknown, that B_{12} is critical for this transient fasting period and later for the proper utilization of fat and protein provided to the infant by the milk.

Returning to iodine, the thyroid hormones play important roles in fetal development from early in gestation onward, and have been associated with the appearance and increase in a number of enzymes needed for metabolism by the fetus (see Greengard[34,35]).

3.9. Selenium

Proof that selenium is an essential element for life and health was provided by McCoy and Weswig in 1969,[71] using rats, although its essentiality was first suggested by studies of Schwarz and Foltz[105] in 1957 (others have verified its importance for the chick). The crucial question bandied about in the intervening time was whether its effect was simply as a substitute for vitamin E, so that if adequate amounts of vitamin E were given, no selenium

would be needed. This possibility is no longer of concern, and the independent essentialness of selenium has been established.[71] (Reviews of these problems and of selenium metabolism as a whole are provided by Hoekstra[47,48] and Diplock.[24])

Despite the finding of symptoms in selenium deficiency that are not prevented or alleviated by vitamin E, the only well-established role of selenium so far discovered is as a cofactor in the functioning of glutathione peroxidase, a nonheme enzyme that metabolizes peroxides and reduced glutathione. This action prevents destructive effects of both substrates on lipids of cell membranes, inhibits mitochondrial swelling, and replenishes oxidized glutathione needed for electron transfer reactions.[104] Glutathione peroxidase is widely distributed in tissues, including the liver, lung, kidney, and erythrocytes, where it plays a role in maintenance of cell integrity (turnover of red blood cells is enhanced in selenium deficiency). This function is analogous to that of superoxide dismutase, the copper- and zinc-containing enzyme that destroys superoxide anions in erythrocytes and elsewhere (see Sections 2.2.2 and 3.2).

It cannot be concluded at this time whether symptoms of selenium deficiency that are not responsive to vitamin E (including reproductive failure and poor growth) have anything to do with glutathione peroxidase, or whether they reflect other functions of this trace element not yet discovered. The former seems unlikely, since new selenium-containing proteins have already been discovered and others may be found. One protein appears in the plasma some hours after tissue uptake of radioactive selenium from the blood.[15] Selenium is transported on LDLs and vLDLs.[15] Another appears to be a microsomal cytochrome of muscle and heart,[128] and there are additional reports that selenide-containing proteins in rat liver microsomes and mitochondria are involved in electron transport for drug metabolism.[25] Indeed, uptake of selenium by endoplasmic reticulum proteins is stimulated by pentabarbital, a drug that increases drug-metabolizing enzyme activities. Recent results suggest that glutathione peroxidase of liver is much more responsive to dietary selenium deficiency and excess than that of erythrocytes and other tissues,[38,48] although decreases occur in all cases. Glutathione peroxidase is present in fetal and newborn erythrocytes and perhaps in other tissues to perform similar basic functions in gestation and thereafter.

In conclusion, it should be recalled that while no evidence of selenium deficiency in the human or animal has been reported,[122] selenium toxicity has been of some concern, especially for farm animals.[123] Along with fluorine, it is one of the few trace elements for which toxicity and essentiality go almost hand in hand, and doses for optimal health and for toxicity are not widely separated. The exact mechanisms by which selenium is toxic are not clear, but may in part involve interactions with other trace elements, notably copper, cadmium, and mercury.[46]

3.10. Fluorine

Fluorine is the third member of the halogens accepted as essential for life and health. Despite membership in this elemental group, the little known about its functioning within the body does not appear to be analogous to that of chlorine or iodine, which in turn have quite different functions. Among the problems encountered in attempting to demonstrate fluorine's essentiality has been the difficulty of removing it from foodstuffs. Comparisons have thus been made between the effects of diets very low and quite high in the element.

Using such diets, three kinds of rather general effects have been observed in experiments involving rats or mice: (1) growth retardation, (2) progressive infertility, and (3) enhancement of the anemias of pregnancy and infancy (newborns from deficient mothers do not initially show anemia). (For a review of the essentiality and function of fluorine, see Messer et al.[74]) With the exception of the growth-retardation effect, which was only partly reversed by fluorine supplementation, the other two effects were completely abolished after refeeding of the element. Experiments on fertility indicated that with increasing time on a low-fluorine diet, the percentage of mice having litters gradually fell off. In addition, pups from low-fluorine mothers raised on the low-fluorine regimen showed an even more depressed capacity for producing litters (see Messer et al.[74]). Mother mice on low-fluorine diets showed a more marked anemia of pregnancy, and their offspring a more severe anemia than controls, 5–20 days after birth. These kinds of general effects on growth and health often occur with deficiencies of trace elements or vitamins, and it is difficult to say whether they are direct and what mechanisms are involved. They point, however, to an involvement in processes crucial to the perinatal period.

Although there has been much interest in fluorine

for its preventive effects on dental caries and also osteoporosis, a lack of fluorine intake has not been shown to result in skeletal and dental abnormalities despite numerous animal experiments. These effects of fluoride could thus be viewed as nonessential and fortuitous. Certainly they cannot be ignored, and their desirability is self-evident. There is no longer any question that fluorine at a level of 1 ppm in the drinking water in children during development of the permanent teeth markedly reduces the incidence of dental caries.[123] The central reaction involved both in the hardening of the tooth enamel and the stabilizing of the bone matrix appears to be formation of fluoroapatite from hydroxyapatite. Nucleation by fluorine of the "crystallizing-out" of hydroxyapatite (during mineralization) may also be important.

Aside from its beneficial actions on teeth and bones during growth, a high fluorine content of the diet may have adverse effects. The recommendation of 1 ppm fluorine in the drinking water as optimal for caries prevention and health represents a compromise between (1) the benefits of even higher levels for caries prevention and (2) the adverse effects of higher concentrations, including mottling of tooth enamel. The latter is an unsightly and permanent effect produced when growing children are exposed to excess dietary fluorine.

Like selenium, fluorine is an element that has essential and beneficial effects at lower concentrations but toxic and damaging ones at concentrations less than 1 order of magnitude higher. In farm animals, in which it has been most frequently observed, fluorosis may occur at levels of 3–5 ppm in the drinking water, not much higher than the optimum 1 ppm recommended for the human. The basis for the toxic effects, such as loss of appetite, weakness, and gastroenteritis, is not difficult to conjecture, since fluorine is a potent inhibitor of cell respiration, and a potent activator of adenyl cyclase, which mediates the actions of many hormones in their target tissues.

The beneficial effects of fluorine on bone and tooth formation probably require higher levels than those for prevention of anemia of infancy, which goes along with a limited transfer of this element to the fetus in gestation and the infant through the milk (see Tables II and V). It would seem that fluorine availability becomes important only well after infancy, in midchildhood, when permanent teeth are growing, and later on, when growth and the reformation of bone cease and bone becomes more mineralized. As mentioned early on, bone is the major depot site for fluorine within the body, and the element is deposited there in increasing amounts, starting after birth and continuing throughout life. In man, it has been estimated that a continuous fluoride intake of 8 ppm in the total diet for 35 years would exhaust the storage capacity of the skeleton, so excess fluorine would spill out into the rest of the body, with toxic effects.[123] Initially, however, such intake in the human probably has no overt deleterious effects (aside from mottling the teeth), but it does eventually lead to fluorosis.

3.11. Silicon

Along with fluorine and selenium, silicon is a recent addition to the roster of essential elements. Again, as with fluorine, its ubiquity in foods has made it difficult to exclude from the diet, but deficiency symptoms have been produced by placing rodents and chickens on food containing 1 ppm. The resulting symptoms were deformation and incomplete development of the skeleton, as well as growth retardation. From the considerable work of Schwarz and Carlisle and their colleagues, it appears that the primary and perhaps only defect in metabolism is the formation of mucopolysaccharides, which are essential for connective tissue function and cartilage formation (for reviews, see Schwarz[102,103] and Carlisle[19,20]). Schwarz[102] showed that silicon is bound to various glycosaminoglycans, including hyaluronic acids, heparan, and chondroitin sulfates isolated from cartilage, lung, umbilical cord, and intestinal mucosa, and even from bovine corneal tissue and vitreous humor.[125] On the basis of chemical evidence, he has postulated that silicon acts to form cross-linkages for these molecules, of etherlike configuration (e.g., R–O–Si–O–R).[102] Unlike most of the other trace elements, therefore, silicon appears to be integral to the structure of some molecules, rather than a dissociable cofactor in enzyme reactions.

Because of the vast importance of connective tissue and cartilage formation in embryonic growth, and in growth after birth into the teens, it is very likely that this element plays a crucial role at early stages of development. Exact information on this role is not yet available, although recent findings indicate that most tissues, especially those rich in connective tissue, have much more silicon in early life than later on. In the rabbit, silicon is 9 times more concentrated in fetal skin than in skin from the adult animal.[19] In contrast to fluorine, therefore, silicon is especially associated with processes that are most active in the earliest stages of development.

3.12. Nickel

Even less is known about the actions of nickel in metabolism than about those of most other newer trace elements. It is present in many tissues, with highest concentrations in bone, both in the marrow (where it is 20-fold more concentrated than in plasma) and in the mineral portion, where it is part of the insoluble matrix.[81,82] Liver and muscle appear to be the most responsive to changes in dietary intake,[75] however, and it is rapidly absorbed from the diet and cleared from the body.[83] Deficiency of nickel decreases the viability of the fetus, as shown by experiments with rats, and newborns are abnormally lethargic, have sparse and rough hair, and grow slower than supplemented controls. The basis for these effects is not known, but a common feature of deficiency shown in three species is an abnormality of the hepatocytes, with dilatation of the endoplasmic reticulum cisternae and mitochondrial membranes, and changes in respiration and lipid content. (For reviews, see Nielson and Ollerich[78] and Nielson et al.[79]) Nickel has been found bound firmly to one plasma protein made in the liver and designated *nickeloplasmin* by Sunderman et al.[116] The function of this α_2-globulin is completely unknown, but it accounts for only 1% of the nickel in plasma, the rest being loosely attached to albumin or in free form.[82]

3.13. Tin

Classification of tin as an essential element has been made on the basis, not of the presence of deficiency signs in its absence, but rather on the basis of dramatic growth-enhancing effects when tin is added to purified amino acid diets of rats.[102,103] This effect was reproducible, showed a dose–response relationship, and occurred with levels of tin normally found in foodstuffs. The bases for these effects are far from understood, although Schwarz[102] postulates that tin, like carbon and silicon, could be incorporated into the structure of many molecules. It is one of the few elements that is capable, like carbon, of forming truly covalent linkages, and can form coordination complexes with four to six ligands. Schwarz also suggests that tin could be involved as a cofactor in oxidation–reduction reactions.

From the present vantage point, tin appears to be the only "essential" element in the roster that is not transferred to the fetus,[99,103] at least in detectable amounts, a finding that Schroeder[99] interpreted early on as indicating that it served no useful biological function in the mammal. Transfer and retention of tin occur immediately after birth with the beginning of suckling, however, and it is not unreasonable to suppose that it serves some basic biochemical role later on in life. At the same time, it is not entirely innocuous, and may decrease longevity when fed in larger amounts.[100]

4. Interactions of Trace Elements

Throughout this chapter, we have touched on the interactions of trace elements in all areas of metabolism, and evidence has been presented suggesting that the ratios of these elements to each other may at times be more important than their absolute quantities, e.g., zinc/copper in relation to heart disease and blood cholesterol. Certain elements tend to interact more frequently than others. Thus, for example, zinc, copper, and iron accumulate in the liver before birth and, with cadmium, interact in absorption in attachment to metallothionein like proteins and at the level of heme synthesis.[87] With manganese, iron, copper, and zinc are excreted in the bile, and manganese and iron are both transported via transferrin (along with chromium and vanadium). Zinc and cadmium have a special relationship as regards metallothionein, and cadmium (with mercury) may substitute for zinc in superoxide dismutase and stimulate release of adrenal catecholamines.[42] Copper also has a special relationship to molybdenum, interacting directly at the level of absorption and less directly in iron mobilization. Copper also substitutes for molybdenum in some forms of xanthine oxidase.

Several elements have effects on cholesterol metabolism, including vanadium and chromium as well as zinc and copper. Others have special roles in connective tissue, including zinc and copper, i.e., amine oxidase, manganese and silicon, i.e., mucopolysaccharides. Vanadium as well as fluorine, manganese, and lead congregate in the mineral portions of bone, and selenium toxicity is counteracted by mercury.[16]

Of special interest are the findings that blood levels of these elements may change together in diseases. Thus, in infection, copper and manganese may be increased, while iron and zinc fall.[135] Other parallel changes occur in normal conditions such as pregnancy. It is likely that studies of the interrelationships of these elements in the body and their effects at different ratios to each other in the diet will yield especially useful information for optimal health, growth, and development of the human and animal organism.

5. References

1. AGABABYAN, A. A., 1973, Dynamics of trace elements in the colostrum of cows, buffaloes, and sheep, *Tr. Stavrop. Skh. Inst.* **4**:203 (*Chem. Abstr.* **81**:102260z).
2. AL-RASHID, R. A., AND SPANGLER, J., 1971, Neonatal copper deficiency, *N. Engl. J. Med.* **285**:841.
3. ARNEIL, G. C., 1969, Some metabolic implications of strontium-90 in children, in: *Mineral Metabolism in Paediatrics* (D. Barltrop and W. J. Burland, eds.), pp. 71–81, Blackwell Scientific Publications, Oxford.
4. ASHKENAZI, A., LEVIN, S., DJALDETTI, M., FISHEL, E., AND BENVENISTI, D., 1973, The syndrome of neonatal copper deficiency, *Paediatrics* **52**:525.
5. BAGGS, R. B., AND MILLER, S. A., 1973, Nutritional iron deficiency as a determinant of host resistance in the rat, *J. Nutr.* **103**:1554.
6. BAGLAN, R. J., BRILL, A. B., SCHUBERT, A., WILSON, D., LARSEN, K., DYER, N., MANSOUR, M., SCHAFFNER, W., HOFFMAN, L., AND DAVIES, J., 1974, Utility of placental tissue as an indicator of trace element exposure to adult and fetus, *Environ. Res.* **8**:64.
7. BARLTROP, D., 1969, Transfer of lead to the human fetus, in: *Mineral Metabolism in Paediatrics* (D. Barltrop and W. J. Burland, eds.), pp. 135–150, Blackwell Scientific Publications, Oxford.
8. BEEM, K. M., RICH, W. E., AND RAJAGOPALAN, K. V., 1974, Total reconstitution of copper–zinc superoxide dismutase, *J. Biol. Chem.* **249**:7298.
9. BRAMBELL, F. W. R., 1970, *The Transistion of Passive Immunity from Mother to Young,* North-Holland Publishing Co., Amsterdam.
10. BREMNER, I., 1974, Copper and zinc proteins in ruminant liver, in: *Trace Element Metabolism in Animals—2* (W. G. Hoekstra, J. W. Suttie, H. E. Ganther, and W. Mertz, eds.), pp. 489–491, University Park Press, Baltimore.

11. BREMNER, I., AND DAVIES, N. T., 1974, Studies on the appearance of a copper binding protein in rat liver, *Biochem. Soc. Trans.* **2**:425.

12. BREMNER, I., AND DAVIES, N. T., 1974, Zinc proteins in rat liver, in: *Trace Element Metabolism in Animals—2* (W. G. Hoekstra, J. W. Suttie, H. E. Ganther, and W. Mertz, eds.), pp. 493–495, University Park Press, Baltimore.

13. BULLEN, J. J., ROGERS, H. J., AND LEIGH, L., 1972, Iron-binding proteins in milk and resistance to *E. coli* infection in infants, *Br. Med. J.* **1**:69.

14. BURCH, R. E., WILLIAMS, R. V., HAHN, H. K. J., JETTON, M. M., AND SULLIVAN, J. F., 1975, Serum and tissue enzyme activity and trace-element content in response to zinc deficiency in the pig, *Clin. Chem.* **21**:568.

15. BURK, R. F., 1974, *In vivo* [75]Se binding to human plasma proteins after administration of [75]SeO$_3^{2-}$, *Biochem. Biophys. Acta* **372**:255.

16. BURK, R. F., FOSTER, K. A., GREENFIELD, P. M., AND KIKER, K. W., 1974, Binding of simultaneously administered inorganic selenium and mercury to a rat plasma protein, *Proc. Soc. Exp. Biol. Med.* **145**:782.

17. BURT, R. L., AND DAVIDSON, W. F., 1974, Carbohydrate metabolism in pregnancy. Possible role of chromium, *Acta Diabetol. Lat.* **10**:770.

18. BUTT, E. M., NUSBAUM, R. E., GILMOUR, T. C., AND DIDIO, S. L., 1964, Trace metal levels in human serum and blood, *Arch. Environ. Health* **8**:52.

19. CARLISLE, E. M., 1974, Silicon as an essential element, *Fed. Proc. Fed. Amer. Soc. Exp. Biol.* **33**:1758.

20. CARLISLE, E. M., 1974, Essentiality and function of silicon, in: *Trace Element Metabolism in Animals—2* (W. G. Hoekstra, J. W. Suttie, H. E. Ganther, and W. Mertz, eds), pp. 407–423, University Park Press, Baltimore.

21. CHESTERS, J. K., 1974, Biochemical functions of zinc with emphasis on nucleic acid metabolism and cell division, in: *Trace Elements Metabolism in Animals—2* (W. G. Hoekstra, J. W., Suttie, H. E. Ganther, and W. Mertz, eds.), pp. 39–49, University Park Press, Baltimore.

22. CURRAN, G. L., AND BURCH, R. E., 1968, Biological and health effects of vanadium, in: *Trace Substances in Environmental Health* (D. D. Hemphill, ed.), pp. 96–105, University of Missouri, Columbia.

23. DICKSON, R. C., AND TOMLINSON, R. H., 1967, Selenium in blood and human tissues, *Clin. Chim. Acta* **16**:311.

24. DIPLOCK, A. T., 1974, The nutritional and metabolic roles of selenium and vitamin E, *Proc. Nutr. Soc.* **33**:315.

25. DIPLOCK, A. T., 1974, Possible stabilizing effect of vitamin E on microsomal, membrane-bound, selenide-containing proteins and drug-metabolizing enzyme systems, *Amer. J. Clin. Nutr.* **27**:995.

26. EVANS, G. W., 1973, Copper homeostasis in the mammalian system, *Physiol. Rev.* **53**:535.

27. EVANS, G. W., AND WIEDERANDERS, R. E., 1968, Effect of hormones on ceruloplasmin and copper concentrations in the plasma of the rat, *Amer. J. Physiol.* **214**:1152.

28. EVANS, G. W., WOLENTZ, M. L., AND GRACE, C. I., 1975, Copper-binding proteins in neonatal and adult rat liver soluble fraction, *Nutr. Rep. Int.* **12**:261.

29. FINELLI, V. N., MURTHY, L., PEIRANO, W. B., AND PETERING, H. G., 1974, δ-Aminolevulinate dehydratase, a zinc dependent enzyme, *Biochem. Biophys. Res. Commun.* **60**:1418.

30. FOGEL, P. I., 1972, Effect of estrogenic hormones and serotonin on trace elements in uterine muscle and placenta, *Akush. Ginekol. (Kiev)* **2**:163 (*Chem. Abstr.* **81**:58557a).

31. FURUGOURI, K., 1974, Copper and hemoglobin status in newborn piglets, *Jpn. J. Vet. Sci.* **36**:255.

32. GARNER, C. W., AND BEHAL, F. J., 1974, Human liver aminopeptidase. Role of metal ions in mechanism of action, *Biochemistry* **13**:3227.

33. GRANICK, S., 1946, Protein apoferritin and ferritin in iron feeding and absorption, *Science* **103**:107.

34. GREENGARD, O., 1971, Enzymic differentiation in mammalian tissues, in: *Essays in Biochemistry,* Vol. 7 (P. N. Campbell and F. Dickens, eds.), pp. 159–198, Academic Press, New York.

35. GREENGARD, O., 1972, The developmental formation of enzymes in rat liver, in: *Biochemical Actions of Hormones,* Vol. I (G. Litwack, ed.), pp. 53–85, Academic Press, New York.

36. GRIGORYAN, A. S., MANASYAN, A. O., ARUTYUNYAN, D., AND OGANESYAN, E. P., 1975, Changes of trace element contents in cow colostrum, *Izv. Skh. Nauk* **18**:54 (*Chem. Abstr.* **83**:111780n).

37. GUENTHER, VON T., RUHE, B., SCHMALBECK, J., AND TEHRANI, N., 1974, Zur Biochemie der Spurenelemente Zink, Kupfer, Mangan, Molybdaen, Chrom und Kobalt: Verteilung, Bindung, und Regulation durch Nebennierenrindenhormone, *Z. Klin. Chem. Klin. Biochem.* **12**:327.

38. HAFEMAN, D. G., SUNDE, R. A., AND HOEKSTRA, W. G., 1974, Effect of dietary selenium on erythrocyte and liver glutathione peroxidase in the rat, *J. Nutr.* **104**:580.

39. HAHN, P. F., BALE, W. F., ROSS, J. F., BALFOUR, W. M., AND WHIPPLE, G. F., 1943, Radioactive iron absorption by gastrointestinal tract, *J. Exp. Med.* **78**:169.

40. HALSTEAD, J. A., SMITH, J. C., JR., AND IRWIN, M. I., 1974, A conspectus of research on zinc requirements of man, *J. Nutr.* **104**:345.

41. HAMBIDGE, K. M., 1974, Zinc deficiency in children, in: *Trace Element Metabolism in Animals—2* (W. G. Hoekstra, J. W. Suttie, H. E. Ganther, and W. Mertz, eds.), pp. 171–183, University Park Press, Baltimore.

42. HART, D. T., AND BOROWITZ, J. L., 1974, Adrenal catecholamine release by divalent mercury and cadmium, *Arch. Int. Pharmacodyn. Ther.* **209**:94.

43. HELLERSTEIN, S., KAISER, C., DARROW, D. D., AND DARROW, D. C., 1960, The distribution of bromide and chloride in the body, *J. Clin. Invest.* **39**:282.

44. HENKIN, R. I., 1971, Newer aspects of copper and zinc metabolism, in: *Newer Trace Elements in Nutrition* (W. Mertz and W. E. Cornatzer, eds.), Marcel Dekker, New York.

45. HERSHKO, C., COOK, T. D., AND FINCH, C. A., 1973, Storage iron kinetics. III. Study of desferrioxamine action by selective radioiron labels of RE and parenchymal cells, *J. Lab. Clin. Med.* **81**:876.

46. HILL, C. H., 1974, Reversal of selenium toxicity in chicks by mercury, copper, and cadmium, *J. Nutr.* **104**:593.

47. HOEKSTRA, W. G., 1974, Biochemical role of selenium, in: *Trace Element Metabolism in Animals—2* (W. G. Hoekstra, J. W. Suttie, H. E. Ganther, and W. Mertz, eds.), pp. 61–76, University Park Press, Baltimore.

48. HOEKSTRA, W. G., 1975, Biochemical function of selenium and its relation to vitamin E, *Fed. Proc. Fed. Amer. Soc. Exp. Biol.* **34**:2083.

49. HOPKINS, L. L., JR., 1974, Essentiality and function of vanadium, in: *Trace Element Metabolism in Animals—2* (W. G. Hoekstra, J. W. Suttie, H. E. Ganther and W. Mertz, eds.), pp. 397–405, University Park Press, Baltimore.

50. HOPKINS, L. L., JR., AND MOHR, H. E., 1974, Vanadium as an essential element, *Fed. Proc. Fed. Amer. Soc. Exp. Biol.* **33**:1773.

51. HOPKINS, L. L., AND SCHWARZ, K., 1964, Chromium (III) binding to serum proteins, specifically siderophilin, *Biochem. Biophys. Acta* **90**:484.

52. JIRKA, M., BLANICKY, P., AND CERNA, M., 1974, The Zn-α_2-glycoprotein level in human serum during ontogenesis, *Clin. Chim. Acta* **56**:31.

53. KAEGI, J. H. R., HIMMELHOCH, S. R., WHANGER, P. D., BETHUNE, J. L., AND VALLEE, B. L., 1974, Equine hepatic and renal metallothioneins, *J. Biol. Chem.* **249**:3537.

54. KARPEL, J. T., AND PEDEN, V. H., 1972, Copper deficiency in long-term parenteral nutrition, *J. Pediatr.* **80**:32.

55. KLEVAY, L. M., 1973, Hypercholesterolemia in rats produced by an increase in the ratio of zinc to copper ingested, *Amer. J. Clin. Nutr.* **26**:1060.

56. KLEVAY, L. M., 1975, The ratio of zinc to copper of diets in the United States, *Nutr. Rep. Int.* **11**:237.

57. KLEVAY, L. M., 1975, Coronary heart disease: The zinc/copper hypothesis, *Amer. J. Clin. Nutr.* **28**:764.

58. KOLDOVSKÝ, O., 1972, Hormonal and dietary factors in the development of digestion and absorption, in: *Nutrition and Development* (M. Winick, ed.), pp. 135–199, Wiley-Interscience, New York.

59. KOVALSKY, V. V., VOROTNITSKAYA, I. E., AND TSOI, G. G., 1974, Adaptive changes of the milk xanthine oxidase and its isoenzymes during molybdenum and copper action, in: *Trace Element Metabolism in Animals—2* (W. G. Hoekstra, J. W. Suttie, H. E. Ganther, and W. Mertz, eds.), pp. 161–170, University Park Press, Baltimore.

60. LEACH, R. M., JR., 1974, Biochemical role of manganese, in: *Trace Element Metabolism in Animals—2* (W. G. Hoekstra, J. W. Suttie, H. E. Ganther, and W. Mertz, eds.), pp. 51–59, University Park Press, Baltimore.

61. LEE, C. R., CARTWRIGHT, G. E., AND WINTROBE, M. M., 1968, Heme biosynthesis in copper deficient swine, *Proc. Soc. Exp. Biol. Med.* **127**:977.

62. LINDER, M. C., AND MUNRO, H. N., 1973, Iron and copper metabolism during development, *Enzyme* **15**:111.

63. LINDER, M. C., DUNN, V., ISAACS, E., JONES, D., LIM, S., VAN VOLKOM, M., AND MUNRO, H. N., 1975, Ferritin and intestinal iron absorption: Pancreatic enzymes and free iron, *Amer. J. Physiol.* **228**:196.

64. LINDER, M. C., MOOR, J. R., SCOTT, L. E., AND MUNRO, H. N., 1972, Prenatal and postnatal changes in the content and species of ferritin in rat liver, *Biochem. J.* **129**:455.

65. LIPSCHITZ, D. A., COOK, J. D., AND FINCH, C. A., 1974, A clinical evaluation of serum ferritin as an index of iron stores, *N. Engl. J. Med.* **290**:1213.

66. MAJUMDAR, A. P. N., AND WADSWORTH, G. R., 1974, The influence of the level of protein in the diet of the pregnant mouse on transfer of iron to the fetus, *Nutr. Rep. Int.* **9**:47.

67. MANSOUR, M. M., SCHUBERT, A. R., AND GLASSER, S. R., 1972, Mechanism of placental iron transfer in the rat, *Amer. J. Physiol.* **222**:1628.

68. MASSON, P. L., AND HEREMANS, J. F., 1971, Lactoferrin in milk from different species, *Comp. Biochem. Physiol.* **39B**:119.

69. MAZUR, A., AND CARLETON, A., 1965, Hepatic xanthine oxidase and ferritin iron in the developing rat, *Blood* **26**:317.

70. MCCONNELL, K. P., HSU, J. M., HERRMAN, J. L., AND ANTHONY, W. L., 1974, Parallelism between sulfur and selenium amino acids in protein synthesis in the skin of zinc deficient rats, in: *Trace Element Metabolism in Animals—2* (W. G. Hoekstra, J. W. Suttie, H. E. Ganther, and W. Mertz, eds.), pp. 736–738, University Park Press, Baltimore.

71. MCCOY, K. E. M., AND WESWIG, P. H., 1969, Some selenium responses in the rat not related to vitamin E, *J. Nutr.* **98**:383.

72. MERTZ, W., 1974, Chromium as a dietary essential for man, in: *Trace Element Metabolism in Animals—2* (W. G. Hoekstra, J. W. Suttie, H. E. Ganther, and W. Mertz, eds.), pp. 185–197, University Park Press.

73. Mertz, W., Roginski, E. E., Feldman, F. J., and Thurman, D. E., 1969, Dependence of chromium transfer into the rat embryo on the chemical form, *J. Nutr.* **99**:363.

74. Messer, H. H., Armstrong, W. D., and Singer, L., Essentiality and function of fluoride, in: *Trace Element Metabolism in Animals—2* (W. G. Hoekstra, J. W. Suttie, H. E. Ganther, and W. Mertz, eds.), pp. 425–435, University Park Press, Baltimore.

75. Moiseeva, S. Z., 1973, Level of nickel in the organs and tissues of rabbits when its content in their rations is varied, *Sb. Rab. Leningr. Vet. Inst.* **33**:122 (*Chem. Abstr.* **81**:1680 98j).

76. Munro, H. N., Linder, M. C., Haberman, M., and Catsimpoolas, N., 1975, Ferritins from normal and malignant human tissues, in: *Proteins of Iron Storage and Transport* (R. R. Crichton, ed.), pp. 223–230, North-Holland Publishing Co., Amsterdam.

77. Murray, M. J., and Stein, W., 1970, Contribution of maternal rat iron stores to fetal iron in rats, *J. Nutr.* **100**:1023.

78. Nielson, F. H., and Ollerich, D. A., 1974, Nickel: A new essential trace element, *Fed. Proc. Fed. Amer. Soc. Exp. Biol.* **33**:1767.

79. Nielson, F. H., Myron, D. R., Givand, S., Zimmerman, T. J., and Ollerich, D. A., 1975, Nickel deficiency in rats, *J. Nutr.* **105**:1620.

80. Nishimura, H., Hirota, S., Tanaka, O., Ueda, M., and Uno, T., 1974, Normal mercury level in human embryos and fetuses, *Biol. Neonate* **24**:197.

81. Nomoto, S., 1974, Determination and pathophysiological study of nickel in humans and animals II. Measurement of nickel in human tissues by atomic absorption spectrometry, *Shinshu Igaku Zasshi* **22**:39.

82. Nomoto, S., 1974, Determination and pathophysiological study of nickel in humans and animals III. *In vivo* labeling and separation of nickeloplasmin in rabbit serum and its immunological study, *Shinshu Igaku Zasshi* **22**:45.

83. Onkelinx, C., Becker, J., and Sunderman, F. W., Jr., 1974, Compartmental analysis of nickel (II) 63 metabolism in rodents, in: *Trace Element Metabolism in Animals—2* (W. G. Hoekstra, J. W. Suttie, H. E. Ganther, and W. Mertz, eds.), pp. 560–563, University Park Press, Baltimore.

84. Owen, C. A., Jr., 1971, Metabolism of copper 67 by the copper deficient rat, *Amer. J. Physiol.* **221**:1722.

85. Parisi, A. F., and Vallee, B. L., 1969, Zinc metalloenzymes: Characteristics and significance in biology and medicine, *Amer. J. Clin. Nutr.* **22**:1222.

86. Perry, H. M., Tipton, I. H., Schroeder, H. A., Steiner, R. L., and Cook, M. J., 1961, Variation in the concentration of cadmium in human kidney as a function of age and geographic origin, *J. Chron. Dis.* **14**:259.

87. Petering, H. G., The effect of cadmium and lead on copper and zinc metabolism, in: *Trace Element Metabolism in Animals—2* (W. G. Hoekstra, J. W. Suttie, H. E. Ganther, and W. Mertz, eds.), pp. 311–325, University Park Press, Baltimore.

88. Pribluda, L. A., 1963, The chromium content of hollow bones of the human fetus, *Dokl. Akad. Nauk. Belorussk. SSR* **7**:135 (*Chem. Abstr.* **59**:3142d).

89. Quarterman, J., 1973, Factors influencing the amount and availability of trace elements in human food plants, *Qual. Plant.—Plant Foods Hum. Nutr.* **23**:171.

90. Quarterman, J., Mills, C. F., and Humphries, W. R., 1966, The reduced secretion of, and sensitivity to, insulin in zinc-deficient rats, *Biochem. Biophys. Res. Commun.* **25**:354.

91. Riordan, J. R., and Gower, I., 1975, Purification of low molecular weight copper proteins from copper loaded liver, *Biochem. Biophys. Res. Commun.* **66**:678.

92. Robbins, E., and Pederson, T., 1970, Iron: Its intracellular localization and possible role in cell division, *Proc. Natl. Acad. Sci. U.S.A.* **66**:1244.

93. Rodgers, G. M., Fisher, J. W., and George, W. J., 1974, Elevation of renal cyclic GMP concentrations and plasma lysosomal enzyme activity following cobalt treatment in rats, *Biochem. Biophys. Res. Commun.* **59**:979.

94. Roeser, H. P., Lee, G. R., Nacht, S., and Cartwright, G. E., 1970, The role of ceruloplasmin in iron metabolism, *J. Clin. Invest.* **49**:2408.

95. Sapota, A., Piotrowski, J. K., and Baranski, B., 1974, Metallothionein levels in certain tissues of pregnant rats exposed to mercury vapors, *Med. Press* **25**:192 (*Chem. Abstr.* **82**:26721d).

96. Schroeder, H. A., 1966, Essential trace metals in man: Manganese, *J. Chron. Dis.* **19**:573.

97. Schroeder, H. A., 1973, *The Trace Elements and Man*, The Devin-Adair Co., Old Greenwich, Connecticut.

98. Schroeder, H. A., Balassa, J. J., and Tipton, I. H., 1962, Abnormal trace elements in man: Chromium, *J. Chron. Dis.* **15**:941.

99. Schroeder, H. A., Balassa, J. J., and Tipton, I. H., 1964, Abnormal trace metals in man: Tin, *J. Chron. Dis.* **17**:483.

100. Schroeder, H. A., Kanisawa, M., Frost, D. V., and Mitchener, M., 1968, Germanium, tin and arsenic in rats: Effects on growth, survival, pathological lesions and life span, *J. Nutr.* **96**:37.

101. Schroeder, H. A., Nason, A. P., Tipton, I. H., and Balassa, J. J., 1967, Essential trace metals in man: Zinc. Relation to environmental cadmium, *J. Chron. Dis.* **20**:179.

102. Schwarz, K., 1974, Recent dietary trace element research, exemplified by tin, fluorine, and silicon, *Fed. Proc. Fed. Amer. Soc. Exp. Biol.* **33**:1748.

103. SCHWARZ, K., 1974, Newer essential trace elements (Sn, V, F, Si): Progress report and outlook, in: *Trace Element Metabolism in Animals—2* (W. G. Hoekstra, J. W. Suttie, H. E. Ganther, and W. Mertz, eds.), pp. 355–405, University Park Press, Baltimore.

104. SCHWARZ, K., 1976, Essentiality and metabolic functions of selenium, *Med. Clin. North Amer.,* in press.

105. SCHWARZ, K., AND FOLTZ, O. M., 1957, Selenium as an integral part of factor 3 against dietary necrotic liver degeneration, *J. Amer. Chem. Soc.* **79**:3292.

106. SCHWARZ, K., MILNE, D. B., AND VINYARD, E., 1970, Growth effects of tin compounds in rats maintained in a trace element controlled environment, *Biochem. Biophys. Res. Commun.* **40**:22.

107. SEELIG, M. S., 1973, Proposed role of copper–molybdenum interaction in iron-deficiency and iron-storage diseases, *Amer. J. Clin. Nutr.* **26**:657.

108. SHIRLEY, R. L., JETER, M. A., FEASTER, J. P., McCALL, J. T., CUTLER, J. C., AND DAVIS, G. K., 1954, Placental transfer of Mo^{99} and Ca^{45} in swine, *J. Nutr.* **54**:59.

109. SHOKEIR, M. H. K., 1971, Investigations on the nature of ceruloplasmin deficiency in the newborn, *Clin. Genet.* **2**:223.

110. SIIMES, M. A., AND DALLMAN, P. R., 1974, New kinetic role for serum ferritin in iron metabolism, *Br. J. Haematol.* **28**:7.

111. SIIMES, M. A., KOERPER, M. A., LICKO, V., AND DALLMAN, P. R., 1975, Ferritin turnover in plasma: An opportunistic use of blood removed during exchange transfusion, *Pediatr. Res.* **9**:127.

112. SIRIVECH, S., FRIEDEN, E., AND OSAKI, S., 1974, The release of iron from horse spleen ferritin by reduced flavins, *Biochem. J.* **143**:311.

113. SMITH, J. E., BROWN, E. D., AND SMITH, J. C., 1974, The effect of zinc deficiency on the metabolism of retinol-binding protein in the rat, *J. Lab. Clin. Med.* **84**:692.

114. SMITH, R. J., AND CONTURA, J. F., 1974, Cobalt-induced alterations in plasma proteins, proteases, and kinin system of the rat, *Biochem. Pharmacol.* **23**:1095.

115. STURGEON, P., AND SHODEN, A., 1971, Storage iron in normal populations, *Amer. J. Clin. Nutr.* **24**:469.

116. SUNDERMAN, F. W., JR., DECSY, M. I., AND McNEELY, M. D., 1972, Nickel metabolism in health and disease, *Ann. N. Y. Acad. Sci.* **199**:300.

117. SUTTLE, N. F., 1974, The effect of dietary molybdenum on hypocupraemic ewes treated by subcutaneous copper, *Vet. Rec.* **95**:165.

118. SUTTLE, N. F., 1974, Recent studies of the copper–molybdenum antagonism, *Proc. Nutr. Soc.* **33**:299.

119. TAVES, D. R., 1968, Electrophoretic mobility of serum fluoride, *Nature (London)* **220**:582.

120. TERAO, T., AND OWEN, C. A., JR., 1974, Copper in supernatant fractions of various rat tissues, *Mayo Clin. Proc.* **49**:376.

121. TIPTON, I. H., AND COOK, M. J., 1963, Trace elements in human tissue. Part II. Adult subjects from the United States, *Health Phys.* **9**:89.

122. TUMAN, R. W., AND DOISY, R. J., 1975, The role of trace elements in human nutrition and metabolism, in: *Physiological Effects of Food Carbohydrates* (A. Jeanes and J. Hodges, eds.), pp. 156–178, American Chemical Society, Washington, D.C.

123. UNDERWOOD, E. J., 1971, *Trace Elements in Human and Animal Nutrition,* Academic Press, New York.

124. VALLEE, B. L., 1954, Serum copper in patients recovering from myocardial infarction, *Metabolism* **1**:420.

125. VARMA, R., VARMA, R. S., ALLEN, W. S., AND WARDI, A. H., 1974, On carbohydrate protein linkage groups in vitreous humor hyaluronate, *Biochem. Biophys. Acta* **362**:584.

126. VULIMIRI, L., LINDER, M. C., MUNRO, H. N., AND CATSIMPOOLAS, N., 1977, Structural features of rat cardiac ferritins, *Biochem. Biophys. Acta* **491**:67–75.

127. WEINBERG, E. D., 1974, Iron and susceptibility to infectious disease, *Science* **172**:952.

128. WHANGER, P. D., PEDERSON, N. D., AND WESWIG, P. H., 1973, Selenium proteins in ovine tissues II. Spectral properties of a 10,000 molecular weight selenium protein, *Biochem. Biophys. Acta* **53**:1031.

129. WHEBY, M. S., AND CROSBY, W. H., 1963, Gastrointestinal tract and iron absorption, *Blood* **22**:416.

130. WHITE, A., HANDLER, P., AND SMITH, E. L., 1973, *Principles of Biochemistry* (5th Ed.), McGraw-Hill, New York.

131. WIDDOWSON, E. M., 1969, Trace elements in human development, in: *Mineral Metabolism in Paediatrics,* pp. 85–97, Blackwell Scientific Publications, Oxford.

132. WIDDOWSON, E. M., AND SPRAY, C. W., 1950, Chemical development *in utero, Arch. Dis. Child.* **5**:205.

133. WIDDOWSON, E. M., DAUNCY, J., AND SHAW, J. C. L., 1974, Trace elements in fetal and early postnatal development, *Proc. Nutr. Soc.* **33**:275.

134. WINTROBE, M. M., CARTWRIGHT, G. E., AND GUBLER, C. J., 1953, Studies on the function and metabolism of copper, *J. Nutr.* **50**:395.

135. WOLFF, H. P., 1956, Untersuchungen zur Pathophysiologie des Zincstoffwechsels, *Klin. Wochenschr.* **15**:409.

CHAPTER 21

Heat Production and Temperature Regulation

Kurt Brück

1. Introduction

Heat production is a side product of metabolic processes, the continuous occurrence of which provides the energy basis of life. This heat production necessarily increases the temperature of an organism above that of the environment. In the majority of the members of the animal kingdom, the metabolic rate does not allow an increase in body temperature of more than some 1/10 of a degree (*bradymetabolism*). In all these animals, body temperature shows wide fluctuations that depend on changes in the environmental temperature; they are therefore called *poikilothermic* animals.

Two groups of the animal kingdom, birds and mammals, differ from the poikilothermic animals in that, first, their minimum metabolic rate is much higher (*tachymetabolism*), and, second, they possess certain mechanisms that enable them to maintain body temperature more or less accurately at a constant level despite changes in the environmental temperature.

One of the mechanisms for maintaining a stable body temperature consists in the precisely controlled variation of heat production. Thus, in the *homeothermic* organism, heat production is not to be considered a side product of metabolism; rather, it needs particular consideration regarding its thermoregulatory function. A detailed description of this function will be presented in this chapter. In large organisms that have a relatively small surface volume ratio and an effective heat-insulation layer (such as a subcutaneous layer of fat, a coat of feathers, or hair), the most important function of the temperature-regulatory system is to dissipate the metabolic heat, the rate of which is inevitably increased with physical activity. In contrast, small organisms are much more likely to be menaced by the excess of heat loss over heat production than by an overproduction of heat. Consequently, the thermoregulatory consideration must be focused on possibilities of producing additional heat to keep body temperature stable.

2. Heat Production

2.1. Methods of Measurement

In the resting organism, the energy generated by oxidative degradation of nutrients is completely transformed into heat. Essentially, then, heat pro-

Kurt Brück · Institute of Physiology, Justus Liebig University, D63 Giessen, West Germany

duction can be determined by either direct or indirect calorimetry, i.e., either by measuring the amount of heat transferred from the body to the surroundings, provided that thermal steady-state conditions exist (no positive or negative heat storage), or by measuring the O_2 consumed during a certain period of time. From O_2 consumption and the caloric equivalent per liter O_2, the heat production can be calculated either in watts (W) or in kilocalories (kcal) per time unit.[30]*

2.1.1. Direct and Indirect Calorimetry

The direct determination of heat production (direct calorimetry) has rarely been used in the past because the older methods were rather complicated and inconvenient. Technical problems have been overcome, however, with the gradient layer calorimeter designed by Benzinger and Kitzing[22] and a similar system specially adapted to human neonates.[184] Although indirect calorimetry will still be preferred for many purposes, direct calorimetry is necessary for the investigation of several problems of temperature regulation, such as heat balance, heat storage, and heat exchange; it may also be noted that the employment of direct calorimetry in combination with indirect calorimetry made it possible to prove the validity of the first law of thermodynamics in the living organism.

Indirect calorimetry employs the determination of O_2 consumption per unit of time. Two different methods are used: the closed and the open system.

In the closed system, a gas mixture with an O_2 content larger than that of air is aspirated from a spirometer. After absorption of CO_2, the expired air is returned into the spirometer, and the change in gas volume serves as a measure of O_2 consumption. With special devices, the amount of expired CO_2 can be determined for the same period of time. The closed-system method has some disadvantages that must be avoided by careful experimentation. First, volume changes due to temperature changes or changes in the resting level of respiration will lead to faulty results. Second, even a small gas leak in the system will cause inaccurate results. Errors of this

kind are particularly likely to arise with the use of a respiratory chamber in which the subject is enclosed. Finally, it must be taken into account that if pure O_2 or O_2 concentrations exceeding that of air are used, during a transient period, some O_2 will shift to the tissues, while the N_2 content of the tissues will decrease. It may require 30 min or more to reach equilibrium.[154] Thus, when a closed system is used, a relatively long period of equilibration must precede the measuring period.

In the open system, normal room air is used. In modern systems, the air is circulated by a pump in such a way that the fresh air passes through a flowmeter and enters a respiratory chamber or a respiratory hood; the outflowing air is led to a gas analyzer, which monitors the O_2 and CO_2 content. In an open system, equilibrium is attained much faster than in a closed system. In contrast to the closed system, the use of respiratory chambers presents no problem because minor gas leakage does not falsify the results.

Infants must be placed in a respiratory chamber, because a mouthpiece cannot be used as it can in adults. The respiratory chamber must be carefully climatized, because small temperature changes have a great influence on heat production (see Section 3.2.2) Furthermore, it is particularly important to use methods that allow a continuous record of O_2 uptake and CO_2 production; from such tracings, one can evaluate whether the infant was quiet and relaxed during the period of measurement. If one is interested in the real heat production, CO_2 measurements should not be omitted, since the respiratory quotient changes considerably in the postnatal period, even under resting conditions (see Section 2.2.2).

During the last few decades, two systems have been described in the literature, a closed system[112] and an open system,[32] which are both specially adjusted for small infants, particularly in that temperature can be exactly regulated to maintain thermal neutrality.

2.1.2. Calculation of Metabolic Rate and Heat Production from Oxygen Uptake—Respiratory Quotient

The O_2 uptake measured must be reduced to standard conditions (STPD—standard temperature, pressure, dry: 0°C, 760 torr, water vapor eliminated). This reduced O_2 uptake must be multiplied by the caloric equivalent of O_2, which is in the range of

---

* The units used throughout this article follow the IUPS-approved "Proposed standard system of symbols for thermal physiology,"[80] which is based on the Système international d'unités. The technical terms and definitions follow the IUPS-approved "Glossary of terms for thermal physiology."[30] In some cases, the more popular units or terms are given in addition, although they are no longer officially approved (e.g., calorie).

19.7 to 21.15 kJ (4.71–5.05 kcal) per liter O_2, depending on the respiratory quotient (RQ). Theoretically, the RQ can vary between 0.7 and 1.0; 0.7 is the quotient of pure fat, 1.0 of pure carbohydrate, utilization. Under certain conditions, i.e., long-term carbohydrate fattening in animals, the RQ may become larger than 1.0. On the other hand, the RQ would become smaller than 0.7 if fat were converted into carbohydrates. RQs smaller than 0.7 have actually been reported, but in view of the difficulties of determining O_2 uptake and CO_2 production in small subjects, such results might be due to incorrect measurements.

Under certain circumstances, highly accurate measurements might be desired; for such accuracy, a correction must be made for the heat produced by protein combustion. It can be calculated from the nitrogen excretion in the urine. On the other hand, it may be sufficient for many purposes to calculate heat production under the assumption that the RQ is 0.85 and the caloric equivalent is 20.4 kJ (4.86 kcal) per liter O_2.

2.1.3. Determination of Fetal Heat Production

In small species, fetal O_2 uptake can be measured by placing a section-delivered fetus in a Warburg apparatus.[136] This method is based on the dubious assumption that all fetal tissues are sufficiently supplied with O_2 by way of diffusion through the body surface. With the instrumentation now available, however, much more satisfactory methods can be applied: by monitoring the arterial and venous umbilical O_2 content and the umbilical blood flow (with an electronic flowmeter), it is possible to calculate the O_2 uptake of the fetus under conditions comparable to the normal intrauterine conditions because the fetus remains attached to the mother by the umbilical cord during the measurements. The fetus can be prevented from breathing by submerging the head in thermostatically controlled water. Recently, the determination of umbilical blood flow has been approached by use of the diffusion-equilibrium technique (Fick's principle), in which no flowmeter arrangement is needed; thus, fetal O_2 uptake can be measured in a chronic preparation, i.e., with the uterus remaining in the closed abdomen.[62] Another approach to estimating fetal O_2 uptake has been made by determining O_2 uptake ($\dot{V}_{O_2}$) in the ewe before and after occlusion of the umbilical circulation with the fetus *in utero*. Fetal $\dot{V}_{O_2}$ prior to occlusion was assumed to be represented by the decrease in maternal $\dot{V}_{O_2}$ after cord-clamping.[1,58]

2.2. Standard Metabolic Rate (Minimum Observed Metabolic Rate)

The metabolic rate depends on factors such as stage of activity, environmental temperature, feeding (calorigenic or specific dynamic action of nutrients), and time of day. For comparison of measurements, the conditions for the measurement of metabolic rate must be standardized. Such standard conditions were first defined in 1906 by Magnus-Levy. The metabolic rate measured under these conditions is called the *basal metabolic rate* (BMR). Infants and children up to 2 years, and particularly neonates, are not likely to fulfill two of the required conditions at the same time: (1) to be awake and fasted for 12 hr and (2) to be fully relaxed. The infant "is always digesting one meal or actively anticipating the next."[187] Thus, special conditions must be defined for the neonate and the young infant. In more recent studies,[32,36,112,153,187] the following conditions are suggested: (1) The infant should remain on the normal feeding schedule. This suggestion is based not only on the arguments presented above, but also on the fact that in infants, the maximum increase in energy metabolism is only of the order of 4–10% after an ordinary feeding[145]; with a special protein-rich formula, however, the specific dynamic action may amount to more than 25% of fasting metabolic rate within 2–3 hr after feeding.[152] (2) The measurements must be made over a period of 5–10 min during which the infant is fully relaxed; in contrast to the BMR standard conditions, it is not required that the infant be awake. The determination may even be made during postprandial sleep.[36] It is recommended that O_2 uptake be continuously recorded over a period of at least 1 hr to ensure that the minimum O_2 uptake has actually been reached during the period of determination (see Sections 2.2.1 and 4.3). (3) An environment of thermal neutrality (defined in Section 2.3.3) should be provided. The "range of thermal neutrality" varies during postnatal development, and it depends on body size. Thus, in each individual case, a series of measurements at various environmental temperatures might be necessary to determine the range of thermal neutrality.

The minimum metabolic rate measured in this way is called the *standard metabolic rate* (SMR).[cf. 30,130] The term "basal metabolic rate"

(BMR) should be used only for determinations performed under standard conditions as employed in adults.

2.2.1. Standard Metabolic Rate in Relation to Body Mass and Age

The SMR is related to body size; i.e., the SMR of a sheep can be anticipated to be larger than that of a rabbit. It can also be anticipated, based on some considerations concerning heat balance,[135] that the metabolic rate per kilogram body mass will be larger in the rabbit than in the sheep. Kleiber[135] found a quantitative relationship: $SMR = 3.29 \times W^{0.75}[W](= 68 \times W^{0.75}$ kcal/day). This equation has proved valid for a wide range of species, including the mouse and the elephant. The biological relationship has also been called the *law of metabolic reduction*.[140]

Although the Kleiber[135] equation can be very useful for predicting metabolic rates when comparing different species, an attempt to arrive at a more precise prediction for a group of individual organisms of the same species but of different body sizes discloses its limited applicability. A number of deviations of the law of metabolic reduction must be introduced. Sex, body shape, and body composition affect the metabolic rate. Age is an even more important factor. The age dependency of the metabolic rate makes it impossible to delineate the metabolic rate for individual species so that it includes neonates as well as adults with a single exponential function of weight, even if a higher exponent than Kleiber's is used.[32]

As illustrated in Fig. 1, in newborn infants up to 1 week of age, the SMR is lower than predicted by Kleiber's equation; i.e., the SMR is lower in a 3-kg human newborn than in a 3-kg rabbit. In the weight range of 5–20 kg, on the other hand, the SMR is higher in human infants than in adult animals of the same weight group. In this period, the SMR is nearly linear in relation to body weight; mathematically, this relationship could be expressed by an exponent of $b = 1$ in the equation $SMR = a \times W^b$. During the period that corresponds to the weight range of 20–70 kg, the SMR approaches the Kleiber curve.

An exponent close to 1, or somewhat larger than 1, would also have to be used to calculate the SMR for infants weighing 1–4 kg, i.e., the range that includes premature infants. This means that in

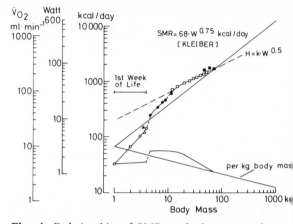

Fig. 1. Relationship of SMR to body mass and age. Top curves: SMR and the corresponding $\dot{V}_{O_2}$ in relation to body mass. Bottom curves: The same data, but expressed in relation to unit of body mass. (———) SMR according to Kleiber's equation; (— · —) heat production that would yield equal temperature differences between body core and environment (see Section 3.2.4). (○) Newborn and premature infants, first week of life[32]; (△) 0–6 hr, full-term infants[112]; (▲) 18–30 hr; (●) boys and girls, 1–36 months[139]; (□) boys, 13–15 years[142]; (■) men, 14–30 years.

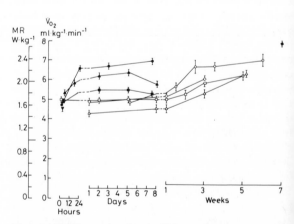

Fig. 2. SMR expressed as milliliters O_2 per minute in relation to age. Data from various authors for full-size (solid symbols) and low-body-mass (open symbols) infants. Vertical brackets denote S.E. ▲[20]; ■[32]; ●[112]; ▼[2]; ◆[139]; □[32]; (△) 1000–1500 g birth weight[150]; (◇) 1500–2000 g birth weight[150]; (○) <1500 g birth weight.[187]

he neonatal period, the SMR per body mass unit is almost independent of weight, whereas a decrease should be expected with increasing weight according to Kleiber's equation (Fig. 1).

Figure 2 compiles the data on metabolic rates in the neonatal period as determined by six different groups of authors; for the sake of easier comparison, O_2 consumption is given instead of heat production. In contrast to Fig. 1, metabolic rates are plotted against age instead of body mass, emphasizing the importance of the age factor. The values for the first hours of life, including premature infants, are within the range of 4.6 to 5 ml/kg · min, and they are, to the satisfaction of all investigators working in this field, surprisingly close together. As for the values for the following days and weeks, the agreement among authors may be considered less satisfactory. During this period, the SMR increases, according to all authors, but there is a great variance in the slopes of the curves representing the SMR–age relationship (Fig. 2), even among full-size infants. These inconsistent results obtained in the first week of life were a great challenge for restudying the SMR several times. The values measured by Hill and Rahimtulla[112] came close (except for the first few hours of life) to the highest values reported in the literature, (see 130) while more recently published data by Levison and Swyer[141] for the first week of life, and by Znamenáček and Přibylová[217] for the first 3 days of life, are very similar to the values reported by Brück,[32] which are the lowest values for the SMR in full-size infants yet published (see Fig. 2). It must be considered, however, that O_2 uptake shows cyclic changes (see Section 4.3), with amplitudes that increase with age.[174] Thus, it is much more likely that an elevated value of the SMR will be measured in older infants than in those in the first day of life. This problem can be eliminated only by continuously recording O_2 uptake over a period of 30–60 min and selecting the 5-min period with the lowest O_2 uptake. Authors who reported the lowest SMRs expressly stated that they had used this procedure.

In a recent study, the authors expressly distinguish between "basal" (equal to SMR in the strictest sense) and resting metabolism. They also emphasize the large variation of SMR due to the nutritional status and other factors.[183]

According to the data summarized in Fig. 2, in premature infants, the SMR does not increase markedly before the second week of life. According to Mestyán et al.,[150] the SMR per unit weight is somewhat lower in infants of less than 1500-g body weight (Fig. 2). The slope of the postnatal increase in the SMR is dependent on birth weight according to Scopes and Ahmed,[187] but no such dependence was observed by Mestyán et al.[150] In the studies by Hill and Robinson,[113] $\dot{V}_{O_2}$ increased from 5–6.5 during the first 2 weeks of life, and continued to rise until values around 9 ml/kg · min had been reached by the age of 1–2 months.

The quantitative changes in the SMR during early postnatal development can be summarized as follows: (1) Immediately after birth, the SMR per kilogram body mass is lower in human infants than in adult animals of the same weight (see Fig. 1). (2) After birth, the SMR per kilogram body weight increases and eventually attains a value that is up to 50% higher in infants than in adult animals of the same body mass. The time factor of this process appears to be variable; it may take from 2 days to a few weeks (particularly in premature infants) to attain the final values that are characteristic for the postneonatal period (see Figs. 1 and 2). A similar deviation of the SMR from the Kleiber curve has been demonstrated for the guinea pig,[41] and can be delineated for the rhesus monkey,[65] the rat,[204] and the pig.[160] In the lamb, the postnatal increase in SMR may occur within the first few hours of life, as demonstrated by Dawes and Mott[64] and confirmed by Andrews et al.[14] In the latter study, O_2 consumption rose from 9.44 in 1- to 6-hr-old lambs to 13.6 in 15- to 20- and to 15.3 ml/kg · min in 30- to 36-hr-old lambs; the latter value is about twice the maximum value in human neonates of the same size. (see Fig. 2). This rapid rise in SMR does not occur in starved lambs. It was thus suggested that the rapid postnatal metabolic rise could be caused, at least in part, by the onset of digestion and absorption.[15]

The violation of the law of metabolic reduction (see above) may be only a fictive problem if one takes into account the considerable changes in extracellular water content (extracellular fluid, ECF) that occur from the early fetal to the adult stage. It is for this reason that Sinclair et al.[192] suggested the use of body weight minus ECF as the reference value in metabolic reference standards. According to their calculations, ECF would make up as much as 44% in a 4000-g newborn and even 58% in a 1000-g premature, whereas the corresponding value for the

Table I. Relationship Between Extracellular Fluid (ECF), Metabolic Rate, Age, and Body Weight

Body weight (kg)	Age	ECF (%)	ECF (liters)	Active tissue mass (kg)	Active tissue mass + 16% ECF (fictive body weight) (kg)	(ml/min)	Oxygen consumption related to: Body weight (ml/kg · min)	Active tissue mass (ml/kg · min)[a]	Fictive body weight (ml/kg · min)
1	0–6 hr	58[b]	0.580	0.42	0.487	5.0[c]	5.0	11.90	10.3
4	0–6 hr	44[b]	1.76	2.24	2.60	20.0[c]	5.0	8.94	7.7
10	1 year	25[d]	2.50	7.50	8.62	82.0[e]	8.2	10.90	9.5
70	Adult	16[f]	11.20	58.80	70.00	245.0[e]	3.5	4.16	3.5

[a] Body weight minus ECF, according to Sinclair *et al.*[192]
[b] Data from Sinclair *et al.*[192]
[c] From Fig. 3 (rounded off).
[d] Data from Friis-Hansen.[79]
[e] From Fig. 1.
[f] Data from *Documenta Geigy*.[70]

adult is only 16%. Since the ECF certainly does not participate in the oxidative metabolism, the expression body weight minus ECF may be considered as representative for the active tissue mass. Thus, it seems theoretically justified to relate metabolic rate to this active tissue mass rather than to total body weight. In contrast, the lean body mass (i.e., total body mass minus fat mass) has not been found to be a suitable reference value.

Going a step further, one may relate metabolic rate to the expression "active tissue mass plus 16% ECF," i.e., to a body mass that corresponds in composition to that of the adult organism. Metabolic rates related to this fictive body mass have been calculated for subjects of different developmental stages (Table I). These metabolic values are plotted against the actual body weight in Fig. 3. As can easily be seen, the neonatal metabolic rate related to this fictive body mass (active body mass + 16% ECF) closely approximates the Kleiber curve, whereas the metabolic rate related to the actual body weight remains below the predicted values. On the other hand, the violation of Kleiber's law by the elevated metabolic rate at an older age cannot be accounted for by alterations in the proportion of ECF. Relating metabolic rate to the fictive body mass, one would obtain even larger deviations from the Kleiber curve. To interpret these high values of metabolic rate, two factors can be discussed here: (1) the high BMR of the so-called "brown fat" and (2) some peculiarities in the function of the endocrine system.

With regard to the first factor, it can be inferred from studies in the rabbit[92] that the resting metabolism of the brown fat may make up in the neonate as much as 30% of the SMR (see Fig. 18).

As for the second factor, the thyroid function must be considered. Its relationship to metabolic rate has long been known. Only a very few studies, however, are actually pertinent to the problem we are interested in here. After thyroidectomy, the SMR is reduced more in juvenile than in adult rats.[86] This finding would mean that at least part of the SMR exceeding the figure predicted by the Kleiber curve (see Figs. 1 and 3) may be related

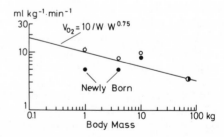

Fig. 3. Minimum O_2 uptake per kilogram body mass (●) and fictive body mass (○). The line follows the equation O_2 uptake = $10/W^{0.75}$ (ml/kg · min), which was derived from Kleiber's equation (see the text for details).

to a particularly high thyroid function. In 3- to 9-year-old children, thyroid activity has indeed been shown to be increased by about 75% when thyroid turnover was compared with the adult.[87] More recent studies have confirmed this view.[76] Many more factors would have to be considered for an interpretation of the postnatal development of metabolic rate. At present, we can only speculate about those factors. The field is a wide one for further investigation.

2.2.2. Respiratory Quotient

Benedict and Talbot[20] showed in 1915 that in the newborn infant, the RQ ranges between 0.9 and 1.0 immediately after birth, and that it decreases to about 0.7 during the first few days of life. Thereafter, it rises toward the end of the first week and attains a value around 0.85 as in the adult. This postnatal change of the RQ was confirmed by more recent studies.[32] It has been concluded that immediately after birth, carbohydrate is the main fuel, while on the second and third days of life, fat utilization prevails. The low RQ during the first few days of life coincides with a low glucose turnover and a high plasma level of free fatty acids.[207]

2.2.3. Fetal Metabolic Rate

The measurement of fetal O_2 uptake has attracted great interest for many decades (cf. Dawes[63]). The large number of data available show a wide range due to serious technical difficulties in obtaining the measurements (see Section 2.1). This range of variation is too large to resolve the question posed by the following two alternatives: either (1) fetal O_2 uptake is in the range of the mother's average O_2 uptake, and it is only immediately after birth that O_2 uptake reaches the higher values found in the neonate, or (2) fetal O_2 uptake is in the same range as that found in the neonate after birth; i.e., it comes close to the value predicted by Kleiber's equation (see Fig. 1).

The lower values found in the literature would be in favor of the first proposition; taking these values for the best approach to the actual values, we must assume that a dramatic metabolic alteration occurs at birth to explain the sudden transition to the increased postnatal rate of O_2 uptake. Recent data substantiating larger values[62,149] favor the second proposition.

2.3. Metabolic Rate and Heat Production in Relation to Body and Environmental Temperature

2.3.1. Van't Hoff–Arrhenius' Law

In a living organism, O_2 consumption may be thought of as being governed by a chemical master reaction, which must, of course, obey the Van't Hoff–Arrhenius law. According to this law, we would expect the O_2 uptake and body temperature of a poikilothermic animal, such as a frog or a lizard, to decrease with falling environmental temperature. This decrease has in fact been demonstrated in biological experiments without exception. In general, O_2 uptake changes by a factor of 2–3 per 10°C change in body temperature (Fig. 4, bottom curve). Briefly, this relationship is expressed by the so-called "Q_{10}" value, which would be 2–3 according to the foregoing.

In contrast, in homeothermic or warm-blooded animals, O_2 consumption is minimal under certain environmental conditions, i.e., within the range of thermal neutrality (see Section 2.3.3) (Fig. 5). O_2 consumption increases when the environmental

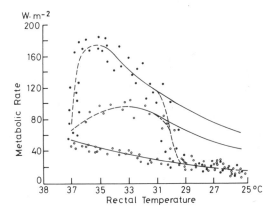

Fig. 4. Relationship between metabolic rate and rectal temperature in anesthetized dogs. Top curve: Light anesthesia; hence, there is a marked cold-induced increase in heat production with decreasing body temperature. Middle curve: Moderate anesthesia; the response of heat production to cooling is reduced. Lower curve: Deep anesthesia; no cold defense reaction. After having reached a maximum, heat production follows the Van't Hoff–Arrhenius law. Note that the upper and middle curves tend to approach the lower curve as soon as the rectal temperature drops below a critical temperature (about 30°C). Reproduced from Behmann and Bontke.[18]

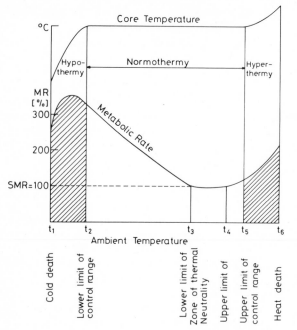

Fig. 5. Schematic representation of the relationship between metabolic rate and ambient temperature in homeotherms: zone of thermal neutrality ($t_3 \cdots t_4$) and zone of tolerated ambient temperature ($t_2 \cdots t_5$). See the text for further explanation. Reproduced from Hensel *et al.*[98]

temperature is either reduced below the lower limit of this range or increased to an extent that body temperature increases. The first is considered part of a cold defense reaction (see Section 2.3.2), the latter an increase according to the Van't Hoff–Arrhenius law.

The cold-induced increase in heat production prevents the body temperature from falling as long as the steady-state heat loss does not exceed the heat production. As soon as this balance becomes disturbed, the body temperature necessarily begins to decrease.

As shown by Fig. 4 (top curve), this cold-induced heat production as well as the basal heat production (Fig. 4, bottom curve) is subjected to the Van't Hoff–Arrhenius law; i.e., it decreases with falling body temperature, the slope of the curve again corresponding to a Q_{10} of 2–3. Heat production may deviate from this curve, however, and approach the "poikilothermic" curve (Fig. 4, bottom curve) as indicated by the dashed line. This can be taken as an indication that the thermoregulatory drive as generated in the thermointegrative area of the CNS is reduced—more or less gradually—

with increasing hypothermia. The body-temperature range at which this reduction occurs may be different depending on the species and on other as yet undefined circumstances. In the rats studied by Andjus and Smith,[13] for example, no reduction in the thermoregulatory drive was seen as long as the body temperature did not fall below 20°C.

The thermoregulatory drive may be entirely blocked by certain drugs, in particular by anesthetics (Fig. 4, bottom curve). The use of such drugs combined with body cooling is generally known as *induced hypothermia* or *artificial hibernation*.

According to more recent studies,[72,150,151,153] the Van't Hoff–Arrhenius law is masked not only by thermoregulatory reactions, but possibly also by a CNS regulation of the metabolic rate that tends to lessen the temperature-dependent changes according to the law. Such stabilization of the metabolic rate against the Van't Hoff–Arrhenius law has been shown to occur to some extent in poikilothermic species if they are subjected to a new thermal environment for a prolonged period of time (references in Precht *et al.*[178]).

2.3.2. Metabolic Rate and Environmental Temperature—Summit Metabolism

Except for the neonates of two species, the ground squirrel[83] and the golden hamster,[115] the neonates of all mammalian species studied thus far do show a cold-induced metabolic response immediately after birth. In adults, the average maximum cold-induced increase in metabolic rate is about 5 times the SMR. In Fig. 6, the maximum cold-induced O_2 uptake, $\dot{V}_{O_2,S(summit)}$, is plotted in relation to age and body mass. During the first few hours or even days of life, $\dot{V}_{O_2,S}$ does not reach the average value (top curve) in all species, particularly in the human infant. $\dot{V}_{O_2,S}$ exceeds the summit curve only in the lamb.

The influence of postnatal age on the cold-induced metabolic rate (or O_2 uptake) in the human neonate is illustrated in Fig. 7. Cold exposure increases metabolic rates in full-term infants by 100% on the first day of life, but by 170% at the end of the first week. The 100% response in heat production has been observed as soon as 15–30 min after birth.[2,32,50,217]

In premature infants, the cold-induced response in O_2 uptake remains behind that of full-term infants in the first days after birth (Fig. 7). Premature infants do not approach the values of full-size infants any earlier than 2–4 weeks after birth.

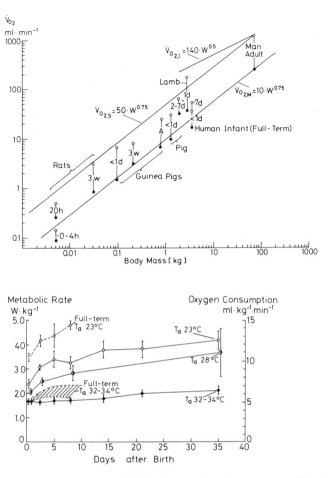

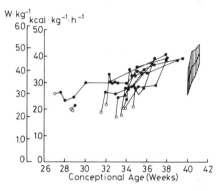

Fig. 6. Minimum and summit metabolic rate ($\dot{V}_{O_2,M}$ and $\dot{V}_{O_2,S}$) related to body mass and age after birth in a number of homeothermic species. The lower line represents Kleiber's allometric equation; the parallel line represents a summit metabolic rate 5 times the minimum metabolic rate. The line designed $\dot{V}_{O_2,I}$ represents the metabolic rate in man that would yield the same width of the zone of tolerated ambient temperature at all given body masses. Data for rats: Taylor[204]; guinea pigs: Brück and Wünnenberg[41]; lamb: Alexander[11]; pig: Mount[163]; human infant: Brück.[32]

Fig. 7. Metabolic rate in full-size (— — —) and premature (———) infants in relation to environmental temperature and age. Mean values ± 2 S.E. Reproduced from Brück.[32]

Fig. 8. Maximum metabolic rate in 10 premature infants exposed to a cool environment (23°C), in relation to conceptional age and age from birth. The first point on each curve (○) shows the maximum metabolic value obtained immediately after birth; the consecutive points show the results during the first postnatal days and weeks. Hatched area at right: Normal range of heat production in full-term newborn infants (mean ± 2 S.D.). Reproduced from Brück.[32]

Gestational age has surprisingly little influence on cold-induced O_2 consumption, as shown in Fig. 8. Neither the metabolic values recorded immediately after birth at an environmental temperature of 23°C nor the steepness of their rise during the first few days of life showed a clear relation to gestational age in a study by Brück.[32] As a result of the rapid rise during the first few days of life, the metabolic values for preterm infants approach the normal range for term-born infants long before they have reached the normal term age and have exceeded their birth weight after the initial weight loss. It has been assumed that the reduced cold-induced metabolic response on the first day of life is partly due to birth stress.[32,51]

According to the studies presented in Fig. 7, the maximum O_2 uptake in 1-week-old full-term infants is about 15 ml/kg · min at 23°C ambient temperature. This value is only slightly greater than the values found at 28°C; it may thus be considered as summit O_2 uptake. The value agrees well with studies by Hey[101] in which the summit O_2 uptake was 16.8 ml/kg · min at 26°C ambient temperature in a comparable group of infants, and with other studies.[173] In the adult, summit O_2 uptake amounts

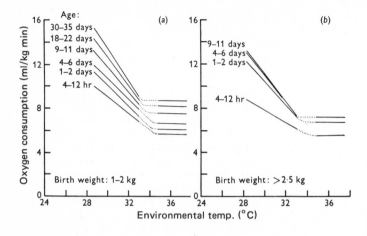

Fig. 9. Metabolic rate (O_2 consumption) in relation to environmental temperature and age after birth. (a) Gradually increasing slope of response with increasing age in low-birth-weight infants. The critical temperature (lower limit of the TNZ) decreases with increasing SMR. (b) Rapid increase in slope of response during the first day of life in normal-sized infants. Reproduced from Hey.[101]

to no more than 20 ml/kg · min,[7,19] but these values are obtained only when the environmental temperature is maintained for a while at about the freezing point.

2.3.3. Thermoneutral Zone

The term *thermoneutral zone* (TNZ), which is used synonymously with "thermal neutrality," "neutral temperature range," and similar terms, was originally defined solely with respect to metabolic rate, and some problems arose concerning its use in perinatal physiology.[104,164] The TNZ is now defined as "the range of ambient temperature within which metabolic rate is at a minimum, and within which temperature regulation is achieved by nonevaporative physical processes alone."[30] This range is delineated by the symbols t_3 and t_4 in Fig. 5. While in the unclothed resting adult, the lower limit of the TNZ, t_3, is 26–28°C [50% relative humidity (RH), still air], it is 32–34°C [operative temperature (see Section 3.2), 50% RH, still air] in the naked full-size newborn infant.[32,69,104,108,159] This difference is of great importance, since it shows that environmental temperature conditions that do not require any thermoregulatory effort in the adult may seriously overtax the metabolic thermoregulatory system of the neonate.

In small premature infants (1 kg), the lower limit of the TNZ may be as high as 35°C,[104,108,150] as shown by Fig. 9. It must be taken into account that with small changes in the sensitivity of the thermoregulatory system (see Section 5.3) as they occur during postnatal development,[39,52] and depending on body size,[188] the lower limit of

thermal neutrality, i.e., the "critical temperature" (cf. Hey[104]) at which thermoregulatory heat production starts, will be shifted accordingly. It is thus extremely difficult to provide exact standard values for the TNZ (see also Sections 5.3 and 6.3) This difficulty could be overcome by extending the definition of TNZ as follows: "TNZ is the range of ambient temperature within which metabolic rate is at a minimum, sweat gland activity is zero, and the deep-body temperature is maintained at a level that is typical for the species under consideration", (cf. Brück[36]). This definition, however, would raise the question whether the deep-body temperature is to be considered a constant quantity during postnatal development (cf. Section 5.3).

2.4. Modes of Extra Heat Production

The ability to produce extra heat in a cool environment is one of the characteristic features of homeothermy. There are three principal modes of heat production that are responsible for the increase of heat production with decreasing environmental temperature: (1) voluntary muscle activity. (2) Involuntary tonic or rhythmic muscle activity, which may be invisible and detectable only by electromyography; with higher intensity, however, the rhythmic activity is accompanied by a characteristic visible tremor known as "shivering." (3) Nonshivering thermogenesis (NST). The existence of this mode of heat production was originally evidenced by the demonstration of a cold-induced increase in oxygen uptake persisting after administration of curare, which blocks the neuromuscular transmission in skeletal muscle and hence prevents shivering.

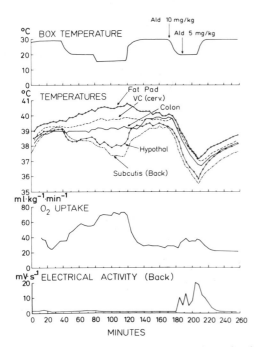

Fig. 10. Course of study in a newborn guinea pig. Age: 0 days; body mass: 101 g. In the first part of the experiment, only NST occurs during cold exposure. After blockade of NST by administration of pronethalol (Alderlin: Ald), shivering takes place and can be recognized by the increased electrical activity of the back muscles. Note the increasing temperature in the area of the interscapular adipose tissue (Fat Pad) and in the cervical part of the vertebral canal [VC (cerv)] before, but the parallel decrease of all temperatures after, blockade of NST. See the text for further explanation. Reproduced from Brück and Wünnenberg.[45]

2.4.1. Shivering and Nonshivering Thermogenesis

Normally, in adult man and in larger adult mammals, shivering is quantitatively the most important involuntary mechanism of thermoregulatory heat production. NST develops to a greater extent only after long-term cold exposure (i.e., cold adaptation), as was first shown by Hart et al.[91] in the rat. Evidence for the development of NST by cold adaptation in mammalian species has been provided; NST is an important and effective mechanism of heat production in the neonates of many mammalian species,[44,66,156,158] including the human infant[32,50,67] (for a review, see Brück[35]).

The elicitation of NST is mediated by the sympathetic nervous system (for a review, see

Himms-Hagen[114]). Evidence for this mediation has been obtained by the demonstration of an inhibition of NST through sympathectomy,[78] through ganglionic blockade,[117,156–158] and by sympathetic stimulation.[122] In this respect, the classic studies by Hsieh et al.[117] are of particular importance. In the cold-adapted, curarized rat, cold-induced O_2 consumption, after suppression by ganglionic blocking agents, can be restored by noradrenaline (NA). NST can also be blocked by adrenergic β-receptor blocking agents such as pronethalol (Alderlin) and propranolol.[43,93] An interesting phenomenon has been observed in studies of the blockade of NST in the newborn guinea pig: when NST was blocked, shivering occurred in place of it, even at environmental temperatures at which normally no shivering was seen (Fig. 10). This observation led to the supposition that shivering is suppressed by NST[42,45] (see also Section 4.2.1).

In comparison with NST, shivering is a less economical form of heat production, since it inevitably increases convective heat loss due to the body oscillations; moreover, it interferes with body movement. This economic aspect becomes more important the smaller the organism (high surface/

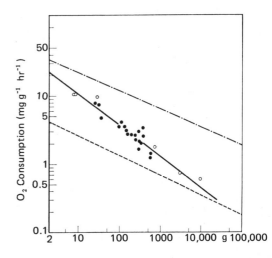

Fig. 11. Maximum amount of NST, measured as increase in O_2 uptake following noradrenaline injection, in relation to body mass (various species in the adult age). (— — —) Minimum O_2 uptake at neutral temperature; (— · —) calculated maximum O_2 uptake for exercise. (●) Rodents: *Clethrionomys glareolus*, NMRI-mouse, *Phodopus sungorus*, *Mesocricetus auratus*, *Glis glis*, rat, guinea pig, *Meriones shawi*; (○) other mammals: *Myotis lucifugus*, *Myotis myotis*, *Erinaceus europaeus*, dog, rabbit. Reproduced from Heldmaier.[94]

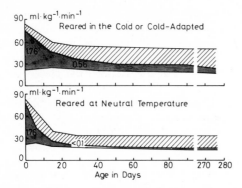

Fig. 12. Reduction of the maximum extent of NST (as determined by two methods) with increasing age and the dependence of this process on the environmental temperature at which the guinea pigs were reared. White area: minimal oxygen consumption; shaded area: NST; striped area: shivering. The inset figures indicate the percentage mass of brown interscapular adipose tissue, which is closely related to the maximum extent of NST. Based on data from Zeisberger et al.[216]

mass ratio; cf. Section 3.2.4) and the poorer its thermal insulation. Thus, it is satisfying, from a teleological point of view, to find that the maximum extent of NST available in one species is inversely related to its order of body size (Fig. 11).[94] Extrapolating the regression line in Fig. 11, one would arrive at the conclusion that subjects with body weights above 10 kg lack the capacity for NST [see also Section 2.4.1(b)].

The existence of NST and brown adipose tissue at the time of birth may be thought of as a compensatory mechanism for the smaller body size, since the thermoregulatory efficiency of NST is greater than that of shivering, as noted above.

(a) Loss of Nonshivering Thermogenesis. In relatively mature newborns, such as the guinea pig, the extent of NST is greatest at the time of birth; it vanishes within a few weeks (Fig. 12). This involution of NST can be retarded and partly inhibited by rearing the animals in a cold environment. After it has disappeared through exposure to a warm environment, NST can again be evoked by exposing the older or even adult guinea pig to a cool environment (cf. Section 5.3) As for the maximum extent of NST, it does not make any difference whether the animal was exposed to a cool or warm environment during the newborn period. With increasing age, however, the extent of evocable NST becomes smaller and smaller.

Glass et al.[84] obtained some results that permit us to assume that a postnatal diminution of NST comparable to that described for the guinea pig occurs in newborn infants. Similar results have been obtained in the calf and in the lamb.[12]

By contrast, in the rat, the maximum extent of NST increases during the first 2–3 weeks of age.[123] Such behavior may be expected to occur in other neonates that, like the rat, are born in a relatively immature stage. This would explain the gradual increase in the maximum cold-induced heat production (shown in Fig. 7) that can be observed during the first few weeks of life of premature infants.

(b) Lack of Nonshivering Thermogenesis. There is at least one example of a species the neonates of which though small, do not possess nonshivering thermogenesis—the pig. Thus, according to Mount,[162,163] the piglet shivers vigorously when it is cold-exposed even on the first day of life. Studies in miniature piglets have shown that there is no NST demonstrable either in neonates immediately after birth or in animals that were reared for a few weeks in a cold environment.[54]

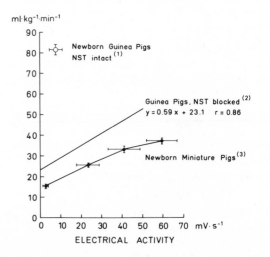

Fig. 13. Relationship between O_2 uptake and electrical activity of the skeletal musculature (as a measure of shivering). Three groups of data are compared, obtained from (1) intact, unanesthetized newborn guinea pigs tested at 8°C; (2) guinea pigs with their NST blocked by pronethalol (Alderlin); and (3) intact, unanesthetized miniature pigs. Vertical and horizontal brackets denote S.E. Note: In the intact guinea pigs, NST prevails. In the miniature pigs as well as in the treated guinea pigs, a strict correlation between O_2 uptake and electrical activity exists; i.e. there is no indication of NST. Reproduced from Brück et al.[54]

The difference in the behavior of these piglets and guinea pigs is illustrated in Fig. 13. It can be seen that O_2 uptake is a strict function of muscle electrical activity in the miniature pig, whereas in the guinea pig, O_2 uptake may increase up to 80 ml/kg · min without an appreciable increase in muscle electrical activity. After NST blockage, however, the behavior of the guinea pig is essentially the same as that of the untreated miniature pig; accordingly, no response to NA could be demonstrated in the miniature pig or in the common piglet.[137] In agreement with the rule expressed by Fig. 11, in a larger neonate, the calf, neither a metabolic response to NA nor the existence of brown adipose tissue could be demonstrated in a study by Jenkinson *et al.*[125]

By contrast, in a more recent study, Alexander and co-workers (references in Alexander[12]) did demonstrate a considerable metabolic increase following NA infusion in the newborn calf. They also demonstrated the existence of "brown fat cells." It remains to be shown that the NA-induced metabolic response is actually due to the activity of the demonstrated adipose tissue, and that NST is used as a cold defense mechanism in the calf. Species are known in which NST is evoked by exogenous NA, but not by cold exposure[123] (references in Brück[38]).

2.4.2. Brown Adipose Tissue and Its Significance for Nonshivering Thermogenesis

From its first description in 1551 by Gesner (quoted in Smith and Roberts[196]) until rather recently, the function of brown adipose tissue was obscure (for a review, see Johannson[128]). For some time, it was preferably studied in hibernators and was denoted "hibernating gland" by many authors, although no evidence had been obtained that it possesses an endocrine function.

Only in the early 1960s was it shown that the *in vitro* metabolic activity of brown adipose tissue was much higher than that of white fat,[126,195] and that the arousal of hibernators is preceded

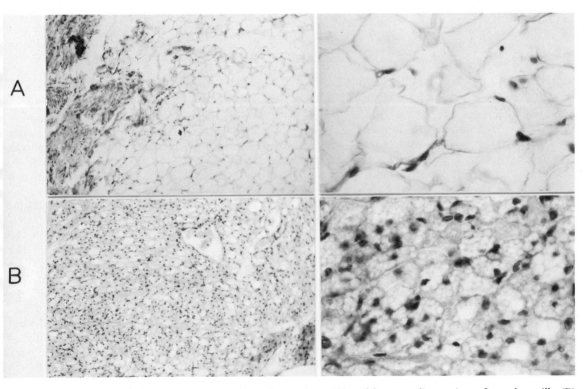

Fig. 14. Photomicrographs of subcutaneous white adipose tissue (A) and brown adipose tissue from the axilla (B) of a 10-day-old infant. Hematoxylin–eosin. Original magnification: ×100 (left) and ×450 (right).

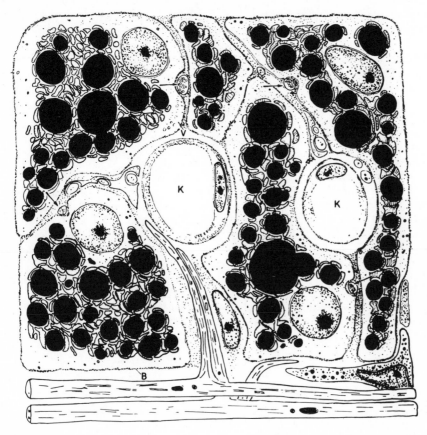

Fig. 15. Innervation of brown fat tissue. Paravascular nerves are at the lower margin. (B) Basal membrane; (K) capillaries; (V) vesiculation. In the intercellular space, sections of axons are shown, some with Schwann sheath cells or their processes (stippled). Arrows denote epicellular nerve endings with synaptic vesicles. For a clearer view, the intercellular collagen fibrils were not drawn in. Reproduced from Bargmann *et al.*[17]

by a local temperature rise in brown adipose tissue.[127,193,194] Thus, it was assumed that the main function of this tissue is to be seen in thermoregulatory heat production. At the same time, it has been found again that the occurrence of brown adipose tissue is by no means restricted to the hibernators, but that it can be found in many nonhibernating mammalian species, mainly in the neonatal stage. In adult animals, it can be observed after cold acclimatization.[195]

The cells of brown adipose tissue (Fig. 14) are characterized by a more centrally located round nucleus, which is surrounded by a large number of small droplets. In contrast, the white fat cell is much larger and has only one large fat droplet with a small plasma skirt that contains the nucleus (signet ring form). Thus, on the basis of light microscopy, we can distinguish "unilocular" and "multilocular" adipose tissue.

Using the electron microscope (Fig. 15), two more functionally important features can be recognized:

(1) the richness in mitochondria,[88] which surround the single fat droplets; and (2) the synaptic contact between sympathetic nerve terminals and the cell membranes.[17,167]

In the hibernator, brown adipose tissue has a brown appearance that gave it its name. In the nonhibernator, the color may be paler and more reddish-yellow.

During the fetal stage, the later unilocular adipose tissue may show a multilocular fat distribution. The embryonic adipose tissue can be distinguished from the persisting multilocular adipose tissue by differences in the number and appearance of the mitochondria.[119]

(a) Location and Mass of Brown Adipose Tissue. In rodents, most of the brown adipose tissue is located around the neck and on the back between the scapulae; other locations are in the axillae, on the surface of the heart and kidneys, and adjacent to the large vessels within the thoracic cavity. In the newborn kitten, as well as in the

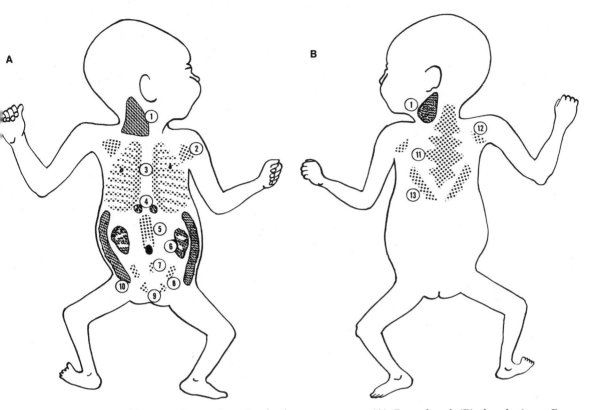

Fig. 16. Distribution of brown adipose tissue in the human neonate. (A) Frontal and (B) dorsal views. From Merklin.[148]

human neonate (Fig. 16), there is no compact interscapular fat pad, but the adipose tissue in this region is more diffusely distributed between the sheets of the musculature. Otherwise, it is distributed as in rodents.

The mass of brown adipose tissue in the newborn rabbit and guinea pig makes up as much as 5–7% of the body weight.[35,44,66] In adult rats, brown adipose tissue amounts to much less than in the neonate. In cold-adapted adult rats, the total amount of brown adipose tissue has been found to be about 1%,[196] and in adult cold-adapted guinea pigs, less than 1%.[35,216] The postnatal involution of adipose tissue, as well as the reduction of NST [see Section 2.4.1(a)], depends on the environmental temperature at which the animals are reared (see Fig. 12).

No brown adipose tissue has been found in the newborn piglet[66,137,163] or in the newborn miniature pig.[54]

Of particular importance for the function of the interscapular adipose tissue are the vascular connections to other organs. According to studies in the rat by Smith and Roberts,[196] the venous blood of the cervical and thoracic interscapular adipose tissue is partly drained into the inner vertebral sinus (plexus venosus vertebralis internus), which surrounds the spinal cord like a heat exchanger (Fig. 17). A similar vascular connection between the interscapular adipose tissue and the vertebral canal has been found in the human neonate.[9] The thermoregulatory significance of these connections is discussed in Section 4.2.1.

The thermogenic function of brown adipose tissue can be shown by a continuous recording of the temperature within the adipose tissue during decreasing environmental temperatures. As shown by Fig. 10, the temperature in the interscapular adipose tissue of a newborn guinea pig rises while the other temperatures fall during the decrease of the environmental temperature. Since a simultaneous blood flow increase has been demonstrated in this

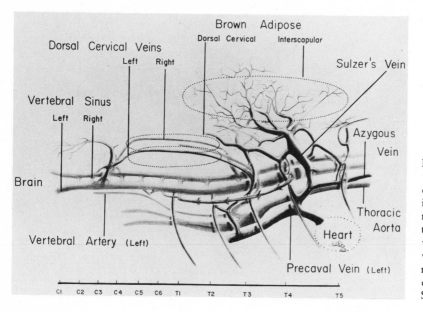

Dorsal Cervical Veins

Left   Right

Brown Adipose

Dorsal Cervical   Interscapular

Sulzer's Vein

Vertebral Sinus

Left   Right

Brain

Azygous Vein

Vertebral Artery (Left)

Heart

Thoracic Aorta

Precaval Vein (Left)

C1 C2 C3 C4 C5 C6 T1   T2   T3   T4   T5

Fig. 17. Lateral view of a polyvinyl replica of the vascular drainage from brown fat pads of interscapular and dorsal cervical regions. Note the venous connections between the fat pads and the vertebral sinus (plexus venosus vertebralis internus), which surrounds the spinal cord like a heat exchanger. Reproduced from Smith and Roberts.[196]

tissue.[43,92] it can be concluded that extra heat is produced in this tissue under cold exposure.

The question arises whether the brown adipose tissue can fully account for the extent of NST observed or whether there are other organs that contribute to NST (skeletal muscle[123,124,202]; liver[213]; white fat—see Section 2.4.3). Recently, to answer this question, Heim and Hull[92] made direct measurements of the blood flow through the interscapular adipose tissue of the newborn rabbit by measuring the arteriovenous difference. These authors found that during cold exposure, the mean blood flow through brown adipose tissue increased from 87 to 304 ml/100 g · min. In individual cases, values of over 700 ml/100 g · min were reached, demonstrating an extremely large blood flow. It was calculated that the blood flow to the brown adipose tissue under resting conditions makes up as much as 10%, and under cold exposure as much as 25%, of the total cardiac output, although the mass of brown adipose tissue accounts for only 5–7% of total body weight.

The O_2 content in the venous blood of less than 3 ml/dl blood indicates a very high O_2 utilization. From these values, Heim and Hull[92] calculated that the O_2 consumption of the brown adipose tissue may account in the newborn rabbit for about two-thirds of the total NST, as observed under maximum stimulation by cold or NA. A similar proportion (Fig. 18) was found in the newborn guinea pig if

the calculation was based on the data from the rabbit and on the maximum amount of NST that was observed in previous studies in the guinea pig.[35,44] It can also be seen from Fig. 18 that brown adipose tissue seems to contribute a considerable part of the standard O_2 uptake.

(b) Mechanism of Extra Heat Production in Brown Adipose Tissue. The mechanism of heat production in brown adipose tissue has been thoroughly studied during the last few years, and has been described in several reviews.[123,181,195] The biochemical sequence of reactions is discussed in detail in Chapter 19 and in several articles.[88,116,143,182]

As a consequence of the oxidation of free fatty acids within brown adipose tissue, the plasma glycerol level increases when NST is evoked (references in Hull and Hardman[120]).

Since brown adipose tissue is an important site of the oxidative processes involved in NST, one would expect the capacity for NST to be quantitatively related to the amount of brown adipose tissue available in an organism. The calculations (Fig. 18) agree with the concept, and also with the fact that the miniature pig is entirely lacking NST and does not possess any brown adipose tissue.[53] Furthermore, they agree with experimental studies in which brown fat was surgically removed from newborn rabbits.[121]

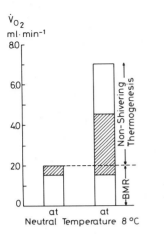

Fig. 18. Schematic representation of the fraction of O_2 uptake that could be accounted for by brown-fat thermogenesis (hatched areas) in a newborn guinea pig weighing 100 g with the brown adipose tissue making up 5% of the body mass. Left: At neutral temperature; right, in a cool environment with maximum cold-induced O_2 uptake. Data from Heim and Hull,[92] Brück,[35] and Brück and Wünnenberg.[44]

2.4.3. Nonshivering Thermogenesis and Brown Adipose Tissue in the Human Neonate

As already mentioned, the human newborn infant is able to increase its heat production without shivering and without physical activity when it is exposed to temperatures below thermal neutrality.[32] From more recent studies,[101,104] it may be roughly calculated that the cold-induced O_2 uptake unaccompanied by shivering and physical activity may be as great as 100% of the minimum O_2 uptake. More direct proof for the existence of NST in the human newborn infant has been obtained by the following experimental results:

1. The newborn infant responds to intravenous administration of NA (0.4 $\mu g/kg \cdot min$) with an increase in O_2 consumption, but without an appreciable increase in physical activity.[131,132] The extra heat production caused by injection of NA reached values of up to 60% of the SMR.

2. Free fatty acids (FFA) are liberated on cold exposure of the neonate and also after NA infusion[186]; however, glycerol liberation exceeds FFA liberation, indicating that part of the FFA is immediately oxidized at the site of liberation, i.e., in the brown adipose tissue.[66,67,120]

3. Renal NA excretion increases simultaneously with the increase in O_2 uptake in cold-exposed newborn infants, while adrenaline excretion remains small,[197] indicating that cold defense reactions are mediated by the excitation of the sympathetic nervous system, and that activation of the adrenal medulla is unimportant for this reaction. Secretion of adrenaline is considered a second-line cold defense reaction that occurs only during severe cold stress.[99,138,177]

4. Skin temperature in the dorsal interscapular area, compared with that in other skin areas, is relatively increased in the human infant when cold-induced O_2 consumption is provoked.[190] This finding supports the view that brown adipose tissue is a site of NST in human neonates as well as in the experimental animals. According to recent studies,[148] brown adipose tissue amounts to about 1.5% of the body mass in full-term newborn infants. The distribution of brown adipose tissue in human neonates is shown in Fig. 16. On the basis of the calculation demonstrated [Section 2.4.2(a) and Fig. 18], one would arrive at a rate of 60 ml O_2 uptake/100 g brown adipose tissue. Taking into account the law of metabolic reduction (i.e., the Kleiber function of metabolic rate; see Fig. 1), one would have to reduce this figure by about half, i.e., to 30 ml/100 g. Thus, 15 g brown adipose tissue per kilogram body weight might account for a nonshivering heat production of 4.5 ml/kg body mass · min, which would be the order of magnitude that is actually observed [see above].

According to these investigations, there is no doubt that the newborn infant is able to employ NST for cold defense, and that the mechanism is not different from that studied in detail in experimental animals. No successful attempts have been made, however, to estimate the relative contribution of NST and shivering to the total cold-induced O_2 consumption during the early postnatal period in human infants. It would be interesting to know whether the extent of NST is at its maximum in the early postnatal period, as is the case in the guinea pig (see Fig. 12), or whether the maximum is not reached until some days or weeks after birth (see Section 2.4.1a). Differences between full-size and premature infants may be expected.

More recent electron-microscopic studies have revealed that the (white) subcutaneous adipose tissue from human neonates contains at least two types of cells. One type is large and has one large fat vacuole and small mitochondria; it thus resembles closely the cells found in adult white adipose tissue. The other cell type is small and has several fat vacuoles and contains numerous mitochondria, thus resembling the cell type found in typical brown adipose tissue.[88,170] Another similarity to brown adipose tissue is to be seen in the fact that carnitine enhances the O_2 consumption of mitochondria isolated from neonatal but not from adult subcutaneous adipose tissue.[171] It is thus tempting to assume that the small neonatal adipocytes found in the (white) subcutaneous adipose tissue contribute to NST[208,171] (cf. results in the calf[12]), but no proof that they do has yet been obtained.

On closer examination, morphological differences between brown adipocytes and the small polyvacuolar cells from human newborn subcutaneous adipose tissue are found. The small polyvacuolar cells have an extensive cytoplasmic membranous system and basement membranes typical of human adult white adipose tissue but not seen in brown adipocytes.[169]

3. Heat Exchange with the Environment

Under steady-state conditions (no positive or negative heat storage) with external work being equal to zero, the metabolic rate (MR) is equal to the heat flow from the interior of the body surface—the internal heat flow, H_{int}—and to the heat flow from the body surface to the environment—the external heat flow, H_{ext}:

$$MR = H_{int} = H_{ext} \qquad (1)$$

The equation for internal heat flow is

$$H_{int} = A \cdot C(T_{re} - \bar{T}_s) \text{ in } [W] \text{ or } [\text{kcal h}^{-1}] \qquad (2)$$

and that for the external heat flow is

$$H_{ext} = A \cdot [h(\bar{T}_s - T_a) + E] \text{ in } [W] \qquad (3)$$

where T_{re} is the deep-body (rectal) temperature, $\bar{T}_s$ is the mean skin temperature, T_a is the ambient temperature, C is the thermal conductance (i.e., the reciprocal of the thermal resistance or thermal insulation, I), h is the combined (see Section 3.2) heat transfer coefficient, and E is the evaporative heat transfer.

Minimum steady-state heat flow will be encountered under conditions of thermal neutrality, since according to the definition (see Section 2.3.3),

the MR and thus heat production is minimal under these conditions. Heat flow may be considerably increased over minimal steady-state flow with increasing heat production, as occurs in a cold environment. Heat flow can be adjusted to heat production at least to a certain extent, by changing the thermal conductance C (see Section 3.1).

A detailed discussion of the biophysics of heat flow is beyond the scope of this chapter; the reader is referred to monographs and reviews.[16,55,89,155,161,163] Here, the considerations are confined to a few elementary facts that are prerequisite to understanding the peculiarities of neonatal temperature regulation.

3.1. Heat Transfer within the Body— Thermal Conductance and Insulation

According to equation (2), heat transfer to the body surface is determined by the internal temperature gradient $(T_{re} - \bar{T}_s)$ and thermal conductance C. This compound quantity C is determined mainly by three factors: (1) the specific heat conductivity of the tissues; (2) the absolute thickness of these tissues, particularly the thickness of the subcutaneous fat, which has relatively low heat conductivity; and (3) the blood flow rate to the surface of the trunk and the extremities.

It follows that the variability of thermal conductance due to blood flow changes depends to a great extent on body size. In a large organism with a thick layer of subcutaneous fat, maximum

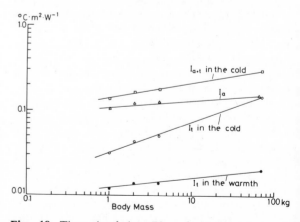

Fig. 19. Tissue insulation (I_t) under cold and warm environmental conditions, ambient insulation (I_a), and total insulation (I_{a+t}) in relation to body mass. Based on data from Hey *et a.*[110] and Hardy.[89]

eduction of blood flow will reduce thermal conductance considerably more than in a small organism. In other words, vasoconstriction as a cold defence reaction would be much less effective in the neonate than in the adult due merely to differences in body mass. This difference is quantitatively shown by Fig. 19, in which maximum and minimum thermal tissue insulation (thermal resistance of the tissues), I_t, is plotted against body mass, based on data determined in neonates.[110] As can be seen from Fig. 19, maximum insulation or thermal resistance in the 4-kg infant is less than one-third that in the adult; in the 1-kg infant, it is only one-fifth. On the other hand, no such great difference exists between the adult and neonate minimum thermal resistance, and no theoretical reasons would lead us to expect such a difference.

3.2. Heat Transfer from the Body to the Environment

Heat transfer from the body to its surroundings is a complex process. For a quantitative consideration, we distinguish four components, namely, heat transfer by conduction, by convection, by radiation, and by water evaporation, as expressed by

$$H_{ext} = H_k + H_c + H_r + H_e \qquad (4)$$

The relative importance of each component depends on environmental conditions such as the temperature of the surroundings, water vapor tension, and wind velocity. Furthermore, the significance of the different components of heat flow varies among species due to factors such as type and length of fur, water diffusion through the skin, and the ability to sweat or to pant.

In dealing with temperature regulation, it is necessary to separate the nonevaporative heat loss, $H_c + H_r$, from the evaporative heat loss, H_e. The latter is subjected to great alterations due to sweat secretion and, in some species, to changes in respiratory rate. The nonevaporative heat loss cannot be influenced by physiologic measures in man, but in animals, it can be influenced by piloerection.

The nonevaporative heat loss may be described by

$$H_{c,r} = A \cdot h(\overline{T}_s - T_o) \cdot [W] \qquad (5)$$

where $\overline{T}_s$ is the mean skin temperature, T_o is the operative temperature [weighted mean of ambient air and wall (radiating) temperature; see Section 3.2.2], and h is the combined nonevaporative heat transfer coefficient. The reciprocal value of h is called

the *air insulation*, or better (cf. Hey and Katz[107]), the *ambient insulation*, I_a. The ambient insulation is largely determined by the heat insulation of the layer of still air, which is also called the *boundary layer*. The thickness of this boundary layer varies with wind speed, and also depends on the properties of the surface to which it adheres; e.g., a rough surface favors formation of a boundary layer. Furthermore, the thickness of this layer depends on the curvature radii of the heat-producing body. Thus, this layer is much thinner on the fingers than on the trunk; for the same reason, it must be thinner on an infant's trunk than on an adult's. Figure 19 shows the alteration of I_a occurring with increasing body mass.

Total Insulation. In adding tissue insulation, I_t, and ambient insulation, I_a, one obtains (for the naked subject) the total insulation, I_{a+t}. As shown in Fig. 19, this overall heat insulation is about 70% greater in the adult than in the human neonate; i.e., at a given difference between rectal temperature, T_{re}, and (operative) environmental temperature, T_o, the heat loss per unit body surface must be correspondingly larger in the neonate than in the adult. For special problems, it may be necessary to consider separately the several avenues of non-evaporative heat loss. The partitional heat loss is therefore treated briefly in the following few paragraphs.

3.2.1. Conductive and Convective Heat Loss

Conductive heat loss occurs, for example, in the small area of the back where the infant is in contact with the support. The amount of this part of heat loss depends on the heat conductivity of the material of which the support is made. This heat flow can be calculated by

$$H_k = h_k/x(\overline{T}_s - T) \cdot A[W] \qquad (6)$$

where h_k is the thermal conductivity of the supporting material, x is the thickness of the material, A is the size, T_s is the mean skin temperature of the area that is in contact with the support, and T is the temperature in the distance x from the skin. Depending on the heat insulation of the support, conductive heat loss may account for up to one-fourth of the observed nonevaporative heat loss in naked babies, but it may be so small as to be negligible if the baby is laid on a well-insulating mattress.[110]

Those parts of the body that are neither in contact

with the support nor covered by clothes are enveloped in a layer of still air that is also called the "boundary layer." Outside this layer, which may be as thick as 4–8 mm if there is no wind, the air is moving, thereby carrying heat by mass flow. This phenomenon is called *heat transport by convection.* Within the boundary layer, heat is transported by conduction. The combined conductive and convective heat flow across the boundary layer is described by

$$H_c = A \cdot h_c (\overline{T}_s - T_a) \ [W] \qquad (7)$$

where $\overline{T}_s$ is the mean skin temperature, T_a is the environmental air temperature outside the boundary layer, h_c is the convective heat transfer coefficient, and A is the surface area; h_c varies with wind velocity.

3.2.2. Heat Loss by Radiation

Heat loss by radiation is given by the Stefan–Boltzmann equation:

$$H_r = \sigma \cdot \varepsilon_s \cdot (\overline{T}_s{}^4 - T_r{}^4) \cdot A \ [W] \qquad (8)$$

where σ is the Stefan–Boltzmann constant, $\overline{T}_s$ is the mean body surface temperature, T_r is the mean radiant temperature of the surrounding walls (not of the air), and ε is the emissivity (i.e., the ratio of the emission of a perfect black body and the emission of the surface under consideration, with the surface temperature being equal in both cases); the subscript s refers to the emissivity of the body surface of the subject. ε_s, also called *emittance*, comes very close to 1, i.e., to the emissivity of a perfect black body; the emissivity of the surrounding walls, ε_r, may become smaller than 1, e.g., in the case of highly polished metal walls. This does not appreciably influence radiative heat loss if the wall area is considerably larger than the body surface area. However, if A_r (area of the surrounding walls) approximates A_b (area of the body surface), as is the case when a baby is enclosed in a small incubator, the following equation[74,100] must be employed:

$$H_r = A_b \left[\frac{1}{\varepsilon_s} + \frac{A_b}{A_r} \left(\frac{1}{\varepsilon_r} - 1 \right) \right]^{-1} \cdot \sigma \cdot (\overline{T}_s{}^4 - T_r{}^4) \ [W]$$
$$(9)$$

As can be seen from equations (8) and (9), heat loss will increase considerably if the mean radiant temperature decreases, which may occur without any change in air temperature. Such conditions

have frequently been encountered when simple incubators were used. In these incubators, the air temperature can be kept fairly constant, but the wall temperature depends on the room temperature. As shown by Hey and Mount,[109] the wall temperature of an incubator may be 7°C lower than the air temperature inside the incubator, if, for example, the latter is adjusted to 34°C and the room temperature averages 17°C. This difference may increase the overall heat loss of the newborn by as much as 25% in comparison with experimental conditions with equal air and wall temperatures.[2,109] Such uncontrolled radiant heat loss can be avoided by placing suitable thin baffles (opaque to long-wave black-body radiation) inside the incubator between the infant and the incubator walls.[109]

Considerable heat stress may be imposed on the infant by the so-called "greenhouse effect" in incubators that are exposed to direct sunlight. The short-wave infrared radiation of the sun passes the Plexiglas incubator walls and is absorbed by the infant and the mattress, while the long-wave radiation emitted from the child is absorbed by the walls, thereby increasing wall temperature $[(T_r$ in equations (8) and (9)] and air temperature. A dangerous hyperthermia of the child may result. To measure mean radiant temperature in restricted surroundings, a small globe thermometer may be used, as described by Hey.[100]

3.2.3. Evaporative Heat Loss

In adult man under conditions of thermal neutrality, about 20–25% of the total heat loss is due to evaporation from the skin and respiratory tract (insensible water loss). Similar values have been found in 2- to 10-day-old human neonates when they were exposed to neutral temperature and a RH of 50%.[106,201] About 10% of the insensible water loss can be accounted for by respiratory water loss.[199]

The driving force for evaporation is the difference between the vapor pressure on the body surface and the vapor pressure in the environment. Evaporative heat flow from the skin is described by

$$H_e = h_e \ (\overline{P}_s - P_a) \cdot A \ [W] \qquad (10)$$

where H_e is the rate of evaporative heat loss, $\overline{P}_s$ is the mean vapor pressure at the skin, P_a is the vapor pressure in the air, A is the body surface area, and h_e is the evaporative heat transfer coefficient, which depends on the curvature radius of the skin surface (as in the case of heat flow by conduction and convection), barometric pressure, and wind velocity.

The influence of RH on heat loss at neutral temperature has been studied in full-term human neonates. It increased from 0.24 W/kg to 0.54 W/kg when the RH was decreased from 80 to 20%. The MR was found to be at a minimum at 50% RH under these temperature conditions.[201]

Evaporative heat loss can be increased considerably by sweat secretion and by increasing respiratory rate. In a hot environment, evaporative heat loss may represent the only, but very effective, avenue of heat loss. Evaporation of 1 liter of sweat dissipates about 2430 kJ (580 kcal) from the body.

3.2.4. Heat Exchange and Thermal Demand in Relation to Body Size

At a given ambient and body temperature, heat loss per unit of body mass is inversely related to body size; the reason is that the (1) body surface body mass quotient A/W (Fig. 20), (2) absolute thickness of the heat insulating body shell, and (3) radii of curvature of the body are functions of the body size. Factors (2) and (3) account for the size-dependent alteration of overall insulation, I_{a+t}, as shown in Fig. 19. Thus, to maintain the same difference between body core temperature, T_{re}, and

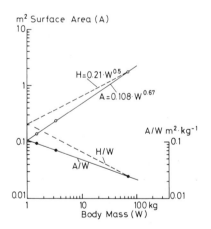

Fig. 20. Body surface area (A) as a function of body mass (W) and the body surface/mass quotient (A/W) as a function of body mass. (- - -) Curve derived by equation $(H = 0.21 \cdot W^{0.5})$ that predicts the heat production (in arbitrary units) required to maintain a constant difference between body core and environment for body masses in the range 1–70 kg, based on the size-dependent total maximum heat insulation according to Fig. 19.

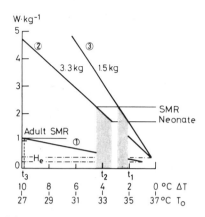

Fig. 21. Schematic representation (based on data given by Figs. 19 and 20) of heat production per unit body mass required to maintain the temperature differences ΔT between body core (= 37°C) and environment (T_0 = operative temperature; see the text) in the adult (1) and in a 3.3-kg (2) and a 1.5-kg (3) infant (with maximum vasoconstriction). With the actual SMR given, the temperature differences t_1, t_2, and t_3 can be maintained under conditions of thermal neutrality; conversely, the neonates require an environmental temperature of about 33°C (2) or even 34–35°C (1) to maintain a deep-body temperature of 37°C, while in the adult, this figure is much lower, 27°C (t_3). (H_e) Minimum evaporative heat loss. For the intercept of zero nonevaporative heat loss with the T_0 scale, see Hey and Katz.[107]

operative ambient temperature, T_o, the small individual would have to produce more heat per unit of body mass, and the increment of MR with decreasing ambient temperature would have to be larger. As shown by Fig. 20, the surface area per body mass unit, A/W, is about 2.7 times and 4 times greater in the full-sized and 1-kg neonate, respectively, than in the adult. Accordingly, the neonate's heat production per unit body mass would have to be increased by at least these factors to compensate for the greater heat loss. Considering the different values of maximum overall heat insulation, I_{a+t} (Fig. 19), however, these factors must be correspondingly increased. As shown by Fig. 21, the slope of the heat-exchange curves as based on experimental data (taken from Fig. 19) is about 4.5 and 7 times greater in the 3.3- and 1.5-kg neonate, respectively, than in the adult. The equation

$$H = 0.21 \cdot W^{0.5} \text{ [arbitrary units]} \qquad (11)$$

approximately predicts (see also Fig. 20) the heat production that would be required to yield a given temperature difference between body core and air in the body mass range of 1–70 kg. In view of the so-called "surface rule of metabolic rate" as well as the empirical Kleiber equation (see Fig. 1), it should be emphasized that the exponent of equation (11) is much smaller than 0.67 and 0.75, respectively, and that the postnatal development of the SMR follows this equation except for the first few months of life (see Fig. 1). In this early period of life, the SMR is by no means sufficient to compensate for the increased heat loss; thus, the temperature differences that can be maintained with the SMR are considerably smaller in the neonate than in the adult (compare t_1 and t_2 with t_3 in Fig. 21).

Furthermore, it is a disadvantage for the newborn that heat content in relation to surface area is smaller than in the adult. Consequently, in the newborn, a short-term change in environmental temperature must result in a much greater deviation from normal body temperature than in the adult. In neonates, therefore, even small and short-term changes in the thermal environment will become significant; i.e., the thermal demand of the environment on the heat-producing metabolism is much greater in the neonate than in the adult.

The thermal demand of an environment cannot be characterized by only one single climatic value such as the temperature of the surrounding air. The given climatic condition must be specified by a number of data, such as air temperature, humidity, radiant temperature, and wind velocity, if one wants to describe precisely the thermal characteristics of an environment, i.e., to predict its thermal demand on the subject. To overcome these problems, some so-called "complex climatic measures" have been proposed, such as the *standard operative temperature*, the *effective temperature* (cf. Burton and Edholm[55] and Mount[161,162]), and the *humid operative temperature*.[168] In a strict sense, however, all such measures can be valid only for one and the same subject or, at most, for a group of subjects who are very similar in shape and size. We thus need special studies in the neonate for establishing such complex climatic measures.

3.3. Control of Heat Loss and Heat Dissipation

3.3.1. Skin Blood Flow

Thermal conductance varies with blood flow to the body surface. Control can therefore be exerted on heat loss by vasomotor reactions that change the blood flow to the body surface. In the past, it was assumed that the newborn infant was not able to change the blood flow to the body surface adequately. This assumption was based on the fact that the neonate's skin is rosy during early life. Skin color, however, is not necessarily a reliable indication of skin blood flow rate. In neonates and in adults, a combination of flushed and cool skin, as well as a combination of pale and warm skin, can be observed.[73] From such phenomena, it has been assumed that the heat transfer to the body surface is determined mainly by the blood flow through deeper blood vessels, which do not influence the color of the skin, whereas the small subpapillar capillaries that determine the color do not contribute much to the heat transfer.[71]

The first experimental studies on vasomotor control of heat loss were made in 1943 by Day et al.,[69] who determined thermal conductance (C in equation 2) in young premature infants. They found that thermal conductance varied with changing environmental temperature by a factor of 2–3. This variation was confirmed in a more recent extensive study by Hey et al.[110] The variation of the conductance in relation to birth weight as derived from the data of these authors is shown in Fig. 19 (compare I_t, the reciprocal value of C, in the cold and in the warmth). The variability of the overall insulation (I_{a+t}; see Section 3.2) resulting from

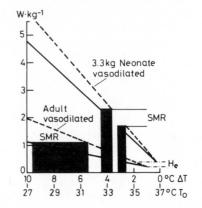

Fig. 22. Schematic representation (based on data given by Figs. 19 and 20) of the effect of vasomotor reactions on heat loss/body mass in a neonate and an adult (‐‐‐) Vasodilated; (——) vasconstricted. Note that the width of the temperature range (stippled fields) within which heat loss can be adjusted by means of vasomotor actions is much smaller in the neonate than in the adult (H_e) Minimum evaporative heat loss.

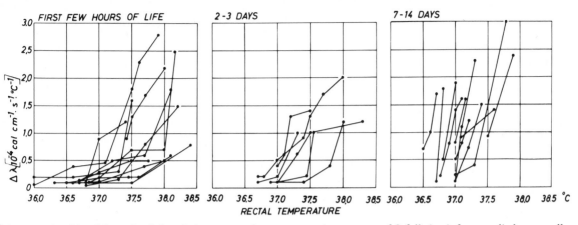

Fig. 23. Skin blood flow (heel) in relation to rectal temperature in a group of 9 full-size infants studied repeatedly during the first few weeks of life. The infants were warmed in a heatable crib to increase rectal temperature. Note the delayed vasodilatation in the first few days of life. Reproduced from Brück.[32]

blood flow changes is shown by the change of slope of the heat-flow curves in Fig. 22. While the change in insulation enables the adult to increase the temperature difference that can be maintained at a given MR by a factor of 2, the increase in this difference due to vasoconstriction is no more than 30% in the neonate.

The so-called "heated thermocouple technique"[85] allows estimation of skin blood flow [expressed in units of heat conductivity: cal (sec · cm · °C)$^{-1}$] in any small area of the body surface. With the use of this method, it has been shown that external temperature changes produce marked cutaneous vasomotor reactions in various areas of the body surface, such as the thigh, the lower leg, the abdominal wall, the palm, and the heel.[32,49] At temperatures below the TNZ, marked vasoconstriction can be demonstrated in all these regions even during the first hours of life. Skin

blood flow increases with increasing environmental temperature (Fig. 23). Only during the first few days of life is a vasoconstriction sustained, particularly in the appendages (heel), even in neutral environmental conditions. Vasodilatation takes place, however, in infants exposed to an environment that is warm enough to increase the deep-body temperature. Vasodilatation occurs in the youngest babies with body temperatures above 37.5°C, whereas in older infants, full vasodilatation is found in the temperature range between 36.5 and 37.5°C. The initially delayed vasodilatation indicates an increased sympathetic tonus, which has been ascribed to birth stress, because delayed vasodilatation was found to be particularly pronounced in infants who had suffered from laborious delivery.[32,51,57,212]

Using the thermal circulation index,[55] Hey and Katz[107] related blood flow for the whole body in naked babies to environmental temperature (Fig. 24).

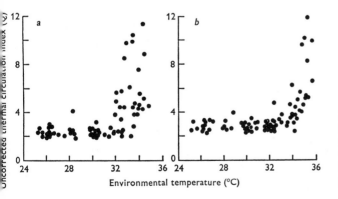

Fig. 24. Peripheral blood flow (expressed as the thermal circulation index[55] related to environmental temperature in (a) 14 infants, 2–4 kg birth weight, 2–14 days old; (b) 12 infants, 1–2 kg birth weight, 2–14 days old. Reproduced from Hey and Katz.[107]

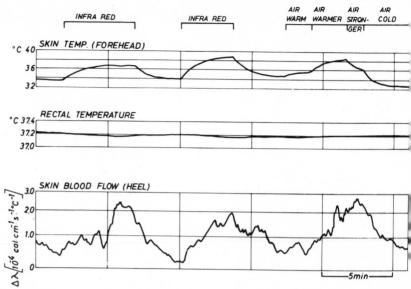

Fig. 25. Vascular reactions induced by thermal stimulation of the facial skin in a 15-hr-old full-size infant. For thermal stimulation, either an infrared lamp or a warm-air fan was used. Note the constancy of the rectal temperature. Only the surface temperature of the skin was altered by the stimulus, while deep-body temperature remained constant. Reproduced from Brück.[32]

As can be seen, peripheral blood flow is sharply reduced when the environmental temperature is decreased below 32–33°C (see also Fig. 32).

Effects of Local Thermal Stimulation. As in adults, vasoreactions can also be produced in full-size and premature infants merely by local cooling or warming of the face using infrared radiation or a cold or warm air flow. A deep-body temperature of 36.5–37.5°C is necessary for obtaining such reflex reactions, as illustrated by Fig. 25. In cases with delayed vasodilatation, such reflex vasoreactions may be difficult or impossible to demonstrate.

Rhythmic fluctuations in blood flow (Traube–Hering–Mayer waves), which have been described in adults, can be observed in neonates as early as in the first hour of life (Fig. 25).

3.3.2. Sweat Secretion and Respiratory Evaporative Heat Loss

At an environmental temperature above the upper limit of the thermal neutral range (t_4 in Fig. 5), thermal equilibrium can be obtained only by increasing evaporative heat dissipation. A regulatory metabolic decrease that is conceivable as a measure of heat defense has been repeatedly assumed, but there is no experimental evidence for it.

In the adult, the increase in evaporative heat loss is due mainly to sweat secretion, not to an increase in respiratory rate, as is the case in many non-sweating species. In the neonate, the respiratory rate may increase sharply, some minutes before the onset of sweating, from 43 (mean resting level) to 50–80/min.[201] In comparison with other species, however, the most effective heat-dissipation mechanism is sweat secretion in the human neonate as well as in the adult. Figure 26 demonstrates the increasing evaporative heat loss that is due to sweat secretion. Maximum sweat secretion is slightly different in full-term (mean body mass 3.4 kg) and in small-for-date (2.5-kg) and slightly premature (2.4-kg) infants.[200] There is a considerable difference in the

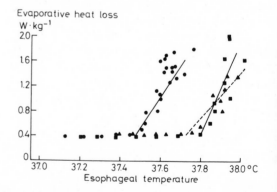

Fig. 26. Evaporative heat loss in relation to esophageal temperature in 22 full-term (●), 9 small-for-date (■), and 8 premature (▲) infants. Note the equal maximum response but increased threshold in the small-size infants. Reproduced from Sulyok *et al.*[200]

hreshold esophageal temperature for the onset of sweating in the smaller and larger infant groups. Fig. 26). These results agree well with the previous studies by Hey and Katz.[106] In addition, these authors showed that the threshold body temperature for sweating in premature infants decreased in the first few postnatal days. No sweating to thermal stimuli could be detected in infants of less than 210 days' postconceptional age, even when the rectal temperature rose as high as 37.8°C. In such infants, the sweat glands did not even respond to intradermal injection of acetylcholine. It is thus assumed that the failing sweating response is due mainly to an immaturity of the sweat glands.[77]

In comparison with the adult, the maximum sweating response is small in the neonate. Thus, in the (non-heat-acclimatized) adult, the maximum evaporative heat loss may amount to 200–300 watt/m², whereas this figure is only about 25 watt/m² in the neonate (recalculated from the data by Hey and Katz[106] and Sulyok et al.[200]). In other words, in the neonate, the maximum evaporative heat loss is in the range of the SMR, whereas in the adult, it is 5 times the SMR (compare Fig. 26 with Fig. 2, in which W/kg is used to express evaporative heat loss and SMR, respectively).

It is interesting in this context that the number of active sweat glands per square centimeter of thigh skin was found to be 6 times greater in the neonate than in the adult. The mean peak sweat rate to chemical stimulation was, however, 3 times lower in the neonate that in the adult.[77]

By contrast, in the newborn calf, the maximum evaporative heat loss from the skin was found to be larger than in 1-year-old animals, and it was concluded that the newborn calves were more heat-tolerant than the 1-year-old calves due to their greater sweating capacity.[23,24] According to the data reported above, the human neonate must be considered to be markedly less heat-resistant than the adult.

4. Regulation of Body Temperature

4.1. Principles of Physiologic Temperature Regulation

In the homeothermic organism, heat production, skin blood flow, sweating, and respiration are balanced in such a way that the body temperature remains constant despite changing environmental temperatures. This balance is achieved by a number of mechanisms which constitute the thermoregulatory system. As shown in the preceding sections, the human newborn infant responds qualitatively like the adult to a changing environment by varying its heat production, skin blood flow, and sweat secretion. It remains to be shown whether these reactions fulfill the criteria of a complete thermoregulatory system.

Some theoretical considerations are needed for this purpose. The first consideration of physiologic temperature regulation may be: Which temperature is regulated? Or, in terms of control engineering, what is the controlled variable in this regulatory system? These questions cannot be readily answered because of the complicated temperature field within the body, which varies with alterations in environmental conditions. Until recently, a circumscribed temperature within the body core was thought to be the controlled variable. The hypothalamic temperature appeared to be the best representation of this controlled variable; the deep rectal, esophageal, sublingual, and tympanic[21] temperatures were taken to be more or less good approximations to the controlled variable.

On the basis of more recent studies, a new concept of temperature regulation has been developed, and this concept is represented by Fig. 27. The central controller receives temperature information from more than one site of the body, and it has thus been characterized as a "multiple input sys-

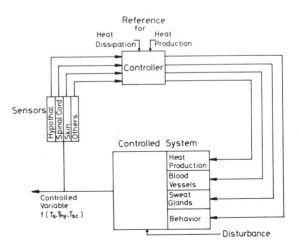

Fig. 27. Diagram representing the concept of temperature regulation in man.

tem"[31,47,198] (references in Hensel *et al.*[98]) in which the controlled variable is a function of several local temperatures, rather than the temperature of a representative area within the body core. In addition to the cutaneous thermal receptors and the well-known thermal receptors of the preoptic area of the hypothalamus,[96,166] thermosensors that affect the final control elements have been demonstrated in the spinal cord[47,210] (references in Hensel *et al.*[98] and Simon[191]) and in the abdominal cavity (references in Simon[191]). Further, there is evidence that thermal receptors may be located in the mucosa of the respiratory ways.[61,179]

In the system described, the activity of cutaneous cold receptors is the main driving force for eliciting and sustaining extra heat production as well as vasoconstriction; these reactions are counteracted by the activity of internal warm receptors, which, in turn, are the driving forces for stimulating the heat-dissipation mechanisms (sweat secretion, vasodilation); conversely, the latter responses are inhibited by cutaneous cold receptors.

Since the system proposed tends to maintain an approximately constant average body temperature, rather than a constant temperature of a limited area of the body core, the "set-point temperature" would have to be stated in terms of an average body temperature, not as a single local temperature. One would then characterize the normal temperature level at which the thermoregulatory system is supposed to operate by the threshold temperatures (T_{th}) for extra heat production, vasoconstriction/vasodilatation, and sweat secretion/heat polypnea. The "set-point" temperature would then be that

body core temperature, or any integrated body temperature (which must be conventionally defined) that is maintained while the output signals of the controller are zero, i.e., the temperature that is maintained without activating the thermoregulatory effector system. Deviations from this temperature state above or below the respective thresholds would actuate one or more appropriate effector systems which in turn would tend to restore the temperature field at which the outputs of the controller become zero or attain values as close as possible to zero. Thus, temperature control is based on a closed-loop or a negative-feedback system.

4.2. Activity of the Effector Systems in Relation to Body Surface and Core Temperature

4.2.1. Control of Shivering and Nonshivering Thermogenesis

As shown by studies in the newborn guinea pig, NST may be described quantitatively by relating it to the temperature of two populations of thermosensors, the cutaneous and the hypothalamic thermosensors, as shown by

$$\text{NST} = k \, (\overline{T}_{\text{hy, o}} - T_{\text{hy}}) \cdot (\overline{T}_{\text{s, o}} - \overline{T}_{\text{s}}) - a \quad (12)$$

where T_{hy} and $\overline{T}_{\text{s}}$ are the hypothalamic temperature and the subcutaneous temperature in the back respectively; $T_{\text{hy, o}}$ and $\overline{T}_{\text{s, o}}$ are the respective "reference temperatures," which are represented by the two asymptotes in Fig. 28; and k and a are

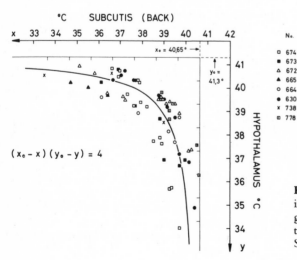

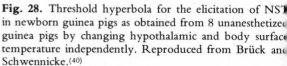

Fig. 28. Threshold hyperbola for the elicitation of NST in newborn guinea pigs as obtained from 8 unanesthetized guinea pigs by changing hypothalamic and body surface temperature independently. Reproduced from Brück and Schwennicke.[40]

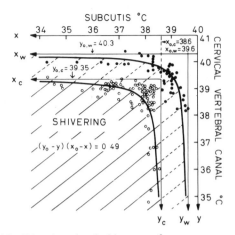

Fig. 29. Shivering threshold curves for two groups of guinea pigs (aged 4–8 weeks) reared at different environmental temperatures. The values were obtained by independent changes of the body-surface temperature and the temperature in the cervical vertebral canal. This diagram shows, for instance, that at a certain body-surface temperature, which corresponds to a subcutaneous temperature of 37°C, shivering begins in warm-adapted animals (●) if the hypothalamic temperature drops below 40°C. In the cold-adapted animals (○), however, shivering does not occur until the hypothalamic temperature has reached a value slightly below 39°C. Reproduced from Brück and Wünnenberg.[42]

constants. As can be derived from equation (12), the threshold curve for NST (NST = 0) follows a hyperbola, as shown by Fig. 28. Shivering can be described, in the guinea pig, by an equation analogous to equation (12) if hypothalamic temperature is replaced by the cervical spinal cord temperature[47]; thus, the shivering threshold curve also follows a hyperbola (Fig. 29).

The cervical spinal cord is the region that preferentially receives, via vascular connections (see Fig. 17), the heat that is generated in the interscapular brown adipose tissue as described in Section 2.4.2. In this manner, the two effector systems, NST and shivering, are interlocked. This interlocking readily explains observations such as that illustrated in Fig. 10: with external cooling, NST is initiated by the cooling of temperature sensors in the skin. This NST leads to an increase of the temperatures in the interscapular adipose tissue and in the cervical vertebral canal. The direction of the temperature gradient between the interscapular adipose tissue and the cervical vertebral canal indicates that heat flows from the adipose tissue to the spinal

cord. As a result of the spinal cord temperature being maintained at a high level, shivering remains suppressed throughout the experimental period. However, shivering starts as soon as the cervical spinal cord temperature begins to fall following the blocking of NST. Thus, under natural conditions, shivering would occur only after NST was evoked to its full extent. The neonate can therefore display shivering only under severe cold stress.

The interlocked control of the two heat-production mechanisms in the neonate is represented schematically in Fig. 30. A controller is thought to be localized in the posterior hypothalamus.[98,209,211] It receives information (E_s, E_{sc}, E_{hy}) on the temperature of at least three sites of the organism: the body surface ($\overline{T}_s$), the cervical spinal cord (T_{sc}), and the anterior hypothalamus (T_{hy}). It is assumed, as indicated in Fig. 30, that the impulse frequency is reciprocally related to the temperature in the cutaneous receptors, as one would expect from cutaneous cold receptors. For the internal receptors, a direct proportionality to the temperature could be demonstrated.

The input signals from the skin, E_s, activate the effector neurons, EF, whereas those from the internal receptors, E_{hy} and E_{sc}, activate the inhibitory interneurons, R, thus yielding the signals I_{hy} and I_{sc}, which act inhibitorily on the effector neurons, EF. The output signals (manipulated variables) y_{NST} and y_{SH} would then control the extent of nonshivering and shivering thermogenesis according to the following equations:

$$y_{NST} = f[E_s \cdot (1/I_{hy} - A)] \qquad (13)$$

$$y_{SH} = f[E_s \cdot (1/I_{sc} - A')] \qquad (14)$$

Thus, formally, a multiplication of the excitatory skin receptor signals, E_s, by the reciprocal values of the inhibitory signals I_{hy} and I_{sc} occurs in the controller. It follows that when I_{hy} and I_{sc} become larger, as is the case with high internal temperature, y_{NST} and y_{SH} approach zero (A and A' are values that are thought to be smaller than 1), even if the temperature of the body surface is low, and vice versa (for details, see Brück and Wünnenberg[47]).

The manipulated variables y_{SH} and y_{NST} may represent the impulse traffic in the motor nervous system that passes through the shivering tracts[97] and the spinal motor neurons (in the case of y_{SH}), and in the sympathetic nervous system (in the case of y_{NST}), respectively.

The relevance of this concept for the newborn

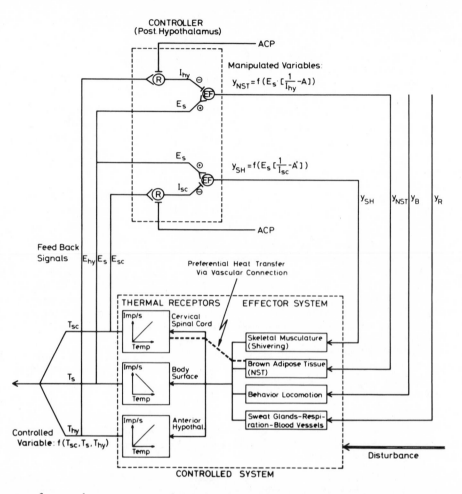

Fig. 30. Diagram of neonatal temperature regulation, based on studies in the guinea pig. In particular, the interlocked control of shivering and nonshivering thermogenesis, as well as the special feedback mechanism through preferential vascular heat transfer from the interscapular adipose tissue to the spinal cord receptor area, are shown. The central integrative mechanisms for heat dissipation and behavioral control (see y_B and y_R) have not yet been worked out in the neonate. The symbols + and −, as well as —< and —⊣, indicate facilitation and inhibition, respectively. (T) Temperature; (Imp) impulse frequency in nerves; (E) facilitatory or excitatory impulses; (I) inhibitory impulses; subscripts: (R) interneurons the spontaneous activity of which is thought to influence the reference signal (see Fig. 27), (EF) effector neuron, (ACP) ascending catecholaminergic pathway influencing the level of reference signals.

infant and for other species remains to be discussed. To a large extent, the concept is based on experimental results obtained from the guinea pig. One may question whether shivering is as little influenced by hypothalamic thermal receptors in species other than guinea pigs, since in the adult dog, cat, goat, and others[29] (references in Hensel et al.[98]), the hypothalamic temperature has been shown to be closely related to the control of shivering, and since the hypothalamic thermosensitive structures were until recently the only ones known to exist in the body core. The concept changed after it was shown that in the adult dog, thermosensitive structures exist in the spinal cord (references in Simon[191]), in addition to the previously known hypothalamic thermal receptors. Both groups of receptors influence shivering in the dog.

On the basis of these findings, we present the following hypothesis: Subjects that exhibit NST to a great extent use one group of internal receptors, the hypothalamic receptors, for separate control of NST, while those species that possess only the shivering mechanism use the two groups of internal receptors jointly for the control of shivering. We assume, consequently, that the function of the hypothalamic thermal receptors changes during postnatal development in species that possess considerable NST only during the neonatal period. Man seems to belong to this group.[54]

Nevertheless, the model shown in Fig. 30 can be adequately applied to certain observations in the human newborn:

1. The rectal temperature of a newly born infant drops during delivery. Due to the great heat loss from the wet body surface or to air draft, it may decrease to 35°C. This condition evokes maximum cold defense reactions; i.e., O_2 uptake increases and vasoconstriction takes place. Soon after the infant is transferred into a heated crib, his O_2 uptake diminishes to the minimum, although it may take the colon temperature several hours to reach 36–37°C. This termination of the cold defense reaction is anticipated from our model, since E_s approaches zero with increasing skin temperature.

2. External cooling induces heat production before the body-core temperature begins to drop (see Fig. 32). It has even been observed that O_2 uptake can be increased by merely cooling the facial skin.[151,179]

3. Shivering in neonates who exhibit NST does not occur before NST has been induced to its full extent (see Fig. 10).

4.2.2. Control of Skin Blood Flow

On the basis of the concept discussed above, we are able to interpret neonatal skin blood flow changes as well as cold-induced heat production. It was demonstrated that skin blood flow changes can be stimulated at various remote body sites. This response depends, however, on the deep-body temperature. Thus, we can conclude that in the neonate (as well as in the adult[59,206]), skin blood flow is determined by both the temperature of the body surface and the temperature of an internal region that contains thermoreceptive structures, i.e., either the hypothalamus or the cervical spinal cord, or both.

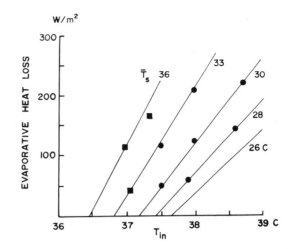

Fig. 31. Evaporative heat loss in relation to esophageal temperature (T_{in}) and mean skin temperature ($\overline{T}_s$) in the human adult as a comparison of threshold temperatures and maximum sweat rate of the neonate (see Fig. 26 and the text) and the adult. Reproduced from Nadel et al.[165]

4.2.3. Control of Sweat Secretion

In the adult, both mean skin and core temperature contribute, additively, to the central drive for sweat gland activity; moreover, the sweat gland activity is dependent on the local temperature, and this effect is probably due to an effect of temperature on the neuroglandular junction between the terminals of the cholinergic sympathetic nerve fibers and the sweat glands.[165,172] The dependence of sweat rate on surface and core temperature, as found in the adult, can be seen in Fig. 31. The sweat secretion rate in the neonate remains to be studied in this way. It may be inferred from the studies carried out so far,[32,106,200] however, that the sweat rate must be described as a function of the integrated body temperature in the neonate as well as in the adult.

4.2.4. Behavioral Measures and Temperature Regulation

Besides the autonomic control actions such as extra heat production, vasomotion, and sweat secretion, behavioral measures must not be neglected in considering the constancy of body temperature.[90] In adults, particularly in man, behavioral measures play a perhaps more important part in temperature constancy than the autonomic reactions, and they are the only means of remaining in thermal comfort.

Civilized man is rarely seen to shiver; he would rather raise the set point of his air conditioner, or lower it before he begins to sweat. Animal neonates with a well-developed motor system make considerable use of behavioral measures; e.g., piglets reduce heat loss by huddling together.[163] Since human neonates are born singly and with poorly developed motor abilities, they cannot make much use of behavioral measures. All they can do is cry, thereby inducing indirect behavioral regulation through the parent.

4.3. Circadian Rhythms of Body Temperature and Other Rhythmic Changes

It is commonly known that the deep-body temperature shows regular daily fluctuations of about 1°C.[98] These circadian rhythms have not been observed in the neonate,[95] but cyclic changes in physical activity of shorter duration do exist. These periods of activity do not necessarily interrupt sleep; they are accompanied by changes in O_2 uptake, respiratory rate, and rectal temperature.[174] The cyclic increase in O_2 uptake that occurs concomitantly with physical activity increases with age. These cyclic changes may interfere with the determination of the SMR (cf. Section 2.2.1).

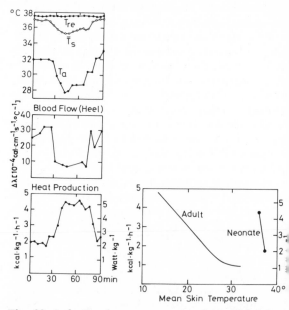

Fig. 32. Left: Simultaneous response of skin blood flow (heel) and heat production to a slight drop in mean skin temperature ($\overline{T}_s$) evoked by a decrease in ambient temperature (T_a) from 32 to 28°C. Study in a 7-day-old infant, 3290 g. Right: Relationship between $\overline{T}_s$ and heat production in adults and newborn infants. Data from Adolph and Molnar[7] for adults and Brück[32] for neonates.

5. Ontogenetic and Adaptive Alterations in the Thermoregulatory System

5.1. Temperature Regulation and Body Size

If we were to design a thermoregulatory system for the neonate that follows our knowledge of the adult system, we would have to make some changes for adjusting it to the neonate's smaller body size.[33]

The mean skin temperature in the small neonate is higher than that in the adult at any environmental temperature that allows steady-state heat flow. We have already shown that this difference is due to the high thermal conductance of the body shell in small subjects (see Section 3.1 and Fig. 19). Thus, in the newborn, we must adjust the temperature characteristics of the cutaneous thermal receptors in such a manner that changes in the skin temperature, at various environmental temperatures, evoke the full

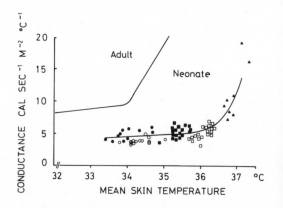

Fig. 33. Thermal conductance (peripheral blood flow) related to mean skin temperature, $\overline{T}_s$, in neonates[184] and in adults.[90] The neonates were studied at the following ambient temperatures: (●) 28°C; (○) 30°C; (■) 32°C; (□) 34°C; (▲) 36°C. Note that vasoconstriction/vasodilatation occurs at a much higher mean skin temperature in neonates than in adults.

response of the respective effector systems at an elevated skin-temperature level. Such altered characteristics can indeed be recognized in Figs. 32 and 33. Extra heat production and maximum vasoconstriction are elicited and maintained in the newborn at a much higher skin temperature than in the adult. Moreover, the increment of O_2 uptake in relation to average skin temperature is larger in the neonate than in the adult; this difference corresponds to the higher increment of heat loss related to environmental temperature (see Fig. 21).

This increased relative weight of the cutaneous thermal input in neonates might be explained in two ways: (1) Due to the increased body surface/mass quotient, the number of cutaneous cold receptors per unit body mass is increased (assuming that the density of the distribution of cold receptors is the same in adults and neonates). (2) The central processing of thermal input signals (see Fig. 30) is different in the neonate from that in the adult (see Section 4.2.1).

In any case, the increased cutaneous sensitivity is a prerequisite for enabling the newborn infant to maintain its body temperature—within a limited range of environmental temperature—at the same level with the same accuracy as does the adult.

5.1.1. Tolerated Ambient Temperature Range

This term, which is used synonymously with "control range," refers to the range of environmental temperatures at which the body temperature can be kept constant by means of regulatory processes[30] over a defined period of time (say 1 hr). If the neonate were to have the same range of tolerated ambient temperature as its parent, its maximum heat production would have to lie well above that exponential curve, $\dot{V}_{O_2,s}$ (see Fig. 6), that represents the parental summit metabolism; in the case of man, it would have to conform approximately to the exponential curve, $\dot{V}_{O_2,I}$. Except for the lamb, the maximum MR of which exceeds slightly the $\dot{V}_{O_2,s}$ curve,[11] the maximum metabolism in all other neonates, including man, is far out of this required range. Thus, generally, the lower limit of tolerated ambient temperature range will be found at higher temperature values in the neonate than in the adult. In the human full-term neonate, this lower limit is about 23°C (see Section 2.3.2). Since it seems that the maximum MR per unit body mass can be increased only to a very limited degree within one species, the lower limit

of the range of tolerated ambient temperature will be closer to the adult values for neonates that are large in proportion to their parents than for those of smaller birth size. The body mass ratios between adults and neonates vary considerably from species to species. In the guinea pig, this ratio may be as low as 1:7 to 1:10, while it is 1:20 in the human full-size, and only 1:70 in the very small premature infant.

NST as an additional mechanism of thermoregulatory heat production is an important means of adjusting the neonate's metabolic capacity more or less completely to the requirements of the smaller body size. The newborn guinea pig is unique in combining the advantages of being relatively large and having a well-developed coat of fur and a high capacity for NST. These three factors result in a lower limit of its tolerated ambient temperature, approaching that of the adult.[41]

5.1.2. Threshold Temperature for Extra Heat Production in Small and Young Premature Infants

In small premature infants, in particular during the first few days of life, the SMR per unit body mass is no greater than in full-term neonates[32,39,101,103] (see Fig. 7). Consequently, small prematures would have to produce extra heat at a higher environmental temperature (see Fig. 21) to maintain a core temperature of 37°C. Further, this requirement would mean that the cutaneous sensitivity must be increased even more than in the full-size infant (see Section 5.1) to yield the required thermal input for the controlling system (see Fig. 30). Actually, this is not, or not generally, the case. As shown by Fig. 34, thermoregulatory heat production may not occur before the rectal temperature falls below 34.5°C during the first few hours of life, while on the second day, this threshold temperature is 36°C. According to equation (12), both skin and core temperature are determinants for the onset of nonshivering and shivering heat production, but since the studies demonstrated in Fig. 34 were made under steady-state conditions, it can be inferred that skin temperature was below rectal temperature in both cases. Similar observations were made in a study in which a group of small (below 1500 g) and young premature infants was compared with older and larger ones. In the small group, minimum O_2 uptake was compatible with rectal temperatures in the range of 35–36°C.[52]

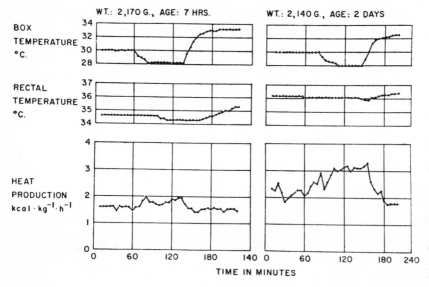

Fig. 34. Thermoregulatory increase of MR in relation to ambient and deep body temperature in a premature infant on the first and second days of life. Note that on the first day, the threshold for the elicitation of the metabolic reaction is decreased; thus, deep-body temperature can be maintained below 35°C without evoking a metabolic reaction. Reproduced from Brück and Brück.[39]

As judged from the time spent in quiet sleep, these babies did not show signs of thermal discomfort; thus, one may state that the discomfort threshold was also shifted to a lower level of (integrated) body temperature. Moreover, a slight tendency to vasodilatation indicated that there was also a decreased threshold for vasomotor temperature control. By contrast, Hey[104] concludes from his studies with Katz[108] that the critical temperature (operative environmental temperature) is adjusted to body size and SMR in such a way that even small and young (low-SMR) infants tend to maintain a deep-body temperature of 37°C; i.e., the critical temperature would be higher the smaller and younger the infant is (cf. Fig. 9). As already mentioned, the critical temperature seems to be a variable that is subjected to many influences; thus, these different results are not necessarily at variance (see also Section 5.3.2).

5.1.3. Sweating Threshold

The sweating threshold appears to be shifted to a higher body-temperature level in small and young premature infants and to decrease with maturation and postnatal age.[106,200] In any case, no sweat gland activity was seen with rectal temperatures below 37.2°C. These findings are discussed in the context of thermoadaptive modifications in the thermoregulatory system (Section 5.3) that have been described as a widening of the interthreshold zone.[37,54]

5.2. Stage of Maturity of the Thermoregulatory System at Birth

The newborn infant develops many functional systems.[6] Temperature regulation is frequently referred to as being "not fully developed" at the time of birth. We should be very cautious, however, in asserting immaturity of the control centers, even though the neonate shows more fluctuations in body temperature than the adult. In regard to responses of the effector systems, which may be in part adjusted to the smaller body size (see Section 5.1), we have no indication for asserting general immaturity of the nervous or hormonal systems that are involved in the transfer and integration of temperature-control information. Even in the very small premature, we find metabolic and vasomotor control responses developed. Thus, instability of the body temperature seems to be due, to a large extent, to the discrepancy between the efficiency of the effector systems and body size; growth alone will slowly enlarge the control range. According to the criteria mentioned above, we may distinguish three groups of mammals with respect to the functional stage of temperature regulation immediately after birth.

The first group exhibits a thermoregulatory system more or less completely adjusted to the smaller body size. The body temperature is stable within a certain control range, this range being narrower, however, than in the adult. Members of this group are the full-term human neonate, the guinea pig,[41] the pig,[163] the miniature pig,[53] the lamb,[10–12] and larger mammals such as the calf.[23]

The second group has the following characteristics: Thermoregulatory responses can be evoked at birth, but the capacity and efficiency of the effector system are not sufficiently adjusted to the small body size, so that body temperature drops on exposure to environmental temperatures that are only slightly below thermal neutrality. In this group, we find, for example the low-birth-weight human newborn,[32,153] the kitten, the rabbit,[118] the puppy,[82] the rat,[204] and others.

In a third group, thermoregulatory responses are not evocable, and O_2 uptake does not increase with decreasing environmental temperatures, but follows the Van't Hoff–Arrhenius law. Thus, these animals, among which are the ground squirrel (*Citellus citellus*[83]), and the golden hamster,[115] behave like poikilothermic animals. This type is presumably restricted to the neonates of hibernators.

5.3. Thermal Adaptation and Postnatal Modifications in the Thermoregulatory System

The adult thermoregulatory system may be modified, through repeated or sustained exposure to cold or hot environmental conditions, so that the "range of tolerated ambient temperature" (see Section 5.1.1) is increased and the thermal discomfort evoked by thermal stressors is relieved.[4,5,37] As far as cold is concerned, the development of NST has been demonstrated to be an important adaptive modification in smaller organisms (see Section 2.4.1). As long as the neonatal temperature control system was looked on merely as a deficient system, it was thought that thermal adaptation, in addition to developmental processes, improved this system postnatally.

5.3.1. Loss of NST

Since the extent of NST is already at its maximum at birth, according to the studies in guinea pigs (see Fig. 12), there is no possibility of improving cold resistance by adaptive modifications in the metabolic system. On the contrary, we come to the following conclusion: Regarding the preponderance of NST, the newborn resembles a cold-adapted adult more than a warm-adapted one, although the intrauterine environment has protected the fetus from experiencing cold stimuli. On the other hand, we may conclude that cold adaptation in the adult organism (insofar as it produces brown adipose tissue and NST) is based partly on the reestablishment of a neonatal functional mechanism.

5.3.2. Cold-Adaptive Deviation of the Shivering Threshold

As shown in Fig. 29, in guinea pigs reared in the cold, the shivering threshold is shifted to a temperature level about 1°C lower than in controls reared at neutral temperature.[46,47,53] This shift enables these animals to make full use of NST before the less economical shivering mechanism is evoked. A similar shift in the shivering threshold can be produced in adult man by repeated short-term cold exposure.[48] Linked with the change in shivering threshold in man is a shift in the threshold temperature for the experience of thermal discomfort. Depending on the modalities of cold exposure (intermittent vs. permanent cold exposure), the shift of shivering threshold was accompanied in the guinea pig either by a corresponding shift in the threshold for heat dissipation or by no such change. In the former case, the controlled variable (an integrated body temperature; see Fig. 30) is maintained at a lower level, and this occurrence may be called, according to the present conventions, *set-point shift*. In the latter case, however, the "set point" remains unaffected. This type of adaptation may be called *tolerance adaptation*, since there is an increase in the deviations in body temperature that are tolerated before the actuation of the appropriate thermoregulatory effectors occurs. In other words, the precision in temperature regulation is reduced, but this reduction produces at the same time a gain in economy of temperature regulation.[37]

As for the underlying mechanism, it has been shown that a similar shift in the threshold for shivering and nonshivering thermogenesis can be brought about by microinjections of NA into a circumscribed area of the hypothalamus in which the interneurons designated R in Fig. 30 are presumed to lie.[214] Furthermore, the threshold could be changed in the opposite direction by microinjection of an α-receptor blocking agent,[215] and it could also be altered by electrical stimulation of an area in the lower brainstem in which an ascending catecholaminergic pathway originates (ACP in Fig. 30).[203] It is thus no longer difficult to conceive that alterations in threshold temperatures occur under nonpathologic conditions.

Now one may ask whether the deviations in the thresholds for the various effector systems as found in young and small premature infants (see Section 5.1.2) are due to adaptation or to an inherent peculiarity. The threshold change in the adult described above requires no more than 3–5 1-hr cold exposures within a few days. Thus, in a 2- or 3-day-old premature infant, a cold-induced threshold deviation may well have developed. The deviations found immediately after birth must be taken as inherent.

Since no downward shift in sweating threshold has been found, the small-size human neonate resembles (with respect to the position of thresholds for actuation of thermoregulatory effectors) the intermittently cold-exposed guinea pig in which a widening of the interthreshold zone (see above) has been demonstrated.

The biological significance of this phenomenon may be seen in the avoidance of an undue exploitation of energy reserves by the quick metabolic responses to cold loads, which can be eventually compensated for by heat obtained from the environment, such as sun radiation, by heat exchange with the mother, or from other external heat sources (see also Section 6.3).

6. Pathophysiology and Clinical Aspects

6.1. Hypothermia

Hypothermia occurs in the homeothermic organism when heat loss exceeds the maximum heat production. Due to the large body surface/volume ratio, cooling occurs much more quickly in the neonate than in the adult once the endogenous heat production has been overtaxed, and it occurs at ambient temperatures that are nearly comfortable for the adult, i.e., at temperatures below 25–23°C (cf. Section 5.1.1). The CNS control system for temperature regulation seems to be much more susceptible to various disturbances in the neonate than in the adult. In particular, birth trauma plays an important part in disturbing normal neonatal temperature regulation, thus leading to hypothermia.[39,153] Moreover, respiratory deficiency leading to hypoxia and hypercapnia may contribute

to a rapid development of hypothermia; it is known that the metabolic response in neonates is inhibited by a degree of hypoxia that does not affect the resting MR.[111] It was inferred from these and other experiments[25] that the extra heat production in the brown adipose tissue is especially susceptible to hypoxia. Heat production by shivering may go on in adult species, even with reduction of O_2 to 8% in the inspired air.

Hypercapnia has long been known to suppress the thermoregulatory metabolic reactions, and it has thus been used to induce artificial hypothermia.[13] Recently, it was shown that with increasing P_{CO} in the inspired air, the shivering threshold decreases.[185]

On the other hand, the neonate is generally thought to be less susceptible to the dangerous corollaries of hypothermia, such as cardiac arrest and respiratory trouble. Thus, according to Adolph,[3] cardiac activity ceases at a rectal temperature of 5–10°C in the kitten, but at 15–20°C in the adult cat. Newborn dogs could be revived after the body temperature had dropped to an average of 3°C, while in 2.5-month-old dogs, this critical temperature was found to be 11.5°C.[180] A shift in age-dependent cold tolerance could also be demonstrated in the cat and rat, whereas no difference was found between newborn and adult guinea pigs.[3,176] Since the guinea pig is born in a more mature stage than the rat, it was assumed that a relationship exists between cold tolerance and degree of maturity at birth. Accordingly, we must not expect an increased cold tolerance in the human neonate in comparison with that in the adult, because the human full-size neonate is relatively advanced in its developmental stage at the time of birth, particularly with regard to its thermoregulatory abilities. The premature infant is more likely to have such an increased cold tolerance. Knowledge of basic functional differences among species with respect to cold tolerance is lacking. An elucidation of this problem requires insight into pathophysiologic processes underlying cold death that are not yet fully revealed.[147,205]

Thermal Exhaustion—Cold Injury. Even a mild cold exposure that does not lead immediately to deep hypothermia may result in severe disturbance of the neonate if it is extended over a prolonged period of time. Neither the neonatal nor the adult control system is capable of coping with environmental conditions requiring sustained metabolic cold defense reactions. The disturbances observed in newborns after prolonged cold exposure have been described by Mann and Elliot[144] as "neonatal cold injury." The essential symptoms are (besides a fall of rectal temperature): edema of the extremities, rhinitis, apathy, refusal of food, and hypoglycemia. Another characteristic symptom is an erythema that may simulate skin with good circulation and mislead us into underestimating the dangerous situation. According to McCance and Widdowson,[146] the newborn pig is able to maintain its body temperature for 6–8 hr in an environmental temperature of 12°C. With continuation of this cold stress, the rectal temperature drops to 20°C within the following 12 hr. The phenomena observable at this time closely resemble those denoted as "cold injury" in the human neonate. Blood glucose is decreased to 15 mg/dl (controls, 93 mg/dl), and the glycogen content of cardiac and skeletal muscle, as well as that of the liver, is considerably reduced. These phenomena seem to be a direct result of the prolonged cold-induced increase of the energy metabolism. An increased nitrogen excretion and a reduction of the total fat content are indicative of an increased degradation of protein and utilization of fat. Furthermore, Na^+ is shifted into the intracellular, and K^+ into the extracellular, compartment.

Hey and Katz[105] described a temporary loss of thermogenesis in young premature infants that might have resulted from the depletion of fat stores available to the calorigenic brown adipose tissue. In this context, the classic studies by Silverman[189] must be mentioned. Before much was known about neonatal temperature regulation and "exhaustion of the regulatory system by sustained cold defense reactions," he found that the survival rate could be significantly increased by maintaining (naked) premature infants during a control period of 5 days at 31.6°C rather than at 28.9°C (the temperature figures have been converted from degrees Fahrenheit). Eventually, it was shown that even warmer environmental conditions further increase the survival rate in premature infants.[56,68] Even the drop in the environmental temperature during the relatively short period of delivery can cause significant functional effects.[81] Gandy et al.[81] observed that the increased energy expenditure in the usual thermal environment of the delivery room aggravates the metabolic acidosis of the newborn. Thus, the question of the optimum environmental temperature has received tremendous interest in neonatal care (see Section 6.3).

6.2. Hyperthermia

(a) Hyperthermia due to Disturbed Heat Balance.

Like the development of hypothermia, the development of hyperthermia in the neonate is favored by its large surface/volume ratio and by the lack of a capacity for heat storage due to the relatively high temperature of the body shell. In addition, there is the relatively small capacity for evaporative heat dissipation (cf. Section 3.3.2), which makes the neonate susceptible to hypothermia. In contrast to the tolerance to hypothermia, tolerance to high body temperature is scarcely greater in the neonate than in the adult.[8]

The neonate's respiratory system is particularly susceptible even to slight increases in deep-body temperature and to rapidly increasing environmental temperatures. Due to these environmental changes, even apneic spells are to be expected.[39,102,104,129,132]

(b) Fever.

It is well known that newborn infants may suffer severe infections, e.g., meningitis, enteritis, and sepsis, without an increased body temperature. Newborn lambs do not respond with fever to the injection of bacterial pyrogen or endogenous pyrogen (leukocyte pyrogen) within the first few days of life.[60] Newborn guinea pigs have been shown to react to bacterial pyrogen no sooner than after the fourth day of life.[26]

According to the current hypothesis[60,98] leukocyte pyrogen affects some thermointegrative neuronal mechanism within the anterior hypothalamus, thereby shifting the set point of the thermoregulatory system to a higher level. This action on the thermointegrative system seems to be mediated by release of prostaglandin E (PGE) and NA (see Section 5.3.2). The elevation of the temperature level is finally brought about by activation of the heat-conserving mechanism (vasomotor system) and the thermogenetic mechanisms (in the neonate; NST[27]).

Since neonates are able to activate these effector mechanisms in response to cold, the failure to respond to bacterial pyrogen (or to infectious diseases) cannot be ascribed to a defective thermoregulatory system. It may be due in part to an immunologic defect, the inability to form leukocyte pyrogen; since lamb leukocyte pyrogen does not evoke fever in the newborn (see above), however, there must be an additional interruption in the chain of events leading to the shift of set point. Current studies on the PGE–NA system in the brainstem may finally elucidate this problem.

As this chapter was being completed, new studies were reported which show that the newborn guinea pig *is* able to form endogenous pyrogen, and that it does respond with fever to leukocyte pyrogen when this pyrogen is administered at 10 times the standardized adult dose. The reported neonatal unresponsiveness to pyrogen may thus turn out to be a quantitative difference in the hypothalamic sensitivity to leukocyte pyrogen.[28]

6.3. The Optimum Thermal Environment

The investigation of the neonatal thermoregulatory system has provided a much safer basis for the evaluation of optimum thermal conditions for the neonate than was possible two decades ago. At that time, the newborn infant was thought of as a more or less poikilothermic being whose metabolic rate follows the bottom curve in Fig. 4. Consequently, environmental conditions resulting in low body temperatures appeared not only tolerable but even beneficial for the neonate, since a small O_2 demand would lessen the problems of oxygen supply due to any kind of respiratory insufficiency.

6.3.1. Thermal Neutrality As an Optimum Temperature Condition

On the basis of the concept of neonatal temperature regulation now available, the environment that must be considered optimum is, as a first approximation, an environment that requires the least thermoregulatory effort, i.e., an environment that corresponds to the thermoneutral zone as defined in Section 2.3.3. This concept was strongly supported by (1) a series of clinical studies[56,68,189] that showed empirically that survival rate increases as the environmental conditions approach the zone of thermal neutrality and by (2) the fact that in the (resting) adult, the zone of thermal neutrality is identical with the zone of "thermal comfort" (cf. Brück et al.[52]).

6.3.2. Thermal Comfort Zone

The condition of *thermal comfort* as defined for the adult is used synonymously with "optimum temperature."[75] During a given physical activity, thermal comfort is experienced in the adult when, under stationary temperature conditions, the values for skin temperature and sweat secretion are within narrow limits. Under resting (comfort) conditions, both the sweat rate and the thermoregulatory extra heat production are zero, whereas during physical activity, moderate sweat secretion is necessary for thermal comfort (environments so cold that sweat secretion is completely suppressed would be considered much too cool for physically active persons).[75]

Thus, with respect to resting conditions, the zone of thermal comfort is identical to the zone of thermal neutrality. With increasing physical activity, the zone of thermal comfort is shifted gradually to temperature levels below the neutral temperature range.

6.3.3. Clothing vs. Incubator

Thermoneutral conditions may be established in different ways; if one accepts the neutral temperature range as the optimum temperature range for resting neonates, the question arises whether one regimen may be preferable to another. High conductance, or poor thermal insulation, appears to be the most serious handicap of the newborn. The most reasonable and rational aid for establishing thermal stability for the neonate would be to improve its thermal insulation, thereby increasing the lower limit of the thermal neutral range. In earlier times, pediatricians wrapped the babies in swaddling clothes and covered them with eiderdown. This method was effective, but it interfered with continuous observation of the infant's behavior and with light therapy.[102,104] To solve this problem, the transparent incubator with its regulated microenvironment was developed. Two factors were changed by introducing the incubator: (1) the infant's face and respiratory tract were exposed to much higher temperatures than before, and (2) the surface of the rest of the body, formerly wrapped in swaddling clothes, was directly exposed to the surrounding air; thus, much smaller changes in air temperature than before became significant as far as heat loss was concerned [see Section 6.3.3(a) below].

It is commonly known that the adult prefers environmental temperatures that keep the head cooler than the trunk. Discomfort is experienced if the inspired air is too warm. There is also evidence that the autonomic centers must be stimulated continuously to be kept active. The output of the cutaneous thermal receptors in the face appears to play an important part in this respect (references in Brück et al.[51]). At present, there is no experimental evidence to show that these objections against conditions in which the face is exposed to warm air do not also apply to the care of premature infants.

(a) Overheating. According to the concept of thermal neutrality, the most serious problem in providing the optimum temperature for neonates is to be seen in the *narrow* zone of neutrality in neonates. As shown by Fig. 22, the ambient temperature range (T_0) at which deep-body temperature may be maintained at 37°C by means of vasomotor control alone (i.e., without thermoregulatory heat production and without sweating) becomes smaller and smaller with decreasing body size (a change that is reflected by the increased slopes of the heat-loss curves). In other words, the zone of thermoneutrality (the zone between t_3 and t_4 in Fig. 5) is small in the neonate in comparison with the adult. As a consequence, a slight increase in metabolic rate due to increased physical activity will evoke sweating and rapidly result in hyperthermia, since the capacity for sweat secretion is poor in neonates (in particular, in premature infants). In the example of Fig. 22, a 20% increase in metabolic rate would require the onset of sweating in the neonate, whereas in the adult, a metabolic rise of 100% could be compensated for by vasodilatation before there is a need for sweating. It is thus not surprising to see that small animals prefer an environment slightly below the zone of thermal neutrality,[175] apparently making an allowance for extra heat produced by intermittent physical activity.

The problem of overheating due to physical activity may menace the wrapped infant in the cot as well as the infant in the incubator. In the former condition, however, physical activity may be reduced by the restricting effect of the swaddles,[102] whereas in the latter, much smaller changes in the environment surrounding the infant will have a significant effect on deep-body temperature and the thermoregulatory effectors. This difference can be easily seen in Fig. 21: the steeper the slope of the heat-loss curves, the larger the percentage change in ΔT and thus in dry heat loss with the same absolute change in T_0. Thus, very high accuracy in incubator temperature control is required.

(b) Incubator Techniques. It is technically difficult to cope with the problem of temperature control by means of the air-conditioned incubator. A better answer to this problem is the incubator that provides a variable environmental (operative) temperature (T_0; see Section 3.2.1) by a radiating heat source, which is controlled by the neonate's skin temperature.[8,56]

6.3.4. Variable Threshold for Cold Defense Reactions

In Section 5.3.2, a thermoadaptive deviation in the threshold for the elicitation of thermoregulatory metabolic reactions was described, and it was shown that this deviation led to a "widening of the interthreshold zone." This widening would result in an enlargement of the zone of thermal neutrality. The finding that the threshold for the metabolic cold defense reaction is so low in some small and young premature infants as to yield the maintenance of a deep-body temperature between 35 and 36°C might thus no longer be looked on as an "abnormal" regulatory phenomenon,[103,104] but as a beneficial physiologic adjustment of the small infants. If they were kept at the lower end of the enlarged neutral zone, they would be less menaced by dangerous hyperthermia. In fact, some pediatricians[129,133,134] maintained premature infants under such conditions, and they reported no detrimental effects. Other observers, however, obtained quite different results.[56,68,189] According to these studies, keeping deep-body temperature above 36°C is the decisive factor in increasing survival chances. This finding has been strictly reemphasized on the basis of clinical experience.[102,104] These conflicting results and viewpoints might be due to differences in the thermoregulatory behavior of the premature infants studied, differences that depended on some external or internal, as yet undefined, factors. Further experimental and clinical studies may finally solve these puzzling discrepancies.

6.3.5. Uniform vs. Fluctuating Environment

Assuming all the technical prerequisites are fulfilled, could the zone of thermal neutrality then be considered the optimum environment for the neonate, at least as long as the neonate is physically inactive?[51,104] It could be argued, as has been argued in the case of the human adult comfort zone, that a uniform environment may have some as yet undefined negative effects that could be counteracted by providing a slightly fluctuating thermal environment.[34,104] This idea has not been supported, however, by more recent studies in the adult.[75]

6.3.6. Clinical Application

Considering the differences in SMR and in the threshold temperature for the thermoregulatory metabolic reactions, which are influenced by a number of factors in addition to postnatal age and size, it is difficult to predict exactly the temperature range that corresponds to thermal neutrality, to say nothing of the "optimum temperature," for the individual case. In regard to this subject, the evaluation of additional clinical criteria is required. For details, the reader is referred to the excellent reviews by Hey.[102–104]

7. References

1. ABRAMS, R., CATON, D., CLAPP, J., AND BARRON, D. H., 1970, Thermal and metabolic features of life *in utero, Clin. Obstet. Gynecol.* **13**:549–564.

2. ADAMSONS, K., JR., GANDY, G. M., AND JAMES, L. S., 1965, The influence of thermal factors upon oxygen consumption of the newborn human infant, *J. Pediatr.* **66**:495–508.

3. ADOLPH, E. F., 1951, Responses to hypothermia in several species of infant mammals, *Amer. J. Physiol.* **166**:75–91.

4. ADOLPH, E. F., 1956, General and specific characteristics of physiological adaptations, *Amer. J. Physiol.* **184**:18–28.

5. ADOLPH, E. F., 1964, Perspectives of adaptation: Some general properties, in: *Handbook of Physiology* (D. B. Dill, ed.), Sect. 4, pp. 27–35, American Physiological Society, Washington, D. C.

6. ADOLPH, E. F., 1968, *Origins of Physiological Regulations,* Academic Press, New York and London.

7. ADOLPH, E. F., AND MOLNAR, G. W., 1946, Exchanges of heat and tolerances to cold in men exposed to outdoor weather, *Amer. J. Physiol.* **146**:507–537.

8. AGATE, F. J., AND SILVERMAN, W. A., 1963, The control of body temperature in the small newborn infant by low energy infrared radiation, *Pediatrics* **31**:725–733.

9. AHERNE, W., AND HULL, D., 1964, The site of heat production in the newborn infant, *Proc. R. Soc. Med.* **57**:1172, 1173.

10. ALEXANDER, G., 1961, Temperature regulation in the newborn lamb. III. Effect of environmental temperature on metabolic rate, body temperatures and respiratory quotient, *Aust. J. Agric. Res.* **12**: 1152–1174.

11. ALEXANDER, G., 1962, Temperature regulation in the newborn lamb. V. Summit metabolism, *Aust. J. Agric. Res.* **13**(1):100–121.

12. ALEXANDER, G., 1975, Body temperature control in mammalian young, *Br. Med. Bull.* **31**:62–68.

13. ANDJUS, R. K., AND SMITH, A. U., 1955, Reanimation of adult rats from body temperatures between 0 and +2°C, *J. Physiol.* **128**:446–472.

14. ANDREWS, J. F., MERCER, J. B., RYAN, E. M., AND SZÉKELY, M., 1973, Metabolic changes in the lamb during the first 36 hr of life related to body weight and to environmental temperature, *J. Physiol.* **236**:35, 36.

15. ANDREWS, J. F., MERCER, J. B., RYAN, E. M., AND SZÉKELY, M., 1975, The post-natal increase in minimum metabolic rate in the lamb, in: *Depressed Metabolism and Cold Thermogenesis* (L. Janský, ed.), Charles University, Prague.

16. ASCHOFF, J., AND KRAMER, 1971, Temperature regulation, in: *Physiologie des Menschen,* Vol. 2 *Energiehaushalt und Temperaturregulation* (Gauer Kramer, and Jung, eds.), Urban and Schwarzenberg, Munich.

17. BARGMANN, W., VON HEHN, G., AND LINDNER, E. 1968, Über die Zellen des braunen Fettgewebes und ihre Innervation, *Z. Zellforsch.* **85**:601–613.

18. BEHMANN, F. W., AND BONTKE, E., 1958, Die Regelung der Wärmebildung bei künstlicher Hypothermie. I. Experimentelle Untersuchungen über den Einfluss der Narkosetiefe, *Pflügers Arch. ges. Physiol.* **266**:408–421.

19. BEHNKE, A. R., AND YAGLOU, C. P., 1951, Physiological responses of men to chilling in ice water and to slow and fast rewarming, *J. Appl. Physiol.* **3**:591–602.

20. BENEDICT, F. G., AND TALBOT, F. B., 1915, *The Physiology of the Newborn Infant: Character and Amount of the Catabolism,* Carnegie Institution of Washington Publication No. 233, Washington D.C.

21. BENZINGER, T. H., 1964, The thermal homeostasis of man, *Symp. Soc. Exp. Biol.* **18**:49–80.

22. BENZINGER, T. H., AND KITZING, C., 1963, Gradient layer calorimetry and human calorimetry, in: *Temperature—Its Measurement and Control in Science and Industry,* Vol. 3, Part 3, pp. 87–109, Reinhold Publishing Corp., New York.

23. BIANCA, W., 1970, Animal response to meteorological stress as a function of age, *Int. J. Biometeorol. Suppl.* **14**:119–131.

24. BIANCA, W., AND HALES, J. R. S., 1970, Sweating panting and body temperatures of newborn and one-year-old calves at high environmental temperatures, *Br. Vet. J.* **126**:45–52.

25. BLATTEIS, C. M., 1971, Shivering and nonshivering thermogenesis during hypoxia, in: *Proceedings of the International Symposium on Environmental Physiology Dublin, 1971,* pp. 151–160, Federation of American Societies for Experimental Biology.

26. BLATTEIS, C. M., 1975, Postnatal development of pyrogenic sensitivity in guinea pigs, *J. Appl. Physiol.* **39**:251–257.

27. BLATTEIS, C. M., 1976, Effect of propranolol on endotoxin-induced pyrogenesis in newborn and adult guinea pigs, *J. Appl. Physiol.* **40**:35–39.

28. BLATTEIS, C. M., 1976, A possible cause of the

pyrogenic insensitivity of neonates to endotoxin, *Fed. Proc. Fed. Amer. Soc. Exp. Biol.* **35**:(3):482, abstract of a paper presented at the 60th Physiological congress, Anaheim, California, April 11–16, 1976. (Full-length article: Comparison of endotoxin and leukocyte pyrogenicity in newborn guinea pigs, *J. Appl. Physiol.* **42**:355–361, 1977.)

9. BLIGH, J., 1973, *Temperature Regulation in Mammals and Other Vertebrates,* North-Holland Publishing Co., Amsterdam and London; American Elsevier Publishing Co., New York.

0. BLIGH, J., AND JOHNSON, K. G., 1973, Glossary of terms for thermal physiology, *J. Appl. Physiol.* **35**:941–961.

1. BROWN, A. C., AND BRENGELMANN, G. L., 1970, The temperature regulation control system, in: *Physiological and Behavioral Temperature Regulation* (J. D. Hardy, A. P. Gagge, and J. A. J. Stolwijk, eds.), Charles C. Thomas, Springfield, Illinois.

2. BRÜCK, K., 1961, Temperature regulation in the newborn infant, *Biol. Neonate* **3**:65–119.

3. BRÜCK, K., 1964, General aspects of temperature regulation of small subjects, in: *The Adaptation of the Newborn Infant to Extra-uterine Life* (J. H. P. Jonxis, H. D. A. Visser, and J. A. Troelstra, eds.), pp. 229–247, H. E. Stenfert Kroese, Leiden, South Holland.

4. BRÜCK, K., 1968, Which environmental temperature does the premature infant prefer?, *Pediatrics* **41**: 1027–1030.

5. BRÜCK, K., 1970, Non-shivering thermogenesis and brown adipose tissue in relation to age, and their integration in the thermoregulatory system, in: *Brown Adipose Tissue* (O. Lindberg, ed.), American Elsevier Publishing Co., New York.

6. BRÜCK, K., 1970, Heat production and temperature regulation, in: *Physiology of the Perinatal Period,* Vol. I (U. Stave, ed.), Appleton-Century-Crofts, New York.

7. BRÜCK, K., 1976, Cold adaptation in man, in: *Regulation of Depressed Metabolism and Thermogenesis* (L. Janský and X. J. Mussacchia, eds.), Charles C. Thomas, Springfield, Illinois.

8. BRÜCK, K., 1976, Temperature regulation and catecholamines, *Isr. J. Med. Sci.* **12**(9):924–933.

9. BRÜCK, K., AND BRÜCK, M., 1960, Der Energieumsatz hypothermer Frühgeborener, *Klin. Wochenschr.* **38**: 1125–1130.

0. BRÜCK, K., AND SCHWENNICKE, H. P., 1971, Interaction of superficial and hypothalamic thermosensitive structures in the control of nonshivering thermogenesis, *Int. J. Biometeorol.* **15**:156.

1. BRÜCK, K., AND WÜNNENBERG, B., 1965, Über die Modi der Thermogenese beim neugeborenen Warmblüter. Untersuchungen am Meerschweinchen, *Pflügers Arch. ges. Physiol.* **282**:362–375.

2. BRÜCK, K., AND WÜNNENBERG, B., 1965, Blockade der chemischen Thermogenese und Auslösung von Muskelzittern durch Adrenolytica und Ganglienblockade beim neugeborenen Meerschweinchen, *Pflügers Arch. ges. Physiol.* **282**:376–389.

43. BRÜCK, K., AND WÜNNENBERG, B., 1965, Untersuchungen über die Bedeutung des multiloculären Fettgewebes für die Thermogenese des neugeborenen Meerschweinchens, *Pflügers Arch. ges. Physiol.* **283**: 1–16.

44. BRÜCK, K., AND WÜNNENBERG, B., 1966, The influence of ambient temperature in the process of replacement of non-shivering by shivering thermogenesis during postnatal development, *Fed. Proc. Fed. Amer. Soc. Exp. Biol.* **25**:1332–1336.

45. BRÜCK, K., AND WÜNNENBERG, W., 1966, Beziehung zwischen Thermogeneses im "braunen" Fettgewebe, Temperatur im cervicalen Anteil des Vertebralkanals und Kältezittern, *Pflügers Arch. ges. Physiol.* **290**: 167–183.

46. BRÜCK, K., AND WÜNNENBERG, W., 1967, Eine kälteadaptative Modifikation: Senkung der Schwellentemperaturen für Kältezittern, *Pflügers Arch. ges. Physiol.* **293**:226–235.

47. BRÜCK, K., AND WÜNNENBERG, W., 1970, Meshed control of two effector systems: Non-shivering and shivering thermogenesis, in: *Physiological and Behavioral Temperature Regulation* (J. D. Hardy, A. P. Gagge, and J. A. J. Stolwijk, eds.), Charles C. Thomas, Springfield, Illinois.

48. BRÜCK, K., BAUM, E., AND SCHWENNICKE, H. P., 1976, Cold adaptive modifications in man induced by repeated short-term cold-exposures and during a 10-day and -night cold-exposure, *Pflügers Arch. ges. Physiol.* **363**:125–133.

49. BRÜCK, K., BRÜCK, M., AND LEMTIS, H., 1957, Hautdurchblutung und Thermoregulation bei neugeborenen Kindern, *Pflügers Arch. ges. Physiol.* **265**:55–65.

50. BRÜCK, K., BRÜCK, M., AND LEMTIS, H., 1958, Thermoregulatorische Veränderungen des Energiestoffwechsels bei reifen Neugeborenen, *Pflügers Arch. ges. Physiol.* **267**:382–391.

51. BRÜCK, K., BRÜCK, M., AND LEMTIS, H., 1960, Die Temperaturregelung Neugeborener und Frühgeborener nach spontaner und pathologischer Geburt, *Geburtshilfe Frauenheilkd.* **20**:461–472.

52. BRÜCK, K., PARMELEE, A. H., AND BRÜCK, M., 1962, Neutral temperature range and range of "thermal comfort" in premature infants, *Biol. Neonate* **4**:32–51.

53. BRÜCK, K., WÜNNENBERG, W., GALLMEIER, H., AND ZIEHM, B., 1970, Shift of threshold temperature for shivering and heat polypnea as a mode of thermal adaptation, *Pflügers Arch. ges. Physiol.* **321**:159–172.

54. BRÜCK, K., WÜNNENBERG, W., AND ZEISBERGER, E., 1969, Comparison of cold-adaptive metabolic modifications in different species with special reference to the miniature pig, *Fed. Proc. Fed. Amer. Soc. Exp. Biol.* **28**:1035–1041.

55. Burton, A. C., and Edholm, O. G., 1969, *Man in a Cold Environment,* Hafner Publishing Co., New York and London.

56. Buetow, K. C., and Klein, S. W., 1964, Effect of maintenance of "normal" skin temperature on survival of infants of low body weights, *Pediatrics* **34:**163–170.

57. Celander, O., 1960, Blood flow in the foot and calf of the newborn, *Acta Paediatr. Scand.* **49:**488–496.

58. Clapp, J. F., and Abrams, R. M., 1976, The postpartum chill, *Isr. J. Med. Sci.* **12:**1131–1133.

59. Cooper, K. E., 1970, Studies of the human central warm receptor, in: *Physiological and Behavioral Temperature Regulation* (J. D. Hardy, A. P. Gagge, and J. A. J. Stolwijk, eds.), Charles C. Thomas, Springfield, Illinois.

60. Cooper, K. E., Pittman, Q. J., and Veale, W. L., 1975, Observations on the development of the "fever" mechanism in the fetus and newborn. Temperature regulation and drug action, in: *Proceedings of a Symposium, Paris 1974,* pp. 43–50, S. Karger, Basel.

61. Cort, J. H., and McCance, R. A., 1953, The neural control of shivering in the pig, *J. Physiol. (London)* **120:**115–121.

62. Crenshaw, C., Huckabee, W. E., Curet, L. B., Mann, L., Barron, D. H., 1968, A method for the estimation of the umbilical blood flow in unstressed sheep and goats with some results on its application, *J. Exp. Physiol.* **53:**65–75.

63. Dawes, G. S., 1968, *Foetal and Neonatal Physiology,* Year Book Medical Publishers, Chicago.

64. Dawes, G. S., and Mott, J. C., 1959, The increase in oxygen consumption of the lamb after birth, *J. Physiol. (London)* **146:**295–315.

65. Dawes, G. S., Jacobson, H. N., Mott, C., and Shelley, H. J., 1960, Some observations of foetal and newborn rhesus monkeys, *J. Physiol. (London)* **152:**271–298.

66. Dawkins, M. J. R., and Hull, D., 1964, Brown adipose tissue and the response of the newborn rabbit to cold, *J. Physiol. (London)* **172:**216–238.

67. Dawkins, M. J. R., and Scopes, J. W., 1965, Non-shivering thermogenesis and brown adipose tissue in the human newborn infant, *Nature (London)* **206:**201, 202.

68. Day, R. L., Caliguiri, L., Kamenski, C., and Ehrlich, F., 1964, Body temperature and survival of premature infants, *Pediatrics* **34:**171–181.

69. Day, R. L., Curtis, J., and Kelley, M., 1943, Respiratory metabolism in infancy and in childhood. XXVII. Regulation of body temperature of premature infants, *Amer. J. Dis. Child.* **65:**376–398.

70. *Documenta Geigy,* 1960, *Wissenschaftliche Tabellen* (J. R. Geigy, ed.), J. R. Geigy, Basel.

71. Doerr, F. F., and Heite, H. J., 1957, Farbe und Wärmeabgabe der Haut nach Einwirkung von Nikotinsäurebenzylester insbesondere bei Neurodermitikern, *Arch. Klin. Exp. Dermatol.* **204:**543–553.

72. Donhoffer, S., 1966, The regulation of energy metabolism and van't Hoff's rule in the homeotherm animal, *Helgol. Wiss. Meeresunters.* **14:**541–558.

73. Ebbecke, U., 1917, Die lokale vasomotorische Reaktion (L.V.R.) der Haut und der inneren Organe, *Pflügers Arch. ges. Physiol.* **169:**1–81.

74. Eckert, E., 1959, *Wärme- und Stoffaustausch,* 2d Ed., Springer-Verlag, Berlin.

75. Fanger, P. O., 1972, *Thermal Comfort. Analysis and Applications in Environmental Engineering,* McGraw-Hill Book Co., New York.

76. Fisher, D. A., and Dussault, J. H., 1974, Development of the mammalian thyroid gland, in: *Handbook of Physiology* (R. O. Greep and E. B. Astwood, eds.), Sect. 7, pp. 21–38, American Physiological Society, Washington, D.C.

77. Foster, K. G., Hey, E. N., and Katz, G., 1969, The response of the sweat glands of the new-born baby to thermal stimuli and to intradermal acetylcholine, *J. Physiol. (London)* **203:**13–29.

78. Freund, H., and Jansen, S., 1923, Über den Sauerstoffverbrauch der Skelettmuskulatur und seine Abhängigkeit von der Wärmeregulation, *Pflügers Arch. ges. Physiol.* **200:**96–118.

79. Friis-Hansen, B., 1959, Changes in body water compartments during growth, in: *Die physiologische Entwicklung des Kindes* (F. Linneweh, ed.), pp. 196–203, Springer-Verlag, Berlin.

80. Gagge, A. P., Hardy, J. D., and Rapp, G. M., 1969, Proposed standard system of symbols for thermal physiology, *J. Appl. Physiol.* **27:**439–446.

81. Gandy, G. M., Adamsons, K., Jr., Cunningham, N., Silverman, W. A., and James, L. S., 1964, Thermal environments and acid–base homeostatis in human infants during the first few hours of life, *J. Clin. Invest.* **43:**751–758.

82. Gelineo, S., 1957, Développement ontogénétique de la thermorégulation chez le chien, *Bull. Acad. Serbe Sci.* **18:**97–102.

83. Gelineo, S., and Sokic, P., 1953, La naissance et le développement de la thermorégulation chimique chez le spermophile (*Citellus citellus*), *Bull. Acad. Serbe Sci.* **12:**1–11.

84. Glass, L., Silverman, W. A., and Sinclair, J. C., 1968, Effect of the thermal environment on cold resistance and growth of small infants after the first week of life, *Pediatrics* **41:**1033–1046.

85. Golenhofen, K., Hensel, H., and Hildebrandt, G., 1963, *Durchblutungsmessung mit Wärmeleitelementen,* Verlag Georg Thieme, Stuttgart.

86. Grad, B., 1953, Changes in oxygen consumption and heart rates of rats during growth and ageing: Role of the thyroid gland, *Amer. J. Physiol.* **174:**481–486.

87. Haddad, H. M., 1960, Studies on thyroid hormone metabolism in children, *Pediatrics* **57:**391–398.

88. Hahn, P., and Novak, M., 1975, Development of brown and white adipose tissue, *J. Lipid Res.* **16**:79–91.

89. Hardy, J. D., 1961, Physiology of temperature regulation, *Physiol. Rev.* **41**:521–606.

90. Hardy, J. D., Gagge, P. A., and Stolwijk, J. A. J. (eds.), 1970, *Physiological and Behavioral Temperature Regulation,* Charles C. Thomas, Springfield, Illinois.

91. Hart, J. S., Héroux, O., and Dépocas, F., 1956, Cold acclimation and the electromyogram of unanesthetized rats, *J. Appl. Physiol.* **9**:404–408.

92. Heim, T., and Hull, D., 1966, The blood flow and oxygen consumption of brown adipose tissue in the newborn rabbit, *J. Physiol. (London)* **186**:42–55.

93. Heim, T., and Hull, D., 1966, The effect of propranolol on the calorigenic response in brown adipose tissue of newborn rabbits to catecholamines, glucagon, corticotrophin and cold exposure, *J. Physiol. (London)* **187**:271–283.

94. Heldmaier, G., 1971, Zitterfreie Wärmebildung und Körpergrösse bei Säugetieren, *Z, Vgl. Physiol.* **73**:222–248.

95. Hellbrügge, T., 1960, The development of circadian rhythms in infants, *Cold Spring Harbor Symp. Quant. Biol.* **25**:311.

96. Hellon, R. F., 1970, Hypothalamic neurons responding to changes in hypothalamic and ambient temperatures, in: *Physiological and Behavioral Temperature Regulation,* (J. D. Hardy, A. P. Gagge, and J. A. J. Stolwijk, eds.), Charles C. Thomas, Springfield, Illinois.

97. Hemingway, A., 1963, Shivering, *Physiol. Rev.* **43**:397–422.

98. Hensel, H., Brück, K., and Raths, P., 1973, Homeothermic organisms, in: *Temperature and Life* (H. Precht, J. Christophersen, H. Hensel, and W. Larcher, eds.), Springer-Verlag, Berlin—Heidelberg—New York.

99. Héroux, O., 1955, Acclimation of adrenalectomized rats to low environmental temperature, *Amer. J. Physiol.* **181**:75–78.

100. Hey, E. N., 1968, Small globe thermometers, *J. Sci. Instrum. Ser. 2* **1**:955–957, 1260.

101. Hey, E. N., 1969, The relation between environmental temperature and oxygen consumption in the new-born baby, *J. Physiol. (London)* **200**:589–603.

102. Hey, E. N., 1972, Thermal regulation in the newborn, *Br. J. Hosp. Med.,* July, pp. 51–64.

103. Hey, E. N., 1974, Physiological control over body temperature, in: *Heat Loss from Animals and Man* (J. L. Monteith and L. E. Mount, eds.), Butterworths, London.

104. Hey, E. N., 1975, Thermal neutrality, *Br. Med. Bull.* **31**:69–74.

105. Hey, E. N., and Katz, G., 1969, Temporary loss of a metabolic response to cold stress in infants of low birthweight, *Arch. Dis. Child.* **44**:323.

106. Hey, E. N., and Katz, G., 1969, Evaporative water loss in the new-born baby, *J. Physiol. (London)* **200**:605–619.

107. Hey, E. N., and Katz, G., 1970, The range of thermal insulation in the tissues of the newborn baby, *J. Physiol. (London)* **207**:667–681.

108. Hey, E. N., and Katz, G., 1970, The optimum thermal environment for naked babies, *Arch. Dis. Child.* **45**:328–334.

109. Hey, E. N., and Mount, L. E., 1967, Heat losses from babies in incubators, *Arch. Dis. Child.* **42**:75–84.

110. Hey, E. N., Katz, G., and O'Connell, B., 1970, The total thermal insulation of the newborn baby, *J. Physiol. (London)* **207**:683–698.

111. Hill, J. R., 1959, The oxygen consumption of newborn and adult mammals: Its dependence on the oxygen tension in the inspired air and on the environmental temperature, *J. Physiol. (London)* **149**:346.

112. Hill, J. R., and Rahimtulla, K. A., 1965, Heat balance and the metabolic rate of newborn babies in relation to environmental temperature, and the effect of age and of weight on basal metabolic rate, *J. Physiol. (London)* **180**:239–265.

113. Hill, J. R., and Robinson, D. C., 1968, Oxygen consumption in normally grown, small-for-dates and large-for-dates new-born infants, *J. Physiol. (London)* **199**:685–703.

114. Himms-Hagen, J., 1967, Sympathetic regulation of metabolism, *Pharmacol. Rev.* **19**:367–461.

115. Hissa, R., 1968, Postnatal development of thermoregulation in the Norwegian lemming and the golden hamster, *Ann. Zool.* **5**:345–383.

116. Horwitz, B. A., 1975, Pathways underlying nonshivering thermogenesis in peripheral tissues, in: *Proceedings of an International Symposium on Depressed Metabolism and Cold Thermogenesis, Prague* (L. Jansky, ed.), pp. 127–132, Charles University, Prague.

117. Hsieh, A. C. L., Carlson, L. D., and Gray, G., 1957, Role of the sympathetic nervous system in the control of chemical regulation of heat production, *Amer. J. Physiol.* **190**:247–251.

118. Hull, D., 1965, Oxygen consumption and body temperature of newborn rabbits and kittens exposed to cold, *J. Physiol. (London)* **177**:192–202.

119. Hull, D., 1966, The structure and function of brown adipose tissue, *Br. Med. Bull.* **22**:92–96.

120. Hull, D., and Hardman, M. J., 1970, Brown adipose tissue in newborn mammals, in: *Brown Adipose Tissue* (O. Lindberg, ed.), American Elsevier Publishing Co., New York.

121. Hull, D., and Segall, M. M., 1965, The contribution of brown adipose tissue to heat production in the newborn rabbit, *J. Physiol. (London)* **181**:449–457.

122. Hull, D., and Segall, M. M., 1965, Sympathetic nervous control of brown adipose tissue and heat

production in the newborn rabbit, *J. Physiol. (London)* **181**:458–467.

123. JANSKÝ, L., 1973, Non-shivering thermogenesis and its thermoregulatory significance, *Biol. Rev.* **48**: 85–132.

124. JANSKÝ, L., AND HART, J. S., 1963, Participation of skeletal muscle and kidney during non-shivering thermogenesis in cold-acclimated rats, *Can. J. Biochem.* **41**:953–964.

125. JENKINSON, D. M., NOBLE, R. C., AND THOMPSON, G. E., 1968, Adipose tissue and heat production in the newborn ox (*Bos taurus*), *J. Physiol. (London)* **195**:639–646.

126. JOEL, C. D., 1965, The physiological role of brown adipose tissue, in: *Handbook of Physiology* (A. E. Renold and G. F. Cahill, Jr., eds.), Sect. 5, pp. 59–85, American Physiological Society, Washington, D.C.

127. JOEL, C. D., TREBLE, D. H., AND BALL, E. G., 1964, On a major role for brown adipose tissue in heat production during arousal from hibernation, *Fed. Proc. Fed. Amer. Soc. Exp. Biol.* **23**:271.

128. JOHANNSON, B., 1959, Brown fat: A review, *Metabolism* **8**:221–240.

129. JOPPICH, G., AND SCHÄFER, H., 1955, Unterkühlung bei Frühgeborenen, *Dtsch. Med. Wochenschr.* **80**: 73–75.

130. KARLBERG, P., 1952, Determination of standard energy metabolism (basal metabolism) in normal infants, *Acta Paediatr. (Uppsala)* **41**(*Suppl. 89*):3–151.

131. KARLBERG, P., MOORE, R. E., AND OLIVER, T. K., 1962, The thermogenic response of the newborn infant to noradrenaline, *Acta Paediatr. (Uppsala)* **51**:284–292.

132. KARLBERG, P., MOORE, R. E., AND OLIVER, T. K., 1965, Thermogenic and cardiovascular response of the newborn baby to noradrenaline, *Acta Paediatr. (Uppsala)* **54**:225–238.

133. KINTZEL, H. W., 1957, Zur Frage der Warm- oder Kalthaltung der Frühgeborenen, *Arch. Kinderheilkd.* **154**:238–247.

134. KINTZEL, H. W., 1968, Untersuchungen über die Auswirkungen langanhaltender Hypothermie auf das Frühgeborene, *Dtsche. Gesundheitswes.* **15**:710.

135. KLEIBER, M., 1961, *The Fire of Life: An Introduction to Animal Energetics,* John Wiley & Sons, New York.

136. KLEIBER, M., COLE, H. H., AND SMITH, A. H., 1943, Metabolic rate of rat foetuses *in vitro, J. Cell. Comp. Physiol.* **22**:167–176.

137. LEBLANC, J., AND MOUNT, L. E., 1968, Effects of noradrenaline and adrenaline on oxygen rate and arterial blood pressure in the newborn pig, *Nature (London)* **217**:77, 78.

138. LEDUC, J., 1961, Catecholamine production and release in exposure and acclimation to cold, *Acta Physiol. Scand.* **53**:(*Suppl. 183*):1–101.

139. LEE, V. A., AND ILIFF, A., 1956, The energy metabolism of infants and young children during postprandial sleep, *Pediatrics* **18**:739–749.

140. LEHMANN, G., 1956, Das Gesetz der Stoffwechselreduktion (Oberflächengesetz), in: *Handbuch der Zoologie* (J. G. Helmcke and H. von Lengerken, eds.), Vol. 8, Part 4, Chapt. 4, pp. 1–32, Walter de Gruyter & Co., Berlin.

141. LEVISON, H., AND SWYER, P. R., 1964, Oxygen consumption and the thermal environment in newly born infants, *Biol. Neonate New Ser.* **7**:305–312.

142. LEWIS, R. C., DUVAL, A. M., AND ILIFF, A., 1943, Standards for the basal metabolism of children from 2 to 15 years of age, inclusive, *J. Pediatr.* **23**:1.

143. LINDBERG, O. (ed.), 1970, *Brown Adipose Tissue,* American Elsevier Publishing Co., New York.

144. MANN, T. P., AND ELLIOT, R. J. K., 1957, Neonatal cold injury due to accidental exposure to cold, *Lancet* **1**:229–234.

145. McCANCE, R. A., AND STRANGEWAYS, W. M. B., 1954, Protein catabolism and oxygen consumption during starvation in infants, young adults and old men, *Br. J. Nutr.* **8**:21–31.

146. McCANCE, R. A., AND WIDDOWSON, E. M., 1959, The effect of lowering the ambient temperature on the metabolism of the newborn pig, *J. Physiol. (London)* **147**:124–134.

147. MENDLER, N., REULEN, H. J., AND BRENDEL, W., 1972, Cold swelling and energy metabolism in the hypothermic brain of rats and dogs, in: *Hibernation and Hypothermia, Perspectives and Challenges* (F. E. South, J. P. Hannon, J. R. Willis, E. T. Pengelley, and N. R. Alpert, eds.), Elsevier Publishing Co., Amsterdam—London—New York.

148. MERKLIN, R. J., 1974, Growth and distribution of human fetal brown fat, *Anat. Rec.* **178**:637–646.

149. MESCHIA, G., COTTER, J. R., MAKOWSKI, E. L., AND BARRON, D. H., 1967, Simultaneous measurement of uterine and umbilical blood flows and oxygen uptakes, *Q. J. Exp. Physiol.* **52**:1–18.

150. MESTYÁN, J., JÁRAI, I., BATA, G., AND FEKETE, M., 1964, The basal metabolic rate of premature infants, *Biol. Neonate* **7**:11–25.

151. MESTYÁN, J., JÁRAI, I., BATA, G., AND FEKETE, M., 1964, The significance of facial skin temperature in the chemical heat regulation of premature infants, *Biol. Neonate* **7**:243–254.

152. MESTYÁN, J., JÁRAI, I., KEKETE, M., AND SOLTÉSZ, G., 1969, Specific dynamic action in premature infants kept at and below the neutral temperature, *Pediatr. Res.* **3**:41–50.

153. MESTYÁN, J., VARGA, F., FOHL, E., AND HEIM, T., 1962, Oxygen consumption of hyper- and hypothermic premature infants, *Arch. Dis. Child.* **37**: 466–469.

154. MOLL, W., AND BARTELS, H., 1960, Eine kritische Prüfung der offenen und der geschlossenen Methode zur Bestimmung des O_2-Verbrauches nach Veränder-

ung der inspiratorischen Sauerstoffkonzentration, *Pflügers Arch. ges. Physiol.* **271**:583–594.

155. MONTIETH, J. L., AND MOUNT, L. E. (eds.), 1974, *Heat Loss from Animals and Man,* Butterworths, London.

156. MOORE, R. E., AND UNDERWOOD, M. C., 1960, Possible role of noradrenaline in control of heat production in the newborn mammal, *Lancet* **1**:1277, 1278.

157. MOORE, R. E., AND UNDERWOOD, M. C., 1962, Hexamethonium, hypoxia and heat production in newborn and infant kittens and puppies, *J. Physiol. (London)* **161**:30–53.

158. MOORE, R. E., AND UNDERWOOD, M. C., 1963, The thermogenic effects of noradrenaline in newborn and infant kittens and other small mammals. A possible hormonal mechanism in the control of heat production, *J. Physiol. (London)* **168**:290–317.

159. MORDHORST, H., 1933, Über die chemische Wärmeregulation frühgeborener Säuglinge, *Monatsschr. Kinderheilkd.* **55**:174–191.

160. MOUNT, L. E., 1959, The metabolic rate of the newborn pig in relation to environmental temperature and to age, *J. Physiol. (London)* **147**:333–345.

161. MOUNT, L. E., 1964, Radiant and convective heat loss from the newborn pig, *J. Physiol. (London)* **173**:96–113.

162. MOUNT, L. E., 1966, Basis of heat regulation in homeotherms, *Br. Med. Bull.* **22**:84–87.

163. MOUNT, L. E., 1968, *The Climatic Physiology of the Pig,* Edward Arnold, London.

164. MOUNT, L. E., 1974, The concept of thermal neutrality, in: *Heat Loss from Animals and Man* (J. L. Monteith and L. E. Mount, eds.), pp. 425–439, Butterworths, London.

165. NADEL, E. R., BULLARD, R. W., AND STOLWIJK, J. A. J., 1971, Importance of skin temperature in the regulation of sweating, *J. Appl. Physiol.* **31**:80–87.

166. NAKAYAMA, T., HAMMEL, H. T., HARDY, J. D., AND J. D., AND EISENMAN, J. S., 1963, Thermal stimulation of electrical activity of single units of the preoptic region, *Amer. J. Physiol.* **204**:1122–1126.

167. NAPOLITANO, L., 1965, The fine structure of adipose tissues, in: *Handbook of Physiology* (A. E. Renold and G. F. Cahill, Jr., eds.), Sect. 5, pp. 109–123, American Physiological Society, Washington D.C.

168. NISHI, Y., AND GAGGE, A. P., 1971, Humid temperature. A biophysical index of thermal sensation and discomfort, *J. Physiol. (Paris)* **3**:365–368.

169. NOVAK, M., AND HAHN, P., 1975, Early development of fat metabolism, in: *Childhood Obesity* (P. J. Collipp, ed.), Publishing Sciences Group, Acton, Massachusetts.

170. NOVAK, M., HAHN, P., PARDO, V., MONKUS, E., AND ALZAMORA, D., 1975, The effect of carnitine on respiration of mitochondria obtained from newborn

and adult human subcutaneous white adipose tissue, *Int. J. Biochem.* **5**:223–234.

171. NOVAK, M., PENN-WALKER, D., AND MONKUS, E. F., 1975, Oxydation of fatty acids by mitochondria obtained from newborn subcutaneous (white) adipose tissue, *Biol. Neonate* **25**:95–107.

172. OGAWA, T., 1970, Local effect of skin temperature on threshold concentration of sudorific agents, *J. Appl. Physiol.* **28**:18–22.

173. OLIVER, T. K., 1965, Temperature regulation and heat production in the newborn, *Pediatr. Clin. North Amer.* **12**:765–779.

174. PARMELEE, A. H., JR., BRÜCK, K., AND BRÜCK, M., 1962, Activity and inactivity cycles during the sleep of premature infants exposed to neutral temperature, *Biol. Neonate* **4**:317–339.

175. PICHOTKA, J., 1958, Behaglichkeitstemperaturen und Minimalumsätze bei Meerschweinchen, *Pflügers Arch. ges. Physiol.* **268**:9, 10.

176. POPOVIC, V., 1960, Survival time of hypothermic white rats (15°C) and ground squirrels (10°C), *Amer. J. Physiol.* **199**:463–466.

177. POULIOT, M., 1966, Catecholamine excretion in adrenodemedullated rats exposed to cold after chronic guanethidine treatment, *Acta Physiol. Scand.* **68**:164–168.

178. PRECHT, H., LAUDIEN, H., AND HAVSTEEN, B., 1973, The normal temperature range, in: *Temperature and Life* (H. Precht, J. Christopherson, H. Hensel, and W. Larcher, eds.), Springer-Verlag, Berlin—Heidelberg—New York.

179. PRIBILOWÁ, H., 1968, The importance of thermoreceptive regions for the chemical thermoregulation of the newborn, *Biol. Neonate* **12**:13–22.

180. PROKOPEVA, E. M., 1960, The limits of overcooling and survival in puppies, in: *The Problem of Acute Hypothermia* (P. M. Starkov, ed.), pp. 226–236, Pergamon Press, New York.

181. PRUSINER, S., CANNON, B., AND LINDBERG, O., 1970, Mechanisms controlling oxydative metabolism in brown adipose tissue. in: *Brown Adipose Tissue* (O. Lindberg, ed.), American Elsevier Publishing Co., New York—London—Amsterdam.

182. RAFAEL, J., KLAAS, D., AND HOHORST, H. J., 1968, Mitochondrien aus braunem Fettgewebe: Enzyme und Atmungskettenphosphorylierung während der prä- und postnatalen Entwicklung des interscapularen Fettkörpers des Meerschweinchens, *Hoppe-Seyler's Z. Physiol. Chem.* **349**:1711–1724.

183. RUBECZ, I., AND MESTYAN, J., 1975, The partition of maintenance energy expenditure and the pattern of substrate utilization in intrauterine malnourished newborn infants before and during recovery, 1975, *Acta Paediatr. Acad. Sci. Hung.* **16**:335–350.

184. RYSER, G., AND JÉQUIER, E., 1972, Study by direct calorimetry of thermal balance on the first day of life, *Eur. J. Clin. Invest.* **2**:176–187.

185. SCHAEFER, K. E., AND WÜNNENBERG, W., 1976, Threshold temperatures for shivering in acute and chronic hypercapnia, *J. Appl. Physiol.* **41**:67–70.

186. SCHIFF, D., STERN, L., AND LEDUC, J., 1966, Chemical thermogenesis in newborn infants: Catecholamine excretion and the plasma non-esterified fatty acid response to cold exposure, *Pediatrics* **37**:577–582.

187. SCOPES, J. W., AND AHMED, I., 1966, Minimal rates of oxygen consumption in sick and premature newborn infants, *Arch. Dis. Child.* **41**:407–415.

188. SCOPES, J. W., AND AHMED, I., 1966, Range of critical temperatures in sick and premature newborn babies, *Arch. Dis. Child.* **41**:417–419.

189. SILVERMAN, W. A., 1959, The physical environment and the premature infant, *Pediatrics* **23**:166–171.

190. SILVERMAN, W. A., ZAMELIS, A., SINCLAIR, J. C., AND AGATE, F. J., JR., 1964, Warm nape of the newborn, *Pediatrics* **33**:984–986.

191. SIMON, E., 1974, Temperature regulation: The spinal cord as a site of extrahypothalamic thermoregulatory functions, *Rev. Physiol. Biochem. Pharmacol.* **71**:1–76.

192. SINCLAIR, J. C., SCOPES, J. W., AND SILVERMAN, W. A., 1967, Metabolic reference standards for the neonate, *Pediatrics* **39**:724–732.

193. SMALLEY, R. L., AND DRYER, R. L., 1963, Brown fat: Thermogenic effect during arousal from hibernation in the bat, *Science* **140**:1333, 1334.

194. SMITH, R. E., AND HOCK, R. J., 1962, Brown fat: Thermogenic effector of arousal in hibernators, *Science* **140**:190, 200.

195. SMITH, R. E., AND HORWITZ, B. A., 1969, Brown fat and thermogenesis, *Physiol. Rev.* **49**:330–425.

196. SMITH, R. E., AND ROBERTS, J. C., 1964, Thermogenesis of brown adipose tissue in cold-acclimated rats, *Amer. J. Physiol.* **206**:143–148.

197. STERN, L., LEES, M. H., AND LEDUC, J., 1965, Environmental temperature, oxygen consumption and catecholamine excretion in newborn infants, *Pediatrics* **36**:367–373.

198. STOLWIJK, J. A. J., AND HARDY, J. D., 1966, Temperature regulation in man—A theoretical study, *Pflügers Arch. ges. Physiol.* **291**:129–162.

199. SULYOK, E., JÉQUIER, E., AND PROD'HOM, L. S., 1973, Respiratory contribution to the thermal balance of the newborn infant under various ambient conditions, *Pediatrics* **51**:641–650.

200. SULYOK, E., JÉQUIER, E., AND PROD'HOM, L. S., 1973, Thermal balance of the newborn infant in a heat-gaining environment, *Pediatr. Res.* **7**:888–900.

201. SULYOK, E., JÉQUIER, E., AND RYSER, G., 1972, Effect of relative humidity on thermal balance of the newborn infant, *Biol. Neonate* **21**:210–218.

202. SZEGVÁRI, G., VÁRNAI, J., AND DONHOFFER, S., 1963, The effect of environmental temperature, hypoxia and hypercapnia on total heat production and the electrical activity of muscle in the rat: Shivering and non-shivering thermogenesis and the site of non-shivering thermogenesis, *Acta Physiol. Acad. Sci. Hung.* **23**:49–62.

203. SZÉLENYI, Z., ZEISBERGER, E., AND BRÜCK, K., 1976, Effects of electrical stimulation in the lower brainstem on temperature regulation in the unanesthetized guinea-pig, *Pflügers Arch. ges. Physiol.* **364**:123–127.

204. TAYLOR, P. M., 1960, Oxygen consumption in newborn rats, *J. Physiol. (London)* **154**:153–168.

205. THAUER, R., AND BRENDEL, W., 1962, Hypothermie, *Prog. Surg.* **2**:73–271.

206. WENGER, C. B., ROBERTS, M. F., NADEL, E. R., AND STOLWIJK, J. A. J., 1975, Thermoregulatory control of finger blood flow, *J. Appl. Physiol.* **38**:1078–1082.

207. WOLF, H., AND MELICHAR, V., 1968, Determinations of turnover of triglycerides, FFA and free glycerol following triglyceride infusion in preterm and full-term newborns, *Z. Klin. Chem.* **7**:205, 206.

208. WOLF, H., STAVE, U., NOVAK, M., AND MONKUS, F., 1974, Recent investigations on neonatal fat metabolism, *J. Perinat. Med.* **2**:75.

209. WÜNNENBERG, W., 1976, Thermointegrative activity of hypothalamic structures, *Isr. J. Med. Sci.* **12**(9):1050–1051.

210. WÜNNENBERG, W., AND BRÜCK, K., 1968, Single unit activity evoked by thermal stimulation of the cervical spinal cord in the guinea pig, *Nature (London)* **218**:1268–1269.

211. WÜNNENBERG, W., AND HARDY, J. D., 1972, Response of single units of the posterior hypothalamus to thermal stimulation, *J. Appl. Physiol.* **33**(5):547–552.

212. YOUNG, I. M., 1962, Vasomotor tone in the skin blood vessels of the newborn infant, *Clin. Sci.* **22**:325–332.

213. ZEISBERGER, E., 1966, Liver oxygen consumption of cold- and warm-acclimated rats and factors regulating liver oxidative metabolism, *Helgol. Wiss. Meeresunters.* **14**:528–540.

214. ZEISBERGER, E., AND BRÜCK, K., 1972, Effects of intrahypothalamically injected noradrenergic and cholinergic agents on thermoregulatory responses, in: *The Pharmacology of Thermoregulation* (E. Schönbaum and P. Lomax, eds.), pp. 232–243, S. Karger, Basel.

215. ZEISBERGER, E., AND BRÜCK, K., 1976, Alteration of shivering threshold in cold- and warm-adapted guinea pigs following intrahypothalamic injections of noradrenaline and of an adrenergic alpha receptor blocking agent, *Pflügers Arch. ges. Physiol.* **362**:113–119.

216. ZEISBERGER, E., BRÜCK, K., WÜNNENBERG, W., AND WIETASCH, C., 1967, Das Ausmass der zitterfreien Thermogenese des Meerschweinchens in Abhängigkeit vom Lebensalter, *Pflügers Arch. ges. Physiol.* **296**:276–288.

217. ZNAMENÁČEK, K., AND PŘIBYLOWÁ, H., 1964, Some parameters of respiratory metabolism in the first three days after birth, *Acta Paediatr. Scand.* **53**:241–246.

CHAPTER 22

Liver Enzymes

Uwe Stave

1. Introduction

The metabolic activity of the liver is multifarious, and a discussion of perinatal changes in hepatic enzyme patterns embraces many areas of physiology and biochemistry. Most of the chapters in this Part III on metabolism and several chapters of the remaining parts of this volume deal with functions that proceed predominantly in the liver. Specific enzyme activities are discussed in connection with those different topics. In this chapter, an attempt will be made to present a survey of metabolic potentials in the perinatal liver, and to elucidate the developmental formation of hepatic enzymes. As much as it would be desirable to survey all liver enzymes, and preferably those of the human fetus and newborn, there are good ethical reasons for the restricted research on normal human tissues obtained in the perinatal period. The data that are available from human liver, however, demonstrate trends and principles very similar to those studied in subhuman mammals.

2. Growth, Structure, and Composition of the Liver in the Perinatal Period

The liver is the largest organ, comprising about 4% of the body weight (Tables I and II; see also Fig. 5); differences among species are considerable. Earlier in gestation, the percentage of liver weight is even greater than at term; toward the end of the second trimester (menstrual age of 24 weeks) Gruenwald and Minh[34] found the liver comprising 5.2% of the body weight. Some changes in the ratio of the weight of the right to that of the left liver have been observed in the perinatal period. In the last trimester, the human fetal liver has a right/left ratio of 0.89; at the first postnatal day, the lobes are of equal weight; by the end of the 5th day and for several weeks thereafter, the R/L ratio reverses and becomes 1.1–1.16.[64] In the newborn baby, the left lobe of the liver seems to be more prone to circulatory deficiencies; most probably in consequence of this susceptibility, thrombi, necrotic lesions, and calcification are far more frequently found in the left lobe.[17] A more pronounced cell vacuolization in the right lobe has been ascribed to hypoxia fetalis or neonatorum.[33]

Uwe Stave · Mailman Center for Child Development and Department of Pediatrics, University of Miami School of Medicine, Miami, Florida 33152

Table I. Liver Weight as Percentage of Body Weight in the Human Fetus and Newborn[a]

Sex	Gestation 90% completed	Newborn (0–7 days)	4 weeks
Male	3.68 (62)[b]	4.07 (91)	3.36 (56)
Female	3.88 (52)	4.25 (55)	3.65 (28)

[a] Data from Schulz et al.[100]
[b] Number of samples in parentheses.

Table II. Liver Weight as Percentage of Body Weight in Human Newborns by Gestational Age (Sexes Combined)[a]

Gestational (menstrual) age (weeks)	Number of cases	Body weight (g)	$\dfrac{\text{Liver} \times 100}{\text{Body weight}}$
28	139	1020	4.50
30	148	1230	4.31
32	150	1488	4.40
34	104	1838	4.03
36	87	2165	4.02
38	102	2678	4.15
40	220	3163	4.11
42	112	3263	4.25

[a] Data from Gruenwald and Minh.[34]

Before birth, the umbilical vein supplies the liver with highly oxygenated blood that also provides nutrients. The left lobe receives the arterialized blood firsthand and unaltered, whereas the right lobe receives a mixture of blood from the umbilical vein and the vena porta; consequently, the blood supplied to the right lobe has a lower oxygen content. Lind[59] stated that hemodynamically speaking, the liver undergoes a major shock at birth. With cessation of the placental circulation, the liver receives most of its blood supply from the portal vein and the hepatic artery; the oxygen deficiency at and immediately after birth seems to be greater for the liver than for other organs (see also Chapter 8).

Cytological changes in the fetal and neonatal liver can be divided into alterations of the tissue cell composition and changes within cell type. Because of our interest in hepatic enzyme activities, the question of how many other than parenchymatous cells are present at a given stage of development is of great importance, since the developmental change in the parenchymatous liver cell is the immediate object of the enzymatic analysis. After birth, the parenchymatous cells outnumber all other types of cells in the liver. The cells that form the hepatic vascular system, bile canaliculi, and ducts, and the connective tissue with its few fibroblasts, represent a rather small amount of the total hepatic tissue. Cytomorphometric studies in developing rat liver[32] revealed marked changes in the quantitative distribution of cells and in changes of specific cell volumes over age. The event of birth is clearly marked by each parameter of these cell studies. At term, 85% of rat liver volume is occupied by parenchymal cells. The lining of the hepatic sinusoids consists of a thin layer of cells that differ from typical endothelial cells. One type forms with its cytoplasm a thin film in the wall of the sinusoid; the other is a fixed macrophage, the stellate cell of von Kupffer. These cells never represent more than 2% of rat liver volume.[32]

The most important cell type other than the parenchymatous cell is the hemopoietic cell because of its abundant presence during gestation and its gradual disappearance after birth. In fetal rat liver, hydrocortisone accelerates the involution of hematopoietic tissue.[32] During the third trimester of gestation, the hemopoietic cells are so diffusely integrated into the parenchyma that the lobulation of the hepatic tissue is not visible. In prematurely born infants, this abundance of hemopoietic cells cause the impression of a diffuse structure that is typical for this age group.[5] The postnatal decrease in hemopoietic cells is rapid during the first 10 days (Fig. 1), but in two-thirds of all infants, some clusters of hemopoietic cells can be found for

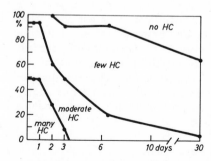

Fig. 1. Frequency of occurrence of hemopoietic cells (HC) in the liver of 260 newborn human infants at ages 1–30 days. Data from Sarrut and Nezelof.[97]

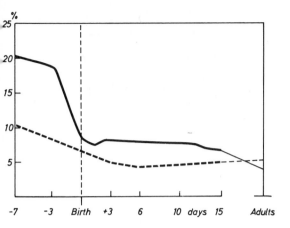

Fig. 2. Blood content in rabbit liver (——) and guinea pig liver (– – –) in percentage of liver wet weight. Data from Theile and Frank.[121]

several months. This widely varying amount of a profoundly different cell type in the newborn liver affects the analysis of enzyme activities, and it definitely results in a particular distortion of the hepatic enzyme pattern.

In newborn infants, the hepatic parenchymatous cells are approximately half the size of those in adults; the nuclei are relatively bigger, resulting in a considerably smaller cytoplasmic volume in the newborn. Postnatally, about 5% of the parenchymal cells are binucleated, whereas in adults, approximately one-fourth of these cells have two nuclei. A comparison of the number of mitochondria in hepatic cells of 4-week-old rats and adult animals showed a doubling of their number per cell with age.[96]

The *blood content* of liver samples can be altered by the sampling technique insofar as well-blotted, small samples contain much less blood than unblotted, bigger tissue samples. With the use of a standard sampling technique, the hemoglobin content of newborn rat and guinea pig livers was revealed to be slightly higher than that of adult animals (Fig. 2); in fetal liver, the hemoglobin content is much higher.[121]

Some other developmental changes in liver composition can be essential for the evaluation of enzyme patterns analyzed in different age groups. The concentration of extracted or total protein is used as a reference basis for tissue enzyme activities to express the units measured as "specific activity.' Frequently, authors refer to the "protein con-

centration" of the high-speed supernatant of the homogenate instead of the "total protein"; however, the latter is highly dependent on the degree of disruption of the subcellular structures. In this regard, ultrasonic disintegration of tissues has proved to be most effective, and hence this method of tissue homogenization is satisfactory.

The *protein content* of rat liver does not increase parallel with total organ weight, but shows a steeper increase at birth (Fig. 3). The same kind of changes were observed in perinatal rabbit liver (Fig. 4). A comparison of rat and rabbit liver protein content with that in newborn pigs (Table III) provides an example of important species differences. In rabbit liver extracts, the free amino acids were measured by column chromatography,[112] and marked changes in individual amino acid concentration were recorded. The total amount of hepatic free amino acids decreases immediately after birth, with a recovery and continuous increase after 3 days of age (Table IV). Glutathione, a peptide that is important for oxidation–reduction reactions, doubles its concentration in the perinatal period (Table IV).

The *DNA content* of a tissue reflects the number of cells or, more precisely, the number of nuclei.[18] A comparison between the rate of increase in total protein and in total DNA of the liver reveals an important discrepancy, as shown in Fig. 3. As mentioned above, the percentage of binucleate cells in liver tissue increases soon after birth, and the DNA content per cell increases accordingly. Enesco

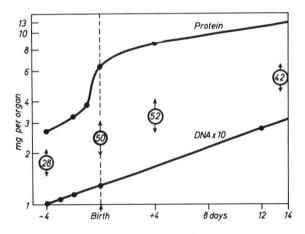

Fig. 3. Rat liver total protein and DNA content on semilogarithmic scale. Circled figures: Protein/DNA ratios. Data from Winick and Noble.[139]

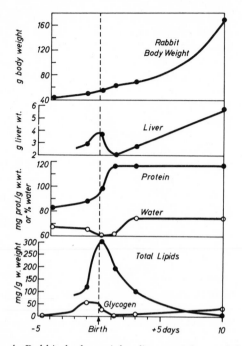

Fig. 4. Rabbit body weight, liver weight, and liver content of protein, water, lipids, and glycogen. Average values from New Zealand whites.

Table III. Composition of Newborn Pig Liver[a]

Age:	At birth (n = 12)	24 hr (n = 11)	10 days (n = 13)
Liver weight as percentage of body weight:	3.00%	3.14%	3.65%
Protein[b]	71.7	93.5	115.1
DNA[b]	3.6	3.3	2.4
Protein/DNA ratio	20.5	28.3	50.3
Fat[b]	34.0	47.2	—
Carbohydrate[b]	100.4	43.5	38.4

[a] Calculated from data by Widdowson and Crabb.[137] Animals were suckled from birth on.
[b] Values in milligrams per gram liver weight.

and Leblond[18] calculated the mean DNA content of the rat liver cell at age 7 days as being 6.2×10^{-12}g and that at age 95 days as being 9.5×10^{-12}g; no such data are available for fetal liver. Two important conclusions can be drawn from the experiments of Winick and Noble[139]: First, the increasing DNA content of a tissue is indicative of its growth by cell division, and, as shown in Fig. 3, liver growth follows a logarithmic function in the perinatal period, as demonstrated by the linear increase of the total DNA content on a semilogarithmic scale. Second, the protein/DNA ratio can be used to compare functional cell sizes in growing organs (regardless of depositions such as fat or glycogen, both of which contribute considerably to total liver weight or reduce the protein and DNA content per unit of organ weight). During the immediate perinatal period, the enlargement of rat liver cells is clearly indicated by the increased protein/DNA ratio (circled numbers in Fig. 3). The protein/DNA ratio increases similarly in perinatal pig liver, though with a delay of a few days (Table III).

Figure 4 demonstrates the perinatal changes in total body and liver weight of rabbits in connection with water, protein, total lipid, and glycogen concentrations in the liver. The sudden decrease in

Table IV. Free Amino Acids and Glutathione in Neonatal Rabbit Liver (μmol/g Weight)[a]

Age	Fetuses (30th day of gest.)	Newborns			
		0–3 hr	12–30 hr	3 days	10 days
Sum of 23 amino acids	24,892	20,822	19,222	24,526	26,034
Sum of essential amino acids	2,955	1,646	2,394	2,547	2,760
Total glutathione[b]	3,500	3,537	4,234	5,311	7,567

[a] From Stave and Armstrong.[112]
[b] Oxidized and reduced forms were measured separately; the total is calculated as reduced GSH.

liver weight after birth is the effect of the combined decrease of fat and glycogen. The sharp increase in liver protein seems to be independent of other changes, and it might well be a reflection of the high rate of synthesis of enzyme protein that is similar to enzyme activity increases. Figure 5 shows perinatal changes in the rat liver weight as a percentage of the body weight, and in the water content. These changes in liver growth and composition must be taken into consideration if reference values for enzyme activities must be selected. Species differences are considerable and to a certain degree dependent on the stage of maturation at birth. For instance, neonatal pig liver has considerably less fat than rabbit liver, but twice as much carbohydrate (Table III).

3. Enzyme Activities and Metabolic Potentials

3.1. General

It is generally accepted that demonstration of the occurrence of a certain enzyme activity in a tissue allows a conclusion as to the presence of that enzyme. A conclusion that goes one step further is that the enzyme activity measured reveals some clue to the metabolic potential of the tissue analyzed. A third step in evaluating tissue enzyme activities is the hypothesis that the units of a specific enzyme activity measured *in vitro* closely reflect the amount of a specific, enzymatically active protein in the tissue. Some of the objections to the latter statement will be discussed below. We need not disregard substantial or possible objections to the former statements entirely in bringing forward an additional hypothesis that is based only partially on the three statements mentioned before. The fourth step speculates that enzyme activities occur in tissues in certain characteristic patterns, and that such a selected pattern of representative enzyme activities allows conclusions as to the metabolic potentials of certain pathways, cycles, or reactions. The application of such a hypothesis would greatly promote the understanding of age-specific changes in the dynamics of the tissue metabolism. It is easy to accept the conclusion that missing or no enzyme activities of, for instance, the gluconeogenetic pathway in fetal rat liver (see Fig. 11) means that very little or no gluconeogenesis occurs in that organ. More details will be discussed below.

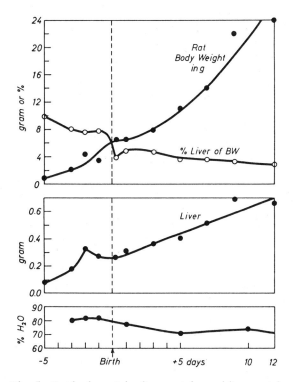

Fig. 5. Rat body weight, liver weight, and liver weight in percentage of body weight (Holtzman rats). Data from Auerbach and Waisman.[1] Liver water in grams per 100 grams liver. Data from Theile.[120]

In recent years, the determination of the molecular identity of enzyme proteins has been perfected by utilizing subtle immunochemical methods. The structure of these proteins, however, remains obscure in most cases or is restricted to some areas of the molecule's surface and concerns binding sites. Consequently, the understanding and prediction of function by unraveling the enzyme structure will need a lot of future research. On the same road, we might learn to identify gene codes for specific enzyme proteins.

At present, three different measures exist for the determination of specific enzyme proteins: the *molecular concentration,* the *weight of the enzyme protein,* and the *catalytic activity.*[8] The measurement of enzyme activity is of practical importance for serial tissue or plasma determinations, whereas the molar activity or the turnover number of enzymes (i.e., moles of substrate converted per mole enzyme protein per minute) is based on the molecular weight of the enzyme protein, and is used in biochemistry for kinetic studies. For some time, the expression *specific activity* has been used to express the amount of substrate that is converted per minute and per unit of tissue protein content. A recent trend analysis[51] showed that 56% of all tissue enzyme activities were expressed per tissue wet weight, and only 37% per soluble or total protein. The activity can also be related to other reference values, such as tissue dry weight, fat-free dry weight, total nitrogen content, or DNA, and it can also be calculated per total organ weight or per unit of body weight. The *in vitro* enzyme analysis must be performed under optimum and standardized conditions at, preferably, 25°C; however, the comparability of results obtained by different laboratories is frequently not satisfactory.

It is generally assumed that the *in vitro* measurement of enzyme activities reflects rather closely the amount of enzyme protein in the particular tissue[8,89]; occasionally, a cautious statement can be found saying that the activity of an enzyme is "presumably a measure of the amount present."[125] Even if a consistent relationship between enzyme activity and amount of enzyme protein has been proved to exist under certain conditions in a standard tissue extract,[19,102] it must remain an assumption that such a correlation applies to all tissue extracts under all conditions.[89] Granted that a certain amount of enzyme protein yields a fairly constant value of activity, however, we still cannot neglect the possibility that during the procedure of extracting the tissue and measuring the activity under *in vitro* conditions, the expected relationship between actual amount and activity becomes distorted. Steadily improved procedures, however, such as cell fractionation and the use of ultrasonic cell disruption and the most critical use of analytic methods, seem to stabilize this relationship and increase the repeatability. The customary use of enzyme activities to learn about the metabolic potentials of a tissue indicates a good amount of confidence in enzymatic tissue analysis. The investigation of inherited metabolic diseases in general and the study of metabolic effects in tissues with enzyme deficiencies can be taken as proof of this concept of a metabolic potential that depends on enzyme activities as measured *in vitro*.

Thus far, we have looked on enzyme activity as a result of an *in vitro* measurement, but naturally, the enzyme activity *in vivo* should be of greater importance. Our knowledge of the range of actually used catalytic activity of a specific enzyme protein within its intracellular location, and, in addition,

the intracellular kinetics of enzyme reactions, is still very limited. For each enzyme, or for certain functional groups of enzymes, the need and the environmental condition for their activity varies, and many regulatory mechanisms affect the actual turnover that is catalyzed by the particular enzyme or group of enzymes. The discrepancy between an enzyme activity at its intracellular location (even if we assume a steady state of metabolism) and the enzyme activity measured *in vitro* can at best be an assumption or a roughly calculated value. However, we want to measure *in vitro* the full catalytic potential of the enzyme. Under these assumptions, the *in vitro* activity would be a measure of the *in vivo* catalytic potential of the enzyme. Numerous investigations of tissue enzyme activities, especially those in which the rates of enzyme synthesis and degradation[128] or other simultaneous measurements of enzyme activity and content of enzyme were studied,[19] have revealed a surprisingly close relationship among enzyme activity, amount of enzyme, and metabolic potential. This relationship is also relevant to studies of tissue and cell enzyme activities in inherited metabolic diseases. This finding is of special importance for ontogenetic studies of tissue enzyme activities, in which the enzyme activities may reveal clues about developmental changes of the tissue metabolism. Such clues have frequently been obtained, as is shown by examples cited in the following sections.

3.2. Regulation

The *in vivo* activity of an enzyme protein can be altered in two ways: by factors that influence the enzyme activity and by factors that influence the amount of enzyme protein.[133] Both factors are subject to a complicated network of regulation.[28,74,116,135]

The developmental changes are thought to occur on the level of the amount of enzyme protein present in the tissue; consequently, these regulatory factors are of special interest to us. The regulating factors affect the rate of synthesis as well as the breakdown of enzyme protein.[82,99] In some cases, the formation of the apoenzyme occurs quite independently of the enzyme protein.[21] The genetic information for the proper construction of a specific enzyme protein originates from the DNA of the structural gene, is transcribed to the messenger RNA, and then goes to the template RNA of the ribosomes, where activated amino acids are synthesized to the specific protein molecule. This final process needs energy from the ATP pool.[45] The enzyme protein synthesis is regulated at both levels—the synthesis (ribosomes) and the genes (release of information).[135]

The master plan of the cellular metabolism discloses a schematic organization with surprising similarities among cells from virtually all animals; this master plan was called an *archetype* by Pette.[81] The basic qualitative order of cell metabolism shows modifications that we ascribe to cell differentiation and specialization; i.e., special cells lose certain metabolic capacities, other cells develop special functions by enhancing certain reactions. The growing knowledge of the network of intermediary reactions has shown that certain reactions are rate-limiting for a pathway, and the respective enzymes play a key role. Hexokinase, for instance, regulates the entry of glucose into the Embden–Meyerhof pathway.[55] Key enzymes unlock and regulate (or restrict) metabolic pathways. Furthermore, some enzymes represent a directional pathway because of their preference for catalyzing the conversion of a substrate into a product with practically no reversibility; frequently, such enzymes circumvent a thermodynamic barrier. These particular enzymes also have a key function,[135] but for practical reasons, they will be referred to here as *representative* enzymes. For example, phosphofructokinase represents the glycolytic pathway, while fructose-1,6-diphosphatase and phosphopyruvate carboxylase are representative of the gluconeogenetic pathway; other glycolytic enzymes are bifunctional, such as glucosephosphate isomerase, glyceraldehydephosphate dehydrogenase, and phosphopyruvate hydratase.[134] There are many other enzyme activities that can be representative of certain pathways, cycles, or reactions, but for many of these activities, the validity and specificity remain to be proved on a broader basis and by combined studies with labeled substrates. Among others, the following enzyme activities have been used: the citrate synthase (condensing enzyme) reflects the Krebs cycle,[81] the 3-hydroxyacyl-CoA dehydrogenase is indicative of the fatty acid oxidation,[81] the cytochrome c oxidase (or the cytochrome c content) represents the endoxidation in the respiratory chain,[81] and ATP citrate lyase (CL: EC 4.1.3.8) is considered to be of rate-controlling significance for the formation of fatty acids from carbohydrates via citrate.[123] ATP citrate lyase is the first of three sequential key enzymes for fatty acid synthesis,[56] with acetyl-CoA carboxylase[79] being in a central position and fatty acid

synthetase of final importance. Enzyme kinetics, inhibition, feedback mechanisms, rates of synthesis and degradation, and hormone sensitivity are among the characteristics that must be known for full understanding of key enzymes and their use for quantitation of metabolic capacities of tissues and organs.

3.3. Activity Ratios and System Correlations

The discovery of fixed ratios among certain groups of enzyme activities in cells and tissues of a wide variety of origin has added a new aspect to tissue enzymology.[82,83] Bücher[8] and his associates called these groups of enzymes *constant proportion groups,* and the first of this kind was found to exist in all animal cells examined and consisted of the following glycolytic enzymes: triosephosphate isomerase, glyceraldehydephosphate dehydrogenase, glycerate phosphomutase, phosphoglycerate kinase, and enolase. The existence of such groups has led to the speculation that their structural relationship within the cell must be close. Certain functionally related groups of enzymes have been shown to occur in organized aggregates.[27,93] Such macromolecular organizations of enzymes had first been hypothesized, and their existence was later confirmed.[62]

If representative enzyme activities reflect the metabolic potential of a system, such as glycolysis, gluconeogenesis, Krebs cycle, fatty acid oxidation, and so forth, then we can bring them into relationship to each other by comparing activity ratios; these comparisons were made by Pette,[81] and were called *system-correlations.* The cell metabolism passes through many changes during ontogenesis, and for the study of characteristic differences among organs and tissues, system-correlations were shown to be of value.[82,111,113]

For example, the activity ratios of phosphofructokinase and 3-hydroxyacyl-CoA dehydrogenase (PFK/HAD) provides information about relative tissue preference for utilizing glycolysis or fatty acid oxidation. Glucose utilization can be put in relationship to the Krebs cycle activity by forming the ratio PFK/CS (citrate synthase). Glycolysis (PFK) and gluconeogenesis (fructosediphosphatase, FD-Pase) can be compared by using the PFK/FDPase ratio. Table V demonstrates the relative constancy of the four metabolic pathways (systems) over age in the liver; in contrast, heart and skeletal muscle

Table V. System Correlations in Perinatal and Adult Rabbit Liver, Heart, and Skeletal Muscle[a]

Organ and system correlation	Representative enzyme activities	Fetus (last day)	Newborn (first day)	Adult
Liver: $\dfrac{\text{Glycolysis}}{\text{Fatty acid oxidation}}$	$\dfrac{\text{PFK}}{\text{HAD}}$	0.14	0.25	0.11
$\dfrac{\text{Glycolysis}}{\text{Krebs cycle}}$	$\dfrac{\text{PFK}}{\text{CS}}$	3.5	3.1	2.9
$\dfrac{\text{Glycolysis}}{\text{Glyconeogenesis}}$	$\dfrac{\text{PFK}}{\text{FDPase}}$	1.0	1.1[b]	1.1
Heart: $\dfrac{\text{Glycolysis}}{\text{Fatty acid oxidation}}$	$\dfrac{\text{PFK}}{\text{HAD}}$	4.7	4.1	1.9
Muscle: $\dfrac{\text{Glycolysis}}{\text{Fatty acid oxidation}}$	$\dfrac{\text{PFK}}{\text{HAD}}$	10.0	9.8	155.0

[a] From Stave.[111]

[b] At age 2 hr; the ratio drops to 0.7 at age 24 hr.

change the preference for oxidizing glucose or fatty acids markedly and in opposite directions postnatally.

3.4. Isoenzymes

The discovery of multiple forms of enzymes was of great benefit for the study of enzyme activities in growing tissues.[65] Isoenzymes are biochemically and physically separable enzyme proteins with qualitatively identical but quantitatively distinct catalytic activities. The age-dependent changes of isoenzyme patterns in different tissues made us aware of the different kinetic properties we must consider for the composition of reaction mixtures when we analyze tissue extracts from different organs and from animals of different age groups.[110] The isoenzymes of lactate dehydrogenase (LDH) have been investigated most frequently and most intensively. While, in general, the LDH activity is referred to as the *anaerobic potential* of a tissue, it was an interesting observation of Richterich et al.[95] that cells with high oxygen consumption contain predominantly fast-migrating LDH isoenzymes, and cells with high glycolytic activity contain more of the slow-migrating fractions.

Cahn et al.[10] discovered the hybrid nature of LDH, and they developed an immunologic method for separate measurements of the two basic subunits, which they called the *H-unit* (since it occurs in a pure form in the adult chicken heart) and the *M-unit* (which is found pure in chicken breast muscle). The H- and M-subunits occur only in tetramers, and the five bands that appear on electrophoretic separation of LDH from various sources have been shown to be the five possible combinations: MMMM, MMMH, MMHH, MHHH, and HHHH.[10,16] The LDH isoenzymes are synthesized within the same cell, and all serve the same general function, but the two subunits are governed by different genes, or the type of hybrid formed is an expression of "differential regulation of genes."[16] The same authors demonstrated that monkey heart cells cultured in an anaerobic environment produced more M-subunits than did aerobically grown cells. Similarly, Lindy and Rajasalmi[60] analyzed significantly more M-subunits in chicken liver, heart, and breast muscle after anaerobic incubation of eggs than in organs from air-incubated chicken embryos. In these experiments, the total LDH activity did not change significantly. Blatt et al.[6] speculated that the H-subunits are more prone to work under aerobic conditions, since high pyruvate concentrations inhibit their activity, and that, vice versa, the M-subunits are more appropriate for an oxygen-deficient environment, since they are less inhibited by high pyruvate concentrations. The few examples mentioned above and the kinetics of the purified H- and M-subunits[129] lead to the conclusion that the oxygen-dependent metabolism has a regulatory effect on the synthesis of H- and M-subunit peptides, and hence on the LDH isoenzyme pattern.

The LDH isoenzyme pattern of the liver shows characteristic differences among species. Wiggert and Villee[138] did not find any appreciable change in the pattern of fetal, neonatal, and adult rat liver, but Blatt et al.[6] measured more M-subunits of LDH in fetal rat liver than in the adult. In human liver, Fine et al.[20] found more than 99% H-subunits in a 6-week-old fetus, 73.6% in a 7-month-old fetus, and 2.7–14.1% in the adult. These values agree well with measurements in the human liver published by Pfleiderer and Wachsmuth,[84] which are shown in Fig. 6. The big differences among species are well documented by many authors. Fine et al.[20] analyzed the amount of H-subunits and found 12.5% in fetal rabbit liver, but 67% in bovine fetal liver; in adult rabbit liver, the H-subunits account for 63% and in adult beef for 97.4% of total LDH activity. A more detailed description of sequential alterations in LDH isoenzymes during development was published by Vesell and Philip.[124]

The "electrophoretic variation in enzymes"[105] provides a major tool for genetics and for developmental research. The LDH isoenzymes have been used here as an example, but for many more enzymes, the occurrence of multiple forms has been demonstrated. Shaw[105] listed 16 groups of isoenzymes in diploid organisms, but since then that number has grown considerably. Among the more recently identified isoenzymes are phosphorylase,[98] aldolases of the L- and M-types,[41] pyruvate kinase,[70] and alanine aminotransferase.[108] The high-resolution zymogram is now in frequent use for the study of genetic alterations. In developmental studies, the kinetic changes that are due to changing isoenzyme patterns are of great importance.

3.5. Oxygen Consumption

Since the beginning of the analysis of metabolic development, the *in vitro* measurement of oxygen uptake in tissue slices, homogenates, and cell suspensions has been an important source of information about the activity of the cell metabolism.

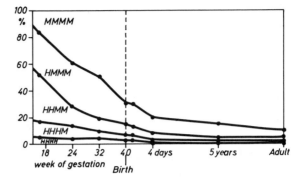

Fig. 6. Percent distribution of human liver LDH isoenzymes during pre- and postnatal development. Data from Pfleiderer and Wachsmuth.[84]

Warburg's methodological refinements and his many comparative measurements were essential contributions.[131,132] A review of early investigations of embryonic, fetal, and neonatal tissues was published by Needham in 1931.[75] The rate of oxygen consumption is regarded as an equivalent of tissue energy production. In addition to many technical difficulties, such as preparing tissue slices of exact thickness and providing optimum environmental conditions, the correct measurement of oxygen consumption is highly dependent on the concentration of substrates and energy-rich phosphates, which can both be easily reduced or destroyed during preparation, especially of homogenates. Many times, the question has been raised whether the oxygen uptake actually corresponds to the energy production.[38] The varying levels of tissue oxygen consumption during gestation, especially, raised the question of the functional significance of such data.[44] With the use of glucose as substrate, human liver slices from fetuses and adults were revealed to have the same oxygen consumption of 28 μmol oxygen/g wet tissue per hr[126]; the respiratory quotient was 1.31 in fetal and 0.95 in adult liver.

The basal oxygen consumption in developing sheep tissues was discussed in detail by Barcroft[4] in 1947. In the liver, the oxygen uptake per unit of body weight is lower in the last quarter of gestation than earlier and also lower after birth. The oxygen uptake per unit of liver dry weight shows an approximately linear decline from midterm gestation through adulthood. A very interesting calculation was performed by Barcroft for all major organs and tissues. Table VI shows the organs in order of their

Table VI. Organs in Order of Their Contribution to the Oxygen Uptake by the Body in Fetal, Neonatal, and Adult Sheep[a]

Fetal age (days)					Lamb (6 days)	Adult sheep
78	99	112	130	144		
Cartilage	Cartilage	Muscle	Skin	Skin	Skin	Muscle
31	32	38	31	23	26	50
Liver	Muscle	**Liver**	**Liver**	**Liver**	Muscle	Gut
28	26	20	20	18	15	23
Muscle	**Liver**	Skin	Muscle	Muscle	Gut	**Liver**
15	17	18	18	13	14	12
Kidney	Gut	Lung	Gut	Gut	**Liver**	Cartilage
3	4	7	7	7	12	3

[a] Data from Barcroft.[4] Oxygen taken up by the organ is expressed as a percentage of that taken up by the whole body.

contribution to the oxygen uptake by the body. The table shows that the liver ranges in second place through the second half of gestation, drops to fifth place in the newborn lamb, and comes back to third position in adult sheep, in which 12% of the whole-body oxygen consumption is taken up by the liver.

4. Enzyme Development

The literature on developmental changes in enzyme activities in mammalian liver has become quite extensive within the last decade,[29,38,51] and this survey does not claim to be complete in regard to all liver enzyme activities in mammals. We have tried to cover a wide range of enzyme activities, however, and we present the data for the perinatal period in a uniform manner to make comparisons possible. The protein concentration in the liver has been used as reference whenever it was available, and the term "specific activity" is used accordingly. The best comparability seems to be achieved by referring to the average adult enzyme activity as 100, thus expressing developmental values in percentages of adult levels. The obvious disadvantage of this method is that no absolute data for enzyme activities are presented, but since the absolute values published by different laboratories still differ frequently, this method of comparing percentages is an acceptable compromise. By comparing percentages, we learn as much about the principles of change as we would learn from

absolute values. Most data deal with rat liver, since information is most complete for this animal.[51] Some values for the human liver and some for other mammals are included, thus allowing comparison of hepatic development among species.

Carbohydrate metabolism is discussed in Chapter 17. Additional information on glycolytic enzyme activities in the liver will be presented here to complete the picture of developmental changes in the hepatic enzyme pattern. Developmental changes in 16 glycolytic enzymes in rat liver were investigated by Hommes and Wilmink.[42]

Glycogen synthesis and mobilization are discussed in Chapter 17 (especially Fig. 1 and Table III). The three key glycolytic enzymes[135]—hexokinase (HK) phosphofructokinase (PFK), and pyruvate kinase (PK)—are shown in Fig. 7. It is of interest to observe that they decline concordantly in the perinatal period; however, the further down they are located in the Embden–Meyerhof pathway, the lower is their activity in comparison with the adult level and the less marked is their decline. This pattern leads to the speculation that the amount of substrate flow along this chain of glycolytic reactions is further reduced by branching-off pathways before birth than after. The declining activities of glucose-6-phosphate dehydrogenase (G-6-PDH) and phosphogluconate dehydrogenase (PGDH) are demonstrated in Figs. 8 and 9. The G-6-PDH activity in guinea pig liver (Fig. 9) is calculated per body weight, and by this frame of reference, it is much higher before birth. Details on the hexose monophosphate shunt are discussed in Chapter 17. However, the activity of another important sideway, catalyzed by glycerol-3-phosphate dehydrogenase (GDH), is no higher at birth than later in life (Figs. 10 and 11). Such comparisons are still speculative, because we do not know the actual flux through the respective reaction chains.

The four *key gluconeogenetic enzymes*[135] increase from very low prenatal to high postnatal activities (Fig. 12). The overall shape of the activity curves during perinatal development is uniform, and this uniformity seems to be typical for a close functional relationship. The same observation was made for human newborn liver.[66]

In rat liver, the phosphorylation of galactose is revealed to have a high potential even before birth,

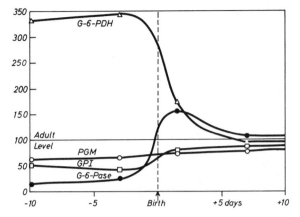

Fig. 9. Guinea pig liver. Enzyme activities calculated per unit of body weight and expressed as percentages of adult levels. G-6-PDH (see Fig. 8), phosphoglucomutase (PGM: EC 2.7.5.1), glucosephosphate isomerase (GPI: EC 5.3.1.9), and glucose-6-phosphatase (G-6-Pase: EC 3.1.3.9). Data from Lea and Walker.[58]

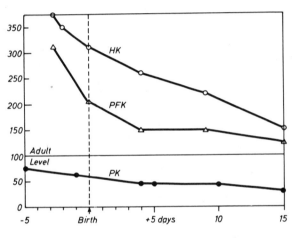

Fig. 7. Rat liver. Perinatal changes in specific enzyme activities expressed as percentages of adult level. Data for hexokinase (HK: EC 2.7.1.1) and phosphofructokinase (PFK: EC 2.7.1.11) from Burch *et al.*[9] Data for pyruvate kinase (PK: EC 2.7.1.40) from Vernon and Walker.[123]

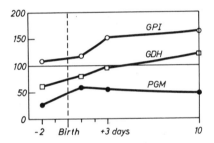

Fig. 10. Rabbit liver. Specific enzyme activities expressed as percentages of adult levels. PGM (see Fig. 9), GPI (see Fig. 9), and glycerol-3-phosphate dehydrogenase (GDH: EC 1.1.1.8).

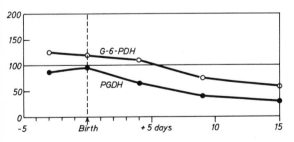

Fig. 8. Rat liver. Specific enzyme activities expressed as percentages of adult levels. Glucose-6-phosphate dehydrogenase (G-6-PDH: EC 1.1.1.49) and phosphogluconate dehydrogenase (PGDH: EC 1.1.1.44). Data from Burch *et al.*[9]

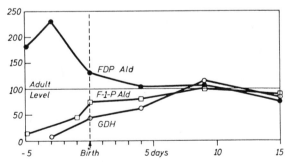

Fig. 11. Rat liver. Specific enzyme activities expressed as percentages of adult levels. Fructose-1,6-diphosphate aldolase (FDP Ald: EC 4.1.2.13), GDH (see Fig. 10), and fructose-1-phosphate aldolase (F-1-P Ald: EC 4.1.2.7). Data from Burch *et al.*[9]

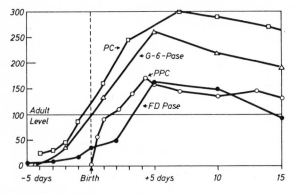

Fig. 12. Rat liver. Specific enzyme activities expressed as percentages of adult levels. Data for pyruvate carboxylase (PC: EC 6.4.1.1), phosphopyruvate carboxylase (PPC: EC 4.1.1.32), and fructose-1,6-diphosphatase (FDPase: EC 3.1.3.11) from Yeung *et al.*[144] Data for G-6-Pase (see Fig. 9) from Vernon and Walker.[123]

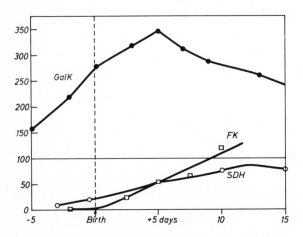

Fig. 13. Rat liver. Specific enzyme activities expressed as percentages of adult levels. Data for galactokinase (GalK: EC 2.7.1.6) from Cuatrecasas and Segal.[13] Data for fructokinase (FK: EC 2.7.1.3) from Walker.[130] Data for sorbitol dehydrogenase or L-Idit DH (SDH: EC 1.1.1.14) were calculated in units per liver nitrogen from the data of Theile.[120]

and 5 days after birth, the activity reaches a peak value. The phosphorylation of fructose follows a distinctively different pattern (Fig. 13); before birth, no activity is found; after birth, it increases quickly and reaches the adult level around the 10th day or later after weaning, according to Sillero *et al.*[107] The development of sorbitol-dehydrogenase (L-Idit DH; SDH) is also shown in Fig. 13. This activity increases slowly after birth, and remains below the adult level for more than 15 days.

The four enzyme activities that are involved in the immediate metabolism of glucose-6-phosphate are glucose-6-phosphatase (G-6-Pase), phosphoglucomutase (PGM), glucosephosphate isomerase (GPI), and G-6-PDH. Their development is shown in Fig. 9 for the guinea pig liver, based on a calculation of enzyme units per unit of body weight. The high G-6-PDH activity before birth and the steep increase in G-6-Pase at birth are the most impressive changes. The G-6-Pase activity of the human fetal liver was found to be much lower than that measured in adult liver, but significant changes were observed between the 5th and 9th months of gestation.[2] For rabbit liver calculated per protein, the GPI and PGM activities are shown in Fig. 10. The PGM activity develops very similarly in both species, whereas PGI is considerably higher in rabbits during the perinatal period.

The activity of GDH increases steadily in rabbits (Fig. 10), and steadily but at a lower level in rats (Fig. 11). The ketose-1-phosphate aldolase activity measured with fructose-1-phosphate as substrate increases in a manner similar to that of GDH (Fig. 11).

The so-called "bifunctional enzymes" of the glycolytic pathway[135] have little or no similarities in their developmental patterns except for those five enzymes that form a constant-proportion group and of which glyceraldehydephosphate dehydrogenase (GAPDH) and triosephosphate dehydrogenase (TPI) are shown for rat liver in Fig. 14 and for rabbit liver in Fig. 15; these two enzymes have nearly identical values in the perinatal period, and the other three enzymes can be expected to show the same pattern. However, fructose-1,6-diphosphate aldolase (FDP Ald) (Fig. 11), LDH (Figs. 14

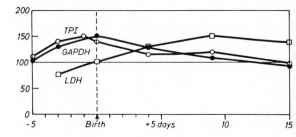

Fig. 14. Rat liver. Specific enzyme activities expressed as percentages of adult levels. Lactate dehydrogenase (LDH: EC 1.1.1.27), glyceraldehydephosphate dehydrogenase (GAPDH: EC 1.2.1.12), and triosephosphate isomerase (TPI: EC 5.3.1.1). Data from Burch *et al.*[9]

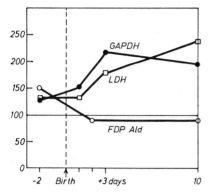

Fig. 15. Rabbit liver. Specific enzyme activities expressed as percentages of adult levels. GAPDH (see Fig. 14), LDH (see Fig. 14), and FDP Ald (see Fig. 11). Data from Stave.[109]

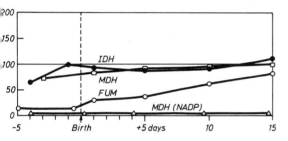

Fig. 16. Rat liver. Specific enzyme activities expressed as percentages of adult levels. Data for isocitrate dehydrogenase (NADP) (IDH: EC 1.1.1.42), malate dehydrogenase (MDH: EC 1.1.1.37), and fumarase (FUM: EC 4.2.1.2) from Vernon and Walker.[123] Data for dehydrogenase (decarboxylating, NADP) [MDH(NADP): EC 1.1.1.40] from Taylor et al.[117]

and 15), and GPI (Fig. 9) all demonstrate quite different perinatal changes in rats. In perinatal pig liver, the changes in glycolytic enzyme activities are different from those in rats, and are very dependent on early postnatal feeding.[115] In 10- to 20-week-old human fetuses, PK, PFK, GAPDH, and GDH were measured in liver tissue.[37]

Some enzyme activities of the *tricarboxylic acid cycle* (Krebs cycle) for rats are shown in Fig. 16. The activities of isocitrate dehydrogenase (NADP) (IDH) and malate dehydrogenase (NAD-specific) (MDH) develop perinatally at the same level with respect to adult values, and they both reach the adult potential at birth. Fumarase (FUM) is very low before birth, and postnatally it increases rapidly. The NADP-specific MDH activity [MDH (NADP)] is below the level of measurability for the entire

perinatal period, but it increases sharply between the 20th and 30th days in rats.[123]

The next group of enzyme activities to be discussed serves in pathways that connect glycolytic or Krebs cycle reactions with the amino acid pool. The glutamate dehydrogenase (GlDH) activity is shown for rabbit liver (Fig. 17) and the aspartate aminotransferase (AspAT) activity for rat liver (Fig. 18). Both activities are low before birth and increase above adult level at birth (rabbit) or within the first few days (rats). The same metabolites, glutamate, aspartate, 2-oxoglutarate, and oxaloacetate, are involved in both enzyme reactions. However, alanine aminotransferase (AlAT) and glutamine synthetase (GS) activities are low or not detectable during the perinatal period in rats, despite their close relationship and the involvement of some of the metabolites mentioned for the former two enzymes.

In Fig. 19, the low activities and the slow increase

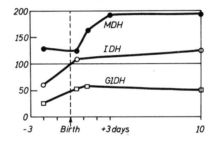

Fig. 17. Rabbit liver. Specific enzyme activities expressed as percentages of adult levels. MDH (NAD) (see Fig. 16), IDH (NADP) (see Fig. 16), and glutamate dehydrogenase (GlDH: EC 1.4.1.2).

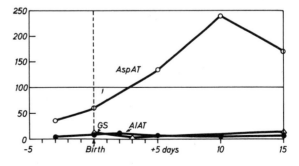

Fig. 18. Rat liver. Specific enzyme activities expressed as percentages of adult levels. Data for aspartate aminotransferase (AspAT: EC 2.6.1.1) and alanine aminotransferase (AlAT: EC 2.6.1.2) from Yeung and Oliver.[142] Data for glutamine synthetase (GS: EC 6.3.1.2) from Wu.[141]

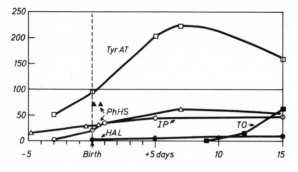

Fig. 19. Rat liver. Enzyme activities calculated in units per gram tissue wet weight and expressed as percentages of adult level. Data for tyrosine aminotransferase (Tyr AT: EC 2.6.1.5) from Kenney and Kretchmer.[48] Data for histidine ammonia-lyase (HAL: EC 4.3.1.3) and imidazolonepropionase (IP: EC 3.5.2.7) from Makoff and Baldridge.[63] The phenylalanine hydroxylating system (PhHS) represents more than one enzyme, and was calculated on the basis of tissue protein: (△) values from Freedland et al.[22]; (▲) values from Brenneman and Kaufman.[7] Data for tryptophan oxygenase (TO: EC 1.13.1.12) were calculated per unit of liver dry weight from the data of Auerbach and Waisman.[1]

in three enzymes of *amino acid metabolism* are shown. Histidine ammonia-lyase (HAL) and imidazolone proprionase (IP) remain low in rat liver within the first 15 days after birth. The activity of histidine decarboxylase per total rat liver is shown in Fig. 23; the highest activity is found at birth, with a decrease to almost zero on the second day after birth. The prenatal increase in this enzyme activity was also demonstrated to occur in fetal human liver.[72] Glutamine-dependent asparagine synthetase declines from prenatal values of approximately 20 to around 4 nmol/min per g liver wet weight on the 6th day of life, and to 2 nmol/min per g in adult rats.[43]

The phenylalanine hydroxylating system (PhHS) was first shown to be negligibly low in livers of fetal rats near term and rats less than 24 hr old[94]; later, it was found that liver preparations from fetal rats, rabbits, pigs, and a human premature infant were incapable of forming tyrosine from phenylalanine unless the reaction mixture was supplemented by a cofactor from adult liver extracts.[48] In newborn rats, the activity of the PhHS, measured without additions, was found to be about 30%[22] or 70%[7] of the adult level. Another study[67] showed no enzyme in the liver of a 20-day-old rat fetus; at birth, 20% of the adult level was reached, and 40% in the second week of life. The PhHS has been measured in human fetal liver[11,91] and in children.

The mean value of PhHS in human fetal liver was 14.7 μmol/hr per g wet weight and 29.2 μmol/hr per g in the liver of children[68]; in these studies, the cofactor and the complementing enzyme were not measured. In animal experiments, the analysis of cofactors and *in vivo* conditions revealed that the specific enzyme protein is present at birth at about the same level as in adult male rats, and that the prenatally missing cofactor reaches adult level within the first day of life.[7] The same authors found that the activity of dihydropteridine reductase was low before birth; later, it was reported[23] that there exist two strikingly different patterns of development in the rat on one hand and the human and guinea pig on the other. In rats, the PhHS is inactive before birth and rises to above adult levels at birth; in the human, the hydroxylase was detectable in the second trimester.

The tyrosine aminotransferase (Tyr AT) activity in rats (Fig. 19) develops in a pattern very similar to that of AspAT (Fig. 18). A more recent analysis of the ontogenetic development of rat liver showed that this aminotransferase, together with *p*-hydroxyphenylpyruvate hydroxylase and homogentisate oxygenase, increases from 10% of adult level at birth to about 25% on the second day and a plateau around 45% between the 10th and 20th days of life.[25]

Another shunt between the amino acid pool and the glycolytic pathway is represented by D-glycerate and D-3-phosphoglycerate dehydrogenases. The first one increases steeply in the perinatal period, and the second one decreases in the perinatal period and is below measurability in adult rat liver.[47]

The metabolism of *fatty acids* and lipids is discussed in Chapter 19. In the liver, three initial reactions for acetate and acetyl-CoA formation are catalyzed by ATP citrate-lyase (CL), acetyl-CoA synthetase (ACoAS), and pyruvate dehydrogenase (PDH: EC

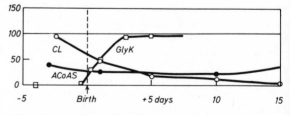

Fig. 20. Rat liver. Specific enzyme activities expressed as percentages of adult levels. Data for ATP citrate-lyase (CL: EC 4.1.3.8) from Vernon and Walker.[123] Data for acetyl-CoA synthetase (ACoAS: EC 6.2.1.1) from Hahn and Drahota.[36] Data for glycerol kinase (GlyK: EC 2.7.1.30) from Theil.[119]

Table VII. ATP Citrate-Lyase (CL) and 3-Hydroxyacyl-CoA Dehydrogenase (HAD) in Rabbit Liver (Calculated on Soluble Protein Base and Expressed in Percentages of Adult Values)

Rabbits	CL[a]	HAD[b]
Fetuses		
(1 day before term)	472	68
Newborns		
1–3 hr old	393	68
24–30 hr old	164	123
3 days old	239	100

[a] From Wolf et al.[140]
[b] From Stave and Wolf.[113]

1.2.4.1). The first two enzyme activities are shown for rat liver in Fig. 20. The activity of the PDH complex in these animals increases from around 3 μmol/min per g protein in fetal liver to about 10 U/g in adult liver.[50] CL and 3-hydroxyacyl-CoA dehydrogenase (HAD) in perinatal rabbit liver are presented in Table VII. The high activity of CL in perinatal rabbit liver is remarkable. A 2-fold post-natal increase in fatty acid oxidation capacity supports the general observation of a high dependence of newborns on fatty acid oxidation. At the same time, the formation of acetyl-CoA from citrate drops to less than half, which leads us to speculate that the fatty acids for oxidation originate from extrahepatic sources, such as brown adipose tissue.

Before birth, no phosphorylation of glycerol seems to occur, but at birth the glycerol kinase (GlyK) activity increases steeply in rat liver and reaches the adult level within 3 days (Fig. 20; see also Chapter 19, Fig. 11). Glycerol is a product of triacylglycerol hydrolysis that is catalyzed by lipases, and since the latter group of hydrolyzing enzymes is low during prenatal development, the enzyme for glycerol utilization by phosphorylation is not needed before birth.

The activity of the *respiratory chain* and enzymes involved in the oxidoreduction of cytochromes is essential for every living cell. During gestation and even after birth, however, rather drastic changes of respiratory enzymes have been observed.[14,57] The alteration in activities during the perinatal period in rat liver is shown in Fig. 21. The increases occur rather linearly and almost parallel to each other. This phenomenon supports the hypothesis proposed by Green[27] that the electron transport of the endoxidation is located in a macroenzyme complex in the elementary particle. Mino and Takai[71] studied the activities of cytochrome c oxidase and succinate dehydrogenase in fetal human liver and other organs.

The developmental pattern of enzymes involved in urea synthesis is covered in Chapter 24.

Some other hepatic enzyme activities are demonstrated in the following figures. Figure 22 shows the slow but steady perinatal increase of two enzymes involved in the metabolism of sialic acid. The activity of alcohol dehydrogenase (ADH) in rat liver increases linearly from very low fetal values to about 75% of the adult level at age 15 days (Fig. 23). In human liver, the development is similarly linear, but adult values are not attained before 5 years of age.[86] Sulfate conjugation is an important mechanism for detoxifying phenols and compounds of steroid structure (see Chapter 25). Before birth, this function would have little meaning; accordingly, the activity of sulfate conjugation tested with p-nitrophenol is negligibly low in rat liver. However, it increases at birth and slowly thereafter (Fig. 23). Some measurements have been performed in human perinatal liver.[90] Cystathionine synthase activity in rat liver increases by more than an order of magnitude shortly before birth and much less postnatally.[127]

Histidine decarboxylase (HD) activity increases steeply before birth in rat liver, and reaches a peak value at birth. This development, as shown in Fig. 23, is interrupted after birth, and during days 2–4, only

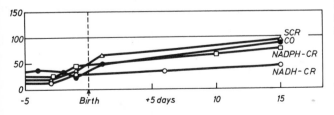

Fig. 21. Rat liver. Specific enzyme activities expressed as percentages of adult levels. Succinate dehydrogenase or succinate cytochrome c reductase (SCR: EC 1.3.99.1), cytochrome c oxidase (CO: EC 1.9.3.1), NADPH–cytochrome c reductase (NADPH-CR: EC 1.6.99.1), and NADH–cytochrome c reductase (NADH-CR: EC 1.6.99.3). Data from Lang.[57]

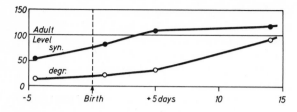

Fig. 22. Rat liver. Specific enzyme activities expressed as percentages of adult levels. Two enzymes involved in sialic acid metabolism that synthesize (syn.) or degrade (degr.) cytidine 5'-monophospho-*N*-acetyl neuraminic acid are shown. Data from Shoyab and Bachhawat.[106]

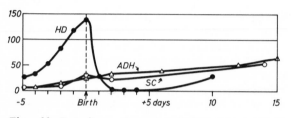

Fig. 23. Rat liver. Enzyme activities expressed as percentages of adult levels. Data for histidine decarboxylase (HD: EC 4.1.1.22) were calculated per total liver from the data of Telford and West.[118] Data for alcohol dehydrogenase (ADH: EC 1.1.1.1) were calculated per gram liver wet weight from the data of Räihä et al.[92] The sulfate conjugation (SC) was measured with *p*-nitrophenol as substrate and was calculated per gram liver wet weight from the data of Pulkkinen.[90]

traces of activity can be detected[118]; thereafter, HD activity increases slowly.

The enzyme activities of *nucleic acid metabolism* in perinatal liver have long escaped a systematic investigation.[54] Purine and adenine phosphoribosyl transferase activities decrease markedly in postnatal mouse liver,[88] while RNA polymerase I and II activities more than double during the first 30 days after birth.[3]

Three key enzymes of the *synthesis of phospholipids* show perinatal increases.[136] In rat liver, choline kinase (EC 2.7.1.3.2) increases steeply (about 50%) at birth, cholinephosphate cytidyltransferase (EC 2.7.7.15) increases even before birth, and choline phosphotransferase (EC 2.7.8.2) increases in a delayed fashion for 5 days after birth; the amount of increase in all three enzyme activities is quite similar. The functional significance of perinatal activity changes of these enzymes is discussed in Chapter 7.

5. Initiation of Enzyme Formation in the Perinatal Period

In the preceding section, it was shown that several enzyme activities first appear at, or immediately after, birth; other enzymes change markedly at birth, and many enzyme activities do not change significantly during the time of transition from intrauterine to extrauterine life. The initiation of activity within the immediate perinatal period was observed for tryptophan oxygenase (TO) by Nemeth,[77] for G-6-Pase by Nemeth[76] and Dawkins,[15] for Tyr AT by Litwack and Nemeth,[61] and for phosphopyruvate carboxylase by Yeung et al.[144]; more recently, other enzymes have been added to this "cluster"[29] of enzyme activations after birth.

The degree of maturity at birth, as usually determined by the functional state of the CNS, differs markedly among mammalian species. In analogy, differences in the biochemical maturation of liver function can be observed by comparing enzyme activities in the perinatal period. For example, in maturely born guinea pigs, liver TO activity begins to appear shortly before birth, and rises to the adult level immediately after birth. In rabbits, which are born at a less mature stage, this enzyme appears immediately after birth, and rises within 24 hr to the adult level (cf. Fig. 24.) Finally, in the liver of immature rats, TO appears around the 15th postnatal day[77] (Fig. 19). Certain differences in perinatal changes among the species mentioned have been observed for many other liver enzymes; e.g., compare the activity of GDH in rabbits (Fig. 10) and rats (Fig. 11), or the activities of MDH and IDH in rats (Fig. 16) and rabbits (Fig. 17). This phenomenon reveals that the developmental change in certain enzyme activities follows an ontogenetic time schedule that governs independently the time of birth as well as biochemical cell functions such as the activity of enzymes.

Premature delivery of rabbits or rats resulted in a postnatal increase in those enzyme activities listed in the first paragraph of this section similar to the increase in term newborn animals. Delayed delivery prevented the rise until birth. Nemeth[77] introduced this experimental technique of premature or delayed delivery for the study of tissue enzyme initiation in the perinatal period (by sectioning rabbits on the 27th day of gestation, or on the 35th day after hormonal stimulation of corpus luteum formation for prolonging the gestation period). Figure 24

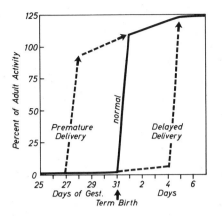

Fig. 24. Schematic presentation of the perinatal development of tryptophan oxygenase activity in rabbit liver and the effect of premature and delayed delivery. Data from Nemeth.[77]

shows schematically the results of the investigation by Nemeth[77] of liver TO in rabbit liver as influenced by premature or delayed delivery. Subsequent studies of this effect on other enzyme activities, such as Tyr AT[61] and phosphopyruvate carboxylase,[142] confirmed Nemeth's original observation. In 1959, Nemeth[77] considered a "factor associated with birth" and, later,[78] "a repressive factor in the uterine environment from which release is obtained at birth" and that triggers the initiation of enzyme activity at birth.

Substrate induction of specific enzymes has been shown to occur in adult animals as well as in some embryonic tissues.[52] In adult rabbits and rats, tryptophan administration results in a 6- to 8-fold adaptive increase of liver TO.[53] In rabbit fetal liver, however, which has no detectable enzyme activity, tryptophan injection failed to induce this activity[77]; as soon as TO begins to appear postnatally, it also becomes sensitive to a substrate-induced adaptive increase. The controversial results of experiments dealing with substrate induction of other enzyme activities in embryonic or fetal tissues might not rule out the possibility of substrate induction of enzymes before birth, but they make it rather unlikely for the majority of enzymes (for a review, see Moog[73]).

Hormones play an essential role in the regulatory system of the metabolism. The hormonal control of enzyme protein has been the object of many studies, and evidence has been presented that some hormonal control of protein synthesis occurs at the translational level,[87,122] and some on the level of the genetic material.[103]

Jacquot and Kretchmer[46] changed the endocrine status of the rat fetus drastically by decapitation on the 18th day of gestation. The application of such a procedure prevented the physiologic increase of liver G-6-Pase and uridine diphosphoglucose-glycogen-transglucosylase activity, while PGM was significantly decreased and G-6-PDH considerably higher in decapitated fetuses than in controls at birth. These changes occurred within 2–3 days, and were associated with a negligible deposition of liver glycogen. These results supported the hypothesis that the prenatal development of liver enzyme activities is influenced by hormones. Injection of adrenocortical hormone into guinea pig or rabbit fetuses did not induce a precocious induction of TO, nor did this treatment initiate an earlier appearance of this enzyme activity in 7-day-old rats.[77] The same lack of prenatal responsiveness was found for Tyr AT.[61,104] The administration of hydrocortisone acetate to fetal rats did not increase the activities of G-6-Pase or NADPH dehydrogenase.[31] Injection of estradiol into rat fetuses on the 19th day of gestation did not induce precocious development of ornithine aminotransferase in either liver or kidney, although estradiol induces a sharp increase of this enzyme activity in young and adult rats.[39] Injection of triamcinolone did not result in premature appearance of phosphopyruvate carboxylase[144] in fetal rat liver.

Many experiments have shown that enzyme activation, e.g., increase in activity stimulated by adrenocortical hormones, appears shortly after birth; in this context, the 3.5-fold increase in the corticosterone blood level that occurs within the first 5 hr after birth in rats is most important.[40] Adrenalectomized newborns suffer from a significantly slower postnatal increase of those enzyme activities that normally increase rapidly.[61,104] Liver Tyr AT activity can be markedly increased by corticosteroids in adult mammals, birds, and reptiles, but not in amphibia or fish,[12] and by interpreting these results, Litwack and Nemeth[61] speculated that "the late evolutionary development of the response to hydrocortisone may bear some relationship to the late appearance of the response in the development of mammals."

The hormones that are phylogenetically older than corticosteroids, such as thyroxine and glucagon, have a decisive influence on prenatal regulation, and probably also on prenatal induction of enzyme activities. Greengard and Dewey[31] observed a marked acceleration of the developmental increase of G-6-Pase and NADPH dehydrogenase in rat liver after administration of thyroxine; similarly, glucagon treatment increased G-6-Pase and Tyr AT. The latter enzyme was not affected by thyroxine, however, and hydrocortisone did not increase the level of any of these enzyme activities. The authors discuss the possibility that a successful experimental stimulation of enzyme activities in fetal tissues might identify the natural developmental stimulus for enzyme induction, especially if the beginning of hormone formation and the first appearance of certain enzyme activities coincide during ontogeny; this seems to be true for the enzymes and hormones studied by the authors. Furthermore, Greengard and Dewey[31] provided evidence that the hormonal regulation of the enzyme profile in fetal tissues and their maturational increases of activity seem to proceed rather independently of structural changes on the subcellular level.

The hormonal effect at the translational or DNA level became more likely when Yeung and Oliver[143] presented their study on phosphopyruvate carboxykinase induction; this enzyme appeared prematurely in the fetus after injection of glucagon or adrenaline, and could be prevented from appearing by treatment with actinomycin D. Final proof was published in 1972 by Philippidis et al.,[85] when the increase in enzyme activity was proved to be activation of enzyme synthesis; in fetal rat liver, only traces of enzyme protein could be detected by an antibody precipitation technique. Yeung and Oliver[143] showed that prenatal treatment with glucagon, adrenaline, or noradrenaline induces precocious enzyme activity, as does premature delivery. The physiologic hypoglycemia after birth and, similarly, the prenatally produced drop in the blood glucose level triggers the appearance of this enzyme; moreover, the prevention of postnatal hypoglycemia by administration of glucose, mannose, galactose, lactate, pyruvate, or glycerol repressed the postnatal development of this enzyme. Since adrenaline, noradrenaline, and glucagon promote the production of 3′,5′-(cyclic)-AMP (cAMP) in liver, Yeung and Oliver[143] suggested that this compound may act as a critical effector that derepresses the synthetic system for phosphopyruvate carboxylase when an appropriate concentration is reached.

These important and revealing animal experiments of the 1960s have demonstrated that specific hormones and messenger substances regulate the development of enzyme patterns. More recent investigations helped to understand the interplay between hormones and cAMP, and also to point out species differences.[24,30] It seems to be most important, however, to point to the few studies performed with *human fetal liver* explants. Schwartz et al.[101] analyzed G-6-Pase (EC 3.1.3.9) in fetal liver, and found 25–35% of the level measured in adult human liver between the 8th and 28th weeks of gestation. In organ culture, this level could be maintained for 2–3 days. In such a culture, incubation with dibutyryl cAMP increased the G-6-Pase activity 4–8 times within 24 hr, an effect that could be completely abolished by simultaneous administration of actinomycin D.

Kirby and Hahn[49] cultured human fetal liver (7–21 weeks' gestation) and used the following four enzymes for induction studies: PK, G-6-PDH, phosphoenolpyruvate carboxykinase (PEPK), and tyrosine transanimase (TTA). After correction for any losses from culture aging, it was shown that cAMP raised the activities of PEPK and TTA by 35 and 50%, respectively; no activity change was observed for PK or G-6-PDH. A special observation seems to be important: The aborted fetus of a mother who was treated with 20 mg prednisolone/day for 8 days prior to abortion was examined. The liver PEPK activity was 10 times higher than in any other fetus, the TTA and PK activities were not affected, and G-6-PDH was below normal. In this respect, it is an important finding that the adenyl cyclase in human fetal liver is sensitive to stimulation by fluoride ions, epinephrine, and glucagon.[69]

The existence of *regulator genes* was claimed by Jacob and Monod[45]; however, it remains to be proved whether timing factors or time-controlling elements can be identified as part of the genetic code. The sensitive phase that is frequently defined as the beginning of potential enzyme induction[35,38] might be identical with a derepression of a regulator gene, while the biosynthesis of active enzyme protein might eventually be dependent on a sufficient amount of hormonally stimulated effectors or other cofactors.

The combined genetic and enzymologic studies of inherited metabolic diseases provide ample evidence that enzyme formation in man and mammals is controlled by Mendelian genes.[114] However, experimental proof to this effect is scarce. Paigen[80] provided very instructive experimental results by comparing the postnatal development of β-glucuronidase activity in several tissues of two strains of mice that showed distinctive differences in enzyme development. Cross-breeding experiments led to the conclusion that controlling elements might act to determine when during development the structural genes become sensitive to diffusible factors. The author concluded that the controlling element seems to act as derepressor. The studies by Garn *et al.*[26] of the genetic action on the timing of tooth formation and on tooth size strongly support the hypothesis of a genetic timing factor that affects the timing of formation and development.

The genetic basis of enzyme development will remain an area of intensive investigation. At the same time, we need to learn more about the many regulatory mechanisms involved in enzyme protein synthesis.

6. Conclusions

In the immediate perinatal period, the liver shows marked biochemical and morphologic changes, of which the increase in protein content and the drastic decrease in lipids and glycogen are the most obvious chemical changes. The disappearance of hemopoietic cells occurs over a longer period of time. Simultaneously, with the rapidly rising total liver protein, and with the lowering of all essential free amino acid concentrations, several new enzyme activities are formed, many of them showing steep increases after birth. Several of the enzyme activities that have been present before birth reveal no or only minor changes perinatally. Comparison of the enzyme patterns of mammals that are born at different stages of maturity, such as rats, rabbits, and guinea pigs, allows us to distinguish two types of groups of enzymes: One type is induced by the process of birth, no matter whether parturition occurs physiologically or is artifically performed at an early or late stage of maturation (e.g., phosphopyruvate carboxykinase). The second type appears independent of the timing of birth and obviously according to a genetic control element (e.g., aspartate aminotransferase). We might speculate that there exists a genetic clock that seems to determine the time of birth as well as the initiation of specific protein synthesis by starting several regulatory mechanisms for which hormones act as humoral transmitters. Evidence is now accumulating that the activation on the translational and ribosomal level is dependent on the presence, or on the sufficient accumulation, of effectors or messengers. Finally, the lack of specific compounds for the prosthetic group or of certain cofactors can delay the development of the catalytic activity of an enzyme protein. These developmental and regulatory mechanisms need to be investigated to a greater extent in the future in order to utilize their positive, life-preserving action in clinical medicine.

7. References

1. AUERBACH, V. H., AND WAISMAN, H. A., 1959, Tryptophan peroxidase–oxidase, histidase, and transaminase activity in the liver of the developing rat, *J. Biol. Chem.* **234**:304–306.
2. AURICCHIO, S., AND RIGILLO, N., 1960, Glucose-6-phosphatase activity of the human foetal liver, *Biol. Neonate* **2**:146–148.
3. BAGSHAW, J. C., AND BOND, B. H., 1974, Postnatal development of mouse liver: Increasing RNA polymerase activity and orotic acid incorporation, *Differentiation* **2**:269–273.
4. BARCROFT, J., 1947, *Researches on Pre-natal Life*, Charles C. Thomas, Springfield, Illinois.
5. BECKER, V., AND KOSEGARTEN, A., 1963, Die texturelle perinatale Leberreifung, *Acta Hepato-Splenol. (Stuttgart)* **10**:145–153.
6. BLATT, W. F., BLATTEIS, C. M., AND MAGER, M., 1966, Tissue lactic dehydrogenase isoenzymes: Developmental pattern in the neonatal rat, *Can. J. Biochem.* **44**:537–543.
7. BRENNEMAN, A. R., AND KAUFMAN, S., 1965, Characteristics of the hepatic phenylalanine-hydroxylating system in the newborn rat, *J. Biol. Chem.* **240**:3617–3622.
8. BÜCHER, T., 1962, Enzyme unter biologischem Aspekt, in: *Erbliche Stoffwechselkrankheiten* (F. Linneweh, ed.), pp. 125–141, Urban und Schwarzenberg, Munich.
9. BURCH, H. B., LOWRY, O. H., KUHLMAN, A. M., SKERJANCE, J., DIAMANT, E. J., LOWRY, S. R., AND VON DIPPE, P., 1963, Changes in patterns of enzymes of carbohydrate metabolism in the developing rat liver, *J. Biol. Chem.* **238**:2267–2273.
10. CAHN, R. D., KAPLAN, N. O., LEVINE, L., AND ZWILLING, E., 1962, Nature and development of lactic dehydrogenases, *Science* **136**:962–969.
11. CARTWRIGHT, E. C., CONNELLAN, J. M., AND DANKS, D. M., 1973, Some properties of phenylalanine hydroxylase in human foetal liver, *Aust. J. Exp. Biol. Med. Sci.* **51**:559–563.
12. CHAN, S. K., AND COHEN, P. P., 1964, A comparative study of the effect of hydrocortisone injection on tyrosine transaminase activity of different vertebrates, *Arch. Biochem.* **104**:335–337.

13. CUATRECASAS, P., AND SEGAL, S., 1965, Mammalian galactokinase, *J. Biol. Chem.* **240**:2382–2388.

14. DAWKINS, M. J. R., 1959, Respiratory enzymes in the liver of the newborn rat, *Proc. R. Soc. Biol.* **150**:284–298.

15. DAWKINS, M. J. R., 1963, Glycogen synthesis and breakdown in fetal and newborn rat, *Ann. N. Y. Acad. Sci.* **111**:203–211.

16. DAWSON, D. M., GOODFRIEND, T. L., AND KAPLAN, N. O., 1964, Lactic dehydrogenases: Functions of the two types, *Science* **143**:929–933.

17. EMERY, J. L., 1963, Functional asymmetry of the liver, *Ann. N. Y. Acad. Sci.* **111**:37–44.

18. ENESCO, M., AND LEBLOND, C. P., 1962, Increase in cell number as a factor in the growth of the organs and tissues of the young male rat, *J. Embryol. Exp. Morphol.* **10**:530–562.

19. FEIGELSON, P., AND GREENGARD, O., 1962, Immunochemical evidence for increased titers of liver tryptophan pyrrolase during substrate and hormonal enzyme induction, *J. Biol. Chem.* **237**:3714–3717.

20. FINE, I. H., KAPLAN, N. O., AND KUFTINEC, D., 1963, Developmental changes of mammalian lactic dehydrogenase, *Biochemistry* **2**:116–121.

21. FINEBERG, R. A., AND GREENBERG, D. M., 1955, Ferritin biosynthesis. II. Acceleration of synthesis by the administration of iron, *J. Biol. Chem.* **214**:97–106.

22. FREEDLAND, R. A., KRAKOWSKI, M. C., AND WAISMAN, H. A., 1962, Effect of age, sex, and nutrition on liver phenylalanine hydroxylase activity in rats, *Amer. J. Physiol.* **202**:145–148.

23. FRIEDMAN, P. A., AND KAUFMAN, S., 1971, A study of the development of phenylalanine hydroxylase in fetuses of several mammalian species, *Arch. Biochem. Biophys.* **146**:321–326.

24. GIRARD, J. R., CAQUET, D., BAL, D., AND GUILLET, I., 1973, Control of rat liver phosphorylase, glucose-6-phosphatase, and phosphoenolpyruvate carboxykinase activities by insulin and glucagon during the perinatal period, *Enzyme* **15**:272–285.

25. GOSWAMI, M. N., ROSENBERG, A. J., AND MEURY, F., 1973, A comparative analysis of the ontogenic development of rat liver sequential enzymes—tyrosine α-ketoglutarate aminotransferase, *p*-hydroxyphenylpyruvate hydroxylase, and homogentisate oxygenase, *Dev. Biol.* **30**:129–136.

26. GARN, S. M., LEWIS, A. B., AND VICINUS, J. H., 1963, Third molar polymorphism and its significance to dental genesis, *J. Dent. Res.* **42**:1344–1363.

27. GREEN, D. E., 1959, Electron transport and oxidative phosphorylation, *Adv. Enzymol.* **21**:73–130.

28. GREENGARD, O., 1967, The quantitative regulation of specific proteins in animal tissues; words and facts, *Enzymol. Biol. Clin. (Basel)* **8**:81–96.

29. GREENGARD, O., 1973, The developmental formation of enzymes in rat liver, in: *Biochemical Aspects of Hormones* (G. Litevack, ed.), pp. 53–87, Academic Press, New York.

30. GREENGARD, O., 1973, Effect of hormones on development of fetal enzymes, *Clin. Pharmacol. Ther.* **14**:721–726.

31. GREENGARD, O., AND DEWEY, H. K., 1968, The developmental formation of liver glucose-6-phosphatase and reduced nicotinamide adenine dinucleotide phosphate dehydrogenase in fetal rats treated with thyroxine, *J. Biol. Chem.* **243**:2745–2749.

32. GREENGARD, O., FEDERMAN, M., AND KNOX, W. E., 1972, Cytomorphometry of developing rat liver and its application to enzymatic differentiation, *J. Cell. Biol.* **52**:261–272.

33. GRUENWALD, P., 1949, Degenerative changes in the right half of the liver resulting from intrauterine anoxia, *Amer. J. Clin. Pathol.* **19**:801–813.

34. GRUENWALD, P., AND MINH, H. N., 1960, Evaluation of body and organ weights in perinatal pathology. I. Normal standards derived from autopsies, *Amer. J. Clin. Pathol.* **34**:247–253.

35. HADORN, E., 1958, Role of genes in developmental processes, in: *The Chemical Basis of Development* (W. D. McElroy and B. Glass, eds.), pp. 779–791, The Johns Hopkins Press, Baltimore.

36. HAHN, P., AND DRAHOTA, Z., 1966, The activities of citrate cleavage enzyme, acetyl-CoA synthetase and lipoprotein lipase in white and brown adipose tissue and the liver of the rat during development, *Experientia* **22**:706.

37. HAHN, P., AND SKALA, J., 1970, Some enzymes of glucose metabolism in the human fetus, *Biol. Neonate* **16**:362–369.

38. HERRMANN, H., AND TOOTLE, M. L., 1964, Specific and general aspects of the development of enzymes and metabolic pathways, *Physiol. Rev.* **44**:289–371.

39. HERZFELD, A., AND KNOX, W. E., 1968, The properties, developmental formation, and estrogen induction of ornithine aminotransferase in rat tissue, *J. Biol. Chem.* **243**:3327–3332.

40. HOLT, P. G., AND OLIVER, I. T., 1968, Plasma corticosterone concentrations in perinatal rat, *Biochem. J.* **108**:339–341.

41. HOMMES, F. A., AND DRAISMA, M. I., 1970, The development of L- and M-type aldolases in rat liver, *Biochim. Biophys. Acta* **222**:251, 252.

42. HOMMES, F. A., AND WILMINK, C. W., 1968, Developmental changes of glycolytic enzymes in rat brain, liver and skeletal muscle, *Biol. Neonate* **12**:181–193.

43. HUANG, Y. Z., AND KNOX, E. W., 1975, Glutamine-dependent asparagine synthetase in fetal, adult and neoplastic rat tissue, *Enzyme* **19**:314–328.

44. IMMERS, S. J., AND RUNNSTROM, J., 1960, Release of respiratory control by 2,4-dinitrophenol in different stages of sea urchin development, *Dev. Biol.* **2**:90–104.

45. JACOB, F., AND MONOD, J., 1961, On the regulation

of gene activity, *Cold Spring Harbor Symp. Quant. Biol.* **26**:193–211.

46. JACQUOT, R., AND KRETCHMER, N., 1964, Effect of fetal decapitation on enzymes of glycogen metabolism, *J. Biol. Chem.* **239**:1301–1304.

47. JOHNSON, B. E., WALSH, D. A., AND SALLACH, H. J., 1964, Changes in the activities of D-glycerate and D-3-phosphoglycerate dehydrogenase in the developing rat liver, *Biochim. Biophys. Acta* **85**:202–205.

48. KENNEY, F. T., AND KRETCHMER, N., 1959, Hepatic metabolism of phenylalanine during development, *J. Clin. Invest.* **38**:2189–2196.

49. KIRBY, L., AND HAHN, P., 1973, Enzyme induction in human fetal liver, *Pediatr. Res.* **7**:75–81.

50. KNOWLES, S. E., AND BALLARD, F. J., 1974, Pyruvate dehydrogenase activity in rat liver during development, *Biol. Neonate* **24**:41–48.

51. KNOX, W. E., 1972, *Enzyme Patterns in Fetal, Adult and Neoplastic Rat Tissues,* S. Karger, Basel and New York.

52. KNOX, W. E., AND MEHLER, A. H., 1951, The adaptive increase of the tryptophan peroxidase-oxidase system of the liver, *Science* **113**:237, 238.

53. KNOX, W. E., AUERBACH, V. H., AND LINN, E. C. C., 1956, Enzymatic and metabolic adaptations in animals, *Physiol. Rev.* **36**:164–254.

54. KÖHLER, E., 1972, Activity of some enzymes of nucleic acid metabolism in developing rat liver, *Naunyn-Schmiedeberg's Arch. Pharmacol.* **274**:385–393.

55. KREBS, H. A., 1956, Die Steuerung der Stoffwechselvorgänge, *Dtsch. Med. Wochenschr.* **81**:4–8.

56. LANE, M. D., AND MOSS, F., 1971, Regulation of fatty acid synthesis in animal tissues, in: *Metabolic Pathways,* Vol. 5, 3rd Ed., (H. J. Vogel, ed.), p. 23, Academic Press, New York.

57. LANG, C. A., 1965, Respiratory enzymes in the heart and liver of the prenatal and postnatal rat, *Biochem. J.* **95**:365–371.

58. LEA, M. A., AND WALKER, D. G., 1964, The metabolism of glucose-6-phosphate in developing mammalian tissues, *Biochem. J.* **91**:417–424.

59. LIND, J., 1963, Changes in the liver circulation at birth, *Ann. N. Y. Acad. Sci.* **111**:110–120.

60. LINDY, S., AND RAJASALMI, M., 1966, Lactate dehydrogenase isozymes of chick embryo: Response to variations of ambient oxygen tension, *Science* **153**:1401.

61. LITWACK, G., AND NEMETH, A. M., 1965, Development of liver tyrosine aminotransferase activity in the rabbit, guinea pig, and chicken, *Arch. Biochem.* **109**:316–320.

62. LYNEN, F., 1967, The role of biotin-dependent carboxylations in biosynthetic reactions, *Biochem. J.* **102**:381–400.

63. MAKOFF, R., AND BALDRIDGE, R. C., 1964, The metabolism of histidine: Liver enzyme changes during development, *Biochim. Biophys. Acta* **90**:282–286.

64. MALL, F. P., 1906, A study of the structural unit of the liver, *Amer. J. Anat.* **5**:227–308.

65. MARKERT, C. L., AND MØLLER, F., 1959, Multiple forms of enzymes: Tissue, ontogenetic, and species specific patterns, *Proc. Natl. Acad. Sci. U.S.A.* **45**:753–763.

66. MARSAC, C., SAUDUBRAY, J. M., MONCION, A., AND LEROUX, J. P., 1976, Development of gluconeogenic enzymes in the liver of human newborns, *Biol. Neonate* **28**:317–325.

67. MCGEE, M. M., GREENGARD, O., AND KNOX, W. E., 1972, The quantitative determination of phenylalanine hydroxylase in rat tissues. Its developmental formation in liver, *Biochem. J.* **127**:675–680.

68. MCLEAN, A., MARWICK, M. J., AND CLAYTON, B. E., 1973, Enzymes involved in phenylalanine metabolism in the human fetus and child, *J. Clin. Pathol.* **26**:678–683.

69. MENON, K. M. J., GIESE, S., AND JAFFE, R. B., 1973, Hormone and fluoride sensitive adenylate cyclases in human fetal tissues, *Biochem. Biophys. Acta* **304**:203–209.

70. MIDDLETON, M. C., AND WALKER, D. G., 1972, Comparison of the properties of two forms of pyruvate kinase in rat liver and determination of their separate activities during development, *Biochem. J.* **127**:721–731.

71. MINO, M., AND TAKAI, T., 1966, Enzymatic development of human fetus: Studies on cytochrome oxidase and succinic dehydrogenase in developing human fetus, *Acta Paediatr. Jpn. (Overseas)* **8**:1–6.

72. MITCHELL, R. G., 1963, Histidine decarboxylase in the newborn human infant, *J. Physiol. (London)* **166**:136–144.

73. MOOG, F., 1965, Enzyme development in relation to functional differentiation, in: *The Biochemistry of Animal Development* (R. Weber, ed.), Vol. 1, pp. 307–365, Academic Press, New York.

74. MOYED, H. S., AND UMBARGER, H. E., 1962, Regulation of biosynthetic pathways, *Physiol. Rev.* **42**:444–466.

75. NEEDHAM, J., 1931, *Chemical Embryology,* Cambridge University Press, London.

76. NEMETH, A. M., 1954, Glucose-6-phosphatase in the liver of the fetal guinea pig, *J. Biol. Chem.* **208**:773–776.

77. NEMETH, A. M., 1959, Mechanisms controlling changes in tryptophan peroxidase activity in developing mammalian liver, *J. Biol. Chem.* **234**:2921–2924.

78. NEMETH, A. M., 1963, Initiation of enzyme formation by birth, *Ann. N. Y. Acad. Sci.* **111**:199–202.

79. NUMA, S., NAKANISHI, S., HASHIMOTO, T., IRRITANI, N., AND OKAZAKI, T., 1970, Role of acetyl coenzyme A carboxylase in the control of fatty acid synthesis, *Vitam. Horm. (N.Y.)* **28**:213–243.

80. PAIGEN, K., 1961, The genetic control of enzyme activity during differentiation, *Proc. Natl. Acad. Sci. U.S.A.* **97**:1641–1649.

81. PETTE, D., 1965, Plan und Muster im zellulären Stoffwechsel, *Naturwissenschaften* **52**:597–616.

82. PETTE, D., AND DÖLKEN, G., 1975, Some aspects of regulation of enzyme levels in muscle energy-supplying metabolism, *Adv. Enzyme Regul.* **13**: 355–377.

83. PETTE, D., LUH, W., AND BÜCHER, T., 1962, A constant-proportion group in the enzyme activity pattern of the Embden–Meyerhof chain, *Biochem. Biophys. Res. Commun.* **7**:419–424.

84. PFLEIDERER, G., AND WACHSMUTH, E. D., 1961, Die Heterogenität der Lactatdehydrogenase in Entwicklungsgeschichte und Pathologie des Menschen, *Klin. Wochenschr.* **39**:352–354.

85. PHILIPPIDIS, H., HANSON, R. W., RESHEF, L., HOPGOOD, M. F., AND BALLARD, F. J., 1972, The initial synthesis of proteins during development, *Biochem. J.* **126**:1127–1134.

86. PIKKARAINEN, P. H., AND RÄIHÄ, N. C. R., 1967, Development of alcohol dehydrogenase activity in the human liver, *Pediatr. Res.* **1**:165–168.

87. PITOT, H. C., 1964, The regulation of enzyme synthesis in mammalian tissues, in: *Sixth International Congress on Biochemistry, New York, Abstracts*, Vol. 9, p. 682.

88. PLANET, G., AND WILLEMOT, J., 1974, Changes in purine phosphoribosyltransferase activities in mouse brain, liver, and muscle with age, *Biochim. Biophys. Acta* **364**:236–242.

89. POLLUCK, M. R., 1959, Induced formation of enzymes, in: *The Enzymes* (P. D. Boyer, H. Lardy, and K. Myrbäck, eds.), Vol. 1, p. 628, Academic Press, New York.

90. PULKKINEN, M. O., 1966, Sulfate conjugation during development in human, rat, and guinea pig, *Acta Physiol. Scand.* **66**:115–119.

91. RÄIHÄ, N. C. R., 1973, Phenylalanine hydroxylase in human liver during development, *Pediatr. Res.* **7**:1–4.

92. RÄIHÄ, N. C. R., KOSKINEN, M., AND PIKKARAINEN, P., 1967, Developmental changes in alcohol dehydrogenase activity in rat and guinea pig, *Biochem. J.* **103**:623–626.

93. REED, L. J., AND COX, D. J., 1966, Macromolecular organization of enzyme systems, *Ann. Rev. Biochem.* **35**:57–84.

94. REEM, G. H., AND KRETCHMER, N., 1957, Development of phenylalanine hydroxylase in liver of the rat, *Proc. Soc. Exp. Biol. Med.* **96**:458.

95. RICHTERICH, R., SCHAFROTH, P., AND FRANZ, H. E., 1961–1962, Das isolierte Glomerulum der Rattenniere. III. Heterogenität der Lactat-Dehydrogenase in Nierenrinde, Nierenmark und Glomerulum, *Enzymol. Biol. Clin. (Basel)* **1**:114–122.

96. ROSS, M. H., AND ELY, J. O., 1954, Aging and enzyme activity, *J. Franklin Inst.* **258**:63.

97. SARRUT, S., AND NEZELOF, C., 1959, La maturation hépatique ses aspects histologiqués, *Rev. Int. Hepatol.* **9**:425–471.

98. SATO, K., MORRIS, H. P., AND WEINHOUSE, S., 1972, Phosphorylase: A new isozyme in rat hepatic tumors in fetal liver, *Science* **178**:879–881.

99. SCHIMKE, R. T., SWEENEY, E. W., AND BERLIN, C. M., 1964, An analysis of the kinetics of rat liver tryptophan pyrrolase induction: The significance of both enzyme synthesis and degradation, *Biochem. Biophys. Res. Commun.* **15**:214–219.

100. SCHULZ, D. M., GIORDANO, D. A., AND SCHULZ, D. H., 1962, Weights of organs of fetuses and infants, *Arch. Pathol. (Chicago)* **74**:244–250.

101. SCHWARTZ, A. L., RÄIHÄ, N., AND RALL, T. W., 1974, Effect of dibutyryl cyclic AMP on glucose-6-phosphatase activity in human fetal liver explants, *Biochim. Biophys. Acta* **343**:500.

102. SEGAL, H. L., ROSSO, R. G., HOPPER, S., AND WEBER, M. M., 1962, Direct evidence for an increase in enzyme level as the basis for the glucocorticoid-induced increase in glutamic alanine transaminase activity in rat liver, *J. Biol. Chem.* **237**:PC 3303, 3304.

103. SEKERIS, C. E., 1967, Wirkung der Hormone auf den Zellkern, in: *Wirkungsmechanismen der Hormone* (P. Karlson, ed.), pp. 126–157, Springer-Verlag, Berlin.

104. SERENI, F., KENNEY, F. T., AND KRETCHMER, N., 1959, Factors influencing the development of tyrosine α-ketoglutarate transaminase activity in rat liver, *J. Biol. Chem.* **234**:609–612.

105. SHAW, C. R., 1965, Electrophoretic variation in enzymes, *Science* **149**:936–943.

106. SHOYAB, M., AND BACHHAWAT, B. K., 1967, Age dependent changes in the level of cytidine 5′-mono-phospho-N-acetyl-neuraminic acid synthesizing and degrading enzymes and bound sialic acid in rat liver, *Indian J. Biochem.* **4**:142–145.

107. SILLERO, A., SILLERO, M. A. G., AND SOLS, A., 1970, Development of the enzymes of fructose and glyceraldehyde metabolism in liver, *Enzymol. Biol. Clin.* **11**:563–566.

108. SNELL, K., AND WALKER, D. G., 1972, The adaptive behavior of isoenzyme forms of rat liver alanine aminotransferases during development, *Biochem. J.* **128**:403–413.

109. STAVE, U., 1964, Age dependent changes of metabolism. I. Studies of enzyme patterns of rabbit organs, *Biol. Neonate* **6**:128–147.

110. STAVE, U., 1967, Importance of proper substrate concentrations for enzyme assays in tissue homogenates for developmental studies, *Enzymol. Biol. Clin. (Basel)* **8**:21–32.

111. STAVE, U., 1975, Perinatal changes of interorgan differences in cell metabolism, *Biol. Neonate* **26**: 318–332.

112. STAVE, U., AND ARMSTRONG, M. D., 1973, Tissue free amino acid concentrations in perinatal rabbits, *Biol. Neonate* **22**:374–387.

113. STAVE, U., AND WOLF, H., 1971, Enzyme studies in

perinatal tissues of normal, hypothermic, hypotrophic, and hypoxic rabbits, *Biol. Neonate* **19**:434–450.

114. STRAUSS, B. S., 1960, *An Outline of Chemical Genetics,* W. B. Saunders Co., Philadelphia.

115. SWIATEK, K. R., CHAO, K.-L., CHAO, H.-L., CORNBLATH, M., AND TILDON, J. T., 1970, Enzymatic adaptation in newborn pig liver, *Biochim. Biophys. Acta* **222**:145–154.

116. TATA, J. R., 1970, Regulation of protein systhesis by growth and developmental hormones, *Biochemical Action of Hormones* (G. Litwack, ed.), Vol. I, pp. 89–133, Academic Press, New York.

117. TAYLOR, C. B., BAILEY, E., AND BARTLEY, W., 1967, Changes in hepatic lipogenesis during development of the rat, *Biochem. J.* **105**:717–722.

118. TELFORD, J. M., AND WEST, G. B., 1961, The effect of age on the formation of histamine in the rat, *J. Physiol. (London)* **157**:303–314.

119. THEIL, S., 1966, Die Aktivität der Glycerokinase in Placenta, mütterlicher und fötaler Leber bei Ratten, *Naturwissenschaften* **53**:436.

120. THEILE, H., 1965, Die prä- und postnatale Entwicklung einiger Leberenzyme beim Tier, *Paediatr. Grenzgeb.* **4**:57–66.

121. THEILE, H., AND FRANK, M., 1964, Der Blutgehalt der Leber im Verlaufe der prä- und postnatalen Entwicklung und seine Bedeutung für Enzymbestimmungen in Leberhomogenaten, *Acta Biol. Med. Ger.* **13**:317–324.

122. TOMKINS, G. M., AND THOMPSON, E. B., 1967, Hormonal control of protein synthesis at the translational level, in: *Wirkungemechanismen der Hormone* (P. Karlson, ed.), pp. 107–125, Springer-Verlag, Berlin.

123. VERNON, R. G., AND WALKER, D. G., 1968, Changes in activity of some enzymes involved in glucose utilization and formation in developing rat liver, *Biochem. J.* **106**:321–331.

124. VESELL, E. S., AND PHILIP, J., 1963, Isozymes of lactic dehydrogenase: Sequential alterations during development, *Ann. N. Y. Acad. Sci.* **111**:243–256.

125. VILLEE, C. A., 1966, Differentiation and enzymatic heterogeneity, *Fed. Proc. Fed. Amer. Soc. Exp. Biol.* **25**:874–878.

126. VILLEE, C. A., HAGERMAN, D. D., HOLMBERG, N., LIND, J., AND VILLEE, D. B., 1958, The effects of anoxia on the metabolism of human fetal tissues, *Pediatrics* **22**:953–970.

127. VOLPE, J. J., AND LASTER, L., 1973, Transulfuration in fetal and postnatal mammalian liver and brain. Cystathionine synthase, its relation to hormonal influences and cystathionine, *Biol. Neonate* **20**:385–403.

128. VOLPE, J. J., LYLES, T. O., RONCARI, D. A. K., AND VAGELOS, P. R., 1973, Fatty acid synthetase of developing brain and liver, *J. Biol. Chem.* **248**:2502–2513.

129. WACHSMUTH, E. D., AND PFLEIDERER, G., 1963, Biochemische Untersuchungen an kristallinen Isozymen der Lactatdehydrogenase aus menschlichen Organen, *Biochem. Z.* **336**:545–556.

130. WALKER, D. G., 1963, The postnatal development of hepatic fructokinase, *Biochem. J.* **87**:576–581.

131. WARBURG, O., 1925, Manometrische Messung des Zellstoffwechsels im Serum, *Biochem. Z.* **164**:481–503.

132. WARBURG, O., 1948, *Wasserstoffübertragende Fermente,* Springer-Verlag, Berlin.

133. WEBER, G., LEA, M. A., CONVERY, H. J. H., AND STAMM, N. B., 1967, Regulation of gluconeogenesis and glycolysis: Studies of mechanisms controlling enzyme activity, *Adv. Enzyme Regul.* **5**:257–298.

134. WEBER, G., LEA, M. A., FISHER, E. A., AND STAMM, N. B., 1966, Regulatory pattern of liver carbohydrate metabolizing enzymes: Insulin as inducer of key glycolytic enzymes, *Enzymol. Biol. Clin. (Basel)* **7**:11–24.

135. WEBER, G., SINGHAL, R. L., STAMM, N. B., AND SRIVASTAVA, S. K., 1965, Hormonal induction and suppression of liver enzyme biosynthesis, *Fed. Proc. Fed. Amer. Soc. Exp. Biol.* **24**:745–754.

136. WEINHOLD, P. A., SKINNER, R. S., AND SANDERS, R. D., 1973, Activity and some properties of choline kinase, cholinephosphate cytidyltransferase, and choline phosphotransferase during liver development in the rat, *Biochem. Biophys. Acta* **326**:43–51.

137. WIDDOWSON, E. M., AND CRABB, D. E., 1976, Changes in the organs of pigs in response to feeding for the first 24 h after birth. I. The internal organs and muscles, *Biol. Neonate* **28**:261–271.

138. WIGGERT, B. O., AND VILLEE, C. A., 1964, Multiple molecular forms of malic and lactic dehydrogenases during development, *J. Biol. Chem.* **239**:444–451.

139. WINICK, M., AND NOBLE, A., 1965, Quantitative changes in DNA, RNA and protein during prenatal and postnatal growth in the rat, *Devel. Biol.* **12**:451–466.

140. WOLF, H., STAVE, U., NOVAK, M., AND MONKUS, E., 1974, Recent investigation on neonatal fat metabolism, *J. Perinat. Med.* **2**:75–87.

141. WU, C., 1964, Glutamine synthetase. III. Factors controlling its activity in the developing rat, *Arch. Biochem.* **106**:394–401.

142. YEUNG, D., AND OLIVER, I. T., 1967, Gluconeogenesis from amino acids in neonatal rat liver, *Biochem. J.* **103**:744–748.

143. YEUNG, D., AND OLIVER, I. T., 1968, Factors affecting the premature induction of phosphopyruvate carboxylase in neonatal rat liver, *Biochem. J.* **108**:325–331.

144. YEUNG, D., STANLEY, R. S., AND OLIVER, I. T., 1967, Development of gluconeogenesis in neonatal rat liver, *Biochem. J.* **105**:1219–1227.

CHAPTER 23

Bilirubin Metabolism

Thomas R. C. Sisson

1. Introduction

It was pointed out by With[122] in his exhaustive monograph on bile pigments that we are indebted to the work of Hans Fischer and his colleagues for much of our knowledge of the bile pigments. Their metabolism, principally that of bilirubin IXa, is of importance to the pediatrician because hyperbilirubinemia is singular among the common symptoms appearing in the newborn in that it in itself, regardless of cause, can produce severe and irrevocable damage to the developing CNS.

To understand why plasma levels of bilirubin in the fetus are low but may rise rapidly to high concentrations after birth, it is necessary to review those mechanisms responsible for the formation of this pigment, its transport in the body, its conjugation, and its ultimate excretion. Against this background, certain pathologic conditions of importance in the neonate that may result in the most severe consequence of bilirubin toxicity—kernicterus—will then be reviewed.

The few methods available to prevent the appearance of hyperbilirubinemia in the newborn or to correct the condition once it has appeared will be discussed. Since the appearance of the first edition of this volume, the use of photo-therapy has not only gained universal acceptance, but also has spawned a variety of biochemical and clinical studies of interest in bilirubin metabolism.

2. Bilirubin Metabolism

2.1. Formation

The bile pigments found among the higher animals are derivatives of protoporphyrin IX, and it was shown by Gray et al.[40] that the previous assumption that all natural tetrapyrrole bile pigments have such a derivative structure is correct. Thus, the pigment with which we are concerned is identified as *bilirubin IXa* under currently accepted nomenclature. The prosthetic group of hemoglobin from which bilirubin is derived is shown in Fig. 1. It is not yet certain whether the hemoglobin molecule splits into a globin portion, the remainder forming an iron–protoporphyrin intermediate moiety, such as hemin, which subsequently loses its ferric iron portion before converting to bilirverdin, or whether the molecule of hemoglobin changes to a bilirverdin–iron–globin complex (the ring tetrapyrrole having become linear) from which the globin and iron portions are separated, leaving biliverdin. Whichever sequence of events takes place, the biliverdin remnant is then changed to bilirubin,

Thomas R. C. Sisson · Department of Pediatrics, Obstetrics, and Gynecology (Perinatology), Neonatal Research Laboratory, Temple University School of Medicine, Philadelphia, Pennsylvania 19140

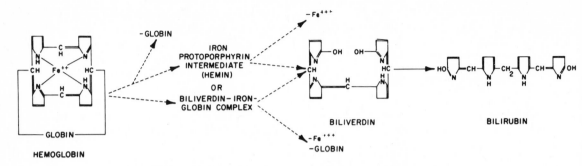

Fig. 1. Formation of bilirubin from hemoglobin catabolism.

and the iron and the globin amino acids are reutilized.

Many investigators have studied the formation of bilirubin *in vitro* and *in vivo*, and a variety of theories have been advanced to delineate the process. The work of Goldstein and Lester,[39] in which radiochemically pure [14C] biliverdin was injected into rats and 54–95% of the injected radioactivity was rapidly excreted in the bile as conjugated [14C]bilirubin, confirmed the view that biliverdin is the principal and primary degradation product of hemoglobin and the important intermediate pigment in the formation of bilirubin.

Ostrow et al.[86,87] studied the efficiency of the conversion of hemoglobin to bilirubin by injecting sensitized red cells, labeled with 14C and either 59Fe or 51Cr, or solutions of labeled hemoglobin in equivalent doses. In this manner, they were able to measure the rate of removal of heme pigment from the circulation and the excretion of [14C]bilirubin in bile from formed fistulae. The radioactive bilirubin appeared in bile within 30 min of the sequestration of heme. Of the labeled pigment, 50% was excreted within 3 hr. When sensitized red cells were injected, 63–80% of the heme was recovered as [14C]bilirubin. When smaller doses of hemoglobin were thus administered, in amounts calculated not to exceed the binding capacity of plasma haptoglobin, the conversion of heme to [14C]bilirubin was found to be nearly complete. From these investigations and others, it seems clear that the breakdown of erythrocytes precedes the formation of bilirubin, and that the relationship is direct, with only necessary intermediate steps intervening, among them the important enzymatic conversion of biliverdin to bilirubin by biliverdin reductase.[103]

Although hemoglobin is the major source of bilirubin, other nonhemoglobin sources of heme are known and contribute, perhaps significantly in some instances, to the general pool of bilirubin in the body. An "early-labeled pigment" has been demonstrated[41,68] and found to appear earlier than would be the case were it derived from hemoglobin released from the breakdown of circulating red cells. This pigment may be derived from other erythropoietic elments, from tissue heme such as hepatic cytochrome P450,[62] or from the direct combination of monopyrroles. The contribution of bilirubin from these sources, from ineffective erythropoiesis, and possibly from short-lived reticulocytes, may indeed influence increased bilirubin production in the newborn.

2.2. Transport

Bilirubin is transported in plasma bound to albumin, to red blood cells, and to some small degree to β-lipoproteins.[19] The bulk of the circulating pool of bilirubin is bound to albumin at two sites on that molecule, a primary binding site to which most of the pigment is attached by a strong bond, and a secondary site at which the binding is much weaker. The studies of Ostrow and Schmid,[85] in which serum supplemented with [14C]bilirubin was subjected to continuous–flow and starch-block electrophoresis, demonstrated that at concentrations of pigment ranging from physiologic levels to those of the binding capacity of serum protein, the 14C labeled bilirubin migrated only with albumin (Fig. 2.). In the human, 1 mole albumin can bind 2 mol bilirubin.[3] Jacobsen[53] showed that the dissociation constants of the 2 mol bilirubin are approximately 7×10^{-9} M and 2×10^{-6} M, respectively. When the concentration of bilirubin exceeds available binding sites on albumin, red cells, or β–lipoproteins, it will circulate

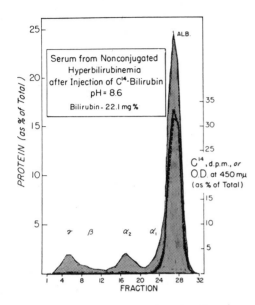

Fig. 2. Continuous-flow electrophoresis of human serum containing 1.7 mg bilirubin-C¹⁴/dl. It can be seen that all radioactive pigment is bound to albumin. Reproduced from Ostrow and Schmid.[85]

in a free or unbound state. It is this fraction of unconjugated, lipid-soluble bilirubin that will contribute significantly to the migration of the pigment to cells of the brain. It was pointed out by Brown[16] that "the occurrence of bilirubin encephalopathy appears to be ... closely related to the concentration of diffusible, loosely-bound, bilirubin in extracellular fluids..." and to the availability of binding sites rather than to serum concentrations of total bilirubin.

2.3. Transfer from Blood to Bile

Bilirubin is transferred from the blood into liver cells, then across their plasma membranes, where the pigment is subsequently stored or moves through the cell cytoplasm to endoplasmic reticulum. In this location, bilirubin is conjugated, and from thence it is excreted. The transfer is affected by proteins that have a specificity for binding organic anions. These proteins have been termed *Y* and *Z*, or *ligandin*.[66] The major and functionally more important fraction, *Y*, is of particular concern in dealing with jaundice of the newborn.[2] Ligandin is an acceptor of bilirubin in plasma, and apparently is involved in the efflux of bilirubin from the liver cell back to the plasma, both influx and efflux being related to the amount and binding affinity of albumin

in the plasma and the amount and binding affinity of ligandin in the cytoplasm, to the dissociation of anions from blood protein and the nonionic diffusion of these substances across the liver cell plasma membrane, and to the total available binding sites on either side of the membrane.[3]

Fleischner and Arias[31a] have outlined the three possibilities that exist for the selective extraction of bilirubin and other organic anions:

1. Saturable, non-energy-dependent, facilitated diffusional transport.
2. Transport by specific active systems.
3. Transfer by nonionic diffusion across hepatic cell plasma membrane, which faces the sinusoid.

It is most likely, according to our present knowledge, that ligandin may be part of a non-energy-dependent transport system that permits liver cells to take up certain substances selectively. It is thought that, in man, ligandin may play a role in liver detoxification mechanisms.

Ligandin is a basic protein of two monomeric subunits, the combined molecular weight of which is 46,000. It is induced by phenobarbital and other drugs that also induce P450 cytochrome. This protein has been found to maintain the net flux of organic ions in their transfer from plasma to liver cells; it binds both heme and GSH.

Recently, ligandin was further identified as glutathione transferase B[41a] and was found to have at least five times the activity of all other GSH transferases combined.

The mechanism for the intracellular transfer of bilirubin from ligandin to the membranes of the endoplasmic reticulum is poorly understood. In any event, bilirubin is transferred by some means to this locus, where it is converted into an ester glucuronide through enzymatic action.

2.4. Conjugation

It has been suggested[11,120] that bilirubin, having entered the hepatic cell, binds to the microsomal fraction, in particular to the smooth membrane subfraction. These studies suggest that glucuronyl transferase may provide a site for the binding of bilirubin in respect to the endoplasmic reticulum membranes.

The conjugation of bilirubin to form bilirubin glucuronide requires a hepatic microsomal enzyme, UDP-glucuronyl transferase, which acts as a catalyst in the transfer of glucuronic acid from UDP-glucuronic acid to various receptors. Numerous drugs, thyroxine, and steroid hormones are conjugated in this manner. By this mechanism, bilirubin, too, is conjugated, as was demonstrated by Schmid[96] and by Billing et al.[13]:

$$\text{bilirubin} + 2\ \text{UDPGA} \xrightarrow{\text{UDP-glucuronyl transferase}}$$
(indirect-reacting)

bilirubin diglucuronide
(direct-reacting)
+ 2 UDP

Bilirubin itself is very nearly insoluble in aqueous media at physiologic pH, being instead a more nearly lipid-soluble compound. To react with diazotized sulfanilic acid in the van den Bergh reaction, it requires the addition of alcohol or other organic solvents; it is therefore referred to as *indirect-reacting* bilirubin. Bilirubin diglucuronide, on the other hand, is water-soluble and will couple with diazo reagent in the absence of alcohol; it is therefore referred to as *direct-reacting* bilirubin.

The conversion of bilirubin to its ester conjugate, bilirubin diglucoronide, requires the transfer of glucuronic acid from the nucleotide uridine diphosphate glucuronic acid (UDPGA) to the carboxyl receptors of the pigment. This transfer is achieved by a sequence of enzymatic actions similar to the steps in hepatic detoxification of some drugs and hormones. UDPGA is the product of the oxidation of UDP glucose, which is itself the result of preceding enzymatic steps:

$$\text{UDP} + \text{ATP} \xrightarrow[\text{diphosphokinase}]{\text{nucleoside}} \text{UTP} + \text{ADP}$$

$$\text{UTP} + \text{glucose-1-PO}_4 \xrightarrow{\text{UDPG pyrophosphorylase}} \text{UDP glucose} + \text{PP}$$

$$\text{UDP glucose} + 2\ \text{DPN} \xrightarrow{\text{UDPG dehydrogenase}} \text{UDP glucuronic acid} + 2\ \text{DPNH} + 2\ \text{H}^+$$

$$\text{UDP glucuronic acid} + \text{bilirubin} \xrightarrow[\text{transferase}]{\text{UDP-glucuronyl}} \text{bilirubin diglucuronide} + \text{UDP}$$

The UDPG dehydrogenase is derived from the soluble fraction of liver, while the UDP-glucuronyl transferase is derived from the lipoprotein microsomal fraction. The overall reaction is thus a stepwise process, as shown in Fig. 3.

It should be noted that there may be a number of UDP-glucuronyl transferase enzymes responsible for the catalytic formation of various glucuronides.[52,77]

2.5. Excretion

In normal situations, the conjugation of bilirubin is essential for its biliary excretion,[6,98] a rate-limiting phenomenon in the transfer of bilirubin from blood to bile, at least in the newborn animal.[35] However, the mechanism by which conjugated bilirubin (and, for that matter, unconjugated as well) is rapidly excreted by the liver cell into the bile is unknown. Increased ratio of bile to plasma bilirubin probably results from energy-dependent hepatic cell excretory processes rather than from solute reabsorption by biliary epithelium, as Arias[3] has remarked. Anatomically, the site of excretion is first the bile canaliculi, from there to the major ducts, and to the intestine.

The integrity and efficiency of the excretory process depends on the availability of mechanisms to prevent or to limit intestinal absorption of bilirubin or its derivatives. The excretion of bilirubin in its conjugated form as the glucuronide seems to fill this requirement, since unconjugated bilirubin is readily absorbed from both small and large

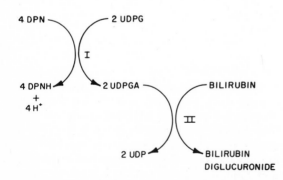

Fig. 3. Conversion of bilirubin to bilirubin diglucuronide with involvement of two requisite enzymes: (I) UDPG dehydrogenase (soluble fraction) and (II) UDP-glucuronosyl transferase (microsomal fraction).

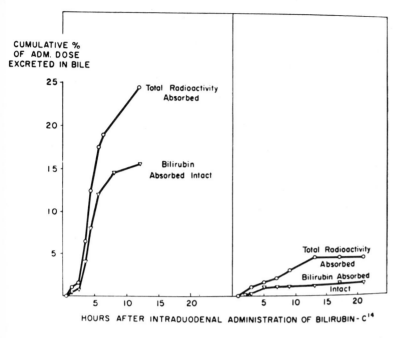

Fig. 4. Pigment absorption after administration of unconjugated (left) and conjugated (right) C^{14}-labeled bilirubin. Reproduced from Lester and Schmid.[60]

intestines, whereas the absorption of conjugated bilirubin is minimal.[60,61] This is illustrated by the experiments represented graphically in Fig. 4. When 4.4 mg unconjugated ^{14}C-labeled bilirubin in a volume of 13 ml was infused into the duodenum (left panel), biliary excretion of the isotope became evident within 2.5 hr and continued at an accelerated rate over the next 10 hr. It was estimated that over a total of 12.5 hr, 24.5% of the labeled bilirubin infused into the duodenum was absorbed, excreted, and recovered in the bile. About 60% of the total biliary radioactivity was found in bilirubin crystallized from the bile collected during the period of study.

When 3.2 mg conjugated ^{14}C-labeled bilirubin in a total of 5 ml rat bile was infused in like fashion into the duodenum (right panel), only 4.4% of the radioactivity was found in bile collected over 21 hr, and less than one-third of this radioactivity was in the form of conjugated [^{14}C]-bilirubin. This amount was in marked contrast to the large amount of unconjugated bilirubin so rapidly absorbed intact.

3. Bilirubin Metabolism in the Fetus

It is an accepted dictum that plasma concentrations of bilirubin are low in the fetal circulation except in unusual circumstances, such as in severe erythro-blastosis foetalis, and that plasma concentrations rise sharply in the newborn infant shortly after birth if the production of bilirubin is exaggerated beyond the liver's capacity to manage its uptake, conjugation, and excretion. Plasma concentrations rise more gradually during the first 3 days of life, in most instances.[23,31,47] Inasmuch as UDPG dehydrogenase, glucuronyl transferase, and ligandin are very low in the fetal liver,[17,28,33,59] one can assume that conjugation of bilirubin to its glucuronide and its prior uptake in the liver cell by proteins Y and Z cannot occur in the fetus at a normal rate. It follows, then, that bilirubin must be transferred from the fetal circulation across the placenta to enter the maternal circulation, and from there taken up by the maternal liver, conjugated, and excreted in her bile.

In 1959, Schmid et al.[99] investigated the placental transfer of bilirubin in pregnant guinea pigs in the last week of gestation. A uterine vein was cannulated, permitting continuous sampling of venous blood from an individual placenta. On the fetal side, an umbilical artery was cannulated, its accompanying umbilical vein was severed, and the cord was clamped between fetus and cannula. Unconjugated bilirubin and iodinated albumin were injected into the umbilical artery on the fetal side. It was observed that both the unconjugated bilirubin and the albumin appeared in the maternal uterine vein

FETUS   PLACENTA   MATERNAL LIVER

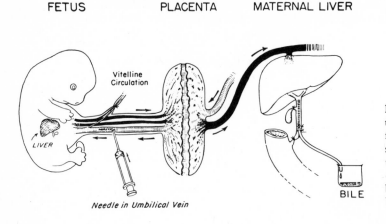

Vitelline
Circulation

LIVER

Needle in Umbilical Vein

BILE

Fig. 5. Diagram of the experimental set-up used to study bilirubin metabolism in the fetus. Fetus, placenta, and uterus were submerged in isotonic saline at 37°C. For the injection into the umbilical vein, a loop of the umbilical cord was transiently brought above the surface of the saline bath. Reproduced from Schenker *et al.*[95]

within 2–4 min. When unconjugated bilirubin was injected into the maternal circulation, it then appeared in the fetal blood.

The experiment was repeated, but this time conjugated bilirubin (glucuronide) prepared from human bile and iodinated albumin were injected into the umbilical artery of the fetus. Although the radioactive albumin rapidly appeared in the maternal blood, transfer of the bilirubin glucuronide was minimal.

Subsequently Schenker and Schmid[94] repeated these studies using [14C]bilirubin. The experimental setup is illustrated in Fig. 5. When unconjugated

[14C]bilirubin was infused into living fetal guinea pigs, a major portion of the labeled pigment was transferred across the placenta and appeared in the maternal bile. Between 43 and 101% of the radioactivity in the maternal bile was excreted in the form of conjugated bilirubin. Figure 6 shows graphically that there was a very rapid rise in the amount of radioactivity in the bile within 15 min of injection into the fetal umbilical artery; the maximum radioactivity was reached in 30 min and it decreased gradually thereafter.

Contrary to these observations, less than 2% of the injected radioactive label was recovered from

RADIOACTIVITY IN BILE
% OF ADM. DOSE

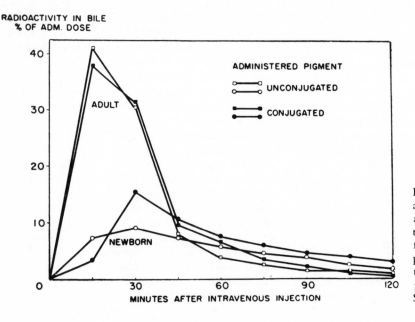

ADMINISTERED PIGMENT

□—□ UNCONJUGATED

○—○ UNCONJUGATED

●—● CONJUGATED

ADULT

NEWBORN

MINUTES AFTER INTRAVENOUS INJECTION

Fig. 6. Excretory rate of radio-activity in the maternal bile after administration of bilirubin-C14 to the fetus. In one instance, the fetus was removed from the placental circulation 15 min after the intrafetal infusion of the pigment. Reproduced from Schenker *et al.*[95]

Table I. Transfer of Unconjugated [¹⁴C]Bilirubin Across the Placenta As Measured by Excretion of Radioactive Bilirubin in the Maternal Bile[a]

| | Recovery of radioactivity in maternal bile in 2 hr (expressed as % of administered dose) | | | |
| | Unconjugated [¹⁴C]bilirubin | | Conjugated [¹⁴C]bilirubin | |
[¹⁴C]Bilirubin given per fetal weight	In whole bile	In crystallized bilirubin	In whole bile	In crystallized bilirubin
4.1	—	35.4[b]	—	—
4.5	—	—	2.2	—
5.5	—	—	0.8	0.3
7.2	18.8[c]	—	—	—
13.2	58.0	46.4	—	—
13.8	—	—	5.7	3.8

[a] Data from Schenker *et al.*[95]
[b] 60 min.
[c] 40 min.

fetal bile during the 2 hr after infusion of unconjugated [¹⁴C]bilirubin. Similarly, when unconjugated [¹⁴C]bilirubin was injected intravenously into the maternal circulation, there was a rapid rise and fall of fetal serum bilirubin concentration. This result demonstrated the rapid transfer of pigment from the maternal circulation across the placenta to the fetus and its almost equally rapid removal from the fetal circulation back across the placenta.

The experiments were again repeated, using conjugated ¹⁴C-labeled bilirubin. Unlike the previous results, only a small fraction of the radioactive bilirubin injected into the fetus was transferred across the placenta to appear in the maternal bile, as shown in Table I. A slower rate of disappearance of conjugated bilirubin from fetal plasma was found, indicating that instead of being excreted in bile, the pigment was distributed in extravascular spaces.

Lester *et al.*[63] found essentially the same response in studies of pregnant rhesus monkeys. Studies by Gartner and Lane,[36] also in the rhesus monkey, demonstrated that in the newborn of this species during the first 36 hr of life, maximum bilirubin uptake by the liver and the hepatic conjugation of bilirubin, as well as the amount of hepatic excretion of bilirubin, is far less than in the adult. These studies indicate that at least in the animal species that most closely approximates the human in this metabolic aspect, the limiting factor in the ability

to dispose of bilirubin in the first day or so after birth is the capacity of the fetal–neonatal liver to conjugate bilirubin with glucuronic acid.

One must assume that bilirubin is easily transported across the placenta in its unconjugated, nonpolar state, while the heavier, polar molecules of bilirubin glucuronide are hardly transferred at all across this biological membrane structure. Since the maternal liver is efficient both in conjugating bilirubin to form the glucuronide and in the hepatic excretion of this conjugate into the bile, the transplacental gradient favors the movement of bilirubin from the fetus to its mother. The result is a nearly normal plasma concentration of bilirubin during intrauterine life. Even in conditions of rapid erythrocyte breakdown and consequent accelerated bilirubin production—as is seen in severe maternal–fetal blood group incompatibility—the cord blood bilirubin rarely exceeds 5 ml/dl. These situations attest to the rapidly efficient transfer of the pigment across the placenta and the equally efficient disposal of fetal bilirubin by the mother.

4. Bilirubin Metabolism in the Neonate

On delivery of the fetus and as soon as the cord is cut, the newly born infant loses the placental mechanism by which bilirubin is removed through the maternal liver and biliary system. As a result, there is a modest accumulation of unconjugated bilirubin in the plasma. This accumulation is usually referred to as "physiologic" or, as Gartner has so felicitously suggested, "developmental" jaundice. Since the appearance of jaundice in most newborns seems to be related to limited uptake, enzymatic conversion, and excretion of bilirubin by the immature liver, it is more truly a developmental phenomenon than a physiologic one: common occurrence of an abnormal state does not make it physiologic, in the usual though inexact sense of that word.

4.1. Formation

Pearson[88] made an estimate of the contribution of the breakdown of normal red blood cells to the development of jaundice in the newborn. His calculations were based on three factors: (1) the life span of the fetal erythrocyte, (2) the bilirubin space of the newborn, and (3) the glucuronide conjugating capacity of the liver. He estimated the average weight of the newborn infant to be 3.4 kg, and the blood volume to be 85 ml/kg, with an average hemoglobin concentration of 17 g/dl. From these values, he calculated the mean circulating hemoglobin mass to be

$$3.4 \text{ kg infant} \times 85 \text{ ml/kg} \times 17 \text{ g/dl} = 49 \text{ g Hb} \quad (1)$$

Data derived from the study of ^{51}Cr-tagged erythrocytes led to Pearson's estimate that the life span of the fetal red blood cell is about 70 days. Thus, about 1.4% of the circulating red cell mass is hemolyzed each day. The quantity of hemolgobin released by hemolysis and broken down each day is calculated as

$$49 \text{ g Hb} \times 1.4\%/\text{day} = 0.69 \text{ g Hb/day} \quad (2)$$

Since each gram of hemoglobin catabolized will yield 35 mg bilirubin, the amount of bilirubin formed by hemolysis during the first 3 days of life would be

$$0.69 \text{ g Hb/day} \times 35 \text{ mg bili/g Hb} \times 3 \text{ days}$$
$$= 72 \text{ mg bili/3 days} \quad (3)$$

The bilirubin space of the newborn has not been determined, but in the adult, it is equivalent to the albumin space, and is approximately twice the plasma volume. If this equivalency holds for the neonate, then the bilirubin space for a 3.4-kg infant would

be approximately 280 ml. If no hepatic conjugation and excretion occurred in the first 3 days of life, the serum bilirubin concentration would rise to a theoretical level of

$$72 \text{ mg bilirubin/280 ml plasma} = 26 \text{ mg/dl} \quad (4)$$

The average term infant who does not exhibit excessive hemolysis develops a peak serum bilirubin concentration, at 3 days of age, of only about 6–7 ml/dl. This value suggests that the neonatal liver is capable of conjugating and excreting approximately two-thirds to three-quarters of the bilirubin circulating through its body in these first few days of life. A marked increase in unconjugated bilirubin during this period indicates an excessive bilirubin production, related principally to red cell hemolysis, or a decreased ability to conjugate or excrete a normal bilirubin load, or both.

In this regard, the mechanism by which bile pigment is overproduced may compromise otherwise barely adequate hepatic conjugating and excretory capacity, most particularly in the premature infant. Studies of the induction mechanisms for bile pigment formation have offered some interesting speculations on the incidence of hyperbilirubinemia in the immature newborn, the infant of the diabetic mother, and the small-for-gestational-age infant, all of whom have an increased predilection for jaundice. Heme catabolism is mediated by microsomal heme oxygenase, which is present in hepatic parenchymal and sinusoidal cells, in splenic cells, in macrophages, and in the kidney.[93,114,115] This enzyme converts heme to biliverdin, which, in turn, is enzymatically converted to bilirubin by the catalytic activity of biliverdin reductase. Microsomal heme oxygenase is influenced by the rate of heme synthesis (e.g., release of hemoglobin by red cells), by phagocytosed red cells, by the fasting state,[8] by some hormones, and by the availability of glucose to macrophages. It has been shown[116] that there is an increase of heme oxygenase activity in newborn rats by 10 hr of age, which reaches a peak of activity by 7 days of age, and declines thereafter. There is speculation that this increase in the activity of hepatic heme oxygenase is the result of the loss of maternal glucose supply to the fetus at birth, leading to low liver glycogen content. The subsequent hypoglycemia, of relative degree, may induce hepatic heme oxygenase by the stimulated release of glucagon and epinephrine.[8,116] This sequence of events may also occur in the human newborn either fasted or for other reasons hypoglycemic. It is worth noting that both epinephrine and glucagon cause a marked increase in carbon monoxide production from nonerythrocytic sources of heme, thus possibly contributing to the total bilirubin pool without hemolysis having played a role.[24] Interestingly enough, it has been shown[73] that fasting increases carbon monoxide production in man.

4.2. Transport

Unconjugated bilirubin is transported in a complex with albumin in the newborn just as in the adult; however, several important factors complicate the matter during the neonatal period.

The studies of Odell[79,80] demonstrated that unconjugated bilirubin may be present in the plasma in two distinct forms. The great bulk of circulating bilirubin is bound to albumin in a complex that has an absorption peak (in serum) at 460 nm. Since unconjugated bilirubin may also circulate in a free state, it can be identified by spectroscopy, which shows an absorption peak at 420 nm, and a mobility different from that of albumin-bound bilirubin on Sephadex gel column chromatography.[15,57] During the neonatal period, three processes may augment the amount of free bilirubin:

(1) There may be an absolute or relative hypoalbuminemia in the newborn. For example, immature and low-birth-weight infants often have low levels of serum albumin, which would lead to a smaller proportion of bound bilirubin and a detectable increase of bilirubin in the free form. Rapid shifts of plasma from vascular to extravascular compartments in the neonatal period may reduce the amount of circulating albumin available for binding with bilirubin.

(2) Electrophoretic studies have shown that bilirubin dissociates completely from protein at pH 7.0 and below. Since moderate to severe degrees of acidosis are not uncommon in the newborn, particularly in association with respiratory distress syndrome and hemolytic disease of the newborn, more free bilirubin in relation to bound may appear in the plasma.

(3) Several organic anions, such as salicylates, sulfisoxazole, and some antibiotic stabilizers,[9,55] may competitively displace bilirubin from its albumin binding sites and thereby increase the unbound pigment fraction.

Free bilirubin acts on the CNS in two ways: (1) by penetrating the blood–brain barrier, and (2) by transfer to brain cells with mitochondrial uptake. Diamond and Schmid[25] showed that only unbound bilirubin can cross the blood–brain barrier; in consequence, the amount of bilirubin transferred from the plasma into the brain is determined by the magnitude of the unbound fraction, rather than by the concentration of total bilirubin circulating. As shown in Fig. 7, when newborn guinea pigs were infused with [^{14}C]bilirubin in taurocholate, and subsequently treated with human albumin, the amount of bilirubin in the brain remained at a low

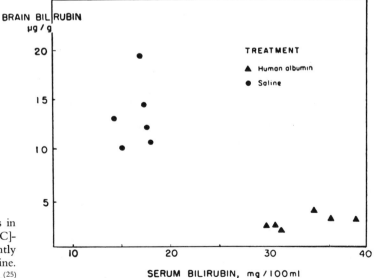

Fig. 7. Brain and serum bilirubin levels in newborn guinea pigs infused with [^{14}C]-bilirubin in taurocholate and subsequently treated with either human albumin or saline. Reproduced from Diamond and Schmid.[25]

Table II. Distribution of Bilirubin Between Mitochondria and the Sucrose Suspension Medium Containing Different Bovine Albumin Concentrations[a]

Suspension bilirubin (μg)	Added albumin (mg)	Molar ratio bilirubin/albumin	Bilirubin recovery (μg)	
			Mitochondria	Supernatant
276	0		184	54
287	6	5.8	64	190
315	15	2.3	24	256
309	30	1.1	8	308
308	45	0.8	2	300
324	60	0.6	2	294
291	75	0.4	2	296
300	90	0.3		

[a] From Odell.[81]

level, and the serum bilirubin concentration remained high. In contrast, when these animals were infused with bilirubin and subsequently treated with saline, to which the bilirubin would not bind, the quantity of bilirubin in brain increased, and the serum concentration became much lower. These data indicated that bilirubin had been able to penetrate the blood–brain barrier when in an unbound state, but when in complex with albumin, it remained in the serum and did not transfer into brain tissue.

Odell[81] demonstrated in a series of *in vitro* experiments that mitochondria suspended in an aqueous solution containing albumin and bilirubin preferentially sequestered the bilirubin fraction of such suspensions. The effect was prevented by the addition of protein in adequate concentrations. As shown in Table II, there is virtually no association between bilirubin and mitochondria as long as the molar ratio of bilirubin to albumin remains below 1:1. As the proportion of bilirubin increases and the molar ratio exceeds 1:1, however, a linear relationship between mitochondrial uptake of bilirubin and the molar ratio of the pigment to albumin is revealed. Salicylates and other organic anions enhance the association of bilirubin and mitochondria at the expense of bilirubin bound to albumin. It can be seen from Table III that organic anions exert a negligible effect when the molar ratio of bilirubin

Table III. Distribution of Bilirubin Between Mitochondria and the Suspension Medium Containing Different Bovine Albumin Concentrations[a]

Molar ratio bilirubin/albumin	Bilirubin recovery (μg)			
	Without salicylates		With salicylates	
	Mitochondria	Supernatant	Mitochondria	Supernatant
4.1	163	68	178	58
2.0	128	124	161	74
1.4	85	140	142	104
1.0	56	188	102	136
0.7	33	216	67	178

[a] From Odell.[81]

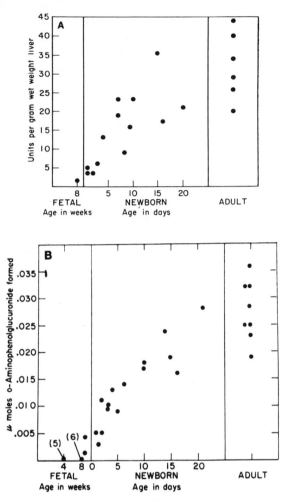

Fig. 8. Comparison of (A) UDPG dehydrogenase and (B) glucuronyl transferase in fetal, newborn, and adult guinea pigs. (A) The enzyme fraction from liver homogenate that precipitated between 50 and 70% ammonium sulfate saturation was used. One unit of UDPG dehydrogenase activity equaled a change in transmittance at 340 mμ of 0.001/min. (B) Microsomal fraction from 200 mg liver with added UDPGA was incubated with 0.66 μM o-aminophenol for 30 min at 37°C. Reproduced from Brown and Zuelzer.[17]

to albumin is below 1:1. As the bilirubin concentration rises, however, there is a greater mitochondrial uptake of bilirubin when the salicylates are present. These observations were of importance in the later studies of Odell, which led to the technique of salicylate saturation index determination in jaundiced sera.[83]

4.3. Conjugation

In 1958, Brown and Zuelzer[17] reported a marked decrease of UDPG dehydrogenase and glucuronyl transferase activity in the fetal and newborn guinea pig, as shown in Fig. 8. These observations have been confirmed in several species, including man,[28,33,59] but other observations indicate that more than one glucuronyl transferase may be present.[29] This possibility has led to much speculation on the precise role that inhibitors and inducers may play in neonatal bilirubin metabolism, especially the glucuronyl transferase enzyme system.

In the past, most investigators have assumed that the enzyme that conjugates bilirubin, o-aminophenol, and p-nitrophenol in different mammalian species was identical in each. More recent studies, however, have presented evidence that the enzyme that conjugates bilirubin is not the enzyme that conjugates other substrates, and furthermore that there may be a difference in their developmental patterns in the liver, as illustrated in Fig. 9.[30,32,42,117]

Lathe and Walker[58] first reported that serum from pregnant women inhibited the conjugation of bilirubin by liver slices, and demonstrated a similar effect with progestational steroids *in vitro*. Hsia *et al.*,[48] using a test system of o-aminophenol conjugation in rat liver homogenate, observed that

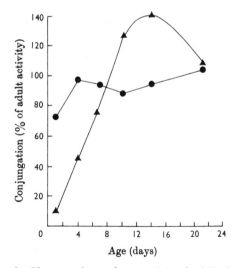

Fig. 9. Glucuronyl transferase activity for bilirubin (▲) and p-nitrophenol (●) in liver homogenates from rabbits of different ages. Reproduced from Tomlinson and Yaffe.[117]

serum from pregnant women inhibited this conjugation by 64%, and that serum from women in the immediate *postpartum* period inhibited by 42%. They further observed that serum from newborn infants caused an inhibition of 48%. On the other hand, serum from adult males had but 1% inhibition, and serum from nonpregnant women produced only 26% inhibition. Serum from pregnant women was pooled and purified, and the predominant fraction of inhibiting substance was identified as pregnanediol.

Later investigations[4,5] demonstrated that pregnane-3(α),20(β)-diol isolated from breast milk and perhaps from some maternal sera was the agent that inhibited glucuronyl transferase in these experiments, and they suggested that pregnanediol might be responsible for the appearance of excesive and prolonged jaundice in some otherwise normal term infants. Kinetic studies have shown that pregnanediol is a potent inhibitor of glucuronyl transferase.[5,12, 49,56] Although pregnanediol exerts a significant inhibiting effect on the activity of this enzyme, it does not remain in high concentration in breast milk for longer than a few weeks postpartum, and any causative effect it may have on neonatal hyperbilirubinemia is self-limited.

It was long believed impossible to stimulate the production of a hepatic microsomal enzyme such as glucuronyl transferase. In 1960, however, Inscoe and Axelrod[51] showed that when benzpyrene was injected into newborn rats, there was a significant increase in glucuronyl transferase in liver slices compared with that in livers of untreated litter mates. Benzpyrene injected into pregnant rats produced no increase in the enzyme activity of the fetuses, only in that of the dams. Shortly thereafter, Hart et al.[45] found that by injecting phenobarbital into a pregnant doe prior to delivery or into newly born rabbits, significant increase of hepatic microsomal enzyme activity would result. With this background in mind, Catz and Yaffe[18] investigated the effect on newborn mice of intraperitoneal administration of sodium phenobarbital in a dose of 50 mg/kg for 3 days, beginning on the day of birth. This treatment resulted in a 3.5-fold increase in bilirubin glucuronide formation compared with untreated littermates used as controls. These same effects were also obtained by injecting the pregnant female with barbital for 6 consecutive days prior to delivery. This treatment produced a 2-fold increase in bilirubin conjugation in the offspring, but did not affect the conjugating capacity in the mother.

Our knowledge of the conjugation of bilirubin in the neonate increases slowly, but piecemeal, and there remain gaps in the information we have and many unresolved questions. Although it is apparent, and reasonably well documented, that there is a decrease of glucuronyl transferase and UDPG dehydrogenase in the fetal and newborn liver, we are still uncertain about many factors leading to decreased conjugation in the newborn and the clinical expression of jaundice that results.

4.4. Excretion

Relatively little is known about the enterohepatic circulation of bilirubin in the newborn period. The principal fraction of bilirubin that appears in the bile after leaving the liver cells and enters the bile canaliculi is in the conjugated form. It is known, however, that a more or less minor portion of bilirubin in the bile is unconjugated, and that this portion is a normal excretory component in newborns. Lund and Jacobsen[72] showed that the excretion of unconjugated bilirubin can be markedly increased during phototherapy of neonatal jaundice, although it is not yet clear whether this increase is directly light-induced or a phenomenon related to increased gut-transit time or to some effect on the biliary system by the presence of photoproducts of bilirubin breakdown.

Our simple acceptance of this excretory phenomenon was justified, but recent studies offer a more satisfactory reason for Lund and Jacobsen's observations. Zenone et al.[126] have demonstrated that three polar isomers are produced by the photodecomposition of bilirubin in the body. Two of these are excreted unchanged in the bile; the third reverts to bilirubin after passage into the bile. Thus it seems clear, from this new information, that photoisomerization of bilirubin may account for the principal photoproduct found in bile and the observed increase of unconjugated bilirubin appearing in bile as a consequence of phototherapy.

Having been expelled into the lumen of the small intestine, bilirubin glucuronide may be deconjugated by the action of β-glucuronidase produced in the gut mucosa. Once having been converted to its unconjugated form, bilirubin may then be readily reabsorbed by the mucosa of both the small and the large bowel and so reenter the circulation.

Studies have been made[94,95] of the biliary excretion of conjugated and unconjugated [^{14}C]-bilirubin injected into 1-day-old and adult guinea

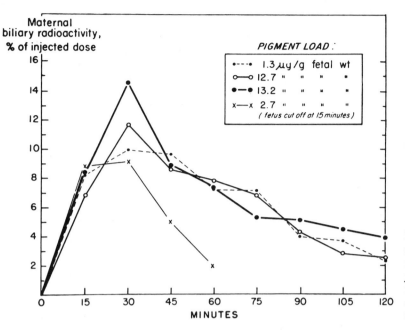

Fig. 10. Comparative rates of biliary isotope excretion after intravenous administration of unconjugated or conjugated [^{14}C]bilirubin to newborn (1-day-old) and adult guinea pigs. Reproduced from Schenker and Schmid.[194]

pigs. As shown in Fig. 10, the elimination of unconjugated pigment in the newborn was less than half that of the adult, and the elimination of conjugated bilirubin but two-thirds of the adult value. These data suggest that although impaired conjugation was the major defect, there was also a defect in excretion present during the neonatal period. The investigations of Gartner and Lane[36] on the rhesus monkey support this view.

Since the transport of bilirubin to the liver and its uptake, conjugation, and then excretion may be considered a single process comprising several progressively related steps, a deficiency in the excretory capacity of the liver may act to limit the preceding events in the chain, and thus lead to a significant accumulation of unconjugated bilirubin in the plasma and transfer of excess to the tissues.

4.5. Cause of "Physiologic" Jaundice in the Neonate

There is only a slight decrease in the life span of red blood cells in the healthy term newborn of normal birth weight, and hence a slight increase in the formation of bilirubin from this erythroid source. Under normal circumstances, this excess could be easily conjugated and excreted by the liver without the clinical appearance of jaundice. The efficiency of the conjugating mechanism is clearly reduced in the first days of life, however, resulting in a reduced conversion of bilirubin to its glucuronide. The presence of physiologic inhibitors, such as steroid hormones, and the lack of inducers of enzyme activity might contribute to the decreased efficiency. Moreover, there appears to be an excretory defect in the disposal of conjugated bilirubin that may even further inhibit its conversion and removal. Restriction of these mechanisms ultimately leads to an accumulation of unconjugated bilirubin in the plasma, and eventually to accumulation in other body tissues, notably fat and collagen. Excess of unconjugated bilirubin together with an absolute or relative hypoalbuminemia, acidosis, or the presence of organic anions in competition with bilirubin may lead to an increase in free, unbound bilirubin. Since free unconjugated bilirubin is nonpolar and lipid-soluble, it will readily cross the blood–brain barrier, after which it may be preferentially sequestered by neuronal mitochondria. The pigment is toxic to the brain cell. These considerations make the newborn infant, particularly the prematurely born, highly susceptible to the deposition of bilirubin in the brain and to the development of bilirubin encephalopathy.

5. Pathologic Hyperbilirubinemia in the Neonate

Excessive jaundice and toxic damage to the brain by bilirubin can be caused by abnormal processes occurring at the five sites shown in Fig. 11. These processes include: (1) increased breakdown of red blood cells, (2) interference with conjugation, (3) deficient excretion, (4) alteration of protein binding, and (5) susceptibility of brain cells to bilirubin deposition. The first four processes are discussed in this section; prevention of bilirubin encephalopathy is discussed in Section 6.

5.1. Increased Red Blood Cell Breakdown

The most common cause of excessive hemolysis during the neonatal period is maternal–fetal blood group incompatibility. Formerly, the major abnormality was found in the Rhesus factor when the Rh-negative mother of an Rh-positive fetus produced antibodies that invaded the fetus and caused continuous hemolysis of the fetal red blood cells. With the wide use of passive immunization of Rh(−) mothers before they become sensitized, improvements in blood-banking, and better techniques for the management of affected infants, this abnormality is less of a problem. There remains, however, the continued risk of hemolytic disease of the newborn from maternal–fetal incompatibility in the major A-B-O blood groups. The clinical expression of this condition is usually much less severe than with Rh incompatibility, but it adds significantly to the incidence of neonatal hyper-

Table IV. Antibodies Causing Hemolytic Disease of the Newborn During a 3-Year Period[a]

Antibody	Number of cases	Percentage of total
Anti-D	345	82.14
Anti-C + D	45	10.71
Anti-C	14	3.33
Anti-E	9	2.14
Anti-Ce	2	0.48
Anti-K	2	0.48
Anti-Fy[a]	1	0.24
Anti-JK[a]	1	0.24
Anti-U	1	0.24
Total	420	100

[a] Data from Giblett.[38]

bilirubinemia. Although about 100 different blood group antigens can be distinguished by their reactions to specific antibodies, only a few are responsible for causing hemolytic disease. Their occurrence is shown in Table IV.

Three approaches have been taken to reduce the morbidity and mortality associated with maternal isoimmunization: (1) early termination of pregnancy; (2) readings of the optical density of amniotic fluid obtained by amniocentesis to determine the bilirubin concentration of the fluid, and intrauterine transfusion in cases at risk of fetal demise; and (3) prevention of Rh immunization of mothers by administration of potent anti-D γ-globulin after the delivery of an Rh(+) infant to a mother not previously sensitized. Because of the large number of abortions that are now being done on demand, obstetricians recognize the risk of sensitization of such women by the procedure, and passive immunization by the anti-D γ-globulin is frequently performed in these circumstances.

Widespread population studies throughout the world indicate an association between glucose-6-phosphate dehydrogenase (G-6-PDH) deficiency and severe neonatal jaundice among Greeks,[27] Chinese,[69] and Bantus,[65] but not among non-Ashkenazi Jews[112] or American Negroes.[84,123] The reason for the selective occurrence of severe jaundice in some ethnic groups but not others is the large number of variants of the enzyme deficiency with differing molecular and clinical expressivity.

Excessive hemolysis during the newborn period

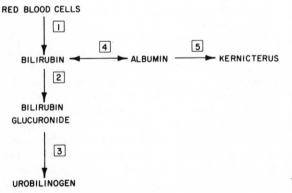

Fig. 11. Diagram of sites at which processes responsible for pathologic hyperbilirubinemia in the newborn infant can occur.

can occur because of genetic factors alone, environmental factors alone, or both. Aside from isoimmunization and G-6-PDH deficiency, susceptible to oxidative challenge by drugs or infections, other causes of hemolysis leading to hyperbilirubinemia are: congenital or neonatal infections, viral or bacterial sepsis; drug-induced hemolysis; inborn errors of red cell metabolism, such as pyruvate kinase deficiency and hereditary spherocytosis; transient defects in red cell metabolism; infantile pyknocytosis; and light-induced hemolysis (reduction of riboflavin in erythrocytes?).

There are at least a dozen genetically determined disturbances of the glycolytic cycle of the red blood cells.[46] Theoretically, a congenital nonspherocytic hemolytic anemia with any of these defects could result in excessive jaundice during the newborn period. Clinically, this condition has been described in several variants of G-6-PDH deficiency and in hereditary absence of glutathione. Glutathione deficiency induced by visible light irradiation has been reported[14] in relation to phototherapy, although the studies were performed *in vitro* and *in vivo* occurrence has not been documented. Excessive hemolysis can also occur if enzyme-deficient but nonhemolyzing infants or their mothers are exposed to certain drugs, such as vitamin K, primaquine, and sulfamethoxypyridazine (Kynex).[127] Meyer and Angus[75] described hyperbilirubinemia in premature infants receiving large doses of menadione (Synkavite).

5.2. Interference with Conjugation of Bilirubin

The hepatic metabolism of bilirubin in the neonate may be impaired by (1) insufficient intrahepatic transport proteins (ligandin); (2) glucuronyl transferase deficiency due to prematurity or a congenital defect (Crigler–Najjar); (3) suppression of conjugation from hormones or drugs, such as pregnanediol in breast milk, maternal steroids, or novobiocin; (4) hepatic cell damage from infection, drugs, or hypoxia; or (5) certain metabolic factors, such as maternal diabetes, hypoglycemia, hypothyroidism, acidosis, or dehydration.

Since liver glucuronyl transferase is commonly decreased in the normal newborn at term, it is difficult to explain why some term infants are more jaundiced than others. Premature infants tend to be more jaundiced than full-term infants and the incidence of hyperbilirubinemia is greater among them, and we assume the reason to be the very much more immaturely functioning liver in the premature. Leaving out the question of inhibitors and inducers in the term infant, one must postulate that there is a relatively greater degree of functional immaturity in the more jaundiced infants. This greater immaturity could be caused by a difference in the rate of development of the bilirubin-conjugating form of glucuronyl transferase of the bilirubin-conjugating form of glucuronyl transferase compared with the similar transferase(s) that conjugate *o*-aminophenol or *p*-nitrophenol. It is quite likely that such infants have a deficiency of UDPGA caused by a less mature UDPG dehydrogenase system.[32] In any event, a greater degree of immaturity of glucuronyl transferase or its related enzyme, UDPG dehydrogenase, would account for most of the hyperbilirubinemia encountered in the newborn—in particular, in the prematurely born infant.

Crigler and Najjar[22] reported their studies of a group of infants with a previously undescribed congenital abnormality characterized by marked elevation of plasma unconjugated bilirubin levels. All the initial patients were from a large kindred in western Maryland, and the families had closely inbred for several generations. Since extrapyramidal tract involvement was a prominent feature of the disease, the condition was named *congenital nonhemolytic jaundice with kernicterus*. Later, Schmid and Hammaker[97] showed through the use of [^{14}C]-bilirubin that a patient with this condition cannot excrete unconjugated bilirubin, although excretion of conjugated bilirubin is normal. This finding indicates that the patient with the Crigler–Najjar form of hyperbilirubinemia has a genetically determined absence of UDP glucuronyl transferase. These patients do excrete bilirubin to some extent by mediation of other conjugating pathways. Odell (personal communication) observed a bilirubin glycinate fraction in the bile of one such patient. Those with the Crigler–Najjar syndrome can be divided into two types, one responsive to the administration of phenobarbital (Type II), and one unresponsive to this enzyme inducer (Type I). Arias[1] showed that certain patients with familial nonhemolytic jaundice, an autosomal dominant that appears in children at about 10 years of age, also have a complete or partial deficiency of glucuronyl transferase. This condition, too, responds to the administration of phenobarbital.

Several investigations have shown an association

between inhibitors of glucuronyl transferase and hyperbilirubinemia. As mentioned earlier, serum from pregnant women, and particularly progestational hormones, are potent inhibitors of this enzyme. In 1965, Arias et al.[7] found that sera from 8 mothers and their newborn infants who exhibited transient familial neonatal hyperbilirubinemia inhibited direct-reacting bilirubin and o-aminophenol glucuronide formation by rat liver slices and homogenates 4–10 times more than was observed with control sera from pregnant women. While the serum inhibitory factor in these women was not identified at the time, that the inhibitor was found in pregnancy serum suggested that it might be a progestational steroid that would inhibit glucuronyl transferase activity in neonatal liver. This inhibition of conjugation could explain markedly elevated plasma bilirubin concentrations in some infants with no blood group incompatibilities or G-6-PDH deficiency or other reason for excessive levels of unconjugated pigment.

Arias et al.,[5] Gartner and Arias,[34] and others[78,110] described a syndrome of prolonged unconjugated hyperbilirubinemia occurring in full-term, breast-fed newborns. Two-thirds of the breast-fed siblings of these infants also had a history of prolonged jaundice, whereas none of the siblings fed cow's milk formulas had such a history. Breast milk from the mothers of the jaundiced infants was found to inhibit glucuronyl transferase activity in vitro. Pregnane-3(α),20(β)-diol was isolated from the milk

of 4 mothers of infants with prolonged unconjugated hyperbilirubinemia, but was not isolated from normal human milk. Because of these findings, Arias and Gartner[4] gave this steroid to healthy, full-term infants starting at 6, 8, 34, and 66 days of age. Jaundice was not observed in the older infants who received the steroid for 12 days, but was found in the two younger infants. Ramos et al.[90] repeated these studies in 20 term newborns fed either pregnane-3(α),20(α)-diol or pregnane-3(α),-20(β)-diol, and were unable to confirm an elevation of serum unconjugated bilirubin in any of the infants.

Sutherland and Keller[111] showed that administration of novobiocin caused hyperbilirubinemia in newborn infants. They found that jaundice appeared in 60 of 688 infants (9%) who received 50 mg novobiocin 3 times a day, an incidence far higher than occurred in infants who did not receive the drug. When novobiocin was injected into newborn rats, the rats become jaundiced. A decreased excretion of bilirubin was noted in rabbits after the administration of novobiocin. Lokietz et al.[67] and Hargreaves and Holton[43] demonstrated that novobiocin is a potent inhibitor of glucuronyl transferase, as is shown in Table V.

The induction of glucuronyl transferase has been applied to three clinical situations. Crigler and Gold[21] showed that when phenobarbital was administered to a patient with the Crigler–Najjar syndrome at a dose of 15 mg twice daily, the

Table V. Glucoronyl Transferase Activity and Inhibition Levels of Young Rats Given 500 mg Novobiocin per kg Body Weight[a]

Hours after injection	Litters (number)	Serum bilirubin levels[b]		Activity (%)[b,c]
		Control (mg/dl)	Experimental (mg/dl)	
2–4	4	0.3 ± 0.1	1.1 ± 0.9	44 ± 19
4–8	5	0.3 ± 0.1	0.9 ± 0.5	39 ± 11
8–18	4	0.5 ± 0.3	5.1 ± 1.8	69 ± 25
24	8	0.6 ± 0.3	4.0 ± 0.9	85 ± 15
48	5	0.4 ± 0.1	1.4 ± 0.9	115 ± 15
72	4	0.4 ± 0.1	0.7 ± 0.2	109 ± 21

[a] From Lokietz et al.[67]
[b] Mean and standard deviation are given.
[c] Using rat liver homogenate and o-aminophenol as substrate and expressed as percentage of activity over controls.

serum bilirubin concentration was reduced from 17.9 to 6.0 mg/dl. This reduction has not been observed in all patients with the syndrome, which accounts for the division of this syndrome into two types, as previously noted. Yaffe et al.[125] gave phenobarbital in a dose of 15 mg 3 times a day to a 9-month-old female infant with persistent jaundice. This treatment reduced the serum bilirubin level from 8 to 3 mg/dl. When therapy was discontinued, the serum bilirubin rose again to previous levels. Readministration of phenobarbital resulted in a decrease in bilirubin concentration.

Trolle[118] investigated the serum bilirubin levels in 98 infants born of mothers treated with phenobarbitone during the last weeks of pregnancy, and compared them with nearly 1500 controls. He found that the infants of treated mothers had a significantly lower incidence of hyperbilirubinemia than controls.

Sereni et al.[101] reported that diethylnicotinamide (Coramine) lowered serum bilirubin concentrations, but this finding is of biochemical, not clinical, interest.

These observations on the effect of enzyme inducers on the metabolism of bilirubin should be tempered by the realization that they are not specific for glucuronyl transferase alone, but affect other liver enzyme systems—which may not be desirable. Robinson et al.,[91] for instance, observed that in addition to reducing serum bilirubin concentrations, inhibitors can also markedly enhance early pigment formation, probably by increasing the turnover rate of microsomal heme enzymes (oxygenase) and cytochromes b_5 and P450.[100]

5.3. Disturbances of Bilirubin Excretion

The excretion of bilirubin in the newborn is complicated by the reabsorption of the deconjugated pigment in the gut. Details of the mechanisms involved are scant, and attempts to apply reasonable theoretical measures to prevent or inhibit intestinal reabsorption have been less than successful. In 1962, Lester et al.[64] showed that administration of cholestyramine resin to icteric Gunn rats resulted in a significant reduction of serum bilirubin levels, due to the fact that cholestyramine is a chelating agent with high affinity for bilirubin. Schmid and Hammaker[97] were not able to produce this same reduction in premature infants. Ulstrom and Eisenklam[119] undertook a controlled trial of the oral administration of activated charcoal, an adsorbant

that can bind bilirubin firmly to itself in the intestinal lumen, preventing its reabsorption. This treatment was effective only if begun in the first 4 hr of life. Poland and Odell[89] reported the successful interruption of the enterohepatic recirculation of bilirubin in nine infants with hyperbilirubinemia by the administration of agar by mouth in infant feed. They were able to reduce the concentration of plasma bilirubin in their patients by the binding of excreted biliary pigment in the bowel, preventing reabsorption, and removal of the bound bilirubin in the normal intestinal evacuation. On both practical and theoretical grounds, this mode of treatment was successful, but unfortunately it has not been so in other hands.

5.4. Alteration of Protein Binding

In 1956, Silverman et al.[102] carried out a controlled study on the relative effectiveness of two prophylactic antibacterial drugs, tetracycline and penicillin with sulfisoxazole (Gantrisin). Quite unexpectedly, they found 29 instances of kernicterus among 141 necropsies, and of these, 27 were among infants who received penicillin and sulfisoxazole. Some years later, the studies of Odell[79] and Ostrow and Schmid[85] showed that organic anions, such as sulfisoxazole, will cause a dissociation of the albumin–bilirubin complex and thus increase the concentration of free bilirubin in plasma, making the infant more susceptible to bilirubin encephalopathy. Other compounds are known to produce this effect by competitively displacing bilirubin from its binding sites on albumin, among them a variety of stabilizers in preparations of antibiotic drugs for parenteral administration.[9] It is also well known that nonesterified fatty acids, which are commonly elevated in the plasma of premature infants, will compete with bilirubin for protein-binding sites.

Since the premature infant is hypoalbuminemic, compared with the full-term, available binding sites are diminished for him. It has been found useful to inject human serum albumin in such infants who are hyperbilirubinemic in order to provide binding sites and prevent the accumulation of free unconjugated bilirubin in the plasma, at least on a temporary basis until a more permanent and definitive treatment can be accomplished.

Odell et al.[82] advocated the administration of 1 g albumin/kg body weight 1 or 2 hr prior to exchange transfusion. The purpose of this regimen is to provide extra available binding sites in plasma to reverse the plasma–tissue gradient of bilirubin and thus to reduce the total pool of pigment in the body. It has been found that on the average, 41% more bilirubin is removed during exchange transfusion when this method of "albumin-priming" is followed.

6. Prevention of Bilirubin Encephalopathy

The ultimate objective of investigations on the pathogenesis of neonatal jaundice is the prevention of bilirubin encephalopathy. Johnson and Boggs[54] reported that peak concentrations of bilirubin in the serum of full-term newborns as low as 15 mg/dl were associated with some degree of neurological damage determined on examination at 4–7 years of age. This finding has caused a rethinking of criteria for the treatment of hyperbilirubinemia, since it is no longer possible to consider the term infant safe from damage to the brain at concentrations below 20 mg/dl. The situation for the small premature infant is even more chancy, for the histological proof of kernicterus in such infants at low levels of serum bilirubin (10 mg/dl) has been documented repeatedly.[37,44,109]

6.1. Clamping of the Cord

A number of studies have shown a possible association between delayed clamping of the umbilical cord, producing increased red cell volume, and increased neonatal jaundice. While there is agreement that late clamping of the cord results in red cell hypervolemia, that this results in an increase of serum bilirubin levels is still presumptive. Taylor et al.[113] found that the weighted mean bilirubin concentrations were greater in late-clamped than in early-clamped premature infants—but not in full-term infants. This finding, of course, may have been related to the greater conjugative and excretory capacity of the infants born at term.

6.2. Early Feeding

Several investigations have shown that early feeding of the neonate results in a decreased incidence of jaundice. Some years ago, Hubbel et al.[50] found that if infants born of diabetic mothers were fed at 4 hr of age, rather than fasted for 48 hr, as was usual at the time, they had significantly less jaundice. This finding was later confirmed by the studies of Wennberg et al.[121] in full-term infants and of Wu and Hodgman[124] in premature infants. Moreover, the early feeding of distilled water, 5% glucose in saline, and 15% glucose solutions was equally effective in reducing serum bilirubin levels.[121] There are two possible explanations for these observations: (1) that dehydration and consequent hemoconcentration was prevented by the early administration of fluids or (2) that hypoglycemia was prevented, thus inhibiting the stimulation of microsomal heme oxygenase and accelerated bilirubin production.

6.3. Exchange Transfusion

Despite advances in the management of neonatal bilirubinemia in the last few years, exchange transfusion is still the most effective and certain method of reducing dangerously elevated concentrations of unconjugated bilirubin in the plasma of the newborn to prevent bilirubin encephalopathy. It is preferred in the treatment of moderately severe hemolytic disease of the newborn because it serves not only to remove excessive bilirubin, but also to remove offending antibodies and red blood cells, replacing them with cells unaffected by remaining antibody. Exchange transfusion is also a preferred treatment of rapidly raising serum bilirubin levels in sick newborns and some prematures whose immaturity and illness will not brook delay in the correction of hyperbilirubinemia. The risk of morbidity or mortality from this procedure is small, probably less than 1% today, in experienced hands and with the ancillary service of a competent blood bank.

Although one cannot truly assess the risk of brain damage by measurement of the serum bilirubin concentration, this determination remains the most widely useful guide for clinical management of jaundice. Its serious limitations must be recognized, however, and traditional criteria for intervention with exchange transfusion should probably be discarded in favor of earlier transfusion, at somewhat lower levels of serum bilirubin than has been the custom. In the small premature infant, most particularly if he is ill with respiratory distress, and acidotic or septic or both, exchange at levels below 15 mg/dl is certainly a conservative practice. In the term infant, although the usual serum bilirubin level indicating treatment has been 20 mg/dl, institution of exchange at a level of about 18 mg/dl does not seem too cautious. A rate of rise in serum bilirubin concentration greater than 0.5 mg/dl per hr indicates unusually rapid bilirubin production, and in hemolytic disease, exaggerated red cell breakdown. In such a case, one might expect that high levels of bilirubin will be reached in hours rather than two or three days, and transfusion may be indicated.

Since reliance on serum bilirubin concentrations cannot be complete because it is imprecise and, in part, intuitive, other laboratory tests have been advocated. Among them are the reserve binding capacity of albumin (HBABA), measurement of albumin binding capacity by fluorescence, and Sephadex gel separation of bound and unbound bilirubin from plasma.

6.4. Phototherapy

Other than exchange transfusion, the only method of treating neonatal hyperbilirubinemia that not only has had success but also has remarkable utility is phototherapy. First described and proposed in 1958 in the classic paper by Cremer et al.,[20] this essentially noninvasive (in the mechanical sense)

mode of therapy has become a universally accepted method for the reduction of elevated levels of serum bilirubin. Its rationale depends on the fact that bilirubin is a photochemically active substance, both in vitro and in vivo. The pigment breaks down under visible light—which emits in the range of its absorption peak (about 460 nm in serum)—to a variety of photoproducts that include photolabile elements themselves, but are not known to be toxic.[26] It has been shown that there is a dose–response relationship between bilirubin and the energy of the light to which it is exposed.[76,106] This relationship accounts for some of the varied response to phototherapy that has been observed.

It has not been proved that phototherapy actually prevents bilirubin encephalopathy, but since this condition results from the toxic effect of bilirubin on brain cells, any method that will prevent entry of the pigment into the brain must be assumed to occasion this benefit. There is evidence in support of this assumption.[70,105]

In addition to causing the photooxidation of bilirubin in vivo by mechanisms that are not yet fully understood, but are probably related to the action of singlet oxygen,[74] phototherapy increases the

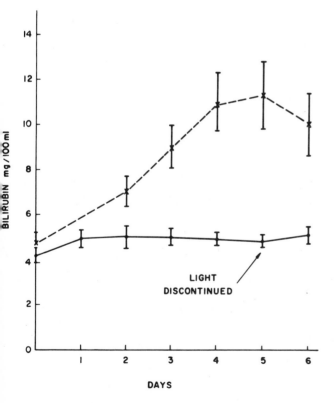

Fig. 12. Serum bilirubin levels in the phototherapy group (× — — — ×) and the control group (● ——— ●). The values given represent mean ± S.E. for each day. Reproduced from Hsia, D. Y.-Y., and Porto, S., 1970, Bilirubin metabolism, in: *Physiology of the Perinatal Period* (Uwe Stave, ed.), 1st Ed., Chapter 18, p. 618, Appleton-Century-Crofts, New York.

hepatic excretion of unconjugated bilirubin,[71] increases gut transit time,[92] alters the biorhythm of plasma human growth hormone,[104] and reduces the amount of whole blood riboflavin in the neonate.[107]

The optimum radiant energy for the application of phototherapy is not yet known, nor is the correct means of exposure, constant or intermittent (though both are effective). The light sources in common use are either broad-spectrum "daylight" fluorescent lamps, broad-spectrum "blue" fluorescents, or relatively monochromatic "blue-violet" lamps. A quartz halide white light with tungsten filament that has a significant output in the range of absorption of the bilirubin molecule is also in use, but not generally available at this time.[107]

There is some concern about possible unwanted sequelae from the use of phototherapy, and to uncover the many possible consequences and the many other photobiological effects of visible light radiation of the newborn, a large number of investigators are exploring the chemical and biological effects of phototherapy. Until significant deleterious effects are found, this form of treatment will enjoy wide use, for its effectiveness is acknowledged. Figure 12 illustrates the results of a controlled study of phototherapy that typifies the many clinical reports in the literature. A more complete discussion of phototherapy of neonatal hyperbilirubinemia may be found in two recently published sources.[10,108]

7. Conclusion

An attempt has been made in this chapter to review bilirubin metabolism in the newborn infant to point out the unique physiologic and biochemical events that take place in the developing fetus during intrauterine life and in the infant during the neonatal period. These events are interpreted to give some explanation for the causes and rational management of jaundice in the newborn full-term and premature infant and the jaundice of pathologic degree encountered in this period of life.

8. References

1. ARIAS, I. M., 1962, Chronic unconjugated hyperbilirubinemia without overt signs of hemolysis in adolescents and adults, *J. Clin. Invest.* **41**:2233.

2. ARIAS, I. M., 1970, The pathogenesis of "physiologic" jaundice of the newborn: A re-evaluation, in: "Bilirubin Metabolism in the Newborn," *Birth Defects: Orig. Artic. Ser.* **6**:55.

3. ARIAS, I. M., 1972, Transfer of bilirubin from blood to bile, *Semin. Hematol.* **9**:55.

4. Arias, I. M., AND GARTNER, L. M., 1964, Production of unconjugated hyperbilirubinemia in full-term new-born infants following administration of pregnane-3(α),20(β)-diol, *Nature (London)* **203**:1292.

5. ARIAS, I. M., GARTNER, L. M., SEIFTER, S., AND FURMAN, M., 1964, Prolonged neonatal unconjugated hyperbilirubinemia associated with breast feeding and a steroid, pregnane-3(alpha),20(beta)-diol, in maternal milk that inhibits glucuronide formation *in vitro*, *J. Clin. Invest.* **43**:2037.

6. ARIAS, I. M., JOHNSON, L., AND WOLFSON, S., 1961, Biliary excretion of injected conjugated and unconjugated bilirubin by normal and Gunn rats, *Amer. J. Physiol.* **200**:1091.

7. ARIAS, I. M., WOLFSON, S., LUCEY, J. F., AND McKAY, R. J., 1965, Transient familial neonatal hyperbilirubinemia, *J. Clin. Invest.* **44**:1442

8. BAKKEN, A. F., THALER, M. M., AND SCHMID, R., 1972, Metabolic regulation of heme catabolism and bilirubin production: I. Hormonal control of hepatic heme oxygenase activity, *J. Clin. Invest.* **51**:530.

9. BALLOWITZ, L., AND HANEFELD, F., 1976, Effect of drugs on infant Gunn rats under phototherapy, in: "Bilirubin Metabolism in the Newborn (II)," (D. Bergsma and S. H. Blondheim, eds.), *Birth Defects: Orig. Artic. Ser.* **12**:61.

10. BERGSMA, D., AND BLONDHEIM, S. H. (eds.), 1976, "Bilirubin Metabolism of the Newborn (II)," *Birth Defects: Orig. Artic. Ser.* **12**, American Elsevier, New York.

11. BERNSTEIN, L. H., BEN EZZER, J., GARTNER, L. M., AND ARIAS, I. M., 1966, Hepatic intracellular distribution of tritium-labeled unconjugated and conjugated bilirubin in normal and Gunn rats, *J. Clin. Invest.* **45**:1194.

12. BEVAN, B. R., HOLTON, J. B., AND LATHE, G. H., 1965, The effect of pregnanediol and pregnanediol glucuronide on bilirubin conjugation by rat liver slices, *Clin. Sci.* **29**:353.

13. BILLING, B. H., COLE, P. G., AND LATHE, G. H., 1957, The excretion of bilirubin as a diglucuronide giving the direct van den Bergh reaction, *Biochem. J.* **65**:774.

14. BLACKBURN, M. G., ORZALESI, M. M., AND PIGRAM, P., 1972, Effect of light on fetal red cells *in vivo*, *J. Pediatr.* **80**:641.

15. BLONDHEIM, S. H., KAPITULNIK, J., VALAES, T., AND KAUFMAN, N. A., 1972, Use of a sephadex column to evaluate the bilirubin-binding capacity of the serum of infants with neonatal jaundice, *Isr. J. Med. Sci.* **8**:22.

16. Brown, A. K., 1976, Bilirubin metabolism in the fetus and newborn, in: *The Physiology of the Newborn Infant* (C. A. Smith and N. M. Nelson, eds.), p. 338, Charles C. Thomas, Springfield, Illinois.

17. Brown, A. K., and Zuelzer, W. W., 1958, Studies on neonatal development of glucuronide conjugating system, *J. Clin. Invest.* **37**:332.

18. Catz, C., and Yaffe, S. J., 1962, Pharmacological modification of bilirubin conjugation in the newborn, *Amer. J. Dis. Child.* **104**:516.

19. Cooke, J. R., and Roberts, L. B., 1969, The binding of bilirubin to serum proteins, *Clin. Chim. Acta* **26**:425.

20. Cremer, R. J., Perryman, P. W., and Richards, D. H., 1958, Influence of light on the hyperbilirubinaemia of infants, *Lancet* **1**:1094.

21. Crigler, J. F., Jr., and Gold, N. I., 1967, Effect of sodium phenobarbital on the metabolism of bilirubin ^{3}H and ^{14}C in an infant with congenital nonhemolytic jaundice and kernicterus, *J. Clin. Invest.* **46**:1047.

22. Crigler, J. F., Jr., and Najjar, V. A., 1952, Congenital familial nonhemolytic jaundice with kernicterus, *Pediatrics* **10**:169.

23. Davidson, L. T., Merritt, K. K., and Weech, A. A., 1941, Hyperbilirubinemia in the newborn, *Amer. J. Dis. Child.* **61**:958.

24. Dawber, N. H., Bakken, A., and Schmid, R., 1974, Stimulation of bilirubin production by epinephrine and glucagon, *Gastroenterology* **66**:881.

25. Diamond, I., and Schmid, R., 1966, Experimental bilirubin encephalopathy. The mode of entry of bilirubin-^{14}C into the central nervous system, *J. Clin. Invest.* **45**:678.

26. Diamond, I., and Schmid, R., 1968, Neonatal hyperbilirubinemia and kernicterus, experimental support for treatment by exposure to visible light, *Arch Neurol.* **18**:699.

27. Doxiades, S. A., Fessas, P., and Valaes, T., 1960, Erythrocyte enzyme deficiency in unexplained kernicterus, *Lancet* **2**:44.

28. Dutton, G. J., 1959, Glucuronide synthesis in foetal liver and other tissue, *Biochem. J.* **71**:141.

29. Dutton, G. J., 1963, Foetal and infant liver function and structure: IV. Bilirubin and related compounds. Comparison of glucuronide synthesis in developing and mammalian and avian liver, *Ann. N. Y. Acad. Sci.* **111**:259.

30. Dutton, G. J., Langelaan, D. E., and Ross, P. E., 1964, High glucuronide synthesis in newborn liver: Choice of species and substrate, *Biochem. J.* **93**:4P.

31. Fashena, G. J., 1948, Mechanism of hyperbilirubinemia in the newborn infant, *Amer. J. Dis. Child.* **76**:196.

31a. Fleischner, G. M., and Arias, I. M., 1976, Structure and function of ligandin (Y protein, GSH transferase B) and Z protein in the liver: A progress report, in: *Progress in Liver Disease,* Vol. 5 (H. Popper and F. Schaffner, eds.), pp. 172–182, Grune and Stratton, New York.

32. Flodgaard, H. J., and Broderson, R., 1967, Bilirubin glucuronide formation in developing guinea pig liver, *Scand. J. Clin. Lab. Invest.* **19**:149.

33. Gartner, L. M., and Arias, I. M., 1963, Developmental pattern of glucuronide formation in rat and guinea pig liver, *Amer. J. Physiol.* **20**:633.

34. Gartner, L. M., and Arias, I. M., 1966, Studies of prolonged neonatal jaundice in the breast-fed infant, *J. Pediatr.* **68**:54.

35. Gartner, L. M., and Arias, I. M., 1969, The transfer of bilirubin from blood to bile in the neonatal guinea pig, *Pediatr. Res.* **3**:171.

36. Gartner, L. M., and Lane, D., 1971, Hepatic metabolism and transport of bilirubin during physiologic jaundice in the newborn rhesus monkey, *Pediatr. Res.* **70**:166.

37. Gartner, L. M., Snyder, R. N., Chabon, R. S., and Bernstein, J., 1970, Kernicterus. High incidence in premature infants with low serum bilirubin concentrations, *Pediatrics* **45**:906.

38. Giblett, E. R., 1964, Blood group antibodies causing hemolytic disease of the newborn, *Clin. Obstet. Gynecol.* **7**:1044.

39. Goldstein, G. W., and Lester, R., 1964, Reduction of biliverdin-C^{14} *in vivo*, *Proc. Soc. Exp. Biol. Med.* **117**:681.

40. Gray, C. H., Nicholson, D. C., and Nicolaus, R. A., 1958, The IXa structure of the common bile pigments, *Nature (London)* **181**:183.

41. Gray, C. H., Neuberger, A., and Sneath, P. H. A., 1950, Studies in congenital porphyria: II. Incorporation of ^{15}N in the normal and in the porphyric, *Biochem. J.* **47**:87.

41a. Habig, W., Pabst, M., Fleischner, B., Gatmaitan, Z., Arias, I. M., and Jakoby, W., 1974, The identity of glutathione transferase B with ligandin, a major binding protein of liver, *Proc. Natl. Acad. Sci. U.S.A.* **71**:3879.

42. Halac, E., Jr., and Reff, A., 1967, Studies on bilirubin UDP-glucuronyltransferase, *Biochim. Biophys. Acta* **139**:328.

43. Hargreaves, T., and Holton, J. B., 1962, Jaundice of the new-born due to novobiocin, *Lancet* **1**:839.

44. Harris, R. C., Lucey, J. F., and MacLean, J. R., 1958, Kernicterus in premature infants associated with low concentrations of bilirubin in plasma, *Pediatrics* **21**:875.

45. Hart, G., Adamson, R. H., Dixon, R. L., and Fouts, J. R., 1962, Stimulation of hepatic microsomal drug metabolism in the newborn and fetal rabbit, *J. Pharmacol. Exp. Ther.* **137**:103.

46. Hsia, D. Y.-Y., 1966, *Inborn Errors of Metabolism. I. Clinical Aspects,* 2nd Ed., Year Book Medical Publishers, Chicago.

47. Hsia, D. Y.-Y., Allen, F. H., Diamond, L. K., and Gellis, S. S., 1953, Serum bilirubin in the newborn infant, *J. Pediatr.* **42**:277.

48. Hsia, D. Y.-Y., Dowben, R. M., Shaw, R., and Grossman, A., 1960, Inhibition of glucuronosyl transferase by progestational agents from serum of pregnant women, *Nature (London)* **187**:693.

49. Hsia, D. Y.-Y., Riabov, S., and Dowben, R. M., 1963, Inhibition of glucuronosyl transferase by steroid hormones, *Arch. Biochem.* **103**:181.

50. Hubbel, J. P., Jr., Drorbaugh, J. E., Rudolph, A. J., Auld, P. A. M., Cherry, R. B., and Smith, C. A., 1961, "Early" versus "late" feeding of infants of diabetic mothers, *N. Engl. J. Med.* **265**:835.

51. Inscoe, J. K., and Axelrod, J., 1960, Some factors affecting glucuronide formation *in vitro*, *J. Pharmacol. Exp. Ther.* **129**:128.

52. Isselbacher, K. J., 1968, Evidence for the multiplicity of glucuronyl transferases, in: *Ikterus* (K. Beck, ed.), Schattauer, Stuttgart and New York.

53. Jacobsen, J., 1969, Binding of bilirubin to human serum albumin, determination of the dissociation constants, *FEBS Lett.* **5**:112.

54. Johnson, L., and Boggs, T. R., Jr., 1974, Bilirubin dependent brain damage: Incidence and indications for treatment, in: *Phototherapy: An Overview* (G. B. Odell, R. Shaffer, and A. Simopoulos, eds.), pp. 121–149, National Academy of Science, Washington, D.C.

55. Johnson, L., Sarmiento, F., Blanc, W. A., and Day, R. L., 1959, Kernicterus in rats with an inherited deficiency in glucuronyl transferase, *Amer. J. Dis. Child.* **97**:591.

56. Jones, B., 1964, Glucuronyl transferase inhibition by steroids, *J. Pediatr.* **64**:815.

57. Kapitulnik, J., Valaes, T., Kaufman, N. A., and Blondheim, S. H., 1974, Clinical evaluation of Sephadex gel filtration in the estimation of bilirubin binding in serum in neonatal jaundice, *Arch. Dis. Child.* **97**:591.

58. Lathe, G. H., and Walker, M., 1958, Inhibition of bilirubin conjugation in rat liver slices by human pregnancy and neonatal serum and steroids, *Q. J. Physiol.* **43**:257.

59. Lathe, G. H., and Walker, M., 1958, The synthesis of bilirubin glucuronide in animal and human liver, *Biochem. J.* **70**:705.

60. Lester, R., and Schmid, R., 1963, Intestinal absorption of bile pigments. I. The enterohepatic circulation in the rat, *J. Clin. Invest.* **42**:736.

61. Lester, R., and Schmid, R., 1963, Intestinal absorption of bile pigments. II. Bilirubin absorption in man. *N. Engl. J. Med.* **269**:178.

62. Lester, R., and Troxler, R., 1969, Recent advances in bile pigment metabolism, *Gastroenterology* **56**:143.

63. Lester, R., Behrman, R. E., and Lucey, J. F., 1963, Transfer of bilirubin C14 across monkey placenta, *Pediatrics* **32**:416.

64. Lester, R., Hammaker, L., and Schmid, R., 1962, A new therapeutic approach to unconjugated hyperbilirubinemia, *Lancet* **2**:1257.

65. Levin, S. E., Charlton, R. W., and Freiman, I., 1964, Glucose-6-phosphate dehydrogenase deficiency and neonatal jaundice in South African Bantu infants, *J. Pediatr.* **65**:757.

66. Litwak, G., Ketterer, B., and Arias, I. M., 1971, Ligandin: A hepatic protein which binds steroids, bilirubin, carcinogens, and a number of exogenous organic anions, *Nature (London)* **234**:466.

67. Lokietz, H., Dowben, R. M., and Hsia, D. Y.-Y., 1963, Studies on the effect of novobiocin on glucuronosyl transferase, *Pediatrics* **32**:47.

68. London, I., West, R., Shemin, D., and Rittenberg, D., 1950, On the origin of bile pigment in normal man, *J. Biol. Chem.* **184**:359.

69. Lu, T. C., Wei, H. Y., and Blackwell, R. W., 1966, Increased incidence of severe hyperbilirubinemia among newborn Chinese infants with G-6-PD deficiency, *Pediatrics* **37**:994.

70. Lucey, J. F., Hewitt, J. R., Emery, E. S., Goldstein, S., and Collins, S., 1973, Controlled follow-up study of low birth weight infants at 4–6 years of age treated with phototherapy, *Pediatr. Res.* **7**:313.

71. Lund, H. T., and Jacobsen, J., 1972, Influence of phototherapy on unconjugated bilirubin in duodenal bile of newborn infants with hyperbilirubinemia, *Acta Paediatr. Scand.* **61**:693.

72. Lund, H. T., and Jacobsen, J., 1974, Influence of phototherapy on the bilirubin excretion pattern in newborn infants with hyperbilirubinemia, *J. Pediatr.* **85**:262.

73. Lundh, B., Johansson, B., and Mercke, C., 1972, Enhancement of heme catabolism by caloric restriction in man, *Scand, J. Lab. Clin. Med.* **30**:421.

74. McDonagh, A. F., 1971, The role of singlet O_2 in bilirubin photooxidation, *Biochim. Biophys. Res. Commun.* **44**:1306.

75. Meyer, T. C., and Angus, J., 1956, The effect of large doses of "Synkavite" in the newborn, *Arch. Dis. Child.* **31**:212.

76. Mims, L. C., Estrada, M., Gooden, D. S., Caldwell, W. R., and Kotas, R. V., 1973, Phototherapy for neonatal hyperbilirubinemia—a dose: response relationship, *J. Pediatr.* **83**:658.

77. Mowat, A. P., and Arias, I. M., 1970, Observations of the effect of diethylnitrosamine on glucuronide formation, *Biochim. Biophys. Acta* **212**:65.

78. Newman, A. J., and Gross, S., 1966, Hyperbilirubinemia in breast-fed infants, *Pediatrics* **32**:995.

79. Odell, G. B., 1959, Dissociation of bilirubin from albumin and its clinical implications, *J. Pediatr.* **55**:286.

80. Odell, G. B., 1959, Studies in kernicterus. I. The protein binding of bilirubin, *J. Clin. Invest.* **38**:823.

81. Odell, G. B., 1966, The distribution between albumin and mitochondria, *J. Pediatr.* **68**:164.

82. Odell, G. B., Cohen, S. N., and Gordes, E. H.,

1962, Administration of albumin in the management of hyperbilirubinemia by exchange transfusion, *Pediatrics* **30**:613.

83. ODELL, G. B., COHEN, S. N., AND KEELY, P. C., 1969, Studies in kernicterus. II. The determination of the saturation of serum albumin with bilirubin, *J. Pediatr.* **74**:214.

84. O'FLYNN, M. E. D., AND HSIA, D. Y.-Y., 1963, Serum bilirubin levels and glucose-6-phosphate dehydrogenase deficiency in newborn American negroes, *J. Pediatr.* **63**:160.

85. OSTROW, J. D., AND SCHMID, R., 1963, The protein binding of C^{14}-bilirubin in human and murine serum, *J. Clin. Invest.* **42**:1286.

86. OSTROW, J. D., HAMMAKER, L., AND SCHMID, R., 1961, The preparation of crystalline bilirubin-C^{14}, *J. Clin. Invest.* **40**:1442.

87. OSTROW, J. D., JANDL, J. H., AND SCHMID, R., 1962, The formation of bilirubin from hemoglobin *in vivo, J. Clin. Invest.* **41**:1628.

88. PEARSON, H. A., 1967, Life-span of the fetal red blood cell, *J. Pediatr.* **70**:166.

89. POLAND, R. L., AND ODELL, G. B., 1971, Physiologic jaundice: The enterohepatic circulation of bilirubin, *N. Engl. J. Med.* **284**:1.

90. RAMOS, A., SILVERBERG, M., AND STERN, L., 1966, Pregnanediols and neonatal hyperbilirubinemia, *Amer. J. Dis. Child.* **111**:353.

91. ROBINSON, S. H., LESTER, R. CRIGLER, J. J., AND TSONG, M., 1967, Early-labeled peak of bile pigment in man, *N. Engl. J. Med.* **277**:1323.

92. RUBALTELLI, F. F., AND LARGAJOLLI, G., 1973, Effect of light exposure on gut transit time in jaundiced newborn infants, *Acta Paediatr. Scand.* **62**:146.

93. SCHACTER, B. A., 1975, Induction mechanisms for bile pigment formation, in: *Hepatology—Research and Clinical Issues*, Vol. 2, *Jaundice* (C. A. Goresky and M. M. Fisher, eds.), pp. 85–102, Plenum Press, New York.

94. SCHENKER, S., AND SCHMID, 1964, Excretion of C^{14} bilirubin in newborn guinea pigs, *Proc. Soc. Exp. Biol. Med.* **115**:466.

95. Schenker, S., DAWBER, N. H., AND SCHMID, R., 1964, Bilirubin metabolism in the fetus, *J. Clin. Invest.* **43**:32.

96. SCHMID, R., 1956, Direct-reacting bilirubin, bilirubin glucuronide in serum, bile, and urine, *Science* **124**:76.

97. SCHMID, R., AND HAMMAKER, L., 1963, Metabolism and disposition of C^{14}-bilirubin in congenital non-hemolytic jaundice, *J. Clin. Invest.* **42**:1720.

98. SCHMID, R., AXELROD, J., HAMMAKER, L., AND SWARM, R. L., 1958, Congenital jaundice in rats due to a defect in glucuronide formation, *J. Clin. Invest.* **37**:1123.

99. SCHMID, R., BUCKINGHAM, S., MENDILLA, G. A., AND HAMMAKER, L., 1959, Bilirubin metabolism in the fetus, *Nature (London)* **183**:1823.

100. SCHMID, R., MARVER, H. S., AND HAMMAKER, L.,

101. SERENI, F., Perletti, L., AND MARINI, A., 1967, Influence of diethylnicotinamide on the concentration of serum bilirubin of newborn infants, *Pediatrics* **39**:446.

102. SILVERMAN, W. A., ANDERSEN, D. H., BLANC, W. A., AND CROZIER, D. N., 1956, A difference in mortality rate and incidence of kernicterus among premature infants allotted to two prophylactic antibacterial regimens, *Pediatrics* **18**:614.

103. SINGLETON, J., AND LASTER, L., 1965, Biliverdin reductase of guinea pig liver, *J. Biol. Chem.* **244**:6388.

104. SISSON, T. R. C., 1977, Phototherapy of neonatal jaundice: Effect on blood biorhythm, in: *Research in Photobiology* (A. Castellani, ed.), p. 431, Plenum Press, London.

105. SISSON, T. R. C., GOLDBERG, S., AND SLAVEN, B., 1974, The effect of visible light on the Gunn rat: Convulsive threshold, bilirubin concentration, and brain color, *Pediatr. Res.* **8**:647.

106. SISSON, T. R. C. KENDALL, N., SHAW, E., AND KECHAVARAZ-OLIAI, L., 1972, Phototherapy of jaundice in the newborn. II. Effect of various light intensities, *J. Pediatr.* **81**:35.

107. SISSON, T. R. C., SLAVEN, B., AND HAMILTON, P. B., 1976, Effect of broad and narrow spectrum fluorescent light on blood constituents, in: *Bilirubin Metabolism in the Newborn (II)* (D. Bergsma and S. H. Blodehim, eds.), *Birth Defects: Orig. Artic. Ser.* **12**:122–133, American Elsevier, New York.

108. SMITH, K. C. (ed.), 1976, *Photochemical and Photobiological Reviews,* Vol. 1, Plenum Press, New York.

109. STERN, L., AND DENTON, R. L., 1965, Kernicterus in small premature infants, *Pediatrics* **35**:483.

110. STIEHM, E. R., AND RYAN, J., 1965, Breast-milk jaundice, *Amer. J. Dis. Child.* **109**:212.

111. SUTHERLAND, J. M., AND KELLER, W. H., 1961, Novobiocin and neonatal hyperbilirubinemia, *Amer. J. Dis. Child.* **101**:447.

112. SZEINBERG, A., OLIVER, M., SCHMIDT, R., ADAM, A., AND SHEBA, C., 1963, Glucose-6-phosphate dehydrogenase deficiency and hemolytic disease of the newborn in Israel, *Arch. Dis. Child.* **38**:23.

113. TAYLOR, P. M., BRIGHT, N. H., BIRCHARD, E. L., DERINOZ, M. N., AND WATSON, D. W., 1963, The effect of race, weight loss, and the time of clamping of the umbilical cord on neonatal bilirubinemia, *Biol. Neonate* **5**:299.

114. TENHUNEN, R., 1972, The enzymatic degradation of heme, *Semin. Hematol.* **9**:19.

115. TENHUNEN, R., MARVER, H. S., AND SCHMID, R., 1968, The enzymatic conversion of heme to bilirubin by microsomal heme oxygenase, *Proc. Natl. Acad. Sci. U.S.A.* **61**:748.

116. THALER, M. M., GEMES, D. L., AND SCHMID, R.,

1972, Enzymatic conversion of heme to bilirubin in normal and starved fetuses and newborn rats, *Pediatr. Res.* **6**:197.

117. TOMLINSON, G. A., AND YAFFE, S. J., 1966, The formation of bilirubin and *p*-nitrophenyl glucuronides by rabbit liver, *Biochem. J.* **99**:507.

118. TROLLE, D., 1968, Phenobarbitone and neonatal icterus, *Lancet* **1**:251.

119. ULSTROM, R. A., AND EISENKLAM, E., 1964, The enterohepatic shunting of bilirubin in the newborn infant, *J. Pediatr.* **65**:27.

120. WEISS, J., AND ARIAS, I. M., 1967, Hepatic glucuronyl transferase: Submicrosomal distribution and role in intracellular transport of bilirubin, *J. Clin. Invest.* **46**:1130.

121. WENNBERG, R. P., SCHWARTZ, R., AND SWEET, A. Y., 1966, Early versus delayed feeding of low birth weight infants: Effects on physiologic jaundice, *J. Pediatr.* **68**:860.

122. WITH, T. K., 1968, *Bile Pigments, Chemical, Biological and Clinical Aspects,* p. 1, Academic Press, New York.

123. WOLFF, J. A., GROSSMAN, B. H., AND PAYA, K., 1967, Neonatal serum bilirubin and glucose-6-phosphate dehydrogenase, *Amer. J. Dis. Child.* **113**:251.

124. WU, P. Y. K., AND HODGMAN, J., 1967, "Early" versus "late" feeding of low birth weight neonates: Effect on serum bilirubin, blood sugar, and responses to glucagon and epinephrine tolerance tests, *Pediatrics* **39**:733.

125. YAFFE, S. J., LEVY, G., MATSUZAWA, T., AND BALIAH, T., 1966, Enhancement of glucuronide-conjugating capacity in a hyperbilirubinemic infant due to apparent enzyme induction by phenobarbital, *N. Engl. J. Med.* **275**:1461.

126. ZENONE, E. A., STOLL, M. S., AND OSTROW, J. D., 1977, Mechanism of unconjugated bilirubin during phototherapy, *Gastroenterology* **72**:1180 (abstr).

127. ZINKHAM, W. H., 1967, The selective hemolytic action of drugs: Clinical and mechanistic considerations, *J. Pediatr.* **70**:200.

CHAPTER 24

Development of the Ornithine-Urea Cycle

Niels C. R. Räihä and Martti Kekomäki

1. Introduction

One of the fundamental facts about mammals is that they are intolerant to even modest concentrations of ammonium ion in the cellular environment. Simpler organisms living in a water environment have little problem with nitrogen disposal, since ammonia diffuses freely and is thereby diluted to a very low concentration. During evolution, when a movement from marine to terrestrial environment occurred, a more efficient detoxication mechanism for ammonia was needed, and the formation of urea developed.

The human placenta is virtually impermeable to protein molecules, and all the fetal nitrogen is therefore originally derived from unbound amino acids from the maternal plasma. The concentrations of free amino acids are generally high in fetal plasma and tissues as compared with their concentrations in the mother,[18,25] and the placental transport of amino acids has to overcome a considerable concentration gradient. The high plasma and tissue concentrations of amino acids in the fetus have been

interpreted as a sign of rapid growth and protein synthesis.[3]

The placenta does not, however, control the transfer of amino acids to the fetus accurately enough to eliminate the need for transformation and degradation of amino acids. Thus, despite the anabolic character of fetal metabolism, requirements for catabolic activities do exist.

The production of urea is predominantly a function of the liver, although many other mammalian tissues contain some of the enzymes involved in urea biosynthesis. There are five enzymes involved in the conversion of CO_2 and ammonia to urea, as shown in Fig. 1.

The first two enzymes, carbamyl phosphate synthetase and ornithine transcarbamylase, are located in the mitochondria, and the other three, the argininosuccinate condensing enzyme, the cleavage enzyme (comprising the arginine synthetase system), and arginase, are all found in the soluble fraction of the cell.[24] Transport of the urea cycle intermediates to and from the mitochondria in the course of urea synthesis is therefore necessary. The argininosuccinate synthetase or condensing enzyme has the lowest relative activity of the five urea cycle enzymes[12] in adult human liver, and is considered to be the rate-limiting enzyme of the cycle. Apart

Niels C. R. Räihä · Departments of Obstetrics and Gynecology and Pediatrics Martti Kekomäki · Department of Pediatric Surgery, University of Helsinki, Helsinki, Finland

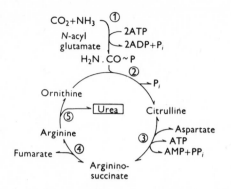

Fig. 1. The ornithine–urea cycle. Enzymes and cofactors of the urea cycle. ① Carbamyl phosphate synthetase; ② ornithine transcarbamylase; ③ arginine synthetase, condensing enzyme; ④ arginine synthetase, cleavage enzyme; ⑤ arginase.

from the activity and capacity of the enzymes, the rate of urea synthesis is regulated by the availability of substrates. This regulation applies not only to the whole cycle, where "substrate" means ammonia and aspartate, but also to the intermediate steps in the cycle. The rate of synthesis of citrulline from carbamyl phosphate and ornithine is limited by the availability of ornithine. This was clearly demonstrated by Krebs et al.[14] in perfused rat liver preparations in that when there is a high concentration of precursor such as ammonia or alanine in the medium, addition of ornithine greatly accelerates the rate of urea synthesis. The availability of acetylglutamate, which is the cofactor for the mitochondrial carbamylphosphate synthetase, may also regulate the formation of urea, especially during development.

Our present knowledge about urea synthesis of the human fetus is based on observations on the levels of urea in the fetal tissues and fluids, on the production of urea in vitro by human fetal liver, and on the measurement of the activities of the urea cycle enzymes in fetal liver preparations.

2. Concentrations of Urea in the Fetus and the Fetal Fluids

The concentration of urea in the amniotic fluid exceeds that of the maternal serum after the second trimester.[6] Recent studies by Teoh et al.[28] also showed a steady increase in the urea concentration of amniotic fluid with increasing gestational age.

Colombo and Richterich[4] found high concentrations of urea (30 mg/g) in the fetal liver even during the first trimester of pregnancy. These observations indicate that the human fetus produces urea at a very early stage of gestation, in contrast to some other mammalian species such as the rat,[22] which does not produce urea until the end of gestation.

3. Overall Synthesis of Urea by the Human Fetal Liver

The first report concerning direct measurements of urea production by human fetal liver is that of Manderscheid[15] in 1933. Using the tissue slice technique developed by Krebs and Henseleit,[13] she found urea production in the presence of an excess of ammonia and ornithine in the livers of 3- to 4-month-old fetuses. More recently,[21] we have studied the overall capacity of human fetal liver slices to synthesize urea from ammonia and bicarbonate in the presence of optimal concentrations of ornithine. Urea was produced under these conditions by 16- to 20-week fetal livers at the rate of about 4 μmol/g liver per hr. Kennan and Cohen[12] estimated the amount of urea that could be produced in the fetus in a 24-hr period from the activity of the rate-limiting enzymatic step (the arginine synthetase). The estimated urea production was 0.021, 0.321, and 3.19 g for a 12-, 20-, and 40-week fetus, respectively.

An adult liver would be able to produce over 100 g urea, according to these authors.[12] Barlow and McCance[1] estimated the daily output of urea by adults on a normal diet to be about 20 g. These data suggest that the adult human has a very large reserve capacity to synthesize urea, and is using only about one-fifth of this potential ability under normal conditions.

In the term newborn infant on breast milk, the daily excretion is 140–250 mg from the first to the sixth days of life.[1] Further studies on overall urea production by the fetal liver were carried out in liver perfusion experiments by Kekomäki et al.[11] An intact isolated human fetal liver of 14 weeks of gestation, perfused in a recirculating system with oxygenated saline buffer, releases urea into the perfusion media. The rate of urea release remains constant for several hours. The addition to the perfusion medium of buffered solutions of L-alanine, L-glutamate, or L-aspartate in high concentrations (10 mM) does not, however, increase the rate of

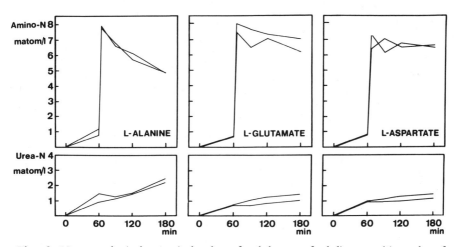

Fig. 2. Urea synthesis by an isolated perfused human fetal liver at 16 weeks of gestation. At 60 min from the start of the perfusion, amino acids were added to a calculated final concentration of 10 mmol/liter.

urea production, as shown by Fig. 2 (Kekomäki *et al.*, unpublished observations). In similar perfusion experiments using adult rat liver, Krebs *et al.*[14] found increased urea formation in response to the addition of alanine to the perfusion medium. These findings suggest that although the fetal human liver is capable of synthesizing urea at an early stage of development, the capacity to expand urea synthesis is limited.

During human pregnancy, the urea formed by the fetus is excreted by the mother. The relatively small amounts of fetal urea nitrogen would be within the normal variation of nitrogen excretion of the mother; thus, nitrogen balance studies would not reflect the contribution of the fetus to the maternal nitrogen excretion.

4. Development of the Urea Cycle Enzymes in the Human Liver

The availability of methods developed by Brown and Cohen[2] for assaying all the urea cycle enzymes in extracts of liver made it possible to study the developmental aspects of these enzymes. The first report on the development of the urea cycle enzymes in human fetal tissues was published by Kennan and Cohen.[12] All the measured enzymes, carbamyl phosphate synthetase, ornithine transcarbamylase, arginine synthetase (measured as the combined activity of both the condensing and cleavage enzymes), and arginase, were present in the livers of three

fetuses of 12, 20, and 40 weeks' gestation that were studied. The arginine synthetase system had the lowest relative activity per liver weight, and the liver of the youngest fetus had about 25% of the activity found in adult livers, whereas the term fetus had 41% of the adult activity.

Subsequent studies from our laboratory[21] and by Colombo and Richterich[4] and Guha and Mukherjee[8] confirmed the presence of all urea cycle enzymes in human fetal liver at an early stage of development. We studied liver samples from fetuses with gestational ages ranging from 3 to 25 weeks of gestation and from postnatal and adult liver biopsy samples. The postnatal development of the urea cycle enzyme activities is shown in Fig. 3. The arginine synthetase activity in 10- to 20-week-old fetuses ranges from 5 to 15 μmol/g liver per hr, and is similar to that reported by Kennan and Cohen.[12] In general, the fetal enzyme activities are only about 25%, and the activities at term are about 50%, of the adult activities.

Observations on the kinetic characteristics of arginine synthetase indicate that the K_m for citrulline is similar in magnitude in both fetal and adult human liver enzyme preparations.[21]

4.1. Hormonal Control of Urea Cycle Enzyme Activities

In adult rats, the activities of the urea cycle enzymes are directly proportional to the daily con-

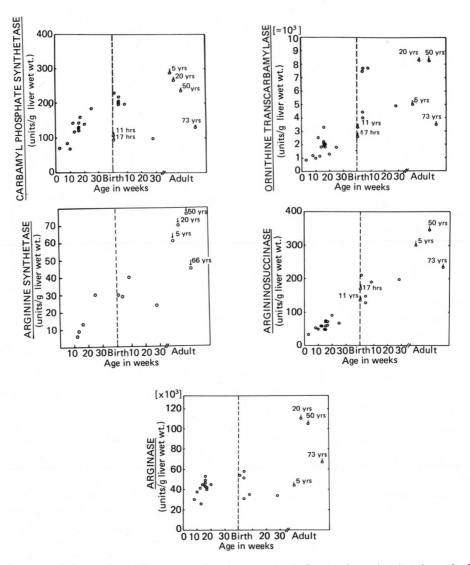

Fig. 3. Development of the activity of the urea-synthesizing enzymes in human liver. 1 unit = 1 μmol of product produced per hour. Data from Räihä and Suihkonen.[21] Reproduced with permission from *Acta Paediatr. Scand.* **57:**121–124 (1968).

sumption of protein of the animal, as shown by Schimke.[26] The urea cycle enzyme activities can also be altered in adult rats by corticosteroids and by glucagon and insulin.[16,17]

Adrenalectomy performed in newborn rats causes an almost complete inhibition of the normal postnatal increase of the arginine synthetase system.[22] The administration of corticosteroids to the adrenalectomized rats prevents the decrease

in enzyme activity caused by the removal of the adrenals. Thus, corticosteroids seem to be important for the normal postnatal development of the arginine synthetase system in the rat. *In vitro* studies on fetal rat liver explants in organ culture have also shown that the arginine synthetase system activity can be induced by the addition of corticosteroids and cyclic AMP (cAMP) to the culture medium.[19]

Preliminary data in our laboratory[19] indicated

that the activity of the arginine synthetase system cannot be stimulated in human fetal liver explants (14–16 weeks) in organ culture by the addition of cAMP or dexamethasone. Schwartz,[27] however, observed an increase in the incorporation of ureido carbon of citrulline into urea when cAMP or glucagon was added to human fetal liver explants in organ culture.

4.2. Clinical Implications

On the basis of the enzymatic data discussed previously, a full-term newborn infant has the capacity to produce about 3 g urea/day.[12] This amount would correspond to a degradation of about 4.5 g amino acids/day. If 50% of the total nitrogen intake were to be excreted as urea by a newborn—a fair overestimation—this amount would set an upper limit for protein intake of about 9 g/day. For an infant weighing 3.5 kg, a protein intake of more than 2.5 g/kg per day may thus theoretically overload the urea-synthesizing capacity of the liver. For a low-birth-weight infant, the urea-synthesizing capacity would be even smaller per unit body weight.

There has been considerable controversy among pediatricians regarding the optimum quantity of protein that should be administered to premature newborn infants. Some previous studies[5,7] indicated that preterm infants gain weight better and retain more nitrogen when fed high-protein diets. These studies were followed by a widely accepted use of high-protein formulas, and intakes of 4–6 g/kg per day were used and are still used in some centers.

In a recent study on the effects of variations of milk protein quantity as well as quality on physical growth and metabolic homeostasis in preterm infants, we showed that high-protein diets, especially casein-predominant protein, produce marked metabolic imbalances without an increased rate of growth. These metabolic changes were not seen in infants fed on breast milk or low-protein (2.25 g/kg per day) whey-predominant formula.[23] A casein-predominant bovine protein formula administered at 4.5 g/kg per day produced considerable late metabolic acidosis, strikingly elevated blood urea nitrogen levels, and hyperammonemia. In addition, the essential amino acids were markedly elevated in blood and urine. In particular, there was hyperphenylalaninemia, hypertyrosinemia, and hypermethioninemia, which lasted for several weeks. The blood urea nitrogen values correlated with the

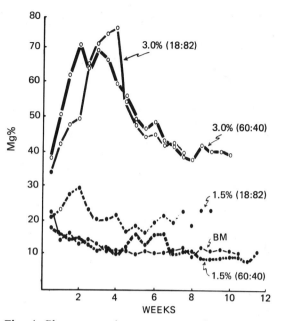

Fig. 4. Plasma urea nitrogen concentrations in preterm infants fed with diets varying in the quality and quantity of milk protein. (BM) Human breast milk; 1.5% (60 : 40): whey-predominant milk formula fed at 2.25 g/kg per day; 1.5% (18 : 82): casein-predominant milk formula fed at 2.25 g/kg per day; 3.0% (60 : 40): whey-predominant milk formula fed at 4.5 g/kg per day; 3.0% (18 : 82): casein-predominant milk formula fed at 4.5 g/kg per day. Data from Räihä et al.[23] Reproduced with permission from *Pediatrics* **57**:659–674 (1976).

quantity of protein in the diet as shown in Fig. 4. These data indicate that premature infants can increase the formation of urea in response to an increased load of dietary protein, as was also observed by Johnson et al.,[10] and are in agreement with the presence of the urea cycle enzymes in the liver of the human fetus at a relatively early stage of development. It was of interest, however, to find that the blood ammonia was also significantly elevated in the infants fed a casein-predominant formula, whether high or low in protein quantity. The infants on a high-protein whey-predominant formula also had significantly higher blood ammonia concentrations than the infants on breast milk or low-protein whey-predominant formula, as shown in Fig. 5. These findings are consistent with a somewhat limited capacity of the immature human infant for expansion of urea production. Mild to moderate hyperammonemia in the immature human infant in addition to other metabolic imbal-

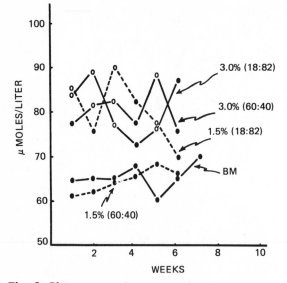

Fig. 5. Plasma ammonia concentrations in preterm infants fed with diets varying in the quality and quantity of milk protein. (BM) Human breast milk; 1.5% (60 : 40): whey-predominant milk formula fed at 2.25 g/kg per day; 1.5% (18 : 82): casein-predominant milk formula fed at 2.25 g/kg per day; 3.0% (60 : 40): whey-predominant milk formula fed at 4.5 g/kg per day; 3.0% (18 : 82): casein-predominant milk formula fed at 4.5 g/kg per day. Data from Räihä et al.[23] Reproduced with permission from *Pediatrics* **57**:659–674 (1976).

caution and careful biochemical monitoring of the blood.

Amino acid mixtures for intravenous use that correspond both quantitatively and qualitatively to human milk are currently available and should be used in newborn infants (Lindblad, personal communication).

5. Conclusion

In the adult human and also in the full-term infant, the urea-producing capacity of the liver exceeds the catabolic load produced by a normal dietary protein intake. Although the enzymes of the urea cycle are present in human fetal liver at an early stage of development, the activities before term are less than half the adult activities, and the capacity of the fetal liver to expand urea biosynthesis seems to be limited. This is confirmed by clinical studies on the metabolic effects of variations in protein intake in preterm infants. The results of these studies indicate that although blood urea is increased in response to high protein intake, hyperammonemia is also produced. This limited metabolic capacity should be considered when dietary regimens or parenteral amino acid infusions are planned for the care of small premature infants.

ances may affect the long-term outcome of these infants. It must also be remembered that most children with congenital deficiencies of the urea cycle enzymes and resulting hyperammonemia are mentally retarded.

Hyperammonemia may also complicate parenteral nutrition with protein hydrolysates, especially in preterm infants, as shown by Johnson et al.,[10] Heird et al.,[9] and Touloukian.[29] The hyperammonemia may be produced by several mechanisms. One possibility is the limited capacity of the liver to respond by increase in the urea-synthesizing capacity to the increased load of amino acids, especially if the infused hydrolysate produces an amino acid imbalance and a deficiency of arginine or ornithine. A second cause might be the presence of ammonia in the amino acid solution used. If amino acid hydrolysates are to be used in preterm infants, it is suggested that the infusion be initiated with very low concentrations (less than 2 g/kg per day). An increase in the dosage should be approached with utmost

6. References

1. BARLOW, A., AND McCANCE, R. A., 1948, The nitrogen partition in newborn infants' urine, *Arch Dis. Child.* **23**:225.
2. BROWN, G. W., AND COHEN, P. P., 1959, Comparative biochemistry of urea synthesis. I. Methods for the quantitative assay of urea cycle enzymes in liver, *J. Biol. Chem.* **234**:1769.
3. CHRISTENSEN, H. N., AND STREICHER, J. A., 1948, Association between rapid growth and elevated cell concentrations of amino acids, *J. Biol. Chem.* **175**:95.
4. COLOMBO, J. P., AND RICHTERICH, R., 1968, Urea cycle enzymes in the developing human fetus, *Enzymol. Biol. Clin.* **9**:68.
5. DAVIDSON, M., LEVINE, S. Z., BAUER, C. H., AND DUNN, M., 1967, Feeding studies in low-birth weight infants, *J. Pediatr.* **70**:695.
6. FRIEDBERG, V., 1955, Untersuchungen über die fetale Urinbildung, *Gynaecologia* **140**:34.
7. GORDON, H. H., LEVINE, S. Z., AND McNAMARA, H., 1947, Feeding of premature infants. A comparison of human and cow's milk, *Amer. J. Dis. Child.* **73**:442.

8. GUHA, S. K., AND MUKHERJEE, K. L., 1974, Urea biosynthesis in normal human fetuses, *Biochem. Biophys. Acta* **372**:285.

9. HEIRD, W. C., NICHOLSON, J. F., DRISCOLL, J. M., SCHULLINGER, J. N., AND WINTERS, R. W., 1972, Hyperammonemia resulting from intravenous alimentation using a mixture of synthetic L-amino acids: A preliminary report, *J. Pediatr.* **81**:162.

10. JOHNSON, J. D., ALBRITTON, W. L., AND SUNSHINE, P., 1972, Hyperammonemia accompanying parenteral nutrition in newborn infants, *J. Pediatr.* **81**:154.

11. KEKOMÄKI, M., SEPPÄLÄ, M., EHNHOLM, C., SCHWARTZ, A. L., AND RAIVIO, K., 1971, Perfusion of isolated human fetal liver: Synthesis and release of α-fetoprotein and albumin, *Int. J. Cancer* **8**:250.

12. KENNAN, A. L., AND COHEN, P. P., 1961, Ammonia detoxication in liver from humans, *Proc. Soc. Exp. Biol. Med.* **106**:170.

13. KREBS, H. A., AND HENSELEIT, K., 1932, Untersuchungen über die Harnstoffbildung in Tierkörper, *Hoppe-Seylers Z. Physiol. Chem.* **210**:33

14. KREBS, H. A., HEMS, R., AND LUND, P., 1973, Some regulatory mechanisms in the synthesis of urea in the mammalian liver, *Adv. Enzyme Regul.* **11**:361.

15. MANDERSCHEID, H., 1933, Über die Harnstoffbildung bei den Wirbeltieren, *Biochem. Z.* **263**:245.

16. MCLEAN, P., AND GURNEY, M. W., 1963, Effect of adrenalectomy and growth hormone on enzymes concerned with urea synthesis in rat liver, *Biochem. J.* **87**:96.

17. MCLEAN, P., AND NOVELLO, F., 1965, Influence of pancreatic hormones on enzymes concerned with urea synthesis in rat liver, *Biochem. J.* **94**:410.

18. RÄIHÄ, N. C. R., AND KEKOMÄKI, M., 1975, Developmental aspects of amino acid metabolism in the human, in: *Total Parenteral Nutrition* (H. Ghadimi, ed.), pp. 199–211, John Wiley & Sons, New York.

19. RÄIHÄ, N. C. R., AND SCHWARTZ, A. L., 1973, Enzyme induction in human fetal liver in organ culture, *Enzyme* **15**:330.

20. RÄIHÄ, N. C. R., AND SCHWARTZ, A. L., 1973, Development of urea biosynthesis and factors influencing the activity of the arginine synthetase system in perinatal mammalian liver, in: *Inborn Errors of Metabolism* (F. A. Holmes and C. J. Van den Berg, eds.), pp. 221–237, Academic Press, New York.

21. RÄIHÄ, N. C. R., AND SUIHKONEN, J., 1968, Development of urea-synthesizing enzymes in human liver, *Acta Paediatr. Scand.* **57**:121.

22. RÄIHÄ, N. C. R., AND SUIHKONEN, J., 1968, Factors influencing the development of urea-synthesizing enzymes in rat liver, *Biochem. J.* **107**:793.

23. RÄIHÄ, N. C. R., HEINONEN, K., RASSIN, D. K., AND GAULL, G. E., 1976, Milk protein quality and quantity in low birth weight infants: 1. Metabolic responses and effects on growth, *Pediatrics* **57**:659.

24. RATNER, S., 1973, Enzymes of arginine and urea synthesis, *Adv. Enzymol.* **39**:1.

25. RYAN, W. L., AND CARVER, M. J., 1966, Free amino acids in human foetal and adult liver, *Nature (London)* **212**:292.

26. SCHIMKE, R. T., 1962, Adaptive characteristics of urea cycle enzymes in the rat, *J. Biol. Chem.* **237**:459.

27. SCHWARTZ, A. L., 1974, Hormonal regulation of glucose production in human fetal liver, Thesis, Department of Pharmacology, Case Western Reserve University, pp. 1–220, Cleveland, Ohio.

28. TEOH, E. S., LAU, Y. K., AMBROSE, A., AND RATMAN, S. S., 1973, Amniotic fluid creatinine, uric acid and urea as indices of gestational age, *Acta Obstet. Gynecol. Scand.* **52**:323.

29. TOULOUKIAN, R. J., 1975, Isoosmolar coma during parenteral alimentation with protein hydrolysate in excess of 4 mg/kg/day, *J. Pediatr.* **86**:270.

CHAPTER 25

Hepatic Drug Metabolism

Ross C. de Belle and Roger Lester

1. Introduction

Drugs represent a heterogeneous group of compounds acquired by an organism that usually require metabolic transformation before they can be eliminated. The main site of mammalian drug metabolism is the liver, where the parent drug is rendered more polar, thereby enhancing its biliary and renal excretory properties. The next section of this chapter will review mechanisms by which drugs are taken up, metabolized, and excreted by liver cells. Section 3 will describe how these mechanisms are operant in the fetus and neonate. Section 4 will outline clinicopharmacological aspects of abnormalities or immaturity of these mechanisms and briefly discuss modes of therapeutic manipulation.

2. Mechanisms of Drug Transport and Metabolism

Since most drugs are poorly soluble in water at physiologic pH, a mechanism must exist for their solubilization and transport in blood from their site of absorption to their sites of action and transformation. This process is accomplished by

reversible binding to plasma proteins, of which albumin is the most important fraction.[20] The nature of drug–protein interactions was recently reviewed[2]: the solubility of lipophilic substances in plasma is related to (1) the quantity of serum protein available for drug binding and (2) the chemical affinity between protein and drug. Most drugs interact with plasma proteins by weak bonds (ionic, hydrogen, and van der Waals types), and the rate of dissociation of drug–protein complexes is rarely rate-limiting in overall drug metabolism.[16]

The precise nature of hepatocellular uptake and transport of drugs is poorly understood. In general, the possible mechanisms by which substances cross cell membranes include simple diffusion, facilitated diffusion, active transport, and special processes. Most lipid-soluble drugs are thought to penetrate the liver cell membrane by simple diffusion, which probably represents the rate-limiting step in their metabolism.[9] The rate of hepatocellular sequestration of some lipophilic compounds is too rapid to be accounted for by simple diffusion alone, however, and facilitated diffusion along a concentration gradient has therefore been postulated.[20] Small, ionized molecules are believed to enter liver cells by diffusion through aqueous channels in the membrane.[21] Polar compounds of greater molecular weight have classically been considered unable to cross lipoid cell membranes. Recent evidence indicates, however, that some highly charged (cationic) quaternary ammonium compounds can

Ross C. de Belle · McGill University, Montreal Children's Hospital, Montreal, PQ Canada   Roger Lester · University of Pittsburgh School of Medicine, Pittsburgh, Pennsylvania 15261

rapidly cross the presinusoidal membrane of rodent hepatic parenchymal cells by processes that probably require active transport.[52] It is also possible that drug-binding proteins in the cytoplasm of liver cells may participate in maintaining concentration gradients across hepatocyte membranes and increase the amount of drug available to enzymes more centrally located within the cell.[17] For example, Y and Z proteins have been postulated to act as carriers of sulfobromophthalein and other organic anions in hepatic cells,[34] and drug interaction with intracellular macromolecules such as mucopolysaccharides, nucleoproteins, and phospholipids has been demonstrated.[51]

Drugs thus transported to enzyme sites within hepatocytes may then dissociate from their protein or macromolecular carrier and enter into a number of different types of metabolic transformations. These transformations have characteristically included the chemical reactions of oxidation, reduction, hydrolysis, and conjugation, resulting in polarization of the compound, thereby enhancing excretion in bile or urine. Since conjugation reactions usually result in biological inactivation of drugs, they are also referred to as *detoxification reactions*. The enzyme systems associated with drug metabolism are located in various subcellular compartments of hepatic parenchymal cells, including the mitochondria, the soluble fraction of the cell (cytosol), and the endoplasmic reticulum.[24] In recent years, attention has been focused on the metabolism of drugs by an important group of nonspecific enzymes in hepatocyte endoplasmic reticulum: the hepatic microsomal mixed-function oxidase system.

When tissues are homogenized, thereby disrupting the cells, the subcellular components may be separated by differential centrifugation. Isolation by this technique of the cell fraction containing the endoplasmic reticulum results in the endoplasmic reticulum itself breaking into small, closed fragments, or vesicles, bounded by an intact membrane called microsomes.

The microsomal fraction derived from the smooth endoplasmic reticulum contains a number of enzymes associated with biological oxidations that are characterized by an unusual requirement for NADPH, NADH, molecular oxygen, and a hemoprotein electron transport system for their action (Fig. 1). In hepatic microsomes, the drug first combines with oxidized cytochrome P450, forming a drug-oxidized cyt P450 complex. This complex is then reduced by electron flux through associated electron transport systems, forming first a drug-reduced cyt P450 complex, which in turn reacts with molecular oxygen. A second electron flow is believed to reduce the drug–cyt P450–O_2 complex to an active oxygen intermediate, which decomposes, forming oxidized cyt P450 and the oxidized drug product. Oxidized cyt P450 may then be recycled in the system, and the final drug product is ready either for further transformation, i.e., conjugation, or for excretion from the liver cell. Recent evidence suggests that NADPH, in association with cytochrome c reductase, preferentially donates electrons for the reduction of the drug-

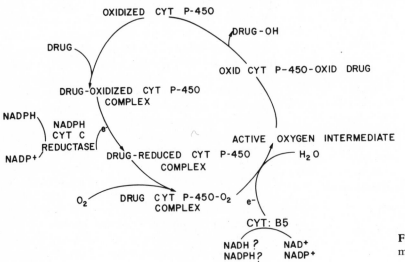

Fig. 1. The hepatic microsomal mixed-function oxidase system.

oxidized cyt P450 complex, and that either NADPH or NADH, mediated by cytochrome b_5 reductase, donates the second electron required by the mixed-function oxidase system.[18] Most studies indicate that enzymes associated with hepatic microsomal drug metabolism are located in parenchymal cells and in high quantities in hepatocytes clustered around central veins.[13] Thus, not all liver cells have these systems, and even within a given cell type, not all cells are equally active.

The factors that determine whether a metabolized drug product is secreted from the liver cell into the plasma or the bile canaculi are poorly understood. The secretion of drugs into the bile is now receiving considerable attention, however, and was recently reviewed.[50] It is evident that the relative importance of the biliary secretion route depends on the species and the drugs concerned. For those substances for which bile is an important excretory route, alterations in this pathway apparently have profound effects on the depth and duration of drug action. For example, the toxicity of ouabain is markedly increased in mice, the bile ducts of which have been occluded.[15] Interest is also developing in elucidating the mechanisms involved in bile secretion[43] and the transfer of substances into bile. For drugs actively excreted via the biliary route, three distinct transport systems have been characterized: (1) Organic anions secreted from liver cells and transported into bile against a concentration gradient by a mechanism that may be closely related to Y and Z proteins.[12] (2) Organic cations, in particular quaternary ammonium compounds, can be secreted into bile in high concentrations by a transport system that appears to differ from that associated with the excretion of organic acids.[23] (3) Finally, many nonionized drugs, e.g., ouabain, are actively secreted unchanged into bile by a third transport mechanism.[23] If the properties of the drug metabolite are favorable for intestinal absorption, there results an *enterohepatic cycle* in which biliary secretion and intestinal reabsorption continue until renal excretion finally eliminates the drug. This cycle is typical for certain cardiac glycosides.

3. Perinatal Drug Metabolism and Excretion

One of the unique characteristics of the mammalian fetus is that all exogenous compounds must be maternally derived and cross the placenta. Placental transfer of substances has importance not only in the maternal–fetal direction, but also in the fetal–maternal direction. The latter relationship is important for fetal elimination of most toxic substances and waste products, including metabolized drugs. Information concerning *in vivo* bidirectional placental transport mechanisms has been limited due to lack of an appropriate experimental model. Recently, the development of surgical techniques that permit maternal/fetal measurements in near-term dogs while preserving fetal homeostasis[27] has enabled characterization of certain fetal hepatic metabolic and excretory mechanisms,[28,49] thereby providing a new method to study bidirectional placental transport and maternal–placental–fetal interactions *in vivo*.

The transplacental passage and maternal–fetal distribution of a number of drugs of different classes have been investigated.[19] Most exogenous compounds appear to cross the placenta by simple diffusion in accordance with their lipid solubility; facilitated diffusion and active transport, the primary modes of maternal–fetal transfer of vital substances, are considered to apply only in rare instances in which drugs are structurally similar to endogenous substances. For example, active transport mechanisms are postulated to account for fetal accumulation of 5-fluorouracil and α-methyldopa because of the similarity of these drugs to pyrimidines and amino acids.[35] Polar drugs have classically been considered unable to cross the placental barrier.

Recent studies, however, are providing notable exceptions to these generalizations. When tubocurarine, a highly ionized drug with low lipid solubility, is maternally administered in large amounts, enough drug crosses the placenta to produce a curarized infant at birth.[41] In fact, it is becoming apparent that *any* substance present in sufficient maternal concentration will eventually reach the fetus.[19] Furthermore, investigations in dogs have shown that equilibrium between maternal and fetal concentrations of sodium barbital (a relatively polar long-acting barbiturate) and sodium pentobarbital (a lipophilic short-acting barbiturate) is established early, implicating a process of facilitated diffusion for both these compounds, irrespective of their duration of action or physicochemical properties.[7] In other studies of the maternal–fetal distribution of lidocaine[48] and thiopental,[45] it was demonstrated that the placenta

Table I. Factors That Influence Placental Transfer

Factor	Example
Simple diffusion	Maternal–fetal transfer of most drugs; fetal–maternal transfer of unconjugated bilirubin
Facilitated diffusion	Maternal–fetal transfer of certain exogenous compounds, e.g., 5-fluorouracil, that are structurally similar to endogenous substances (pyrimidines)
Active transport	Maternal–fetal transfer of essential nutrients, e.g., glucose, amino acids, vitamins
Special processes	Maternal–fetal transfer of antibodies
Placental size and thickness	Impaired amino acid transfer in toxemia of pregnancy[57]
Placental blood flow	—
Placental metabolism	Hydrolysis of endogenous steroids, sulfated in fetal tissues, by placental sulfatases[29]
Binding to placental macromolecules	Placental binding of nicotine, which apparently retards maternal–fetal transfer[54]
Differential fetal–maternal protein binding	Enhanced maternal binding of diphenylhydantoin in pregnant goats[47]

may act as a functional "barrier" to the diffusion of these lipophilic drugs. It is therefore evident that generalizations concerning the nature of placental drug transport mechanisms are inappropriate.

Unfortunately, the majority of these studies are based on experimental determinations of net drug concentration (or radiolabel transfer) in the "fetus" after birth or termination of pregnancy. It has been demonstrated that in a dynamic maternal–placental–fetal unit, a number of interrelated factors regulate transfer across the placenta at any given time

(Table I), so that the ultimate disposition of substances between the mother and fetus generally represents the integrated result of many events. It is clear that further investigations using in vivo experimental models that will permit kinetic maternal–fetal determinations are urgently required to define mechanisms of placental drug transport more specifically.

The majority of exogenous chemical substances are transported in fetal and neonatal circulation bound to albumin and other plasma proteins. There is a paucity of data relating to perinatal drug–protein interactions, but it has been established that serum protein concentrations are diminished in the newborn infant compared with the adult.[31] Investigations of the effect of differential protein binding on the maternal–fetal distribution of diphenylhydantoin in pregnant goats demonstrated that the total protein level of goat fetal serum (3.1 g/dl) was lower than that of maternal serum (6.4 g/dl) due mainly to a reduction in the albumin and γ-globulin fractions of fetal serum.[47] Further, it was found that goat maternal albumin had a greater binding affinity for the drug than fetal albumin, which, together with the increased concentration of maternal serum protein, was considered a major factor responsible for the very low fetal serum levels measured after steady-state infusions into the mother. Other studies showed that thiopental binds to the same extent with either maternal or fetal plasma,[11] as does iophenoxic acid.[36]

Another important factor that affects drug disposition and metabolism in the fetus is related to the unique characteristics of the fetal circulation, one of which is that the quantity of drug delivered to any organ will be a function of the blood flow to it.[38] Drug access to the fetal liver is unusual in that exogenous compounds enter the fetal circulation via umbilical venous flow and pass through the liver prior to entering the inferior vena cava and thence the arterial system. Umbilical venous flow to the fetal liver, however, may be diverted into the portal system to perfuse hepatic parenchymal cells, or it can bypass the liver altogether through the ductus venosus.[38] It is therefore possible that selective partitioning of blood flow to the ductus would increase the proportion of drug metabolized immediately following its placental transfer to the fetal circulation, but this effect would diminish when circulatory redistribution was established. Exogenous compounds in the perinatal circulation are thought to pass readily into liver cells for a number of reasons: (1) The permeability of cell membranes is generally increased during the fetal and early neonatal period; consequently, high concentrations of pharmacologically active compounds may be sequestered in all tissues, including those that are not the primary target organ for the drug.[38] (2) In view of the lipophilic properties of most drugs, the relatively high proportion of lipid in liver (also fetal ovary and adrenal) as compared with the relatively high water content of other fetal tissues[58] means that these drugs will tend to concentrate in the liver. (3) Binding to certain receptor proteins (ligandin) may constitute a mechanism for selective hepatocellular uptake of certain organic anions; however, evidence suggests that hepatocyte carrier proteins are virtually absent in fetal primate and guinea pig liver, and are markedly deficient in human perinatal liver.[4]

3.1. Hepatic Microsomal Function in the Fetus and Newborn

Biochemical and morphological studies in experimental animals have shown conclusively that fetal and newborn animals have a deficient capacity to metabolize drugs.[14] Similarly, the lack of significant metabolism of drugs such as diazepam in the human fetus[26] and the higher blood level and prolonged serum half-life of diazepam in premature infants relative to older children[30] suggests the possibility of deficient drug-oxidative function in the human neonatal period. In fact, a possible biochemical basis for this deficiency in drug metabolism has been demonstrated in human fetuses by decreased enzyme activity within the hepatic microsomal mixed-function oxidase system relative to adult liver microsomes.[42] In addition, a recent study showed that hepatic microsomal enzyme titers are lower in premature and full-term newborn infants compared with adult enzyme titers.[3] This study also provided evidence that there is a progressive increase in the activity of the hepatic microsomal drug-metabolizing enzymes during the last trimester of gestation and in the neonatal period.

It should be noted that in all studies in human fetuses and newborn infants, there is marked variability in the activities of various enzymes comprising the mixed-function oxidase system. Furthermore, although the rate of NADPH oxidase activity has not been measured in human liver microsomes, the activity of this enzyme measured in one full-term infant was approximately 70% of that obtained from adult rat microsomes.[3] In this regard, it is of interest that the apparent subcellular distribution of the various components of the mixed-function oxidase system is different in fetal hepatocytes as compared with adults because of differences in sedimentation properties of the subcellular organelles.[1] The time at which the fetal hepatic subcellular localization of drug-metabolizing enzymes approaches adult patterns is not established. Since measurements of perinatal drug-metabolizing enzymes are done primarily on the microsomal fraction, and since the smooth endoplasmic reticulum may not have sedimented optimally in the microsomal fraction, it is possible that the levels of enzyme activity reported may be lower than the actual values. On the other hand, biochemical and morphological studies have clearly demonstrated that the microsomal drug-metabolizing enzymes are exquisitely sensitive to the influence of drugs and environmental pollutants. For example, adult patients who have received phenobarbital show remarkable induction of drug metabolism, and similar therapy in two infants with normal hepatic parenchyma[53] resulted in a 100–150% increase in the activity of NADPH cytochrome c reductase from hepatic microsomes concomitant with proliferation of the endoplasmic reticulum. For this reason, and because of the ubiquitous nature of these drugs and chemicals, one can raise the question whether the reported presence, and the high levels of activity in certain instances, of mixed-function oxidase enzyme systems in the human fetus and newborn infant may not result from the pregnant woman's exposure to such enzyme inducers. Further studies are needed to clarify this problem.

The factors that regulate the development of fetal hepatic enzyme systems are poorly understood. Some of the explanations that have been proposed to account for the low rates of mixed-function oxidation and glucuronidation observed in perinatal hepatic tissues can be summarized: (1) the low proportion of hepatic parenchymal cells to reticulo-endothelial cells in fetal liver[13]; (2) the quantitative reduction of smooth endoplasmic reticulum in hepatocytes before birth[33]; (3) the presence of relatively high levels of maternal inhibitory factors (female gonadal hormones) in the fetal circulation[10]; (4) the inability of inducing agents to bind to critical proteins in fetal hepatic tissues[13]; (5) the presence of repressor substances in fetal liver[30]; and

(6) the influence of growth hormone on rapidly growing tissues.[63] Various aspects of these possibilities were recently reviewed[13]; it would seem that many of these factors may interact in contributing to decreased microsomal drug metabolism in the prenatal and perinatal periods.

3.2. Perinatal Drug Excretion

Exogenous compounds metabolized by the liver are usually made more polar, thereby preventing their pharmacological effect and enhancing their capacity to be excreted in urine or bile. In the fetus, polar metabolites would be expected to remain within the fetal compartment, in either the amniotic fluid, the intestine, or the blood, since selective fetal–maternal transfer of polar compounds has not been demonstrated. It is worth noting, however, that the presence of sulfatases in the placenta has been postulated as a mechanism to account for the fetal–maternal transfer of certain endogenous steroids, which have presumably been sulfated in fetal tissues to block their action on fetal target organs.[29] Further investigations are required to determine whether polar drug metabolites in the fetal circulation are metabolized in the placental unit, allowing their transfer into the maternal circulation for excretion.

It is well known that renal function in the newborn infant is decreased compared with the adult, even when corrected for differences in body size.[61] Drugs that are not significantly metabolized and depend on renal excretion for termination of their action, e.g., most antibiotics, will therefore have a noticeably longer effect in the newborn infant, and drugs that have been metabolized in the liver will have a prolonged rate of urinary excretion. However, much less information is available on the biliary route of excretion of polar metabolites.

It has been demonstrated in adults that bile acids play a central role in the formation and secretion of bile.[62] One can therefore raise the question whether there is sufficient bile acid formation and excretion in the perinatal period to provide the basic apparatus for the fetal hepatic elimination of drugs and toxic metabolites transferred from mother to fetus or administered to the newborn infant. Primary and secondary bile acids are found in fetal bile and meconium.[5,46] The presence of secondary bile acids in the fetus strongly suggests the existence of maternal–fetal bile acid transfer. Recent studies have established that the near–term fetal dog has an efficient mechanism for the uptake, conjugation, and excretion of primary bile acids and immense reserve capacity for the excretion of a bile acid load.[28,49] Placental transfer appears to play a minor excretory role, and it has been shown that the bile acids that are secreted are reabsorbed from the intestine, thereby undergoing a fetal enterohepatic circulation. Preliminary evidence indicates that the metabolism and excretion of bile acids are less efficient in the primate fetus. The full-term human neonate has been shown to be capable of *de novo* bile salt synthesis, but the bile salt pool size and rate of primary bile acid synthesis are only half the average values obtained for adults, compared on the basis of body surface.[59] Furthermore, the formation of an enterohepatic circulation of bile salts is even further reduced in premature infants.[60]

4. Clinical Pharmacology of Perinatal Hepatic Drug Metabolism

It is apparent from the foregoing discussion that there is an intact but deficient drug-oxidizing enzyme system in human fetal liver, and that enzyme activity increases during the latter part of gestation and the neonatal period. Unfortunately, however, the oxidative metabolism of only a limited number of drugs has been studied in preparations of human fetal liver and in newborn infants (Table II). All these compounds had decreased oxidation or delayed excretion. Many more drugs must be studied to elucidate how compounds with different physicochemical and structural properties are metabolized by the hepatic microsomal mixed-function oxidase system during the perinatal period.

With regard to other detoxification processes, the most widely studied example is hepatic conjugation of bilirubin. While the occurrence of jaundice in the newborn infant has been ascribed to a diminished capacity to eliminate bilirubin via conjugation with glucuronic acid, it should be emphasized that elimination also involves hepatic uptake and secretion into bile. Both these processes have been shown to be deficient in newborn animals. In studies of an *exogenous* compound that is conjugated with different amino acids and glutathione in the liver, the plasma half-life of sulfobromophthalein (BSP) was investigated in a large number of healthy full-term and premature newborn infants. Half-lives were twice as long

Table II. Drugs Tested for Which Human Perinatal Liver Has Decreased Oxidative Capacity[a]

Acetanalid	Desmethylimipramine
Aminopyrine	Diazepam
Aniline	Ethylorphine
Chlorpromazine	Tolbutamide

[a] From Lane et al.[32] and Yaffe and Juchau.[54]

compared with half-lives in older children and adults. The reason for the delayed elimination of BSP is not clear, although it has been suggested that secretion of the dye into bile is deficient.[56] Another contributing factor might include deficiency of hepatocyte transport protein. Such differences in the metabolism of BSP decrease its usefulness in the evaluation of hepatic function in newborn infants, and probably contribute to the increased incidence of allergic manifestations by increasing the exposure time of the infant's immune system to the antigen.

Recently, increasing attention has been focused on the metabolic activation of certain drugs to toxic metabolites by the liver.[39] In particular, it has been shown that certain drug-induced tissue lesions may be related to the formation of highly reactive epoxides—metabolic intermediates formed during oxidation of aromatic hydrocarbons.[6] For this reason, there is considerable concern about the possible teratogenic effects of diphenylhydantoin in humans, since certain metabolites in the urine of neonates suggest that epoxides are formed.[37] Another example of the possible oxidation of a drug to toxic intermediates is provided by in vitro studies of the metabolism of aniline in human fetal liver.[44] It was shown that methemoglobin was formed from the hemoglobin present in the incubates, a reaction due to certain aniline metabolites, predominantly the N-oxidized forms.

A wide variety of drugs and environmental chemicals are known that can induce the synthesis or inhibit the activity of hepatic detoxification and drug-metabolizing enzymes. Significant increases in bilirubin glucuronide conjugating activity were demonstrated in newborn mice after pre-treatment of the pregnant female with phenobarbital for 4–6 days prior to delivery, and striking increases in the activity of this enzyme were produced on the 4th day after administration of the barbiturate directly to the newborn mouse for the first 3 days

after birth.[8] In humans, retrospective studies demonstrated that infants born to epileptic mothers treated with phenobarbital throughout pregnancy had low serum bilirubin levels during the neonatal period.[55] With regard to other pathways of detoxification, both oxidation and reduction reactions have been shown to be increased following pretreatment of newborn rabbits with phenobarbital for 3 or 4 days.[25] It is of interest that the capacity for bile salt synthesis and pool size expansion could be enhanced in premature infants whose mothers were treated with adrenocortical steroids and phenobarbital during pregnancy.[60] These studies raise the intriguing possibility of the pharmacological modification of the formation and secretion of bile, a function that is clearly deficient in the human perinatal period. The molecular events responsible for the inductive effect of phenobarbital and other drugs during the perinatal period have not been completely elucidated. In addition to its effect on glucuronidation in the neonate, phenobarbital also results in increased bile flow and enhanced hepatocyte anion uptake.[8]

The importance of understanding these mechanisms is underlined, however, by considering the apparent differences between man and animals in the perinatal development of drug-metabolizing enzymes. The human being is continuously exposed to foreign compounds such as drugs, food constituents, cigarette smoke, and air pollutants, many of which, as described above, have been demonstrated to be effective in enzyme induction. Furthermore, the human gestational period is much longer than that of commonly studied animal species, thus providing more time for an induction process to occur. It is clear that such species differences must be considered when evaluating the teratogenicity of any new drug.

ACKNOWLEDGMENT

This work was supported in part by the United States Public Health Service, National Institute of Health, Grants AM17847 and HD08954, and the Medical Research Council of Canada.

5. References

1. ACKERMAN, E., RANE, A., AND ERICSSON, J. L. E., 1972, The liver microsomal monooxygenase system in the human fetus: Distribution in different centrifugal fractions, Clin. Pharmacol. Ther. 13:652.

2. ANTON, A. H., AND SOLOMON, H. M., 1973, Drug–protein binding, *Ann. N. Y. Acad. Sci.* **226.**

3. ARANDA, J. V., MACLEOD, S. M., RENTON, K. W., AND EADE, N. R., 1974, Hepatic microsomal drug oxidation and electron transport in newborn infants, *J. Pediatr.* **85:**534.

4. ARIAS, I. M., 1970, The pathogenesis of physiologic jaundice of the newborn: A re-evaluation, in: "Bilirubin Metabolism in the Newborn," *Birth Defects: Orig. Artic. Ser.* **6:**55.

5. BONGIOVANNI, A. M., 1965, Bile acid content of gallbladder of infants, children and adults, *J. Clin. Endocrinol. Metab.* **25:**678.

6. BRODIE, B. B., 1971, Possible mechanisms of drug-induced tissue lesions, *Chem.-Biol. Interact.* **3:**247.

7. CARRIER, G., HUME, A. S., DOUGLAS, B. H., AND WISER, W. L., 1969, Disposition of barbiturates in maternal blood, fetal blood and amniotic fluid, *Amer. J. Obstet. Gynecol.* **105:**1069.

8. CATZ C., AND YAFFE, S. J., 1968, Barbiturate enhancement of bilirubin conjugation and excretion in young and adult animals, *Pediatr. Res.* **2:**361.

9. COHN, V. H., 1971, Transmembrane movement of drug molecules, in: *Fundamentals of Drug Metabolism and Drug Disposition* (B. N. La Du, H. G. Mandel, and E. L. Way, eds.), Williams and Wilkins Co., Baltimore.

10. FEUER, G., AND LISCIO, A., 1969, Origin of delayed development of drug metabolism in the newborn rat, *Nature (London)* **223:**68.

11. FINSTER, M., MARK, L. C., AND MORISHIMA, H. O., 1966, Plasma thiopental concentrations in the newborn following delivery under thiopental–nitrous oxide anesthesia, *Amer. J. Obstet. Gynecol.* **95:**621.

12. FLEISCHNER, G., AND ARIAS, I. M., 1970, Recent advances in bilirubin formation, transport, metabolism and excretion, *Amer. J. Med.* **49:**576.

13. FOUTS, J. R., 1973, Microsomal mixed-function oxidases in the fetal and newborn rabbit, in: *Fetal Pharmacology* (L. Boreus, ed.), Raven Press, New York.

14. FOUTS, J. R., AND ADAMSON, R. H., 1959, Drug metabolism in the newborn rabbit, *Science* **129:**897.

15. GIBSON, J. E., AND BECKER, B. A., 1967, Demonstration of enhanced lethality of drugs in hypoexcretory animals, *J. Pharm. Sci.* **56:**1503.

16. GILLETTE, J. R., 1973, Overview of drug–protein binding, *Ann. N. Y. Acad. Sci.* **226:**6.

17. GILLETTE, J. R., 1973, Overview of drug–protein binding, *Ann. N. Y. Acad. Sci.* **226:**11.

18. GILLETTE, J. R., DAVIS, D. C., AND SASAME, H. A., 1972, Cytochrome P450 and its role in drug metabolism, *Annu. Rev. Pharmacol.,* **12:**57–84.

19. GINSBURG, J., 1971, Placental drug transfer, *Annu. Rev. Pharmacol.* **11:**387–408.

20. GOLDSTEIN, A., ARONOW, L., AND KALMAN, S. M. (eds.), 1974, *Principles of Drug Action: The Basis of Pharmacology,* p. 159, John Wiley & Sons, New York.

21. GOLDSTEIN, A., ARONOW, L., AND KALMAN, S. M. (eds.), 1974, *Principles of Drug Action: The Basis of Pharmacology,* p. 171, John Wiley & Sons, New York.

22. GOLDSTEIN, A., ARONOW, L., AND KALMAN, S. M. (eds.), 1974, *Principles of Drug Action: The Basis of Pharmacology,* p. 159, John Wiley & Sons, New York.

23. GOLDSTEIN, A., ARONOW, L., AND KALMAN, S. M. (eds.), 1974, *Principles of Drug Action: The Basis of Pharmacology,* p. 219, John Wiley & Sons, New York.

24. GOODMAN, S. L., AND GILMAN, A. (eds.), 1970, *The Pharmacological Basis of Therapeutics,* 4th Ed., MacMillan, New York.

25. HART, L. G., ADAMSON, R. H., DIXON, R., AND FOUTS, J. R., 1962, Stimulation of hepatic microsomal drug metabolism in the newborn and fetal rabbit, *J. Pharmacol. Exp. Ther.* **137:**103.

26. IDAMPAAN-HEIKKILA, J. E., JOUPPILA, P. I., PAULAKKA, J. O., AND VORNE, M. S., 1971, Placental transfer and fetal metabolism of diazepam in early human pregnancy, *Amer. J. Obstet. Gynecol.* **199:**1011.

27. JACKSON, B. T., AND EDGALL, R. H., 1950, The performance of complex fetal operations *in utero* without amniotic fluid loss or other disturbances of fetal–maternal relationships, *Surgery* **48:**564.

28. JACKSON, B. T., SMALLWOOD, R. A., PIAŚECKI, G. J., BROWN, A. S., RAUSCHECKER, H. F. J., AND LESTER, R., 1971, Fetal bile salt metabolism. I. The metabolism of sodium cholate-^{14}C in the fetal dog, *J. Clin. Invest.* **50:**1286.

29. KLEIN, G. P., CHAN, S. K., AND GIROUD, C. J. P., 1969, Urinary secretion of 17-hydroxy- and 17-deoxysteroids of the pregnene-4 series by the human newborn, *J. Clin. Endocrinol.* **29:**1448.

30. KLINGER, W., ZWACKA, G., AND ANKERMANN, H., 1958, Untersuchungen zum Mechanismus der Enzyminduktion, *Acta Biol. Med. Ger.* **20:**137.

31. KRASNER, J., GIACOIA, G. P., AND YAFFE, S. J., 1973, Drug–protein binding in the newborn infant, *Ann. N. Y. Acad. Sci.* **226:**101.

32. LANE, A., VON BAHR, C., ORRENIUS, S., AND SJOVQUIST, F., 1973, Drug metabolism in the human fetus, in: *Fetal Pharmacology* (L. Boreus, ed.), Raven Press, New York.

33. LESKES, A., SICKEVITZ, P., AND PALADE, G. E., 1971, Differentiation of endoplasmic reticulum in hepatocyte microsomes. II. Glucose-6-phosphatase, *J. Cell. Biol.* **49:**288.

34. LEVI, A. J., GATMAITEN, Z., AND ARIAS, I. M., 1969, The role of two cytoplasmic proteins (Y and Z) in the transfer of sulfobromophthalein (BSP) and bilirubin from plasma into the liver, *J. Clin. Invest.* **48:**2156.

35. LONG, R. F., AND MARKS, J., 1969, The transfer of drugs across the placenta, *Proc. R. Soc. Med.* **62:**318.

36. MILLER, R. K., FERM, V. H., AND MUDGE, G. H., 1972, Placental transfer and tissue distribution of iophenoxic acid in the hamster, *Amer. J. Obstet. Gynecol.* **114:**259.

47. MIRKIN, B. L., 1971, Diphenylhydantoin: Placental transport, fetal localization, neonatal metabolism and possible teratogenic effect, *J. Pediatr.* **78**:329.

48. MIRKIN, B. L., 1974, Fetal pharmacology, in: *Modern Perinatal Medicine* (L. Gluck, ed.), Year Book Medical Publishers, Chicago.

49. MITCHELL, J. R., AND JOLLOWS, D. J., 1975, Metabolic activation of drugs to toxic substances, *Gastroenterology* **68**:392.

40. MORSELLI, P. L., PRINCIPE, N., TOGNONI, G., KEALL, E., BELVEDERE, G., STANDEN, S. M., AND SERENI, F., 1973, Diazepam elimination in premature and full-term infants and children, *J. Perinat. Med.* **1**:133.

41. OLDER, P. O., AND HARRIS, J. M., 1968, Placental transfer of tubocurarine, *Br. J. Anaesthiol.* **40**:459.

42. PELKONEN, O., KALTILIA, E. H., LARMI, T. K., AND KARKI, N. T., 1973, Comparison of activities of drug metabolizing enzymes in human fetal and adult livers, *Clin. Pharmacol. Ther.* **14**:840.

43. PLAA, G. L., 1971, Biliary and other routes of excretion of drugs, in: *Fundamentals of Drug Metabolism and Drug Disposition* (B. N. La Du, H. G. Mandel, and E. L. Way, eds.), Chapt. 9, Williams and Wilkins, Baltimore.

44. RANE, A., AND ACKERMAN, E., 1977, Metabolism of ethylmorphine and aniline in human fetal liver, *Clin. Pharmacol. Ther.,* in press.

45. SCHECTER, P. J., AND ROSS, L. J., 1967, The distribution of thiopental-2-C^{14} in maternal and fetal tissues of the rat, *J. Pharmacol. Exp. Ther.* **158**:164.

46. SHARP, A. L., PELLER, J., CAREY, J. B., AND KRIVIT, W., 1971, Primary and secondary bile acids in meconium, *Pediatr. Res.* **5**:274.

47. SHOEMAN, D. W., KAUFFMAN, R. E., AZARNOFF, D., AND BOULOS, B. M., 1972, Placental transfer of diphenylhydantoin in the goat, *Biochem. Pharmacol.* **21**:1237.

48. SHNIDER, S. M., AND WAY, E. L., 1968, The kinetics of transfer of lidocaine (xylocaine) across the human placenta, *Anesthesiology* **29**:944.

49. SMALLWOOD, R. A., LESTER, R., PIASECKI, G. J., KLEIN, P. D., GRECO, R., AND JACKSON, B. T., 1972, Fetal bile salt metabolism. II. Hepatic excretion of endogenous bile salts and of a taurocholate load, *J. Clin. Invest.* **51**:1388.

50. SMITH, R. L., 1971, Excretion of drugs in bile, in: *Handbook of Experimental Pharmacology* (B. B. Brodie and J. R. Gillette, eds.), Chapt. 19, Springer-Verlag, Berlin.

51. SOMANI, S. M., 1974, Binding of ^{14}C-neostigmine and ^{14}C-3-hydroxyphenyl-trimethyl ammonium to chondroitin sulfate, human serum albumin and liver subcellular fractions, *Fed. Proc. Fed. Amer. Soc. Exp. Biol.* **33**:514.

52. SOMANI, S. M., AND ANDERSON, J. H., 1975, Sequestration of neostigmine and metabolites by perfused rat liver, *Drug Metab. Dispos.* **3**(4):275–282.

53. THALER, M. M., DALLMAN, P. R., AND GOODMAN, J., 1972, Phenobarbital-induced changes in NADPH-cytochrome C reductase and smooth endoplasmic reticulum in human liver, *J. Pediatr.* **70**:302.

54. TJALVE, H., HANNSSON, E., AND SCHMITERLOW, C. G., 1968, Passage of ^{14}C-nicotine and its metabolites into mice foetuses and placentae, *Acta Pharmacol. Toxicol.* **26**:339.

55. TROLLE, D., 1968, Phenobarbital and neonatal icterus, *Lancet* **1**:251.

56. VEST, M. F., 1962, Conjugation of sulfobromophthalein in newborn infants and children, *J. Clin. Invest.* **41**:1013.

57. VILLEE, C. A., 1952, Metabolism of the placenta, *Amer. J. Obstet. Gynecol.* **74**:1684.

58. WADDELL, W. J., AND MIRKIN, B. L., 1971, Distribution of diphenylhydantoin C^{14} in fetal and maternal tissues of the pregnant mouse, *Biochem. Pharmacol.* **21**:547.

59. WATKINS, J. B., INGALL, D., KLEIN, P. D., AND LESTER, R., 1973, Bile salt metabolism in the newborn: Measurement of pool-size and synthesis by stable isotope technique, *N. Engl. J. Med.* **288**:431.

60. WATKINS, J. B., SZCZEPANIK, P., GOULD, J. B., KLEIN, P. D., AND LESTER, R., 1975, Bile salt metabolism in the human premature infant: Preliminary observations of pool-size and synthesis rate following prenatal administration of dexamethasone and phenobarbital, *Gastroenterology* **69**:706.

61. WEST, J. R., SMITH, H. W., AND CHASSIS, H., 1948, Glomerular filtration rate, effective renal blood flow, and maximal tubular excretory capacity in infancy, *J. Pediatr.* **32**:10.

62. WHEELER, H. O., 1972, Secretion of bile acids by the liver and their role in the formation of hepatic bile, *Arch. Intern. Med.* **130**:353.

63. WILSON, J. T., 1970, Alteration of normal development of drug metabolism by injection of growth hormone, *Nature (London)* **225**:861.

64. YAFFE, S. J., AND JUCHAU, M. R., 1974, Perinatal pharmacology, *Annu. Rev. Pharmacol.* **14**:219.

CHAPTER 26

Electrolyte and Water Metabolism

Edmund Kerpel-Fronius

1. The Fetal Fluids

1.1. Amount and Composition of Intrauterine Fluids

According to measurements during the last trimester of pregnancy, fluid retention is associated with a mean increase of 756 meq exchangeable sodium and of 171 meq potassium.[70] In this chapter, we are concerned with the fraction of retained water and electrolytes that accumulates during fetal development in the uterine cavity. The intrauterine water content in the primate may be divided into three compartments: fetal, placental, and amniotic fluid. Estimates of the water, sodium, and potassium content of these compartments are shown in Table I. If the data in Table I are compared with the total amount of electrolytes retained during pregnancy, it is obvious that the increase of sodium is divided equally between the intrauterine fluid pools and the expanding maternal extracellular fluid space, while most of the retained potassium is used for the formation of fetal tissues.

The composition of fetal fluids has been thoroughly studied in many mammalian species. One of the aims of these studies was to compare the composition of these fluids with that of the maternal blood plasma. It was hoped that similarities and deviations in composition and the study of concentration gradients between maternal and fetal fluids might reveal clues for the understanding of the mechanisms and principles of intrauterine fluid accumulation. A survey of data from such a comparative study in the lamb is presented in Table II.

1.2. Fetomaternal Relationship of Total Osmolarity and of Solute Concentrations

Total Osmolar Concentrations. Some authors found a higher osmolar concentration in fetal blood plasma compared with that in maternal blood. When sampling of fetal and maternal blood was performed with a minimum of interference with placental circulation, the osmotic pressure was the same in both fluids.[77] Delayed sampling, i.e., clamping of the cord, caused a rise in osmolar concentration of the fetal plasma. The data in Table II show the same osmolar concentration in the blood plasma of the ewe and the fetal lamb. The same holds

Edmund Kerpel-Fronius · Department of Pediatrics No. II, University Medical School, Budapest IX, Hungary

Table I. Water, Sodium, and Potassium Content of Intrauterine Fluids[a]

Compartment	Water (g)	Sodium (meq)	Potassium (meq)
Fetus (3.5 kg)	2400	243	150.0
Placenta (0.5 kg)	433	49	20.0
Amniotic fluid (0.7 kg)	700	88	2.8
TOTALS:	3533	380	172.8

[a] From Widdowson and Dickerson.[108]

true for the human. Battaglia[13] found average values for maternal and fetal plasma of 289.1 and 292.7 mosmol/liter, respectively.

Plasma Sodium Concentration. In the ewe and the fetal lamb at term, these levels are equal (Table II). The data presented in Table III show, however, that it is somewhat embarrassing to take a firm stand with regard to the human fetus and newborn. The range of variations was found to be even greater for measurements performed on the plasma of young fetuses: 134–188 meq/liter.[105] This great range conveys the impression that extremely high values may be due to shortcomings of the sampling technique or to pathology. On the other hand, very low values may reflect maternal hyponatremia, a condition that is frequently found in mothers treated with a low-sodium diet, diuretics, and glucose solutions prior to delivery. The concentration of sodium in the blood plasma of the human fetus near term is practically the same as in the maternal plasma.[13,14,24] The latter is frequently a few milliequivalents lower and occasionally is much lower than the accepted normal values for older infants or adults.

According to Bengtsson *et al.*,[14] the sodium concentration in the blood plasma from fetuses and newborns lies within the normal range. These authors found a sodium concentration of 140.0 ± 0.7 meq/liter in the blood plasma of midterm fetuses, as compared with 135.1 ± 0.9 meq in the maternal plasma. The sodium concentration in the red cells of the fetus was slightly lower than that of the mother, 5.55 ± 0.21 as compared with 7.26 ± 0.45 meq/liter, while in the newborn it was somewhat higher than in the mother, 9.63 ± 0.58 as compared with 7.63 ± 0.28 meq/liter.

Plasma Potassium Concentration. This level in the newborn has been a much-discussed problem ever since Widdowson and McCance[109] reported very

high values in the human fetus and in the fetal pig. The relevant information that serves as a base for discussion is summarized in Table IV.

In early fetal life, very high plasma potassium concentrations were reported. In the previable fetuses of Westin *et al.*,[105] the range was 8.0–12.8 meq/liter, and Widdowson and McCance[109] found a mean value of 10.2 meq/liter in the human and 17.5 meq/liter in the pig fetus. Before the somewhat contradictory data presented can be evaluated, some pitfalls of methodology must be discussed. The conceivable causes of real or apparent hyperkalemia are: (1) intrauterine hypoxia and acidosis; (2) escape of potassium from the red cells, since the cells of the newborn and fetus give up their potassium with great speed *in vitro*[56]; (3) hemolysis, which occurs easily during sampling of blood from fetal vessels; (4) delayed sampling of cord blood, causing potassium gain from the hypoxic placental tissue; (5) a genuine ability of the fetus to maintain an uphill gradient for potassium between maternal and fetal circulation. Hyperkalemia in the first condition is pathologic, while a sampling technique that is open to criticism may also have caused artifacts. Finally, an uphill gradient would imply some form of active potassium transport from mother to fetus.

A critical inspection of the values shown in Table IV leads to the suggestion that some authors may have included in their material some severely acidotic cases, or that their sampling technique was not absolutely perfect. The means of all authors were found to be 0.5–1 meq/liter higher than the corresponding maternal values, and concentration certainly increased with decreasing maturity of the fetus. This thesis is also supported by evidence from comparative physiology. The somatic immaturity at birth of certain species of animals is reflected by a higher hyperkalemia. The immaturely born rat, pig, and dog exhibit consistently higher plasma potassium concentrations relative to maternal plasma, in contrast to more mature newborns such as the guinea pig and the lamb. The dog is a particularly suitable animal for such studies, since the sodium and not the potassium is the dominant cation in canine erythrocytes. This situation excludes the possibility of a high plasma potassium concentration being an artifact in this species.

The conclusive proof that the fetus can maintain a transplacental uphill gradient against maternal blood was given by experiments of Serrano *et al.*[95] In potassium-deficient pregnant bitches, plasma

Table II. Comparison of Maternal and Fetal Fluids in the Lamb[a]

Measure	Maternal arterial blood	Fetal umbilical blood	Fetal tracheal fluid	Amniotic fluid	Allantoic fluid	Fetal urine
Osmolality (mosmol/liter)[b]	302 ±6.0	300 ±6.0	300 ±6.0	275 ±14.0	278 ±14.0	264 ±7.6
Sodium (meq/liter)[b]	143 ±4.9	140 ±3.4	142 ±4.6	110 ±2.0	35.0±27.0	—
Chloride (meq/liter)[b]	108 ±3.1	105 ±4.9	144 ±7.1	94 ±9.6	39.0±21.0	—
Potassium (meq/liter)	4.7	4.4	6.6	10.7	51.4	—
Total CO_2 (meq/liter)[b]	22.6 ±3.6	22.1 ±1.9	4.4 ±1.6	18.4	16.9	18.8
pH[b]	7.44±0.55	7.34±0.65	6.43±0.13	7.07±0.22	6.9± 0.25	6.84±0.4
Urea (mg/dl)	—	—	46.0	118	112	—
Sugar (mg/dl)	135	152	113	304	300	—
Protein (mg/dl)	6509	4439	327	699	1691	—

[a] From Adams et al.(2,3)
[b] Mean ± S.D.

Table III. Plasma Sodium Concentration in Cord Blood (meq/liter)

Number of samples	Mean	Range	S.D.	References
14	146.8	126–166	±8.1	Archarya and Payne[1]
19	139.0	130–158	±8.0	Oliver et al.[81]
10	140.1	137–145	—	Battaglia et al.[13]
12	135.0	127–142	±5.0	Pincus et al.[86]
62	135.0	—	±6.1	Crawford[25]

potassium concentration fell from 4.1 to 2.7 meq/liter, while the fetal concentration remained unchanged and was 5.3 meq/liter in controls and 5.4 meq/liter in newborns of potassium-deficient mothers. The uphill gradient of striking proportions in the experimental group, and the important fact that carcass potassium did not decrease in these newborns, strongly suggest some form of active transport for this ion through the placental barrier. This remarkable ability of the fetus to resist maternal potassium deficiency was also shown to be true for the rat.[26] In maternal plasma, the potassium level decreased on a potassium-deficient diet from 4.61 to 2.3 meq/liter, while fetal potassium concentration did increase slightly from 5.5 ± 0.15 to 6.0 ± 0.27 meq/liter. Resistance to potassium depletion is also shown by the maintained potassium concentration in the muscles of the fetus as contrasted with the low values found in the depleted mother.

Plasma Magnesium Concentration. By the use of advanced methodology, the plasma concentration of magnesium was found to be in the normal range of adults.[10,100] Jukarainen[55] gives a mean value for term newborns of 1.70 ± 0.25 meq/liter, while values for prematures are somewhat higher: 1.91 ± 0.31 meq/liter. Plasma magnesium concen-

Table IV. Plasma Potassium Concentration in Cord Blood and During the First Hours of Life (meq/liter)

Species	Number	Mean	Range	S.D.	Mean in maternal plasma	References
Human						
Term	40	9.10	6.8–14.3	±2.0	—	Oliver et al.[81]
Term	5	8.00	4.8–12.9	—	—	Widdowson and McCance[109]
Term	14	7.79	5.6–12.0	±2.0	—	Acharya and Payne[1]
Term	7	4.47	3.1– 5.8	—	3.85	Battaglia et al.[13]
Term	62	4.50	—	±0.61	3.50	Crawford[25]
Term	12	5.40	4.5– 6.8	±0.7	—	Pincus et al.[86]
Most premature	—	6.10	5.6– 7.2	±0.6	—	Pincus et al.[86]
Premature	12	5.80	—	±0.35	—	Nicolopoulos and Smith[79]
Most premature	4	7.50	—	±0.97	—	Nicolopoulos and Smith[79]
Midterm fetus	—	4.81	—	±0.20	4.31 ± 0.09	Bengtsson et al.[14]
Term infant	—	4.59	—	±0.12	3.66 ± 0.07	Bengtsson et al.[14]
One-day-old infant	—	4.65	—	±0.04	—	Bengtsson et al.[14]

tration, in analogy to the situation with potassium, increases by interference with placental circulation and by acidosis. Hemolytic jaundice of the newborn may double plasma magnesium concentration.[52]

There is evidence that the somatic immaturity of certain species of animals at birth is reflected by higher magnesium levels. Higher values were observed in the fetal pig than in the sow.[32] A similar concentration gradient between fetus and mother was also found in the rat.[27] Most interesting is the observation[27] that in magnesium deprivation of the mother, the fetus, in sharp contrast to the situation in potassium deprivation, remains unprotected during pregnancy; few fetuses survived until term. In later pregnancy, magnesium deficiency abolishes the concentration gradient between fetus and mother, the plasma magnesium levels falling in both to extremely low figures. The fetuses insufficiently supplied with this important intracellular constituent were small, feeble, and obviously affected by the deficient diet.

Plasma Calcium and Phosphorus Concentrations. These are discussed in Chapter 28.

Plasma Chloride and Total CO$_2$ Concentrations. According to unanimous opinion, there are only slight differences in the plasma chloride concentrations between term infants and adults.[45,86] In premature infants, the range of variation is greater, and the mean chloride concentration is higher.

The total CO$_2$ content is low at birth, which reflects a variable degree of metabolic acidosis. The range of variation increases immediately after birth. At 24 hr after birth, healthy full-term infants exhibit an average CO$_2$ value of 21 meq/liter, with a range of 16.1–24.9 meq/liter, the corresponding concentrations for adults being 24 meq/liter, with a range of 21.4–26.4 meq/liter.[45]

Plasma pH. According to *in utero* measurements by the scalp-sampling technique,[90] the pH in fetal blood is only a few hundredths of a unit lower than that in maternal blood before the onset of labor. With labor in progress, the fetal pH decreases very slowly. Values below 7.2 are generally considered to reflect intrauterine asphyxia.[66,90] As will be discussed later, premature infants exhibit a conspicuous tendency to develop acidosis.

1.3. Origin of Intrauterine Fluid Accumulation

During fetal development, a net quantity of 3.5 liters water, 380 meq sodium, and 173 meq potas-

sium must have been transferred from the mother to the intrauterine cavity (as shown in Table I). The mechanism of this transfer still remains obscure. Isotope studies revealed exchange rates that exceeded by far the net transfer rates; the net transfer rate is defined as the transfer of water or of electrolytes in one direction in excess of the transfer in the reverse direction. The two directional transfer rates appear to be enormously high (Table V).[87] Exchange rates for water between mother and fetus increase 10 times between midpregnancy and term, while the initially high exchange rates between mother and amniotic fluid and between fetus and amniotic fluid increase at a much slower rate as term approaches. The turnover rates for sodium and potassium were found to be much smaller than those for water.

The reported isotope studies do not solve the problem of the driving forces of the net transfers, which result in the accumulation of intrauterine fluids. The net fluid transfer from the mother to the intrauterine pools cannot be explained simply by osmotic, colloid osmotic, or hydrostatic pressure differences between fetal and maternal blood.[94] For the time being, we must be satisfied with the assumption of Seeds[94] that gradients that are too small or infrequent for accurate measurements by present techniques may supply small daily fluid amounts that are necessary for the normal intrauterine development. Temperature differences within the vascular beds of the placenta may also be considered as a possible force. As for potassium and probably also for magnesium, some hitherto unknown mechanism for active transport must be sought.

Table V. Transfer Rates for Water (ml/hr) Between Mother and Fetus[a]

	Weeks of pregnancy	
Transfer	20	40
Mother–fetus	302	3657
Fetus–mother	259	3682
Mother–amniotic fluid	79	265
Amniotic fluid–mother	107	247
Fetus–amniotic fluid	70	149
Amniotic fluid–fetus	37	165

[a] From Plentl.[87]

1.4. Effects on the Fetus of Changes in Volume and Composition of Maternal Extracellular Fluid

Although the problem of the mechanism of net fluid transfer across the placenta remains unsolved, it has been shown that acute changes in maternal extracellular fluid volume and composition lead to predictable changes in the fetal fluids. In a series of impressive experiments, Battaglia et al.[13] created osmotic gradients between human maternal and fetal blood by infusion of mannitol, hypertonic saline, or isotonic glucose solutions into the maternal circulation. The hypertonic expansion of maternal extracellular fluid was accompanied by a similar but smaller rise in osmolarity in the fetal blood plasma, while increasing plasma protein concentration indicated net movement of fluid from the fetus to the mother. Dilutional hyponatremia was induced in the mother by injecting 5% glucose solution, and the injection produced a decrease of the osmolar concentration in fetal blood. This result indicated a transfer of water from the mother to the fetus or a transfer of sodium in the opposite direction, or both. These observations in the human were supplemented by similar experiments in animals. Burns et al.[15] induced water depletion in rabbit fetuses by an intravenous infusion of hypertonic mannitol solution into pregnant rabbits. The resulting decrease in fetal extracellular fluid was 18%, and the loss of cell fluid was calculated to be 15%. These high amounts of fluids were transferred from the fetus to the mother through the placenta. The increase in osmotic pressure in the fetal blood was less marked than in the maternal, and about half the increase in osmolarity in the fetal fluids could be ascribed to the transfer of mannitol. Osmotic gradients that were experimentally produced among fetal, maternal, and amniotic fluid pools by injection of sucrose solution into the amniotic sac of pregnant monkeys also led to fetal dehydration; the placental water content remained unchanged in these experiments.[16]

In addition to such short-duration experiments, it was shown that chronic salt depletion also affects the fetal fluid pools. Phillips and Sundaram[85] induced sodium depletion in pregnant ewes by draining the saliva from one parotid gland for a period of 6 days. Fetal sodium concentration showed a smaller reduction than either maternal or amniotic sodium concentration. The authors assumed that some still unidentified mechanism must have provided some degree of independence to the fetal sodium plasma level from the maternal plasma level. Furthermore, it was assumed that these fetuses responded to sodium deficiency by restricting their renal sodium loss.

These assumptions seem to hold true only for the type of hyponatremia that is accompanied by dehydration of some days' duration. In the clinical cases of Altstatt,[7] in which iatrogenic transplacental hyponatremia was caused by a low-salt diet and by administering large amounts of 5% glucose solutions to the mother, changes in fetal sodium concentration exhibited a close parallelism to maternal concentrations. In the 4 cases observed, maternal sodium concentrations of 119, 118, 117, and 119 meq/liter were accompanied by the following neonatal values: 120, 119, 122, and 114 meq/liter. In experimental dialysis, maternal and fetal plasma sodium concentration changes were also practically identical.

For potassium, a genuine independence of fetal from maternal plasma concentration was shown to exist. As mentioned in Section 1.2, hypokalemia induced in bitches[95] or in rats[26] decreased neither the fetal plasma potassium level nor the total carcass potassium of the fetus. There appears to be, however, no protection of the fetus against magnesium deprivation. The placenta is relatively ineffective against maternal hyperkalemia or hypermagnesiemia.[26,27]

Concerning hydrogen ion concentration, an increasing maternal acid accumulation during labor is reflected by a parallel increase in fetal negative base excess, as shown by studies carried out with the fetal scalp-sampling technique. In fetal asphyxia, however, base excess in fetal blood decreases out of proportion to maternal values.[66]

1.5. Volume, Composition, Origin, and Disposal of Amniotic Fluid

Amniotic fluid appears in all mammalian species early in pregnancy. In the human, a few milliliters of this fluid have been found as early as in the 8th week of gestation. Figure 1 shows the rate of accumulation of this fluid during pregnancy. The peak value of 1000 ml is reached at about 2 weeks before term. Thereafter, the amount of fluid decreases slowly until the 40th week. This decrease is accelerated as soon as normal term is passed; the average fluid volume decreases to about one-fourth of its peak value after 43 weeks of gestation. This decrease in fluid volume may occur in consequence

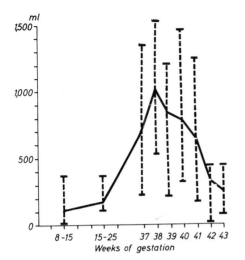

Fig. 1. Rate of accumulation of amniotic fluid during pregnancy. Averages and ranges of variation in milliliters. Data from Seeds.[94]

of diminishing functional efficiency of the placenta, which begins after the normal term is passed.

The individual variations of fluid volume are large even in normal pregnancies. Extreme values exceeding 1.5–2 liters (hydramnios) or volumes below 0.5 liter (oligohydramnios), however, are frequently associated with fetal pathology.

Progressive distension of the uterus is thought to be necessary for normal uterine, placental, and fetal development. The removal of amniotic fluid at about midpregnancy causes death of the fetuses; however, near-term survival without amniotic fluid is possible.[4]

In the first half of gestation, the composition of amniotic fluid is similar to that of extracellular fluid. Later in pregnancy, osmolarity and sodium concentration fall below the fetal or maternal levels in blood plasma.[44] Other conspicuous changes are the increases in potassium, urea, uric acid, creatinine, and acidity.

Concerning the provenance of amniotic fluid, we have to accept the hypothesis of Lind et al.[68] that in the first half of pregnancy it should be considered an extension of the fetal extracellular fluid space. These authors showed that in the first half of pregnancy, amniotic fluid volume is more closely related to fetal weight than to length of gestation, and that in terms of its composition, it is more closely related to the extracellular fluid composition of the fetus than to that of the mother. They also showed that the fetal skin is freely permeable to

sodium and water in the first 20 weeks of pregnancy, and thus fetal skin may act as a diffusing surface. In keeping with this hypothesis are some observations made after the intraamniotic infusion of hypertonic saline, a procedure used clinically to terminate pregnancy after midgestation. The sodium content of the bodies of fetuses exposed to this procedure at gestational ages of 14–19 weeks is 3 times higher than that reported in fetuses of corresponding gestational ages.[103] It was assumed that the sodium entered the fetal body through the skin.

Later in pregnancy, the problem becomes more complicated, since the secretions of the fetal kidneys and lungs appear to participate to a large extent in the formation of this fluid. The convincing proof that amniotic fluid is modified by a steadily increasing admixture of fetal urine is, in addition to the decreasing osmolarity and sodium concentration, the accumulation of fetal waste products in the amniotic fluid. Table II shows that fetal urine is hypotonic and that the amniotic fluid of the lamb has a high urea and potassium content. In the human, urea concentration in amniotic fluid at term varies between 24 and 44 mg/dl, creatinine levels are between 2 and 3.7 mg/dl, and uric acid reaches a value of 6.8 mg/dl. These values are considerably higher than those in fetal plasma. The important role of the fetal kidneys in the formation and regulation of amniotic fluid is supported by clinical observations. Bain and Scott[12] reviewed 50 cases of fetal urinary tract malformations with the common feature that no fetal micturition could have occurred. Among these cases, bilateral renal agenesis was present in 28 cases, severe cystic dysplasia in 17, and congenital urethral atresia in 5. In all but 1 case, fluid was recorded as being absent, deficient, or suggestive of liquor deficiency. Fluid was present in 1 anencephalic case, in which no amniotic fluid could have been swallowed. A unique clinical observation of Mauer et al.[76] points to the significance of fetal urination, and the importance of oligohydramnios in the genesis of Potter's syndrome. One of monoamniotic, monochorionic twins was born with absence of kidneys, but had none of the manifestations of Potter's syndrome. His twin had a single kidney and was capable of preventing oligohydramnios by producing a normal amount of urine. This observation supports the thesis that Potter's syndrome is due to oligohydramnios secondary to absence of intrauterine urine production. The extensive literature on the relationship of renal agenesis and oligohydramnios permits the general conclusion that if the mechanisms for the disposal of amniotic fluid are operating normally, the absence of fetal urination is associated with oligohydramnios. Thus, the absence of fetal micturition disturbs the steady state of amniotic fluid formation and disposal.

The same conclusions can be drawn when the problem of amniotic fluid formation is evaluated from available data on fetal urine formation. In general, fetal urine flow was found to be surprisingly high. Alexander et al.[6] measured amounts of 1.9 ml/min per kg at 61 days of gestation and 0.04 ml at term in sheep, the latter value being still twice as high as in adults. The authors concluded that the rate of urine formation is more than enough to account for the total volume of fetal fluids observed. It was admitted, of course, that several factors are involved in the formation of fetal fluids.[5] Wright and Nixon[111] calculated that the total volume of fluid that is absorbed by the gut of fetal sheep between 80 days of gestation and term was about 32 liters, which is in the same range as the volume of urine produced during this time (about 40 liters). Comparably high volumes of urine are passed by the human fetus. Wladimiroff and Campbell[110] measured the hourly fetal urine production rate in 92 normal cases by an ultrasonic technique. There was a rapid and linear rise in the mean values from 9.6 ml at 30 weeks' to 27.3 ml at 40 weeks' gestational age.

Another source of amniotic fluid is the fetal tracheal fluid. This fluid has the same total osmolar and sodium concentration as fetal blood plasma (see Table II), and it appears to be an ultrafiltrate of the latter. The reason for certain differences in composition, such as the very low pH and total CO_2 content and the high chloride concentration, remains at present unexplained, but the origin of the fetal tracheal fluid and its direction of flow are known. The fluid produced by the fetal airways flows out of the trachea and pharynx into the esophagus, and part of it enters the amniotic cavity. The rate of flow was found to be 1–2 ml/min in fetal lambs at term,[2] and such an amount should contribute appreciably to the volume of amniotic fluid.

Filtration and diffusion through the fetal membranes and their secretions may be additional sources of amniotic fluid.

The gut of the fetus is believed to play an important role in the disposal of amniotic fluid. In 54 of 169 cases of hydramnios,[93] the excessive accumulation of amniotic fluid could be ascribed to conditions in which there had probably been a failure of the fetal swallowing mechanism, or in which the fetus was mechanically incapable of swallowing. All cases of esophageal atresia are accompanied by hydramnios except those in which both segments of the esophagus communicate with the trachea, thus providing a route for swallowing. Anencephaly and other severe neurological anomalies frequently interfere with swallowing, and are therefore associated with hydramnios. Further evidence that the inability to swallow is certainly one of the causes of hydramnios comes from the findings of Moya et al.,[78] who reviewed 1745 cases from the literature and found esophageal malformations in 26.7% and other pathologic conditions interfering with swallowing in 17.7% of all cases.

As an interesting clinical fact, it should be mentioned that maternal hydramnios is a constant feature in the perinatal anamnesis of a rare disease, congenital chloride diarrhea.[84] The difficulty in absorbing chloride might be the explanation for this phenomenon.

Fluid exchange relies on a finely tuned system of production and removal. There are many sites for interference. An imbalance of only a few milliliters per hour in transfer rates could result in the formation of hydramnios.

1.6. Regulation of Volume and Composition of Fetal Fluids

The placenta, the fetal and maternal kidneys, the fetal skin, the fetal membranes, and the fetal lung and intestine play certain roles in maintaining the volume and composition of the fetal fluids. The ways in which these multiple processes are ultimately integrated still elude our full understanding. Osmolarity and sodium concentrations are evidently in equilibrium with maternal concentrations, but no convincing results are available to prove that the regulation of electrolyte levels could be absolutely independent of the mother. It is not fully known how much the fetal kidney function contributes to the regulation of these concentrations. A decreasing sodium concentration in fetal urine during gestation speaks for a sodium-saving ability of the fetal kidneys. Whether the fetal urine volumes vary with changing sodium concentrations in fetal plasma remains to be investigated. Similarly, potassium and magnesium regulation remains problematic. It is known that normal potassium concentration can be maintained in fetal fluids despite maternal potassium depletion.

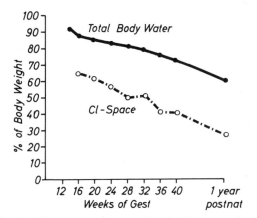

Fig. 2. Changes in TBW and chloride space during intrauterine development in man. Data from Iob and Swanson.[53]

2. Changes in Body Water Compartments and Electrolyte Contents During Growth

2.1. Fluid Spaces During Growth

It has been known for many years that progressive decrease in water and chloride content of the body is a characteristic of growth and development. These processes are understood to occur as a consequence of the decrease in extracellular body fluid volume and of the increase in fat and in proteins. Figure 2 reflects the impressive extent of these changes during intrauterine development and their continuation through early infancy. The developmental changes in electrolyte contents and in the size of the fluid spaces have been studied in detail by dilution methods. Values obtained with deuterium oxide or antipyrine, which are both frequently used to measure total body water (TBW), agree with those obtained by direct postmortem analysis. with those obtained by direct postmortem analysis.

The measurement of extracellular fluid volume is a controversial problem. The substances used for this purpose measure different spaces. According to the size of space they measure in adults, these substances can be divided into two groups: (1) chloride, bromide, and thiocyanate; and (2) inulin, mannitol, and thiosulfate. The volume of extracellular water (ECW) measured with substances of group 1 is about 25% of the body weight, while the volume of ECW measured with the second group (inulin) is considerably smaller—about 16% of the body weight. The "battle of the boundaries," as Gamble (personal communication) called the discussion on the significance of parameters measured by the various substances, is of importance, since intracellular water (ICW) is usually calculated by subtracting ECW from TBW. If the calculation is based on ECW measured by any substance of group 2, ICW is considerably greater, and consequently the calculated concentration of intracellular solutes is considerably lower than if substances of group 1 are used. In the first case, large amounts of exchangeable sodium and chloride would be assigned to ICW. Since inulin penetrates dense connective tissue water, bone water, and transcellular fluid only partially, and since these compartments of the sodium- and chloride-containing fluids evidently have to be assigned to ECW, in practice, the "inulin space" refers only to the "mobile" fraction of ECW. We agree with those authors[20,37] who consider the corrected bromide space (i.e., the space corrected for intracellular chloride) in adults as the extracellular fluid space.

The foregoing discussion has less bearing on the newborn period, since at this age the spaces measured with any of the substances of either group 1 or group 2 are more similar than in adults (Fig. 3). In searching for the reason for this age-dependent difference, i.e., the inequality of the inulin and chloride spaces in the adult, we agree with Friis-Hansen[40,41] that it reflects the increasing heterogeneity of the extracellular fluid during development, i.e., the increasing proportion of dense

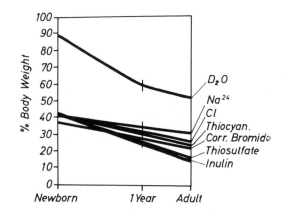

Fig. 3. Comparison of the relative volumes of distribution of various substances used for measuring fluid spaces in the human newborn, at 1 year of age, and in adults. Adapted from Friis-Hansen.[40]

Table VI. TBW, ECW, and Calculated Volume of ICW (% of Body Weight) in the Human Newborn and Adult

Age	TBW D$_2$O space	ECW	ICW	ICW measured by:	References
23- to 54-yr–old males	54.3	23.4	30.9	Corrected bromide space	Parker et al.[82]
0–11 days	76.4	41.6	34.8	Thiosulfate	Parker et al.[82]
1-day term	78.4	44.5	33.9	Thiosulfate	Friis-Hansen[40]
1-day term	77.4	38.7	39.8	Corrected bromide space	Clapp et al.[22]
1-day term	—	35.8	—	Corrected bromide space	Fink and Cheek[34]
1–6 days (prematures)	85.8	40.5	44.8	Corrected bromide space	Fink and Cheek[34]

connective tissue water in total ECW with growth. An additional comment is necessary regarding the volume of ECW measured with substances belonging to either group 1 or group 2 in the newborn. Friis-Hansen[40] found a mean value for ECW of 44.5% of the body weight; this measurement was made with thiosulfate, and it is appreciably higher than the corrected bromide space of the newborn. For the latter, mean values of $35.8 \pm 6\%$[34] and $38.7 \pm 3.4\%$[22] were measured on the first day of life. The correction factor used for intracellular chloride might thus be either somewhat too high, or, as seems more likely, the exclusion of the brain from the volume of distribution of bromide introduces a larger error in the measurement of ECW in the newborn than in the adult. This assumption is supported by the fact that the brain of the newborn contains 11.2% of the TBW, while that of the adult accounts for only 2.2%. Furthermore, the chloride concentration is higher in the brain of the newborn than in that of the adult.

Table VII. Fluid Spaces of the Adult Human Being Compared with Those of a Newborn (g/kg Fat-Free Body Weight)

Age	TBW	ECW[a]	ICW[a]
Adult	720	305	415
Newborn	823	448	375

[a] ECW and ICW are recalculated from the data of Parker et al.[82] presented in Table VI.

It appears reasonable to conclude that in the adult, the difference between the corrected bromide space and the inulin space should be ascribed to that part of the extracellular fluid system that has an organized structure. Hence, for the calculation of the volume of ICW in the adult, the difference between TBW and corrected bromide space (and certainly not the difference between TBW and inulin or thiosulfate space) should be used, while for the calculation of ICW in the newborn, the difference between TBW and thiosulfate space seems to be more appropriate. Table VI summarizes some data on the size of the fluid compartments. If fluid volumes are calculated on a fat-free basis, differences in ECW between the newborn and the adult appear to be smaller, and ICW in the adult is higher than in the newborn (Table VII).

2.2. Electrolyte Content of the Body During Growth

Developmental changes in the total electrolyte content of the body are summarized in Table VIII.

2.3. Changes in Composition of Organs and Tissues During Growth

The typical developmental changes in water content and size of fluid spaces in the peripheral muscle are illustrated in Fig. 4. The peculiarities of immature human muscle compared with adult muscle are the high proportion of ECW per 100 g dry substance and the much less expanded ICW. In the fresh muscle of the premature infant, the ECW

Table VIII. Chloride, Sodium, and Potassium Content of the Human Fetus and Newborn Compared with Values of Adults (meq/kg)

Age	Cl	Na	K	Method	References
Fetus (271 g)	76.0	96.0	46.0	Chemical analysis	Widdowson and Dickerson[108]
Newborn	49.7	73.7	40.4	Chemical analysis	Camerer[17]
Newborn	48.0	—	—	Bromide	Cheek[19]
Newborn	—	80.0	40.0	^{24}Na, ^{42}K	Corsa et al.[23]
Adult man	33.2	62.3	51.5	Chemical analysis	Forbes and Lewis[38]
Adult man	31.6	—	—	Bromide	Dunning et al.[31]
Adult man	—	41.9 (+30%)[a]	—	^{24}Na	Forbes and Lewis[38]
Adult man	—	—	46.3 (+5%)[b]	^{42}K	Corsa et al.[23]

[a] Amount of nonexchangeable sodium.
[b] Amount of nonexchangeable potassium.

accounts for about half the weight of the muscle, while the content in dry matter and in ICW is smaller than in the newborn. A very similar order of increasing maturity is seen when the fluid spaces of the very immaturely born rat are compared with those of the more mature puppy and newborn pig. The composition of the muscle of the newborn rat shows a considerably less mature pattern than that of the human premature of 1.6 kg.

Table IX presents data that demonstrate the maturational trends for some organs.[107,108] The water and chloride content of the heart, in contrast with the great changes occurring in skeletal muscle, shows only minor changes with age. Widdowson and Dickerson[107] related this difference in chemical maturation to variations in the rate of functional maturation: the heart matures functionally earlier

than the skeletal muscle. The decrease in the water content of the skin is due to an increase in collagen; it is associated with an increase of the connective tissue water fraction of total ECW. Parallel with these changes, the Na:Cl ratio falls, indicating an increase in connective tissue chloride. The proportion of ICW is low in all age groups, as could be suggested from the low potassium content. The skin certainly is the main depot of ECW of the body. The decrease of the water and chloride content of the brain is a characteristic phenomenon of growth.

Another important depository for ECW is the skeleton (see Chapter 4). The water content of bone decreases, while its sodium content rises, during growth. The diminishing exchangeability of bone sodium with age is a further interesting feature of the growth process.[38] As already mentioned, the radio-

Table IX. Developmental Changes of the Electrolyte Content of Some Organs[a]

Organ	Fetus (20–22 weeks)				Newborn				Adult			
	H_2O	Na	K	Cl	H_2O	Na	K	Cl	H_2O	Na	K	Cl
Muscle[b]	887	90.6	57.6	65.6	804	60.1	57.7	42.6	792	36.3	92.2	22.1
Heart[b]	860	46.1	81.1	41.0	841	64.2	54.3	49.3	827	57.8	66.5	45.6
Skin[c]	901	120.0	36.0	96.0	828	87.1	45.0	66.9	694	79.3	23.7	71.4
Brain[b]	922	91.7	52.0	72.6	897	80.9	58.2	66.1	774	55.2	84.6	40.5

[a] From Widdowson and Dickerson.[108]
[b] In g or meq/kg fresh tissue.
[c] In g or meq/kg fat-free skin.

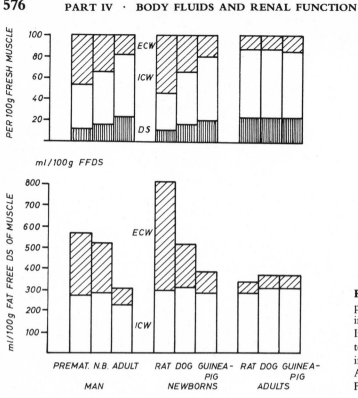

Fig. 4. Changes in volume of water compartments in the skeletal muscle during growth in man and in newborn animals. Premature: Infant weighing 1.6 kg; (NB) newborn full-term infant. (ECW) Extracellular and (ICW) intracellular water; (DS) dry substance. Adapted from Kerpel-Fronius[57] and Kerpel-Fronius et al.[62]

sodium space in the newborn is about the same size as the thiosulfate space, while in the adult, the amount of sodium found by chemical analysis is approximately 30% higher than the exchangeable sodium, and much higher than the fraction of sodium allocated to ECW. These changes indicate that during maturation, a rising amount of bone sodium is bound in a rather inaccessible form in the crystalline bone structure.

2.4. Role of Changing Organ Proportions in the Decrease of Extracellular Fluid Volume During Growth

That proportion of the body weight that accounts for major tissues and organs undergoes great changes during growth and maturation. The relative contribution of these tissues to TBW and total ECW and ICW in each stage of maturation depends on both the changing size in relation to body weight and the changes in composition.

Organs rich in ECW, such as skin and brain,

account for a much higher percentage of body weight, and hence of TBW, in the newborn than in the adult, while the muscle mass is not only less in the newborn, but also contains a much higher percentage of ECW. The differences of those three organs, which represent more than 60% of TBW, and the higher water content of the skeleton easily explain the higher ECW content of the immature body. The decrease in ECW during growth obviously results from two maturational processes: (1) the decreasing proportion of body weight that accounts for tissues rich in ECW and (2) the decrease in the percentage of ECW in the skeletal muscle.

2.5. Intracellular Solutes During Growth

The potassium concentration in the ICW space of the muscle of the human embryo was found to be very high; in the newborn, it appeared to be somewhat lower compared with the adult.[107] The differences of intracellular potassium concentrations between newborn and adult animals are insignificant. Intracellular fluid volume and potassium content expressed per 100 g fat-free dry matter

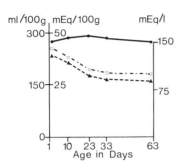

Fig. 5. Changes in intracellular fluid volume per 100 g FFDM (— · —), in potassium content per 100 g FFDM (▲---▲), and in potassium concentration per liter intracellular water (●—●—●) during the development of the rat. Ordinate: left outside—ICW, ml/100 g FFDM; left inside—potassium content, meq/100 g FFDM; right—potassium concentration. Adapted from Jelinek.[54]

(FFDM) decrease in a parallel manner in the rat during development, and intracellular potassium concentration remains practically unchanged (Fig. 5).

The high ICW volume (expressed per unit of FFDM in the newborn) is partially due to the low concentration of intracellular protein. It was calculated that the concentration of intracellular protein in muscle per kilogram of intracellular water increases during extrauterine growth from 32.2 g in the newborn to 44.4 g in the adult.[107] Accordingly, the ratio meq K/g protein N in muscle tissue is higher in the newborn than in the adult. This ratio is of some importance for clinical investigations, since it is used in balance experiments to calculate a loss or gain of intracellular potassium above or below the amount derived from protoplasmic catabolism or anabolism, respectively.

In summary, the main features of the maturational processes are a considerable decrease in TBW, ECW, and chloride content, and an increase in potassium, nitrogen (protein), and fat contents; these are the main differences between the newborn and the adult when compared on the basis of body weight. The main change in the composition of ECW is its increasing heterogeneity, as judged by the increasing difference between the chloride space and the inulin space. Plasma potassium concentration shows a moderate decrease, and total CO_2 a small increase.

The age-dependent difference in the exchangeable fraction of total sodium is due to the increasing

amounts of sodium that are deposited in the bone crystalline structures.[39] In ICW, a considerable increase in intracellular protein concentration takes place, while no such differences seem to occur in the potassium concentration during postnatal development.

3. Body Fluid Homeostasis in the Newborn

3.1. Overall Efficiency and Maturation Patterns of Homeostatic Defense Mechanisms

Disturbances in the volume and composition of body fluids occur more frequently in infancy than at other ages. These disturbances are due partially to the high incidence of diseases that primarily endanger the body fluid homeostasis and partially to a less efficient defense mechanism. The latter can be illustrated by the observation that diets such as milk evaporated to one-fourth its original volume, or salt- and protein-free food, produce extreme changes in the osmolarity and volume of the body fluids within a very short time. After the first challenge, the osmolarity of the blood plasma in puppies rose to 526 mosmol/liter; after the second, it decreased to 232 mosmol/liter. Dehydration occurred in the first experiment, while in the second, an increase in the water content of all organs was observed (Fig. 6).

The newborn has a limited capacity to excrete a water, electrolyte, or hydrogen-ion load, a limited ability to produce a concentrated urine or to react to antidiuretic and aldosterone hormones, and a small glomerular filtration rate. In a stress situation, the functional immaturity of these performances will be fully exposed. Serial studies of these functions during growth yield so-called "maturation curves." These curves reveal that the various functions mature at quite individual rates, and that a low initial performance does not allow one to predict the later rate of maturation. Figure 7 shows that the capacity to excrete a water load, which in the newborn is only 10% of that of adults, reaches maturity within 1 month, while the concentrating mechanism matures at 3 months and the glomerular filtration rate at 12–18 months of age.

Such timetables of maturation may be of assistance to the clinician, since these data expose the weak points of the defense mechanisms in each age group.

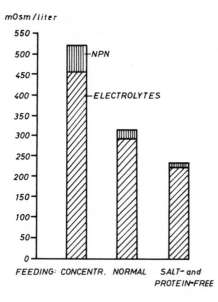

Fig. 6. Lability of osmotic regulation in plasma of 10-day-old puppies after feeding of concentrated milk, normal diet, or a salt- and protein-free diet. Adapted from Kerpel-Fronius.[58]

3.2. Water Output

3.2.1. Renal Water Expenditure

The ability of the newborn to excrete excess water or to save water when the intake is low is less efficient than in the adult. Both maximum and minimum urine volumes are dependent on the amount of solutes that must be excreted by the

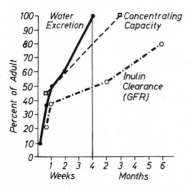

Fig. 7. Maturation of some renal functions. Data in percentages of adult values. Water excretion according to Ames[9]; GFR in the newborn from Strauss *et al.*[98]; remaining data from Kerpel-Fronius.[59]

kidneys. When the solute load is small, only a limited diuretic response to a water load is possible, while high solute loads increase the obligatory urine volume. The solute load is an inseparable determinant of renal water expenditure, and the latter is integrated with the infant's metabolic rate, nutritional state, and stage of development.

The spectacular effects of nutrition and growth on water expenditure were demonstrated in experiments by the Cambridge group.[72] Newborn puppies were fed an amount of water equivalent to the water that their normal supply of milk contains. Without the milk solids, no cell growth was possible, and the kidneys of these puppies were unable to excrete the water that was not incorporated into growing tissues.

Water retention causes dilutional hyponatremia, a condition that is not uncommon in early infancy. On the other hand, in fast-growing animals, such as the piglet or the rabbit, a high fraction of electrolytes and nitrogen from food is incorporated into the structures of growing tissues. Assuming a failure of growth without a reduction in food intake, the totality of the molecules derived from food would burden the excretory mechanisms. Under such circumstances, the osmolar load that requires excretion would be 4-fold compared with that in the normally growing animal.[28] Such an enormous solute load would either greatly increase urine volume and lead to dehydration or, if entirely retained, increase NPN by 318 mg/dl. The presentation of this problem here is, of course, hypothetical and suitable only to point out the powerful homeostatic effect of growth.

In the slowly growing human premature, the effect of the growth failure would be much smaller. Assuming a daily incorporation of 10 g isotonic fluid and of 250 mg N/kg, the failure to thrive would increase the load to be excreted by 40% when cow's milk providing an intake of 4.4 g protein/kg in 24 hr is fed. The load of solutes presented to the kidneys by feeding cow's milk is higher than the load in an equal amount of human breast milk. With an intake of 200 ml/kg per day, the solute load in the first case is 60.9 mosmol/kg, and in the second, only 14.0 mosmol/kg.[8]

The ability of the newborn to economize the renal water expenditure during hydropenia is a much-discussed question. It was axiomatic that the maximum concentration of the urine in young infants does not exceed 700 mosmol/liter, i.e., about half the value observed in adults. Low concentrating ability was attributed to a target-organ insensitivity to antidiuretic hormone (ADH) due to functional or anatomic immaturity. Newborn rats certainly do not respond to the injection of pitressin.[48]

The newborn infant, however, is able to respond to an injection of hypertonic saline with a decrease in urine flow rate and an increase in urinary osmolarity. Following the infusion of isotonic dextran, the reverse changes consistent with ADH inhibition were observed.[35] Such observations indicate that the newborn has a certain potential for ADH release and renal response. It is interesting to note, however, that despite the application of stimuli known to mobilize ADH, antidiuretic activity in blood plasma can be detected only rarely during the first 2 months of life, while it is found regularly during the 3rd month following the same stimuli.[71] With the assumption that in terms of countercurrent multiplier mechanism, the young infant may not achieve a satisfactory gradient of urea between cortex and papilla, the effect of high-protein feeding on the ability to concentrate the urine was studied by Edelman and Barnett.[33] After an initial period of feeding 9 g protein/kg per day, they observed during thirsting that a 25-day-old infant concentrated his urine up to 1139 mosmol/liter. The effect of high-protein intake on the renal concentrating mechanism was enhanced by a low-volume diet providing 115 ml water/kg per 24 hr (Fig. 8).

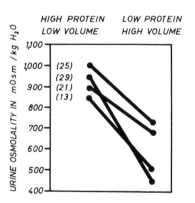

Fig. 8. Concentrating ability of young infants as influenced by various diets. High-protein diet provided 9 g and low-protein diet 2.5 g protein/kg body weight per day. High-volume diet provided 220 ml and low-volume diet 115 mg/kg body weight per day. Numbers in parentheses: age in days. Adapted from Edelman and Barnett.[33]

Experiments with young and newborn rabbits provided evidence that the cortex-to-papilla gradient of urea is markedly different between hydropenic newborn and adult animals.[36,113] The low urea content of the primary urine and of the papilla is due to the large retention of nitrogen for growth. Premature infants between 1 and 3 days of age were found, however, to be unable to increase osmolarity above 552 mosmol/liter after fasting, thirsting, or high-protein diet.[97] The author attributed this failure to achieve a higher concentration to the fact that the loop of Henle had not reached its mature length at that stage of development and thus impaired the efficient function of the countercurrent mechanism. Although it must be admitted that the osmolarity in the urine of young infants can be raised to higher levels than previously thought, it must be emphasized that this increase can be achieved only by an amount of protein intake that is never used in practice.

In conclusion, the renal concentrating mechanism in infancy is dependent on both nutritional and developmental factors.

3.2.2. Extrarenal Water Expenditure

Extrarenal water losses vary with maturity, total metabolic rate, food intake, motor activity, ambient temperature, environmental humidity, and respiratory minute volume.

Under usual environmental conditions at rest, the insensible perspiration reflects the level of the basal metabolic rate. According to the higher value of the latter in young infants, Levine et al.[67] calculated a mean value of water loss by the skin and lungs of 1 g water/kg per hr, i.e., about twice as much as in adults. Immediately after birth, however, the mean extrarenal loss was found to be considerably lower: 0.7 ml/kg per hr.[69] This finding is in accordance with data that oxygen consumption in the human infant is rather low immediately after birth, and increases during the first few days of life.[49,92] In 48 newborns of both sexes younger than 28 hr, even lower basal values of 390–460 mg/kg per hr[115] were found. Insensible perspiration was measured recently by Wu and Hodman[112] in 170 healthy preterm infants with birth weights ranging from 800 to 2000 g, who were appropriate for gestational age. They found an interesting effect of maturity: insensible perspiration increased with decreasing birth weight from a mean of 0.7 ml/kg per hr in infants weighing 1751–2000 g to 2.67 ml/kg per hr in infants weighing less than 1000 g. In the more immature newborns, insensible water expenditure decreased with postnatal age, while it increased in the 2nd week in the more mature ones, remaining stable in the 3rd week. The authors concluded that the large differences in extrarenal water expenditure in neonates of varying maturity should be taken into account in the calculation of water requirements.

Other factors to be considered are the effects of activity: long-sleeping infants lose much less water than short-sleeping ones. According to Zweymüller and Preining,[115] the value of water expenditure should be increased by a factor of at least 1.7. High-caloric feeding may double the insensible losses,[30] as may a rise in ambient temperature from 21 to 34°C.[8] Motor activity increases insensible perspiration more in infants than in adults.[51] During normal perspiration, pulmonary water loss alone accounts for about one-third of the total insensible loss, i.e., 0.35 ml/kg per hr.[50] Hyperventilation greatly increases pulmonary water loss. In a severe case of primary hyperventilation, Kerpel-Fronius[59] measured a loss of 4.5 ml/kg per hr, i.e., an increase of more than 10-fold above the basal value measured by Hooper et al.[50] Pulmonary water loss may be almost completely prevented by keeping infants in an atmosphere of 100% relative humidity.[80]

3.3. Effects of Water and Food Deprivation

The first challenge imposed in the body fluid homeostasis of the neonate, neglecting early acidosis, is the low water intake. The weight loss of 5–6% of the initial body weight during the first few days of life is accompanied by the loss of some sodium, chloride, and potassium. This loss is due in part to the correction of initial overhydration, not to real dehydration.[35,101] Cheek et al.[21] made serial measurements of the bromide space in newborn infants. On the 5th day of life, the weight loss reached its maximum of 50 g/kg, and the ECW loss was 20 ml/kg. The decrease of the ECW volume continued during the following days and reached 40 g/kg at about 10 days of age, at which time the weight loss was already restored. The comment of the authors seems to be justified in that with the acceleration of tissue growth, the loss of ECW is replaced by new tissue protein, ICW, and possibly some fat. Thus, the initial loss of some ECW and sodium appears to be part of the physiologic

maturation in that the decrease of ECW proceeds most rapidly during the first 10 days of life and continues at a slower rate during early infancy. Despite an observed weight loss of 6% during the first 3 days of life, Fisher et al.[35] found a mean urinary osmolarity of only 187 mosmol/kg. If this weight loss were due to dehydration, it would have been expected to stimulate the secretion of ADH with a subsequent rise of the urinary solute concentration. Some most interesting observations on "neonatal hyperosmolarity"[29,44] can be reconciled with the hypothesis[35,101] that weight and ECW loss in early-fed infants is often not directly related to dehydration. Furthermore, we like to speculate that the rise in osmolarity that occurs during the first few days of life may in some cases be due to a correction of an initial hypotonic expansion of the ECW compartment. This assumption is supported by the fact that the mean value of maternal osmolarity and the corresponding osmolarity in cord blood in the material of Gautier[43] were rather low (280 mosmol/liter), while the osmolarity after 48 hr rose to about 294 mosmol/liter and was in correspondence with normal values of older infants.

The range of variation of the initial plasma sodium values is 108–142 meq/liter (Fig. 9). We suggest that some cases of transplacental hyponatremia must have been included in this material[29]; 48 hr later, the mean value reaches 142 meq/liter, while at 168 hr of life, at a time when the ascending weight curve excludes dehydration, plasma sodium becomes stabilized at a mean level of 140 meq/liter, which is definitely higher than the initial value and is very close to the value found at 48 hr. Of course, it must be admitted that a number of the newborns in this series must have suffered from genuine hyper-

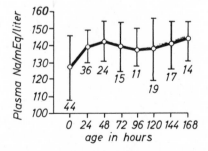

Fig. 9. Plasma sodium concentration in the normal human newborn. Means of the normal and ranges of variation (±2 S.D.) are shown. The number beneath each range is the number of estimations on that day. Adapted from Davis et al.[29]

osmolarity, probably due to low fluid intake in these cases. This hyperosmolarity might be due not only to hypernatremia, but also to an increase of other blood constituents[29] or water depletion due to low fluid intake, or both.

In term or premature infants, withholding of food and water results in a considerable increase in weight loss in excess of that noted in early-fed infants. This dehydration is accompanied by hypernatremia. After 72 hr of fasting and thirsting, term infants lose 10–15%, and premature infants lose 14–19%, of their body weight.[46] In term infants, the ensuing dehydration was not accompanied by a substantial increase in sodium excretion. In these cases, it might be surmised that a rapidly progressing dehydration has stimulated the secretion of mineralocorticoids, which affected the tubular reabsorption of sodium despite a rising plasma sodium concentration. The same effect can be observed in adults during water deprivation that leads to dehydration of comparable severity. The response of the aldosterone secretion rate to a low-sodium diet, although smaller in the first days of life, was found to be normal between 8 and 15 days of age.[104] The assumption of Visser et al.[101] that physiologic weight loss in early-fed and non-dehydrated infants will not stimulate the secretion of aldosterone during this period seems likely. Such an effect could be expected only in the case of the stimulus of a more severe water depletion. The important role of aldosterone in neonatal sodium homeostasis is supported by observations in infants with salt-losing syndrome due to adrenal hyperplasia. The onset of symptoms as late as the 2nd week of life may be due to the fact that this is the age when the sodium balance should become positive in the normal infant.[101] The delayed onset of renal salt excretion may also be associated with the initially very low GFR, which increases sharply during the first week of life.

Water depletion due to water deprivation proceeds at a faster rate in the newborn than in the adult. An apparently equal rate of loss was found only when body surface was used as a basis of comparison. Since the newborn's TBW content expressed per unit of surface area is very low compared with that of the adult, this basis of comparison leads to erroneous conclusions with regard to the magnitude of water loss (Fig. 10). Equal losses of, for instance, 5 liters referred to the body surface of the adult turn out to be of a very different order of magnitude if they are calculated

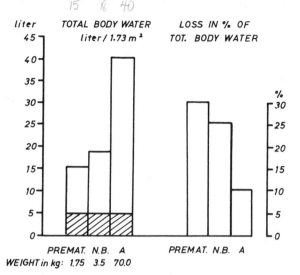

Fig. 10. Significance of equal losses expressed per unit of body surface. (NB) Newborn; (A) adult. Water loss ☐: 5 liter/1.73 m². Adapted from Kerpel-Fronius.[58]

as percentages of individual total water content. The premature would lose about one-third and the newborn more than one-fourth of his total body water, but an adult person would lose only 10% of his total water.

Dehydration due to water deprivation occurs faster in infants than in adults, since water reserves in infants are low in relation to the metabolic rate and consequently to obligatory urine volume and to dermal and pulmonary losses of water. Infants develop a serious degree of water depletion within 1½ days similar to that developed by adults in the course of 5 days of thirsting.[99]

3.4. Effects of Electrolyte Loads

In the case of a salt load, the adjustment of output and intake will require a time interval during which retention will ensue. This retention after a salt load is greater in newborn infants than in adults. Gamble et al.[42] found in older infants that the accumulation of surplus electrolytes in the body continued through almost 8 days and amounted to about 15% of the initial body content of electrolytes.

McCance and Widdowson[73] observed that under certain conditions, the relationship of sodium to water intake may be such that a hypertonic expansion of extracellular fluid ensues. According to these authors: "Hypertonic expansion of the extracellular fluid must take place under the following conditions: (1) an intake of sodium chloride greater than excreted by the kidneys; (2) an intake of water greater than that required to maintain the normal volume of extracellular fluid, but insufficient to meet the amounts being excreted by all channels and the maintenance of a normal internal concentration of electrolytes." The authors observed this type of disturbance in piglets fed evaporated cow's milk. The same observations were made in piglets and in premature infants fed a rather large addition of sodium chloride to their food. The sodium concentration of the blood plasma rose, and there was an increase in body weight. Most probably, an intracellular dehydration must accompany the rise in extracellular sodium concentration. McCance and Widdowson[75] also studied the excretion of sodium chloride and of sodium and potassium bicarbonate loads in newborn piglets. During the 40 hr of the experiment, the sodium was not excreted when administered as chloride, and sodium retention was accompanied by water retention. If the sodium was given as bicarbonate, about half the sodium was excreted; however, hypokalemia, hypochloremia, and severe alkalosis ensued. More than 90% of the potassium was excreted following potassium bicarbonate loads, together with a great amount of sodium and chloride. The observed disturbances in homeostasis were dehydration, hyperkalemia, and moderate alkalosis.

Aperia et al.[11] recently published comparative studies concerning the natriuretic response to an oral salt load in newborn term and preterm infants. The extent of the response following the loading was in all neonates merely a fraction of that found in older children. A somewhat unexpected finding was the considerably higher natriuretic response in the group of neonates of 29–35 weeks' gestational age as compared with that found in term infants. One factor of importance for the difference between the response of the very early preterm and the full-term neonates might be the anatomic development: in comparison with the adult kidney, the immature kidney has relatively larger glomerular than tubular mass. A further curious finding of the authors was that in the preterm infants, there occurs a reduction of the natriuretic response during early postnatal development. The peculiarities of the natriuretic response of the preterm infants go far in explaining the old observation of Hansen and

Smith[46] that preterm neonates lose more sodium during water deprivation than do term babies.

Potassium is readily excreted by prematures; however, a higher intake increases the plasma potassium concentration. This concentration was found to be directly correlated with the potassium intake.[56]

3.5. Effects of Diet on Body Fluid Homeostasis and on Body Composition

Feeding concentrated milk may cause hypernatremia in young infants.[18] This fact is in keeping with the low capacity of the newborn to excrete a sodium load. The renal defense response to induced acidosis is limited in the term infant and even more limited in the premature neonate.[83,89] Under the stimulus of the higher acid load generated by feeding of cow's milk, the newborn infant is capable of increasing hydrogen ion excretion above the level observed in the breast-fed term infant.[34] The percentage of hydrogen ions that was excreted by the newborn following the administration of NH_4Cl, however, was considerably less than that excreted by the adult.[47] Despite this limited ability to excrete hydrogen ions, the newborn infant is fully capable of maintaining a constant pH with a range of variation not exceeding that found in adults.

As known since the pioneer work of Yllpö,[115] however, most premature infants fail to achieve such adjustment. Kildeberg[63] distinguishes two types of acidosis in premature neonates: the early and the late form. The "early" type is a dangerous perinatal complication and a consequence of intrauterine or perinatal asphyxia. It is also associated with the respiratory distress syndrome. The "late" or benign type of acidosis develops in the second half of the first week, reaches its maximum during the second week of life, and disappears during the third or fourth week.[64,65,88] The incidence of late metabolic acidosis is high. Schain and O'Brien[91] found a blood pH below 7.29 in 33% of their infants with birth weights below 2500 g.

Acidosis results from the interaction of many factors: the acidogenic type of diet with a high protein or acid content, the slowing down of growth, a certain inadequacy in the respiratory response to acidosis, and the limited capacity of the kidneys to excrete hydrogen ions. Net acid excretion even at low levels of total CO_2 in blood is considerably lower in premature than in term or in older infants.[61,96] These observations are suggestive of a maturation of the capacity to excrete hydrogen ions. Late metabolic acidosis appears at an age when this function is small, and it disappears spontaneously with its improvement. Svenningsen and Lindquist[96] claim that at 4–6 weeks of postnatal age, when the premature would reach the normal gestational age, the hydrogen ion excretory capacity reaches the degree found in the term newborn. There is also a certain sluggishness of respiratory compensation of metabolic acidosis. Although relatively slight changes in base deficit do not elicit consistent respiratory responses, the latter increase with ever-increasing negative base excesses, reaching or approaching in prematures of 2 weeks of age the degree observed in older infants.[60]

Higher food intake during the early suckling period of animals can accelerate the chemical maturation of the tissue in terms of an earlier replacement of certain amounts of the extracellular fluid by protein and intracellular fluid.[106] In the long run, the percentage composition of the body, with the exception of the fat and calcium, cannot be changed by higher food intake.[37] Differences may be noted, however, when values are expressed on a per-animal basis. Animals fed with a high-protein and -electrolyte diet may become larger, and thus accumulate more protein and solids over a period of time, than if they were fed a diet that contained less of these constituents. These observations may also hold true for the human infant on a high-protein and -calorie intake.

4. Conclusions

Osmolar gradients between mother and fetus or fetus and amniotic fluid effectuate considerable shifts of water between fetal and maternal fluid pools. The fetus may be dehydrated or overhydrated by fluid shifts. Parallel with maternal changes such as changes in sodium concentration, the fetal fluids may become hyper- or hypotonic, causing damage to the fetus by water intoxication, hypernatremia, or dehydration. The possibility of fetal damage due to maternal magnesium deprivation must be considered, while the fetus seems to be more resistant to maternal potassium deprivation.

A diagnosis of hydramnios or oligohydramnios must alert the physician to search for disturbances of the swallowing mechanism or abnormalities of the urinary tract.

The defense mechanisms of the newborn for maintaining body fluid homeostasis are fully capable of meeting normal demands. Under stress conditions, however, the fragility of the system becomes exposed. The ability of the newborn to excrete excess water or to save water when the intake is low is less efficient than that of the adult, and salt loads are excreted at a much slower rate. These limitations may lead to hypo- or hypernatremia and to dehydration or overhydration. The limited capacity of the premature neonate to excrete hydrogen ions should discourage the use of a very high protein intake and the use of strongly acidified formulas. Although late metabolic acidosis is without clinical significance, except for flattening the weight curve, it certainly limits the margin of safety of humoral homeostasis. Furthermore, intercurrent diseases such as enteral infections aggravate the already existing acidosis.

5. References

1. ACHARYA, P. T., AND PAYNE, W. W., 1965, Blood chemistry of normal full-term infants in the first 48 hours of life, *Arch. Dis. Child.* **40:**430–441.
2. ADAMS, F. H., FUJIWARA, T., AND ROWSHAN, S., 1963, The nature and origin of the fluid in the fetal lamb lung, *J. Pediatr.* **63:**881–888.
3. ADAMS, F. H., MOSS, A. J., AND FAGAN, L., 1963, The tracheal fluid in the fetal lamb, *Biol. Neonate* **5:**151–158.
4. ADOLPH, E. F., 1967, Ontogeny of volume regulations in embryonic extracellular fluids, *Q. Rev. Biol.* **42:**1–38.
5. ALEXANDER, D. P., AND NIXON, D. A., 1961, The fetal kidney, *Br. Med. Bull.* **17:**112–117.
6. ALEXANDER, D. P., NIXON, D. A., WIDDAS, W. F., AND WOHLZOGEN, F. X., 1958, Renal function in the sheep foetus, *J. Physiol. (London)* **140:**14–22.
7. ALSTATT, L. B., 1965, Transplacental hyponatremia in the newborn infant, *J. Pediatr.* **66:**985–988.
8. AMERICAN ACADEMY OF PEDIATRICS, 1957, Report Committee on Nutrition: Water requirement in relation to osmolar load as it applies to infant feeding, *Pediatrics* **19:**339–341.
9. AMES, R. G., 1953, Urinary water excretion and neurohypophyseal function of full term and premature infants shortly after birth, *Pediatrics* **12:**272–282.
10. ANAST, C. S., 1964, Serum magnesium levels in the newborn, *Pediatrics* **33:**969–974.

11. APERIA, A., BROBERGER, O., THODENIUS, K., AND ZETTERSTRÖM, R., 1974, Developmental study of the renal response to an oral salt load in preterm infants, *Acta Paediatr. Scand.* **63**:517–524.

12. BAIN, A. D., AND SCOTT, J. S., 1960, Renal agenesis and severe urinary tract dysplasia. A review of 50 cases with particular reference to the associated anomalies, *Br. Med. J.* **1**:841–846.

13. BATTAGLIA, F., PRYSTOWSKY, H., SMISSON, C., HELLEGERS, A., AND BRUNS, P., 1960, Fetal blood studies. XIII. The effect of administration of fluids intravenously to mothers upon the concentration of water and electrolytes in plasma of human fetuses, *Pediatrics* **25**:2–10.

14. BENGTSSON, B., GENNSER, G., AND NILSSON, E., 1970, Sodium, potassium and water content of human fetal and maternal plasma and red blood cells, *Acta Paediatr. Scand.* **59**:142–148.

15. BRUNS, P. D., LINDER, R. O., DROSE, V. E., AND BATTAGLIA, F., 1963, The placental transfer of water from fetus to mother following the intravenous infusion of hypertonic mannitol to the maternal rabbit, *Amer. J. Obstet. Gynecol.* **86**:160–167.

16. BRUNS, P. D., HELLEGERS, A. E., SEEDS, A. E., JR., BEHRMAN, R. E., AND BATTAGLIA, F. C., 1964, Effects of osmotic gradients across the primate placenta upon fetal and placental water contents, *Pediatrics* **34**:407–411.

17. CAMERER, W., 1900, Die chemische Zusammensetzung des Neugeborenen, *Z. Biol. (Munich)* **xxi**:173–193.

18. CHAMBERS, T. L., AND STEEL, A. E., 1975, Concentrated milk feeds and their relation to hypernatraemic dehydration in infants, *Arch. Dis. Child.* **50**:610–615.

19. CHEEK, D. B., 1954, Observations on total body chloride in children, *Pediatrics* **14**:5–10.

20. CHEEK, D. B., 1961, Extracellular volume: Its structure and measurement and the influence of age and disease, *J. Pediatr.* **58**:103–125.

21. CHEEK, D. B., MADDISON, T. G., MALINEK, M., AND COLDBECK, J. H., 1961, Further observations on the corrected bromide space of the neonate and investigation of water and electrolyte status in infants born of diabetic mothers, *Pediatrics* **21**:861–869.

22. CLAPP, W. M., BUTTERFIELD, L. J., AND O'BRIEN, D., 1962, Body water compartments in the premature infant with special reference to the effects of the respiratory distress syndrome and of maternal diabetes and toxemia, *Pediatrics* **29**:883–889.

23. CORSA, L., JR., GRIBETZ, D., COOK, C. D., AND TALBOT, N. B., 1956, Total body exchangeable water, sodium, potassium in "hospital normal" infants and children, *Pediatrics* **17**:184–191.

24. CORSA, L., JR., OLNAY, J. M., STEENBURG, R. N., BALL, M. R., AND MOORE, I. D., 1950, The measurement of exchangeable potassium in man by isotope dilution, *J. Clin. Invest.* **29**:1280–1295.

25. CRAWFORD, J. S., 1965, Maternal and cord blood at delivery. IV. Glucose, sodium, potassium, calcium and chloride. *Biol. Neonate* **8**:222–237.

26. DANCIS, J., AND SPRINGER, D., 1970, Fetal homeostasis in maternal malnutrition: Potassium and sodium deficiency, *Pediatr. Res.* **4**:345–351.

27. DANCIS, J., SPRINGER, D., AND COHLEN, S. Q., 1971, Fetal homeostasis in maternal malnutrition. II. Magnesium deprivation, *Pediatr. Res.* **5**:131–136.

28. DAVIES, J. S., WIDDOWSON, E. M., AND McCANCE, R. A., 1964, The intake of milk and the retention of its constituents while the newborn rabbit doubles its weight, *Br. J. Nutr.* **18**:385–392.

29. DAVIS, J. A., HARVEY, D. R., AND STEVENS, J. F., 1966, Osmolality as a measure of dehydration in the neonatal period, *Arch. Dis. Child.* **41**:448–450.

30. DE RUDDER, B., 1928, Die Perspiratio insensibilis beim Säugling. II. Ihre Abhängigkeit von der Calorienzufuhr, *Z. Kinderheilkd.* **46**:384–390.

31. DUNNING, M. F., STEELE, J. M., AND BERGEN, A. Y., 1951, The measurement of total body chloride, *Proc. Soc. Exp. Biol. Med.* **77**:854–858.

32. ECONOMOU-MAVROU, C., AND McCANCE, R. A., 1958, Calcium, magnesium and phosphorus in foetal tissues, *Biochem. J.* **68**:573–580.

33. EDELMAN, C. M., JR., AND BARNETT, H. L., 1960, Role of the kidney in water metabolism in young infants, *J. Pediatr.* **56**:154–179.

34. FINK, C. W., AND CHEEK, D. B., 1960, The corrected bromide space (extracellular volume) in the newborn, *Pediatrics* **26**:397–401.

35. FISHER, D. A., *et al.*, 1963, Control of water balance in the newborn, *Amer. J. Dis. Child.* **106**:137–146.

36. FLEISHAKER, G. H., GESINK, O. J., AND McCRORY, W. W., 1960, Effect of age on distribution of urea and electrolyte in kidneys of young rabbits, *Amer. J. Dis. Child.* **100**:558.

37. FORBES, G. B., 1962, Methods for determining composition of the human body: With a note on the effect of diet on body composition, *Pediatrics* **29**:477–494.

38. FORBES, G. B., AND LEWIS, A. M., 1956, Total sodium, potassium and chloride in adult man, *J. Clin. Invest.* **35**:596–600.

39. FORBES, G. B., MIZNER, G. L., AND LEWIS, A., 1957, Effect of age on radiosodium exchange in bone (rat), *Amer. J. Physiol.* **190**:152–156.

40. FRIIS-HANSEN, B., 1961, Body water compartments in children: Changes during growth and related changes in body composition, *Pediatrics* **28**:169–181.

41. FRIIS-HANSEN, B., 1971, Body composition during growth. *In vivo* measurements and biochemical data correlated to differential anatomical growth, *Pediatrics* **47**:264–274.

42. GAMBLE, J. L., *et al.*, 1951, Effects of large loads of electrolytes, *Pediatrics* **7**:305–320.

43. GAUTIER, E., 1964, Neonatal hyperosmolarity, an instance of unresponsiveness to antidiuretic hormone,

in: *The Adaptation of the Newborn Infant to Extra-uterine Life* (J. H. P. Jonxis, H. K. A. Visser, and J. A. Troelstra, eds.), pp. 83–94, H. E. Stenfert Kroese, Leiden, South Holland.

44. GILLIBRAND, P. N., 1969, Changes in the electrolyte, urea and osmolality of the amniotic fluid with advancing pregnancy, *J. Obstet. Gynecol. Br. Commonw.* **76**:898–905.

45. GRAHAM, B. D., *et al.*, 1951, Development of neonatal electrolyte homeostasis, *Pediatrics* **8**:68–78.

46. HANSEN, J. D. L., AND SMITH, C. A., 1953, Effects of withholding fluid intake in immediate postnatal period, *Pediatrics* **12**:99–113.

47. HATEMI, N., AND McCANCE, R. A., 1961, Renal aspects of acid–base control in the newly born. III. Response to acidifying drugs, *Acta Paediatr. Scand.* **50**:603–616.

48. HELLER, H., AND LEDERIS, K., 1959, Maturation of the hypothalamoneurohypophysial system, *J. Physiol. (London)* **147**:299–314.

49. HILL, J., AND RAHIMTULLA, K. A., 1965, Heat balance and the metabolic rate of newborn babies in relation to environmental temperature; and the effect of age and of weight on basal metabolic rate, *J. Physiol. (London)* **180**:239–265.

50. HOOPER, J. M. D., EVANS, I. W. Y., AND STAPLETON, T., 1954, Resting pulmonary water loss in the new-born infant, *Pediatrics* **13**:206–210.

51. HUNGERLAND, H., 1954, Wasserhaushalt, in: *Biologische Daten für den Kinderarzt*, 2nd Ed. (J. Brock, ed.), pp. 480–542, Springer-Verlag, Berlin.

52. ILTER, O., EZER, G., HATEMI, N., AND TÜMAY, S. B., 1973, Le magnesium sérique au cours des ictères du nouveau-né, *Pediatrie* **28**:297–301.

53. IOB, V., AND SWANSON, W. W., 1934, Mineral growth of the human fetus, *Amer. J. Dis. Child.* **47**:302–306.

54. JELINEK, J., 1961, Changes in water and electrolyte distribution in the body of rats during development, in: *The Development of Homeostasis*, pp. 267–278, Publishing House of the Czechoslovak Academy of Sciences, Prague.

55. JUKARAINEN, E., 1972, Plasma magnesium in the newborn, *Acta Paediatr. Scand.* **61**:489, 490.

56. KEITEL, H. G., 1959, The concentration of potassium in the plasma, *Amer. J. Dis. Child.* **97**:583–590.

57. KERPEL-FRONIUS, E., 1937, Über die Besonderheiten der Salz- und Wasserverteilung im Säuglingskörper, *Z. Kinderheilkd.* **58**:726–738.

58. KERPEL-FRONIUS, E., 1958, Clinical consequences of the water and electrolyte metabolism peculiar to infancy, in: *Ciba Found. Coll. on Aging* Vol. 4 (G. E. W. Wolstenholme and M. O'Connor, eds.), Churchill, London.

59. KERPEL-FRONIUS, E., 1959, *Pathologie und Klinik des Salz- und Wasserhaushaltes*, Publishing House, Hungarian Academy of Sciences, Budapest.

60. KERPEL-FRONIUS, E., AND HEIM, T., 1964, Efficiency of respiratory compensation for metabolic acidosis in premature infants, *Biol. Neonate* **7**:203–213.

61. KERPEL-FRONIUS, E., HEIM, T., AND SULYOK, E., 1970, The development of the renal acidifying processes and their relation to acidosis in low-birth-weight infants, *Biol. Neonate* **15**:267–278.

62. KERPEL-FRONIUS, E., NAGY, L., AND MAGYARKA, B., 1964, Volume and composition of fluid compartments in peripheral and cardiac muscles of animals born at different stages of maturity, *Biol. Neonate* **6**:177–196.

63. KILDEBERG, P., 1964, Disturbances of hydrogen ion balance occurring in premature infants. II. Late metabolic acidosis, *Acta, Paediatr. Scand.* **53**:517–526.

64. KILDEBERG, P., 1968, *Clinical Acid–Base Physiology. Studies in Neonates, Infants, and Young Children*, Munksgaard, Copenhagen.

65. ENGEL, K., AND WINTERS, R. W., 1969, Balance of net acid in growing infants, *Acta Paediatr. Scand.* **58**:321–329.

66. KUBLI, F., 1966, *Fetale Gefahrenzustände und ihre Diagnose*, Georg Thieme, Stuttgart.

67. LEVINE, S. Z., KELLY, M., AND WILSON, J. R., 1930, Insensible perspiration in infancy and childhood. II. Proposed standards for infants, *Amer. J. Dis. Child.* **39**:917–929.

68. LIND, T., KENDALL, A., AND HYTTEN, F. E., 1972, The role of the fetus in the formation of amniotic fluid, *J. Obstet. Gynecol. Br. Commonw.* **79**:289–298.

69. LITTLE, J. A., BRODSZKY, W. A., AND GREATHOUSE, R., 1955, The insensible weight loss of newborns and of older infants, *Amer. J. Dis. Child.* **90**:630, 631.

70. MacGILLIVRAY, I., AND BUCHANAN, T. J., 1958, Total exchangeable sodium and potassium in non-pregnant women and in normal and preeclamptic pregnancy, *Lancet* **2**:1090–1093.

71. MARTINEK, J., JANOVSKY, M., AND STANINCOVA, V., 1963, Concentration mechanism in young infants, *Excerpta Med. Int. Congr. Ser. No. 78*, pp. 647–652.

72. McCANCE, R. A., 1961, Mineral metabolism of the fetus and the newborn, *Br. Med. Bull.* **17**:132–136.

73. McCANCE, R. A., AND WIDDOWSON, E. M., 1957, Hypertonic expansion of the extracellular fluids, *Acta Paediatr. Scand.* **46**:337–353.

74. McCANCE, R. A., AND WIDDOWSON, E. M., 1960, Renal aspects of acid–base control in the newly born. I. Natural development, *Acta Paediatr. Scand.* **49**:409–414.

75. McCANCE, R. A., AND WIDDOWSON, E. M., 1963, The effect of administering sodium chloride, sodium bicarbonate, and potassium bicarbonate to newly-born piglets, *J. Physiol. (London)* **165**:569–574.

76. MAUER, S. M., DOBRIN, R. S., AND VERNIER, R. L., 1974, Unilateral and bilateral renal agenesis in mono-amniotic twins, *J. Pediatr.* **84**:236–238.

77. MESCHIA, G. F. C., BATTAGLIA, F., AND BARRON, D. H., 1957, A comparison of the freezing points of

fetal and maternal plasmas of sheep and goat, *Q. J. Exp. Physiol.* **42**:163–170.

78. MOYA, F., APGAR, V., ST. JAMES, L., AND BERRIEN, C., 1960, Hydramnios and congenital anomalies, *J. Amer. Med. Assoc.* **173**:1552–1556.

79. NICOLOPOULOS, D. A., AND SMITH, C. A., 1961, Metabolic aspects of idiopathic respiratory distress (hyaline membrane syndrome) in newborn infants, *Pediatrics* **28**:206–222.

80. O'BRIEN, D., HANSEN, J. D. L., AND SMITH, C. A., 1954, Effect of supersaturated atmospheres on insensible water loss in the newborn infant, *Pediatrics* **13**:126–132.

81. OLIVER, F. K., JR., DENNIS, J. A., AND BATES, G. D., 1961, Serial blood–gas tensions and acid–base balance during the first hour of life in human infants, *Acta Paediatr. Scand.* **50**:346–360.

82. PARKER, H. W., OLESEN, K. H., McMURREY, J., AND FRIIS-HANSEN, B., 1958, Body water compartments throughout the life span, in: *CIBA Foundation Colloquia on Aging* (G. E. W. Wolstenholme and U. O'Connor, eds.), Vol. 4, Churchill, London.

83. PEONIDES, A., LEVIN, B., AND YOUNG, W. F., 1965, The renal excretion of hydrogen ions in infants and children, *Arch. Dis. Child.* **40**:33–39.

84. PERHEENTUPA, J., HOLMBERG, C., AND LAUMIALEN, K., 1974, Congenital chloride diarrhea. I. Clinical experience with 17 cases, *Acta Paediatr. Scand.* **63**:665, 666.

85. PHILLIPS, G. D., AND SUNDARAM, S. K., 1966, Sodium depletion of pregnant ewes and its effect on foetuses and foetal fluids, *J. Physiol. (London)* **184**:889–897.

86. PINCUS, J. G., GITTLEMAN, I. F., SAITO, M., AND SOBEL, A. E., 1956, A study of the plasma values of sodium, potassium, chloride, CO_2-tension, sugar, urea, the protein base-binding power, pH and hematocrit in prematures on the first day of life, *Pediatrics* **18**:39–49.

87. PLENTL, A. A., 1959, The dynamics of amniotic fluid, *Ann. N. Y. Acad. Sci.* **75**:746–761.

88. RANLOW, P., AND SIGGAARD-ANDERSEN, O., 1965, Late metabolic acidosis in premature infants, *Acta Paediatr. Scand.* **54**:531–540.

89. RUBEN, B. L., CALCAGNO, P. L., RUBIN, M. I., AND WEINTRAUB, D. H., 1956, Renal defense response to induced acidosis in premature infants: Ammonia production and titratable acid excretion, *Amer. J. Dis. Child.* **92**:513.

90. SALING, E., 1966, *Das Kind in der Geburtshilfe,* Georg Thieme, Stuttgart.

91. SCHAIN, R. J., AND O'BRIEN, K. O., 1957, Longitudinal studies of acid–base status in infants with low birth weight, *J. Pediatr.* **70**:885–890.

92. SCOPES, J. W., 1966, Metabolic rate and temperature in the human baby, *Br. Med. Bull.* **22**:88–91.

93. SCOTT, J. S., AND WILSON, L. K., 1957, Hydramnios as an early sign of oesophageal atresia, *Lanc* **2**:569–572.

94. SEEDS, A. E., JR., 1965, Water metabolism of th fetus, *Amer. J. Obstet. Gynecol.* **92**:727–745.

95. SERRANO, C. V., TALBERT, L. M., AND WELT, L. G 1964, Potassium deficiency in the pregnant dog *J. Clin. Invest.* **43**:27–31.

96. SVENNINGSEN, N. W., AND LINDQUIST, B., 197 Postnatal development of renal hydrogen io excretion capacity in relation to age and protei intake, *Acta Paediatr. Scand.* **63**:721–731.

97. STRAUSS, J., 1960, Urinary concentration in newbor premature infants, *Amer. J. Dis. Child.* **100**:635.

98. STRAUSS, J., ADAMSONS, K., JR., AND JAMES, L. S 1965, Renal function of normal full-term infants i the first hours of extrauterine life. I. Infants delivere naturally and given a placental transfusion, *Amer. J Obstet. Gynecol.* **91**:286–290.

99. TALBOT, N. B., AND RICHIE, R., 1958, The effect o age on the body's tolerance for fasting, thirsting an for overloading with water and certain electrolytes in: *CIBA Foundation Colloquia on Aging* (G. E. W Wolstenholme and U. O'Connor, eds.), Vol. 4 pp. 139–149, Churchill, London.

100. TSANG, R. C., 1972, Neonatal magnesium dis turbances, *Amer. J. Dis. Child.* **124**:282–293.

101. VISSER, H. K. A., DEGENHART, H. J., COST, W. S. AND CROUGHS, W., 1964, Adrenocortical contro of renal sodium and potassium excretion in the new born period, in: *Nutricia Symposium on The Adapta tion of the Newborn Infant to Extra-uterine Lif* (J. H. P. Jonxis, H. K. A. Visser, and J. A. Troelstra eds.), pp. 45–123, H. E. Stenfert Kroese, Leiden South Holland.

102. WALLACE, W. W., WEIL, W. B., AND TAYLOR, A. 1958, Effect of variable protein and mineral intak upon the body composition of the growing animal in: *Ciba Found. Colloq. on Aging* (G. E. W Wolstenholme and M. O'Connor, eds.), Vol. 4 Churchill, London.

103. WANG, J., ROUFA, A., MOORE, T. J., TOWELL H. M. M., AND PIERSON, R. N., JR., 1973, Body composition studies in the human fetus after intra amniotic injection of hypertonic saline, *Amer. J Obstet. Gynecol.* **117**:57–63.

104. WELDON, V. V., KOWALSKI, A., AND MIGEON, C. J. 1967, Aldosterone secretion rates in normal subject from infancy to adulthood, *Pediatrics* **39**:713–723.

105. WESTIN, B., KAISER, G. H., LIND, J., NYBERG, R. AND TEGER-NILSSON, A. C., 1959, Some constituent of umbilical venous blood of previable fetuses *Acta Paediatr. Scand.* **48**:609–613.

106. WIDDOWSON, E. M., 1958, Discussion, in: *CIBA Foundation Colloquia on Aging* (G. E. W. Wolstenholme and M. O'Connor, eds.), Vol. 4, p. 136 Churchill, London.

107. WIDDOWSON, E. M., AND DICKERSON, J. W. T., 1960,

The effect of growth and function on the chemical composition of soft tissues, *Biochem. J.* **77**:30–43.

08. WIDDOWSON, E. M., AND DICKERSON, J. W. T., 1964, Chemical composition of the body, in: *Mineral Metabolism* (C. F. Connor and F. Bronner, eds.), Vol. 2, Part A, Academic Press, New York and London.

09. WIDDOWSON, E. M., AND MCCANCE, R. A., 1956, The effect of development on the composition of the serum and extracellular fluid, *Clin. Sci.* **15**:361–371.

10. WLADIMIROFF, J. W., AND CAMPBELL, S., 1974, Fetal urine production rates in normal and complicated pregnancies, *Lancet* **1**:151–154.

11. WRIGHT, G. H., AND NIXON, D. A., 1961, Absorption of amniotic fluid in the gut of foetal sheep, *Nature (London)* **190**:816.

112. WU, P. Y. K., AND HODMAN, J. E., 1974, Insensible water loss in preterm infants: Changes with postnatal development and non-ionizing radiant energy, *Pediatrics* **54**:704–712.

113. YAFFE, S. J., AND ANDERS, T. F., 1960, Renal solute content in young rabbits, *Amer. J. Dis. Child.* **100**:558–559.

114. YLLPÖ, A., 1916, Neugeborene, Hunger und Intoxicationsacidosis in ihren Beziehungen zueinander, *Z. Kinderheilkd.* **14**:268.

115. ZWEYMÜLLER, E., AND PREINING, O., 1970, The insensible water loss of the newborn infant, *Acta Paediatr. Scand. Suppl.* **205**:1–29.

CHAPTER 27

The Kidney

Leonard I. Kleinman

1. Introduction

The primary function of the mammalian kidney is to maintain water and electrolyte homeostasis. The kidney carries out this function by selectively excreting or retaining water and solutes as the condition dictates. In the fetus, body water and electrolyte balance are maintained largely by the placenta, so that renal maturation *in utero* is geared primarily to prepare the kidney for its extrauterine role. As a result, the functional capabilities of the fetal kidney are much greater than its normal functional requirements. Indeed, fetuses without functioning kidneys often manifest no water and electrolyte abnormalities. The major responsibility for water and electrolyte homeostasis is suddenly thrust upon the perinatal kidney as soon as the infant is born. Yet, as we shall see in subsequent portions of this chapter, renal maturation does not suddenly accelerate after the infant is born. Indeed, renal anatomic maturation is essentially complete in the human at the time of birth.

The physiologic capability of the perinatal kidney during a given stage of maturation is not merely a function of the state of its anatomic maturity at that period. Rather, there is a complex interrelationship between intrinsic renal factors (anatomic, chemical, and physical) and extrinsic factors (hemodynamic and environmental) that regulate the function of the kidney during any stage of development. This interrelationship will be stressed in this chapter. Emphasis will be placed on physiologic mechanisms that govern renal function and the relevance of these mechanisms to the particular renal function and developmental stage of the perinatal animal under discussion.

2. Technical Problems of Studying Perinatal Renal Function

Although the basic techniques used in studying renal function are the same for the perinatal animal as they are for the adult, the very nature of the perinatal animal introduces problems that are not encountered in the adult. The most important of these problems is, of course, the inaccessibility of the fetus.

Studies of renal function dealing directly with the human fetus have been semiquantitative at best, since they have by necessity been limited to analyses of bladder urine obtained from aborted fetuses. Studies utilizing nonhuman fetuses have been per-

Leonard I. Kleinman · Departments of Pediatrics, Physiology, and Environmental Health, University of Cincinnati College of Medicine, Cincinnati, Ohio 45229

formed with acute or chronic *in situ* preparations[20,27,48,100,102] or in acute experiments with the fetuses exteriorized.[2,4,110] The major advantage of the *in situ* technique is that results are more likely to represent the true physiologic condition of the fetus, since there has been minimal interference with its natural intrauterine environment. In addition, the same fetus can be utilized many times to study maturation of renal function in individual animals. The advantage of the exteriorization technique is that more sophisticated studies may be performed (exteriorization of the fetus permits placement of catheters in almost any vessel desired). The limitations of exteriorization of the fetus lie in its unphysiologic state.

Problems also arise in studying renal function of postnatal animals. In humans, there is the ethical dilemma of subjecting babies to certain risks that are necessitated by the experimental protocol. Studies in newborn infants, especially when the rights of experimental subjects have been rigorously adhered to, have been largely descriptive rather than mechanistic. The small size of the newborn baby, or the newborn animal for that matter, also limits somewhat the degree to which certain renal function studies can be carried out.

The difficulties involved in the use of human subjects in perinatal renal research necessitates reliance on data gathered from animal studies for understanding renal physiologic maturation. Results obtained from animal model experimentation must be interpreted with caution, however, because not only are there the usual difficulties of extrapolating animal data to the human situation, but also there is the added complication that renal maturation, both anatomic and physiologic, has different patterns in different species.

That the perinatal animal is continuously growing creates the special problem of normalizing the particular function that is being studied. For example, does the increase in glomerular filtration rate as the animal matures reflect merely growth of the whole animal, or is there a *real* change in glomerular function? Should glomerular filtration rate, or any renal function for that matter, be normalized to body weight, body surface area, kidney weight, total body water, or extracellular body water? Different investigators studying perinatal renal function have used one or another of these factors to normalize their data. This difference makes it difficult for a reviewer to compare the results from one laboratory with those from another.

3. Anatomic Maturation of the Mammalian Kidney

This chapter will give only a brief summary of the anatomic maturation of the mammalian kidney merely sufficient for an understanding of the discussion of the physiology of the perinatal kidney. Readers who desire a more detailed knowledge of renal anatomic maturation are referred to standard textbooks of embryology and to a recent and excellent monograph on developmental nephrology.[85]

The mammalian kidney develops through three successive but overlapping stages: the pronephros, the mesonephros, and the metanephros. The functional significance of the three stages of renal development is not the same in all species. The mesonephros, for example, is a functional organ in the cow, sheep, pig, cat, and rabbit. In rodent and man, the mesonephros appears early and then degenerates rapidly, developing little, if any, functional capabilities.

The definitive mammalian kidney, the metanephros, develops from the union of the cranial part of the ureteral bud with the metanephric blastema. The ureteral bud arises from an offshoot of the mesonephric duct and ultimately forms the ureter, renal pelves, major and minor calyces, and collecting ducts. The nephroblastic cells of the metanephric blastema, on contact with the ureteral bud, eventually develop into the glomerulus, proximal convoluted tubule, loop of Henle, and distal convoluted tubule.

In those animals with a functional allantoic sac (rabbit, pig, sheep), the fetal urine first passes into the allantois and later (during gestation) into the amniotic sac. In rodent and man, the urine always passes into the amnion.

In the human fetus, by the 5th month of gestation, the demarcation of the renal cortex and medulla is apparent. At this time, the kidney contains only one-third of its final number of nephrons. Prior to the 5th month of gestation, the major renal growth is of the inner medullary section containing primarily collecting ducts. From the 5th to the 9th months, major renal growth is cortical and outer medullary, with formation of new nephrons.

The first nephrons to develop are those the glomeruli of which will be found in the juxtamedullary region of the mature kidney. At 22 weeks gestation, all the glomeruli in the human fetus are juxtamedullary glomeruli. Since nephron develop ment starts in the juxtamedullary region and progresses toward the capsule, at any time during development, there is a greater percentage of mature nephrons in the juxtamedullary region than in the outer cortex.

In the human fetus, nephrogenesis ceases at about 36 weeks' gestation, although some of the more recently formed nephrons manifest anatomic immaturity. This anatomic immaturity disappears within several weeks, however, and renal development from this stage on consists solely of nephron growth.[75] Nephrogenesis does not cease prenatally in all mammalian species. In the rat,[10] dog,[59,69] and pig,[130] which are animals that are used frequently in perinatal renal function studies, new nephrons continue to be formed for some weeks after birth, although in the guinea pig, nephrogenesis is complete before the animal is born.[113]

The size of all parts of the nephron continues to increase as the infant matures. The rate of growth of the tubules, however, especially that of the proximal tubules, is much greater than that of the glomerulus. In humans at birth, the ratio of glomerular surface area to proximal tubular volume is about 27. This ratio rapidly falls to 8 at 6 months of age, and then gradually approaches the adult level of 3 during late adolescence.[42] This anatomic glomerular preponderance suggests that the neonate may have greater potential for glomerular than for tubular function, assuming that glomerular surface area can be equated with functional glomerular potential and proximal tubular volume with functional tubular potential. As will be discussed in subsequent sections of this chapter, however, there is some question concerning the functional relevance of the anatomic glomerular preponderance in the perinatal kidney.

Although the mean ratio of glomerular surface area to proximal tubular volume is 27 in the neonate and 3 in the adult, not all nephrons in the respective age groups have identical ratios. The range of ratios for the neonate is from 4.7 to 97.5, and that for the adult from 1.9 to 6.6.[42] The greater variability of the ratio in the newborn signifies a greater anatomic heterogeneity of glomerular–tubular relationships during this period of development. The physiologic significance of this large degree of nephron heterogeneity will be discussed in subsequent sections of this chapter.

Maturation of glomeruli and proximal tubules is not the same in all sections of the kidney. At birth, the glomeruli in the outer cortex are smaller than in the inner cortex, a finding that is not surprising, since the outer cortical glomeruli are younger. In the adult, glomeruli are the same throughout the cortex. In the newborn, proximal tubules are shorter in the outer cortex than in the inner cortex. By the time the human reaches adulthood, however, the length of outer cortical proximal tubules exceeds that of tubules from the inner cortex.

In addition to the growth of the glomeruli and proximal tubules, there is an increase in the length of Henle's loop during maturation. In the human kidney at birth, 20% of the loops of Henle are too short to reach into the medulla. Even though the total thickness of the cortex is increasing, due largely to growth of glomeruli and proximal tubules, the loops of Henle are growing at an even more rapid rate, so that by adulthood, only 1 or 2% of all loops of Henle are too short to reach into the medulla.[41] The physiologic significance of the length of Henle's loop is discussed in Section 8.

4. Renal Hemodynamics in the Perinatal Kidney

In adult man, about 20–25% of the cardiac output goes to the kidneys, even though the kidneys constitute less than $\frac{1}{2}$% of the total body weight. This large flow per unit organ weight, the largest of any organ in the body, is necessary because the kidney receives blood, not merely for its nutrient and oxygen supply as do all other organs, but also in order to alter the water and electrolyte content of the blood.

Renal blood flow can be measured directly by means of flow meters attached to the renal artery or indirectly by utilizing radioactive microspheres or measuring the clearance of p-aminohippurate (PAH).

When microspheres (15–50 μm) are injected into the circulation, they are trapped in the capillaries in proportion to the blood flowing to that particular area. If cardiac output is measured and the ratio of microspheres trapped in the kidney to that trapped in the rest of the body is then determined (radioactive labeling facilitates the determination), the blood flow to the kidney can be calculated by multiplying this ratio by the cardiac output. The limitations of this technique lie in the necessity for accurate measurements of cardiac output, good mixing of the microspheres within the circulation, absence of plasma skimming, and total trapping by all organs of the body. Unfortunately, not all these conditions have been verified in all the studies utilizing the microsphere technique to measure renal blood flow in perinatal animals. The microsphere technique can also be used to measure distribution of blood flow within an organ, and indeed this technique has been used to measure intrarenal blood flow distribution in both perinatal and adult animals.

The most commonly used technique to measure renal blood flow is to equate renal plasma flow with the clearance of PAH. The basis for this equation is the Fick principle, which implies that plasma flow to the kidney is equal to the amount of any substance (as long as it is not metabolized or synthesized by the kidney) excreted into the urine divided by the concentration difference of that substance between renal artery and vein plasma. In algebraic form, $\text{RPF} = (U_x \cdot \dot{V})/(P_{a_x} - P_{v_x})$, where RPF is the renal plasma flow, U_x is the urinary concentration of substance x, $\dot{V}$ is the urine flow rate, and P_{a_x} and P_{v_x} are the concentrations of x in the renal artery and vein plasma, respectively. In adult animals, PAH is almost completely (90%) extracted as it passes through the kidney, so that the term P_{v_x} may be neglected. In that case $\text{RPF} = U_{\text{PAH}} \dot{V}/P_{a\text{PAH}}$ (or $U_{\text{PAH}} \dot{V}/0.9 \, P_{a\text{PAH}}$ if P_{v_x} is calculated as $0.1 \, P_{a_x}$, i.e., 90% extraction). The term $U_x \dot{V}/P_x$ is known as the renal clearance of x, or C_x, so that $\text{RPF} = C_{\text{PAH}}$ (or more accurately $C_{\text{PAH}}/0.9$). The concentration of PAH in the renal artery is essentially the same as it is in any other blood vessel of the body (except for the renal vein), so that $P_{a\text{PAH}}$ may be obtained from a peripheral vein sample.

The use of PAH clearance avoids the technical difficulties of sampling from the renal vein, which must be done if the complete Fick principle formula is to be used. If PAH extraction is much less than 90% and is also variable, however, renal PAH clearance will give an inaccurate estimate of renal plasma flow, and the complete Fick principle formula must be used. For example, if C_{PAH} is 2 ml/min in each of two animals, but in one animal PAH extraction is 0.95 and in the other it is 0.50, then the true renal plasma flow of the first animal will be 2.1 ml/min and that of the second, 4 ml/min.

The newborn human,[28] rat,[57] and dog[68] have renal PAH extractions that are variable and that quantitatively are considerably lower than 0.9. This circumstance should negate the use of renal PAH clearance as an indicator of renal blood flow in the perinatal animal unless simultaneous renal PAH extractions are measured. Unfortunately, many of the earlier studies on perinatal renal function used PAH clearance as the indicator of renal plasma flow, and interpretation of the results of these studies must be made in light of the present knowledge of the incomplete extraction of PAH.

Results of various studies using either the PAH clearance technique (with or without correction for renal PAH extraction), the electromagnetic flow meter technique, or the radioactive microsphere technique have all indicated that renal blood flow is lower in the perinatal animal than in the adult of that species on an absolute basis, and in most cases even if values were normalized to body or kidney weight.[6,12,18,28,49,67,131] Moreover, the fraction of the cardiac output going to the kidney is usually lower in the perinatal animal than in the adult. In the fetus, of course, the largest part of the cardiac output goes to the placenta (about 40–50% of the combined right and left heart output). In the baboon fetus, for example, less than 5% of the combined cardiac output goes to the kidney, a fraction less than that going to the GI tract.[92] The postnatal distribution of cardiac output varies with the species studied. In the rat, the kidney receive 3.6% of the cardiac output at birth and 16.6% at maturity.[99] In the monkey, there is no difference between the newborn and adult in the renal fraction of cardiac output.[18]

Although renal blood flow is unquestionably low in the perinatal animal, it is difficult to describe the maturational patterns of perinatal renal blood flow, particularly in the fetus, because of the unreliability of the techniques used in the various studies. For example, some studies have utilized the exteriorized lamb fetus preparation, which in itself must have affected renal hemodynamics. Moreover, most studies used PAH clearance without correction for PAH extraction as the indicator of renal blood flow. The difficulties of interpreting maturational patterns of renal blood flow in the perinatal animal are further exemplified by conflicting reports of apparently well-designed and -executed experiments using the same animal species. One group of investigators reported that in newborn rats there was no maturational increase in renal blood flow (measured by PAH clearance with correction for PAH extraction) normalized to kidney weight.[57] Another group reported that such an increase did exist in the rat when they measured renal blood flow with the microsphere technique.[6]

Renal blood flow is directly proportional to arterial blood pressure and inversely proportional to renal vascular resistance. Theoretically, then, the lower renal blood flow found in the perinatal animal could be due to a low blood pressure or a high renal vascular resistance or both. There is some experimental evidence that low arterial blood pressure contributes to the low renal blood flow in the perinatal animal. First, blood pressure during the perinatal period is significantly below that of the adult.[88] In addition, there is good correlation between maturation of mean arterial blood pressure and that of RPF.[67] Finally, when blood pressure is raised acutely in the newborn dog, renal blood flow increases.[67]

Alternatively, the low renal blood flow in the perinatal animal could be due to a high renal vascular resistance. Renal vascular resistance, corrected for kidney or body weight, has been found to be elevated in the newborn pig,[49] guinea pig,[114] dog,[63] and lamb.[12] Renal vascular resistance, however, is not elevated in the newborn of all species under all conditions. In the newborn dog undergoing mannitol diuresis, renal blood flow is lower than in the adult, although renal vascular resistance is the same.[67] In the rhesus monkey, renal vascular resistance is slightly *lower* in the neonate than it is in the adult.[18]

Not only does total renal blood flow in the perinatal animal differ from that in adults, but it is also differently distributed in the kidney. In the adult, most of the blood flowing through the kidney is distributed to superficial nephrons. In the kidney of perinatal animals, a smaller fraction of the total blood flow is distributed to the superficial nephrons than it is in that of the adult.[62,69,91] This difference is, of course, not surprising, since the more superficial nephrons are more immature and presumably require less blood flow. Since perfusion pressure is essentially the same in all regions of the kidney, the lower flow to the superficial nephrons indicates a higher renal vascular resistance in this region compared with deeper layers.

In the newborn dog during the first 2 weeks of life, blood flow per unit regional kidney weight remains approximately constant to deeper nephrons, while it increases to more superficially situated nephrons.[69] Thus, during this period, the ratio of blood flow to inner nephrons divided by blood flow to outer nephrons decreases (Fig. 1). After 2 weeks of age, blood flow to inner and outer nephrons increases proportionately, so that the flow distribution ratio thereafter remains relatively constant. Since the arterial blood pressure is rising during the 2-week period of the falling flow-distribution ratio, the constancy of blood flow to inner nephrons indicates that renal vascular resistance is rising there. Conversely, the vascular resistance to the outer nephrons is gradually falling as these nephrons are becoming anatomically more mature.

Thus, there is a complicated interplay of renal pressure and resistances during kidney maturation. Fortunately, this interplay provides blood to those nephrons that are most mature and presumably those that function best. As new nephrons mature, intrarenal vascular resistances are altered so that more

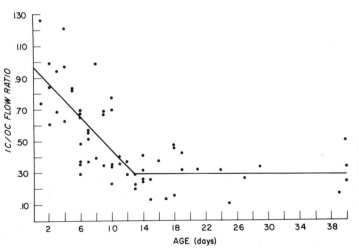

Fig. 1. Intrarenal blood flow distribution in newborn dogs. IC/OC flow ratio: Ratio of inner cortical blood flow per gram inner cortical tissue to outer cortical blood flow per gram outer cortical tissue. The ratio declines during the first 2 weeks of life, and then remains constant. Reproduced from Kleinman and Reuter.[69]

blood can be distributed to these nephrons. This process results in a reasonable degree of nephron–perfusion balance throughout the renal maturational period. Factors that control and regulate the intrarenal distribution of vascular resistance still need to be studied. There is enhanced activity of the renin–angiotensin system during the perinatal period, [47,71,93,94,123] and this increased activity may contribute to the generally high renal vascular resistance usually found in the perinatal animal. Conceivably, a changing intrarenal pattern of the synthesis and release of renin during the perinatal period may account for the changing intrarenal distribution of vascular resistances. Alternatively, renal vascular response to catecholamine release, through either humoral or neural mechanisms, may be responsible for the changing pattern of renal hemodynamics in the perinatal animal. In the newborn dog, there is a greater renal vascular sensitivity to epinephrine than exists in the adult.[63] Finally, changes in other humoral agents known to affect renal hemodynamics, such as the prostaglandins, may contribute to the changing pattern of renal blood flow.

5. Glomerular Filtration Rate in the Perinatal Animal

In the adult animal, approximately 20–25% of the plasma flowing through the kidney is filtered at the glomerulus. The kidney of an average-size man filters about 120 ml of water every minute.

The glomerular filtration rate (GFR) is usually measured as the renal clearance of a substance that is freely filterable, not reabsorbed, not secreted, not metabolized, and not synthesized by the renal tubules. Inulin fulfills these criteria and has been used extensively and most reliably for the measurement of GFR. Creatinine is also frequently employed, especially since it has the advantage of being an endogenous substance and therefore does not need to be infused as does inulin. There are, however, limitations to the use of creatinine clearance as an indicator of GFR. One of the limitations is technical and is related to the chemical determination of creatinine. If noncreatinine chromagens are not removed from the serum during the analytic procedure, spurious values for serum creatinine, and thus creatinine clearance, will be obtained. Such spurious values are most likely to be obtained when the true serum creatinine level is low, as during the

neonatal period. The other limitation to the use of creatinine clearance as an indicator of GFR is that creatinine is transported by the renal tubules, and therefore does not fulfill the criteria of an ideal glomerular marker. Creatinine clearance has been found to differ from simultaneously measured inulin clearance in infants and children even when "true" creatinine (without noncreatinine chromagens) has been measured in plasma.[36,60] Data utilizing creatinine clearance as the index of GFR must therefore be interpreted with caution.

Recently, radiolabeled [^{125}I]sodium iothalamate has been found useful as a glomerular marker for perinatal renal studies based on the fact that its renal clearance equals that of inulin.[30,102]

Most measurements of fetal glomerular filtration have been carried out in sheep,[20,24,27,48,100,102,110] although there are reports of GFR in fetal guinea pigs[25] and dogs.[98] In all species studied, the GFR of the fetus is lower than that of the adult. There is, however, some controversy concerning the maturational pattern of glomerular filtration. Initial studies by investigators using an acute exteriorized fetal lamb preparation and creatinine or urea as the glomerular marker suggested that the GFR, normalized to body weight, actually *decreased* with gestational age.[4] More recent studies from the same laboratory, utilizing essentially the same surgical preparation but using the preferable glomerular marker inulin, revealed that the GFR per gram body weight *increased* with gestation.[2] On the other hand, a more recent study using an acute intrauterine lamb preparation and iothalamate as the glomerular marker revealed that although the GFR increased on an absolute basis during gestation, there was no maturational change when the GFR was normalized to body or kidney weight.[102]

In newborn animals, the GFR is lower than it is in the adult on an absolute basis or when normalized to body weight, body surface area, extracellular fluid volume, or kidney weight.[3,6,7,25,40,53,57,58,67,80,95,131] The maturational pattern of the GFR depends, however, on the parameter used for normalization. The GFR increases, of course, as the animal grows. When comparison is made on the basis of kidney weight (or estimated kidney weight in the human), the GFR reaches mature levels at 4–5 months of age in the human,[104] 10 weeks in the dog,[58] 4–5 weeks in the rat,[95] and not before 2 months in the lamb.[7] Most studies on humans report the GFR normalized to body surface area. With such normalization, the GFR at

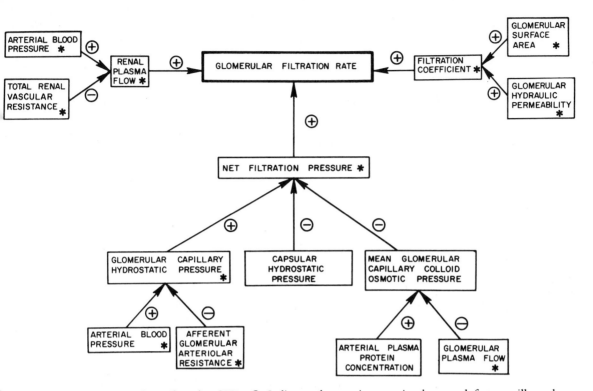

Fig. 2. Scheme of factors that affect the GFR. ⊕ Indicates that an increase in the causal factor will produce an increase in the resultant factor; ⊖ indicates that an increase in the causal factor will produce a decrease in the resultant factor; (＊) indicates a factor that may contribute to low GFR in the perinatal kidney. Reproduced from Loggie et al.[74]

birth amounts to about 15–30% of adult values and increases asymptotically to reach mature values at about 1–3 years of age.[9,85,131] During the first 3 weeks of life, the GFR increases linearly from 10 ml/min per M² to 30 ml/min per M².[50]

There are many discrepancies and wide variations in reported values describing maturation patterns of the GFR, even when it is normalized to a single variable such as body surface area. These discrepancies and variations are related to a number of factors, including the use of different glomerular markers, varying levels of hydration and motor activity of the infant at the time of study, different techniques used for collecting urine and sampling blood, and probably the great lability of the GFR in the newborn infant.

Analysis of the underlying mechanisms contributing to the low GFR in the immature kidney can be made more clearly if the physiologic factors that affect the GFR in any kidney are first presented (Fig. 2). The GFR is a function of the amount of plasma reaching the glomeruli and the physical forces aiding or opposing filtration at the glomerulus. The amount of plasma reaching the glomerulus is directly related to arterial blood pressure and inversely proportional to the total renal vascular resistance. The net filtration pressure is the difference between forces aiding and those opposing glomerular filtration. Forces aiding filtration are the hydrostatic pressure in the glomerular capillary, the glomerular hydraulic permeability, and the surface area available for filtration (the latter two factors combined are known as the filtration coefficient, K_F). The capillary hydrostatic pressure is related directly to the arterial blood pressure and inversely related to the resistance of the afferent glomerular arteriole. Forces opposing filtration are the mean colloid osmotic pressure of the capillary plasma and the hydrostatic pressure in Bowman's capsule. The mean capillary colloid osmotic pressure is a function of the protein concentration in arterial plasma as well as of glomerular plasma flow. If flow is high, a smaller increase in plasma colloid osmotic pressure will result from a given filtration rate, and the mean colloid osmotic pressure will be lower than if flow were low, even though the initial osmotic pressure is the same in either instance.

Low arterial blood pressure is one explanation for the low GFR in the perinatal kidney. Evidence supporting the important role of blood pressure in GFR maturation includes the good statistical correlation of blood pressure with GFR and the experimental results that show that acute changes in blood pressure in the newborn animal result in parallel changes in the GFR.[67] Some investigators have minimized the importance of the relationship between blood pressure and GFR in the perinatal animal on the grounds that blood pressure changes during maturation are much smaller than the concomitant increases in GFR. This argument would be valid, however, only if the relationship between GFR and blood pressure were direct. The GFR is not directly related to arterial blood pressure, however, but rather to net filtration pressure (see Fig. 2), which in turn is a function of the difference between a forward-acting glomerular capillary pressure (related to arterial blood pressure and preglomerular arteriolar resistance) and a back pressure (related to mean colloid osmotic pressure and capsular pressure). When glomerular capillary pressure is low, small changes in forward-acting pressure could theoretically produce relatively large changes in net filtration pressure and therefore in GFR. For example, if glomerular capillary pressure were 30 mm Hg and the back pressure were 25 mm Hg, then the net filtration pressure would be 5 mm Hg.

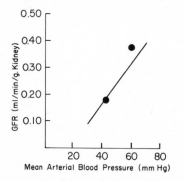

Fig. 3. Relationship between GFR and mean arterial blood pressure. The straight line represents the statistical regression equation relating GFR to mean arterial blood pressure in newborn dogs over their physiologic blood pressure range[67]; (●) GFR of adult dogs when their blood pressures were lowered to 42 and 60 mm Hg.[89]

If the blood pressure doubled and afferent glomerular arteriolar resistance remained constant, glomerular capillary pressure would double to 60 and the net filtration pressure (if back pressure did not change) would increase to 35 mm Hg Thus, a 2-fold increase in arterial blood pressure could theoretically lead to a 7-fold increase in GFR.

This theoretical relationship is supported by experimental evidence in adult dogs.[89] When the blood pressure in these animals was lowered to 42 mm Hg, the GFR was 0.18 ml/min per g. At a blood pressure of 60 mm Hg, an increase of less than 50%, the GFR was 0.38 ml/min per g, an increase of more than 100%. Moreover, at these blood pressures, the GFR in the adult dog is similar to that in the newborn dog, the physiologic blood pressures of which are in this range (Fig. 3). This finding further supports the importance of blood pressure to GFR maturation.

At blood pressure levels normally found in adults, changes in arterial blood pressure result in little if any change in the GFR. The reason is that preglomerular arteriolar resistance increases as arterial blood pressure increases, resulting in a relative constancy of glomerular capillary hydrostatic pressure. This phenomenon is known as *autoregulation of GFR.* At blood pressures below 80 mm Hg, however, there is little change in preglomerular arteriolar resistance, so that the GFR varies with blood pressure. In newborn animals the physiologic blood pressures of which are below 80 mm Hg, therefore, it is not surprising that increases in arterial pressure result in increases in GFR.[67]

In addition to low blood pressure, most perinatal animals have a high renal vascular resistance. If this high resistance is located in the preglomerular arterioles, then glomerular capillary pressure would be low at any arterial blood pressure, and the GFR would be impeded. Such a situation has been found to exist in the newborn guinea pig.[114]

The combination of low arterial blood pressure and high renal vascular resistance would limit not only glomerular capillary hydrostatic pressure, but also glomerular plasma flow. As discussed previously, renal blood flow and consequently glomerular plasma flow are low in the perinatal animal. Furthermore, studies have implicated the low glomerular plasma flow as a major contributor to the low GFR in newborn lambs[7] and rats.[6]

Hemodynamic factors therefore play a major role in the maturation of glomerular filtration. In humans, the importance of these hemodynamic factors is supported by studies that demonstrate the relationship between GFR and the timing of umbilical cord clamping. Newborn infants whose umbilical cords are clamped relatively late after delivery have higher circulating blood volumes than do those infants whose umbilical cords are clamped earlier. The later-cord-clamped infants have GFR (inulin clearance) 40–50% higher than the earlier-cord-clamped infants.[90]

There is also evidence that nonhemodynamic factors, particularly a low filtration coefficient, may contribute to the low GFR in the perinatal kidney. A large part of the absolute maturational increase in the GFR is undoubtedly due to the increasing glomerular volume occurring with kidney growth. The low glomerular volume of the perinatal kidney, however, would not explain the low GFR normalized to kidney size. There is evidence, nevertheless, that surface area available for filtration may be lower per unit glomerular volume in the newborn than in the more mature kidney.[113]

A low filtration coefficient could also be due to a lowered glomerular hydraulic permeability. Studies utilizing the clearance of dextran of different molecular sizes indicated that the pore radii of the glomerular membrane of the neonatal human were relatively small and increased as the infant matured.[11]

Analysis of factors affecting the maturation of the GFR is complicated by the fact that renal maturation as a whole and that of the glomeruli in particular is not homogeneous. As discussed previously, nephrons in the juxtamedullary region of the kidney are more mature than those in the periphery. In view of this difference, it is not surprising to find that maturation of the GFR varies in different segments of the kidney. In the newborn guinea pig, the early maturational increase in the GFR is due primarily to an increase in function of the deep glomeruli, whereas the later increase is due to the increasing filtration rate of the superficial nephrons.[113]

The perinatal kidney therefore seems to compensate for any anatomic immaturity it may have by utilizing its hemodynamic factors optimally. Despite the low blood pressure and high renal vascular resistance, which are the major limitations to renal blood flow and GFR, the blood that does flow to the kidney goes to those nephrons best able to utilize it, and glomerular filtration occurs in those nephrons that are most mature. As anatomic maturation progresses, blood is distributed to those newly matured nephrons, and the GFR increases in these nephrons accordingly.

6. Tubular Transport in the Perinatal Kidney

The function of the kidney tubules is to alter the glomerular filtrate by transporting solutes and water across the tubular epithelium. Transport from the tubular lumen to interstitial fluid or peritubular capillaries is termed *reabsorption*, and transport from capillary to tubular lumen is called *secretion*. Transport can be either passive (along an electrochemical gradient and requiring no metabolic energy) or active (against an electrochemical gradient and requiring metabolic energy).

Classically, renal tubular function has been evaluated by measuring rates of transport of various substances between tubular lumen and peritubular capillary. Transport rates of certain substances appear to be limited by a transport maximum (T_m); measurement of the T_m for these substances has been utilized as an index of tubular function. The T_m for glucose (T_{mG}), a substance that is transported from proximal renal tubule to peritubular capillary, and the T_m for PAH (T_{mPAH}), a substance that is transported from peritubular capillary to proximal renal tubule, have both been used as a measure of renal tubular potential. More recent studies have indicated, however, that the T_m for each of these substances is a function of the GFR (i.e., T_m increases as GFR increases).[34,73,106,121,128]

Absolute values for T_{mPAH} are low in newborn animals, including human beings.[56,104,125] The low values for T_{mPAH} apply even when corrected for body weight or surface area, kidney weight, and, more importantly, GFR. Glucose T_m is also lower in the neonate than in the adult when comparison is made on a body-weight or surface-area basis.[124,125] Early investigators found the ratio T_{mG}/GFR to be lower in the newborn infant than in the adult,[125] but more recent investigations have found the ratio to be the same in the adult and newborn infant.[26] Perhaps one source of the difficulty in measuring the T_{mG}, or even the T_{mG}/GFR, which is more appropriate, is that proximal tubular glucose transport appears to be a function of proximal tubular sodium reabsorption.[73] When a large fraction of the filtered sodium is reabsorbed, the T_{mG}/GFR is large and vice versa. Studies of the

T_{mG}/GFR in newborn dogs initially indicated that tubular transport of glucose might be limited.[13] More recent studies, however, suggest that the low T_{mG}/GFR was due to the lower fractional sodium reabsorption in the proximal tubule that occurred in the newborn animal during glucose loading.[14] At any level of sodium reabsorption, the T_{mG}/GFR was the same for the newborn and adult.

The earlier studies indicating that the T_{mG}/GFR and T_{mPAH}/GFR were low in neonatal animals suggested that tubular function was more immature than glomerular function. These *in vivo* physiological studies were consistent with the *in vitro* studies showing a limitation in the transport capacities of isolated immature kidney slices to PAH[54,65,101] and nonmetabolizable sugars.[107] In addition, as discussed previously, anatomic studies revealed that the ratio of glomerular surface area to proximal tubular volume was greater in the neonate than in the adult,[42] signifying that in the newborn infant, the anatomic potential for proximal tubule transport appeared to be less than that for glomerular filtration. Unfortunately, *in vitro* and *in vivo* correlates may not be so precise. Although both T_{mPAH} and *in vitro* PAH uptake by kidney slices are low in the newborn infant, their maturational characteristics are quite different. In addition, the more recent studies showing that the T_{mG}/GFR may be similar in newborn and adult animals cast some doubt on the functional relevance of the anatomic findings of glomerular preponderance in the immature kidney.[14,26]

The constancy of the T_{mG}/GFR ratio throughout maturation is a reflection of the balance of glomerular and tubular function of the whole kidney. The kidney, however, consists of a million nephrons, and it is as important for each of these individual nephrons to maintain glomerular tubular balance as it is for the kidney as a whole. Thus, if there exist certain nephrons with tubules of a low transport capability, it would be beneficial to have these tubules attached to glomeruli with low filtration rates; conversely, tubules that function well should be matched with glomeruli that filter well. Such a situation would result in functional glomerular–tubular balance, with a homogeneous population of nephrons with similar ratios of glomerular to tubular function. If the opposite situation occurs, i.e., poorly functioning glomeruli with well-functioning tubules (high T_m/GFR) or vice versa (low T_m/GFR), there would result functional glomerular–tubular imbalance, with a hetero-

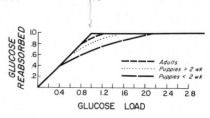

Fig. 4. Relationship between filtered glucose load and tubular reabsorption of Glucose. The 45° solid-line segment is a hypothetical line representing complete reabsorption of glucose; the horizontal solid-line segment represents constant maximum glucose reabsorption when the load is greater than T_m. The two dashed lines and the dotted line represent the actual titration curves for puppies and adult dogs, as indicated in the legend. Based on data from Baker and Kleinman.[13]

geneous population of nephrons with different ratios of glomerular to tubular function.

Functional analysis of homogeneity or heterogeneity of glomerular–tubular balance may be made by examining a titration curve of a substance such as glucose that has a transport maximum or overall T_{mG}/GFR (Fig. 4). As the filtered glucose load is progressively increased by raising plasma glucose, all the glucose in each nephron will be reabsorbed until the T_{mG}/GFR for that nephron is reached; additional reabsorption will then cease, and the excess filtered glucose will be excreted. If the T_{mG}/GFR were identical for each nephron (perfect nephron homogeneity), reabsorption would cease at the same glucose load for each nephron and for the kidney as a whole. This situation is represented by the solid line in Fig. 4, which shows a continuing increase in total kidney glucose reabsorption equal to that of the filtered load (the line has a slope of 45°), and then a cessation of reabsorption when the transport maximum is reached (the line becomes horizontal). If some nephrons have a lower T_{mG}/GFR than others, glucose reabsorption will cease in these tubules before it does in the others, and there will be a deviation from the solid line. This deviation is referred to as "splay," and is shown in Fig. 4 as the curved dashed lines connecting the two segments of the solid line. The degree of splay is largely a function of the degree of nephron heterogeneity. As can be seen from Fig. 4, there is a progressive decline in the degree of splay as the newborn dog matures. This physiologic nephron heterogeneity in the newborn animal is consistent with the anatomic nephron heterogeneity discussed previously.

Nephron heterogeneity not only produces splay

in a glucose titration curve, but also lowers the plasma threshold for glucose, i.e., the plasma glucose level at which glucose first appears in the urine. As soon as glucose reabsorption ceases in the tubule, the excess glucose that is filtered will be excreted in the urine. Thus, as soon as the function in Fig. 4 deviates from the 45° straight line, it represents the point at which glucose will appear in the urine. This situation is made more apparent in Fig. 5, in which urinary glucose excretion is plotted against plasma glucose. In the adult dog, no glucose appears in the urine until plasma glucose is well above 200 mg/dl. In puppies less than 2 weeks old, however, glucose is excreted when the plasma glucose is only 100 mg/dl. This degree of depression of the glucose threshold in the perinatal animal means that the immature kidney will excrete glucose at blood levels only slightly above the physiologic level for the adult.

Teleologically, functional heterogeneity with its resultant lowered plasma glucose threshold is not too detrimental to the normal fetus or newborn. Fetal and neonatal blood glucose values are lower than those of the adult, and consequently are below the renal glucose threshold. In certain circumstances, however, such as may exist in fetuses of diabetic mothers or in fetuses of mothers receiving large glucose infusions, fetal glucose plasma levels may rise to levels exceeding the renal glucose threshold, and glucose will be excreted in the urine. Non-reabsorbed glucose acts as an osmotic diuretic, and urine flow will consequently be enhanced. This effect probably accounts for the polyhydramnios seen in infants of diabetic mothers. Postnatally, newborn infants are prone to glucose diuresis if they receive glucose infusions that raise their plasma glucose levels above the low renal threshold. The subsequent loss of water and electrolytes might in these infants result in dehydration.

As discussed previously, T_{mPAH} and renal extraction of PAH are considerably lower in the perinatal kidney than in that of the adult. The lowered T_{mPAH} can be explained on a cellular basis, since the capacity of cells from perinatal kidneys to transport PAH appears to be limited.[54,65,101] The low renal extraction of PAH cannot be explained by the lowered renal PAH transport capabilities or the low T_{mPAH}, since even when tracer amounts of PAH are used, PAH extraction is low.[68] An intriguing explanation for the low PAH extraction is that perhaps in the perinatal animal, postglomerular blood bypasses those sections of the nephron involved in PAH transport. The different intrarenal distribution of blood flow in the perinatal kidney would seem to support this possibility. However, in the only study done to determine systematically the relationship between PAH extraction and intrarenal blood flow distribution in the newborn animal, no correlation could be found between these two functions.[69] Thus, other explanations for the low PAH extraction in perinatal kidneys need to be sought.

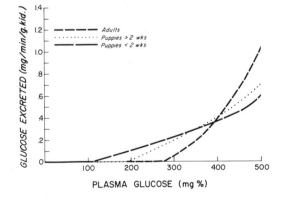

Fig. 5. Relationship between plasma glucose and glucose excreted in the urine. The plasma level at which glucose first appears in the urine is referred to as the *plasma threshold for glucose*. Based on data from Baker and Kleinman.[13]

7. Excretion of Sodium by the Perinatal Kidney

In the adult, under antidiuretic conditions, more than 99% of filtered sodium is reabsorbed by the tubules. Micropuncture studies reveal that about 70% of filtered sodium is reabsorbed in the proximal convoluted tubule; the rest is reabsorbed more distally, largely in the ascending limb of the loop of Henle. Sodium reabsorption in the proximal tubule is due primarily to the active transport of sodium. Nevertheless, the net proximal reabsorption of sodium is also a function of the physical forces of the peritubular environment such as colloid osmotic and hydrostatic pressures and the integrity of the intercellular tight junctions.

In the adult animal, under most circumstances, as the filtered load of sodium is increased, proximal tubular sodium reabsorption is proportionately increased, and as filtered sodium falls, proximal sodium reabsorption decreases. As a result, the fraction of filtered sodium reabsorbed proximally remains relatively constant, testifying to the existence of glomerular tubular balance for sodium reabsorption.

In the newborn dog and guinea pig, the fractional reabsorption of water (and presumably sodium) at the end of the proximal tubule has been found to be relatively constant during maturation and similar to that for the adult.[58,113] In these animals, the GFR increases as the animal matures; concomitantly, there is a proportional increase in proximal tubular size and consequently in water reabsorption. Similarly, in the newborn rat, as single nephron glomerular filtration rate increases with maturation, proximal tubular sodium reabsorption increases proportionately.[112] The maturational increase in proximal tubular sodium reabsorption in the rat is due partly to the improved anatomic geometry of the maturing proximal tubule providing greater surface area for reabsorption and partly to a greater intrinsic reabsorptive capacity in the maturing tubules.[112] In newborn dogs, acute changes in filtered sodium result in proportional changes in proximal tubular sodium reabsorption.[66] Thus, glomerular–tubular balance for sodium occurs in the perinatal as well as in the mature kidney. The fractional proportionality of glomerular and proximal tubular function during maturation further questions the functional importance of the previously described anatomic findings of glomerular preponderance in perinatal kidneys.

When exposed to a glucose osmotic diuresis, proximal tubular sodium reabsorption in the neonatal animal decreases more than in the adult.[14] Thus, more sodium and water are excreted for any given osmotic load in the perinatal kidney. The reason for this greater sensitivity to osmotic diuresis is still unclear. Perhaps at the rapid proximal tubular flow rates that occur during osmotic diuresis, the proximal tubule of the immature kidney cannot reabsorb as much sodium as can that of the adult. This hypothesis is contradicted by the finding that in newborn rats undergoing mannitol diuresis,[111] and in newborn dogs with glucose diuresis,[14] the sodium concentration gradient between tubular lumen and peritubular blood is approximately the same as that for the adult of the species. Alternatively, the greater osmotic effect of glucose in the perinatal kidney may have been due to greater back-leak of sodium and water, perhaps through leaky intercellular tight junctions. Thus, although the same amount of sodium and water may have been reabsorbed from the proximal tubules of the perinatal kidney, the osmotic effect of glucose in the tubular lumen was permitted to draw back more of this reabsorbate.

Although the mechanism of this osmotic phenomenon is still unclear, its implications for fluid and electrolyte management of newborn infants are more apparent. Because of the low glucose threshold, newborn infants are more prone to excrete glucose and thus to undergo osmotic diuresis. For any degree of glucose excretion, moreover, the newborn infant will lose more sodium and water and become more easily dehydrated than will the adult.

One physiologic mechanism thought by some investigators to influence sodium excretion is the distribution of intrarenal blood flow,[16] which is different in newborn animals from that in adults. As discussed previously, in the immature animal compared with the adult, there is a relatively greater fractional blood flow to the inner renal nephrons.[62,69,91] Increased blood flow to inner renal nephrons in the adult is believed by some investigators to be associated with a state of sodium retention.[15] However, since the level of maturity of inner renal nephrons differs from that of outer renal nephrons in the immature animal,[69,75,96] extrapolation of results from adult animals may not apply to the immature animal. In addition, more recent studies in adult animals and human beings have brought into question the significance of the role of the distribution of intrarenal blood flow in sodium excretion by the mature kidney.[22,29,55,117]

The primary purpose of renal sodium excretion is to maintain body sodium and water homeostasis and, since sodium is limited primarily to the extracellular fluid compartment, to maintain extracellular sodium and water content. Regulation of extracellular sodium and water content, however, appears to be less efficient in the perinatal than in the adult animal. When an adult is given a large sodium load, there is an immediate expansion of the extracellular fluid space. This expansion stimulates the kidney to increase its GFR and to decrease tubular sodium reabsorption, resulting in increased excretion of sodium and a relatively rapid return of the extracellular fluid space to preload conditions. When newborn infants and animals are given a sodium load, they experience a rise in serum sodium levels, abnormal increases in weight, and generalized edema.[81] Newborn infants given an oral sodium load excrete the sodium at much lower rates than do older children given an equivalent sodium load (per body surface area). The poor renal response of the infant to the sodium load is due to its low GFR and to its relatively high fractional tubular sodium reabsorption during the sodium loading.[8,9] The ability to excrete the sodium load increases linearly with age throughout the first year of life. This maturational increase in sodium excretion is due both to the increase in filtered sodium (due to the maturational increase in the GFR) and to an increase in fractional sodium excretion.[9]

An exception to this maturational response to sodium loading is the prematurely born infant. Infants born before 36 weeks' gestation have a better sodium excretory response to sodium loading than do infants born later in gestation.[8a] As the premature infants mature over the first few weeks of life, their ability to excrete the sodium load declines rather than improves. Premature infants also excrete more sodium than do full-term infants, even if they do not receive a sodium load.[9a] Thus, full-term infants can maintain net zero total body sodium balance when given sodium intakes of 1.5–2 meq/kg per day and net positive sodium balance (sodium retention) at sodium intakes of 3–4 meq/kg per day, while premature infants will have net negative sodium balance (sodium excretion) at both these levels of sodium intake. The reasons for the relatively large sodium excretory ability of the kidney of premature infants is still unclear and limited to the realm of speculation. Conceivably, the same processes involved in the relatively large excretion of sodium during osmotic diuresis in newborn animals (discussed above) are operating at a more exaggerated level in the premature infant, so that sodium reabsorption is limited even without an osmotic diuresis. It is difficult to determine the mechanisms involved in renal sodium excretion of premature infants because of the lack of an appropriate animal model.

The newborn dog has been used as a model for studying maturation of renal function, since its renal response to sodium loading is similar to that of the term newborn infant. Newborn dogs excrete only 5% of a sodium load administered intravenously after 2 hr, compared with 30% excretion of an equivalent load (per body weight) administered to adult dogs. Both puppies and adult dogs have equivalent increases in GFR following the salt load, but the adult dog excretes 6% of the filtered sodium compared with only 1% excreted by the puppy (under control conditions, both adult and newborn dogs excrete about 0.2% of the filtered sodium).[70]

The ability to excrete a sodium load can be modified in the newborn dog by previous dietary salt intake. Puppies that had been maintained on a relatively high-sodium diet prior to the imposition of the large sodium load excreted a larger fraction of the imposed sodium load than did those puppies maintained on a relatively low-sodium diet.[116]

In the adult animal, extracellular fluid volume expansion decreases fractional sodium reabsorption in the proximal tubule. The increased sodium escaping proximal reabsorption is largely reabsorbed in more distal segments of the nephron, especially in the loop of Henle. However, a significant portion of this distal nephron sodium load escapes reabsorption, particularly in the collecting duct, resulting in an increased fractional and total renal sodium excretion. In the newborn dog, however, although fractional sodium reabsorption is decreased in the proximal tubule to approximately the same degree as it is in the adult on sodium loading, the distal nephron almost totally reabsorbs the increased sodium load presented to it.[66] The result is a small increase only in fractional and total renal sodium excretion.

The mechanism involved in the response of the kidney to a salt load or to extracellular volume expansion are still controversial. Factors that have been suggested to influence sodium excretion during extracellular volume expansion include: changes in the physical properties (hydrostatic and colloid osmotic pressures) of the peritubular environment; changes in the permeability of the tubules; changes in intrarenal distribution of blood flow or of the glomerular filtrate; production of a humoral salt-losing factor; and changes in renal autonomic nervous activity. To evaluate critically the evidence for or against each of these mechanisms is beyond the scope of this chapter. Relevant to this discussion, however, is an evaluation of proposed mechanisms as they relate to the response of the perinatal kidney to a salt load.

Except for intrarenal blood flow, to date none of the previously mentioned mechanisms has been studied directly in perinatal animals. Although there is a definite change in the distribution of intrarenal blood flow after sodium expansion in newborn dogs, there is no correlation between this change and sodium excretion.[70] In addition, the ability of puppies to respond to salt loading is not affected by the maturational change in intrarenal blood flow distribution. The intrarenal distribution of blood flow therefore does not play an important role in the inability of the perinatal kidney to respond to expansion of extracellular volume.

As previously discussed, the lack of response of the immature kidney appears to relate to the distal rather than the proximal tubule. Further investigations into this problem in perinatal animals should therefore be directed at examining factors that influence sodium reabsorption in the loop of Henle, distal convoluted tubule, and collecting ducts.

Under most circumstances, the perinatal animal is not exposed to sodium loads, and so the poor ability of its kidney to respond to such loads is not a teleological mistake. In the fetus, sodium and water homeostasis is largely regulated by the placenta. Postnatally, the newborn infant suckles his mother, and therefore receives nutrition containing small amounts of sodium. The kidneys of newborns of different species have different abilities to excrete a sodium load. The newborn pig, for example, responds better than a newborn human, and not surprisingly, the sodium content of sow's milk is greater than that of human milk. When the infant of one species receives milk from another species, however, it is possible that the sodium load may be excessive for its kidneys. Such is the case of the human infant receiving cow's milk, which has four times the sodium content of human milk. It is not unusual, therefore, to see infants who are receiving cow's-milk formula developing signs of fluid and salt retention.

Renal tubular sodium reabsorption can be influenced by a number of humoral agents. Among these is aldosterone, a steroid hormone secreted by the adrenal cortex and responsible for part of the sodium reabsorption in the distal convoluted tubule. In human beings, aldosterone secretion rates are low at birth and increase to adult values by 2 weeks of age.[132] Aldosterone blood levels, however, are higher in the newborn infant than in the adult,[19,108] and respond to changes in sodium balance. In terms of renal tubular response, the important criterion would be either the amount of aldosterone reaching the kidney or the level of aldosterone circulating in the blood. The high aldosterone blood levels in the newborn infant suggest that the renal tubules of the immature kidney are exposed to a greater salt-retaining stimulus than are those of the more mature kidney. Although aldosterone is in-

volved in distal sodium reabsorption, the high circulating levels of this hormone found in perinatal animals probably are not responsible for the poor renal response to salt loading, since in the adult animal, there is a good response to saline loading even in those animals that have been pretreated with salt-retaining adrenal cortical hormones.

As discussed previously, there is enhanced activity of the renin–angiotensin system in the fetus and newborn. Although the high renin and angiotensin levels could theoretically contribute by themselves to the high levels of circulating aldosterone in the neonate, the report that aldosterone secretion rates are low[132] suggests that aldosterone levels may be high in part because of diminished excretion or metabolic breakdown of aldosterone in the newborn. The renin–angiotensin system is stimulated, in part at least, by low intrarenal vascular pressure[21] and by low sodium delivery to the distal tubule.[127] As these physiologic factors pertain during the newborn period, both probably contribute to the enhanced renin–angiotensin activity in the newborn infant.

8. Excretion and Conservation of Water in the Perinatal Kidney

Although the concentration of solutes in human plasma is held fairly constant at about 300 mosmol/liter, the concentration of solutes in the urine of an adult human varies from 50 to 1500 mosmol/liter depending on the amount of water intake.

All mammalian fetuses studied excrete urine hypotonic to plasma. The fetal lamb at 81–93 days' gestation excretes urine with a solute concentration of 239 mosmol/liter, and the urine becomes progressively more dilute with gestation, so that at 130–142 days, urinary solute concentration has fallen to 166 mosmol/liter.[1] Interestingly enough, while the urine is becoming more and more dilute, the urinary urea concentration is increasing.

The infant of a few days of age is not able to excrete a water load as well as can an adult. Infants given a water load of 3% of their body weight excreted only 10% of the load in the first 3 hr, whereas an adult excreted all of it during this time.[5] Infants of 6–18 days excreted 57% of a water load equal to 5% of body weight, compared with an adult who excreted 100% of an equivalent water load in that time.[84] The ability to respond to a water load improves rapidly during the first few weeks of life, reaching adult capabilities by 1 month of age.[5]

Newborn animals also have a limited renal response to water loading. Newborn dogs given a water load of 5% of their body weight excrete only 56% of the dose in 4 hr, compared with an 85% excretion of a similar dose in the adult. In addition, maximum urine flow rate per unit body weight in the puppies was only 65% of that in adults.[79]

The ability to excrete a water load is a function of the amount of water presented to the diluting segment (ascending limb of the loop of Henle and early distal convoluted tubule) and the ability of this segment to dilute the urine (Fig. 6). The amount of water presented to the diluting segment is a function of the GFR and of proximal tubular water reabsorption. Diluting ability, in turn, is a function of the ability of the ascending limb of the loop of Henle to transport chloride against a concentration gradient and the ability of the distal convoluted tubule and the collecting duct to remain impermeable to water. Newborn infants can dilute their urine to the same degree as can adults (to 50 mosmol/liter).[17,84] The reason for the poor response of the newborn animal to a water load is therefore likely to be the decreased load presented to the diluting segment; this decrease, in turn, is most likely due to the low GFR.

The newborn animal and infant are not as capable of responding to dehydration or hypertonic solute loading by excreting as concentrated a urine as the adult.[35,40,77] An adult man normally excretes a urine of about 800–1000 mosmol/liter, and is able to increase the concentration of solutes to 1400 mosmol/liter under conditions of dehydration. A newborn infant usually excretes urine hypotonic to plasma, and can concentrate his urine to only 600–700 mosmol/liter under conditions of water deprivation.

The ability to produce a concentrated urine is a function of the ability to produce and maintain a solute concentration gradient in the interstitial fluid of the kidney from the inner medulla to the corticomedullary junction, and also of the ability of the fluid, within the collecting duct, to equilibrate with the interstitial fluid of the medullary region (Fig. 7). The ability to produce the renal medullary interstitial solute gradient is a function of: (1) the ability of the thick portion of the ascending limb of the loop of Henle to transport chloride; (2) the length of the loops of Henle; (3) the selective permeability characteristics of the various segments of the loops of Henle to sodium, chloride, water, and urea; and (4) the amount of urea presented to the medullary portion of the kidney. The ability of the kidney to maintain the medullary solute gradient is a function of the blood flow to the renal medulla and the ability of the water in the medullary vasculature to be shunted from descending to ascending limbs of the vasa recta (therefore, less water reaches the deep medullary tissue to dissipate the solute gradient).

The ability of the collecting duct to equilibrate with the interstitial fluid of the renal medulla is a function of the amount of antidiuretic hormone (ADH) present, the ability of the collecting duct to respond to ADH, and the amount of urine flow in the collecting duct.

The major reason an immature animal cannot excrete urine as concentrated as that of an adult is that the kidneys of newborn animals have smaller medullary solute gradients than do those of adult animals[105,115,122] There is relatively little change in the medullary *sodium* gradient as the animal

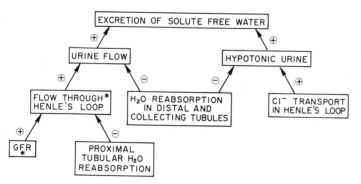

Fig. 6. Scheme of factors that affect the excretion of solute free water. (+) Indicates that an increase in the causal factor will produce an increase in the resultant factor; (−) indicates that an increase in the causal factor will produce a decrease in the resultant factor (*) indicates a factor found to contribute to the decreased ability of the perinatal kidney to respond to a water load.

matures, but there is usually a small *urea* gradient in immature kidneys, and it is this gradient that increases as the animal matures. The reasons for the small urea gradient in the immature kidney may be related to the low renal excretion of urea (due primarily to the positive nitrogen balance in maturing animals) and to the anatomic immaturity of the loop of Henle, which might retard cycling of urea in the medulla.[35,122] Infants on high-protein diets or urea supplements can concentrate their urine to a greater degree than can infants on low-protein diets,[37,38] further emphasizing the importance of renal delivery of urea to the concentrating mechanism in maturing animals. Newborn infants on high-protein or urea diets and newborn animals receiving urea loads, however, cannot increase the concentration of urinary nonurea solutes,[37,122] as can adult animals.[32] Moreover, urea loads given to immature animals do not produce increases in the renal medullary solute gradients (for either urea or nonurea solutes), as they do in more mature animals.[122] These findings support the concept of the immaturity of the medullary urea-cycling mechanism.

There are factors other than urea that may play a role in the poor concentrating ability of the kidney of the immature infant. Newborn animals and infants have shorter loops of Henle than do more mature animals.[23,35,41] Relative blood flow to the medullary region of the kidney is greater in immature than in mature animals,[62,69,91] which may increase the dissipation of the medullary solute gradient. In addition, immaturity of the vasa recta may retard countercurrent water recycling.[122] All these factors may theoretically contribute to the low renal medullary solute gradient found in immature

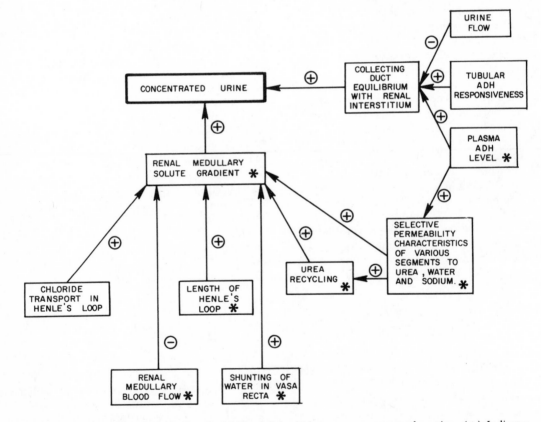

Fig. 7. Scheme of factors that affect the ability of the kidney to concentrate the urine. (+) Indicates that an increase in the causal factor will produce an increase in the resultant factor; (−) indicates that an increase in the causal factor will produce a decrease in the resultant factor; (*) indicates a factor that may contribute to the poor concentrating ability in the perinatal kidney. Reproduced from Loggie *et al.*[74]

animals, but their actual roles remain to be determined.

There is still some controversy about the importance of ADH in limiting the urinary concentrating ability of immature animals. Early reports suggested that ADH activity was diminished during the newborn period. These reports were based on observations that the ADH content was low[52] and that less ADH was released from the pituitaries of immature than from those of mature animals. In addition, ADH activity was undetectable by bioassay (less than 0.5 μU/ml plasma) in plasma from infants 16 days to 5 months of age.[61] When these infants were loaded with sodium chloride, antidiuretic activity was noted in the infants $2\frac{1}{2}$–5 months of age, but not in younger infants. Plasma from infants older than 5 months contained antidiuretic activity in the presence or absence of an osmotic stimulus. That release of ADH and plasma ADH levels may be lower in the young infant than in the adult is not, however, conclusive evidence that lack of ADH is important to the poor concentrating ability of the immature kidney of the infant. Normally, only small amounts of ADH are necessary to achieve adequate equilibration of the collecting duct fluid with the renal medullary interstitium.[43] Moreover, it has been shown that urine osmolality equals inner medullary osmolality in neonatal puppies.[58] Thus, there is adequate equilibration between collecting duct and medullary interstitium in immature animals, even though ADH levels may be less in these animals. On the other hand, the low ADH levels might contribute significantly to the poor concentrating ability of the immature kidney if it were to limit urea permeability in the collecting duct and thus retard urea recycling in the renal medulla. The importance of ADH to collecting duct urea permeability is still controversial, however, since there are studies that have found that ADH increases collecting duct permeability to urea[24] and studies that have found no effect of ADH on collecting duct urea permeability.[103]

Differences in urinary solute concentration between perinatal and adult animals largely reflect their different needs. Adult mammals usually excrete a concentrated urine, since there is need to conserve free water (water without solutes). They usually have a low intake of water, and in addition, they excrete free water through the skin and lungs. The fetus, of course, does not excrete free water through its skin or through its lungs. In-

gestion of hypotonic amniotic fluid requires excretion of hypotonic urine; this the fetal kidneys are apparently well designed to do. The newborn animal subsists largely on a hypotonic liquid intake, and it too needs to excrete a dilute urine. As it matures and as nitrogen excretion (in the form of urea) increases, urine-concentrating ability improves. During the period of low urea output, however, the kidneys are unable to maximally concentrate urine, and are consequently unable to conserve free water. Under conditions of water deprivation or hypotonic solute loading, the neonatal animal is thus extremely prone to hypertonic dehydration.

9. Acid Excretion by the Perinatal Kidney

Normally, the average human adult produces approximately 13,000 meq acid (hydrogen ions) per day. Most of this acid is produced from tissue respiration in the form of carbon dioxide or carbonic acid. The nonrespiratory acid production, usually derived from metabolism of ingested food, amounts to only 30–100 meq hydrogen ions per day, depending, of course, on the diet and metabolic state of the individual. During steady state, all the acid produced is excreted. The respiratory acid is excreted by the lungs and the nonrespiratory acid by the kidneys.

The kidney assists in the maintenance of body acid base homeostasis in two fundamental ways: (1) it regulates extracellular bicarbonate ion concentration and (2) it excretes the nonrespiratory acid produced by metabolism. Both these mechanisms involve active secretion of hydrogen ions into the tubular lumen.

Under normal circumstances, all filtered bicarbonate is reabsorbed by the tubules, about 90% proximally and the rest in the distal convoluted tubule and collecting duct. Under certain circumstances, the load presented to the tubules may be too large, and bicarbonate will consequently be excreted in the urine. It was previously believed that a tubular maximum (T_m) existed for bicarbonate, but more recent evidence suggests that the apparent T_m was an artifact of the experimental conditions used to measure bicarbonate excretion.[72,97]

There is general agreement that at least some, if not all, of the bicarbonate ions are reabsorbed as a consequence of the active secretion of hydrogen ions by the tubules, although some investigators have postulated an additional mode of bicarbonate reabsorption entailing direct reabsorption of the bicarbonate ion itself.[76] Bicarbonate reabsorption via the hydrogen secretory mechanism occurs in the following manner (Fig. 8): Within the tubular cell, CO_2 is converted to hydrogen and bicarbonate ions. This reaction is accelerated by the enzyme carbonic anhydrase. The hydrogen ion is actively pumped out of the cell into the tubular lumen in exchange for sodium. Once in the tubular lumen, the hydrogen ion combines with the bicarbonate to form CO_2, which then diffuses back into the cell. In the cell, the CO_2 is converted to hydrogen and bicarbonate ions. The bicarbonate ion diffuses into the peritubular blood, and the hydrogen ion is resecreted into the tubular lumen. The net effect, therefore, is the reabsorption of bicarbonate.

In the proximal tubule, along the brush border, there is carbonic anhydrase, so that the production of CO_2 from hydrogen and bicarbonate ions is accelerated in the tubular lumen. This acceleration permits a rapid lowering of the hydrogen ion concentration in the tubular lumen toward its equilibrium concentration. Consequently, the pH of proximal tubular fluid is lowered only slightly (to approximately 7.0), and the active transport of hydrogen ions from cell to lumen occurs against only a small concentration gradient, resulting in more efficient hydrogen ion secretion and bicarbonate reabsorption. There is no evidence of intraluminal carbonic anhydrase in the distal hydrogen secreting sites, although there is ample activity of this enzyme within the cells at this locus.

Bicarbonate reabsorption can be influenced by the following factors (Fig. 9): (1) GFR—increases of GFR result in increases of bicarbonate reabsorption; (2) arterial P_{CO_2}—increases of $P_{a_{CO_2}}$ result in increases of bicarbonate reabsorption; (3) body potassium—decreases of body potassium result in increases of bicarbonate reabsorption; (4) activity of renal carbonic anhydrase—substantial decreases of carbonic anhydrase activity decrease bicarbonate reabsorption; (5) extracellular fluid volume—increases of extracellular fluid volume decreases bicarbonate reabsorption; (6) sodium reabsorption—increases of sodium reabsorption result in increases in bicarbonate reabsorption.

Acid is excreted by the kidney as free hydrogen ions and hydrogen bound to certain buffers in the urine. There are two classes of urinary buffers: (1)

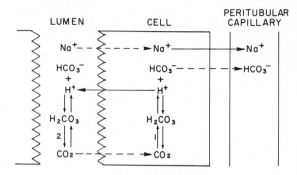

Fig. 8. Diagrammatic representation of bicarbonate reabsorption and hydrogen secretion in the renal tubule. (→) Active transport; (--→) passive diffusion. Note that the net effect of this process is the transport of sodium and bicarbonate from tubular lumen to peritubular capillary. In the proximal and distal tubules, intracellular carbonic anhydrase increases reaction rate 1. In the proximal tubule, intraluminal brush border carbonic anhydrase increases reaction rate 2. In the absence of intraluminal carbonic anhydrase, the dehydration of carbonic acid is slowed, and the intraluminal hydrogen ion concentration increases.

those filtered by the glomerulus, the most important being phosphate, and (2) the buffer produced by the tubular cells, ammonia. The amount of acid excreted as free hydrogen ion plus the hydrogen bound to the filtered buffers is known as the titratable acid, since it is measured by titrating the urine back to a pH of 7.4. Net renal acid secretion is the acid excreted as urinary titratable acid plus urinary ammonia minus urinary bicarbonate excretion.

The maximum amount of acid that can be excreted by the kidney is limited by the maximum gradient for hydrogen ions that can be maintained between the tubular lumen and the tubular cell and the amount of buffer present in the urine. In man, the maximum urine/blood free hydrogen ion gradient is about 1000 : 1, which means that the kidney of man can lower its urinary pH to about 4.4. If the kidney had to excrete all its hydrogen ions in the free ionic form, then the normal kidney would be able to excrete less than 1% of the body's normal nonrespiratory acid production. Therefore, practically all the hydrogen excreted by the kidney must be buffered.

The basic cellular mechanisms involved in acid excretion are essentially the same as that for bicarbonate reabsorption (see Fig. 8). Hydrogen ions are actively secreted into the tubular lumen. Those ions not utilized for bicarbonate reabsorption are then buffered by one of the two classes of buffers. The amount of hydrogen ions excreted is therefore related to the amount of bicarbonate remaining in the tubules. At the end of the proximal tubule, approximately 10% of the filtered bicarbonate remains unreabsorbed, and the pH of the tubular fluid is about 7.0. The free hydrogen ions in this segment are buffered by the filtered buffer with a relatively high pK, phosphate, and the renal buffer ammonia. In the distal acid-secreting sites, the remainder of the bicarbonate ions are usually reabsorbed, and the urine is acidified to a degree dependent on the excess of free hydrogen ions secreted up to the production of a urine with a minimum pH of 4.4. The hydrogen ions here are buffered primarily by ammonia and the filtered buffers with a low pK such as creatinine and β-hydroxybutyrate. Under conditions of high bicarbonate filtered loads or decreased tubular reabsorption of bicarbonate or both, less acid will be

excreted. Indeed, if there is significant excretion of bicarbonate, then the pH of the urine will rise to values above that of blood, and there will be a net excretion of base, not acid. Under conditions of decreased renal phosphate load or decreased synthesis of ammonia, net acid excretion will also be impaired.

Ammonia is synthesized in the tubular cells from a nitrogen pool of amino and amide groups contributed to by tubular intracellular as well as renal arterial glutamine and other amino acids. The ammonia synthesized from this nitrogen pool passively diffuses across the tubular cell membrane into the tubular lumen; there it combines with the free hydrogen ion to form ammonium ion (NH_4^+). The charged ammonium ion cannot diffuse back into the cell because the cell membrane is impermeable to it, in contradistinction to its high permeability to the noncharged ammonia molecule. The ability of the tubular cells to secrete ammonia therefore depends on the ability of the kidney cells

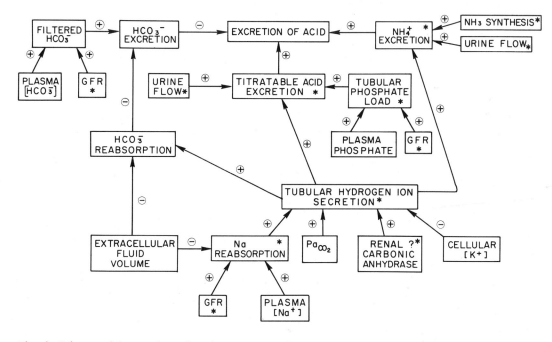

Fig. 9. Scheme of factors that affect the excretion of acid. (+) Indicates that an increase in the causal factor will produce an increase in the resultant factor; (−) indicates that an increase in the causal factor will produce a decrease in the resultant factor; (*) indicates a factor that may contribute to the decreased ability of the perinatal kidney to respond to an acid load. Renal carbonic anhydrase is low in the perinatal kidney, but the significance of this low enzyme activity with respect to the decreased hydrogen ion secretion in the perinatal kidney is questionable.

to synthesize ammonia and on the amount of free hydrogen ions present in the tubular lumen to trap the ammonia as ammonium ions. Synthesis of ammonia by the renal tubular cells depends on a complex interplay of substrate availability (primarily glutamine), various enzyme activities, and intracellular pH. Since the amount of hydrogen ions in the tubules is a function of both hydrogen ion concentration and urine volume, the ability of the tubular fluid to trap ammonia will depend on the pH of this fluid as well as on urine flow. A schematic diagram of factors that affect the excretion of hydrogen ions is presented in Fig. 9.

The fetus is capable of acidifying its urine. In the fetal pig, the pH of the allantoic fluid (consisting primarily of urine) decreases progressively from 7.0 at 22 days' gestation to 5.8 at 90 days'. Titratable acidity and ammonia concentration of this fluid both increase progressively during this period.[82] The human infant is born with a bladder filled with a urine at a pH of about 6.3.[83] Although the fetus is clearly capable of excreting an acid urine, its renal acidifying capacity, estimated by measuring response to acid loading, is not as efficient as that of the adult. When fetal lambs were infused with small to moderate amounts of hydrochloric acid, there was little change in urine pH and total acid excretion.[129] With infusion of larger amounts of hydrochloric acid, there was a greater fall in urine pH (to about 5.8) and a significant increase in urinary titratable acidity and ammonia concentration, but not to the same degree as that obtained in adults.[109,129] Similar results were obtained from a recent study[33] in which lactic acid was infused over a 90-min period into *in situ* fetal lambs. Blood pH fell to 7.13 during the infusion, but urinary pH fell no lower than 6.25, and net acid excretion by the kidney over a 3-hr period following initiation of the acid infusion amounted to only a small fraction of the acid load. Although much of the infused acid must have been excreted by extrarenal mechanisms (the rise in extracellular pH and buffer base during the recovery period could not be accounted for by renal excretion of acid), the small amount of renal acid excretion accompanied by depression of extracellular pH during the acid infusion indicates that a relative inefficiency of one or more of the mechanisms of renal acid secretion exists in the fetus.

The newborn animal and infant are also unable to adequately excrete an imposed acid load.[31,44,51,64,78,118–120,129] In the human neonate, the more pre-maturely born infants respond less well than do more mature infants to acid loading.[118,120] The ability to excrete acid in the newborn human improves rapidly over the first few weeks of life. By 1 month of age, the infant can excrete as much hydrogen ion on acid loading as can the older child.[39] The relatively poor response to acid loading in the newborn includes a low total acid excretion, titratable acid excretion, ammonia excretion, and usually a relatively high minimum urinary pH.

Factors that affect the renal excretion of acid are schematized in Fig. 9, and the following discussion will be presented from the perspective of the relevance of these factors to perinatal acid excretion. The relatively poor ability of the perinatal kidney to excrete an imposed acid load could be due to the limited ability of its tubules to secrete hydrogen ions against a large concentration gradient or to the inadequate excretion of urinary buffers or to both factors. In favor of the first hypothesis is the finding that in most studies of urinary acidification in perinatal animals, the minimum urinary pH is much higher than in the adult. This finding does not apply to all species under all conditions, however. The newborn dog, for example, is capable of lowering its urinary pH to 4.8,[31] a value approaching that of the adult. Moreover, when fetal lambs were infused with sodium sulfate, which resulted in an increase of tubular sodium reabsorption without an accompanying anion reabsorption, and consequently in an enhancement of tubular sodium–hydrogen exchange, the urinary pH was lowered to a minimum of 4.7, and urinary titratable acidity and ammonia concentration were significantly enhanced.[86] These findings suggest that if the tubular cells of the perinatal kidney were presented with sufficient sodium ions for exchange with hydrogen, then they might be able to acidify the urine to the same or almost the same extent as the adult kidney. Further support for the hypothesis that poor response of the perinatal kidney to acid loading may be related to a limited tubular sodium–hydrogen exchange is the finding that in newborn infants, as the ability to excrete hydrogen ions increases with maturation, urinary sodium excretion decreases.[118]

Theoretically, a deficient renal tubular carbonic anhydrase enzyme activity could impair the active secretion of hydrogen ions. Carbonic anhydrase activity is lower in the perinatal than in the adult kidney.[76] This lower enzyme activity may not contribute to the lower hydrogen ion secretion, however, since carbonic anhydrase activity may have to be decreased to levels much lower than those found in the perinatal animal before hydrogen ion secretion will be affected.[76] On the other hand, carbonic anhydrase has not yet been localized in the perinatal kidney, so that if the moderate deficiency of the total enzyme activity of the kidney represents a severe deficiency of enzyme activity in only one locus (e.g., distal tubule or proximal brush border) and little or no change in another area, then hydrogen ion secretion may indeed be affected.

There is good evidence that the relatively poor ability of the perinatal kidney to respond to acid loading is related to inadequate excretion of urinary buffers. The amount of filtered buffers presented to the tubules depends on the glomerular filtration rate, which is low in the perinatal kidney. In addition, the amount of phosphate presented to the tubules is also related to the amount of phosphate ingested. In the human infant before feeding commences, only 10–25% of the acid is excreted as titratable acid.[83] In babies fed cow's milk, a formula containing large amounts of phosphate, total acid excretion is high, and 60% of the urinary acid is titratable acid. In breast-fed babies, both total acid excretion and the proportion of acid excreted as titratable acid are lower.[83] Total acid excretion is lower in these babies because the lower protein content of human breast milk decreases the metabolic production of acid, and the lower phosphate content of this milk decreases the titratable acid excretion.

When 1-week-old infants were given an acid load of ammonium or calcium chloride, they were not as able to excrete as much titratable acid or ammonia as were adults. Babies loaded with phosphate before the acid load demonstrated a marked increase in urinary titratable acidity and excreted $2\frac{1}{2}$ times as much acid in 8 hr as did infants not receiving phosphate.[51,78] That low phosphate excretion is not the complete explanation for the poor response of the newborn infant to acid loading can be deduced from the finding that adults excreted twice as much acid as did the phosphate-loaded infants.

Inadequate excretion of ammonia also plays an important role in the inability of the perinatal kidney to excrete an acid load. All studies reveal a lower secretion of ammonia on acid loading in the immature than in the mature kidney. As mentioned previously, the ability of the tubular cells to secrete ammonia will depend on the ability of the kidney to synthesize ammonia and on the amount of free hydrogen ions present in the tubular lumen to trap the ammonia. One reason for the low ammonia secretion is the relatively high urinary pH of most acid–loaded perinatal animals. However, since ammonia excretion is also diminished in cases of good urinary acidification,[31] the low ammonia excretion must also be related to decreased synthesis by renal tubular cells.

Factors that affect the renal synthesis of ammonia that may play an important role in the inability of the perinatal kidney to adequately secrete ammonia include:

1. Renal concentration of glutamine, the major substrate used for renal ammonia production: In newborn rats, renal glutamine concentration is lower than it is in adults.[45]

2. Activity of glutaminase, the enzyme involved in the deamidation of glutamine to ammonia and glutamate: Glutaminase activity is lower in newborn than in adult kidneys.[45]

3. Renal glutamate concentration: Glutamate, in addition to being one of the products of glutamine deamidation, acts as an inhibitor of the enzyme glutaminase. During acidosis in adult animals, renal glutamate concentrations are lower than normal, and this lowering is believed by some investigators to be largely responsible for the increased renal ammonia secretion during acidosis. Although renal glutamate concentrations are lower in newborn than in adult rats (which would lead to *increased* ammonia production), it is not as relatively low as glutamine and glutaminase.[45] Moreover, there is no lowering of the renal glutamate concentration in response to acid loading in newborn rats.[45]

4. NAD+/NADH ratio in renal tubular mitochondria: A large ratio of these pyridine nucleotides increases the deamination of glutamate (and consequently decreases the inhibition of glutaminase); the ratio is low in newborn rats.[46]

5. Renal gluconeogenic activity: Gluconeogenesis influences the rate of conversion of glutamate to glucose. Renal gluconeogenesis is low in newborn animals.[46]

It should be emphasized that the mechanisms involved in renal ammonia synthesis are not yet clearly understood, and that there is a great deal of controversy among investigators in the field. Thus, the findings of a different renal glutamine concentration, glutaminase activity, glutamate concentration, NAD+/NADH ratio, and rate of gluconeogenesis in newborn animals should not necessarily be interpreted as evidence for the definite implication of one or all of these factors in the inadequate renal ammonia response to acid loading. In addition, extrapolation of results of *in vitro* experiments to *in vivo* phenomena is fraught with dangers. These dangers become apparent when one recognizes that the pattern of *in vivo* maturation of renal ammonia secretion does not correlate well with the measurement of the *in vitro* maturation of some of the factors mentioned above.

As discussed previously, renal tubular bicarbonate reabsorption is dependent largely on active secretion of hydrogen ions by the kidney cells, and any difference in bicarbonate reabsorptive capacity between adult and perinatal animals will be largely a function of the difference in hydrogen ion secretion. Hydrogen ion secretion appears to be limited in the perinatal kidney, but the degree of the limitation has not yet been completely ascertained, and the limitation may be largely due to a low reabsorption of exchangeable sodium ions. The degree of restriction of hydrogen ion secretion is important, since the first hydrogen ions secreted will be utilized for bicarbonate reabsorption, and only the remainder will be excreted. Thus, a modest limitation of hydrogen ion secretion may not affect bicarbonate reabsorption, but may have a pronounced affect on net excretion of acid and the production of a maximally acid urine.

Earlier reports investigating bicarbonate reabsorption in the perinatal kidney utilized the T_m as the index for bicarbonate reabsorptive capacity. The T_m for bicarbonate, however, is largely the result of an experimental artifact. As the bicarbonate concentration in the blood is raised, the extracellular volume of the experimental animal is also changed, and this change influences the reabsorption of bicarbonate. Nevertheless, the T_m for bicarbonate, corrected for GFR, has been found to be the same for newborn infants as for the adult[126] (the T_m for bicarbonate, corrected for body weight or surface area, is, of course, much lower in the newborn). This finding of a normal bicarbonate T_m/GFR in newborn infants is consistent with the suggestion that tubular hydrogen ion secretion is limited only slightly, if at all, in the perinatal kidney. Again, the reader must be cautioned in his interpretations when utilizing the T_m as an indicator of bicarbonate reabsorptive capacity of the renal tubule.

The plasma threshold for bicarbonate has been found to be lower in the newborn dog and human than in the adult of the species.[87,126] However, even more caution must be given to the utilization of plasma bicarbonate threshold as an index of bicarbonate reabsorptive capacity than was given to T_m. Plasma threshold is a function not only of reabsorptive capacity, but also depends, as we have seen for glucose, on the degree of nephron heterogeneity. The large degree of nephron heterogeneity in the perinatal kidney would itself result in a low plasma threshold for bicarbonate. Moreover, techniques used to measure threshold also influence the extracellular volume of the animal, which in turn influences bicarbonate reabsorption and consequently plasma threshold for bicarbonate. In newborn dogs, when extracellular volume expansion was kept at a minimum during threshold studies, the plasma threshold for bicarbonate was 25 mmol/liter compared with 18 mmol/liter under standard experimental conditions where extracellular volume was increased.[87] Thus, the lower threshold for bicarbonate in the newborn animal is due either to greater nephron heterogeneity or to a different response to extracellular volume expansion, but it is unlikely that it represents a lower bicarbonate reabsorptive capacity.

In summary, the kidney of the perinatal animal is well capable of handling the normal acid loads presented to the fetus and the newborn. Hydrogen ion secretion is sufficiently effective to reabsorb all the bicarbonate filtered and to permit excretion of the normal metabolic acid production. Phosphate is filtered and ammonia is synthesized in amounts adequate to buffer hydrogen ion secretion, so that the acid may be excreted without taxing the secretory capacity of the tubular cells. Under conditions of excessive acid load, however, the perinatal kidney cannot maintain acid–base homeostasis. The tubules secrete enough hydrogen ions to reabsorb bicarbonate, but they may not be able to secrete sufficient hydrogen ions as excretable acid because there is insufficient sodium available for exchange. In addition, there may not be sufficient phosphate filtered or ammonia synthesized to buffer the hydrogen ions that are secreted.

10. Summary and Conclusions

The primary function of the kidney is to maintain water and electrolyte homeostasis within the body. The perinatal kidney has the ability to excrete the loads of sodium, water, and acid that are normally presented to it, and can thus maintain water and electrolyte balance. The perinatal kidney is well adapted for the normal needs of the fetus and newborn.

When the perinatal kidney is taxed with excessive water and electrolyte stresses, however, it cannot compensate as well as can the adult kidney. Perinatal body water and electrolyte content are therefore often thrown out of balance. If the perinatal animal is given an excessive load of acid, it will not excrete the load as efficiently as would the adult, with the result that the perinatal animal becomes acidotic. If the perinatal animal is given large amounts of sodium, its serum sodium concentration will rise, and it will become edematous. If water is restricted, the perinatal animal will easily become dehydrated, and its plasma will be hyperosmotic. On the other hand, if large amounts of free water are given to the perinatal animal, it will retain a greater fraction than will the adult.

The relative inefficiency of the perinatal kidney to respond to excessive water and electrolyte stresses should not, however, be interpreted as a serious defect in its functional design. An important factor in the inability of the perinatal kidney to respond to excessive stresses is its low GFR. In water loading, the low GFR of the perinatal kidney is responsible for the low flow rate in the diluting segments of the tubules. During sodium loading, the low GFR limits the amount of sodium that can be filtered. As a result, although fractional sodium reabsorption is lowered in the proximal tubule and fractional sodium load is enhanced to more distal segments, the absolute load of sodium to the distal segments of the tubule is not as great as it is to those of the adult on sodium loading. In acid loading, the low GFR limits the amount of phosphate that can be filtered to buffer the hydrogen ions secreted by the tubules. Moreover, tubular hydrogen ion secretion is limited by the low amounts of filtered sodium available for exchange. Yet, under most circumstances, the perinatal kidney requires a low rate of filtration to function properly. The tubules of the developing kidney have low active reabsorptive and secretory capacities, due largely to their small size. Thus, the low GFR assures a reasonable degree of glomerular tubular balance in the perinatal kidney, a characteristic most important for its proper functioning. If the immature tubular transport system were presented with excessive loads of sugar and electrolytes, as would occur if the GFR were high, then it would not be capable of reabsorbing these substances appropriately, and excessive amounts of sugar, water, and electrolytes would be excreted in the urine. Under these conditions, water and electrolyte homeostasis would be difficult to maintain. The inability to respond to excessive water and electrolyte stresses appears to be the price that the developing kidney pays for the maintenance of a more important functional capability, glomerular–tubular balance.

Proper functioning of the perinatal kidney depends not only on the intrinsic anatomic, chemical, and physical properties at any stage of maturation, but also on certain extrarenal factors. An appropriate GFR is extremely important for the proper functioning of the kidney. In the perinatal animal, the GFR is largely dependent on hemodynamic factors such as mean arterial blood pressure and renal vascular resistance. Anatomically, the perinatal kidney exhibits glomerular preponderance, and if the hemodynamic factors were not such as to limit the GFR, functional glomerular–tubular balance would be upset.

In the maturing kidney, there are nephrons at different stages of development. The more mature nephrons are usually situated in the juxtamedullary region and the less mature nephrons in the periphery. To maintain appropriate glomerular tubular balance, and appropriate nephron–perfusion balance, blood flow is selectively directed to the mature nephrons. As the kidney matures, more blood is eventually directed to the nephrons in the periphery as these nephrons become more capable of utilizing it.

The process of renal maturation is therefore largely one of maintaining a maximum (albeit imperfect) degree of functional glomerular–tubular and nephron–perfusion balance. This balance is achieved partially by a fair degree of morphological matching of glomerular and tubular size and largely hemodynamically by appropriate distribution of blood flow and limitation of glomerular filtration.

ACKNOWLEDGMENT

Preparation of this chapter was supported in part by the Children's Hospital Research Foundation, Cincinnati, Ohio, and by NIEHS grant ES-00159.

11. References

1. ALEXANDER, D. P., AND NIXON, D. A., 1961, The foetal kidney, *Br. Med. Bull.* **17**:112.

2. ALEXANDER, D. P., AND NIXON, D. A., 1962, Plasma clearance of *p*-aminohippuric acid by the kidneys of foetal, neonatal and adult sheep, *Nature (London)* **194**:483.

3. ALEXANDER, D. P., AND NIXON, D. A., 1963, Reabsorption of glucose, fructose and mesoinositol by the foetal and post-natal sheep kidney, *J. Physiol.* **167**:480.

4. ALEXANDER, D. P., NIXON, D. A., WIDDAS, W. F., AND WOHLZOGEN, F. X., 1958, Renal function in the sheep fetus, *J. Physiol.* **140**:14.

5. AMES, R. G., 1953, Urinary water excretion and neurohypophyseal function in full term and premature infants shortly after birth, *Pediatrics* **12**:272.

6. APERIA, A., AND HERIN, P., 1975, Development of glomerular perfusion rate and nephron filtration rate in rats 17–60 days old, *Amer. J. Physiol.* **228**:1319.

7. APERIA, A., BROBERGER, O., AND HERIN, P., 1974, Maturational changes in glomerular perfusion rate and glomerular filtration rate in lambs, *Pediatr. Res.* **8**:758.

8. APERIA, A., BROBERGER, O., THODENIUS, K., AND ZETTERSTRÖM, R., 1972, Renal response to an oral sodium load in newborn fullterm infants, *Acta Paediatr. Scand.* **61**:670.

8a. APERIA, A., BROBERGER, O., THODENIUS, K., AND ZETTERSTRÖM, R., 1974, Developmental study of the renal response to an oral salt load in preterm infants, *Acta Paediatr. Scand.* **63**:517.

9. APERIA, A., BROBERGER, O., THODENIUS, K., AND ZETTERSTRÖM, R., 1975, Development of renal control of salt and fluid homeostasis during the first year of life, *Acta Paediatr. Scand.* **64**:393.

9a. APERIA, A., BROBERGER, O., THODENIUS, K., AND ZETTERSTRÖM, R., 1975, Renal control of sodium and fluid balance in newborn infants during intravenous maintenance therapy, *Acta Paediatr. Scand.* **64**:725.

10. ARATAKI, M., 1926, Postnatal growth of kidney with special reference to number and size of glomeruli (albino rat), *Amer. J. Anat.* **36**:399.

11. ARTURSON, G., GROTH, T., AND GROTTE, G., 1971, Human glomerular membrane porosity and filtration pressure: Dextran clearance data analyzed by theoretical models, *Clin. Sci.* **40**:137.

12. ASSALI, N. S., BEKEY, G. A., AND MORRISON, L., 1968, Fetal and neonatal circulation, in: *Biology of Gestation* (N. S. Assali, ed.), Vol. 2, p. 51, Academic Press, New York.

13. BAKER, J. T., AND KLEINMAN, L. I., 1973, Glucose reabsorption in the newborn dog kidney, *Proc. Soc. Exp. Biol. Med.* **142**:716.

14. BAKER, J. T., AND KLEINMAN, L. I., 1974, Relationship between glucose and sodium excretion in the newborn dog, *J. Physiol.* **243**:45.

15. BARGER, A. C., 1966, Renal hemodynamic factors in congestive heart failure, *Ann. N.Y. Acad. Sci.* **139**:276.

16. BARGER, A. C., AND HERD, J. A., 1971, The renal circulation, *N. Engl. J. Med.* **284**:482.

17. BARNETT, H. L., VESTERDAL, J., McNAMARA, H., AND LAUSON, H. D., 1952, Renal water excretion in premature infants, *J. Clin. Invest.* **31**:1069.

18. BEHRMAN, R. E., AND LEES, M. H., 1971, Organ blood flows of the fetal, newborn and adult rhesus monkey, *Biol. Neonate* **18**:330.

19. BEITENS, I. Z., BAYARD, F., LEVITSKY, L., ANCES, I. G., KOWARSKI, A., AND MIGEON, C. J., 1972, Plasma aldosterone concentration at delivery and during the newborn period, *J. Clin. Invest.* **51**:386.

20. BERNSTINE, R. L., 1970, A chronic renal model for the fetus, *Lab. Anim. Sci.* **20**:949.

21. BLAINE, E. H., DAVIS, J. O., AND PREWITT, R. L., 1971, Evidence for a renal vascular receptor in control of renin secretion, *Amer. J. Physiol.* **220**:1593.

22. BLANTZ, R. C., KUTZ, M. H., RECTOR, F. C., AND SELDIN, D. W., 1971, Measurement of intrarenal blood flow. II. Effect of saline diuresis in the dog, *Amer. J. Physiol.* **220**:1914.

23. BOSS, J. M., DLOUHA, H., KRAUS, M., AND KRECEK, J., 1963, The structure of the kidney in relation to age and diet in white rats during the weaning period, *J. Physiol.* **168**:196.

24. BOWMAN, F. J., AND FOULKES, E. C., 1970, Antidiuretic hormone and urea permeability of collecting ducts, *Amer. J. Physiol.* **218**:231.

25. BOYLAN, J. W., COLBURN, E. P., AND McCANCE, R. A., 1958, Renal function in the foetal and newborn guinea-pig, *J. Physiol.* **141**:323.

26. BRODEHL, J., FRANKEN, A., AND GELLISSEN, K., 1972, Maximal tubular reabsorption of glucose in infants and children, *Acta Paediatr. Scand.* **61**:413.

27. BUDDINGH, F., PARKER, H. R., ISHIZAKI, G., AND TYLER, W. S., 1971, Long term studies of the functional development of the fetal kidney in sheep, *Amer. J. Vet. Res.* **32**:1993.

28. CALCAGNO, P. L., AND RUBIN, M. I., 1963, Renal extraction of PAH in infants and children, *J. Clin. Invest.* **43**:1632.

29. CARRIERE, S., FRIBORG, J., AND GUAY, J. P., 1971, Vasodilators, intrarenal blood flow and natriuresis in the dog, *Amer. J. Physiol.* **221**:92.

30. COHEN, M. L., SMITH, F. G., JR., MINDELL, R. S., AND VERNIER, R. L., 1969, A simple, reliable method of measuring glomerular filtration rate using single, low dose sodium iothalamate I^{131}, *Pediatrics* **44**:905.

31. CORT, J. H., AND McCANCE, R. A., 1954, The

renal response of puppies to an acidosis, *J. Physiol.* **124**:358.

32. CRAWFORD, J. D., DOYLE, A. P., AND PROBST, J. H., 1959, Service of urea in renal water conservation, *Amer. J. Physiol.* **196**:545.

33. DANIEL, S. S., BOWE, E. T., LALLEMARD, R., YEH, M. N., AND JAMES, L. S., 1975, Renal response to acid loading in the developing lamb fetus, intact *in utero, J. Perinat. Med.* **3**:34.

34. DEETJEN, P., AND SONNENBERG, H., 1965, Der tubuläre Transport von PAH. Microperfusionsversuche am Einzelnephron der Rattenniere *in situ, Pfluegers Arch.* **285**:35.

35. DICKER, S. E., 1970, Renal function in the newborn mammal, in: *Mechanisms of Urine Concentration and Dilution in Mammals* (S. E. Dicker, ed.), p. 133, The Williams & Wilkins Company, Baltimore.

36. DODGE, W. F., TRAVIS, L. B., AND DAESCHNER, L. W., 1967, Comparison of endogenous creatinine clearance with inulin clearance, *Amer. J. Dis. Child.* **113**:638.

37. EDELMANN, C. M., JR., BARNETT, H. L., AND STARK, H., 1966, Effect of urea on concentration of urinary nonurea solute in premature infants, *J. Appl. Physiol.* **21**:1021.

38. EDELMANN, C. M., JR., BARNETT, H. L., AND TROUPKOV, V., 1960, Renal concentrating mechanisms in newborn infants. Effect of dietary protein and water content, role of urea and responsiveness of antidiuretic hormone, *J. Clin. Invest.* **39**:1062.

39. EDELMANN, C. M., JR., SORIANO, J. R., BOICHIS, H., GRUSKIN, A. B., AND ACOSTA, M. I., 1967, Renal bicarbonate reabsorption and hydrogen ion excretion in normal infants, *J. Clin. Invest.* **46**:1309.

40. FALK, G., 1955, Maturation of renal function in adult rats, *Amer. J. Physiol.* **181**:157.

41. FETTERMAN, G. H., SHUPLOCK, N. A., PHILIPP, F. J., AND GREGG, H. S., 1963, The postnatal growth and maturation of the glomeruli and proximal convolutions in the human kidney with a note on cortical nephrons: Studies by microdissection, in: *Excerpta Medica International Congr. Ser. No. 78, Proceedings of the Second International Congress of Nephrology* (August, 1963), p. 32.

42. FETTERMAN, G. H., SHUPLOCK, N. A., PHILIPP, F. J., AND GREGG, H. S., 1965, The growth and maturation of human glomeruli and proximal convolutions from term to adulthood, *Pediatrics* **35**:601.

43. GAUER, D. H., AND TATA, P. S., 1968, Vasopressin studies in the rat. IV. The vasopressin-water-equivalent and vasopressin clearance by the kidneys, *Pfluegers Arch.* **298**:241.

44. GOLDSTEIN, L., 1970, Renal ammonia and acid excretion in infant rats, *Amer. J. Physiol.* **218**:1394.

45. GOLDSTEIN, L., 1971, Ammonia metabolism in kidneys of suckling rats, *Amer. J. Physiol.* **220**:213.

46. GOLDSTEIN, L., AND HARLEY-DEWITT, S., 1973, Renal gluconeogenesis and mitochondrial NAD$^+$/NADH ratios in nursing and adult rats, *Amer. J. Physiol.* **224**:752.

47. GRANGER, P., ROJO-ORTEGA, J. M., CASADO PEREZ, S., BOUCHER, R., AND GENEST, J., 1971, The renin–angiotensin system in newborn dogs, *Can. J. Physiol. Pharmacol.* **49**:134.

48. GRESHAM, E. L., RANKIN, J. H. G., MAKOWSKI, E. L., MESCHIA, G., AND BATTAGLIA, F. C., 1972, An evaluation of fetal function in a chronic sheep preparation, *J. Clin. Invest.* **51**:149.

49. GRUSKIN, A. B., EDELMANN, C. M., JR., AND YUAN, S., 1970, Maturational changes in renal blood flow in piglets, *Pediatr. Res.* **4**:7.

50. GUIGNARD, J. P., TORRADO, A., DACHUNHA, O., AND GAUTIER, E., 1975, Glomerular filtration rate in the first three weeks of life, *J. Pediatr.* **87**:268.

51. HATEMI, N., AND MCCANCE, R. A., 1961, Renal aspects of acid base control in the newly born. III. Response to acidifying drugs, *Acta Paediatr. Scand.* **50**:603.

52. HELLER, H., AND LEDERIS, K., 1959, Maturation of the hypothalamoneurohypophyseal system, *J. Physiol.* **147**:299.

53. HELLER, J., AND CAPEK, K., 1965, Changes in body water compartments and inulin and PAH clearance in the dog during post-natal development, *Physiol. Bohemoslov.* **14**:433.

54. HIRSCH, G. H., AND HOOK, J. B., 1970, Maturation of renal organic acid transport: Substrate stimulation by penicillin and *p*-aminohippurate (PAH), *J. Pharmacol. Exp. Ther.* **171**:103.

55. HOLLENBERG, N. K., ADAMS, D. F., SOLOMON, H. S., ABRAMS, H. L., AND MERRILL, J. P., 1972, What mediates the renal vascular response to a salt load in normal man, *J. Appl. Physiol.* **33**:491.

56. HOOK, J. B., WILLIAMSON, H. E., AND HIRSCH, G. H., 1970, Functional maturation of renal PAH transport in the dog, *Can. J. Physiol. Pharmacol.* **48**:169.

57. HORSTER, M., AND LEWY, J. E., 1970, Filtration fraction and extraction of PAH during neonatal period in the rat, *Amer. J. Physiol.* **219**:1061.

58. HORSTER, M., AND VALTIN, H., 1971, Postnatal development of renal function: Micropuncture and clearance studies in the dog, *J. Clin. Invest.* **50**:779.

59. HORSTER, M., KEMLER, B. J., AND VALTIN, H., 1971, Intracortical distribution of number and volume of glomeruli during postnatal maturation in the dog, *J. Clin. Invest.* **50**:796.

60. IKKOS, D., AND STROM, L., 1955, A comparison of the endogenous creatinine and inulin clearance in children, *Acta Paediatr.* **44**:426.

61. JANOVSKY, M., MARTINEK, J., AND STANINCOVA, V., 1965, Antidiuretic activity in the plasma of human infants after a load of sodium chloride, *Acta Paediatr. Scand.* **54**:543.

62. Jose, P. A., Logan, A. G., Slotkoff, L. M., Lilienfield, L. S., Calcagno, P. L., and Eisner, G. M., 1971, Intrarenal blood flow distribution in canine puppies, *Pediatr. Res.* **5**:335.

63. Jose, P. A., Slotkoff, L. M., Lilienfield, L. S., Calcagno, P. L., and Eisner, G. M., 1974, Sensitivity of neonatal renal vasculature to epinephrine. *Amer. J. Physiol.* **226**:796.

64. Kerpel-Fronius, E., Heim, T., and Sulyok, E., 1970, The development of the renal acidifying processes and their relation to acidosis in low-birth-weight infants, *Biol. Neonate* **15**:156.

65. Kim, J. K., Hirsch, G. H., and Hook, J. B., 1972, *In vitro* analysis of organic ion transport in renal cortex of the newborn rat, *Pediatr. Res.* **6**:600.

66. Kleinman, L. I., 1975, Renal sodium reabsorption during saline loading and distal blockade in newborn dogs, *Amer. J. Physiol.* **228**:1403.

67. Kleinman, L. I., and Lubbe, R. J., 1972, Factors affecting the maturation of glomerular filtration rate and renal plasma flow in the newborn dog, *J. Physiol.* **223**:395.

68. Kleinman, L. I., and Lubbe, R. J., 1972, Factors affecting the maturation of renal PAH extraction in the newborn dog, *J. Physiol.* **223**:411.

69. Kleinman, L. I., and Reuter, J. H., 1973, Maturation of glomerular blood flow distribution in the newborn dog, *J. Physiol.* **228**:91.

70. Kleinman, L. I., and Reuter, J. H., 1974, Renal response of the newborn dog to a saline load: The role of intrarenal blood flow distribution, *J. Physiol.* **239**:225.

71. Kotchen, T. A., Strickland, A. L., Rice, T. W., and Walters, D. R., 1972, A study of the renin–angiotensin system in newborn infants, *J. Pediatr.* **80**:938.

72. Kurtzman, N. A., 1970, Regulation of renal bicarbonate reabsorption by extracellular volume, *J. Clin. Invest.* **49**:586.

73. Kurtzman, N. A., White, M. G., Rodgers, P. W., and Flynn, J. J., III, 1972, Relationship of sodium reabsorption and glomerular filtration rate to renal glucose reabsorption, *J. Clin. Invest.* **51**:127.

74. Loggie, J. M. H., Kleinman, L. I., and Van Maanen, E. F., 1975, Renal function and diuretic therapy in infants and children. Part I, *J. Pediatr.* **86**:485.

75. MacDonald, M. S., and Emery, J. L., 1959, The late intrauterine and postnatal development of human renal glomeruli, *J. Anat.* **93**:331.

76. Maren, T. H., 1967, Carbonic anhydrase: Chemistry, physiology, and inhibition, *Physiol. Rev.* **47**:595.

77. McCance, R. A., 1948, Renal function in early life, *Physiol. Rev.* **28**:331.

78. McCance, R. A., and Hatemi, N., 1961, Control of acid base stability in the newly born, *Lancet* **1**:293.

79. McCance, R. A., and Widdowson, E. M., 1955, The response of puppies to a large dose of water, *J. Physiol.* **129**:628.

80. McCance, R. A., and Widdowson, E. M., 1956, Metabolism, growth and renal function of piglets in the first days of life, *J. Physiol.* **133**:373.

81. McCance, R. A., and Widdowson, E. M., 1957, Hypertonic expansion of the extracellular fluids, *Acta Paediatr. Scand.* **46**:337.

82. McCance, R. A., and Widdowson, E. M., 1960, The acid base relationships of the foetal fluids of the pig, *J. Physiol.* **151**:484.

83. McCance, R. A., and Widdowson, E. M., 1960, Renal aspects of acid base control in the newly born. I. Natural development, *Acta Paediatr. Scand.* **49**:409.

84. McCance, R. A., Naylor, N. S. B., and Widdowson, E. M., 1954, The response of infants to a large dose of water, *Arch. Dis. Child.* **29**:104.

85. McCrory, W. W., 1972, *Developmental Nephrology*, Harvard University Press, Cambridge, Massachusetts.

86. Moore, E. S., DeLannoy, L. W., Paton, J. B., and Ocampo, M., 1972, Effect of Na_2SO_4 on urinary acidification in the fetal lamb, *Amer. J. Physiol.* **218**:1394.

87. Moore, E. S., Fine, B. P., Satrasook, S. S., Vergel, Z. M., and Edelmann, C. M., Jr., 1972, Renal reabsorption of bicarbonate in puppies: Effect of extracellular volume contraction on the renal threshold for bicarbonate, *Pediatr. Res.* **6**:859.

88. Mott, J. C., 1966, Cardiovascular function in newborn mammals, *Br. Med. Bull.* **22**:66.

89. Navar, L. G., 1970, Minimal preglomerular resistance and calculation of normal glomerular pressure, *Amer. J. Physiol.* **219**:1658.

90. Oh, W., Oh, M. A., and Lind, J., 1966, Renal function and blood volume in the newborn infant related to placental transfusion, *Acta Paediatr. Scand.* **56**:197.

91. Olbing, H., Blaufox, M. D., Aschinberg, L. C., Silkalns, G. I., Bernstein, J., Spitzer, A., and Edelmann, C. M., Jr., 1973, Postnatal changes in renal glomerular blood flow distribution in puppies, *J. Clin. Invest.* **52**:2885.

92. Paton, J. B., Fisher, D. E., DeLannoy, C. W., and Behrman, R. E., 1973, Umbilical blood flow, cardiac output and organ blood flow in the immature baboon fetus, *Amer. J. Obstet. Gynecol.* **117**:560.

93. Pipkin, F. B., Kirkpatrick, S. M. L., Lumbers, E. R., and Mott, J. C., 1974, Renin and angiotensin-like levels in foetal newborn and adult sheep, *J. Physiol.* **241**:575.

94. PIPKIN, F. B., MOTT, J. C., AND ROBERTON, N. R. C., 1971, Angiotensin II-like activity in circulating arterial blood in immature and adult rabbits, *J. Physiol.* **218**:385.

95. POTTER, D., JARRAH, A., SAKAI, T., HARRAH, J., AND HOLLIDAY, M. A., 1969, Character of function and size in kidney during normal growth of rats, *Pediatr. Res.* **3**:51.

96. POTTER, E. L., 1965, Development of the human glomerulus, *Arch. Pathol.* **80**:241.

97. PURKERSON, M. L., LUBOWITZ, H., WHITE, R. W., AND BRICKER, N. S., 1969, On the influence of extracellular fluid volume expansion on bicarbonate reabsorption in the rat, *J. Clin. Invest.* **48**:1754.

98. RAHILL, W. J., AND SUBRAMANIAN, S., 1973, The use of fetal animals to investigate renal development, *Lab. Anim. Sci.* **23**:92.

99. RAKUSAN, K., AND MARCINEK, H., 1973, Postnatal development of the cardiac output distribution in rat, *Biol. Neonat.* **22**:58.

100. RANKIN, J. H. G., GRESHAM, E. L., BATTAGLIA, F. C., MAKOWSKI, E. L., AND MESCHIA, G., 1972, Measurement of fetal renal inulin clearance in a chronic sheep preparation, *J. Appl. Physiol.* **32**:129.

101. RENNICK, B., HAMILTON, B., AND EVANS, R., 1961, Development of renal tubular transports of TEA and PAH in the puppy and piglet, *Amer. J. Physiol.* **201**:743.

102. ROBILLARD, J. E., KULVINSKAS, C., SESSIONS, C., BURMEISTER, L., AND SMITH, F. G., 1975, Maturational changes in the fetal glomerular filtration rate, *Amer. J. Obstet. Gynecol.* **122**:601.

103. ROCHA, A. S., AND KOKKO, J. P., 1974, Permeability of medullary nephron segments to urea and water: Effect of vasopressin, *Kidney Int.* **6**:379.

104. RUBIN, M. I., BRUCH, E., AND RAPOPORT, M., 1949, Maturation of renal function in childhood: Clearance studies, *J. Clin. Invest.* **28**:1144.

105. SAKAI, F., AND ENDOV, H., 1971, Postnatal development of urea concentration in the newborn rabbit's kidney, *Jpn. J. Pharmacol.* **21**:677.

106. SCHULTZE, R. G., AND BERGER, H., 1973, The influence of GFR and saline expansion on T_{mG} of the dog kidney, *Kidney Int.* **3**:291.

107. SEGAL, S., REA, C., AND SMITH, I., 1971, Separate transport systems for sugars and amino acids in developing rat kidney cortex, *Proc. Natl. Acad. Sci. U.S.A.* **68**:372.

108. SIEGEL, S. R., FISHER, D. A., AND OH, W., 1974, Serum aldosterone concentrations related to sodium balance in the newborn infant, *Pediatrics* **53**:410.

109. SMITH, F. G., AND SCHWARTZ, A., 1970, Response of the intact lamb fetus to acidosis, *Amer. J. Obstet. Gynecol.* **106**:52.

110. SMITH, F. G., JR., ADAMS, F. H., BORDEN, M., AND HILBURN, J., 1966, Studies of renal function in the intact fetal lamb, *Amer. J. Obstet. Gynecol.* **46**:240.

111. SOLOMON, S., 1974, Maximal gradients of Na + K across proximal tubules of kidneys of immature rats, *Biol. Neonate* **25**:327.

112. SOLOMON, S., 1974, Absolute rates of sodium and potassium reabsorption by proximal tubule of immature rats, *Biol. Neonate* **25**:340.

113. SPITZER, A., AND BRANDIS, M., 1974, Functional and morphologic maturation of the superficial nephrons and relationship to total kidney function, *J. Clin. Invest.* **53**:279.

114. SPITZER, A., AND EDELMANN, C. M., JR., 1971, Maturational changes in pressure gradients for glomerular filtration, *Amer. J. Physiol.* **221**:1431.

115. STANIER, M. W., 1972, Development of intrarenal solute gradients in foetal and post-natal life, *Pfluegers Arch.* **336**:263.

116. STEICHEN, J. J., AND KLEINMAN, L. I., 1975, Influence of dietary sodium intake on renal maturation in unanesthetized canine puppies, *Proc. Soc. Exp. Biol. Med.* **148**:748.

117. STEIN, J. H., BOONJARERN, S., WILSON, C. B., AND FERRIS, T. F., 1973, Alterations in intrarenal blood flow distribution. Methods of measurement and relationship to sodium balance, *Circ. Res.* **32**(*Suppl. I*):1.

118. SULYOK, E., HEIM, T., SOLTESZ, G., AND JASZAI, V., 1972, The influence of maturity on renal control of acidosis in newborn infants, *Biol. Neonate* **21**:418.

119. SVENNINGSEN, N. W., 1974, Renal acid–base titration studies in infants with and without metabolic acidosis in the postnatal period, *Pediatr. Res.* **8**:659.

120. SVENNINGSEN, N. W., AND LINDQUIST, B., 1974, Postnatal development of renal hydrogen ion excretion capacity in relation to age and protein intake, *Acta Paediatr. Scand.* **63**:721.

121. TORELLI, G., MILLA, E., KLEINMAN, L. I., AND FAELLI, A., 1973, Effect of hypothermia on renal reabsorption, *Pfluegers Arch.* **342**:219.

122. TRIMBLE, M. E., 1970, Renal response to solute loading in infant rats: Relation to anatomical development, *Amer. J. Physiol.* **219**:1089.

123. TRIMPER, L. E., AND LUMBERS, E. R., 1972, The renin–angiotensin system in foetal lambs, *Pfluegers Arch.* **336**:1.

124. TUDVAD, F., 1949, Sugar reabsorption in prematures and full-term babies, *Scand. J. Clin. Lab. Invest.* **1**:281.

125. TUDVAD, F., AND VESTERDAL, J., 1953, The maximal tubular transfer of glucose and para-aminohippurate in premature infants, *Acta Paediatr. Scand.* **42**:337.

126. TUDVAD, F., MCNAMARA, H., AND BARNETT, H. L., 1954, Renal response of premature infants to

administration of bicarbonate and potassium, *Pediatrics* **13**:4.

127. VANDER, A. J., AND MILLER, R., 1964, Control of renin secretion in the anesthetized dog, *Amer. J. Physiol.* **207**:537.

128. VAN LIEW, J. B., DEETJEN, P., AND BOYLAN, J. W., 1967, Glucose reabsorption in the rat kidney, *Pfluegers Arch.* **295**:232.

129. VAUGHN, D., KIRSCHBAUM, T. H., BERSENTES, T., DILTS, P. V., JR., AND ASSALI, N. S., 1968, Fetal and neonatal response to acid loading in the sheep, *J. Appl. Physiol.* **24**:135.

130. VOGH, B., AND CASSIN, S., 1966, Stop flow analysis of renal function in newborn and maturing swine, *Biol. Neonate* **10**:153.

131. WEIL, W. B., JR., 1955, Evaluation of renal function in infancy and childhood, *Amer. J. Med. Sci.* **229**:678.

132. WELDON, V. V., KOWARSKI, A., AND MIGEON, C. J., 1967, Aldosterone secretion rates in normal subjects from infancy to adulthood, *Pediatrics* **39**:713.

CHAPTER 28

Calcium and Phosphorus Metabolism

William H. Bergstrom and
Margaret L. Williams

1. Introduction

During normal human pregnancy, the fetus accumulates approximately 30 g calcium and 24 g phosphorus, most of which is deposited in the skeleton, and is born with approximately 11 mg calcium and 5.6 mg phosphorus/dl serum.[36] These figures are independent of maternal intakes of calcium, phosphorus, and calciferol ("vitamin D") over rather wide ranges. In the neonatal period, especially in premature infants, clinically significant fluctuations in serum calcium and phosphorus concentration are common. In this chapter, we shall discuss the factors that contribute to intrauterine stability and *postpartum* perturbations of calcium and phosphorus metabolism.

2. The Antenatal Period

Our understanding of antenatal mineral metabolism is derived chiefly from animal data and from a small number of analyses of human material. The common laboratory animals have rates of maturation so different from our own (and from each other) that the amount of information transferable from species to species is quite limited. Systematic antenatal chemical descriptions of the primates are not yet available.

In human embryos prior to the appearance of the skeleton, calcium and phosphorus together comprise about 0.2% of the total body mass. Figure 1 shows the accretion of these substances during gestation. At birth, more than 90% of the total body content of calcium and phosphorus is in the form of hydroxyapatite, or "bone salt."[48] Bone at term is relatively undermineralized, having approximately half the adult normal ash weight/dry weight ratio.

The factors that govern antenatal osteogenesis are probably similar to those that are operative after birth. Prerequisites include orderly cartilage growth, calcification of cartilage, osteoclastic remodeling, osteoid synthesis, and final mineralization. The work of Abdul-Karim *et al.*[1,2] indicates that estrogen may be essential to normal fetal bone growth. These authors were able to inhibit orderly cartilage growth and osteoid synthesis by administering an antiestro-

William H. Bergstrom and Margaret L. Williams · Department of Pediatrics, State University of New York Upstate Medical Center, Syracuse, New York 13210

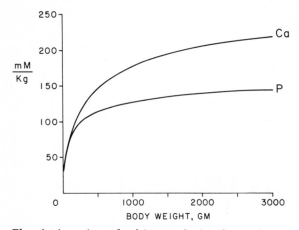

Fig. 1. Accretion of calcium and phosphorus during gestation. Data from Fee and Weil[18] and Kelly *et al.*[28]

genic compound (ethamoxytriphetol) to pregnant ewes and to prevent these adverse effects by simultaneous estrogen therapy.

Disorders of antenatal osteogenesis are for the most part related to substrate synthesis, rather than to calcium and phosphorus metabolism. Thus, in achondroplasia, dyschondroplasia, osteogenesis imperfecta, and osteopetrosis, the skeleton may be grossly deformed or the total bone mass much larger or smaller than usual, but the concentrations of calcium and phosphorus in body fluids are normal, and such bone as is present is normally mineralized. In hypophosphatasia, unmineralized osteoid may simulate rickets both grossly and microscopically, but serum calcium and phosphorus are characteristically normal at birth. The disorder is thought to result from the synthesis of an abnormal, uncalcifiable organic matrix. Among the infectious diseases, syphilis and rubella affect bone *in utero*, producing characteristic diaphyseal and periosteal lesions without influencing mineral metabolism.[38]

Congenital rickets has been seen only in association with severe maternal osteomalacia. In the series reported by Maxwell[33] from North China, mothers of the affected infants were multiparous, had bone pain, and had been almost totally deprived of calcium and calciferol by dietary and cultural patterns. Elsewhere, very wide variations in maternal nutrition have had little or no effect on fetal skeletal development.[10,27] Drastic alterations in the calcium and phosphorus intake of pregnant rats produce only minor changes in the bones of the offspring.[51] From these clinical and laboratory findings, it has been inferred that fetal calcium and phosphorus requirements may be met, if necessary, almost entirely at the expense of maternal stores. The calcium and phosphorus content of the newborn at term represents only 3–4% of his mother's skeletal content. The amounts of calcium and phosphorus normally supplied to the fetus from the mother's diet as compared with those contributed by her skeleton and soft tissues are not well defined.[36]

In postnatal life, at least five factors affect calcium and phosphorus homeostasis; there may well be others as yet undefined. Those recognized include diet, calciferol, parathyroid hormone (PTH), thyrocalcitonin, estradiol, and cortisol. Calciferol[43] facilitates intestinal absorption of calcium and phosphate. It enhances bone mineralization and renal tubular calcium and phosphate transport and facilitates the mobilization of bone calcium by PTH.

Two forms of calciferol are equally effective in mammals. Cholecalciferol results from ultraviolet irradiation of endogenous 7-dehydrocholesterol in the skin. Ergocalciferol, produced commercially by irradiation of ergosterol, is the familiar "vitamin D" dietary supplement. Both these steroids are hydroxylated at the 25 position (in the liver) and the 1 position (in the kidney), with consequent marked increases in physiologic activity. Hillman and Haddad[25,26] and Rosen *et al.*[44] showed a close correspondence between maternal and cord blood concentrations of the 25–OH derivative over a wide range, including low and supernormal levels. Their data indicate that neonatal levels of this steroid depend on passive (or perhaps facilitated) placental transfer. Similar information regarding the 1,25 $(OH)_2$ metabolite is not yet available.

PTH mediates intestinal calcium transport, though to a lesser degree than calciferol. In the bone, it stimulates resorption by osteoclasts and lysis by osteocytes. In the kidney, it promotes the reabsorption of calcium and the excretion of phosphorus. These various actions together determine serum calcium and phosphorus concentrations. Calcitonin (CT), which is secreted by the interstitial "c" cells of the thyroid, has an effect on osteoclastic and osteolytic activity opposite that of PTH. Although its hypocalcemic efficacy is established, its physiologic significance is undefined. Cortisol and estradiol also inhibit osteoclasis, and are thus PTH antagonists.[11,21]

The amounts of calcium and phosphorus available for diffusion or transport across the placenta depend on the simultaneous operation of these maternal regulatory factors. It is therefore very difficult to assess fetal homeostatic mechanisms; indeed, it is possible that the fetus is normally passive. Disturbances in maternal parathyroid function can evoke adaptive responses in the fetal glands, probably by altering the availability of calcium. It is unlikely that PTH crosses the placenta.[36] Independent operation of the other regulatory factors has not yet been shown in the fetus.

Bodansky and Duff[9] showed that rats on low-calcium diets regularly lost skeletal calcium and phosphate during pregnancy. Parathyroidectomy prevented maternal demineralization and resulted in poorly calcified fetuses. In mothers on high-calcium diets, however, maternal skeletons were unchanged during pregnancy, and neither mothers nor fetuses were affected by parathyroidectomy. Evidently the parathyroids are essential for the transfer of calcium and phosphate from mother to fetus when dietary calcium is restricted. No transfer is necessary when calcium is abundant. It is not clear, however, how the low- and high-calcium intakes selected for these studies correspond to those of rats in their natural state, and the data are therefore hard to interpret in terms of human nutrition. Normal bone structure and composition are maintained by human populations whose calcium intake varies from 200 to 1200 mg/day,[10,27] suggesting a wide range of efficiency of intestinal absorption. This efficiency has been confirmed by balance studies. Adaptation to low-calcium diets is achieved over a period of several months by most persons; a few are unable to increase their intestinal absorption appropriately and remain in negative balance, presumably at the expense of skeletal mineral.[32] In the chick, adaptive enhancement of calcium absorption involves synthesis of a specific calcium-binding protein (CaBP) found only in the intestinal mucosa and in the kidney.[58,59] Mammals also possess this protein; its physiologic regulation in the higher forms has not yet been studied, but is probably consistent throughout the vertebrates, as are the other known factors in calcium homeostasis. CaBP synthesis is calciferol-dependent, but seems not to require estrogen or PTH. The laying hen, which has a high calcium requirement, has more CaBP than the pullet. A similar adaptive increase in maternal CaBP during mammalian pregnancy has not yet been established.

Heaney and Skillman[24] studied calcium and phosphorus metabolism in a group of young mothers. They found that calcium and phosphorus retention exceeded that of nonpregnant controls as early as the 20th week of pregnancy, a time at which fetal mineralization is negligible.[36] Increased maternal skeletal accretion was defined. The authors advanced the interesting hypothesis that human chorionic somatomammotropin (HCS), acting in conjunction with estrogen and PTH, may be responsible for these anticipatory changes in mineral metabolism. Increased absorption persisted for several weeks after delivery whether lactation was present or not.

Cushard et al.[14] found that maternal serum PTH levels began to rise after the 24th week; by 36–40 weeks, 17 of 20 subjects showed PTH concentrations above the range for nonpregnant controls. *Postpartum* measurements, including those in 13 of 14 lactating women, were all within the normal range. These data, in accord with those of other groups,[29,39] indicate temporary adaptive maternal hyperparathyroidism in pregnancy. It is not clear what stimulates the parathyroids at a time when maternal ionized calcium is within the normal range.[36]

Samaan et al.[45] measured CT in term maternal plasma and in samples from the umbilical artery and vein. Surprisingly, maternal levels exceeded those of nonpregnant adults; umbilical vein levels were still higher, and umbilical arterial values highest of all. The data define a brisk rate of CT production by the fetus; in combination with a continuous transplacental calcium and phosphorus influx, this high production should promote skeletal mineralization.

It thus appears that mothers who are provided adequate calciferol can adapt to a wide range of calcium intakes so as to assure normal fetal mineralization. When dietary calcium is inadequate, the fetus is supplied at the expense of the maternal skeleton; this process is parathyroid-dependent. Since ideal allowances of calcium and calciferol during pregnancy have not been defined, it is difficult to evaluate supplementation of calcium or phosphate or both during pregnancy in terms of maternal or fetal benefit; animal data do not support the practice, and controlled studies in human beings are not available. Calciferol deficiency should be avoided; 400 U/day is the present standard recommendation.[22]

Maternal parathyroid disease induces transient functional changes in the offspring after delivery. Tetany lasting for several weeks has been seen in the infants of hyperparathyroid mothers.[17,23] Whether the tetany is due to suppression of the fetal parathyroids or to stimulation of CT secretion has not been determined; the former possibility is more consistent with the observed hyperphosphatemia. Conversely, hyperparathyroidism has been reported in the offspring of a hypoparathyroid mother.[3] This circumstance is rare, since hypoparathyroidism is a less common disease, and untreated mothers rarely carry babies to term. Fetal response in both disorders is probably evoked by abnormal calcium ion concentrations rather than by placental transfer of maternal hormone, although the latter factor cannot be excluded. Thus, continuous exposure to excessive calcium ion concentration *in utero* may suppress fetal parathyroid function, whereas calcium lack may serve as a stimulus. This hypothesis is based on the assumption that fetal parathyroids, at least near term, respond in the same fashion as do those of postnatal subjects and explants in tissue culture. The studies by Scothorne[46] of human parathyroid explants suggest that the glands are functional by the 12th week of gestation. Sinclair[49] was able to alter fetal parathyroid size in the rat by manipulating the maternal diet. It is likely that the fetal parathyroids are minimally stimulated during normal pregnancy, since the calcium and phosphorus concentrations of their circumambient fluids are regulated by maternal parathyroid and renal function and possibly by the placenta as well. Widdowson et al.[61] found that urine collected immediately after birth contained very little phosphorus (0.24 mg/dl). Since these samples were formed *in utero*, it may be inferred that prenatal parathyroid activity was minimal.

3. The Postnatal Period

It has long been known that calcium and phosphorus concentrations in human cord blood at term exceed those of simultaneously taken maternal venous samples.[16] In the case of calcium, most of the difference is due to a higher fetal level of the ionized portion. In 317 paired analyses, the fetal/maternal calcium ratio was 1.11:1.00.[36] This phenomenon has led to the general conclusion that the placenta actively transports calcium and phosphorus. Studies in a few previable fetuses, however,[60] showed no transplacental gradient for calcium in the fetal weight range from 50 to 750 g. As we noted above, the normal ranges of fetal serum

calcium and phosphorus concentrations are defined by very sparse data. Nevertheless, there is indirect evidence that intrauterine hypercalcemia may occur. Beuren et al.[8] found the typical stigmata and vascular lesions of idiopathic hypercalcemia in the offspring of mothers who had received massive doses of calciferol (12.5 mg or 500,000 U) repeatedly during pregnancy. It has since been possible to reproduce the vascular lesions in the offspring of calciferol-treated rabbits.[19] These findings strongly suggest that intrauterine hypercalcemia may have been present.

Mean *serum calcium concentration* in the cord blood has been reported as 10.4–11.0 mg/dl.[36,50,15] Over the first day, this level falls progressively. Full-term infants show mean calcium concentrations of 8.8–9.1 mg/dl at 24 hr.[50] The mean serum phosphorus concentration in the cord blood is 5.7 mg/dl; this concentration increases within a few hours of birth, reaching 6–6.5 mg/dl at 24 hr and 7–8 mg/dl at the end of a week.[50]

In comparison with the full-term infant, the premature shows a greater decrease in serum calcium over the first day, with 24- to 48-hr concentrations often falling below 7.0 mg/dl.[53] Between 12 and 72 hr of age, serum calcium levels correlate significantly with gestational age, but not with birth weight in infants who are small for gestational age.[55] Symptoms of this early hypocalcemia rarely occur with serum calcium levels greater than 7. mg/dl and are generally not those of classic tetany, e.g., carpopedal spasm, Chvostek's sign, or inspiratory stridor. Instead, the clinical picture is one of rapid, shallow respirations, apneic episodes, and poor color, followed by increasing agitation, tachycardia, and finally flaccidity suggesting exhaustion.[13] Grand mal seizures are occasionally seen.[41]

Symptomatology in hypocalcemia relates more closely to plasma ionized calcium concentration than to total calcium. Ionized calcium concentration is influenced by a variety of factors, including pH, serum protein, inorganic phosphate, and other calcium-binding substances, but in general it represents 0.40–0.45 of total calcium.[37] Sorrell and Rosen[52] showed that wide variations from these values exist in individual cases, and suggested that symptomatology occurs below a critical Ca^{2+} level of about 2.5 meq/liter.

A relationship between neonatal hypocalcemia and a transient state of hypoparathyroidism in the first day of life was first suggested by Bakwin[6] in 1939. Evidence for this hormonal deficiency appears in the experiments of Connelly *et al.*,[12] who compared the responses of newborns to PTH given on the 1st and 3rd days of life. These authors found enhancement of renal phosphate excretion at both ages, with an increase in the proportion of phosphate clearance/creatinine clearance. The change at 3 days was greater than that seen at 1 day. Untreated infants also showed a decrease in tubular reabsorption of phosphorus over the period of study. Thus, both endogenous parathyroid activity and renal tubular responsiveness increased within the first 3 days. In full-term infants, Linarelli[31] found that urinary cyclic AMP increased 3- to 4-fold and phosphate clearance more than 30-fold between the 1st and 3rd days of life. When PTH was infused, both urinary cyclic AMP and phosphate clearance increased; the change was much greater on the 3rd than on the 1st day, but still far below the mean for adult controls. The data indicate partial maturation of renal tubular phosphaturic response to PTH within the first 3 days of life. McCrory *et al.*[34] found that tubular phosphate reabsorption was increased when intestinal phosphate absorption was reduced by oral aluminum hydroxide gel. The ability of an infant so treated to excrete exogenous phosphate was markedly reduced, since tubular reabsorption established during phosphate deprivation persisted throughout the acute loading period. Adult rats[42] kept on a low-phosphorus diet for 2 weeks showed fatal tetany following parenteral phosphate loads well tolerated by animals on the standard high-phosphate ration. Injection of PTH prior to loading was protective, and phosphate tolerance was reestablished by 5 days on the standard diet. It seems likely that these experiments are analogous to those of McCrory *et al.*

Tsang *et al.*[57] studied the calcemic response of 23 newborn infants to exogenous PTH during the first 3 days of life. They found no relationship between this response and gestational age, concluding that hypocalcemia was related to immature or suppressed parathyroid function rather than to end-organ unresponsiveness. Their data did not bear, however, on the questions of phosphorus homeostasis considered by Linarelli[31] and by Connelly *et al.*[12]

Direct evidence of decreased parathyroid function was presented by David and Anast.[15] They demonstrated undetectable or low serum immunoreactive PTH (iPTH) levels associated with decreased plasma calcium concentrations in normal newborns in the first 48 hr of life, with parallel increases in both iPTH and plasma calcium thereafter. A group of sick infants, some of low gestational age, showed significantly lower plasma calcium levels than well babies, but an equal or greater serum iPTH. However, infants with plasma calcium of 7.5 mg/dl had generally undetectable iPTH. No significant differences in plasma phosphorus levels were detected and hyperphosphatemia was uncommon as opposed to other investigators' reports.[57] The authors contrasted the relatively similar distribution of iPTH levels in the groups of well and sick infants with the significantly differing calcium concentrations and suggested that factors other than PTH deficiency contribute to the lowered calcium in the newborn period.

Both hormonal and nutritional status may represent such modifying influences. For example, cortisol is known to oppose PTH in calcium homeostasis through inhibition of bone resorption. Thus, the tendency of newborns with the respiratory distress syndrome to be hypocalcemic may be due in part to their increased plasma cortisol levels.[4,5,40] The authors[21] have data indicating that estrogen administration lowers serum calcium concentration in newborn rats. It is possible that high estrogen levels at birth may contribute to hypocalcemia in human infants as well.

The variable undernutrition of the first days of life, particularly common in the premature infant, may also play a modifying role. Fasting releases endogenous phosphate from protein catabolism, and has in fact been shown to bring about healing of active rickets in both human and animal subjects. Deposition of bone calcium in infants with minimal calcium intake and abundant undermineralized osteoid could establish hypocalcemia by the same mechanism as that in rapidly healing rickets.

In addition to low gestational age, three other neonatal problems are closely associated with hypocalcemia in the first days of life. Tsang *et al.*[54] pointed out the high incidence of low serum calcium concentrations in infants who have suffered birth asphyxia, postulating that functional hypoparathyroidism, bicarbonate therapy, and hyperphosphatemia may all be contributory factors.

The second group of neonates predisposed to hypocalcemia are infants of diabetic mothers (IDM), irrespective of gestational age or perinatal complications.[13,56] Serum calcium levels in diabetic mothers are higher than in nondiabetic mothers; serum calcium is lower and serum phosphate higher in infants of insulin-dependent diabetic mothers up to 72 hr of age. These data suggest an increased suppression of fetal parathyroid function in IDM related to maternal calcium level, which in turn may result from relative hyperparathyroidism. Tsang et al.[56] demonstrated failure of serum PTH values to increase appropriately in the face of marked hypocalcemia in these infants. Their response to exogenous PTH was unimpaired.

Intravenous administration of bicarbonate to correct acidosis is a third situation frequently associated with hypocalcemia.[35] Urinary calcium excretion is not increased, and it would appear that the hypocalcemia reflects increased calcium deposition in bone.

As opposed to hypocalcemia in the early postnatal days, the occurrence of the classic "tetany of the newborn" at approximately 1 week of life appears to be linked to the presence of excessive dietary phosphate, and is probably related more to renal than to parathyroid immaturity. An early study by McCrory et al.[34] demonstrated that the proportion of excreted phosphorus to filtered phosphorus was as high in infants by 6 days of age as in fasting adults, and the response of their subjects to exogenous PTH was similar to that of adults. They concluded that the higher serum phosphate and intolerance of phosphate loading of these infants could be attributed to their lower glomerular filtration rate (GFR). It can be assumed that both the parathyroid glands and renal tubules are hypoactive during the first 2 or 3 days of postnatal life, when hyperphosphatemia is established. Thereafter, the relatively low GFR of early infancy may maintain the serum phosphorus above the level found in older children.

Decreased renal phosphorus excretion, whatever its cause, has the clinical correlate of susceptibility to tetany in the presence of excessive dietary phosphate. Cow's milk contains approximately 5 times as much phosphorus as human milk and a calcium/phosphorus ratio of 1:1 instead of 2:1. Most commonly used dilutions of whole or evaporated milk therefore impose a phosphate load on the formula-fed infant. Gardner[20] demonstrated parathyroid hyperplasia, hyperphosphatemia, and an increased incidence of neonatal tetany in formula-fed as compared with breast-fed infants. The composition of commercial formulas has since been altered to decrease phosphorus and increase the calcium/phosphorus ratio, with the result that tetany is now uncommon in normal full-term, formula-fed infants.

Calcium absorption increases with both gestational and postnatal age.[47] The influence of dietary fat on calcium absorption appears to depend more on the saturation of the fatty acids and their position on the triglyceride molecule than on the absolute amount of fat fed. There is no evidence, however, that normal infants become calcium-depleted as a result of the fat ingested in commonly used formulas.[47]

Shaw[47] found that premature infants 30–70 days old absorbed less calcium, even with calciferol supplements of 688–760 IU/day, than would correspond to intrauterine accretion rates for fetuses of equivalent weights. On cow's milk, retention was 40% of the estimated antenatal accretion; on human milk, it was 20%. Barltrop[7] reported negative calcium balances in premature formula-fed infants 6–22 days old; the calciferol supplement was unspecified.

These studies suggest that inadequate calcium absorption may contribute to hypocalcemia in premature infants.

Several other causes of hypocalcemia are recognized. One is congenital hypomagnesemia, in which available magnesium does not suffice for PTH secretion,[15] and secondary hypocalcemia ensues. A more frequent association of hypocalcemia and hypomagnesemia results from deficiency of PTH, the major homeostatic determinant of both ions. In the DiGeorge syndrome, hypoparathyroidism occurs in association with thymic aplasia as a manifestation of abnormal branchial arch development.

In 11 of 15 hypocalcemic premature infants, Rosen et al.[44] found subnormal levels of serum 25-OHD corresponding to similarly depressed maternal levels. The authors suggest that maternal calciferol deficiency may on occasion contribute to neonatal hypocalcemia. Lewin et al.[30] reported rickets as early as 2 months of age in premature infants receiving 100–150 U calciferol/day; on the same calcium intake, comparable infants receiving 400 U/day did not develop rickets. Finally, congenital hypoparathyroidism may follow maternal hyperparathyroidism, as discussed above.

4. Summary

It appears that the neonate is functionally hypoparathyroid as a result of either immaturity or lack of intrauterine stimulation of parathyroids and kidneys. This tendency is exaggerated by prematurity and by maternal hyperparathyroidism. Birth asphyxia and maternal diabetes predispose to early hypocalcemia, as does alkali administration. Hyperphosphatemia as a result of high phosphorus intake may cause hypocalcemia in the first weeks of life. Clinical signs of hypocalcemia are nonspecific, and a high index of suspicion is appropriate for the clinician.

5. References

1. ABDUL-KARIM, R., 1967, Fetal endocrinology—a review, *J. Med. Liban.* **20**:201.
2. ABDUL-KARIM, R., NESBITT, E. L., JR., AND PRIOR, J. T., 1966, Study of the effects of experimentally induced endocrine insults upon pregnant and non-pregnant ewes, *Fertil. Steril.* **17**:637.
3. ACETO, T., JR., BATT, R. E., AND BRUCK, E., 1966, Intrauterine hyperparathyroidism: A complication of untreated maternal hypoparathyroidism, *J. Clin. Endocrinol.* **26**:487.
4. BACON, G. E., GEORGE, R., KOEFF, S. T., AND HOWATT, W. F., 1975, Plasma corticoids in the respiratory distress syndrome and in normal infants, *Pediatrics* **55**:500.
5. BADEN, M., BAUER, C. R., COLLE, E., KLEIN, G., PAPAGEORGIOU, A., AND STEIN, L., 1973, Plasma corticosteroids in infants with the respiratory distress syndrome, *Pediatrics* **52**:782.
6. BAKWIN, H., 1939, Tetany in newborn infants: Relation to physiologic hypoparathyroidism, *J. Pediatr.* **14**:1.
7. BARLTROP, D., 1975, Neonatal hypocalcemia, *Postgrad. Med. J.* **51**(Suppl. 3) : 7.
8. BEUREN, A. J., APITZ, J., STOERMER, J., SCHLANGE, H., KAISER, B., VAN BERG, W., AND JÖRGENSON, G., 1966, Vitamin-D-hypercalcamische Herz und Gefasserkrankung, *Dtsch. Med. Wochenschr.* **91**:881.
9. BODANSKY, M., AND DUFF, V. B., 1941, Dependence of fetal growth and storage of calcium and phosphorus on the parathyroid function and diet of pregnant rats, *J. Nutr.* **22**:25.
10. BOOHER, L. E., AND HAUSMANN, G. H., 1931, Studies on the chemical composition of the human skeleton. I. Calcification of the tibia of the normal newborn infant, *J. Biol. Chem.* **94**:195.
11. CANAS, F. M., BERGSTROM, W. H., AND CHURGIN, S. J., 1967, Effects of the adrenal on calcium homeostasis in the rat, *Metabolism* **16**:670.
12. CONNELLY, J. P., CRAWFORD, J. D., AND WATSON, J., 1962, Studies of neonatal hyperphosphatemia, *Pediatrics* **43**:425.
13. CRAIG, W. S., 1958, Clinical signs of neonatal tetany: With especial reference to their occurrence in newborn babies of diabetic mothers, *Pediatrics* **22**:297.
14. CUSHARD, W. G., JR., CREDITOR, M. A., CANTERBURY, J. M., AND REISS, E., 1972, Physiologic hyperparathyroidism in pregnancy, *J. Clin. Endocrinol. Metab.* **34**:776.
15. DAVID, L., AND ANAST, C. S., 1974, Calcium metabolism in newborn infants, *J. Clin. Invest.* **54**:287.
16. ECONOMU-MAVROU, C., AND MCCANCE, R. A., 1958, Calcium, magnesium and phosphorus in foetal tissues, *Biochem. J.* **68**:573.
17. ERTEL, N. H., REISS, J. S., AND SPERGEL, G., 1969, Hypomagnesemia in neonatal tetany associated with maternal hyperparathyroidism, *N. Engl. J. Med.* **280**:260.
18. FEE, B. A., AND WEIL, W. B., 1963, Body composition of infants of diabetic mothers by direct analysis, *Ann. N. Y. Acad. Sci.* **110**:869.
19. FRIEDMAN, W. F., AND MILLS, L. F., 1969, The relationship between vitamin D and the craniofacial and dental anomalies of the supravalvular aortic stenosis syndrome, *Pediatrics* **43**:12.
20. GARDNER, L. I., 1952, Tetany and parathyroid hyperplasia in the newborn infant: Influence of the dietary phosphate load, *Pediatrics* **9**:534.
21. GOTTUSO, M. A., NERVEZ, C. T., JACOBS, R. D., SHOTT, R. J., WILLIAMS, M. L., AND BERGSTROM, W. H., 1975, Steroid effects on serum calcium in the rat, *Pediatr. Res.* **9**:290 (abstract).
22. GREENGARD, P., 1975, The vitamins, in: *The Pharmacological Basis of Therapeutics* (L. S. Goodman and A. Gilman, eds.), pp. 1544–1598, Macmillan, New York.
23. HARTENSTEIN, H., AND GARDNER, L. I., 1966, Tetany of the newborn associated with maternal parathyroid adenoma, *N. Engl. J. Med.* **274**:266.
24. HEANEY, R. P., AND SKILLMAN, T. G., 1971, Calcium metabolism in normal human pregnancy, *J. Clin. Endocrinol. Metab.* **33**:661.
25. HILLMAN, L. S., AND HADDAD, J. G., 1974, Human perinatal vitamin D metabolism I: 25-Hydroxyvitamin D in maternal and cord blood, *J. Pediatr.* **84**:742.
26. HILLMAN, L. S., AND HADDAD, J. G., 1975, Perinatal vitamin D metabolism, *J. Pediatr.* **86**:928.
27. JACKSON, W. P. U., 1961, Effects of altered nutrition on the skeletal system: The requirement of calcium in man, in: *Recent Advances in Human Nutrition* (J. S. Brock, ed.), p. 293, Little Brown & Co., New York.
28. KELLY, H. J., SLOAN, R. E., HOFFMAN, W., AND SAUNDERS, C., 1951, Accumulation of nitrogen and six minerals in the human fetus during gestation, *Hum. Biol.* **23**:61.
29. LEQUIN, R. M., HACKENG, W. H. L., AND SCHOPMAN, W., 1970, *Acta Endocrinol. (Copenhagen)* **63**:611.
30. LEWIN, P. K., REID, M., REILLY, B. J., SWYER, P. R., AND FRASER, D., 1971, Iatrogenic rickets in low-birth-weight infants, *J. Pediatr.* **78**:207.
31. LINARELLI, L. G., 1972, Newborn urinary cyclic AMP and developmental renal responsiveness to parathyroid hormone, *Pediatrics* **50**:14.
32. MALM, O. J., 1963, Adaptation to alterations in calcium intake, in: *The Transfer of Calcium and Strontium Across Biological Membranes* (R. H. Wasserman, ed.), pp. 143–173, Academic Press, New York.

33. MAXWELL, J. P., 1930, Further studies in osteomalacia, *Proc. R. Soc. Med.* **23**:19.

34. McCRORY, W. W., FORMAN, C. W., McNAMARA, H., AND BARNETT, H. L., 1952, Renal excretion of inorganic phosphate in newborns, *J. Clin. Invest.* **31**:357.

35. NERVEZ, C. T., SHOTT, R. J., BERGSTROM, W. H., AND WILLIAMS, M. L., 1975, Prophylaxis against hypocalcemia in low-birth-weight infants requiring bicarbonate infusion, *J. Pediatr.* **87**:439.

36. PITKIN, R. M., 1975, Calcium metabolism in pregnancy: A review, *Amer. J. Obstet. Gynecol.* **121**:724.

37. RADDE, J. C., PARKINSON, D. K., HOFFKEN, B., APPIA, K. E., AND HANLEY, W. B., 1972, Calcium ion activity in the sick neonate: Effect of bicarbonate administration and exchange transfusion, *Pediatr. Res.* **6**:43.

38. REED, G. B., JR., 1969, Rubella bone lesions, *J. Pediatr.* **74**:208.

39. REITZ, R. E., DAANE, T. A., WOODS, J. D., AND WEINSTEIN, R. L., 1972, in: *Fourth International Congress of Endocrinology*, Washington, D. C., *Excerpta Med. Int. Congr. Ser.* No. 256, p. 208. Excerpta Medica Foundation, Amsterdam.

40. REYNOLDS, J. W., 1973, Serum total corticord and cortisol levels in premature infants with respiratory distress syndrome, *Pediatrics* **51**:884.

41. ROBERTON, N. R. C., AND SMITH, M. A., 1975, Early neonatal hypocalcemia, *Arch. Dis. Child.* **50**:604.

42. ROGERS, M. C., AND BERGSTROM, W. H., 1971, Diet-induced hypoparathyroidism: A model for neonatal tetany, *Pediatrics* **47**:207.

43. ROOT, A. W., AND HARRISON, H. E., 1976, Recent advances in calcium metabolism, *J. Pediatr.* **88**:1.

44. ROSEN, J. F., ROGINSKY, M., NATHENSON, G., AND FINBERG, L., 1974, 25-Hydroxyvitamin D, *Amer. J. Dis. Child.* **127**:220.

45. SAMAAN, N. A., ANDERSON, G. D., AND ADAM-MAYNE, M. E., 1975, Immuno-active calcitonin in the mother, neonate, child, and adult, *Amer. J. Obstet. Gynecol.* **121**:622.

46. SCOTHORNE, R. J., 1964, Functional capacity of fetal parathyroid glands with reference to their clinical use as homografts, *Ann. N. Y. Acad. Sci.* **120**:669.

47. SHAW, J. C. L., 1976, Evidence for defective skeletal mineralization in low birthweight infants: The absorption of calcium and fat, *Pediatrics* **57**:16.

48. SHOHL, A. T., 1939, *Mineral Metabolism,* Reinhold Publishing, New York.

49. SINCLAIR, J. G., 1942, Fetal rat parathyroids as affected by changes in maternal serum and phosphorus through parathyroidectomy and dietary control, *J. Nutr.* **23**:141.

50. SNODGRASS, G. J. A. I., STIMMLER, L., WENT, J., ABRAMS, M. E., AND WILL, E. J., 1972, Interrelations of plasma calcium inorganic phosphate, magnesium, and protein over the first week of life, *Arch. Dis. Child.* **48**:279.

51. SONTAG, L. W., MUNSON, P., AND HUFF, E., 1936, Effects on the fetus of hypervitaminosis D and calcium and phosphorus deficiency during pregnancy, *Amer. J. Dis. Child.* **51**:302.

52. SORRELL, M., AND ROSEN, J. F., 1975, Ionized calcium: Serum levels during symptomatic hypocalcemia, *J. Pediatr.* **87**:67.

53. TSANG, R. C., AND OH, W., 1970, Neonatal hypocalcemia in low birthweight infants, *Pediatrics* **45**:773.

54. TSANG, R. C., CHEN, I., HAYES, W., ATKINSON, W., ATHERTON, H., AND EDWARDS, N., 1974, Neonatal hypocalcemia in infants with birth asphyxia, *J. Pediatr.* **84**:428.

55. TSANG, R. C., GIGGER, M., OH, W., AND BROWN, D. R., 1975, Studies in calcium metabolism in infants with intrauterine growth retardation, *J. Pediatr.* **86**:936.

56. TSANG, R. C., KLEINMAN, L. I., SUTHERLAND, J. M., AND LIGHT, I. J., 1972, Hypocalcemia in infants of diabetic mothers, *J. Pediatr.* **80**:384.

57. TSANG, R. C., LIGHT, I. J., SUTHERLAND, J. M., AND KLEINMAN, L. I., 1973, Possible pathogenetic factors in neonatal hypocalcemia of prematurity, *J. Pediatr.* **82**:423.

58. WASSERMAN, R. H., AND TAYLOR, A. N., 1968, Vitamin D-dependent calcium-binding protein: Response to some physiologic and nutritional variables, *J. Biol. Chem.* **243**:3987.

59. WASSERMAN, R. H., CORRADINO, R. A., AND TAYLOR, A. N., 1968, Vitamin D-dependent calcium-binding protein: Purification and some properties, *J. Biol. Chem.* **243**:3978.

60. WESTIN, B., KAISER, I. H., LIND, J., NYBERG, R., AND TEGER-NILSSON, A. C., 1959, Some constituents of umbilical venous blood of previable human fetuses, *Acta Paediatr. Scand.* **48**:609.

61. WIDDOWSON, E. M., McCANCE, R. A., HARRISON, G. F., AND SUTTON, A., 1962, Metabolism of calcium, strontium, and other minerals in the perinatal period, *Lancet* **2**:373.

CHAPTER 29

Physiology and Pharmacology of the Central Nervous System

Williamina A. Himwich

1. Introduction

The maturity of the neonatal animal of any species depends on its rate of development *in utero*. The young animal requires additional development and integration of behavior before reaching the adult state. The growth and development of the brain, including the attainment of the adult level of various chemical constituents as well as of metabolism, proceeds in generally the same fashion in all species of animals from the time of the appearance of the neural streak until maturity. The chronological relationship of this maturation to physiologic events, e.g., implantation, birth, opening of the eyes, varies in different species of animals. The problem of comparison and the difficulties of drawing generalizations from one species to another have been emphasized by many authors.[40,41] Among the mammalian species, the young at birth may be deemed

either relatively mature (precocial), such as lamb and guinea pig, or relatively immature, such as rat, mouse, and man (nonprecocial). In general, such a classification describes the entire behavior and physical condition of the animal, rather than that of individual systems. In mammals born relatively mature, not only the CNS but also the muscular and bony structures are sufficiently developed to allow the young to subsist with a minimum of maternal care.

It was pointed out by Anokhin[8] and by Brown,[23] in their elegant studies of systemogenesis, that even in the young born immature, some CNS nuclei have reached relative maturity at birth. Which nuclei these are depends on which parts of the CNS are necessary for the survival of the young. In fact, some neurons in a specific nucleus may mature earlier than adjacent neurons in the same nucleus. Similarly, other areas of less importance to the survival of the neonate may be less mature at the same chronological age. If we are to attempt to relate human development to that

Williamina A. Himwich · Nebraska Psychiatric Institute, University of Nebraska Medical Center, Omaha, Nebraska 68105

of the young animals from other species, we must discard attempts to fit the total human organism logically into the scale of development of the other animals, but rather attempt to correlate specific systems or areas or both. In some ways, the human infant is born more mature than a baby rabbit; e.g., the visual system is more mature in human infants, with the eyes open and beginning to function. After birth, on the other hand, the brain of the baby rabbit develops at a much faster rate.[19] For these reasons, it is exceedingly important that we consider the maturity of the young of one species as compared with another in terms of specific functions and systems such as the visual system and the auditory sytem.

In this chapter, we shall attempt to examine what is known of the physiology of the CNS of the human newborn, as indicated by biochemical and electrophysiological analyses. In addition, we will also discuss the rapidly developing field of fetal and neonatal pharmacology.

2. Brain Constituents

There is widespread interest in the biochemical development of the human brain, but unfortunately the data are scarce. The outstanding difficulty in biochemical studies of the human newborn is that the brain can be sampled only after death. While certain parameters may show little or no change, the influence of hypoxia on such relatively simple measures as brain weight and moisture content have been well documented in experimental animals.[49] It is necessary in this field to scrutinize carefully all the data available, especially at any points at which they do not conform to values or trends obtained on the newborn of experimental animals. Where the data on human beings diverge, we are always faced with the question whether the divergence is a true species difference, a difference in developmental rate, or an artifact due to the condition of the neonate. This problem becomes increasingly complex, since except for those who lose their lives suddenly in an accident, most persons suffer from a longer or shorter period of deranged metabolism, anoxia, or other complicating factors before death. These factors are especially difficult to pinpoint in the case of the neonate, since it is impossible to document how long an infant may have been in distress before birth or how abnormal his condition may have been. Nonetheless, we can only proceed

to examine what data are available on the human brain, keeping these doubts firmly in mind.

The general picture is essentially the same in all species of animals, but timing is different. If we look at graphs of changes in growth rate in various species when the chronological time is ignored (Fig. 1), the graphs illustrate very clearly the before and after birth differences in the rate of brain growth. The monkey most nearly approaches man, but the fetal period of growth in the monkey corresponds best to the perinatal infant.[83]

Such data on the general composition of the human brain as are available were published in the first edition, and will not be repeated here because of space limitations. Much of these data is bits of information not yet ready to be woven into a pattern.

2.1. Enzymes

Papers from Japan on the enzymatic content of the human brain have considerably enriched the literature. Although published in the later 1960s, these papers were not available to the author at that time. The enzymes studied are those related to the carbohydrate metabolism of fetal tissue.[172] Among these enzymes were LDH and the LDH/aldolase ratio,[111] data applicable to the brain as well as to the liver. In the human brain, there is a sharp rise in aldolase activity after birth (Fig. 2). Hexokinase appears to occur in different forms in various human tissue; e.g., there is a considerable difference between the enzyme from the brain, which electrophoretically shows only one band; those found in the liver and the heart, each of which yields two; and the one from the placenta, which yields three. The hexokinase in the brain shows considerable activity even before birth, but increases dramatically as the brain matures (Fig. 3).[172] These authors confirm that the brain metabolism does not appear to be greatly dependent on aerobic conditions. Succinic dehydrogenase and cytochrome oxidase have developed the major portion of their adult level of activity before birth, and no major change occurs after that (Fig. 4).[110,172] Their basic conclusion is that developing brain hexokinase and aldolase show an abrupt increase following birth, while both forms of LDH remain low in activity throughout the period, suggesting that glycolysis occurs at an even higher rate following birth than immediately prior to birth.

The critical period for the activity of fructose-1,6-diphosphate aldolase in developing human tissue

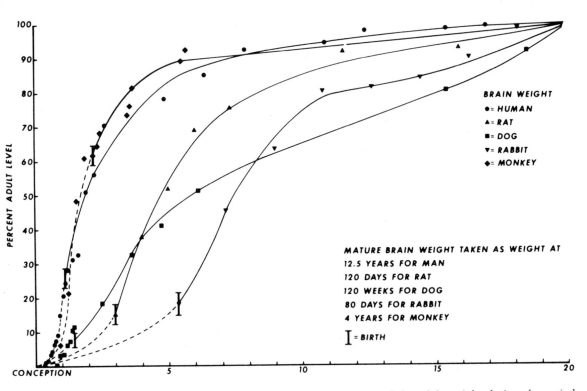

Fig. 1. Weight of the brain in various species expressed as a percentage of the adult weight during the period from conception to the attainment of adult brain weight. From Himwich.[83]

seemed to be the 5th month of gestation, but the changes in the developing brain are small compared with those that occur in liver and muscle.[172]

Animal studies are necessary to extend our knowledge of pre- and perinatal development of enzymes, especially brain enzymes. A study of DNA polymerase in the developing brain of the rat[31] showed that the polymerase activity in the various parts of the brain depends on age, and at certain ages is 20–50 times greater in the cerebellum than in the cortex. In the cerebellum, it peaked around 6 days of age and then dropped. The activity in the cortex was highest immediately after birth, and then decreased gradually.

The esterases characteristic of adult white matter do not appear to occur in the infant brain until about 4 months postnatally.[13] At about the same time, between 1 and 4 months of age, the acetylcholinesterase and butyrylcholinesterase zymograms become identical to those of the adult.

The enzymes necessary for the utilization of ketone bodies in the human brain become extremely important as we become more aware of the use made by the infant human brain of various ketone bodies.[132] The activities of the enzymes involved in ketone body utilization in the human brain are, however, quite a bit lower than those that have been described for the rat brain. Since only age spans are given for the human brain, it is difficult to be sure how these data apply in the neonate (Table I).

In essential fructosuria, there is a deficiency of fructokinase activity. In hereditary fructose intolerance, on the other hand, there are some abnormal properties of aldolase in liver as related to aldolase of muscle and brain,[154] which are normally synthesized by the embryo and persist without change. Hereditary fructose intolerance appears to the authors to be due to the mutation of a structural gene.

In perinatal and adult rabbit cortex, diencephalon, and cerebellum, Stave[168] measured enzymes representing glycogenolysis, glucose phosphorylation, glycolysis, oxidation of fatty acids, and quick energy yield. The perinatal brain has a relatively higher ability to utilize fatty acids for generating energy,

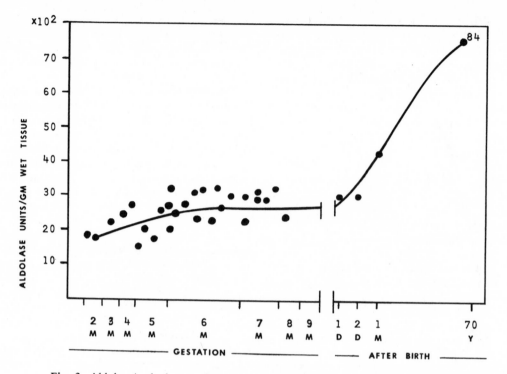

Fig. 2. Aldolase in the human fetus during development. From Mino and Takai.[111]

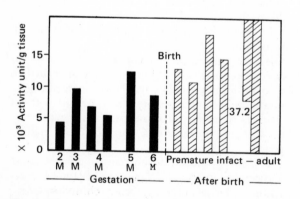

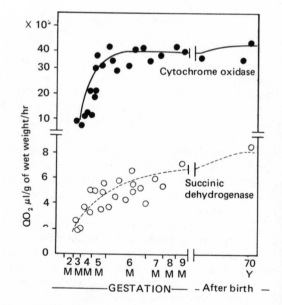

Fig. 3. Changes in hexokinase in the human brain during development. From Takai and Mino.[172]

Fig. 4. Changes in cytochrome oxidase and succinic dehydrogenase during development of the brain. From Takai and Mino.[172]

Table I. Changes in the LDH/Aldolase Ratio During Development of the Human Brain[a]

Age	M-LDH/ALD	H-LDH/ALD	Total LDH/ALD
Gestational			
2 months	7.1	10.8	17.9
4 months	7.5	9.6	17.1
5 months	3.5	6.4	9.9
6 months	2.9	5.3	8.2
7 months	3.9	5.9	9.8
Neonatal	3.4	5.8	9.2
Adult	3.3	6.9	10.2

[a] From Mino and Takai.[111]

and the cortex and cerebellum are better equipped in this respect than the diencephalon. The latter structure seems to be the most dependent on plasma glucose. Severe hypoxia of 24-hr duration causes the newborn brain to shift even more to fatty acid oxidation, but the adult brain increases its glycolytic capacity. Creatine kinase activity decreases by 20% in hypoxic adult brain, while it remains unaltered in the newborn brain.

3. The Blood–Brain Barrier

The whole area of interpretation of hematoencephalic exchange is fraught with difficulty because we do not understand the mechanisms involved. Certainly no generalizations can be drawn, and data cannot be assumed to apply to any species except the one studied and only under the *specific* experimental conditions observed.

The chief clinical observations on which the condition of the blood–brain barrier in human infants can be based are cases of kernicterus.[182,184] The lesions in the brain associated with this condition have been well documented (Fig. 5). Attempts to reproduce this syndrome in experimental animals suggest that hypoxia may be necessary for the entrance of bilirubin into the brain.[27,28,151,152] In man, the work of Gröntoft[74] also supports this thesis.

Many reviews of the blood–brain barrier phenomena[39] as they apply to animals of all ages have been published. In general, the younger the animal, the greater the hematoencephalic exchange. Among the best animal studies are those of Roth and his colleagues[12,150,155] and of Lajtha.[99–101] The latter studied the penetration of individual amino acids in young and adult animals. Although again each amino acid must be considered individually, the general rule of better penetration in the younger animals held. The most exciting finding is that one amino acid can inhibit the entry of others.[75]

Domek et al.[42] demonstrated that myelin offers a barrier to the entrance of phenobarbital into the brain. The same probably applies to urea[155] and thiopental,[12] but not to acetazolamine-S.[35,150] The lack of myelin in young brains may explain the

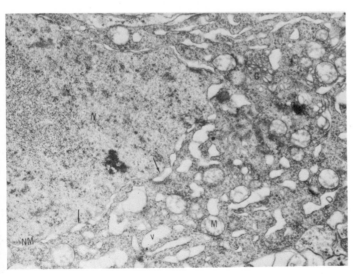

Fig. 5. A neuron undergoing preicteric changes. Vascuolar alteration of the endoplasmic reticulum is conspicuous. The mitochondria (M) are swollen, and their interiors have become electron-lucid. The inner and outer nuclear membranes (NM) are separated, showing a tendency to vacuole (V) formation (arrow). × 14,000. From Chen et al.[27a]

relatively faster penetration of some materials Barlow et al.[12] state: "It would seem that a series of factors can and do affect the distribution of compounds in brain. Consideration of the physical properties of the substance (fat or water solubility, dissociation, etc.), the blood–brain barrier, water compartmentation of brain tissues, and probably local biochemical and metabolic factors in specific anatomical units of brain is necessary."

The recent work of Oldendorf[127,128] using a bolus of labeled material for adult animals has not yet been extended to young animals. The only comprehensive investigation of which the author is aware is that of Baños et al.,[11] who compared the entry rates into brain of various amino acids in rats under 14 days of age and 10–20 weeks old. The "nonessential" amino acids had the highest rates. Presumably, in the young animal, they are used to facilitate protein synthesis.

4. Metabolism

The most important new development in the metabolism of the human brain, especially that of the neonate, is the growing concept that ketone bodies can form an important foodstuff for the brain.[1,6,81] From 1929, when Himwich and Nanhum[82] established that glucose is the main foodstuff for the brain, the use of ketone bodies was considered of minor importance and to be more applicable in vitro[89,90,96] than in vivo.[78,166]

The studies of Cahill and his colleagues[25,131] on starving obese patients sparked the current interest in the ability of ketone bodies to enter the brain and to be oxidized. During the 5th to 6th weeks of starvation, 33 g glucose at the most would be available to the brain, which would be expected to use 110–145 g/24 hr.[95,131] In both the infant and the adult, the three key enzymes 3-hydroxybutyrate dehydrogenase, 3-oxoacid CoA transferase, and acetoacetyl–CoA thiolase are present from 32 weeks' gestational age through 69 years of life.[131]

The capacity for ketone body formation before birth has been detected in liver.[169] Postnatally, acetoacetate and β-hydroxybutyrate are present in the blood of the umbilical artery. These ketone bodies in the cord blood of the healthy newborn seem to have been transferred from the maternal circulation, since there is a rather constant correlation of 2:1 between the maternal and fetal ketone body blood levels.

A full-term newborn human infant weighing 3500 g contains approximately 550 g of lipids, mainly triglycerides.[180] On the 3rd and 4th days after birth, the ketone body concentration reaches markedly high values, which decrease toward the end of the first week of life.[146] The rising levels of fatty acids and glycerol in the plasma may indicate an increased utilization of neutral fat during this period.

Under normal conditions, the fetus does not seem to oxidize ketone substances to any extent,[44] but during intrauterine hypoxia, lipolysis does seem to occur, for a high cord blood arteriovenous free fatty acid difference, especially the higher concentration in the umbilical artery, revealed that the fatty acids present originated from the fetus, not from the mother.

The studies of Adam et al.[2] on the oxidation of glucose and β-hydroxybutyrate in the human fetal brain were foreshadowed by those of Page and Williamson,[132] who found that the brain of a human fetus of 32 weeks' gestation and the brains of infants from 0 to 2 years of age possessed the three

Table II. Activities of Enzymes Involved in Ketone Body Utilization in the Cortex and the Cerebellum in Relation to the Age of the Subject[a,b]

Age	Cortex			Cerebellum		
	Dehydrogenase	Transferase	Thiolase	Dehydrogenase	Transferase	Thiolase
Fetal (32 weeks' gestation)	0.12	0.64	1.82	0.12	0.45	1.49
0–2 years	0.30 (4)	1.66 (4)	1.25 (4)	0.27 (4)	1.32 (3)	1.31 (4)
3–10 years	0.34 (3)	1.93 (3)	1.66 (3)	0.36 (3)	1.53 (3)	1.68 (3)
37–69 years	0.29 (5)	1.31 (3)	2.68 (4)	0.34 (5)	1.35 (3)	2.93 (4)

[a] From Page and Williamson.[132]

[b] Activities are expressed in micromoles of substrate removed or formed per minute per gram fresh weight of brain at 25°C. The results are mean values, with the number of observations in parentheses.

key enzymes necessary for the oxidation of the ketone bodies (Table II). Moreover, the observations of Persson et al.[143] demonstrated that the brains of infants and children between 6 weeks and 12 years of age oxidized ketone bodies in vivo. Adam et al.[2] studied the brains of 12 previable human fetuses obtained at 12–21 weeks' gestation by means of abdominal hysterotomy. On a molar basis, labeled β-hydroxybutyrate was taken up at a rate 1.47 times that of labeled glucose. The rate of conversion of β-hydroxybutyrate was equal to its rate of consumption and exceeded the conversion of glucose to CO_2 because 45% of the glucose was converted to lactate. Adam et al.[2] showed that early in gestation, the oxidation of β-hydroxybutyrate may replace that of glucose in the isolated human fetal brain during temporary privation, and that β-hydroxybutyrate potentially may provide a large proportion of the fuel for the oxidative metabolism of the human fetal brain.

Himwich et al.[84] attempted to duplicate studies of the oxygen consumption of animal brains in human babies for purposes of comparison with similar data from experimental animals. The data on more than 50 babies who showed no marked pathology and whose mothers were free of complications of pregnancy have been reported. Obviously, these infants could not have been normal, since they all died either at birth or shortly thereafter. The actual data on the oxygen consumption of the parts were widely scattered, so regression equations were prepared using the method of least

squares, and lines were drawn on the graph from these equations (Fig. 6). These lines suggest that at 140 days' gestation, i.e., at approximately the 20th week, the oxygen consumption of the medulla oblongata is well above that of the other brain parts. The oxygen consumption of this part remained at approximately the same level as the fetus matured, whereas the oxygen consumption of other areas increased markedly. The pathway of glucose metabolism in the human fetal cortex appears to be mainly the Embden–Meyerhof glycolytic pathway.[178]

In the adult brain (rat), isotopic carbons present in glucose rapidly become incorporated into amino acids. This characteristic pattern appears first at the critical period of development when enzymes are developing rapidly, and is probably dependent on changes in the enzyme systems controlling glycolysis and the oxidation of glucose. These changes are accompanied by a 3-fold increase of decarboxylic amino acids (Fig. 7).[70] Some labeled glutamate may go via the oxoglutarate shunt into fatty acids. Even in developing brain, however, this pathway appears to be of little quantitative significance.[35] DeVivo and colleagues[4,37,38] showed that before 21 days of age in the rat, ketone bodies were better precursors of amino acids, as well as of cholesterol.[3,37,48]

All these rapidly changing metabolic patterns in the brain during development are dependent on enzyme changes. The lack of data on human infants and the various species of animals used, with their different rates of maturation, makes it difficult to predict exactly what the metabolic pattern in the human brain in the perinatal period will be. Nonetheless, a knowledge of what is happening in general in the developing brain is necessary for an understanding of the period.

The development of the theory of compartmentation of glutamic acid metabolism[179] has contributed greatly to our understanding of amino acid metabolism. In the cortex of the cat, at least, this compartmentation follows a developmental pattern,[17] appearing between the 3rd and 6th weeks of life. As the pattern becomes definitive, the pool available for glutamine formation contracts, and the other pool or pools enlarge. In kittens, the glutamine synthetase activity[18] of the neocortex correlates well with the compartmentation data. In other areas, the correlation is poor. Possibly, as suggested by Salganicoff and De Robertis,[153] the subcellular distribution of the enzyme may be of more importance than the total concentration.

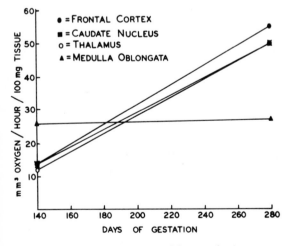

Fig. 6. Oxygen consumption of human brain parts at various periods of gestation. Values for 140 days and 280 days calculated from regression equations. From Himwich et al.[84]

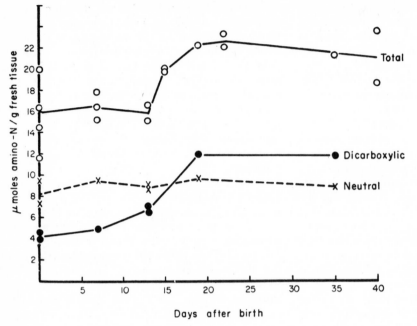

Fig. 7. Amino acid content of the developing rat brain. From Gaitonde and Richter.[70]

5. Electrophysiologic Activity

5.1. Spontaneous

One physiologic measurement that can be made readily on the newborn infant is the electrical activity of the brain. Since Lindsley[102] published his historic paper on the EEG of the fetus, there has been no doubt that the fetus as well as the newborn shows spontaneous electrical activity from the brain. It is no wonder, therefore, that a great volume of data is available on studies at many ages and under many conditions. Ellingson,[52] Kellaway and Petersén,[94] and recently Parmelee et al.[136] in this country, Dreyfus–Brisac and Blanc,[45] Monod and Pajot,[117] and Passouant and Cadilhac[139] in France, and Arshavsky et al.[9] in Russia, to mention a few, have published much excellent material on this subject (Fig. 8). In the normal, full-term child, the EEG appears to be of little diagnostic value as far as future evidence of

neurologic damage is concerned. This point is thoroughly discussed by Ellingson,[56] and also by Monod and Ducas.[116] As Ellingson points out, in the absence of pathology of the nervous system, the importance of an abnormal EEG can be determined only by longitudinal studies. Unfortunately, such studies are few. Monod and Ducas[116] reported continued paroxysmal activity in apparently normal children followed for 8 years. Investigations of epilepsy in the newborn were conducted by Passouant and Cadilhac[139] and of cerebral palsy by Lesný.[103] Ellingson and colleagues[54,59] followed up a number of children for as long as 8 years, their records extending as far into fetal life as the 24th week of conceptual age. Records of the premature infants were also made by Parmelee and colleagues[134,135] and Dreyfus–Brisac and colleagues.[44,46]

Lombroso[105] gives a number of generalizations in regard to "dysmaturity" of the bioelectrical

Fig. 8. EEGs of a premature newborn. Gestational age at birth, 30 weeks. Birth weight, 1558 g. (A) EEG No. 1: 65 hr after birth; weight 1490 g. Note asynchrony and sporadic sharp transients. (B) EEG No. 2: Gestational age, 31 weeks; weight, 1500 g. There has been striking change in the 7 days since EEG No. 1; the pattern is that typically seen several weeks later. (C) EEG No. 7: Gestational age, 36 weeks; weight, 2268 g. The transition from wakefulness to sleep, seen for the first time, is characterized by an increase in the prominence of the slower components. (D) EEG No. 8: Gestational age, 37 weeks, 2590 g. The pattern is typical of the full-term infant. From Ellingson.[54]

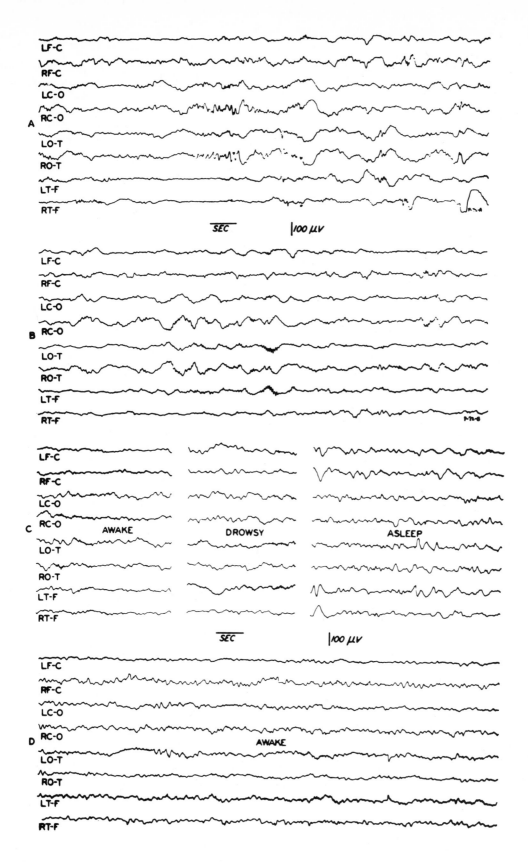

behavioral organizations, and an interpretation of these items in terms of the current physical well-being of the child and its maturation, with sick babies showing a regression to more immature patterns. Although bioelectrical maturity is primarily a function of conceptual age, exceptions occur both in sick babies and in those who have suffered CNS injury.[105,134]

The work of Vaughan[177] attempted to analyze the regional maturation of the cortex through EEG analysis. He points out that the major block to understanding how the brain matures is our lack of understanding of maturation of the anatomic structures. Opinion is now divided between the studies of Conel,[33] which were widely interpreted as indicating that little cortical function was present at birth,[174] and the more recent studies of Molliver et al.[115] which suggest that synapses develop in the fetal cortex as early as the 23rd week.

Eeg-Olofsson and his colleagues[50,51,144] presented three papers on the EEG development in children, dividing their subjects into those with paroxysmal activity and those showing 14 and 16 H_2 positive spike phenomenon. These papers, together with that of Schulte and Bell[156] on the EEG power spectra in infants and young children, have contributed to the data usable by clinicians. Schulte et al.[157,158] also published patterns from neonates born to diabetic mothers. Such patterns tend to be immature for gestational age.

Shepovalnikov[160] believed that alpha activity was present in newborns and was an intrinsic activity of the brain. Lindsley,[102] as well as Ellingson and Lindsley,[57] believed that alpha waves develop from the slow waves of infancy. Churchill et al.[32] in studying the effects of birth condition (such as presentation or drug administration) on the newborn EEG, came to the conclusion that Shepovalnikov's thesis should be further investigated before a decision is made.

Parmelee et al.[137] coded the EEG patterns between 28 and 20 weeks of conceptional age with a three-digit code, and they find these codes useful, for example, in differentiating premature from small-for-date infants (Table III). Attempts at quantifying the EEG data in the neonate were also made by Bartoshuk[14] and Bartoshuk and Tennant.[15] Quiet sleep increased as the infant matured, while active (rapid eye movement; REM) sleep decreased. Quiet sleep, which was 10% of the total at 31 to 32 weeks of gestational age, increased to approxi-

mately 50% at 3 months of age, while active sleep decreased from 68% at 33 to 34 weeks of gestational age to 36% at 3 months. These data apply to records visually scanned. Dreyfus-Brisac,[43] in a study of previable infants (24–27 weeks of gestational age), showed that such infants had neither quiet nor active sleep patterns.

There appear to be differences in the EEG during development in various ethnic groups.[133] Alpha activity developed earlier in African Negro children than in European and Indian children. Before alpha, there appeared a well-defined sinusoidal rhythmic activity at 5 or 6 cycles/sec in the occipital area on eye closure. This pattern was also seen earlier in African Negro children than in others.

The current surge of interest in paradoxical sleep and its function[148] has led to a reexamination of young infants, both premature and full-term[138] (Figs. 9 and 10). Dreyfus-Brisac[44] collected records from a group of previable infants of 24–28 weeks of gestational age, and tabulated the changes that occur in the normal ontogenesis of sleep organization from conceptual age of 32 weeks through 3 years of age. As might be expected, many factors influence sleep–wake patterns in the infant, e.g., the stress of circumcision,[62] sound,[120] length of gestation,[73,107] and diabetes in the mother.[157,158] An excellent review of the subject was published by Sterman and Hoppenbrouwers.[170] Monod et al.[118] as well as Lombroso[105] and Ornitz et al.,[129] followed sleep patterns in the young suffering from pathology. Newborn mongols appear to have longer periods of non-REM sleep than do normal infants, and tracings during sleep show more low-amplitude slow activity.[60,72]

5.2. Evoked Potential

Responses can be evoked in any of the sensory areas by use of the appropriate stimuli. In general, this technique measures the ability of the tract being stimulated to transmit stimuli from the point of input to the area in which the response is being monitored, e.g., from the retina to the visual cortex. The latency from the time of stimulation and the complexity of the wave forms have been used to measure the ontogeny of the evoked potential. The wave form progresses from a simple form in which a negative wave is the first response to a sharply defined positive–negative form. The typical longitudinal sequence is similar for all mammals studied, but is more complex in primates.[149] In human

Table III. Percentage of Each Sleep State at Each Gestational Age As Obtained by Computer Sorting of Coded Data from Polygraphic Recordings[a]

Gestational age (weeks)	Number	Active sleep		Transitional sleep		Quiet sleep	
		Mean %	Range	Mean %	Range	Mean %	Range
Premature infants							
30	2	15	14–17	67	63–70	18	15–20
31–32	5	27	7–44	63	43–83	10	4–17
33–34	4	45	36–57	46	35–53	10	6–14
35–36	7	42	29–61	46	38–60	11	8–24
37–38	8	32	15–55	43	30–66	24	9–47
39–40 (term)	9	32	12–46	38	21–63	31	21–48
53 (3 months past term)	8	25	15–37	29	13–36	45	30–59
Term infants							
39–40 (term)	6	38	19–48	34	24–42	28	18–40
53 (3 months past term)	6	23	15–34	30	19–37	47	38–59

[a] From Parmelee et al.[137]

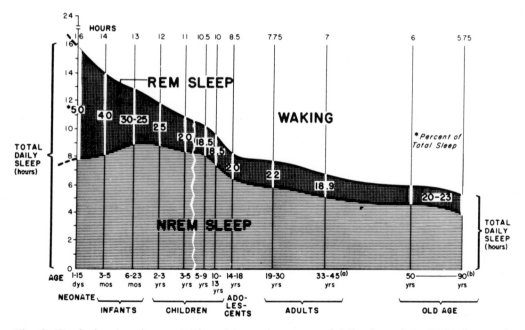

Fig. 9. Graph showing changes (with age) in total amounts of daily sleep, daily REM sleep, and percentage of REM sleep. Note the sharp diminution of REM sleep in the early years. REM sleep falls from 8 hr at birth to less than 1 hr in old age. The amount of non-REM sleep (NREM) throughout life remains more constant, falling from 8 hr to 5 hr. In contrast to the steep decline of REM sleep, the quantity of NREM sleep is undiminished for many years. Although total daily REM sleep falls steadily during life, the percentage rises slightly in adolescence and early adulthood. This rise does not reflect an increase in amount; it is due to the fact that REM sleep does not diminish as rapidly as total sleep. From Roffwarg et al.[148]

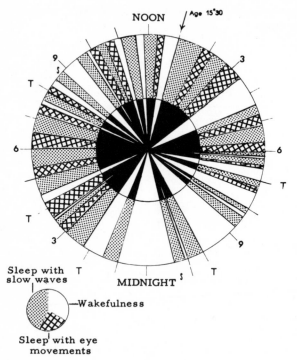

Sleep with
slow waves

—Wakefulness

Sleep with eye
movements

Fig. 10. Cycles in the course of a night and a day (24 hr) in a newborn, recorded from 15 hr and 30 min to 39 hr and 30 min after birth. Inner circle: periods of sleep (black) and wakefulness (white); outer circle: calm sleep (dotted area) and sleep with eye movements (hatched area); lower circle: total duration of wakefulness, of sleep with slow waves (calm or slow sleep), and of sleep with eye movements (during the 24-hr period). From Passouant.[138]

infants, Ellingson[52] reported a positive–negative form after birth at full-term and only an electronegative response in the premature infant.

The evoked potential offers a means of evaluating the status of the various sensory systems in the neonate. It was even proposed as a means of determining the degree of prematurity. Engel[63] and Engel and Butler[64] found the latency of the visual evoked potential to be as good a criterion of conceptual age as birth weight. The auditory evoked potential was similarly evaluated by Graziani et al.[73] and others.[5,58,79,130] In general, the evoked responses in the infant are simple in wave form with a longer latency, a great fatigability, and a more discrete topographic localization than in the adult.

The visual evoked potential can always be seen in the neonate, although averaging techniques may be required.[55,65,88,175] Responses have been recorded at 24 weeks[63] and 28 weeks of gestational age.[53] Dustman and Beck[47] discussed the maturational aspects of the visual evoked potential. Unfortunately, real longitudinal studies have not yet been finished.[66] The wave form may be adult in shape as early as the first month of postnatal life, or maturation may be delayed until 2–3 years of age.[56] The response may be variable not only between sessions, but also during a session.[61] There appears to be little agreement on the incidence of responses in normal as compared with neurologically abnormal infants. Hrbek and Mareš[88] obtained differences, but neither Engel and Butler[64] nor Ellingson[54] could confirm these differences.

The following response has been studied with many divergent results, but under suitable conditions, Ellingson[56] found a high incidence of following in infants. The optimum frequency appears to be 3/sec. With age, the following response can be elicited at higher frequencies, and the optimum frequency seems to be close to the dominant rhythm during wakefulness.[71]

The auditory and somesthetic responses have been less thoroughly studied than the visual. The auditory responses are probably nonspecific responses to auditory stimuli, not primary responses. The nonspecific character of the response makes it difficult to relate it to maturation. Dreyfus–Brisac and Blanc[45] found such responses only after 8 months of conceptual age. Graziani et al.,[73] however, obtained responses from 30-week-old prematures that correlated well with estimated postconceptual age, but not with birth weight or postnatal age.

Somesthetic responses have been little studied. Desmedt et al.[36] reported interesting differences in adult and newborn responses to stimulation of the hand. The extension of such studies will increase our ability to interpret the maturation of the CNS in the neonate.

5.3. Drug Effects

The ease of recording the EEG in the newborn has led to many investigations of the effects on the infant's EEG of drugs given either to the mother or to the child in the neonatal period. Children whose mothers had received barbiturate were reported by Ellingson[52] to show a transient depression

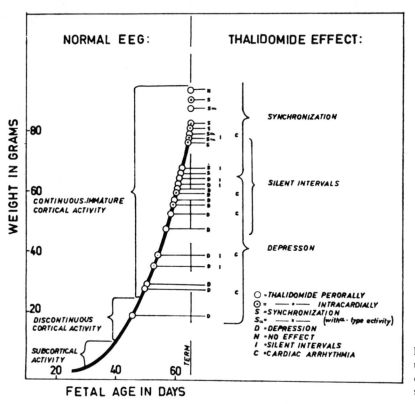

Fig. 11. Effects of thalidomide on the EEG of the guinea pig fetus at different fetal stages. From Bergström *et al.*[16]

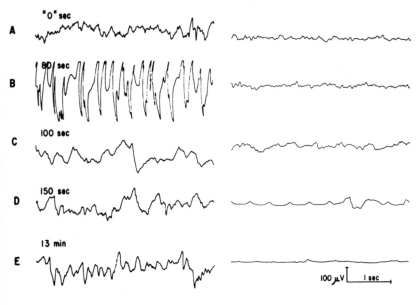

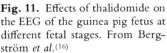

Fig. 12. Convulsive–depressive response to meperidine (17 mg/ kg). (A) Control EEGs of mother (left) and fetus (right) sampled during the minute before injection of the drug into a maternal vein. (B) At 80 sec after the injection, the maternal EEG shows sharp waves. Fetal EEG changes are not yet apparent. (C) At 100 sec, the maternal epileptiform activity has ceased, and the fetal EEG shows increased voltage and slowing. (D) At 150 sec, the maternal EEG shows increased activity, and the fetal EEG shows flattening. (E) At 13 min, the maternal EEG has begun to return to the preinjection pattern; the fetal EEG continues flat. From Bleyer and Rosen.[20]

Table IV. Effect of Drugs on the Duration of Single Episodes of Both Phases of Sleep in Growing Kittens[a]

Age (days)		Control	Imipramine (5 mg/kg)	Chlorpromazine (10 mg/kg)	Propericiazine (3 mg/kg)	Haloperidol (5 mg/kg)
1–3	Slow-wave sleep	0.6±0.2	0.9±0.1*	1 1±0.4*	1.2±0.2†	0.8±0.3
	Activated sleep	2.4±0.3	0.5±0.2†	1.4±0.4†	1.8±0.2†	2.7±0.7
6–8	Slow-wave sleep	1.2±0.3	1.4±0.5	2.2±0.6*	1.8±0.1*	1.2±0.3
	Activated sleep	3.1±0.6	0.5±0.5†	1.4±0.5†	1.9±0.5*	2.3±0.6
11–13	Slow-wave sleep	1.6±0.3	4.2±1.5†	4.3±0.7†	3.0±0.7†	1.8±0.4
	Activated sleep	4.4±0.5	0.8±1.1†	1.5±1.1†	2.9±1.1*	3.2±1.1
16–18	Slow-wave sleep	2.3±0.6	9.2±1.9†	9.1±1.7†	5.2±1.9*	4.2±0.5*
	Activated sleep	5.2±1.3	0.2±0.4†	2.1±1.1†	3.1±1.1*	6.2±1.5
21–23	Slow-wave sleep	3.2±0.6	11.3±3.5†	18.2±8.6†	6.5±1.0†	9.2±2.9†
	Activated sleep	5.5±1.5	0±0†	2.7±1.3†	4.0±1.5	6.3±2.0
26–28	Slow-wave sleep	4.7±1.2	22.3±9.0†	21.0±6.7†	10.6±2.7†	9.0±2.2†
	Activated sleep	6.4±1.4	0±0†	3.9±1.9*	4.2±1.5*	7.2±1.0

[a] From Shimizu and Himwich.[164] Each figure indicates the mean in minutes ±S.D. In the control study, 6 or 7 kittens were used in each age group, and 5 kittens in each age group for each of the drug studies. Superscript symbols show that the differences are statistically significant as calculated with the Student's t test: *$P < 0.05$; †$P < 0.005$.

of the EEG. Borgstedt and Rosen[21] also found transient behavioral and electroencephalographic changes in newborns at birth that could be correlated with the sedative–hypnotic or narcotic medications given to their mothers during labor.

Thalidomide given to the pregnant guinea pig causes changes in the EEG of the fetus—largely electrical silence.[16] These data suggest that thalidomide is a sedative, being narcotic in the younger fetuses and neurotoxic in the youngest ones (Fig. 11). Bleyer and Rosen[20] found that in the guinea pig, meperidine had a convulsant effect in the mother and a depressant effect in the fetus. The effect in the mother was short-lived, but continued longer in the fetus (Fig. 12).

An extensive study of the sleep cycle in the developing kitten and rabbit and of the effects of various drugs administered to the young animal was conducted by Shimizu and Himwich[161–164] (Table IV). The drugs include LSD, which diminishes REM sleep in the kitten.[161] In animals younger than 6–8 days, however, the decrease was less than in the older animal. Similar data were found on the phenothiazines,[162] imipramine, and haloperidol.[165] The reasons for these differences may be found in the absorption, excretion, and metabolism of the drugs, or in the fact that in the younger animal, the cerebral structures involved in sleep are still too immature to respond to the drugs. With amphetamine, the period of wakefulness in the kitten was increased, with a concomitant diminution in activated (REM) sleep. As with the other drugs, these effects became more significant after the kittens were 2 weeks old. Propériciazine did not affect the percentage of wakefulness in the kittens as chlorpromazine did. The propériciazine animals were also more playful than were those receiving chlorpromazine.

Few studies have yet been done on the effects of postnatal behavior of the young of drugs given to the mother. Monod et al.[118] noted differences in sleep–wakefulness patterns in neonates whose mothers received chlorpromazine during the latter part of pregnancy. Chlorpromazine given to pregnant rats was also reported to influence postnatal behavior.[91]

6. Pharmacology of the Neonate

Drugs may exert their influence on the fetus and newborn in a number of ways: (1) ingestion of drugs by the mother during her pregnancy, (2) administration of drugs to the mother during labor (3–26 different drugs have been given to the same patient[87]), and (3) administration of drugs to the neonate.

The effects that many drugs given to the mother will have on the fetus are illustrated in Table V. Drugs may affect the cardiac output of the mother, or her blood pressure, and hence exert an indirect effect on the fetus irrespective of their direct effect. Placental transfer of drugs is still not well understood. The concept that the placenta is a protective barrier appears to be unfounded, since equilibrium between fetal and maternal circulation is exceedingly rapid.[87] Although many drugs are thought to cross the placenta by simple diffusion, transfer mechanisms, solubility, degree of ionization, and related factors are undoubtedly of importance (Table VI). Variations of placental blood flow (both fetal and maternal) as well as placental metabolism[113] all make the prediction of how much of a specific drug will reach the fetus a matter of speculation rather than quantitation (see Chapter 25).

The brain of the fetus is particularly vulnerable to drugs, in part because of the unique aspects of fetal circulation. The fetal heart and the brain can be expected to receive a higher concentration of any drug than the rest of the body. Total elimination from the fetus must, in general, await placental transfer and maternal elimination.[176] Obviously, the experiments necessary to clear up these points are untenable in pregnant human beings.

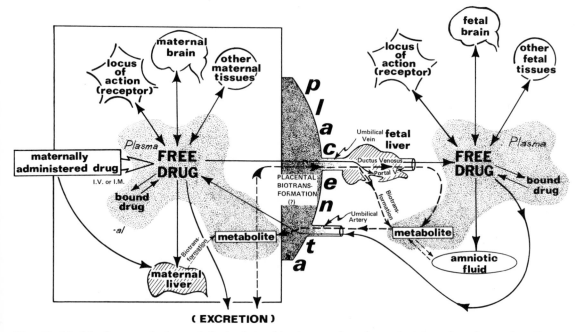

Fig. 13. Model of maternal–placental–fetal relationships in regard to drug administered to the mother. From Mirkin.[13]

Table V. Effects of Medication on the Intrauterine and Newborn Patient[a]

Maternal medication	Fetal or neonatal effect[b]	Maternal medication	Fetal or neonatal effect[b]
Oral progestins Androgens Estrogens	Masculinization and advanced bone age	Reserpine	Nasal congestion and drowsiness
Potassium iodide Propylthiouracil Methimazole	Goiter	Hexamethonium bromide	Neonatal ileus
		Intravenously administered fluids (excessive amounts)	Fluid and electrolyte abnormalities
Iophenoxic acid (Teridax)	Elevation of serum protein-bound iodine	Heroin and morphine	Neonatal death, convulsions and tremors
Aminopterin Amethopterin Chlorambucil	Anomalies and abortions	Phenobarbital (excessive amounts)	Neonatal bleeding
		Smoking	Premature births
Bishydroxycoumarin (Dicumarol)	Fetal death	Orally administered hypo-glycemic agents:	
Ethyl bicoumacetate	Hemorrhage	Sulfonylurea derivatives	Anomalies (?)
Salicylates (large amounts)	Neonatal bleeding	Phenformin (D.B.I.)	Lactic acidosis (?)
		Phenothiazines	Hyperbilirubinemia (?)
	Deposition in bone	Diazepams	Retarded development
Tetracyclines	Inhibition of bone growth in premature infants	Meprobamate	Retarded development (?)
	Discoloration of teeth	Chloroquine	Retinal damage or death (?)
		Quinine	Thrombocytopenia
Sulfonamides	Kernicterus	Thalidomide	Phocomelia and fetal death; hearing loss.
Chloramphenicol	Death ("gray" syndrome)		
Novobiocin	Hyperbilirubinemia	Vaccination	Fetal vaccinia
Erythromycin	Liver damage (?)	Influenza vaccination	Increased anti-A and anti-B blood-group titers in mother (?)
Nitrofurantoin (Furadantin)	Hemolysis		
Vitamin K analogues (excessive amounts)	Hyperbilirubinemia	Antihistamines	Anomalies (?) Prevention of pregnancy (?)
Ammonium chloride	Acidosis	Insulin shock	Fetal loss

[a] From Van Petten.[176]

[b] (?) Indicates that results are based on animal studies only.

The fetal–placental–maternal unit can be modeled (Fig. 13) to show probable drug distribution and metabolite formation, and such a model can serve as the base for experimental design.

Once the drugs have been absorbed, differences in metabolism or in detoxication may be evident. Some of these differences are due to the low activity of specific enzyme systems of the neonate. The enzyme systems require time to mature, just as do other physiologically and biochemically important parameters. Data obtained from different animal species suggested to Pelkonen and Kärki[141] that certain generalizations may be made: (1) oxidative and reductive transfer motions are uniformly

Table VI. Determinants of Drug Disposition in the Fetoplacental Unit[a]

I. Factors that may influence the transplacental passage of drugs
  A. Lipid solubility
  B. Degree of ionization
  C. Molecular weight
  D. Placental blood flow
  E. Placental metabolism of drugs
  F. Aging of placenta

II. Factors that may influence the distribution of drugs in the fetus
  A. Permeability of specialized membranes
  B. Selective tissue uptake of drug
    1. Nonspecific lipid solubility
    2. Specific binding to cellular constituents
      a. Binding protein
      b. Enzyme–substrate interaction
    3. Active secretion by yolk sac [rodents; human (?)]
  C. Distribution of fetal circulation

---

[a] From Mirkin.[113]

deficient; (2) most conjugative processes are deficient, although less uniformly so than the oxidative and reductive ones; (3) some hydrolytic reactions are fairly well developed; and (4) postnatal increase depends on such factors as species, and compounds being studied. As one example, the toxicity of chloramphenicol in newborn and premature infants is probably due to an immature stage of enzymatic development, which does not allow the efficient removal of the drug. Tolbutamide is another drug that is metabolized very slowly in the newborn.[123] After the first few days of life, the rate of metabolism of this compound approaches that of the adult. Among the anesthetic agents, sodium-4-hydroxybutyrate appears to cross the placenta, at least in the guinea pig, and to produce depression in the fetus.[34] Such depression, however, has not been noted in human infants whose mothers were given this compound before birth, a fact that underlines the hazards of extrapolating data from one species to another. The newborn rat has been reported to be more susceptible to pentobarbital than the adult.[86]

Nyhan[124] and Nyhan and Lampert[125] point out that the responses to drugs in the very young are

sufficiently novel to warrant establishment of a systematic developmental pharmacology. Even when quantitative adjustments are made for the size of the patient, impressive qualitative differences still occur. It is never safe to extrapolate to the neonate pharmacological results obtained in later life, and fetal effects in particular are completely unpredictable. Optimally, the therapeutic responses to drugs of the newborn and of the fetus should be determined experimentally before the drug is used clinically. Alcohol has different effects on the young animal than on the adult or the fetus, the young being more resistant to the toxic effects.[29] The same relative resistances were shown by the animals to morphine.[30] Divergent results were found by Kupferberg and Way,[98] who noted the greatest toxicity to morphine in the young animals and ascribed this difference to greater brain permeability in the young.

Immature or newborn mice and guinea pigs showed a marked inability to metabolize many drugs, being particularly unable to form glucuronides as a means of detoxication. It is of interest that the newborn guinea pig, which is in many ways quite mature, nevertheless shows an immature pattern of drug metabolism. In this respect, the degree of immaturity of an enzyme system in the guinea pig born relatively mature seems to equal that in the newborn mouse, an animal born at a very immature stage.[92] Young rabbits show a marked lack of enzymes necessary to metabolize hexabarbital, pyramidon, and amphetamine, among other drugs. Fouts and Adamson[68] suggest in this regard that in the young animal, some inhibitors may be present.

Drugs given during the first trimester have the greatest risk of causing malformations. The horrible example of thalidomide has created a lasting impression that forces us to regard with suspicion any drug given during the early months of pregnancy. It is still not widely appreciated, however, that many over-the-counter drugs used for self-medication, as well as prescription drugs given by the physician before the woman realizes she may be pregnant, are an unpredictable hazard.[67]

An excellent review on the effects of drugs commonly used in obstetrics on fetuses and newborns was written by Meester.[106] He points out that almost any drug given to a pregnant woman and consequently found in her blood must be assumed to pass into the infant's circulation. Our

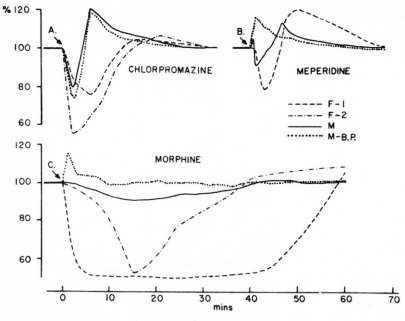

Fig. 14. Effects of drugs on fetal and maternal brain αO_2 and maternal blood pressure in three experiments. In each experiment, brain αO_2 was recorded simultaneously from two fetuses (F-1 and F-2) and the mother (M). Blood pressure (M-BP) was recorded from the maternal carotid artery. Drugs were injected intravenously at the arrow. The curves were plotted from continuous recordings. Abscissa: time in minutes; ordinate: blood pressure and αO_2 in percentage (100% represents average during control period). Control averages (μA = diffusion current = oxygen availability) for experiment with: *chlorpromazine*: F-1, 0.27 μA ($\pm 5\%$); F-2, 0.115 μA ($\pm 0\%$); M, 0.28 μA ($\pm 5\%$); M-BP; 70 mm Hg ($\pm 0\%$); *meperidine*: F-1, 0.20 μA ($\pm 0\%$); M, 0.15 μA ($\pm 3\%$); M-BP, 60 mm Hg ($\pm 3\%$); *morphine* (0.15 mg/kg): F-1, 0.75 μA ($\pm 7\%$); F-2, 0.026 μA ($\pm 8\%$); M, 0.144 μA ($\pm 3\%$); M-BP, 68 mm Hg ($\pm 3\%$). From Misrahy et al.[114]

knowledge as to what effects these drugs may have on the baby is only fragmentary. Some information has been obtained from animal experimentation. The effects of drugs during pregnancy on fetal cerebral oxygen in guinea pigs[114] (Fig. 14) and on response to anoxia and resuscitation in rabbits[26] have been studied. It must be remembered, also, that some drugs can inhibit or in some cases even facilitate the action of other drugs given simultaneously.[112]

Placental drug metabolism imposes another variable in our understanding of fetal drug responses. Placental enzymes are apparently induced by maternal ingestion of drugs (e.g., cigarette smoking)[142] at least in man. What effect does the presence of placental enzymes have on the concentration of "toxic" material reaching the fetus?[141,142] Juchau et al.[93] published an excellent review of this subject.

Stimulus to the liver by the compound in question appears to be necessary for the induction of fetal liver enzymes.[68,77] Pelkonen and Kärki[141] raised a number of interesting and as yet unanswered questions and pointed out that certain aspects of enzyme induction in the human fetus appear unique in the animal species studied.

The amounts and nature of the drugs used seem to be as closely related to the information and intuition of the obstetrician in relation to each individual patient as to any other factors.[24] Meperidine and barbiturates are the two drugs most commonly used. Meperidine has been studied in the guinea pig fetus near term to determine its effects on oxygen tension and blood pressure in mother and fetus[114] and for comparison of these effects with those of chlorpromazine and morphine (see Fig. 14). The formation of epoxide intermediates can lead not only to inactivation of the drugs, but also to their activation.[141]

Among the well-known drugs prescribed routinely by physicians and continued during pregnancy is diphenylhydantoin (DPH). Other anticonvulsant drugs can be included in this category of drugs necessary for the health of the mother but potentially hazardous to the fetus. Hill et al.[80] studied the effects of such drugs in 28 infants for the first 3 years of life. In general, there were more malformations, either disfiguring or life-threatening, as well as more failure to develop normally (low-level Gesell developmental quotients), in infants exposed prenatally to anticonvulsant drugs than in "normal" infants. Seip[159] came to the conclusion that DPH is the prime agent causing changes in blood coagulation.[119] These problems can be overcome with the administration of vitamin K. Stamp et al.[167] felt that DPH was responsible for the osteomalacia he saw in both adults and infants. Seip[159] recommended extra vitamin D as well as larger doses of other vitamins for pregnant women.

Drugs are often administered as analgesics and to allay anxiety during labor, e.g., barbiturates, meperidine, the diazepams,[65] and chlorpromazine.[126,141]

Heroin, morphine, and methadone all produce withdrawal symptoms in babies born to addicted mothers. Zelson et al.[183] reported withdrawal effects from methadone, and in some cases even convulsions and jaundice.[122] On a low-dose program, there was no increase in mortality or prolonged morbidity despite the withdrawal symptoms.[76] No congenital abnormalities were noted, but approximately one-fourth of those born were less than 2500 g in weight.[104] Of 30 infants born to heroin addicts 80% had withdrawal symptoms for as long as 3–6 months. Even at 1 year of age, some of the babies showed behavioral disturbances—predominantly hyperactive.[181] Naeye et al.[121] reported evidence of fetal stress in babies of heroin-addicted mothers. Friedler and Cochin[69] showed: "Morphine had a depressant effect on antenatal growth, even if the maternal exposure was before mating."

In rats treated with morphine, the young showed decreased response to nociceptive stimuli if morphine was given on day 17, 18, 19, or 20 of gestation. No abnormalities were noted at birth, but appeared by 12 or 13 days and as late as the 21st day. The young also showed a tolerance to morphine as late as the 12th to 13th day of life. These data are confirmed by Friedler and Cochin,[69] who found that the effects of premating morphine on the growth of the offspring could not be eradicated by cross-fostering.

Alcohol addiction gives rise to interesting problems in its possible effects on the newborn. Withdrawal symptoms have been noted in the newborn, and congenital malformations have also been reported.

The French authors Auroux and Dehaupas[10] reported that behaviorally, young rats from alcoholic mothers tend to be hyperactive. Such hyperactivity leads to faster learning in various test situations. Himwich et al.[85] found that young cats the mothers of which received chronic doses of alcohol grew more slowly and also had a slower reflex development.

Drugs taken early in pregnancy, even before the woman is aware of the pregnancy, can cause changes in fetal development. Such changes appear to be caused by meprobamate, chlordiazepoxide, haloperidol,[97] imipramine, valium and countless others.[108] Aspirin taken as late as the last week of pregnancy can influence the blood-clotting pattern in the newborn. Moreover, many drugs will displace bilirubin from albumin, an important factor in the prevention of kernicterus.[171]

Nicotine from cigarette smoking appeared to affect birth weight and length adversely.[109] Amphetamine, on the other hand, had no effect.[22]

Infants exposed to methylmercury in their mothers' milk appeared to lose the compound only slowly from their bodies after a single exposure of the mothers to methylmercury. It required 6 months for the blood levels in the infants to reach those of the mother.[7]

The fetal liver gradually develops the ability to detoxify drugs. The necessary microsomal enzymes have been detected at 8–13 days' gestational age in the human fetus.[140] However, even intermediate products may still be toxic; e.g., thalidomide is hydroxylated to a compound teratogenic to the developing chick.

The ability of hormones given during pregnancy to change the hormone levels in the fetus is well known. Combinations of drugs or hormones or both appear more dangerous than either alone.[106]

Tanimura[173] followed the teratogenic properties of drugs thought to be harmful in human embryos. Marked species differences were found with thalidomide, quinine, aminopterins, and acetylsalicyclic acid.

Imipramine produced fetal abnormalities in rabbit fetuses in a study by Robson and Sullivan.[147] There is at the moment apparently no evidence that imipramine can produce human fetal abnormalities.

Richards[145] listed salicylates, antiemetics, and poor diet among the factors of greatest importance in the production of congenital malformations in South Wales.

Meprobamate at doses of 280 mg/kg showed no effect on offspring of mice given the drug both during and before pregnancy.[21a]

7. References

1. ABOOD, L. G., AND GEIGER, A., 1955, Breakdown of proteins and lipids during glucose-free perfusion of the cat's brain, *Amer. J. Physiol.* **182**:557–560.

2. ADAM, P. A. J., RÄIHÄ, N., RAHIALA, E.-L., AND KEKOMÄI, M., 1975, Oxidation of glucose and D-β-OH-butyrate by the early human fetal brain, *Acta Paediatr. Scand.* **64**:17–24.

3. AGRAWAL, H. C., AND PRENSKY, A. L., 1973, Differential incorporation of ^{14}C derived from glucose and acetate into proteins of developing brain, Fourth Meeting of the International Society for Neurochemistry, Tokyo, Japan, p. 550.

4. AGRAWAL, H. C., PRENSKY, A. L., FISHMAN, M. A., AND BURTON, R. M., 1974, Amino acids and myelin proteins, *Mod. Probl. Pediatr.* **13**:1–13.

5. AKIYAMA, Y., SCHULTE, F. J., SCHULTZ, M. A., AND PARMELEE, A. H., JR., 1969, Acoustically evoked responses in premature and full term newborn infants, *Electroencephalogr. Clin. Neurophysiol.* **26**:371–380.

6. ALLWEIS, C., LANDAU, T., ABELES, M., AND MAGNES, J., 1966, The oxidation of uniformly labelled albumin-bound palmitic acid to CO_2 by the perfused cat brain, *J. Neurochem.* **13**:795–804.

7. AMIN-ZAKI, L., ELHASSANI, S., MAJEED, M. A., CLARKSON, T. W., DOHERTY, R. A., AND GREENWOOD, M. R., 1974, Studies of infants postnatally exposed to methylmercury, *J. Pediatr.* **85**(1):81–84.

8. ANOKHIN, P. K., 1964, Systemogenesis as a general regulator of brain development, *Prog. Brain Res.* **9**:54–86.

9. ARSHAVSKY, I. A., AKHUNDKI, M., AND SOLOMATIN, S. S., 1966, Characteristics of electrical activity and steady potential of the brain cortex in children under three months of age during sleep and wakefulness, *Byull. Eksp. Biol. Med.* **9**:8–12.

10. AUROX, M., AND DEHAUPAS, M., 1971, Influence de la nutrition de la mère sur le dévelopement tardif du système nerveux central de la progeniture (rats). II. Evolution de l'accroissement, des capacités d'apprentissage de la progeniture par alcoolisation de la mère pendant la gestation et la lactation, *C. R. Soc. Biol.* **165**:1534–1537.

11. BAÑOS, G., DANIEL, P. M., MOORHOUSE, S. R., AND PRATT, O. E., 1970, The entry of amino acids into the brain of the rat during the postnatal period, *J. Physiol.* **213**:45–46P.

12. BARLOW, C. F., SCHOOLAR, J. C., DOMEK, N. S., BENSON, D. W., AND ROTH, L. J., 1959, Observations on isotope-labeled drugs in the central nervous system, in: *Proceedings of the Second International United Nations Conference of the Peaceful Uses of Atomic Energy, Geneva 1958,* pp. 243–247, Pergamon Press, New York.

13. BARRON, K. D., AND BERNSOHN, J., 1968, Esterases

14. BARTOSHUK, A. K., 1964, Human neonatal EEG: Frequency analysis of awake and asleep samples from four areas, *Psychon. Sci.* **1**:281–282.

15. BARTOSHUK, A. K., AND TENNANT, J. M., 1964, Human neonatal EEG correlates of sleep–wakefulness and neural maturation, *J. Psychiatr. Res.* **2**:73–83.

16. BERGSTRÖM, R. M., BERGSTRÖM, L., PUTKONEN, P., AND SAINIO, K., 1963, The effects of thalidomide on the electrical activity of the brain in the intrauterine guinea pig foetus, *Med. Exp.* **11**:119–127.

17. BERL, S., 1965, Compartmentation of glutamic acid metabolism in developing cerebral cortex, *J. Biol. Chem.* **240**:2047–2054.

18. BERL, S., 1966, Glutamine synthetase. Determination of its distribution in brain during development, *Biochemistry* **5**:916–922.

19. BISHOP, E. J., 1950, The strychnine spike as a physiological indicator of cortical maturity in the postnatal rabbit, *Electroencephalogr. Clin. Neurophysiol.* **2**:309–315.

20. BLEYER, W. A., AND ROSEN, M. G., 1968, Meperidine-induced changes in the maternal and fetal electroencephalogram of the guinea pig, *Electroencephalogr. Clin. Neurophysiol.* **24**:249–258.

21. BORGSTEDT, A. D., AND ROSEN, M. G., 1968, Medication during labor correlated with behavior and EEG of the newborn, *Amer. J. Dis. Child.* **115**:21–24.

21a. BRAR, B. S., 1969, The effect of meprobamate on fertility, gestation, and offspring viability and development of mice, *Arch. Int. Pharmacodyn. Ther.* **177**(2):416–422.

22. BRIGGS, G. C., SAMSON, J. H., AND CRAWFORD, D. J., 1975, Lack of abnormalities in a newborn exposed to amphetamine during gestation, *Amer. J. Dis. Child.* **129**:249, 250.

23. BROWN, J. W., 1973, Differentiation of neurons in subnucleus caudalis of the nucleus of the spinal tract of V in human and rabbit embryos, *Prog. Brain Res.* **40**:67–90.

24. BROWN, W. A., MANNING, T., AND GRODIN, J., 1972, The relationship of antenatal and perinatal psychologic variables to the uses of drugs in labor, *Psychosom. Med.* **34**(2):119–127.

25. CAHILL, G. F., JR., OWEN, O. E., AND MORGAN, A. P., 1968, The consumption of fuels during prolonged starvation, *Adv. Enzyme Regul.* **6**:143–150.

26. CAMPBELL, A. G. M., MILLIGAN, J. E., AND TALNER, N. S., 1968, The effect of pretreatment with pentobarbital, meperidine, or hyperbaric oxygen on the response to anoxia and resuscitation in newborn rabbits, *J. Pediatr.* **72**:518–527.

27. CHEN, H.-C., LIEN, I.-N., AND LU, T.-C., 1965,

Kernicterus in newborn rabbits, *Amer. J. Pathol.* **46**:331–343.

27a. CHEN, H.-C., LIN, C.-S., AND LIEN, I.-N., 1966, Ultrastructural studies in experimental kernicterus, *Amer. J. Pathol.* **48**:683–711.

28. CHEN, H.-C., LIN, C.-S., AND LIEN, I.-N., 1967, Vascular permeability in experimental kernicterus: An electron-microscopic study of the blood–brain barrier, *Amer. J. Pathol.* **51**:69–99.

29. CHESLER, A., LABELLE, G. C., AND HIMWICH, H. E., 1942, The relative effects of toxic doses of alcohol on fetal, newborn and adult rats, *Q. J. Stud. Alcohol* **3**:1–4.

30. CHESLER, A., LABELLE, G. C., AND HIMWICH, H. E., 1942, A study of the comparative toxic effects of morphine on the fetal, newborn and adult rats, *J. Pharmacol. Exp. Ther.* **75**:363–366.

31. CHIU, J.-F., AND SUNG, S. C., 1970, DNA nucleotidyltransferase activity of the developing rat brain, *Biochim. Biophys. Acta* **209**:34–42.

32. CHURCHILL, J. A., GRISELL, J., AND DARNLEY, J. D., 1966, Rhythmic activity in the EEG of newborns, *Electroencephalogr. Clin. Neurophysiol.* **21**:131–139.

33. CONEL, J. L., 1939–1963, in: *The Postnatal Development of the Human Cerebral Cortex*, Vols. 1–7, Harvard University Press, Cambridge, Massachusetts.

34. COSMI, E. V., MORISHIMA, H. O., DANIEL, S. S., AND JAMES, L. S., 1968, Effect of sodium-4-hydroxybutyrate (gamma-OH) on fetal and newborn guinea pigs, *Amer. J. Obstet. Gynecol.* **100**:72–75.

35. D'ADAMO, A. F., JR., AND D'ADAMO, A. P., 1968, Acetyl transport mechanisms in the nervous system: The oxoglutarate shunt and fatty acid synthesis in the developing rat brain, *J. Neurochem.* **15**:315–323.

36. DESMEDT, J. E., MANIL, H., CHORAZYNA, H., AND DEBECKER, J., 1967, Potentiel évoqué cérébral et conduction corticipète pour une volée d'influx somesthesique chez le nouveau-né normal, *C. R. Soc. Biol. (Paris)* **161**:205.

37. DEVIVO, D. C., LECKIE, M. P., AND AGRAWAL, H. C., 1973, The differential incorporation of β-hydroxybutyrate and glucose into brain glutamate in the newborn rat, *Brain Res.* **55**:485–490.

38. DEVIVO, D. C., LECKIE, M. P., AND AGRAWAL, H. C., 1974, The differential incorporation of β-hydroxybutyrate and glucose into brain amino acids during rat development, *Trans. Amer. Soc. Neurochem. (New Orleans)*, p. 88.

39. DOBBING, J., 1961, The blood–brain barrier, *Physiol. Rev.* **41**:130–188.

40. DOBBING, J., AND SANDS, J., 1973, Quantitative growth and development of human brain, *Arch. Dis. Child.* **48**(10):757–767.

41. DOBBING, J., AND SMART, J. L., 1973, Early undernutrition, brain development and behavior, in:

Ethology and Development (S. A. Barnett, ed.), pp. 16–36, Spastics International Medical Publications with Heinemann Medical Books, London.

42. DOMEK, N. S., BARLOW, C. F., AND ROTH, L. J., 1960, An ontogenetic study of phenobarbital-C^{14} in cat brain, *J. Pharmacol. Exp. Ther.* **130**:285–293.

43. DREYFUS-BRISAC, C., 1968, Sleep ontogenesis in early human prematurity from 24 to 27 weeks of conceptional age, *Dev. Psychobiol.* **1**:162–169.

44. DREYFUS-BRISAC, C., 1975, Neurophysiological studies in human premature and full-term newborns, *Biol. Psychiatry* **10**(5):485–496.

45. DREYFUS-BRISAC, C., AND BLANC, C., 1956, Electroencéphalogramme et maturation cerebrale, *Encephalé* **45**:205–241.

46. DREYFUS-BRISAC, C., FLESCHER, J., AND PLASSART, E., 1962, L'électroencéphalogramme: Critère d'âge conceptionnel du nouveau-né à terme et prématuré, *Biol. Neonate* **4**:154–173.

47. DUSTMAN, R. E., AND BECK, E. C., 1969, The effects of maturation and aging on the wave form of visually evoked potentials, *Electroencephalogr. Clin. Neurophysiol.* **26**:2–11.

48. EDMOND, J., 1974, Ketone bodies as precursors of sterols and fatty acids in the developing rat, *J. Biol. Chem.* **249**:72–80.

49. EDSTROM, R. F. S., AND ESSEX, H. E., 1956, Swelling of the brain induced by anoxia, *Neurology* **6**:118–124.

50. EEG-OLOFSSON, O., 1971, The development of the electroencephalogram in normal children from the age of 1 through 15 years, *Neuropädiatrie* **4**:405–427.

51. EEG-OLOFSSON, O., PETERSÉN, I., AND SELLDÉN, U., 1971, The development of the electroencephalogram in normal children from the age of 1 through 15 years, *Neuropädiatrie* **4**:375–404.

52. ELLINGSON, R. J., 1958, Electroencephalograms of normal, full term newborns immediately after birth with observations on arousal and visual evoked responses, *Electroencephalogr. Clin. Neurophysiol.* **10**:31–50.

53. ELLINGSON, R. J., 1960, Cortical electrical responses to visual stimulation in the human infant, *Electroencephalogr. Clin. Neurophysiol.* **12**:663–677.

54. ELLINGSON, R. J., 1964, Studies of the electrical activity of the developing human brain, *Prog. Brain Res.* **9**:26–53.

55. ELLINGSON, R. J., 1966, Development of visual evoked responses in human infants recorded by a response averager, *Electroencephalogr. Clin. Neurophysiol.* **21**:403–404.

56. ELLINGSON, R. J., 1967, The study of brain electrical activity in infants, in: *Advances in Child Development and Behavior* (L. P. Lipsitt and C. C. Spiker, eds.), Vol. 3, pp. 53–97, Academic Press, New York.

57. ELLINGSON, R. J., AND LINDSLEY, D. B., 1949, Brain waves and cortical development in newborns and young infants, *Amer. J. Physiol.* **4**:248–249.

58. ELLINGSON, R. J., DANAHY, T., NELSON, B., AND LATHROP, G. H., 1974, Variability of auditory evoked potentials in human newborns, *Electroencephalogr. Clin. Neurophysiol.* **36**:155–162.

59. ELLINGSON, R. J., DUTCH, S. J., AND McINTIRE, M. S., 1974, EEG's of prematures: 3–8 year follow-up study, *Dev. Psychobiol.* **7**(6):529–538.

60. ELLINGSON, R. J., EISEN, J. D., AND OTTERSBERG, G., 1973, Clinical electroencephalographic observations on institutionalized mongoloids confirmed by karyotype, *Electroencephalogr. Clin. Neurophysiol.* **34**:193–196.

61. ELLINGSON, R. J., LATHROP, G. H., DANAHY, T., AND NELSON, B., 1973, Variability of visual evoked potentials in human infants and adults, *Electroencephalogr. Clin. Neurophysiol.* **34**:113–124.

62. EMDE, R. N., HARMON, R. J., METCALF, D., KOENIG, K. L., AND WAGONFELD, S., 1971, Stress and neonatal sleep, *Psychosom. Med.* **33**(6):491–497.

63. ENGEL, R., 1964, Electroencephalographic responses to photic stimulation, and their correlation with maturation, *Ann. N. Y. Acad. Sci.* **117**:407–412.

64. ENGEL, R., AND BUTLER, B. V., 1963, Appraisal of conceptual age of newborn infants by electroencephalographic methods, *J. Pediatr.* **63**:386–393.

65. ERKKOLA, R., KANTO, J., AND SELLMAN, R., 1974, Diazepam in early human pregnancy, *Acta Obstet. Gynecol. Scand.* **53**(2):135.

66. FERRISS, G. S., DAVIS, G. D., HACKETT, E. R., AND DORSEN, M. M., 1966, Maturation of visual evoked responses in human infants, *Electroencephalogr. Clin. Neurophysiol.* **21**:404.

67. FORFAR, J. O., AND NELSON, M. M., 1973, Epidemiology of drugs taken by pregnant women: Drugs that may affect the fetus adversely, *Clin. Pharmacol. Ther.* **14**(4):632–642.

68. FOUTS, J. R., AND ADAMSON, R. H., 1959, Drug metabolism in the newborn rabbit, *Science,* **129**:897–898.

69. FRIEDLER, G., AND COCHLIN, J., 1972, Growth retardation in offspring of female rats treated with morphine prior to conception, *Science* **175**:654–655.

70. GAITONDE, M. K., AND RICHTER, D., 1966, Changes with age in the utilization of glucose carbon in liver and brain, *J. Neurochem.* **13**:1309–1318.

71. GLASER, G. H., AND LEVY, L. L., 1965, Photic following in the EEG of the newborn, *Amer. J. Dis. Child.* **109**:333–337.

72. GOLDIE, L., CURTIS, J. A. H., SVENDSEN, U., AND ROBERTSON, N. R. C., 1968, Abnormal sleep rhythms in mongol babies, *Lancet* **1**:229–230.

73. GRAZIANI, L. J., WEITZMAN, E. D., AND VELASCO, M. S. A., 1968, Neurologic maturation and auditory evoked responses in low birth weight infants, *Pediatrics* **41**:483–494.

74. GRÖNTOFT, O., 1954, Intracranial haemorrhage and blood–brain barrier problems in the newborn, *Acta Pathol. Microbiol. Scand. Suppl.* **100**:5–109.

75. GUROFF, G., AND UDENFRIEND, S., 1962, Studies on aromatic amino acid uptake by rat brain *in vivo*: Uptake of phenylalanine and of tryptophan; inhibition and steroselectivity in the uptake of tyrosine by brain and muscle, *J. Biol. Chem.* **237**:803–806.

76. HARPER, R. G., SOLISH, G. I., PUROW, H. M., SANG, E., AND PANEPINTO, W. C., 1974, The effect of a methadone treatment program upon pregnant heroin addicts and their newborn infants, *Pediatrics* **54**(3):1–6.

77. HART, L. G., ADAMSON, R. H., DIXON, R. L., AND FOUTS, J. R., 1962, Stimulation of hepatic microsomal drug metabolism in the newborn and fetal rabbit, *J. Pharmacol. Exp. Ther.* **137**:103–106.

78. HAWKINS, R. A., WILLIAMSON, D. H., AND KREBS, H. A., 1971, Ketone-body utilization by adult and suckling rat brain *in vivo, Biochem. J.* **122**:13–18.

79. HECOX, K., AND GALAMBOS, R., 1974, Brain stem auditory evoked responses in human infants and adults, *Arch. Otolaryngol.* **99**:30–33.

80. HILL, R. M., VERNIAUD, W. M., HORNING, M. G., McCULLEY, L. B., AND MORGAN, N. F., 1974, Infants exposed *in utero* to antiepileptic drugs, *Amer. J. Dis. Child.* **127**:645–653.

81. HIMWICH, H. E., 1976, Foodstuffs of the brain: Ketone bodies, in: *Brain Metabolism and Cerebral Disorders* (H. E. Himwich, ed.), pp. 33–63, Spectrum Publications, New York.

82. HIMWICH, H. E., AND NAHUM, L. H., 1929, The respiratory quotient of brain, *Amer. J. Physiol.* **90**:389–390.

83. HIMWICH, W. A., 1975, Forging a link between basic and clinical research: Developing brain, *Biol. Psychiatry* **10**:125–139.

84. HIMWICH, W. A., BENARON, H. B. W., TUCKER, B. E., BABUNA, C., AND STRIPE, M. C., 1959, Metabolic studies on perinatal human brain, *J. Appl. Physiol.* **14**:873–877.

85. HIMWICH, W. A., HALL, J. S., AND MACARTHUR, W., 1977, Maternal alcohol and neonatal health, *Biol. Psychiatry*, in press.

86. HOMBERGER, E., ETSTEN, B., AND HIMWICH, H. E., 1947, Factors influencing the susceptibility of rats to barbiturates, *Fed. Proc. Fed. Amer. Soc. Exp. Biol.* **6**:131.

87. HORNING, M. G., BUTLER, C. M., NOWLIN, J., AND HILL, R. M., 1975, Mini-review—Drug metabolism in the human neonate, *Life Sci.* **16**:651–672.

88. HRBEK, A., AND MARÈS, P., 1964, Cortical evoked responses to visual stimulation in full term and premature newborns, *Electroencephalogr. Clin. Neurophysiol.* **16**:575–581.

89. IDE, T., STEINKE, J., AND CAHILL, G. F., JR., 1969, Metabolic interactions of glucose, lactate and β-hydroxybutyrate in rat brain slices, *Amer. J. Physiol.* **217**:784–792.

90. ITOH, T., AND QUASTEL, J. H., 1970, Acetoacetate

metabolism in infant and adult rat brain *in vitro,* *Biochem. J.* **116**:641–655.

91. JEWETT, R. E., AND NORTON, S., 1966, Effect of tranquilizing drugs on postnatal behavior, *Exp. Neurol.* **14**:33–43.

92. JONDORF, W. R., MAICKEL, R. P., AND BRODIE, B. B., 1958–1959, Inability of newborn mice and guinea pigs to metabolize drugs, *Biochem. Pharmacol.* **1**:352–355.

93. JUCHAU, M. R., PEDERSEN, M. G., FANTEL, A. G., AND SHEPARD, T. H., 1973, Drug metabolism by placenta, *Clin. Pharmacol. Ther.* **14**(4[2]):673–679.

94. KELLAWAY, P., AND PETERSÉN, I., 1964, *Neurologic and Electroencephalographic Correlative Studies in Infancy,* Grune & Stratton, New York.

95. KETY, S. S., 1957, The general metabolism of the brain *in vivo,* in: *The Metabolism of the Nervous System* (D. Richter, ed.), pp. 221–236, Pergamon Press, London.

96. KLEE, C. B., AND SOKOLOFF, L., 1967, Changes in D(-)-β-hydroxybutyric dehydrogenase activity during brain maturation in the rat, *J. Biol. Chem.* **242**:3880–3883.

97. KOPELMAN, A. E., McCULLAR, F. W., AND HEGGENESS, L., 1975, Limb malformations following maternal use of haloperidol, *J. Amer. Med. Assoc.* **231**(1):62–64.

98. KUPFERBERG, H. J., AND WAY, E. L., 1963, Pharmacologic basis for the increased sensitivity of the newborn rat to morphine, *J. Pharmacol. Exp. Ther.* **141**:105–112.

99. LAJTHA, A., 1961, Exchange rates of amino acids between plasma and brain in different parts of the brain, in: *Regional Neurochemistry* (S. S. Kety and J. Elkes, eds.), pp. 19–24, Pergamon Press, Oxford.

100. LAJTHA, A., AND FORD, D., 1968, Conclusions, *Prog. Brain Res.* **29**:535–537.

101. LAJTHA, A., LAHIRI, S., AND TOTH, J., 1963, The brain barrier system. IV. Cerebral amino acid uptake in different classes, *J. Neurochem.* **10**:765–773.

102. LINDSLEY, D. B., 1939, A longitudinal study of the occipital alpha rhythm in normal children: Frequency and amplitude standards, *J. Genet. Psychol.* **55**:197–213.

103. LESNÝ, I., 1964, Electroencephalographic study of infantile cerebral palsy with special regard to electroclinical correlations, *Acta Univ. Carol. Med. (Prague), Monogr.* 15.

104. LIPSITZ, P. J., AND BLATMAN, S., 1974, Newborn infants of mothers on methadone maintenance, *N. Y. State J. Med.* **74**:994–999.

105. LOMBROSO, C. T., 1975, Neurophysiological observations in diseased newborns, *Biol. Psychiatry* **10**(5):527–558.

106. MEESTER, W. D., 1964, The effects on the fetus of drugs given during pregnancy, *Marquette Med. Rev.* **30**(4):147–154.

107. METCALF, D. R., 1969, The effect of extrauterine experience on the ontogenesis of EEG sleep spindles, *Psychosom. Med.* **31**(5):393–399.

108. MILKOVICH, L., AND VAN DEN BERG, B. J., 1974, Effects of prenatal meprobamate and chlordiazepoxide hydrochloride on human embryonic and fetal development, *N. Engl. J. Med.* **291**:1268–1271.

109. MILLER, H. C., AND HASSANEIN, K., 1964, Maternal smoking and fetal growth of full term infants, *Pediatr. Res.* **8**:960–963.

110. MINO, M., AND TAKAI, T., 1966, Enzymatic development of human fetus; studies on cytochrome oxidase and succinic dehydrogenase in developing human fetus, *Acta Paediatr. Jpn.* **8**(16):1–6.

111. MINO, M., AND TAKAI, T., 1967, Enzymatic development of the human fetus: LDH/aldolase ratio in developing human fetus, *Acta Paediatr. Jpn.* **9**(18):14–21.

112. MIRKIN, B. L., 1970, Effects of drugs on the fetus and neonate, *Postgrad. Med.* **47**(1):91–96.

113. MIRKIN, B. L., 1973, Drug distribution in pregnancy, in: *Fetal Pharmacology* (L. O. Boréus, ed.), pp. 6–22, Raven Press, New York.

114. MISRAHY, G. A., BERAN, A. V., AND PRESCOTT, E. J., 1963, Effects of drugs used in pregnancy on availability of fetal cerebral oxygen, *Anesthesiology* **24**:198–202.

115. MOLLIVER, M. E., KOSTOVIC, I., AND VAN DER LOOS, H., 1973, The development of synapses in cerebral cortex of the human fetus, *Brain Res.* **50**:403.

116. MONOD, N., AND DUCAS, P., 1968, The prognostic value of the electroencephalogram in the first two years of life, in: *Clinical Electroencephalography of Children* (P. Kellaway and I. Petersén, eds.), pp. 61–76, Grune & Stratton, New York.

117. MONOD, N. J., AND PAJOT, N., 1965, Le sommeil du nouveau-né et du prématuré. I. Analyse des études polygraphiques (mouvements oculaires, respiration et E.E.G.) chez le nouveau-né à terme, *Biol. Neonate* **8**:281–307.

118. MONOD, N. J., ELIET-FLESCHER, J., AND DREYFUS–BRISAC, C., 1967, The sleep of the full-term and premature infant. III. The disorders of the pathological newborn sleep organization: Polygraphic studies, *Biol. Neonate* **11**:216–247.

119. MOUNTAIN, K. R., HIRSH, J., AND GALLUS, A. S., 1970, Neonatal coagulation defect due to anticonvulsant drug treatment in pregnancy, *Lancet* **1**:265.

120. MURRAY, B., AND CAMPBELL, D., 1971, Sleep states in the newborn: Influence of sound, *Neuropädiatrie* **3**:335–342.

121. NAEYE, R. L., BLANC, W., LEBLANC, W., AND KHATAMEE, M. A., 1973, Fetal complications of maternal heroin addiction: Abnormal growth, infections, and episodes of stress, *J. Pediatr.* **83**(6):1055–1061.

122. NEWMANN, R. G., 1974, Pregnancies of methadone

patients—Findings in New York City Methadone Maintenance Treatment Program, *N. Y. State J. Med.* **74**(1):52–54.

123. NITOWSKY, H. M., MATZ, L., AND BERZOFSKY, J. A., 1966, Studies on oxidative drug metabolism in the full-term newborn infant, *J. Pediatr.* **69**:1139–1149.

124. NYHAN, W. L., 1961, Toxicity of drugs in the neonatal period, *J. Pediatr.* **59**:1–20.

125. NYHAN, W. L., AND LAMPERT, F., 1965, Response of the fetus and newborn to drugs, *Anesthesiology* **26**:487–500.

126. O'DONOGHUE, S. E. F., 1971, Distribution of pethidine and chlorpromazine in maternal, foetal and neonatal biological fluids, *Nature (London)* **229**:124–125.

127. OLDENDORF, W. H., 1970, Measurements of brain uptake of radiolabeled substances using a tritiated water internal standard, *Brain Res.* **24**:372–376.

128. OLDENDORF, W. H., 1973, Stereospecificity of blood–brain barrier permeability to amino acids, *Amer. J. Physiol.* **224**:967–969.

129. ORNITZ, E. M., 1972, Development of sleep patterns in autistic children, in: *Sleep and the Maturing Nervous System* (C. D. Clemente, D. P. Purpura, and R. E. Mayer, eds.), pp. 363–381, Academic Press, New York.

130. ORNITZ, E. M., RITVO, E. R., LEE, Y. H., PANMAN, L. M., WALTER, R. D., AND MASON, A., 1969, The auditory evoked response in babies during REM sleep, *Electroencephalogr. Clin. Neurophysiol.* **27**:195–198.

131. OWEN, O. E., MORGAN, A. P., KEMP, H. G., SULLIVAN, J. M., HERRERA, M. G., AND CAHILL, G. F., JR., 1967, Brain metabolism during fasting, *J. Clin. Invest.* **46**:1589–1595.

132. PAGE, M. A., AND WILLIAMSON, D. H., 1971, Enzymes of ketone-body utilisation in human brain, *Lancet* **2**:66–68.

133. PAMPIGLIONE, G., 1965, Brain development and the E.E.G. of normal children of various ethnical groups, *Br. Med. J.* **2**:573–575.

134. PARMELEE, A. H., 1975, Neurophysiological and behavioral organization of premature infants in the first months of life, *Biol. Psychiatry* **10**(5):501–512.

135. PARMELEE, A. H., AKIYAMA, Y., SCHULTZ, M. A., WENNER, W. H., SCHULTE, F. J., AND STERN, E., 1968, The electroencephalogram in active and quiet sleep in infants, in: *Clinical Electroencephalography of Children* (P. Kellaway and I. Petersén, eds.), pp. 77–88, Almquist and Wiksell, Stockholm.

136. PARMELEE, A. H., JR., SCHULTE, F. J., AKIYAMA, Y., WENNER, W. H., SCHULTZ, M. A., AND STERN, E., 1968, Maturation of EEG activity during sleep in premature infants, *Electroencephalogr. Clin. Neurophysiol.* **24**:319–329.

137. PARMELEE, A. H., WENNER, W. H., AKIYAMA, Y.,

138. PASSOUANT, P., 1964, Influence de l'âge sur l'organisation du sommeil de nuit et la période de sommeil avec mouvements oculaires, *J. Psychol. Norm. Pathol.* **3**:257–279.

139. PASSOUANT, P., AND CADILHAC, J., 1962, EEG and clinical study of epilepsy during maturation in man, *Epilepsia* **3**:14–43.

140. PELKONEN, O., 1973, Drug metabolism in the human fetal liver—relationship to fetal age, *Arch. Int. Pharmacodyn. Ther.* **202**(2):281–287.

141. PELKONEN, O., AND KÄRKI, N. T., 1973, Drug metabolism in human fetal tissues, *Life Sci.* **13**:1163–1180.

142. PELKONEN, O., JOUPPILA, P., AND KÄRKI, N. T., 1972, Effect of maternal cigarette smoking on 3,4-benzpyrene and N-methylaniline metabolism in human fetal liver and placenta, *Toxicol. Appl. Pharmacol.* **23**:399–407.

143. PERSSON, B., SETTERGREN, G., AND DAHLQUIST, G., 1972, Cerebral arteriovenous difference of acetoacetate and D-β-hydroxybutyrate in children, *Acta Paediatr. Scand.* **61**:273–278.

144. PETERSÉN, I., AND EEG-OLOFSSON, O., 1971, The development of the electroencephalogram in normal children from the age of 1 through 15 years, *Neuropädiatrie* **3**:247–304.

145. RICHARDS, I. D. G., 1969, Congenital malformations and environmental influences in pregnancy, *Br. J. Prev. Soc. Med.* **23**:218–225.

146. ROBERTSON, A. F., AND SPRECHER, H., 1968, A review of human placental lipid metabolism and transport, *Acta Paediatr. Scand. Suppl.* **183**:1–18.

147. ROBSON, J. M., AND SULLIVAN, F. M., 1963, The production of foetal abnormalities in rabbits by imipramine, *Lancet* **1**:638, 639.

148. ROFFWARG, H. P., MUZIO, J. N., AND DEMENT, W. C., 1966, Ontogenetic development of the human sleep–dream cycle, *Science* **152**:604–619.

149. ROSE, G. H., AND ELLINGSON, R. J., 1970, Ontogenesis of evoked potentials, in: *Developmental Neurobiology* (W. A. Himwich, ed.), pp. 393–440, Charles C. Thomas, Springfield, Illinois.

150. ROTH, L. J., SCHOOLAR, J. C., AND BARLOW, C. F., 1959, Sulfur-35 labeled acetazolamide in cat brain, *J. Pharmacol. Exp. Ther.* **125**:128–136.

151. ROZDILSKY, B., AND OLSZEWSKI, J., 1960, Permeability of cerebral vessels to albumin in hyperbilirubinemia: Observations in newborn animals, *Neurology* **10**:631–638.

152. ROZDILSKY, B., AND OLSZEWSKI, J., 1961, Experimental study of the toxicity of bilirubin in newborn animals, *J. Neuropathol. Exp. Neurol.* **20**:193–205.

53. SALGANICOFF, L., AND DE ROBERTIS, E., 1965, Subcellular distribution of the enzymes of the glutamic acid, glutamine and γ-aminobutyric acid cycles in rat brain, *J. Neurochem.* **12**:287–309.

54. SCHAPIRA, F., NORDMANN, Y., AND GREGORI, C., 1972, Hereditary alterations of fructose metabolizing enzymes, *Acta Med. Scand.* **542**:77–83.

55. SCHOOLAR, J. C., BARLOW, C. F., AND ROTH, L. J., 1960, The penetration of carbon-14 urea into cerebrospinal fluid and various areas of the cat brain, *J. Neuropathol. Exp. Neurol.* **19**:216–227.

56. SCHULTE, F. J., AND BELL, E. F., 1973, Bioelectric brain development. An atlas of EEG power spectra in infants and young children, *Neuropädiatrie* **4**:30–45.

57. SCHULTE, F. J., MICHAELIS, R., NOLTE, R., ALBERT, G., PARL, U., AND LASSON, U., 1969, Brain and behavioural maturation in newborn infants of diabetic mothers. Part I: Nerve conduction and EEG patterns, *Neuropädiatrie* **1**:24–35.

58. SCHULTE, F. J., LASSON, U., PARL, U., NOLTE, R., AND JÜRGENS, U., 1969, Brain and behavioural maturation in newborn infants of diabetic mothers, Part II: Sleep cycles, *Neuropädiatric* **1**:36–43.

59. SEIP, M., 1973, Effects of antiepileptic drugs in pregnancy on the fetus and newborn infant, Review article, *Ann. Clin. Res.* **5**:205–207.

60. SHEPOVALNIKOV, A., 1962, Rhythmic components of the infant EEG, *Zh. Vyssh. Nervn. Deyat. im. I. P. Pavlova* **12**:797–808.

61. SHIMIZU, A., AND HIMWICH, H. E., 1968, Effect of LSD on the sleep cycle of the developing kitten, *Dev. Psychobiol.* **1**:60–64.

62. SHIMIZU, A., AND HIMWICH, H. E., 1968, Effects of phenothiazine derivatives on the sleep–wakefulness cycle in growing kittens, *Folia Psychiatr. Neurol. Jpn.* **22**:297–305.

63. SHIMIZU, A., AND HIMWICH, H. E., 1968, The effects of amphetamine on the sleep–wakefulness cycle of developing kittens, *Psychopharmacologia* **13**:161–169.

64. SHIMIZU, A., AND HIMWICH, H. E., 1969, Effects of psychotropic drugs on the sleep–wakefulness cycle of the developing kittens, *Dev. Psychobiol.* **2**:161–169.

65. SHIMIZU, A., BOST, K., AND HIMWICH, H. E., 1968, Electroencephalographic studies of haloperidol, *Int. Pharmacopsychiatry* **1**:134–142.

66. SPITZER, J. J., 1973, CNS and fatty acid metabolism, *Physiologist* **16**:55–68.

67. STAMP, T. C. B., ROUND, J. M., ROWE, D. J. F., AND HADDAD, J. G., 1972, Plasma levels and therapeutic effect of 25-hydroxycholecalciferol in epileptic patients taking anticonvulsant drugs, *Br. Med. J.* **4**:9.

68. STAVE, U., 1971, Perinatal brain metabolism in normal and hypoxic rabbits, in: *International Congress of Pediatrics*, pp. 19–87, Verlag der Wiener.

169. STAVE, U., AND WOLF, H., 1970, Metabolic effects in hypoxia neonatorum, in: *Physiology of the Perinatal Period* (U. Stave, ed.), Vol. 2, pp. 1043–1088, Appleton-Century-Crofts, New York.

170. STERMAN, M. B., AND HOPPENBROUWERS, T., 1971, The development of sleep–waking and rest–activity patterns from fetus to adult in man, in: *Brain Development and Behavior* (M. B. Sterman, D. J. McGintz, A. M. Adinolfi, eds.), pp. 203–227, Academic Press, New York.

171. STERN, L., 1972, Pharmacology for the pediatrician—Drug interactions. Part II. Drugs, the newborn infant, and the binding of bilirubin to albumin, *Pediatrics* **49**(6):916–918.

172. TAKAI, T., AND MINO, M., 1967, Enzymatic development of the human fetus, *SABCO J.* **4**:76–101.

173. TANIMURA, T., 1972, Effects on macaque embryos of drugs reported or suspected to be teratogenic to humans, *Acta Endocrinol.* **166**:293–308.

174. TANNER, J. M., 1970, Physical growth, in: *Carmichael's Manual of Child Psychology* (P. H. Mussen, ed.), 3rd. Ed., Vol. 1, pp. 77–155, John Wiley & Sons, London.

175. UMEZAKI, H., AND MORRELL, F., 1970, Developmental study of photic evoked responses in premature infants, *Electroencephalogr. Clin. Neurophysiol.* **28**:55–63.

176. VAN PETTEN, G. R., 1975, Pharmacology and the fetus, *Br. Med. Bull.* **31**(1):75–77.

177. VAUGHAN, H. G., JR., 1975, Electrophysiologic analysis of regional cortical maturation, *Biol. Psychiatry* **10**(5):513–527.

178. VILLEE, C. A., AND LORING, J. M., 1961, Alternative pathways of carbohydrate metabolism in foetal and adult tissues, *Biochem. J.* **81**:488–494.

179. WAELSCH, H., 1961, Compartmentalized biosynthetic reactions in the central nervous system, in: *Regional Chemistry: Physiology and Pharmacology of the Nervous System* (S. S. Kety and J. Elkes, eds.), pp. 57–64, Pergamon Press, New York.

180. WIDDOWSON, E. M., 1964, Changes in the composition of the body at birth and their bearing on function and food requirements, in: *Symposium on the Adaptation of the Newborn Infant to Extra-Uterine Life* (J. H. P. Joxis, H. K. A. Visser, and J. A. Troelstra, eds.), pp. 1–13, Charles C. Thomas, Springfield, Illinois.

181. WILSON, G. S., DESMOND, M. M., AND VERNIAUD, W. M., 1973, Early development of infants of heroin-addicted mothers, *Amer. J. Dis. Child.* **126**:457–462.

182. ZACHAU-CHRISTIANSEN, G., AND VOLLMOND, K., 1965, The relation between neonatal jaundice and

the motor development in the first year, *Acta Paediatr. Scand. Suppl.* **159**:26–29.

183. ZELSON, C., LEE, S. J., AND CASALINO, M., 1973, Neonatal narcotic addiction—comparative effects of maternal intake of heroin and methadone, *N. Engl. J. Med.* **289**:1216–1220.

184. ZUELZER, W. W., 1960, Neonatal jaundice and mental retardation, *Arch. Neurol.* **3**:127–135.

CHAPTER 30

Function of the Nervous System During Prenatal Life

Tryphena Humphrey†

1. Introduction

That the nervous system begins to function early during prenatal life is demonstrated only by the movements resulting from its activity. The skeletal muscle reflexes of the fetus are one manifestation of function, and constitute its overt behavior.[35] Another way that function is revealed is through visceral reactions, such as cardiac action, intestinal activity due to smooth muscle contraction, or glandular secretion. The neural regulation of the heart is probably the earliest evidence for function of the nervous system in visceral reactions, for nerve fibers invade the heart at about 16–19 mm,[60] and ECGs have been obtained as early as at 9.5 weeks of menstrual age [36.0 mm crown–rump length (CR), Hooker fetal series].[30]

In lower vertebrates such as fishes, there is

evidence that the motor neurons of the spinal cord can function before the reflex arc is completed.[29] The same does not hold true for higher mammals and for man. The earliest proof of function of the human nervous system, therefore, is provided by the elicitation of a reflex. What part of the reflex arc matures last is still a matter for conjecture.

The function of the neuromuscular system in the development of the overt behavior of the human fetus is the major concern of this chapter. Although the title of this book mentions only the physiology of the perinatal period, it should be remembered that the functional capacities of the nervous system at that time are dependent on the morphological development earlier in fetal life. Far more attention has been given to the capabilities of premature and perinatal infants than to the functional capacities of the fetus before the age of viability is attained. Indeed, until the last 35–40 years, there had been relatively little reliable objective information available on the reactions of human fetuses during the first half of fetal life.

Tryphena Humphrey · †Deceased. Department of Anatomy, The University of Alabama in Birmingham, The Medical Center, Birmingham, Alabama

2. Historical Background of the Investigations of Human Fetal Activity

The early comments on human fetal activity, some of which date back to 1885[84] and even before, are casual notes, not carefully planned observations. These accounts were reviewed in the 1944 and 1952 papers of Hooker.[35,36] The extensive and detailed investigations of Minkowski[67–69] were also based on dictated records. Fitzgerald and Windle[25] used motion-picture recording for the few human embryos they studied, but the methods of stimulation were not uniform, and no photographic documentation was published. Likewise, no photographic records are as yet available from the observations of the Soviet investigators such as Golubewa et al.[28] The early literature on human prenatal activity was treated extensively in the papers of Hooker,[35,36,38] and will not be considered further. Likewise, the literature concerned with subhuman mammalian prenatal activity was discussed in some detail by Hooker[35,36] and by Hamburger.[29] Reference will be made to it only insofar as it is relevant to the interpretation of human fetal reflex activity.

2.1. Basis of this Account

In this account, the function of the nervous system, as manifested by the overt activity of the fetus, is based primarily on the work of Hooker and his co-workers, with some ancillary material from the work of other investigators. Consequently, brief mention will be made of the methods utilized in his work. Fetuses removed by cesarean section, when the therapeutic termination of pregnancy was deemed necessary by a committee of consulting obstetricians, were placed under a motion-picture camera in an isotonic fluid bath as soon as possible (usually normal mammalian saline or Tyrode's solution). The solution was maintained as near to normal body temperature as feasible. The time lapse between beginning placental separation and the initial observations was usually about 1.5–2 min.[35]

Most of the motion pictures were taken at 16 frames/sec. A few records were made at 24 frames/sec. Some slow-motion recordings were made, but they proved extremely costly and added relatively little to the information provided by the photographs at normal speed. Color film, also an expensive method, was not employed. The motion-picture camera used for most of the work was a 35-mm World War I surplus camera, motor-driven and operated by a foot switch to leave the hand of the observer free to move the fetus and to stimulate it with the esthesiometer.

The major observations were made by touching the cutaneous surfaces of the fetus with hair esthesiometers similar to the von Frey hairs used by neurologists. These esthesiometers were calibrated to exert a pressure no greater than 10, 25, 50, and 100 mg and 2 g. To prevent penetration of the delicate epithelium of the young fetuses and so stimulate the underlying muscles directly, the tip of the hairs were coated with a droplet of smooth, transparent, inert material. Stroking the skin surface provided the more effective stimulation, since both spatial and temporal summation resulted, whereas punctate or spot stimuli would seldom elicit reflex activity. Movements caused by unknown stimuli, the so-called "spontaneous movements," were photographed when they occurred.

3. Effects of Anoxia, Asphyxia, Narcotics, and Anesthetics on Fetal Reflexes

After placental separation, reflexes can be elicited from fetuses only until the oxygen supply is depleted. During the first few weeks after activity begins, the movements occur for about 5–8 min. As the fetus becomes older, the time increases to 10, then to 15–20 min or even more. With depletion of the oxygen supply, anoxia develops, and asphyxia takes over as the carbon dioxide and lactic acid accumulate. All overt activity then ceases, although heart action continues for some time.[42,96] Many anesthetics and various drugs administered to the mother preoperatively cross the placental barrier and influence the activity of the fetus. These drugs include general anesthetics such as chloroform, ether, nitrous oxide and sodium amytal, and drugs such as morphine, codeine, barbiturates, and tranquilizers. For the limited preoperative period involved, demerol does not affect the fetus. Similarly, neither spinal novocaine nor local anesthetics influence fetal reflexes.

Observations of activity based on mammals that have the fetal circulation maintained and drug and anesthetic effects eliminated vary from those on human fetuses, as is to be expected. The surprising thing, of course, is that there should be so little difference in the sequence of development of activity or the different mammals studied. Nevertheless, at least some of the differences were attributed to the effects of progressive anoxia and asphyxia on the human fetus, or to the influence of drugs and anesthetics. Consequently, several investigators of lower mammalian reflexes considered the activity of human fetuses observed by Hooker and others to be so much affected by asphyxia that it could not be the normal sequence of behavioral development,[25,97,99] and even considered that the reflexes themselves were abnormal.[98]

The effects of narcotics and anesthetics on reflex activity are similar to those of anoxia. In all instances, however, the reflex is either elicited or suppressed. Because a higher oxygen level is required for newly functioning reflex arcs, the reflexes that become active first in development are the last to disappear when asphyxia arrests all reflexes (Table I). The most recently functional reflex arcs can be activated only when the conditions are optimal. Consequently, until large amounts of data are collected, it is always possible that any given reflex may not have been elicited at as early an age as it may be demonstrated when more data become available. As demonstrated in the experimental literature, a reflex does not change its character and become abnormal.[42] *It is not the reflex that is abnormal, but the morphological/or functional conditions, or both, under which it is obtained.*[53] Thus, the Babinski reflex, for example, indicates abnormality in the nervous system when

elicited from an adult, but is a part of normal development both prenatally and postnatally.

4. Significance of Different Types of Stimuli

Two types of general somatic afferent stimuli may be used to elicit reflexes—exteroceptive and proprioceptive stimuli. The light stroking stimuli with hair esthesiometers used by Hooker and his co-workers are exteroceptive stimulations, although there is a minor amount of superficial pressure. Proprioceptive stimuli result from deep pressure or from stretching a muscle. These types of stimulation were commonly used by Windle and his collaborators in their investigations. Tapping on the amnion, which was also employed by these observers, produces a considerable amount of diffuse pressure on widely spread areas. Stretching muscles by lifting and releasing a limb also elicits proprioceptive reflexes of a type that is always local in character, even in the adult.[42] It is quite impossible to make comparisons between such proprioceptive reactions and exteroceptive reflexes elicited by light stroking of cutaneous surfaces. Neither the age of origin nor the course of development would be alike, for different neuronal arcs are utilized. Cinematographic recording has been found essential if all—or even most of—the actions of the reflex responses

Table I. Example of the Sequence of Suppression of Fetal Reflexes by Anoxia and Asphyxia[a]

Reflex elicited	Order and time of appearance	Order of suppression
Total pattern contralateral flexion reflexes	Earliest in development; 7.5 weeks—beginning, 8.5 weeks—fully developed	Last of all of reflexes that disappear with asphyxia
First of local reflex, orbicularis oculi contraction (action not accompanied by trunk and extremity movements)	10.5 weeks—2 weeks after total pattern contralateral flexion reflexes are fully developed	Before total pattern contralateral flexion reflexes are suppressed by asphyxia
Later-developing local reflexes such as tongue movements	12.5 weeks for earliest motion-picture evidence; 4 weeks after total pattern reflexes are fully developed	Prior to first local reflex as well as before total pattern reflexes are lost through asphyxia

[a] Note that progressive action of anoxia and asphyxia suppresses the reflexes elicited by cutaneous stimulation in the reverse order of their appearance in development.

to cutaneous stimuli are seen. Such recording will be even more necessary in evaluating the time of onset and the later developmental history of reflexes evoked by stretch and pressure stimuli.

5. Theories on the Development of Fetal Behavior

Differences in the sequence observed in the development of motor activity among the different mammals studied produced two major views concerning the manner in which behavior develops. From his studies on *Amblystoma,* Coghill[21] developed the concept that all the neuromuscular system capable of responding to the stimulus reacts when a reflex is first elicited during development. When well developed, these reflexes involved head, trunk, and extremity movements. Coghill referred to these reactions of *Amblystoma* as *total pattern reflexes,* and stated that partial patterns, e.g., the local movements of a single limb, individuated out of the total pattern reflexes. Coghill found that even mouth-opening begins as part of a forward–jumping movement following a visual stimulus.[21]

From his observation of early human fetal activity, Hooker[35] concluded that the exteroceptive stimuli utilized in his studies elicited reflexes of the total pattern type described by Coghill, i.e., a lateral flexion of the head (muscle action in the cervical region) that extended to include the upper extremities, the lower trunk, the rump, and the lower extremities in that general order as the fetus increased in age. He found that the local reflexes elicited by these light stroking stimuli appeared later in development than did the total pattern reflexes. Reference was also made in these studies to the union of some local reflexes with others later in development of functional combinations of reflexes, some of which are retained in late fetal life and postnatally.[40,45]

Although they accept Coghill's interpretation for tailed amphibians, some workers on mammalian fetuses, including Windle,[97] have considered that the proprioceptive local reflexes, such as those observed on lifting a limb and releasing it, develop first of all in mammals. Consequently, they advanced the theory that behavior evolves by the addition and integration of local reflexes to build up complex functional activity.

Other interpretations of the manner of behavioral development have been proposed by the Soviet investigators and by Kuo[63] In his concept of behavioral gradients, Kuo emphasizes that for any given response and in any given stage of development, the entire organism is involved either actively or passively.[63] Many Soviet investigators[7,28] stress the importance of heterochronic maturation of individual parts of a functional system in early development and systemogenesis in later fetal life. It could be said for all these viewpoints that their proponents have concentrated attention on some facets of behavioral development to the relative exclusion of certain other aspects.

6. Determination of Fetal Age

The age of the human fetus has been expressed in different ways. For the observations made by Hooker and his co-workers from 1932 to 1962, menstrual age based on the data accumulated by Streeter[95] was used. Since this account is based on the records and publications of Hooker and his co-workers, menstrual age taken from these records is used throughout the discussion unless stated otherwise. Menstrual age was determined from the crown–rump length (CR) as compared with the curve constructed from Streeter's data (Fig. 1), not from the history secured from the mother, which is often incorrect. The curve for menstrual age given by Mall[65] has been added to Fig. 1, since the ages determined from Mall's data differ from those based on the Streeter data. The most accurate information obtainable is the CR of the fetus, if it is taken carefully before fixation while the fetus is still immersed in fluid so that the normal curvature of the spine is retained. Fixation changes the size of the fetus, either through swelling of the tissues (as with formalin) or through shrinkage (especially with alcohol).

Because ovulation occurs at about the middle of the menstrual cycle and fertilization takes place within a day or two after ovulation, fertilization age (or rather presumptive fertilization age)[8,78] is in theory approximately 2 weeks less than menstrual age.[8,78] The data from Patten's curve for fertilization age have therefore been added to Fig. 1 and extended to the 30-week age level. It is possible to determine the time of ovulation quite accurately with the cooperation of an intelligent mother because of the change in body temperature that occurs at that time, but even when it is obtained, this date simply provides a better estimate of fertilization age

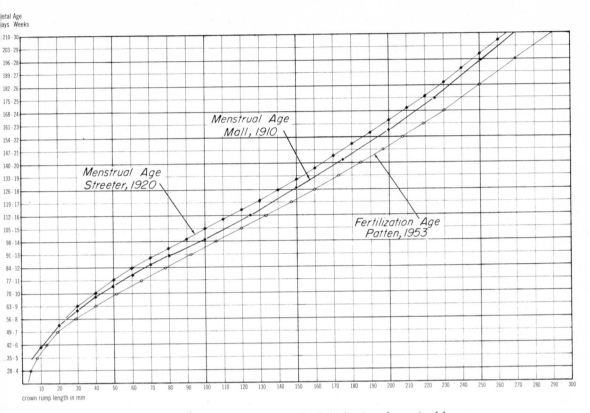

Fetal Age
Days Weeks

crown rump length in mm

Fig. 1. Three curves showing fetal age from 3 to 30 weeks (21–210) days) as determined by crown–rump measurements expressed in millimeters.[65,78,95]

Ovulation age is sometimes used, but it is an unfortunate term, because embryonic development begins with fertilization. *Gestation age*, although sometimes erroneously used as synonymous with menstrual age, is the equivalent of fertilization age. It is evident, then, that there is no truly accurate way of determining the exact age of any fetus.

7. First Reflexes Elicited by Exteroceptive Stimulation: Contralateral Total Pattern Flexion Reflexes

The first reflex observed consists of bending the head to the side opposite the perioral area stimulated (contralateral head flexion). The muscles involved are limited to the cervical and possibly the upper thoracic level of the trunk.[36,38] This reflex was first noted by Hooker for a 20.7-mm embryo and

by Fitzgerald and Windle[25] for a 20.0-mm embryo, i.e., at 7.5 weeks of menstrual age (Fig. 1). Although the extent of the muscle contraction in this reflex is restricted to the cervical and upper thoracic regions, the reflex itself meets the requirements for the total pattern reflexes described by Coghill because all the neuromuscular structures capable of reacting to the stimulus participate.

It has been suggested[41–45] that the neuronal arc functioning for this reflex of the human embryo at this time has for its sensory limb the trigeminal nerve fibers that transmit impulses from about the mouth to the upper cervical spinal cord levels and for its motor limb the spinal accessory neurons and nerve fibers that supply the sternocleidomastoid muscle and probably the cervical part of the trapezius. Perhaps the upper cervical motor neurons that innervate neck muscles also participate, although these nerve cells are less well differentiated. The

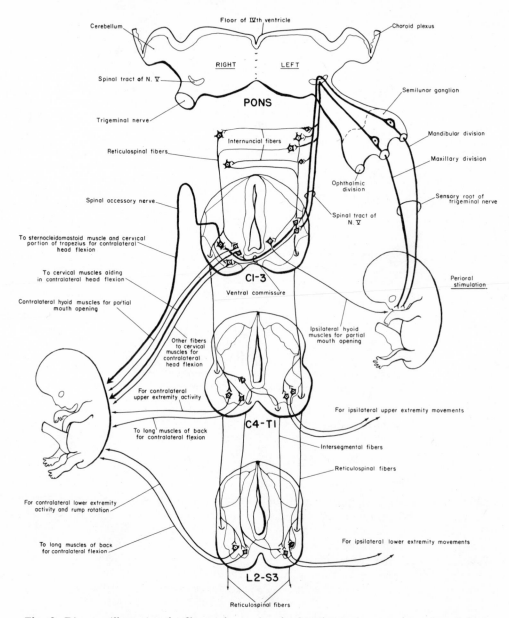

Fig. 2. Diagram illustrating the fiber pathways involved in the total pattern contralateral flexion reflexes that include extremity movements bilaterally and active mouth-opening like that illustrated in Figs. 4A–C. The sensory limb of these reflexes and the internuncial and motor fibers of the earliest functioning reflex arc are drawn in *heavy* lines. Other internuncial fibers and the additional efferent fibers for mouth-opening and the other parts of the fully developed contralateral total pattern reflex are shown by the lighter lines. The drawing of the fetus on the right side of the figure is an enlargement from Fig. 4A (27.1-mm fetus) and shows the position of the fetus at the time of stimulation. On the left side, the drawing is from Fig. 4B and illustrates the position of the fetus at the peak of the reflex action. The muscles that open the mouth in the midline region at this age, but not all the way to the corners, are probably supplied by the first three cervical nerves (C_1–C_3), and are indicated in this diagram as hyoid muscles. These muscles include the sternohyoid,[70] the omohyoid, and the thyrohyoid,[70,87] which act indirectly, and the geniohyoid, which acts directly.[43] The outlines for the pons and spinal cord levels were drawn from sections of the nervous system of a fetus of the same age.

axons of commissural neurons constitute the internuncial fibers that cross in the ventral white commissure at upper cervical spinal cord levels (Fig. 2).

Maturation of the embryo is rapid, and the lateral flexion reflexes soon extend to the remaining thoracic and the lumbosacral levels, so that as early as 25.0 mm,[38] the contralateral flexion reflex following perioral stimulation includes bending the head, trunk, and pelvis to the opposite side. Movements of the extremities are then added to the lateral flexion reflexes, beginning with extension of both arms at the shoulders. The lower extremities soon participate enough in the reflex so that the soles of the feet separate slightly. The extension of the arms is usually sufficient to pull the hands away from over the mouth for two or three motion-picture frames before the fetus returns to the resting position. With this increased involvement of the neuromuscular system, the reticulospinal pathways[11] and propiospinal fibers (fasciculus proprius) also become active (Fig. 2).

7.1. Development of Mouth-Opening as Part of the Contralateral Flexion Reflexes

At 26.0 mm, some rotation of the pelvis (or rump rotation) is added to the contralateral flexion reflexes. When the more forceful extension of the arms pulls the hands downward to uncover the mouth, the mandible is often actively lowered and the mouth partially opened, i.e., opened in the midline region, but not all the way to the corners (Figs. 3A, B). At this time also, the lower extremities participate in this reaction, and the soles of the feet, facing each other when the fetus is at rest, are pulled apart. For this 26.0-mm fetus, the motion-picture records show that mouth-opening accompanied 9 of the 16 contralateral total pattern flexion reflexes elicited, or 56.2%. One of these reflexes took place when the hair esthesiometer was drawn over the face area while the fetus was still in the amniotic sac. More details about body and extremity movements of these contralateral flexion reflexes are given in the papers of Hooker.[35-39] The oral activity is discussed further in the accounts of the author.[49,53,54]

During the period from 26.0 mm to 28.0 mm CR, the contralateral flexion reflexes increase in frequency and in the extent of the movements. Both the upper and the lower extremities soon begin to move asymmetrically in the reflex, the digits spread apart, and the hands flex, but the mouth still opens only partially (Figs. 4A–C). Rotation of the rump to the contralateral side becomes marked. A week later (Fig. 4D), the movements of the pelvis and the upper and lower extremities are even greater in amplitude, and the mouth-opening that constitutes part of the reflex is complete; i.e., the lips are

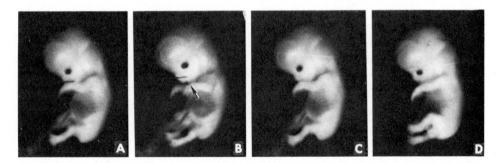

Fig. 3. Contralateral (A,B) and ipsilateral (C,D) total pattern flexion reflexes elicited by stimulating the perioral region of a 26.0-mm human fetus (No. 24, 8.5 weeks' menstrual age, Fig. 1). (A) Resting position before action begins. (B) Contralateral flexion of head, trunk, and pelvis, the arm extension that pulls the hands downward off the face and separates them, the abduction of the legs that separates the soles of the feet, and the partially open mouth (arrow) $\frac{1}{6}$ sec later. The black line passing across the nose and ending near the corner of the mouth is the 100-mm hair esthesiometer. (C) Resting position before the ipsilateral reflex. (D) Height of the action. At this time, the head, the trunk, and the pelvis are bent ipsilateralward, and the soles of the feet are also separated, but the mouth remains covered by the hands. The marked ipsilateral pelvic flexion shown here took place $\frac{3}{8}$ sec after the movement began. The photographs are about 1.2 times the size of the fetus.

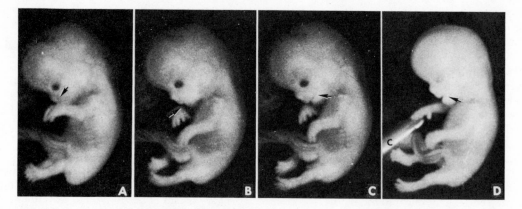

Fig. 4. A–C illustrate a contralateral flexion reflex elicited by stimulating the left perioral area from the corner of the mouth upward across the nose of a 27.1-mm fetus (No. 116, 8.5 weeks' menstrual age, Fig. 1). (A) The curved linear shadow across the nose (arrow) is the stimulator as it was being removed before the reflex began. (B) The arrow points to the partially open mouth revealed when the arms extend unequally (left more than right), and the soles of the feet separate as the legs abduct. (C) The lips are well apart only in the middle, although lateral to this area, the beginning separation of the lips is shown by the dark line (arrow) at the corner of the mouth. The left hand at this time is rather sharply flexed, and the digits of the hands and feet are spread apart. The photographs are about 1.6 times actual size. Six motion picture frames are spanned by the illustrations (16 frames/sec). (D) A contralateral flexion reflex of a 34.3-mm CR fetus (No. 134, 9.5 weeks' menstrual age, Fig. 1). The mouth is wider open, with the lips separated as far as the corners. Other parts of the reflex, such as head flexion and rump rotation, are more pronounced than in A–C. The photograph is approximately 1.2 times actual size. This single photograph, like that in C, illustrates the peak of activity in the reflex. The right hand and foot are near the clamp on the umbilical cord (c).

separated at the corners as well as in the midline (Fig. 4D). The total pattern type of contralateral flexion reflex continues throughout the 10-week age period and may be seen even later as well, but then it is often combined with other movements such as head extension or turning the chin ipsilaterally. In the reflexes that include mouth-opening at 11 weeks, the mandible is lowered less far, the mouth does not open so widely, and the lips are separated no farther in the midline than at the corners (Figs. 5B–D). Later on in development, e.g., at 11.5 weeks, the mouth again opens all the way to the corners as part of a combined head extension and contralateral flexion reflex.[53]

7.2. Relationship of Mouth-Opening Reflexes to Palatal Closure

It is perhaps worthy of mention that when the first mouth-opening reflexes develop as part of the total pattern contralateral flexion reflexes, the palate has not yet formed to separate the common oral-nasal space into the nasal and oral cavities. These mouth-opening reflexes begin concomitantly with the period of change of the palatal processes from the vertical to the horizontal position that is essential for palatal closure. This active lowering of the mandible undoubtedly plays a major role in withdrawing the tongue from between the vertical palatal processes and their immediate change to the horizontal position and closure.[50,51] Unless closure takes place, the resulting cleft palate interferes with the sucking and swallowing reflexes that are essential for normal feeding postnatally.

8. Ipsilateral Total Pattern Flexion Reflexes

Ipsilateral responses to stroking of the surface of the perioral area with the tip of the stimulator have not been elicited as early in development as have the contralateral reflexes. The first was cinematographically recorded at 22.6 mm, approximately half a week later than the first contralateral total pattern reaction was seen as reported in the papers of Hooker.[36] For this embryo, only one ipsilateral flexion reflex (limited to cervical levels) was recorded in the motion pictures, whereas five more extensive contralateral reflexes (some with beginning arm extension) were photographed. Ipsilateral total pattern reflexes are far less frequent throughout early development than those contralateral to the stimulus. Of the eighteen reflexes photographically recorded for a 26.0-mm fetus, however, two were ipsilateral to the side stimulated. Both were as vigorous as the contralateral reflexes. One was elicited by a perioral stimulus (Figs. 3C, D), and the other followed a contralateral reflex without an intervening perioral stimulation. Throughout the early period of reflex activity when the total pattern type of reflex is dominant, these ipsilateral reactions constitute only a small percentage (5.4%; Table II) of the total number of lateral flexion reflexes cinematographically recorded.[36,38,49,53]

Although mouth-opening is frequently seen as part of the contralateral flexion reflexes, it has not been seen with an ipsilateral response to perioral stimulation until 10 weeks of menstrual age (38.2 mm CR), and then only once.[49,53] The ipsilateral reflexes are often less vigorous than the contralateral ones. In connection with the forceful ones, however, where mouth-opening would be expected, the face is usually turned away from the camera, so that it is not possible to see the mouth adequately. In a strong reflex (Figs. 3; compare A and B with C and D), the action is as vigorous as in the contralateral reflexes and includes the marked rump rotation and the separation of the soles of the feet that are usually present on mouth-opening, but the mouth is completely obscured by the ipsilateral hand when the head bends ipsilateralward.

9. Classification of Reflexes as Negative and Positive Reactions

The contralateral flexion reflexes were referred to in the early studies of mammalian fetal activity as *avoiding* reactions[6,20,40,41] because the area touched by the stimulator is removed from the stimulating agent. They are also known as *negative*

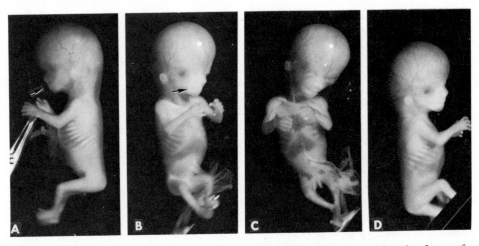

Fig. 5. Photographs showing extension of the head, trunk, and pelvis and oral reflexes of a fetus of 11 weeks' menstrual age (No. 65, 48.5 mm CR length, Fig. 1), reproduced at about 0.9 times actual size. The stimulus eliciting the two reflexes in B–D appears to have been along the back as the fetus was pulled over the underlying cloth surface. (A) Peak of an extension reflex resulting from touching the midline perioral area with the clamp (c) on the umbilical cord. The lips (arrow) are tightly closed or compressed. (B,C) Fetus just before movement began (B) and later (C) at the peak of the reflex, when the head, trunk, and pelvis are bent lateralward, the lower extremities are extended, one arm is extended at the shoulder and the elbow of the other arm is flexed, and the mouth is open to the corners but with little separation of the lips even at the midline. (D) Photograph at the crest of the activity of another mouth-opening reflex showing a profile view of the separation of the lips to about the same degree laterally as in the midline. There is little indication of upper extremity movement, and the lower extremities are not completely in the field of view.

Table II. Lateral Flexion Reflexes Cinematographically Recorded in Fetuses of 20.7–40.7 mm CR [a]

CR (mm)	Menstrual age (weeks) (Fetus no.)	Reflexes contralateral to area of stimulation	Reflexes ipsilateral to area of stimulation
20.7	7.5 (93A)	1	0
22.6	8− (131)	5	1
25.0	8+ (4)	13	0
26.0	8.5 (24)	16	2
27.1	8.5 (99)	7	0
27.1	8.5 (116)	14	4
27.7	8.5 (61)	10	0
28.0	8.5 (29)	20	0
32.7	9+ (94)	7	1
34.3	9.5 (134)	27	0
34.8	9.5 (127A)	13	2
35.0	9.5 (16)	18	0
36.0	9.5 (18)	9	0
37.5	10.0 (105)	18	0
38.2	10.0 (101)	8	1
40.7	10.0 (103)	8	0
	Totals:	194 (94.6%)	11 (5.4%)

[a] Menstrual age is based on the tables of Streeter[95] and taken from the records of Hooker.

After the total pattern types of reflexes have largely disappeared, head movements occur in association with other reflexes to form combinations either protective in their functional potential or related to feeding. Adequate functioning of the full-term newborn infant for nursing depends on turning the face toward the nipple that stimulates the lips, as well as on mouth-opening. This reflex occurs whether the lips are touched at the corners of the mouth or at the middle of the upper or lower lip.[54,82] For premature infants, the positive response to lip stimulation has not developed as satisfactorily as for normal full-term infants.[54]

As estimated by the number of motion-picture frames involved, the contralateral flexion reflexes are executed more rapidly than are the ipsilateral ones. Both the ipsilateral flexion reflex of the 26.0-mm fetus elicited by touching the face (Figs. 3C, D) and that following a contralateral flexion reflex consumed far more time, for example, than did the forceful contralateral flexion reflexes of this fetus (more than 1 sec as compared with $\frac{1}{2}$ sec or less). Thus, the avoiding or negative type of lateral flexion reflex is quicker than the positive one. When reflexes appear that are more restricted in their action and when functional combinations are formed, the protective or avoiding reactions are again completed more rapidly than are the positive reflexes of equivalent complexity that are related to feeding.[49]

or *nociceptive* reflexes,[45,46,61] and are referred to as protective in their functional potential. Ipsilateral responses are classed as positive in character.[45,46] They have been considered to be the initial reflexes in the development of reactions related to feeding,[45,53] since the perioral area that is touched approaches the stimulator (Table II).

Like the contralateral and ipsilateral flexion reflexes just mentioned, the more complicated head movements that develop later in fetal life are both negative and positive. The negative reactions again precede the positive ones in their order of appearance. Thus, head extension, which quickly moves the face away from the stimulus, develops before ventral head flexion, which brings the fetal face toward the source of stimulation.[45,46,53] Likewise, rotation of the face, either combined with trunk movements, or later as face rotation alone, is first directed away from the source of stimulation and only later toward it.

10. Pathways and Areas Involved in the Total Pattern Reflexes

The pathway suggested by the author[41] for the first contralateral flexion reflexes of human fetuses in response to perioral stimulation is illustrated in Fig. 2. At the time when flexion is limited to the cervical region (20–21 mm), the fibers of the maxillary and mandibular divisions of the trigeminal nerve can be traced through the first cervical levels of the spinal cord,[41,43] and differentiation has begun in this portion of the spinal trigeminal nuclear complex.[17] Both the commissural fibers that carry the impulses to the opposite side and the motor root fibers have developed at these levels much earlier. These reflexes are therefore probably mediated over a typical three-neuron reflex arc, with the major action dependent on the sternocleidomastoid and the cervical part of the trapezius muscles (see Fig. 2). The motor neurons of the spinal accessory nerve that supply these muscles are the best-developed motor neurons in the upper cervical region at this time. Undoubtedly, the reticulospinal pathways, which develop early embryologically and phylogenetically, participate in the reflex as soon as it extends farther caudalward. Likewise, neurons that connect different segments of the spinal cord through the fasciculus proprius (or propriospinal fibers) must also take part. In addition, the motor neurons at all levels obviously function as soon as the extremities are included in the reflex activity. When the mouth begins to open by lowering of the mandible (see Fig. 3B), at least part of the muscles supplied by the first two cervical nerves are involved in the mouth-opening.[43,49] The anterior belly of the digastric muscles probably also participates early, for both this muscle[26] and the neurons believed by some investigators to supply it also differentiate early.[59] When the mouth opens completely about a week later in development (see Fig. 4D), no doubt all the muscles that participate in mouth-opening are involved to some degree in the action.

The only cutaneous surface that has been shown to be sensitive to stimulation during this early period of activity is the face in the areas innervated by the sensory fibers of the maxillary and mandibular nerves (Table III). During the first 7.5–8.5 weeks, no nerve fibers have grown near enough to the surface to touch the basement membrane of the cutaneous epithelium.[31,48] All these nerve fibers terminate as naked, growing nerve tips, a few of which touch the basement membrane of the mucosa, although none has been identified in cutaneous areas nearer than 5 μm, even in the lips.[48] By 9.5 weeks, however, when the mouth opens widely, some maxillomandibular fibers penetrate the mucosal basement membrane inside the lips, and a few touch this membrane in the perioral cutaneous areas. By 10 weeks, more maxillary and mandibular fibers contact the basement membrane periorally. On the mucosal surfaces, a few fibers already end on large, basally located epithelial cells to form primitive Merkel's end disks, the first specialized nerve terminations to appear in development.[48] For the cutaneous surfaces, these receptors develop somewhat later, but Hogg[31] found them at 12 weeks (63.5 mm CR). During this 10- to 12-week age period, also, differentiation is taking place in the subnucleus interpolaris portion of the spinal trigeminal nuclear complex[18] that is especially concerned with the mediation of reflexes over motor cranial nerves.[52]

11. Characteristics of Reflexes from 8.5 to 10 Weeks of Menstrual Age (26.0–41.0 mm CR)

From the 8.5- through the 10-week age level, the reflexes elicited by perioral cutaneous stimulation are stereotyped in nature[35,36,38]; i.e., they vary only in vigor and magnitude of the reaction. Almost identical movements may be seen several times in succession. The reflexes elicited are either contralateral or, more rarely, ipsilateral flexion reflexes. If the contralateral reflex is a strong one even at 8.5 weeks, it usually includes mouth-opening (during the time that the hands uncover the mouth), asymmetrical upper and lower extremity movements, separation of the soles of the feet, spreading of the digits of both hands and the feet, and flexion of the hands (see Fig. 4). If the reflex elicited is a weak one, it is not accompanied by mouth-opening, the upper extremity movements are symmetrical and less extensive, and separation of the soles of the feet does not occur. Instead, only head, trunk, and pelvic flexion, with or without rump rotation, may take place. The strength of the stimulus, the adequacy of the oxygen supply, the number of times the area has already been stimulated, and other factors all enter into the determination of the forcefulness and duration of the reflex elicited.

By 9.5 weeks, it is possible to observe stages in opening and closing of the mouth while it is uncovered by the hands during the contralateral flexion reflexes.[49,53] Since mouth closure at this age requires more time than lowering the mandible to open it, closure is evidently due to a passive return to position, rather than to active muscle contraction. At 10 weeks, the mouth appears to be opening less wide as a part of the contralateral flexion reflexes. Head and trunk extension then begin to replace the earlier lateral flexion reflexes, and are the dominant action for a brief interval, with peak activity at about 11 weeks. The extension reflexes are likewise elicited less often after a brief period of maximum frequency. Mouth-opening then occurs as a part of mixed contralateral flexion and head and trunk extension reflexes elicited by perioral stimulation by 11.5 weeks,[49,50] but trunk and

Table III. Sequence of Development of Sensitivity of Cutaneous Surfaces and Oral Mucosa[a]

Surface areas shown sensitive to stimulation	Menstrual age (weeks)[b]
Rima oris (or vermilion border) of the lips and adjacent perioral areas (maxillary and mandibular branches of trigeminal nerve)	7.5
More peripheral perioral areas, including the alae of the nose and the chin	8–9.5
Bridge of nose, lower eyelid, and area below it	10.5
Palms of hands	10–10.5 (possibly earlier)
Upper eyelid (ophthalmic division of trigeminal nerve)	10.5 (possibly earlier)
Genital areas and genitofemoral sulcus[c]	10.5 (possibly earlier)
Shoulder area	10.5
Soles of the feet	10.5–11
Eyebrows and forehead	11
Upper arm and forearm	11
Back (probably)	11
Upper chest	11.5
Thighs and legs	11–12
Remaining chest areas	13
Tongue anteriorly	14 (probably earlier)
Back, scapular area, lateral wall of trunk	14
Abdominal wall	15
Buttocks[c]	17
External auditory canal	17.5
Dorsal surface of hand	18.5
Posterior tongue areas (possibly posterior pharyngeal wall)	17–18.5 (probably earlier)
Inside of nostrils[d]	24

[a] The data are mainly from Hooker[36] and Humphrey,[45] with unpublished supplementary information from the film analysis records of Hooker.
[b] Determined from the tables of Streeter,[95] as recorded by Hooker.
[c] From dictated records only, and not cinematographically verified.
[d] Reported by Golubewa et al.[28]

extremity movements continue to decrease in both extent and frequency during later development.

12. Development of Head and Trunk Extension Reflexes

After having attained a peak of development by 9.5–10 weeks, the contralateral (and ipsilateral) total pattern reflexes decrease in number and in vigor. By 10.5–11 weeks, the responses to stimulation of the maxillomandibular areas of the face are changing to an extension of the head, trunk, and pelvis (see Fig. 5), rather than the lateral flexion reflexes elicited earlier. Stimulation at or near the midline is the most effective. When the extension reflex is vigorous, the head is hyperextended. Neither the upper

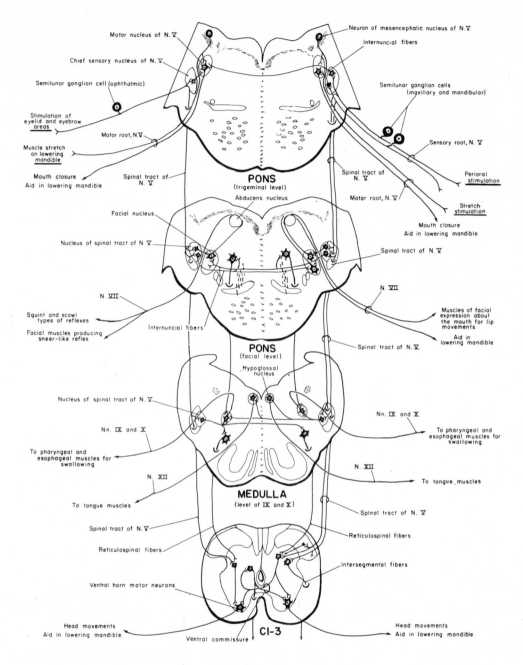

Fig. 6. Diagram illustrating some of the neuronal pathways involved in the more limited reactions of the combined head, arm, and face movements and in the local reflexes that appear following stimulation of the cutaneous facial areas from 10 to 10.5 weeks onward. The fiber paths for such reflexes as mouth-opening and closure, swallowing, tongue movements, and contraction of the eyelid and corrugator muscles are shown. The outlines for the levels through the pons, medulla, and spinal cord were drawn from sections of the brainstem of a fetus of 107.5 mm CR (15.5 weeks' menstrual age).

extremities nor the lower extremities always participate in the same manner or to the same extent that
they act in the contralateral flexion elicited earlier.
When the extremities take part in the extension
reflexes, the extension at the proximal joints (shoulder
and elbow, hip and knee) is greater for distal joints
of the lower extremities.[49]

The mouth does not open with the extension
reflexes, but at their peak, the lips are often
compressed. As a result, the vermilion borders
almost disappear for the very brief interval that the
head is maximally extended in this rapidly executed
reflex (see Fig. 5A).

Except for minor variations in the amplitude and
duration of the movement, the extension reflexes
are essentially alike, or sterotyped. Almost indentical
movements may be elicited repeatedly. Because not
all the neuromuscular mechanisms that participate
earlier in the total pattern lateral flexion reflexes act
in these extension reflexes, even when the latter are
the most vigorous, these reactions cannot be considered true total pattern reflexes in the sense that
the term was used by Coghill.[21]

The essential changes that give rise at this time
to the extension reflexes include the contraction of
the dorsal longitudinal axial muscles bilaterally
instead of unilaterally. The bilateral muscle action
is undoubtedly due largely to the development of
ipsilateral as well as contralateral connections between the reticulospinal pathways and the spinal
cord motor neurons (Fig. 6). A degree of inhibitory
effect from higher centers over the neurons acting in
the contralateral flexion reflex must also be effective
by this time.

When the trunk extension reflexes first appear,
there is a period of transition from the contralateral
flexion reflexes. Consequently, a reaction may begin
with head extension, then go over into flexion at
the lower levels of the trunk, and include rump
rotation. As development progresses, these mixed
reactions decrease in frequency and tend to disappear.
Sometimes, however, a reflex begins with head
extension, then passes over into the contralateral
flexion type of reflex, especially if the stimulus is
applied more peripherally or the same area has
been stimulated several times in succession. Also,
when the oxygen supply is becoming exhausted,
often only the contralateral flexion reflexes can be
elicited before all activity is abolished (see Table I).
This situation is an example of reversion to
the earlier-developed type of reflex when anoxia
develops.

13. Development of Local Reflexes in Response to Stimulation of the Face

In the papers of Hooker[36,38] and in the earlier
ones of the author,[43,45] active mouth-opening was
given as the first local reflex to be elicited by
stimulating facial areas supplied by the trigeminal
nerve. As now demonstrated, however, lowering of
the mandible develops initially as part of the total
pattern contralateral flexion reflex. The orbicularis
oculi reflex in response to stimulation of the
opthalmic fibers of the trigeminal nerve is evidently
a true local reflex. This reflex was reported by
Hooker[36,38] and by Humphrey[45] as early as 10–10.5
weeks, and verified recently from the cinematographic records at 10.5 weeks (46.5 mm CR).
According to Hooker,[36] it is not combined with
head movements until later. Swallowing was
reported at 10.5 weeks by Hooker[37,38] and by
Hooker and Humphrey[40] from dictated records,
but has not been verified from the motion-picture
records before 12–12.5 weeks.[36] Thus, the earliest
truly local reflexes from facial stimulation are evidently orbicularis oculi (10–10.5 weeks) and corrugator reactions (11 weeks), both set off by stimulation of the ophthalmic fibers of the trigeminal nerve.
Because both these actions are protective in their future potential, the earliest local reflex verified thus
far, as well as the first total pattern flexion reflexes,
belong in the category of avoiding, or protective
(also negative or nociceptive), reflexes. Figure 6
illustrates the neuronal pathways for some of the
local reflexes and their combination with head
movements.

14. Mouth-Opening and -Closing Reflexes at 11 Weeks of Menstrual Age and Later

As already mentioned, the character of mouth-
opening changes from its first appearance at 8.5
weeks through the 10-week period. At 11 weeks,
when compression of the lips rather than mouth-
opening accompanies marked head extension,
mouth-opening of a different type was seen (see
Figs. 5B–D). The lips separated about equally in the
midline and at the corners. Closure as well as
opening was so rapid that the entire reflex required

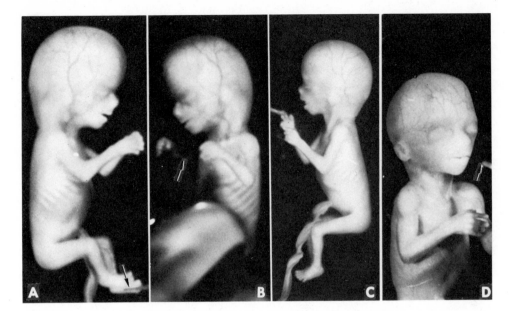

Fig. 7. Photographs of oral area reflex activity of four different fetuses showing different types of mouth-opening and, for three of the reflexes, evidence for tongue movements. (A,B) No. 110, 12.5 weeks, 70.0. mm CR, 0.8 times actual size; (C) No. 37, 14 weeks, 85.5 mm CR, 0.6 times actual size; (D) No. 135, 15.5 weeks, 107.5 mm CR, 0.6 times actual size. In each case, the photograph illustrates approximately the stage of maximum movement in the reflex. (A) Stimulation of the sole of the left foot (arrow points to stimulator being removed), followed by a rapid mouth-opening and -closing reflex in which the separation of the lips lasted only $\frac{1}{8}$ sec. Slight ipsilateral bending of the head accompanied the jaw movement, which was followed by a rapid kick of the leg of the side stimulated. (B) Stimulation of the volar surface of the right forearm by the observer's finger (arrow), followed by ipsilateral bending of the head, extension of the contralateral arm with flexion of the forearm, and mouth-opening with the tongue elevated to obscure the lateral part of the space between the lips. (C) Stimulation of the left hand resulting in a greater degree of lowering of the mandible than shown in B, accompanied by elevation, protrusion, and then retraction of the tongue. In this photograph, the tongue is elevated and is easily noted between the lips laterally. Only finger closure of the stimulated hand and a little head movement accompanied the oral activity. (D) Lip and tongue movements elicited by drawing the stimulator (arrow) across the lips and tongue from the midline region lateralward to the corner of the mouth. In addition to the separation of the lips shown here, the dark zone inside the lips at the midline is the longitudinal groove in the tongue formed by lifting of its two sides. At the end of the reflex, the lips closed on the stimulator. The lips in this reflex are separated and brought together by the action of the muscles of facial expression, not by depressing of the jaw.

only about half a second. One reflex accompanied a contralateral body flexion reflex in which the head rotated as well as flexed (see Figs. 5B, C); another included very little movement aside from quick opening and closing of the mouth (see Fig. 5D). These two reflexes, both of which were elicited when the position of the fetus was changed so that its back brushed along the underlying cloth surface, are the earliest mouth-opening reflexes elicited by other than perioral stimuli.

As development progresses, stimulation of a wide variety of areas of the body may produce mouth-opening at times.[49,53] It was observed after touching of the volar surface of the forearm at 12.5 weeks (70.0 mm CR) as part of a reflex that included bending of the head toward the forearm stimulated. The fingertips of the two hands moved apart, then returned to position. When the mouth was wide open, the tongue could be seen between the lips (Fig. 7B).

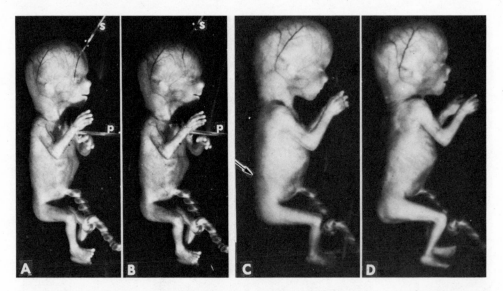

Fig. 8. Photographs illustrating two reflexes elicited by stimulating the cutaneous surfaces of a fetus of 14 weeks of menstrual age (No. 13, 88.5 mm CR, Fig. 1). The fetus shown at about half (A,B) and three-fifths (C,D) actual size. (A,B) Simultaneous eyelid and oral reflexes elicited by drawing the stimulator(s) across the cheek, over the eyelids, and off the forehead. With this reflex, the head bent contralateralward. (A) The fetus is shown at rest. (B) The contraction of the eyelid muscle has flattened the eyeball and obscured the fusion line between the lids. The upper lip has lifted near the corner and the corner has pulled lateralward. Neither trunk nor extremity action accompanied this reflex, although these movements may be present with such reflexes. The action shown involved about half a second. A pipette (p) squirted hot saline against the fetus at this time, but no specific effect was demonstrable. (C,D) Reaction elicited by drawing the stimulator (arrow in C) upward along the back. The head and trunk extended, the mouth opened, and the chest and abdominal muscles contracted to elevate the rib cage and flatten the abdominal wall in an inspiratory gasp accompanied by shoulder and other movements to give a response characteristic for a tickling reaction such as is seen postnatally. The total reflex, including the return to the resting position, lasted about 3 sec. The duration of the part shown was slightly more than 1 sec.

For this same 70.0-mm fetus, stimulation of the sole of the foot in one instance elicited an extremely rapid mouth-opening and -closing reflex. It was accompanied only by an exceedingly slight ipsilateral bending of the head at the same time (Fig. 7A), but was followed at once by a kick of the leg on the side stimulated.

In addition to forearm and foot-sole stimulation, mouth-opening was elicited from this fetus both by eyelid and by perioral stimuli. None of the reflexes from these four areas was like any other. It is evident, then, that by 12.5 weeks oral reflexes may already be elicited from a wide range of cutaneous surfaces and be accompanied by quite different movements. From about 13 weeks onward,[36,38] the reflexes become remarkably variable, rather than stereotyped.

Stimulation of still other cutaneous areas has been found to evoke oral reflexes for somewhat older fetuses. These areas include the palm of the hand (Fig. 7C), the eyelids, and the back (Fig. 8) at 14 weeks.[49,53] The movements that are associated with these oral reflexes are variable. Tongue action accompanied the mouth-opening from palmar stimulation (Fig. 7C). Squintlike action from the eyelid muscle contraction and sneerlike lip elevation (Figs. 8A, B) were part of a head, trunk, and extremity reflex combination following eyelid stimulation.[33,49] Lip and tongue stimulation elicited mouth-opening and closure with the appearance of a groove or furrow in the tongue at 15.5 weeks (Fig. 7D). As the lip and tongue movements that are essential for sucking make their appearance, the sensitive area for the elicitation of oral reflexes becomes limited mainly to the tongue, the lips, and the perioral zone adjacent to the lips.

Until 11 weeks, mouth closure has been considered passive because it requires more time than does depression of the lower jaw in opening it. The mouth-opening reflexes at 11 weeks (see Figs. 5B–D) are followed by a quick closure, one of them described as snaplike in character.[49,53] A mouth-opening reflex elicited by stimulating the sole of the foot at 12.5 weeks was also followed by an equally rapid closure (see Fig. 7A). The quick closure in these instances is active. Undoubtedly, it is due to stretching the masticatory muscles like the masseter and so activating the two neuron reflex arcs that mediate stretch reflexes[49,53] over the neurons and fibers of the mesencephalic root of the trigeminal nerve and the motor nerve cells of this nerve (see Fig. 6).

Before the earliest sneerlike reflex is noted at 14 weeks (see Figs. 8A, B), mouth closure is due to elevation of the mandible, at first passively (a relatively slow return to position), then actively (due to muscle contraction set off by stretch stimuli). The sneerlike facial expression results from elevation of the upper lip near the corner of the mouth, and may include lifting of the ala of the nose. These actions are mediated over the motor fibers of the facial nerve, like those of the earlier-appearing squint and scowl type reflexes. From 14 weeks onward, more and more of the muscles of facial expression participate in the local reflexes such as moving the lips. When tongue movements begin, the hypoglossal nerve constitutes the motor limb of these reflex arcs (see Fig. 6). One sensory limb of these reflex arcs continues to be the trigeminal nerve fibers, but other sensory fibers also function in these reflexes as soon as activity in the oral area can be elicited by stimulation of the sole of the foot (see Fig. 7A), the palm of the hand (see Fig. 7C), and other areas (see Figs. 7B, 8C, and 9C).

Both mouth-opening and head movements have a dual functional relationship in mammals. Although mouth-opening was reported earlier to be an isolated local reflex when it first appears,[37,38,40,43,45,46] photographic prints from the motion pictures of these reflexes (see Figs. 3 and 4) clearly demonstrate that they begin as part of the total pattern contralateral flexion reflexes.[49,53,54] Thus, mouth-opening develops initially as part of an avoiding reflex, and so belongs with the defense or protective reactions early in development, only later becoming part of the development reflex sequence for feeding.

When the mouth-opening reflex is no longer an integral part of the contralateral flexion reflex, it also becomes associated with ipsilateral head responses, tongue movements, and other oral activity, such as swallowing, all of which are clearly feeding reactions. Postnatally, mouth-opening and closure continue to serve in both capacities. The fetal reflexes involving oral activity, like those postnatally, are more rapid as part of the avoiding reflexes of protective or negative character than when they are associated with the positive feeding ones, such as swallowing and tongue movements.

15. Tongue Movements

Until the mouth opens wide, there is opportunity neither to see the tongue nor to touch it without stimulating the lips at the same time. Consequently, the exact time that active tongue movements begin has never been determined.[38,45,49,53] Examination of microscopic sections shows that such extrinsic tongue muscles as the genioglossus and hyoglossus of the 11-week fetus are clearly able to contract. However, no photographic proof of tongue movement has been observed until 12.5 weeks, a week and a half later. In the reflex mouth-opening of this 12.5-week fetus (see Fig. 7B), elevation of the tongue has taken place, for it is visible near the corner of the wide-open mouth. As part of a reflex of one 14-week fetus, the tongue was not only elevated but thrust forward, then retracted before the mouth closed (see Fig. 7C). In the mouth-opening and -closing reflex of a 15.5-week fetus (see Fig. 7D), there was a longitudinal groove or furrow in the elevated tongue. When the upper lip puckered and the lower lip protruded at 20 weeks (Figs. 10B, C), the tongue was also visible just behind the lips, and hence must have both elevated and moved forward. In the crying of a resuscitated nonviable premature infant of 23.5 weeks, the elevated tongue with the tip turned backward has the same position as is usually seen when a newborn infant cries.

16. Swallowing Reflexes

Reflex swallowing has been observed fairly early in development from stimulation of the lips. It was thought at one time to begin as early as 10.5 weeks,[37,38,40] but no motion pictures were secured,

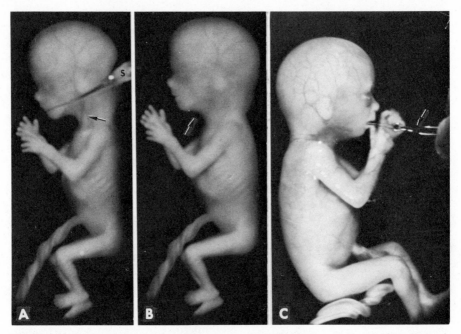

Fig. 9. A and B illustrate a swallowing reflex at 13 weeks of menstrual age (No. 45, 75.0 mm CR). C shows a gag reflex at 18.5 weeks (No. 111, 144.5 mm CR). (A) The area of the lower lip stroked by the stimulator(s) and the sharp outline of the sternocleidomastoid muscle (arrow) are illustrated. (B) The mouth has opened and the head extended slightly as the larynx moved upward, thus rounding the contour beneath the chin (arrow) and obscuring the border of the sternocleidomastoid muscle. No movements of the extremities or of the trunk accompanied this reflex. The photographs are about 0.8 times actual size. (C) The fullness in the floor of the mouth and one phase in the facial expression accompanying a gag reflex that was elicited by inserting a glass rod (arrow) far into the mouth so that it stimulated the back of the tongue and possibly the posterior wall of the pharynx. No trunk or extremity movements accompanied the reflex. Almost 3 sec elapsed after the glass rod was inserted before the rapid action began. The photograph is slightly less than half the size of the fetus.

and swallowing has not been demonstrated photographically until 12.5 weeks. This difference is mentioned here partly to emphasize the hazards of attempting to interpret fetal movements without motion-picture records that can be viewed repeatedly and studied from photographic prints as well. It may be, however, that stimulation of the mucosa elicits swallowing before it can be elicited by touching the lips.

Inasmuch as amniotic fluid must enter the oral cavity as soon as the mouth opens wide (and be retained when it closes), possibly this fluid in the mouth stimulates the oral mucosa and leads to swallowing earlier in development than the motion-picture records have shown it to occur. This concept is supported by the fact that the nerve fibers make

contact with the basement membrane of the oral mucosa by 8.5 weeks (27.1 mm), when mouth-opening is frequent although partial, and terminate on the basal epithelial cells as primitive Merkel's disks at 10 weeks (37.0 mm CR), after the mouth opens more completely (see Section 10). Adequate sensory receptors for such reflexes are therefore present before 10.5 weeks.[48] Indeed, nerve fibers contact the basement membrane of the mucosal epithelium a week earlier than that of the lips, and the primitive Merkel's disks appear 2 weeks before they have been identified for the cutaneous surfaces at 12 weeks.[31]

The first part of a swallowing reflex at 13 weeks is reproduced in Figs. 9A and B. It was accompanied by slight head extension as the larynx elevated and the mouth opened (Fig. 9B), then some ventral head flexion as the mouth partly closed and the larynx descended in completing the swallowing act. In this swallowing reflex, the mouth remained partly open. In a swallowing reflex recorded at 14 weeks,[49] the mouth closed completely when the head flexed ventralward (88.5 mm CR). Then the mouth reopened again.

Fetal swallowing reflexes normally occur *in utero*. They were demonstrated at 12 weeks' gestation by Davis and Potter.[23] It has been estimated that as much as 500 ml of amniotic fluid may be swallowed by the normal near-term human fetus in 24 hr,[3,85] although none was swallowed by anencephalic fetuses of comparable age.[85] The frequency of fetal swallowing and other factors that influence it *in utero* are unknown, according to Adams *et al.*[3] Arshavsky[9] suggested a nutrient function for the substances in the amniotic fluid, a view held by Preyer in 1885.[84] At least these reflexes must strengthen the pharyngeal and esophageal musculature. Adequate strength of swallowing is just as essential for nursing by the newborn infant as is the integration of tongue and lip reflexes for the complex activity of sucking.

17. Gag Reflexes

A prolonged stimulation of the inside of the mouth with a glass rod, which probably included the back of the tongue and perhaps the pharynx as well, was followed by a rapidly executed gag reflex at 18.5 weeks (see Fig. 9C). The action included closure of the mouth on the stimulator, its reopening, an inspiratory gasp with contraction of the diaphragm, and a second partial mouth closure.[49,53] The gag reflex is almost always present in premature infants,[79] even if the infant is unable either to suck or to swallow. It seems unlikely, however, that gag reflexes would ever occur *in utero* under normal conditions.

18. Lip Movements and Sucking

Before 13.5–14 weeks,[36] the reflex opening and closing of the mouth has been due to lowering and lifting of the mandible, not to movements of the lips. At 14 weeks (see Figs. 8A, B), however, there is clear evidence of upper lip movement of quite a different sort. The stimulus producing the reflex was

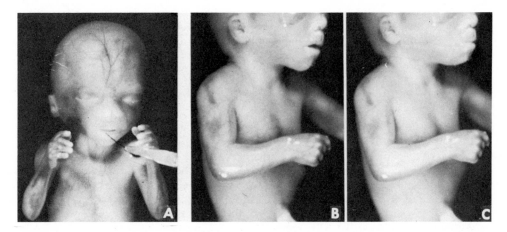

Fig. 10. (A) Depression of the lower lip of a fetus of 15.5 weeks (No. 53, 110.5 mm CR, Fig. 1) following stimulation of the vermilion border from the lateral side toward the middle. The tongue shows between the parted lips. No other action took place. The photograph is about 0.7 times the size of the fetus. (B,C) Puckering of the upper lip *(vertical lines)* and protrusion of the lower lip following stimulation of the lower lip of a fetus of 20 weeks (No. 55, 166.0 mm CR, Fig. 1). The tongue elevated and was thrust forward, since it fills the space between the lips in C where the borders of the mentalis muscle are accentuated by its contraction. Before the movement began (B), the open mouth was held with the upper lip elevated near the corner. The photographs are about 0.4 times the size of the fetus. The lip action, both in the reflex in A and in that in B and C, is produced by the muscles of facial expression.

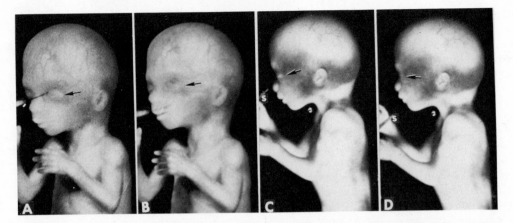

Fig. 11. Photographs illustrating reflex contraction of the orbicularis oculi muscle (squintlike reflex) in two different combinations with other reflex activity. (A, B) Photographs of a fetus of 15.5 weeks (No. 135, 107.5 mm CR). (C, D) A different reflex combination from a fetus of 16 weeks (No. 27, 114.0 mm CR). The fertilization age as given by Patten[78] and the menstrual age based on the data of Mall[65] may be checked against those stated here by consulting Fig. 1. (A, B) The stimulator is touching the upper eyelid near the inner canthus in A, where the action has not yet begun, and is being lifted away from the face in the upper lip area in B. The contraction of the eyelid muscle is shown by the disappearance of the fusion line (arrow in A) between the eyelids in B (arrow) and by the flattening of the eyeball. In combination with this reflex, there is a slight separation of the lips, so that the tongue shows immediately behind them. The head is extended slightly, and the fingers on the ipsilateral hand are extended at the interphalangeal joints and flexed slightly at the metacarpophalangeal joints, but there was no other muscle activity. The photographs are about 0.7 times the size of the fetus. (C, D) The stimulator(s) that elicited this reflex was drawn down over the eyebrows on the left as well as along the inner canthus of the eye. As in the reflex shown in A and B, the lips were slightly parted before action began, but in this case, they came together a little, rather than parting more. In this reflex, both the orbicularis oculi and the corrugator supercilii contracted, so that not only a squintlike reflex but also a scowl-like reflex appeared. As in the reflex in A and B, the fusion line between the eyelids almost disappeared, and the eyeball flattened (compare line at arrow in C with that in D). The slight movement caused by contraction of the corrugator is demonstrated only by the decrease in the size of the highlight in the eyebrow area in the two photographs, which are reproduced here at about half the size of the fetus.

an upward stroke of the stimulator from the angle of the jaw across the eyelids. The upper lip was raised ipsilaterally near the corner of the mouth, and in one reflex, the ala of the nose also elevated. In addition, the face rotated away from the side stimulated. Extemity movements also occurred with one of these reflexes, but not with the other. An oral reflex of this type involves the muscles of facial expression about the mouth. These muscles develop later than those that depress the mandible, but have attained a degree of differentiation that enables them to act at this age.[26]

In response to stimulation of the lower lip (see Fig. 10A), this lip alone may be depressed as early as 15.5 weeks.[49] Stimulation of the upper lip may give rise to its protrusion at 17 weeks.[36,45] Stimulation of the lower lip may result in its protrusion by 20 weeks (see Figs. 10B, C), and also in puckering of the upper lip. Puckering of the lower lip has been seen at 22 weeks, when both lips may both pucker and protrude.[36,45] According to Golubewa et al.,[28] sucking reflexes have been observed at 24 weeks. Sucking sufficiently strong to be audible was reported by Hooker[38] at 29 weeks for one of the viable premature infants studied.

Popular publications, such as those of Nilsson[73] and Nilsson et al.,[74] refer to fetal thumb sucking in utero as early as 18 weeks. Their photographs show the thumb between the lips, but without the lip-puckering that is an essential part of sucking. As just mentioned, both lips have not been shown to protrude and pucker simultaneously before 22 weeks, and sucking reflexes, even weak ones, have not been reported in scientific papers before 24 weeks. At 8.5 weeks of menstrual age (see Figs. 3A and 4A) and later, however the hands are often close to the face after the fetus is removed from the amnion. Within the confined space of the amniotic sac, the hands often touch the face, as shown in the photographs of Nilsson et al.[74] Because the mouth often remains open or partly open from 14 weeks onward when the fetus is not moving (see Figs. 8A, 10B, 11A, C, 12D), the thumb probably enters it earlier than true sucking is possible. Definite blisters on the thumb and other parts of the hands and lower forearms at birth were interpreted by Murphy and Langley[72] as the result of sucking of these areas before birth. Inasmuch as sucking is often too weak in small premature infants to be adequate for nursing,[64] strong sucking must take place only

during the last part of gestation. However, the close positional relationship of the hands and the face *in utero* provides ample opportunity for self-stimulation of the face during a large part of prenatal life.

19. Respiratory Reflexes

Windle et al.[100] reported respiratory movements in a fetus of 62.0 mm CR (12 weeks' menstrual age), and isolated respiratory chest contractions were mentioned by Hooker[38] as early as 13 weeks of menstrual age. At 14 weeks (see Figs. 8C, D), drawing of the stimulator upward along the back of the fetus resulted in a complex series of movements resembling the postnatal reaction to tickling. This reflex included an inspiratory gasp with flattening of the abdominal wall as well.[49,53] At 18.5 weeks,[38] weak chest contractions have been seen both spontaneously and in response to chest stimulation, and at 22 weeks, diaphragmatic con-

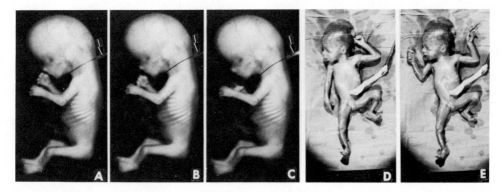

Fig. 12. (A–C) Photographs of a fetus of 11 weeks of menstrual age (No. 26, 48.5 mm CR, Fig. 1) illustrating the position of the fingers when the stimulator (arrows) touched the palm (A), the partial closure of the fingers (B), and the flexion of the hand and arm movement with the added finger flexion (C). No other action accompanied this reflex. The photographs are approximately 0.8 times actual size. (D, E) Photographs of a fetus of 23.5 weeks of menstrual age (No. 56, 205.0 mm CR, Fig. 1) that was resuscitated with a respirator, but was unable to maintain respiration adequately. (D) The characteristic position for the symmetric tonic neck reflex is demonstrated, with the face turned toward the side on which the extremities are extended. Although the fetus is not crying, the mouth is open. The digits of the hand of the extended arm are also extended, whereas the fingers of the flexed arm are tightly closed with the thumb outside. (E) Both upper extremities are in the flexion position, although the face is turned toward the side of the extended lower extremity in one of the asymmetrical tonic neck reflex patterns. The fingers of the hand near the face are flexed with the thumb inside the index finger. All the digits of the other hand are extended, and the hand itself is adducted. The fetus is beginning to cry, as indicated by the wider separation of the lips, the tightening of the eyelids, and the increased depth of the nasolabial fold. The disappearance of the border of the sternomastoid muscle is due to laryngeal movement upward, and the depression of the xiphoid process that often occurs with intake of air at this age can be seen. The photographs show this fetus at only about 0.1 times its actual size.

tractions have been noted. It is at this age also that fetal hiccups, which are due to spasmodic contractions of the diaphragm, were first recorded by Norman.[75] When fetuses are artificially resuscitated at 23.5 weeks,[38] and possibly earlier, deep respiratory movements occur for a time, with contraction of the diaphragm and of the abdominal and chest muscles. In the series of premature infants observed by Hooker, however, effective respiration could not be maintained until 27 weeks of menstrual age, although it could be artifically established much earlier on a temporary basis.

There is considerable evidence that respiratory movements may occur *in utero*.[23,96,97,100] It has been suggested that these movements are a normal part of intrauterine development that bring amniotic fluid into the developing lungs and so aid in the expansion of the alveolar spaces.[14,91] The experimental evidence now available on subprimates demonstrates, however, that fluid present in the fetal respiratory passages is secreted by the lungs of the fetus, possibly some by the alveoli.[2] After being expelled into the amniotic cavity, it is swallowed with the amniotic fluid or, to a lesser degree, passes directly into the pharynx and is swallowed. Only under conditions of fetal stress have respiratory movements been demonstrated to take place *in utero*. The evidence for this conclusion and the current views on its significance are discussed in the papers of Adams[1] and Adams *et al.*[3,4]

20. Crying

According to Peiper,[79] premature infants weighing only 650 g cry audibly. This is approximately the size of the nonviable premature of 23.5 weeks for which the tonic neck reflex is illustrated (Figs. 12D, E). Audible crying with the mouth wide open and the tongue movements typical of a crying infant were photographed for this fetus. The preliminary puckering up to cry is shown in Fig. 12E. Scowling and tight contraction of the eyelid muscles accompany crying at this time, although the eyelids ordinarily remain fused until the 7th month.[8,78] A single cry was reported by Golubewa *et al.*[28] before 22 weeks, and a series of cries by 22 weeks. Minkowski[67] found crying at a comparable age (21 weeks).

On different occasions, obstetricians have heard infants cry before delivery but after the membranes had ruptured,[19,88,89] so that air probably entered the uterus. Since the emission of sound, and consequently crying, depends on the expulsion of air as well as on the development of adequately maintained diaphragmatic and chest contractions, it will not take place *in utero* under normal circumstances. On the delivery of a premature infant with a respiratory system sufficiently developed to enable breathing to be established even temporarily, crying should be expected.

21. Reflexes Associated with the Eyes

As mentioned earlier, contraction of the orbicularis oculi muscle when it first occurs (10–10.5 weeks) on stimulation of the upper eyelid is not accompanied by other movements.[36,38] The corrugator supercilii reflex is also independent of other movements when it begins at 11 weeks. A week later, the two reflexes (squint and scowl in type) may be seen together. These reflexes were not observed in conjunction with neck and trunk movements (see Figs. 8A, B) until 13 to 14 weeks.[45] Still later (15.5 weeks), a quick mouth-opening with the tongue behind the lips was seen along with the squintlike reflex (see Figs. 11A, B). A slight brief mouth closure may accompany the combination of squint and scowl type reflexes by 16 weeks (see Figs. 11C, D).

Reflexes have not been elicited by stimulating the ophthalmic fibers before the fibers touch the basement membrane, whereas they have been elicited by stimulating the maxillomandibular fibers when these fibers are as much as 13 μm from the epithelium. The ophthalmic nerve fibers do not make contact with the basement membrane of the upper eyelid epithelium until 10 weeks (37 mm CR), about a week later (9–9.5 weeks, 32 mm CR) than the maxillomandibular fibers reach the same level of the cutaneous epithelium of the lips, and 1.5 weeks later (8.5 weeks, 27.1 mm CR) than they touch this membrane of the oral mucosa.[48] In the spinal tract of the trigeminal nerve, likewise, the ophthalmic fibers arrive at their adult caudal level about a week later than the maxillomandibular fibers reach it.[43] These differences in growth centrally and peripherally may account in part for the fact that the orbicularis oculi and corrugator reflexes are local in character when they appear, and the head and trunk movements accompany them only later.

Downward movements of both eyes were reported by Hooker[36] following eyelid stimulation of two fetuses at 12.5 weeks, although at this age the eyelids are fused.[78] Conjugate lateral movements of the eyes were noted first at 25 weeks with the eyelids open, and such movements were also seen thereafter. Eye movements undoubtedly occur during prenatal life in response to changes in position,[19] but proof that they do is lacking. The neurons of the vestibular nuclei that mediate such reflexes are sufficiently differentiated at 13.5 weeks to function.[47] Inasmuch as the other parts of the essential reflex arcs mature early, eye movement reflexes of vestibular origin may begin relatively early in development.

22. Reflexes Elicited by Stimulation of the Genital and Anal Regions

Reflexes have been elicited by stimulation of the genital area of fetuses as early in development as 10.5 and 11 weeks, and have also been seen at 17 and 18.5 weeks.[45,56,57] The region of the genito-femoral sulcus as well as the phallus reacted to stimulation in the youngest fetus mentioned. The older fetuses reacted to stimuli over the penis and scrotum, as well as to stroking of the genitofemoral sulcus. By 32 weeks, stimulation of the inside of the thigh may elicit the cremasteric reflex,[38] but Robinson[86] found it present more often after that for infants of normal weight as compared with those low in weight for their age.

Thus far, the reflexes reported from genital stimulation have been lower trunk and lower extremity movements. Motion-picture records were secured for only one of the fetuses listed above (18.5 weeks), so details of the reactions of the other fetuses were not secured. Bilateral flexion of the thighs on the pelvis was seen for the youngest fetus (10.5 weeks), however, as well as for all the older ones. Stimulation of the genitofemoral sulcus, or sometimes of the genital area (laterally), elicited an ipsilateral flexion of the thigh on the pelvis that, at 18.5 weeks, included flexion at the knee joint as well. At this age, the bilateral reflex may include flexion at the hips, extension at the knees, and dorsiflexion of the feet and toes with toe-fanning, as well as ventral flexion of the lower back and rotation of the pelvis to one side. Although action of the upper extremities and head has not been recognized with these reflexes, they are general body and extremity reflexes, not local reactions. Undoubtedly, head and upper extremity movements will also be found when additional data are studied.

The cremasteric reflex is the first local reflex, and the only one, that has been reported from genital stimulation as yet.

Fewer reactions have been seen from anal stimulation than from stimulation of the genital areas.[45] At 10.5 weeks, flexion of the pelvis on the trunk was noted. Later (17 weeks), with the fetus prone rather than supine, the reflex included flexion at the hips and knees as well as flexion of the pelvis on the trunk. For these reflexes, stroking the anal surface with the esthesiometer was the effective stimulus. Introducing a glass rod into the anal canal was a less adequate stimulus.

23. Tonic Neck Reflexes

In the symmetrical tonic neck reflex, the upper and lower extremities are extended on the side toward which the face is turned and flexed on the side toward the occiput when the infant is in the supine position (see Fig. 12D). Asymmetrical tonic neck reflexes like that illustrated in Fig. 12E are more common for nonviable premature infants, at least. Gesell and Amatrude[27] indicate that the tonic neck reflex is present in the newborn infant, and consider it a characteristic feature at 4 postnatal weeks. Some observers believe that the symmetrical form of this reflex occurs only rarely[5,58] and has little significance, whereas the asymmetrical reaction is often seen. Others[83] state that it may be present or absent at birth.

24. Extremity Reflexes

24.1. Origin and Early Developmental History

Extremity reflexes, like active mouth-opening reflexes, first appear in development as part of the total pattern lateral flexion reflexes. The backward movement of the arms at the shoulders (beginning arm extension, 25 mm) appears before there is any evidence that the lower extremities move as part of these contralateral reflexes. Almost at once, however, the separation of the soles of the feet (normally facing each other and in contact when the fetus is in the rest position) demonstrates a primitive sort of abduction at the hip joints. This movement has begun at 26.0 mm (see Fig. 3), but the separation of the soles of the feet is slight, brief, and part of the reflex only when the action is forceful. As early as 27.1 mm, the two upper extremities may no longer move in exactly the same way, and by 34.3 mm, a considerable difference between the arm movements on the two sides has been seen. During this period when the extremity movements are an integral part of the contralateral flexion reflexes following perioral stimulation (see Fig. 4), the digits of both the hands and the feet appear to spread apart.[49,53]

When the total pattern type of contralateral (and ipsilateral) flexion reflexes disappears, beginning at 10–10.5 weeks, the lower extremity movements commence to drop out of the reactions to perioral stimulation, whereas the upper extremity movements are still present.[49] The arm on the side ipsilateral to the stimulus may react to the facial stimulus after both upper extremities no longer participate. Obviously, both upper and lower extremity movements begin in response to perioral stimulation. Likewise, they are suppressed as part of these reflexes after the extremities themselves (palms and soles) become sensitive.

24.2. Reflexes Elicited by Stimulation of the Upper Extremity

24.2.1. Areas Sensitive to Stimulation

The palm of the hand (see Table III) is both the most sensitive area of the upper extremity for eliciting reflexes and the one that responds to stimulation earliest.[36,38] Only rarely has stimulation over the shoulder areas resulted in extension of the upper arm or brachium at 10.5 weeks[38] or caused abduction by 11.5 weeks.[38] The reflexes elicited from palmar stimulation often involve only the fingers, but sometimes the hand, forearm, and upper arm are involved, and occasionally an oral area reflex is elicited as well (see Fig. 7C).[53,54]

24.2.2. Reflexes Elicited

Partial finger closure is the earliest reflex elicited by palmer stimulation. At about 10.5 weeks, "and possibly a little before,"[38] stimulation of the palm of the hand occasionally elicits quick, partial finger closure, without flexion of the thumb. By 11 weeks, the partial finger closure is quite consistently evoked by palmar stimulation (see Figs. 12A–C); it is usually accompanied by participation of the hand, sometimes by forearm flexion, and less commonly by pronation of the forearm and rotation of the upper

arm medialward. Finger closure becomes more complete by 13 weeks, and the thumb may come into apposition with the fingers, but only rarely. Finger closure is also more variable, with the third to fifth digits shut more tightly and the index finger remaining extended.[54] By 13.5–14 weeks, finger closure may be complete (see Fig. 7C). Finger closure is maintained for a longer time by 15–15.5 weeks, and Hooker found that by 18.5 weeks, the fingers grasped a rod. The grasp of nonviable premature infants has become stronger by 23.5 weeks and is more variable (see Figs. 12D, E). The thumb is sometimes folded inside the fingers (see Fig. 12E), but more often lies alongside the index finger (see Fig. 12D). In a fetus of 27 weeks that proved viable, the grasp on one hand was apparently sufficiently strong to support most of the weight of the body when it was lifted almost entirely away from the surface of the bed. The preceding account is based on the 1938, 1952, and 1958 papers of Hooker.[32,36,38] The illustrations of Hooker's that show the development of finger movements and grasping and photographs of finger movements are included in other papers.[45,54]

24.2.3. Hand–Mouth Interrelationships

When the total pattern types of flexion reflexes are suppressed by the development of inhibitory connections from higher centers,[54] arm and hand movements ipsilateral to the side of the face stimulated are seen after bilateral upper extremity movements following such stimuli have disappeared. Conversely, stimulation of one hand may be followed not only by some ipsilateral hand and finger action, but also by turning of the face ipsilaterally, and by oral activity such as mouth-opening, mouth closure, and tongue movements. This linkage of upper extremity and ipsilateral head movements (see Figs. 7B, C) was seen at 12.5 weeks and at 14 weeks.[49,53] It was demonstrated after 13.5–14 weeks by the fetal double simultaneous stimulation tests of face and ipsilateral hand. Before this age, when both face and palm are stimulated simultaneously, the hand reflex tends to be suppressed. After this age, the reflexes from both palmar and facial stimuli are more often elicited when the two stimuli are simultaneous.[37,55]

At 14 weeks, the close hand–mouth association has been seen following palmar stimulation. In one instance, a quite prolonged mouth-opening with tongue protrusion and retraction occurred, as well as tongue elevation, all combined with turning of

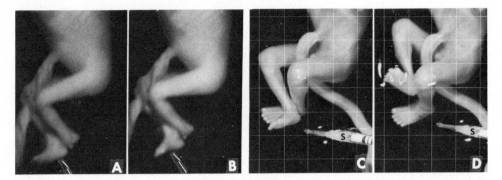

Fig. 13. Reflexes in response to stimulation of the sole of the foot at 13 weeks (No. 45, 75.0 mm CR) (A, B) and at 16.5 weeks (No. 43, 121.0 mm CR) (C, D). (A) Position of the foot before this planter flexion reflex began. (B) Both the toes and the adjacent part of the foot are plantar-flexed. The arrow points to the area of stimulation in A and the region of change in position in B. With this reflex, no other action took place, even for the lower extremities. The photographs are slightly smaller than actual size. (C, D) A Babinski reflex. On stroking of the sole of the right foot with a 2-g stimulator(s), a rapid dorsiflexion of all toes took place, accompanied by dorsiflexion of the foot and flexion at the knee and at the hip joints. In D, however, neither dorsiflexion of the great toe nor toe-fanning is complete, but both occurred a little later. There was no movement of the other lower extremity and no action elsewhere. The photographs are about half the size of the fetus. The grid overlay was placed over these two photographs in an attempt to demonstrate the action more effectively.

the face toward the hand stimulated (see Fig. 7C). This reflex has been suggested as the fetal forerunner of the Babkin reflex,[54] which is elicited more frequently from premature than from newborn infants.[10,77,79] The intimate relationship between the hand and the mouth is seen postnatally in the close association between grasp and sucking.[54,79,81] Another fetus of 14 weeks (No. 13, 88.5 mm CR) reacted to palmer stimulation by turning the head toward the midline, elevating the ipsilateral upper lip near the corner and pulling the corner laterally, contracting the eyelid muscles in the squintlike reaction, and elevating the lower lip slightly. This reflex appears to be the fetal forerunner of the palmomental reflex[54] that was described by Marinesco and Radovici[66] for premature and term infants[76] and is seen occasionally in normal adults[13] as well as fairly often in young children.[79]

24.3. Reflexes Elicited by Stimulation of the Lower Extremity

24.3.1. Areas Sensitive to Stimulation

The sole of the foot becomes sensitive to stimulation by 10.5 weeks, very shortly after reflexes are elicitable from the palm of the hand.[36] Although

there is very little difference in their time of onset if the age group is considered (see Table III), the palmar response for any single fetus is well established when the plantar reaction is first elicited. The retention of reflex finger closure after anoxia suppresses the plantar reflex also demonstrates that the palmar reflex develops earlier (see Table I), for the longer-established reflexes function later than newly matured reflex arcs under such conditions. The cutaneous areas of the leg and thigh do not become sensitive until later than the sole of the foot. At 17 weeks, stroking the surface of the buttock elicits a reflex.[45] Probably other surfaces, such as the dorsum of the foot, also become sensitive, but adequate testing has not been done. By 32 weeks, the medial surface of the thigh is also sensitive. However, the sole of the foot not only is the first lower extremity surface to become sensitive, but also remains reflexogenous throughout both fetal and postnatal life.

24.3.2. Reflexes Elicited

The initial response to plantar stimulation was found by Hooker[38] to be plantar flexion of all the toes (Figs. 13A, B), as originally reported by Minkowski.[68] Dorsiflexion of the great toe and toe-fanning were elicited by 11.5–12 weeks by

Hooker.[38] At 12.5 weeks, however, plantar stimulation may elicit either reflex, i.e., plantar flexion of the toes or dorsiflexion of the great toe with toe-fanning (Figs. 13C, D). Either reflex may be accompanied by flexion at the ankle, knee, and hip, and sometimes by rotation and abduction of the thigh.[36,38] The tabulations of reflexes by Hooker from the motion-picture records show that plantar flexion continues to be elicited occasionally even as late as 18.5–20 weeks, although it occurs less frequently.[54] However, dorsiflexion of the great toe with fanning of the other toes becomes more common during this period. The essential parts of the Babinski reflex, according to DeJong,[24] are dorsiflexion of the toes, particularly the great toe, with spreading (or fanning) of the other digits. The Babinski reflex therefore develops in fetal life after plantar flexion has appeared. The plantar toe flexion reflex is comparable to the finger closure elicited by palmar stimulation. It has been suggested that it is the equivalent of the foot-grasp reflex present phylogenetically.[45]

Perinatally, especially in premature infants, plantar flexion is elicited more often by scratching of the lateral aspect of the sole of the foot than is dorsiflexion of the great toe and toe-fanning. Plantar flexion is also elicited during this period by pressure on the ball of the foot, however, and the two reflexes are frequently confused in the literature.[54]

25. Sequence of Development of Sensitivity to Light Touch

In human development, the areas about the mouth are the first to become sensitive to stimulation by light stroking of the surface with a hair. For small fetuses that are not influenced by narcotics or anesthetics or both, like those in Figs. 3 and 4, 25- or 50-mg stimulators are adequate to elicit reflexes before the oxygen supply is sufficiently depleted to suppress all reactions. As the amount of oxygen diminishes, stronger stimuli are necessary. In older fetuses that have a thicker surface epithelium, stronger stimuli are also needed. Although these stimulators exert very little pressure, even a 10-mg stimulator is easily felt when drawn across the palm of the hand. Because the growing nerve tips do not yet touch the basement membrane of the thin epithelium when sensitivity is first demonstrable,

even the light stroking stimulus is thought to deform the nerve tips enough by displacement of the surrounding tissues to cause their excitation.[31]

The nerves functioning when the lips and adjacent perioral areas become sensitive to stimulation at 7.5 weeks (20–21 mm) are the maxillary and mandibular divisions of the trigeminal or fifth cranial nerve. Table III gives the chronologic order in which the surfaces of the body and oral cavity become sensitive to stimulation as far as it can be determined from the data available at present. Hooker[36,38] found some indication that the maxillary fibers respond earlier than the mandibular fibers. There has been little difference shown between the distance of the nerve tips from the epithelium in the upper and lower lips (13–14 μm in the rima oris region), however, when they become sensitive at 7.5 weeks.[48] The sensitive area widens to cover the more peripheral perioral zones, including the alae of the nose and the chin, by 9.5 weeks, and the lower eyelids, the bridge of the nose, and the region below the lower eyelid by 10.5 weeks. None of the areas supplied by the opthalmic division of the trigeminal nerve becomes sensitive until 10–10.5 weeks, when the upper eyelids are responsive to stimulation.[38] The supercilliary ridges (eyebrow areas) and the forehead are added a little later (11 weeks),[38] but the forehead rarely responds to stimulation. No reflexes have been reported from stroking of the surface areas of the scalp that are supplied by ophthalmic fibers or of the other areas of the scalp that are supplied by cervical nerves.

It might be expected that surface sensitivity would spread regularly from the perioral facial areas peripheralward over the body and extremities. Such a regular sequence has not been demonstrated, however (see Table III). The palms of the hands, the genital areas, and the areas supplied by the ophthalmic fibers apparently become responsive to stimuli at approximately the same time. Touching the genital areas produces reflex action before stimulation of the back, the chest, or the abdominal wall becomes effective. The palms react to stimulation earlier than do the more centrally located shoulder, upper arm, and forearm areas. Likewise, the soles have been found to be sensitive earlier than either the thighs or the legs.

These functional sequences do not necessarily mean that nerve fibers have not arrived as close to the surface of these intermediate regions as to the finger tips, for example. There are far fewer nerves terminating in these intermediate areas.[31] Consequently, there is little summation, and evidence of their functional capacity is therefore difficult to obtain. Reflexes elicited by cutaneous stimulation perinatally and postnatally are likewise mainly from the palms and soles, not from either the shoulder-to-wrist or the buttock-to-ankle area.

Although the ages given in Table III are subject to change as more data are accumulated, certain trends are clear. One is that the anterior end (oral area) and the posterior end (genital region) of the fetus become sensitive to external stimulation before the intervening regions. Likewise, the palmar and plantar surfaces of distal portions of the extremities become sensitive earlier than the proximal ones. From the morphological viewpoint, it is evident at once that these areas—lips, genitalia, palms, and soles—are the cutaneous areas of the adult that contain both the greatest concentration of sensory nerve endings and the most highly specialized varieties of sensory receptors.[45]

26. Other Types of General Sensation

Relatively little is known concerning the function of the other types of sensory stimuli during fetal life. The literature on function of premature and full-term infants is discussed by Carmichael[19] and Peiper,[79] and cannot be included here. Stretch reflexes such as the localized reactions elicited by Windle[97] by rapidly lifting and releasing a limb undoubtedly develop early, even though Cuajunco[22] found the receptors (muscle spindles) only beginning to develop by 11 weeks of menstrual age in the biceps brachii. Whether these reflexes precede those elicited by light stroking of the skin remains an unsettled question. Two points, at least, favor the earlier functioning of the cutaneous reflexes: (1) They do not require specialized receptors, only naked end bulbs, even in the adult. (2) Until muscle contracts, there can be no stretch stimuli, and in higher mammals, skeletal muscle does not contract before the reflex arcs function, although in birds, for example, spontaneous movements appear before reflexes can be elicited.[29]

Sensations interpreted postnatally as painful have relatively little effect.[19,79] However, as soon as the fetus responds to perioral stimulation positively (turning toward) as well as negatively (turning away or avoiding), distinction is made on a reflex level. This discrimination occurs at 22.6–26.0 mm (see Fig. 3). It is not possible to say whether this difference

is due to the strength of stimulation (strong stimuli being nociceptive), as some believe, or is on some other basis. Whether the area stimulated is peripherally or centrally situated may also be a factor.

Newborn infants and probably prematures also react more vigorously to stimuli colder than the body than to those warmer.[19] In the observations of Hooker[33,35–38] on fetuses, the temperature of the fluid bath was kept as near normal body temperature as possible. A stream of hot saline directed against the body of the fetus was tried a few times, but no definite information was obtained. Cold saline was not tried. If the saline bath became overheated by 3 or 4°F, reflexes were not obtained. However, reflexes were elicited from fetuses of 11 weeks of menstrual age and older with the usual hair esthesiometers when the temperature was as low as 80°F.[57] This finding may indicate that sensitivity to temperatures colder than the body is also greater than that to warmth in fetal life. There is some evidence to indicate that temperature from the face is mediated through the rostral part of the spinal trigeminal nuclear complex.[52] If so, then temperature sensitivity may be developing at the time that this region starts differentiation at 11 weeks,[18] the age mentioned above.

So far as the other general sensory modalities mentioned are concerned, it is only possible to say that if they are related in any way to the development of the special receptors, such as Meissner's corpuscles and pacinian corpuscles, they may make their appearance in fetal life when these receptors begin to differentiate. This time would probably be as the age of viability is approached, or attained, for cholinesterase activity has been demonstrated for pacinian corpuscles at 24 weeks and for Meissner's corpuscles at 28 weeks.[12]

27. Special Senses During Intrauterine Life

Space does not allow more than brief comments on the questions of vestibular, gustatory, auditory, olfactory, and visual function in prenatal life. The reflex circuits that act at brainstem levels—vestibular, gustatory, and auditory reflex arcs—will mature earliest, since differentiation proceeds from cervical levels cephalad as well as caudad.[62] This order of maturation has been shown in human fetuses for the spinal trigeminal nuclear complex.[16–18] It is indicated also for some reflex arcs.[43,54] The vestibular ganglion cells mature early, and the neurons of the lateral[67,69] and inferior vestibular nuclei are sufficiently mature to function at 9.5 weeks of menstrual age.[47] Both Minkowski[69] and Hooker[34] suggested that some movements observed by them might be due to vestibular stimulation. Abundant vestibular stimuli are certainly present *in utero*. Minkowski[69] suggested that the almost weightless status of the fetus *in utero* provided a particularly advantageous medium for vestibular reflexes.

Concerning taste, Bradley and Stern[15] concluded that taste buds are mature enough to function during the 13.5- to 15-week age period (their reference was apparently to fertilization age). This age is later than the time that tongue movement has been demonstrated in our investigations. Swallowing begins at about the same age level as tongue movement, and undoubtedly amniotic fluid enters the mouth as it opens completely (9.5 weeks' menstrual age). The addition of saccharine to amniotic fluid has been shown to result in increased swallowing by fetuses near term with hydramnios, but it is possible that other taste stimuli, such as bitter, or saccharine for that matter, may be effective in eliciting reflexes much earlier. The literature on taste sensitivity of premature and newborn infants is controversial,[79] but at least two types of reactions occur: grimacing and rejection, as with quinine, for example, and swallowing and sucking movements, as with sugar.

Fetal reactions to auditory stimuli have been demonstrated both by an increase in reflex activity and by an increase in fetal heart rate. The increase in heart rate has been shown at "about the beginning of the 29th week"[94] to "30 postconception weeks"[71] and is present until birth.[94] Sontag and Wallace[92] also report that both the mother's emotion (such as anger or fear) and fatigue increase the fetal heart rate. Increased movements in response to sound were first observed a little later than the change in heart rate, i.e., at the "beginning of the 31st week of intrauterine life."[93] Other literature on this subject is discussed by Carmichael,[19] Pratt,[80] and Peiper.[79]

As succinctly stated by Windle,[96] there can be no visual stimulation during intrauterine life. The information on the light reflexes of premature infants[19] is controversial, but it is probably safe to say that the elicitation of this reflex is the first evidence of retinal function.

Because the olfactory portions of the telencephalon are relatively large in lower vertebrates, it is some-times assumed that olfactory sensitivity develops early embryologically. There is no evidence to support this view. Differentiation of the nervous system takes place from cervical levels cephalad, and the efferent pathways must reach the brainstem for reflexes to occur. Even if the necessary maturation occurs relatively early and there were an adequate stimulus, until the nasal plugs of epithelium in the external nares have resolved and disappeared, which may not be until 4–6 months,[90] no currents of fluid pass across the nasal epithelium. Therefore, until the infant is born, there is little likelihood that there is any olfactory function taking place. The literature concerning the olfactory capacities of premature and full-term infants is extensive and controversial,[19,79] in part due to the use of irritants that stimulate the trigeminal endings in the nose, rather than only the olfactory cells. It appears justifiable, however, to conclude that when olfactory function begins, the reflex activity will indicate that the odor is either agreeable or disagreeable.

28. Closing Comments

The development of nervous system function is an orderly process that is integrated from the beginning of the first reflex. Each added function is incorporated with the existing ones when it makes its appearance. Regardless whether one reflex is suppressed and another performed, or whether two or more reflexes are combined, the reactions are integrated when they occur.

In response to cutaneous stimulation, at least, behavior begins with a reaction of the embryo as a whole. At first, the reflex is limited, because only the earliest-matured portions of the neuromuscular system have attained the capacity to respond. When additional regions have matured sufficiently, the whole fetus reacts to the same stimulus—the head and trunk, the four extremities, including the hands and the digits, and even the mandible to open the mouth—all in response to a perioral stimulation (see Fig. 4). Such reflexes meet all the qualifications for the total pattern reflexes of Coghill. They constitute the only reflexes that have been recognized from known cutaneous stimuli of human fetuses until 10–10.5 weeks of menstrual age.

As cutaneous surfaces other than the perioral areas become sensitive to stimulation, inhibitory reactions develop. Local reflexes then begin to appear and increase in frequency. At the same time, the total pattern reflexes begin to disappear. The suppression of the total pattern reflexes elicited by facial stimulation takes place in a definite order. The lower extremity, lower trunk, and pelvic activity drop out of the responses first, and the bilaterality of arm movements becomes an ipsilateral arm reaction. The reflex activity that most often remains is ipsilateral head movement, usually in combination with oral reflexes. Other head movements form functional combinations of reflexes such as the head extension and ventral flexion that accompany mouth-opening, mouth closure, tongue movements, and raising and lowering the larynx in swallowing.[49,53,54]

In the total pattern lateral flexion reflexes, the activity is stereotyped and varies only in vigor and extent. Each extremity moves as a part of the general body and extremity reflex, not separately, although there may be action at all major joints— e.g., shoulder, elbow, and wrist. Movement of some part of an extremity alone makes its appearance only when some surface area of that extremity becomes responsive to stimulation. This sequence is true for both the upper and the lower extremities.

It is of some interest that mouth-opening reflexes, although elicited earliest by stimulation in the perioral region, may be elicited (usually in combination with other activity) by stroking widely separated surfaces of the body, including the sole, the back, the forearm, the palm, and the external auditory canal. However, oral reflexes during later development are usually limited to stimulation of maxillomandibular zones of the face, although stimulation of the palm may be effective. Active mouth-opening reflexes by lowering the jaw are also linked initially with contralateral flexion reflexes (avoiding reactions). Later, they are associated with the reflexes related to feeding. The mouth-opening reflexes elicited from areas distal to the mouth (and hand) are avoiding in type, and some of them appear comparable to snapping and biting. Like mouth-opening accompanying the total pattern lateral flexion reflexes, they disappear almost entirely, whereas the positive responses, such as turning toward the stimulus (and the actions associated with it), remain and increase in strength, in number, and in the variety of combinations that develop.

Throughout the preceding discussion, specific correlations have been made between the functional changes that take place during development and known morphological changes in related areas of the nervous system. For the most part, however, it is only possible to speculate concerning what levels of the CNS that are responsible for the activity described. On the one hand, both nuclear groups and fiber tracts in the telencephalon, for example, are identifiable long before there is any evidence that they become functional. On the other hand, in the development of the reflex arc mediating the first reflex that develops (see Fig. 2), there appears to be an almost immediate onset of function.[41,43] The author's speculations are that the reflex activities that have been demonstrated before 20 weeks of menstrual age are executed through the mesencephalon, the lower brainstem, and the spinal cord (see Fig. 6), and do not involve diencephalic and telencephalic centers. After approximately 20 weeks, neural circuits through the diencephalon and striatal complex (or basal ganglia) become functional to an increasingly greater degree. In premature infants, the lack of adequate temperature regulation indicates incomplete functional development of the hypothalamus. In both premature and newborn infants, the activity of the extremities is typically striatal in type. Electroencephalographic studies demonstrate that there is cortical activity in the brain during the perinatal period, but according to Gesell and Amatruda,[27] there is no indication that cortical function results in movements until the eyes of the postnatal infant are able to fix on a moving object and follow it at 4 weeks. Function of additional extrapyramidal areas of the cortex probably begins when the infant endeavors to reach for the object on which the eyes are fixed. Much later, when fine finger movements make it possible to pick up, say a small pellet, the hand area of the motor cortex (area 4) is undoubtedly active.

Some mention should be made of the fact that activity sequences seen in fetal life are repeated perinatally or postnatally or both when higher levels of the nervous system, such as the striatal region, control activity. Likewise, when regulation is taken over by the cerebral cortex and becomes voluntary, the same general sequences may be repeated again, but with greater variability and complexity. The development of fetal hand movements provides one example. Other instances are discussed by the author elsewhere,[54] and explanations are proposed as to the neuroembryological background for this repetition.

ACKNOWLEDGMENTS

This investigation was supported by Public Health Service research career program award NB-K6-16716 from the National Institute of Neurological Diseases and Blindness, and was aided by grant HD-00230, National Institute of Child Health and

Human Development, National Institutes of Health. This chapter is publication No. 54 in a series of physiological and morphological studies on human prenatal development begun in 1932 under the direction of Dr. Davenport Hooker. The data on which this paper is based were collected during periods of support in the past by grants from The Penrose Fund of the American Philosophical Society, The Carnegie Corporation of New York, The University of Pittsburgh, The Sarah Mellon Scaife Foundation of Pittsburgh, and Grant B-394 from the National Institute of Neurological Diseases and Blindness, National Institutes of Health, to Davenport Hooker or the author or both.

29. References

1. ADAMS, F. H., 1966, Functional development of the fetal lung, *J. Pediatr.* **68**:794–801.

2. ADAMS, F. H., AND FUJIWARA, T., 1963, Surfactant in fetal lamb tracheal fluid, *J. Pediatr.* **63**:537–542.

3. ADAMS, F. H., DESILETS, D. T., AND TOWERS, B., 1967, Control of flow of fetal lung fluid at the laryngeal outlet, *Respir. Physiol.* **2**:302–309.

4. ADAMS, F. H., DESILETS, D. T., AND TOWERS, B., 1967, Physiology of the fetal larynx and lung, *Ann. Otol.* **76**:735–743.

5. ANDRÉ-THOMAS Y. C., AND SAINT-ANNE DARGASSIES, S., 1960, *The Neurologic Examination of the Infant,* Wm. Heinemann Medical Books, London.

6. ANGULO Y GONZALES, A. W., 1932, The prenatal development of behavior in the albino rat, *J. Comp. Neurol.* **55**:395–442.

7. ANOKHIN, P. K., 1964, Systemogenesis as a general regulator of brain development, *Prog. Brain Res.* **9**:54–86 (discussion: 99–102).

8. AREY, L. B., 1965, *Developmental Anatomy,* 7th Ed., W. B. Saunders Co., Philadelphia and London.

9. ARSHAVSKY, I. A., 1959, Mechanisms of the development of nutritional functions during the intrauterine period and following birth, *J. Gen. Biol.* **20**:104–114 (transl. from Russian).

10. BABKIN, P. S., 1960, The establishment of reflex activity in early postnatal life, in: *Central Nervous System and Behavior. Translations from Fiziol. Zh. (Kiev)* **44**:922–927, Scientific Translation Program, National Institutes of Health, Bethesda, Maryland.

11. BARCROFT, J., AND BARRON, D. H., 1939, Movement in the mammalian foetus, *Ergeb. Physiol.* **42**:107–152.

12. BECKETT, E. B., BOURNE, G. H., AND MONTAGNA, W., 1956, Histology and cytochemistry of human skin: The distribution of cholinesterase in the finger of the embryo and the adult, *J. Physiol. (London)* **134**:202–206.

13. BLAKE, J. R., AND KUNKLE, E. C., 1951, The palmomental reflex: A physiological and clinical analysis, *Arch. Neurol. (Chicago)* **65**:337–345.

14. BONAR, B. E., BLUMENFELD, C. M., AND FENNING, C., 1938, Studies of fetal respiratory movements. I. Historical and present day observations, *Amer. J. Dis. Child.* **55**:1–11.

15. BRADLEY, R. M., AND STERN, I. B., 1967, The development of the human taste bud during the foetal period, *J. Anat. (London)* **101**:743–752.

16. BROWN, J. W., 1956, The development of the nucleus of the spinal tract of V in human fetuses of 14 to 21 weeks of menstrual age. *J. Comp. Neurol.* **106**:393–424.

17. BROWN, J. W., 1958, The development of subnucleus caudalis of the nucleus of the spinal tract of V, *J. Comp. Neurol.* **110**:105–134.

18. BROWN, J. W., 1962, Differentiation of the human subnucleus interpolaris and subnucleus rostralis of the nucleus of the spinal tract of the trigeminal nerve, *J. Comp. Neurol.* **119**:55–75.

19. CARMICHAEL, L. (ed), 1954, The onset and early development of behavior, in: *Manual of Child Psychology,* pp. 60–185, John Wiley & Sons, New York.

20. COGHILL, G. E., 1916, Correlated anatomical and physiological studies of the growth of the nervous system of Amphibia. II. The afferent system of the head of *Amblystoma, J. Comp. Neurol.* **26**:247–340.

21. COGHILL, G. E., 1929, *Anatomy and the Problem of Behaviour,* Cambridge University Press, Cambridge, England; reprinted 1964, Hafner Publishing Co., New York.

22. CUAJUNCO, F., 1940, Development of the neuromuscular spindle in human fetuses, *Carnegie Inst. Washington Contrib. Embryol.* **28**:95–128.

23. DAVIS, M. E., AND POTTER, E. L., 1946, Intrauterine respiration of the human fetus, *J. Amer. Med. Assoc.* **131**:1194–1201.

24. DEJONG, R. N., 1967, *The Neurologic Examination,* 3rd Ed., Hoeber Medical Division, Harper and Row, New York.

25. FITZGERALD, J. E., AND WINDLE, W. F., 1942, Some observations on early human fetal movements, *J. Comp. Neurol.* **76**:159–167.

26. GASSER, R. F., 1967, The development of the facial muscles in man, *Amer. J. Anat.* **120**:357–376.

27. GESELL, A., AND AMATRUDA, C. S., 1947, *Developmental Diagnosis: Normal and Abnormal Child Development,* 2nd Ed., Hoeber Medical Division, Harper and Row, New York.

28. GOLUBEWA, E. L., SHULEJKINA, K. V., AND VAINSTEIN, I. I., 1959, The development of reflex and spontaneous activity of the human fetus during embryogenesis, *Obstet. Gynecol. (USSR)* **3**:59–62.

29. HAMBURGER, V., 1963, Some aspects of the embryology of behavior, *Q. Rev. Biol.* **38**:342–365.

30. HEARD, J. D., BURKLEY, G. G., AND SCHAEFER, C. R., 1936, Electrocardiograms derived from eleven fetuses through the medium of direct leads, *Amer. Heart J.* **11**:41–48.

31. HOGG, I. D., 1941, Sensory nerves and associated structures in the skin of human fetuses of 8 to 14 weeks of menstrual age correlated with functional capability, *J. Comp. Neurol.* **75**:371–410.

32. HOOKER, D., 1938, The origin of the grasping movement in man, *Proc. Amer. Philos. Soc.* **79**:597–606.

33. HOOKER, D., 1939, *A Preliminary Atlas of Early Human Fetal Activity,* published by the author.

34. HOOKER, D., 1942, Fetal reflexes and instinctual processes, *Psychosom. Med.* **4**:199–205.

35. HOOKER, D., 1944, *The Origin of Overt Behavior,* University of Michigan Press, Ann Arbor.

36. HOOKER, D., 1952, *The Prenatal Origin of Behavior. 18th Porter Lecture,* University of Kansas Press, Lawrence; Reprinted 1969, Hafner Publishing Co., New York.

37. HOOKER, D., 1954, Early human fetal behavior, with a preliminary note on double simultaneous fetal stimulation, *Res. Publ. Assoc. Res. Nerv. Ment. Dis.* **33**:98–113.

38. HOOKER, D., 1958, *Evidence of Prenatal Function of the Central Nervous System in Man. James Arthur Lecture on The Evolution of the Human Brain for 1957,* American Museum of Natural History, New York.

39. HOOKER, D., 1960, Development reaction to environment, *Yale J. Biol. Med.* **32**:431–440.

40. HOOKER, D., AND HUMPHREY, T. 1954, Some results and deductions from a study on the development of human fetal behavior, *Gaz. Med. Port.* **7**:189–197.

41. HUMPHREY, T., 1952, The spinal tract of the trigeminal nerve in human embryos between $7\frac{1}{2}$ and $8\frac{1}{2}$ weeks of menstrual age and its relation to early fetal behavior, *J. Comp. Neurol.* **97**:143–209.

42. HUMPHREY, T., 1953, The relation of oxygen deprivation to fetal reflex arcs and the development of fetal behavior, *J. Psychol.* **35**:3–43.

43. HUMPHREY, T., 1954, The trigeminal nerve in relation to early human fetal activity, *Res. Publ. Assoc. Res. Nerv. Ment. Dis.* **33**:127–154.

44. HUMPHREY, T., 1955, Pattern formed at upper cervical spinal cord levels by sensory fibers of spinal and cranial nerves, *Arch. Neurol. (Chicago)* **73**:36–46.

45. HUMPHREY, T., 1964, Some correlations between the appearance of human fetal reflexes and the development of the nervous system, *Prog. Brain Res.* **4**:93–135.

46. HUMPHREY, T., 1964, Embryology of the central nervous system: With some correlations with functional development, *Ala. J. Med. Sci.* **1**:60–64.

47. HUMPHREY, T., 1965, The embryologic differentiation of the vestibular nuclei in man correlated with functional development, in: *International Symposium on Vestibular and Ocular Problems,* Tokyo, Japan, pp. 51–56, Society of Vestibular Research, University of Tokyo.

48. HUMPHREY, T., 1966, The development of trigeminal nerve fibers to the oral mucosa, compared with their development to cutaneous surfaces, *J. Comp. Neurol.* **126**:91–108.

49. HUMPHREY, T., 1968, The development of mouth opening and related reflexes involving the oral area of human fetuses, *Ala. J. Med. Sci.* **5**:126–157.

50. HUMPHREY, T., 1968, The dynamic mechanism of palatal shelf elevation in human fetuses, *Anat. Rec.* **160**:369.

51. HUMPHREY, T., 1969, The relation between human fetal mouth opening reflexes and closure of the palate, *Amer. J. Anat.* **125**:317–344.

52. HUMPHREY, T., 1969, The central relations of the trigeminal nerve, in: *Correlative Neurosurgery,* 2nd Ed. (E. A. Kahn, E. C. Crosby, R. C. Schneider, and J. A. Taren, eds.), pp. 477–492 and 501–508, Charles C. Thomas, Springfield, Illinois.

53. HUMPHREY, T., 1969, Reflex activity in the oral and facial area of human fetuses, in: *Second Symposium on Oral Sensation and Perception* (J. F. Bosma, ed.), Charles C. Thomas, Springfield, Illinois.

54. HUMPHREY, T., 1969, Postnatal repetition of human prenatal activity sequences with some suggestions on their neuroanatomical basis, in: *Brain and early Behaviour: Development in the Fetus and Infant* (R. J. Robinson, ed.), pp. 43–84, Academic Press, New York.

55. HUMPHREY, T., AND HOOKER, D., 1959, Double simultaneous stimulation of human fetuses and the anatomical patterns underlying the reflexes elicited, *J. Comp. Neurol.* **112**:75–102.

56. HUMPHREY, T., AND HOOKER, D., 19c1, Reflexes elicited by stimulating perineal and adjacent areas of human fetuses, *Trans. Amer. Neurol. Assoc.* **86**:147–152.

57. HUMPHREY, T., AND HOOKER, D., 1961, Human fetal reflexes elicited by genital stimulation, in: *Transactions of the 7th International Neurological Congress,* Rome, Italy, Vol. 2, pp. 587–590.

58. ILLINGWORTH, R. S., 1966, *The Development of the Infant and Young Child, Normal and Abnormal,* 3rd Ed., The Williams & Wilkins Co., Baltimore.

59. JACOBS, M. J., 1970, The development of the human motor trigeminal complex and accessory facial nucleus and their topographic relations with the facial and abducens nuclei, *J. Comp. Neurol.* **138**:161–194.

60. JORDAN, H. E., AND KINDRED, J. E., 1942, *Textbook of Embryology,* 4th Ed., Appleton-Century-Crofts, New York.

61. KAPPERS, C. U., ARIËNS, HUBER, G. C., AND

CROSBY, E. C., 1936, *The Comparative Anatomy of the Nervous System of Vertebrates, Including Man,* The Macmillan Co., New York; reproduced 1960 without revision by Hafner Publishing Co., New York.

62. KINGSBURY, B. F., 1924, The significance of the so-called law of cephalocaudal differential growth, *Anat. Rec.* **27**:305–321.

63. KUO, Z. Y., 1967, *The Dynamics of Behavior Development: An Epigenetic View,* Random House, New York.

64. LUNDEEN, E. C., AND KUNSTADTER, R. H., 1958, *Care of the Premature Infant,* J. B. Lippincott Co., Philadelphia.

65. MALL, F. P., 1910, Determination of the age of human embryos and fetuses, in: *Manual of Human Embryology* (F. Keibel and F. P. Mall, eds.), Vol. 1, pp. 180–201, J. B. Lippincott Co., Philadelphia.

66. MARINESCO, G., AND RADOVICI, A., 1920, Sur un réflexe cutané nouveau à réflexe palmomentonnier, *Rev. Neurol. (Paris)* **27**:237–240.

67. MINKOWSKI, M., 1922, Über frühzeitige Bewegungen Reflexe und muskuläre Reaktionen beim menschlichen Fötus, und ihre Beziehungen zum fötalen Nerven- und Muskelsystem, *Schweiz. Med. Wochenschr.* **52**:721–724, 751–755.

68. MINKOWSKI, M., 1923, Zur Entwicklungsgeschichte, Lokalisation und Klinik des Fussohlenreflexes, *Schweiz. Arch. Neurol. Psychiatr.* **13**:475–514.

69. MINKOWSKI, M., 1928, Neurobiologische Studien am menschlichen Foetus, in: *Handbuch der Biologischen Arbeitsmethoden* (E. Abderhalden, ed.), Abt. V, Teil 5B, Heft 5, Leif **253**:511–618.

70. MOYERS, R. E., 1950, An electromyographic analysis of certain muscles involved in temporomandibular movement, *Amer. J. Orthod.* **36**:481–515.

71. MURPHY, K. P., AND SMYTH, C. N., 1962, Response of foetus to auditory stimulation, *Lancet* **1**:972–973.

72. MURPHY, W. F., AND LANGLEY, A. L., 1963, Common bullous lesions—presumably self-inflicted—occurring *in utero* in the newborn infant, *Pediatrics* **32**:1099–1101.

73. NILSSON, L., 1965, Drama of life before birth, *Life* **58**:54–69.

74. NILSSON, L., INGELMAN-SUNDBERG, A., AND WIRSEN, C., 1966, *A Child Is born: The Drama of Life Before Birth,* Delacorte Press, New York.

75. NORMAN, H. N., 1942, Fetal hiccups, *J. Comp. Psychol.* **34**:65–73.

76. PARMELEE, A. H., JR., 1963, The palmomental reflex in premature infants, *Dev. Med. Child Neurol.* **5**:381–387.

77. PARMELEE, A. H., JR., 1963, The hand–mouth reflex of Babkin in premature infants, *Pediatrics* **31**:734–740.

78. PATTERN, B. M., 1953, *Human Embryology,* 2nd Ed., The Blakiston Division, McGraw-Hill Book Co., New York.

79. PEIPER, A., 1963, *Cerebral Function in Infancy and Childhood* (J. Wortis, ed.), Consultants Bureau, New York; Translation of *Die Eigenart der kindlichen Hirntätigkeit,* 3rd Ed., 1961, Georg Thieme Verlag, Leipzig.

80. PRATT, K. C., 1954, The neonate, in: *Manual of Child Psychology,* 2nd Ed. (L. Carmichael, ed.), pp. 215–291, John Wiley & Sons, New York and London.

81. PRECHTL, H. F. R., 1953, Über die Koppelung von Saugen und Greifreflex beim Säugling, *Naturwissenschaften* **12**:347–348.

82. PRECHTL, H. F. R., 1958, The directed head turning response and allied movements of the human baby, *Behaviour* **13**:212–242.

83. PRECHTL, H. F. R., AND BEINTEMA, D., 1964, *The Neurological Examination of the Full Term Newborn Infant,* W. Heinemann Medical Books, London.

84. PREYER, W., 1885, *Specielle Physiologie des Embryo,* Th. Grieben's Verlag, Leipzig.

85. PRICHARD, J. A., 1965, Deglutition by normal and anencephalic fetuses, *Amer. J. Obstet. Gynecol.* **25**:289–297.

86. ROBINSON, R. J., 1966, Assessment of gestational age by neurological examination, *Arch. Dis. Child.* **41**:437–447.

87. ROOT, R. W., 1946, The mechanics of the temporomandibular joint: Illustrated by two cases, *Amer. J. Ortho.* **32**:113–119.

88. RUSSELL, P. M. G., 1957, Vagitus uterinus: Crying *in utero, Lancet* **272**:137–138.

89. RYDER, G. H., 1943, Vagitus uterinus, *Amer. J. Obstet. Gynecol.* **46**:867–872.

90. SCHAFFER, J. P., 1910, The lateral wall of the cavum nasi in man, with especial reference to the various developmental stages, *J. Morphol.* **21**:613–707.

91. SNYDER, F. F., AND ROSENFELD, M., 1937, Direct observation of intrauterine respiratory movements of the fetus and the role of carbon dioxide and oxygen in their regulation, *Amer. J. Physiol.* **119**:153–166.

92. SONTAG, L. W., AND WALLACE, R. F., 1934, Preliminary report of the Fels Fund: Study of fetal activity, *Amer. J. Dis. Child.* **48**:1050–1057.

93. SONTAG, L. W., AND WALLACE, R. F., 1935, The movement response of the human fetus to sound stimuli, *Child Dev.* **6**:253–258.

94. SONTAG, L. W., AND WALLACE, R. F., 1936, Changes in the rate of the human fetal heart in response to vibratory stimuli, *Amer. J. Dis. Child.* **51**:583–589.

95. STREETER, G. L., 1920, Weight, sitting height, head size, foot length, and menstrual age of the human embryo, *Carnegie Inst. Washington Contrib. Embryol.* **11**:143–170.

96. WINDLE, W. F., 1940, *Physiology of the Fetus. Origin and Extent of Function in Prenatal Life,* W. B. Saunders Co., Philadelphia.

97. WINDLE, W. F., 1944, Genesis of somatic motor

function in mammalian embryos: A synthesizing article, *Physiol Zool.* **27**:247–260.

98. WINDLE, W. F., 1950, Reflexes of mammalian embryos and fetuses, in: *Genetic Neurology,* (P. Weiss, ed.), pp. 214–222, University of Chicago Press.

99. WINDLE, W. F., AND BECKER, R. F., 1940, Relation of anoxemia to early activity in the fetal nervous system *Arch. Neurol. (Chicago)* **43**:90–101.

100. WINDLE, W. F., DRAGSTEDT, C. A., MURRAY, D. E., AND GREENE, R. R., 1938, A note on the respiration-like movements of the human fetus, *Surg. Gynecol. Obstet.* **66**:987–988.

CHAPTER 31

Neonatal Brain Mechanisms and the Development of Motor Behavior

Franz J. Schulte

1. Introduction

In the adult mammal, including the human, motor control has its representation at different levels of the CNS. A short review of motor control in the mature organism will precede each section of this chapter dealing with the various brain mechanisms of neonatal motor behavior. Since the turn of the century, a great wealth of data on spinal functions has been accumulated, thus allowing a detailed description of motor control at the spinal level. For neonatal studies, this description is particularly advantageous, since the motor behavior of the newborn seems to be mainly under the control of the spinal cord and the medulla. On the other hand, our sparse knowledge of the neurophysiologic mechanisms of higher motor control, even in the adult, may

well account for a tremendous overestimation of the significance of the spinal cord in neonatal motoricity.

2. Spinal Cord and Peripheral Nerves

The segmental efferent innervation of skeletal muscle (Fig. 1) is furnished by motoneurons with different axonal calibers of the Aα type. The larger neurons prefer a more phasic, the smaller ones a more tonic, discharge pattern.[57,87,97] The smallest motoneurons, with axons belonging to the Aγ group, are not directly engaged in muscle contraction and limb movement. Activating the intrafusal muscle fibers inside the muscle spindle stretch receptors, the γ or fusimotoneurons increase the afferent discharge frequency of the receptors and their sensitivity to stretch.[107,114,123] The fusimotoneurons can be subdivided by means of different

Franz J. Schulte · Department of Pediatrics, University of Göttingen, Göttingen, Germany

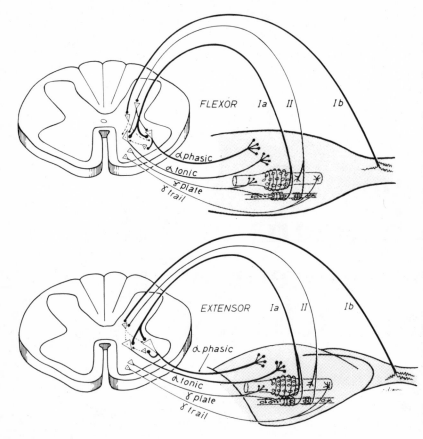

FLEXOR   Ia   II   Ib

α phasic
α tonic
γ plate
γ trail

EXTENSOR   Ia   II   Ib

α phasic
α tonic
γ plate
γ trail

Fig. 1. Diagram of important pathways in the spinal motor system for flexor muscles (top) and for extensor muscles (bottom). (———) Excitatory connections; (———) inhibitory connections. (α phasic) Phasic α-motoneurons that activate skeletal muscles and generally cause fast movements by means of short bursts of action potentials; (α tonic) tonic α-motoneurons that activate skeletal muscles for longer periods of contraction by means of a series of repetitive action potentials. While still within the gray matter, axon collaterals of the α-motoneurons activate Renshaw cells, which act as inhibitors of α-motoneurons. (γ-plate and γ-trail) Fusimotoneurons innervating muscle fibers within the muscle spindles (intrafusal muscle fibers). (Ia, II, Ib) Sensory afferent nerve fibers of muscle receptors activated by stretch. Reproduced from Schulte.[192a] Courtesy of Hippokrates Verlag, Stuttgart.

endings into γ-plate and γ-trail fibers, the former producing static, the latter producing dynamic, changes in the afferent discharge pattern.[14,15,35]

Two different types of intrafusal muscle fibers act on the sensory end-organ from the inside of the receptor: the nuclear bag and the nuclear chain muscle fibers.[29] Spiral or semispiral endings of the group Ia and group II fiber afferents are twisted around both. Group Ia fiber afferents produce monosynaptic excitation of the homonymous α-motoneurons while inhibiting motoneurons of antagonistic muscles, thus forming the proprioceptive reflex arc.[56,106,127,135,136] The group II fiber afferents, however, are monosynaptically connected only with flexor motoneurons, whereas even homonymous extensor motoneurons are inhibited via interneurons.[63,118] The Golgi tendon organ or group Ib afferents are connected with homonymous α-motoneurons via inhibitory interneurons, thus producing what is called "autogenetic inhibition."[76]

The α-motoneurons, before leaving the gray matter of the spinal cord, branch out into collaterals, activating inhibitory interneurons called "Renshaw cells."[59,173,174] Both Renshaw cells and Golgi tendon organs comprise the main parts of two negative feedback systems, limiting the discharge frequency and the recruitment of spinal motoneurons (see Section 2.6).

2.1. Immature α-Motoneurons

The differences between immature and mature motoneurons become evident in the two bioelectric properties of nerve cells: (1) the computational process of synaptic excitation or inhibition and (2) the conduction of impulses along myelinated axons.

2.1.1. Synaptic Transmission

No direct information on the biochemical or electrophysiologic process of intracentral impulse transmission in human infants is available. Eccles and Willis[64] showed that in kittens, the postsynaptic potentials of immature motoneurons are greater than in adult cats. Thus, with an afferent volley produced by an electric stimulus to certain dorsal root fibers, a pool of motoneurons can easily be activated. In adult cats, however, an even greater number of ventral horn cells, although reached by the afferent volley, is not activated, since the depolarization does not reach the threshold. These motoneurons in the subliminal fringe can easily be coactivated either by additional, excitatory impulses after a slight delay, i.e., temporal summation, or by other afferent sources, i.e., spatial summation. The subliminal fringe of preactivated motoneurons is considerably smaller in newborn kittens compared with adult cats.[64] If this difference holds true for human infants as well, the recruitment of motoneurons, i.e., the increasing strength of muscle contraction, would occur stepwise, rather than smoothly.

2.1.2. Impulse Conduction

If the motoneuron membrane is depolarized to a certain degree by a sufficient amount of excitatory, postsynaptic potentials, a spike potential or "all-or-none" action potential is generated at the axon hillock of the nerve cell. This spike potential progresses along the myelinated axon by means of saltatory conduction, the action potential being regenerated at each Ranvier node.[147,214] The conduction velocity is dependent on the thickness of the myelin sheath,[66,180] which probably is positively related to the distance between the Ranvier nodes. Since myelination increases with age from conception,[41,65,207] measuring the impulse conduction speed in peripheral nerves of human infants is a rather simple method of determining the menstrual age[26,54,180,203] (Fig. 2). Nerve conduction velocity, in contrast to many other parameters, seems to be almost independent of abnormal influences.[196] Infants of either diabetic or toxemic mothers, dysmature and small-for-date, or hydropic babies and infants with moderate to severe but nonfatal degrees of intranatal hypoxia have a conduction velocity normal for conception age (Tables I and II). The slow conduction rate of the immature nerve has little bearing on the functional incapacity of the newborn infant.[192] The interneuron and the neuromuscular distances are shorter, thus more than compensating for the low speed (Fig. 3). Other characteristics of the nerve, however, such as maximum spike frequency, afterpotentials, oscillation of the membrane potential, and excitability,

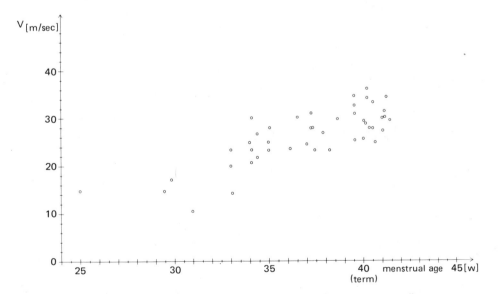

Fig. 2. Ulnar motor nerve conduction velocity in relation to menstrual age. Nerve conduction velocity increases with age. Reproduced from Schulte.[192] Courtesy of Springer-Verlag, Berlin.

Table I. Statistical Analysis (Student's *t* Test) of Nerve Conduction Velocity in Normal, Full-Term, and Preterm Small-for-Date Infants[a,b]

| | | | | N. ulnaris | | | | | | N. tibialis | |
| | | | | | Conduction velocity | | | | | | Conduction velocity | |
Group	n	Menstrual age (weeks)	Weight (g)		(m/sec)	β (P = 0.05)	n	Menstrual age (weeks)	Weight (g)		(m/sec)	β (P = 0.05)
Term	19	40.6 ± 0.61	3345 ± 349	★	30.4 ± 3.40	31.87 / 28.82	15	40.5 ± 0.20	3355 ± 316	★	25.8 ± 2.0	26.85 / 24.82
Small-for-dates	16	40.3 ± 1.58	2064 ± 183	▲	32.4 ± 7.25	35.95 / 28.85	24	40.7 ± 1.78	2139 ± 231	▲	23.68 ± 4.02	25.29 / 22.07
Preterm	17	35.8 ± 1.64	2129 ± 243	★▲	25.9 ± 4.08	27.87 / 24.0	20	36.3 ± 1.56	2224 ± 219	★▲	18.6 ± 3.71	20.26 / 17.0

N. ulnaris:
★ t = 4.520, P < 0.001
▲ t = 3.360, P < 0.005

N. tibialis:
★ t = 5.934, P < 0.001
▲ t = 6.516, P < 0.001

[a] From Schutte *et al.*[203]

[b] In each group, the mean values and first S.D.s are given for conceptional ages and body weights at the time of examination and for both ulnar and tibial nerve conduction velocities. In addition, the confidence interval for the mean value of the conduction velocities is indicated under β when the probability is 95% (P = 0.05). Statistically significant differences in ulnar or tibial nerve conduction velocities among the three groups of infants are indicated by (★) and (▲) with the corresponding *t* values and the level of probability (P).

Table II. Regression and Correlation Coefficients for Ulnar Nerve Conduction Velocity in Relation to Menstrual Age [a,b]

| Group | Number | Menstrual age (weeks) | | b_{yx} | r | $P<$ | $\bar{y}_i$(m/sec) |
		Range	Mean				
Normal infants	38	25–42	37.5	1.08	0.78	0.001	29.6 ± 3.4
Abnormal infants	43	34–47	39.5	1.07	0.63	0.001	30.9 ± 3.9

b_{yx} = regression coefficient
r = correlation coefficient (Pearson)
$\bar{y}_i$ = conduction velocity extrapolated at 40 weeks (mean and 1 S.D.)

$$y_i = y - b_{yx}(x - x_i)$$

→ 40 weeks
→ actual menstrual age
→ regression coefficient
→ actual conduction velocity
→ conduction velocity, extrapolated at 40 weeks' menstrual age

[a] From Schulte *et al.*[196]
[b] Both coefficients, as well as the conduction velocity, extrapolated to 40 weeks of menstrual age, are strikingly similar in normal, newborn infants and in those under various abnormal influences during pregnancy, birth, and the postnatal period.

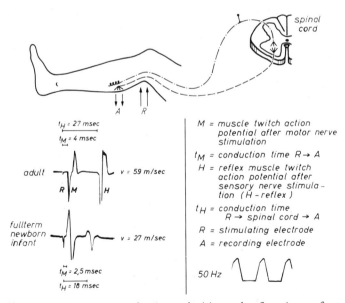

Fig. 3. Motor nerve conduction velocities and reflex times of an adult human subject compared with those of a normal, full-term newborn infant. Although motor nerve conduction velocity is significantly lower in the newborn infant, reflex times are shorter than in the adult because of the smaller distances. Reproduced from Schulte.[192] Courtesy of Springer-Verlag, Berlin.

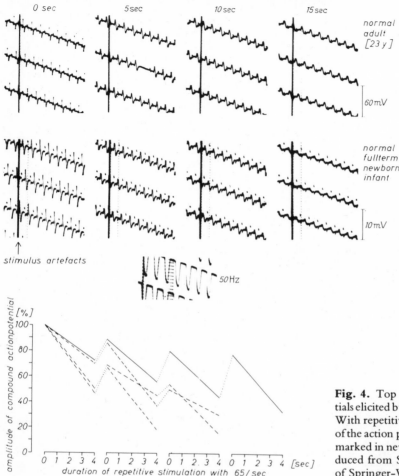

Fig. 4. Top and bottom: Muscle action potentials elicited by repetitive motor nerve stimulation. With repetitive motor stimulation, the amplitude of the action potential decreases; this effect is more marked in newborn infants than in adults. Reproduced from Schulte and Michaelis.[194] Courtesy of Springer-Verlag.

also vary with myelination.[106,128] We have, as yet, no information about the significance of these parameters in the course of development toward a greater complexity of nervous functions.

2.2. Neuromuscular Transmission

The nerve action potential is transmitted to the muscle at the neuromuscular synapses by means of a chemical transmitter, acetylcholine.[48] Whereas the maximum spike frequency electrically imposable on the neuronal axon is about several hundreds per second, being limited only by the refractory period, which is on the order of 1 msec, the neuromuscular transmission, including its recovery cycle, is a more time-consuming process with a tendency to fatigue, the latter being more marked in newborn

infants than in adults.[45,194] Neuronal spike frequencies of 50/sec are not transmitted to the muscle without decay.[43,90] The higher the frequency, the more motor end-plates become refractory, and the resulting compound muscle action potential decreases (Fig. 4). It is still debatable whether the more limited neuromuscular transmission in the newborn infant is due to the immaturity of the enzyme systems of acetylcholine metabolism, or whether it is due merely to differences in the distribution of electrolytes on both sides of the membrane. Both hypocalcemia and hyperpotassemia, i.e., a decreased potassium gradient from intracellular to extracellular fluid, are able to impair the neuromuscular transmission of impulses.[43,44,69,213]

In preterm newborn infants, the neuromuscular transmission capacity is unknown, and particularly in very immature infants, it may be too limited to allow maximum muscle contraction over a longer period of time. In full-term newborn infants, however, neuromuscular transmission is not an important factor limiting muscle power.

2.3. α-Motoneurons and Muscle Spindles of the Neonate

2.3.1. Intrafusal Innervation

As shown in Fig. 1, the intrafusal muscle fibers of the spindle stretch receptors are activated by γ-motoneurons. No information is available about γ-motoneuron and intrafusal activity in human infants, the data being extremely sparse even for adult humans. In kittens, the intrafusal activity maintained by γ-motoneuron innervation seems to be less tonic than that in adult cats.[208] This would imply decreased afferent muscle spindle activity, the depolarization pressure, i.e., the excitatory drive on motoneurons, being diminished.[206]

The lack of γ-motoneuron support might be responsible for the absence of tonic, myotatic reflexes in preterm infants of less than 34 weeks of menstrual age (see Section 2.4.2).[2,183,184,200]

2.3.2. Group I Muscle Spindle Afferent Fibers

Sensory nerve fibers with the highest conduction velocity, originating from spiral structures winding around intrafusal muscle cells, form the afferent pathway of the proprioceptive feedback circuit illustrated in Fig. 1. The peripheral endings of these fibers, being the transducer membrane of the receptor, are depolarized by stretching of the muscle.

This generator potential is transformed quantitatively by means of frequency modulation into spike potentials at the first Ranvier node. Maximum muscle spindle discharge frequency and its maintenance over a long period of time are severely restricted in the newborn kitten compared with the adult animal.[208] Both the absence of the tonic γ-motoneuron activity described above and particular membrane properties of the immature, receptive end-organ may account for the lack of tonicity in the afferent muscle spindle discharge pattern, which, in turn, implies low γ-motoneuron activity and skeletal muscle hypotonia.

2.4. Proprioceptive Reflexes of Newborn Infants

2.4.1. Phasic T and H Reflexes

A brisk tap on the tendon stretches the muscle, thereby exciting muscle spindles, which, in turn, activate spinal α-motoneurons, which give rise to a quick muscle twitch, called the *T (tendon) reflex*. The receptors responsible for this reflex are located in the muscle, rather than in the tendon.[100,101] The same reflex can be elicited by an electrical stimulus to the afferent nerve, and it is then called the *H (Hoffmann) reflex*. Both types of phasic, proprioceptive reflexes can already be obtained in the newborn infant, provided the infant is not asleep, and particularly not in active, or rapid eye movement (REM), sleep (see Section 2.5). In both animal and human, adult as well as newborn, muscle stretch reflexes are diminished or even abolished during active sleep.[82,83,98,99,169] That it is has led to considerable confusion in pediatric textbook literature

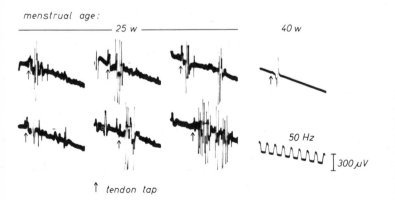

menstrual age:

————————— 25 w ————————— 40 w

50 Hz

↑ *tendon tap*

300 μV

Fig. 5. Monosynaptic stretch reflex elicited by a tendon tap in a preterm infant (25 weeks of menstrual age). The reflex consists in a burst of impulses, rather than of one compound muscle action potential. Reproduced from Schulte *et al.*[196a] Courtesy of Academic Press, London.

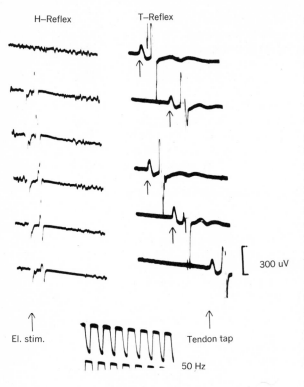

H–Reflex   **T–Reflex**

El. stim.

Tendon tap

50 Hz

300 uV

Fig. 6. Monosynaptic reflex of m. gastrocnemius in a 1–day–old neonate. Left: H (Hoffman) reflex elicited by electrical stimulation of sensory nerve fibers of the n. tibialis; right: T (tendon) reflex elicited by tendon tap. Reproduced from Schulte and Schwenzel.[195] Courtesy of S. Karger.

about stretch reflexes. Since the examination of the newborn infant is sometimes accidentally carried out while the subject is asleep, many authors have erroneously assumed that some neonates do not have certain stretch reflexes. Even in the youngest preterm infant that we were able to study (25 weeks of menstrual age), proprioceptive reflexes in the quadriceps could be elicited by tendon tap.[205] The reflex response, however, consisted of a burst of desynchronized impulses (Fig. 5), rather than of a single compound muscle action potential, as is usually seen in newborn infants above 30 weeks of menstrual age (Fig. 6).

2.4.2. Tonic Myotatic Reflexes

In the normal adult human, a slow, gradual muscle stretch does not lead to an increased resistance against passive movement. In this case, the afferent

drive from the muscle stretch receptors remains subthreshold, and motoneurons are not activated to a substantial degree. Contrarily, in healthy, full-term newborn infants, tonic myotatic reflexes, i.e., an increasing resistance against gradual stretch, can be elicited in almost all flexor and many extensor muscles.[3,4,6,157] A great number of the so-called "primitive" reflexes depend on the tonic, myotatic reflex activity of the newborn—in the awake, full-term infant, an extension of the lower arms is followed by a rather quick recoil into the flexed position (Fig. 7). If an infant lying on his back is pulled by his hands into the sitting position, the arms remain flexed (Fig. 8, top). The palmar grasp can be reinforced by gradually extending the baby's fingers (see Section 2.5). A newborn infant standing on his legs usually activates hip and knee extensors if the body weight is allowed to act on these muscles (see Section 2.7.1). The motoneuron activity demonstrated electromyographically during the recoil maneuver provides clear evidence that this phenomenon is a spinal reflex, rather than being caused by mere elastic properties of muscles and ligaments only.

Tonic myotatic reflexes are more easily obtained in flexor than in extensor muscles. They can hardly be demonstrated in infants of less than 34 weeks of menstrual age, and are normally present at 36 weeks.[2,140,183,184] One of the most characteristic behavioral patterns in newborn infants is posture. During both waking and sleeping in full-term infants, the arms and legs are usually flexed. In preterm infants of less than 34 weeks of gestational age, the arms and legs quite frequently remain extended (Fig. 9). Since at rest no predominant flexor muscle activity could be detected electromyographically, some authors speculated that neonatal flexor posture is due to mechanical factors such as gravity and tissue structure, rather than to innervational muscle tone.[52,129,198] As documented in Chapter 30, however, there is ample evidence from neonatal reflex behavior that with increasing gestational age, tonic myotatic flexor reflexes strongly increase. Any stretching of flexor muscles leads to a tonically sustained flexor motoneuron activity. Despite the aforementioned speculations, no one can seriously doubt that palmar and plantar responses, closure of the fist, and the so-called "second phase" of the Moro reflex are due to tonic flexor activity. Furthermore, one cannot possibly explain abnormally strong flexor posture in neonates with CNS damage on the basis of mechanical

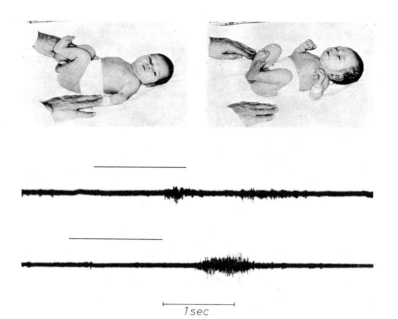

Fig. 7. Stretch and release of the forearms followed by a quick recoil due to biceps muscle activity. Stretching of the elbows is indicated by a horizontal line over each of the biceps electromyograms of two recoils given below.

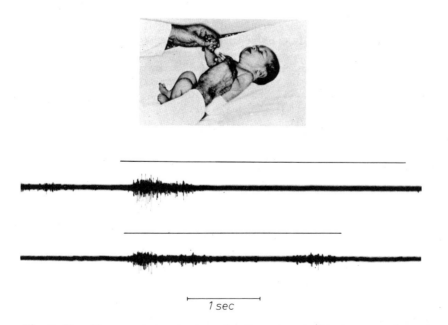

Fig. 8. Top: Photograph showing how the elbows remain flexed while the infant is pulled to a sitting position. Bottom: Electromyograms of biceps muscle activity during two traction responses (traction indicated by a horizontal line over each tracing).

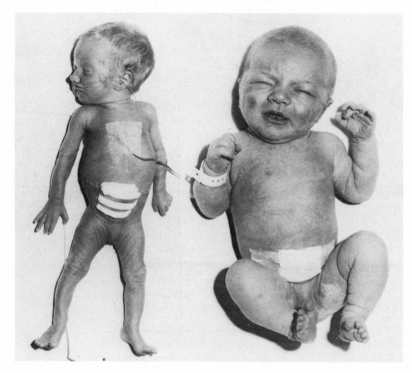

Fig. 9. Right: In the healthy, awake full-term newborn infant, the arms and legs are flexed and return immediately to this position when extended. Left: In the healthy, awake preterm infant of 34 weeks of gestational age, the arms and legs frequently remain extended for a certain period of time.

factors only. Thus, we must assume that with increasing gestational age, flexor muscles become more easily activated. This might, additionally, have some influence on tissue structure—as it has in spastic adults—which in turn promotes flexor posture even at rest.

2.5. Cutaneous Afferents and Exteroceptive Reflexes of the Newborn Infant

Stimulation of cutaneous receptors leads to a more or less stereotyped activation of spinal motoneurons via many interneurons—exteroceptive polysynaptic reflexes. Reactions of this type are numerous, and they are an essential part of the neurological examination of infants as well as of adults. In general, for all exteroceptive reflexes, the tendency to irradiate is greater in more immature subjects.[23,104]

In the newborn, there seems to be a principal difference in the behavior of proprioceptive and exteroceptive reflexes during sleep. Whereas proprioceptive reflexes are diminished in active, i.e., REM, sleep, exteroceptive reflexes are either diminished in quiet sleep (non-REM) or equally strong during wakefulness and both sleep states.[124,169] In particular, motor responses to nociceptive stimuli, namely, the abdominal skin, and the Babinski reflex were found to be surprisingly independent of the infant's behavioral state.[124]

The palmar and plantar *grasp reflexes* were first described by Robinson[177] and von Woerkom,[225] respectively, and were more extensively investigated by Peiper.[157] The response can already be elicited in the fetus (see Chapter 30), and is present in every healthy newborn infant, both preterm and full-term.[49,161,212] The afferent stimulus consists of a light touch on the palmar or plantar surface of the infant's hands and feet with the examiner's finger or with a pencil.[160] The infant closes his fingers in the following order: 3, 4, 5, 1, 2.[163] This exteroceptive reflex can easily be reinforced by an additional proprioceptive stimulus, i.e., stretching of the flexor muscles of the fingers. The grasp is stronger during sucking.[163]

The *withdrawal reflex* is elicitable in every healthy newborn infant, both preterm and full-term, from any point on the skin. A semiquantitative assessment of the response strength and speed is most easily obtained, however, when the stimulus is applied to the sole of the foot.[9] The leg is held in the flexed position as long as the stimulus lasts.[157] In newborn infants born in breech presentation, the flexion response is hardly visible, and, paradoxically, a vigorous extension occurs.[165]

The *Babinski reflex,* which is already present in the preterm newborn infant, is part of the withdrawal reflex. Richards and Irwin[176] described seven different response patterns ranging from flexion to extension of one to five toes. Stimulating the skin of the foot only at the lateral and posterior part of the sole or at the instep avoids the grasp response and usually leads to the well-known extension of the big toe while the other toes are spread. In the newborn infant, however, this response might have a significance different from that in older children and adults. Wartenberg[224] suggested that the spread of four toes is part of a climbing pattern, and according to Schoch,[189,190] the extension of the first toe is the release part of a grasp reflex. This author is still inclined to believe that the true Babinski reflex pattern in the newborn infant, as well as in abnormal adults, is due to the lack of certain supraspinal influences mediated via the pyramidal tract, although Peiper[157] disagreed with this hypothesis.

The *magnet response* is elicited by light pressure on the sole of the foot while the leg is flexed. The response consists of a continuous slow extension as long as the examiner maintains contact with the infant's foot.[12] Peiper[157] states that the magnet response can be elicited in only 20% of newborn infants, and Lenard *et al.*[124] found a positive response in the awake and quiet, healthy, full-term infant only occasionally.

The *palmomental reflex* was first described by Marinesco and Radovici.[134] Scratching of the infant's hypothenar with the fingernail sometimes leads to a muscle contraction with lifting of the chin.

The *Babkin reflex*[9,126] is present with particular strength in preterm infants.[151] While the examiner applies firm pressure to the infant's palms, the neonate opens his mouth and occasionally lifts or turns his head.

The *lip tap reflex* was first described by Escherich.[67] Some authors believed this reflex to be abnormal, occurring only with hypocalcemia.[216] Many authors, however, confirmed the original observation, noting that this reflex occurs in almost every healthy, full-term infant.[77,109,217] A sharp tap on the upper or lower lip is followed by a protrusion of the lips. Prechtl *et al.*[169] showed electromyographically that the lip tap response consists of two components with different latencies and duration. The first quick component is probably proprioceptive in origin, whereas the following long-lasting contraction of the orbicularis oris is supposed to be an exteroceptive reflex.

The *rooting reflex,* apparently first described by Pepsy,[159] as well as by Gentry and Aldrich,[79] was later studied by many authors.[157] Tickling of the skin at the corner of the infant's mouth is followed by a rotation of the head to the side of the stimulus. The same stimulus applied to the upper lip leads to mouth-opening and retroflection of the head; applied to the lower lip, it leads to mouth-opening and jaw-dropping. This response is particularly strong when the infant is hungry.[167,168] If the stimulus is painful, the infant turns his head in the opposite direction.[7] The lip tap reflex and the rooting response are incorporated in the mechanism of food uptake. The main parts of this complex behavior, sucking and swallowing, are described in Chapter 30.

The *glabella reflex* is elicitable in newborn infants of more than 32–34 weeks of menstrual age through a sharp tap on the glabella.[178] The stimulus response is a blink with a short-lasting, tight closure of the eyelids.[72,79,115,118] Like the lip tap, this response probably consists of two components; the short blink is a monosynaptically mediated proprioceptive reflex of the m. orbicularis occuli, and the following tonic contraction is maintained by polysynaptic activation of the same motoneurons.

A similar type of *blink reflex* can be elicited by tactile stimulation of the eyelashes and the cornea, as well as with sound and with bright light.[164] A tonically sustained contraction of the eyelids can easily be obtained through strong and unpleasant stimuli to the taste buds.[157]

The *pupil reaction to light,* an exteroceptive reflex in a broader sense, appears between 29 and 31 weeks of menstrual age.[27,178] The dilatation of the pupils after painful skin stimuli was regularly found by Bartels[16] and Bach[11] in full-term and occasionally in preterm newborn infants.[155]

The *abdominal skin reflexes,* contrary to the assertions of several authors, are always present in full-term newborn infants, providing the subjects are not crying heavily with vigorous contraction of the abdominal muscles.[89,124]

The *Galant reflex,*[76] or incurvation of the trunk,

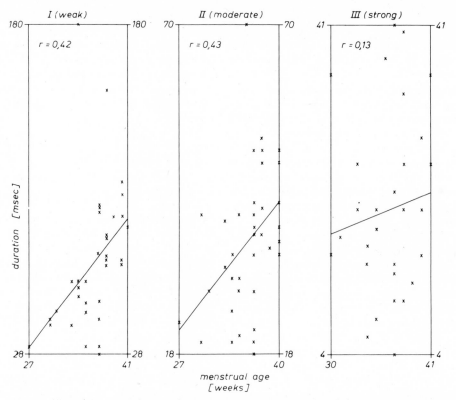

Fig. 10. Dependence of the duration of the postreflex silent period (m. quadriceps) on background muscle activity (weak, moderate, or strong), and its slight increase with conceptional age. The Pearson correlation coefficient *r* is 0.42 during weak and 0.43 during moderate background activity. However, the duration of the silent period, subsequent to a monosynaptic reflex and elicited during strong muscle contraction, shows only little variation with age.

first described by Bertolotti,[24] is present in all normal full-term and most preterm infants.[110] A skin stimulus along a line parallel to the spine is followed by an extension of the lower trunk and an incurvation toward the side of the stimulus. Concomitantly, the contralateral hip and knee joints are extended.

The *cremaster reflex* is present in all full-term, and most preterm, newborn boys,[157] and is apparently not different from the same response in adults.

The *anal retraction response* is an important test for infants with spina bifida.

Vlach[219,220] was able to demonstrate some principal rules for the occurrence of numerous exteroceptive reflexes in the newborn infant. Skin stimuli above flexors usually activate the motoneurons of the underlying muscles. The corresponding extensor activation from the skin is hardly

visible or at least weak. The same results were obtained in newborn cats.[65] For the trunk and the proximal part of the extremities, the sensitive area is located over the muscle bulk. For the distal part of the extremities, the exteroceptive reflexes are usually elicitable from skin areas over the tendons.

2.6. Spinal Inhibition

"No excitation without inhibition": this basic rule of CNS activity holds for neonatal, spinal motoricity as well. The monosynaptic, compound reflex action potential, as well as any synchronous burst of motoneuron activity, is followed by a short period of more or less complete inhibition, indicated by a silent period in the background activity called "Innervationsstille."[100] In newborn infants, the duration of the silent period is dependent on the amount of background activity, i.e., the depolarization pressure on spinal motoneurons.[195] The duration of the silent period decreases with increasing background activity (Fig. 10), indicating that spinal inhibitory mechanisms can in part be outweighed by supraspinal, excitatory drive.[150]

The duration of the silent period, i.e., the amount of inhibitory influences on spinal motoneurons subsequent to the monosynaptic stretch reflex, increases with menstrual age (Fig. 10). However, the minimum duration of the silent period after the monosynaptic reflex is almost equal for all ages during very strong supraspinal motoneuron excitation.[201] This observation is consistent with the hypothesis that a minimum of postexcitatory inhibition, possibly due to basic membrane phenomena, is well developed in preterm infants of 30 weeks of menstrual age. Surplus inhibition, however, due to more complex, computational synaptic mechanisms in the spinal cord, proceeds with menstrual age.

Spinal motoneuron inhibition is guaranteed by several mechanisms (see Fig. 1):

1. Each spike potential is followed by membrane hyperpolarization due to a postexcitatory increase of potassium membrane permeability. This membrane potential shift is called "positive after potential."[96,154]

2. Each motoneuron action potential, before leaving the gray matter of the spinal cord, activates interneurons called "Renshaw cells," which inhibit the surrounding motoneurons. This pathway represents an intraspinal, inhibitory feedback mechanism, and is already active in newborn kittens.[144]

3. The reflex muscle twitch activates Golgi tendon organs, the afferent impulses of which inhibit spinal motoneurons via interneurons. This pathway represents a musculospinal inhibitory feedback mechanism (see Section 2).

4. Muscle spindle afferents are silenced by the reflex shortening of the muscle; thus, part of the continuous afferent drive of spinal motoneurons from peripheral sources is eliminated for the short period of time while the muscle is contracting.

5. Afferent fibers from both supraspinal and peripheral sources, before reaching spinal motoneurons, branch into collaterals with end-organs located at presynaptic excitatory nerve fibers. Action potentials reaching these presynaptic end-organs depolarize the underlying nerve fibers, thus diminishing the amplitude of the action potentials traveling along these fibers and thereby also the amount of transmitter secreted at the axodendritic motoneuron synapses. This mechanism is called "presynaptic inhibition."[58,60–62,64] Thus, synaptic excitation of spinal motoneurons simultaneously produces presynaptic inhibition of the surrounding ventral horn cells.

2.7. Complex Motor Phenomena of the Newborn Infant

2.7.1. Placing and Standing Response

If an infant is lifted while its insteps are touching the edge of a table, the feet are lifted and placed on the table.[182] When the trunk of the infant is lowered after this placing response, a proprioceptive, tonic myotatic stretch reflex is produced, and the leg extensors become activated. This standing response is variable but usually present in healthy, full-term newborn infants.[140]

2.7.2. Walking

If the infant is held in an upright position, and the soles of the feet are allowed to touch the surface of the table, stepping movements occur. The steps usually cross each other.[156,211] The same movements can be elicited in any position of the body, horizontal or vertical, head up or head down, or even without the soles of the feet touching the table.[6,157]

2.7.3. Crawling

If the infant is awake and lying on his abdomen, crawling movements occur that can be reinforced by a light push on the soles of the feet.[18,25,211]

2.7.4. Asymmetrical Tonic Neck Reflex

This reflex, first described in animals by Magnus,[130] can sometimes be demonstrated in newborn infants.[37,81,110,116,117,186] If the infants head is turned to the right and left, after a few seconds the extremities become extended on the side to which the face is turned, whereas the contralateral arm and leg remain flexed. In many normal newborn infants, this response can hardly be seen because of interfering spontaneous movements. Electromyographically, however, an ipsilateral increase of

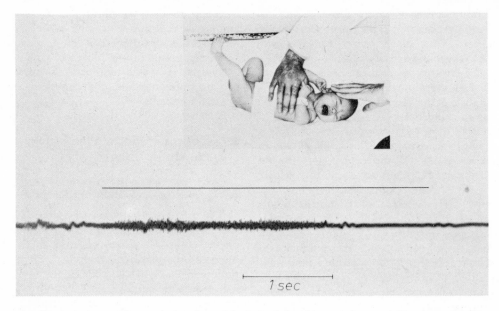

Fig. 11. Asymmetrical tonic neck reflex. If the infant's head is turned to one side, the extremities on that side are stretched. Even if this reflex cannot be detected visually, an increase of extensor muscle activity can usually be recorded electromyographically, as the tracing illustrates. The head-turning is indicated by the horizontal line over the tracing.

extensor muscle activity can always be demonstrated while the face is turned to one side (Fig. 11). The receptors of this reflex are very likely to be located in the muscles and joints of the neck.

2.7.5. Righting Response

If the head of a healthy, full-term newborn infant is turned to one side, the trunk follows.[178] Again, the afferent sources of the righting reflex are located in the muscles and joints of the neck.

2.7.6. Moro Response

The Moro reflex is a well-known phenomenon in newborn human infants. The motor pattern was first observed by Magnus and Kleijn[131] during dorsal flexion of the infant's head. Moro[142] elicited the reaction with a blow to the infant's mattress. At present, a brief head drop is most commonly used to elicit the Moro response.[164] It is still a matter of controversy whether under normal conditions the main afferent pathway of the reflex originates in the neck muscle[5,6,73,152] or in the labyrinthine receptors.[157,166]

The characteristics of the observed Moro response

pattern are dependent on the infant's gestational age.[10,30,183,184,200] In preterm infants of less than 35 weeks of menstrual age, the reaction consists of a brisk extension and abduction of the upper extremities. The subsequent flexion and abduction component is missing or incomplete (Fig. 12). After 35 weeks of menstrual age, the infant develops the characteristic flexion posture of the full-term neonate. Concomitantly, in the Moro response, extension and abduction decrease, whereas flexion and adduction become increasingly prominent.

Despite the high variability of the Moro response pattern, a statistically significant decrease with age of the triceps/biceps activity ratio can be demonstrated. Electromyographic analysis indicates that flexor predominance, which is dependent on age, is due to an increase of flexor, rather than a decrease of extensor, activity (Fig. 13).

2.7.7. Rhythmic Motoneuron Activity

In some infants, part of the Moro reaction pattern consists of rhythmic, instead of tonic, motoneuron activity (Fig. 14). Frequently, similar rhythms occur spontaneously, particularly when the infant is crying. It is not absolutely clear whether all these

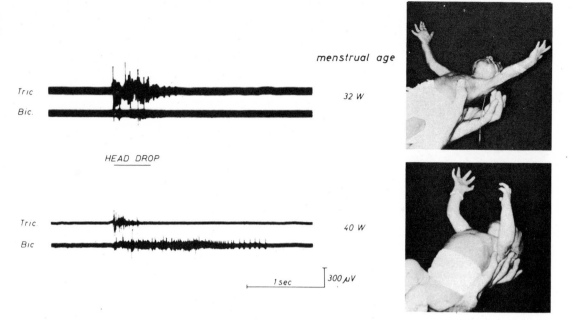

Fig. 12. Moro response at 32 weeks of menstrual age, consisting in extension and abduction of the upper extremities. With increasing maturity, both extension and abduction decrease, while adduction and flexion become more prominent. EMG activity, subsequent to the head drop, starts in the triceps muscle and is outlasted by the biceps in full-term newborn infants. Reproduced from Schulte et al.[200] Courtesy of John Wiley and Sons.

rhythmic motoneuron activities have an identical neurophysiologic background. Most of our own experiments are based on rhythmic activities occurring with the Moro reflex and subsequent to muscle stretch. These rhythms show all the characteristics of a clonus rather than a tremor.[195] In preterm infants of less than 34 weeks of menstrual age, the rhythmic activity in the arm and leg muscles is quite irregular, whereas interval histograms show increasing regularity, i.e., predominating discharge frequencies in more mature infants (Fig. 15). Under abnormal conditions, both the amount and the regularity of rhythmic activity increase. Particularly in hypertonic and hyperexcitable infants, rhythmic motoneuron activity predominates. The clonus frequency is higher in the jaw compared with arm and leg muscles.[191] This difference might have something to do with the length of the reflex arc. On the other hand, the spontaneous discharge frequency of single motoneurons is higher in cranial than in spinal motor nuclei.[185]

3. The Rhombencephalic Reticular Formation and the Neuronal Control of Breathing

The reticular formation, as defined by anatomists,[32] consists of more or less diffuse aggregations of nerve cells and a great wealth of fibers. The reticular formation extends rostrally into the thalamic nuclei, forming part of the midbrain and hypothalamic gray matter. Caudally, the reticular substance ends below the medullary pyramids, the interneuron network of the spinal cord usually not being referred to as reticular formation. As to function, the reticular neurons influence (1) the behavioral state in the sleep/wakefulness cycle[132,144–146]; (2) spinal motoneuron activity, i.e., muscle tone and contraction[133,175,210]; and (3) sensory perception.[19,20,55,187]

In this chapter, we are dealing only with the influence of the reticular formation on muscle tone and contraction.

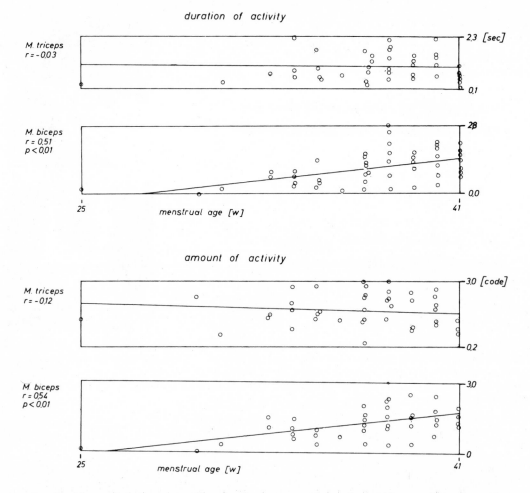

duration of activity

amount of activity

Fig. 13. Moro reflex. Regression lines for the amount and duration of biceps activity rise with increasing menstrual age; the product-moment correlation is significant. Triceps activity shows no significant alteration with age. Reproduced from Schulte et al.[200] Courtesy of John Wiley and Sons.

The comparatively large neurons of the ventro-medial and caudal parts of the rhombencephalic reticular formation give rise to descending, inhibitory pathways to spinal extensor moto-neurons, while at the same time facilitating flexor motoneurons. Laterally, a more extensive part of the reticular formation, reaching from the subthalamus to the rhombencephalon, consists of smaller neurons with excitatory influence on spinal extensor and inhibitory influence on flexor motoneurons.[80,210] The reticulospinal tract is very likely to act via chains on interneurons, predominantly on γ-moto-neurons, but probably on α-motoneurons as well.[86]

The reticular formation receives afferent impulses from almost all structures of the nervous system, both central and peripheral. Descending from the cortex and the basal ganglia as well as from the cerebellum, and ascending from cutaneous as well as from proprioceptive receptors, axon collaterals feed into the rhombencephalic reticular formation. A main source of excitatory afferents for the reticular activating system is provided by the chemo-receptors, their influence on rhombencephalic respiratory neurons being only one part of their alerting influence on the reticular formation.[105,197] Baroreceptor afferents, on the other hand, inhibiting

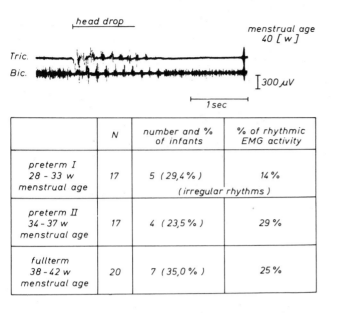

	N	number and % of infants	% of rhythmic EMG activity
preterm I 28 - 33 w menstrual age	17	5 (29,4%)	14%
		(irregular rhythms)	
preterm II 34 - 37 w menstrual age	17	4 (23,5%)	29%
fullterm 38 - 42 w menstrual age	20	7 (35,0%)	25%

Fig. 14. Differences in the Moro reflex. In some newborn infants, particularly in hyperexcitable babies, the response consists in rhythmic, rather than tonic, motoneuron discharges.

the reticular activation system or facilitating the de-activating system, decrease γ-motoneuron activity and muscle tone.[113,199,205]

Little is known about the development of dendrites in the brainstem reticular formation, particularly in structures responsible for respiration, muscle tone, and the control of heart rate and blood pressure. Although the myelination of reticular axons is not complete for 10 years after birth, the influence of supraspinal structures on muscle tone is already quite obvious in the newborn period. Traumatic or hemorrhagic transection of the spinal cord immediately causes skeletal muscle hypotonia, which is followed by spasticity after some days or weeks. For the immature infant, it seems to be particularly difficult to maintain a strong enough depolarization pressure, i.e., excitatory drive on respiratory neurons. Thus, periodic breathing and apneic spells frequently occur in preterm infants of less than 36 weeks of gestational age.[47,70,153]

Apneic spells, together with bradycardia and decreased spinal motoneuron excitability, i.e., skeletal muscle hypotonia, seem to occur more often in active or REM sleep than in the other behavioral states, since in REM sleep, strong descending inhibitory influences act on spinal motoneurons including respiratory neurons.[75,198] Furthermore, the stability of the thoracic wall, which depends heavily on tonic intercostal muscle reflex activity, collapses during REM sleep.[36]

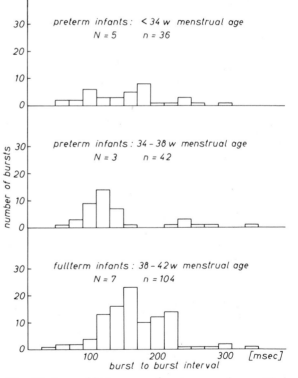

Fig. 15. Interval histograms of motoneuron bursts. The rhythmic motoneuron discharges in the course of a Moro reflex are more regular in full-term than in very immature preterm infants.

4. The Vestibular System and the Nucleus Ruber

Spinal and cranial nerve motoneuron activity is heavily influenced by afferents arising in the vestibular organ, which act via the vestibulospinal and the rubrospinal tract and produce both acceleratory and righting reflexes. In the adult human, these reflexes are partly masked by voluntarily controlled movements, but they are easily elicitable in newborn infants and in animals.

4.1. Acceleratory Reflexes

Linear acceleration and gravity activate the macula receptors of the otolith organs, mainly in the utricle.[39] The corresponding receptors in the saccule are currently believed to be involved in the perception of slow vibration.[137] If the animal is suddenly lowered, the legs become extended and the toes spread. Toward the end of the movement, the legs become flexed. If the animal, standing on its legs, is lifted upward, the legs become flexed and later extended. These reflexes are particularly marked in the forelegs if the animal is in the vertical position, head pointed downward or upward.

Rotatory acceleration of the body around a vertical, a horizontal, or a sagittal axis activates receptors of the christa ampullaris, located in the ampulla of the semicircular canals.[39] The reflex responses are identical in adults and newborn infants. If the infant is held in the upright position and spun around facing the examiner, the head and finally the trunk turn in the direction opposite to that of rotation, and nystagmus is induced with its quick, or refixation, component in the same direction as the rotation. The vestibular organ responds only to a change in the rate of movement, rather than to a steady movement itself. When the rotation is suddenly discontinued, the same motor phenomena occur once again, but in the opposite direction.[1,13,17,55,204] Corresponding head and eye movements can be obtained while turning the infant around each one of the three axes. These are sensitive tests for both eye muscle and vestibular function, but the responses are negative when the infant is asleep.[122]

Thornval,[218] Schur,[204] and Berberich and Wiechers[22] found eye muscle responses similar to those in adults following caloric stimulation of the auditory canal.

If the head is turned slowly to one side or upward and downward, the eyes move in the opposite direction (doll's eye test).[17,68] As for the afferent source of the Moro reflex, it is still debatable whether neck muscle or vestibular receptors are responsible for the doll's eye reflex phenomenon. If the head is turned more rapidly, particularly in hyperexcitable infants, clonic eye muscle activity occurs.[202]

4.2. Righting Reflexes

The head always tends to turn back into the normal or resting position; this righting reflex is guaranteed by certain afferent impulse patterns from the macula receptors, probably in the utricle. If a cat is dropped with its legs upward, the head is immediately rotated and is followed by the upper and in turn by the lower body.[130,171,172] These latter, neck-righting reflexes are guaranteed by the activity of neck and trunk muscle proprioceptors.

5. The Cerebellum

The archicerebellum (nodulus and flocculus) is connected to the vestibular nuclei by both afferent and efferent fibers.[74] Lesions in these structures lead to ataxia of the trunk, even in the sitting position.[51]

The paleocerebellum, or anterior lobe, comprised of the lingula, the lobulus centralis, and culmen, receives afferent inflow from muscle, joint, and skin receptors via the spino- and bulbocerebellar tract.[50,88,209] Most of the efferent fibers originating in the Purkinje cells are interrupted at the cerebellar nuclei, such as the nucleus emboliformis, the nuclei globosi, and primarily the larger cells of the dentate nucleus.[34] Their efferents, in turn, project to the nucleus ruber and the reticular formation. Electrical stimulation of the anterior lobe decreases muscle tone and decerebrate rigidity, while destruction of the lobe leads to increased proprioceptive reflexes, opisthotonus, and tremor.[46,162]

The neocerebellum, or posterior lobe, receives afferent fibers from the contralateral motor cortex as well as from sensory areas of the parietal and occipital cortex. The different parts of the body are topically represented at the cerebellar cortex.[88,92,179] The efferent Prukinje cell fibers in turn project back to the area 4 motor cortex with synaptic relays both at the smaller neurons of the dentate nucleus and at the ventral nucleus of the thalamus.[91,143] The neocerebellum is part of the voluntary motor control system. Its destruction is followed by adiadochokinesis, hypotonia, dysmetria, ataxia, and intention tremor.[51,102,103]

The cerebellum as a whole has no direct connection with the spinal motoneurons. Its influence, therefore, is only a regulating and stabilizing one, rather than an executing one. Complete absence of the organ might be asymptomatic, but its destruction usually implies dysregulation of muscle tone, posture, walking, and an inability to perform voluntary, skilled movements. As far as one can judge from the literature, the cerebellum is of little significance for neonatal motor behavior. Complete absence of the cerebellum, not easy to detect even later in life, can be asymptomatic in the newborn period.

6. The Basal Ganglia

According to anatomic classification, the subcortical nuclei of the forebrain, the caudate nucleus, the putamen, and the pallidum are called "basal ganglia." Modern physiological concepts of a reconsidered, extrapyramidal motor system include such structures as the subthalamic nucleus (corpus Luys), certain parts of the thalamus, the substantia nigra, the nucleus ruber, the cerebellar dentate nucleus, the brainstem reticular formation, and parts of the prefrontal cortical motor area. Hassler[94] showed that this system works by means of several feedback circuits, modifying and adding to the voluntary corticospinal output.[112] The main circuit seems to be formed by connecting fibers from the motor cortex to the putamen,[84] from the putamen to the external and to the internal pallidum, from the pallidum to the nucleus ventralis oralis of the thalamus, and from the thalamus to cortical motor area 6. This positive feedback circuit represents an activating system for corticospinal influences. In addition, there are other direct connections from the motor cortex to the putamen, to the external pallidum, as well as to the rostral nuclei of the thalamus, forming, at least in part, inhibitory short circuits.

The efferent fibers of the basal ganglia to the spinal motoneurons can be considered as two main tracts. From the putamen and the caudate nucleus, the nucleus niger is reached by inhibitory afferents influencing the nitrospinal and reticulospinal activity.[112,222] Lesions in this strionigroreticulospinal system lead to rigidity, alkinesis (poverty of movement), and resting tremor.

A second descending system, originating in the external pallidum, discharges to the subthalamic nucleus (corpus Luys), the nucleus ruber, and the reticular formation influencing rubrospinal activity. Lesions in the striopallidorubroreticulospinal system imply athetosis, chorea, and other forms of hyperkinesis. From each of these brainstem structures— the nucleus ruber, the corpus Luys, and the substantia nigra—reafferent connections feed back into the pallidum.[42,84]

The functional significance of single parts of the extrapyramidal system is still obscure, perhaps because this system works by means of circuits rather than centers. In birds, the basal ganglia, together with the spinal cord, form a motor system capable of producing flying. Highly skilled movements can be obtained from striatal animals (cortex removed),[223] and stimulation of the caudate nucleus can produce both stereotyped movements and an immediate arrest of cortically induced movements that is called the "holding response."[121,139]

Ever since 1913, when Foerster[71] coined the word "Pallidumwesen," neonatal motor behavior has been supposed to be under the exclusive influence of the pallidal neurons. Flexor posture, climbing movements, and grasp and palmomental reflexes recurring in adults with cortical and striatal lesions probably represent the pallidal influences on spinal motoneurons. It is widely assumed that these motor phenomena disappear when the pallidum comes under striatal control.[157] Orthner and Roedar[149] suggested a fascinating comparison of infantile motor development with extrapyramidal motor disturbances before and after stereotactic operations. These authors hypothesize that the choreoathetotic kicking-about of the newborn infant is a pallidum pattern that is replaced some weeks later by more ballistic movements under the influence of the corpus Luys. Interestingly enough, although myelination already occurs at 2–3 months after birth at term, the nucleus niger becomes pigmented only when the extrapyramidal motor skill is almost fully developed at about 3–4 years of age. According to Hassler,[95] the nucleus niger has a direct regulating and desynchronizing effect on spinal motoneurons.

7. The Cerebral Motor Cortex

7.1. Primary Motor Area

In the precentral gyrus (area 4), the nerve cells of the central motoneurons are arranged in a relationship to each other similar to that of the muscles that can be activated by them. This somatotopic organization was postulated by Jackson in 1870,[215] and has been proved by several authors.[28,33,40,158,215,221] It is primarily the pyramid-shaped Betz cells that give rise to descending fibers that activate single spinal motoneurons and, thereby, muscles in a volitional act of movement.

7.2. Supplementary Cortical Motor Areas

Muscle contraction and movement can be obtained by electrical stimulation of areas other than the precentral gyrus. In fact, movement can be elicited from almost the entire surface of the cerebral cortex.[125] Gross movements can be elicited particularly from areas 6 and 8 of the frontal lobe. However, motor nerve cells with pyramidal tract efferents become sparse in passing forward from the central fissure. Area 6 and 8 neurons are part of the extrapyramidal motor system (cortical extrapyramidal system; COEPS), with both efferent and afferent connections to the basal ganglia, the thalamus, and the cerebellum.

7.3. The Pyramidal Tract

Of the fibers of this tract, 31% belong to area 4 motoneurons and only 3% to Betz cells.[119,138] The cellular origin of 20% lies in the 6th area, and of 40% in the postcentral 5th and 7th areas. The majority of the pyramidal tract fibers reach lower motoneurons via interneurons in the segmental level of the spinal cord.

7.4. Evidences of Cortical Motor Control in the Newborn Infant

Peiper[157] thought that neonatal motor behavior was entirely subcortical, but he was constantly searching for cortical nerve cell activity.

Electroencephalographic and evoked response studies have shown that bioelectrical brain activity changes with certain behavioral states and reactions to stimuli, thus indicating that the cortex at least takes part in these states and response patterns.

Dendritic arborization of Betz cells, although occurring predominantly after birth, has already started before birth, particularly in the motor area of the trunk.[170] The myelination of pyramidal tract fibers has started before birth, and we were able to elicit isolated movements of the toes and fingers by electrical stimulation of unclassified cortical brain tissue in newborn infants with exencephaly.

Cortical lesions, due to pre- or perinatal injury and later confirmed by radiographic studies, sometimes present themselves as early as in the newborn period if the infant is carefully examined.

Finally, in neonatal convulsions, cortical convulsive potentials occur synchronously with peripheral massive muscle contractions.

Admittedly, all these factors are not convincing evidence of cortical influence on normal neonatal behavior. However, in view of our present knowledge that behavioral mechanisms are the result of all computational processes in a countless number of neuronal feedback circuits, it is illogical to assume that well-documented cortical activity should have no influence on the infant's behavior.

8. Clinical Applications

8.1. Milestones in Motor Development and the Assessment of Gestational Age

During the past decade, a number of neurophysiological studies of the newborn, although aiming at diagnostic clues, have revealed the great variability of neonatal motor behavior with menstrual age. Both reflexes and complex motor phenomena appear or change at a certain time of the gestational period. A summary of these relationships between menstrual age and behavior compiled by R. Michaelis (Fig. 16) relies mainly on the work of Saint Anne-Dargassies,[183,184] Robinson,[178] Babson and McKinnon,[10] Amiel-Tison,[2] and Michaelis and Shulte.[140]

8.2. Developmental Profile of Preterm and Full-Term Newborn Infants

The relationship between menstrual age and behavior was so striking that several authors suggested the assessment of menstrual age by means

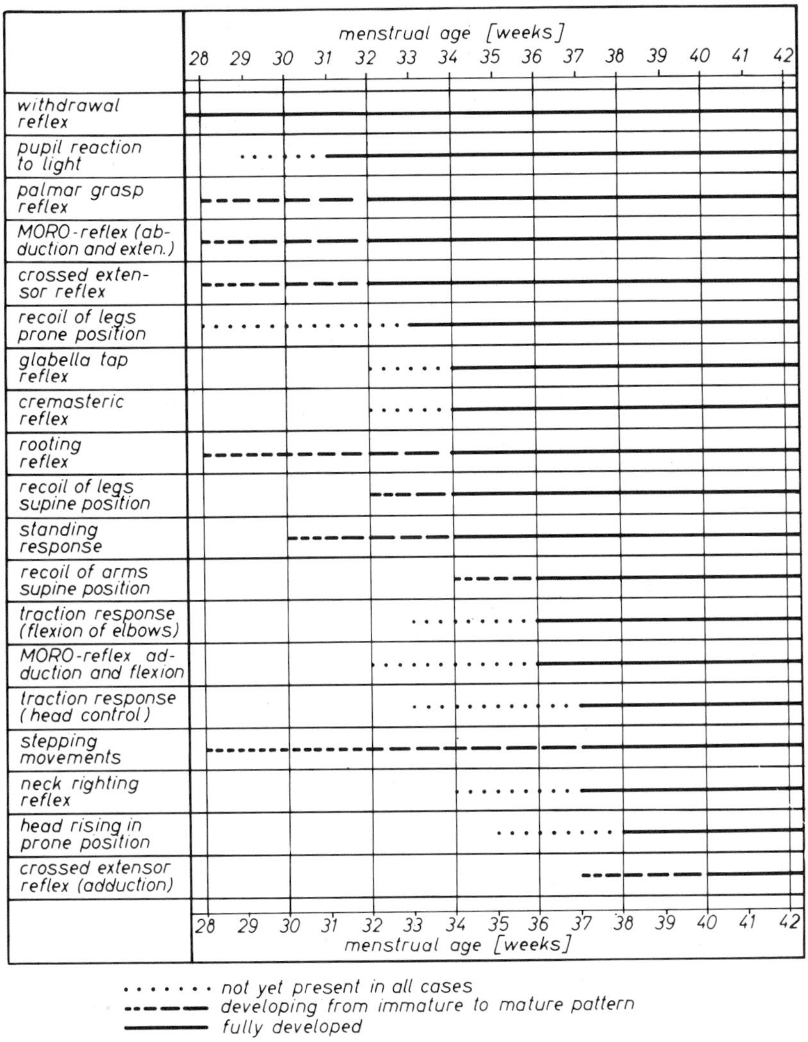

menstrual age [weeks]

	28	29	30	31	32	33	34	35	36	37	38	39	40	41	42

- withdrawal reflex
- pupil reaction to light
- palmar grasp reflex
- MORO-reflex (abduction and exten.)
- crossed extensor reflex
- recoil of legs prone position
- glabella tap reflex
- cremasteric reflex
- rooting reflex
- recoil of legs supine position
- standing response
- recoil of arms supine position
- traction response (flexion of elbows)
- MORO-reflex adduction and flexion
- traction response (head control)
- stepping movements
- neck righting reflex
- head rising in prone position
- crossed extensor reflex (adduction)

menstrual age [weeks]

· · · · · · not yet present in all cases
- - - - - developing from immature to mature pattern
———— fully developed

Fig. 16. Developmental sequence of various reflexes and motor automatisms. Data compiled by R. Michaelis according to Amiel-Tison,[2] Babson and McKinnon,[10] Michaelis *et al.*,[141] Robinson,[178] and Saint Anne-Dargassies.[185,184]

of a neurological examination. Neurophysiological parameters, however, being dependent on menstrual age as well as on pathology, seem to be unreliable for both a neurological diagnosis and an age estimate, if one of these factors is not known. According to our own experience, the problem is even greater, since abnormal motor phenomena frequently mimic immature behavior. An infant supposed to be 32 weeks of menstrual age and having no pupil reaction to light is either younger or abnormal. Thus, every neurological examination becomes an equation with two unknown factors. As shown in Fig. 13, the triceps/biceps ratio of the Moro response decreases with menstrual age, since the flexor component gets stronger when the infant

matures. Flexor motoneuron activity, however, is diminished or even abolished under many abnormal influences; thus, the resulting triceps/biceps Moro response activity ratio increases and may become identical with the ratio of preterm infants.

Thus, estimation of gestational age becomes difficult just in those cases in which it is most urgently needed, i.e., when the infant is abnormal. None of the gestational age estimate scores published thus far can totally overcome this problem.[53] In small-for-dates-infants, for example, gestational age is usually underestimated, since the development of motor behavior, of the EEG, and of somatic parameters is frequently abnormal or retarded or both.[193]

8.3. General Principles for the Neurological Examination of the Newborn Infant

It is not the purpose of this chapter to provide the reader with another scheme for the neurological examination; such schemes have already been published by several authors.[111,164] All of the reflex and motor phenomena described above can be used in a routine or scientific study.

During the examination, the infant should be in a specified behavioral state to make the results comparable from one infant to another. Preferably, the infant should be awake but quiet. The examiner should be familar with the following characteristics of different behavioral states worked out by Wolff[226] and Prechtl and Beintema[164]:

1. Eyes closed, regular respiration, no movements—quiet sleep (non-REM sleep).
2. Eyes closed, irregular respiration, many small movements—active sleep (REM sleep).
3. Eyes open, no gross movements—awake but quiet.
4. Eyes open, gross movements, no crying—awake active.
5. Eyes open or closed, crying.
6. Other states that have to be described.

It is particularly important to know that during active (REM) sleep, proprioceptive reflexes, and during quiet (non-REM) sleep, some exteroceptive reflexes, are diminished or even abolished. During the examination, the infant should be kept in a neutral environmental temperature, i.e., 32°C.

The stimuli and the reflex responses should be quantified as much as possible and controlled by interscorer reliability studies.

Beintema[21] described in detail slight physiologic changes in the motor behavior of the full-term newborn infant during the first days after birth. There is ample evidence now that during the first 3 days of life, many behavioral parameters are less stable than thereafter. Thus, a routine neurophysiological examination should be done between 4 and 8 days after birth, provided the infant is not severely ill and in urgent need of neurological evaluation. Gross abnormalities are obvious at any time.

The results of all single tests can be summarized in order to classify the infant's motor behavior as normal, hyperexcitable, apathetic, hypertonic, hypotonic, hemilateral or focal, convulsive, or comatose. This classification is far from being a diagnosis. Some of these groupings, however, although not specific, are typical for certain perinatal complications.[202] Infants of diabetic mothers are usually hyperexcitable, dysmature, small-for-date infants are frequently hypertonic, and infants with traumatic or inflammatory encephalopathies are usually found to have hemilateral, focal, or convulsive abnormalities.

The neurophysiological classification of the newborn infant, by means of a quantitative assessment of each reflex response, gives little information about the nature of the underlying disease, but indicates the degree and sometimes the localization of the functional disturbance.

9. Perspectives

The historical development of research into the nervous system of newborn infants, both normal and abnormal, is marked by three milestones, and for contemporary researchers, the direction of the fourth step seems already to have been outlined.

The first effort was an anatomic approach linked with the names of Flechsig, Yllpö, and Schwartz. Second were the behavioral motor observations culminating in the work of Peiper and Andre-Thomas. Their work was carried further by a number of eminent authors who determined the third step, which is characterized by a great wealth of quantitative data that were obtained through behavioral observations as well as electrophysiological methods and that were subjected to statistical analysis. This approach can be called "brain engineering" (Prechtl).

Undoubtedly, the fourth phase will be dominated by biochemical results, which will have to be combined with structural, behavioral, and electrophysiological findings as a true correlative study of the neonatal nervous system. Quantification of nerve cell multiplication by DNA and total protein measurement (Dobbing), Goldi technique studies of the development of synaplies (Purpura), combined with behavioral studies with environmental influences as a variable, have hitherto not been applied to CNS motor areas, including respiratory centers.

10. References

1. ALEXANDER, G., 1911, Die Reflexerregbarkeit des Ohrlabyrinthes am menschlichen Neugeborenen, *Z. Sinnesphysiol. Abt. 2* **45**:153–196.

2. AMIEL-TISON, C., 1968, Neurological evaluation of the maturity of newborn infants, *Arch. Dis. Child.* **43**:89–93.

3. ANDRÉ-THOMAS, Y. C., AND AJURIAGUERRA, J., 1949, *Étude Sémiologique du Tonus Musculaire,* Flammarion, Paris.

4. ANDRÉ-THOMAS, Y. C., AND AUTGAERDEN, G., 1959, *Psycho-affectivité des Premiers Mois,* pp. 23 and 96, University Press, Paris.

5. ANDRÉ-THOMAS, Y. C., AND HANON, F., 1947, Les premiers automatismes, *Rev. Neurol. (Paris)* **79**:641.

6. ANDRÉ-THOMAS, Y. C., AND SAINT ANNE-DARG-ASSIES, S., 1952, *Études Neurologiques sur le Nouveau-né et le Jeune Nourrisson,* Masson et Cie, Paris.

7. ANDRÉ-THOMAS, Y. C., CHESNI, Y., AND AUTGAERDEN, S., 1954, A propos de quelques points de sémiology nerveuse du nouveau-né et du jeune nourrisson. Exploration de quelques afférences. Réactions aux excitations digitales et palmaires. Rythme; inhibitions de réflexes. Aptitude statique et locomotrice des membres supérieurs. Affect et affectivité, *Presse Med.* **62**:41–44.

8. BABINSKI, J., 1922, Réflexes de defense, *Rev. Neurol. (Paris)* **28**:1049–1081.

9. BABKIN, P. S., 1955, Jaw-rotating reflex of the head in infants, *Zh. Nevropatol. Psikhiatr. im. S. S. Korsakova* **53**:692–696.

10. BABSON, S. G., AND McKINNON, C. M., 1965, A preliminary report on the neuromuscular milestones in premature infant development, 13th Annual Meeting of the Western Society for Pediatric Research, Portland, Oregon.

11. BACH, L., 1908, *Pupillenlehre. Anatomie, Physiologie und Pathologie. Methodik der Untersuchung,* p. 72, S. Karger, Berlin.

12. BALDUZZI, O., 1932, Die Stützreaktionen beim Menschen in physiologischen und pathologischen Zuständen, *Z. Neurol.* **141**:1–29.

13. BÁRÁNY, R., 1918, Über einige Augen-, und Halsmuskelreflexe bei Neugeborenen, *Acta Otolaryngol. (Stockholm)* **1**:97–102.

14. BARKER, D., 1962, The structure and distribution of muscle receptors, *Symposium on Muscle Receptors,* University of Hong Kong Press.

15. BARKER, D., 1966, The motor innervation of the mammalian muscle spindle, in: *Proceedings of the First Nobel Symposium,* p. 51, Almquist & Wiksell, Stockholm.

16. BARTELS, M., 1904, Pupillenverhältnisse bei Neugeborenen, *Z. Augenheilkd* **12**:638–644.

17. BARTELS, M., 1910, Das Puppenaugenphänomen, *Graefes Arch. Opthalmol.* **76**:1–8.

18. BAUER, J., 1926, Das Kriechphänomen des Neugeborenen, *Klin. Wochenschr.* **4**:1468.

19. VON BAUMGARTEN, R., 1956, Koordinationsformen einzelner Ganglienzellen der rhombencephalen Atemzentren, *Pfluegers Arch. Gesamte Physiol. Menschen Tiere* **262**:573–594.

20. VON BAUMGARTEN, R., MOLLICA, A., AND MORUZZI, G., 1954, Modulierung der Entladungsfrequenz einzelner Zellen der substantia reticularis durch corticofugale und cerebelläre Impulse, *Pfluegers Arch. Gesamte Physiol. Menschen Tiere* **259**:56–78.

21. BEINTEMA, D. J., 1968, *A Neurological Study of Newborn Infants,* Spastics International Medical Publication No. 28, W. Heinemann Medical Books, London.

22. BERBERICH, J., AND WIECHERS, A., 1924, Symptomatologie des Geburtstraumas, *Z. Kinderheilkd.* **38**:59–102.

23. BERGSTRÖM, R. M., HELLSTRÖM, P. E., AND STENBERG, D., 1962, Über die Entwicklung der elektrischen Aktivität im Grosshirn des intrauterinen Meerschweinchen-Fetus, *Ann. Chir. Gynaecol. Fenn.* **51**:460.

24. BERTOLOTTI, M., 1904, Étude sur la diffusion de la zone réflexogène chez les enfants; quelques remarques sur la loi à l'orientation des réflexes cutanés à l'état normal et à l'état pathologique, *Rev. Neurol. (Paris)* **12**:1160–1166.

25. BLANTON, M. G., 1917, The behaviour of the human infant during the first thirty days of life, *Psychol. Rev.* **24**:456–483.

26. BLOM, S., AND FINNSTRÖM, O., 1968, Motor conduction velocities in newborn infants of various gestational ages, *Acta Paediatr. Scand.* **57**:377–384.

27. BOLAFFIO, M., AND ARTOM, G., 1924, Richerche sulla fisiologia del sistema nervosa del feto umano, *Arch. Sci. Biol. (Bologna)* **5**:457–487.

28. VON BONIN, G., AND BAILEY, P., 1947, *The Neocortex of Macaca mulatta,* University of Illinois Press, Urbana.

29. BOYD, J. A., 1962, The nuclear-bag fibre and nuclear-chain fibre systems in the muscle spindles of the cat, in: *Symposium on Muscle Receptors* (R. Granit, ed.), University of Hong Kong Press.

30. BRETT, E. A., 1966, The estimation of foetal maturity by the neurological examination of the neonate, in: *Clinics in Developmental Medicine* (M. Dawkins and B. MacGregor, eds.), pp. 105–117, Publication No. 19 of the Spastics Society for Medical Education, W. Heinemann Medical Books, London.

31. BRETT, E. M., 1966, Measurement of cerebrospinal fluid pressure in infants without puncture, *Dev. Med. Child Neurol.* **8**:207–210.

32. BRODAL, A., 1957, *The Reticular Formation of the Brain Stem. Anatomical Aspects and Functional Correlations,* Oliver and Boyd, London.

33. BRODMANN, K., 1909, Vergleichende Lokalisationslehre der Großhirnrinde in Prinzipien dargestellt auf Grund des Zellenbaues, J. A. Barth, Leipzig.

34. BROOKHARDT, J. M., 1961, The cerebellum, in: *Handbook of Physiology* (J. Field, ed.), Sect. I, Chapt. 51, American Physiological Society, Washington, D.C.

35. TEN BRUGGENCATE, H. G., HENATSCH, H. D., AND

BOSSMANN, H., 1964, Reduction of dynamic sensitivity of primary muscle spindle endings in experimental tremor, *Experientia* **20**:554.

36. BRYAN, A. C., AND BRYAN, M. H., 1974, Respiratory control in newborn infants, read before the Congress for Perinatal Medicine, Berlin.

37. BYERS, R. K., 1938, Tonic neck reflexes in children considered from prognostic standpoint, *Amer. J. Dis. Child.* **55**:696–742.

38. RAMÓN Y CAJAL, S., 1949, *Histologie du Système Nerveuse de l'Homme et des Vertébrés,* p. 949, University Press, Paris.

39. CAMIS, M., 1930, *The Physiology of the Vestibular Apparatus* (R. S. Creed, trans.), Oxford University Press, London.

40. CAMPBELL, A. W., 1905, *Histological Studies on the Localisation of Cerebral Function,* Cambridge University Press.

41. CARPENTER, F. G., AND BERGLAND, R. M., 1957, Excitation and conduction in immature nerve fibers of the developing chick, *Amer. J. Physiol.* **190**:371–376.

42. CARPENTER, M. B., CORREL, J. W., AND HINMEN, A., 1960, Spinal tracts mediating subthalamic hyperkinesia: Physiological effects of selective partial cordotomies upon physikinesia in rhesus monkey, *J. Neurophysiol.* **23**:288–304.

43. CASTILLO, J. DEL, AND KATZ, B., 1954, The effect of magnesium on the activity of motor nerve endings, *J. Physiol. (London)* **124**:553–559.

44. CASTILLO, J. DEL, AND STARK, L., 1952, The effect of calcium ions on the motor end-plate potential, *J. Physiol. (London)* **116**:507–515.

45. CHURCHILL-DAVIDSON, H. C., AND WISE, R. P., Neuromuscular transmission in the newborn infant, *Anesthesiology* **24**:271–278.

46. CONNOR, G. J., 1941, Functional localization within anterior cerebellum, *Proc. Soc. Exp. Biol. Med.* **47**:205–207.

47. DAILY, W. I. R., KLAUS, M., AND MEYER, H. B. P., 1969, Apnea in premature infants: Monitoring incidence, heart rate changes, and an effect of environment temperature, *Pediatrics* **43**:510–519.

48. DALE, H. H., FELDBERG, W., AND VOGT, M., 1936, Release of acetylcholine at voluntary motor nerve endings, *J. Physiol. (London)* **86**:353–380.

49. DIETRICH, H. F., 1957, A longitudinal study of the Babinski and plantar grasp reflexes in infancy, *Amer. J. Dis. Child.* **94**:265–271.

50. DOW, R. S., 1942, Cerebeller action potentials in response to stimulation of cerebral cortex in monkeys and cats, *J. Neurophysiol.* **5**:121–136.

51. DOW, R. S., AND MORUZZI. G., 1958, *The Physiology and Pathology of Cerebellum,* University of Minnesota Press, Minneapolis.

52. DREXLER, L., AND WENGRAF, F., 1959, Die Schlafstellung des Säuglings, *Nord Österr. Z. Kinderheilkd.* **4**:27–38.

53. DUBOWITZ, L. W. S., DUBOWITZ, V., AND GOLDBERG, C., 1970, Clinical assessment of gestational age in the newborn infant, *J. Pediatr.* **77**:1–11.

54. DUBOWITZ, V., WHITTACKER, Ö. F., BROWN, B. H., AND ROBINSON, A., 1968, Nerve conduction velocity, *Dev. Med. Child Neurol.* **10**:741–749.

55. DUENSING, F., AND SCHAEFER, K. P., 1957, Die Neuronenaktivität in der Formatio reticularis des Rhombencephalon beim vestibulären Nystagmus, *Arch. Psychiatr. Nervenkr.* **196**:265–290.

56. ECCLES, J. C., 1964, *The Physiology of Synapses,* Springer-Verlag, Berlin—Göttingen—Heildelberg.

57. ECCLES, J. C., ECCLES, R. M., AND LUNDBERG, A., 1957, The convergence of monosynaptic excitatory afferents on the many different species of alpha motoneurons, *J. Physiol. (London)* **137**:22–50.

58. ECCLES, J. C., ECCLES, R. M., AND MAGNI, F., 1961, Ventral inhibitory action attributable to presynaptic depolarisation produced by muscle afferent volleys, *J. Physiol. (London)* **159**:147–166.

59. ECCLES, J. C., FATT, P., AND KOKETSU, K., 1954, Cholinergie and inhibitory synapses in a pathway from motor-axon collaterals to motoneurones, *J. Physiol. (London)* **126**:524–562.

60. ECCLES, J. C., KOSTYUK, P. G., AND SCHMIDT, R. F., 1962, Presynaptic inhibition of the central actions of flexor reflex afferents, *J. Physiol. (London)* **161**:258–281.

61. ECCLES, J. C., MAGNI, F., AND WILLIS, W. D., 1962, Depolarisation of central terminals of Group I afferent fibres from muscle, *J. Physiol. (London)* **160**:62–93.

62. ECCLES, J. C., SCHMIDT, R. F., AND WILLIS, W. D., 1962, Presynaptic inhibition of the spinal monosynaptic reflex pathway, *J. Physiol. (London)* **161**:282–297.

63. ECCLES, R. M., AND LUNDBERG, A., 1959, Synaptic actions in motoneurones by afferents which may evoke the flexion reflex, *Arch. Ital. Biol.* **97**:199–221.

64. ECCLES, R. M., AND WILLIS, W. D., 1962, Presynaptic inhibition of the monosynaptic reflex pathway in kittens, *J. Physiol. (London)* **165**:403–420.

65. EKHOLM, J., 1967, Postnatal changes in cutaneous reflexes and in the discharge pattern of cutaneous and articular sense organs: A morphological and physiological study in the cat, *Acta Physiol. Scand. Suppl.* **297**:1.

66. ERLANGER, J., AND GASSER, H. S., 1924, Compound nature of action current of nerve as disclosed by cathode-ray oscilloscope, *Amer. J. Physiol.* **70**:624–666.

67. ESCHERICH, T., 1888, Über die Saugbewegungen beim Neugeborenen, *Muench. Med. Wochenschr.* **1**:687–689.

68. ESENTE, L., 1958, *Physiologie de la Vision chez le Prématuré et le Nourrisson Normal*, p. 22, University Press, Paris.

69. FATT, P., AND KATZ, B., 1951, An analysis of the end-plate potential recorded with an intra-cellular electrode, *J. Physiol. (London)* **115**:320–370.

70. FENNER, A., SCHALK, U., AND HOENICKE, H., 1973, Periodic breathing in premature and neonatal babies: Incidence, breathing pattern, respiratory gas tensions, response to changes in the composition of ambient air, *Pediatr. Res.* **7**:174–183.

71. FOERSTER, O., 1913, Das phylogenetische Moment in der spastischen Lähmung, *Klin. Wochenschr.* **1**:1217–1255.

72. FRA, L., AND GANDIGLIO, G., 1966, Risposte faciali reflessi da percussione dei distretti mimici. Studio EMG, *Boll. Soc. Ital. Biol. Sper.* **42**:978–980.

73. FREUDENBERG, E., 1931, in: *Pfaundler-Schloßmanns Handbuch der Kinderheilkunde*, 4th Ed., Vol. 1, p. 785, Springer-Verlag, Berlin.

74. FULTON, J., 1952, *Physiologie des Nervensystems*, p. 483, Georg Thieme, Stuttgart.

75. GABRIEL, M., AND ALBANI, M., 1976, Cardial slowing and respiratory arrest in preterm infants, *Z. Kinderheilkd., Eur. J. Pediatr.* **122**:257.

76. GALANT, S., 1917, Der Rückgratreflex, Dissertation, Basel.

77. GAMPER, E., AND UNTERSTEINER, T. R., 1924, Über eine komplex gebaute postencephalitische Hyperkinese und ihre möglichen Beziehungen zu dem oralen Einstellautomatismus des Säuglings, *Arch. Psychiatr. Nervenkr.* **71**:282–303.

78. GANDIGLIO, G., FRA, L., AND BERGAMASCO, B., 1965, Risposte faciali reflessi da stimolazione elettrica delle tre branche terminali del trigemino. Studio EMG, *Boll. Soc. Ital. Biol. Sper.* **42**:385–388.

79. GENTRY, E. F., AND ALDRICH, C. A., 1948, Rooting reflex in the newborn infant. Incidence and effect on it of sleep, *Amer. J. Dis. Child.* **75**:528–539.

80. GERNANDT, B. E., AND THULIN, C. A., 1955, Reciprocal effects upon spinal motoneurones from stimulation of bulbar reticular formation, *J. Neurophysiol.* **18**:113–129.

81. GESELL, A., 1938, Tonic neck reflex in human infant, morphogenetic and clinical significance, *J. Pediatr.* **13**:455–464.

82. GIAQUINTO, S., POMPEJANO, O., AND SOMOGYI, J., 1964, Supraspinal modulation of heteronymous monosynaptic and of polysynaptic reflexes during natural sleep and wakefulness, *Arch. Ital. Biol.* **102**:245–281.

83. GIAQUINTO, S., POMPEJANO, O., AND SOMOHYI, J., 1964, Descending inhibitory influences on spinal reflexes during natural sleep, *Arch. Ital. Biol.* **102**:282–307.

84. GLEES, P., 1944, Anatomical basis of cortico–striate connexions, *J. Anat.* **78**:47–51.

85. GRANIT, R., 1950, Reflex self-regulation of muscle contraction and autogenetic inhibition, *J. Neurophysiol.* **13**:351–372.

86. GRANT, R., AND KAADA, B., 1952, Influence of stimulation of central nervous structures on muscle spindles in cat, *Acta Physiol. Scand.* **27**:130–160.

87. GRANIT, R., HENATSCH, H. D., AND STEG, G., 1956, Tonic and phasic ventral horn cells, differentiated by post-tetanic potentiation in cat extensors, *Acta Physiol. Scand.* **37**:114–126.

88. HAMPSON, J. L., 1949, Relationships between cat cerebral and cerebellar cortices, *J. Neurophysical.* **12**:37–50.

89. HARLEM, O. K., AND LÖNNUM, A., 1957, A clinical study of the abdominal skin reflexes in newborn infants, *Arch. Dis. Child.* **32**:127–130.

90. HARVEY, A. M., AND MASLAND, R. L., 1941, A method for the study of neuromuscular transmission in human subjects, *Bull. Johns Hopkins Hosp.* **68**:81–93.

91. HASSLER, R., 1950, Über Kleinhirnprojektionen zum Mittelhirn und Thalamus beim Menschen, *Dtsch. Z. Nervenheilkd.* **163**:629–671.

92. HASSLER, R., 1953, Erkrankungen des Kleinhirns, in: *Handbuch der Inneren Medizin* (H. Schwiegk, ed.), 4th Ed., pp. 620–668, Springer-Verlag, Berlin.

93. HASSLER, R., 1953, Extrapyramidalmotorische Syndrome und Erkrankungen, in: *Handbuch der Inneren Medizin* (H. Schwiegk, ed.), 4th Ed., pp. 676–904, Springer-Verlag, Berlin—Göttingen—Heidelberg.

94. HASSLER, R., 1956, Die extrapyramidalen Rindensysteme und die zentrale Regelung der Motorik, *Dtsch. Z. Nervenheilkd.* **175**:233–258.

95. HASSLER, R., 1964, Pathologische Grundlagen der Klinik und Behandlung extrapyramidaler Erkrankungen, *Klin. Wochenschr.* **42**:404.

96. HENATSCH, H. D., 1962, Allgemeine Elektrophysiologie erregbarer Strukturen, in: *Lehrbuch der Physiologie des Menschen* (H. V. Landau-Rosemann, ed.), 28th Ed., Vol. 2, Urban & Schwarzenberg, Munich.

97. HENATSCH, H. D., SCHULTE, F. J., AND BUSCH, G., 1959, Wandelbarkeit des tonischen und phasischen Reaktionstyps einzelner Extensor-Motoneurone bei Variation ihrer Antriebe, *Pfluegers Arch. Gesamte Physiol. Menschen Tiere* **270**:161–173.

98. HODES, R., AND DEMENT, W. C., 1964, Depression of electrically induced reflexes in man during low voltage EEG sleep, *Electroencephalogr. Clin. Neurophysiol.* **17**:617–629.

99. HODES, R., AND GRIBETZ, J., 1962, H-reflex in normal human infants; depression of these electrically induced reflexes in sleep, *Proc. Soc. Exp. Biol. Med.* **110**:577–580.

100. HOFFMANN, P., 1922, *Untersuchungen über Eigenreflexe*

(*Sehnenreflexe*) *menschlicher Muskeln,* Springer-Verlag, Berlin.

101. HOFFMANN, P., 1934, Die physiologischen Eigenschaften der Eigenreflexe, *Ergeb. Physiol.* **36**: 15–108.

102. HOLMES, G., 1922, Clinical symptoms of cerebellar disease and their interpretation, *Lancet* **1**:1177–1182, 1231–1237; **2**:59–65, 111–115.

103. HOLMES, G., 1939, Cerebellum of man. Hughlins Jackson Memorial Lecture, *Brain* **62**:1–30.

104. HOPF, H. C., HUFSCHMIDT, H. J., AND STRÖDER, J., 1964, Über die "Ausbreitungsreaktion" nach Trigeminusreifung beim Säugling, *Ann. Paediatr. (Basel)* **203**:89–100.

105. HUGELIN, A., BONVALET, M., AND DELL, P., 1959, Activation réticulaire et corticale d'origine chimoreceptie au cours de l'hypoxie, *Electroencephalogr. Clin. Neurophysiol.* **11**:325–340.

106. HUNT, C. C., 1954, Relation of function to diameter in afferent fibers of muscle nerves, *J. Gen. Physiol.* **38**:17–131.

107. HUNT, C. C., AND PAINTAL, A. S., 1958, Spinal reflex regulation and fusimotor neurones, *J. Physiol. (London)* **143**:195–212.

108. HURSH, J. B., 1939, The properties of growing nerve fibres, *Amer. J. Physiol.* **127**:140–153.

109. INGRAM, T. T. S., 1960, Little Club Summer Meeting, Groningen.

110. ISBERT, H., AND PEIPER, A., 1927, Über die Körperstellung des Säuglings, *Jahrb. Kinderheilkd.* **115**:142–176.

111. JOPPICH, G., AND SCHULTE, F. J., 1968, *Neurologie des Neugeborenen,* Springer-Verlag, Berlin.

112. JUNG, R., AND HASSLER, R., 1960, The extrapyramidal motor system, in: *Handbook of Physiology* (J. Field, ed.), Sect. I, Vol. 2, pp. 863–927, American Physiological Society, Washington, D.C.

113. KOCH, E., 1932, Die Irradiation der pressoreceptorischen Kreislaufreflexe, *Klin. Wochenschr.* **11**:225–227.

114. KUFFLER, S. W., HUNT, C. C., AND QUILLIAM, J. P., 1951, Function of medullated small-nerve fibres in mammalian ventral roots: Efferent muscle spindle innervation, *J. Neurophysiol.* **14**:29–54.

115. KUGELBERG, E., 1952, Facial reflexes, *Brain* **75**:385–396.

116. LANDAU, A., 1923, Über einen tonischen Lagereflex beim älteren Säugling, *Klin. Wochenschr.* **2**:1253–1255.

117. LANDAU, A., 1925, Über motorische Besonderheiten des zweiten Lebenshalbjahres, *Monatsschr. Kinderheilkd.* **29**:555–558.

118. LAPORTE, Y., AND BESSOU, P., 1959, Modification d'excitabilité de motoneurones homonymes provoqueś par l'activation physiologique de fibres afférentes d'origine musculaire du group II, *J. Physiol. (Paris)* **51**:897–908.

119. LASSEK, A. M., 1942, Human pyramidal tract; study of mature myelinated fibres of pyramid, *J. Comp. Neurol.* **76**:217–225.

120. LAURSEN, A. M., 1962, Movements evoked from the region of the caudate nucleus in cats, *Acta Physiol. Scand.* **54**:175–184.

121. LAURSEN, A. M., 1962, Inhibition evoked from the region of the caudate nucleus in cats, *Acta Physiol. Scand.* **54**:185–190.

122. LAWRENCE, M. M., AND FEIND, C. R., 1953, Vestibular responses to rotation in newborn infants, *Pediatrics* **12**:300–305.

123. LEKSELL, L., 1945, The action potential and excitatory effects of the small ventral root fibres to skeletal muscle, *Acta Physiol. Scand.* **10**(*Suppl. 3*):1–84.

124. LENARD, H. G., BERNUTH, H. VON, AND PRECHTL, H. F. R., 1968, Reflexes and their relationship to behavioural state in the newborn, *Acta Paediatr. Scand.* **57**:177.

125. LILLY, J. C., 1958, in: *Biological and Biochemical Bases of Behavior* (H. F. Harlow and C. N. Woolsey, eds.), University of Wisconsin Press, Madison.

126. LIPPMANN, C., 1958, Über den Babkin'schen Reflex, Dissertation, Leipzig, 1958; *Arch. Kinderheilkd.* **157**:234.

127. LLOYD, D. P. C., 1944, Functional organization of the spinal cord, *Physiol. Rev.* **24**:1–17.

128. LLOYD, D. P. C., AND CHANG, H. T., 1948, Afferent fibres in the muscle nerves, *J. Neurophysiol.* **11**:199–207.

129. MAEKAWA, K., AND OCHIAI, Y., 1975, Electromyographic studies on flexor hypertonia of the extremities of newborn infants, *Dev. Med. Child Neurol.* **17**:440–446.

130. MAGNUS, R., 1924, *Körperstellung,* Fischer Verlag, Berlin.

131. MAGNUS, R., AND KLEIJN, A. DE, 1912, Die Abhängigkeit des Tonus der Extremitätenmuskulatur von der Kopfstellung, *Pfluegers Arch. Gesamte Physiol. Menschen Tiere* **145**:455–548.

132. MAGOUN, H. W., 1954, *The Waking Brain,* Charles C. Tomas, Springfield, Illinois.

133. MAGOUN, H. W., AND RHINES, R., 1946, Inhibitory mechanism in the bulbar reticular formation, *J. Neurophysiol.* **9**:165–171.

134. MARINESCO, G., AND RADOVICI, A., 1920, Sur une réflexe cutané nouveau réflex palmomentonier, *Rev. Neurol. (Paris)* **27**:237–240.

135. MATTHEWS, B. H. C., 1933, Nerve endings in mammalian muscles, *J. Physiol. (London)* **78**:1–53.

136. MATTHEWS, P. B. C., 1964, Muscle spindles and their motor control, *Physiol. Rev.* **44**:219–288.

137. MCNALLEY, W. J., AND STUART, E. A., 1942, Physiology of labyrinth reviewed in relation to seasickness and other forms of motion sickness, *War Med. (Chicago)* **2**:683–771.

138. METTLER, F. A., 1944, An origin of fibres in

pyramid of primate brain, *Proc. Soc. Exp. Biol. Med.* **57**:111–113.

139. METTLER, F. A., ADES, H. W., LIPMAN, E., AND CULLER, A. A., 1939, Extrapyramidal system; experimental demonstration of function, *Arch. Neurol. (Chicago)* **41**:984–995.

140. MICHAELIS, R., AND SCHULTE, F. J., 1969, Neurological examination and estimation of postmenstrual age in abnormal newborn infants, *Pediatrics* **42**:26–35.

141. MICHAELIS, R., SCHULTE, F. J., AND NOLTE, R., 1970, Motor behavior of small for gestational age newborn infants, *J. Pediatr.* **76**:208–213.

142. MORO, E., 1918, Das erste Trimenon, *Muench. Med. Wochenschr.* **65**:1147–1150.

143. MORUZZI, G., 1950, *Problems in Cerebellar Physiology,* Charles C. Thomas, Springfield, Illinois.

144. MORUZZI, G., 1960, Synchronizing influences of the brain stem and the inhibitory mechanisms underlying the production of sleep by sensory stimulation, in: Moscow Collokquim, 1958 (H. H. Jasper and G. D. Smirnov, eds.), *Electroencephalogr. Clin. Neurophysiol.* **12**(*Suppl. 13*): 231.

145. MORUZZI, G., 1964, Reticular influences on the EEG, *Electroencephalogr. Clin. Neurophysiol.* **16**:2–17.

146. MORUZZI, G., AND MAGOUN, H. W., 1949, Brain stem reticular formation and activation of the EEG, *Electroencephalogr. Clin. Neurophysiol.* **1**:455–473.

147. VON MURALT, A., 1958, *Neue Ergebnisse der Nervenphysiologie,* Springer-Verlag, Berlin.

148. NAKA, K. J., 1964, Electrophysiology of the fetal spinal cord. II. Interaction among peripheral and recurrent inhibition, *J. Gen. Physiol.* **47**:1023–1038.

149. ORTHNER, H., AND ROEDER, F., 1969, Die Entwicklung der Motorik beim Menschen, personal communication.

150. PAILLARD, J., 1954, Eléments d'une étude psycho-physiologique du "Tonus musculaire," *Bull. Psychophysiol. (Paris)* **12**:653.

151. PARMELEE, A. H., 1963, The palmomental reflex in premature infants, *Dev. Med. Child Neurol.* **5**:381–387.

152. PARMELEE, A. H., 1964, A critical evaluation of the Moro reflex, *Pediatrics* **33**:773–788.

153. PARMELEE, A. H., STERN, E., AND HARRIS, M. A., 1972, Maturation of respiration in premature and young infants, *Neuropädiatrie* **3**:294–304.

154. PATTON, H. D., 1965, Special properties of nerve trunks and tracts, in: *Physiology and Biophysics* (T. C. Ruch and H. D. Patton, eds.), pp. 73–94, W. B. Saunders Co., Philadelphia.

155. PEIPER, A., 1926, Über das Pupillenspiel des Säuglings, *Jahrb. Kinderheilkd.* **112**:179–183.

156. PEIPER, A., 1928, Die Hirntätigkeit des Säuglings, Fisher Verlag, Berlin.

157. PEIPER, A., 1963, Die Eigenart der kindlichen Hirntätigkeit, VEB Thieme, Leipzig.

158. PENFIELD, W., AND JASPAR, H., 1954, *Epilepsy and the Functional Anatomy of the Human Brain,* Little, Brown and Co., Boston.

159. PEPSY, S., 1933, cited in: *Murchison's Handbook of Psychology* (K. C. Pratt, ed.), 2nd Ed., Clark University Press, Worchester, Massachusetts.

160. POECK, K., 1968, Die Bedeutung der Reizqualität für die Greifreflexe beim menschlichen Neugeborenen und Säugling, *Dtsch. Z. Nervenheilkd.* **192**:317–327.

161. POLLACK, S. L., 1960, The grasp response in the neonate: Its characteristics and interaction with the tonic neck reflex, *Arch. Neurol. (Chicago)* **3**:547–581.

162. POLLOCK, L. J., AND DAVIS, L., 1927, Influence of Cerebellum upon reflex activities of decerebrate animal, *Brain* **50**:277–312.

163. PRECHTL, H. F. R., 1953, Über die Kopplung von Saugen und Greifreflex beim Säugling, *Naturwissenschaften* **40**:347.

164. PRECHTL, H. F. R., AND BEINTEMA, D., 1964, *The Neurological Examination of the Newborn,* William Heinemann Medical Books, London.

165. PRECHTL, H. F. R., AND KNOL, A. R., 1958, Der Einfluß der Beckenendlage auf die Fußsohlenreflexe beim neugeborenen Kind, *Arch. Psychatr. Nervenkr.* **196**:542.

166. PRECHTL, H. F. R., AND LENARD, H. G., 1968, Verhaltensphysiologie des Neugeborenen, in: *Fortschritte der Paedologie* (F. Linneweh, ed.), Springer-Verlag, Berlin.

167. PRECHTL, H. F. R., AND SCHEIDT, W. M., 1950, Auslösende und steuernde Mechanismen des Säuglings. I, *Z. Vgl. Physiol.* **32**:257–262.

168. PRECHTL, H. F. R., AND SCHEIDT, W. M., 1951, Auslösende und steuernde Mechanismen des Saugaktes. II, *Z. Vgl. Physiol.* **33**:53–62.

169. PRECHTL, H. F. R., VLACH, V., LENARD, H. G., AND GRANT, P. K., 1967, Exteroceptive and tendon reflexes in various behavioural states in the newborn infant, *Biol. Neonate* **11**:159–175.

170. RABINOWICZ, T., 1964, The cerebral cortex of the premature infant of the 8th month, *Prog. Brain Res.* **4**:39–86.

171. RADEMAKER, G. G. J., 1931, Das Stehen, Springer-Verlag, Berlin.

172. RADEMAKER, G. G. J., AND TER BRAAK, J. W. G., 1936, Das Umdrehen der fallenden Katz in der Luft, *Acta Otolaryngol. (Stockholm)* **23**:313–343.

173. RENSHAW, B., 1941, Influence of discharge of motoneurons upon excitation of neighboring motoneurons, *J. Neurophysiol.* **4**:167–183.

174. RENSHAW, B., 1946, Central effects of centripedale impulses in axons of spinal ventral roots, *J. Neurophysiol.* **9**:190–204.

175. RHINES, R., AND MAGOUN, H. W., 1946, Brain stem facilitation of cortical motor response, *J. Neurophysiol.* **9**:219–229.

176. RICHARDS, T. W., AND IRWIN, O. C., 1935, *Iowa Studies in Child Welfare,* Vol. 11, No. 1, Iowa.

177. ROBINSON, L., 1891, Darwinismus in the nursery, *Nineteenth Century* **30**:831.

178. ROBINSON, R. J., 1966, Assessment of gestational age by neurological examination, *Arch. Dis. Child.* **41**:437–447.

179. ROSSI, G., 1912, Singli effetti consequenti alla stimulazione contemporanea della corteccia cerebrale e di quella cerebellare, *Arch. Fisiol.* **10**:389–399.

180. RUPPERT, E. S., AND JOHNSON, E. W., 1968, Motor nerve conduction velocities in low birth weight infants, *Pediatrics* **42**:255–260.

181. RUSHWORTH, G., 1962, Observations on blink reflexes, *J. Neurophysiol.* **25**:93–108.

182. SAINT ANNE-DARGASSIES, S., 1954, Méthode d'examin neurologique sur la nouveau-né, *Etud. Neo-Natales* **3**:101.

183. SAINT ANNE-DARGASSIES, S., 1955, La maturation neurologique du premature, *Rev. Neurol. (Paris)* **93**:331–340.

184. SAINT ANNE-DARGASSIES, S., 1966, Neurological maturation of the premature infant of 28–42 weeks gestational age, in: *Human Development* (F. Faulkner, ed.), W. B. Saunders Co., Philadelphia.

185. SCHAEFER, K. P., 1965, Die Erregungsmuster einzelner Neurone des Abducens-Kernes beim Kaninchen, *Pfluegers Arch. Gesamte Physiol. Menschen Tiere* **284**:31–52.

186. SCHALTENBRAND, G., 1925, Normale Bewegungs und Lagereaktionen bei Kindern, *Dtsch. Z. Nervenheilkd.* **87**:23–59.

187. SCHERER, H., AND HERNÁNDEZ-PÉON, R., 1955, Inhibitory influence of reticular formation upon synaptic transmission in facialis nucleus, *Fed. Proc. Fed. Amer. Soc. Exp. Biol.* **14**:132.

188. SCHLOON, H., O'BRIEN, M. J., SCHOLTEN, C. A., AND PRECHTL, H. F. R., 1976, Muscle activity and postural behaviour in newborn infants, *Neuropädiatrie* **4**:384–415.

189. SCHOCH, E. O., 1948, Über die stammesgeschichtliche Bedeutung und die biologische Zusammengehörigkeit der Fußsohlenreflexe, *Grenzgeb. Med.* **1**:111–113.

190. SCHOCH, E. O., 1949, Die Fußsohlenreflexe als phylogenetisch bedingte Greif- und Loslassreflexe, *Homo 1* **1**:148–149.

191. SCHULTE, F. J., 1964, Reflex activation and inhibition of spinal motoneurones of the newborn, in: Symposium on Neurology of the Newborn, Rome, April 1964.

192. SCHULTE, F. J., 1968, Gestation, Wachstum und Hirnentwicklung, in: *Fortschritte der Paedologie* (F. Linneweh, ed.), Vol. II, pp. 46–64, Springer-Verlag, Berlin.

192a. SCHULTE, F. J., 1968, Elektromyographie, in: *Chirurgie des Gehirns und Rückenmarks im Kindes- und Jugendalter* (K. A. Bushe and P. Glees, eds.), pp. 171–191, Hippokrates Verlag, Stuttgart.

193. SCHULTE, F. J., 1974, Fetal malnutrition and brain development, in: *Size at Birth. Ciba Found. Symp.* **27**, Elsevier—Excerpta Medica—North-Holland, Amsterdam.

194. SCHULTE, F. J., AND MICHAELIS, R., 1965, Zur Physiologie und Pathophysiologie der neuromuskulären Erregunsübertragung beim Neugeborenen, *Klin. Wochenschr.* **43**:295–300.

195. SCHULTE, F. J., AND SCHWENZEL, W., 1965, Motor control and muscle tone in the newborn period. Electromyographic studies, *Biol. Neonate* **8**:198–215.

196. SCHULTE, F. J., ALBERT, G., AND MICHAELIS, R., 1969, Gestationsalter und Nervenleitgeschwindigkeit bei normalen und abnormalen Neugeborenen, *Dtsch. Med. Wochenschr.* **94**:599–601.

196a. SCHULTE, F. J., LINKE, I., MICHAELIS, R., AND NOLTE, R., 1969, Excitation, inhibition, and impulse conduction in spinal motoneurone of preterm, term, and small-for-dates newborn infants, in: *Brain and Early Behaviour* (R. J. Robinson, ed.), pp. 87–89, Academic Press, London.

197. SCHULTE, F. J., BUSCH, G., AND HENATSCH, H. D., 1959, Antriebssteigerungen lumbaler Extensor-Motoneurone bei Aktivierung der Chemoreceptoren im Glomus caroticum, *Pfluegers Arch. Gesamte Physiol. Menschen Tiere* **269**:580–592.

198. SCHULTE, F. J., BUSSE, C., AND EICHHORN, W., 1976, REM sleep, motoneurone inhibition and apneic spells in preterm infants, in preparation.

199. SCHULTE, F. J., HENATSCH, H. D., AND BUSCH, G., 1959, Über den Einfluß der Carotissinus-Sensibilität auf die spinalmotorischen System, *Pfluegers Arch. Gesamte Physiol. Menschen Tiere* **269**:248–263.

200. SCHULTE, F. J., LINKE, J., MICHAELIS, R., AND NOLTE, R., 1968, Electromyographic analysis of the Moro-reflex in term, preterm and small-for-date newborn infants, *Dev. Psychobiol.* **1**:41–47.

201. SCHULTE, F. J., LINKE, J., MICHAELIS, R., AND NOLTE, R., 1968, Excitation, inhibition and impulse conduction in spinal motoneurones of preterm, term, and small-for-date newborn infants, in: *Ciba Found. Study Group* (R. Robinson, ed.), London, February 12–16, 1968.

202. SCHULTE, F. J., MICHAELIS, R., AND FILIPP, E., 1965, Neurologie des Neugeborenen. I. Ursachen und klinische Symptomatologie von Funktionsstörungen des Nervensystems bei Neugeborenen, *Z. Kinderheilkd.* **93**:242–263.

203. SCHULTE, F. J., MICHAELIS, R., LINKE, J., AND NOLTE, R., 1968, Motor nerve conduction velocity in term, preterm, and small-for-date newborn infants, *Pediatrics* **42**:17–26.

204. SCHUR, E., 1922, Studien über das statische Organ normaler Säugling und Kinder, *Z. Kinderheilkd.* **32**:227–239.

205. SCHWEITZER, A., AND WRIGHT, S., 1937, Effects on knee jerk of stimulation of the central end of the vagus and of various changes in the circulation and respiration, *J. Physiol. (London)* **88**:459–475.

206. SKOGLUND, S., 1960, On the postnatal development of postural mechanisms as revealed by electromyography and myography in decerebrate kittens, *Acta Physiol. Scand.* **49**:299–317.

207. SKOGLUND, S., 1960, The spinal transmission of proprioceptive reflexes and the postnatal development of conduction velocity in different hindlimb nerves in the kitten, *Acta Physiol. Scand.* **49**:318–329.

208. SKOGLUND, S., 1960, The activity of muscle receptors in the kitten, *Acta Physiol. Scand.* **50**:203–221.

209. SNIDER, R. S., AND STOWELL, A., 1944, Receiving areas of tactile, auditory and visual systems in cerebellum, *J. Neurophysiol.* **7**:331–357.

210. SPRAGUE, J. M., AND CHAMBERS, W. W., 1954, Control and posture by reticular formation and cerebellum in intact, anesthetized and unanesthetized, and in decerebrated cat, *Amer. J. Physiol.* **176**:52–54.

211. STIRNIMANN, F., 1938, Das Kriech- und Schreitphänomen der Neugeborenen, *Schweiz. Med. Wochenschr.* **68**:1374–1376.

212. STIRNIMANN, F., AND STIRNIMANN, W., 1940, Der Fussgreifreflex bei Neugeborenen und Säuglingen. Seine diagnostische Verwendbarkeit, *Ann. Paediatr. (Basel)* **154**:249–264.

213. TAKEUCHI, N., 1963, Effects of calcium on the conductance change of the end plate membrane during the action of transmitter, *J. Physiol. (London)* **167**:141–155.

214. TASAKI, J., 1953, *Nervous Transmission,* Charles C. Thomas, Springfield, Illinois.

215. TAYLOR, J., (ed.), 1956, *Selected Writings of John Huglings Jackson,* Basic Books, New York.

216. THIEMICH, M., 1900, Über Tetanie und tetanoide Zustände im ersten Kindesalter, *Jahrb. Kinderheilkd.* **51**:222.

217. THOMSON, J., 1903, On the lip-reflex of newborn children, *Rev. Neurol. Psychiatr.* **1**:145–148.

218. THORNVAL, A., 1920–1921, L'épreuve laborique chez les nouveau-nés, *Acta Otolaryngol. (Stockholm)* **2**:451–454.

219. VLACH, V., 1966, Exteroceptive trunk reflexes in the newborn infant, *Cesk. Neurol.* **29**:240–247.

220. VLACH, V., 1968, Some exteroceptive skin reflexes in the limbs and trunk in newborn, in: *Clinics in Developmental Medicine,* Spastics International Medical Publication No. 27, W. Heinemann Medical Books, London.

221. VOGT, C., AND VOGT, O., 1919, Allgemeine Ergebnisse unserer Hirnforschung, *J. Psychol. Neurol. (Leipzig)* **25**:279–461.

222. VOGT, O., 1903, Zur anatomischen Gliederung des Cortex cerebri, *J. Psychol. Neurol. (Leipzig)* **2**:160–180.

223. WANG, G. H., AND AKERT, K., 1962, Behaviour and reflexes of chronic striadal cats, *Arch. Ital. Biol.* **100**:48–85.

224. WARTENBERG, R., 1952, Die Untersuchung der Reflexe, cited by PEIPER.[157]

225. VON WOERKOM, W., 1912, Sur la signification physiologique des réflexes cutanés des membres inférieurs; quelques considerations à propos de l'article de Marie et Foix, *Rev. Neurol. (Paris)* **20**:285–291.

226. WOLFF, P. H., 1959, Observations on newborn infants, *Psychosom. Med.* **21**:110–118.

CHAPTER 32

Biochemistry of Muscle Development

Jean Claude Dreyfus and Fanny Schapira

1. Introduction

Among the factors that govern the development of muscle in young animals, many remain unknown. Advances in recent years have aimed at a better definition of the various types of muscle and a better knowledge of the enzymatic pattern of muscular tissue and of the synthesis of specific proteins. The development of tissue culture has given a new impetus to the study of myogenesis.

2. Myogenesis

The striated musculature of vertebrates is of mesodermal origin. Boyd[7] named the first stage of embryonic muscle cell the "premyoblast." This cell cannot be distinguished from the associated fibroblast.

The next stage of development following the premyoblast is the myoblast, which is elongated but does not exhibit transverse striation. The cell then becomes multinucleated with the nucleus still centrally situated, and at that stage the striation

appears, forming the myotube. Progressively, the pale axial cytoplasmic core of the myotube disappears, while the nucleus migrates under the sarcoplasmic membrane. The mature muscle fiber is characterized by the transverse striation and peripheral nuclei.

Extensive histochemical studies have been performed on the development of human skeletal muscle.[30,47] From the 5th through the 8th weeks of gestation, the muscle shows a syncytium of premyoblasts without mitotic figures. Multiple nuclei are located in the central region, and mitochondria are concentrated beneath the sarcolemma. Mitochondrial enzyme activities and glycogen are intense in regions of myofibrillar formation. From the 10th to the 20th weeks of gestation, the number of myotubes increases. At 20 weeks of gestation, the myocytes become mature. There are differences among species regarding the fiber differentiation at birth. There exist two distinct types of fibers[24,25]: in newborn infants, in guinea pigs, and in rabbits, the fibers are fully differentiated at birth; in the rat, however, the differentiation into two types of fibers occurs between the 7th and 10th postnatal days.[23]

During the later stages of embryonic development and during fetal life, the number of muscle fibers

Jean Claude Dreyfus and Fanny Schapira · Institute of Molecular Pathology, University of Paris, Paris, France increases considerably. This increase is due to the differentiation of fibroblastlike cells that surround the muscle fibers.[12]

Konigsberg[48] studied myogenesis in tissue cultures of chick embryos. Multinucleated myotubes seem to be formed through a process of successive cell fusions that is the predominant or even the sole mechanism to produce multinuclearity. Mintz and Baker[62] showed that in skeletal muscle of allophenic mice, which consists of a mosaic of cells, a hybrid isoenzyme form of isocitrate dehydrogenase occurred, and they demonstrated that in each muscle cell, nuclei of diverse origin are at work. They have consequently confirmed the origin of the syncytium by myoblast fusion. A phenomenon that is not well understood is that of cell death during embryogenesis. In human embryos, it takes place in muscle, as well as in other tissue, between weeks 10 and 16.[93]

3. Nucleic Acids and Protein Synthesis

3.1. Deoxyribonucleic Acid

In adult muscle, no gross synthesis of DNA exists. In embryonic and in growing muscle, both synthesis and differentiation of DNA occur. The sequence of events has been better worked out *in vitro*. In myoblast cell cultures, early myogenic cells proliferate[98]; they are assumed to be myoblasts. As soon as several myogenic cells fuse to build a myotube, however, synthesis of DNA stops.[86]

Two DNA polymerases have been found in chick muscle prior to differentiation, one in the nucleus and the other in the cytoplasm. Of the latter, 90% is lost during differentiation.[94]

The *messenger RNA* (mRNA) specific for myofibrillar proteins seems to be transcribed very early in embryonic muscle, both *in vivo* and *in vitro*.[8,38] Myosin RNA might be stored in the cytoplasm and bound to protein. This ribonucleoprotein contains a 26S RNA that is probably the messenger for myosin. In normal muscle cells, fusion and synthesis of specific proteins are linked. Synthesis of specific messengers, however, seems to precede fusion. It is possible to uncouple the two phenomena *in vitro*: if presumptive myoblasts are treated with drugs such as cytochalasin B, fusion is prevented, while specific muscle proteins are synthesized.[17,71]

Protein synthesis is very active in developing muscle. Ribosomes in chick muscles at 11–17 days are 90% polysomal, and degrading activity is low as judged from proteolytic activity of cell supernatant fractions.[64] The role of nonhistone chromosomal proteins is likely to be important in muscle differentiation, as in other tissues.[52]

Cyclic AMP (cAMP), adenyl cyclase, and protein kinase all increase in chick embryo between the 7th and 10th days.[101] The maximum values of the three parameters coincide with the onset of cell fusion in the tissue. Subsequently, adenylate cyclase and protein kinase decrease in activity. The developmental changes of protein kinase may be obscured by the existence of several isozymes, which do not follow the same pattern.[69] The suggestion has been made that cAMP levels control the expression of myoblast differentiation.

3.2. Sarcoplasmic Reticulum

In muscle microsomes of newly hatched chicks, a rapid rise in the rate and extent of calcium accumulation is accompanied by increases in total and Ca-sensitive ATPase activity and concentration of phosphoprotein. The changes were apparent in sarcoplasmic reticulum membranes with a concomitant decrease of phospholipids.[6]

The volume of sarcoplasmic reticulum and of the transverse tubular system increases in mouse muscle from birth to adult stage. In all ages, this increase is twice as great in fast muscles as it is in slow muscles.[51]

4. Muscle Proteins

The soluble sarcoplasmic fraction of muscle protein is relatively greater in fetuses than in adults. In the skeletal muscle of 16-day-old rabbit fetuses, the sarcoplasmic nitrogen concentration was found to be higher than myofibrillar nitrogen. During gestation, the percentage of the sarcoplasmic nitrogen fraction decreases, while the myofibrillar fraction increases (see Chapter 22 for an age comparison of total muscle protein).

4.1. Myofibrillar Proteins

Striated myofibrils may be detected very early; however, a contractile reaction in response to direct electrical stimulation cannot be demonstrated before the 16th day in the rabbit fetus. At the end of gestation, the relative amount of myofibrillar protein suddenly increases. Csapo and Herrmann[14,36] initiated these studies. By measuring the decrease in viscosity, the authors found a sharp increase in the actomyosin content starting at the 12th day of gestation, but some myosin was already present before the 9th day. Actin appears later than myosin, but its rate of increase is faster. The formation of other extractable proteins seemed to be slower.

In the chick embryo, traces of myosin have been detected as early as 16 hr after the beginning of incubation by an immunologic technique, and actin and myosin in skeletal muscle were found after 3 days of incubation. As noted in Section 3.1, the mRNA for myosin is probably present in inactive form before synthesis of the protein in high amounts begins.

In the last few years, much has been learned about differences in myosin of various types of muscles. It has also been shown that myosin is present in other cells, although in smaller amounts; however, this myosin differs from that of skeletal muscle.[100] Embryonic myosin differs from adult muscle in light chains[80] and contains no methyl histidine, in contrast to adult myosin.[49,67,89] It appears likely that the various myosins are coded by different genes. In contrast, actin is probably the same in all tissues. Despite all these differences, however, common trends for myosin can be observed during development of chick muscle.[70] They include a decrease in RNA-binding capacity and in specific activity, an increase in thermostability and sensitivity to Ca^{2+}, and a decrease in activity in the presence of Mg^{2+}.[9] ATPase activities were found to be higher in fast than in slow muscle and heart[3]; this difference may be the biochemical basis for the histoenzymological difference between fast and slow muscle.

Marcaud-Raeber[53−55] described a specific myofibrillar protein in fetal rabbit muscle, the metamyosin, which almost completely disappears after birth. The abnormal protein of the rods found in nemaline myopathy resembles metamyosin.[27]

4.2. Myoglobin

Myoglobin is less abundant in fetal than in adult muscle.[44] It increases more in slow "red" than in fast "white" muscle. The breast muscles of flying birds (e.g., the pigeon) are considerably richer in myoglobin than those of nonflying birds (e.g., the chicken). The normal increase in myoglobin during development does not take place in muscular dystrophy.

The existence of a specific fetal form of myoglobin[43,66] has now been disproved. This heme protein is identical to fetal hemoglobin.[97]

Synthesis of myoglobin was detected in the chick embryo heart as early as 6 days of age, and at age 10 days in skeletal muscle.[45]

4.3. Sarcoplasmic Proteins

The soluble proteins are more acidic in fetal than in adult muscle. On the 16th day of gestation, the basic fraction accounts for about 16% in fetal rabbit muscle. It increases to 30% at birth and reaches 80% several months after birth. Starch gel electrophoresis reveals more cathodic bands in adult than in fetal rabbit muscle.[34] Chromatography on diethylaminoethyl cellulose revealed that fetal sarcoplasmic proteins are more similar in composition to heart proteins than to skeletal muscle proteins of adults. Further studies have confirmed these facts and, moreover, have shown that some analogies exist between red (slow) adult muscle and fetal muscle; however, the latter contains little myoglobin.

4.4. Enzymes

The enzymatic pattern of muscle sarcoplasm has been studied by histochemical and biochemical techniques. Histoenzymological methods have culminated in the description of two major types of fibers.[22,24,26] This description is based on the reciprocal relationship that exists between phosphorylase (representative for glycogenolysis) and succinic dehydrogenase (an example of oxidative enzyme). Type I fibers are "red," contain a high number of mitochondria, and are rich in oxidative and poor in glycolytic enzymes. Type II fibers are "white," poor in mitochondria and oxidative enzymes, and have intense glycolytic activity and a faster twitch than that of type I fibers. Subclasses have been described, especially in human muscle and for type I fibers. In a normal human muscle, both types of fibers are generally mixed, in an apparently random manner. The most frequently used histoenzymological test is that of alkaline ATPase, which heavily stains only type II fibers. Histological observations have now been completed by direct enzymatic determinations.[68] The level of glycolytic enzymes is 3–10 times higher in white than in red muscles in the rat and the rabbit.

The onset of differentiation into the two types of fibers varies in different species. Cosmos[10] and Cosmos and Butler[11] studied the ontogenic differentiation in chick muscle. In chick embryo, the development of red fibers (slow contraction) precedes that of white fibers (fast contraction). Phosphorylase activity is low in the embryo, and phosphorylase a is almost absent. Phosphorylase activity increases rapidly in white fibers after hatching, and reaches the adult value at 6 weeks of age. In embryonic breast muscle, glycerol-3-phosphate dehydrogenase and lactate dehydrogenase activities are low, while the other enzyme increase. Fenichel[30] studied muscle development in human fetuses. From 5 to 8 weeks of gestation, the majority of cells form a syncytium of premyoblasts. From 8 to 10 weeks, myotubes predominate, and they have central nuclei and a positive ATPase reaction (type II fibers); mitochondrial enzyme activity is intense, but type I fibers remain small. From 10 to 20 weeks, the nuclei are migrating, and at 20 weeks, the two fiber types become equal in number; the type I fibers are growing larger than the type II ones. Fenichel[30] compared this evolution to the development of the same fibers in fetal mice, as studied by Wirsen and Larsson.[96] Dubowitz[21,22] studied this enzymatic ontogeny more extensively in the human fetus by histochemical methods. Before the 18th week of gestation, the pattern does not show fiber differentiation; skeletal muscles do not display different enzyme patterns. From 20 to 26 weeks, a differentiation occurs between the two types of fibers, the majority of which belong to the phosphorylase-rich type. At the end of gestation, the distribution of the two types is approximately equal, and the pattern resembles that of the adult.

Experimental cross-innervation of slow and fast muscles showed not only an interconvertibility of muscle types, but also consequent enzyme changes. Yellin[99] and Guth and Watson[33] performed these experiments in adult rats and demonstrated the important role of innervation in physiologic and biochemical differentiation. Dubowitz[23] performed cross-innervation experiments in newborn animals; fast or mixed muscles show a transformation to a pattern resembling the m. soleus pattern, but in the m. soleus of newborns, the changes were less extensive.

Postnatal changes leading to fiber differentiation are essentially due to modifications of fast muscles.[2,50] While the enzymatic level remains rather stable in slow muscle after birth, the activity of glycolytic enzymes increases and oxidative activity decreases.

Postnatally, aldolase increases in rabbit white muscles[2]; this increase is entirely due to aldolase A.[50] In red muscle, there is no increase after birth. In contrast, succinate dehydrogenase remains unchanged in red muscle, but decreases considerably in white.

Scattered results have been obtained from various species that corroborate the increase in glycolytic enzyme activities during development.

Eppenberger et al.[29] studied a series of cytoplasmic enzymes in chick embryos and found that in the first days glycolysis is the only source of energy in most tissues, including muscle. Their data do not indicate, however, that glucose is the only source of substrate for glycolysis. It seems that amino acids are another important source of metabolic fuel.

Bocek and Beatty[5] found that glycogenolysis is especially high in muscles from monkey fetuses near term (on the 150th day of gestation), and this finding may explain, partially, the increased resistance of the fetus to anoxia.

Little is known about the postnatal development of muscle enzymes in man. Hooft et al.[40] studied 14 muscle biopsies from children between birth and 14 years of age. The activities of sarcoplasmic enzymes, such as creatine kinase, aldolase, and lactate dehydrogenase, increase with age. The mitochondrial malate dehydrogenase, however, seems to decrease postnatally.

The perinatal changes of glycolytic and Krebs cycle enzyme activities were studied by biochemical methods in m. psoas major of the rabbit[81] (see Table I). There is a low specific activity of glycolytic enzymes in the perinatal period. Hexokinase, however, was found to be up to 27 times higher immediately after birth than in adults. Postnatally, it decreases rapidly. This observation might explain the very active prenatal glycogen deposition in skeletal muscles, since the blood glucose is channeled into the muscle cells by this phosphorylation process. In Fig. 1, some enzyme activities of Krebs cycle and related reactions are shown for the perinatal period. All these reactions increase in the immediate perinatal period, and all are several times higher in fetal and newborn than in adult muscle. From this observation, the simultaneous low glycolytic enzyme activities, and the exceptionally high concentrations of amino acids (see Section 6), one might speculate that perinatal skeletal muscle utilizes amino acids for energy production.[83]

4.5 Glycogen and Periglycogenic Enzymes

The glycogen concentration in the muscle as well as in the liver of various mammals increases rapidly during the later period of gestation[79] (see also Chapter 17). The carbohydrate reserve is 3–4 times higher at birth than in the adult. Bocek and Beatty[5] followed the glycogen content of muscle in the perinatal period; in the rhesus monkey, it rises from 0.8 g/100 g fresh tissue at 20 days of gestational age to 2.8 g/100 g at 160 days. The glycogen level in skeletal muscle is not significantly decreased during hypoxia, while the liver becomes depleted of glycogen. Work of the last few years has attempted to correlate the fluctuations of glycogen with the evolution of periglycogenic enzymes.[82,83]

Glycogen synthetase increases through the 17th–19th days of fetal life in rat muscle,[92] and its appearance is demonstrated before nerves begin to contact the muscle cells.[56] A second increase is observed during the first 2 weeks after birth. In contrast, the degrading enzymes, phosphorylase and kinase, are extremely low prenatally, and increase throughout the first 30 postnatal days. The basic level of phosphorylase, therefore, does not explain the postnatal decrease in glycogen content.[63]

Table I. Free Amino Acids in Rabbit Skeletal Muscle (m. psoas major)[a,b]

Amino acid	Fetuses ($n = 5/19$)[c]	Newborns, first day ($n = 6/9$)[c]	3-Day rabbits ($n = 6$)	Adults ($n = 9$)
Taurine	4.443 ± 1.594	7.040 ± 2.329	7.519 ± 2.044	0.272 ± 0.076
Aspartic acid	0.614 ± 0.173	0.068 ± 0.123	0.552 ± 0.201	0.212 ± 0.096
Threonine	0.261 ± 0.046	0.445 ± 0.184	0.561 ± 0.321	0.230 ± 0.096
Serine	1.429 ± 0.376	0.979 ± 0.251	0.878 ± 0.375	0.372 ± 0.133
Glutamine plus Asn	6.595 ± 0.676	4.529 ± 0.977	3.020 ± 0.448	1.026 ± 0.366
Proline	0.822 ± 0.280	0.510 ± 0.120	0.679 ± 0.360	0.355 ± 0.117
Glutamic acid	5.791 ± 0.407	2.896 ± 0.723	2.357 ± 1.194	0.487 ± 0.309
Glycine	2.965 ± 0.303	3.468 ± 0.785	2.329 ± 1.093	1.707 ± 0.576
Alanine	2.955 ± 0.286	2.900 ± 0.795	1.991 ± 0.613	1.244 ± 0.580
Butyrine	0.009 ± 0.012	0.051 ± 0.031	0.050 ± 0.007	0.023 ± 0.024
Valine plus half-Cys	0.112 ± 0.022	0.215 ± 0.092	0.377 ± 0.160	0.256 ± 0.084
Methionine	0.042 ± 0.038	0.116 ± 0.035	0.108 ± 0.059	0.085 ± 0.038
Isoleucine	0.088 ± 0.018	0.184 ± 0.104	ND[d]	0.107 ± 0.050
Leucine	0.116 ± 0.040	0.198 ± 0.083	0.217 ± 0.075	0.166 ± 0.076
Tyrosine	0.116 ± 0.021	0.199 ± 0.057	0.179 ± 0.069	0.117 ± 0.036
Phenylalanine	0.124 ± 0.054	0.103 ± 0.030	0.074 ± 0.020	0.091 ± 0.035
β-Alanine	0.468 ± 0.226	1.217 ± 0.049	1.649 ± 0.470	0.335 ± 0.230
Citrulline	0.126 ± 0.027	ND[d]	0.175 ± 0.054	0.076 ± 0.038
Ornithine	0.783 ± 0.117	0.694 ± 0.133	0.436 ± 0.339	0.035 ± 0.013
Lysine	1.161 ± 0.227	1.509 ± 0.361	0.415 ± 0.181	0.142 ± 0.104
1-Methylhistidine	0.049 ± 0.040	0.079 ± 0.080	0.016 ± 0.010	0.044 ± 0.040
Histidine	0.310 ± 0.032	0.257 ± 0.067	0.179 ± 0.061	0.117 ± 0.036
3-Methylhistidine	0.030 ± 0.010	0.050 ± 0.043	0.023 ± 0.034	<0.010
Tryptophan	0.135 ± 0.050	ND[d]	ND[d]	0.045 ± 0.011
Arginine	1.102 ± 0.266	0.627 ± 0.404	0.177 ± 0.107	0.097 ± 0.016

[a] From Stave and Armstrong.[85]

[b] Data in micromoles per gram tissue wet weight, expressed as means ± S.D.

[c] The first number is the number of analyses; the second number is the total number of animals used for pooling samples.

[d] Not determined for technical reasons.

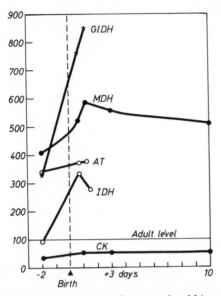

Fig. 1. Enzyme activities of perinatal rabbit muscle. (GlDH) Glutamate dehydrogenase (EC 1.4.1.2.); (MDH) malate dehydrogenase EC 1.1.1.37); (AT) aspartate aminotransferase (EC 2.6.1.1.); (IDH) isocitrate dehydrogenase (EC 1.1.1.42); (CK) creatine kinase (EC 2.7.3.2.). Data from Stave.[81] Revised and supplemented, courtesy of Dr. Stave.

4.6. Other Enzymes

The *pentose phosphate cycle* is more active in fetal than in adult muscle; this difference has been shown for several species,[41] especially the monkey[4] and the rabbit.[14] *Glucose-6-phosphate dehydrogenase* and *6-phosphogluconate dehydrogenase* are high in fetal muscle, while these activities are very low in adult muscle, particularly in white fibers.

Cholinesterase is found in myoneural junctions, and it plays a fundamental role in the transmission of nervous stimulation to the muscle fiber; histochemically, this role was detected by Couteaux.[13] Cholinesterase appears first along the nerve fibers at 6 weeks of gestation, and then in the neuromuscular junction[61]; in the beginning, it shows a diffuse pattern, and later it becomes more localized. The appearance of cholinesterase activity coincides with the first movements.[88]

Creatine kinase is very specific for muscle, and its ontogeny is of great interest. In a tissue culture of chick embryo, Konigsberg[48] detected no creatine kinase activity before the 7th day; its later increase correlates well with the initiation of contraction. Stave[81] found that the activity is much lower in

rabbit fetuses at the end of gestation and in newborn than in adult muscles. In skeletal muscle of chick embryo, the development of creatine kinase activity is similar in comparison to actomyosin appearance[28]; the authors defined four stages of development:

1. Creatine kinase synthesis begins in the myoblast, but the phosphocreatine level (substrate) is very low, and consequently it seems that the enzyme cannot function.
2. Cross-striation and contractile proteins appear, but phosphocreatine remains low.
3. On the 13th day, true myofibrils appear. Actomyosin and creatine kinase concentrations increase sharply, as soon as phosphocreatine becomes abundant.
4. After the chick is hatched, the concentration of specific proteins and enzymes increases.

Cathepsins A and D are highest in the prenatal period in chick embryo. Their activities then decline for the first 2 or 3 months of life. Cathepsin B reaches a maximum after 1 week postnatally and then decreases. The overall autolytic activity, therefore, is maximal at birth and diminishes progressively postnatally.[42]

4.7. Isoenzymes

A considerable amount of work has been devoted to the evolution of isoenzymes in developing muscle. During ontogeny, a typical fetal or embryonic pattern is gradually substituted by another pattern that is characteristic of the adult muscle. Initial studies have been devoted to lactic dehydrogenase (LDH); however, many other enzymes possess specific muscle forms. Besides LDH, important changes of isoenzyme patterns have been reported for aldolase and creatine kinase.

Fine *et al.*[31] showed that the isoenzyme pattern of lactate dehydrogenase changes during ontogeny in human or animal tissues.[1,9,57,58] Two basic types of LDH subunits exist, the muscle type (M) and the heart type (H). Each LDH isoenzyme is composed of four of these subunits, and the random combination leads to the formation of five different isoenzymes of the same molecular weight, but of different charge. The five LDH isoenzymes can be separated by electrophoresis (on starch gel, agar, cellulose acetate, and other media). At alkaline pH, the most anodic isoenzyme (1) is a pure tetramer of H-subunits; the most cathodic isoenzyme (5) is a pure tetramer of M-subunits. The intermediary isoenzymes are hybrids. The different methods[19] of isoenzyme differentiation are in good agreement. A distinct ontogenetic evolution can be observed in muscles of some species, especially man: of the LDH isoenzyme subunits, type M is predominant in adult muscle, while type H predominates in fetuses. This difference was first noted by Dreyfus et al.[20] for man. Chick embryo and rabbit fetal muscle show an analogous development.[31,46] In cattle and sheep, the same evolutionary change from the H type toward the M type occurs.[59] In contrast, in rat and mouse muscle[76] no specific LDH isoenzyme pattern changes occur, and fetal and adult muscle contain almost exclusively type M. Goodfriend et al.[32] showed that oxygen represses the biosynthesis of M-subunits; however, it remains difficult to explain all differences of ontogenic evolution of isoenzymes in species. The overall level of LDH activity increases notably after birth.[84]

The histochemical difference between the two types of muscle fibers also applies to the isoenzyme pattern. The rabbit m. soleus with slow contraction (a "red" muscle) has a predominant H-type pattern (similar to the heart), while white muscles, such as the m. gastrocnemius or the breast muscles of chicken, have both fast contraction and a predominant type-M pattern. The isoenzyme pattern of red muscles is similar to the isoenzyme pattern of fetal white muscles.

In long-term tissue cultures, Vesell et al.[91] showed that various tissues eventually assume a similar LDH isoenzyme pattern: the sequential alteration is the same for fetal muscles of different species, and it always develops into a predominantly M-type form (effect of aging in culture or lack of oxygen or both).

Takasu and Hughes[87] emphasized that the isoenzyme pattern varies considerably in the various muscles of human adults. This variation is in contrast to young fetuses, which have a more uniform pattern; at term, the pattern is less different from adults.

The isoenzymes of several other enzymes also show an ontogenic development. Creatine kinase, for example, has been shown to be a dimer.[15,16,29] Each subunit is either muscle type (M) or brain type (B); electrophoretically separated at an alkaline pH, type B is the most anodic. The hybrid "MB" has an intermediate position. In embryonic chicken, Eppenberger et al.[29] found only the "BB" (pure brain type) isoenzyme; later, the BB isoenzyme disappeared slowly, and the hybrid BM type appeared.

Finally, at hatching, only the pure muscle type MM was found.

In rats, the ontogenic evolution is similar but much slower. In fetuses (gestational age 11 days), only the brain type BB exists. In 10-day-old rats, the BB isoenzyme is replaced by the MB type, and in adults, the hybrid disappears and only the MM type remains.

Schapira et al.[77] studied the ontogenic evolution of creatine kinase in some other species. In the rabbit, the developmental changes are slow; on the 25th day of life, the muscle isoenzymes of creatine kinase are still of brain type. In mice, however, no difference was found between the adult and fetal isoenzyme patterns. In man, the evolutionary changes occur very early; isoenzyme BB was found only in the first trimester.

Aldolase isoenzymes have also been studied.[37,60,72,74,78] In fetal rabbit muscle, an aldolase isoenzyme was separated that revealed kinetic and electrophoretic characteristics similar to brain type aldolase (aldolase C). Furthermore, embryonic chick muscle contains primarily this aldolase isoenzyme C; later, the type "AC" isoenzymes appear.

There appears to be a coordinated increase in several muscle isoenzymes during myogenesis: aldolase, creatine kinase, phosphorylase, and phosphofructokinase. This view is supported by evidence obtained both in vivo and in vitro.[18,90]

Among other muscle enzymes with multiple molecular forms, the ontogenic evolution of the intracellular distribution of two forms of malate dehydrogenase[95] and of carboxyl and aryl esterases[39] might be worth mentioning. Recently, interesting results were obtained with pyruvate kinase.[65] In rat skeletal muscle, as in most tissues, the fetal isoenzyme PK_3 is present before birth. After birth, a rapid shift toward the muscle isozyme (PK_2 or PKM_1) is taking place.

It is noteworthy that in muscle diseases of either myopathic or neurogenic origin,[73] a shift toward the fetal pattern was observed for LDH,[20] creatine kinase, and aldolase isoenzymes.[72,75]

5. Water and Electrolytes

Skeletal muscle from newborn animals contains as much as 90% water. The percentage decreases to approximately 75% in the mature animal. The macromolecules therefore increase during development at the expense of tissue water. In addition, sodium, which is higher than potassium at birth, decreases very fast in the first weeks of postnatal life, while potassium concentration increases[35] (see also Chapter 26).

6. Peptides and Amino Acids

The typical muscle dipeptides anserine and carnosine are low in concentration in fetal skeletal muscle of rabbits. The postnatal increase is more pronounced for anserine than for carnosine. The glutathione content is about the same shortly before and after birth, but adult muscle contains less glutathione than that of the newborn rabbit.[85] Glutathione might have a specific function in protecting SH groups of several enzymes, and it also might function as an enzyme activator.[82] The perinatal changes of free amino acids in rabbit skeletal muscle (m. psoas major) are shown in Table I. Compared with adult muscle, the high concentrations in perinatal muscle are of special significance.

7. Conclusions

The biochemical composition of muscle varies considerably during pre- and postnatal development. The general trend is toward a more differentiated pattern after birth. The factors governing the biosynthesis of constituents that are specific for the adult muscle remain to be explored; however, the onset of a purposeful use of muscles and the respective nervous stimulation after birth seem to accelerate the maturation of the skeletal muscle, directly or indirectly, to a great extent.

ACKNOWLEDGMENTS

This work was supported by l'Institut National de la Santé et de la Recherche Médicale, le Centre National de la Recherche Scientifique, and the Muscular Dystrophy Associations of America.

8. References

1. APPELLA, E., AND MARKERT, C. L., 1961, Dissociation of lactate dehydrogenase units with guanidine hydrochloride, *Biochem. Biophys. Res. Commun.* **6**:971.
2. BACOU, F., 1972, Evolution quantitative de l'aldolase, asparate transaminase, succinate deshydrogénase et acétylcholinésterase dans les muscles blancs et rouges de lapin au cours de la période postnatale, *C. R. Soc. Biol. (Paris)* **166**:1037.
3. BARANY, M., GAETJENS, E., BARANY, K., AND KARP, E., 1964, Comparative studies of rabbit cardiac and skeletal myosins, *Arch. Biochem.* **106**:280.
4. BEATTY, C. H., BASSINGER, G. M., AND BOCEK, R. M., 1965, Pentose cycle activity in muscle from fetal, neonatal and infant rhesus monkeys, *Arch. Biochem.* **117**:275.
5. BOCEK, R. M., AND BEATTY, C. H., 1967, Glycogen metabolism in fetal, neonatal and infant muscle of the rhesus monkey, *Pediatrics* **40**:412.
6. BOLAND, R., MARTONOSI, A., AND TILLACK, T. W., 1974, Developmental changes in the composition and function of sarcoplasmic reticulum, *J. Biol. Chem.* **249**:612.
7. BOYD, J. O., 1960, Development of striated muscle, in: *The Structure and Function of Muscle* (G. H. Bourne, ed.), Vol. I, p. 63, Academic Press, New York.
8. BUCKINGHAM, M. D., CAPUT, D., COHEN, A., WHALEN, R. G., AND GROS, F., 1974, The synthesis and stability of cytoplasmic messenger RNA during myoblast differentiation in culture, *Proc. Natl. Acad. Sci. U.S.A.* **71**:1466.
9. CAHN, R. D., KAPLAN, N. O., LEVINE, L., AND ZWILLING, E., 1962, Nature and development of lactic dehydrogenase, *Science* **136**:962.
10. COSMOS, E., 1966, Enzymatic activity of differentiating muscle fibers, *Dev. Biol.* **13**:163.
11. COSMOS, E., AND BUTLER, J., 1967, Differentiation of fiber types in muscle of normal and dystrophic chickens, in: *Exploratory Concepts in Muscular Dystrophy* (A. T. Milhorat, ed.), p. 197, Excerpta Medica Foundation, New York.
12. COUTEAUX, R., 1941, Recherches sur l'histogénèse du muscle strié des mammifères et la formation des plaques motrices, *Bull. Biol. Fr. Belg.* **75**:101.
13. COUTEAUX, R., 1955, Localization of cholinesterases at neuromuscular junctions, *Int. Rev. Cytol.* **4**:604.
14. CSAPO, A., AND HERRMANN, H., 1951, Quantitative changes in contractile proteins of chick skeletal muscle during and after embryonic development, *Amer. J. Physiol.* **165**:701.
15. DANCE, N., AND WATTS, D. C., 1962, Comparison of creatine phosphotransferase from rabbit and brown-hare muscle, *Biochem. J.* **84**:114.
16. DAWSON, D. M., EPPENBERGER, M., AND KAPLAN, N. O., 1965, Creatine kinase: Evidence for a dimeric structure, *Biochem. Biophys. Res. Commun.* **21**:346.
17. DELAIN, D., AND WAHRMANN, J. P., 1975, Is fusion a trigger for myoblast differentiation?, *Exp. Cell Res.* **9**:495.
18. DELAIN, D., MEIENHOFER, M. C., PROUX, D., AND SCHAPIRA, F., 1973, Studies in myogenesis in vitro: Changes of creatine kinase, phosphorylase and phosphofructokinase isozymes, *Differentiation* **1**:349.
19. DREYFUS, J. C., AND SCHAPIRA, F., 1967, Lactic de-

hydrogenase isozymes, in: *Methods and Achievements in Experimental Pathology* (C. Bajusz, ed.), Harvard University Press, Cambridge, Massachusetts.

20. DREYFUS, J. C., SCHAPIRA, F., SCHAPIRA, G., AND DEMOS, J., 1962, La lactico-déshydrogénase musculaire chez le myopathe: Persistance apparente du type foetal, *C. R. Acad. Sci. Ser. D (Paris)* **254**:4384.

21. DUBOWITZ, V., 1963, Enzymic maturation of skeletal muscle, *Nature (London)* **197**:1215.

22. DUBOWITZ, V., 1966, Enzyme histochemistry of developing human muscle, *Nature (London)* **211**:884.

23. DUBOWITZ, V., 1967, Cross innervation of fast and slow muscle: Histochemical, physiological and biochemical studies, in: *Exploratory Concepts in Muscular Dystrophy* (A. T. Milhorat, ed.), p. 164, Excerpta Medica Foundation, New York.

24. DUBOWITZ, V., AND PEARSE, A. G. E., 1960, Reciprocal relationship of phosphorylase and oxidative enzymes in skeletal muscle, *Nature (London)* **185**:701.

25. DUBOWITZ, V., AND PEARSE, A. G. E., 1961, Enzymic activity of normal and dystrophic human muscle: A histochemical study, *J. Pathol. Bacteriol.* **81**:365.

26. ENGEL, W. K., 1962, The essentiality of histo- and cytochemical studies of skeletal muscle in the investigation of neuromuscular diseases, *Neurology (Minneapolis)* **12**:778.

27. ENGEL, W. K., WANKO, T., AND FENICHEL, G., 1964, Nemaline myopathy, *Arch. Neurol. (Chicago)* **11**:22.

28. EPPENBERGER, H. M. K., VON FELLENBERG, R., RICHTERICH, R., AND AEBI, H., 1962–1963, Die Ontogenese von zytoplasmitischen Enzymen beim Hühner Embryo, *Enzymol. Bio. Clin. (Basel)* **2**:139.

29. EPPENBERGER, H. M. K., RICHTERICH, R., AND AEBI, H., 1964, The ontogeny of creatine kinase isozymes, *Dev. Biol.* **10**:1.

30. FENICHEL, G. M., 1966, A histochemical study of developing human skeletal muscle, *Neurology (Minneapolis)* **16**:741.

31. FINE, I. H., KAPLAN, N. O., AND KUFTINEC, D., 1963, Developmental changes of mammalian lactic dehydrogenases, *Biochemistry* **2**:116.

32. GOODFRIEND, T. L., SOKOL, D., AND KAPLAN, N. O., 1966, Control of synthesis of lactic acid dehydrogenases, *J. Mol. Biol.* **15**:18.

33. GUTH, L., AND WATSON, P. K., 1967, The influence of innervation on the soluble proteins of slow and fast muscles of the rat, *Exp. Neurol.* **17**:107.

34. HARTSHORNE, D. J., AND PERRY, S. V., 1962, A chromatographic and electrophoretic study of sarcoplasm from adult and fetal rabbit muscles, *Biochem. J.* **85**:171.

35. HAZLEWOOD, C. F., AND NICHOLS, B. L., 1969, Changes in muscle sodium, potassium, chloride, water and voltage during maturation in the rat: An experimental and theoretical study, *Johns Hopkins Med. J.* **125**:119.

36. HERRMANN, H., 1952, Studies of muscle development, *Ann. N. Y. Acad. Sci.* **55**:99.

37. HERSKOVITZ, J., MASTERS, C. J., WASSARMAN, P. M., AND KAPLAN, N. O., 1967, On the tissue specificity and biological significance of aldolase C in the chicken, *Biochem. Biophys. Res. Commun.* **26**:24.

38. HEYWOOD, S. M., KENNEDY, D. S., AND BESTER, A. J., 1975, Stored myosin messenger in embryonic chick muscle, *FEBS Lett.* **53**:69.

39. HOLMES, R. S., AND MASTERS, C. J., 1967, The developmental multiplicity and isoenzyme status of rat esterases, *Biochim. Biophys. Acta* **146**:138.

40. HOOFT, C., DE CAEY, P., AND LAMBERT, Y., 1966, Etude comparative de l'activité enzymatique du tissu musculaire de l'enfant normal et d'enfants atteints de dystrophie musculaire progressive aux différents stades de la maladie, *Rev. Fr. Etud. Clin. Biol.* **11**:510.

41. ILYIN, V., 1965–1966, Central regulation of enzyme activity and synthesis in embryonal and adult mammalian tissues, *Biol. Neonate* **9**:215.

42. IODICE, A. A., CHIN, S., PERKER, S., AND WEINSTOCK, I. M., 1972, Cathepsins A, B, C, D and autolysis during development of breast muscle of normal and dystrophic chickens, *Arch. Biochem. Biophys.* **152**:166.

43. JONXIS, J. H. P., AND WADMAN, S. K., 1952, A fetal form of myoglobin, *Nature (London)* **169**:884.

44. KAGEN, L. J., AND CHRISTIAN, C. L., 1966, Immunologic measurement of myoglobin in human adult and fetal skeletal muscle, *Amer. J. Physiol.* **211**:655.

45. KAGEN, L. J., AND FREEDMAN, A., 1973, Embryonic synthesis of myoglobin *in vivo* estimated by radioimmunoassay, *Dev. Biol.* **31**:295.

46. KAPLAN, N. O., AND CAHN, R. D., 1962, Lactic dehydrogenases and muscular dystrophy in the chicken, *Proc. Natl. Acad. Sci. U.S.A.* **48**:123.

47. KARPATI, G., AND ENGEL, W. K., 1968, Correlative histochemical study of skeletal muscle, *Neurology (Minneapolis)* **18**:681.

48. KONIGSBERG, J. R., 1963, Clonal analysis of myogenesis, *Science* **140**:1273.

49. KUELH, W. M., AND ADELSTEIN, R. S., 1970, The absence of 3-methylhistidine in red, cardiac and fetal myosin, *Biochem. Biophys. Res. Commun.* **39**:956.

50. LEBHERZ, H. G., 1975, Ontogeny and regulation of fructose diphosphate aldolase isoenzymes in red and white skeletal muscles of the chick, *J. Biol. Chem.* **250**:5976.

51. LUFF, A. R., AND ATWOOD, H. L., 1971, Changes in the sarcoplasmic reticulum and transverse tubular system in fast and slow skeletal muscles of the mouse during postnatal development, *J. Cell Biol.* **51**:369.

52. MAN, N. T., MORRIS, G. E., AND COLE, R. J., 1975, Gene activation during muscle differentiation and the role of non-histon chromosomal protein phosphorylation, *Dev. Biol.* **47**:81.

53. MARCAUD-RAEBER, L., 1959, Sur une nouvelle protéine myofibrillaire: La métamyosine. Observation et isolement, *Bull. Soc. Chim. Biol. (Paris)* **41**:283.

54. Marcaud-Raeber, L., 1959, Hetérogénéité de la métamyosine, *Bull. Soc. Chim. Biol. (Paris)* **41**:297.

55. Marcaud-Raeber, L., 1959, Comparaison de la métamyosine avec les autres protéines myofibrillaires, *Bull. Soc. Chim. Biol. (Paris)* **41**:315.

56. Margreth, A., Di Mauro, S., Tartarini, A., and Salviati, G., 1971, Glycogen synthetase in developing and adult skeletal muscle, *Biochem. J.* **122**:597.

57. Markert, C. L., and Møller, F., 1959, Multiple forms of enzymes: Tissues, ontogenetic, and species specific patterns, *Proc. Natl. Acad. Sci. U.S.A.* **45**:753.

58. Markert, C. L., and Ursprung, H., 1962, The ontogeny of isozyme pattern of lactate dehydrogenase in the mouse, *Dev. Biol.* **5**:363.

59. Masters, C. J., 1964, The developmental progression of ruminant lactate dehydrogenase, *Biochim. Biophys. Acta* **89**:1.

60. Masters, C. J., 1968, The ontogeny of mammalian fructose-1,6-diphosphate aldolase, *Biochim. Biophys. Acta* **167**:161.

61. Mavrenskaya, I. F., 1963, Histochemical study of cholinesterase during development of somatic musculature in the human fetus, *Fed. Proc. Fed. Amer. Soc. Exp. Biol. (Transl. Suppl.)* **22**:T597.

62. Mintz, B., and Baker, W. B., 1967, Normal mammalian muscle differentiation and gene control of isocitrate dehydrogenase synthesis, *Proc. Natl. Acad. Sci. U.S.A.* **58**:592.

63. Novak, M., Drummond, G. I., Skala, J., and Hahn, P., 1972, Developmental changes in cyclic AMP, protein kinase, phosphorylase kinase, and phosphorylase in liver, heart, and skeletal muscle in the rat, *Arch. Biochem. Biophys.* **150**:511.

64. Nwagwu, M., and Nana, M., 1974, Quantitative measurement of active polysomes in developing chick muscle, *Dev. Biol.* **41**:1.

65. Osterman, J., Fritz, P. J., and Werntch, T., 1973, Pyruvate kinase isozymes from rat tissues. Developmental studies, *J. Biol. Chem.* **248**:1011.

66. Perkoff, G. T., 1966, Evidence for a specific human fetal muscle heme protein, *J. Lab. Clin. Med.* **67**:685.

67. Perrie, W. T., and Perry, S. V., 1970, An electrophoretic study of the low molecular weight components of myosin, *Biochem. J.* **119**:31.

68. Peter, J. B., Barnard, R. J., Edgerton, V. R., Gillespie, C. A., and Stempel, K. E., 1972, Metabolic profiles of three fiber types of skeletal muscle in guinea pigs and rabbits, *Biochemistry* **11**:2627.

69. Piras, M. M., Staneloni, R., Leiderman, B., and Piras, R., 1972, Protein phosphokinases of chick muscle: Changes during embryonic development, *FEBS Lett.* **23**:199.

70. Radha, E., 1974, Embryonic differentiation in the nucleoside triphosphatase activities of myosin from the fast, slow and cardiac muscles of chick, *Enzyme* **18**:327.

71. Sanger, J. W., Holtzer, S., and Holtzer, H., 1971, Effects of cytochalasin B on muscle cells in tissue culture, *Nature (London) New Biol.* **229**:121.

72. Schapira, F., 1965, Modification de spécificité de l'aldolase musculaire au cours de l'atrophie expérimentale, *C. R. Soc. Biol. (Paris)* **159**:2189.

73. Schapira, F., 1966, Modification des isozymes de la créatine kinase musculaire au cours de l'atrophie, *C. R. Acad. Sci. Sér. D (Paris)* **262**:2291.

74. Schapira, F., 1967, Type embryonnaire de l'aldolase musculaire chez le poulet myopathe, *C. R. Acad. Sci. Sér. D (Paris)* **264**:2654.

75. Schapira, F., 1968, Ontogenetic evolution and pathogenic modifications of multiple forms of lactate dehydrogenase, creatine kinase and aldolase, in: *Homologous Enzymes and Biochemical Evolution* (U. V. Thoai and J. Roche, eds.), Gordon and Breach, New York.

76. Schapira, F., and Dreyfus, J. C., 1965, Différence de comportement au cours de l'atrophie des isozymes de la lactico-deshydrogénase musculaire selon l'espèce animale, *Bull. Soc. Chim. Biol. (Paris)* **47**:2261.

77. Schapira, F., Dreyfus, J. C., and Allard, D., 1968, Les isozymes de la créatine kinase et de l'aldolase du muscle foetal et pathologique, *Clin. Chim. Acta* **20**:439.

78. Schapira, F., Dreyfus, J. C., and Schapira, G., 1965, Fetal-like patterns of lactic dehydrogenase and aldolase isozymes in some pathological conditions, *Enzymol. Biol. Clin. (Basel)* **7**:98.

79. Shelley, H. J., 1960, Blood sugars and tissue carbohydrate in fetal and infant lambs and rhesus monkeys, *J. Physiol. (London)* **153**:527.

80. Sreter, F., Holtzer, S., Gergely, J., and Holtzer, H., 1972, Some properties of embryonic myosin, *J. Cell Biol.* **55**:586.

81. Stave, U., 1964, Age dependent changes of metabolism, *Biol. Neonate* **6**:128.

82. Stave, U., 1965, Age dependent changes of metabolism: Influence of hypoxia on tissue enzyme patterns of newborn and adult rabbits, *Biol. Neonate* **8**:114.

83. Stave, U., 1967, Age dependent changes of metabolism: The effect of prolonged hypoxia upon tissue enzyme activities of newborn and adult rabbits, *Biol. Neonate* **11**:310.

84. Stave, U., 1967, Importance of proper substrate concentration for enzyme assays in tissue homogenates for developmental studies, *Enzymol. Biol. Clin. (Basel)* **8**:21.

85. Stave, U., and Armstrong, M. D., 1973, Tissue free amino acid concentrations in perinatal rabbits, *Biol. Neonate* **22**:374–387.

86. Stockdale, F. E., and O'Neill, M. C., 1972, Deoxyribonucleic acid synthesis, mitosis, and skeletal muscle differentiation, *In Vitro* **8**:212.

87. TAKASU, T., AND HUGHES, B. P., 1966, Lactate dehydrogenase isoenzymes in developing human muscle, *Nature (London)* **212**:609.

88. TENNYSON, V. M., BRZIN, M., AND SOLTWINER, P., 1972, The appearance of acetylcholinesterase in the myotome of the embryonic rabbit, *J. Cell Biol.* **51**:703.

89. TRAYER, J. P., HARRIS, C. J., AND PERRY, S. V., 1968, 3-Methyl histidine and adult and fetal forms of skeletal muscle myosin, *Nature (London)* **217**:452.

90. TURNER, D. C., AND EPPENBERGER, H. M., 1973, Developmental changes in creatine kinase and aldolase isoenzymes and their possible function in association with contractile elements, *Enzyme* **15**:224.

91. VESELL, E. S., PHILIP, J., AND BEARN, A. G., 1962, Comparative studies of the isozymes of lactic dehydrogenase in rabbit and man, *J. Exp. Med.* **116**:797.

92. WAHRMANN, J. P., LUZZATI, D., GROS, F., AND MEYER, F., 1971, Evolution de quelques enzymes du métabolisme énergétique au cours du développement embryonnaire et post-natal des muscles squelettiques du rat, *Biochimie* **53**:1023.

93. WEBB, J. N., 1974, Muscular dystrophy and muscle cell death in normal foetal development, *Nature (London)* **252**:233.

94. WICHA, M., AND STOCKDALE, F. E., 1972, DNA-dependent DNA polymerases in differentiating muscle cells, *Biochem. Biophys. Res. Commun.* **48**:1079.

95. WIGGERT, C., AND VILLEE, C. A., 1964, Multiple molecular forms of malic and lactic dehydrogenase during development, *J. Biol. Chem.* **239**:444.

96. WIRSEN, C., AND LARSSON, K. S., 1964, Histochemical differentiation of skeletal muscle in fetal and newborn mice, *J. Embryol. Exp. Morphol.* **12**:759.

97. WOLFSON, R., YAKULIS, V., COLEMAN, R. G., AND HELLER, P., 1967, Studies on fetal myoglobin, *J. Lab. Clin. Med.* **69**:728.

98. YAFFE, D., 1971, Developmental changes preceding cell fusion during muscle differentiation *in vitro*, *Exp. Cell Res.* **66**:33.

99. YELLIN, H., 1967, Neural regulation of enzymes in muscle fibers of red and white muscle, *Exp. Neurol.* **19**:92.

100. YOUNG, U., 1969, The molecular basis of muscle contraction, *Annu. Rev. Biochem.* **38**:913.

101. ZALIN, R. J., AND MONTAGUE, W., 1975, Changes in cyclic AMP, adenylate cyclase and protein kinase levels during the development of embryonic chick skeletal muscle, *Exp. Cell Res.* **93**:55.

CHAPTER 33

The Autonomic Nervous System

Mark C. Rogers and Julius B. Richmond

1. Introduction

Since clinical medicine is organized with specialties in specific organ systems, it is understandable that a disparate system that regulates and affects virtually all other organs but that performs no independent function of its own could be left without representation in the vast array of clinical specialties. Such is the case with the autonomic nervous system, which is a system more in concept than in function. Nevertheless, the autonomic nervous system has effects of such protean nature that most complex activities of the human organism are dependent on the integrating and regulating function of this system.

Any factor that causes a change in the basic homeostatic nature of autonomic nervous system function ultimately results in some alteration in necessary body function. This change in the autonomic nervous system can be the result of disease or of maturational changes such as are seen in the newborn period. In the past 20 years, immaturity of the autonomic nervous system has been implicated in an increasing number of complex clinical conditions occurring in the newborn period, ranging from alteration in breathing patterns to alterations in response to thermal stress. The purpose of this chapter is to review the more recent developments in understanding the intricate nature of autonomic nervous system function, with specific regard to the clinical significance of altered autonomic function in the neonate.

2. Control of Cardiac Function

2.1. Autonomic Innervation of the Heart

Various early pharmacological studies performed on the neonate appeared to demonstrate that there was an increased sensitivity in the newborn to various parasympathetic agents, particularly pilocarpine.[84] This exaggerated vagotonic response to large and sometimes toxic doses of pilocarpine was matched with an apparent decreased sensitivity of neonates to sympathomimetic drugs such as ephedrine.[44] Since these pharmacological findings corroborated isolated clinical observations on the

Mark C. Rogers · Departments of Pediatrics and Anesthesia, The Johns Hopkins Hospital, Baltimore, Maryland 21205
Julius B. Richmond · The Judge Baker Guidance Center, Boston, Massachusetts 02115

frequency of bradycardia in newborns,[88] it was assumed that the newborn had a normal parasympathetic innervation, but was lacking in sympathetic innervation. Nevertheless, more recent studies by Unna *et al.*[84] on the effects of atropine and by Patterson *et al.*[62] on the effects of neostigmine in infants and children have failed to show that there is a parasympathetic hyperactivity in this age group. Recent studies[19] have helped to explain these phenomena by the use of pharmacological and histochemical techniques designed to demonstrate the degree of sympathetic and parasympathetic innervation of the heart in the fetus and in the newborn.

By use of the monamine fluorescence technique of Flack and Owman,[18] histochemical observation has been made[20] on the distribution of sympathetic nerves within the hearts of animals of different ages. The results show that sympathetic innervation is incomplete in the fetal and early newborn heart. With the use of techniques that cause norepinephrine to fluoresce under the microscope, it is apparent that in adult hearts, the sympathetic nervous system innervation is represented by a dense network of fibers. Conversely, in the fetal heart, there is a much lower density of sympathetic fibers.[19] In addition, the fetal hearts have most norepinephrine granules only in the large preterminal nerve trunks found surrounding the coronary arteries and in the connective tissue among cardiac muscle bundles. In the mature hearts, the norepinephrine granules are more widely spread. Comparison of the distribution of parasympathetic fibers by staining for pseudocholinesterase using the thiocholine technique has failed to demonstrate any difference between fetal and adult hearts.[35] As a result, these studies make it possible to say that the newborn myocardium does lack full sympathetic innervation, but does have full parasympathetic innervation.

Functionally, it may be anticipated that fetal and early newborn myocardium should demonstrate supersensitivity to exogenous norepinephrine if fetal myocardium lacks full sympathetic innervation. In fact, average norepinephrine dose–response curves in fetal, newborn, and adult lambs show that fetal cardiac muscle is 3-fold more sensitive to norepinephrine than is adult myocardium.[19] The degree of sensitivity shown by newborn myocardium gradually decreases over the first few days to weeks of life until it approaches adult levels. The extent to which this changed sensitivity to catecholamines affects the force of contraction of newborn hearts is

still being defined.[39] In adult hearts, it has been shown that the myocardial contractile state is not affected by changes in endogenous cathecholamines. Nevertheless, in the perinatal period, it is possible that catecholamines[76] have a significant effect on contractility, since the myocardium in this period appears to be more sensitive to catechols because of its partially denervated state.[19] While the effect of developing autonomic innervation of the heart on cardiac contractile state remains unclear, the effect on possible alterations in heart rate has been more thoroughly investigated.

2.2. Autonomic Control of Heart Rate

Perhaps the most widely made observation suggesting autonomic nervous system control of heart rate in the fetus and newborn is the one documenting wide swings in heart rate that have been noted in the perinatal period. In the fetus, for example, the cardiotachometer and the fetal ECG have documented wide fluctuation in fetal heart rate and rhythm in response to a wide variety of stimuli.[43] Over 30 years ago, observations were made on the incidence and nature of fetal arrhythmias.[75] The application of vibratory stimuli to the maternal abdomen was also shown to result in fetal tachycardias and extrasystoles.[2] These observations have been confirmed and expanded,[55] but they have not differentiated between direct fetal and maternal stimulation in the generation of these heart rate changes. The observations of the effects of fetal hypoxia are much more clear. Severe fetal hypoxia results in a transient tachycardia, followed by a profound bradycardia.[98] Moreover, this bradycardia can be reversed by atropine, and these changes become more clear as the fetus approaches term.[29,31] For example, Stern *et al.*[83] injected atropine into the umbilican vein of 6 human fetuses weighing 100–525 g. None of these very young fetuses developed significant heart rate changes, even though when atropine is injected nearer term,[33] heart rate changes are obtained. This finding implies a maturation of cardiac parasympathetic innervation during the last trimester.

Fetal electrocardiography has been especially useful in documenting the frequency of alterations in fetal heart rate in response to a wide variety of stimuli.[40] It is now apparent that fetal heart rate and rhythm are subject to a wide variety of fluctuations in the newborn period, though it is not yet clear how all these changes are mediated. For example, the fetal bradycardia resulting from head and umbilical cord compression during uterine contraction is now thought to be mediated by the vagus nerve and to be the direct result of hypoxia.[29,31] The work of Phillips *et al.*,[65] in particular, suggests that the primary stimulus for the bradycardia of head compression is via pressure on the anterior fontanel with a resultant vagal reflex. The complex reflexes postulated to be responsible for fetal heart rate changes are difficult to verify, but it is clear, at least, that the fetal autonomic nervous system is part of the pathway by which these changes are mediated.

Following birth, the wide fluctuations in heart rate appear, if anything, to increase. Bradycardia has been noted, in particular, to occur following a sneeze,[89] a hiccup, or a yawn.[43] Nasogastric intubation or gavage feeding has also been noted to result in bradycardia in both premature and full-term infants.[43] Cotton and O'Meara[15] showed that a sigh also resulted in cardiac slowing in infants under 12 hr of age, and they attributed this result to a reflex initiated by the sudden increase in negative intrapleural pressure from the sigh.

The difficulty of making generalizations about the heart rate effects of various stimuli is shown, however, by the investigation done on the effect of sucking. There has long been general disagreement on the heart rate effect of sucking, with some investigators reporting a resultant tachycardia[23,25,28] while other investigators were reporting a resultant bradycardia.[65,93] In 1968, however, Boschan and Steinschneider[6] documented that sucking initially results in an increase and cessation of sucking in a decrease in heart rate. In addition, to further complicate matters, the magnitude and direction of any given change are dependent on the initial heart rate, a phenomenon reported as the "law of initial value."[91]

If graded external stimulation is applied to the newborn, predictable heart rate changes are observed. With the use of sound stimulation in newborns, an increase in heart rate is noted with increasing intensity of sound stimulation.[3,82] The effect of external tactile or noise stimulation can be changed by altering the duration as well as the magnitude of the stimulus.[38,78] More important, the site of stimulation may determine the direction and magnitude of heart rate change, as demonstrated by the fact that tactile abdominal stimulation results almost exclusively in tachycardia, while similar stimulation at the anus could produce tachycardia or bradycardia. Perhaps most important of all, the effect of stimuli on heart rate can change following repeated stimuli. Repeated application of the stimulus results in progressive decrease of the heart rate change—a phenomenon called *habituation*.[81] Since a small change in stimulating conditions results in a prompt return of the heart rate response to the stimulus,[38] habituation may not be a form of fatigue, but rather may be a form of learning.

2.3. Arrhythmias

For many years, it was felt that children had a very low incidence of arrhythmias, but this viewpoint has had to be revised in recent years. To begin with, sinus arrhythmia has now been noted to occur in virtually all premature and full-term infants.[88] While this arrhythmia may not be evident at fast heart rates,[100] it is now clear that sinus arrhythmia is the predominant rhythm found in the newborn. What is more surprising is the high incidence of ectopic beats and supraventricular tachycardias in the newborn. While routine ECGs obtained in the newborn period showed the high incidence of sinus arrhythmia and occasional ectopic ventricular beats, the development of a transistorized electrocardiographic tape recorder documented a much higher incidence of arrhythmias than had previously been suspected.[72] With the use of this device, several hours of continuous recording could be obtained, and it was possible to obtain a more accurate reflection of the incidence of arrhythmias. Morgan and Gunteroth[49] reported the results of studies of 20 normal newborns who demonstrated occasional nodal beats. Subsequent studies[12] demonstrated ectopic atrial activity and premature ventricular contractions in prematures and suggested autonomic immaturity as the cause. More recently,[88] a higher incidence of ectopic atrial and ventricular beats was reported, with a tendency for the more serious arrhythmias to occur in premature or asphyxiated infants. Moreover, experimental studies have shown that in young mammals, ectopic atrial beats may pass through the atrioventricular node and result in serious ventricular arrhythmias.[24,66] As a result, it has been suggested[36] that atrial arrhythmias conducted to the ventricle may be responsible for some of the fatalities in the sudden infant death syndrome. Even if this is not so, it is now apparent that serious arrhythmias do occur in otherwise healthy children, and there may be severe or even life-threatening complications. Furthermore, that the physiologic basis of these arrhythmias is autonomic in nature is supported by the observation that infants and children are more susceptible to bradycardia from stimuli such as ocular pressure and intubation.[67]

3. Peripheral Vascular Regulation

3.1. Peripheral Vasomotor Control

Experimental studies done on vasomotor regulation in the fetal and neonatal lamb[8,74] and in the newborn piglet[22] demonstrated that there is a progressive increase in the baroreflex sensitivity as term is approached. Nevertheless, in these complex experimental studies, it was felt that while cardiovascular regulatory centers are functional at birth, they are not fully matured.[22]

Most studies of vasomotor control in human neonates have naturally been simpler in design, and have been done using the effect of applied temperature changes on blood flow to a limb. Both generalized temperature stress and localized application of temperature changes have been utilized in these studies. The use of digital plethysmographic tracings has allowed investigators[42] to study the effect of applied cold stimulus on digital pulse volume and total digital volume in neonates. Following infants through the first weeks of life, these investigators showed a lack of reflex vasoconstriction to cold in small prematures as well as a delayed response in term infants. They concluded that the vasoconstrictor response to local cold application matures postnatally, and that adult responses are present only after several months. In contrast, Brück[9] demonstrated vasoconstriction in response to low ambient temperatures in both premature and full-term infants from the first day of life. Heat-induced reflex vasodilatation was studied by Bower,[7] who showed a different pattern in infants and adults. He documented that following the heating of an upper extremity, the resultant rise in skin temperature in the foot in infants was slower and failed to achieve as high a skin temperature as did a similar stimulus in an adult. By age 3 months, an adult response pattern was observed. Similar results were also seen with the use of body-warming during the first 3 days of life.[97] Warming in newborns failed to produce vasodilatation. After 3 days of age, an adult

pattern was observed. Richmond and Lustman[68] provided confirmatory observations, but, importantly, demonstrated a marked subject variation in reflex vasocilatation. Of 31 infants studied between 3 and 4 days of age, 10 failed to demonstrate any change in temperature response of the left toe following immersion of the right foot in warm water.

Dickins and Richmond[17] showed that lumbar sympathetic block results in vasodilatation in the premature infant. This finding is consistent with the increase in peripheral blood flow in response to an increase in ambient temperature observed by Brück[9] in premature and full-term infants. He demonstrated clearly that peripheral blood flow could be augmented by heating in all age groups. In younger newborns, however, higher rectal temperatures were required before an increase in blood flow became apparent. Using a venous occlusion plethysmograph to measure blood flow in the calf and foot in response to reactive hyperemia in sleeping newborns, he found that resting blood flow (adjusted for size) was higher in premature infants than in full-term infants, but both were higher than in adults.[11] Following release of venous occlusion, flow during reactive hyperemia increased to its highest levels in premature infants, but the ratio of hyperemic flow to resting flow was similar in all three groups. If the infants had suffered from asphyxia during delivery, blood flow was markedly reduced because of peripheral vasoconstriction.

Using an entirely different approach, Wilkes *et al.*[92] observed the reflex vasodilatation in response to varying doses of intradermal histamine both in adults and in full-term infants less than 49 hr of age. Higher histamine concentrations were required in the infants, and this finding suggested that either there was a higher resting vasoconstrictor tone in infants or the vascular smooth muscle of infants was less responsive to the histamine-produced reflex vasodilatation.

It is apparent from these studies that the newborn full-term and premature infant is born with a considerable degree of peripheral vasomotor tone. However, infant vasomotor responsiveness differs from that in adults on the basis of unknown factors.

3.2. Blood Pressure

A wide variety of techniques using the sphygmomanometer cuff have been utilized to record blood pressure in infants. Auscultation,[50] flush,[53] visual oscillometry,[58] and digital palpation[51] blood pressure measurements in newborns demonstrated a wide variety of systolic pressures ranging from 41 mm Hg[53] to 92 mm Hg.[2] One of the reasons for this wide range of values was the problem of cuff size in small infants. The standard 2.5-cm cuff designed for small infants is often of inappropriate width for newborns, and the inflatable balloon may not always occlude the artery without unnecessarily high pressures. These pressures, in turn, may be interpreted as artificially high systolic pressures. Nevertheless, Moss and Adams[51] convincingly demonstrated that blood pressure in newborns is higher in the upper extremities than in the lower extremities, and that both values climb significantly in the first few weeks of life. The recent popularization of the Doppler technique for blood pressure recordings in infants[46] and the widespread[37] use of the intraaortic umbilical artery catheter confirmed a narrower range of pressures in normal infants, in keeping with the 80/46 mm Hg reported by Woodbury *et al.*[95] and the 72/47 mm Hg reported by Moss *et al.*[52] Corresponding umbilical artery pressure measurements in premature infants[52] were 64/39 mm Hg. Both size and weight were of importance in predicting blood pressure in the premature, however, and there was a wide range of values for both mature and premature infants. In addition, the effect of various stimuli on blood pressure in both the premature and full-term remains somewhat confused.

Contis and Lind[14] demonstrated a rise in blood pressure during the first few hours of life, with a subsequent drop as temperature fell. Such factors as cesarean section or fetal distress were found to alter circulating blood volume and blood pressure,[96] as may immediate clamping of the umbilical cord.[60] In addition, that complex circulatory adjustments such as closure of the ductus venosus and the ductus arteriosus are taking place in the neonatal period makes detailed interpretation of blood pressure measurements in this period nearly impossible. In few, if any, of the studies are the neonates comparable in age, maturation, blood volume, temperature, metabolic state, and so forth. This is reflected in the conflict in experimental results. Nevertheless, there are several stimuli associated with changes in blood pressure that are of interest.

The effect of crying on systolic blood pressure was originally described to be minimal in the first 3 days of life, and to result in systolic pressure elevation only after that age.[99] Subsequent investigation[51] showed, conversely, that in both premature and full-term infants, crying produced an elevation in both systolic and diastolic pressure, even in the first days of life. As in so many of these studies, part of the reason for the difference in results was in the use of different methods of blood pressure recording. Young and Holland[99] used palpation, while Moss *et al.*[52] used umbilical artery pressure measurements. Subsequently, Gupta and Scopes[26] demonstrated increases in blood pressure recordings with crying, even in the first 24 hr of life.

Contradictory results have also been found in experiments testing the blood pressure adjustment of newborns to changes in position. Using indirect blood pressure recordings, original reports[27,99] did not find a change in blood pressure associated with a change from supine to upright body position until infants were older than 3 days of age. However, it was possible[52] with the use of indwelling arterial catheters to record an increase in systolic pressure following an upright tilt. This increase was immediately followed by a systolic pressure drop and then by a return to control values, and these results were entirely consistent with an adult pattern. A subsequent report[51] confirmed these results, but Gupta and Scopes,[26] as well as Young and Cotton,[98] found a persistent increase in both systolic and diastolic pressures with tilting. Once again, the latter investigators found large variability in response. A more prolonged tilt of 30–36 min produced a fall in right atrial and aortic pressure, and suggested that the degree of tilting and the duration of the tilt were important in determining the response.[59]

To remove the uncertainty found using a tilting stimulus, hemorrhage was used to provoke a fall in arterial pressure. These experiments demonstrated[90] that during exchange transfusion, when a volume of blood was removed, the pressure fell, but when an equal volume was returned, the pressure rose above control values. Removal of 20 ml of blood over 15 sec[98] was observed to produce an increase in heart rate and a decrease in blood pressure that persisted over 40 sec until the blood was returned. Mott[54] suggested that a simulated Valsalva maneuver could be used to test baroreceptor function by observing blood pressure changes. He also suggested, however, that the test would be easier to perform than it would be to interpret. The same comment could be made with regard to all regulation of systemic blood pressure.

4. Pulmonary Vascular Regulation

During the last trimester of gestation, pulmonary arterial muscle thickness markedly increases, and at the time of birth, it is largely responsible for the high pulmonary vascular resistance found in neonates.[69] Autopsy data on humans[56] demonstrated that the ratio of the area of the pulmonary artery media to the pulmonary artery intima doubles in the last 10 weeks of gestation, so that at birth this ratio is highest. Over the first 8–10 weeks of life, the percentage of the pulmonary artery that is composed of muscle rapidly falls, until by age 3 months, it approaches the value found in adults.[57] This morphological change in the pulmonary arteries is matched by a corresponding physiologic change in calculated pulmonary vascular resistance.[69] Just prior to birth, when the pulmonary arterial muscle thickness is greatest and pulmonary blood flow is low, pulmonary vascular resistance is highest. With the onset of breathing and the large increase in blood flow to the lungs, pulmonary vascular resistance is still very high, but gradually falls over the first 8–10 weeks of life.[70] As a result, the drop in pulmonary vascular resistance markedly parallels the drop in pulmonary arterial muscle.

Even though this gradual drop in pulmonary vascular resistance is the predominant pattern in the first few weeks of life, the pulmonary vasculature remains very labile in the fetus and neonate. Postnatally, the pulmonary vessels are very responsive to a wide range of mechanical,[41] metabolic,[70] pharmacological,[47] and neurological[13] stimuli. Lauer[41] demonstrated that expansion of the lung in fetal lambs with a gas mixture that produced no alteration in blood gases still resulted in a marked fall in pulmonary vascular resistance. These studies, conducted on lambs near term delivered by cesarean section while the umbilical circulation was intact, also demonstrated that ventilation with 100% O_2 produced a marked drop in pulmonary arterial resistance that was not blocked by the administration of atropine. Rudolph[69] stated that although expansion of the lungs by introduction of air is a factor in the drop in pulmonary vascular resistance, the major factor is an increase in the P_{O_2} to which the newborn is exposed. Rudolph and Yuan[70] demonstrated in newborn calves the interrelationship of alterations in P_{O_2} and acidemia on pulmonary vascular resistance. With arterial P_{O_2} below 30 mm Hg, pulmonary arterial resistance increases. Similarly, acidemia alone can produce increases in resistance in the pulmonary circuit, but the combination of acidemia and low P_{O_2} produces marked increases in pulmonary vascular resistance greater than either stimulus can produce by itself. Additional studies[47] demonstrated that bradykinin can produce changes in arteriolar tone in the pulmonary vessels and, in particular, in the ductus arteriosus of the newborn. Other studies[61] demonstrated that prostaglandin E_2 has a vasodilatory effect on pulmonary vasculature and on the ductus arteriosus. With specific reference to the effect of the autonomic nervous system on pulmonary vasculature, the data are somewhat confusing. The work of Lauer[41] and of Colebatch,[13] both studying fetal lambs, tended to show a lack of autonomic control. Colebatch, in particular, demonstrated that bilateral vagotomy and thoracic sympathectomy failed to alter the vascular response to positive pressure ventilation or acute asphyxia. This lack of dramatic autonomic nervous system influence on fetal pulmonary vasculature did not mean, however, that there was absolutely no neural control. Rather, some degree of neural control of pulmonary vasculature was demonstrated in fetal lambs by Colebatch.[13] He showed that electrical stimulation of the cervical vagus resulted in an increase in pulmonary blood flow secondary to vasodilatation that was blocked by the administration of atropine. In contrast, comparable stimulation of the thoracic sympathetic system produced pulmonary vasoconstriction and a decrease in pulmonary blood flow. Campbell et al.[10] helped resolve some of these apparent conflicts when they suggested that neural control of pulmonary vasculature becomes more manifest in later fetal life. Employing a technique of cross-circulation between twins as a means of maintaining constant blood gases, these authors showed that compression of the umbilical cord in lambs of 91 to 92 days' gestation had no influence on the pulmonary vasculature, providing the arterial blood supply from the twin donor was maintained intact. A comparable procedure performed on lambs of 98–143 days' gestation was associated with a small pulmonary vasoconstriction. Significantly, this latter effect was abolished following surgical interruption of the left sympathetic supply to the left lung. As a result of these studies, the effect of autonomic nervous system function on pulmonary vasculature in the newborn is as complex and unclear as is the effect on systemic vasculature.

5. The Cardiorespiratory Unit and the Sudden Infant Death Syndrome

If the etiology of the sudden infant death syndrome (SIDS) is primarily a respiratory arrest, there must be something unique about the respiratory pattern of infants, particularly that of prematures, that makes them susceptible to sudden and prolonged apnea. In fact, there is a good deal of evidence to indicate that this is true. Knowledge of the physiology of the cardiorespiratory unit will therefore benefit from a discussion of this syndrome.

There appears to be general agreement that the incidence of the SIDS is consistent throughout Europe and North America. Epidemiogical studies performed in Northern Ireland,[21] in Czechoslovakia,[34] in Canada,[77] and in the United States[4] all concluded that the incidence is 2–3 cases per 1000 live births. Unfortunately, there is no matching general agreement as to the etiology of the SIDS.

Innumerable hypotheses have been proposed to explain the SIDS, and explanations as divergent as cortisol insufficiency, milk allergy, and viremia have all been considered.[85] Recently, there has been a growing consensus that the ultimate cause of the SIDS is a sudden cardiorespiratory arrest. Nevertheless, there still remains a good deal of uncertainty about the cause and mechanism of such an arrest. It has been recognized for some time that infants who have sustained a neurological insult often display irregular breathing patterns that may, in turn, produce hypoxia and further neurological damage.[64] The development of the impedance plethysmographic respiratory monitor allowed investigators to record and to quantify over long intervals the frequency and severity of apnea in otherwise healthy newborns. When this technique was first used in the nursery in the late 1960s, the incidence of apnea was found to be much higher than had previously been suspected.[73] In fact, apneic episodes of greater than 30 sec occurred in 25% of premature infants studied in the first 10 days of life,[16] and these episodes often resulted in bradycardia as well.[73] Furthermore,

these episodes of apnea appeared to be increased in the face of environmental stresses such as high ambient temperature.[64] Subsequent studies have indicated[73] that infants with apnea show a decreased CO_2 response curve that is the result of a defect in the respiratory center, rather than in the lungs or in the peripheral chemoreceptors. These episodes of apnea could be abolished by the use of theophylline, which stimulated the central respiratory center and prevented the apnea.[73] Despite these impressive studies, there still remained a big gap between the observations made in prematures and the possible role of apnea in otherwise healthy children who succumb to the SIDS at several weeks of age.

Steinschneider[79] suggested that the SIDS is caused by an abnormal autonomic discharge that, in turn, results in the sudden development of a respiratory arrest or a cardiovascular catastrophe. In 1972, he presented data on 5 patients, 3 of whom were approximately 1 month of age and had previously had an episode of sudden cyanosis of unknown etiology.[80] The infants demonstrated frequent periods of apnea, which were most frequent during rapid eye movement (REM) sleep and often resulted in cyanosis requiring resuscitation. These infants were studied serially, and observations confirmed the relationship between the onset of REM sleep and the development of apnea. Most impressively, 2 of these infants were subsequently found dead of SIDS. Steinschneider's data supported the hypothesis that prolonged apnea is a physiologic component of REM sleep during the first month or two of life, and that this apnea is part of the final pathway resulting in the SIDS.

If sleep apnea is part of the final pathway of the SIDS, it is not universally accepted as the only pathway. The same physiologic stimuli that result in apnea may cause severe bradycardia or tachycardia. Under the right circumstances, these heart rates may result in the development of life-threatening arrhythmias. Unfortunately, these circumstances are known to exist in the neonate. Whereas the adult is protected from the development of ventricular fibrillation following premature atrial beats by the slow conduction times of the specialized conduction tissue, this is not the case in the young mammal.[66] The specialized conduction tissue of the heart, particularly the atrioventricular node, is designed to prevent the spread of premature atrial impulses into the ventricle during the electrical recovery phase of ventricular muscle. During this period, premature impulses find the ventricle partially depolarized, and may cause repetitive ventricular impulses or even ventricular fibrillation. Infants can conduct rapid supraventricular rhythms up to 400 per min because their specialized conduction tissue is not physiologically developed.[24] While there is some disagreement concerning the anatomic state of the newborn atrioventricular node,[1,87] it is true that atrial premature beats in the newborn may result in repetitive ventricular beats or in ventricular fibrillation.[24] Furthermore, infants have wide fluctuations in heart rate associated with defacation, micturition, and sucking,[44] and fluctuations, when combined with the high frequency of atrial premature beats observed in these patients,[88] increase the risk of serious arrhythmias. Maron et al.[45] have resuscitated patients with classic signs of SIDS in whom the underlying etiology for the episodes was repetitive ventricular fibrillation.

This relationship between bradyarrhythmias, premature atrial beats, and ventricular fibrillation becomes far more intriguing when it is appreciated that infants are known to have a diving reflex. This reflex occurs when the body is immersed in water, and it results in a decrease in metabolic demands brought about largely by a redistribution of blood flow so that only flow to the heart and brain is preserved. Shared by all diving vertebrates, this reflex is designed to decrease oxygen consumption, and it results in significant changes in cardiac rhythm. Profound sinus bradycardia and even sinus arrest is often seen, with resultant ventricular escape beats and idioventricular rhythm. While immersion in water will produce this response, it may also be mimicked by immersion of the face only or by direct cold facial stimuli.[63] Since the diving response can be elicited in neonates by a variety of maneuvers and results in profound bradycardia or arrhythmias, Wolf[94] postulated that this reflex is responsible for the SIDS. This hypothesis holds appeal because the incidence of the SIDS is highest in the winter,[4] and the potential significance of cold facial stimuli provoking profound bradycardia, apnea, and cardiac arrhythmias cannot be overlooked.

While no exact sequence of events may be responsible for all cases of SIDS, it does appear that the concept of a visceral or environmental stimulus resulting in an autonomic-reflex-induced apnea or cardiac arrhythmia or both will probably be the final common pathway for the production of the SIDS.

6. Conclusion

In the past 20 years, there have been significant advances in understanding the role that disorders of the autonomic nervous system play in producing disease states in the newborn. Moreover, it has become apparent that there are a variety of clinical problems in the neonate that may be viewed, at least conceptually, as disorders of autonomic neural control. It is clear, at least, that the autonomic nervous system is not completely developed in the neonate, and that the lack of autonomic development may be particularly significant in the premature infant. What effect this immaturity may have on the maturation and regulation of neonatal GI, hormonal, and metabolic functions, for instance, remains speculative for the present. Areas in which active investigation is currently proceeding include studies on the role of the autonomic nervous system in the development of hypothermia of the newborn, in the genesis of cystic fibrosis, and in the disorders of GI motility of the neonate. Undoubtedly, this list will and should continue to grow.

7. References

1. ANDERSON, R. H., 1974, Sudden death in infancy: A study of cardiac specialized conduction tissues, *Br. Med. J.* **2**:135.
2. ASHMAN, A. M., AND NELIGAN, G. A., 1959, Changes in the systolic blood pressure of normal babies during the first twenty-four hours of life, *Lancet* **1**:804.
3. BARTOSHUK, A. K., 1964, Human neonatal cardiac responses to sound: A power function, *Psychon. Sci.* **1**:151.
4. BERGMAN, A. B. (ed.), 1970, Sudden infant death syndrome in King County, Washington: Epidemiologic aspects, in: *Sudden Infant Death Syndrome*, pp. 47–54, University of Washington Press, Seattle.
5. BERNARD, J., AND SONTAG, L. W., 1947, Fetal reactivity to tonal stimulation: A preliminary report, *J. Genet. Psychol.* **70**:205.
6. BOSCHAN, P. J., AND STEINSCHNEIDER, A., 1968, Cardiac rate and bottle feeding in the neonate, Unpublished data presented at the annual meeting of the American Psychosomatic Society, Boston, Massachusetts, March 29, 1968.
7. BOWER, B. D., 1954, Pink disease: The autonomic disorder and its treatment with ganglionic blocking agents, *Q. J. Med.* **23**:215.
8. BRINKMAN, C. P., LADNER, C., WESTON, P., AND ASSALI, N. S., 1969, Baroreceptor function in the fetal lamb, *Amer. J. Physiol.* **217**:1346.

9. Brück, K., 1961, Temperature regulation in the newborn infant, *Biol. Neonate* **3**:65.

10. Campbell, G. M., Cockburn, F., Dawes, G. S., and Milligan, J. E., 1966, Pulmonary blood flow and cross-circulation between twin foetal lambs, *J. Physiol. (London)* **186**:96.

11. Celander, O., and Marild, K., 1962, Reactive hyperemia in the foot and calf of the newborn infant, *Acta Pediatr.* **51**:544.

12. Church, S. C., Morgan, B. C., Oliver, T. K., and Guntheroth, W. G., 1967, Cardiac arrythmias in premature infants: An indication of autonomic immaturity?, *J. Pediatr.* **71**:542.

13. Colebatch, H. J. H., Dawes, G. S., Goodwin, J. W., and Nadeau, R. A., 1965, The nervous control of the circulation in the foetal and newly expanded lungs of the lamb, *J. Physiol. (London)* **178**:544.

14. Contis, G., and Lind, J., 1963, Study of systolic blood pressure, heart rate, body temperature or normal newborn infants through first week of life, *Acta Paediatr. Suppl.* **146**:41.

15. Cotton, E. K., and O'Meara, O. P., 1964, Cardiovascular response to sighing in newborn infants, Presented at the annual meeting of the American Pediatric Society, June 16–18, 1964.

16. Daily, W. J. R., Klaus, M., and Meyer, H. B., 1969, Apnea in premature infants: Monitoring, incidence, heart rate changes, and an effect of environmental temperature, *Pediatrics* **43**:510.

17. Dickens, R., and Richmond, J. B., 1944, Lumbar sympathetic block in a premature infant, *J. Amer. Med. Assoc.* **126**:1149.

18. Falck, B., and Owman, C., 1965, A detailed methodological description of the fluorescence method for the cellular demonstration of biogenic monoamines, *Acta Univ. Lund.* **2**:7.

19. Friedman, W. F. (ed.), 1973, The intrinsic physiologic properties of the developing heart, in: *Neonatal Heart Disease,* pp. 21–49, Grune & Stratton, New York.

20. Friedman, W. F., Pool, P. E., Jacobowitz, D., Seagram, S. C., and Braunwald, E., 1968, Sympathetic innervation of the developing rabbit heart, *Circ. Res.* **23**:25.

21. Froggatt, P., Lynas, M. A., and Marshall, T. K., 1968, Sudden death in babies: Epidemiology, *Amer. J. Cardiol.* **22**:457.

22. Gootman, N., Gootman, P. M., Buckley, N. M., Cohen, M. I., Levine, M., and Spielberg, R., 1972, Central vasomotor regulation in the newborn piglet *Sus scrofa, Amer. J. Physiol.* **222**:994.

23. Gottlieb, G., and Simner, M. L., 1966, Relationship between cardiac rate and nonnutritive sucking in human infants, *J. Comp. Physiol. Psychol.* **61**:128.

24. Gough, W. B., and Moore, E. M., 1975, The difference in atrioventricular conduction of pre-

mature beats in young and adult goats, *Circ. Res.* **37**:48.

25. Greenberg, N. H., Cekan, P. R., and Loesch, J. G., 1963, Some cardiac rate and behavioral characteristics of sucking in the neonate, Presented at the annual meeting of the American Psychosomatic Society, April 27–28, 1963.

26. Gupta, J. M., and Scopes, J. W., 1965, Observations on blood pressure in newborn infants, *Arch. Dis. Child.* **40**:637.

27. Hakulinen, A., Hirvoner, L., and Peltoner, T., 1962, Response of blood pressure to sucking and tilting in the newborn infant, *Ann. Paediatr. Fenn.* **8**:56.

28. Halverson, H. M., 1941, Variation in pulse and respiration during different phases of infant behavior, *J. Genet. Psychol.* **59**:259.

29. Hellman, L. M., Johnson, H. L., Tolles, W. E., and Jones, E. H., 1961, Some factors affecting the fetal heart rate, *Amer. J. Obstet. Gynecol.* **82**:1055.

30. Herrington, R. T., Harned, H. S., Ferreiro, J. I., and Griffin, C. A., 1971, The role of the central nervous system in perinatal respiration: Studies of chemoregulatory mechanisms in the term lamb, *Pediatrics* **47**:857.

31. Hon, E. H., 1962, Electronic evaluation of fetal heart rate. VI. Fetal distress—working hypothesis, *Amer. J. Obstet. Gynecol.* **83**:333.

32. Hon, E. H., 1963, The fetal heart rate, in: *Modern Trends in Human Reproductive Physiology* (H. M. Cavey, ed.), pp. 245–256, Butterworth and Co., New York.

33. Hon, E. H., Bradfield, A. H., and Hess, O. W., 1961, The electronic evaluation of the fetal heart rate. V. The vagal factor in fetal bradycardia, *Amer. J. Obstet. Gynecol.* **82**:291.

34. Houstek, J., and Holy, J., 1968, Respiratory viruses and sudden and unexpected death in babies and small infants, *Cesk. Pediatr.* **23**:243.

35. Jacobowitz, D., and Koelle, G. B., 1965, Histochemical correlations of acetylcholine-esterase and catecholamines in postganglionic autonomic nerves of the cat, rabbit, and guinea pig, *J. Pharmacol. Exp. Ther.* **148**:225.

36. James, T. N., 1968, Sudden death in babies, *Amer. J. Cardiol.* **22**:456.

37. Kafka, H. L., and Oh, W., 1971, Direct and indirect blood pressure measurements in newborn infants, *Amer. J. Dis. Child.* **122**:426.

38. Keen, R. E., Chase, H. H., and Graham, F. K., 1965, Twenty-four hour retention by neonates of a habituated heart rate response, *Psychon. Sci.* **2**:265.

39. Kirkpatrick, S. E., Covell, J. W., and Friedman, W. F., 1973, A new technique for continuous assessment of fetal and neonatal cardiac performance, *Amer. J. Obstet. Gynecol.* **116**:963.

40. Larks, S. D., 1964, Resemblance of fetal ECG

complex to standard lead II ORS of newborn, *Obstet. Gynecol.* **24**:1.

41. LAUER, R. M., EVANS, J. A., AOKI, H., AND KITTLE, C. F., 1965, Factors controlling pulmonary vascular resistance in fetal lambs, *J. Pediatr.* **67**:568.

42. LAUPUS, W. E., BILSEL, Z., COLLINS, L. W., AND STUBBS, J. T., JR., 1963, Vasoconstrictor responses in the young infant, *Circulation* **28**:755.

43. LIPTON, E. L., STEINSCHNEIDER, A., AND RICHMOND, J. B., 1964, Autonomic function in the neonate. VIII. Cardio-pulmonary observations, *Pediatrics* **33**:212.

44. LIPTON, E. L., STEINSCHNEIDER, A., AND RICHMOND, J. B., 1965, The autonomic nervous system in early life, *N. Engl. J. Med.* **273**:147.

45. MARON, B. J., CLARK, C. E., GOLDSTEIN, R. E., FISCHER, R. B., AND EPSTEIN, S. E., 1975, Sudden infant death syndrome, *Circulation (Suppl. II)* **52**:II-44.

46. McLAUGLIN, G. W., KIRBY, R. A., KEMMERER, W. T., AND DELEMOS, R. A., 1971, Indirect measurement of blood pressure in infants utilizing Doppler ultrasound, *J. Pediatr.* **79**:300.

47. MELMON, K. L., CLINE, M. J., AND HUGHES, T., 1968, Kinins: Possible mediation of neonatal circulatory changes in man, *J. Clin. Invest.* **47**:1295.

48. MORGAN, B. C., AND GUNTEROTH, W. G., 1965, Cardiac arrhythmias in premature infants, *Pediatrics* **35**:658.

49. MORGAN, B. C., AND GUNTEROTH, W. G., 1965, Cardiac arrhythmias in normal newborn infants, *J. Pediatr.* **67**:1199.

50. MORSE, R. L., BROWNELL, G. L., AND CURRENS, J. H., 1960, The blood pressure of normal infants, *Pediatrics* **25**:50.

51. MOSS, A. J., AND ADAMS, F. H., 1965, *Problems of Blood Pressure in Childhood,* Charles C. Thomas, Springfield, Illinois.

52. MOSS, A. J., DUFFIE, E. R., AND EMMANOUILIDES, G. C., 1963, Blood pressure and vasomotor reflexes in the newborn infant, *Pediatrics* **32**:175.

53. MOSS, A. J., LIEBLING, W., AND ADAMS, F. H., 1958, The flush method for determining blood pressure in infants. II. Normal values during the first year of life, *Pediatrics* **21**:950.

54. MOTT, J. C., 1966, Cardiovascular function in newborn mammals, *Br. Med. Bull.* **22**:66.

55. MURPHY, K. P., AND SMYTH, C. N., 1962, Letters to the editor, *Lancet* **1**:972.

56. NAEYE, R. L., 1961, Arterial changes during the perinatal period, *Arch. Pathol.* **71**:121.

57. NAEYE, R. L., 1973, Pulmonary arterial abnormalities in sudden-infant-death syndrome, *N. Engl. J. Med.* **289**:1167.

58. NELIGAN, G., 1959, The systolic blood pressure in neonatal asphyxia and the respiratory distress syndrome, *Amer. J. Dis. Child.* **98**:460.

59. OH, W., ARCILLA, R. A., OH, M. A., AND LIND, J., 1966, Renal and cardiovascular effects of body tilting in the newborn infant, *Biol. Neonate* **56**:197.

60. OH, W., LIND, J., AND GESSNER, I. H., 1966, The circulatory and respiratory adaptation to early and late cord clamping in newborn infants, *Acta Paediatr.* **55**:17.

61. OLLEY, P. M., AND COCEANI, F., 1975, Prostaglandin E_2 in cyanotic congenital heart disease: A new therapeutic approach, *Circulation (Suppl.)* **52**:II-66.

62. PATTERSON, P. R., LIPTON, E. L., UNNA, K. R., AND GLASER, K., 1956, Dosage of drugs in infants and children. III. Neostigmine, *Pediatrics* **18**:31.

63. PAULEV, P. E., 1968, Cardiac rhythm during breath holding and water immersion in man, *Acta Physiol. Scand.* **73**:139.

64. PERLSTEIN, P. H., EDWARDS, N. K., AND SUTHERLAND, J. M., 1970, Apnea in premature infants and incubator-air-temperature changes, *N. Engl. J. Med.* **282**:461.

65. PHILLIPS, S. J., AGAFE, F. J., SILVERMAN, W. A., AND STEINER, P., 1964, Autonomic cardiac reactivity in premature infants, *Biol. Neonate* **6**:225.

66. PRESTON, J. B., McFADDEN, S., AND MOE, G. K., 1959, AV transmission in young mammals, *Amer. J. Physiol.* **197**:236.

67. RACKOW, H., SALANITRE, E., AND GREEN, L. T., 1961, Frequency of cardiac arrest associated with anesthesia in infants and children, *Pediatrics* **28**:697.

68. RICHMOND, J. B., AND LUSTMAN, S. L., 1955, Autonomic function in the neonate. I. Implications for psychosomatic theory, *Psychosom. Med.* **17**:269.

69. RUDOLPH, A. M., 1970, The changes in the circulation after birth, *Circulation* **61**:343.

70. RUDOLPH, A. M., AND YUAN, S., 1966, Response of the pulmonary vasculature to hypoxia and H^+ ion concentration changes, *J. Clin. Invest.* **45**:399.

71. SALK, L., 1974, Sudden infant death. Normal cardiac habituation and poor autonomic control, *N. Engl. J. Med.* **291**:219.

72. SALMI, T., HANNINEN, P., AND PELTONEN, T., 1960, Electrocardiogenesis of premature infants in first month of life, *Biol. Neonate* **2**:149.

73. SHANNON, D. C., GOTAY, F., STEIN, I. M., ROGERS, M. C., TODRES, I. D., AND MOYLAN, F. M. B., 1975, Prevention of apnea in low birth weight infants, *Pediatrics* **55**:589.

74. SHINEBOURNE, E. A., VAPAAVUORI, E. K., WILLIAMS, R. L., HEYMAN, M. A., AND RUDOLPH, A. M., 1972, Development of baroreflex activity in unanesthetized fetal and neonatal lambs, *Circ. Res.* **31**:710.

75. SONTAG, L. W., AND NEWBERRY, H., 1941, Incidence and nature of fetal arrythmias, *Amer. J. Dis. Child.* **62**:991.

76. SPANN, J. F., JR., SONNENBLICK, E. H., COOPER, T.,

CHIDSEY, C. A., WILLNAN, V. L., AND BRAUNWALD, E., 1966, Cardiac norepinephrine stores and the contractile state of heart muscles, *Circ. Res.* **19**:317.

77. STEELE, R., KRAUS, A. S., AND LANGWORTH, J. T., 1967, Sudden unexpected death in infancy in Ontario, *Can. J. Public Health* **58**:369.

78. STEINSCHNEIDER, A., 1966, Sound intensity and respiratory responses in the neonate: Comparison with cardiac rate responsiveness, *Psychosom. Med.* **30**:534.

79. STEINSCHNEIDER, A., 1970, Possible cardiopulmonary mechanisms, in: *Sudden Infant Death Syndrome* (A. B. Bergman, ed.), pp. 181–205, University of Washington, Seattle.

80. STEINSCHNEIDER, A., 1972, Prolonged apnea and the sudden infant death syndrome; clinical and laboratory observations, *Pediatrics* **50**:646.

81. STEINSCHNEIDER, A., AND RICHMOND, J. B., 1970, The autonomic nervous system. in: *Physiology of the Perinatal Period* (U. Stave, ed.), pp. 859–873, Appleton-Century-Crofts, New York.

82. STEINSCHNEIDER, A., LIPTON, E. L., AND RICHMOND, J. B., 1966, Auditory sensitivity in the infant: Effect of intensity on cardiac and motor responsivity, *Child Dev.* **37**:233.

83. STERN, L., LIND, J., AND KAPLAN, B., 1961, Direct human fetal electrocardiography, *Biol. Neonate* **3**:49.

84. UNNA, K. R., GLASER, K., LIPTON, E., AND PATTERSON, P. R., 1950, Dosage of drugs in infants and children. I. Atropine, *Pediatrics* **6**:197.

85. VALDES-DAPENA, M. A., 1967, Sudden and unexpected death in infancy, a view of the world literature 1954–1966, *Pediatrics* **39**:123.

86. VALDES-DAPENA, M., AND HUMMELER, K., 1963, Sudden and unexpected death in infants. II. Viral infections as causative factors, *J. Pediatr.* **63**:398.

87. VALDES-DAPENA, M. A., GREENE, M., BASAVANNAND, N., CATHERMAN, R., AND TRUEX, R. C., 1973, The myocardial conduction system in sudden death in infancy, *N. Engl. J. Med.* **289**:1179.

88. VALIMAKI, I., 1969, Tape recordings of the electrocardiogram in newborn infants, *Acta Paediatr. Scand. (Suppl.)* **199**:1.

89. VALLBONA, C., 1963, Cardiodynamic studies in the newborn. II. Regulation of the heart rate, *Biol. Neonate* **5**:159.

90. WALLGREN, G., BAUR, M., AND RUDHE, U., 1964, Hemodynamic studies of induced hypo- and hypervolemia in the newborn infant, *Acta Paediatr.* **53**:1.

91. WILDER, J., 1967, *Stimulus and Response: The Law of Initial Value,* John Wright and Sons, Bristol.

92. WILKES, T., FRIEDMAN, R. I., HODGMAN, J., AND LEVAN, N. E., 1966, The sensitivity of the axon reflex in term and premature infants, *J. Invest. Dermatol.* **47**:491.

93. WINTER, S. T., 1966, Neonatal cardiac deceleration on suckle feeding, *Amer. J. Dis. Child.* **112**:11.

94. WOLF, S., 1964, The bradycardia of the dive reflex—a possible mechanism of sudden death, *Trans. Amer. Clin. Climatol. Assoc.* **76**:192.

95. WOODBURY, R. A., ROBINOW, M., AND HAMILTON, W. F., 1958, Blood pressure studies on infants, *Amer. J. Physiol.* **122**:472.

96. YOUNG, I. M., 1961, Blood pressure in the newborn baby, *Br. Med. Bull.* **17**:154.

97. YOUNG, I. M., 1962, Vasomotor tone in the skin blood vessels of the newborn infant, *Clin. Sci.* **22**:325.

98. YOUNG, I. M., AND COTTON, D., 1966, Arterial and venous blood pressure responses during a reduction in blood volume and hypoxia and hypercapnia in the first two days of life, *Pediatrics* **27**:733.

99. YOUNG, I. M., AND HOLLAND, W. W., 1958, Some physiological responses of neonatal arterial blood pressure and pulse rate, *Br. Med. J.* **2**:276.

100. ZIEGLER, R. F., 1951, *Electrocardiographic Studies in Normal Infants,* Charles C. Thomas, Springfield, Illinois.

CHAPTER 34

The Visual System

David S. Walton

1. Introduction

Visual behavior dominates early neonatal development. The wakefulness of the neonate is closely correlated with visual activity.[26] At birth, he responds to light, possesses reactive pupils, demonstrates conjugate eye movements, and opens his lids to see.

Within hours of birth, the neonate may be observed to fixate on a near object. This state, which is often uniocular, may be associated with slowing of body movement, raising of the eyelids, and cessation of crying. If the visual stimulus is moved, it may be briefly pursued, a chase characterized by coarse conjugate refixation movements.

The month following delivery is characterized by rapid ocular development. Periods of visual activity become longer, fixation and following become refined, binocularity becomes the rule, and the range of visual interest expands outward. In the weeks that follow, visual activity accelerates, mirrored by facial expressions of interest, curiosity, and joy.

It is the purpose of this chapter to describe the functional characteristics of the visual system of the newborn and infant.

David S. Walton · Massachusetts Eye and Ear Infirmary, Boston, Massachusetts 02114

2. Visual Function

2.1. Visual Acuity

The clinical concept of visual acuity is the measurement of visual performance based on the determination of the resolution threshold of distant target forms of decreasing size. It is employed as an expression of overall ocular function, and its measurement may be influenced by many factors, such as target contrast and illumination, pupillary size, clarity of ocular media, and refractive error, as well as by retinal factors, which include retinal sensitivity and stage of histological development. The ability of the retina to initiate the recognition of separate points or components of an object is dependent on the number of photoreceptors per unit area in the retina. Visual acuity is the most useful expression of visual achievement. An acuity of 20/20 indicates the resolution of 1' of arc detail.

Measurement of visual acuity in the newborn period has required the use of objective techniques. Optokinetic nystagmus has been utilized, the angular size of the moving targets being varied. By correlation of the onset of nystagmus in the infant with the angular size of the moving targets, the visual acuity of premature and term infants has been estimated. This technique showed good correlation with Snellen visual acuity values when the tests were conducted with older subjects.[64,70] Gorman *et al.*[29] found 93 of 100 newborns responsive to a pattern equivalent to 20/670. Dayton *et al.*[13] concluded from results with 18 full-term infants that the expected visual acuity in this age group is at least 20/150. Kiff and Lepard,[45] in examining premature infants, estimated a visual acuity of 20/820 for such infants, with the earliest such response occurring in an infant weighing 1418 g.

Measurement of visual evoked occipital potentials in infants has also been utilized to measure visual acuity while avoiding problems of behavioral or oculorotary development or attention. Visual evoked potential response to form correlates well with psychophysical threshold acuity measurements. It has seemed reasonable that results are as valid for infants as in adults. Results of visual evoked potential acuity in infants revealed acuity of 20/600 at less than 4 weeks of age, with rapid improvement to 20/20 by 4–6 months of age.[56] Pattern reversal visually evoked potential stimuli recorded in infants 2–6 months of age also indicated a rapid improvement in acuity, so that infants 6 months of age showed responses similar to those of adults with 20/20 acuity.[67]

Application of the optokinetic nystagmus technique to rhesus monkeys demonstrated the development of visual acuity in the first postnatal months in 8 neonates from approximately 20/400 after birth to 20/80 at age 1 month.[61] Visual acuity development in kittens measured by visual evoked potentials is completed by 3 months of age.[25]

2.2. Visual Perception

Visual perception is that associative cortical function that gives meaning and significance to the visual stimuli received by the primary central visual centers. When 40 newborn infants were tested with a series of moving stimuli, responsiveness was significantly greater to a proper face pattern than to two scrambled versions. These results suggest that visual discriminations can be made at an early age, and that organized visual perception is at least in part an unlearned capacity.[28] With pupillary measurements as indicative of interest and arousal, infants 1–4 months of age showed greater response (pupillary dilation) to social stimuli (faces) than to nonsocial patterns.[23] The greater attention of infants to black and white patterns than to plain

surfaces has been felt to be indicative of the newborns' probable innate ability to perceive form.[22]

Observation of infants from the newborn period through 6 months of age has given insight into the human infant's perception of objects.[6] Tested with a virtual object created by viewing through polaroid lenses, these infants showed no surprise when they encountered a solid object to touch, but the absence of solidity in the virtual object caused a significant startle response. These findings suggest that this quality of the solidity of objects is not a learned sense from previous tactile experiences. Object permanence also was found to be an endowed quality given to objects by infants of at least 10 days of age. When the reaction of infants to object movement was studied, the results suggested that infants less than 4 months of age do not attach significance to size, shape, or color, but rather to the motion characteristics and the position of objects.

2.3. Fixation

Fixation is the visual reflex that maintains the image of the object of regard on the retinal area of maximum visual acuity. In the normal eye, this area is the fovea centralis. Successful following of an object, such as optokinetic nystagmus test objects or an examiner's light, depends on the integrity of this fundamental ocular mechanism. Blindness should be suspected in the infant who does not soon locate and fixate his mother and nearby attractive objects.

Examination of full-term newborn infants less than 10 days of age demonstrated the presence of an intact fixation reflex in 17 of 30 subjects alert enough for testing.[14] A qualitative evaluation of the fixation reflex in 163 normal infants from birth to 6 months of age described the refinement of the reflex through this period.[12] The amplitude of readjustment movements during periods of successful following of a moving object was found to decrease markedly during the first 10 days of life, followed by a more gradual decrease in the frequency of such movements over the first 6 months of life.

Haith (personal communication) demonstrated preferential fixation in the newborn for certain types of objects. A vertical edge induced many fixations, while a horizontal edge induced essentially none. Fixations on an acute angle were seen to be concentrated at its apex. Such studies suggest that fixation in the newborn infant is not only present, but also has become complex and refined.

2.4. Accommodation

Accommodation of the ocular lens is the adjustment that occurs in the lens to focus an object of regard on the retina when the object is located closer than infinity. The lens of a young adult's eye can change so as to focus the eye on an object located at points from 10 cm to optical infinity. The nearpoint of focus recedes with normal aging, so that a near spectacle optical aid is often required by 45 years of age. Accommodation is largely involuntary, and is accomplished by the contraction and relaxation of the ciliary muscle, which produces the necessary adjustment in the shape of the lens.

Study of the accommodative performance of 22 normal infants ranging in age from 6 days to 4 months was accomplished employing the technique of dynamic retinoscopy.[34] Before 1 month of age, the infants' accommodative response was found not to adjust to change of target distances. The system appeared locked at one focal distance, the median value of which was 19 cm. Although the lens system was apparently incapable of adjustment for object distance, significant relaxation of the system occurred in 11 sleeping infants compared with its state when the infants were awake and alert. During the 2nd month of infancy, the accommodative system was found to respond adaptively to change in target distance. By 3 months of age, this development appeared complete, with accommodative responses similar to those of an adult.

3. Retinal Development

In the 16th century, the retina was established as the light-sensitive element of the eye. In the centuries that have followed, investigators have studied the retina in search of answers to many questions, including those related to understanding visual capacity of the newborn.

The retina is an appendage of the CNS. Impulses initiated in its photosensitive cells (rods and cones) are relayed by axons of the ganglion cell layer to an intracranial relay center. The histological development of the human neonatal retina approximates that of an adult; however, the visually important foveal region at its center must continue its development after birth. Its relative under-

development, and its subsequent rapid differentiation during the first 4 postnatal months, have historically provided support for the belief that neonates should have little visual acuity.[17]

3.1. Microscopy

Use of thin sections embedded in plastic has made possible the reevaluation of human fetal retinal development by light microscopy. With the use of this technique and electron microscopy, early development of the human fetal retina was described.[36] The sequential early fetal development of the retinal pigment epithelium featuring the evolution of pigment granules followed by surface synthesis was associated with simultaneous development of a multilayered retina. By the 4th fetal month, the posterior retina exhibited all the layers of the adult retina, and the retinal pigment epithelium possessed mature melanosomes, and there was marked undulation of its inner border.

Wiedman and Kuwabara[69] used electron microscopy to illustrate the fetal developmental stages of the rat retina. This important work, describing retinal development paralleling human prenatal development, demonstrates the early formation of the outer segments (rods and cones) of the photoreceptors concomitant with the development of the retinal cellular layers and their synaptic unions in the outer plexiform layer. The electroretinographic quiet present at this stage was shown to end with the development of synapses with inner retinal cells with the ganglion cell layer.

Light microscopy of the retina of the newborn human and thesus monkey demonstrates fully structured rods and cones, pigment epithelium, and inner adult retinal layers. Thinning of the retina at the fovea with spread of the ganglion cells away from the central foveal depression has already begun. Further refinement occurs in the postnatal period. The foveal cones increase in number concomitant with elongation and thinning of their outer segments. The fovea's high density of cones is the anatomic basis for its selective high visual acuity. These changes are completed by the 5th postnatal month.[17]

The neonatal retinal architecture of the human[17] and the rhesus monkey[61] is similar and markedly more advanced at birth than that of the dog and rat, the retinas of which correspond at birth to the level achieved by the human fetus during the 5th gestational month. The subsequent retinal development in these animals is rapid, with a level equivalent to the human and monkey neonates reached by the end of their first postpartum month. Electron microscopy of the important cone outer segments in the foveal region of the newborn rhesus monkey shows well-developed bimembraneous lamellar plates closely resembling those seen in the adult.[61]

3.2. Electrophysiology

The electroretinogram (ERG) is a recording of the change in corneoretinal potential evoked by a light stimulus and occurring secondary to retinal synaptic electrical activity. The ERG is influenced by the wavelength of the light, the state of light adaptation of the eye, the intensity of light reaching the retina, and the maturation of the retina. Since 1951, electroretinography has been applied to the interpretation of the visual performance of the newborn.[52] Suspected absence of an ERG response in term and premature newborns, followed by progressive development during the first 6 months of life, was felt to be consistent with the suspected low level of visual function in the neonate.[52,53]

In 1960, Horsten and Winkelman[37] reported the appearance of the ERG in the developing dog retina at a stage comparable to the human during the 7th fetal month. The appearance of the response was found at considerably higher intensity than was required for a mature retina, and it was also favorably affected by prolongation of dark adaptation. Examination of newborn rhesus monkeys revealed discernible ERG potentials on the day of birth, followed by rapid maturation to adult responses during the first 2 months of life.[61] Reexamination of term and premature infants followed, employing higher-intensity stimuli. It was shown that the ERG is present in the newborn, and that it does not differ in form from that of the adult.[38] Action potentials were increased by dark adaptation, and reached adult size over the first 3 months.[52] In a study of 50 newborns and 10 infants between 1 month and 1 year of age, an ERG was elicited in all subjects, and was adult in form except for diminished amplitudes (Haith, personal communication). Electroretinographic evidence of fusion of repeated light flashes at adult frequencies is also indicative that cone vision is functional in the neonate.[38]

4. Lower and Central Visual Pathways

The lower visual pathway is formed by the axons of retinal ganglion cells directed to central thalamic and tegmental centers. This pathway is recognized grossly by its three anatomic divisions: the optic nerves, chiasm, and optic tracts. The central visual pathway is formed by the paired lateral geniculate subcenters in the thalami, their projections in the cerebral cortex, and the association tracts arising in the occipital lobes.

4.1. Morphology

By the end of the first fetal trimester, the lower visual pathway is well developed, with recognizable nerve fibers extending posteriorly to the chiasm, where partial decussation occurs, followed by extension to the embryologic thalami. During the middle trimester, septal vessels grow into the optic nerve, and the dural, arachnoid, and pial sheaths are completed. The final trimester is characterized by cellular differentiation and myelin formation. Myelination is initiated and then proceeds distally from the geniculate bodies, becoming evident in the optic tracts in the 6th month, in the optic nerves in the 7th month, and reaching the eye during the 9th gestational month.[18] This process was found to be completed in the optic tract of term newborns, but present only in the axial fibers of the optic nerve.[60] The macular fibers are those first myelinated in the optic nerve.[5] There appeared to be no acceleration of myelination in premature infants compared with term newborns of similar gestational age.[60]

It might be well to recall that nerve function is thought to be poorly correlated with myelination; pupillary responsiveness to light has been seen at 6 months in premature infants, long before the completion of myelination.[54]

Development of the upper visual pathways and primary and association neuronal centers in the occipital lobe may be the limiting link in the visual system of the newborn. Myelination in these pathways is first seen at about the time of birth, occurring first in the cortical projection system, which carries the primary visual stimulus from the geniculate bodies to area 17 in the occipital lobe. Myelination proceeds forward centrifugally from the occipital centers, and is later seen in the association tracts. Not until the 4th postnatal month is myelination of all the main visual fiber tracts completed.[19]

Functional correlation with this histological evidence of early visual tract development is provided by the presence in the newborn of the optokinetic reflex, location and fixation of an object, following of an object, pupillary reactivity, and other signs of visual responsiveness. The behavior of the normal seeing newborn is in marked contrast to that of the blind infant.[47]

4.2. Electrophysiology

Light-evoked cortical potentials have been examined in the newborn. In a group of 120 human newborns, including 58 prematures, responses were obtained from the occipital regions following light stimulus in all but 3 of the prematures.[40] Responses differed from those of older children and adults in the shape of the wave response, fatigability, and time lapse (latency) between the stimulus and initial positive wave response registered in the occipital region. The shape of evoked potentials in prematures resembled full-term responses. Absent response in a 1700-g premature became present after 10 days. The latency period was greatest in the prematures, and decreased progressively with age in all the newborn subjects. The amplitude of the visually evoked potential in infants increases in size during the first 5 months of life, and then decreases. During this period, it is larger than adult responses.[67] The latency of the cortically evoked potential responses and wave shape reach adult form by age 1 year.[24] It was suggested that the fatigability of the responses at relatively low stimulus frequencies (3/sec) is due to the slowness of the metabolic process in newborn nerve cells.[40] Occipital evoked potential measurements have been employed to measure infant visual acuity objectively (see Section 2.1).

Similar examinations using newborn rhesus monkeys demonstrated progressive diminution of the latency period, adult values being reached by the 3rd month of life.[61]

Hubel and Wiesel[41] studied single occipital cortical cell responses to patterned retinal stimuli in visually inexperienced and experienced newborn kittens and compared their receptive field organization, cellular binocular interaction, and functional architecture with results from similar studies using adult cats. The responses from kitten cortical cells were found to be strikingly similar to those of the adult cat, suggesting that highly complex neural connections are developed in the newborn and do not await the arrival of light stimulation or other visual experience.[41]

5. Ocular Motility

Each eye acquires motility within its respective facial socket by the action of six extraocular muscles. The higher the mammal is in the phylogenetic scale, the more highly developed are the extraocular muscles and eye movements.[9] An increased range of movement allows for the preservation of a wide visual field, despite the developmental shift of the eyes from the side to the front of the head associated with the climb up the phylogenetic scale.

From an early embryonic stage, the four muscles are seen in the orbit in their adult arrangement, directed to the globe from their origin at the apex of the orbit. The medial rectus appears more fully developed than the lateral rectus muscle during embryological development. The development of the oblique muscles parallels that of the rectus muscles. During the course of fetal development, the muscles lengthen and narrow until at term they resemble the mature state.

The extraocular muscles are voluntary, and within the family of striated muscles, they have unique pharmacological, histological, and physiologic characteristics that have been well described.[1,2,10] One of the unique features of these muscles is their constant state of electrical activity, even when the eye is in the straight-ahead position, which contrasts with the electrical quiet of a relaxed skeletal muscle.

The position of an eye or its velocity of movement is determined by the relative innervation received by opposing pairs of ocular muscles. Centers that control this innervation are as follows: from the labyrinth in response to body position or acceleration; from the retina in response to light intensity, eccentric fixation, and disparateness of retinal immages (i.e., not falling on corresponding retinal receptor areas); and from cerebral centers participating in voluntary, object-elicited eye movements, or following or pursuit eye movements. These centers work simultaneously to determine the momentary resultant ocular muscle equilibrium.

It has often been the custom, in describing the ocular movements of the newborn and their development, to speak of their "sequential development."[44] Vestibular movements were conceded to be present at birth, followed by the appearance of random movements, followed at age 2 weeks by (object) optically elicited movements. Following movements were said then to occur at age 4 months, followed later by acoustically elicited eye movements and voluntary movements at age 5 months. The loss of oculomotor function in the reverse order in progressive deterioration of the CNS with the uncovering of the various stages of development may be indirect evidence to support this sequential pattern of development.[42] Recent studies have at least moved the timetable ahead by demonstrating a complex system of eye movements to be already present in the neonate. These movements are described below in the order in which they were named above.

Forced conjugate deviation of the eyes in response to vestibular stimulation is perhaps the first and simplest eye movement in the developmental hierarchy. These movements are analogous to the residual doll's head movements seen with rotation of the head in the presence of acquired paralysis of the other sources of conjugate gaze. Forced deviation of the eyes appeared to be the only type of induced eye movement present in resting premature infants of 32–34 weeks of gestational age.[63]

Premature infants first demonstrated the onset of postrotatory vestibular nystagmus at 33 weeks of gestational age, and at later ages, regularly demonstrated vestibular nystagmus similar to that seen in full-term infants subjected to body rotation. Vestibular nystagmus consists of forced deviation secondary to the effect of rotation on the semicircular vestibular end-organs and of a reflex quick return component of uncertain origin but probably utilizing pathways related to voluntary gaze. Vestibular nystagmus, in response to rotation, is best seen as a postrotatory phenomenon, and is a constant finding in the awake, full-term neonate. Its absence is a sensitive sign of a normal or pathologic variation in the state of consciousness. Vestibular nystagmus in response to caloric stimulation in the newborn has been variously reported as present or absent. Its presence should be expected in the alert neonate.

During the clinical examination, object-elicited movements are difficult to initiate in response to a hand light or other objective until about 3 weeks of age. Their association with head movements appears soon after this time. In contrast, following movements to either side can usually be demon-

strated in the immediate postnatal period with the use of simple targets by beginning the test in the center of the field.

Following movements have been shown to be well developed in the neonate,[12] and to possess a high degree of conjugation. The difference between the following movements of infants and those of older children is in the number and amplitude of necessary refixations required to correct the tendency of the following eye to fall behind the moving target. Refinement of these following movements occurs over the first year of life, with the amplitude of the refixations decreasing rapidly during the first 2 neonatal weeks. The angular velocity of the refixation movements is very rapid compared with the relatively slow following or pursuit movement. There is both anatomic and neurophysiological support for the presence of independent rapid (saccadic) and slow (pursuit or following) oculomotor systems.[58] Their integrated activity produces successful following movements.

It is interesting that normal voluntary eye movements are never slow eye movements, but rather resemble the rapid saccadic refixations or the object-elicited type movement. It is a moot question when the neonate first shows voluntary eye movement. The presence of the rapid phase of vestibular nystagmus, and the saccadic refixation with following movements in the term and premature neonate, suggest that the initiation of voluntary gaze movements await only the development of an intellectual desire for them.

When 36 full-term newborn infants were examined with respect to their response to central or laterally placed lights, significant divergence of each eye with respect to the central light was observed.[68] Frequent conjugate movement was seen with respect to lateral stimuli, but convergence was consistently absent. Convergence and divergence eye movements are first seen during the 3rd month (Haith, personal communication).

6. Intraocular Pressure

An important characteristic of an eyeball is its internal pressure. Among body organ systems, only arterial pressure is greater than the intraocular pressure. The chief function of intraocular pressure is to maintain the optical shape of the cornea. Adequate ocular pressure also inhibits distortion of the globe, which would cause significant injury secondary to minor trauma. Variation from normal

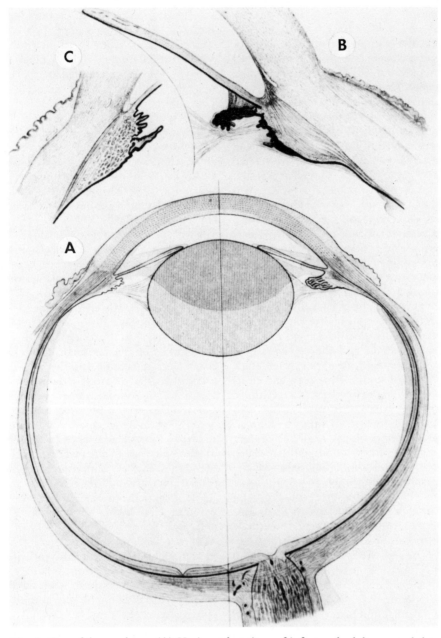

Fig. 1. Eye of the newborn. (A) Horizontal sections of infant and adult eyes scaled to equal size and superimposed. (B) Adult corneoscleral angle. (C) Newborn corneoscleral angle. Note position of Schlemm's canal and retention of mesodermal tissue, compared with B. Reproduced from Merkel and Orr.[57]

pressure causes a decrease in corneal transparency: increased pressure causes edema and clouding of the cornea, and decreased pressure allows corneal wrinkling to occur.

The eye may be considered a sphere of constant volume, with relatively little elasticity. The anterior chamber, behind the cornea, is shallow in the newborn, and communicates with the posterior chamber through the pupil. These chambers are filled with an aqueous solution. Although intraocular pressure is affected momentarily by arterial pulsation and external pressure, it is chiefly determined by the balance between aqueous humor formation and rate of outflow. The aqueous humor is secreted from the ciliary processes of the ciliary body, exists in equilibrium with iris blood vessels, and is finally filtered out through the trabecular meshwork to reach the extraocular venous network. Alteration in aqueous formation and drainage occurs to produce normal and abnormal variations in the intraocular pressure (see Fig. 1).

The development of the filtration area begins at the 5th gestational month. At birth, the filtration angle of the anterior chamber is well developed. Throughout childhood, its development continues with circumferential migration of its apex, widening of the corneoscleral angle, and the appearance of pigmentation. These stages have been well illustrated.[20] Histological study of the fetal and postnatal corneoscleral angle showed the intimate relationship of the ciliary body musculature and filtering trabecular meshwork.[50] Scanning electron microscopy of the iridocorneal angle of fetuses, premature and mature infants, and adults revealed a marked separation of the lining cells of the endothelial membrane at approximately 8 months of gestational age.[33] This separation, it would seem, represents an adaptive change to allow freer exit of fluid.

Tonometric pressure readings in the premature newborn were first reported by Brockhurst,[7] who examined 59 premature infants under topical anesthesia. Of these infants, 3 born nearly 3 months prematurely demonstrated hypotony, while the others had an average pressure of 24 mm Hg (1948 Friedenwald Standard Tonometer Scale). A total of 32 tonometer readings in 1-hr-old, full-term neonates revealed high normal pressures.[27] Examination of 100 eyes in full-term newborns during the first week of life using topical anesthesia revealed an average pressure of 16 mm Hg, with values ranging between 11 and 24 mm Hg (1955 Friedenwald Scale).[39] In this study, lower pressure

determinations correlated with newborns of greater birth weight. When electronic tonometry was performed on 504 newborns without any drugs, an average pressure of 12.4 mm Hg was determined.[15] The intraocular pressure of 356 normal eyes of children from age 1 day to age 10 years was measured under ether general anesthesia.[49] Of these eyes, 96 examined in the first year had an average pressure of 21 mm Hg (1955 scale). The effect of general anesthesia causing the lowering of intraocular pressure must be considered in the interpretation of these results.[48] Later childhood years correlated with a progressive diminution of the intraocular pressure. Ocular pressure measurements in 30 normal infants under 1 year were taken under light Fluothane anesthesia.[16] With the use of applanation tonometry, a mean of 9.6 mm Hg was determined.

Most clinical problems related to intraocular pressure occur secondary to an elevation of pressure caused by increased resistance to aqueous outflow. Measurement of the facility of outflow of aqueous humor by tonographic methods offers the opportunity to study this important determinant of intraocular pressure.[4,32]

It has been the experience of most clinical investigators that measurement of the facility of outflow in infants is difficult technically and unreliable even when the infants are prepared with general anesthesia.[35] A study of 96 children between 11 and 13 years of age revealed values for facility of outflow within the range considered normal for adults.[30] Enucleated eyes from fetuses of 20 weeks of gestational age to term were studied to determine the coefficient of outflow employing constant-pressure perfusion.[51] For 13 eyes from fetuses of 22–28 weeks, the mean outflow was 0.16 μl/min per mm Hg (facility of outflow, C, μl/min per mm Hg). For 10 eyes from fetuses 31 weeks or older, the facility of outflow was 0.24 μl/min per mm Hg. This increased facility of aqueous outflow measured in the eyes from infants closer to term was correlated theoretically with the perforation of the continuous lining of the filtration angle that occurs late in gestation.

7. The Pupil

The pupil is the round aperture seen in the center of the iris annulus. Functional iris components include a central sphincter muscle and a peripheral dilator muscle. The sphincter fibers appear in an early embryological stage and give the pupil movement in response to light as early as the 6th gestational month. The dilator muscle does not make its appearance until the 6th month, and is not fully formed and fuctional until after birth.

At birth, the pupil is usually small and shows only moderate movement in response to light. Enlargement of the resting pupil may occur early in the postnatal period, or it may be delayed until 1 year of age. Its size then progresses to reach a maximum size during adolescence.

8. The Lacrimal System

The function of the lacrimal system is the maintenance of a normal precorneal and conjunctival tear film. Tears act as a lubricant, possess antibacterial properties, and enhance the optical characteristics of the front of the cornea. To accomplish these functions and others, tears have a complex composition and organized layering.[1,59]

The basic physiologic tear fluid seen under usual conditions is mostly the secretion of accessory lacrimal glands associated intimately with the conjunctival fornices. These glands are present at birth, but are incompletely developed. Excessive tear production, as seen secondary to corneal irritation or to psychic stimulation, is produced by the main lacrimal gland. This structure appears early in embryological development and, though well formed at birth, does not reach full development until age 3–4 years.[46]

Obstruction of the lacrimal drainage passage is a common clinical problem in pediatric ophthalmology. The development of the nasolacrimal passages has been well described and illustrated.[8,21,65] Canalization of the system begins early at its ocular end. The lacrimal puncta open on the lid margins during the 7th month; however, the lower end of the nasolacrimal duct, even at birth, is frequently separated from the nasal cavity. This block consists of a membrane formed by the opposed mucosal linings of the nasal fornix and lacrimal duct. An investigation of 15 full-term stillborn fetuses revealed this abnormality in 73% of their lacrimal ducts.[8]

When basic tear production was examined in 65 noncrying, premature newborns using Schirmer litmus paper, secretion was found to be proportionate to body weight.[3] Only 14% of prematures of less than 1500 g had normal tear production, while 63% of those weighing between 2000 and 2500 g had normal lacrimation. Tear secretion increases progressively during the first postnatal month following premature birth.[65] Lacrimation in the premature newborn is increased with crying.[3]

Lacrimation in the full-term newborn is usually normal. Of 140 eyes of noncrying, 1-day-old newborns, 82% demonstrated normal secretion using the adult Schirmer standard.[3] This percentage increased with the crying state or with retesting at 1 week of age. More recently, 212 newborns were examined for quantitative evidence of tear secretion.[62] Of this group, 90% showed normal secretion rates compared with older children when examined with Schirmer standardized sterile filter strips.

Tear samples from 8 newborns examined by paper electrophoresis demonstrated normal globulin, albumin, and lysozymal concentration when compared with adult tear fluid.[3] Assay for the presence of lysozymal antibacterial activity was also in an adult normal range.[3]

Psychic weeping is usually delayed until the 3rd or 4th postnatal month.

9. Refractive State

Vision depends on the production of focused images on the retina. The anterior surface of the cornea is the principal refracting surface, and is aided by the lens inside the eye. The lens can vary its power, and so can function as the fine-focusing component. Refraction in the eye is a function of the corneal and lens curvatures (lens power), the distance between these lenses, and their distance from the retina.

Compared with the body, the eye grows little, increasing its volume only 3-fold from birth to maturity. Of this increment, however, 70% is attained by age four.[43] The main growth occurs in the posterior segment.

The cornea of the newborn is proportionately larger than that of the mature eye, and is geometrically similar to that of an adult.[55] The radius of curvature of its center is about 1 mm less than that of an adult cornea.[55] The flattening of the cornea with postnatal growth helps to mask the myopic effect of axial elongation (see Fig. 1).

The lens also flattens with continued postnatal growth and occupies proportionately less volume.

The total refractive error of full-term newborns was found to be hyperopic and between 1 and 4 diopters in 80% of infants tested.[11] Astigmatism is found more frequently in the hyperopic newborn than in the myopes.[11] With postnatal growth, the eye becomes more hyperopic in early childhood, followed by a progressive myopic growth pattern.[66]

Examination of 150 premature infants found a predominance of emmetropia or myopia.[31]

10. Summary

Visual behavior in the newborn is active and develops rapidly. The visual acuity of the newborn is about 20/600 and improves steadily. Fixation occurs, and evidence of visual perception is present. Retinal development is advanced at birth, awaiting only macular refinement in the neonatal period. Electroretinography indicates the presence of a well-developed visual cone system. Myelination of the optic pathways is completed after birth.

In the neonate, eye movements can be induced in response to vestibular stimuli, moving objects, displaced still objects, and optokinetic stimuli.

Structures that control aqueous humor dynamics are well developed in the newborn. The intraocular pressure in newborns is within the range of normal for older children and adults.

The pupil is small and reactive in the newborn, but accommodation is not active until the 2nd month of life.

Basic tear production is qualitatively and quantitatively normal in the neonate. Tearing occurs later in infancy.

The newborn refractive error is usually hyperopic. The eye is proportionately large at birth, compared with the body as a whole, and shows rapid growth in infancy.

ACKNOWLEDGMENT

The author is indebted to Mrs. Jean Wong and Ms. Susan Oxford for their editorial assistance.

11. References

1. ADLER, F. H., 1975, *Physiology of the Eye,* 6th Ed., pp. 18–22, C. V. Mosby Co., St. Louis.
2. ADLER, F. H., 1975, *Physiology of the Eye,* 6th Ed., pp. 86–121, C. V. Mosby Co., St. Louis.
3. APT, L., AND CULLEN, B. F., 1964, Newborns do secrete tears, *J. Amer. Med. Assoc.* **189**:951–953.
4. BECKER, B., 1958, The decline in aqueous secretion and outflow facility with age, *Amer. J. Ophthalmol.* **46**:731–736.
5. BEMBRIDGE, B. A., 1956, The problem of myelination of the central nervous system with special reference to the optic nerve, *Trans. Ophthalmol. Soc. U. K.* **76**:311.
6. BOWER, T. G. R., 1971, The object in the world of the infant, *Sci. Amer.* **224**:30–38.
7. BROCKHURST, R. J., 1955, The intraocular pressure of premature infants, *Amer. J. Ophthalmol.* **39**:808–11.
8. CASSIDY, J. V., 1952, Developmental anatomy of the nasolacrimal duct, *Arch. Ophthalmol. (Chicago)* **47**:141–158.
9. COGAN, D. G., 1956, *Neurology of the Ocular Muscles,* p. 7, Charles C. Thomas, Springfield, Illinois.
10. COGAN, D. G., 1956, *Neurology of the Ocular Muscles,* Chapt. 3, Charles C. Thomas, Springfield, Illinois.
11. COOK, R. C., 1951, Refractive and ocular findings in the newborn, *Amer. J. Ophthalmol.* **34**:1407.
12. DAYTON, G., AND JONES, M., 1964, Analysis of characteristics of fixation reflex in infants by use of direct current electrooculography, *Neurology* **14**:1152–1156.
13. DAYTON, G., JONES, M., RAWSON, R., STEELE, B., AND ROSE, M., 1964, Developmental study of coordinated eye movements in the human infant. I. Visual acuity determined by electrooculography, *Arch. Ophthalmol. (Chicago)* **71**:865–870.
14. DAYTON, G., JONES, M., STEELE, B., AND ROSE, M., 1964, Developmental study of coordinated eye movements in the human infant. II. Fixation reflex, *Arch. Ophthalmol. (Chicago)* **71**:871–875.
15. DOMINGUEZ, A., ALVAREZ, M. G., AND SANCHEZ, B., 1975, Electronic tonometry in the newborn, *Adv. Ophthalmol.* **29**:88–125.
16. DOMINGUEZ, A., BANOS, M. S., ALVAREZ, M. G., CONTRA, G. F., AND QUINLETA, F. B., 1974, Intraocular pressure measurements in infants under general anesthesia, *Amer. J. Ophthalmol.* **78**:110–116.
17. DUKE-ELDER, W. S. (ed.), 1963, *System of Ophthalmology,* Vol. 3, Part 1, pp. 96–99, C. V. Mosby Co., St. Louis.
18. DUKE-ELDER, W. S. (ed.), 1963, *System of Ophthalmology,* Vol. 3, Part 1, p. 119, C. V. Mosby Co., St. Louis.
19. DUKE-ELDER, W. S. (ed.), 1963, *System of Ophthalmology,* Vol. 3, Part 1, p. 125, C. V. Mosby Co., St. Louis.
20. DUKE-ELDER, W. S. (ed.), 1963, *System of Ophthalmology,* Vol. 3, Part 1, pp. 171–179, C. V. Mosby Co., St. Louis.
21. DUKE-ELDER, W. S. (ed.), 1963, *System of Ophthalmology,* Vol. 3, Part 1, pp. 241–246, C. V. Mosby Co., St. Louis.

22. FANTZ, R. L., 1963, Patterned vision in newborn infants, *Science* **140**:296.

23. FITZGERALD, H. E., 1968, Autonomic pupillary reflex action during early infancy and its relation to social and non-social visual stimuli, *J. Exp. Child Psychol.* **6**:470.

24. FOGARTY, T. P., AND REUBEN, R. N., 1969, Light-evoked cortical and retinal responses in premature infants, *Arch. Ophthalmol. (Chicago)* **81**:454.

25. FREEMAN, D. N., AND MARG, E., 1975, Visual acuity development coincides with sensitive period in kittens, *Nature (London)* **254**:614.

26. GESELL, A., 1949, *Vision: Its Development in Infant and Child,* Paul B. Hoeber, New York.

27. GILES, G. L., 1959, Tonometer tensions in the newborn, *Arch. Ophthalmol. (Chicago)* **61**:517–519.

28. GOREN, C. C., SARTY, M., AND PAUL, Y. K., 1975, Visual following and pattern discrimination of face-like stimuli by newborn infants, *Pediatrics* **56**:544–549.

29. GORMAN, J. J., COGAN, D. G., AND GELLIS, S. S., 1957, An apparatus for grading the visual acuity of infants on the basis of optokinetic nystagmus, *Pediatrics* **19**:1088–1092.

30. GRAFF, E., AND DYSON, C., 1965, Outflow studies in children, *Arch. Ophthalmol. (Chicago)* **74**:36, 37.

31. GRAHAM, M. V., AND GRAY, O., 1963, Refraction of premature babies' eyes, *Br. Med. J.* **1**:1452–1454.

32. GRANT, W. M., 1950, Tonographic method for measuring the facility and rate of aqueous flow in human eyes, *Arch. Ophthalmol. (Chicago)* **44**:204–214.

33. HANSSON, H. A., AND JERNDAL, T., 1971, Scanning electron microscopic studies on the development of the iridocorneal angle in human eye, *Invest. Ophthalmol.* **10**:252–265.

34. HAYNES, H., WHITE, B. L., AND HELD, R., 1965, Visual accommodation in human infants, *Science,* **148**:528–530.

35. HETHERINGTON, J., AND SHAFFER, R. N., 1968, Tonometry and tonography in congenital glaucoma, *Invest. Ophthalmol.* **7**:134, 137.

36. HOLLENBERG, M. J., AND SPIRA, A. W., 1972, Early development of the human retina, *Can. J. Ophthalmol.* **7**:472–491.

37. HORSTEN, G. P. M., AND WINKELMAN, J. E., 1960, Development of the ERG in relation to histological differentiation of the retina in man and animals, *Arch. Ophthalmol. (Chicago)* **63**:232–242.

38. HORSTEN, G. P. M., AND WINKELMAN, J. E., 1962, Electrical activity of the retina in relation to histological differentiation in infants born prematurely and at full-term, *Vision Res.* **2**:269–276.

39. HORVEN, I., 1961, Tonometry in newborn infants, *Acta Ophthalmol. (Copenhagen)* **39**:911–918.

40. HRBEK, A., AND MARES, P., 1964, Cortical evoked responses to visual stimulation in full-term and premature newborns, *Electroencephalogr. Clin. Neurophysiol.* **16**:575–581.

41. HUBEL, D. H., AND WIESEL, T., 1963, Receptive fields of cells in striate cortex of very young, visually inexperienced kittens, *J. Neurophysiol.* **26**:994–1002.

42. JAMPEL, R. S., AND QUAGLIO, N., 1961, Eye movements in Tay–Sachs disease, *Neurology* **11**:1013–1019.

43. KAISER, J. H., 1926, Die Grösse und das Wachstum der Hornhaut im Kindesalter, *Arch. Ophthalmol.* **116**:288–311.

44. KESTENBAUM, A., 1961, *Clinical Methods of Neuro-ophthalmologic Examinations,* Grune & Stratton, New York.

45. KIFF, R., AND LEPARD, C., 1966, Visual response of premature infants, *Arch. Ophthalmol. (Chicago)* **75**:631–633.

46. KIRCHSTEIN, F., 1894, Ueber die Tränendrüse der Neugeborenen, Dissertation, Berlin, cited in *Acta Ophthalmol.* Copenhagen 1955, **33**:557.

47. KNOX, L., 1964, Cortically blind infants, *Amer. J. Ophthalmol.* **58**:617–621.

48. KORNBLUETH, W., 1959, Influence of general anesthesia on intraocular pressure in man, *Arch. Ophthalmol. (Chicago)* **61**:84–87.

49. KORNBLUETH, W., ALADJEMOFF, L., MAGRA, F., AND GABBAY, A., 1964, Intraocular pressure in children measured under general anesthesia, *Arch. Ophthalmol. (Chicago)* **72**:489, 490.

50. KUPFER, C., 1962, Relationship of ciliary body meridional muscle and corneoscleral trabecular meshwork, *Arch. Ophthalmol. (Chicago)* **68**:818–822.

51. KUPFER, C., AND ROSS, K., 1971, The development of outflow facility in human eyes, *Invest. Ophthalmol.* **10**:513–517.

52. LETTERSTROM, B., 1951, The clinical electroretinogram. IV. The electroretinogram in children during the first year of life, *Acta Ophthalmol. (Copenhagen)* **29**:295–304.

53. LETTERSTROM, B., 1952, The electroretinogram in prematurely born children, *Acta Ophthalmol. (Copenhagen)* **30**:405–408.

54. MAGITOT, A., 1909, l'Apparition précoce du réflexe photo-moteur au cours du développement foetal, *Ann. Oculist (Paris)* **141**:161.

55. MANDELL, R. B., 1967, Corneal contour of the human infant, *Arch. Ophthalmol. (Chicago)* **77**:345–348.

56. MARG, E., FREEMAN, D. N., PELTZMAN, P., AND GOLDSTEIN, P. I., 1976, Visual acuity development in human infants: Evoked potential measurements, *Invest. Ophthalmol.* **15**:150–153.

57. MERKEL, F., AND ORR, W., 1892, Das Auge des Neugeborenen an einem schematischen Durchschnitt erläutert, *Anat. Hefte* **1**:273–296.

58. MILLER, D., 1968, Saccadic and pursuit systems: A review, *J. Pediatr. Ophthalmol.* **5**:39–43.

59. MISHIMA, A., 1965, Some physiological aspects of the

precorneal tear film, *Arch. Ophthalmol. (Chicago)* **73**:233–241.

60. NAKAYAMA, K., 1968, Studies on the myelination of the human optic nerve, *Jpn. J. Ophthalmol.* **11**:132–140.

61. ORDY, J. M., SAMORAJSKI, T., COLLINS, R. C., AND NAGY, A. R., 1965, Postnatal development of vision in a subjuman primate, *Arch. Ophthalmol. (Chicago)* **73**:674–686.

62. PATRICK, R. K., 1974, Lacrimal secretion in full-term and premature babies, *Trans. Ophthalmol. Soc. U. K.* **93**:283–290.

63. PENDLETON, M. E., AND PAINE, R., 1961, Vestibular nystagmus in newborn infants, *Neurology* **11**:450–458.

64. REINECKE, R., AND COGAN, D., 1958, Standardization of objective visual acuity measurements, *Arch. Ophthalmol. (Chicago)* **60**:418–421.

65. SJÖGREN, H., 1955, Lacrimal secretion in newborn premature and fully developed children, *Acta Ophthalmol. (Copenhagen)* **33**:557–560.

66. SLATAPER, F. J., 1950, Age norms of refraction and vision, *Arch. Ophthalmol. (Chicago)* **43**:466–481.

67. SOKOL, S., AND DOBSON, V., 1976, Pattern reversal visually evoked potentials in infants, *Invest. Ophthalmol.* **15**:58–61.

68. WICKELGREN, L. W., 1969, The ocular response of human newborns to intermittent visual movement, *J. Exp. Child Psychol.* **8**:469–482.

69. WIEDMAN, T. A., AND KUWABARA, T., 1968, Postnatal development of the rat retina, *Arch. Ophthalmol. (Chicago)* **79**:470–484.

70. WOLIN, I., AND DILLMAN, A., 1964, Objective measurement of visual acuity, *Arch. Ophthalmol. (Chicago)* **71**:822–826.

CHAPTER 35

The Auditory Response

John Bench

1. Introduction

The author has deliberately chosen the term "auditory response" in this discussion of auditory function in the fetus and neonate, and has eschewed the use of "hearing." The reason for the choice is that the word "hearing" used with reference to the fetus, neonate, and even the older infant could give rise to a conceptual hazard. A little thought will show that "hearing" is normally used in relation to a complex adult activity whereby the hearer elaborates, consciously or unconsciously, the connotations of certain acoustic properties of sounds on the basis of previous auditory experience. In other words, when the adult hears, he interprets sounds by making use of what he has heard previously, even long previously, and this interpretation can be regarded as part of hearing. Also, "hearing" may refer to listening, to perceiving, and so on. Thus, the word can have different meanings, but if it is used to refer to babies' responses to sounds, the meaning must be different even from these meanings. The baby, especially the fetus, cannot have had many of the adult kinds of auditory experiences. Even if he had, he does not possess the ability to process them in the same way as an adult. These conceptual difficulties can be finessed

if we reject the use of "hearing" with reference to the fetus and infant and use instead the expression "auditory behavior," or, more specifically, "auditory response." We can thus limit the discussion that follows to a more objective account of responses to sound stimuli and thereby avoid the inference of higher-order perceptual skills that the fetus or neonate does not possess.

2. Fetal Auditory Response

The study of fetal auditory response may be conveniently separated into two aspects: prenatal (especially the third trimester of pregnancy) and perinatal. Clearly, the neurological, psychological, and physiologic nature of the baby will be different in these different stages of development, but there are other factors concerned with the reliability and ease of investigation that reinforce the case for discussing them separately.

2.1. Prenatal Aspects

Several brief notes describing responses of the human fetus to sound or vibratory stimuli were published some 50 years ago. These reports suggested that the fetus may respond to stimuli in the audiofrequency range, but they could not be relied on too greatly because the observations were made on a small number of cases and lacked a

John Bench · Audiology Unit, Royal Berkshire Hospital, Reading, England

number of controls (e.g., for spontaneous or false positive "responses"). Also, these studies were accidental or occasional, and in some instances relied only on the mother's reports of fetal movement. This situation changed in the 1930s and 1940s with the pioneering work of Sontag,[46–48] who elected to study fetal heart rate and objectively recorded movement responses and thus obtained more reliable response data. Sontag's approach has since been adopted and extended by investigators throughout the world.[17,21,28,39] There is thus a body of opinion that regards the human fetus as responsive to audiofrequency stimuli before birth, and this opinion is in accord with the view that the fetal ear is anatomically complete well before birth.[6,53] However, although the reported investigations have been worldwide, they have been relatively few, and have occasionally been questioned. In part, the reason is probably that the technical and procedural difficulties involved both in stimulating and in recording responses from the human fetus *in utero* are formidable. It will be salutary to consider these difficulties briefly. The reader is referred to Bench and Mentz[8] for a more exhaustive account.

The technique generally used is to stimulate the fetus with audiofrequency stimuli via a transducer (a loudspeaker or vibrator) placed on the mother's abdomen above the fetal head. The position of the latter is, of course, discovered by palpation or, more reliably, by ultrasonic methods. The use of a vibrator in contact with the mother's skin[28] is usually a more efficient way of introducing sounds into maternal tissues than the use of a loudspeaker, since the sound from the latter is reflected considerably at the air–maternal skin interface. Although we can measure the intensity and other properties of the sound stimuli at the transducer, it is difficult to ascertain the level and type of sound that impinges on the fetus itself. To overcome this problem, several workers passed small microphones into the uteri of women just after they had given birth[28] or, following amniotomy, during birth.[23,54] Although there is some disagreement over the details of calibration and placement of the microphone, this method gives a useful estimate of the sound stimulus levels near the fetal head, and at the same time yields data on the background noise levels in the uterus. The latter appear to be of the order of 85 dB SPL, are mainly composed of low-frequency sounds, and probably originate in turbulent blood flow, muscle movement, and

borborygmi from the mother. Hence, it is advisable to use sound stimuli that are either loud (100–110 dB SPL) or middle-to-high-frequency or both to avoid masking of the sound stimulus by internal background noises. Heart rate responses may be measured by monitoring changes in fetal heart rate (FHR) computed from the fetal ECG (via maternal abdominal electrodes), phonocardiogram, or, more recently, by an ultrasonic FHR monitor.[21] Fetal movement responses are recorded by a displacement transducer on the mother's body.[21] None of the techniques is completely satisfactory, since all are affected to some degree by maternal artifacts, and hence there has been recourse to some work with animals[9,42] for more direct recording. Lindsley[35] attempted to record fetal EEG (FEEG) potentials via maternal abdominal electrodes, but his work does not seem to have been replicated.

Other problems arise when the alert investigator wishes to prevent the mother from hearing the fetal sound stimulus, and to allow for variations in the psychological state of the mother.[8] It is likely that both aspects will have some effect on the overall levels of maternal physiology, and hence will affect the responsivity of the fetus via humoral mediation. In a well-conducted study, note should also be taken of uterine contractions and maternal geometry or posture. Both are likely to have some effect on the transduction of sounds through the maternal body wall, may affect movement responses by the fetus, and, in the case of uterine contractions, produce effects ranging from pressure and tactile stimuli on the fetal body to changes of fetal state related to variations in the blood supply caused by pressure on the umbilical cord.[8]

The comments made above provide ample evidence that work on human fetal auditory responses is far from easy. Although the relative isolation of the fetus during pregnancy protects it from the outside world, and, in the case of auditory response studies, from a variety of adventitious factors that may complicate the interpretation of the experiment, this advantage is offset both by problems of conveying auditory stimuli to the fetus and by difficulties in measuring fetal responses of sufficient magnitude at the maternal skin surface. The latter issue has meant that studies of the human fetus have usually had to be confined to the last trimester of pregnancy, when fetal signals are sufficiently large to be measured.

It is not possible to give anything like a full description of fetal responses to sounds in this third trimester, because workers in the field have been few (see above), and different workers have used different sound stimuli, ranging from pure tones to noisebands, and with various estimates (or no estimates) of such factors as sound pressure level and rise/decay times. There is general agreement, however, that with a variety of such stimuli there is usually a movement response detected within a second or so of the sound-stimulus onset. This movement is usually accompanied by, and perhaps at least partly causes, a FHR change that is usually monophasic and accelerative, but appears to be of longer latency-to-peak change than for, say, the neonate. This property may reflect the immature state of aspects of the fetal nervous system. It was also shown,[28] however, that in a few cases, the FHR response was also of longer latency than that seen in older infants, young children, and adults.

2.2. Perinatal Aspects

Very recently, there has been some change of emphasis in the study of fetal auditory responses from work in the last trimester of pregnancy to work in the puerperium. The reason is that the accessibility of the fetal scalp during birth permits more reliable measures to be made of such parameters as FEEG and FHR. This easier accessibility, together with a recent increase in the use of sophisticated electrophysiological monitoring equipment and computer-assisted data analysis by obstetricians, has opened up a new field for measuring fetal auditory responses. The work of Scibetta and Rosen,[42] who developed a method for FEEG recording from the brain of fetal guinea pigs, has already been mentioned. They and their colleagues[40,43] recently extended aspects of this work by using scalp electrodes to measure human FEEG changes during labor, after ruption of the amniotic membranes, in response to both maternal medications and sound stimuli. They have also developed a small sound-emitting transducer that can be placed alongside the fetal ear, so that the entire experiment can be conducted without the problems arising from obstruction by the maternal body wall and other maternal structures, including the uterus. Their results suggest that FEEG responses to audiofrequency stimuli are broadly similar to those recorded from the neonate. This point is important because, as is well known, it is all too easy to record an "EEG" signal that on closer investigation turns out to be an artifact produced by physiologic or other noise.

Bench and Mentz[8] reported on FHR responses to sound stimuli during birth. They found, on averaging the FHR responses of each of 14 fetuses to 38 sound stimuli, a biphasic response pattern of long latency (taking place over 60 interbeat intervals). The first phase was accelerative, and was followed by a decelerative phase. This response pattern seems to be more characteristic of the older infant and the child than of that of the fetus before birth or of the neonate, although a biphasic response was noted[28] in individual fetuses before birth, and in the response of neonates less than 24 hr old to a "thumping on the foot" stimulus.[52] It seems possible that for certain patterns and strengths of stimulation, the FHR response appears (first) in the third trimester of pregnancy as a monophasic accelerative response, which changes at or near birth to a biphasic accelerative/decelerative pattern. A few hours after birth, the response again becomes monophasic accelerative, and in later infancy, it becomes biphasic accelerative/decelerative once more. This schema is very tentative, and much more work is required before it can be fully accepted. If valid, it may be explained (see Section 3.2) on the basis of changes in the autonomic nervous or limbic system function or both.[8]

3. Neonatal Auditory Response

In contrast to studies of the fetus, there is an enormous amount of published material relating to auditory responses in the neonate. A variety of auditory stimuli have been used to elicit responses studied electrophysiologically and by direct observation. It is quite impossible in this brief chapter to do justice to all this material, which ideally requires a large volume of its own. Hence, in what follows, the author has had to be very selective, and has attempted to concentrate on the more salient aspects. Most of the work outlined below deals with neonates up to 1 week old, but occasional reference is made to studies of babies up to 1 month of age.

For convenience, the field of neonatal auditory response may be considered under the following headings: (1) end-organ function; (2) electrophysiologic response; (3) behavioral response; and (4) habituation of auditory response.

3.1. End-Organ Function

In this section, we consider work that has as its specific aim the study of the neonatal end-organ, namely, the middle ear and the cochlea. Although much of the work described in Sections 3.2 and 3.3 is, of course, relevant to the investigation of end-organ function, its main concern is with "higher-order" aspects of auditory response, involving the central auditory pathways.

Keith[29] obtained measures of acoustic impedance, tympanometry, and crossed stapedial reflexes in neonates. His findings suggested that newborn middle ear structures are in a relatively flaccid or elastic state. This suggestion implies to this author that neonatal middle ears tend to act as low pass filters, a view that is supported by observations that neonates seem to be rather more responsive to low than to high audiofrequencies. In attempting to measure stapedial reflexes, Keith encountered difficulties with the neonates' frequent changes in states of alertness and activity—a recurring problem in neonatal work—and obtained positive reflexes to less than 50% of 500- and 2000-Hz test tones presented at 100 dB SPL. Other data from Keith[30] suggest that the newborn middle ear is largely free of mucus, embryonic connective tissue, or mesenchyme by 2.5 hr after birth. In a similar area of inquiry, Vasiliu[53] documented a number of cases suggesting that the mastoid and middle ear are pneumatized by about the 4th or 5th month of gestation. Early morphological and functional changes in other aspects of the peripheral auditory system were discussed by Bosher.[12]

Very recently, attempts were made to estimate aspects of cochlear function in young children and infants by electrocochleography—the recording, usually with computer averaging—of the compound action potential of the cochlea nerve via a promontory, meatal skin surface, or earlobe electrode.[1,55] This technique was used by Leiberman et al.[34] in a study of 19 normal newborn infants presented with click stimuli, with electrodes on the earlobes and scalp. The neonates were studied during spontaneous sleep periods (without sedation). The evoked responses were similar to those seen in adults except for slightly higher thresholds, longer latencies, and smaller amplitudes. The responses arise mainly from the basal coil of the cochlea, and it is difficult to obtain data with low-audiofrequency stimuli. An advantage of electrocochleography with computer averaging is that it is unlikely to offer false positive results.

Douek et al.[15] recently described their application of observations reported by Kiang et al.[31] on the postauricular myogenic response to newborns and to young children (Douek, personal communication). This muscle response from the postaural region is generally accepted as being purely cochlear in origin, and mediated through a brainstem pathway that does not involve the cortex. The responses, in the microvolt range, generally require computer averaging methods of analysis. Only audiofrequencies above 1 KHz have been found effective, and click stimuli (with a sudden onset) are required for consistent elicitation. This method of assessing auditory responses is quick and easy to perform on newborns, and like the electrocochleogram, it does not give rise to false positive responses when used with computer averaging.

3.2. Electrophysiologic Response

Electrophysiologic responses, including those mediated via central auditory pathways, comprise electrodermal, electrocardiographic (ECG), electroencephalographic (EEG), and other bioelectrical responses. Since most of the more recent literature has been concerned with ECG, usually dealt with in terms of heart rate (HR), and EEG responses, this brief review will be concerned only with these responses.

Bartoshuk[5] measured HR responses in neonates presented with four sound pressure levels (48.5, 58, 62.5, and 78 dB) of a 1 KHz tone in five ascending and descending cycles. He found an approximately linear relationship between the logarithm of HR change on sound stimulation and the stimulus sound pressure level, consistent with the power function between sensory magnitude and physical intensity as found in psychoacoustic work with adults. This study also suggested that neonates showed much finer sensitivity to sounds than had previously been supposed.

Steinschneider et al.[49] studied both HR and motor responses in a group of newborns presented with broad-spectrum noise stimuli of 55–100 dB SPL and no-sound (control) stimuli. Their results showed that the percentage of motor responses, defined as any detectable alteration in subjectively observed motor activity following stimulation, increased, and their latency decreased, as the SPL of the stimulus was raised. This finding was associated with a progressive increase in the duration and a decreasing latency of the primary accelerative phase of the HR response as the stimulus SPL increased. Also, the magnitude of the primary accelerative and secondary return (return to baseline) phases of the HR response increased with SPL. Individual differences were noted among neonates, reflecting their ability to respond differentially to stimulus changes and providing evidence of stimulus intensity (loudness) discrimination. All the 9 newborns in this study responded to a stimulus SPL of 70 dB, and 3 to an SPL of 55 dB.

Graham and Jackson[20] pointed out that work on neonatal HR responses to a variety of stimuli, including sounds, has usually found relatively prolonged, short-latency accelerative responses with no secondary decelerative phase (apart from a return to baseline HR). This neonatal HR response pattern differs from the biphasic (acceleration followed by deceleration to below baseline) or decelerative response generally found in older infants, children, and adults. In other words, neonatal HR decelerations following accelerations are generally small and very much the exception. Moreover, Jackson et al.[27] designed an experiment to optimize the occurrence of a decelerative HR response, but failed to obtain reasonable evidence for such a response, which appears reliably in infants a few weeks or a few months old.[38] Graham and Jackson[20] argued that work on neonates has generally used intense stimuli with sudden onsets, offered while the baby was in a drowsy or sleepy state. Even when awake or alert, however, neonates do not show the decelerative HR responses to stimuli that will produce HR decelerations in older infants.

The newborn accelerative HR responses to sound and other stimuli may be at least partly explained by reference to Sokolov,[45] who described two general reflex systems. These are the defensive reflex, which occurs in response to intense stimuli and functions to contain the effects of stimulation, and the orienting reflex, which is elicited by "novel" or "interesting" stimuli and acts to enhance the effects of stimulation. Routtenberg[41] discussed two mutually inhibiting arousal systems that may be related to the defensive and orienting reflexes. One of Routtenberg's systems is related to the reticular activating system, is excited by intense stimulation, and limits the effects of stimulation, while the other relates to the limbic system and enhances the effects of stimulation. If the view of Lacey[32] that HR acceleration occurs when stimulation is to be rejected, and HR deceleration is found when stimulation is accepted, then the fact that HR responses in neonates are usually accelerative may imply that, for the newborn, sound stimuli usually elicit defensive reactions, associated with the reticular activating system. This argument is supported by the common finding of startle responses accompanying accelerative HR responses when neonates are stimulated with sounds, since startle reflexes may be regarded as aversive responses. On the other hand, it would seem that the function of the limbic system is immature or inhibited in the newborn.

The neonatal EEG consists mainly of slow waves below 2 Hz in states of regular and irregular sleep, and in wakefulness. Frequencies above 4 Hz are present in insignificant proportions. The auditory-evoked EEG response was studied in neonates by Ellingson,[18] who found that 2–5 sec after a loud auditory stimulus, the EEG tracing may flatten out for a period of 7–8 sec, after which the slow waves reappear. Of Ellingson's 52 subjects, 54% showed the flattening (arousal) response to some but not all stimuli. In 10 cases, this response was preceded by a diffuse burst of waves similar to the K complex.[14] In two cases, the K-type response occurred alone, without the subsequent flattening. Ellingson regarded his evoked response data as evidence of the physiologic immaturity of the newborn's nervous system. More recently, Barnet et al.[2] presented sets of 100 click stimuli to normal and Down's syndrome (DS) infants aged 8 days to 13 months and measured computer-averaged EEG responses. They found that in both normal and DS infants, the first stimuli only (cf. Ellingson[18]) were followed by a few seconds of EEG flattening and desynchronization that had the characteristics of an electrocortical orienting response.

3.3. Behavioral Response

Studies of neonatal behavioral responses to auditory stimuli have tended to develop in two phases. In the first phase, early workers were concerned to describe the type or pattern of the behavioral response in morphological terms. Thus, Ewing and Ewing[19] described newborn responses as reflex blinking, screwing up the eyes, jumping, and twitching of the fingers. Suzuki et al.[50] extended this type of list to include:

1. Blinking of the open eyes or further tightening of the lids if the eyes are closed
2. Jerking of the trunk, jerking of the extremities and the face, or both
3. Grimace, or wrinkling of the forehead
4. Opening or closing of the eyelids

5. Fixation of the eye position, or turning of the eye toward the source of the sound stimulation
6. Turning of the head
7. Opening, closing, or twisting the mouth or beginning to cry
8. Relative slow movement of the trunk, the extremities, or both

Responses 1 and 2 were used most often by Suzuki's observers. Since the other responses were almost evenly distributed between the 40- and 80-dB sound stimuli presented to the babies, the authors assumed that response cues apart from 1 or 2 were not reliable as criteria of neonatal auditory response. This situation was also encountered by Hardy et al.,[23] who reduced an original list of 15 response cues to four:

1. Head turn
2. Eye response (except blinks)
3. Startle response and eye blink
4. Other, e.g., cessation of activity, disturbance of sleep, or stopping crying

From these and other reports, it seems to be generally agreed that the most easily observed behavioral response, elicited by loud, complex stimuli, is a gross startle or jumping reaction. With less loud and less complex stimuli, the response is less gross, but there is little evidence to suggest that the response is patterned. Eye blinks (the auropalpebral reflex) have often been observed in response to stimuli with sudden onsets, e.g., click stimuli. The literature frequently describes the newborn startle response as a Moro or Moro-like reflex, which implies that the response shows abduction of the upper arms from the shoulders, extension of the forearm at the elbows, and extension of the fingers, followed by return movements, all of which are symmetrical as regards right and left arms. In a detailed comparison of the sound-evoked startle response and the head-drop (Moro) reflex, however, Bench et al.[10] found that the two responses were quite different. Far from being a symmetrical response related mainly to the arms, the sound-evoked startle was a gross paroxysmal movement involving all or most of the limbs in a relatively diffuse way. The authors concluded that the term "Moro reflex" as applied to newborn auditory responses has been used too loosely, or that there has been insufficient observational expertise.

In the second phase, more recent work has been devoted to distinguishing sound-evoked behavioral responses from ongoing, spontaneous activity. There has also been a shift away from morphological approaches—the descriptive categories of which are difficult to compare because of different kinds and levels of description—toward use of more objectively defined segments of the body (e.g., use of "mouth movement" rather than "smile" or "grimace"). At the same time, rather more experimental approaches were adopted (e.g., Ling et al.[37] and Bench et al.[11]). In this more recent work, closer attention was paid to careful measurement of sound stimuli, assessment of the babies' prestimulus state of activity and alertness, and, particularly important, controls for "spontaneous" responses. It seems that the distribution of sound-evoked behavioral responses tends to follow that of general movements, suggesting that what is normally spontaneous movement can be augmented in some way by a sound stimulus.

This recent work has also shown clearly that newborns are not very responsive behaviorally to pure tones, nor to narrow-band noise stimuli. Generally, responsivity is evoked only by relatively loud, broad-spectrum noise stimuli. A possible explanation, suggested by Hutt et al.[25] is that broad-spectrum auditory signals energize a greater proportion of the basilar membrane than do narrow-spectrum sounds. Both the findings and the explanation are unfortunate in the sense that they do not help us in assessing responses for pure tones or other tonal stimuli, and hence it is difficult to measure pure tone behavioral audiograms for neonates. As Turkewitz et al.[51] argued: "If we are to devise effective forms of early stimulus intervention simple auditory stimuli such as pure tones are likely to be of little use (for newborns) and we should opt in favour of more complex auditory stimuli that are likely to be effective."

3.4. Habituation of Auditory Response

Although there has been some work on newborn classic (Pavlovian) conditioning and also on operant (rewarded) conditioning involving sound stimulation, most of the emphasis in this work has been on studying early learning as a component of behavior. There has thus been little by way of special reference to the auditory modality, and this work will not be discussed further. On the other hand, there has been considerable interest in the possibility of studying the more "primitive" learning aspect of habituation, e.g., by Bridger,[13] who defined habituation as decrement and cessation of a response with the repeated application of a constant stimulus. This work suggested insights into the way in which the neonate may organize repetitive sound inputs, and may make various auditory discriminations, such as intensity and especially pitch discriminations.

Following closely on Bridger's work, Bartoshuk[3] presented 120 neonates with 40 85-dB sound stimuli of 1-sec duration over repeated trials and measured HR change response. He found a significant HR decrement across stimulus trials when the decrement was expressed as a proportion of the initial response. The response decrement curves were independent of age (days 1–4), initial responses, or interstimulus intervals (14, 30, and 60 sec). Bartoshuk argued that the response decrement could not be explained away as an epiphenomenon of some gradual reduction in overall activation level during the course of his experiment because the mean HR was higher before the 40th than before the 1st stimulus, and also the response decrement was found in babies with identical HRs before the first and last stimuli. He also argued that the response decrement was unlikely to be due to auditory fatigue because similar decrements occurred across trials for all three interstimulus intervals. If neural fatigue had been present, the decrement should have been more rapid for the 15-sec interstimulus interval stimulus series than for the 60-sec interval series. In a second paper describing similar experiments, Bartoshuk[4] presented further evidence of response decrement and described a dishabituation or recovery of response produced by changing the tonal properties of his stimuli. He again presented evidence suggesting that auditory fatigue could not account for the observed response decrements, which he interpreted as selective habituation probably related to a kind of discrimination learning.

Hutt et al.,[26] however, took issue with aspects of Bartoshuk's work. For example, they argued that the increase in prestimulus HR between the 1st and 40th trials in the first study[3] neither supports nor refutes the claim that the response decrement was not due to a change in activation level during the experiment, and that the decrement was probably due to a change in overall behavioral state, toward lower states (deeper sleep) than at the outset of the experiment. They also argued[26] that a similar problem arises in considering dishabituation. Following response decrement, Bartoshuk[4] introduced one stimulus 11 dB greater than that during

the decrement trials, and then reverted to the original sound level. Since the responses to the six stimuli following Bartoshuk's intense stimulus were all somewhat greater than to the six stimuli preceding the intense stimulus, it would seem that the effect of the intense stimulus was to produce a change in the babies' behavioral state. It is interesting that in a study of their own, Hutt et al.[24] found no evidence for response decrement other than that associated with a state change. However, they analyzed their data in blocks of trials, and hence may have missed a response decrement that might have occurred, without an endogenous state change, very early in their experiment.

Barnet et al.,[2] whose auditory evoked EEG study has already been noted, compared the individual evoked responses preceding the EEG flattening across stimulus trial numbers. They found that their normal neonates and DS subjects of all ages showed no response decrement, whereas the older normal infants showed a progressive decrease in the amplitude of the auditory evoked potentials with repeated stimulation. They remarked, however, that behavioral (startle) responses were observed occasionally in their younger normal and DS infants following the first one or two stimuli. Apparently these startle responses disappeared with repeated stimulation.

In view of the work of Barnet et al.[2] cited above and other data from Bartoshuk,[4] the writer's opinion is that some response decrement that is not due to endogenous state changes may occur over the first few sound stimulus trials. Thereafter, continued response decrement is probably largely associated with changes of behavioral state toward (deep) sleep. Further work is required to explore this area more fully.

4. Clinical Aspects

This chapter concludes with a brief account of some of the more important points from a variety of clinical studies seeking to assess the hearing status of the fetus and neonate.

4.1. Fetal Screening

For reasons given above, fetal screening audiometry is difficult to study, and the field has attracted few investigators. Murphy and Smyth[39] and Johansson et al.,[28] however, performed feasibility studies partly with a view toward screening for aspects of hearing loss before birth. Their work has not been pursued by others, mainly because of problems in achieving reliable and valid fetal responses to sounds, and because the technology is relatively expensive. At best, responses to relatively loud sound (90–110 dB SPL) can be demonstrated. There is little evidence that absence of response is necessarily associated with impaired hearing, since it seems probable that the false negative response rates are rather high.

4.2. Newborn Screening

In recent years, several workers have implemented screening, diagnostic, and even therapeutic programs for young infants, arguing from the critical period concept.[44] They have remarked that the experience of auditory stimuli during critical periods in infancy has profound long-lasting and irreversible effects on subsequent auditory and other behavior, and that deprivation of this experience has deleterious and irreversible effects on the acquisition of speech and language.[33]

This is an important viewpoint, and many of its aspects are valid, but in their anxiety to emphasize the potential value of early diagnosis and treatment, many workers have gone beyond the idea of importance or value to claim scientific proofs, for which the evidence (especially with regard to the irreversibility of critical period effects) is lacking.[7]

Despite certain weaknesses in the arguments, the critical period concept focused considerable effort on behavioral response screening programs for infants in the first year of life. Special emphasis was placed on the newborn period by Downs and Sterrit,[16] using loud complex stimuli, partly because of the apparent feasibility of screening populations of newborn infants, readily accessible in the hospital, for hearing loss. Following Downs and Sterrit's early work, a number of screening clinics were established in North America and in Europe, though not in the United Kingdom. With the screening techniques used, however, the proportion of false-positive and false-negative assessments appears to be unacceptably high, requiring follow-up studies that are not always easy to establish. Those who set up newborn screening programs thus appeared to have identified an area for investigation, but were unable to develop sufficiently

adequate screening methods.[36] At best, it is difficult to obtain reliable responses in newborn behavioral audiometry to stimuli less than about 60–70 dB SPL. The reason seems to be mainly that newborn infants spend most of their time asleep. When it is possible to study them in states of alertness, responses to stimuli as low as 30 dB may be observed,[11] but it is virtually impossible to conduct *population* screening work with stimuli of this type because neonates spend so little of their time awake. Population screening requires relatively quick tests and cannot afford to wait until the babies attain some state of alertness that is especially suitable for testing. It would therefore appear that newborn behavioral screening work was begun before the field was adequately researched.

5. References

1. ARAN, J. M., 1971, The electro-cochleogram; recent results in children and in some pathological cases, *Arch. Ohren-, Nasen-, Kehlkopfheilk.* **198**:128.
2. BARNET, A. B., OHLRICH, E. S., AND SHANKS, B. L., 1971, E.E.G. evoked responses to repetitive auditory stimulation in normal and Down's syndrome infants, *Dev. Med. Child Neurol.* **13**:321.
3. BARTOSHUK, A. K., 1962, Response decrement with repeated elicitation of human neonatal cardiac acceleration to sounds, *J. Comp. Physiol. Psychol.* **55**:1.
4. BARTOSHUK, A. K., 1962, Human neonatal cardiac acceleration to sound: Habituation and dishabituation, *Percept. Mot. Skills* **15**:15.
5. BARTOSHUK, A. K., 1964, Human neonatal cardiac responses to sound: A power function, *Psychonom. Sci.* **1**:151.
6. BAST, T. H., AND ANSON, B. J., 1949, *The Temporal Bone and the Ear,* Charles C. Thomas, Springfield, Illinois.
7. BENCH, R. J., 1971, The rise and demise of the critical period concept, *Sound (Br. J. Audiol.)* **5**:21.
8. BENCH, R. J., AND MENTZ, D. L., 1975, On the measurement of human foetal auditory response, in: *Sound Reception in Mammals (Symp. Zool. Soc. London No. 37)* (R. J. Bench, A. Pye, and J. D. Pye, eds.), pp. 23–40, Academic Press, New York and London.
9. BENCH, R. J., ANDERSON, J. H., AND HOARE, M., 1970, Measurement system for fetal audiometry, *J. Acoust. Soc. Amer.* **47**:1602.
10. BENCH, J., COLLYER, Y., LANGFORD, C., AND TOMS, R., 1972, A comparison between the neonatal sound evoked startle response and the head-drop (Moro) reflex, *Dev. Med. Child Neurol.* **14**:308.
11. BENCH, J., COLLYER, Y., MENTZ, L., AND WILSON, I.,

1976, Studies in infant behavioural audiometry: I. Neonates, *Audiology* **15**:85.

12. BOSHER, S. K., 1975, Morphological and functional changes in the peripheral auditory system associated with the inception of hearing, in: *Sound Reception in Mammals (Symp. Zool. Soc. London No. 37)* (R. J. Bench, A. Pye, and J. D. Pye, eds.), pp. 11–22, Academic Press, New York and London.

13. BRIDGER, W. H., 1961, Sensory habituation and discrimination in the human neonate, *Amer. J. Psychiatry* **117**:991.

14. DAVIS, H., DAVIS, P. A., LOOMIS, A. L., HARVEY, E. N., AND HOBART, G. A., 1939, Electrical reactions of human brain to auditory stimulation during sleep, *J. Neurophysiol.* **2**:500.

15. DOUEK, E., GIBSON, W., AND HUMPHRIES, K., 1974, The crossed acoustic response and objective tests of hearing, *Dev. Med. Child Neurol.* **16**:32.

16. DOWNS, M. P., AND STERRIT, G. M., 1967, A guide to newborn and infant hearing screening programs, *Arch. Otolaryngol.* **85**:15.

17. DWORNICKA, B., JASIENSKA, A., SMOLARZ, W., AND WAWRYK, R., 1964, Attempt of determining the fetal reaction to acoustic stimulation, *Acta Otolaryngol.* **57**:571.

18. ELLINGSON, R. J., 1958, Electroencephalograms of normal full-term newborns immediately after birth with observations on arousal and visual evoked responses, *Electroencephalogr. Clin. Neurophysiol.* **10**:31.

19. EWING, I. R., AND EWING, A. W. G., 1944, The ascertainment of deafness in infancy and early childhood, *J. Laryngol. Otol.* **59**:309.

20. GRAHAM, F. K., AND JACKSON, J. C., 1970, Arousal systems and infant heart rate responses, in: *Advances in Child Development and Behavior* (H. W. Reese and L. P. Lipsitt, eds.), pp. 59–117, Academic Press, New York and London.

21. GRIMWADE, J. C., WALKER, D. W., BARTLETT, M., GORDON, S., AND WOOD, C., 1971, Human fetal heart rate change and movement in response to sound and vibration, *Amer. J. Obstet. Gynecol.* **109**:86.

22. HARDY, J. B., DOUGHERTY, A., AND HARDY, W. G., 1959, Hearing responses and audiologic screening in infants, *J. Pediatr.* **55**:382.

23. HENSHALL, W. R., 1972, Intra-uterine sound levels, *Amer. J. Obstet. Gynecol.* **112**:576.

24. HUTT, C., VON BERNUTH, H., LENARD, H. G., HUTT, S. J., AND PRECHTL, H. F. R., 1968, Habituation in relation to state in the human neonate, *Nature (London)* **220**:618.

25. HUTT, S. J., HUTT, C., LENARD, H. G., BERNUTH, H. V., AND MUNTJEWERFF, W. J., 1968, Auditory responsivity in the human neonate, *Nature (London)* **218**:888.

26. HUTT, S. J., LENARD, H. G., AND PRECHTL, H. F. R., 1969, Psychophysiological studies in newborn infants,

in: *Advances in Child Development and Behavior, 4* (L. P. Lipsitt and H. W. Reese, eds.), pp. 127–172, Academic Press, New York and London.

27. JACKSON, J. C., KANTOWITZ, S. R., AND GRAHAM, F. K., 1971, Can newborns show cardiac orienting?, *Child Dev.* **42**:107.

28. JOHANSSON, B., WEDENBERG, E., AND WESTIN, B., 1964, Measurement of tone response by the human foetus, *Acta Otolaryngol.* **57**:188.

29. KEITH, R. W., 1971, Impedance audiometry with neonates, *Arch. Otolaryngol.* **97**:465.

30. KEITH, R. W., 1975, Middle ear function in neonates, *Arch. Otolaryngol.* **101**:376.

31. KIANG, N. Y.-S., GRIST, A. H., FRENCH, M. A., AND EDWARDS, A. G., 1963, Postauricular electrical response to acoustic stimuli in humans, *M. I. T. Q. Prog. Rep.* **68**:218.

32. LACEY, J. J., 1959, Psychophysiological approaches to the evaluation of psychotherapeutic process and outcome, in: *Research in Psychotherapy* (E. A. Rubinstein and M. B. Parloff, eds.), pp. 160–208, American Psychology Association, Washington, D.C.

33. LENNEBERG, E. H., 1967, *Biological Foundations of Language,* Wiley, New York and London.

34. LEIBERMAN, A., SOHMER, H., AND SZABO, G., 1973, Cochlear audiometry (electro-cochleography) during the neonatal period, *Dev. Med. Child Neurol.* **15**:8.

35. LINDSLEY, D. B., 1942, Heart and brain potentials of human fetuses *in utero, Amer. J. Psychol.* **55**:412.

36. LING, D., 1972, Response validity in auditory tests of newborn infants, *Laryngoscope* **82**:376.

37. LING, D., LING, A. H., AND DOEHRING, D. G., 1970, Stimulus, response and observer variables in the auditory screening of newborn infants, *J. Speech Hear. Res.* **11**:811.

38. LIPTON, E. L., STEINSCHNEIDER, A., AND RICHMOND, J. B., 1966, Autonomic function in the neonate: VII. Maturational change in cardiac control, *Child Dev.* **37**:1.

39. MURPHY, K. P., AND SMYTH, C. N., 1962, Response of foetus to auditory stimulation, *Lancet* **1**:972.

40. ROSEN, M. G., SCIBETTA, J. J., AND HOCHBERG, C. J., 1970, Human fetal electroencephalogram. III. Pattern changes in presence of fetal heart rate alterations and after use of maternal medications, *Obstet. Gynecol.* **36**:132.

41. ROUTTENBERG, S., 1968, The two-arousal hypothesis: Reticular formation and limbic system, *Psychol. Rev.* **75**:51.

42. SCIBETTA, J. J., AND ROSEN, M. G., 1969, Response evoked by sound in the fetal guinea pig, *Obstet. Gynecol.* **33**:830.

43. SCIBETTA, J. J., ROSEN, M. G., HOCHBERG, C. J., AND CHIK, L., 1971, Human fetal brain response to sound during labor, *Amer. J. Obstet. Gynecol.* **109**:82.

44. SCOTT, J. P., 1962, Critical periods in behavioral development, *Science* **138**:949.

45. SOKOLOV, E. N., 1963, *Perception and the Conditional Reflex,* Macmillan, New York.

46. SONTAG, L. W., 1936, Changes in the rate of the human fetal heart in response to vibratory stimuli, *Amer. J. Dis. Child.* **51**:583.

47. SONTAG, L. W., 1944, Differences in modifiability of fetal behavior and physiology, *Psychosom. Med.* **6**:151.

48. SONTAG, L. W., AND WALLACE, R. F., 1935, The movement response of the human fetus to sound stimuli, *Child Dev.* **6**:253.

49. STEINSCHNEIDER, A., LIPTON, E. L., AND RICHMOND, J. B., 1966, Auditory sensitivity in the infant: Effect of intensity on cardiac and motor responsivity, *Child Dev.* **37**:233.

50. SUZUKI, T., JAMIJO, Y., AND KIUCHI, S., 1964, Auditory test of newborn infants, *Ann. Otol.* **73**:914.

51. TURKEWITZ, G., BIRCH, H. G., AND COOPER, K. K., 1972, Responsiveness to simple and complex auditory stimuli in the human newborn, *Dev. Psychobiol.* **5**:7.

52. VALLBONA, C., DESMOND, M. M., RUDOLPH, A. J., PAP, L. F., HILL, R. M., FRANKLIN, R. R., AND RUSH, J. B., 1963, Cardiodynamic studies in the newborn. II. Regulation of the heart rate, *Biol. Neonat.* **5**:159.

53. VASILIU, D. I., 1968, L'enfant est prêt à entendre dans la vie intrauterine. Contributions sur l'embryologenese de l'oreille et la pneumatisation de la mastoide et du rocher, *Int. Audiol.* **7**:181.

54. WALKER, D., GRIMWADE, J., AND WOOD, C., 1971, Intra-uterine noise. A component of the fetal environment, *Amer. J. Obstet. Gynecol.* **109**:91.

55. YOSHIE, N., 1973, Diagnostic significance of the electrocochleogram in clinical audiometry, *Audiology* **12**:504.

CHAPTER 36

Morphological and Functional Development of the Skin

Klaus Dietel

1. Introduction

The physiology of human skin has been amply investigated for the assessment of pathologic processes, with the skin of the adult standing in the forefront of interest. In contrast, while the anatomy of fetal and infantile skin is relatively well understood, there is only fragmentary knowledge of its physiology. Changes taking place in neonatal skin vary over a wide physiologic range, presumably as the expression of the ended intrauterine life, the stress of birth, the adaptation period, or the attainment of postnatal stability.

Changes that occur frequently but are nevertheless to be interpreted as abnormal reactions, such as localized edema on the dorsum of the hand or foot, in the pubic region, or in the form of a caput succedaneum, witch's milk production by the mammary glands, neonatal toxic erythema, and harlequin skin, have received little or no special attention. These phenomena are distinguished by being topically circumscribed and restricted to the

first days of life, and undergoing spontaneous regression.

Skin phenomena, along with other examination findings, are used in neonatology to assess maturity, duration of pregnancy, and neonatal vitality. The human skin is an organ, anatomically built up from various tissues, that covers the body surface and is connected with the other body organs via the blood circulation, lymph stream, and nervous system. It has its characteristic metabolism, forms skin-specific substances, is involved in the body's metabolism, and serves further as an organ for storage and deposition. It plays an important regulatory role.

Being the outer cover of the body, the skin is in constant reciprocal relationship with the environment. As a boundary organ, it is subject to special chemical, physical, and infectious influences.

Along with these physiologic and somatic tasks, the skin as a sense organ plays a role in thermal and tactile perception. As a means of communication, the skin is instrumental in early establishment of the mother–child relationship. In this sense, it fulfills a task of vital importance.

Klaus Dietel · Children's Hospital of the Regional Hospital, Karl-Marx-Stadt, German Democratic Republic

2. Morphology and Embryology of Neonatal Skin

The skin consists of two fundamentally different tissues, namely, the epidermis and dermis. Each exhibits a multiplicity of structures, of which some are transitory while others endure.

2.1. Epidermis

The epidermis develops from the single cell layer of the outer germinal stratum, which is two cells thick as of the 4th embryonic week. The outer stratum (periderm) is formed from the vesicular cells, which later become flat, lose their nuclei, and come to resemble the later stratum corneum. They work like an active membrane between embryo and amniotic surroundings, while at the same time they constitute a barrier.[8] The cells of the inner stratum are strikingly rich in cytoplasm. The inner stratum develops into the stratum germinativum, which up to the 11th week of life forms three to four cell layers and displays differentiation. Protoplasmic fibers and cell bridges develop and form the prickle-cell layer, which shows an abundance of glycogen. The elevated glycogen content is regarded as an energy reserve for the enhanced epidermal growth.[7,14]

At the 18th week of life, along with a decrease of the glycogen reserves, there is a development of keratogenic structures, which lead to regional differences in epidermal thickness.

Further differentiation of the epidermis takes place both in the layers and in the shape and arrangement of the cells, before the definitive adult pattern is attained. These morphological changes, some of which are quite transient, cannot yet be regarded as the integration of a biochemical and physiologic system of skin development in human fetuses.

More is known about the behavior and migration of the keratinocytes deriving from the stratum germinativum. They are deposited through a basement membrane against the dermis, arranged in columnar fashion, and contain the usual organelles and fibrillar substances. Their melanin content is acquired from the contiguous melanocytes.

DNA synthesis is as intensive in fetal as in adult skin.[17] The replacement of the keratinized epithelium from the stratum germinativum can be measured by the number of mitoses occurring. The mitotic coefficient (number of mitoses/1000 cells) is highest in immature and very young infants, with a value of 9.0. In adults, it declines to values between 0.1 and 1.6.[33]

The keratinocytes migrate to the surface in approximately 28 days. In the early stages of this migration, there forms within the keratinocytes a protein-like amorphous substance that later develops into keratohyaline bodies. From the 8th fetal month, the keratinocytes are to be found in the granular layer, which is complete only in the palm and sole and so contributes to the rosy hue of newborns. Losing organelles and intracellular water, which decreases to less than one-fifth of the original amount, the keratinocytes transform into the stratum corneum.

The melanocytes are a second cell type that is located in the germinative layer of the epidermis, though it arises from the neural crest. They migrate as melanoblasts from the dermis, and from the 5th month they transform into melanocytes and become able to produce a pigment that is transported along the dendrites and, after phagocytosis of the dendritic segments, is taken up by the basal cells.[29,43] This process begins to become important after birth. Prenatal pigmentation occurs in the region of the nipples, axillae, and genitalia, and around the anus.

Langerhans' cells are a special type of malanocytes, the function of which remains unknown. They are provided with special organelles.[53]

2.2. Epidermal Appendages

Hairs develop from epidermal invaginations up to the 5th fetal month, the eyebrows appearing as lanugo by the beginning of the 3rd month. It is a characteristic feature of the neonatal period that some 80% of all follicles are in a dormant state.

Nails develop from the primary nail field, likewise as epidermal invaginations. Cornification of the nails takes place in the 5th fetal month. Until the 7th month, the nails are still covered with a thin layer of epidermis. They grow more slowly on the toes than on the fingers, and more slowly on the 5th than on the 3rd phalanx.

The eccrine sweat glands develop deep in the epidermis between the 6th embryonal week and the 5th fetal month. In the early developmental period, they are rich in glycogen, and their phosphorylase activity is also increased.[48]

The apocrine glands develop later than the eccrine glands. They are capable of producing a milky secretion in the 8th fetal month.

In both gland types, the transport of secretions is affected by myoepithelial cells located in the region of the acini. In newborns, these cells are still absent from the periglandular connective tissue capsule of apocrine glands.

Simultaneously with the hair follicles, the sebaceous glands develop in the 4th fetal month from epithelial components, and are capable of secretory activity from the 6th month. While already capable of holocrine secretion in infants, they are still distinctly smaller than those of children and adults, since the lobules do not exhibit any lumina. The time of replacement of a sebaceous gland is about a week.

The epidermis and dermis are separated by an undulating basal membrane that is located beneath the germinative cells and that enhances the resistance of the dermoepidermal junction to shearing stresses.[39]

2.3. Dermis

In the 8-week embryo, the dermis (corium) consists of undifferentiated cells, appears myxedema-like, and contains no fibrillar elements. The latter subsequently appear up to the 4th month. During the time that the early fetal abundance of water, sugar, and hyaluronidase is diminishing, the first elastic and collagen fibers are formed by fibroblasts. At the same time, fibroblastic activity causes the tissue to become enriched with sulfated poly-saccharides. The development of elastic tissue starts to accelerate after birth.

An important cell type in the dermis is the mast cell, which can be observed in fetuses having a crown–rump length of 33 cm. Mast cells reach their highest counts in newborns, and subsequently diminish.[27]

2.4. Adipose Tissue

The subcutaneous adipose tissue (hypodermis) used to be regarded as a "passive" tissue, the function of which consisted exclusively of insulation and storage. The first cells of this "primitive" organ are formed from mesenchymal cells around the 14th fetal week. As cytoblasts, they contain no fat droplets. It is only during their maturation to adipose cells that they become filled with single or multiple fat granules, which displace the nucleus toward the cell wall. The morphological structure remains un-

changed up to the 7th fetal month, and thus is characteristic of small premature infants.

Adipose tissue has a lobulated structure, and is surrounded by connective tissue. Each lobule has its own blood supply down to the individual adipose cell, each of which has its own capillary circulation. "Brown" adipose tissue occurs in fetuses and newborns. Its cells differentiate from the multi-locularly disposed cells of the "primitive" organ until the 28th week of pregnancy. They contain small fat droplets, which only exceptionally coalesce into large fat vacuoles, and an abundance of mitochondria, which envelop the fat vacuoles. In mature neonates, they constitute only about one-tenth of the adipose cells. The brown adipose cells aggregate in the neck, underneath the scapulae, and in the axillae, mediastinum, and perirenal tissues.

2.5. Nervous System

The nervous system of the skin develops from the dermis at a very early stage. In the 3rd embryonal month, the free nerve endings bud off with the papillary ridges on the finger and toe pads. In newborns, they are exceptionally well developed in the region of the lips, sucking pad, and perioral zone. The specific end apparatuses such as Merkel's and Meissner's tactile corpuscles and Vater-Paccini corpuscles, although present in abundance, are not fully functional. Their maturation continues through the entire period of infancy.

3. Physiology of Fetal Skin

The "physiology" of the skin of the prenatal period is determined not only by growth, development, and maturation of the fetus, but also by its environment, i.e., the amniotic fluid.

3.1. Amniotic Fluid

The amniotic fluid guarantees an even distribution of temperature, and it protects against trauma. At the beginning of pregnancy, it is nothing more than a dialysate of maternal or fetal plasma or both,[28] with 135 meq sodium, 4.0 meq potassium, and 109 meq chloride/liter[46] (see Chapter 26). Later, the amniotic fluid becomes a repository for excreta such as urine and secretions emanating from the cavities of the future respiratory tract and the upper sectors of the alimentary canal. With increasing duration of pregnancy, the skin plays an ever greater role in the composition of this aquatic environment.

A great number of investigations have been carried out in recent years concerning the significance of amniotic fluid composition; these investigations have been concerned mainly with the possibility of a prenatal diagnosis of hereditary enzymopathies, fetal emergencies, and fetal lung maturity.

The composition of the amniotic fluid reflects skin function; after the 38th week of gestation, there is an increase in the number of anucleated cells and keratinized lipid-containing skin flakes. These fat-laden cells account for less than 10% of all analyzed cells in the amniotic fluid prior to the 38th week. Subsequently, they can make up more than 50%. The finding of more than 20% of fat-laden cells is an indication of a mature fetus.[5]

3.2. Permeability

There is no evidence for a transepidermal exudation in fetuses; their eccrine glands are still immature or dormant. During the fetal stage, skin permeability seems to be dependent on morphological changes in the epidermis. The fine structure of epidermal cells changes due to sulfhydrylation and accentuated keratinization. This structural change results in a marked decrease of the permeability of skin to water in the last trimester of pregnancy.[40]

Similar conclusions were drawn from investigations on the blanching response of the skin after application of a 10% epinephrine solution, the response being manifestly weaker in mature infants than in 28- to 39-week-old fetuses.[36]

Amniofetal permeation is well recognized from the imbibition of the nails, umbilical cord, and skin with yellow-green staining by meconium-containing amniotic fluid in asphyxiated, postmature, and otherwise damaged fetuses; it is also used for diagnostic grading of the postnatal vital status.[9,10]

3.3. Vernix Caseosa

A role in transepidermal exudation and permeability must be ascribed to the vernix caseosa as well. This substance begins to form as a superficial fatty film after the 5th fetal month. The fat is considered to originate both from the sebaceous glands and from the lipid-laden anucleated superficial cells destined to be shed. It is most intensely developed at birth, and it extends over the face, ears, shoulders, sacral region, and inguinal folds. It accumulates at sites of dense lanugo covering.

The vernix is thought to minimize friction during birth and also to insulate the skin. *In utero*, the vernix helps to prevent water and electrolytes from permeating out of the skin into the amniotic fluid. The vernix caseosa is rich in triglycerides, cholesterol, and unsaponifiable fats (Table I).

In postmature newborns, the vernix caseosa has vanished *in utero*, and this disappearance is accompanied by changes in skin turgor and consistency. The skin is osmotically damaged, and this damage can lead to abnormal development of folds, shedding of large shreds of the horny layer, and areas of maceration. After birth, the skin rapidly shrinks and becomes wrinkled, fissured, and parchmentlike, and undergoes gross desquamation (desquamatio lamellosa).

3.4. Biochemistry

The biochemical development of fetal skin has hitherto been investigated only sporadically.

Table I. Lipid Composition of Human Skin Surface Fat (% of Total Lipids)[a]

Lipids	Skin fat of adults	Scalp fat of boys, 6–12 yr	Vernix caseosa	Cerumen
Free fatty acids	22–32	46.5	2.3– 9.4	14.7
Triglycerides	22–41	2	33.3–42.1	4.3
Total cholesterol	2.9–5.9		19.4–20.6	17.4
Squalen	3.8–8.7	1.6	2.6	
Nonsaponifiable fat	27–36	2.9	27–48.6	57.5

[a] From Dietel.[12]

Table II. Collagen Content of the Skin (g/kg Wet Weight)[a]

Fetus (20–22 weeks)	2.4
Newborn	16.8
Infants (4–7 months)	39.2
Adults	45.7

[a] Data from Geigy's Scientific Tables.[46]

Observations on the glycogen content derive from histological studies. Glycogen was found in skin most actively involved in cell division. It was noted in the stratum spongiosum as early as in the 11th fetal week, and later in the region of the hair follicles and in the clear cells of the sweat glands. By the 8th fetal month, apocrine glands produce a milky substance that is composed of water, protein, lipids, sugar, and ferric ions. The mature glandular cells contain an abundance of mucopolysaccharides and iron.

As already mentioned, the amount of glycogen in the keratinocytes decreases when keratin formation sets in. Later, it is demonstrable only in the germinative cells of the epidermis.

Enzyme studies on embryonal skin have been directed to the activity of glucose-6-phosphate dehydrogenase, which is increased at the time of the development of sweat glands and hairs. In this way, the individual topographic developmental stages can be well differentiated. An enzyme activation with the inception of keratinization is detectable in the epidermis.[23] All cells that are undergoing rapid division and growth show increased alkaline phosphatase and phosphorylase activities. Along with the increase of the mast cells in the course of fetal development,[27] there is a simultaneous increase in the histamine content.[60]

Fetal skin has a high water content; as compared with that of 22-week fetuses, the water content is decreased to 92% in newborns and to 77% in adults. The water decrease has been correlated with the simultaneously occurring increase of collagen (Table II).

The nitrogen content rises from 11.9 to 26.5 g/kg, and the potassium content from 36.0 to 45.0 meq/liter. Increased levels during fetal development have also been found for magnesium, calcium, and phosphorus, while sodium and chloride decrease (Table III).

4. Physiology of Neonatal Skin

During birth, the neonatal skin is subjected directly to the mechanical stress of delivery and to diverse types of changes in the blood circulation, and it is exposed to the bacterial flora of the maternal genital tract. It serves indirectly as a reactive organ for systemic phenomena that in turn can be used for diagnostic purposes.[44,59]

With the separation of the umbilical cord, the phenomena attributable to the transformation of the fetal circulation become evident. Of particular importance, however, are the changes that relate to the adaptation to the new extrauterine environment,

Table III. Composition of Fat-Free Skin (g or meq/kg Wet Weight)[a]

Age	Weight of skin (% of body weight)	Water (g)	N (g)	Na	K	Cl	Mg	Ca	P
						(meq)			
Fetus (14 weeks)	—	917	11.6	—	23.8	90.6	—	4.4	41.8
Fetus (20 weeks)	13	901	11.9	120	36.0	96.0	3.0	6.1	28.2
Newborn	15	828	26.5	87.1	45.0	66.9	4.7	10.0	31.7
Infants (3–5 months)	—	675	54.5	65.4	43.7	72.3	7.4	11.4	34.9
Adults	7	694	53.0	79.3	23.7	71.4	3.1	9.5	14.0

[a] Data from Geigy's Scientific Tables.[46]

the assumption of functions appropriate to the skin organ, and participation in the body's postnatal adaptation. Soon after the cord is cut, the normal neonate develops the vivid red coloration regarded as characteristic of the newborn; it remains unchanged for hours. In a cooler environment, this coloration is replaced by a bluish blotchiness; this mottled appearance (livido reticularis) disappears quickly on rewarming of the infant. Neonatal skin is "red like a lobster," transparent, and smooth-looking, since neither the large skin folds nor the texturing of the skin are as yet sufficiently well developed.

Soon after birth, the skin decreases its moisture content and shows uneven regional temperature distribution compared with the intrauterine period.

During the first few days of life, the insulating layer of vernix caseosa is lost due to routine postnatal skin care procedures. This loss results in a loss of insulation for the stratum corneum, the uppermost layers of which (along with the remains of the periderm, which were adapted to the humid intrauterine medium) peel off, with the result that the skin acquires a grayish-white or yellowish hue. The deeper layers of the stratum corneum are not involved in this desquamation.

After about 7 days, the visible skin desquamation comes to an end and is replaced by invisible flaking off (desquamatio insensibilis), as the expression of postnatal adaptation.

After the loss of the vernix caseosa and the horny lamellae, the skin undergoes a change, and forms a surface adapted to extrauterine conditions. It becomes a dividing barrier between body and environment; it must develop protective functions. This development is assured by a film of lipids, an acid mantle, the discharge of electrolytes and water, certain resorptive capacities, pigmentations, and regulatory processes such as blood circulation and nerve supply.

4.1. Surface Fat

In recent years, considerable attention has been given to surface fat, in order to test, on one hand, the ability to influence dermatoses and, on the other, the effect of modern detergents.

Modern investigational procedures have furthermore confirmed the long-known fact that the amount of lipid can vary considerably at different body sites. It is maximum on nose and forehead, and least on the extensor aspects of the limbs. In

Table IV. Amount of Surface Fat on the Skin (mg/m²)[a]

Skin region	Newborns	Children	Adult	
			Male	Female
Forehead	2200	600	1667	1267
Chest	400	133	1000	800
Epigastrium	467	47	600	533

[a] From Dietel.[12]

childhood, including infancy, the body regions fall roughly into the following sequence with respect to decreasing strength of the lipid film: nasal dorsum and alae, forehead and chin, auricular helices, back, neck, sternum, shoulders, trunk below the umbilicus, extremities, palms of the hands, and soles of the feet. These findings apply to the neonatal age as well (Table IV). The differences are to be explained by the diverse size and topographical density of the sebaceous glands in the body regions. Other factors determining the strength of the fat film that are of significance for adults and children, such as nutritional conditions and influence of the CNS and environmental conditions, are not significant for newborns.

Accordingly, the influence of maternal hormones (androgens or progesterone) may be related to the increased activity of the sebaceous glands. Even through the urinary excretion of 17-ketosteroids is normal in neonates with acne,[55] the association must nevertheless be considered, since newborns with adrenogenital syndrome are more prone to develop acne; otherwise, neonatal acne is to be seen as an idiosyncratic exaggerated response of the sebaceous glands in the neonate.

The composition of the surface fat can be characterized by the triglyceride content and, to a lesser extent, by the content of free fatty acids. As a result of splitting of lipids by *Corynebacteria acnes* and coagulase-positive staphylococci in the postnatal days, the spectrum changes with increase of free fatty acids and decrease of the triglycerides. Cholesterol is released as epidermal lipid from desquamating horny lamellae; it starts to appear in demonstrable quantities in the course of the first month of life, until finally its content increases after complete arrest of the postnatal sebaceous gland stimulation (see Table I).

The physiologic significance of the surface lipids for the neonate lies in the maintenance of the suppleness, the water content of the stratum corneum, and the maintenance of the acid mantle, which must be built up *de novo* in the postnatal days. These lipids also contribute to the development of a normal bacterial flora.

Studies on modifying the skin lipids by modern surfactant detergents, and on the endogenous fat regeneration time, and resultant conclusions for the skin care of newborns are as scanty as are reports on the determination of their emulsifiability or spreading velocity.[30,42,45]

4.2. Acid Mantle

The chemical reaction of the surface designated as the "acid mantle of the skin" is the sum total of all the chemically active substances occurring on the skin surface. They derive from the uppermost horny layers, the sweat, the superficial fat, endogenous transepidermally discharged metabolic products, and external factors such as amniotic fluid, microorganismal metabolism, and cosmetics.

The acid mantle of the skin is measured by the pH in the water-soluble phase of the surface emulsion. Immediately after birth, it has a mean value of pH 6.34, with a range of 3.0 to 8.0. This value is markedly influenced by the alkaline reaction of the vernix caseosa, which is pH 7.4. The surface pH is also dependent on the pH of the amniotic fluid, with normal values between 6.95 and 7.1 (Table V). The acid–base status of the amniotic fluid is regulated by both the maternal and the fetal acid–base metabolism, the latter being thought to exert the stronger influence. Inferences may possibly be derived from these facts for explaining the amniofetal permeation in postmature fetuses.

In the first 4 days after birth, the pH declines to

an average of 4.95. The scatter of individual values ranges from 3.2 to 7.2. These values do not change appreciably during the course of childhood.

The pH value on the neonatal skin is also stabilized by the fat film, as could be ascertained from studies of pH changes after cleansing with water or alcohol[4] (also see Table VI).

The regeneration of the pH after washing with alkaline soap solutions takes longer than an hour in the majority of newborns.[41] The factors that influence the normalization of the extrinsically altered pH remain obscure.

Topographic differences of pH occur, inasmuch as the majority of newborns have a greater acidity in the shoulder region than on the abdominal skin (Table VII). No sex-related or racial differences of pH were found in newborns. In immature infants, the pH undergoes changes similar to those in full-term infants.

4.3. Sweat

From the 28th week of gestation, the eccrine sweat glands are anatomically developed and found over the entire body; their function, however, is somewhat immature in the perinatal period. After stimulation of the sweat gland receptors by acetylcholine and epinephrine, mature neonates showed a marked reaction with sweat formation, while the glands of premature infants showed little or no reaction. Topical application of nicotine, which acts through the pseudomotor axon reflex, produces the same result (Table VIII).

The insufficiency of the sweat glands is important in connection with the maintenance of the body temperature of newborns, since exogenously overheated newborns have a limited capacity to lower the elevated body temperature by increased sweating (see Chapter 21). The maturation of the sweat gland function is completed by the 5th day of life; the final functional capacity of adults, however, is not achieved until the 2nd or 3rd year of life. In prematures, sweating first sets in between the 21st and 33rd days of life.[31] The sweat of the neonate on the first day of life has a pH between 4.0 and 6.8. The chloride content is 39 meq/liter, with a range of 14 to 64; the sodium content is 36 meq/liter, with a range of 10 to 62; and the potassium content is 8 meq/liter (Table IX). The sodium and chlorine concentration decline in the first month to 13.3 and 14.5 meq/liter, respectively, and increase again during childhood.[24]

Table V. pH of Amniotic Fluid in Normal Term Pregnancies[a]

Author and year of publication	pH
Mannherz (1949)	6.95–7.10
Sjöstedt, Rooth, and Caligara (1961)	7.04
Räihä and Kauranimie (1962)	7.04
Schreiner (1964)	7.00 ± 0.16
Kubli (1966)	7.05 ± 0.07

[a] Data compiled by Tosetti and Krause.[54]

Table VI. Skin Surface pH in Different Areas of the Body and After Water or Alcohol Cleansing[a]

Infant no.	Age (hr)	Method of skin cleansing	Right side			Method of skin cleansing	Left side		
			Shoulder	Armpit	Abdomen		Shoulder	Armpit	Abdomen
1	10	Water	4.9	4.8	6.0	Water and alcohol	4.5	5.0	4.8
	34		5.0	4.9	4.3		5.0	5.3	4.8
2	2	Water	6.9	7.2	7.8	Alcohol	6.2	6.5	6.1
	26		5.3	6.8	7.2		6.2	4.3	7.3
	76		4.2	3.8	6.3		4.2	4.5	6.8
3	1	None				None	7.4	7.1	7.5
	2						7.5	7.3	6.9
	25		6.7	6.8	6.6	Alcohol	6.4	6.3	6.9
	74		4.0	3.4	4.9		3.8	3.5	4.6
4	2	None	6.9	7.4	7.2	None	7.0	7.1	7.4
	3.5		7.1	6.4	7.3	Alcohol	5.0	6.8	7.3
	27		6.0	6.2	7.0		4.8	6.8	7.2
	75		3.8	5.0	5.8		4.8	4.8	6.0
5	5	Water	6.7	7.5	7.0	Water	6.9	7.3	7.2
	8		6.8	7.0	7.0	Alcohol	7.3	6.9	6.8
	33		3.8	4.0	6.3		4.0	4.8	6.5
	55		3.6	3.8	5.9		4.3	4.4	6.3
6	2	Water	7.0	6.9	7.2	Water	7.1	7.4	7.4
	3.5		7.4	6.7	7.0	Alcohol	6.3	6.8	6.7
	26		4.8	6.3	7.0		6.0	6.8	7.3
	48		5.0	6.1	6.9		4.8	4.3	5.6

[a] Data from Behrendt and Green.[3]

Table VII. Skin Surface pH at Different Ages and in Different Areas of the Body[a]

Age	Region	Number of infants	Percentage distribution of pH values					
			3–3.9	4–4.9	5–5.9	6–6.9	7–7.9	≥8.0
1–48	Shoulder	87	3	27	20	24	24	2
hours	Armpit	86	3	19	11	24	38	5
	Abdomen	82	0	4	11	35	48	2
3–6	Shoulder	85	25	47	15	12	1	0
days	Armpit	83	9	46	24	19	2	0
	Abdomen	82	2	38	22	27	9	2
7–30	Shoulder	76	21	71	4	3	1	0
days	Armpit	75	11	55	29	4	1	0
	Abdomen	73	3	64	21	8	3	1

[a] Calculated from data by Behrendt and Green.[3]

Table VIII. Drug-Induced Localized Sweating in Full-Size and Low-Birth-Weight Newborns[a]

Newborns	Number	Reaction	Stimulus result and concentration		
			Nicotine (10^{-4} and 10^{-5})	Epinephrine (10^{-3} and 10^{-4})	Acetylcholine (10^{-4} and 10^{-5})
Full-size	14	Positive	12	7	10
		Negative	2	0	0
		Ambiguous	0	7	4
Low-birth-weight	14	Positive	2	2	0
		Negative	12	8	0
		Ambiguous	0	4	3

[a] Data from Behrendt and Green.[4]

4.4. Transepidermal Exudation

The acid mantle is modified by fluid that exudes transepidermally and finds its way, like spring water rising to the surface, via the lymph spaces of the epidermis. In neonates, this transepidermal fluid loss is almost one-third lower than in infants. It is only in recent years that losses of this type have been noted in newborns with hyperbilirubinemia, and they have come increasingly within the focus of medical interest in babies undergoing phototherapy. The water loss has been related to the high water content of the stratum corneum.

The total water loss of a neonate ranges between 0.5 and 1.0 g/kg per hr. The insensible perspiration component of this loss equals about 0.063% of the total body water per hour.

Metabolic products including unconjugated bilirubin and some exogenous substances such as carotene traverse the cutis–epidermis boundary. They penetrate into the intercellular clefts of the epidermis, where they can be chemically bound and phagocytosed and cast off externally with the migrating cells in the course of continuing epidermal regeneration. In this context, each dermal papilla with its capillary and the superjacent epidermis constitutes an excretory unit.

Table IX. Amount of Sweat and Concentration of Electrolytes in Sweat of 1- to 6-day-old Newborns After Pilocarpine Iontophoresis[a]

Electrolytes		Boys (n = 43)	Girls (n = 35)
Total amount (mg)	Mean:	130.4	125.2
	Range:	57–409	47–300
Sodium (meq/liter)	Mean:	36.8	38.0
	Range:	16.3–50.2	28.2–50.1
Potassium (meq/liter)	Mean:	13.4	14.1
	Range:	9.1–22.6	8.9–21.6
Chlorine (meq/liter)	Mean:	36.5	36.3
	Range:	17.5–50.4	20.2–49.4

[a] Data from Shwachman and Mahmoodian.[49]

5. Physiology of the Dermis

The physiology of the dermis is determined by the properties of its ground substance. The latter forms an amorphous gelatinous mass in which cells and fibers are suspended. It consists of water, protein, and mucopolysaccharides, which are represented mainly by hyaluronic acid and chondroitin sulfate B. From the 4th fetal month, the fibrocytes produce collagen fibers, which are distinguished by their high hydroxyproline content. Collagen becomes more stable with increasing fetal age. The capacity for water fixation runs parallel with this increasing stability. It is characterized by dermal instability in newborns and the tendency to cause edemas. After delivery, the water plethora rapidly regresses.

Until recently, the subcutaneous adipose tissue was considered to have thermal insulation as its sole function (see Chapter 21). The investigations of neonatal metabolism made major revisions necessary, and the subcutis in the postnatal period is now considered to be a metabolically extremely active tissue, in contrast to the adipose tissue of the adult. In the first hours of life, glycerol is released in increased amounts, though not accompanied by the commensurate amount of free fatty acids.[37] Simultaneously, the glycogen concentration in the subcutaneous adipose tissue decreases with increasing activity of glycogen phosphorylase.[38]

Brown adipose tissue (for details, see Chapters 19 and 21) reacts during cold exposure with a lipolysis of the neutral fat stored in its cells. The free fatty acids are oxidized or reesterified up to 90% within the adipose tissue cells,[11,25] while the glycerol content in the blood increases. The surface temperature over the nape region increases compared with that of other skin areas[50] during cold exposure.

6. Cutaneous Immunity

The skin assures immunologic protection against extrinsic infections. The amniotic fluid is generally sterile until the membranes rupture; consequently, there is no possibility of exogenous infections of the skin during the fetal period. Hematogenously transferred infections, such as syphilis, listeriosis, herpes simplex, rubella, and cytomegaly, to mention only a few, lead to characteristic symptoms and signs in the neonate.

The skin displays a high degree of natural resistance represented in part by the acid mantle and the lipid film. The acid skin surface medium, with a pH lower than 5, is credited with a bactericidal quality, as are the unsaturated fatty acids of the superficial fat. The horny layer, especially the stratum lucidum, functions as a barrier. In newborns, the vernix caseosa and the enhanced desquamation of the upper horny cell layers contribute to the natural resistance of the early days of life. With lowering of the pH, the acid mantle takes over this protective function. The colonization of the neonatal skin with microorganisms occurs not only during birth by organisms from the maternal vagina, but also by contact with people. Investigations on the colonization of the neonatal skin with yeasts originating from the maternal vagina show that 37% of all investigated newborns display a yeast colonization. Within 3 days, this percentage decreases by one-third. The demonstrable microorganismal species correspond to those of the mother (Table X).

The colonization of the skin with *Staphylococcus aureus* has been the object of numerous investigations. The earlier opinion that the nose represents the most frequent colonization site and reservoir[16] cannot be sustained. Today, the umbilicus, lower abdomen, especially the pubic region, and the axilla are regarded as the foremost colonization sites[21,26] (Table XI).

Within a few days after birth, the colonization increases in intensity and soon attains the known range of adult skin microorganisms. There is still no explanation for the change in the microorganismal colonization. Whether the reduction of the yeasts is

Table X. Distribution of Yeast Colonizing the Skin of Infants and Children (% of Total Colonies in Each Age Group)[a]

Organism	Postpartum	3rd day	Months				Years			
			1	3	6	9	1	1.5	2	3
Candida										
albicans	64	44	63	26	10	4			4	
C. parapsilosis		6	4	25	23	16	32	18	17	19
Rh. mucilaginosa	4		23	16	29	16	15		25	31
Deb. hansenii	4	13			2	8	15	11		4
C. guilliermondii		6	2	6	8	12		16	14	14
Cr. diffluens	14	6								
T. glabrata	4									

[a] Computed from data by Blaschke-Hellmessen.[6]

connected with a change in the glucose content in the skin, as was concluded from findings in adults, is still as open a point as is the predilection to development of staphylococci in skin regions endowed with a "weaker" acid mantle or more alkaline pH.

The skin of prematures is protractedly colonized with staphylococci, likewise primarily in the umbilical region. The relative frequency of gram-negative organisms would appear to be not so much a problem of age-specific immunity as due to topical humidity conditions.

7. Conclusions

Neonatal skin is characterized by changes that result, on one hand, from morphological im-maturity and, on the other, from incompletely developed functional capacities. The transfer from the intrauterine "aquatic" to the extrauterine atmospheric environment enhances and accelerates peri-natal maturation of skin function. While present knowledge about the embryology and morphology of the skin can be regarded as extensive, that concerning the biochemistry and histochemistry is incomplete. The skin has so far been little invest-igated concerning its intrinsic metabolism. Interest has concentrated mainly on its role in the overall body metabolism in the neonate.

In addition to a continuously evolving morpho-logical and functional maturation after birth, there occur adaptive processes that are characterized by attrition of the intrauterine facilities, such as vernix

Table XI. Colonization of Skin and Mucous Membranes of Newborn Infants in Two Hospitals[a]

Site	Hospital "M" determination				Hospital "L" determination			
	Single	Multiple	Sum	%	Single	Multiple	Sum	%
Nose	0	1	1	3	0	7	7	10
Throat	0	0	0	0	1	15	16	23
Eyes	0	1	1	3	2	16	18	26
Navel	3	4	7	10	14	47	61	88

[a] From Hurst.[26]

caseosa, desquamation of the upper lamellae of the stratum corneum, and the formation of corresponding *postpartum* necessities such as development of the acid mantle, sweat secretion, sebum production, collagenization, and cornification.

The skin is readily accessible for diagnostic studies of maturity and vitality of a neonate. More interest should be directed toward the cutaneous intrinsic metabolism and its role in the postnatal adaptation of the body as a whole, e.g., during phototherapy, or temperature regulation.

8. References

1. AHERNE, W., AND HULL, D., 1964, The site of the heat production in the newborn infant, *Proc. Roy. Soc. Med.* **57**:1172, 1173.

2. ANDREWS, B. F., 1970, Amniotic fluid studies to determine maturity, *Pediatr. Clin. North Am.* **17**:49–67.

3. BEHRENDT, H., AND GREEN, M., 1958, Skin pH pattern in the newborn infant, *Am. J. Dis. Child.* **95**:35–41.

4. BEHRENDT, H., AND GREEN, M., 1969, Drug-induced localized sweating in full-size and low-birth-weight neonates, *Am. J. Dis. Child.* **117**:299–306.

5. BISHOP, E. H., AND CORSON, S., 1968, Estimation of fetal maturity by cytologic examination of amniotic fluid, *Am. J. Obstet. Gynecol.* **102**:654–667.

6. BLASCHKE-HELLMESSEN, R., 1970, Zum Vorkommen von Hefepilzen bei Neugeborenen, Säuglingen und Kleinkindern und ihre pathogenetische Bedeutung als Soorerreger, *Kinderaerztl. Prax.* **38**:219–229.

7. BRAUN-FALCO, O., 1961, Histochemie der Haut, in: *Dermatologie und Venerologie* (H. A. Gottron and W. Schönfeld, eds.), Vol. I, Part I, Georg Thieme, Stuttgart.

8. BREATHNACH, A. S., 1971, Embryology of the human skin, *J. Invest. Dermatol.* **57**:133–141.

9. CLIFFORD, S. H., 1945, Clinical significance of yellow staining of vernix caseosa, skin, nails and umbilical cord, *Am. J. Dis. Child.* **69**:327–332.

10. CLIFFORD, S. H., 1957, Postmaturity, *Adv. Pediatr.* **9**:13–63.

11. DAWKINS, M. J. R., AND SKOPES, J. W., 1965, Non-shivering thermogenesis and brown adipose tissue in the human newborn infant, *Nature (London)* **206**:201–202.

12. DIETEL, K., 1974, *Die Haut und ihre Erkrankungen im Kindesalter*, VEB Georg Thieme, Leipzig.

13. DOLD, H., AND THIESSEN, P., 1952, Beitrag zur biologischen Funktion der vernix caseosa, *Geburtshilfe Frauenheilkd.* **12**:368–375.

14. EBLING, F. G., 1970, The embryology of the skin, in: *An Introduction to the Biology of the Skin* (R. T. Champion, T. Gillman, A. J. Rook, and R. T. Sims, eds.), F. A. Davis Co., Philadelphia.

15. EHRING, F., 1965, Die obersten Hautschichten als Ausscheidungs-organ, *Hautarzt* **16**:219–223.

16. ELEK, S. D., 1956, Experimental staphylococcal infections in the skin of men, *Ann. N. Y. Acad. Sci.* **65**:85–89.

17. GERSTEIN, W., 1971, Cell proliferation in human fetal epidermis, *J. Invest. Dermatol.* **57**:262–268.

18. GLEISS, J., AND HERMANNS, M., 1969, Ektodermale Kriterien zur klinischen Reifebestimmung Neugeborener, *Arch. Kinderheilkd.* **179**:266–283.

19. GREEN, M., AND BEHRENDT, H., 1969, Sweating capacity of neonates. Nicotine-induced axon reflex sweating and the histamine flare, *Am. J. Dis. Child.* **118**:725–732.

20. GRIFFITHS, A. D., 1966, Skin desquamation in the newborn, *Biol. Neonate* **10**:127–139.

21. HARDYMENT, A. F., WILSON, R. A., COCKCROFT, W., AND JOHNSON, B., 1960, Observations on the bacteriology and epidemiology of nursery infections, *Pediatrics* **25**:907–927.

22. HARNACK, G. A. VON, AND OSLER, H., 1958, Quantitative Reifebestimmung von Frühgeborenen, *Monatsschr. Kinderheilkd.* **106**:324–328.

23. HASHIMOTO, T., AND LEVER, W. F., 1966, Histochemical demonstration of glucose-6-phosphate-dehydrogenase in the skin of human embryos, *J. Invest. Dermatol.* **47**:421–425.

24. HINKEL, G. K., AND KORTH, G., 1967, Altersabhängigkeit und diagnostische Aussagekraft der Schweisselektrolyte, *Dtsch. Gesundheitwes.* **22**:405–409.

25. HULL, D., 1966, The structure and function of brown adipose tissue, *Br. Med. Bull.* **22**:92–96.

26. HURST, V., 1960, Transmission of hospital staphylococci among newborn infants. II. Colonization of the skin and mucous membranes of the infants, *Pediatrics* **25**:204–214.

27. KEHNSCHERPER, M., 1963, Die Mastzellen der Haut im Kindesalter, *Paediatr. Grenzgeb.* **2**:162–177.

28. KERPEL-FRONIUS, E., 1970, Electrolyte and water metabolism, in: *Physiology of the Perinatal Period* (U. Stave, ed.), pp. 643–678, Appleton-Century-Crofts, New York.

29. KLAUS, S. N., 1969, Pigment transfer in mammalian epidermis, *Arch. Dermatol.* **100**:756–762.

30. KLEINE-NATROP, H. E., 1974, Über Testmethoden der Rückfettung der Haut durch tensidhaltige Badelösungen mit Lipidzusätzen, *Dermatol. Monatsschr.* **160**:873–881.

31. KUNO, Y., 1956, *Human Perspiration*, Charles C. Thomas, Springfield, Illinois.

32. MAJUMDAR, T. D., 1963, Der Zuckergehalt der Haut bei Candida-Infektionen, *Hautarzt* **14**:370–372.

33. MIELER, W., 1963, Der Mitosekoëffizient in der Haut

des gesunden und kranken Kindes, *Paediatr. Grenzgeb.* **2**:71–82.

34. MIESCHER, G., 1957, Die Haut als Organ der Abwehr, *Hautarzt* **8**:88–93.

35. MONTAGNA, W., 1962, *The Structure and Function of the Skin,* 2nd Ed., Academic Press, New York.

36. NACHMAN, R. L., AND ESTERLY, N. B., 1971, Increased skin permeability in preterm infants, *J. Pediatr.* **79**:628–632.

37. NOVAK, M., AND MONKUS, E., 1972, Metabolism of subcutaneous adipose tissue in the immediate postnatal period of the human newborn. I. Developmental changes in lipolysis and glycogen content, *Pediatr. Res.* **6**:73–80.

38. NOVAK, M., MONKUS, E., AND WOLF, H., 1973, The metabolism of subcutaneous adipose tissue in the immediate postnatal period of human neonates. III. Role of fetal glycogen in lipolysis and fatty acid esterification in the first hours of life, *Pediatr. Res.* **7**:769–777.

39. ODLAND, G. F., AND SHORT, J. M., 1971, Structure of the skin, in: *Dermatology in General Medicine* (T. B. Fitzpatrick, K. A. Arnst, W. H. Clark, A. Z. Eisen, E. J. Van Scott, and J. H. Vaughan, eds.), McGraw-Hill-Blackston, New York.

40. PARMLEY, T. H., AND SEEDS, A. E., 1970, Fetal skin permeability to isotopic water (DHO) in early pregnancy, *Am. J. Obstet. Gynecol.* **108**:128–131.

41. PECK, S. M., AND BOTWINICK, J. S., 1964, The buffering capacity of infants' skins against an alkaline soap and neutral detergent, *J. M. Sinai Hosp. N. Y.* **31**:134–137.

42. POSL, H., AND SCHIRREN, C. G., 1966, Beeinflussung des pH der Hautoberfläche durch Seifen, Waschmittel und synthetische Detergentien, *Hautarzt* **17**:37–40.

43. PRUNIERAS, M., 1969, Interactions between keratinocytes and dendritic cells, *J. Invest. Dermatol.* **52**:1–17.

44. SALING, E., 1966, *Das Kind im Bereich der Geburtshilfe,* Georg Thieme Verlag, Stuttgart.

45. SCHIRREN, C. G., AND HONSIG, C., 1968, Über die Lipidregenerationszeit im Bereich der Talgdrüsen der Haut, *Hautarzt* **19**:53–56.

46. SCIENTIFIC TABLES, 1973, Geigy A. G., Basel.

47. SERRI, F., MONTAGNA, W., AND HUBER, W. M., 1963, Studies of skin of fetus and the child. I. The distribution of alkaline phosphatase in the skin of the fetus, *Arch. Dermatol. (Chicago)* **87**:234–245.

48. SERRI, F., MONTAGNA, W., AND MESCONI, H., 1962, Studies of the skin of the fetus and the child. II. Glycogen and amylophosphorylase in the skin of the fetus, *J. Invest. Dermatol.* **39**:199–217.

49. SHWACHMAN, H., AND MAHMOODIAN, A., 1967, Pilocarpine iontophoresis. Sweat testing results of seven years experience, in: *Cystic Fibrosis* (E. Rossi and E. Stoll, eds.), pp. 158–178, S. Karger, Basel and New York.

50. SILVERMAN, W. A., ZAMELIS, A., SINCLAIR, J. C., AND GATE, F. J. A., 1967, Warm nape of the newborn, *Pediatrics* **33**:984–987.

51. SMITH, R. E., AND HORWITZ, B. A., 1969, Brown fat and thermogenesis, *Physiol. Rev.* **49**:330–425.

52. STUR, A., 1967, Discussion, in: *Cystic Fibrosis* (E. Rossi and E. Stoll, eds.), pp. 179 and 180, S. Karger, Basel and New York.

53. TARNOWSKI, W. M., AND HASHIMOTO, K., 1967, Langerhans cell granules in histiocytosis, *Arch. Dermatol.* **96**:298–304.

54. TOSETTI, K., AND KRAUSE, W., 1972, *Der intrauterine Patient. Diagnostik und Therapie intrauteriner Gefahrenzustände,* Steinkopf, Dresden.

55. TROMOVITCH, T. A., ABRAMS, A. A., AND JACOBS, P. H., 1963, Acne in infancy, *Am. J. Dis. Child.* **106**:230–231.

56. VOTTA, R. A., CAGNETTEN, C. B., PARADU, O., AND GIULLIETTI, M., 1968, Cytologic studies of amniotic fluid in pregnancy, *Am. J. Obst. Gynecol.* **102**:571–577.

57. WILDNAUER, R. H., AND KENNEDY, R., 1970, Transepidermal water loss of human newborns, *J. Invest. Dermatol.* **54**:483–468.

58. WU, P. Y. K., AND HODGMAN, J. E., 1972, Changes in insensible water loss in infants with and without phototherapy, *Clin. Res. Proc.* **20**:294–301.

59. WULF, H., 1965, Der Neugeborenenindex, *Z. Geburtshilfe Frauenheilkd.* **163**:270–276.

60. ZACHARIAE, H., 1964, Histamine and mast cells in human fetal skin, *Proc. Soc. Exp. Biol. Med.* **117**:63–65.

CHAPTER 37

Steroid Hormone Formation and Metabolism

Eduardo Orti

1. Introduction

The decade of the 1960s saw the development of knowledge on the steroid synthetic capabilities of the fetal adrenals and the placenta *in vitro* and *in situ*. The important concept of the *fetoplacental unit* emerged in the second half of that decade from the extensive research effort of Diczfalusy, Solomon, and others; it emphasized that both organs have extensive but incomplete steroidogenic capabilities: the adrenal, being poor in 3β-hydroxysteroid dehydrogenase, can carry out extensive steroid hydroxylation, but must use exogenous progesterone to synthesize cortisol; the placenta produces large amounts of this precursor, but not from the basic building block—acetate. It depends on blood cholesterol as a precursor to form progesterone. The concept of fetoplacental unit is also central to the understanding of estrogen formation in pregnancy.

Eduardo Orti · Department of Pediatrics, State University of New York Downstate Medical Center, Brooklyn, New York 11203

The progress since 1970 has been considerable. On one hand, the sensitive and specific methods of steroid and peptide-hormone estimation by competetive protein-binding and radioimmunoassay allowed workers to estimate individual hormones in very small volumes of blood or other biological fluids, an estimate that is essential in studies of the fetus and newborn. On the other hand, the development of techniques of specific hormone-binding sites in end-organs, while it is still in a developmental stage, may in the future identify the specific effector tissue to a given hormone, at each moment in ontogenetic development.

This technique may well be the technical wedge that will open to our understanding the presently dark areas in the physiologic significance of each hormone at each step in development. Which steroids have a physiologic role and which are excretion products or vestigial metabolic pathways may best be understood in the perspective of phylogenetic evolution. Third, some steroids have been shown to inhibit the action of others at the cellular level (i.e., progesterone inhibition of cortico-steroids), and may thereby protect a target organ at a particular point in time. Also, the intracellular action of steroid hormones in the protoplasmic and nuclear machinery of the effector cell, derepressing opera-tional potentialities of the genome at critical moments, promises to bring us closer than ever before to the understanding of this chapter of physiology in terms of molecular biology. The topic of steroid–cell interactions was recently reviewed by King and Mainwaring[66] and Cuatrecasas *et al.*[25]

The adrenal cortex is essential for life in mammals. It is well known that the steroids secreted by the adrenal exert important regulatory actions on carbo-hydrate, lipid, and protein metabolism. The nature of their contribution to the physiologic phenomena that occur during intrauterine life remains to be established. The phylogenetic appearance of adrenal cortical glands is a much earlier phenomenon that placentation. Both the adrenal and the placenta are steroid-secreting organs. It is therefore of con-siderable interest to understand how the biosynthetic function of the placenta has interdigitated itself with that of the adrenal. We have limited this chapter to the human species when available data are adequate, and referred to research done in rodents when information is not available for the human fetus. There is always a considerable risk of error when applying to one species notions obtained in another. For the adrenal and placenta, this general caution cannot be overemphasized. The adrenal bio-synthetic pathways are well known to vary among mammals. As for the placenta, it is probably the organ that has the greatest variability from species to species. Recent reviews of the human placenta and fetal adrenal were published by Gardner[45] and other authors.[102,118,119]

2. Onset of Functional Capability in the Fetal Adrenal

2.1. Embryologic Development of the Adrenal Cortex in Man

In man, the adrenal cortical primordium appears toward the 4th week of gestation when the crown–rump (CR) length is about 6–8 mm. At this time, its dimensions are $0.5 \times 0.3 \times 0.1$ mm,[116] and it is composed mainly of large acidophilic cells. In the 5th

week in the 12-mm CR embryo, the adrenal has doubled in size ($0.8 \times 0.6 \times 0.4$ mm), and a smaller type of basophilic cell has appeared, presumably derived from the coelomic epithelium, as were the earlier acidophilic cells[63] over which the baso-philic cells soon spread. These small cells give rise to the definitive cortex, while the initial migration becomes the distinctive fetal zone. According to this interpretation of Keene and Hewer,[63] which is supported by the work of Uotila,[114] the cells of the fetal and definitive zones of the fetal cortex are cytologically different from the time of their earliest differentiation. The question of their separate origin by a succession of two separate migrations is not accepted by some recent workers.[24,51] What-ever its embryologic origin, the definitive cortex appears on electron-microscopic studies to be in-active, while the mitochondria of the fetal zone studied by Ross[94] appear to be active in fetuses between the 6th and 17th weeks of gestation. In the 20-mm CR embryo (7–8 weeks), when the adrenal dimensions are $1.2 \times 1.0 \times 0.8$ mm, the fetal zone accounts for 30–50% of the cross-sectional area of the cortex. Its relative prominence increases during pregnancy; during the last trimester, it constitutes about 80% of the cortex.[110] During the first month of postnatal life, the involution of the fetal zone is largely completed.

2.2. Onset of Steroidogenic Capability

The functional capabilities for which the human fetal adrenal has been studied to date comprise its steroidogenic capability (spontaneous or with added precursors) by comparison with the known synthetic pathways of the adult cortex, and its enzymatic content as shown by histochemical studies. Studies on DNA, RNA, and protein synthesis of the fetal adrenals still remain to be done. The first studies on the biosynthetic capability of the fetal adrenal were made using *in vitro* incubation of surviving fetal glands. The studies aimed at ascertaining whether the sequence of synthetic reactions known to occur in the adult gland also took place in the fetal gland. In that sequence, as shown in Fig. 1, cholesterol is synthesized from acetate. The side-chain of cholesterol is then broken down by a desmolase to pregnenolone. Pregnenolone, like cholesterol, has a hydroxyl in position 3 and is unsaturated in position 5-6. The next step involves the formation of progesterone and consists in the conversion of the 3–hydroxyl

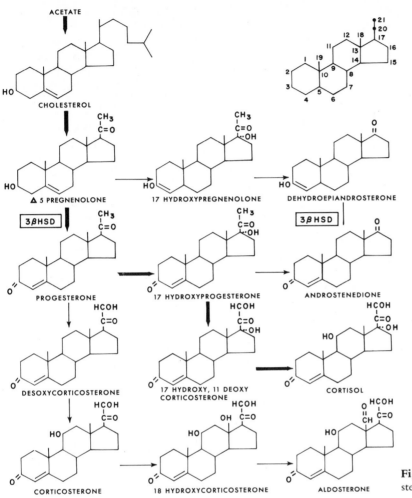

Fig. 1. Biosynthetic pathways of steroid metabolism.

into a 3-ketone and the shift of the double bond from position 5-6 to position 4-5; the first step of dehydrogenation is done by an enzyme called "3β-hydroxysteroid dehydrogenase" (3β-HSD). The second step or shift (isomerization) of the double bond can take place spontaneously *in vitro*; *in vivo* it is believed to be performed by an isomerase. In this chapter, we will refer to both the actions jointly as mediated by 3β-HSD. When this enzyme acts on 5-pregnenolone, the product is progesterone. In the normal sequence of events in the adult adrenal cortex, progesterone is hydroxylated in position 17 by a 17-hydroxylase to produce 17-hydroxyprogesterone. 17-Hydroxyprogesterone is then acted on by 21- and 11-hydroxylases to yield, respectively, 17-hydroxycorticosterone and

cortisol. It is with this sequence of biosynthetic steps known to occur in the adult cortex that the fetal cortex or its two individual zones have been compared.

In 1956, Davis and Plotz[30] demonstrated for the first time that the adrenals from human fetuses in the 3rd–5th months could perform the first step of steroid biosynthesis *in vitro*, converting ^{14}C-labeled acetate to cholesterol.

Lanman and Silverman[73] and Lanman *et al.*[74] showed that the adrenals of fetuses obtained in abortions and those of premature infants had little spontaneous steroidogenic capability, but after the addition of progesterone to the medium, they were able to recover cortisol, corticosterone, and 17-hydroxycorticosterone, thereby demonstrating that at those stages of development, the human adrenal cortex had the capacity to hydroxylate in positions 11, 17, and 21. They were the first to postulate that the 3β-HSD system was either deficient or inhibited in the fetus.

Solomon et al.[109] using material from fetuses obtained in abortions between the 10th and 22nd weeks of gestation, dissected the fetal zone and the definitive type cortex and were able to show that both zones could convert progesterone to 17-hydroxyprogesterone and androstenedione. The latter C_{19} steroid is assumed to derive from 17-hydroxyprogesterone by cleavage of the C_{20-21} side chain. The in vitro capacity of the adrenal cortex to perform the complete synthesis from acetate to cortisol was soon demonstrated[9] for fetuses between 12 and 22 weeks. Products identified after addition of [^{14}C]acetate were dehydroepiandrosterone (DHA), pregnenolone, androstenedione, 11-hydroxyandrostenedione, and cortisol; sought but not found were progesterone 17-hydroxyprogesterone, corticosterone, testosterone, and adrenosterone (Δ^4-androstene 3,11-17 trione). These results showed that capability for complete adultlike synthesis of cortisol from acetate was present in the fetal adrenal cortex as a whole, and brought into the picture the synthesis of DHA; also, these workers confirmed the presence of 11-, 17-, and 21-hydroxylases, and even though the study was qualitative, the authors believed their results pointed to a restricted activity of 3β-HSD. Villee et al.,[121] using human fetuses of 11–26 weeks of age, confirmed that adrenal cortices could transform progesterone to cortisol, but were more efficient if 17-hydroxyprogesterone was the added precursor. They were unable to confirm that Porter Silber chromogens (which include cortisol) appeared after the addition of precursors more primitive than progesterone ($\Delta5$ pregnenolone, cholesterol, and acetate). They again interpreted their findings to indicate either a deficiency or a lability of 3β-HSD activity in the whole fetal cortex. Studies on the secretory capability of the fetal zone were carried out after dissection of the fetal cortex by several authors. Solomon et al.[109] showed that fetal zone tissue essentially free from definitive cortex had the capacity to convert [^{14}C]progesterone to 17-hydroxyprogesterone and androstenedione. These findings were confirmed and extended by Bloch and Benirshke,[9,10] who demonstrated the capability of the fetal zone tissue of embryos 12 weeks or older to synthesize DHA, androstenedione, and

cortisol from [^{14}C]acetate. In these experiments, the amount of androstenedione plus cortisol (4 compounds) produced was only one-fourth to one-sixth the amount of DHA (the major 5 compound isolated). Thus, in early pregnancy, the isolated fetal zone in the human fetus has full corticosteroidogenic capability, and its 3β-HSD activity is as limited as that of the adrenal as a whole.

Villee and Villee[120] used incubations of homogenized adrenals in vitro to study the quantitative developmental changes in enzyme contribution to steroid synthesis. Adrenals of fetuses of less than 10 cm CR length produce in vitro androstenedione, 11β-hydroxyandrostenedione, 16α-hydroxyprogesterone, $16\alpha,17\alpha$-dihydroxyprogesterone, deoxycorticosterone, corticosterone, and cortisol from progesterone. Under their conditions, androstenedione was a major metabolite of progesterone in the fetus of less than 10 cm CR length. Beyond this stage of fetal growth, the adrenal homogenates produced much less if any androstenedione or 11β-hydroxyandrostenedione from the same precursor and increased quantities of corticosterone and cortisol. In the same preparation, pregnenolone was converted largely to DHA, with small amounts of 17-hydroxypregnenolone, 16α-hydroxypregnenolone, and androstenedione.

In summary, very early in fetal development, the adrenal has complete capability for synthesis of cortisol from acetate. The step between 5-pregnenolone and progesterone mediated by 3β-HSD, however, is very restricted in in vitro studies. As a consequence of this block, progesterone must be supplied to the adrenal from an outside source if any significant corticosteroid synthesis is to take place. The major androgen produced in vitro from pregnenolone is DHA, and that produced from progesterone is androstenedione.

2.3. Demonstration of Enzymes in the Fetal Adrenal by Histochemical Methods

Histochemical staining to reveal the presence of enzymes that are known to be implicated in steroid biosynthesis has given some information on the presence of those enzymes at different stages of fetal development. Goldman et al.[49,50] reported 3β-HSD activities in the adrenals of fetuses larger than 15 cm CR. Cavallero and Magrini[17] used DHA, pregnenolone, 17α-hydroxypregnenolone, and androstenediol as substrates for the demonstration of 3β-HSD. This enzyme could not be demonstrated by them in the fetal zone at any gestation age from the 2nd month of intrauterine life to birth. The definitive cortex, on the other hand, showed no evidence of 3β-HSD activity in the first 2–3 months of intrauterine life, but a positive reaction was faintly visible at 4–6 months, and increased to the point of being quite evident in the neocortex of the newborn. The best substrates were found to be DHA and androstenediol.

3. Steroid Metabolism in the Perfused Previable Fetus at Midterm

Further studies of the synthesis and metabolism of adrenal steroids have frequently been made by the perfusion of the previable fetus in cases in which elective legal abortion was performed. Most of the information yielded by this approach concerns the fetus at midpregnancy (15–20 weeks). The results obtained by perfusion of the previable fetus with steroid precursors, followed by isolation of the metabolites from blood and various tissues, are a considerable step forward in the study of the integrated metabolism of steroid hormone.

The work of Solomon in collaboration with the group of Diczfalusy helped greatly in clarifying many aspects of the metabolism of neutral steroids in the fetus and placenta. This work was summarized in three papers.[106–108]

The previable fetus of 18–22 weeks' gestational age, when perfused for 60 min, can synthesize cholesterol from [14C]acetate in its liver and adrenal. When the same preparation was perfused with tritium-labeled cholesterol and 14C-labeled acetate, only minute amounts of Δ5-pregnenolone or 17α-hydroxypregnenolone could be isolated from the adrenal with either label. Perfusion with cholesterol sulfate yielded no transformation products. Solomon et al.[108] concluded from this experiment that the human fetus at midterm must use precursors reaching it from the placenta or the mother to synthesize neutral steroids.

Injection of Δ5-pregnenolone into the umbilical vein in a fetus at 13 weeks' gestation, with clamping of the veins 20 sec after the injection, resulted in the isolation from the adrenal of 14.6% nonmetabolized Δ5-pregnenolone; 2.8% of the radioactivity in the adrenal appeared as DHA sulfate,

and 2.3% as 17α-hydroxypregnenolone sulfate. All tissues studied contained only unmetabolized Δ5-pregnenolone and 20α-dihydropregnenolone sulfate. After perfusion of the previable fetus with progesterone 14C$_4$, extensive metabolism of the precursor occurred, the major sites of which were the adrenal and the liver. Hydroxylated metabolites were recovered exclusively from the adrenal, and included 16α-hydroxyprogesterone, 17α-hydroxyprogesterone, and cortisol. The perfusate contained 16β-hydroxyprogesterone and small amounts of corticosterone and 6β-hydroxyprogesterone. Reduced metabolites were recovered from the adrenal (20α-dihydroprogesterone), but most came from the liver (20α-dihydroprogesterone, 3α15β-pregnan-20-one, and pregnane 3α,20α-diol). Lung, kidney, and intestine contained lesser amounts and numbers of reduced metabolites of progesterone. In all tissues, Δ4-androstenedione was searched for but could not be detected. These experiments were repeated after fetal adrenalectomy to assess the extent to which the hydroxylated and reduced metabolites found in the perfusate and nonadrenal tissues were of adrenal origin. It was concluded that a number of tissues of the fetus can reduce progesterone to a variety of products, but that the adrenals are the main site for the formation of hydroxylated products isolated from the tissues of the intact perfused fetuses.

When 17α-hydroxyprogesterone 14C$_4$ was injected into the umbilical vein of a male fetus (19 weeks' gestation) and a female fetus (8 weeks' gestation), no labeled androstenedione or testosterone could be detected in the adrenal extract. Therefore, as far as this preparation is concerned, there is apparently no functioning 17,20-desmolase in the fetus at midterm. Similar studies with 16α-hydroxyprogesterone, a major product of the perfusion with progesterone, supported the conclusion that the fetal adrenal at midterm does not further hydroxylate this steroid, nor is it extensively metabolized in the fetal tissues.

Aldosterone secretion was considered to be absent at midpregnancy because of the nonsecretory aspect of the zona glomerulosa. Longchamp[80] claimed that the 18-hydroxylase system required for the synthesis of aldosterone develops shortly before term. Pasqualini et al.,[91] however, were able to isolate aldosterone from the adrenal of fetuses at midterm, after perfusion with corticosterone.

Dell'Acqua et al.[34] studied the metabolism of androgens in the perfused fetus. They perfused two male and two female fetuses at midpregnancy with

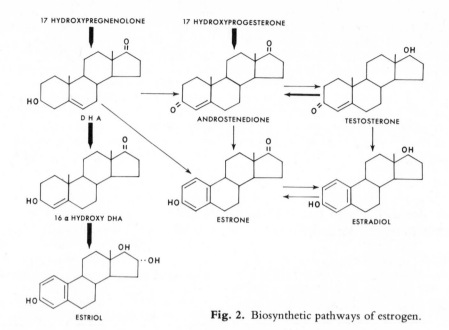

Fig. 2. Biosynthetic pathways of estrogen.

[14]C-labeled androstenedione and tritium-labeled testosterone. Very little interconversion of androstenedione to testosterone was found in any of the fetal tissues studied, with the exception of the liver. In the fetal liver, complete interconversion of these two compounds was found. The resting tissues transform testosterone into androstenedione[6] and both androgens into several metabolites, including etiocholanolone, etiocholanediol, dehydrotestosterone, and etiocholanedione. Androsterone was isolated only from the lung. Fetal aromatization of the two androgens also takes place only in the liver, while the fetal adrenals can produce 11β-, 15α-, and 16α-hydroxylated derivatives.

The fetal circulation contains levels of estrogen about 10-fold those of the maternal blood, estriol being 50–100 times higher in concentration than estrone or estradiol. Yet little if any of this estrogen circulating in the fetus originates in fetal tissues. The contribution of the fetal adrenal to estrogen metabolism consists probably in the synthesis of DHA (Fig. 2), which is a precursor for the placental synthesis of estrone and estradiol and 16α-hydroxydehydroepiandrosterone, which the placenta will cyclize to estriol. Estrogens reaching the fetus from the placenta are conjugated by most fetal tissues to their sulfate derivatives, and once in conjugated form are further transformed by hydroxylation.[35,95]

4. Placental Contribution to the Metabolism of Steroids

The placenta is a very efficient synthesizer within a very limited range of steroid biosynthesis. One might well say that it is a highly specialized organ if one takes as a comparative standard the accepted steroidogenic sequence and scope of the adult human adrenal. Its capability appears to include total synthesis of progesterone from acetate. Evidence from *in vitro* perfusion experiments suggests, however, that synthesis from acetate is quantitatively a very insignificant capability of the placenta.[77,115]

4.1. Partial Biosynthesis of Pregnenolone and Progesterone from Cholesterol

The midterm placenta does have 3β-HSD and is capable of producing progesterone from pregnenolone and 17α-hydroxyprogesterone from 17α-hydroxypregnenolone[92]; most important, it can produce pregnenolone from cholesterol.[57] When placental homogenates were incubated *in vitro* with adequate precursors, Jungmann and Schweppe[62] also found evidence of 16α- and 17α-hydroxylases, which have not been shown to be operational in *in situ* perfusion. The placenta appears to be incapable of metabolizing or further hydroxylating progesterone to corticosteroid compounds. It would therefore seem that its main precursor is cholesterol and its main products are pregnenolone and progesterone. From *in vitro* incubation studies of placental homogenates and mitochondria, Ryan *et al.*[96] concluded that pregnenolone (from the fetus) was also a placental precursor of progesterone, but was quantitatively less important than cholesterol.

Histochemical studies found 3β-HSD activity in the trophoblast amniotic epithelium and in chorion, using DHA and androstenediol as substrates.[17]

The placenta can also resynthesize progesterone from reduced metabolites (20α-hydroxyprogesterone) of that steroid produced in the fetal liver and adrenal when they are recirculated into the placenta.[124]

Arguments were presented by Diczfalusy[36] to support the notion that the main source of cholesterol for placental pregnenolone and progesterone synthesis is maternal blood cholesterol and, to a lesser extent, fetal blood cholesterol. Davis and Plotz[31] had previously shown that administration of tritiated cholesterol to pregnant women resulted in the production of tagged pregnandiol excretion, which implied the synthesis of progesterone from cholesterol. They calculated that 70% of the progesterone elaborated in the placenta came from maternal blood cholesterol. The placenta at term produces daily about 250 mg progesterone, which is distributed in roughly equal amounts between the maternal and fetal compartments.[119]

While the placenta does not have corticosteroid synthetic capability, it can dehydrogenate cortisol to cortisone.[111] This conversion may be of considerable importance, for it has been found that cortisone rather than cortisol predominates in cord blood. This predominance of cortisone might explain the hyperfunction of the fetal pituitary, since only cortisol appears to have biological activity in most target organs,[16] and presumably also in inhibiting the pituitary.

4.2. Partial Biosynthesis of Estrogen

Estriol, the estrogen quantitatively most abundant in fetal and maternal circulation and urine during pregnancy, originates from 16α-hydroxydehydroepiandrosterone (16α-OHDHA) and 16α-hydroxydehydroepiandrosterone sulfate (16α-OHDHAS), which in turn has been formed from DHA and DHAS in the fetal liver. The placenta

reduces ring A of 16α-OHDHA to produce estriol[81] (see Fig. 2).

If DHA rather than the 16-hydroxylated relative is perfused through the placenta, no estriol is formed; only estrone and estradiol appear, indicating that the placenta lacks 16α-hydroxylating ability. Using a different technique, Siiteri and MacDonald[104] demonstrated that maternal DHAS can be a quantitatively important precursor of estradiol; they further showed that in the normal pregnant woman, estriol may be formed by more than one mechanism. The most important is the one already described, which uses 16α-OHDHAS derived from the fetus as a precursor. Estradiol may be further hydroxylated in position 16 by the fetus, and thus make a minor contribution to estriol formation.

4.3. Metabolism of Androgens

This aspect of placental synthetic function was extensively studied by Diczfalusy *et al.*[37] DHA and its sulfate are found in substantial amounts in cord blood.[20] The placenta will cyclize and transform DHA and DHAS to estrone and estradiol[11-13] when they are injected into a uterine artery or perfused into the placenta *in situ*. Synthesis of androgens in the placenta using DHA as a precursor was also suggested by the work of Lamb *et al.*[69] They perfused the fetal side of the midterm placenta with DHA while it was attached to the uterus and isolated testosterone and androstenedione from the perfusate.

4.4. Steroid Transfer Between Mother and Fetus

The placenta allows all steroids that have been studied to cross in both directions. The rate at which this happens, however, varies greatly from steroid to steroid, and depends on the form of conjugation with glucuronic or sulfuric acid or both in which the steroid is present in blood.

This problem was extensively studied at midpregnancy[83] and near term.[85] Originally, Migeon and co-workers, using Nelson and Samuel's method for estimation of total 17-OH-corticosteroids in blood, found the concentration of 17-OH-corticosteroids to be higher in maternal blood than in cord blood by a factor of 2:5, which allowed them to postulate that the latter was derived from the former.[87] In a series of subsequent studies,[83,84] they established unequivocally that cortisol traversed the placental barrier rapidly, and they confirmed for cortisol a mother-to-fetus gradient of the same order of magnitude as that previously shown by them to exist for 17-OH-corticosteroids as a group. These authors interpreted the observed gradient to be a consequence of the high concentration of transcortin in maternal blood during pregnancy, rather than an active placental function. The findings at midpregnancy were similar to those at term. Other steroids studied included ^{14}C-labeled corticosterone, progesterone, estrone, and 17β-estradiol. In all cases, there was a bidirectional transfer of the steroids, the specific rate of transfer for each steroid varying by a factor of more than 3, the rate for cortisol and estrone being the fastest, and the rates for corticosterone, progesterone, and estriol being slower and approximately equal.

Most of the steroids found in cord blood, however, are in conjugated form, mainly as sulfates and also as glucosiduronides.[40] The transference and/or previous deesterification of the steroid by the placenta is probably the most important factor in regulating the retention of steroids in the fetus or their transfer to the mother for external elimination. Dancis et al.[26] and Levitz et al.[77] studied this problem extensively. They demonstrated for estrone and its glucosiduronide, estradiol and its sulfate, and estriol sulfate and its glucosiduronide[76] that the free forms of the hormone go through the placenta many times faster than do the conjugates. The sulfate is transferred at about 3 times the rate of the glucosiduronide, probably because the placenta has a powerful sulfatase activity that liberates the free steroid from its sulfated conjugate. The glucosiduronide is probably not split by the placenta in vivo, even though β-glucuronidase activity has been reported in the placenta in vitro.[42]

4.5. Integrated Steroid Synthesis and Metabolism in the Fetoplacental Unit

The results of the experiments on perfusion of fetuses and placentas in situ and of in vitro incubations led to the understanding that both the fetal adrenal and the placenta are incomplete endocrine organs. The synthetic and metabolic capabilities are complementary except in the synthesis of cholesterol, in which both appear to be defective at midpregnancy. If cholesterol is supplied by the maternal and fetal livers, however, the combined capabilities of both organs cannot only carry out all the synthetic steps

of the adult human adrenal, but also are capable of performing several other synthetic reactions that do not exist in the adult organ. Diczfalusy et al.[36] deserve the credit for having established firmly the notion of the fetoplacental unit as a functional whole.

The methodology of direct study of steroid metabolism in the fetoplacental unit is complicated by the fact that the precursors must be injected while the fetoplacental circulation is still intact, in cases of legal abortion produced by hysterotomy at midterm. The circulation is allowed to continue for some time before the cord is ligated, and the metabolites are extracted from blood, placenta, and fetal tissues, and in some cases from maternal urine. Other important data were obtained by steroid fractionation and identification in cord blood at term,[40] or by the study of quantitative differences of steroid content in blood from the umbilical arteries and umbilical vein.[46]

4.5.1. Neutral Steroids

Synthesis of cholesterol appears to take place in the maternal and fetal livers, rather than in either the placenta or the fetal adrenal. Maternal blood contains a higher cholesterol level and is probably the major contributor.[97] The placenta can produce $\Delta 5$-pregnenolone and progesterone from the cholesterol. These two precursors are secreted into the fetal and maternal circulations. $\Delta 5$-Pregnenolone is sulfonated by the adrenal and is hydroxylated to 17α-hydroxypregnenolone sulfate, which serves within the adrenal as precursor to DHAS. In the fetal liver, the same precursor may be either hydroxylated in position 16 to yield 16α-hydroxypregnenolone sulfate or reduced to 20α-hydroxypregnenolone. The latter steroid may be used, on returning to the placenta, to resynthesize progesterone.

Progesterone produced by the placenta may go into the maternal circulation to the liver, be transformed to pregnandiol, and be excreted by maternal urine. A large amount goes into the fetus. In the fetal adrenal, progesterone may be hydroxylated in positions 17, 21, and 11 to yield corticosteroids—corticosterone sulfate, 11-deoxycorticosterone sulfate, 11-dehydrocorticosterone sulfate, hydrocortisone, and its sulfate. Hydrocortisone will be oxidized in the fetus to cortisone, which is, as such, probably devoid of biological activity and incapable of repressing the pituitary release of ACTH. Other forms of hydroxylation of progesterone in the fetal adrenal that do not enter into the corticosteroid biosynthetic pathway are 16α- and 6α-hydroxylation to 16α-hydroxy-progesterone and to 6α-hydroxyprogesterone, respectively.

In the fetal liver and other tissues, progesterone may be transformed into pregnandiol and its sulfate or reduced to 20α-hydroxyprogesterone.

4.5.2. Androgens and Estrogens

DHAS secreted by the fetal (and maternal) adrenal may undergo, on returning to the placenta, two types of transformations: (1) cyclizing of ring A to yield estrone or estradiol or both, or (2) transformation by the action of placental 3β-HSD into androstenedione, which in turn may be transformed into testosterone by a 17-reductase. Both these androgens can be secreted into the maternal and fetal circulations, or they can be cyclized within the placenta to estrone and estradiol. DHAS may also be hydroxylated by the fetus to 16α-hydroxydehydro-isoandrosterone sulfate, which, on repassage through the placenta, will serve as the main precursor for estriol sulfate and estriol, the quantitatively most important estrogen in pregnancy. Estriol is excreted in maternal urine, but it is also abundantly distributed in all fetal tissues, in which, evidence[54] indicates, it can be further hydroxylated to a tetrol derivative.

Eberlein[40] made an important contribution to the knowledge of steroid content in pooled fetal blood retained in the placenta after vaginal delivery of full-term infants. In this blood, he detected 23 steroids and 5 sterols. Of these steroids, 20 appeared to exist in fetal blood as sulfoconjugates; only 17-hydroxyprogesterone was found in the free state, and the only glucosiduronide detected was 5β-pregnane-3α,20α-diol. This author found two populations of steroids in fetal blood. One group was composed of 4 compounds, including progesterone and its metabolites. The second group included the majority of the steroids and all 5 sterols; they were found to be Δ5,3β-hydroxysteroids. Eberlein believes that these Δ5-hydroxysteroids originate in the fetal zone of the fetal adrenal cortex, which is markedly deficient in 3β-HSD at term as well as at midpregnancy.

4.5.3. Conjugation and Conjugate Hydrolysis in the Fetoplacental Unit

Most fetal tissues, including the skin, have an intense steroidsulfokinase activity, but scarce sulfatase activity. Therefore, steroid sulfates formed by the fetal tissues from circulating free steroids will remain as conjugates as long as they are in the fetal organism. On the other hand, the placenta has powerful sulfatase capable of hydrolyzing most steroid sulfates.[47,48] Glucuronide conjugation is quantitatively less important than sulfate conjugation. Of 23 steroids isolated by Eberlein[40] from cord blood, 20 were recovered by a transesterification method[40] that appears to be specific for sulfates, and only 1 (5β-pregnane-3α,20α-diol) was present as a glucosiduronate. Levitz[76] gave figures for the relative amounts of three types of conjugates of estriol in cord blood: 67% is present as estriol sulfate, 20% as glucosiduronate, and about 10% each as the unconjugated and diconjugated estriols.

5. The Maternal Compartment

The fetoplacental unit is in dynamic equilibrium with the larger continent of the maternal organism. Levels of steroids and their metabolites in the fetoplacental circulation depend, to a considerable extent, on mechanisms that operate in the mother. Maternal secretion, metabolism, and excretion of steroids regulate the composition of the milieu in which the fetoplacental unit extracts precursors and excretes metabolites. While a detailed exposition of steroid metabolism in the pregnant woman is outside the scope of this chapter, some of the pertinent facts will be summarized.

Plasma cortisol and corticosteroids have consistently been found to be elevated in maternal plasma during pregnancy.[1,5,8,19,58] This elevation is probably secondary to the increase in cortisol-binding globulin (CBG).[105] The concentration of CBG is 29–30 mg/liter in the plasma of non-pregnant women. It starts to rise in the 2nd or 3rd month of pregnancy, and reaches a mean level of 70 mg/liter at term. This concentration is much higher than that of cord blood,[28,29] which probably accounts for the lower corticosteroid level found in the fetal circulation. Bound cortisol is probably not biologically active, and pregnant women show no clinical manifestations of hypercorticism.

The half-life of cortisol in the plasma of pregnant women is greatly prolonged,[85] and its glucuronic conjugation in the liver is decreased. This situation, together with the increases of CBG, probably accounts for its increased concentration of blood even though cortisol production rates by the adrenal are decreased in pregnancy except at the time of labor.[86] Testosterone concentration in maternal blood is significantly increased independent of sex in the fetus.[93] Androstenedione and dehydroepiandrosterone are also increased, although only slightly. Pregnancy increases the protein binding of testosterone and DHA, but does not affect binding of androstenedione.

Estriol concentration in maternal plasma increases an average of 5-fold from the 25th to the 40th weeks. Values given by various authors have varied considerably, depending on the techniques used. Nachtigall *et al.*[88] introduced a method in which synthetic conjugated estriol is used to correct for recovery losses. They found values ranging between 9.3 and 56 mg/dl plasma, with a mean of 27 mg/dl in normal late pregnancy. Most of the estriol was in the form of a sulfoglucosiduronate diconjugate.[112]

Serial estimations of unconjugated estrone, estradiol, and estriol[32] showed the sequence in which these extrogens rise in the course of pregnancy: the rise of estriol follows that of the other two estrogens.

Aldosterone is increased progressively during pregnancy, as are renin and angiotensin, but there is a dissociation between these increases that remains unexplained.[123]

6. Function of the Fetal Adrenal Cortex

There is scant information on the function of the adrenal cortex of the human fetus. Forsham[43] discussed the biochemical phenomena in a physiologic perspective. Experimental evidence in rats indicates that adrenalectomy of mother and fetus on day 18.5 does not result in death of the fetus or interruption of pregnancy. In the anencephalic human fetus, in which the adrenals frequently fail to show the usual hypertrophy, mainly at the expense of the fetal zone, no corresponding failure in somatic development results; the fetus develops normally to term. A large number of experiments done by Jost *et al.*[61] in rabbits and rats established that in these species, the fetal adrenal cortex is not required for fetal growth. The main function found by Jacquot[56] for the rat adrenal cortex is that it influences the desposition of glycogen in the fetal liver and fetal myocardium. The size of the fetal

thymus is also influenced by adrenocortical secretions. Jost *et al.*[61] showed that intrauterine decapitation of the fetus at day 17.5 reduces by 90% the medullary activity of the enzyme phenylethanolamine-N-methyl transferase, the enzyme that mediates the synthesis of adrenaline from noradrenaline. These works were summarized by Jost.[59,60]

Present knowledge does not permit a physiological interpretation of many changes in corticosteroid and sex hormone production and metabolism that the biochemists have unveiled in the last decade. Indeed, thinking in terms of what little is known of the biological activities of these steroids, the high circulating levels of androgens and estrogens in fetal blood would appear to be a liability rather than an asset. Nor is it in any way clear that the high levels of androgens and estrogens in the fetoplacental unit play a symbiotic role, the end-organ of which is in the maternal organism, with the possible exception of the maternal elevation of transcortin as a response to placental estrogen. Steroids as well as chorionic gonadotropin or the placenta lactogen have yet to be assigned a convincing role in the physiology of pregnancy. Yet it would be rash to conclude at the present stage of our knowledge that any of these hormones is superfluous. Our understanding of the biological effect of the steroids at the cellular level is rudimentary. The determining factors of tissue differentiation are almost completely unknown. The nonrejection of the placenta by the maternal organism, the successful competition of fetal tissues vs. maternal tissues for available nutrients, and the factors that determine the initiation of labor are all problems that await elucidation.

Steroids may have a role in some of these mechanisms. The fetal adrenal does not appear to be necessary for fetal development in the rat, as shown by Jost *et al.*,[61] or in the human species, as suggested by the normal development of the anencephalic fetus. As for the maternal adrenal, it is well known that Addison's disease in the mother is no impediment to a successful pregnancy.[30] One may therefore surmise that the adrenal plays a role in survival only in extrauterine life, and that the gland is not necessary *in utero*. But unlike the other unused systems, such as the sensory organs, the adrenal is active, and that activity may not be pertinent or may be deleterious to fetal development. Hypercorticism of the mother is known to be detrimental to the fetus,[22] and corticosteroid, progestin, and sex hormone treatments all have adverse side effects on the fetus at certain moments of its development. In this light, the sequence of biosynthetic transformations described may represent a huge dumping operation by which the fetal organism is defended against the noxious steroids.

The lack of 3β-HSD could be understood as the essential block whereby production of corticosteroids is prevented and the superabundant precursors are shifted to the synthesis of more innocuous estriol. It is of considerable interest that this increased estriol formation may be stimulated by estrogens, suggesting the presence of an autoregulatory mechanism. Gurpide[53] and his associates showed that the administration of the synthetic estrogen Stilbestrol results in a marked elevation of 16α-hydroxylation of steroids by the liver.

The inactivity of 3β-HSD itself may be due to a late developmental schedule for this enzyme, or it may be due, as Ville[117] suggested, to inhibition by its normal reaction product, progesterone, originated in the placenta. The reductive pathways of progesterone in the liver would serve a similar purpose by withdrawing progesterone from corticosteroid synthesis. The ubiquitous sulfokinase of fetal tissues would serve to impede the biological action of estrogens, androgens, and progestins alike. Three additional mechanisms would defend the fetus against maternal cortisol: (1) the increased transcortin in maternal blood; (2) the rapid dehydrogenation of free cortisol to cortisone by placental cortisol dehydrogenase; and (3) the fact that progesterone has been shown to be a powerful competitor for costicosteroid binding sites at the cellular level, and may therefore be a cortisol inhibitor[66] in some tissues. However, a possible role for costicosteroids in fetal development was convincingly demonstrated by Liggins and Howie.[78] Corticosteroids will enhance functional maturation of the fetal lung,[33] and the mode of action is partially understood, since Ballard and Ballard[3,4] showed the existence of glucocorticoid receptors in that organ in man. Pharmacological doses of costicosteroids to the mother were recommended for the prevention of the respiratory distress syndrome.[78,79]

7. Control of Fetal Adrenal Secretion

The question of trophic control of the fetal adrenal has intrigued workers in this field for years. Factors suggesting a strong trophic stimulus were the large size of the fetal adrenal relative to body weight and the peculiar pattern of its development in intrauterine life followed by involution in the first 3 weeks after birth. This involution is accounted for mainly by the development followed by the necrosis of the distinctive fetal zone. It appeared probable that this stimulus was due to a trophic hormone different from ACTH, since the anatomic pattern of the hypertrophy was peculiar and the hypertrophy was confined to the duration of pregnancy. It is not surprising that chorionic gonadotropin was considered for some time a likely candidate for the trophic role.[44,46] That both the fetal zone and a luteinizing type of chorionic gonadotropin are peculiar to the human species and restricted to pregnancy made this speculation extremely attractive. Early attempts to stimulate the adrenal *in vivo* or *in vitro* with chorionic gonadotropins failed. The work of Aurtizen et al.,[2] however, gave some evidence for the stimulation by human chorionic gonadotropin of DHA secretion by the newborn adrenal, while ACTH administration stimulated the excretion of cortisol and its metabolites. At this moment, therefore, the possibility of a dual control of the fetal adrenal remains open.

Anencephalic fetuses fail to produce a fetal zone in the second half of pregnancy, probably because of lack of pituitary stimulation. Lanman[71] was able to produce adrenal hypertrophy equivalent in size to that of the normal fetus in these anencephalic fetuses by injection of zinc ACTH, while chorionic gonadotropin did not result in fetal zone stimulation.

Lanman[72] reviewed the available evidence and concluded that in the human fetus, the pituitary is responsible for the maintenance of the fetal zone. The pituitary control of the fetal adrenal is now widely accepted. However, the question of what makes the adrenal involute after birth has not been adequately answered. It would probably be necessary to postulate either hyperactivity of the fetal pituitary in the second half of pregnancy or a partial pituitary insufficiency or adrenal unresponsiveness after birth.

Jost[59] and Jost et al.,[61] working with rats and rabbits, accumulated an impressive body of evidence in support of an active role of the pituitary in the hypertrophy, maintenance, and secretion of the adrenal *in utero*. Evidence was also found in animals that a feedback mechanism exists between the fetal adrenal and the fetal pituitary, unilateral adrenalectomy being followed by enlargement of the remaining gland.[67] This enlargement can be prevented by decapitating the fetus. In humans, the evidence for a feedback is much less explicit. Babies born to mothers who have received large doses of prednisone during the later part of pregnancy may show evidence of adrenal insufficiency after birth,[55] but this type of experience has been neither abundant nor conclusive, and larger series of pregnant women treated with prednisone make no reference to the occurrence of adrenal insufficiency in the neonate.[122] The functional development of the fetal pituitary is covered in Chapter 38.

The studies of steroid production and metabolism in the fetoplacental unit previously outlined suggest that a closed-loop feedback control mechanism between the pituitary and the adrenal probably does not exist in the fetus. Because of the deficient 3β-HSD system in the fetal adrenal, the earlier steps of steroid metabolism that are supposed to be the steps at which the stimulatory effect of ACTH is largely exerted do not result in the formation of corticosteroids. Rather, 5-pregnenolone is used in the pathway leading to the formation of DHA, 16-OHDHA, and estriol, none of which is efficient as far as we know in inhibiting the pituitary. Large amounts of progesterone of placental origin are continuously offered the adrenal. The adrenal has all the enzymatic equipment to transform this progesterone into cortisol, and cortisol can be isolated from the fetal adrenal after progesterone perfusion. But cortisol is probably dehydrogenated in the placenta to cortisone,[40,100] and cortisone is presumably not capable of inhibiting the pituitary. The progesterone that is assumed to be the precursor of hydrocortisone is mainly of placental origin, and pituitary ACTH is not known to stimulate any of the biosynthetic steps leading to the synthesis of progesterone from cholesterol by the placenta. No known feedback exists between the placenta and the pituitary. The remaining possible source of cortisol would be the maternal circulation. This cortisol would presumably also be subject to the conversion to cortisone in the placenta, and in any case, this exogenous cortisol could not explain how the regulatory loop including the fetal adrenal could be closed.

In conclusion, there is little doubt that fetal pituitary ACTH is one of the trophic stimuli to the fetal adrenal. The pituitary may be influenced by the level of circulating cortisol, and because this level is low, the pituitary tends to overstimulate the adrenal. The role of chorionic gonadotropin is not yet established, but it may well be an additional stimulus to the fetal adrenal.

8. Adrenal Function in the Neonatal Period

During the first 3–4 weeks of life, the adrenal is undergoing a dramatic structural reorganization. The fetal zone starts to involute shortly before term, and by the end of the first month has completely regressed. The definitive cortex, on the contrary, develops to adopt the three-zone structure of the adult gland. It is now believed that this structural change does not compromise the function of the neonate's adrenal. The adrenal appears to be competent to carry out its metabolic functions and electrolyte regulation, as well as to react to stress. This physiologic competence does not mean that the quantitative and qualitative patterns of steroids in blood and urine are identical to those of the adult.

Several factors require special caution in interpreting results in the first 48 hr of life. These factors were reviewed by Seely[100,101] and Ulstrom et al.[113] During the first 24 hr, concentrations of plasma and urine corticosteroids probably represent an unknown proportion of corticosteroids of maternal origin.[7]

During delivery, both maternal and fetal adrenals are responding to stress, resulting in elevated values. When the Porter–Silber reaction is used, bilirubin and ketone may interfere with the reaction. The large number of pregnane derivatives present in blood and urine during the first day may also contribute color in several steroid reactions used. The newborn has a circadian rhythm, and the time of day at which the sampling is done must be taken into consideration for the comparison of different sets of blood values.

17-Hydroxycorticosteroids in plasma decrease from the high values found in cord blood (19 μg/dl[7]) to somewhat subnormal values (9 μg/dl[7] and 5.4 μg/dl[98]) during the first 3 weeks of life, and return to normal adult levels in the 4th week and thereafter. During this period, the ratio of blood conjugated to free corticosteroids is 1 : 1.

This decrease of blood corticosteroids is probably not due to a decreased ability of the adrenal to respond to ACTH[7,70] or to a low cortisol production rate. The cortisol production rate in the neonatal period is not lower than that of the adult in terms of milligrams per unit of body surface,[82] but the urinary excretion is lower.[65] The half-life of cortisol has consistently been found to be considerably increased.[14,23,82] On the other hand, the half-life of injected tetrahydrocortisol, the main excretion product of cortisol, is not increased.[14,52] The deficiency is probably in reduction ring A in the liver to form the tetrahydro derivative from cortisol. There is ample evidence for a similar deficiency in glucuro conjugation. The proportion of free to conjugated corticosteroids in plasma shows a disproportionate amount of free corticosteroids when compared with adult blood. ACTH produces an increase of the free corticosteroids and of the conjugated fraction during the first 3 weeks of life.[38] There is some evidence for an alternate pathway of cortisol metabolism postnatally.[27]

Another peculiarity of the neonate consists in the failure of estrogen administration to produce an elevation of blood corticosteroids, probably because the corticosteroid-binding globulin fails to increase at this age. Seely[101] and Eberlein[40] found that corticosteroids in cord blood were mainly in the form of cortisone. This peculiarity of cortisol metabolism in cord blood has been attributed to the presence of an 11-dehydrogenase in the placenta. However, the effect persists for about 3 weeks *postpartum*. It is therefore probable that in the neonatal period, the liver has the capability of transforming most of the secreted cortisol to cortisone, a reaction that takes place normally but to a lesser extent in adult life, which is an important regulatory factor of the half-life of cortisol. In urine, there is a parallel excess of tetrahydro E over tetrahydro F. Thus, the THF/THE ratio is 0.003 : 1 in the infant, while it is 2.0 : 1 in older children.[7]

Another feature of adrenal cortical secretion in the neonatal period is the predominance of corticosterone over cortisol.[41] The physiologic significance of these differences of steroid metabolism in the neonate is poorly understood.

The levels of total blood 17-ketosteroids measured by the Zimmermann reaction rise during and immediately after delivery,[40] remain elevated during the first week of life, and decline thereafter. Using the Zimmermann reaction for total 17-ketosteroids and the Oertel–Eik-Nes[90] reaction for $\Delta 5,3\beta$-hydroxysteroids simultaneously, Eberlein[40] showed that during the first week of life, blood levels of $\Delta 5,3\beta$-hydroxysteroids are higher than those for total 17-ketosteroids, while the reverse is true after the first week.

Finally, 16α-hydroxylated C^{19} steroids were detected in the infant's urine during the neonatal period.[18] They probably represent the persistence during this time of the same mechanisms that are responsible for the production of estriol precursors in the fetus. Infants born to mothers whose estriol excretion during pregnancy was reduced have decreased rates of excretion of the latter compounds. High and rapidly declining levels of unconjugated estrogens are present in blood of the newborn in the first 3 days of life. Kenny *et al.*[64] discussed the implications of these levels being high even though the neonate shows scant clinical evidence of estrogen stimulation. They speculate that this lack of response could in fact be due to incomplete development of estrogen receptors in target tissues.

Aldosterone concentration in blood increases significantly after the 11th day of life, and remains elevated throughout the first year.[68] This increased concentration is due mainly to an increased secretion in relation to size.

9. Conclusion

Both the fetal adrenal and the placenta appear to be very active steroidogenic organs. The steroid spectrum secreted by the fetal adrenal is very different from that secreted by the adult gland. Some of the most important differences can be accounted for by postulating a deficiency of 3β-HSD, a contention that has considerable experimental support. Extensive 16-hydroxylation is also a distinctive capability of the fetal adrenal.

The placenta is a potent synthesizer of pregnenolone and progesterone from maternal and fetal blood circulating cholesterol. These two products are potential precursors for corticosteroid synthesis by the fetal adrenal, and can be catabolized by different reductive reactions in the fetal liver and maternal liver; the catabolic reactions are probably of greater quantitative importance than those of adrenal corticosteroid synthesis. A second placental function is that of steroid transformation. Only some of these transformations are known: 16α-OHDHAS from the fetal adrenal is converted to estriol sulfate, the most abundant estrogen of the fetal circulation. DHA is converted to estrone and estradiol, and possibly to testosterone and androstenedione. Cortisol is dehydrogenated to cortisone. A third important function of the placenta is the transfer of corticosteroids from mother to fetus, and of estrogens and possibly androgens from fetus to mother.

Finally, the fetus conjugates most steroids in its circulation as steroid sulfates. The placenta can split these sulfates and efficiently transfer the steroid to the maternal circulation. It is probable that the estrogens are then responsible for the increase of CBG in the maternal circulation. All these combined activities of the fetal adrenal and placenta result in large amounts of circulating steroids, in both circulations. Corticosteroids are elevated in the mother, but not in the fetus. It is tempting to infer that these unusually high levels are of physiologic consequence to fetal development, but evidence in this direction is conspicuous by its absence. The simplest explanation may be that the fetoplacental unit is functioning to inactivate biologically active steroids.

In the neonatal period, most of the qualitative and quantitative peculiarities of steroid composition of the infant's blood seem to be due to a continuing activity of the fetal pathways during the first few days of life, to the excretion of the large amounts of metabolites accumulated in fetal tissues, and to the stress of labor.

10. References

1. ASSALI, N. S., GARST, J. B., AND VOSIKAN, J., 1955, Blood level of 17 hydroxycorticosteroids in normal and toxemic pregnancy, *J. Lab. Clin. Med.* **46**:385–390.

2. ASSALI, N. S., 1968, *Biology of Gestation,* Vol. 1, p. 185, Academic Press, New York.

3. BALLARD, P. L., AND BALLARD, R. A., 1972, Glucocorticosteroid receptors and the role of glucocorticosteroids in fetal lung development, *Proc. Natl. Acad. Sci. U.S.A.* **69**:2668.

4. BALLARD, P. L., AND BALLARD, R. A., 1974, Cytoplasmic receptor for glucocosteroids in the lung of the human fetus, *J. Clin. Invest.* **53**:477.

5. BAYLISS, R. S., BROWNE, J. M., ROUND, B. P., AND STEINBECK, A. W., 1955, Plasma corticosteroids in pregnancy, *Lancet* **1**:62–64.

6. BENAGIANO, G., KINEL, F. A., ZIELSKE, F., WIQUIST, N., AND DICZFALUSY, E., 1967, Metabolism of C19 steroids in the fetoplacental unit. III. Metabolism of androstenedione and teststerone by previable fetuses at mid pregnancy, *Act. Endocrinol. (Copenhagen)* **56**:203–220.

7. BERTRAND, J., LORAS, B., SAEZ, J. M., AND CANTENET, B., 1965, Hydroxycorticosteroid secretion and metabolism in neonates and infants up to the age of three months, in: *Hormonology of Human Pregnancy* (M. F. Jayle, ed.), pp. 165–187, Pergamon Press, Oxford.

8. BIRKE, G., GEMZELL, C. A., PLAUTIN, L. O., AND ROBBE, H., 1958, Plasma levels of 17 hydroxycorticosteroids and urinary excretion pattern of ketosteroids in normal pregnancy, *Acta Endocrinol. (Copenhagen)* **27**:389–402.

9. BLOCH, E., AND BENIRSCHKE, K., 1959, Synthesis *in vitro* of steroids by human fetal adrenal gland slices, *J. Biol. Chem.* **234**:1085–1089.

10. BLOCH, E., AND BENIRSCHKE, K., 1962, Steroidogenic capacity of fetal adrenal *in vitro,* in: *The Human Adrenal Cortex* (A. R. Currie, T. Symington, and J. K. Grant, eds.), pp. 580–589, The Williams & Wilkins Co., Baltimore.

11. BOLTE, E., MANCUSO, S., ERIKSSON, G., WIQUIST, N., AND DICZFALUSY, E., 1964, Studies on the aromatization of neutral steroids in pregnant women. I. Aromatization of C19 steroid by placentas perfused *in situ,* *Acta Endocrinol. (Copenhagen)* **45**:535–559.

12. BOLTE, E., MANCUSO, S., ERIKSSON, G., WIQUIST, N., AND DICZFALUSY, E., 1964, Studies on the aromatization of neutral steroids in pregnant women. II. Aromatization of dehydroepiandrosterone and of its sulfate administered simultaneously into a uterine artery, *Acta Endocrinol. (Copenhagen)* **45**:560–575.

13. BOLTE, E., MANCUSO, S., ERIKSSON, G., WIQUIST, N., AND DICZFALUSY, E., 1964, Studies on the aromatization of neutral steroids in pregnant women. III. Overall aromatization of dehydroepiandrosterone sulfate circulating in the fetal and maternal compartments, *Acta Endocrinol. (Copenhagen)* **45**:575–599.

14. BONGIOVANNI, A. M., EBERLEIN, W. R., WETPHAL, M., AND BOGS, T., 1958, Prolonged turnover rate of hydrocortisone in the newborn infant, *J. Clin. Endocrinol.* **18**:1127–1130.

15. BOYD, E. M., AND WILSON, K. M., 1935, Exchange of lipids in umbilical circulation at birth, *J. Clin. Invest.* **14**:7–15.

16. BUSH, I. E., 1962, Chemical and biological factors in the action of steroid hormones, in: *The Human Adrenal Cortex* (A. R. Currie, T. Symington, and J. K. Grant, eds.), pp. 138–171, The Williams & Wilkins Co., Baltimore.

17. CAVALLERO, A., AND MAGRINI, U., 1966, Histochemical studies on 3 hydroxysteroid dehydrogenase and other enzymes in the steroid secreting structures of human fetus, in: *Proceedings of the Second International Congress on Hormonal Steroids, Excerpta Med. Int. Congr. Ser.* **132**:667–674.

18. CLEARY, R. E., AND PION, J., 1968, Urinary excretion of 16-hydroxy dehydroepiandrostenedione and 16-keto androstenediol during early neonatal period, *J. Clin. Endocrinol.* **28**:372–378.

19. COHEN, M., STEIFEL, M., REDDY, W. J., AND LAIDLAW, J. C., 1958, The secretion and disposition of cortisol during pregnancy, *J. Clin. Endocrinol.* **18**:1076–1192.

20. COLAS, A. L., HEINRICHS, W., AND TALUM, H., 1964, Pettenkoffer chromogen in the maternal and fetal circulations, *Steroids* **3**:417–434.

21. COPE, C. L., AND BLACK, E., 1959, The hydrocorti-

sone production in late pregnancy, *J. Obstet. Gynaecol. Br. Emp.* **66**:404–408.

22. COPE, O., AND RAKER, J. W., 1955, Cushing's disease: The surgical experience of 46 cases, *N. Engl. J. Med.* **253**:119–127.

23. CRANNY, R. L., VINK, J. F. K., AND KELLEY, V. C., 1960, The half life of hydrocortisone in normal newborn infants, *Amer. J. Dis. Child.* **99**:437–443.

24. CROWDER, R. E., 1957, The development of the adrenal gland in man with special reference to origin and ultimate location of cell types and evidence in favor of the cell migration theory, *Carnegie Inst. Contrib. Embryol.* **36**:195–210.

25. CUATRECASAS, P., HOLLENBERG, M. D., CHANG, K. J., AND BENNETT, V., 1975, Hormone receptor complexes and their modulation of membrane function, in: *Recent Progress in Hormone Research,* p. 37, Academic Press, New York.

26. DANCIS, J., MONEY, W. L., CONDON, G. P., ABD LEVITZ, M., 1958, The relative transfer of estrogens and their glucuronides across the placenta in the guinea pig, *J. Clin. Invest.* **37**:1373–1378.

27. DANIILESEU-GOLDINBERG, D., AND GIROUD, C. J. P., 1974, Metabolism of cortisol by the newborn infant, *J. Clin. Endocrinol. Metab.* **38**:64–70.

28. DAUGHADAY, W. H., 1958, Binding of corticosteroids by plasma proteins. V. Corticosteroid-binding globulin activity in normal human beings and in certain disease states, *Arch. Intern. Med.* **101**:286–290.

29. DAUGHADAY, W. H., 1967, The binding of corticosteroids by plasma protein, in: *The Adrenal Cortex* (A. N. Eisenstein, ed.), pp. 385–403, Little, Brown and Co., Boston.

30. DAVIS, M. E., AND PLOTZ, E. J., 1956, Hormonal interrelationships between maternal adrenal, placenta and fetal adrenal function, *Obstet. Gynecol. Surv.* **11**:1–43.

31. DAVIS, M. E., AND PLOTZ, E. J., 1957, The metabolism of progesterone and its clinical use in pregnancy, *Recent Prog. Horm. Res.* **13**:347–388.

32. DEHERTOGH, R., THOMAS, K., BIETLOT, Y., VANDERHAYDEN, I., AND FERIN, J., 1975, Plasma levels of unconjugated estrone, estradiol and estriol and of HCS throughout pregnancy in normal women, *J. Clin. Endocrinol. Metab.* **40**:93–101.

33. DELEMOS, R. A., 1970, Acceleration of appearance of pulmonary surfactant in the fetal lamb by administration of corticosteroids, *Amer. Rev. Respir. Dis.* **102**:459.

34. DELL'ACQUA, S., MANCUSO, S., BENAGIANO, G., WIQUIST, N., AND DICZFALUSY, E., 1966, Androgen metabolism in the fetoplacental unit at midterm, in: *Proceedings of the Second International Congress on Hormonal Steroids, Excerpta Med. Int. Congr. Ser.* **132**:639–645.

35. DICZFALUSY, E., 1965, *In vivo* biogenesis and metabolism of oestrogens in the fetoplacental unit,

in: *Proceedings of the Second International Congress of Endocrinology, Excerpta Med. Int. Congr. Ser.* **83**:732–736.

36. DICZFALUSY, E., 1967, Endocrinology of the feto-placental unit, in: *Fetal Homeostasis* (R. M. Wynn, ed.), pp. 268–361, New York Academy of Sciences, New York.

37. DICZFALUSY, E., TELLINGER, G., AND WESTMAN, A., 1957, Studies on estrogen metabolism in newborn boys. I. Excretion of oestrone, oestradiol-17 and estriol during the first few days of life, *Acta Endocrinol.* **26**:303–312.

38. DUCHARME, J. R., LEBOEUF, G., AND SANDOR, T., 1970, C21 steroid metabolism and conjugation in the human premature neonate. I. Urinary excretion and the response to ACTH, *J. Clin. Endocrinol. Metab.* **30**:96–101.

39. EBERLEIN, W. R., 1963, Transesterification method for the measurement of plasma 17 ketosteroid sulfates, *J. Clin. Endocrinol.* **23**:990–995.

40. EBERLEIN, W. R., 1965, Steroids and sterols in umbilical cord blood, *J. Clin. Endocrinol.* **25**:1101–1118.

41. EXLEY, D., AND NORYMBERSKI, J. K., 1964, Urinary excretion of 17-deoxy-corticosteroids by man, *J. Endocrinol.* **29**:293–302.

42. FISHMAN, W. H., AND ANLYAN, A. J., 1947, β-Glucuronidase activity in human tissues: Some correlations with the process of malignant growth and with the physiology of reproduction, *Cancer Res.* **7**:808–817.

43. FORSHAM, P. H., 1967, The adrenal cortex in pregnancy, in: *The Human Adrenal Cortex: Its Function Throughout Life, Ciba Found. Study Group No. 27,* pp. 48–59, Little, Brown and Company Boston.

44. GARDNER, L. I., 1956, Adrenocortical metabolism of the fetus, infant and child, *Pediatrics* **17**:897–924.

45. GARDNER, L. I., 1975, Development of the normal fetal and neonatal adrenal, in: *Endocrine and Genetic Diseases of Childhood and Adolescence,* p. 460, W. B. Saunders Co., Philadelphia.

46. GARDNER, L. I., AND WALTON, R. L., 1954, Plasma 17 ketosteroids of the human fetus: Demonstration of concentration gradient between cord and maternal circulation, *Helv. Paediatr. Acta* **4**:311–316.

47. GOEBELSMANN, U., ERIKSSON, G., WIQUIST, N., AND DICZFALUSY, E., 1965, Metabolism of oestriol-3-sulfate and oestriol-16(17)-glucosiduronate in pregnant women, *Acta Endocrinol. (Copenhagen)* **50**:273–288.

48. GOEBELSMANN, U., WIQUIST, N., DICZFALUSY, E., LEVITZ, M., CONDON, G. P., AND DANCIS, J., 1966, Fate of intra-amniotically administered oestriol-15³H-3 sulfate and oestriol-16-¹⁴C-16-glucosiduronate in pregnant women at midterm, *Acta Endocrinol. (Copenhagen)* **52**:550–564.

49. GOLDMAN, A. S., BONGIOVANNI, A. M., TAKOVAC, W. C., AND PRADER, A., 1964, Study on 5 3B hydroxysteroid dehydrogenase in normal, hyperplastic and neoplastic adrenal tissue, *J. Clin. Endocrinol.* **24**:894–909.

50. GOLDMAN, A. S., TAKOVAC, W. C., AND BONGIOVANNI, A. M., 1966, Development of activity of 3B hydroxysteroid dehydrogenase in human fetal tissue and in two anencephalic newborns, *J. Clin. Endocrinol.* **26**:14.

51. GRUENWALD, P., 1946, Embryonic and postnatal development of the adrenal cortex: Particularly the zona glomerulosa and accessory nodules, *Anat. Rec.* **95**:391–422.

52. GRUMBACH, M. M., DUCHARME, J. R., AND NORISHIMA, A., 1959, The metabolism of hydrocortisone and its metabolite in premature and newborn infants: Evidence for defective degradation and impaired laydrolysis of steroidesters, *Amer. J. Dis. Child.* **98**:672, 673.

53. GURPIDE, E., 1973, Stimulation of 16α-hydroxylation of dehydroisoandrosterone sulfate by diethylstilbestrol, *J. Clin. Endocrinol. Metab.* **37**:867.

54. GURPIDE, E., SCHWERS, J., WELCH, M. T., VANDE WIELLE, L. R., AND LIEBERMAN, S., 1966, Fetal and maternal metabolism of estradiol in pregnancy, *J. Clin. Endocrinol.* **26**:1355–1365.

55. VON HOTTINGER, A., 1959, Vorübergehende, passive Nebenniereninsuffizienz beim Neugeborenen, *Schweiz. Med. Wochenschr.* **11**:419–472.

56. JACQUOT, R., 1959, Recherches sur le controle endocrinien de l'accumulation de glycogene dans le foie chez le fetus de rat, *J. Physiol. (Paris)* **51**:655–721.

57. JAFFE, R. B., ERIKSON, G., AND DICZFALUSY, E., 1966, *In situ* perfusion of the midterm human placenta with cholesterol, Proceedings of the International Congress on Hormonal Steroids, *Excerpta Med. Int. Congr. Ser.* **99**:182.

58. JAYLE, M. F., AND PASQUALINI, J. R., 1965, Metabolism of adrenocortical hormones in the course of human pregnancy, in: *Hormonology of Human Pregnancy* (M. F. Jayle, ed.), pp. 127–154, Pergamon Press, Oxford.

59. JOST, A., 1966, Problems of fetal endocrinology: The adrenal glands, *Recent Prog. Horm. Res.* **22**:541–574.

60. JOST, A., 1967, The function of the fetal adrenal cortex, in: *The Human Adrenal Cortex: Its Function Throughout Life*, Ciba Found. Study Group No. 27, pp. 11–28, Little, Brown and Co., Boston.

61. JOST, A., JACQUOT, R., AND COHEN, A., 1962, The pituitary control of the fetal adrenal cortex, in: *The Human Adrenal Cortex* (A. R. Currie, T. Symington, and J. K. Grant, eds.), pp. 569–579, The Williams & Wilkins Co., Baltimore.

62. JUNGMANN, R. A., AND SCHWEPPE, J. S., 1967, Biosynthesis and metabolism of neutral steroids by human midterm placenta and fetal liver, *J. Clin. Endocrinol.* **27**:1151–1160.

63. KEENE, M. F. L., AND HEWER, E. E., 1927, Observations on the development of the human suprarenal gland, *J. Anat.* **61**:302–324.

64. KENNY, F. M., ANGSUSINGHA, K., STINSON, D., AND HOTCHKISS, J., 1973, Unconjugated estrogens in the perinatal period, *Pediatr. Res.* **7**:826–831.

65. KENNY, F. M., PREEYASOMBAT, C., AND MIGEON, C. J., 1966, Cortisol production rate. II. Normal infants, children and adults, *Pediatrics* **37**:34–42.

66. KING, R. J. B., AND MAINWARING, W. I. P., 1974, *Steroid–Cell Interactions*, University Park Press, Baltimore.

67. KITCHELL, R. L., 1950, Compensatory hypertrophy of the intact adrenal of fetal rats subjected to unilateral adrenalectomy, *Proc. Soc. Exp. Biol. Med.* **75**:824–827.

68. KOWARSKI, A., KATZ, H., AND MIGEON, C., 1974, Plasma aldosterone concentration in normal subjects from infancy to adulthood, *J. Clin. Endocrinol. Metab.* **38**:489–491.

69. LAMB, E., MANCUSO, S., DELL'ACQUA, S., WIQUIST, N., AND DICZFALUSY, E., 1967, Studies on the metabolism of C19 steroids in the human faetoplacental unit, *Acta Endocrinol. (Copenhagen)* **55**:263–277.

70. LANMAN, J. T., 1953, Adrenal function in premature infants. II. ACTH treated infants and infants born of toxemic mothers, *Pediatrics* **12**:62–71.

71. LANMAN, J. T., 1960, An interpretation of human foetal adrenal structure and function, in: *The Human Adrenal Cortex* (A. R. Currie, T. Symington, and J. H. Grant, eds.), pp. 547–558, The Williams & Wilkins Co, Baltimore.

72. LANMAN, J. T., 1961, The adrenal gland in the human fetus: An interpretation of its physiology and unusual developmental patterns, *Pediatrics* **27**:140–158.

73. LANMAN, J. T., AND SILVERMAN, L. M., 1957, *In vitro* steroidogenesis in the human neonatal adrenal gland, including observations on the human adult and monkey adrenal glands, *Endocrinology* **60**:433–445.

74. LANMAN, J. T., SOLOMON, S., LIND, J., AND LIEBERMAN, S., 1957, *In vitro* biogenesis of steroids by the human fetal adrenal, *Amer. J. Dis. Child.* **94**:504, 505.

75. LAURITZEN, C., SHACKLETON, C. H. L., AND MITCHELL, F. L., 1969, The effect of exogenous human chorionic gonadotrophin on steroid excretion in the newborn, *Acta Endocrinol.* **61**:83.

76. LEVITZ, M., 1966, Conjugation and transfer of fetal–placental steroid hormones, *J. Clin. Endocrinol.* **26**:773–777.

77. LEVITZ, M., CONDON, G. P., MONEY, W. L., AND DANCIS, J., 1960, The relative transfer of estrogens

and their sulfates across the guinea pig placenta: Sulfurylation of estrogens in the placenta, *J. Biol. Chem.* **235**:973–977.

78. LIGGINS, G. C., AND HOWIE, R. N., 1971, A controlled trial of antepartum glucocorticord treatment for the prevention of the respiratory distress syndrome, *Pediatrics* **50**:515.

79. LIGGINS, G. C., AND HOWIE, R. N., 1974, Prevention of RDS by maternal steroid therapy, in: *Modern Perinatal Medicine* (L. Gluck, ed.), Year Book Publishers, Chicago.

80. LONGCHAMP, J., 1965, Biogenese des steroids par les corticosurrenales foetales, in: *Hormonologie de la Grossesse Humaine* (M. F. Jayle, ed.), pp. 205–218, Gauthiers-Villars, Paris.

81. MAGENDANTZ, H. G., AND RYAN, K. G., 1964, Isolation of an estriol precursor, 16α-hydroxyepiandrosterone, from human umbilical sera, *J. Clin. Endocrinol.* **24**:1155–1162.

82. MIGEON, C. J., 1959, Cortisol production and metabolism in the neonate, *J. Pediatr.* **55**:280–295.

83. MIGEON, C. J., BERTRAND, J., AND GEMZELL, C. A., 1961, The transplacental passage of various steroid hormones in midpregnancy, *Recent Prog. Horm. Res.* **17**:207–248.

84. MIGEON, C. J., BERTRAND, J., AND GEMZELL, C. A., 1962, The transplacental passage of 4C¹⁴ cortisol in midpregnancy, in: *The Human Adrenal Cortex* (A. R. Currie, T. Symington, and J. K. Grant, eds.), pp. 580–588, The Williams & Wilkins Co., Baltimore.

85. MIGEON, C. J., BERTRAND, J., AND WALL, P. E., 1957, Physiological disposition of 4-C¹⁴ cortisol during late pregnancy, *J. Clin. Invest.* **36**:1350–1362.

86. MIGEON, C. J., KENNY, F. M., AND TAYLOR, F. H., 1968, Cortisol production rate. BIII. Pregnancy, *J. Clin. Endocrinol.* **28**:961–968.

87. MIGEON, C. J., PRYSTOWSKY, H., GRUMBACH, M., AND BYRON, M. C., 1956, Placental passage of 17 hydroxycorticosteroids: Comparison of the levels in maternal and fetal plasma and effect of ACTH and hydrocortisone administration, *J. Clin. Invest.* **35**:488–493.

88. NACHTIGALL, L., BASSETT, M., HOGSANDER, U., SLAGLE, S., AND LEVITZ, M., 1966, A rapid method for the assay of plasma estriol in pregnancy, *J. Clin. Endocrinol.* **26**:941–948.

89. NELSON, D. H., AND SAMUELS, L. T., 1952, A method for the determination of 17-hydroxycorticosteroids in blood: 17-Hydroxycortisone in the peripheral circulation, *J. Clin. Endocrinol.* **12**:519–526.

90. OERTEL, G. W., AND EIK-NES, K. B., 1959, Determination of 5-3-beta-hydroxysteroids, *Anal. Chem.* **31**:98–100.

91. PASQUALINI, J. R., WIQUIST, N., AND DICZFALUSY, E.,

1966, Biosynthesis of aldosterone by human fetuses perfused with corticosterone at midterm, *Biochim. Biophys. Acta* **121**:433–460.

92. PION, R., JAFFE, R., ERIKSON, G., WIQUIST, N., AND DICZFALUSY, E., 1965, Studies on the metabolism of C21 steroids in the human placental unit. I. Formation of β unsaturated 3 ketones in midterm placentas perfused *in situ* with pregnenolone and 17 hydroxypregnenolone, *Acta Endocrinol. (Copenhagen)* **48**:234–248.

93. RIVAROLA, M. A., FOREST, M. G., AND MIGEON, C. J., 1968, Testosterone, androstenedione and dehydroepiandrosterone in plasma during pregnancy and at delivery: Concentration and protein binding, *J. Clin. Endocrinol.* **28**:34–40.

94. ROSS, N. H., 1960, Electron microscopy of human foetal adrenal cortex, in: *The Human Adrenal Cortex* (A. R. Currie, T. Symington, and J. K. Grant, eds.), pp. 558–569, The Williams & Wilkins Co., Baltimore.

95. RYAN, K. J., 1965, Estrogens: Blood and placental levels and the factors which control them, in: *Proceedings of the Second International Congress of Endocrinology, Excerpta Med. Int. Congr. Ser.* **83**:727–731.

96. RYAN, K. J., MERGS, R. A., AND PETRO, Z., 1966, Biosynthesis of progesterone in the human placenta, in: *International Congress on Hormonal Steroids, Excerpta Med. Int. Congr. Ser.* **132**:663–666.

97. SCHREIER, K., Studien zur Entwicklungsphysiologie des Fettstoffwechsels. I. Mitteilung über die Serumlipide der Säuglinge, *Z. Kinderheilkd.* **91**:157–162.

98. SCHWEITZER, M., AND GIROUD, C. J. P., 1971, A comparison of the pattern of steroid glucoronide and sulfate in maternal plasma, umbilical cord plasma and amniotic fluid, *J. Clin. Endocrinol. Metab.* **33**:793–798.

99. SCHWEITZER, M., KLEIN, G. P., AND GIROUD, C. J. P., 1971, Characterization of 17 deoxy and 17 hydroxycorticosteroid in human lignor amnii, *J. Clin. Endocrinol. Metab.* **33**:605–611.

100. SEELY, J. R., 1961, Adrenal function in newborns: Methodology and perinatal circulating steroid patterns, *Amer. J. Dis. Child.* **102**:530–533.

101. SEELY, J. R., 1964, Adrenocortical function in newborn humans: Methodology and perinatal circulating patterns, Ph.D. thesis, University of Utah, Salt Lake City.

102. SEELY, J. R., 1974, The fetal and neonatal adrenal cortex, in: *Metabolic, Endocrine and Genetic Disorders of Children* (V. C. Kelley, ed.), p. 225, Harper and Row, New York.

103. SITTERI, P. K., 1974, Steroid hormones in pregnancy, in: *Modern Perinatal Medicine* (L. Gluck, ed.), p. 231, Year Book Medical Publishers, Chicago.

104. SIITERI, P. K., AND MACDONALD, P. C., 1966,

Placental estrogen biosynthesis during human pregnancy, *J. Clin. Endocrinol.* **26**:751–761.

105. SLAUNWHITE, W. R., AND SANDBERG, A. A., 1959, Transcortin, a corticosteroid binding protein of plasma, *J. Clin. Invest.* **38**:384–391.

106. SOLOMON, S., 1966, The formation and metabolism of neutral steroids in the human fetus and placenta, in: *International Congress on Hormonal Steroids, Excerpta Med. Int. Congr. Ser.* **132**:653–662.

107. SOLOMON, S., AND FRIESEN, H. G., 1968, Endocrine relations between mother and fetus, *Annu. Rev. Med.* **19**:399–430.

108. SOLOMON, S., BIRD, C. E., LING, W., IWAMIYA, M., AND YOUNG, P. C. M., 1967, The formation and metabolism of steroids in the fetus and the placenta, *Recent Prog. Horm. Res.* **23**:297–349.

109. SOLOMON, S., LANMAN, J. T., LIND, J., AND LIEBERMAN, S., 1958, The biogenesis of 4 androstenedione and 17 hydroxyprogesterone from progesterone by surviving human fetal adrenals, *J. Biol. Chem.* **233**:1084–1088.

110. SWINEYARD, C. A., 1943, Growth of the human suprarenal glands, *Anat. Rec.* **87**:141–150.

111. SYBULSKI, S., AND VENNING, E., 1961, The possibility of corticosteroid production by human and rat placental tissue under *in vitro* conditions, *Can. J. Biochem.* **39**:203–214.

112. TOUCHSTONE, J. C., GREENE, J. W., McELROY, R. C., AND MURAWEC, T., 1963, Blood estriol conjugation during human pregnancy, *Biochemistry* **2**:653–657.

113. ULSTROM, R. A., COLLE, E., REYNOLDS, J. W., AND BURLEY, J., 1961, Adrenocortical function in newborn infants. IV. Plasma concentrations of cortisol in the early neonatal period, *J. Clin. Endocrinol.* **21**:414–425.

114. UOTILA, U. V., 1940, The early embryological development of the fetal and permanent adrenal cortex in man, *Anat. Rec.* **76**:183–203.

115. VAN LUESDEN, H., AND VILLEE, C. H., 1965, The *de novo* synthesis of steroid and steroids from acetate by preparations of human term placenta, *Steroids* **6**:31–45.

116. VELICAN, C., 1946–1947, Embiogenese de la surrenale humaine, *Arch. Anat. Microsc. Morphol. Exp.* **36**:316–333.

117. VILLEE, D. B., 1966, The role of progesterone in the development of adrenal enzymes, in: *Proceedings of the Second International Congress on Hormonal Steroids, Excerpta Med. Int. Congr. Ser.* **132**:680–686.

118. VILLEE, D. B., 1971, Development of endocrine function in the human placenta and fetus, *N. Engl. J. Med.* **281**:473–484.

119. VILLEE, D. B., 1975, *Human Endocrinology, A Developmental Approach,* W. B. Saunders Co., Philadelphia.

120. VILLEE, D. B., AND VILLEE, C. A., 1964, Synthesis of corticosteroids in the fetoplacental unit, in: *Proceedings of the Second International Congress of Endocrinology, Excerpta Med. Int. Congr. Ser.* **83**:709–714.

121. VILLEE, D. B., ENGEL, L. I., AND VILLEE, C. A., 1959, Steroid hydroxylation in human fetal adrenals, *Endocrinology* **65**:465–474.

122. WARRELL, D. W., AND TAYLOR, R., 1968, Outcome for the fetus of mothers receiving prednisolone during pregnancy, *Lancet* **1**:117, 118.

123. WEIR, R. J., BROWN, J. J., FRASER, R., LEVER, A. F., LOGAN, R. W., McILWAINE, G. M., MORTON, J. J., ROBERTSON, J. I. S., AND TREE, M., 1975, Relationship between plasma renin, renin-substrate, angiotensin II, aldosterone and electrolytes in normal pregnancy, *J. Clin. Endocrinol. Metab.* **40**:108–115.

124. ZANDER, J., 1962, Die Hormonbildung der Placenta und ihre Bedeutung für die Frucht, *Arch. Gynaekol.* **198**:113–127.

CHAPTER 38

The Anterior Lobe of the Hypophysis

José Cara

1. Introduction

Cells in the anlage of the anterior lobe of the pituitary differentiate very early in the human fetus. Basophilic cells can be identified by about the 8th week of gestation, and the acidophils are found 1–2 weeks later.[45] The fine structure of the fetal pituitary at about the 12th week is consistent with a gland that is producing and secreting hormone, and by the 18th week, the anterior lobe of the pituitary resembles the adult organ.[45] The human pituitary gland increases its weight 4-fold between the 10th and 24th weeks of gestation.[97] The anterior lobe of the pituitary in perinatal life contains five or more distinct cells,[142] which secrete at least six independent hormones. The development of more elaborate techniques of histochemistry, immunofluorescence, and electron microscopy has permitted further validation of the concept that each major hormone of the pituitary is produced by a distinct cell type, the "one cell, one hormone theory."[133] The application of radioimmunoassay techniques in recent years has confirmed and expanded the results of bioassay procedures, and has provided important

new information concerning the pituitary content and the circulating levels of pituitary hormones in the fetus and in the newborn.

Much research remains to be done to clarify the time of initiation and the mechanisms that maintain the hypothalamus–pituitary–target gland homeostasis in the fetal life. We will discuss here the physiologic significance of the anterior lobe of the pituitary in perinatal life, with particular attention to the production and secretion of human growth hormone (HGH), adrenocorticotropin (ACTH), thyrotropin (TSH), follicle-stimulating hormone (FSH), luteinizing hormone (LH) or interstitial-cell-stimulating hormone (ICSH), and prolactin (PRL).

2. Human Growth Hormone (HGH)

Human fetal pituitary cells first show signs of staining with anti-HGH antiserum between the 10th and 14th weeks of life, and staining is consistent after the 17th week.[43,131] Kaplan et al.[97] detected immunoreactive HGH in fetal pituitary as early as 68 days of gestation. Release of HGH by fetal pituitaries in vitro was detected as early as in 5-week-old fetuses.[149] Acidophils were reported as early as

José Cara · Department of Pediatrics, Coney Island Hospital, State University of New York Downstate Medical Center, Brooklyn, New York 11235

9–10 weeks of fetal life.[45] Porteous and Beck[131] consider that the probable sequence of differentiation of the acidophils of the fetal pituitary is first the appearance of the HGH antigen and later the development of acidophilic cytoplasmic granules. More than 97% of the HGH-positive cells are acidophils, the remainder being chromophobes and basophils.[43] Presumably, the acidophil granules represent compacted deposits of HGH. Fetal HGH is immunologically indistinguishable from adult HGH in fluorescence tests.[43] At birth, the staining reactions of the acidophils are similar to those of corresponding cells in the adult hypophysis.[131]

2.1. Pituitary Content of Growth Hormone

Growth hormone is the most abundant hormone in the adenohypophysis. Parlow,[127] using a radio-immunoassay method, studied the HGH content of human pituitaries pooled according to age. He found that HGH was detectable in fetal pituitaries of less than 5 months of fetal age and progressively increased with age to a maximum at about 12–18 years. There was, however, no significant difference in HGH content in pituitaries from birth to 6 months of age. Kaplan and Grumback[95] and Kaplan et al.[97] found that the radioimmunoassay-able HGH content of pituitaries obtained from human fetuses between the estimated gestational ages of 68 days and 40 weeks varied from 0.15 to 9.3 μg/mg of gland and correlated well with fetal age and pituitary weight. Significant differences were observed in both the content and the concentration of HGH in human fetal pituitary glands with increasing gestational ages except during the last 2 months of fetal life.[97] The pituitary content of HGH increases 15-fold between the 10th and 24th weeks of gestation.[97] In infants less than 1 year of age, the content and the concentration of HGH were comparable to the levels measured in fetal pituitaries at 32–40 weeks of gestation.[97]

The growth hormone content of pituitaries from various animal species continues to increase through-out intrauterine life, reaching a maximum just before birth.[23] Gershberg[62] and Rice and Ponthier,[138] using a bioassay technique, presented data suggesting the presence of biologically active HGH in human fetal pituitaries obtained during the last trimester. Physicochemical and immunochemical properties of HGH from human fetal pituitary glands and HGH from children and adult pituitary glands were also indistinguishable by disk gel electrophoresis, immunoelectrophoresis, starch gel electrophoresis, and radioimmunoassay techniques.[97]

2.2. Plasma Level of HGH

The plasma concentration of HGH in fetuses and in the newborn is high and shows considerable individual variation.[24,67,79,94,106,164] Kaplan and Grumbach,[95] and later Kaplan et al.,[97] found that HGH in cord blood from aborted fetuses of estimated gestational age of 70–245 days was in the adult acromegalic range, greatly in excess of the plasma HGH of pregnant women at comparable stages of gestation.

At 70 days of gestation, the serum HGH concentration was 14.5 ng/ml; at 10–14 weeks, 65.2 ± 7.6 ng/ml; at 15–19 weeks, 114.9 ± 12.5 ng/ml; at 20–24 weeks, 119.3 ± 19.8 ng/ml; at 25–29 weeks, 72.0 ± 11.5 ng/ml; and at term, 33.5 ± 4.2 ng/ml. Therefore, after a steady rise that peaked at 20–24 weeks of gestation, there was a gradual decrease in the concentration of HGH until birth.[97] At birth, the concentration of HGH is higher in the umbilical artery than in the umbilical vein.[168] No differences were found between the serum levels of HGH in infants born by normal vertex presentation and the levels in infants delivered by cesarean section with or without a trial of labor. The concentration of HGH in the serum or pituitary from fetuses removed by hysterectomy was similar to that of spontaneously aborted fetuses.[97] Furthermore, no correlation was found between the amount of HGH in cord blood and the blood glucose, birth weight, or race.[24] HGH remained high in peripheral venous blood during the first 48 hr of life, after which it decreased rather sharply during the first week.[24,146] In the full-term baby, the decline continued more slowly during the 2nd and 3rd weeks. In the low-birth-weight infant, the decrease during the first week was less marked, and a secondary rise occurred between the 3rd and 4th weeks of life, declining thereafter. Thus, the serum HGH was higher in low-birth-weight infants than in full-term infants in the period between the 2nd and 6th days and again between the 2nd and 8th weeks of life.[24] Male full-term infants and female low-birth-weight infants had significantly higher serum HGH than corresponding babies of the opposite sex. Twins sampled at the same age during the neonatal period showed a wide discrepancy in the plasma levels of HGH.[24] Infants of diabetic mothers were reported to have values of HGH in cord blood in the same range as normal newborns.[67] More recently, however, Westphal[164] found much lower levels of HGH in cord blood in infants of diabetic mothers than in normal newborns.

2.3. Growth Hormone Response to Hypoglycemia

In the simian fetus, hypoglycemia or arginine failed to increase the level of growth hormone.[119] Insulin-induced hypoglycemia greatly increases the serum HGH in the full-term and in the low-birth-weight infant.[24,164] The response is greater than in older children and adults. The absolute increment is considerably greater on the first day than at the end of the first week of life for full-term infants. In the low-birth-weight infant, on the other hand, the increment at the end of the first week of life is even greater than during the first 24 hr. In infants of diabetic mothers, the HGH response to insulin-induced hypoglycemia is less pronounced than in normal newborns.[164]

2.4. Growth Hormone Response to Hyperglycemia

Administration of glucose in the simian fetus did not suppress the high levels of growth hormone.[119] In the human neonate, in contrast to the response in adults, hyperglycemia induced by the injection of glucose produces an increase in levels of HGH during the first 2 weeks of life.[24,164] The increase is greater on the first day of life than at the end of the first week. Like the response to hypoglycemia, the increase is more pronounced in the low-birth-weight than in the full-term infant at the end of the first week of life. After the 2nd week, the induced hyperglycemia results in inhibition of HGH secretion, as it does in older children and adults.[24,164]

2.5. Physiologic Role of Growth Hormone

The role of HGH in fetal and early postnatal life is not yet clear. Although the human pituitary is capable of producing, storing, and secreting HGH as early as 70 days of gestational age, the precise time of the initiation of hypothalamic–pituitary

feedback control is not known. Antigenically, fetal HGH is similar to adult HGH, and it is biologically active, although we do not know the exact relationship between levels of immunoreactive HGH and biologically active HGH in blood. However, newborns with the rare syndrome of absence of the pituitary gland and normal skull are born with normal weight and length.[12,34,135,154] Likewise, human cyclopic fetuses, in whom the pituitary is usually absent, are born with normal body size despite the abnormal hypothalamic–pituitary connections.[37,44,123,158] The somatotrophs in these abnormal pituitaries are not so numerous and heavily granulated as in normal human fetuses,[142] and the level of HGH in cord blood from anencephalics is in the low normal range but higher than in maternal blood.[5,6,70,95] In cases of isolated deficiency of HGH, either sporadic or familial, affected children are born normal in size even when the mother is HGH-deficient.[139] Similarly, other abnormalities in the level of HGH in maternal blood do not appear to affect fetal growth. In one rare case of maternal hypophysectomy during the 26th week of gestation, the body size of the newborn infant was normal for gestational age on delivery at the 35th week.[112] Gemzell[61] reported a hypophysectomized woman treated with human gonadotrophins who conceived and delivered a normal full-term baby despite presumably very low levels of or no HGH in the maternal circulation.

Deprivation of the pituitary in rat fetuses by decapitation *in utero* resulted in some growth retardation that could be prevented by the injection of growth hormone into the headless fetuses.[75] Electrocoagulation of the pituitary in fetal lambs produced some retardation in somatic development.[111] In rabbits, however, decapitated fetuses continued to grow and were born with normal body size and weight.[89] Similarly, hypophysectomy of monkey fetuses did not alter their rate of growth, even when the mothers were hypophysectomized at the same time.[80]

Conversely, infants born of acromegalic mothers are of normal size,[2] and pharmacological doses of growth hormone given to pregnant animals resulted in normal-size offsprings.[169] That levels of circulating maternal HGH are not significant for fetal growth may be partially explained by lack of placental transfer of HGH, as demonstrated by the injection of radioiodinated HGH into women in labor.[66] Even pharmacological doses of HGH injected into the mother between 270 and 10 min before delivery failed to show placental transfer of HGH into the fetus.[108] Children who present the picture of hypopituitarism later in life are usually born with normal weight and length, and no growth retardation is detected during the first few months of life, suggesting that the deficiency of HGH is not important for growth during early postnatal life.[11] Rimoin et al.,[140] however, reported that growth retardation begins shortly after birth in the genetic types of HGH deficiency, even though the infant is born with normal weight and length; impaired growth may not become grossly apparent until late infancy or early childhood. Treatment of premature and full-term infants with HGH failed to elicit changes indicating a physiologic effect, suggesting that they were relatively refractory to the metabolic and growth-promoting effects of HGH early in life.[19,33,161] These observations all support the prevailing concept that HGH from either fetal or maternal pituitary is not a major determinant of growth during fetal and early postnatal life.[140] The high level of HGH found at these times seems paradoxical. The stress of labor is not responsible for the high values immediately after birth, since newborns delivered by cesarean section have comparable values.[24] Furthermore, the clearance rate of exogenous HGH in the newborn is more rapid than in the adult.[24] The high levels of HGH in cord blood, associated with rapid clearance, and the higher levels of HGH in umbilical artery than in umbilical vein, indicate active secretion of HGH by the pituitary of the fetus and neonate. Cornblath et al.[24] calculated that the newborn produces about 4.2 mg HGH in 24 hr, a rate comparable to that expected for a 70-kg man. Gitlin et al.,[66] however, consider this conclusion uncertain because of the difficulties in interpreting the serum disappearance rate of labeled HGH. Several hypotheses have been proposed to explain the high values of circulating HGH during the fetal and perinatal periods, and the different patterns of response to hypo- and hyperglycemia.[97,164] Immaturity of the homeostatic control of HGH secretion has been implicated as responsible for this situation. Diminution of HGH in blood after a few days of life could be interpreted as the result of maturation of feedback control. The lower plasma HGH in infants of diabetic mothers could be considered the result of a more mature feedback control due to the exercise of this mechanism during intrauterine life as a consequence of abnormal maternal glucose homeostasis.[164]

Kaplan et al.[97] interpret the chronology of the development of the CNS–pituitary physiologic relationship as follows: Early in pregnancy, a stage of autonomous secretion by the fetal pituitary may occur. The absence of a contiguous portal system does not eliminate the possibility that HGH secretion can occur at this time by simple diffusion of the growth-hormone-releasing factor (GRF) from the hypothalamus. By midgestation, with the development of the hypothalamic nuclei and portal system and the appearance of electrical activity of the diencephalon, secretion of GRF may occur, with resultant unrestrained release of HGH by the fetal pituitary. In late gestation, the neural inhibitory influences become operative, and can lead to decreased GRF and HGH secretion. Regulatory mechanisms for control of HGH secretion may not become fully functional until infancy, at which time myelination, cortical development, and synchronous EEG activity are at a mature stage.[97]

The ineffectiveness of exogenous HGH in newborns has been considered to be due to the saturation of receptor sites by high levels of endogenous HGH. This point could be explored by administering HGH to cyclopic infants or newborns with the genetic type of isolated deficiency of HGH and then studying its effects, since these infants have low values of endogenous HGH. Another possible explanation for the high levels of HGH and the relative refractoriness to exogenous HGH could be immaturity of the enzymatic systems on which HGH acts, resulting in turn in an inefficient feedback mechanism. Future elucidation of the primary sites of the action of the HGH as well as the neuroendocrine influences on the production and secretion of HGH in the perinatal period might provide answers to these questions. Although direct evidence is still lacking, a close correlation between the plasma level of HGH and the level of biologically active HGH is assumed. Laron et al.,[107] however, described a genetic type of dwarfism with clinical and laboratory data suggesting a deficiency of HGH, but with elevated serum levels of immunoreactive HGH. The metabolic response to exogenous HGH was attenuated, and a defective end-organ response to HGH was postulated.[114] More recently, a generalized HGH receptor deficiency was suggested as an explanation for the failure to generate somatomedin and for the abnormal regulation of fasting HGH levels in this syndrome.[42,82] Merimee et al.[116] also described end-organ subresponsiveness to HGH in African pygmies. These pygmies have normal basal levels of plasma HGH and somatomedin, and are able to respond to provocative stimuli with an increase in plasma HGH concentration, but they show less metabolic effect in response to the injection of HGH than normal controls or HGH-deficient subjects.[115,116,141] In the aforementioned syndrome as well as in the case of the pygmies, the affected infants are born normal in size and weight. Conversely, a considerable rate of growth has been reported in children with low plasma levels of immunoreactive HGH.[77,98] All these observations have raised new questions regarding the exact relationship between growth and circulating levels of HGH as measured by radioimmunoassay techniques.

3. Adrenocorticotropin (ACTH)

Special characteristics of the hypothalamic–pituitary–adrenal axis in the human fetus differentiate it from the same axis in extrauterine life and from that of other species during intra- or extrauterine life.[59,104,151,162] The human fetal adrenal gland at term is about 20 times larger than the adult adrenal in relation to body weight. At birth, about 80% of the adrenal gland is fetal adrenal cortex.[59,104,155] The fetal cortex is a very active steroidogenic organ, as evidenced cytologically,[85] by the large amount of steroids in fetal blood,[36,145] and by the large amount of estriol in maternal urine as a result of the placental transformation of fetal adrenal steroids.[137,150,151,162] Similarly, the blood and urine of infants during the first few days of life contain large amounts of steroids of adrenal origin (Cara, unpublished data, and others[9,18,36,58,136]). Lanman,[105] in a review of available information including his own observations, concluded that the primary adrenocorticotropin factor for the fetal adrenal gland is ACTH from the fetal pituitary, the large size of the fetal adrenal reflecting strong ACTH stimulation. The increased secretion of ACTH by the fetal pituitary would be secondary to relative inability of the fetal adrenal to synthesize cortisol. The resulting negative feedback would in turn increase stimulation to the hypothalamic–pituitary–adrenal axis in the fetus, with the consequent hyperplasia of the adrenal cortex until the needs for cortisol are met.[105] Since most of the steroids secreted by the adrenal gland during late fetal life and early postnatal life in humans have the $\Delta5$-3β-ol configuration,

Eberlein[36] postulated that the impaired ability of the fetal adrenal to produce cortisol is due to relative deficiency of the $\Delta5$-3β-ol hydroxysteroid dehydrogenase system (see Chapter 37).

ACTH was measured by bioassay in fetal pituitary extract as early as the 4th month of intrauterine life,[156] and it seems to increase with advancing fetal age.[63] Stark et al.[153] cultured in vitro combined pituitary and adrenal tissue from human fetuses of both sexes, ranging in body length from 18 cm to 46 cm. Their results indicate that the fetal pituitary is able to produce ACTH independently of hypothalamic stimulation, at least for some time, and that the adrenal is able to secrete hydrocortisone. Siler-Khodr et al.[149] detected ACTH release in vitro by pituitaries from 5-week-old fetuses.

Winters et al.[167] found that the radioimmunoassayable levels of ACTH in cord plasma were 241 ± 33 pg/ml from the 12th to the 34th weeks of gestation, 143 ± 7 pg/ml between the 35th and 42nd weeks, and 120 ± 8.3 pg/ml between the 1st and 7th days postnatally. The manner of delivery did not affect the level of ACTH in cord plasma in term fetuses. The mean ACTH level in fetuses and newborns was higher than the afternoon values in normal adults.

The range of both maternal and fetal plasma ACTH concentrations is considerable, and there is no correlation between the maternal and fetal values.[4] In a woman with Nelson's syndrome secondary to bilateral adrenalectomy, the plasma concentration of ACTH at delivery was 23,400 pg/ml, while the cord plasma ACTH level of her normal offspring was 800 pg/ml.[4] The baby appeared entirely normal, while the mother was markedly pigmented. This observation is concordant with the prevalent concept that no significant placental transfer of maternally derived ACTH occurs in man.[4,167] Plasma levels of ACTH in two anencephalic newborns were below the normal range and much lower than the plasma ACTH concentration of their respective mothers.[4]

In human anencephalic monsters with rudimentary pituitary glands, the fetal adrenal is about normal in size during the first 4 or 5 months of intrauterine life, as though a normal hypothalamic–pituitary system were not necessary for adrenal growth during that period.[124,132,158] After the 5th month of pregnancy, however, atrophy of the fetal adrenal progresses as term approaches.[158] At birth, the adrenal glands of these anencephalics are almost always atrophic,[7,44,56,158] with no ultrastructural evidence of secretory activity,[85] and steroidogenesis is much reduced, as reflected in low levels of steroids in cord blood and in the urine in the newborn period, particularly those steroids with the Δ5-3β-ol configuration.[36,125] Furthermore, the urinary excretion of estriol is diminished in women carrying anencephalic fetuses. Frandsen and Stakemann[56] studied the urinary excretion of estriol in 17 pregnant women carrying anencephalic fetuses and found that in 16 cases, the values were very low; the anencephalic newborns showed marked adrenal atrophy. In the remaining case, the excretion of estriol was normal, and the anencephalic offspring had an almost normal fetal adrenal gland. Since maternal urinary estriol during pregnancy seems to reflect the amount of precursor steroids produced by the fetal adrenal gland, these findings are interpreted as indicating fetal adrenal hypofunction in the anencephalic. Tuchmann-Duplessis and Mercier-Parot[159] attribute the atrophy of the adrenal glands in anencephalics to abnormal hypothalamic-pituitary connections. One may also speculate that the number of pituitary cells present in cases of anencephaly may not be enough to supply the large amount of ACTH necessary to maintain fetal function, causing a state of relative deficiency of pituitary ACTH. Interestingly, Kenny et al.[100] reported that the cortisol production rate in anencephalic newborns they studied was at the lower limit of normal. They postulate that the small amount of pituitary tissue usually present in anencephaly could be sufficient for stimulating subnormal cortisol secretion, but not for maintaining the fetal cortex.

In human newborns with congenital absence of the pituitary gland, the adrenals were reported to be absent[34] or atrophic.[8,135] Brewer[12] reported a case with absence of the anterior lobe of the pituitary, but with a normal posterior lobe and with atrophic adrenal glands. In cyclopic newborns[12] and in cases of cebocephaly with absence of the pituitary gland, the adrenals are very small.[73] Mosier[121] described a case of hypoplasia of the pituitary and of the adrenal glands in a child who died at 4 days of age. Maternal ACTH did not seem to cross the placenta to compensate for the absence of ACTH from the fetal pituitary in any of these cases. Migeon et al.[118] reported 6 patients with congenital adrenocortical unresponsiveness to ACTH, presumably due to an abnormality at the site of ACTH action on cortisol biosynthesis. Experimental hypophysectomy of rabbit[90] and rat fetuses[101] produces atrophy of the fetal adrenal

that can be restored to normal by ACTH given to the fetus. The adrenal atrophy occurs in hypophysectomized fetuses whether the mothers are intact or adrenalectomized, indicating that either no maternal ACTH or insufficient maternal ACTH crosses the placenta to compensate for the lack of fetal ACTH.[90] Hypophysectomy of rabbit fetuses produces more change in size and histology of the fetal adrenal when it is done between the 18th and 20th days of gestation than before or after this critical period.[90] It is possible that the fetal pituitary-adrenal system passes through a period of high activity when it exerts its major physiologic role in the fetus. In the human, the growth rate of the fetal adrenal is greater during the last trimester, while the fetal plasma levels of ACTH are lower during this time than the levels found before the 34th week of gestation.[167] There is no clear explanation for this apparent discrepancy. The question of a trophic factor other than ACTH for the fetal adrenal cortex has been raised for many years.

The hypothalamic-pituitary-adrenal homeostatic mechanism, or at least the pituitary-adrenal feedback mechanism, seems to be operative during fetal life. In the syndrome of congenital adrenal hyperplasia, the impaired synthesis of cortisol by the fetal cortex as a result of an enzymatic defect results in large adrenal glands at birth, presumably through increased production of ACTH by the fetal pituitary. Since the associated malformations of the external genitalia occur before the 12th week of gestation, one could assume that the fetal pituitary-adrenal cortex functional relationship is present from very early in fetal life.

Cortisone injected intraperitoneally in rat and rabbit fetuses results in reduction in size of the fetal adrenals.[90,163] Simultaneous injection of ACTH into the fetus counteracts this effect.[90] In rabbits and rats, the administration of cortisone to pregnant mothers results in reduction in size of the fetal adrenals, presumably because of the placental passage of the steroid and its effects on the fetal pituitary.[90] On the other hand, adrenalectomy of pregnant animals produces enlargement of the fetal adrenal. This enlargement can be prevented by hypophysectomy of the fetus, indicating that the source of ACTH is the fetal pituitary, and that maternal ACTH does not cross the placenta in the rat, at least not in sufficient amounts to stimulate the fetal adrenal.[21,90]

In women, large amounts of prednisone or hydrocortisone administered during pregnancy and labor caused a marked decrease in cord blood levels of C19 steroids produced by the fetal adrenal cortex.[150] Likewise, maternal urinary estrogens, particularly estriol, were lowered, presumably as a result of the decreased production of precursors by the fetal adrenals.[32,143,150] These findings are interpreted as indicating suppression of the fetal pituitary–adrenal axis by the exogenous steroids after they have crossed the placenta. Although adrenal atrophy has been reported in infants born to mothers treated with large doses of glucocorticoids,[105] in the majority of cases, the fetus is apparently not damaged by maternal treatment with corticoids.[10,130] In 2 infants who died a few hours after birth to mothers treated with large doses of glucocorticoids, the adrenals were histologically normal.[150] Furthermore, Kenny et al.[100] reported normal cortisol production rates in such infants when they were studied at less than 48 hr of life.

In newborn dogs studied within the first 24 hr after birth, the feedback control for the hypothalamic–pituitary–adrenal axis appears to be functional, since plasma cortisol rises after ACTH administration and falls to low levels after dexamethasone injection.[122] In the rat, the hypothalamic–pituitary–adrenal axis is relatively unable to respond to experimental stress[40,41,84] or to dexamethasone administered during the first few days of life.[27]

In the human neonate, conflicting results have been reported by different groups of investigators.[1] Eberlein,[36] however, found that plasma total ketosteroids, particularly plasma $\Delta 5$-3β-ol hydroxysteroids, rise after delivery, remain elevated during the first week of life, and decline thereafter. Furthermore, these steroids rise in plasma and in urine in response to medical and surgical stresses.[18,36] Kenny et al.[99] reported that in newborn infants less than 5 days old, the cortisol production rate per square meter of body surface is higher than in older infants, children, and adults. These observations indicate that the pituitary–adrenal axis of the human neonate functions at a higher level and is capable of responding to stress.

The physiologic role of the hypothalamus–pituitary–adrenal system in fetal life has not yet been clearly defined. The adrenocorticotropic function of fetal pituitary is not essential for fetal survival or fetal growth. Anencephalic and cyclopic monsters as well as newborns with absent pituitary glands are born with normal body size. In animals, hypophysectomy or adrenalectomy or combined hypophysectomy and adrenalectomy do not markedly affect fetal growth.[92] In rabbits and rats, however, the pituitary–adrenal axis seems to be necessary for normal glycogen deposition in fetal liver.[83,91] In the human fetus, the physiologic role, if any, of the fetal adrenal in the normal storage of glycogen, deserves more study.

It has been postulated that the fetal adrenal in man may represent a vestigial remnant.[59] However, the large size of the adrenal in fetal and neonatal life, and the active steroidogenesis that occurs during fetal life and shortly after birth, suggest that this gland is important. The steroids with a $\Delta 5$-3β-ol configuration that are so prominent in the secretion of the fetal adrenal may have biological effects of which we are not yet aware.[16] Further investigation of the physiologic effects of these steroids may be necessary before we can understand more clearly the role of the fetal adrenal cortex in fetal and in fetomaternal homeostasis.

4. Thyrotropin (TSH)

The organogenesis of the thyroid gland in early life in rodents does not require the presence of the pituitary gland.[88,92] Near the end of intrauterine life, however, a functional relationship between the pituitary and the thyroid has been established, and fetal hypophysectomy results in retardation of histological development and growth of the fetal thyroid,[88,91] a diminution in the uptake of radioactive iodine,[93] and a decrease in the secretion of thyroxine.[60] The administration of thyrotropin or thyroid-stimulating hormone (TSH) to the fetus corrects these deficiencies.[81,92,144] Conversely, the administration of thyroxine to the fetus inhibits thyroid growth and the secretion of fetal thyroid hormone, presumably by inhibition of TSH secretion.[81] In chick embryos, the evidence also favors self-differentiation of the thyroid gland in the initial stages of development.[113]

In human fetuses, TSH activity was reported both in serum and in pituitary homogenates as early as the 3rd month of gestation.[25,57] In vitro cultures of human fetal anterohypophysis reveal that immunoreactive TSH can be produced as early as at 14 weeks of fetal life.[65] TSH as determined by radioimmunoassay is first detectable in human fetal pituitary at 12 weeks of gestation, and the pituitary content of TSH increases with fetal age. At 32 weeks of gestation, the pituitary content of TSH is about one-tenth that in the control adult pituitaries.[57] Serum TSH levels are low in the 11- to 18-week-old fetuses, with a mean concentration of 2.4 ± 0.14 $\mu U/ml$. The levels rise rather abruptly at about the 20th week of gestation to a value of $9.6 \pm 0.93\,\mu U/ml$ between the 22nd and 34th weeks, and this level is maintained until term.[47,51] The fetal serum TSH levels are consistently higher than the maternal values.[51] On the other hand, the synthesis of thyroxine and triiodothyronine in the human thyroid *in vitro* begins at about 11 weeks of gestation,[147] and studies of *in vitro* cultures of fetal thyroid gland suggest the production of thyroglobulin at or before 29 days of gestation.[64] In man, therefore, TSH does not appear to be necessary for organogenesis of the thyroid gland or for the initiation of thyroid function in early fetal life. However, a functional relationship between pituitary and thyroid is well established later in fetal life. In the rare cases of complete absence of the pituitary gland or of the adenohypophysis with normal skull, the thyroid gland is hypoplastic with small follicles, the majority of which are empty.[12,135] The thyroid is also hypoplastic in cases of cebocephaly[73] and of cyclopy with absence of the pituitary gland.[12] In anencephaly, however, the thyroid gland is not structurally different from that of the normal newborn despite abnormal hypothalamic–pituitary connections.[158] Salazar *et al.*[142] identified thyrotrophs apparently active in adenohypophysis of 2 liveborn anencephalics, suggesting that their differentiation and secretion of TSH is not entirely dependent on hypothalamic activity during fetal life. The fetal thyroid seems to enjoy some degree of autonomy, and is less affected than the adrenal gland by the absence of the pituitary in these syndromes. Isolated deficiency of TSH resulting in hypothyroidism in childhood was described in a few instances.[46] Although deficiency of TSH is presumably present before birth, these children are not clinically hypothyroid at birth. Furthermore, the injection of exogenous TSH elicits radioactive iodine uptake by the thyroid, indicating that organogenesis of the gland took place despite the absence of TSH.[46] TSH was not detected in amniotic fluid in 13 fetuses ranging in age from 11 to 16 weeks.[51]

The time in fetal life at which the fetal pituitary–thyroid feedback system becomes established and its physiologic significance in the relatively protected fetal environment are difficult to ascertain in man. Experimentally, it has been established that the fetal pituitary–thyroid axis has the potential of reacting to conditions that disrupt its homeostasis. Unilateral thyroidectomy in rats in late fetal life produces compensatory hypertrophy of the remaining thyroid tissue, presumably through an increase in production of TSH.[38] The administration of prophylthiouracil to pregnant guinea pigs during the last several weeks of gestation resulted in goitrous offsprings with increased TSH in both plasma and pituitary. The increased TSH was closely correlated with the appearance of enlarged basophils in the fetal pituitary, the basophils containing glycoprotein granulations.[28] Fetal goitrogenesis is prevented only if the fetus itself is hypophysectomized[90]; maternal hypophysectomy has no effect on the development of the goiter. In the human, the administration of propylthiouracil to pregnant women produces enlargement of the thyroid in the fetus as early as the 5th month of pregnancy.[30] This finding is indirect evidence of the capability of the fetal pituitary to produce and secrete TSH in response to a block in the synthesis of thyroid hormone. Shepard and Andersen,[148] however, were unable to produce goiter in fetuses of less than 120 gestational days by the administration of propylthiouracil to pregnant women, suggesting that the pituitary–thyroid functional relationship is not well established before this time. Fisher[47] considers that the pituitary–thyroid axis functions at a hypopituitary level before midgestation, and that the hypothalamic–pituitary control system begins to mature at about 20 weeks of gestation, as evidenced by the rather abrupt increase in pituitary and serum TSH levels, by the increment in fetal thyroidal radioiodine uptake, and by the subsequent rise in T_4 in fetal serum at this time. The increase of other fetal pituitary hormones at this time favors the hypothesis of hypothalamic maturation as discussed in Section 2.5.

Deficiency or excess of thyroid hormone or TSH in the maternal circulation have little or no effect on the pituitary–thyroid axis of the fetus in rodents and in humans. Hypophysectomized women made fertile by the use of human gonadotropins,[61] as well as women hypophysectomized during pregnancy, have delivered infants without noticeable effects on the pituitary–thyroid axis despite the absence of TSH in the maternal circulation.[112] Infants born of mothers with low levels of thyroid hormone due to primary hypothyroidism and with presumably high levels of circulating TSH show no evidence of excessive TSH effects such as hyperthyroidism or thyroid enlargement or both.[76] This and other indirect evidence indicates that maternal TSH does not cross the placenta in the human. More direct evidence is provided by the study of Fisher et al.,[53] which demonstrates a fetomaternal gradient of TSH in blood. In rats[103] and in guinea pigs,[129] it has been well established that TSH does not cross the placenta. On the other hand, long-acting thyroid stimulator (LATS), an immunoglobulin G of extrapituitary origin, can cross the placenta.[14]

Congenital goiter in newborns as a result of placental passage of excessive amounts of iodine has been ascribed to increased production of fetal TSH due to interference with normal pituitary–thyroid homeostasis.[26] Homoki et al.[78] found increased serum TSH concentrations in newborns with congenital goiter and delayed ossification, while the levels were within the normal range when ossification, was normal. Stanbury et al.[152] described a child with hypothyroidism without goiter and with high concentrations of TSH in blood who had no thyroid response to exogenous TSH. They postulated impaired ability of the thyroid to respond specifically to stimulation by TSH with cell divisions and synthesis of thyroglobulin. Here again, the patient did not show evidence of hypothyroidism early in life, although the defect was presumably present in fetal life.

Production of TSH can be suppressed in the human fetus when exceedingly large amounts of thyroid are administered to the mother.[17] In this respect, triiodothyronine (T_3) appears to be more effective, since it crosses the placenta more readily than thyroxine (T_4) because it is more loosely bound to proteins in maternal blood, but even at such high concentration, the transfer is limited.[35,134]

The transitional period from uterus to external environment is marked by abrupt changes in thyroid function.[54] In rodents, experimental studies indicate that the pituitary–thyroid system functions at a higher level in late fetal life than in early postnatal life. The TSH content of the pituitary in newborn guinea pigs is relatively low.[28] Unilateral thyroidectomy in late fetal life in rats caused a significant increase in the size of the remaining lobe of the thyroid. In early postnatal life, however, the compensatory hypertrophy was less marked.[38] Thyroxine administered to normal newborn guinea pigs was effective in suppressing the pituitary–thyroid system and lowering the production of TSH, as indicated by reduction in thyroid and pituitary weights and lowered TSH stores in the latter.[28] However, the administration of propylthiouracil to rodents during the first 2 weeks of life failed to induce significant histological changes in the thyroid or to alter the TSH level in blood or pituitary.[28]

In the human fetus at term and in the neonate at birth, the blood concentration of TSH is high and increases even more after a few minutes of extrauterine life.[160] Fisher et al.[53] found that blood samples obtained from the scalps of human fetuses during the 3 hr immediately preceding delivery showed a higher TSH concentration than in the respective maternal blood samples. Furthermore, paired maternal–cord blood samples at birth demonstrated a significantly higher free thyroxine and TSH concentration in cord blood. This gradient was also present in paired samples obtained from cesarean deliveries. The authors concluded that the human fetus at term, and the newborn immediately after birth, have a relative hyperthyrotropinemia that is not accounted for by extrauterine exposure or the stress of birth, since the gradient is also present in paired samples obtained from cesarean deliveries.[53] Furthermore, a few minutes after birth, a large amount of TSH is released from the fetal pituitary. The mean serum TSH increases from 9.5 μU/ml in cord blood to 60 μU/ml and 86 μU/ml at 10 and 30 min after birth, respectively. The TSH concentration then falls rapidly between 30 min and 3–4 hr, and more gradually thereafter to 13 μU/ml by 48 hr of extrauterine life. This rapid rise and fall in serum TSH concentration may represent a release of stored pituitary TSH. Maternal serum TSH concentrations are low and stable during labor and in the *postpartum* period.[49] The stimulus for this early massive discharge of pituitary TSH is unknown. The early rise is not prevented by warming the newborn infant during the first 3 hr of life. If the newborn infant is exposed to room temperature between the 3rd and 4th hours after birth, however, TSH increases significantly. This second rise in TSH concentration is prevented if the infant is kept warm, and is therefore attributed to cooling of the infant. These high blood levels of TSH in the fetus at term and in the neonate would explain previous observations indicating increased thyroid function in the newborn, such as increased PBI concentration,[29] increased saturation of the thyroxine-binding protein in blood, and the high rate of thyroidal radioiodine clearance at 48 hr of life.[48,52] It would also explain why nonincubated infants were found to have higher PBI values and greater thyroid radioiodine clearances at 48 hr of life than incubated infants.[52] More recently, it was demonstrated that the neonatal surge of TSH is associated with an increase of serum T_4 levels and with a more rapid and marked increase of T_3 and free T_3 concentrations.[50]

Measurement of TSH in cord blood or heel-prick blood between 3 and 6 days of life was proved to be successful for the screening of congenital hypothyroidism.[55,102,109]

The physiologic significance of the increased levels of TSH and thyroid hormone in late fetal life and in early extrauterine life is not yet clear. Increased function of the pituitary–thyroid axis is not required for the high rate of growth of the fetus and newborn, since the absence of this function does not impair fetal growth. It is possible that the hypothalamic–pituitary–thyroid homeostatis mechanism is not well adjusted during the perinatal period, and that the increased production of thyroid hormone does not parallel physiologic needs. However, neither the fetus nor the newborn presents clinical evidence of excessive thyroid hormone. Another possibility is that the peripheral tissues in the fetus and in the newborn do not respond to thyroid hormone in the same manner as a more mature organism, and a higher level of circulating hormone might be needed. During fetal life, the levels of T_3 are low, while the concentrations of reverse T_3 are high, suggesting that a specific β-ring iodothyronine monodeiodinase deficiency may exist in fetal tissues.[20,50] Investigation of the effects of thyroid hormone on the enzymatic systems in tissues of the fetus and newborn, and vice versa, may help to elucidate this question.

5. Gonadotropins

In mammals, the hypothalamic–pituitary–gonadal axis varies greatly in its physiologic significance, among various species. In rabbits, decapitation of the male fetus before differentiation of the genital tract results in such gross developmental abnormalities as reduced prostate and feminine external genitalia.[87,90,91] This result is interpreted as a consequence of eliminating the pituitary, since the interstitial cells of the testis show changes parallel to those of the genital tract, and the genital abnormalities can be prevented if equine gonadotropin is

injected into the decapitated fetuses.[87,91,92] On the other hand, effects of fetal decapitation were almost absent in rat fetuses.[101] Similarly, in man, the fetal pituitary does not appear to be necessary for differentiation of the gonads and organogenesis of the genital tract. Absence of the pituitary in the human is not accompanied by any constant abnormality of the genital tract, although there is a trend toward hypoplasia of the testes and the penis.[8,135] In a case absence of the anterior lobe of the pituitary, the ovaries were normal, with numerous primordial follicles.[12] In anencephaly, the gonads are generally normal, and there are no consistent abnormalities of the genital tract,[7,142,158] although hypoplasia of the penis and of the testes has been described in some cases.[44,158] Zondek and Zondek[171] reported that the mean number of Leydig cells was significantly lower in anencephaly than in normal controls. Salazar et al.[142] described gonadotrophs in pituitaries of anencephalics, suggesting that their differentiation is independent of neurosecretory activity. Perrin and Benirschke[128] consider that cephalic integrity or hypothalamic control is not essential for the differentiation of genetically determined sex in man.

Luteinizing hormone (LH) was studied by bioassay in 48 human pituitaries from male fetuses and in 51 pituitaries from female fetuses ranging in age from 13 to 40 weeks of gestation. LH was found only in pituitaries from female fetuses from the 18th to the 28th weeks of gestation. Before and after this period, no LH could be detected in pituitaries from female fetuses. In pituitaries from males, no LH could be detected at any time during intrauterine life.[120] Clements et al.,[22] using a radioimmunoassay, reported that LH is low or nondetectable in fetal pituitary prior to the 12th week. Between the 12th and 20th weeks of fetal life, the pituitary content of LH increases with age in both sexes, although it is significantly higher in females. Release of LH from fetal pituitaries in vitro was detected in both sexes as early as 5–6 weeks of fetal life.[149]

Serum LH is low or undetectable before the 12th week of fetal life. It rises thereafter, and between the 12th and 20th weeks of gestation, reaches values of 5.1 ± 0.8 ng/ml in the male and 14.5 ± 3.1 ng/ml in the female.[22] Serum LH levels decrease thereafter in both sexes, and at term, the cord blood levels are low or undetectable.[165] In the postnatal period, serum LH levels rise in the male, and by 1 week of age, they are in the adolescent range, declining to the levels seen in prepubertal boys by 4 months of age. A similar pattern occurs in newborn females, but the levels are lower.[165]

The LH concentration in amniotic fluid is low before the 12th week of fetal life (<3 ng/ml). Between the 12th and 20th weeks, the levels increase in both sexes, reaching a value of 3.5 ± 0.5 ng/ml in the male and 10.8 ± 1.1 ng/ml in the female. There is a decrease thereafter, and from the 32nd week to term, the levels are low in both sexes (<1 ng/ml).[22]

FSH synthesis by human fetal pituitary incubated in a medium with ^{14}C-labeled precursors was absent at 10.5 weeks of gestation, but well established at 14 weeks.[65] Siler-Khodr et al.,[149] however, detected release of FSH from fetal pituitary in vitro as early as 5–7 weeks of gestation, in both sexes.

Levina,[110] using a bioassay procedure, reported that FSH was present in human pituitaries of female fetuses at about 13 weeks of gestation, whereas it was found irregularly and in lesser amounts in pituitary of male fetuses. Radioimmunoassay of FSH in human fetal pituitary reveals low or undetectable values before the 12th week of pregnancy, and increasing levels between the 12th and 20th weeks in both sexes. Levels in female fetuses were significantly higher than those in males.[22,96] The FSH concentration in fetal pituitary is lower than the LH concentration at a similar age.[22]

Serum FSH levels are low or undetectable in human fetuses before the 12th week in both sexes, and they remain low in male fetuses during fetal life. In female fetuses, the serum FSH rises between the 12th and 20th weeks to a mean value of 5.4 ± 1.4 ng/ml, although individual values may be as high as those seen in castrated adults.[22] The FSH levels in cord blood at term are low in both sexes, but there is a rapid rise in early postnatal life. In males, it reaches a peak between 1 week and 2 months, with a rapid decline by 4 months of age to levels comparable to those seen in older prepubertal boys. In females, the levels are higher between the 2nd and 3rd month of age and persist elevated longer than in boys.[165]

FSH levels in amniotic fluid are low during the entire pregnancy with a male fetus. In case of a female fetus, amniotic fluid FSH concentrations rise between the 12th and 20th weeks, and then decrease to low levels between the 32nd week and term.[22] The FSH and LH found in the amniotic fluid in all probability represent fetal pituitary hormones, since the maternal FSH and LH concentrations are low or undetectable.[22]

The initiation of the synthesis of gonadotropin by the human fetal pituitary seems to occur too late to account for the initial differentiation and growth of the testis. Leydig cells are already evident in the fetal testis at about the 8th week of gestation, and they increase rapidly in number, reaching a maximum at about 14–16 weeks of gestation.[126] Histochemically, they present maximum evidence of steroidogenic activity at about 12 weeks of gestation, with a decline around the 19th week; by the 23rd week, more than half the interstitial cells are enzymatically inactive, but some fully reactive cells remain visible until the end of gestation.[126,170] Therefore, factors other than gonadotropins from the fetal pituitary should be responsible for the initial development and maintenance of the interstitial cells of the fetal testis. It is generally accepted that chorionic gonadotropin is such a factor. In the placenta, the concentration of chorionic gonadotropin rises rapidly to a peak between the 8th and 12th weeks of pregnancy, after which it falls sharply.[31] Chorionic gonadotropin can be detected in pregnant women as early as 10 days after ovulation,[3] and it is present in fetal tissues in physiologically significant amounts.[13] Levels of chorionic gonadotropin in fetal serum and in amniotic fluid are clearly measurable prior to 12 weeks, with high values at 11–14 weeks.[22] Maintenance of the activity of the interstitial cells of the fetal testis after the decline in the production of chorionic gonadotropin suggests that other stimulating factors, perhaps gonadotropin from the fetal pituitary, act on the testis in late fetal life.[92] This action would explain the hypoplasia of the penis and of the interstitial cells observed at birth in cases of absence of the pituitary gland. Eguchi and Morikawa[39] reported that in the perinatal age in the rat, there appears to be a reciprocal relationship between the pituitary and the testes, and that the Leydig cells are maintained largely by the fetal pituitary. Conversely, the fetal ovary is very active in gametogenesis, but its steroidogenic activity is very limited, especially when compared with the fetal adrenal or the fetal testis. These observations agree well with the rather insignificant role of the human fetal ovary in the differentiation of either the genital ducts or the external genitalia.[69]

Information is scant concerning the role of the CNS in the production and release of pituitary gonadotropins by the fetal hypophysis. Extracts from the median eminence of newborn rabbits and rats and from 1- to 2-month-old calves were found to be very active with regard to gonadotropin-releasing activity, while extracts obtained from

20-day-old rabbit fetuses showed no evidence of such activity.[15]

Luteinizing-hormone-releasing hormone (LH-RH) was detected in human fetal hypothalami as early as 4.5 weeks of gestational age.[166] The human fetal pituitary responds *in vitro* to synthetic LH-RH with the release of FSH and LH.[68]

From their own observations and other evidence, Harris and Levine[72] concluded that rats of both sexes are born with a sexually undifferentiated CNS that is of the female type. This pattern becomes fixed in the female in the first few days of life. In the male during the first few days of life, the testicular secretions are fundamental in the organization of normal mechanisms underlying future patterns of sexual behavior and gonadotropin secretion.[72] On the other hand, pituitaries from human fetuses of either sex ranging from 13 to 18 weeks of gestation, when implanted in the sellar region of mature hypophysectomized male rats, were able to maintain the normal weight and histology of the testes. These results would indicate that in the human fetus, the hypothalamus has undergone a sexual differentiation by 13–18 weeks of gestation and is responsible for the sexual dimorphism found in the secretion of gonadotropins by the fetal pituitary.[110] It is possible that the hypothalamic differentiation is brought about by the secretion of testicular androgens that starts at about the 9th week of gestation.[110] Lower concentrations of both FSH and LH were observed in pituitary, serum, and amniotic fluid between 12 and 20 weeks of fetal age in males compared with females. These lower concentrations may be a result of feedback inhibition by the higher concentrations of testosterone in males at this time. The absence of gonadotropin suppression in the midgestation female fetus, despite high levels of circulating estradiol, suggests that hypothalamic or pituitary receptors for estrogen feedback, or both, have not developed at this time. The subsequent decline in gonadotropin concentrations to low levels by term in both sexes presumably reflects maturation of this feedback mechanism.[22]

The challenging field of neurophysiologic and psychosexual development in fetal and early postnatal life is being explored actively at present.

6. Prolactin (PRL)

The pituitary gland of the human fetus is able to synthesize, store, and secrete PRL early in gestation.

Prolactin as measured by the pigeon crop wall bioassay appears in human fetal pituitary of both sexes at 19–20 weeks of gestation, and increases with fetal age to reach a maximum at term.[120] Immunoreactive PRL was detected in the media of cultures of human pituitary from a 5-week-old fetus.[149] Aubert *et al.*[6] measured PRL by immunoassay in human fetal pituitary as early as 68 days of gestation. The content and the concentration of PRL in human fetal pituitary are low in the first 100 days of gestation, and experience a marked increase between 100 and 160 days. During the last 100 days of gestation, the content of PRL increases slowly, while its concentration remains relatively constant.[6] Lactotrops, which have been described in fetal pituitary as early as 4 months of gestation, increase markedly during the last trimester of gestation. There is a positive correlation of the fetal pituitary content and concentration of PRL with fetal age, but no relation to sex.[6]

Aubert *et al.*[6] could not find any immunochemical difference between the human fetal PRL and the PRL from adult glands.

Serum PRL was detected by immunoassay in the human fetus as early as 88 days of gestation.[6] The serum concentration of PRL in the human fetus remains low for the first 165 days of gestation, with a mean value of 19.5 ± 2.5 ng/ml. After 180 days of gestation, there is a steady rise in concentration, reaching levels of 300–500 ng/ml in the fetus near term.[6] The mean PRL concentration in umbilical vein in the newborn is around 167 ± 14.2 ng/ml, while the mean level in maternal blood is 111.8 ± 12.3 ng/ml.[6] No significant difference was observed in matched arterial and venous cord blood samples. Full-term newborns showed no sex difference in their high serum levels of PRL, while in the premature newborn, the levels were lower in the female than in the male.[71]

The concentration of serum PRL remains elevated in infants for several weeks.[6,71]

In amniotic fluid, the PRL levels are higher than in the fetal and maternal circulations,[157] and bear a positive correlation with the maternal serum levels of PRL, while the correlation with the fetal serum levels is negative.[86] The maternal circulation is apparently the major source of PRL in amniotic fluid.[86]

The steady increase of PRL concentration in fetal blood until the end of pregnancy differs from the pattern of the other anterior pituitary hormones during fetal life. Apparently, a functional hypothalamic–pituitary homeostatic system is not neces-

ESTIMATED GESTATIONAL AGE IN DAYS	70 - 120	120 - 160	160 - 200	200 - 240	240 - 280	Birth
Histology of pituitary	Appearance of acidophile cells	Increase of acidophile cells	Increase in pituitary weight ⟶			
Hypophysial-portal system	Few capillaries present in pituitary	Capillaries 1° plexus portal system	1° and 2° plexus portal system established ⟶			
Hypothalamus	Appearance of first nuclei	All nuclei present. Appearance of neuronal tracts	Increase size of nuclei ⟶ Increase neural tracts ⟶			
EEG	Activity in pons	Appearance of electrical activity in diencephalon	Maturation of cortical electrical activity ⟶			

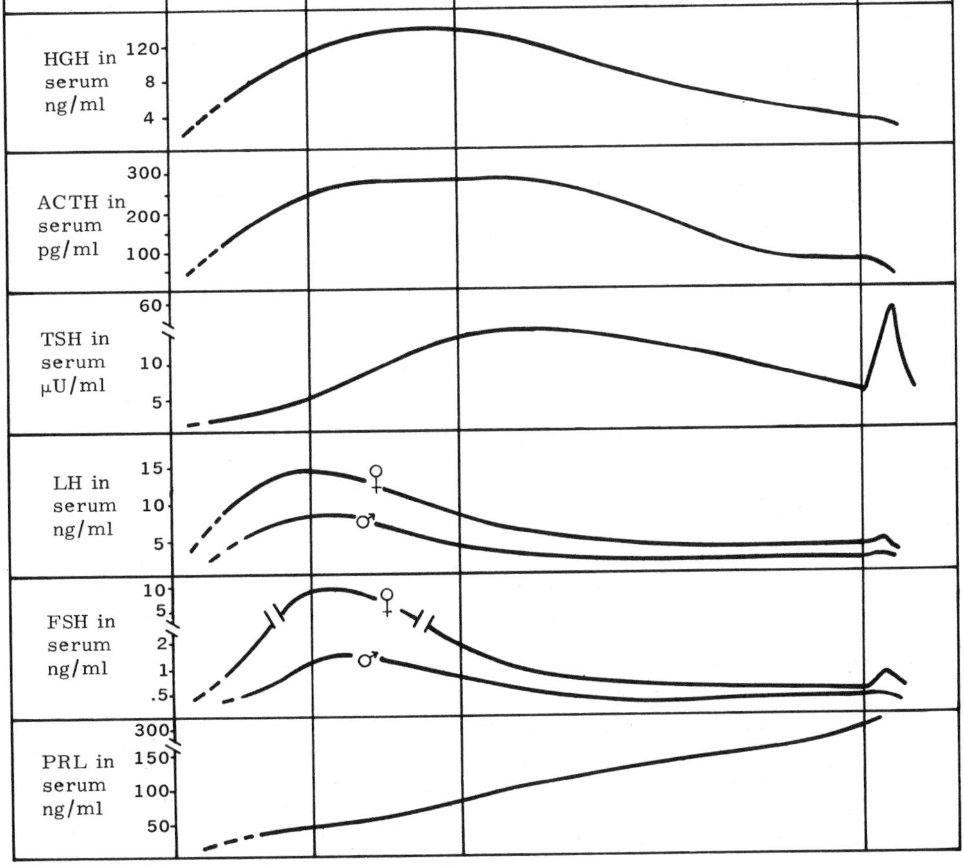

Fig. 1. Ontogeny of the hypothalamic-anterior pituitary system, and the anterior pituitary hormones. Reproduced (with modifications) from Fisher[47] and Kaplan *et al.*[97]

sary for the high levels of PRL in the fetus near term and at birth, since anencephalic newborns have comparable cord blood concentrations of PRL.[6,74] Reviewing the evidence available, Aubert et al.[6] consider that the high concentration of PRL in the fetal and maternal circulations are probably due to the high levels of estrogen in both organisms, since estrogen is known to stimulate the lactotrops.

Placental transfer of PRL is very limited in monkeys,[86] and the available evidence indicates that it is also very limited or absent in humans, although more definite information is necessary.

The biological role of PRL in fetal life is not known. From observations in cases of absent pituitary gland, PRL does not seem to be important for fetal growth.

7. Summary

The human fetal pituitary is able to release HGH, ACTH, LH, FSH, and PRL *in vitro* by the 5th week of gestation, even before the anterior lobe is completely formed. Pituitary content of HGH, TSH, LH, FSH, and PRL has been well documented by the 10th–12th week of pregnancy, and by about the 16th week for ACTH. All the hormones of the anterior pituitary are present in the fetal circulation as early as 10–12 weeks of gestation, and their serum concentration increases during the first part of pregnancy. After midgestation, the serum levels diminish, more or less markedly, for the different hormones. PRL is the exception, since its concentration increases steadily until term (see Fig. 1).

Early in fetal life, absence of the fetal pituitary or the hypothalamus or both does not seem to interfere with organogenesis and functioning of the target glands, or with fetal growth during the entire intrauterine life. In the last trimester, however, the fetal pituitary exerts a trophic effect on the target glands, an effect that is marked for the adrenal cortex, and somewhat less evident for the thyroid and gonads.

The time of initiation and maintenance of the pituitary–target gland feedback mechanism has not been clearly established. Clinical evidence would indicate that the pituitary–adrenal cortex feedback is established before the 12th week of gestation, and that the pituitary–thyroid feedback control is operative as early as the 5th month of pregnancy.

The anterior lobe of the pituitary seems to function autonomously early in gestation. At about midgestation, with the development of the hypothalamic nuclei and tracts, and the hypophyseal portal system, a hypothalamic–pituitary homeostatic system develops. At the beginning, there is an apparently unrestrained stimulation of the pituitary by the hypothalamus, with a resultant increase in the concentration of the anterior pituitary hormones in the fetal circulation. Later in gestation, with the maturation of the CNS, the neurological inhibitory influences become operative, and the levels of hormones in the blood decrease. Refinement of this hypothalamic–pituitary homeostatic mechanism does not become fully effective, however, until infancy.

In the human, there appears to be no intrinsic sex difference in the ability of the fetal pituitary to secrete gonadotropins. The hypothalamus, however, seems to undergo a sexual differentiation around the 13th week of gestation, and would be responsible for the sex differentiation in the secretion of gonadotropins by the fetal pituitary.

8. References

1. Aarskog, D., 1965, Cortisol in the newborn infant, *Acta Pediatr. Scand. Suppl.* **158**:9–91.
2. Abelove, W. A., Rupp, J. J., and Paschkis, K. E., 1954, Acromegaly and pregnancy, *J. Clin. Endocrinol.* **14**:32–44.
3. Albert, A., and Berkson, J., 1951, A clinical bioassay for chorionic gonadotropin, *J. Clin. Endocrinol.* **11**:805–820.
4. Allen, J. P., Cook, D. M., Kendall, J. W., and McGilvra, R., 1973, Maternal–fetal ACTH relationship in man, *J. Clin. Endocrinol. Metab.* **37**:230–234.
5. Allen, J. P., Greer, M. A., McGilvra, R., Castro, A., and Fisher, D. A., 1974, Endocrine function in an anencephalic infant, *J. Clin. Endocrinol. Metab.* **38**:94–98.
6. Aubert, M. L., Grumbach, M. M., and Kaplan, S. L., 1975, The ontogenesis of fetal hormones. III. Prolactin, *J. Clin. Invest.* **56**:155–164.
7. Benirschke, K., 1956, Adrenals in anencephaly and hydrocephaly, *Obstet. Gynecol.* **8**:412–425.
8. Blizzard, R. M., and Alberts, M., 1956, Hypopituitarism, hypoadrenalism and hypogonadism in the newborn infant, *J. Pediatr.* **48**:782–792.
9. Bongiovanni, A. M., 1965, The adrenogenital syndrome with deficiency of 3β-hydroxysteroid dehydrogenase, *J. Clin. Invest.* **41**:2086–2092.
10. Bongiovanni, A. M., and McPadden, A. J., 1960. Steroids during pregnancy and possible fetal consequences, *Fertil. Steril.* **11**:181–186.

11. Brasel, J. A., Wright, J. C., Wilkins, L., and Blizzard, R. M., 1965, An evaluation of seventy-five patients with hypopituitarism beginning in childhood, *Amer. J. Med.* **38**:484–498.

12. Brewer, D. B., 1957, Congenital absence of the pituitary gland and its consequences, *J. Pathol. Bacteriol.* **73**:59–67.

13. Bruner, J. A., 1951, Distribution of chorionic gonadotropin in mother and fetus at various stages of pregnancy, *J. Clin. Endocrinol.* **11**:360–374.

14. Burke, G., 1968, The long-acting thyroid stimulator of Graves' disease, *Amer. J. Med.* **45**:435–450.

15. Campbell, H. J., and Gallardo, E., 1966, Gonadotrophin-releasing activity of the median eminence at different ages, *J. Physiol. (London)* **186**:689–697.

16. Cara, J., 1969, Isolation and identification of 16-OH-pregnenolone (pregn-5-en-3β,16α-diol-20-one) in urine from a patient with adrenocortical carcinoma, *Steroids* **13**:519–527.

17. Carr, E. A., 1959, The effect of maternal thyroid function on fetal thyroid function and development, *J. Clin. Endocrinol.* **19**:1–18.

18. Cathro, D. M., Forsyth, C. C., and Cameron, J., 1969, Adrenocortical response to stress in newborn infants, *Arch. Dis. Child.* **44**:88–95.

19. Chiumello, G. A., Vaccari, A., and Sereni, F., 1965, Bone growth and metabolic studies of premature infants treated with human growth hormone, *Pediatrics* **36**:836–842.

20. Chopra, I. J., Sack, J., and Fisher, D. A., 1975, Reverse T_3 in the fetus and newborn, in: *Perinatal Thyroid Physiology and Disease* (D. A. Fisher and G. N. Burrow, eds.), pp. 33–40, Raven Press, New York.

21. Christianson, M., and Jones, C. I., 1957, The interrelationships of the adrenal glands of mother and foetus in the rat, *J. Endocrinol.* **15**:17–42.

22. Clements, J. A., Reyes, F. I., Winter, J. S. D., and Faiman, C., 1976, Studies on human sexual development. III. Fetal pituitary and serum, and amniotic fluid concentrations of LH, CH, and FSH, *J. Clin. Endocrinol. Metab.* **42**:9–19.

23. Contopoulos, A. N., 1967, Comparative aspects of growth hormone during fetal life, *International Symposium on Growth Hormone,* Milan, Italy, *Excerpta Med. Int. Congr. Ser.* **142**:35.

24. Cornblath, M., Parker, M. L., Reisner, S. H., Forbes, A. E., and Daughaday, W. H., 1965, Secretion and metabolism of growth hormone in premature and full term infants, *J. Clin. Endocrinol.* **25**:209–218.

25. Costa, A., *et al.,* 1965, Thyroid function and thyrotropin activity in mother and fetus, in: *Current Topics in Thyroid Research* (C. Cassano and M. Andreoli, eds.), pp. 738–748, Academic Press, New York.

26. Groughs, W., and Visser, H. K. A., 1965, Familial iodide-induced goiter. Evidence for an abnormality in the pituitary-thyroid homeostatic control, *J. Pediatr.* **67**:353–362.

27. D'Angelo, S. A., 1966, Maturation of pituitary TSH and ACTH mechanism in the guinea pig: Effects of propylthiouracil and dexamethasone on fetus and neonate, *Second International Congress on Hormonal Steroids* (Italy) *Excerpta Med. Int. Congr. Ser* **111**:84.

28. D'Angelo, S. A., 1967, Pituitary–thyroid interrelations in maternal, fetal and neonatal guinea pigs, *Endocrinology* **81**:132–138.

29. Danowski, T. S., Johnston, S. Y., Price, W. C., McKelvy, M., Stevenson, S. S., and McCluskey, E. R., 1951, Protein-bound iodine in infants from birth to one year of age, *Pediatrics* **7**:240–244.

30. Davis, L. J., and Forbes, W., 1945, Thiouracil in pregnancy, effect on foetal thyroid, *Lancet* **2**:740–742.

31. Diczfalusy, E., 1953, Chorionic gonadotrophin and oestrogens in the human placenta, *Acta Endocrinol. (Copenhagen),* Suppl. 12.

32. Driscoll, A. M., 1969, Urinary oestriol excretion in pregnant patient given large doses of prednisone, *Br. Med. J.* **1**:556–557.

33. Ducharme, J. R., and Grumbach, M. M., 1961, Studies on the effects of human growth hormone in premature infants, *J. Clin. Invest.* **40**:243–252.

34. Dunn, J. M., 1966, Anterior pituitary and adrenal absence in a live-born normocephalic infant, *Amer. J. Obstet. Gynecol.* **96**:893, 894.

35. Dussault, J., Row, V. V., Lickrish, G., and Volpe, R., 1969, Studies of serum triiodothyronine concentration in maternal and cord blood: Transfer of triiodothyronine across the human placenta, *J. Clin. Endocrinol.* **29**:595–603.

36. Eberlein, W. R., 1965, Steroids and sterols in umbilical cord blood, *J. Clin. Endocrinol.* **25**:1101–1118.

37. Edmonds, H. W., 1950, Pituitary, adrenal and thyroid in cyclopia, *Arch. Pathol. (Chicago)* **50**:727–735.

38. Eguchi, Y., and Morikawa, Y., 1966, A study of the rat thyroid during perinatal days with observations of compensatory changes following unilateral thyroidectomy, *Anat. Rec.* **156**:415–422.

39. Eguchi, Y., and Morikawa, Y., 1968, Changes in pituitary gonadal interrelations during perinatal days in the rat, *Anat. Rec.* **161**:163–170.

40. Eguchi, Y., and Wells, L. J., 1965, Response of the hypothalamic–hypophyseal adrenal axis to stress: Observations in fetal and caesarean newborn rats, *Proc. Soc. Exp. Biol. Med.* **120**:675–678.

41. Eguchi, Y., Eguchi, K., and Wells, L. J., 1964, Compensatory hypertrophy of right adrenal after left adrenalectomy: Observation in fetal, newborn and week-old rats, *Proc. Soc. Exp. Biol. Med.* **116**:89–92.

42. ELDERS, M. J., GARLAND, J. T., DAUGHADAY, W. A., FISHER, D. A., WHITNEY, J. E., AND HUGHES, E. R., 1973, Laron's dwarfism: Studies on the nature of the defect, *J. Pediatr.* **83**:253–263.

43. ELLIS, S. T., BECK, J. S., AND CURRIE, A. R., 1966, The cellular localization of growth hormone in the human fetal adenohypophysis, *J. Pathol. Bacteriol.* **92**:179–183.

44. EREZ, S., AND KING, T. M., 1966, Anencephaly: A survey of 44 cases, *Obstet. Gynecol.* **27**:601–604.

45. FALIN, L. I., 1961, The development of human hypophysis and differentiation of cells of its anterior lobe during embryonic life, *Acta Anat. (Basel)* **44**:183–205.

46. FINK, C. W., 1967, Thyrotropin deficiency in a child resulting in secondary growth hormone deficiency, *Pediatrics* **40**:881–885.

47. FISHER, D. A., 1975, Thyroid function in the fetus, in: *Perinatal Thyroid Physiology and Disease* (D. A. Fisher and G. N. Burrow, eds.), pp. 21–32, Raven Press, New York.

48. FISHER, D. A., AND ODDIE, T. H., 1964, Neonatal thyroidal hyperactivity. Response to cooling, *Amer. J. Dis. Child.* **107**:574–581.

49. FISHER, D. A., AND ODELL, W. D., 1969, Acute release of thyrotropin in the newborn, *J. Clin. Invest.* **48**:1670–1677.

50. FISHER, D. A., AND SACK, J., 1975, Thyroid function in the neonate and possible approaches to newborn screening for hypothyroidism, in: *Perinatal Thyroid Physiology and Disease* (D. A. Fisher and G. N. Burrow, eds.), pp. 197–209, Raven Press, New York.

51. FISHER, D. A., HOBEL, C. J., GARZA, R., AND PIERCE, C. A., 1970, Thyroid function in the preterm fetus, *Pediatrics* **46**:208–216.

52. FISHER, D. A., ODDIE, T. H., AND MAKOSKI, E. J., 1966, The influence of environmental temperature on thyroid, adrenal and water metabolism in the newborn human infant, *Pediatrics* **37**:583–591.

53. FISHER, D. A., ODELL, W. D., HOBEL, C. J., AND GARZA, R., 1969, Thyroid function in the term fetus, *Pediatrics* **44**:526–535.

54. FLORSHEIM, W. H., FLAIRCLOTH, M. A., CORCORRAN, N. L., AND RUDKO, P., 1966, Perinatal thyroid function in the rat, *Acta Endocrinol. (Copenhagen)* **52**:375–382.

55. FOLEY, T. P., JR., KLEIN, A. H., AGUSTIN, A. V., AND HOPWOOD, N. J., 1975, Screening for congenital hypothyroidism by the determination of thyrotropin levels, in: *Perinatal Thyroid Physiology and Disease* (D. A. Fisher and G. N. Burrow, eds.), pp. 255–261, Raven Press, New York.

56. FRANDSEN, V. A., AND STAKEMANN, G., 1964, The site of production of oestrogenic hormones in human pregnancy. III. Further observations on the hormone excretion in pregnancy with anencephalic foetus, *Acta Endocrinol. (Copenhagen)* **47**:265–276.

57. FUKUSHI, M., TADASHI, I., ABE, H., AND KUMAHARA, Y., 1970, Thyrotropin in human fetal pituitaries, *J. Clin. Endocrinol. Metab.* **31**:565–569.

58. GARDNER, L. I., 1956, Adrenocortical metabolism of the fetus, infant and child, *Pediatrics* **17**:897–924.

59. GARDNER, L. I., (ed.), 1975), Development of the normal fetal and neonatal adrenal, in: *Endocrine and Genetic Diseases of Childhood*, pp. 460–476, W. B. Saunders Co., Philadelphia.

60. GELOSO, J. P., 1958, Récherches préliminares sur la sécrétion de thyroxine par la thyroide du foetus de rat, en fin de gestation, *C. R. Acad. Sci. Ser. D (Paris)* **246**:168–171.

61. GEMZELL, C., 1964, Therapy of gynecological disorders with human gonadotropin, *Vitam. Horm. (N.Y.)* **22**:129.

62. GERSHBERG, H., 1957, Growth hormone content and metabolic actions of human pituitary glands, *Endocrinology* **61**:160–165.

63. GHILAIN, A., AND SCHWERS, J., 1957, Extraction et dosage de l'ACTH dans l'hypophyse foetale humaine, *C. R. Soc. Biol. (Paris)* **151**:1606–1609.

64. GITLIN, D., AND BIASUCCI, A., 1969, Ontogenesis of immunoreactive thyroglobulin in the human conceptus, *J. Clin. Endocrinol.* **29**:849–853.

65. GITLIN, D., AND BIASUCCI, A., 1969, Ontogenesis of immunoreactive growth hormone, follicle-stimulating hormone, thyroid-stimulating hormone, luteinizing hormone, chorionic prolactin and chorionic gonadotropin in the conceptus, *J. Clin. Endocrinol.* **29**:926–935.

66. GITLIN, D., KUMATE, J., AND MORALES, C., 1965, Metabolism and maternofetal transfer of human growth hormone in the pregnant woman at term, *J. Clin. Endocrinol.* **25**:1599–1608.

67. GLICK, S. M., 1968, Normal and abnormal secretion of growth hormone, *Ann. N. Y. Acad. Sci.* **148**:471–487.

68. GROOM, G. V., AND BOYNS, A. R., 1973, Effect of hypothalamic releasing factors and steroids on release of gonadotrophins by organ cultures of human foetal pituitaries, *J. Endocrinol.* **59**:511–522.

69. GRUMBACH, M. M., AND VAN WYK, J. J., 1974, Disorders of sex differentiation, in: *Textbook of Endocrinology* (R. H. Willimas, ed.), pp. 423–501, W. B. Saunders Co., Philadelphia.

70. GRUNT, J. A., AND REYNOLDS, D. W., 1970, Insulin, blood sugar and growth hormone levels in an anencephalic infant before and after intravenous administration of glucose, *J. Pediatr.* **76**:112–116.

71. GUYDA, H. J., AND FRIESEN, H. G., 1973, Serum prolactin levels in humans from birth to adult life, *Pediatr. Res.* **7**:534–540.

72. HARRIS, G. W., AND LEVINE, S., 1965, Sexual differentiation of the brain and its experimental control, *J. Physiol. (London)* **181**:379–400.

73. HAWORTH, J. C., MEDOVY, H., AND LEWIS, A. J., 1961, Cebocephaly with endocrine dysgenesis, *J. Pediatr.* **59**:726–733.

74. HAYEK, A., DRISCOLL, S. G., AND WARSHAW, J. B., 1974, Endocrine studies in anencephaly, *J. Clin. Invest.* **52**:1636–1641.

75. HEGGESTAD, C. B., AND WELLS, L. J., 1965, Experiments on the contribution of somatotrophin to prenatal growth in the rat, *Acta Anat. (Basel)* **60**:348–361.

76. HODGES, R. E., HAMILTON, H. E., AND KEETTEL, W. C., 1952, Pregnancy in myxedema, *Arch. Intern. Med. (Chicago)* **90**:863–868.

77. HOLMES, L. B., FRANTZ, A. G., RABKIN, M. T., SOELDNER, J. S., AND CRAWFORD, J. D., 1968, Normal growth with subnormal growth-hormone levels, *N. Engl. J. Med.* **279**:559–566.

78. HOMOKI, J., BIRK, J., LOOS, U., ROTHENBUCHNER, G., FAZEKAS, A. T. A., AND TELLER, W. M., 1975, Thyroid function in term newborn infants with congenital goiter, *J. Pediatr.* **86**:753–758.

79. HUNTER, W. M., AND GREENWOOD, F. C., 1964, A radio-immunoelectrophoretic assay of human growth hormone, *Biochem. J.* **91**:43–56.

80. HUTCHINSON, D. L., WESTOVER, J. L., AND WILL, D. W., 1962, The destruction of the maternal and fetal pituitary glands in subhuman primates, *Amer. J. Obstet. Gynecol.* **83**:857–865.

81. HWANG, U. K., AND WELLS, L. J., 1959, Hypophysis–thyroid system in the fetal rat: Thyroid after hypophyseoprivia, thyroxin, triiodothyronine, thyrotropin and growth hormone, *Anat. Rec.* **134**:125–141.

82. JACOBS, L. S., SNEID, D. S., GARLAND, J. T., LARON, A., AND DAUGHADAY, W. H., 1976, Receptor-active growth hormone in Laron dwarfism, *J. Clin. Endocrinol.* **42**:403–406.

83. JACQUOT, R., AND KRETCHMER, N., 1964, Effect of fetal decapitation on enzymes of glycogen metabolism, *J. Biol. Chem.* **239**:1301–1304.

84. JAILER, J. W., 1949, The pituitary–adrenal relationship in infant rat, *Proc. Soc. Exp. Biol. Med.* **72**:638–639.

85. JOHANNISSON, E., 1968, Foetal adrenal cortex in human: Its ultrastructure at different stages of development and in different function states, *Acta Endocrinol. (Copenhagen)* **58**:(Suppl. 130):7–107.

86. JOSIMOVICH, J. B., WEISS, G., AND HUTCHINSON, D. L., 1974, Sources and disposition of pituitary prolactin in maternal circulation, amniotic fluid, fetus and placenta in the pregnant rhesus monkey, *Endocrinology* **94**:1364–1371.

87. JOST, A., 1951, Récherches sur la différenciation sexuelle de l'embryon de lapin. IV. Organogenese sexuelle masculine après décapitation du foetus, *Arch. Anat. Microsc. Morphol. Exp.* **40**:247–281.

88. JOST, A., 1953, Sur le developpement de la thyroide

chez le foetus de lapin décapité, *Arch. Anat. Microsc. Morphol. Exp.* **42**:168–183.

89. JOST, A., 1954, Hormonal factors in the development of the fetus, *Cold Spring Harbor Symp. Quant. Biol.* **19**:167–180.

90. JOST., A., 1957, The secretory activities of fetal endocrine glands and their effect upon target organs, in: *Gestation* (C. A. Villee, ed.), pp. 129–171, Josiah Macy, Jr., Foundation, New York.

91. JOST, A., 1961, The role of fetal hormones in prenatal development, *Harvey Lect.* **55**:201–226.

92. JOST. A., 1966, Anterior pituitary function in foetal life, in: *The Pituitary Gland* (G. W. Harris and B. T. Donovan, eds.), Vol. 2, pp. 299–323, University of California Press, Berkeley.

93. JOST, A., MOREL, F. F., AND MAROIS, M., 1952, Nouvelles récherches à l'aide du radioiode I^{131} sur la fonction thyroidienne due foetus de lapin décapité, *C. R. Soc. Biol. (Paris)* **146**:1066–1070.

94. KALKHOFF, R., SCHALCH, D. S., WALKER, J. L., BECK, P., AND KIPNIS, D. M., 1964, Diabetogenic factors associated with pregnancy, *Trans. Assoc. Amer. Physicians* **77**:270–280.

95. KAPLAN, S. L., AND GRUMBACH, M. M., 1967, Growth hormone in the human fetus and in anencephaly, *International Symposium on Growth Hormone* (Italy) *Excerpta Med. Int. Congr. Ser.* **142**:51.

96. KAPLAN, S. L., GRUMBACH, M. M., AND SHEPARD, T. H., 1969, Gonadotropins in serum and pituitary of human fetuses and infants, Society for Pediatric Research, Thirty-ninth Annual Meeting Program and Abstracts, p. 8.

97. KAPLAN, S. L., GRUMBACH, M. M., AND SHEPARD, T. H., 1972, The ontogenesis of human fetal hormones. I. Growth hormone and insulin, *J. Clin. Invest.* **51**:3080–3093.

98. KENNY, F. M., DRASH, A., CARCES, L. Y., AND SUSEN, A., 1968, Iatrogenic hypopituitarism in craniopharyngioma; unexplained catch-up growth in 3 children, *J. Pediatr.* **72**:766–775.

99. KENNY, F. M., PREEYASOMBAT, C., AND MIGEON, C. J., 1966, Cortisol production rate. II. Normal infants, children and adults, *Pediatrics* **37**:34–42.

100. KENNY, F. M., PREEYASOMBAT, C., SPAULDING, J. S., AND MIGEON, C. J., 1966, Cortisol production rate. IV. Infants born of steroid-treated mothers and of diabetic mothers. Infants with trisomy syndrome and with anencephaly, *Pediatrics* **37**:960–966.

101. KITCHELL, R. L., AND WELLS, L. J., 1952, Functioning of the hypophysis and adrenals in fetal rats: Effects of hypophysectomy, adrenalectomy, castration, injected ACTH and implanted sex hormones, *Anat. Rec.* **112**:561–586.

102. KLEIN, A. H., AGUSTIN, A. V., AND FOLEY, T. P., JR., 1974, Successful laboratory screening for congenital hypothyroidism, *Lancet* **2**:77–79.

103. KNOBIL, E., AND JOSIMOVICH, J. B., 1958, Placental

transfer of thyrotrophic hormone, thyroxime, tri-iodothyronine and insulin in the rat, *Ann. N. Y. Acad. Sci.* **75**:895–904.

104. LANMAN, J. T., 1953, The fetal zone of the adrenal gland. Its developmental course, comparative anatomy, and possible physiologic functions, *Medicine* **32**:398–430.

105. LANMAN, J. T., 1962, An interpretation of human foetal adrenal structure and function, in: *The Human Adrenal Cortex* (A. R. Currie, T. Symington, and J. K. Grant, eds.), pp. 547–558, The Williams & Wilkins Co., Baltimore.

106. LARON, Z., AND MANNHEIMER, S., 1966, measurement of human growth hormone, *Isr. J. Med. Sci.* **2**:115–119.

107. LARON, Z., PERTZELAN, A., AND MANNHEIMER, S., 1966, Genetic pituitary dwarfism with high serum concentration of growth hormone. A new error of metabolism?, *Isr. J. Med. Sci.* **2**:152–155.

108. LARON, Z., PERTZELAN, A., MANNHEIMER, S., GOLDMAN, J., AND GUTTMAN, S., 1966, Lack of placental transfer of human growth hormone, *Acta Endocrinol. (Copenhagen)* **53**:687–692.

109. LARSEN, P. R., MERKER, A., AND PARLOW, A. F., 1976, Immunoassay of human TSH using dried blood samples, *J. Clin. Endocrinol. Metab.* **42**:987–990.

110. LEVINA, S. E., 1968, Endocrine features in development of human hypothalamus, hypophysis and placenta, *Gen. Comp. Endocrinol.* **11**:151–159.

111. LIGGINS, G. C., AND KENNEDY, P. C., 1968, Effects of electrocoagulation of the foetal lamb hypophysis on growth and development, *J. Endocrinol.* **40**:371–381.

112. LITTLE, B., SMITH, O. W., JESSIMAN, A. G., SELENKOW, H. A., VAN'T HOFF, W., EGLIN, J. M., AND MOORE, F. D., 1958, Hypophysectomy during pregnancy in a patient with cancer of the breast: Case report with hormone studies, *J. Clin. Endocrinol.* **18**:425–443.

113. MARTINDALE, F. M., 1941, Initiation and early development of thyrotropic function in the incubating chick, *Anat. Rec.* **79**:373–393.

114. MERIMEE, T. J., HALL, J., RABINOWITZ, D., McKUSICK, V. A., AND RIMOIN, D. L., 1968, An unusual variety of endocrine dwarfism: Subresponsiveness to growth in a sexually mature dwarf, *Lancet* **2**:191–193.

115. MERIMEE, T. J., RIMOIN, D. L., AND CAVALLI-SFORZA, L. C., 1972, Metabolic studies in the African pygmy, *J. Clin. Invest.* **51**:395–401.

116. MERIMEE, T. J., RIMOIN, D. L., CAVALLI-SFORZA, L. C., RABINOWITZ, D., AND McKUSICK, V. A., 1968, Metabolic effects of human growth hormone in the African pygmy, *Lancet* **2**:194, 195.

117. MICHIE, E. A., 1966, Oestrogen levels in urine and amniotic fluid in pregnancy with live anencephalic foetus and the effect of intraamniotic injection of sodium dehydroepiandrosterone sulphate on these levels, *Acta Endocrinol. (Copenhagen)* **51**:535–542.

118. MIGEON, C. J., KENNY, F. M., KOWARSKI, A., SNIPES, C. A., SPAULDING, J. S., FINKELSTEIN, J. W., AND BLIZZARD, R. M., 1968, The syndrome of the congenital adrenocortical unresponsiveness to ACTH: Report of six cases, *Pediatr. Res.* **2**:501–513.

119. MINTZ, D. H., CHEZ, R. A., HORGER, E. O., III, 1969, Fetal insulin and growth hormone metabolism in the subhuman primate, *J. Clin. Invest.* **48**:176–186.

120. MITSKEVICH, M. S., AND LEVINA, S. E., 1965, Investigation on the structure and gonadotropic activity of anterior pituitary in human embryogenesis, *Arch. Anat. Microsc. Morphol. Exp.* **54**:129–143.

121. MOSIER, H. D., 1956, Hypoplasia of the pituitary and adrenal cortex: Report of occurrence in twin siblings and autopsy findings, *J. Pediatr.* **48**:633–639.

122. MUELHEIMS, G. H., FRANCIS, F. E., AND KINSELLA, R. A., JR., 1969, Suppression of the hypothalamic–pituitary–adrenal axis in the newborn dog, *Endocrinology* **85**:365–367.

123. NANAGAS, J. C., 1925, A comparison of the growth of the body dimensions of anencephalic human fetuses with normal fetal growth as determined by graphic analysis and empirical formulae, *Amer. J. Anat.* **35**:455–494.

124. NICHOLS, J., 1956, Observations on the adrenal of the premature anencephalic fetus, *Arch. Pathol. (Chicago)* **62**:312–317.

125. NICHOLS, J., LESCURE, O. L., AND MIGEON, C. J., 1958, Levels of 17-hydroxycorticosteroids and 17-ketosteroids in maternal and cord plasma in term anencephaly, *J. Clin. Endocrinol.* **18**:444–452.

126. NIEMI, M., IKONEN, M., AND HERVONEN, A., 1967, Histochemistry and fine structure of the interstitial tissue in the human foetal testis, in: *Endocrinology of the Testis, Ciba Foundation Colloq. Endocrinol. [Proc.]* (G. E. W. Wolstenholme and M. O'Connor, eds.), Vol. 16, pp. 31–52, Little, Brown and Company, Boston.

127. PARLOW, A., 1966, The pituitary content of growth and other hormones during fetal and later life, in: *Human Pituitary Growth Hormone: Report of the Fifty-fourth Ross Conference on Pediatric Research* (R. M. Blizzard, ed.), p. 94, Ross Laboratories, Columbus, Ohio.

128. PERRIN, E. V., AND BENIRSCHKE, K., 1958, Somatic sex of anencephalic infants, *J. Clin. Endocrinol.* **18**:327–328.

129. PETERSON, R. R., AND YOUNG, W. C., 1952, The problem of placental permeability for thyrotrophin, propylthiouracil and thyroxine in the guinea pig, *Endocrinology* **50**:218–255.

130. POPERT, A. J., 1962, Pregnancy and adrenocortical hormones. Some aspects of their interaction in rheumatic diseases, *Br. Med. J.* **1**:967–972.

131. PORTEOUS, I. B., AND BECK, J. S., 1968, The differentiation of the acidophil cell in the human

foetal adenohypophysis, *J. Pathol. Bacteriol.* **96**:455–462.

132. POTTER, E. L., 1961, *Pathology of the Fetus and the Infant,* 2nd Ed., pp.|331 and 332, Year Book Medical Publishers, Chicago.

133. PURVES, H. D., 1966, Cytology of the adenohypophysis, in: *The Pituitary Gland* (G. W. Harris and B. T. Donovan, eds.), Vol. 1, pp. 147–232, University of California Press, Berkeley.

134. RAITI, S., HOLZMAN, G. B., SCOTT, R. I., AND BLIZZARD, R. M., 1967, Evidence for the placental transfer of tri-iodothyronine in human beings, *N. Engl. J. Med.* **277**:456–459.

135. REID, J. R., 1960, Congenital absence of the pituitary gland, *J. Pediatr.* **56**:658–664.

136. REYNOLDS, J. W., 1965, The excretion of two Δ5-3β-OH, 16α-hydroxysteroids by normal infants and children, *J. Clin. Endocrinol.* **25**:416–423.

137. REYNOLDS, J. W., MANCUSO, S., WIQVIST, N., AND DICZFALUSY, E., 1968, Physiological role of 16-keto-androstenediol (16-keto ADL) in the fetoplacental unit, *Pediatr. Res.* **2**:413–414.

138. RICE, B. F., AND PONTHIER, R., JR., 1968, Luteinizing hormone and growth hormone activity of the human fetal pituitary, *J. Clin. Endocrinol.* **28**:1071, 1072.

139. RIMOIN, D. L., MERIMEE, T. J., AND MCKUSICK, V. A., 1966, Growth-hormone deficiency in man: An isolated, recessively inherited defect, *Science* **152**:1635–1637.

140. RIMOIN, D. L., MERIMEE, T. J., AND MCKUSICK, V. A., 1966, Sexual ateliotic dwarfism: A recessively inherited isolated deficiency of growth hormone, *Trans. Assoc. Amer. Physicians* **79**:297–311.

141. RIMOIN, D. L., MERIMEE, T. J., RABINOWITZ, D., MCKUSICK, V. A., AND CAVALLI-SFORZA, L. L., 1967, Growth hormone in African pygmies, *Lancet* **2**:523–526.

142. SALAZAR, H., MACAULAY, M. A., CHARLES, D., AND PARDO, M., 1969, The human hypophysis in anencephaly. I. Ultrastructure of the pars distalis, *Arch. Pathol. (Chicago)* **87**:201–211.

143. SCOMMEGNA, A., NEDOSS, B. R., AND CHATTORAJ, S. C., 1968, Maternal urinary estriol excretion after dehydroepiandrosterone-sulfate infusion and adrenal stimulation and suppression, *Obstet. Gynecol.* **31**:526–533.

144. SEITHRE, A. E., AND WELLS, L. J., 1951, Accelerated growth of the thyroid in normal and "hypophysectomized" fetal rats given thyrotropin, *Endocrinology* **49**:369–373.

145. SHACKLETON, C. H. L., AND MITCHELL, F. L., 1967, The measurement of 3β-hydroxy-Δ5 steroids in human fetal blood, amniotic fluid, infant urine and adult urine, *Steroids* **10**:359–385.

146. SHAYWITZ, B. A., FINKELSTEIN, J., HELLMAN, L., AND WEITZMAN, E. D., 1971, Growth hormone in newborn infants during sleep–wake periods, *Pediatrics* **48**:103–109.

147. SHEPARD, T. H., 1967, Onset of function in the

human fetal thyroid: Biochemical and radioautographic studies from organ culture, *J. Clin. Endocrinol.* **27**:945–958.

148. SHEPARD, T. H., AND ANDERSEN, H. J., 1969, cited in SHEPARD, T. H., 1975, Development of the thyroid gland, in: *Endocrine and Genetic Diseases of Childhood* (L. I. Gardner, ed.), pp. 200–206, W. B. Saunders Co., Philadelphia.

149. SILER-KHODR, T. M., MORGENSTERN, L. L., AND GREENWOOD, F. C., 1974, Hormone synthesis and release from human fetal adenohypophyses *in vitro, J. Clin. Endocrinol. Metab.* **39**:891–905.

150. SIMMER, H. H., DIGNAM, W. J., EASTERLING, W. E., JR., FRANKLAND, M. V., AND NAFTOLIN, F., 1966, Neutral C^{19}-steroids and steroid sulfates in human pregnancy. III. Dehydroepiandrosterone, 16α-hydroxydehydroepiandrosterone sulfate, 16α-hydroxydehydroepiandrosterone sulfate in cord blood and blood of pregnant women with and without treatment with corticoids, *Steroids* **8**:179–193.

151. SOLOMON, S., AND FRIESEN, H. G., 1968, Endocrine relations between mother and fetus, *Annu. Rev. Med.* **19**:399–430.

152. STANDBURY, J. B., ROCMANS, P., BUHLER, U. K., AND OCHI, Y., 1968, Congenital hypothyroidism with impaired thyroid response to thyrotropin, *N. Engl. J. Med.* **279**:1132–1136.

153. STARK, E., GYEVAI, A., SZALAY, K., AND ACS, Z., 1965, Hypophyseal–adrenal activity in combined human foetal tissue cultures, *Can. J. Physiol. Pharmacol.* **43**:1–7.

154. STEINER, M. M., AND BOGGS, J. D., 1965, Absence of pituitary gland, hypothyroidism, hypoadrenalism and hypogonadism in a 17-year-old dwarf, *J. Clin. Endocrinol.* **25**:1591–1598.

155. TAHKA, H., 1951, On the weight and structure of the adrenal glands and the factors affecting them, in children of 0–2 years, *Acta Pediatr. Scand.* **40**(*Suppl. 81*).

156. TAYLOR, N. R. W., LORAINE, J. A., AND ROBERTSON, H. A., 1953, The estimation of ACTH in human pituitary tissue, *J. Endocrinol.* **9**:334–341.

157. TYSON, J. E., HWANG, P., GUYDA, H., AND FRIESEN, H. G., 1972, Studies of prolactin in human pregnancy, *Amer. J. Obstet. Gynecol.* **113**:14–20.

158. TUCHMANN-DUPLESSIS, H., 1959. Étude des glandes endocrines des anencéphales. Déduction sur les correlations hypophyso–nerveuses du foetus humain, *Biol. Neonate* **1**:8–32.

159. TUCHMANN-DUPLESSIS, H., AND MERCIER-PAROT, L., 1963, Étude comparative de la structure de l'hypophyse et de la surrénale des anencéphales et des hydrocéphales humains, *C. R. Soc. Biol. (Paris)* **157**:977–981.

160. UTIGER, R. D., WILBER, J. F., CORNBLATH, M., HARM, J. P., AND MACK, R. E., 1968, TSH secretion in newborn infants and children, *J. Clin. Invest.* **47**:97a (abstract).

161. VEST, J., GIRARD, J., AND BUHLER, U., 1963

Metabolic effects of short term administration of human growth hormone in infancy and early childhood, *Acta Endocrinol. (Copenhagen)* **44**: 613–624.

162. VILLEE, D. B., 1969, Development of endocrine function in the human placenta and fetus, *N. Engl. J. Med.* **281**:473–384, 533–541.

163. WELLS, L. J., 1957, Effect of fetal endocrines on fetal growth, in: *Gestation* (C. A. Villee, ed.), pp. 187–227, Josiah Macy, Jr., Foundation, New York.

164. WESTPHAL, O., 1968, Human growth hormone: A methodological and clinical study, *Acta Pediatr. Scand., Suppl. 182.*

165. WINTER, J. S. D., FAIMAN, D., HOBSON, W. C., PRASAD, A. V., AND REYES, F. I., 1975, Pituitary–gonadal relations in infancy. I. Patterns of serum gonadotropin concentrations from birth to four years of age in man and chimpanzee, *J. Clin. Endocrinol. Metab.* **40**:545–551.

166. WINTERS, A. J., ESKAY, R. L., AND PORTER, J. C.,

1974, Concentration and distribution of TRH and LRH in the human fetal brain, *J. Clin. Endocrinol. Metab.* **39**:960–963.

167. WINTERS, A. J., OLIVER, C., COLSTON, P. C., MACDONALD, P. C., AND PORTER, J. C., 1974, Plasma ACTH levels in the human fetus and neonate as related to age and parturition, *J. Clin. Endocrinol. Metab.* **39**:269–273.

168. YEN, S. S. C., PEARSON, O. H., AND STRATMAN, S., 1965, Growth hormone levels in maternal and cord blood, *J. Clin. Endocrinol.* **25**:655–660.

169. ZAMENHOF, S., MOSLEY, J., AND SCHULLER, E., 1966, Stimulation of the proliferation of cortical neurons by prenatal treatment with growth hormone, *Science* **152**:1396–1397.

170. ZONDEK, L. H., AND ZONDEK, T., 1965, Leydig cells of the foetus and newborn in normal and toxaemic pregnancy, *Biol. Neonate* **8**:1–22.

171. ZONDEK, L. H., AND ZONDEK, T., 1965, Observations on the testis in anencephaly with special reference to the Leydig cells, *Biol. Neonate* **8**:329–347.

CHAPTER 39

Insulin and Glucagon

Mark A. Sperling

1. Introduction

Energy homeostasis requires the integration of nutrient fluxes via appropriate enzymes, the activity of which is modulated by substrates and hormones. Insulin and glucagon, which are produced by, respectively, the β- and α-cells of the pancreas, occupy a key role in this energy homeostasis.

In the mature organism, insulin is secreted in times of fuel abundance, and acts as a major hormone during periods of anabolism; glucagon is secreted in times of fuel deprivation or need, and acts as a major hormone for catabolism. Together, these pancreatic hormones act as a dual push–pull system, directing the disposition of endogenous or exogenous fuels and thus permitting moment-to-moment energy and principally glucose homeostasis during the cyclical alterations of food intake and deprivation.

A relationship between insulin and glucagon exists not only at a functional metabolic level, but also at a subcellular level. Intercellular communications between pancreatic α- and β-cells were recently demonstrated by electron microscopy,[93–95] providing a means whereby the metabolic functions of one cell may modify the activity of the other.

Because of their key role in normal metabolism, and the metabolic disturbances resulting from abnormalities in their secretion or action, insulin and glucagon have been the subject of extensive investigation. Major contributions to the understanding of the processes of synthesis, secretion, and action have resulted from electron microscopy, the availability of pure crystalline preparations, the ability to measure the hormones in biological fluids via radioimmunoassay, elucidation of the "second messenger" concept and the role of cyclic AMP (cAMP) in polypeptide hormone action, the identification and characterization of specific receptors for hormones on target-cell plasma membranes, and the ability to isolate islets for *in vitro* studies. A comprehensive review of the secretion and action of insulin and glucagon is beyond the scope or purpose of this chapter. In-depth reviews are provided in the books edited by Steiner and Freinkel[124] and Lefebvre and Unger,[66] and in papers by Sperling,[118] Kipnis,[62] Lacy,[64] Cahill,[19] and Unger.[130]

2. Synopsis of Insulin and Glucagon Secretion and Action

Briefly, insulin is synthesized in the endoplasmic reticulum of β-cells as proinsulin, a single-chain polypeptide in which the carboxy terminus of the

Mark A. Sperling · Department of Pediatrics, University of California at Los Angeles School of Medicine, Harbor General Hospital Campus, Torrance, California 90509

B-chain is linked to the amino end of the A-chain by a connecting peptide, or C-peptide. The C-peptide is split off in the Golgi apparatus, where insulin granules are packaged in membranes and align themselves along the microtubular microfilamentous system of the cell. Secretion occurs by emiocytosis, a process in which the membranes of insulin granules fuse with the cell membrane. Stimuli to insulin secretion include amino acids, fatty acids, and carbohydrates, principally glucose. A specific glucose receptor exists on the cell surface of the β-cell; evidence for this concept derives from the differential effects of anomeric forms of D-glucose, the α-anomer being more potent in inducing insulin secretion,[49,77] and the stimulating effects of nonmetabolizable sugars such as galactose.[76] Subsequent intracellular glycolytic metabolism of glucose provides the energy source for further insulin synthesis. Thus, insulin secretion in response to stimuli is biphasic, as reflected in *in vitro* or *in vivo* studies, the initial phase representing preformed insulin already aligned on the cell-web, the second phase representing newly synthesized insulin. Translocation of ions, primarily affecting the transfer of calcium into the cell cytoplasm from extra- and intracellular stores, is involved in the process of insulin secretion.[73] Furthermore, insulin secretion is modulated by the autonomic nervous system; α-adrenergic impulses inhibit while β-adrenergic stimuli promote insulin secretion via β-adrenergic receptors of the β-2 type.[70] The system is linked to cAMP. The parasympathetic system, via the vagus, also stimulates insulin secretion.[12,138] Certain GI hormones and glucagon itself directly enhance insulin secretion, as does growth hormone; indirect increases in insulin secretion result from the "antiinsulin" effects of glucocorticoids and sex steroids.[105,118] Insulin action is initiated by specific binding of target cell receptors in tissues such as liver and fat cells[26,110] and the subsequent translation, by mechanisms not yet fully identified, into enzyme action, leading to glycogen and fat synthesis from glucose and protein synthesis from amino acids. Glucagon too is now believed to be synthesized in a larger prohormone form,[90] but the mechanisms of synthesis and release are not well defined. Glucagon secretion is stimulated by amino acids and hypoglycemia; hyperglycemia suppresses glucagon secretion.[130] The autonomic nervous system via epinephrine can stimulate glucagon secretion,[35,138] and parasympathetic impulses also stimulate glucagon release, since truncal vagotomy inhibits glucagon secretion following arginine, or insulin-induced hypoglycemia.[15] The type of adrenergic receptor that modulates glucagon has not been precisely identified.[119]

Glucagon action is primarily on the liver, and is initiated by binding to receptors on cell membranes[109] with stimulation of cAMP.[11] The latter is responsible for glycogenolysis; glucagon also stimulates gluconeogenesis.[29]

In contrast to the situation in the mature organism, knowledge of secretion and action of these hormones in the fetus and newborn is less complete. This chapter focuses on current concepts of the embryogenesis of insulin and glucagon secretion and the possible role of these substances in perinatal glucose homeostasis.

3. Embryonic Development of the Endocrine Pancreas

The pancreas appears at approximately 20–25 somites in most species including man, in whom this stage corresponds to the 4th week of gestation. Development of the pancreatic islets occurs in two phases. The first (primary) transition involves the formation of the pancreatic diverticulum. Although cytodifferentiation of exocrine or endocrine β-cells cannot be recognized, their specific secretory products, namely, certain hydrolytic enzymes and insulin, can be recognized. In contrast, well-differentiated α-cells containing glucagon granules in abundance are already present and account for some 5% of all cells. At this stage, mesenchymal cells accumulate around the primitive gut in proximity to the pancreatic diverticulum.[100] Further epithelial development of the pancreas is dependent on this mesenchymal tissue or a factor extracted from it. The factor is not tissue- or species-specific, since it can be extracted from chick embryos and utilized for rat pancreas, where it acts to stimulate DNA synthesis[67] via cAMP.[101] In addition, the mesenchymal factor influences differentiation, since in its absence, α-cells predominate at the expense of acinar tissue; insulin and β-cells remain constant. Thus, the origin of the α-cells and acinar cells must be from a common stem cell, the differentiation of which can be shifted in one or the other direction by the mesenchymal factor. The origin of the endocrine β-cells is predominantly endodermal, although a neural crest origin for some of the islet endocrine cells is also likely,[98] particularly since the D-cells (α-1 cells) are now known to contain somatostatin,[104] a tetradecapeptide hormone initially isolated from the hypothalamus by its action in inhibiting release of growth hormone,[131] and now known to be capable of inhibiting insulin and glucagon secretion.[131]

The second phase, or secondary transition, is characterized by an increase in the exocrine and endocrine β-cells, the morphological and functional features of which are similar to those of the mature cell. Thus, α-cells predominate early in gestation, while β-cells and insulin synthesis occur later, implying that insulin has no major role in early fetal development.[53,69,100] At birth, the ratio of α-cells to β-cells is approximately 1, while in adult man, the α : β ratio is between 1 : 3 and 1 : 9.[81,84] Because glucagon is so predominant in fetal life, where it appears before any other hormone, and before its specific target cells in liver and fat can respond, a possible role for glucagon in regulating early differentiation of the embryo via cAMP was proposed by Rall et al.[106] The organization as well as the relative numbers of α- and β-cells also change during gestation. Initially, α- and β-cells exist in adjacent clusters. Later, the β-cells become enveloped by α-cells, and after 30 weeks, both cell types are mingled as they are in the adult. The possibility that the endocrine stem cells are pluripotent, permitting interconversion of α- and β-cells is discussed by Picet and Rutter,[100] but apart from the mesenchymal factor, little is known of the regulation of these processes.

3.1. Fetal Insulin Content and Secretion

Pancreatic insulin content is higher in the fetus than in the adult, being 6.3 ± 1.1 U/g between 20 and 32 weeks, and 12.7 ± 3.2 U/g between 34 and 40 weeks; adult values are 2.1 ± 0.3 U/g.[125] A similar high insulin content that increases steadily with gestation was reported by Schaeffer et al.[112] (Table I).

In contrast to this high insulin content, fetal insulin secretion is obtunded, so that release mechanisms rather than synthetic processes are responsible for low circulating levels. There is universal agreement that glucose is at best a weak stimulus to acute insulin secretion in the fetus. Pancreatic islets isolated from human fetuses of 12–16 weeks' gestation failed to respond with a significant increase in insulin secretion during incubation with a high glucose medium[28]; modest increases were reported with pancreas slices of fetuses of 7–20 weeks.[112] Some maturation of this process exists, however, since there is a significant correlation between insulin response to glucose stimulation and gestational age or fetal body weight in the period from 15 to 24 weeks.[6] The amino acids arginine and leucine are effective stimuli for fetal insulin secretion *in vitro*, as are glucagon, the phosphodiesterase inhibitor theophylline, and dibutyryl cAMP; the latter three compounds all raise cAMP levels and are effective even in the presence of low (60 mg/dl) or no glucose in the incubating medium.[28,51,73,81] Tolbutamide is without effect, but certain ions such as potassium and barium, as well as ouabain, are effective.[81] Thus, *in vitro* studies indicate that the β-cell is functional from 14 to 24 weeks, responding to amino acids, ions, and factors that raise intracellular cAMP, but not to glucose.

The *in vivo* situation is more difficult to define in humans because of the potential errors introduced by the stresses of experimental manipulation. In studies preceding hysterotomy, however, it was determined that glucose and arginine are without effect in promoting insulin secretion in the human fetus at midterm.[5,61] Recently, by use of the

Table I. Total Glucagon and Insulin in Human Fetal Pancreas

Gestational age (weeks)	Glucagon concentration (ng/mg tissue)[a]		Insulin (μU/mg tissue)[a]
7–10.0	1.28 ($n = 1$)[b]	4.0 ± 1.2 ($n = 7$)[c]	333 ± 64 ($n = 7$)[c]
10.5–15.5	1.98 ± 0.5 ($n = 2$)[b]	9.7 ± 2.2 ($n = 6$)[c]	1189 ± 359 ($n = 6$)[c]
16–25	5.57 ± 0.86 ($n = 4$)[b]	66.0 ± 15.6 ($n = 5$)[c]	4172 ± 1159 ($n = 5$)[c]

[a] Mean ± S.E.M.
[b] Data adapted from Assan and Boillot,[9] with the authors' permission.
[c] Data adapted from Schaeffer et al.,[112] with the authors' permission.

technique of fetal blood-sampling via scalp capillaries, it was possible to demonstrate that prior to the onset of labor, the normal human fetus is again relatively unresponsive to high glucose concentrations.[91] Similar conclusions were reached in studies employing the subhuman fetal monkey late in gestation, when direct intrafetal injections are possible.[21,85] Neither glucose nor arginine was an effective stimulus for insulin, but as with the *in vitro* studies, glucagon administration caused prompt insulin release. Also, the intravascular administration of glucose and theophylline together into the monkey fetus *in vivo* resulted in a rise in fetal plasma insulin; glucose or theophylline alone was incapable of elevating insulin.[24] These studies are compatible with the concept that the lack of insulin secretion in the intact fetus *in vivo* following glucose is related to a deficiency in the ability to generate cAMP or to its rapid destruction via phosphodiesterase. Indeed, the phosphodiesterase that inactivates cAMP was reported to be very active,[108] and a 2- to 3-fold increase in islet cAMP occurs in newborn rat pups over the initial 72 hr of life.[48,86] Thus, transition from fetal to adult patterns of responsiveness may in part be due to maturation of cAMP systems, and may account for the persistence of poor insulin secretion following glucose in the immediate newborn period in humans. As could be predicted, theophylline or glucagon in pharmacological doses increases insulin secretion in newborn infants.[46]

3.2. Factors That Affect Fetal and Neonatal Insulin Secretion

3.2.1. Source of Fetal Plasma Insulin

Although early data suggested that insulin might be transferred bidirectionally across the placenta,[40] the bulk of evidence now favors lack of any placental permeability to insulin.[81]

3.2.2. Substrates and Hormones

The poor insulin secretory response *in utero* following acute glucose challenge was described in Section 3.1. The nutritional milieu, however, can affect the development of insulin secretion. Thus, hypertrophy and hyperplasia of fetal islets as well as an increased insulin content are seen in infants of diabetic mothers,[20,125] in whom chronic, albeit intermittent, hyperglycemia is reflected in the fetus

by virtue of facilitated diffusion of glucose across the placenta.[17] These infants respond *in utero* to glucose with an adult type of biphasic insulin secretory response,[91] and a similar hypersecretion of insulin relative to normal infants is seen in the immediate neonatal period.[55,129] The insulin responses of infants of gestationally diabetic mothers, who do not require insulin therapy and therefore have less hyperglycemia, are modestly elevated at delivery and following glucose or other stimuli.[102,133] These results suggest that chronic *in utero* hyperglycemia may modify the developmental process of insulin secretion by accelerating the maturation of the secretory mechanism. Similar results were reported in fetal and newborn rats, which serve as a convenient model, although extrapolation to the human is made with caution.[39]

It should be noted that secretion, and not biosynthesis, is accelerated by chronic *in utero* hyperglycemia, since even in normal pregnancy, fetal insulin synthesis is comparable in rate to that of the neonatal period and can be stimulated by glucose.[7,52] Postnatal feeding patterns in rats also can profoundly modify insulin secretion to a glucose challenge; a high-caloric intake favors high insulin secretion and a low intake, low insulin secretion.[7] However, the level of glucose alone cannot totally explain the maturational process, since this process seems to be independent of glucose after birth,[38] and cannot be easily reproduced by prolonged culture of rat islets in a high-glucose medium.[8,59]

As outlined in Section 3.1, amino acids are potent stimuli *in vitro*,[84,112] but are poor stimuli for insulin secretion in the fetus *in vivo*.[85] In contrast to this fetal *in vivo* situation, and to the sluggish insulin response to glucose following delivery, neonatal insulin responsiveness to amino acids is often striking particularly when a mixture of amino acids is used. These stimulatory effects are additive when glucose infusion is combined with amino acids.[45] Since the reported infants were premature, the studies imply that insulin responsiveness to amino acids precedes that of glucose; these findings have further relevance to glucagon secretion, as outlined subsequently. Similar insulin responses to amino acids have now been reported in full-term infants,[61] although the responses were less striking. The role of fatty acids in insulin secretion in the fetus and newborn is undefined.

Certain hormones also affect the development of insulin secretion. In anencephalic infants, the endocrine pancreas develops normally if the mother has unimpaired carbohydrate metabolism. If the mother's glucose tolerance is abnormal, however, hypertrophy and hyperplasia of fetal pancreatic B-cells are found only if the fetal hypothalamic–pituitary system is functional.[132] Similar results were reported in decapitated fetal rabbits,[56] and although unproved, a role for growth hormone was implicated.[84] In rat islets maintained in tissue culture, evidence was presented that glucocorticoids inhibit the proliferation of islet tissue.[65] However, growth hormone and cortisol had no effect on β-cell replication in rat pancreas monolayer culture, although in rats and humans *in vivo,* a stimulatory effect by these hormones on insulin secretion was noted.[25] Thus, any observed effects *in vivo* are probably mediated by indirect rather than direct effects on pancreatic islets.

3.2.3. Miscellaneous Factors

Oral hypoglycemic agents are capable of crossing the placenta and of affecting insulin secretion. Profoundly elevated plasma insulin concentrations have been reported to be present at birth in infants of gestationally diabetic mothers treated with sulphonylureas. These newborn infants show marked hypersecretion of insulin in response to oral glucose, and may suffer severe and prolonged hypoglycemia.[84] Finally, infants with erythroblastosis fetalis may have islet cell hyperplasia, a high pancreatic insulin content, and hyperinsulinemia at birth. This hyperinsulinemia may be associated with severe hypoglycemia, particularly if the infant is premature.[84,113] The mechanism responsible for the islet hyperplasia in erythroblastosis is not entirely clear. Schiff and Lowy[113] suggested that the placenta, an active site of insulin degradation, is even more active in erythroblastosis fetalis, in which placental hyperplasia occurs. Thus, increased destruction would require compensatory hypersecretion of insulin. An alternate hypothesis was provided by Steinke et al.,[126] who suggested that hemolysis provides increased amounts of glutathione, which splits the disulfide bonds of the two insulin chains and thereby promotes compensatory hypersecretion.

4. Metabolic Effects of Insulin *in Utero*

Early in gestation, the pancreatic insulin content is low, and in the rat at least, is sufficient to raise plasma concentrations to approximately 10^{-12} M, a level too low to exert significant metabolic effects.[100] Thus, growth during this stage of gestation must be independent of any anabolic effects of insulin. On the other hand, glucose is the primary energy source of the human fetus,[36] and certainly at term, when the respiratory quotient is close to 1. If glucose were equally important during early gestation, its utilization and disposal would have to be via insulin-independent enzyme systems. The maturation of enzyme systems for glycogen synthesis and breakdown as well as for gluconeogenesis is discussed in detail in Chapter 17. It is of interest that certain key enzymes in glycogen synthesis can be recognized prior to the actual deposition of glycogen. Moreover, the isolated perfused canine liver can switch from net glucose output to net glucose uptake when the perfusing glucose concentration is above a certain concentration, and in the absence of any significant change in the perfusing insulin concentration.[18] Thus, this hepatic process appears to be essentially independent of insulin, and implies at least some capacity for autoregulation of glucose uptake and output by liver. Similar results were reported in rats[42] and in the human fetal liver.[3]

Later in gestation, insulin assumes an important role in fetal metabolism. Cheek and Greystone[21] presented evidence that insulin promotes an increase in cell size by stimulating protein synthesis. Increase in cell size does indeed occur after the 30th week of gestation, a time when pancreatic insulin content would be adequate to exert an influence.[134] *In vitro* experiments with rhesus monkey fetal muscle demonstrate that insulin can increase glucose uptake, glucose oxidation, and incorporation of glucose into glycogen as early as 85 days' gestation, corresponding to approximately 50% of term. In addition, this insulin effect is mediated via cAMP.[16] Despite the utility of the monkey as a model of human metabolism, however, there are limitations, as evidenced by the failure of insulin to exert a significant effect on glycogen synthesis in the isolated near-term fetal monkey liver.[41] Finally, it was recently shown that insulin in pharmacological doses can inhibit the basal and stimulated rate of incorporation of alanine U ^{14}C into glucose and glycogen by human fetal liver explants maintained in cell culture.[115] The high pharmacological doses of insulin, or other agents such as glucagon, required to demonstrate an effect in this system make extrapolations to the *in vivo* physiologic situation tenuous.

By far the most compelling evidence for a significant role of insulin in fetal metabolism exists in the third trimester. The marked increase in fetal growth during this time is due in great part to fat synthesis, which is exaggerated in infants of diabetic mothers.[31] Moreover, there is a positive correlation between birth weight and serum immunoreactive insulin in normal infants and in infants of gestational diabetic mothers.[57] Since infants of diabetic mothers are hyperinsulinemic at birth, and since the transfer of free fatty acids across the human placenta is inadequate for the deposition of fat by the fetus in the last trimester,[27] the data are compatible with the concept that during the period of rapid accumulation of fat in the fetus, insulin promotes lipogenesis from glucose and possibly amino acids.

5. Glucagon in the Fetus

Only recently has the availability of radioimmunoassays for glucagon enabled the documentation of fetal pancreatic glucagon content, circulating fetal plasma glucagon concentrations, and factors that might affect glucagon secretion. Pancreatic glucagon content was studied by two groups, whose results are qualitatively similar.[9,112] These results, which are summarized in Table I, show that immunoreactive pancreatic glucagon is detectable at about the 8th week of gestation, but not before the 6th week. Thereafter, there is a logarithmic increase in glucagon content per unit weight; i.e., the increased content is not due simply to growth of the pancreatic mass. Notably, the pancreatic glucagon content at midgestation is 5–7 ng/mg pancreas tissue, as compared with 1–3 ng/mg in adult pancreas extracted under similar conditions.[9] Gastric and enteric tissues from these fetuses also contain material or materials that cross-react with glucagon antisera and are said to possess glucagonlike immunoreactivity (GLI). The precise nature and function of these substances in man are unknown, but one of the components may represent true glucagon with its full range of biological activity, as recently demonstrated in the dog.[111] Glucagon can be measured in human fetal plasma from 15 weeks' gestation onward; no detectable rise followed intraperitoneal administration or arginine.[9] This plasma glucagon must be fetal in origin, since the placenta is impermeable to glucagon

transfer in either direction in humans early and late in gestation, or in other mammals.[4,23,58,88,121]

Amino acids such as arginine or alanine stimulate release in human pancreas slices *in vitro*,[112] and in the rat or monkey fetus *in vivo*.[23,39] In humans at term, the infusion of alanine into the mother during labor caused a significant increase in neonatal umbilical cord plasma as well as maternal plasma glucagon concentration. Since glucagon does not cross the placenta while amino acids do, the findings imply that at term, human fetal α-cells can respond to amino acids.[137] Acute hypoglycemia cannot, but more prolonged hypoglycemia may, provoke glucagon secretion in the rat fetus. The parasympathetic nervous system stimulates glucagon secretion via acetylcholine; catecholamines, notably norepinephrine, also stimulate glucagon release.[39] Hyperglycemia, however, does not suppress fetal glucagon secretion in rats,[39] monkeys, or lambs.[23,33]

In sum, the human fetal pancreatic glucagon content increases progressively throughout gestation. Secretion, on the other hand, is not affected by acute changes in glucose, the substrate that exerts a major control on glucagon secretion in the normal mature organism, in which maintenance of glucose supply is the major function of glucagon. Amino acids, acetylcholine, and norepinephrine are probably capable of stimulating glucagon release in the fetus *in utero*.

5.1. Metabolic Effects of Glucagon in the Fetus

The metabolic functions of endogenous glucagon in early gestation are unknown, but its high pancreatic concentration prompted the suggestion that it might somehow influence organogenesis via its potent effect on raising cAMP levels.[100] In late gestation, direct infusion of glucagon into the fetal monkey raises the plasma glucose concentration, implying that glycogenolytic mechanisms and phosphorylase can be activated.[23] That the effect is mediated via cAMP is demonstrable in explants of rat fetal liver.[117] In nonphysiologic doses, glucagon can also increase gluconeogenesis from alanine[115] and DNA synthesis in the liver and exocrine pancreas.[74,139] In fetal rats, glucagon in pharmacological doses can induce the early appearance of enzymes involved in gluconeogenesis, including glucose-6-phosphatase, pyruvate carboxylase, p-enolpyruvate carboxykinase (PEPK), and tyrosine amino transferase (TAT).[47,140] Similar enhancement by glucagon of human fetal liver enzyme activity of PEPK and TAT in 20-week-old fetuses was reported.[63] It should be noted that in a variety of mammals, these enzymes are not induced until the time of delivery. Finally, the effects of glucagon in inducing fetal insulin secretion via cAMP were discussed in Section 3.1.

6. Insulin and Glucagon in the Immediate Neonatal Period

The transition from intrauterine to extrauterine life involves the dramatic curtailment of maternal-to-fetal nutrient supply consequent on umbilical-cord cutting. In response to this sudden deprivation of nutrients, there is a fall in the baby's circulating blood glucose concentration, accompanied by a highly significant rise in plasma glucagon concentration, which is maximum within 2 hr of birth.[17,120] Insulin concentrations are low and remain unchanged, although a slight fall from cord levels may be noted if prolonged intravenous infusions of glucose have been employed for the mother during labor (Fig. 1). The fall in glucose and rise in glucagon are significantly correlated, implying a glucagon response to the signal of hypoglycemia.[120] Cord-cutting itself, however, may be a more overriding stimulus, possibly mediated via catecholamines, since in newborn lambs, continuous infusion of somatostatin, a potent inhibitor of glucagon release, cannot prevent this neonatal rise in glucagon. In these experiments, somatostatin infusion was begun *in utero* and continued into the neonatal period; glucagon and glucose levels were low *in utero*, but despite continued somatostatin infusion during delivery, glucagon rose following cord-cutting.[43] In human newborn infants, glucose, insulin, and glucagon levels remain constant from 2 to 24 hr of life. Thereafter, there is a progressive rise in basal postabsorptive glucagon levels from day 1 to day 3 of life, and this rise is associated with, and positively correlated with, the rise of glucose to euglycemic levels, while insulin levels remain unchanged (Fig. 2). Thus, in the immediate neonatal period, the predominant set point of the insulin/glucagon ratio[130] favors glucagon, and thereby glycogenolysis and possibly gluconeogenesis. In addition, this ratio and the absolute levels of glucagon and insulin are in the range shown to markedly enhance the ketogenic capacity of the liver

in experimental animals.[79] On the basis of these hormonal changes and the known biological actions of glucagon, one could postulate that glucose could be provided for the neonatal brain, at least while glycogen stores are adequate in the first few hours. Studies of glucose turnover in neonates suggest that almost all the glucose turnover can be accounted for by brain utilization.[13] A role for glucagon in enhancing gluconeogenesis in neonatal liver is conceivable, and was shown *in vitro*[115]; direct experimental proof *in vivo* was also provided in dogs.[2] If the brain utilized most of the available glucose, an alternate source of fuel is required for muscle metabolism. However, since it is known that free fatty acids also rise in the neonatal period,[22,123] the prevailing substrate as well as the hormonal profile favor ketogenesis, and ketones could provide this source of fuel for muscle metabolism. Finally, since a similar dramatic surge in plasma glucagon was observed in the newborn rat and lamb,[37,38,122] these concepts assign a significant, and perhaps essential, role for glucagon secretion in the homeostatic adjust-

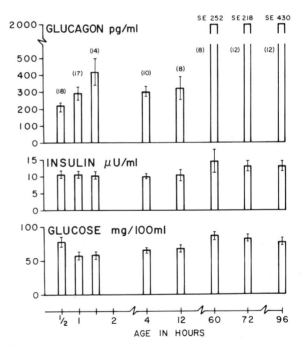

Fig. 1. Cross-sectional studies showing the spontaneous changes in immunoreactive glucagon, insulin, and glucose in the postnatal period. The vertical brackets indicate 1 S.E.M. The numbers in parentheses are the numbers of patients.

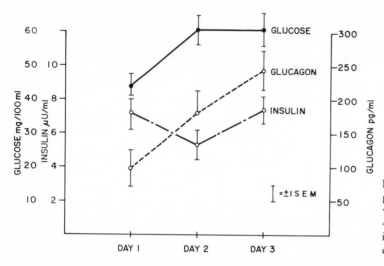

Fig. 2. Sequential changes in glucose, glucagon, and insulin in 8 infants, each of whom was sampled at approximately 24, 48, and 72 hr after birth. The increments in glucose and glucagon are significantly correlated ($r = 1.0$; $P < 0.01$).

ments of the immediate newborn period. That such a role might indeed be played by glucagon secretion is suggested by experiments in newborn lambs.[122] Infusion of somatostatin into neonatal lambs aged 24–72 hr suppressed both insulin and glucagon, and was associated with a fall in glucose. Reinfusion of glucagon to simulate physiologic levels, with maintenance of somatostatin infusion and thereby low insulin concentrations, restored glucose concentrations.

6.1. Factors That Affect Insulin and Glucagon Secretion in Newborn Infants

6.1.1. Glucose

As *in utero*, glucose is a poor stimulus to insulin secretion in the newborn period. Since insulin secretion following glucagon injection is normal, the poor response reflects continued immaturity of insulin secretory mechanisms mediated in part by immaturity of cAMP generation or its rapid destruction. Priming of the β-cell can be achieved by a constant glucose infusion of several hours' duration preceding a further bolus of glucose, which now elicits a striking increase in insulin secretion.[44] These findings clearly have implications for the interpretation of enhanced insulin secretion in infants of diabetic mothers, in whom fetal β-cells may have been "primed" by chronic hyperglycemia *in utero*. Similarly, glucose does not inhibit glucagon secre-

tion in the newborn, akin to the situation *in utero*.[72] When glucose infusion is combined with simultaneous insulin infusion, however, glucagon secretion can be inhibited in neonates.[75] Thus, the data suggest that insulin is required for the suppressive effect of glucose on glucagon secretion, possibly by facilitating the entry of glucose into α-cells. These findings again have implications for glucagon secretion in infants of diabetic mothers, in whom prolonged hyperglycemia and hyperinsulinemia coexist *in utero* (see also Chapter 17).

6.1.2. Amino Acids

In contrast to the lack of glucagon suppression by glucose, amino acids such as arginine or alanine, whether administered intravenously or orally, elicit prompt and significant glucagon secretion in the term fetus and in the initial hours of neonatal life[34,120,137] (Table II and Fig. 3). These glucagon responses are obtunded when levels of glucose are elevated.[34,135] The hyperglycemic effect of endogenous glucagon is also obtunded when plasma glucose levels are greater than 60 mg/dl,[135] and this obtundation of glucagon effect by glucose can be demontrated with exogenously administered glucagon.[103]

Although the effects of breast-feeding on the subsequent pattern of plasma pancreatic glucagon concentration in newborn infants has not been studied, it should be noted that colostrum contains more total protein, almost twice the concentra-

Table II. Response of Newborn Infants to Intravenous Alanine (1 mmol/kg)[a,b]

Substance	Time (minutes postinjection)				
	0	15	30	45	60
Glucose (mg/dl)	47.8 ± 3.1	52.5 ± 3.1	59.3 ± 4.5[c]	53 ± 4.6	56 ± 3.2
Glucagon (pg/ml)	207 ± 27	293 ± 62	262 ± 60	236 ± 45	274 ± 20[c]
Insulin (μU/ml)	6.5 ± 0.7	8.2 ± 1.5	8.6 ± 1.4	8.5 ± 0.5	9.6 ± 1.0

[a] Data from Sperling *et al.*[120]
[a] Concentrations expressed in means ± S.E.M.
[c] $P < 0.05$ in comparison with 0 time.

tion of arginine, and less carbohydrate in the form of lactose than does mature breast milk (see Chapter 16). It might therefore be anticipated that colostrum-feeding would stimulate glucagon secretion more than insulin secretion, and that this pattern of pancreatic hormone secretion would favor maintenance of glucose homeostasis in the newborn infant. Newborn infants release large amounts of GLI materials following feeding,[120] but the significance, if any, and metabolic functions of these GLI materials are entirely unknown. In the infants studied, no correlation existed between the plasma glucagon and GLI concentrations.[120]

6.2. Clinical Correlations

The aforementioned considerations permit a rational explanation of normal perinatal events in the context of glucose–glucagon–insulin interrelationships. The neonatal glucagon surge, consequent on cord-cutting and mediated via interruption of glucose supply or possibly catecholamines, with the accompanying maintenance of low spontaneous or glucose-stimulated insulin secretion, appear to be key events in neonatal homeostasis.

In addition, a surge in plasma catecholamine concentration also occurs, as reflected by a sharp rise in urinary excretion of epinephrine and norepinephrine in the immediate newborn period.[68,127] Since epinephrine and norepinephrine stimulate glucagon secretion and inhibit insulin secretion,[138] as well as activate glycogenolysis and lipolysis, the contribution of catecholamines to neonatal homeostasis is potentially considerable.

These hormonal profiles activate glycogenolysis, possibly gluconeogenesis, and also ketogenesis. Thus, the fall in glucose following interruption of its maternal supply would be arrested and glucose

could be provided for brain utilization while ketone body formation was activated as an alternate fuel source for muscle metabolism. These processes have their framework prepared *in utero*, where, in the last trimester, insulin facilitates deposition of glycogen and fat. In addition, disturbances in perinatal glucose homeostasis can be explained more rationally, though not entirely, on the basis of these hormone–substrate interrelationships.

7. Infants of Diabetic Mothers

Hypertrophy and hyperplasia of fetal islets,[20] as well as an increased insulin content,[125] have been

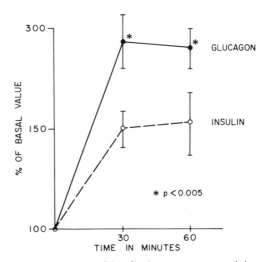

Fig. 3. Glucagon and insulin in response to arginine in newborn infants. Arginine, 0.5 g/kg, was infused and sampled via an umbilical vein catheter. All infants were less than 6 hr old.

found in infants of diabetic mothers. Also, *in utero*, these infants respond to glucose with an adult type of biphasic insulin secretory response.[17,91] Thus, a state of functional hyperinsulinism prevails *in utero*, and its metabolic effects are reflected in increased tissue fat, hepatic glycogen content, and total body size.[31,96,116] At delivery, the umbilical cord plasma insulin concentration is generally higher than in .normal newborns,[57,102] and correlates with total body size. There is a rapid fall in blood glucose concentration in the initial hours after delivery, and about half of infants of insulin-treated diabetic mothers achieve glucose levels below 20 mg/dl.[78,102] This nadir is achieved within the first hour or so, and is maintained for several more hours before glucose rises. A state of functional hyperinsulinism therefore seems to extend into the immediate neonatal period, and this concept is further supported by the finding of lower-than-normal plasma free fatty acid concentrations.[22,99] Furthermore, insulin secretion in response to glucose loading is generally exaggerated as compared with that in normal infants,[10,30,55,91,102] and the glucose disappearance rate following intravenous glucose is also accelerated. Some investigators have reported, however, that plasma immunoreactive insulin concentrations in some infants of gestationally diabetic, non-insulin-treated mothers were similar to levels found in normal infants.[60] In addition, the rate of disappearance of exogenously supplied glucose, administered by constant slow intravenous infusion, was slower in infants of gestational or insulin-treated mothers as compared with normal infants.[60] Thus, the generally accepted concept of hyperinsulinism to explain the disturbed carbohydrate metabolism and lower concentration of free fatty acids in infants of diabetic mothers has been questioned, and the conflicting evidence has been extensively reviewed.[1,99]

Additional insights into understanding the disturbed carbohydrate metabolism of infants of diabetic mothers have been obtained from studies of spontaneous and amino-acid-stimulated glucagon secretion in the immediate newborn period. Bloom and Johnston[14] were the first to show that the spontaneous rise in plasma glucagon observed in normal infants in the first 2 hr of life was markedly obtunded in infants of diabetic mothers, whether the mothers were insulin-treated or not. Williams *et al.*[136] confirmed these findings in the first hour of life, and extended the findings by demonstrating that glucagon secretion in response to an intravenous

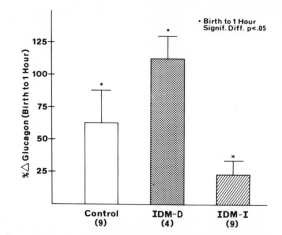

Fig. 4. Spontaneous change in plasma glucagon concentration from birth (umbilical cord) to 1 hr of life, expressed as the percentage change. All infants had a significant change, but spontaneous secretion in infants of insulin-dependent diabetics (IDM-I) was less pronounced than in control infants or infants of mild gestational diabetics treated with diet alone (IDM-D). Data from Williams *et al.*[136]

injection of alanine, 150 mg/kg administered at 1 hr of life, was also significantly inhibited in infants of insulin-treated diabetic mothers. As can be seen from Fig. 4, the spontaneous rise in glucagon in infants whose mothers had mild non-insulin-requiring gestational diabetes did not differ significantly from normal infants. In addition (Fig. 5), following alanine infusion in the normal infants, the increment in glucagon was associated with a significant increment in glucose, while neither plasma constituent changed appreciably in the infants of insulin-treated diabetic mothers. Thus, the suppressed glucagon secretion may contribute significantly to the hypoglycemia in these infants. In addition, urinary excretion of catecholamines is diminished in infants of diabetic mothers.[68,127] The mechanisms responsible for the hypoglucagonemia probably relate to the suppression of pancreatic α-cell function by coexistent hyperglycemia and hyperinsulinemia, as previously discussed.[72,75] Implicit in these results is the suggestion that infusions of glucagon to simulate high physiologic plasma concentrations may avert hypoglycemia in these infants. Failure to demonstrate a beneficial effect in previous studies may have stemmed from the use of massive pharmacological doses of glucagon, which, by elevating cAMP levels, elicit prompt insulin secretion in all newborn infants,

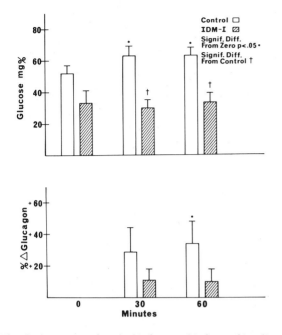

Fig. 5. Response of control infants and infants of insulin-dependent diabetics (IDM-I) to an intravenous bolus of alanine, 150 mg/kg, given at 1 hr of life. Glucose and glucagon rose significantly in controls, but no changes occurred in the IDM-I. Data from Williams et al.[136]

including exaggerated insulin secretion in infants of diabetic mothers.[107] This exaggerated insulin response may cause rebound hypoglycemia, as well as mask a stimulatory effect of glucagon on gluconeogenesis.[107]

8. Transient Hypoglycemia in Premature and Small-for-Gestational-Age Infants

Infants who are small at birth, whether by virtue of prematurity or some disturbance in placental function resulting in intrauterine growth retardation —i.e., small-for-gestational-age (SGA) infants— have an increased incidence of hypoglycemia.[71] This tendency cannot be attributed to disturbance in insulin or glucagon secretion, since both are normal, and glucagon secretion increases after oral alanine feedings.[135]

In addition, plasma concentrations of cortisol and growth hormone are also normal, excluding a hormonal basis.[50] Rather, it would appear that hepatic gluconeogenesis and glycogen reserves are impaired, since plasma lactate and alanine levels are increased in SGA babies in comparison with normal infants,[74,80,135] and the rise in glucagon induced by alanine does not elicit a rise in glucose in SGA babies, although with a similar stimulus, a rise in glucose is seen in premature and normal infants.[135] Observations made in experimental intrauterine growth retardation in the fetal and neonatal rat confirm the impaired gluconeogenesis and diminished glycogen reserves.[89,92]

9. Transient Diabetes of the Newborn

A transient diabetic state with onset during the first week of life was described by several groups.[32,84,97,114] These infants all appear to be small for gestational age, and the tendency to diabetes appears to be familial.[32,84] Although insulin therapy is required initially, spontaneous resolution by 3–4 months of age is the rule. This syndrome probably represents the extension of intrauterine and neonatal immaturity of insulin secretory mechanisms related to delayed maturation of the cAMP system,[48,97] but it is not yet clear whether the underlying defect in humans is due to deficiency in the β-cell adenyl cyclase, which generates cAMP, or to increased activity of the nucleotide phosphodiesterase, which destroys cAMP.[97] Insulin secretion in response to the stimulus of glucose or tolbutamide is absent,[114] but can be augmented by theophylline.[97] Glucagon secretory profiles have not been determined in this condition. Finally, this rare syndrome is distinct from the entity of transient hyperglycemia seen in association with electrolyte disturbance, acidosis, and abnormalities of the CNS. In this condition, euglycemia is rapidly restored by hydration and correction of acid–base balance.[82,128]

10. Erythroblastosis Fetalis

Islet cell hyperplasia, high pancreatic insulin content, hyperinsulinemia at birth, and neonatal hypoglycemia have all been described in infants affected by erythroblastosis fetalis.[81] Plasma glucagon levels in these infants have been found to be higher than normal prior to exchange transfusion. During exchange transfusion with blood preserved with acid citrate and glucose, plasma glucagon levels decline and net glucagon balance is negative, while insulin secretion is prominent and plasma insulin concentrations rise despite negative insulin balance.[83] Thus, with regard to both insulin and glucagon secretion, infants with erythroblastosis fetalis are similar to infants of diabetic mothers in having insulin stimulated and glucagon suppressed by glucose. They differ, however, in that spontaneous glucagon secretion appears to be high in erythroblastotic infants[83] and low in infants of diabetic mothers.[14,135] Addition of glucagon to the donor blood used for exchange transfusion may exert a protective effect on posttransfusion rebound hypoglycemia, despite the concurrent hyperinsulinemia,[82] although the posttransfusion period studied was 1 hr, while rebound hypoglycemia most commonly occurs 2–3 hr posttransfusion.

11. Conclusions

Advances in methodology have allowed quantification of pancreatic insulin and glucagon content during embryonic development as well as delineation of some factors that promote secretion of these hormones *in utero* and in the immediate newborn period. The functional role of these hormones early in development is not yet defined. It seems unlikely that insulin plays a significant role in energy homeostasis early in development; indirect evidence assigns a major role to insulin in fat and glycogen deposition in the third trimester. Similarly, no defined role exists for glucagon in early development, but its high pancreatic content and marked effects on raising cAMP have prompted the intriguing suggestion that it is involved in regulating organogenesis. No other functional effect has been ascribed to glucagon. At birth, there is a surge in glucagon, while insulin secretion remains obtunded. These events appear to be important in the transition to extrauterine life, activating glycogenolysis, gluconeogenesis, and possibly ketogenesis. The manner in which the hormonal changes trigger these events is the subject of considerable research. In addition to the events surrounding birth in normal infants, departures from the norm can be more rationally explained in terms of alterations in insulin and glucagon secretion, as exemplified by infants of diabetic mothers. Further understanding of the secretion and action of these hormones will provide insights into the control of energy homeostasis in the perinatal period.

ACKNOWLEDGMENTS

This work was supported in part by United States Public Health Service Grant HD-07087, and by Research Career Development Award 1-K04-HD-00029. Portions of the quoted work were performed in a Clinical Study Center supported by Grant RR 425. The author gratefully acknowledges the splendid secreterial assistance of Ms. Joy Reynolds.

12. References

1. ADAM, P. A. J., 1971, Control of glucose metabolism in the human fetus and newborn infant, *Adv. Metab. Disord.* **5**:183–275.
2. ADAM, P. A. J., GLAZER, G., AND ROGOFF, F., 1975, Glucose production in the newborn dog: I. Effects of glucagon *in vivo, Pediatr. Res.* **9**:816–820.
3. ADAM, P. A. J., KEROMAKI, M., RAHIALA, E. L., AND SCHWARTZ, A. L., 1972, Autoregulation of glucose production by the isolated perfused human fetal liver, *Pediatr. Res.* **6**:396.
4. ADAM, P. A. J., KING, K. C., SCHWARTZ, R., AND TERAMO, K., 1972, Human placental barrier to ^{125}I-glucagon early in gestation, *J. Clin. Endocrinol. Metab.* **34**:772–782.
5. Adam, P. A. J., TERAMO, K., RAIHA, N., GITLIN, D., AND SCHWARTZ, R., 1969, Human fetal insulin metabolism early in gestation: Response to acute elevation of the fetal glucose concentration and placental transfer of human insulin I^{131}, *Diabetes* **18**:409–416.
6. ASHWORTH, M. A., LEACH, F. M., AND MILNER, R. D. G., 1973, Development of insulin secretion in the human fetus, *Arch. Dis. Child.* **48**:151–152.
7. ASPLUND, K., 1972, Effects of postnatal feeding on the functional maturation of pancreatic islet β-cells of neonatal rats, *Diabetologia* **8**:153–159.
8. ASPLUND, K., ANDERSSON, A., JARROUSSE, C., AND HELLERSTROM, C., 1975, Function of the fetal endocrine pancreas, *Isr. J. Med. Sci.* **11**:581–590.
9. ASSAN, R., AND BOILLOT, J., 1971, Pancreatic glucagon and glucagon-like material in tissues and plasmas from human fetuses 6–26 weeks old, in: *Metabolic Processes in the Fetus and Newborn Infant,* pp. 218 and 219, Williams and Wilkins Co., Baltimore.
10. BAIRD, J. D., AND FARQUHAR, J. W., 1962, Insulin secreting capacity in newborn infants of normal and diabetic women, *Lancet* **1**:71–74.
11. BATAILLE, D., FREYCHET, P., AND ROSSELIN, G., 1974, Interaction of glucagon, gut glucagons, vasoactive intestinal polypeptide and secretin with liver and fat cell plasma membranes. Binding to specific sites and stimulation of adenylate cyclase, *Endocrinology* **95**:713–721.

12. BERGMAN, R. N., AND MILLER, R. E., 1973, Direct enhancement of insulin secretion by vagal stimulation of the isolated pancreas, *Amer. J. Physiol.* **225**:481–486.

13. BIER, D. M., LEAKE, R. D., ARNOLD, K. J., HAYMOND, M., FRUENKE, L. D., SPERLING, M. A., AND KIPNIS, D. M., 1976, Measurement of glucose production in infants and children with deuterium labeled glucose, *Clin. Res.* **24**:186A (abstract).

14. BLOOM, S. R., AND JOHNSTON, D. I., 1972, Failure of glucagon release in infants of diabetic mothers, *Br. Med. J.* **4**:453, 454.

15. BLOOM, S. R., VAUGHAN, N. J. A., AND RUSSELL, R. C. G., 1974, Vagal control of glucagon release in man, *Lancet* **2**:546–549.

16. BOCEK, R. M., YOUNG, M. K., AND BEATTY, C. H., 1973, Effect of insulin and epinephrine on the carbohydrate metabolism and adenylate cyclase activity of rhesus fetal muscle, *Pediatr. Res.* **7**:787–793.

17. BRUDENELL, M., AND BEARD, R., 1972, Diabetes in pregnancy, *Clin. Endocrinol. Metab.* **1**:673–695.

18. BUCOLO, R. J., BERGMAN, R. N., MARSH, D. J., AND YATES, F. E., 1974, Dynamics of glucose autoregulation in the isolated, blood-perfused canine liver, *Amer. J. Physiol.* **227**:209–217.

19. GAHILL, G. F., JR., 1971, Physiology of insulin in man, *Diabetes* **20**:785–799.

20. CARDELL, B. S., 1953, Hypertrophy and hyperplasia of the pancreatic islets in newborn infants, *J. Pathol. Bacteriol.* **66**:325–346.

21. CHEEK, D. B., AND GREYSTONE, J. E., 1969, The action of insulin, growth hormone, and epinephrine on cell growth in liver, muscle and brain of the hypophysectomized rat, *Pediatr. Res.* **3**:77–88.

22. CHEN, C. H., ADAM, P. A. J., LASKOWSKI, D. E., McCANN, M. L., AND SCHWARTZ, R., 1965, The plasma free fatty acid composition and blood glucose of normal and diabetic pregnant women and of their newborns, *Pediatrics* **36**:843–855.

23. CHEZ, R. A., MINTZ, D. H., AND EPSTEIN, M. F., 1974, Glucagon metabolism in non-human primate pregnancy, *Amer. J. Obstet. Gynecol.* **120**:690–696.

24. CHEZ, R. A., MINTZ, D. H., AND HUTCHINSON, D. H., 1971, Effect of theophylline on glucagon and glucose-mediated plasma insulin responses in subhuman primate fetus and neonate, *Metabolism* **20**:805–815.

25. CHICK, W. L., 1973, Beta cell replication in rat pancreatic monolayer cultures, *Diabetes* **22**:687–693.

26. CUATRECASAS, P., HOLLENBERG, M. D., CHANG, K. H., AND BENNETT, V., 1975, Hormone receptor complexes and their modulation of membrane function, *Recent Prog. Horm. Res.* **31**:37–94.

27. DANCIS, J., JANSEN, V., KAYDEN, H. J., SCHNEIDER, H., AND LEVITZ, M., 1973, Transfer across perfused human placenta: II. Free fatty acids, *Pediatr. Res.* **7**:192–197.

28. ESPINOSA, M. M. A., DRISCOLL, S. G., AND STEINKE, J., 1970, Insulin release from isolated human fetal pancreatic islets, *Science* **168**:1111–1112.

29. EXTON, J. H., 1972, Gluconeogenesis, *Metabolism* **21**:945–990.

30. FARQUHAR, J. W., 1970, Islets, insulin and hypoglycemia in infants of diabetic mothers, *Postgrad. Med. J.* **46**:593–599.

31. FEE, B. A., AND WEIL, W. B., JR., 1963, Body composition of infants of diabetic mothers by direct analysis, *Ann. N. Y. Acad. Sci.* **110**:869–897.

32. FERGUSON, A. W., AND MILNER, R. D. G., 1970, Transient neonatal diabetes mellitus in sibs, *Arch. Dis. Child.* **45**:80–83.

33. FISER, R. H., JR., ERENBERG, A., SPERLING, M. A., OH, W., AND FISHER, D. A., 1974, Insulin–glucagon substrate interrelations in the fetal sheep, *Pediatr. Res.* **8**:951–955.

34. FISER, R. H., WILLIAMS, P. R., FISHER, D. A., DeLAMATER, P. V., SPERLING, M. A., AND OH, W., 1975, The effect of oral alanine on blood glucose and glucagon in the human newborn infant, *Pediatrics* **56**:78–81.

35. GERICH, J. E., LANGLOIS, M., NOACCO, C., SCHNEIDER, V., AND FORSHAM, P. H., 1974, Adrenergic modulation of pancreatic glucagon secretion in man, *J. Clin. Invest.* **53**:1441–1446.

36. GIRARD, J. R., 1975, Metabolic fuels of the fetus, *Isr. J. Med. Sci.* **11**:591–600.

37. GIRARD, J., BAL, D., AND ASSAN, R., 1972, glucagon secretion during the early period in the rat, *Horm. Metab. Res.* **4**:168–170.

38. GIRARD, J. R., CUENDET, G. S., MARLISS, E. B., KERVRAN, A., RIEUTORT, M., AND ASSAN, R., 1973, Fuels, hormones, and liver metabolism at term and during the early postnatal period in the rat, *J. Clin. Invest.* **52**:3190–3200.

39. GIRARD, J. R., KERVRAN, A., SOUFFLET, E., AND ASSAN, R., 1974, Factors affecting the secretion of insulin and glucagon by the rat fetus, *Diabetes* **23**:310–317.

40. GITLIN, D., KUMATE, J., AND MORALES, C., 1965, On the transport of insulin across the human placenta, *Pediatrics* **35**:65–69.

41. GLINSMAN, W. H., EISEN, H. J., LYNCH, A., AND CHEZ, R. A., 1975, Glucose regulation by isolated near term fetal monkey liver, *Pediatr. Res.* **9**:600–604.

42. GLINSMAN, W. H., HERN, E. P., AND LYNCH, A., 1969, Intrinsic regulation of glucose output by rat liver, *Amer. J. Physiol.* **216**:698–703.

43. GRAJWER, L. A., SACK, J., SPERLING, M. A., FISHER, D. A., HOBEL, C. J., AND COUSINS, L., 1976, Umbilical cord cutting; the stimulus to the glucagon surge in newborn lambs, Program of Endocrine Society, p. 68, (abstract).

44. GRASSO, S., DiSTEFANO, G., MESSINA, A., VIGO, R., AND REITANO, G., 1975, Effect of glucose priming

on insulin response in the premature infant, *Diabetes* **24**:291–294.

45. GRASSO, S., MESSINA, A., DiStefano, G., Vigo, R., AND REITANO, R., 1973, Insulin secretion in the premature infant: Response to glucose and amino acids, *Diabetes* **22**:349–353.

46. GRASSO, S., MESSINA, A., SAPORITO, N., AND REITANO, G., 1970, Effect of theophylline, glucagon and theophylline plus glucagon on insulin secretion in the premature infant, *Diabetes* **19**:837–841.

47. GREENGARD, O., 1973, Effects of hormones on development of fetal enzymes, *Clin. Pharmacol. Ther.* **14**:721–726.

48. GRILL, V., ASPLUND, K., HELLERSTROM, C., AND CERASI, E., 1975, Decreased cyclic AMP and insulin in response to glucose in isolated islets of neonatal rats, *Diabetes* **24**:746–751.

49. GRODSKY, G. M., FANSKA, R., WEST, L., AND MANNING, M., 1974, Anomeric specificity of glucose stimulated insulin release: Evidence for a gluco-receptor, *Science* **186**:536, 537.

50. HAYMOND, M. W., KARL, I. E., AND PAGLIARA, A. S., 1974, Increased gluconeogenic substrates in the small-for-gestational-age infants, *N. Engl. J. Med.* **291**:322–328.

51. HEINZE, E., AND STEINKE, J., 1972, Insulin secretion during development: Response of isolated pancreatic islets of fetal, newborn and adult rats to theophylline and arginine, *Horm. Metab. Res.* **4**:234–236.

52. HEINZE, E., SCHATZ, H., NIERLE, C., AND PFEIFFER, E. F., 1975, Insulin biosynthesis in isolated pancreatic islets of fetal and newborn rats, *Diabetes* **24**:373–377.

53. HELLMAN, B., 1966, The development of the mammalian endocrine pancreas, *Biol. Neonat.* **9**: 263–278.

54. ISLES, T. E., AND FARQUHAR, J. W., 1967, The effect of endogeneous antibody on insulin-assay in the newborn infants of diabetic mothers, *Pediatr. Res.* **1**:110–115.

55. ISLES, T. E., DICKSON, M., AND FARQUHAR, J. W., 1968, Glucose tolerance and plasma insulin in newborn infants of normal and diabetic women, *Pediatr. Res.* **2**:198–208.

56. JACK, P. M. B., AND MILNER, R. D. G., 1973, Effects of decapitation on the development of insulin secretion in the fetal rabbit, *J. Endocrinol.* **57**:23–31.

57. JOASSIN, G., PARKER, M. L., PILDES, R. S., AND CORNBLATH, M., 1967, Infants of diabetic mothers, *Diabetes* **16**:306–311.

58. JOHNSTON, D. I., BLOOM, S. R., GREENE, K. R., AND BEARD, R. W., 1972, Failure of the human placenta to transfer pancreatic glucagon, *Biol. Neonate* **21**: 375–380.

59. KAUNG, H. L., AND HEGRE, O. D., 1974, *In vitro* development of glucose responsiveness of fetal rat pancreas, *Diabetes* **23**(*Suppl. 1*):375 (abstract).

60. KING, K. C., ADAM, P. A. J., CLEMENTE, G. A., AND

SCHWARTZ, R., 1969, Infants of diabetic mothers; attenuated glucose uptake without hyperinsulinemia during continuous glucose infusion, *Pediatrics* **44**: 381–392.

61. KING, K. C., BUTT, J., RAVIVO, K., RAIHA, N., ROUX, J., TERAMO, K., YAMAGUCHI, K., AND SCHWARTZ, R., 1971, Human maternal and fetal insulin response to arginine, *N. Engl. J. Med.* **285**:607–612.

62. KIPNIS, D. M., 1972, Nutrient regulation of insulin secretion in human subjects, *Diabetes* **21**(*Suppl. 2*): 606–612.

63. KIRBY, L., AND HAHN, P., 1974, Enzyme responses to prednisone and dibutyryl adenosine 3′5′-mono-phosphate in human fetal liver, *Pediatr. Res.* **8**:37–41.

64. LACY, P. E., 1970, Beta cell secretion—from the standpoint of a pathologist, *Diabetes* **19**:895–905.

65. LAZAROW, A., WELLS, L. J., CARPENTER, A. M., HEGRE, O. D., LEONARD, R. J., McEvoy, R. C., 1973, Islet differentiation, organ culture and trans-plantation, *Diabetes* **22**:877–912.

66. LEFEBVRE, P. J., AND UNGER, R. H., 1972, *Glucagon, Molecular Physiology, Clinical and Therapeutic Implications,* Pergamon Press, Oxford.

67. LEVINE, S., PICTET, R., AND RUTTER, W. J., 1973, Control of cell proliferation and cytodifferentiation by a factor reacting with the cell surface, *Nature (London) New Biol.* **246**:49–52.

68. LIGHT, I. H., SUTHERLAND, J. M., LOGGIE, J. M., AND GAFFNEY, T. E., 1967, Impaired epinephrine release in hypoglycemic infants of diabetic mothers, *N. Engl. J. Med.* **277**:394–398.

69. LIU, C. M., AND POTTER, E. L., 1962, Development of the human pancreas, *Arch. Pathol.* **74**:439–452.

70. LOUBATIERES, A., MARIANI, M. M., SOREL, G., AND SAVI, L., 1971, The action of β receptor, *Diabetologia* **7**:127–132.

71. LUBCHENCO, L. O., AND BARD, H., 1971, Incidence of hypoglycemia in newborn infants classified by birth weight and gestational age, *Pediatrics* **47**:831–838.

72. LUYCKX, A. A., MASSI-BENEDETTI, F., FALORNI, A., AND LEFEBVRE, P. J., 1972, Presence of pancreatic glucagon in the portal plasma of human neonates. Differences in the insulin and glucagon responses to glucose between normal infants and infants of diabetic mothers, *Diabetologia* **8**:296–300.

73. MALAISSE, W. J., 1973, Insulin secretion: Multi-factorial regulation for a single process of release, *Diabetologia* **9**:167–173.

74. MALAMUD, D., AND PERRIN, L., 1974, Stimulation of DNA synthesis in mouse pancreas by tri-iodothyronine and glucagon, *Endocrinology* **94**:1157–1160.

75. MASSI-BENEDETTI, F., FALORNI, A., LUYCKX, A., AND LEFEBVRE, P., 1974, Inhibition of glucagon secretion in the human newborn by simultaneous administra-

tion of glucose and insulin, *Horm. Metab. Res.* **6**:392–396.

76. MATCHINSKY, F. M., LANDGRAF, R., ELLERMAN, J., AND KOTLER-BRAJTBURG, J., 1972, Glucoreceptor mechanisms in the' islets of Langerhans, *Diabetes* **21***(Suppl. 2)*:555–569.

77. MATCHINSKY, F. A., PAGLIARA, A. S., HOVER, B. A., HAYMOND, M. W., AND STILLINGS, S. M., 1975, Differential effects of α- and β-D-glucose on insulin and glucagon secretion from the isolated perfused rat pancreas, *Diabetes* **24**:369–372.

78. MCCANN, M. L., 1966, Effects of fructose on hypoglycosemia in infants of diabetic mothers, *N. Engl. J. Med.* **275**:1–7.

79. MCGARRY, J. D., WRIGHT, P. H., AND FOSTER, D. W., 1975, Hormonal regulation of ketogenesis, *J. Clin. Invest.* **55**:1202–1209.

80. MESTYAN, J., SOLTESZ, G., SCHULTZ, K., AND HORVATH, M., 1975, Hyperaminoacidemia due to accumulation of gluconeogenic amino acid precursors in hypoglycemic small-for-gestational-age infants, *J. Pediatr.* **87**:409–414.

81. MILNER, R. D. G., 1971, The development of insulin secretion in man, in: *Metabolic Processes in the Foetus and Newborn Infant,* pp. 193–207, Nutricia Symposium, The Williams and Wilkins Co., Baltimore.

82. MILNER, R. D. G., CHOUKSEY, S. K., AND ASSAN, R., 1973, Metabolic and hormonal effects of glucagon infusion in erythroblastotic infants, *Arch. Dis. Child.* **48**:885–891.

83. MILNER, R. D. G., FEKETE, M., AND ASSAN, R., 1972, Glucagon, insulin, and growth hormone response to exchange transfusion in premature and term infants, *Arch. Dis. Child.* **47**:186–189.

84. MILNER, R. D. G., FERGUSON, A. W., AND MAIDU, S. H., 1971, Aetiology of transient neonatal diabetes, *Arch. Dis. Child.* **46**:724–726.

85. MINTZ, D. H., CHEZ, P. A., AND HORGER, E. O., 1969, Fetal insulin and growth hormone metabolism in the subhuman primate, *J. Clin. Invest.* **48**:176–186.

86. MINTZ, D. H., LEVEY, G. S., AND SCHENK, A., 1973, Adenosine 3′,5′-cyclic monophosphate and phosphodiesterase activities in isolated fetal and neonatal rat pancreatic islets, *Endocrinology* **92**:614–617.

87. MONTELEONE, J. A., AND KEEFE, D. M., 1969, Transient hyperglycemia and aketotic hyperosmolar acidosis with heat stroke, *Pediatrics* **44**:737–741.

88. MOORE, W. M. O., WARD, B. S., AND GORDON, C, 1974, Human placental transfer of glucagon, *Clin. Sci. Mol. Med.* **46**:125–129.

89. NITZAN, M., AND GROFFMAN, H., 1971, Hepatic gluconeogenesis and lipogenesis in experimental intrauterine growth retardation in the rat, *Amer. J. Obstet. Gynecol.* **109**:623–627.

90. NOE, B. D., AND BAUER, G. E., 1975, Evidence for sequential metabolic cleavage of proglucagon to glucagon in glucagon biosynthesis, *Endocrinology* **97**:868–877.

91. OAKLEY, N. W., BEARD, R. W., AND TURNER, R. C., 1972, Effect of sustained maternal hyperglycemia on the fetus in normal and diabetic pregnancies, *Br. Med. J.* **1**:466–469.

92. OH, W., D'AMODIO, D. D., YAP, L. L., AND HOHENAUER, L., 1970, Carbohydrate metabolism in experimental intrauterine growth retardation in rats, *Amer. J. Obstet. Gynecol.* **108**:415–421.

93. ORCI, L., MALAISSE-LAGAE, F., AMBERDT, M., RAVAZZOLA, M., WEISSWANGE, A., DOBBS, R., PERRELET, A., AND UNGER, R., 1975, Cell contacts in human islets of langerhans, *J. Clin. Endocrinol. Metab.* **41**:841–844.

94. ORCI, L., UNGER, R. H., AND RENOLD, A. E., 1973, Structural basis for intercellular communications between cells of the islets of Langerhans, *Experientia (Basel)* **29**:777, 1973.

95. ORCI, L., UNGER, R. H., AND RENOLD, A. E., 1973, Structural coupling between pancreatic islet cells, *Experientia (Basel)* **29**:1025–1018.

96. OSLER, M., AND PEDERSEN, J., 1960, The body composition of newborn infants of diabetic mothers, *Pediatrics* **26**:985–992.

97. PAGLIARA, A. S., KARL, I. E., AND KIPNIS, D. P., 1973, Transient neonatal diabetes: Delayed maturation of the pancreatic beta cell, *J. Pediatr.* **82**:97–99.

98. PEARSE, A. G. E., POLAK, J. M., AND HEATH, C. M., 1973, Development, differentiation and derivation of the endocrine polypeptide cells of the mouse pancreas, *Diabetologia* **9**:120–129.

99. PERSSOM, B., GENTZ, J., AND KELLUM, M., 1973, Metabolic observations in infants of strictly controlled diabetic mothers, *Acta. Pediatr. Scand.* **62**:465–473.

100. PICTET, P., AND RUTTER, W. J., 1972, Development of the embryonic endocrine pancreas, in: *Handbook of Physiology,* Section 7: *Endocrinology,* Vol. 1, *The Endocrine Pancreas* (D. Steiner, and N. Freinkel, eds.), pp. 25–66, The Williams and Wilkins Co., Baltimore.

101. PICTET, R., FILOSE, S., PHELPS, P., AND RUTTER, W. J., 1975, Influences on gene expression, in: *Extracellular Matrix* (R. Greulich and H. C. Slavkin, eds.), p. 531, Academic Press, New York.

102. PILDES, R. S., HART, R. J., WARRNER, R., AND CORNBLATH, M., 1969, Plasma insulin response during oral glucose tolerance tests in newborns of normal and gestationally diabetic mothers, *Pediatrics* **44**:76–83.

103. PILDES, R. S., RAMAMURTHY, R. S., AND PATEL, D. A., 1974, Diminished response to glucagon in the dextrose-primed neonate, *Amer. J. Dis. Child.* **127**:333–335.

104. POLAK, J. M., PEARSE, A. G. E., CRIMELIUS, L., BLOOM, S. R., AND ARIMURA, A., 1975, Growth-hormone release-inhibiting hormone in gastro-intestinal and pancreatic D-cells, *Lancet* **1**:1220–1222.

105. PORTE, D., JR., AND BAGDAGE, J. D., 1970, Human insulin secretion: An integrated approach, *Annu. Rev. Med.* **21:**219–240.

106. RALL, L. B., PICTET, R. L., WILLIAMS, R. H., AND RUTTER, W. H., 1973, Early differentiation of glucagon producing cells in embryonic pancreas: A possible developmental role of glucagon, *Proc. Natl. Acad. Sci. U.S.A.* **70:**3478–3482.

107. REISNER, S. H., ARANDA, J. V., COLLE, E., PAPAGEORGIOU, A., SCHIFF, D., SCRIVER, C. R., AND STERN, L., 1973, The effect of intravenous glucagon on plasma amino acids in the newborn, *Pediatr. Res.* **7:**184–191.

108. RENOLD, A. E., 1970, Insulin biosynthesis and secretion: A still unsettled topic, *N. Engl. J. Med.* **282:**173–180.

109. RODBELL, M., KRANS, H. M. J., POHL, S. L., AND BIRNBAUMER, L., 1970, The glucagon sensitive adenyl cyclase system in plasma membranes of rat liver, *J. Biol. Chem.* **246:**1861–1871.

110. ROTH, J., KAHN, C. R., LESNIAK, M. A., GORDEN, P., DEMEYTS, P., MEGYESI, K., NEVILLE, D. M., GAVIN, J. R., SOLL, A. H., FREYCHET, P., GOLDFINE, D., BAR, R. S., AND ARCHER, J. A., 1975, Receptors for insulin, NSILA-S, and growth hormone: Applications to disease states in man, *Recent Prog. Horm. Res.* **31:**95–139.

111. SASAKI, H., RUBALCAVA, B., BAETENS, D., BLAZQUEZ, E., SRIKANT, C. B., ORCI, L., AND UNGER, R. H., 1975, Identification of glucagon in the gastrointestinal tract, *J. Clin. Invest.* **56:**135–145.

112. SCHAEFFER, L. D., WILDER, M. L., AND WILLIAMS, R. H., 1973, Secretion and content of insulin and glucagon in human fetal pancreas slices *in vitro, Proc. Soc. Exp. Biol. Med.* **143:**314–319.

113. SCHIFF, D., AND LOWY, C., 1970, Hypoglycemia and excretion of insulin in urine in hemolytic disease of the newborn, *Pediatr. Res.* **4:**280–285.

114. SCHIFF, D., COLLE, E., AND STERN, L., 1972, Metabolic and growth patterns in transient neonatal diabetes, *N. Engl. J. Med.* **287:**119–122.

115. SCHWARTZ, A. L., AND RALL, T. W., 1975, Hormonal regulation of incorporation of alanine-U-14-C into glucose in human fetal liver explants, *Diabetes* **24:**650–657.

116. SHELLEY, H. J., AND NELIGAN, G. A., 1966, Neonatal hypoglycemia, *Br. Med. Bull.* **22:**34–39.

117. SHERLINE, P., EISEN, H., AND GLINSMAN, W., 1974, Acute hormonal regulation of cyclic AMP content and glycogen phospharylase activity in fetal liver in organ culture, *Endocrinology* **94:**935–939.

118. SPERLING, M. A., 1973, Control of insulin secretion, in: *The Obese Diabetic, A Symposium on New Developments, Calif. Med.* **119:**17–22.

119. SPERLING, M. A., AND VOINA, S., 1975, Effect of adrenergic blockade on glucagon and growth hormone secretion in normal and diabetic children, *Pediatr. Res.* **9:**748–752.

120. SPERLING, M. A., DELAMATER, P. V., PHELPS, D., FISER, R. H., OH, W., AND FISHER, D. A., 1974, Spontaneous and amino acid stimulated glucagon secretion in the immediate post natal period: Relation to glucose and insulin, *J. Clin. Invest.* **53:**1159–1166.

121. SPERLING, M. A., ERENBERG, A., FISER, R. H., OH, W., AND FISHER, D. A., 1973, Placental transfer of glucagon in sheep, *Endocrinology* **93:**1435–1438.

122. SPERLING, M. A., LEAKE, R., GRAJWER, L., TRYGSTAD, C., AND FISHER, D., 1976, Effects of somatostatin on glucose homeostasis in newborn lambs, *Clin. Res.* **24:**195A (abstract).

123. STAVE, U., 1974, Metabolism of the small-for-gestational-age infant, *N. Engl. J. Med.* **291:**359–360.

124. STEINER, D. F., AND FREINKEL, N. (eds.), 1972, *Handbook of Physiology,* Section 7, *Endocrinology,* Vol. 1, *Endocrine Pancreas,* American Physiological Society, The Williams and Wilkins Co., Baltimore.

125. STEINKE, J., AND DRISCOLL, S. G., 1965, The extractable insulin content of pancreas from fetuses and infants of diabetic and control mothers, *Diabetes* **14:**573–578.

126. STEINKE, J., GRIES, A., AND DRISCOLL, S. G., 1967, *In vitro* studies of insulin inactivation in infants with reference to erythroblastosis fetalis, *Blood* **30:**359–363.

127. STERN, L., RAMOS, A., AND LEDUC, J., 1968, Urinary catecholamine excretion in infants of diabetic mothers, *Pediatrics* **42:**598–605.

128. STEVENSON, R. W., AND BOWYER, F. P., 1970, Hyperglycemia with hyperosmolal dehydration in non-diabetic infants, *J. Pediatr.* **77:**818–823.

129. THOMAS, K., DEGASPARO, M., AND HOET, J. J., 1967, Insulin levels in the umbilical vein and umbilical artery of newborns of normal and gestational diabetic mothers, *Diabetologia* **3:**299–305.

130. UNGER, R. H., 1974, Alpha-and-beta cell interrelationships in health and disease, *Metab. Clin. Exp.* **23:**581–593.

131. VALE, W., BRAZEAU, P., RIVIER, C., BROWN, M., BOSS, B., RIVIER, J., BURGUS, R., LING, N., AND GUILLEMIN, R., 1975, Somatostatin, *Recent Prog. Horm. Res.* **31:**365–397.

132. VAN ASSCHE, F. A., GEPTS, W., AND DEGASPARO, M., 1970, The endocrine pancreas in anencephaly; a histological, histochemical and biological study, *Biol. Neonat.* **14:**374–388.

133. VELASCO, M. S., AND PAULSEN, E. P., 1969, The response of infants of diabetic women to tolbutamide and leucine at birth, *Pediatrics* **43:**546–557.

134. WIDDOWSON, E. M., CRABB, D. E., AND MILNER, R. D. G., 1972, Cellular development of some human organs before birth, *Arch. Dis. Child.* **47:**652–655.

135. WILLIAMS, P. R., FISER, R. H., SPERLING, M. A., AND OH, W. 1975, Effects of oral alanine feeding on blood glucose, plasma glucagon and insulin concentrations

in small-for-gestational-age infants, *N. Engl. J. Med.* **292**:612–614.

136. WILLIAMS, P. R., SPERLING, M. A., AND RACASA, Z., 1975, Blunting of spontaneous and amino acid stimulated glucagon secretion in infants of diabetic mothers, *Diabetes* **24**(*Suppl. 2*):411.

137. WISE, J. K., HENDLER, R., AND FELIG, P., 1973, Evidence of stimulation of glucagon secretion by ananine in the human fetus at term, *J. Clin. Endocrinol. Metab.* **37**:345–348.

138. WOODS, S. C., AND PORTE, D., JR., 1974, Neural control of the endocrine pancreas, *Physiol. Rev.* **54**:596–619.

139. YEOH, G. C. T., AND OLIVER, I. T., 1974, Glucagon stimulation of DNA synthesis in neonatal rat liver, *Eur. J. Biochem.* **34**:474–478.

140. YEUNG, D., AND OLIVER, I. T., 1968, Factors affecting the premature induction of phosphopyruvate carboxylase in neonatal rat liver, *Biochem. J.* **108**:325–331.

CHAPTER 40

Thyroid Hormones

James F. Marks

1. Introduction

The tests of thyroid function that will be referred to in this chapter fall into several groups: (1) direct measurements of the thyroidal hormones and their derivatives in the serum; (2) measurements of unbound circulating thyroid hormones; (3) measurements of thyroid-binding proteins; (4) *in vitro* and *in vivo* isotope studies; and (5) measurements of thyroid-stimulating hormone (TSH) in the serum.

In the first category—direct measurements of thyroidal hormones in serum—are protein-bound iodine (PBI), butanol-extractable iodine (BEI), and levels of thyroxin, triiodothyronine (T_3), and reverse T_3 (3,3',5'-triidothyronine). These last three compounds are now measured by a variety of radioimmunoassay techniques.

The term "free thyroxine" (T_F) is used to refer to that fraction of the circulating thyroxine iodine that is not bound to the plasma proteins. This fraction may represent the critical or biologically active portion of circulating thyroid hormones. It has been measured by a number of techniques involving chomatographic and dialysis procedures.

In the next group of studies are measurements of thyroid-binding globulin (TBG) or TBG capacity. The three plasma proteins that participate in the binding of thyroid hormone are albumin, thyroid-binding prealbumin (TBPA), and TBG.

The *in vitro* [^{131}I]T_3 uptake is an indirect measurement of TBG capacity. A labeled amount of ^{131}I is incubated *in vitro* with either whole blood or serum mixed with a resin sponge. The red cells or the resin acts as an inert surface that picks up labeled T_3 not absorbed by the plasma. Thus, an elevated T_3 uptake correlates with a low TBG capacity, while a decreased T_3 uptake correlates with a high TBG capacity.

The standard ^{131}I *in vivo* uptake has been done using various dosages in the perinatal period. Thyroxine turnover studies using *in vivo* radioisotopes will be referred to specifically where applicable further on in the discussion.

TSH in the serum can be measured by radioimmunoassay. The response of TSH to administered thyrotropin-releasing hormone (TRH), the hypothalamic peptide that modulates TSH release, appears to be a valuable tool in evaluating the hypothalamic–pituitary–thyroid axis.

In this discussion, there is no mention of some old standby techniques, such as the serum cholesterol and the basal metabolic rate. These studies appear to be of very little value in assessing thyroid function in the perinatal period.

James F. Marks · The University of Texas Health Science Center, Dallas, Texas 75235

2. Maternal Thyroid Function

The PBI and similar measurements of circulating thyroid hormone are elevated in the pregnant woman. In 1956, Dowling et al.[13] demonstrated that the TBG capacity of maternal serum was elevated in comparison with that of the nonpregnant adult. It was postulated then that the elevation of TBG could explain the elevation of PBI in the pregnant woman without invoking any basic alteration of thyroid function. The work of these authors was subsequently confirmed by other investigators using different techniques. In addition, Hamolsky et al.[37] had shown that the in vitro [131I]T3 RBC uptake is depressed in the pregnant woman, which would be consistent with the elevation found in TBG capacity.

Clark and Horn[8] demonstrated that the "free thyroxine" index is the same for both pregnant women and nonpregnant normal adults. Sterling and Hegedus,[82] Ingbar et al.,[42] Lee et al.,[50] and Marks et al.,[56] using more specific techniques for the measurement of free thyroxine, demonstrated clearly that the free thyroxine in the pregnant woman is essentially the same as that found in the normal nonpregnant adult.

It has been postulated that some thyroid function tests might be of prognostic value during pregnancy. Nicoloff et al.[66] suggested that measurements of TBG capacity would be helpful. They showed in a group of patients that an abrupt fall in TBG capacity correlates with a sudden unexpected termination of pregnancy.

Using the conventional thyroid function techniques, one would expect the PBI or similar measurements of circulating thyroid hormone to be elevated in the normal pregnant woman. The T3 measured by either the resin or the red cell technique would be depressed. Free thyroxine measured by any of the conventional techniques would be within the normal range. Thyroxine turnover rates in the normal pregnant woman are equivalent to those of the normal nonpregnant adult.[12]

Serum T3 concentrations rise during pregnancy, similar to serum thyroxine concentrations; however, free T3 concentrations are normal.[6] Chopra's data indicate further that the maternal serum levels of reverse T3 are normal during pregnancy.

The TSH response to TRH was studied during pregnancy by a number of investigators. Specifically, there is a greater increment in TSH rise following TRH administration in midpregnancy than there is in nonpregnant adults.[3] This increase is similar to that found in women receiving oral contraceptives. These observations indicate that elevated estrogen or progesterone concentrations in pregnancy could be enhancing the TSH response. An increased TSH response is evidence against increased thyroid function in pregnancy, since a small rise in circulating levels of thyroid hormone leads to a significantly decreased TSH response to TRH. Such a compensation would help maintain normal thyroid function in pregnancy.

The data accumulated thus far indicate that thyroid function during pregnancy is normal.

3. Development of the Fetal Thyroid

Many studies have shown that the human fetal thyroid will pick up iodine at about 12 weeks of fetal life. There is a great deal of variation in many species of mammals with regard to this pickup. The rat will not pick up iodine until nearly the end of gestation, whereas the monkey will pick up iodine at about the beginning of the second trimester of gestation.

Shepard[77] studied thyroxine synthesis in human fetal organ cultures using 125I incubation medium. Fetuses with a length of 22–142 mm and with a gestational age of 45–112 days were studied. In fetuses less than 68 mm, no organic iodine, central colloidal cavity, or tissue binding of 125I could be noted. At 68 mm, or 74 gestational days, and in all later stages, a full spectrum of iodinated thyroidal materials could be found, including monoiodotyrosine, diiodotyrosine, thyroxine, and T3. In addition, 125I tissue binding was apparent on radioautographs. The exact sequences of the biochemical events could not be specifically delineated in the human tissue. Shepard[77] demonstrated that 20-day gestational rat fetuses accumulated 125I, and they showed a gradual reduction of monoiodotyrosine and diiodotyrosine occurring over an 18-hr period. Puromycin inhibited organic binding of 125I, but cyanide did not.

Gitlin and Biasucci[34] showed that synthesis of immunoreactive thyroglobulin is present by the 29th day of human fetal development.

Fisher[20] and Fukuchi et al.[32] showed that the fetal pituitary shows histological differentiation by 10–11 weeks, and that it contains TSH identifiable by radioimmunoassay by 12 weeks. Human fetal serum levels of TSH, T_4, and free T_4 are minimal before 18–20 weeks' gestation.[21] By about 22–26 weeks, there is a progressive increase in pituitary TSH content and concentration and an increase in fetal serum TSH concentration, followed by a progressive increase in fetal serum T_4 levels. These findings would indicate that the fetal hypothalamic pituitary axis is beginning to mature at around 20 weeks' gestation.

Fisher suggests that the development of the fetal thyroid before midpregnancy is not dependent on thyroid hormone or TSH, but that thyroid hormone production and secretion during the second half of gestation are dependent on TSH secretion. He relates this idea to the development of the pituitary portal system and the hypothalamic maturation that can be demonstrated histologically at about 20 weeks' gestation.[21]

There is a progressive rise in human fetal serum T_4 concentrations from about 20 weeks' gestation to term. Fisher et al.[26] further showed in paired maternal and fetal specimens that the fetal T_4 concentration may exceed the paired maternal concentration at term.

A variety of data generated by Fisher and Dussault and their colleagues[15,25,30] show that there is a fetal T_3 deficiency in both the sheep and the human fetus. Data from their group suggest that there is a reduction in monodeiodination of T_4 to T_3 in the sheep fetus. Curiously, the concentration and the daily production rate of reverse T_3 are both increased markedly in the sheep fetus. The serum concentration of reverse T_3 is also elevated in the human newborn.[7] Chopra believes that there may be a specific β-ring iodothyronine monodeiodonase deficiency in fetal tissue to account for the state of fetal T_3 deficiency, but that the α-ring monodeiodonase activity in the fetus is either normal or increased, thus accounting for the increased levels of reverse T_3. Chopra and Crandall[6] recently studied the levels of thyroxine, T_3, and reverse T_3 in the amniotic fluid. They showed that the mean thyroxine and T_3 levels in amniotic fluid were significantly lower and the mean reverse T_3 levels significantly higher than corresponding maternal serum values both at 15–19 weeks and at 36–42 weeks of pregnancy. Sack et al.[74] obtained similar data for thyroxine levels in the amniotic fluid early in pregnancy and near term. In both cases, the amniotic fluid thyroxine level was much less than in fetal or maternal serum. There was a slight, but apparently statistically significant, increase in the amniotic fluid

T_4 from 16–20 weeks to term. Although the significance of Chopra's findings is unclear, it is possible that measurement of amniotic fluid reverse T_3 could provide a means of intrauterine detection of hypothyroidism in selected circumstances.

Thus, by several different methodologies, the time of onset of thyroid activity in the human fetus can be demonstrated. Questions remain unanswered. First, what is the exact sequence of the origination and organization of biochemical events in the human fetal thyroid? Second, what is the significance of the development of hormonogenesis in the human fetus in the overall pattern of fetal development? Third, what is the significance of differences in hormonogenesis among various mammalian species?

4. Fetal–Maternal Relationships

There is a small amount of species variability as to the ways in which various substances related to thyroid biological activity exchange between mother and fetus. Iodine, TSH, the thiourea drugs, thyroxine, and a long-acting thyroid stimulator (LATS) will be considered.

In the rat, guinea pig, rabbit, and monkey, among other species, as well as man, iodine transfer from mother to fetus has been demonstrated. A number of investigators have shown that radioactive iodine administered to mothers prior to therapeutic abortion has appeared localized in the thyroid of human fetuses from about the 12th gestational week. Ample clinical evidence exists as to the toxic effects on the newborn infant of iodine administered to the mother during pregnancy. Thus, there is no question that the human placenta is freely permeable to iodine at least during the second and third trimesters of pregnancy.

In no species studied has there been any demonstration of placental passage of TSH. When Peterson and Young[69] gave TSH to guinea pig mothers, the fetal thyroid was not hyperplastic. On the other hand, such animals given propylthiouracil showed fetal thyroid hyperplasia that was blocked by concomitant thyroid administration to the mother. Knobil and Josimovich[46] showed in the rat that the offspring of hypophysectomized mothers will develop goiter formation from propylthiouracil, presumably due to the fetal production of TSH, and that this effect is similarly blocked by maternal administration of T_3 or thyroxine with suppression of fetal TSH production. Thus, although there is no placental permeability to TSH, the fetal pituitary can respond to environmental stimuli produced by maternal administration of other materials that do appear to cross the placenta.

Many investigators[46,69] have shown that the placenta is freely permeable to the thiourea drugs. Transplacental passage of these drugs produces goiter formation not only in experimental animals, but also in the human fetus.

The problems of placental passage of thyroxine and T_3 form the most interesting aspect of the fetal–maternal thyroid relationship. The type of indirect evidence cited above in the discussion of TSH and the thiourea drugs seems to suggest that thyroxine or T_3 is able to cross the placenta in experimental animals to the extent that it at least partially blocks the TSH stimulation that produces goiters in the offspring of thiourea-treated animals.

Direct studies of transfer of T_3 and thyroxine have been done in a number of species, including man. The work of Fisher and his colleagues[15,16,24] in sheep showed little or no transfer of labeled T_3 or T_4 in either the fetal–maternal or the maternal–fetal direction. Studies done by Pickering[71] in the pregnant monkey indicate that only a small amount of radioactivity from labeled T_4 administered to the mother was present in fetal tissues 24 hr after injection. When the pregnant rhesus monkey received enough T_4 to increase serum levels by 3 times, this amount did not change fetal serum T_4 or block T_4 synthesis in the fetal thyroid.

Studies of placental transfer of ^{131}I-labeled T_3 in the rhesus monkey by Schultz et al.[75] showed that the majority of maternal–fetal placental transfer of radioactivity was in the form of iodine and a chemically unrecognized compound. Only traces of T_3 and thyroxine were detected. In fetal–maternal studies, Schultz et al.[75] felt that the T_3 was more readily transferred into the maternal circulation. Again, small amounts of iodine and a similar unknown compound thought to be a sulfate conjugate of T_3 appeared on chromatography. In their studies, there was a considerably greater concentration gradient from the fetus to the mother than from the mother to the fetus. They suggested that maternal thyroid hormones were not readily available for fetal needs in the later part of pregnancy. In the human, Myant[63] showed that ^{131}I-labeled T_3 and thyroxine injected into mothers scheduled for therapeutic abortion at 10–18 weeks cannot be readily identified in fetal tissues. Fisher et al.[27] studied the effects of administration of intra-venous loads of sodium L-thyroxine on the BEI, T_3, and thyroxine resin uptakes in 15 mothers with uncomplicated pregnancies and their infants. Following such loading, newborn BEI and T_3 uptakes increased progressively with increasing maternal thyroid dose and increasing time. However, such increases were much less than those parallel in the maternal serum even at a maximum load and time. These data suggested that the maternal–fetal transport was limited by maternal thyroid-binding proteins, as well as perhaps by an inherent placental permeability defect with regard to thyroxine. They suggested that the primary gradient in thyroxine transport in the human was from fetus to mother, rather than the other way around.

Although studies[67] showed that there is little or no transfer of labeled T_4 early in pregnancy, there does appear to be limited transfer of labeled thyroid hormones.[35] Administration of large amounts of either thyroxine or T_3 gives rise to a significantly limited transfer. The work of Fisher et al.[27] would indicate that only about 1% of an 8000-μg thyroxine load would reach the fetus, and the work of Raiti et al.[73] would suggest that continuous long-term 300-μg daily doses of T_3 would reduce the fetal serum T_4 to a small and inconsistent extent. Kock et al.[47] suggested that the monkey fetus obtains only about 0.01% of its thyroxine from maternal transfer at term.

Thus, a few conclusions appear applicable in reference to placental transport of thyroxine and T_3. First, transplacental transport of these materials in the human does not appear to occur during early pregnancy. Second, a small but almost certainly physiologically insignificant amount of material crosses at about term. It is clear that not enough would cross to help the fetus unable to make thyroid hormones.

Another interesting substance that should be considered is LATS. This material is a protein, a 7S γ-globulin that readily crosses the placental barrier. The work of Kriss et al.[49] suggests that this material is an antibody to some component of thyroid tissue. In early studies,[83] it was found in congenitally thyrotoxic infants of mothers with Graves' disease. More recent studies cast some doubt on the relationship between the occurrence of LATS and the etiology of congenital thyrotoxicosis.[41]

Thus, the series of compounds relating to thyroid activity have been considered. Iodine apparently crosses quite readily, with evidence of maternal–fetal passage as early as the 12th gestational week in the human fetus. Thyroxine and T_3 seem to cross, but at levels of no physiologic significance. LATS, a 7 S γ-globulin, appears to cross quite readily.

5. Neonatal Thyroid Function

In infants of all birth weights, the various serum protein-bound measures of thyroid hormone are increased in the first week of life. In 1951, Danowski et al.[10] showed that the PBI became elevated shortly after birth, reaching its peak in the first 3 days of life. Man et al.[54] demonstrated similar data using the BEI. The PBI is essentially back to adult values by 3 months of age, although the mean level in the 3-month-old is statistically slightly greater than that in the older child or adult. The PBI returns completely to normal adult values by 1 year of age. In their initial report, Danowski et al.[10] suggested possible reasons for this return. One was an increase in actual circulating thyroid hormone. Others were related to changes in blood volume in the infant or alteration in thyroid-binding proteins in the infant. Table I shows the normal range for serum thyroxine during childhood and adolescence.

In 1956, Dowling et al.[13] showed that the level of TBG in human cord blood was higher than that in normal nonpregnant adults, but lower than that in mothers at term. They suggested that the TBG capacity was elevated but to a lesser degree in the normal full-size infant than in the mother. In 1961, Marks et al.[57] showed that the T_3 uptake increased during the first few days of life, which indicated that the increase in PBI was independent of a change in TBG capacity. If they had been related, one would have expected the binding capacity to increase and the T_3 uptake to decrease when the PBI rose, whereas in fact the reverse occurs.

Using the algebraic approximation of the free thyroxine index,[8] Marks[55] recalculated his data and showed that the free thyroxine index was increased during the first week of life. Subsequently, Marks et al.,[56] using the chromatographic technique described by Lee et al.,[50] indicated that the free thyroxine level was elevated during the first week of life in comparison both with mothers at term and with normal nonpregnant adults and normal children. These data were accumulated on normal infants with birth weights greater than 2500 g. DeNayer et al.[11] showed that the free thyroxine of cord blood was equivalent to the mother's serum level at term. The cord blood TBPA was lower than the maternal.

A number of workers have shown that the ^{131}I uptake in the newborn full-size infant is increased above values for older children and adults. Fisher and Oddie[22] showed that the thyroxine excretion rate during infancy is 18.6 μg/kg per day, or 246 μg/M^2 per day. This value is a marked increase above an adult value of 178 μg/day for the average, 1.73-M^2 adult. On a weight basis, it represents a 7-fold increase in thyroxine turnover in the infant. On a body surface area basis, it represents a 2-fold increase in the thyroxine secretion rate.

Utiger[85] and Fisher et al.[26] showed a rise in plasma TSH during the first 24 hr of life. Fisher showed the cord TSH to be substantially greater than the maternal TSH. There was a significant increase from the cord level of 9.1 μU/ml to a value of 85 μU/ml at 30 min of age. This level fell rapidly to 3–4 hr, and then fell more gradually to 10 μU/ml at 48 hr of age. Although delayed cooling stimulates TSH release in the newborn infant, warming does not prevent the release of TSH, as demonstrated by Fisher et al.[29]

A number of investigators[1,5,18,60] have studied the levels of T_3 immediately following birth. Although the cord level is low, there is a substantial increase in serum levels of T_3 demonstrable from 30 min to 2 hr following birth, with a peak at 24 hr. Erenberg et al.[18] showed concomitant increases in free T_3. The reverse T_3 is substantially elevated at birth and remains elevated for about the first 4–5 days of life, following which it falls into the normal adult range.[7] This pattern is contrasted with the changes in T_3, which show that the T_3 in cord blood is markedly diminished at birth, but rises quite rapidly, peaking at about 24 hr and then falling into the upper part of the normal adult range by about 2 days of age. This would also compare with their parallel data on serum thyroxine levels, which show a mean in the high normal adult range at birth, a peak at 24 hr, and a gradual return to the high normal adult range by 6–30 days of age. Again, these observers suggest that among the various factors responsible for the relationship of the high reverse T_3 and low standard T_3 in the newborn could be differences in specific deiodinase activities. The physiologic significance of these changes is at present unclear.

6. Neonatal Thyroid Pathology

In this section, a few relevant areas of clinical pathologic states in normal full-size and low-birth-weight infants will be considered. Congenital goiters, congenital hyperthyroidism, and hypothyroidism in the infant will be discussed. Emphasis will be placed on those conditions that involve alterations in the maternal–fetal biological unit.

Congenital goiters of multiple etiologies have been described in the newborn infant. Among the causes are: (1) maternal iodide administration; (2) maternal thiourea administration; (3) congenital thyrotoxicosis; (4) congenital defects of thyroxine synthesis; (5) hematomas of the thyroid; and (6) neoplastic change within the thyroid. The pediatric literature indicates that iodine-induced goiter in the newborn is not an uncommon problem. There are reports of infants with strangulation from excessively large goiters of this type. Since the suppression of infantile TSH secretion by exogenous thyroxine or T_3 does not rapidly reduce glandular enlargement in these infants, surgery is a necessity in those infants with significant signs of airway obstruction. In the asthmatic on iodine, the substitution of other therapy during pregnancy would be of great advantage to the unborn infant. Thiourea drugs may also give rise to significant thyroidal enlargement and respiratory embarrassment. It is uncommon for such infants to have a derangement of thyroid function. Treatment of a mother with thyrotoxicosis is complex; however, many authorities feel that reduction of thiourea drugs to the lowest dose compatible with control of the maternal disease reduces the risk of massive goiter formation in the fetus.[76] Goiter has been reported in infants with enzymatic deficiencies of thyroid function at birth; however, it is much more common for such patients to develop goiters later on in infancy and in early childhood. Among the tumors reported to produce thyroidal enlargement in the newborn are hamartomas, hemangiomas, lymphomas, and teratomas.

There are now approximately 50 reports of congenital thyrotoxicosis.[68] The author has an additional 6 unreported cases, and feels sure that the real incidence of this condition is much higher than reported. Although the goiter found in congenital thyrotoxicosis may be present at birth, it is not infrequent to see this occurrence as late as a week following birth.

Congenital hyperthyroidism is seen in a small proportion of infants of mothers with treated and untreated thyrotoxicosis. Although LATS has been found in both the mother and the affected infant in a number of cases, there have been reported circumstances in which LATS has not been detected in either the mother or the affected infant. The work of Hollingsworth[41] casts doubt on the hypothesis that a transplacental humoral factor is necessary for the development of congenital thyrotoxicosis. It should be noted that it is not unusual to find neonatal thyrotoxicosis in infants of mothers who have previously been successfully treated for Graves' disease. Sunshine et al.[83] demonstrated that LATS may persist in the plasma of a thyrotoxic infant for up to 21 days. The specific relationship of this material or any other humoral material to the pathogenesis of thyrotoxicosis and congenital Graves' disease is unclear.

Congenital thyrotoxicosis is an acute, frequently severe, usually self-limiting disease. According to the survey of Sunshine et al.,[83] it has about a 20% mortality rate. Significant symptoms may last up to 6 weeks to 3 months of age. Goiter may frequently be present at birth, but usually does not appear until 3–5 days of age, and may occur as late as 7 or 8 days of age. Exophthalmos is present early, and will persist beyond the actual period of thyrotoxicosis, frequently being apparent up to a year of age. In general, the hypermetabolic state associated with congenital thyrotoxicosis has subsided by 3 months of age. Treatment consists of keeping up with the increased fluid and caloric demands of the infant, an attempt at suppression of the thyrotoxicosis with iodine, and treatment of congestive cardiac failure when present. There have been mixed reports on the use of the thiourea drugs in this disease. It does appear on theoretical grounds, however, that these drugs would not be extremely useful, since their onset of action is too slow for this relatively short-lived disease. There have been several reports now of successful use of propanalol in the treatment of congenital Graves' disease.[38,68,79] More clinical information about infants with congenital Graves' disease treated with beta blocking agents will be necessary to establish firmly the efficacy of this type of agent.

Hypothyroidism in the newborn period should be considered briefly. Basically, there are four types of hypothyroidism that are seen in infancy: (1) congenital athyrotic cretinism; (2) congenital goitrous cretinism; (3) iodine lack cretinism; and (4) cretinism secondary to some type of intrauterine insult. These varieties are discussed quite adequately in the excellent consideration by Wilkins[88] of thyroid problems in children. Several points should be mentioned. Although it is very difficult to make a diagnosis of hypothyroidism in the first weeks or months of life, a diagnosis at that time would prevent a great amount of future morbidity in the affected patient. As mentioned above, infants with congenital goitrous cretinism usually do not have a large palpable goiter in the neonatal period. With the popularity of ^{131}I as a treatment for Graves' disease, one must be alert to the possibility of hypothyroidism in the offspring of mothers who are unknowingly pregnant at the time of their therapy. It is the author's opinion that the infant of any mother who had received ^{131}I at the 12th week of gestation or beyond should be considered hypothyroid and should be so treated.

The most exciting recent information that has come out of the study of thyroid disease and the physiologic alterations of thyroid function in the newborn period is the prospect of detection of cretinism in the newborn period. It has been variously estimated[14,43] that the frequency of congenital hypothyroidism is on the order of 1 in 6000–7000. A recent report by Smith *et al.*[80] would indicate that it is difficult to consistently clinically diagnose congenital hypothyroidism early enough in the newborn period. Since it was shown by Klein *et al.*,[45] Wilkins,[88] and others that the earlier treatment is started, the better the intellectual attainment becomes, it is imperative to make the diagnosis as early as possible.

Two basic approaches have been tried in this regard. One is to measure the level of serum T_4 in the newborn and at various times in the first week of life (Table I). The other is to take advantage of the elevation of TSH that occurs in infants with primary hypothyroidism. The TSH does go up at birth, but the rise of TSH in athyrotic individuals is much greater. Such differences have been shown to be detectable by measurement of the serum TSH, both in the cord blood and at 3 days of age as well as later.[43,44] Thus, the elevation of TSH levels is an excellent screening method. There appears to be much less overlap between normal and hypothyroid individuals using the TSH, rather than the T_4, as the basic screening criterion. Methodologically, however, as of this writing, the performance of T_4 levels on a mass basis was more practicable than the performance of TSH levels. It is to be hoped that the filter paper techniques[44] will in time be sufficiently perfected to be of wide-scale applicability. At present, the T_4 may be used as a primary screen with the TSH as a backup, or the TSH may be used as the primary screening device. Whichever eventually becomes the method of choice, it is clear that screening for hypothyroidism could minimize or eliminate the intellectual and neurological impairment seen with this disease by permitting a diagnosis at a time when its clinical detection would be difficult. Detection and early treatment are obviously better than what has been done historically in the treatment of these infants.

7. Conclusion

A number of significant parameters clearly indicate an increase in thyroid function in the newborn period above that seen in older children and adults. To what extent this increase contributes to the maintenance of day-to-day homeostasis in a small infant with an unfavorable weight/body surface area ratio and to the rapid rate of growth found in the normal newborn infant are questions that at this stage remain unanswered.

Three major aspects of neonatal thyroid pathology in the human infant have been considered: (1) goiter; (2) congenital hyperthyroidism; and (3) congenital hypothyroidism.

In addition, it is apparent from the data presented that an understanding of thyroid physiology in the perinatal period may allow one to prevent the severe intellectual impairment that can be seen with congenital hypothyroidism.

Table I. Normal Range for Serum Total Thyroxine (µg/dl) During Childhood and Adolescence, by Protein-Binding Assay[a]

Age	Mean	Range
Cord blood	11.3	7.3–15.3
1–3 days	15.5	10.1–20.9
1–2 weeks	13.2	9.8–16.6
2–4 weeks	12.4	8.2–16.6
1–4 months	11.4	7.1–15.0
4–12 months	9.6	5.5–13.5
1–6 years	9.1	5.6–12.6
6–10 years	8.3	4.9–11.7
10–16 years	7.2	3.8–10.6
16–20 years	7.5	4.1–10.9
Adult	7.9	4.7–11.1

[a] Adapted from Fisher,[20] with the permission of the author.

8. References

1. ABUID, J., STINSON, A., AND LARSON, P. R., 1973, Serum triiodothyronine and thyroxine in the neonate and the acute increases in these hormones following delivery, *J. Clin. Invest.* **52**:1195.

2. BARKER, S. B., HUMPHREY, M. J., AND SOLEY, M. H., 1951, The clinical determination of protein bound iodine, *J. Clin. Invest.* **30**:55.

3. BURROW, G. N., POLACKWICH, R., AND DONABEDIAN, R., 1975, The hypothalamic–pituitary–thyroid axis in normal pregnancy, in: *Perinatal Thyroid Physiology and Disease* (D. A. Fisher and G. N. Burrow, eds.), p. 1, Raven Press, New York.

4. CHAPMAN, E. M., LORNER, G. W., ROBINSON, D., AND EVANS, R. D., 1948, The collection of radioactive iodine by the human fetal thyroid, *J. Clin. Endocrinol.* **8**:717.

5. CHOPRA, I. J., 1974, A radioimmunoassey for measurement of 3,3′,5′-triiodothyronine (reverse T_3), *J. Clin. Invest.* **54**:583.

6. CHOPRA, I. J., AND CRANDALL, B. F., 1975, Thyroid hormones and thyrotropin in amniotic fluid, *N. Engl. J. Med.* **293**:740.

7. CHOPRA, I. J., SACK, J., AND FISHER, D. A., 1975, Circulating 3,3′,5′-triiodothyronine (reverse T_3) in the human newborn, *J. Clin. Invest.* **55**:1137.

8. CLARK, R., AND HORN, D. B., 1965, Assessment of thyroid function by the combined use of the protein-bound iodine and the resin uptake of ^{131}I-triiodothyronine, *J. Clin. Endocrinol.* **25**:39.

9. DANOWSKI, T. S., *et al.*, 1950, Increases in serum thyroxine during uncomplicated pregnancy, *Proc. Soc. Exp. Biol. Med.* **74**:323.

10. DANOWSKI, T. S., *et al.*, 1951, Protein bound iodine in infants from birth to one year of age, *Pediatrics* **7**:240.

11. DENAYER, P., *et al.*, 1966, Free thyroxine in maternal and cord blood, *J. Clin. Endocrinol.* **26**:233.

12. DOWLING, J. T., APPLETON, W. G., AND NICOLOFF, J. T., 1967, Thyroxine turnover during human pregnancy, *J. Clin. Endocrinol.* **27**:1749.

13. DOWLING, J. T., FREINKEL, N., AND INGBAR, S. H., 1956, Thyroxine binding by sera of pregnant women, newborn infants and women with spontaneous abortion, *J. Clin. Invest.* **35**:1263.

14. DUSSAULT, J. H., COULOMBE, P., LABERGE, C., LETARTE, J., GUYDA, H., AND KHOURY, K., 1975, Preliminary report on a mass screening program for neonatal hypothyroidism, *J. Pediatr.* **86**:670.

15. DUSSAULT, J. H., HOBEL, C. J., AND FISHER, D. A., 1971, Maternal and fetal thyroxine secretion during pregnancy in sheep, *En docrinology* **88**:47.

16. DUSSAULT, J. H., HOBEL, C. J., STEFANO, J. J. D., III, ERENBERG, A., AND FISHER, D. A., 1972, Triiodothyronine turnover in maternal and fetal sheep, *Endocrinology* **90**:1301.

17. DUSSAULT, J. H., ROW, V. V., LICKERISH, G., AND VOLPE, R., 1968, Total triiodothyronine concentration in the serum of pregnant and newborn human subjects: The effect of maternal triiodothyronine administration before parturition, Third International Congress of Endocrinology, Mexico City.

18. ERENBERG, A., PHELPS, D. C., LAM, R., AND FISHER, D. A., 1974, Total and free thyroid concentrations in neonatal blood, *Pediatrics* **53**:211.

19. EVANS, T. C., KRETZCHMAR, R. M., HODGES, R. E., AND SONG, C. W., 1967, Radioiodine uptake studies in human fetal thyroid, *J. Nucl. Med.* **8**:157.

20. FISHER, D. A., 1973, Advances in the laboratory diagnosis of thyroid disease. Part I, *J. Pediatr.* **82**:1.

21. FISHER, D. A., 1974, Fetal thyroid hormone metabolism, *Contemp. Obstet. Gynecol.* **3**:47.

22. FISHER, D. A., AND ODDIE, T. H., 1963, Thyroxine secretion rate during infancy. Effects of estrogen, *J. Clin. Endocrinol.* **23**:811.

23. FISHER, D. A., AND ODELL, W. D., 1969, Acute release of thyrotropin (TSH) in the newborn, *Pediatr. Res.* **3**:378.

24. FISHER, D. A., DUSSAULT, J. H., ERENBERG, A., AND LAM, R. W., 1972, Thyroxine and triiodothyronine metabolism in maternal and fetal sheep, *Pediatr. Res.* **6**:894.

25. FISHER, D. A., DUSSAULT, J. H., AND LAM, R. W., 1973, Serum and thyroid gland triiodothyronine in the human fetus, *J. Clin. Endocrinol. Metab.* **36**:397.

26. FISHER, D. A., HOBEL, C. J., AND ODELL, W. D., 1969, The fetal–maternal gradient of thyroid function, *Pediatr. Res.* **3**:375.

27. FISHER, D. A., LEHMAN, H., AND LACKEY, C., 1964, Placental transport of thyronine, *J. Clin. Endocrinol.* **24**:393.

28. FISHER, D. A., ODDIE, T. H., AND BURROUGHS, J. C., 1962, Thyroidal radioiodine uptake rate measurements in infants, *Amer. J. Dis. Child.* **103**:738.

29. FISHER, D. A., ODELL, W. D., HOBEL, C. J., AND GARZA, R., 1969, Thyroid function in the term fetus, *Pediatrics* **44**:526.

30. FISHER, P. M. S., 1951, Hyperthyroidism in the first year of life, *S. Afr. Med. J.* **25**:217.

31. FISHER, W. D., VOORHESS, M. L., AND GARDNER, L. I., 1963, Congenital hypothyroidism in infant following maternal I-131 therapy with a review of hazards of environmental radioisotope contamination, *J. Pediatr.* **62**:132.

32. FUKUCHI, M., INOUE, T., ABE, H., AND KUMAHARA, Y., 1970, Thyrotropin in human fetal pituitaries, *J. Clin. Endocrinol. Metab.* **31**:564.

33. GALINA, M. P., ANNET, N. L., AND EINHORN, A., 1962, Iodides during pregnancy, *N. Engl. J. Med.* **26**:1124.

34. GITLIN, D., AND BIASUCCI, A., 1969, Ontogenesis of immunoreactive thyroglobulin in the human conceptus, *J. Clin. Endocrinol.* **29**:849.

35. GRUMBACH, M. M., AND WARNER, S. C., 1956, Transfer of thyroid hormone across the human placenta at term, *J. Clin. Endocrinol.* **16**:1392.

36. HAMOLSKY, M. W., GODOLETZ, A., AND FREEDBERG, A. S., 1959, The plasma protein–thyroid hormonal complex in man. III. Further studies of the *in vitro* red blood cell uptake of I¹³¹-I-triiodothyronine as a diagnostic test of thyroid function, *J. Clin. Endocrinol.* **19**:103.

37. HAMOLSKY, M. W., STEIN, M., AND FREEDBERG, A. S., 1957, The thyroid hormone–plasma protein complex in man. II. A new *in vitro* method for study of "uptake" of labeled hormonal components in human erythrocytes, *J. Clin. Endocrinol.* **17**:33.

38. HAYEK, A., AND BROOKS, M., 1975, Neonatal hyperthyroidism following intrauterine hypothyroidism, *J. Pediatr.* **87**:446.

39. HERBST, A. L., AND SELENKOW, H. A., 1965, Hyperthyroidism during pregnancy, *N. Engl. J. Med.* **273**:627.

40. HODGES, R. E., EVANS, T. C., BRADBURY, J. T., AND KEETEL, W. C., 1955, The accumulation of radioactive iodine by human fetal thyroids, *J. Clin. Endocrinol.* **15**:661.

41. HOLLINGSWORTH, D. R., MABRY, C. C., AND ECKERD, J., 1972, Heriditary aspects of Graves' disease in infancy and childhood, *J. Pediatr.* **81**:446.

42. INGBAR, S. H., BRAVERMAN, L. E., DAWBER, D., AND LEE, A. Y., 1964, A simple method for measuring free thyroxine in serum, *Clin. Res.* **12**:271.

43. KLEIN, A. H., AGUSTIN, A. V., AND FOLEY, T. P., JR., 1974, Successful laboratory screening for congenital hypothyroidism, *Lancet* **1**:77.

44. KLEIN, A. H., AGUSTIN, A. V., HOPWOOD, N. J., PERRICELLI, A., JOHNSON, L., AND FOLEY, T. P., JR., 1975, Thyrotropin (TSH) screening for congenital hypothyroidism, *Pediatr. Res.* **9**:291.

45. KLEIN, A. H., MELTZER, S., AND KENNY, F. M., 1972, Improved prognosis in congenital hypothyroidism treated before age three months, *J. Pediatr.* **81**:912.

46. KNOBIL, E., AND JOSIMOVICH, J. B., 1959, Placental transfer of thyrotropic hormone, thyroxine, triiodithyronine and insulin in the rat, *Ann. N. Y. Acad. Sci.* **75**:895.

47. KOCK, H. C., REICHERT, W., STOLTE, L., VAN KESSEL, H., AND SEELEN, J., 1965, Placental thyroxin transfer and foetal thyroxin utilization, *Acta Physiol. Pharmacol. Neerl.* **13**:363.

48. KRISS, J., 1968, Inactivation of LATS by anti-kappa and anti-lambda anti-sera, American Society for Clinical Investigation, 60th Meeting, Atlantic City.

49. KRISS, J., PLESHAKOV, V., AND CHIEN, J. R., 1964, Isolation and identification of the long acting thyroid stimulation and its relation to hyperthyroidism and circumscribed pretibial myxedema, *J. Clin. Endocrinol.* **24**:1005.

50. LEE, N. D., HENRY, R. J., AND GOLUB, O. J., 1964, Determination of the free thyronine content of serum, *J. Clin. Endocrinol.* **24**:486.

51. LINDEGREN, L., AND STARR, P., 1966, Neonatal thyroidology: Correlations of PBI, TBG, bone age and growth, *Acta Endocrinol. (Copenhagen)* **51**:77.

52. MAHONEY, C. B., PYNE, G. E., STAMM, S. J., AND BAKKE, J. L., 1964, Neonatal Graves' disease, *Amer. J. Dis. Child.* **107**:516.

53. MALKASIAN, A. D., AND TAUXE, W. N., 1965, Uptake of L-triiodothyronine I¹³¹ by erythrocytes during pregnancy, *J. Clin. Endocrinol.* **25**:923.

54. MAN, E. G., PICKERING, D. E., WALKER, J., AND COOKE, R. E., 1952, Butanol extractable iodine in the serum of infants, *Pediatrics* **9**:32.

55. MARKS, J. F., 1965, Free thyroxine index in the newborn, *J. Clin. Endocrinol.* **25**:852.

56. MARKS, J. F., HAMLIN, M., AND ZACK, P., 1966, Neonatal thyroid function. II. Free thyroxine in infancy, *J. Pediatr.* **68**:559.

57. MARKS, J. F., WOLFSON, J., AND KLEIN, R., 1961, Neonatal thyroid function. Erythrocyte T uptake in early infancy, *J. Pediatr.* **58**:32.

58. MARTIN, N. M., AND RENTO, R. D., 1962, Iodine goiter with hypothyroidism in two newborn infants, *J. Pediatr.* **61**:94.

59. McKENZIE, J. M., 1964, Neonatal Graves' disease, *J. Clin. Endocrinol.* **24**:660.

60. MONTALVO, J. M., WAHNER, H. W., MAYBERRY, W. E., AND LUM, R. K., 1973, Serum triiodothyronine, total thyroxine and thyroxine to triiodothyronine ratios in paired maternal–cord sera, at one week and one month of age, *Pediatr. Res.* **7**:706.

61. MOSIER, H. D., ARMSTRONG, M. K., AND SCHULTZ, M. A., 1963, Measurements of the early uptake of radio-active iodine by the thyroid gland: A method requiring reduced irradiation, *Pediatrics* **31**:426.

62. MURPHY, B. E. P., AND PATTEE, C. J., 1964, Determination of thyroxine utilizing the property of protein-binding, *J. Clin. Endocrinol.* **24**:187.

63. MYANT, N. B., 1958, Passage of thyroxine and triiodo-thyronine from mother to fetus in pregnant women, *Clin. Sci.* **17**:75.

64. NATAF, B. M., RIVERA, E. M., AND CHAIKOFF, I. L., 1965, Role of thyrotropic hormone in iodine metabolism of embryonic rat thyroid glands in organ culture, *Endocrinology* **76**:35.

65. NAUMAN, J. A., NAUMAN, A., AND WARNER, S. C., 1967, Total and free triiodothyronine in human serum, *J. Clin. Invest.* **46**:1346.

66. NICOLOFF, J. T., NICOLOFF, R., AND DOWLING, J. T., 1962, Evaluation of vaginal smear, serum gonadotropin, protein-binding iodine and thyroxine-binding as measures of placental adequacy, *J. Clin. Invest.* **41**:1998.

67. OSORIO, C., AND MYANT, N. B., 1960, Thyroid hormones in pregnancy, *Br. Med. Bull.* **16**:159.

68. PEMBERTON, P. J., McCONNELL, B., AND SHANKS, R. G., 1974, Neonatal thyrotoxicosis treated with propranolol, *Arch. Dis. Child.* **49**:813.

69. Peterson, R. P., and Young, W. C., 1952, The problem of placental permeability for thyrotropin, propylthiouracil and thyroxine in the guinea pig, *Endocrinology* **50**:218.

70. Pickering, D. E., 1964, Maternal thyroid hormone in the developing fetus, *Amer. J. Dis. Child.* **107**:567.

71. Pickering, D. E., 1968, Thyroid physiology in the developing monkey fetus, *Gen. Comp. Endocrinol.* **10**:182.

72. Pileggi, V. J., Lee, N. D., Golub, O. J., and Henry, R. J., 1961, Determination of iodine compounds in serum. I. Serum thyroxine in the presence of some iodine contaminants, *J. Clin. Endocrinol.* **21**:1272.

73. Raiti, S., Holyman, C. B., Scott, R. L., and Blizzard, R. M., 1967, Evidence for placental transfer of triiodothyronine in human beings, *N. Engl. J. Med.* **277**:456.

74. Sack, J., Fisher, D. A., Hoebel, C. J., and Lam, R., 1975, Thyroxine in human amniotic fluid, *J. Pediatr.* **87**:364.

75. Schultz, M. A., Forsander, J. B., Chez, R. A., and Hutchinson, D. L., 1965, The bidirectional placental transfer of I¹³¹ 3 : 5 : 3′-triiodothyronine in the rhesus monkey, *Pediatrics* **35**:743.

76. Selenkow, H. A., 1975, Therapeutic considerations for thyrotoxicosis during pregnancy, in: *Perinatal Thyroid Physiology and Disease* (D. A. Fisher and G. N. Burrow, eds.), p. 145, Raven Press, New York.

77. Shepard, T. H., 1967, Onset of function in the human fetal thyroid: Biochemical and radioautographic studies from organ culture, *J. Clin. Endocrinol.* **27**:945.

78. Singh, V. N., and Chaikoff, I. L., 1966, Effects of 1-methyl-2-mercaptoimidazole and perchlorate on the insulin-mediated enhancement of I¹³¹ incorp-orated into iodoamino acids by fetal thyroid glands in organ culture, *Endocrinology* **78**:339.

79. Smith, C. S., and Howard, N. J., 1973, Propranolol in treatment of neonatal thyrotoxicosis, *J. Pediatr.* **83**:1046.

80. Smith, D. W., Klein, A. H., Henderson, J. R., and Myrianthopoulos, N. C., 1975, Congenital hypothyroidism—signs and symptoms in the newborn period, *J. Pediatr.* **87**:958.

81. Spafford, N. R., Carr, E. A., Lowrey, G. A., and Beierwaltes, W. H., 1960, I¹³¹ labeled triiodothyronine erythrocyte uptake of mothers and newborn infants, *Amer. J. Dis. Child.* **100**:844.

82. Sterling, K., and Hegedus, A., 1962, Measurements of free thyroxine concentration in human serum, *J. Clin. Invest.* **41**:1031.

83. Sunshine, P., Kusumoto, H., and Kriss, J. P., 1965, Survival time of circulating long-acting thyroid stimulator in neonatal thyrotoxicosis. Implications for diagnosis and therapy of the disorder, *Pediatrics* **36**:869.

84. Tanaka, S., and Starr, P., 1959, The binding of thyroxine analogues by human serum protein, *Acta Endocrinol. (Copenhagen)* **31**:161.

85. Utiger, R. D., 1968, Plasma TSH in health and disease: Immunoassay studies, Third International Congress of Endocrinology, Mexico City.

86. Van Middelsworth, L., 1954, Radioactive iodine uptake of normal newborn infants, *Amer. J. Dis. Child.* **88**:439.

87. White, C., 1912, A foetus with congenital hereditary Graves' disease, *J. Obstet. Gynecol. Br. Emp.* **21**:231.

88. Wilkins, L., 1965, *The Diagnosis and Treatment of Endocrine Disorders in Childhood and Adolescence*, 3rd Ed., Chapts. 6–8, Charles C. Thomas, Springfield, Illinois.

Index